D0788485

Camden House History of German Literature

Volume 4

Early Modern German Literature 1350–1700

The Camden House History of German Literature

Volume 4

The Camden House History of German Literature

Edited by James Hardin

Vol. 1: Early Germanic Literature and Culture
Edited by Brian Murdoch and Malcolm Read,
University of Stirling, UK

Vol. 2: German Literature of the Early Middle Ages
Edited by Brian Murdoch, University of Stirling, UK

Vol. 3: German Literature of the High Middle Ages
Edited by Will Hasty, University of Florida

Vol. 4: Early Modern German Literature 1350–1700
Edited by Max Reinhart, University of Georgia

*Vol. 5: German Literature of the Eighteenth Century:
The Enlightenment and Sensibility*
Edited by Barbara Becker-Cantarino, Ohio State University

Vol. 6: Literature of the Sturm und Drang
Edited by David Hill, University of Birmingham, UK

Vol. 7: The Literature of Weimar Classicism
Edited by Simon Richter, University of Pennsylvania

Vol. 8: The Literature of German Romanticism
Edited by Dennis F. Mahoney, University of Vermont

Vol. 9: German Literature of the Nineteenth Century, 1832–1899
Edited by Clayton Koelb and Eric Downing,
University of North Carolina

*Vol. 10: German Literature of the Twentieth Century:
From Aestheticism to Postmodernism*
Ingo R. Stoehr, Kilgore College, Texas

Early Modern German Literature 1350–1700

Edited by
Max Reinhart

CAMDEN HOUSE

First published 2007
by Camden House

Camden House is an imprint of Boydell & Brewer Inc.
668 Mt. Hope Avenue, Rochester, NY 14620, USA
www.camden-house.com
and of Boydell & Brewer Limited
PO Box 9, Woodbridge, Suffolk IP12 3DF, UK
www.boydellandbrewer.com

ISBN-13: 978–1–57113–247–5
ISBN-10: 1–57113–247–3

Library of Congress Cataloging-in-Publication Data

Early modern German literature 1350–1700 / edited by Max Reinhart.
    p. cm. — (Camden House history of German literature; v. 4)
Includes bibliographical references and index.
ISBN-13: 978–1–57113–247–5 (hardcover : alk. paper)
ISBN-10: 1–57113–247–3 (hardcover : alk. paper)
    1. German literature — Middle High German, 1050–1500 — History
and criticism.   2. German literature — Early modern, 1500–1700 —
History and criticism.   I. Reinhart, Max, 1946–

PT238.E375 2005
830.9′003—dc22

                                                            2007037294

A catalogue record for this title is available from the British Library.
This publication is printed on acid-free paper.
Printed in the United States of America.

Contents

Part I: Transitions

Part II: Formations

Part III: Forms

Part IV: Representations

Part V: Lives

Preface and Acknowledgments

THE ENTERPRISE OF WRITING a literary history of this period under the inclusive nomenclature of "early modern" has only one precedent: Helen Watanabe-O'Kelly's fifty-four-page chapter "The Early Modern Period (1450–1720)" in *The Cambridge History of German Literature* (1997). Volume 4 of the Camden House History of German Literature, however, is the first attempt to give a book-length account of the entire period, from its earliest manifestations in the late Middle Ages to its yielding to the modern aesthetics of individual expression in the Age of Sentimentality. Early modernists disagree somewhat over beginning and end dates. This volume establishes an earliest-possible *terminus a quo* of 1350; the *terminus ad quem* of 1700 allows for a seamless connection to Volume 5 of the series, though 1750 would be closer to the actual transition to modernity. Still, even a volume as ample as this one can make no claim to comprehensiveness. Indeed, the possibility of such a claim expired with the fading, after the First World War, of the nineteenth century's illusions of a single "grand narrative" born among Italian Renaissance princes and bequeathed to a German spiritual prince by the name of Luther, Protestant, whose genius, allegedly, set the great wheel of modernity in motion. The "account" promised here has a rather more modest goal: to represent as thoroughly as possible the current state of scholarship in the field, and to do so across the long duration between 1350 and 1700-plus in order better to observe the essential transitions in mentality, contours in culture, and multiplicities in convention.

To provide some conceptual control over the subjects in this volume, the twenty-six chapters have been arranged in five parts: 1) Transitions: this part includes discussions of the late-medieval-to-early-modern transition itself as well as related studies on the structure of the period and the state of philological-editorial research. 2) Formations: these represent some of the more massive literary-intellectual developments of the period, such as education, which were fundamental to all other aspects. 3) Forms: these include the three classical genres plus the sensational new mixed form of the emblem. 4) Representations: some of these subjects, like the formations, had broad significance, but are placed under this rubric because of their particular nature to reflect, or represent, other interests (for example, literature at or concerning the court). 5) Lives: four parallel-lives studies represent biographical experiences at various stages of the early modern period, from early to late; a fifth study included in this biographical part addresses women's writing of the period, which often tended to be intensely personal in nature.

The term "early modern" in the title of this volume — rather than a reference to "Renaissance" or "Reformation" — may surprise some readers as much as it did the colleague outside the historical disciplines to whom I recently showed a list of the ten titles in the series. After a moment's reflection he responded: "Did Germany not have a Renaissance or a Reformation?" Unwittingly, he had precisely formulated a question that has vexed historians since the second half of the twentieth century and literary historians since about the last quarter. I replied that "early modern" has come to replace the classic categories "Renaissance" and "Reformation" as an explanatory model for the period between the late Middle Ages and the Modern Age. If my explanation did not altogether persuade him, the fault was only mine, for the "early modern" model is by now almost universally accepted by historians across the relevant disciplines.

What difference does it make to conceptualize this enterprise as a unitary subject rather than to divide it into two periods, each with its own volume (1. Renaissance and Reformation, 2. Baroque), as in traditional literary historiography? Let us consider a traditional handling of, say, fool's literature, a prominent genre between Early Humanism and Late Baroque. A scholar assigned this topic for a volume on the Baroque would immediately think of the various foolish types in burlesque drama: the harlequin, the *miles gloriosus*, the *zanni*, *Hanswurst*; or certain characters in Grimmelshausen and Beer and other writers of picaresque fiction; or Reuter's outrageous *Schelmuffsky*, or Riemer's political *Maul-Affen*, "gaping fools," in addition to other related figures and genres. All would then be gathered and explicated against the backdrop of baroque history, morality, aesthetics, and culture. An introductory paragraph would acknowledge the tradition of fool's literature and mention some outstanding titles, such as Erasmus's *Praise of Folly* and Brant's *Ship of Fools*. Then, however, the discussion would necessarily make a giant leap back to the Baroque, leaving decades of generic, social, moral, and confessional development out of sight — the very processes that nourished and transformed the genre in its seventeenth-century forms. Similarly, the separate volume on Renaissance and Reformation would make its obligatory references to the traditions from which fool's literature was derived as well as its continuation into the Baroque, but then settle down to its "own" periodic focus. In both instances, the lingering impression is that fool's literature existed somehow independently in the respective period; that it appeared and disappeared more or less *nolens volens*; and worst, that students may safely ignore the gaps left by these condensed or truncated processes. The present volume, by contrast, seeks to allow the manifestation of the fuller unfolding, or bridging, of genres and forms within the structures of long-term developments in early modern society and culture.

As a practical matter, it was one thing to propose covering the extreme dates of 1350 and 1700 in a single volume, but quite another to find scholars capable of treating assignments across these 350 years. The reasons for this frustration originate within traditional academic structures, and are troubling to the extent that this trammeled thinking still reigns in many places. Notwithstanding all hermeneutical advances in historiography, the organization of literary studies for the fifteenth, sixteenth, and seventeenth centuries in most universities remains mostly locked (a) in the historico-aesthetic periodization scheme of Renaissance, Reformation, and Baroque; (b) in national categories — for German literature, specifically, the Reformation still commonly enjoys the status of founding myth, alternatively of the "German spirit" or a "German early-bourgeois revolution"; and (c) in a pertinacious animadversion toward social and mental history, not to mention a blindness to Latin. As a result, few scholars receive formal training in actual early modern literature — including Neo-Latin studies — in the full chronological sense. The present volume is fortunate to have the participation of some of the preeminent early modernists from Germany, the U.K., and North America. As a result of the pioneering efforts of many of these contributors over the past twenty years or so, early modern literary studies within some universities have gained traction, despite the constant pragmatic tug of "actualizing" or "modernizing" curricula. This development would appear to bode well for the future of the specialization.

The editorial apparatus of this volume conforms in its main features to that of the others in the series. Endnotes accompany each chapter; a bibliography of selected primary works and secondary studies stands in penultimate position, just before the final comprehensive index of names, works, and concepts. A striking one-third of the contributions to this volume were originally written in German — a direct reflection of the publisher's support for recruiting the leading experts, whether their native language was English or German. The volume contains hundreds of German and Latin titles, for which standard English translations are supplied, as known; otherwise, working renderings are provided.

Certain regrets at this final stage of production rise to the surface. Suitable scholars for one or two proposed topics could not be found. Most painful, however, was not being able to accommodate one very fine essay: "Confessionalization and Literature in the Empire, 1555–1700" by Ute Lotz-Heumann and Matthias Pohlig. I am somewhat consoled by its having found a worthy home in *Central European History* 40 (2007): 35–61.

For a work of this size, the list of people who contributed to the production is impossibly long, though a few cannot go unmentioned. At the top of the list I must place the publishers at Camden House and Boydell & Brewer, who believed in the unitary conceptualization of the volume and had the courage to publish it as such — a publishing first. Nothing about this thick, pathbreaking volume was easy, but the sharp editorial staff at CH and B&B managed every step of production with great expertise. I am especially grateful to Jim Walker, the editorial director, for his ever-workable advice and unfailing good humor through countless hours of telephonic brainstorming; to Jane Best, the production editor, for keeping the various editorial stages coordinated and moving forward, and who readied the essays for the typesetter; to Sue Smith, the production manager, for her creative solutions to a host of big and small problems; and to Cheryl Lemmens, the indexer, whose skills were indispensable to the scholarly usefulness of the volume. A personal word of thanks goes to James Hardin, the general editor of the series, for generously sharing his extraordinary editorial wisdom gained over a professional lifetime of editing and publishing.

My sincere appreciation is due the excellent translators of the German-language contributions: Michael Metzger (Professor Emeritus of German, University of Buffalo), Michael Swisher (Chair, Departments of Art and Literature, and of Humanities, Truman College, Chicago), Karl F. Otto Jr. (Professor Emeritus of Germanic Languages and Literatures, University of Pennsylvania), and James Hardin (Professor Emeritus of German, University of South Carolina).

It is, of course, to the individual contributors of this volume that the greatest debt is owed. A number of them were among the first scholars of early modern German studies; without their pioneering efforts, the present volume, which conceptualizes the years between 1350 and 1700 as a unitary period, could not have been imagined. To edit the work of all of these superb contributors has been for me both challenging and rewarding.

And finally, for guidance and inspiration over the years, it is a very special joy to express my gratitude to Klaus Garber, the founder and former director of the Institut für Kulturgeschichte der Frühen Neuzeit (Osnabrück),

> *quo cum sermones poteram conferre suaves,*
> *tutus et in fidum spargere verba sinum.*

Max Reinhart
Athens, Georgia
August 2007

Introduction: German Literature in the Early Modern Period

Max Reinhart

Early Modernity in History and Scholarship

GOETHE'S FAMOUS QUIP to his biographer Johann Peter Eckermann in 1824 that when he was eighteen Germany too was only in its teens was tossed off with a laugh,[1] and was not the sign of historical arrogance that some commentators have made it out to be. Nevertheless, the glib remark can still rankle historians of older literature who research and teach within an academic culture of cost-effectiveness that often seems to have been struck by amnesia for history before Goethe. Taken at face value, it ignores a good 500 years of structural changes that transformed the Middle Ages into modern Europe: politically, the diminution of imperial and papal powers vis-à-vis electors, states, and territories, and the creation of constitutional guarantees; socially, the proliferation of cities and the rise of urban culture, with its officialdom and ideas about citizenship, representation, and social mobility; economically, the advent of industrial capitalism, the invention of the printing press, the marketing of books, and the expansion of international banking; intellectually, humanism, the Copernican revolution, the rise of empirical methodologies, and meritocratic theories of the nobility of mind, which, among other things, inspired co-education and the idea of gender equality; religiously, the Protestant Reformation, the Jesuit renewal of the Catholic faith, and personal expressions of spirituality (mysticism, spiritualism, pietism). This is to say nothing of other kinds of changes that had equal effect on the development of history over this half-millennium: the suppression of heresies, the witch-hunting craze, sectarianism and the wars of religion, the Thirty Years' War (1618–48). All of these events and developments, together with the genre traditions inherited from the Middle Ages and the humanistic forms and styles coming across the Alps from Italy, produced complex, multilayered discourses. These discourses were transmitted by a new university-trained humanist elite and nourished the imaginations of Lessing and Herder and Goethe and Schiller in the Age of Enlightenment. Did it really all begin with Goethe?[2] Only if one does not know one's history.

Where does German literature fit within the big picture of early modernity? If we accept the dominant historiographical paradigm, the history of early modern German literature constitutes a chapter within a much larger unfolding in Europe between the fourteenth and eighteenth centuries, one that manifests four tendencies: (1) the late medieval economic and population depression, followed by a recovery between 1460 and 1500; (2) the gradual weakening after the mid-thirteenth century and then sudden fragmentation in the early sixteenth of Christendom as *una societas christiana* and the formation of independent states and territories; (3) the rise of colonial empires in the fifteenth and sixteenth centuries; and (4) the proto-industrialization of Europe and breaking of the Malthusian barrier as the gateways to modernity.[3] Viewed in these terms, the beginning date of 1350 in the title of volume 4 of the Camden House History of German Literature recalls the inception of the Black Death (from 1347), with its catastrophic effects on population and economy, while the end date of 1700 anticipates the industrial developments of the early eighteenth century.[4] This rather sober account of history between the late Middle Ages and modernity reflects the twentieth century's repudiation of the previous century's revolutionary versions of the Renaissance and the Reformation, most heroically Leopold von Ranke's "grand narrative," which opened with the thunderous *event* of the Protestant Reformation and rumbled its way down to his own time (and would continue until after the First World War).[5] The idea of dramatic revolutions has given way in modern historiography to the observation of epic evolutionary processes.

It is the profound contribution of modern historiography, particularly of the *Annales* method[6] and of the sociohistorical school,[7] to have shifted the focus of historical analysis from great events, or great institutions, or great personalities, or even great works, to their processual and mental contexts.[8] This shift has resulted in paradigmatic changes in the way literary historians view the field of writing in the centuries formerly organized under the epochal categories of "Renaissance," "Reformation," and "Baroque." The nineteenth-century advocates of the Renaissance and Reformation's "modernization" and "liberalization" have been silenced in this scheme, as have those that claimed to find some Germanic essence in the Baroque. Three of their greatest "discoveries" — the Renaissance's discovery of the "subjective" self and the "objective" world (Burckhardt);[9] the Lutheran Reformation's discovery of the "German national spirit" (Treitschke);[10] and the northern Baroque's discovery of the non-Italian, "Germanic qualities" (Wölfflin)[11] — have been exposed as ideological constructs. Gone is the dramatic story of an enchained medieval past that rises to intellectual and spiritual liberation in the Renaissance and the Reformation;[12] gone the fairy tale of an uncouth Baroque transformed at last into Classical Weimar;[13] likewise gone the counter-myth of a reactionary Baroque set on the restoration of an aristocratic, Catholic Europe.[14]

None of this is to suggest, however, that those venerable terms must be discarded in our preference for "Early Modern." They are still useful and desirable, even necessary, as apt metaphors for historical and stylistic *movements*. The balance struck in the mid-1990s by the editors of the *Handbook of European History, 1400–1600* in judging the efficacy of the terms "Renaissance" and "Reformation" in historiography seems as judicious in 2007 as it was then:

"The Renaissance" still means the recovery, adaptation, and expansion of knowledge associated with the neo-classical revival, but it can no longer stand for Burckhardt's birth of modernity in the form of individualism. "The Reformation" still means the transformation and differentiation of western Christianity during the sixteenth century, but it can no longer stand for [John Lothrop] Motley's liberation of the world from priestcraft and superstition. Thus shorn of their former ideological freight, the concepts still retain distinct signatures as aspects of a world which was, at the same time, late medieval and early modern.[15]

To assay a similar judgment for "the Baroque," we may say that it still means a highly rhetorical, nonmimetic, even anticlassicist style (Nietzsche) that tends to the instrumental use of language, perhaps, as some have suggested, in the interest of achieving cultural stability following the chaotic wars of religion.[16] But it can no longer stand for Burckhardt's characterization of the Baroque as a "crude Germanic dialect" as against the "pure language" of the "Renaissance,"[17] or for Wölfflin's implications about a Gothic "manliness" and bold expressivity, as against the alleged effeminacy and subtlety of Italian or French style — a harsh dualism that under National Socialism was turned into a racial distinction between Germanic strength and un-Germanic weakness.

Viewed across the long duration, or *longue durée*, rather than period by period, previously unrecognized or ignored conflicts between political, ecclesiastical, social, and cultural forces become visible in the early modern world and literature. Two of the most powerful of these forces, which both divided and unified European society, were nationalization and confessionalization. Although the autonomous territories that were formed by policy in the Peace of Augsburg (1555)[18] meant that Germany would be politically fractured for the following three centuries, an overarching ideology of the nation, driven especially by humanist patriotism, inspired a search for authentic varieties of German cultural artifacts and experiences. The tide of confessionalization, usually identified with the later century but set in motion in the 1520s with Luther's politicization of theology, which played out most disastrously in the Peasants' Wars, produced deep rifts in sixteenth-century society,[19] but it also brought about solid and positive alliances, not only at the local level, but in ways that overlapped and commonly transcended territorial jurisdictions. This is particularly evident in the early modern history of international Calvinism.[20]

The long perspective can likewise bring into sight previously unnoticed connections, or bridges, between aesthetic, mental, and social phenomena, not as crude causalities but as energies that burst into form (texts, paintings, compositions) at their sites of encounter.[21] By recognizing the proper origins of early modern Europe in the mid-fourteenth century we are able to appreciate both the modern tendencies that were "dawning" in the late Middle Ages[22] and the vernacular medieval forms and attitudes that persisted in the Reformation. The simultaneous arrival of Latin humanistic forms from Italy clashed and meshed with the Germanic medieval forms to produce a formal syncretism that was "perhaps the most conspicuous phenomenon of the late-medieval-to-early-modern transition" [Garber].[23]

Under the epochal categories of traditional literary history, older texts tended to be thought of in a kind of handmaidenly role, as *exempla*, to support religious, philosophical, political, or other ideological interests. This was considered to be less true for allegedly "genuine" literature after about 1750 than for earlier literature, which was understood as functional or rhetorical in the negative sense of being mechanically "imitative," or non-ironic.[24] A great advance in literary interpretation since the 1960s was to give equal value to older texts as individual historical achievements, as representations of real human responses to social circumstances. Hans-Gert Roloff, one of the founders of the early modern philology, reminds us in his chapter in this volume that the transformative fourteenth, fifteenth, sixteenth, and seventeenth centuries were in fact uniquely "rich in human questions about the right way of living, about values, dangers, the need for change, about criticism and affirmation of old and new authorities." Roloff concludes: "The real purpose of a literary history oriented toward human values is to discover and interpret these issues." This reorientation led to a massive rediscovery of texts, both German and Latin; a reevaluation of the canon; the founding of dozens of editorial series; and a revolution in the practice of source scholarship and critical editing. The new texts included many by vernacular writers either unknown to or rejected by Martin Opitz and the seventeenth-century literary reformers. The Opitzian reform aspired to the formal sophistication of foreign, especially French, poetic accomplishments, and therefore rejected most indigenous forms and authors, even literary giants like Martin Luther and Hans Sachs. Elisabeth von Nassau-Saarbrücken, Hermann Bote von Braunschweig, Jörg Wickram, Johann Michael Moscherosch, Christian Weise, and Johann Beer are only a few of the writers — all now considered to be indispensable for a full appreciation of early modern literature — that were recovered by the new *Literaturwissenschaft*. The Neo-Latin tradition too had to be rehabilitated, since it had been marginalized by the nationalistic biases and taste preferences of nineteenth-century philologists, such as Jakob Grimm, who excluded any texts on principle that fell outside of what he called "the Protestant dialect."

This philological renewal contributed moreover to significant innovations in methodology, above all, to comparativism and interdisciplinarity (or multidisciplinarity), which provided a more accurate reflection of how knowledge was organized prior to the departmentalizing reforms of the nineteenth century. The field of early modern studies has adapted and made productive use of these new methods within the humanities and social sciences. Intertextuality, for example, including intermediality, has helped to reveal the ingenious combinational strategies of early modern composition.[25] A related method, known as *Gesellschaftsvergleich* (comparison of societies), was developed in the late 1990s in the social sciences to investigate how structural changes occur in modern economies and industries; it has expanded to embrace historical inquiries across the disciplines and into the early modern period regarding material and other factors (conventions, *habitus*, agendas, confessionalism) that drove organizational changes.[26] Among its possible uses for early modern German studies, the method suggests itself as an approach to long-unanswered questions regarding the internal dynamics and changes in literary societies: for example, concerning the sensitive confessional politics in the Fruchtbringende Gesellschaft (Fruitbringing Society);[27] or the internal causes that led to the dissolution in the early eighteenth century of the older humanist literary societies and the precise motivations behind Leibniz's interest in a national academy of sciences.[28]

The essays in the present volume owe much to these groundbreaking efforts. Indeed, we are pleased to be able to include contributions by several of the outstanding pioneers of early modern German literary studies. One of our goals, of course, is to present the current state of research in the various subjects, although, despite the extraordinary generosity of the publisher, space limitations prevent anything approaching a full inventory of the varieties of research that now occupy the field. On the other hand, while selection was primarily guided by judgments about the readiness or maturity of certain topics for summary in a literary history, contributors were by no means discouraged from taking a "progressive" approach. As a consequence, much new or ongoing research will be found between these covers. Given that early modern literary studies is one of the most active research areas within the humanities and social sciences, it was perhaps inevitable that the *push* of this energy would make itself felt even in a literary history, an essentially conservative genre.

While the topics offered here must be restricted in number, they are often sweeping in breadth and perspective. They range from large historical structures to small aesthetic forms and include, in addition to discussions of literature per se, an overview of early modern German music and an essay on the pictorial "language" of early modern German art. The intent behind the five organizational rubrics is to provide some conceptual control over a potentially unwieldy repertoire. Though other headings might have served as well, together these represent a hermeneutical framework within which the activities of writing and scholarship and living in early modern Germany had their meaning, both historically and aesthetically.

A few words about the headings may be useful. "Transitions" may seem a bit fuzzy given our express certainty that the late Middle Ages was the point of origin for early modernity. In this volume Graeme Dunphy reminds us that the problem is partly a function of how the field is laid out. Because "the early thirteenth and early sixteenth centuries are established coordinates in the discipline of literary history," what lies between leaves the discipline with an apparent transition. However that may be, some solace may be taken in our shared befuddlement with other historians over the question of how periods succeed one another, never more charmingly expressed than by E. H. Gombrich, writing for children: "How nice it would be if, suddenly, heralds were to ride through the streets crying: 'Attention please! A new age is beginning!' But things aren't like that."[29] The next heading, "Formations," stands for fundamental processes that bore everything else along in their own movement. For example, the movement of education in Germany is traced here across the early modern *longue durée* from the late medieval university curriculum to the humanist reforms of Erasmus and Philipp Melanchthon to the pragmatic revisions of seventeenth-century pedagogy. "Forms" includes the classical genres of drama, poetry, and prose, as well as the new mixed form of the emblem. Other mixed forms proliferated in the early modern period too — *Flugblätter* (broadsides), figured poetry, prose eclogue — but none as ubiquitously as the emblem; in fact, many other mixed forms betray essentially emblematic structures. "Representations" pertains to a group of practices or activities that often served, functioned on behalf of, "represented," overriding interests — the making and cataloguing of princely libraries, the application of erotic (especially Petrarchist) imagery to various kinds of discourse, the strategies of writing about magic and witches, the use of travel reports for ideological purposes or for profit. Finally, "Lives" — specifically, "parallel lives," but including an account of women's writing in the context of their lives — reminds us (as does a fascinating subset of early modern research),[30] that men and women experienced life no less vividly in the early modern period than we do today, and that the successes or failures of careers and goals of scholars and artists often hinged on the accidents of fortune or the wisdom of personal choice.

Our main interest in this volume of literary history concerns how *literary* texts had meaning in the early modern period (though "literary" prior to the new organic aesthetics of the later eighteenth century must be defined very broadly). While the organizational headings here provide some assistance, early modern philology has shown that these texts also had meaning individually and within specific discursive traditions. "History," the legal historian Michael Stolleis observes, "essentially relies on texts."[31] But, as he goes on to explain, *how* texts speak is as significant as *what* they speak. Every situation is specific to the text as communicative instrument, and every text has its reception in these situations. Communication and reception occur within specific "sociogenetic" groups (intellectual societies, pietist devotional circles, women's domestic gatherings), as the sociologist Norbert Elias observes: "The originators speak out of a social situation [. . .]; they speak into a very specific situation [. . .] that is characteristic for a specific [. . .] grouping of people."[32] This dynamic of communication and reception can be either affirmative (imitation, mimesis, normative morality, social discipline) or dialogical (negation, alienation, counterfactuality, barbarization[33]). There is also a third, "mental," level — one implied in the *Annales* method — that relates to the semantic forms of communicative structures and patterns of thought not immanent to the texts themselves: traditions, genres, topoi, conventions, occasions, images. These "mentalities" affect textual meaning exogenously but can themselves be transformed in the process of textual interpretation over time.

In this light, events and developments between the mid-fourteenth and the eighteenth centuries constitute not only the backdrop against which all writing took place but are also the stone upon which texts carved their messages. That idea informs the following sketch of the history of German literature between 1350 and 1700.

Early Modern German Literature in Context

Late Medieval and Early Humanism

The early modern period opened in the wake of the imperial crisis provoked by the end of the Hohenstaufen dynasty and the failure to elect a new emperor. The Great Interregnum led in the next century to a formalization (Golden Bull, 1356) of the rights of princely "electors" (seven in number, drawn from both secular and ecclesiastical courts) to choose the emperor. This decentralizing of imperial power ran in near parallel with the erosion of church authority, challenged by the conciliar movement since the early fourteenth century[34] and most starkly manifested in the Great Schism of 1378–1417. After the disasters and anxieties of the thirteenth century, many people expected, well into the fourteenth, the coming of the kingdom of peace prophesied by Joachim of Fiore (ca. 1135–1202). Alas, this hope was shattered by the events of the calamitous fourteenth century, beginning with the Black Death, which within a few years wiped out a quarter of Germany's population.[35]

One reason for the rapid spread of plague was the movement of populations into walled urban settlements over the course of the twelfth and thirteenth centuries. On the eve of the early modern period the number of German towns had quadrupled, most having fewer than 2,000 citizens, but some, like Nuremberg and Augsburg, more than 10,000. Many joined in regional confederations, such as the northern Hanseatic League, for military or economic protection. Some families (the Fuggers, the Welsers, for example) who divined early the potential of the emergent capitalism crossing the Alps from northern Italy, achieved immense wealth in the sixteenth century by lending great sums at interest to ambitious but cash-strapped princes, kings, and emperors.

It was chiefly in the cities that literacy and its attendant skills (especially letter writing, or epistolography), institutions (schools, chanceries), and rewards (social mobility) flourished within the rising apparatus of officialdom and around the new industry of printing. The culture of writing in Germany actually began considerably in advance of the printing press in cities where bureaucratic organization furnished the need and employment for young men skilled in humanistic correspondence. Johannes von Tepl, the author of the first great work in German prose, *Der Ackermann aus Böhmen* (The Plowman of Bohemia, 1400/1), got his start as a notary in the city of Saaz. The first European university north of the Alps and east of Paris was founded in Prague in 1348, followed soon by others in the German-speaking realm: Vienna in 1365, Heidelberg in 1386, Cologne in 1388, Erfurt in 1389, Rostock in 1419, Basel in 1460, Ingolstadt in 1472, Tübingen in 1477, and, as the first of eleven more in the sixteenth century, Wittenberg in 1502, where Luther became a professor of biblical studies. With the gathering into towns came a different ordering of social groupings, reformulations of laws and privileges (Roman law, *ius civitatis*), governing bodies (especially the *Stadtrat*, or city council), and, perhaps most importantly for the arts and literature, a profoundly changed sense of the self with respect to a community of others. This bourgeois self-awareness motivated not only the social satires of a Heinrich Wittenwiler (*Der Ring*, ca. 1410); moral fables like *Reineke Fuchs* (1498); adventurous tales of a new type of hero, the wandering merchant; or the songs of the *Meistersinger*, urbanized mutations of the former singers of courtly love. It also lay behind the psychologically revolutionary self-portraiture of Dürer, or the deeply troubling looks into the realm of social limits and taboos in works like Thüring von Ringoltingen's *Melusine* (1456) [Dunphy].

The epistolary art was not the sole invention of the cities, however, and was in equal demand at the major courts. The courts — estimated to have been around 100 in number during the early modern period [Watanabe-O'Kelly] — exemplified Germany's intimate relationship with Italy in the fourteenth and fifteenth centuries. The cultural intercourse began at the court of Charles IV, who aspired to create an intellectual and aesthetic environment in Prague to rival the finest courts in Europe. Besides founding there the first university and the first botanical garden in the German Empire, Charles was especially keen to absorb the influence of leading Italian scholars, such as the theorist of Roman law Bartolo of Sassoferrato. Apparently at the behest of his chancellor, Johannes von Neumarkt (ca. 1310–80), Charles invited the renowned Petrarch to instruct the chancery in how to cultivate an effective prose style for chancery documents. The result was not only an effective administrative and diplomatic instrument but one distinguished by supple rhythms and lovely concinnity. Beginning in the fifteenth century, leading German courts, notably Vienna and Heidelberg, employed Italian scholars or Germans who had studied in Italy. One of the court's advantages over the cities was its largesse: through patronage it could purchase the creative energies of writers, artists, and musicians in producing a literary, visual, and musical cosmos of "representation." Compared to the courts, cities had a miserly reputation among writers and artists!

Both empire and church were again declaring their respective authority on the eve of the Reformation, and with renewed vehemence. By the late fifteenth century the empire was making the extravagant claim to being the "Heiliges Römisches Reich Deutscher Nation." Grand-scale power politics stormed the European theater in the fifteenth century, from the Ottomans in the Southeast (conquest of Constantinople, 1453; siege of Vienna, 1529), to France (invasion of Italy, 1494) and England in the West (Tudor accession, 1485), to Spain in the Southwest (marriage of Isabella and Ferdinand, 1469), to Sweden in the North (Vasa accession, 1526). Early modern states and monarchies displayed their claims to empire through ambitious seaborne voyages of exploration and discovery (Columbus, Coronado, Da Gama, Cartier, and the rest). The glory days did not fade easily. Even after the Hohenstaufens had become a distant memory, fifteenth-century regent-novelists like Elisabeth von Nassau-Saarbrücken (1393–1456) and Eleonore von Österreich (1433–80) resurrected the old high courtly virtues, not merely for novelistic sentimentality but also to inculcate them as principles of good governance amid the changing sea of embourgeoisement (*Verbürgerlichung*).[36]

The church, for its part, blustered its way past most of its critics with self-entitlements, denunciations, and threats of excommunication. Pope Boniface VIII proclaimed in his bull of 1302, *Unam sanctam ecclesiam*, that all *temporalia* are properly subject to ecclesiastical jurisdiction; in 1329 Pope Johannes XXII, loather of all things German, pronounced Meister Eckhart's teachings, including his disparagement of the Roman Church as a *Mauerkirche* (church of walls), to be heretical.

But it is grossly misleading to paint the late medieval church, as some have done, as ineffectual or unresponsive to its flock or lacking in spiritual heat. Quite the opposite was true. Right up to Luther's repudiation in 1517 of the pope's scriptural authority to sell indulgences for the remission of sins, the church continued to fulfill its basic sacerdotal and totemic functions for the general populace. The production of literary (calendars, plays, hagiographies, celebrations of Mary), artistic (saints, adorations, Christ scenes), and musical (chorale, mass, hymn) works for the special days of the church year reached unprecedented levels in the late medieval period, as did the varieties and fervency of expressions of piety among the laity.[37] Religious poetry was intensely visual and focused much attention on iconographic representations of the exemplary life of Christ. In the late medieval period religious manuscripts outnumbered secular ones by three to one, and this despite the massive increase in secular writings.

Even the literary genius of Luther himself was not unprecedented. The literature produced by the monastic and spiritual traditions (Augustinians, Franciscans, Dominicans, the Teutonic Order) coursed into Luther's world and filled his imagination. Linguistic masters of the stature of Heinrich Seuse or Meister Eckhart or Johannes Tauler were no less gifted than Luther.[38] Nineteenth-century philology established the modern watershed between Middle High German and Early Modern German with Luther and the Reformation. Twentieth-century language scholars, less influenced in their judgment by the brilliance of Luther's accomplishments as a writer and translator, reset the beginning of Early Modern German at a point considerably in advance of the sixteenth century [Born].

Modern research into the vitality of the late medieval church also contradicts the still commonly held belief that the Lutheran Reformation, as the spiritual counterpart to the Renaissance, brought modernity into being in one fell swoop. No doubt, "modern" elements (antischolasticism, individual freedom, secularization) are present in Luther's thought, at least inceptively. However, compared to the rationalist, skeptical brand of religion that arose in the later eighteenth century around Lessing, Luther's Reformation seems more medieval than modern. Scholasticism, allegedly spurned, pervades Luther's thinking; human freedom for him is limited to obedient believers and is hostile to the notion of free will [Carrington]; and while Luther affirms the importance of this world within the plan of salvation, his willingness to place religious enforcement in the hands of secular rulers helped to fuel the confessional politics that not only had a hand in the bloody Peasants' Wars but hastened the coming wars of religion. While the Reformation was indubitably transformational in the history of western religion, it decidedly did not throw open the doors to modernity. What is more, if we again take the long view of early modernity, Luther's was but one, if the most important, among a series of reformations across Europe: Thomas Cromwell's in England, Jean Calvin's in Geneva, Huldrych Zwingli's in Zurich, Thomas Müntzer's in Saxony, the Anabaptists' in Münster, to say nothing of the Catholic Church's own reformation after the birth of the Society of Jesus (1534) and the Council of Trent (1545–63). Indeed, there had been earlier reformation movements, such as Jan Huss's in Bohemia, and there would be later ones as well, such as the Spiritualists' (Sebastian Franck, Kaspar Schwenckfeld) or the Pietists' (Gottfried Arnold, Philipp Spener). All of these shared Luther's goal of reforming the church and deepening spirituality, if by different means.[39]

Still, the church in many ways had indeed failed to reform itself from within, to the dismay of many, and troubling signs of imminent crisis abounded in the decades just prior to the outbreak of the Protestant Reformation. Two Dominican friars in Germany, Heinrich Kramer (known as Institoris) and Jakob Sprenger, were dispatched in the 1480s to seek out alleged enemies of the church known as "witches" and bring them to God's justice. In 1487 Kramer systematized the process of identification and punishment in the infamous *Malleus malleficarum* (The Witches' Hammer) [Scholz Williams]. Another Dominican friar, Savonarola, delivered fiery millenarian sermons in Florence in the 1490s, prophesying the end of the world. Nuremberg, widely admired for its open-mindedness and hospitality, drove the Jews from the city in the 1490s and seized their property and synagogue, a practice that accelerated in these years throughout Europe. The princes of the church enjoyed ever-greater economic prosperity but still sought to rob the poor of their pittance by the sale of *Nachlaßbriefe* (letters of indulgence) that promised remission of sins, an abuse that filled one young monk with such righteous indignation that he dared at last to call Rome to account.

Toward the end of the late medieval period three developments came about that would prove decisive for the flowering of humanism and the advent of the Reformation in Germany. The first was the convocation of two major church councils in German lands, the Council of Constance (1414–18) and the Council of Basel (1431–49). These protracted events brought Italian humanists, who were in the employ of the church, to Germany, where their impact on German intellectuals was nothing less than life changing. The most important of the Italian visitors was Enea Silvio Piccolomini (1405–64, later Pope Pius II), who, after his service at the Council of Basel, was retained by Friederich III to direct the chancery at the new imperial seat of Vienna. It is no exaggeration to say that Enea Silvio introduced the Germans to themselves through his monograph *De ritu, situ, moribus et conditione Germaniae* (On the Customs, Geography, Habits, and Condition of Germany, 1457). Besides describing geographical and other wonders of Germany, Enea Silvio introduced Tacitus, the ancient Roman historian, whose *Germania*, recently rediscovered, sang the praises of the venerable Germanic virtues (modesty, generosity, honesty, loyalty, freedom, perseverance, courage, genius, and nobility). These legendary virtues became weapons for the Germans in the coming cultural and religious wars with Rome.

The second development concerns the model of piety represented by the Devotio Moderna, a Dutch religious movement whose members were known as the Brethren of the Common Life. Their most celebrated member before Erasmus was the German Thomas à Kempis (family name, Hämmerlein), the author of the widely admired *De imitatio Christi* (1420–41). The Brethren cultivated a modest approach to spiritual reform inspired in part by a high regard for classical learning. As a youth in Deventer, Erasmus was introduced to the Brethren's method of textual criticism, which later became for him an instrument of great philological power that allowed him to make significant improvements in how to read and understand the Bible [Rummel].

The third development, the invention of movable type by Johannes Gutenberg in the mid-fifteenth century in Mainz, revolutionized the world of communications [Füssel], contributing fundamentally to the evolution of an essentially oral-based culture to one driven by writing. Scholars have described this transformation as *Verschriftlichung* [Knape].[40] In 1968, at the beginning of the new sociohistorical *Literaturwissenschaft*, Roy Pascal made the astute observation that the printing press was in no small part responsible for the very "consolidation of burgher culture."[41] For the "arch-humanist" Conrad Celtis (1459–1508) it meant that the culture-hungry Germans now had the technological means to overcome their *stolida inertia*, "stupid laziness" (Ode 3,9), and at last to catch up with the Italians.

As we have seen, however, German humanism actually began, if haltingly, some 150 years before Celtis uttered these words; Italian humanism still much earlier. Furthermore, the qualities Emperor Charles and his chancellor recognized in Italian humanism did not spring Minerva-like out of the air but grew from very material social and political roots. The conditions conducive to the formation of an intellectual estate developed in the thirteenth and fourteenth centuries in middle and northern Italy with the rise of a wealthy manufacturing class. While certain of the feudal aristocracy became involved in the early capitalistic enterprises, the rest retired to the countryside.[42] Between the new *haute bourgeoisie* and the old aristocracy a useful estate of civil servants and intellectuals formed over the course of the fourteenth and fifteenth centuries and consolidated its position in part by acquiring access to privileges by virtue of its social proximity to the aristocracy.[43] Petrarch (1304–74), the son of a wealthy merchant and educated in Montpellier and Bologna, belonged to this rising estate, which over the next century forged links across Europe and, by holding in common a set of classically derived ideals and practices known as the *studia humanitatis*, established an identity as the *respublica litteraria* (republic of letters), or *nobilitas literaria*. By 1500 the term *humanista* (humanist) designated a person who shared these features.[44] That humanism eventually took hold north of the Alps owed to the cultivation of similar sociopolitical connections, beginning with its reception at the imperial court in Prague.

Middle Humanism and Reformation

The first signs, in trecento Italy, of an emerging learned aristocracy are visible in the epistolary debate between Dante and the Bolognese grammarian Giovanni del Virgilio over the relative merits of Italian and Latin.[45] The exchange took place in 1319 within the rustic form of the Vergilian eclogue. It has an intensely searching quality that addresses the question of the poet's relationship, or obligation, to his readers. Should one write in the elevated argot of Latin, or should one make a commitment to the humble language of the people, the *lingua volgata*?[46] The unspoken conflict in this ostensibly academic tussle between friends was rooted in social ideology: the value of the people versus the value of the aristocracy. Dante aspired to elevate the *genus humile* by creating a poetic language in the vernacular that was the equal of Latin. For Giovanni, the learned estate should guard its privileges by holding to its hermetic codes. Giovanni reflects the early educated estate's claim to shared privilege with the aristocracy. Thus the aesthetic question raised by Giovanni: What is good? is at base a social question: What is noble? Dante, by insisting that the humble language of the people can be as distinguished as the elevated language of the educated, added an ethical dimension to the question: not, What is good? but What is *truly* good? not, What is noble? but What is *truly* noble? This philosophical distinction would resonate powerfully in the republic of letters for the following half millennium.

This appeal to *vera nobilitas* (true nobility) is coeval with the birth of humanism, for it is predicated not on the privilege of birth but on personally earned merit. Dante pounded this idea home in his *Convivio*, and a massive literature of true nobility followed.[47] It was a cornerstone of republican theory,[48] which asserted the superiority of education and competence over inherited privilege, and is found in many discourses, including political theory and in writers as diverse as Machiavelli (1469–1527) and Hugo Grotius (1583–1645), founder of the modern theory of natural law. Florentine writers of the quinquecento trumpeted the city's record of meritorious civil servants, most notably Coluccio Salutati and Leonardo Bruni, as well as its greatest poets (Dante, Boccaccio, and Petrarch), as living proofs that Florence was the legitimate successor to the ancient republic.[49] The topos can be tracked deep into the eighteenth century with the enlightened middle-class appropriation of natural law and belief in the general perfectibility of humankind, irrespective of social class, race, or gender. It was an ideal of the French Revolution and is deeply embedded in the American Constitution.

It was at about this point in the development of the *respublica litteraria* that humanism personally came to Germany. When Emperor Charles IV and his chancellor Johann von Neumarkt invited Europe's preeminent poet to Prague in 1350 they expected one distinguished visitor; instead, they got two: besides Petrarch, his traveling partner, the revolutionary republican tribune Cola di Rienzi as well. Rienzi had a plan. While the emperor listened with detached amusement and some anxiety, Rienzi laid out a fantastic blueprint for restoring the Roman Republic, under the leadership of Charles himself, to its former glory. Nothing was to come of this except jail time for Rienzi. Petrarch's principles of style, on the other hand, were accepted wholeheartedly; adaptations were made, and a German chancery style was born. Fifty years later it served the notary Johannes von Tepl in composing *Der Ackermann aus Böhmen*, as mentioned earlier. The subsequent wave of anti-Hussite persecution in Bohemia, however, poisoned the environment. Another half century would pass before the *studia humanitatis* would be reintroduced to Germany, by Enea Silvio in the 1640s and in the lectures of the wandering humanist Peter Luder (ca. 1415–72) at the University of Heidelberg in 1456.[50] The idea of *renovatio imperii* (the renewal of the empire) that Rienzi had tried to get across to Charles IV helped to drive a German cultural war against shared adversaries in Rome.[51]

This urge to renew or refashion the world was the fire that welded the ideas of nation and culture for the early German humanists around Conrad Celtis. The private intellectual society, or sodality (*sodalitas*), was the primary institution for the communication of this concept, even more so than the university, court, or church. Here the members "could act according to rules that they themselves had devised. No institution therefore was more suited to the self-expression of the humanists of Europe than these *sodalitates literariae*."[52] The movement of intellectual societies began in quatrocento Italy in Bologna and spread quickly to Florence, Naples, Venice, Rome, and then across Europe over the following three centuries. One of the four societies in Florence, the Accademia della Crusca, inspired a German member, Prince Ludwig von Anhalt-Köthen, to establish the first vernacular literary society on German soil, the Fruchtbringende Gesellschaft, in 1617. Intellectual societies in Germany were founded in the late fifteenth century in important towns, especially those with universities and typically around a respected scholar or distinguished personality: in Heidelberg (Bishop Johann von Dalberg and Celtis), Nuremberg (the patrician Willibald Pirckheimer), Erfurt (the poet-scholar Eobanus Hessus), Augsburg (the antiquarian Conrad Peutinger), Vienna (Celtis and certain court officials). Following in the classical tradition of Giovanni, the common language of these early sodalities was Latin, though the common ethos was Dantean. German humanists on the whole showed greater interest in the natural sciences and mathematics than did their more philosophically minded colleagues in Italy. In the privacy of their gatherings these differences could be mulled over, political issues debated, questions of literary style and taste adjudicated, new writings read aloud, criticism entertained, ideas fostered. A culture of mutual support and high spirits, even a measure of excess, was the order of the day, as we see in a delightful ode by Celtis that recalls an evening at the Sodalitas Rhenana (Rhenish Sodality), which he had founded as a student in Heidelberg in 1484–85. After serious discussions about nature and poetry it is time to eat and drink, and the mood suddenly soars:

> Hinc Bacchi madidis cymbia poculis
> Fervens mensa tulit cum variis iocis,
> Hic nummos nocuam perdit ad aleam,
>   Alter carminibus vacat,

Hic flexu volucri saltibus incites
Exercet variis corpora motibus,
Ut risum eliciat, dum rudis aemulus
Lapsu praecipiti cadit.[53]

[And now quickly to the table! The cups stand running over with Bacchus's draft and call us to merry games. Over there one fellow is gambling away his coins; over there another is singing a song. That fellow is winding up his body to make a great leap, and twists himself about energetically to get his muscles ready. Now laughter ensues as another, competing with him, falls to the floor.]

A century and a half later the cult of friendship in the literary societies could be a shield against the surrounding world of violence. In the amicable warmth of the Kürbishütte in Königsberg, Simon Dach contemplates the blessings and responsibilities of friendship:

Der Mensch hat nichts so eigen
So wol steht ihm nichts an /
Als daß Er Trew erzeigen
Und Freundschafft halten kan;

Wann er mit seines gleichen
Soll treten in ein Band /
Verspricht sich nicht zu weichen
Mit Hertzen / Mund und Hand.

Die Red' ist uns gegeben
Damit wir nicht allein
Vor uns nur sollen leben
Und fern von Leuten seyn;

Wir sollen uns befragen
Und sehn auff guten Raht /
Das Leid einander klagen
So uns betretten hat.[54]

[Nothing is more innate to humankind, nothing more appropriate, than that we should show our loyalty and prove our friendship by joining with others like ourselves in fellowship and promising with heart, mouth, and hand never to fail. Speech has been given us so that we need not live all by ourselves and far from other people. We should ask questions of each other and depend on one another's advice; confess to one another the suffering that afflicts us.]

The scholar Paul Hankamer in 1935, under the "manly Baroque" bias of those years, mocked what he considered a culture of preciosity in the *Sprachgesellschaften*: "In this void they composed often virtuosic congratulations and avowals of friendship and elegant epistles to one another, the dreadful emptiness of which could only be supplemented by mutual assurances of their literary immortality [. . .]."[55] This ill-tempered gibe misses not only the humanity that lay behind the *courteoisie* of the sodalities but its implicit ethical criticism as well. The insistence on deference toward others, the readiness to praise, the avoidance of doctrinal hairsplitting, the cultivation of the correct and the beautiful: in the semantics of humanist discourse these behaviors called attention to their absence in society or, indeed, in the very institutions that ought to know better — the courts, the churches, the universities. The critical potential of panegyrical speech was appreciated in antiquity and exploited in exemplary fashion by Vergil in his eclogues. Within the poetic community of the literary societies it brought forth a type of *Gegenweltsliteratur* (counter-world literature) that, as we shall see, flourished above all in Nuremberg in the 1640s.[56]

The fact that the Rhenish Sodality at Heidelberg enjoyed the patronage of Bishop Johann Dalberg of Worms and Elector Philipp of the Palatinate reminds us of the alliance between intelligence and power in early modern Europe. All major early societies in Italy enjoyed noble benefactors, many of these from the ranks of the *potentes* (wealthy ruling families), such as Cosimo and Lorenzo de' Medici at the Accademia Platonica in Florence. This dependence continued to distinguish the European movement of intellectual societies. In Paris in the seventeenth century the Cabinet Dupuy counted on the protection of no less formidable a figure than Cardinal Richelieu.[57] Through its first generation the Fruchtbringende Gesellschaft was almost completely aristocratic;[58] around 1650, 475 members out of the total of 527 were aristocrats. However, in the next generation this proportion began to shift as memberships in the various societies became predominately bourgeois.[59] Nuremberg's Pegnesischer Blumenorden, founded by the patrician Georg Philipp Harsdörffer (1607–58), consisted almost exclusively of bourgeois members. With the tendency toward refeudalization in the seventeenth century the friction between the learned estate and nobility increased and in some instances culminated in legal confrontations over questions of privilege.[60]

The humanists of Celtis's generation[61] were primarily secular-minded. Most agreed with Celtis that Rome had abandoned its moral and intellectual mandate and that the time had come for those privileges to be transferred to Germany (*translatio artium*) [Füssel], but the church itself was not an issue that aroused them to action. Celtis spoke for most early humanists in his preference for a quasi natural religion —

> est deus in nobis, non est quod numina pictis
> aedibus intuear

[God dwells in us; I have no wish to gad about in painted sanctuaries]

— an attitude that incited some religious leaders, including Luther, to accuse Celtis and his friends of paganism. The focus of these humanists was on the moral qualities of the individual, not on adherence to any particular confession. Even Zwingli (1484–1531), who had received a humanist education, was reproached by Luther's circle for moral leniency; his rejoinder was to fault

Luther's *sola fide* (by faith alone) doctrine, which he said fostered in the faithful a complacency about doing the good works appropriate to a true Christian.

This attitude toward the church changed significantly in the generation of humanists after Celtis. While not doctrinaire, they saw no conflict in a simultaneous commitment to ecclesiastical reform and the reform of human learning and manners;[62] indeed, the two were reckoned as whole cloth. The path to these reforms moved in reverse: *ad fontes,* "to the sources," a method the northern humanists learned from the Italian historians, especially Lorenzo Valla (1406–57). Valla was famous for having proven through meticulous textual analysis that the allegedly fourth-century Donation of Constantine — which purported to confer on the inheritors of St. Peter the city of Rome and the entire Western Roman Empire — was an eighth-century forgery. Erasmus applied this same textual rigor to his 1516 Latin translation of the New Testament (from the Greek original), the edition that Luther would consult assiduously in making his own translation into German in 1521.

This look back to the sources as the way to establish authentic texts and, by extension, authentic Christian theology and behavior was one of the most important practices shared by the humanists and the evangelical church reformers in the early years of the Reformation. Another related practice was the use of criticism. The modern concept of the humanist as *criticus* had been introduced only recently by the Florentine scholar Angelo Poliziano (1454–94), in 1492, to characterize the attitude and method of the new *eruditi* (educated) in their opposition to Scholasticism. Its effectiveness was enhanced by the printing industry, which produced and disseminated books so rapidly and widely that the criticism emanating from, say, remote Wittenberg, was amplified and given the appearance of simultaneity and ubiquity. Luther seized this potential to deliver a devastating blow to the church's foundations in three epochal works from the "Reformation Year" of 1520: *An den christlichen Adel deutscher Nation* (To the Christian Nobility of the German Nation), *Von der babylonischen Gefangenschaft der Kirche* (On the Babylonian Captivity of the Church), and *Von der Freiheit eines Christenmenschen* (On the Liberty of a Christian Individual). There were many types of criticism, of course. One that the humanists and reformers shared was the satirizing of opponents. Several outstanding literary works exemplified this, such as Sebastian Brant's (1457–1521) *Das Narrenschiff* (1494), Erasmus's *Laus Stultitiae* (Praise of Folly, 1511), the *Epistolae obscurorum virorum* (Letters of Obscure Men, 1516 and 1517), written mainly by Ulrich von Hutten (1488–1523) and Crotus Rubeanus (1480–ca. 1545), and Friedrich Dedekind's (1524–98) *Grobianus* (1549). This is to say nothing of the suasive power of *Flugschriften* (pamphlets), one of the deadliest weapons in the vernacular arsenal of the reformers; or of the large generic category of *Narrenliteratur* (literature of fools), which was exploited to hilarious and often brutal effect on all sides. Some of the most effective satirical writings came from the pen of the Franciscan humanist and opponent of the Reformation Thomas Murner (1475–1537), as in his *Von dem großen lutherischen Narren* (On the Great Lutheran Fool, 1522).

Two other behaviors, or traits, are also often mentioned as typical of humanists, though they are found in equal measure among the church reformers: individualism and patriotism. Theories about the "Renaissance man" go back to the ideal of the *uomo universale*.[63] Leonardo da Vinci (1452–1519) is usually thought of in these terms. Burckhardt was particularly in awe of the Dutch humanist Rudolf Agricola (1444–85), poet, painter, sportsman, rhetorician, and musician. The ideal of the "perfected man" was a subject of much speculation in conversational literature (also called literature of dialogues), beginning with Baldassare Castiglione's *Il Libro del Cortegiano* (The Book of the Courtier, 1528) and cultivated through the entire early modern period. Literary examples of the early modern cult of personality are found in many genres, including eulogy — *Leichenpredigten* (eulogies) constitute one of the largest corpora of occasional literature in the early modern period[64] — and autobiography, but especially in painting: Grünewald's attention to expressionistic agony; Hans Holbein the Younger's monumental, sensuous portraits of English royalty and aristocracy; Dürer's penetrating self-portraiture.[65] Here too the printing press and the rapid rise of the publishing industry contributed to the glorification of the individual. The swift appearance of books with one's name on the title page created the potential for sudden fame and enhancement of reputation. Wealthy individuals, such as Willibald Pirckheimer (1470–1530) in Nuremberg, invested heavily in the cultivation of private libraries, the fame of which spread throughout the European republic of letters.

The half century following the printing of Enea Silvio Piccolomini's groundbreaking history of Germany, which advanced the European Tacitean movement — the cult of the Roman historian Tacitus — saw a great outpouring of patriotism among the purveyors of the new learning.[66] This movement grew in intensity in the period of the Reformation as German evangelicals and humanists alike joined in a general *Kulturkampf* against what they considered a decadent Roman culture.[67] It took now a theological or ecclesiological turn, now an intellectual one. Celtis struck a revivalist tone in his inaugural address at the University of Ingolstadt in 1492, haranguing Germans to resist the decadent foreign (read: Roman) strain and affirm their own national genius. To do so will require, he says, nothing less than a "turning," literally a "conversion," to the humanistic studies: "Quamobrem convertite vos, Germani, convertite vos ad mitiora studia!" (Turn then, Germans, turn to more cultured studies!), he cries.[68] Celtis's call was taken up with militant zeal by Hutten in his *Arminius* (ca. 1519). In this Lucian satire Arminius comes before the god of the underworld, Minos, to make his case for his proper place in history. Tacitus appears as Arminius's chief advocate, praising the ancient Germanic conqueror of the Romans as "Germany's Liberator":

> Ohne Zweifel war er Deutschlands Befreier. Er griff das römische Volk nicht in seinen Anfängen an wie andere Könige und Fürsten, sondern in seiner Blütezeit, in Schlachten war sein Erfolg wechselnd, im Kriege blieb

er unbesiegt. 37 Jahre wurde er alt, zwölf davon war er an der Macht, und noch jetzt lebt er in den Liedern der Barbaren.[69]

[Without doubt he was Germany's Liberator. He took on the Roman people, not in its mere beginnings like other kings and princes had, but in its prime. His success was mixed in battles, but in war he remained undefeated. He lived to thirty-seven, twelve of those years as ruler, and he still lives in the songs of the barbarians.]

At the end of the seventeenth century, Daniel Casper von Lohenstein (1635–83) recalled Hutten's work in writing his novel of state of the same name, *Arminius*, in 1689–90 (discussed below). A related hero, Aristarchus, the courageous Greek astronomer and so-called Copernicus of antiquity, was invoked by Martin Opitz in 1617 to make the same appeal to German patriotism as Celtis had: to seize the genius of the German language and create a national poetry in the vernacular.

If the foremost motivation of Celtis's generation was the spread of the *studia humanitatis* through foundings of institutions of learning (schools, universities, sodalities) and the establishment of a humanist curriculum, the next generation was motivated to ensure their lasting success by integrating them within the political and religious structures of authority. In a book that became a model of its kind throughout Europe, *De civilitate* (On Civility, 1530), Erasmus established his pedagogical reform on the ideal of a pure Christian foundation, the *philosophia Christi*. Many religious contemporaries considered *De civilitate* to be more mundane than spiritual, though this impression owed to its subtle method. Erasmus gradually leads the student away from extreme behaviors to that of true modesty, or grace, which he believes to be the true representation of Christ-like behavior. The attitude that should spring from this achievement is the prerequisite for the further pursuit of the *pia philosophia* (pious philosophy). In the seventeenth century this Aristotelian ethic of *modestia* experienced a transformation as *prudentia civilis* (social prudence), by which practice a young man might enhance his chances of success in the political world [Kühlmann, "Education"].

The impact of Erasmus's educational theory was profound across Europe and in England. But it was his younger contemporary, Philipp Melanchthon (1497–1560), who consolidated the humanistic model of erudition and piety and implemented it in the Protestant school system.[70] For his pedagogical accomplishments he became known as the *praeceptor Germaniae* (teacher of Germany). Because Melanchthon established the unity of *eruditio* and *pietas* on biblical precepts, he was able to ensure that Renaissance letters, along with the related humanistic educational goals and methods, would thrive as a staple in the classroom. As a practical matter of importance to all humanists, this also meant that they could count on steady employment.

Even before 1520, however, suspicions had arisen in evangelical as in humanist circles that an irreconcilable difference lay below the surface of their cooperation. In 1524 Erasmus politely raised the essential question in a little publication titled *De libero arbitrio diatribe* (A Disquisition on Free Will), which challenged Luther to state clearly his position on the subject of free will. Luther's reply the following year took the form of a lengthy, vituperative book called *De servo arbitrio* (The Enslaved Will), in which he denies that Scripture gives any evidence to support belief in human volition, and in which he decries Erasmus's willingness to entertain the option of human choice.[71] Clearly, Erasmus and Luther had fundamentally different anthropological perceptions: Erasmus (and most humanists) saw humankind as essentially graceful, that is, able to participate personally in the divine action of grace,[72] whereas Luther (and most evangelicals) held to a view of humankind as hopelessly lost. After this exchange it became apparent to actors on both sides of the issue that their presumed consensus had been illusory and their cooperation only pragmatic. Church historians refer to this tendency toward the leveling of differences between the evangelicals and the humanists in the interest of a common cause (reform) as the confessionalization of humanism.[73] Some humanists, such as Melanchthon, rededicated themselves to the evangelical cause while others, like Pirckheimer, returned to the Catholic fold.

Others did their best to hold the alliance together. Hutten, a brilliant stylist who wrote forcefully on behalf of the new learning (most famously in the *Letters of Obscure Men*), also exploited his family privilege as an imperial knight socially and militarily in support of Luther, whom he continued to value as an indispensable champion of reform. In 1522 Hutten and Franz von Sickingen (1481–1523), another humanist and imperial knight, led a popular crusade on behalf of the Reformation to wrest control of lands belonging to the archbishop of Trier, a quixotic undertaking that failed and spilled over into the Peasants' War of 1524–25. Other individuals employed the pen rather than the sword in this battle. Eobanus Hessus (1488–1540), writing in Latin, and Hans Sachs (1494–1576), writing in German, both celebrated Luther as the *Gottesmann* for the times. Inspired by Luther's courageous stand at the Diet of Worms in 1521, Hessus composed in his honor a cycle of six elegies. In the first elegy Luther is a Christian Moses restoring the truth to Christianity:

> Tu uelut à facie Mosis uelamina ducens
>   Apparere facis quae latuere prius.
> Tu sua Christicolae reddis cognomina plebi,
>   Nomina quae rebus dissona nuper erant.
> Pax iterum coelo redit aurea, & hoste perempto
>   Nocte sub aeterna bella sepulta iacent. (ll. 75–80)[74]

[But you remove the veil, as it were, from the face of Moses and reveal what was formerly hidden. You give back to Christianity its true sign, a name that not long ago was contradictory to reality. Golden peace returns from heaven and, now that the foe has been defeated, wars lie buried in eternal night.]

The same point was made in the vernacular by Nuremberg's famous cobbler, Hans Sachs, best known for his sometimes ribald and always entertaining *Fastnachtspiele* (Shrovetide plays), in a long verse allegory called *Die wittenbergisch Nachtigall* (The Nightingale of Wittenberg). Composed in 1523, it contributed to the local groundswell of support for the Reformation, which was officially adopted in Nuremberg two years later. Like Hessus, Sachs presents Luther as the restorer of true Christianity. Throughout his work he interweaves biblical, creedal, and doctrinal allusions, as in the following passage:

> Die Wahrheit ist kommen ans Licht.
> Deshalb die Christen wieder kehren
> zu den evangelischen Lehren
> unseres Hirten Jesu Christ,
> der unser aller Löser ist,
> des Glaub allein uns selig macht.[75]

[The Truth has come to light. Therefore, Christians return to the evangelical teachings of our Shepherd, Jesus Christ, who is the Redeemer of us all, in whom faith alone makes us righteous.]

These and other attempts notwithstanding, confessional polarization increased as the Reformation spread and had permanent negative implications for the literary societies. The access Celtis had enjoyed to the imperial house in Vienna or the Catholic princely circle in Worms — without feeling co-opted by them! — was eliminated by confessional party formation. Before this time — in Nuremberg, in Augsburg, in Strasbourg, in Basel, in Ingolstadt, in Erfurt — the sodalities pursued, without confessional strictures, the goals of Celtis. Then, suddenly: "Mit dem Einbruch der Reformation kommt der erste Schub der Sodalitätsbewegung in Deutschland zum Stillstand" (With the onset of the Reformation the first impulse of the movement of the literary societies in Germany grinds to a halt).[76] The caesura would last precisely a century, if we measure the onset of the Reformation from Luther's posting of the *Ninety-Five Theses* in 1517 until the founding of the Fruchtbringende Gesellschaft in 1617.

In the second half of the sixteenth century, as Protestant, Catholic, and sectarian camps multiplied, confessional wars engulfed much of Europe. Germany was spared the worst. The settlement of the Peace of Augsburg provided that each of the scores of territories in Germany should have *de facto* authority, which precluded a national political center but led to a pragmatic coexistence of the confessions. In centralized nation-states, such as France, hysteria could run unchecked, as the dreadful fate of the Huguenots in the St. Bartholomew's Day massacre (24 August 1572) attests. Still, many potentially volatile issues remained unresolved in Germany after Augsburg that would fester until at last erupting in the Thirty Years' War.[77] One of the most significant for German literary history was the exclusion of Calvinism from the parties to the Augsburg treaty. Historians have observed that the very success of the Peace of Augsburg guaranteed its ultimate failure. The particularism that came of it only postponed the inevitable confessional explosion. Meanwhile too, the Catholic Church had experienced a reformation of its own, which established or reaffirmed institutional structures and doctrinal positions. Along with the creation of the Jesuits, it gave rise to a militant Counter-Reformation that produced some of the most powerful literature, architecture, and music of the early modern period.[78]

In the midst of the violence and confusion of the late sixteenth century a philosophy of peace, known as irenicism, arose among moderate Lutherans and Calvinists based on Erasmian principles of toleration and conciliation.[79] This movement is sometimes identified with the so-called Second Reformation.[80] The Heidelberg Catechism of 1563, prepared under the auspices of Elector Palatine Friedrich III by two young theologians, Zacharias Ursinus and Caspar Olevianus, was the first major undertaking to reduce conflicts in doctrinal positions to statements of consensus. A generation later, at the threshold of the Thirty Years' War, Ursinus's disciple David Pareus (1548–1622), published a guide for confessional unity called *Irenicum* (The Book of Peace, 1614).[81] Though it could not hold back the coming tide, its Christian-humanist vision inspired others, like the Strasbourg professor Matthias Bernegger (1582–1640)[82] and the poet and dramatist Johann Rist (1607–67),[83] to dare to imagine peace in a peaceless world. A century later similar circumstances would obtain and a new call to understanding and peace would have to be made, as we shall see. But who could have foreseen that prior to the outbreak of the Thirty Years' War?

Late Humanism and Baroque

The devastations and existential dread that accompanied the Second World War reminded many historians of the similar dimensions of horror and loss experienced during the Thirty Years' War, and it is in that context that we must appreciate the impassioned postwar search for the meaning of the Baroque in history. The great scholar of literary topoi Ernst Robert Curtius, known mainly for the inventory of the western literary tradition in his magisterial *Europäische Literatur und Lateinisches Mittelalter* (1948),[84] understood the Baroque as Nietzschean anticlassical "mannerism," a style characterized by contorted, unnatural, artificial effects, by contrast with the stable classical style of the Renaissance and all other "classical" periods. This distinction led to a good deal of tiresome debate over nomenclature reminiscent of the nineteenth-century ideological dualities of Renaissance/Reformation and Renaissance/Baroque. In the late 1950s, however, one of Curtius's students, the journalist Gustav René Hocke, developed a historical typology in two books, *Die Welt als Labyrinth* and *Manierismus in der europäischen Kunst und Literatur*, that have attracted renewed interest since their republication in 1987.[85] For Hocke, the chaotic period of the wars of religion and political fluidity from the late sixteenth century through the Thirty Years' War represented a condition of mannerist insecurity that resulted in a pronounced rhetorical style characterized by singular perspectives and exaggerated poses and colors. By contrast, the period of settlement and nation-building following the Peace of Westphalia (1648) was driven by a search for stability characterized by an intense striving for formal certainties, to which he gave the name Baroque. The utility of this simple scheme helps to bring into focus certain late-sixteenth-century ordering or stabilizing tendencies as early as about 1572[86] — especially the late-humanist pursuit of *ordo*[87] — that led in the following generation to the German literary reform and in the next to grand literary visions of a *pax Europa*.

By 1600, as the idea of modern literary reform was just beginning to be considered seriously in Germany, England already had its Elizabethan Age with Shakespeare, Marlowe, and Sidney; Spain its *siglo de oro* with Cervantes and Lope da Vega; France its classical century with Ronsard, Joachim du Bellay, and Jean-Antoine de Baïf. Germany had its Protestant Reformation and Martin Luther, to be sure, who was revered across the continent for his unparalleled mastery of the German idiom. Unlike the leading vernaculars of Europe, however, the German that fell from the Reformation tree was a plump fruit, cultivated for persuasion and didacticism. Content overwhelmed form; form shaped itself to the demands of the message. German was a polemical hammer (Luther, Müntzer); a satirical catcall (Bote, Murner); a farcical mirror (Sachs, Wickram); a militant pamphlet (*Flugschrift*); an instrument of conversion (Manuel, Rebhun); a Rabelaisian burlesque (Fischart). By the contemporary European standards of *belles lettres*, however, its lack of formal sophistication still marked it as a barbarian language. Opitz's friend Julius Wilhelm Zincgref (1591–1635) complained that to be a German abroad was an embarrassment.

But that is not the whole story. Just as actively as any other nation in the century of the Reformation, Germany participated in the high culture of Latin [Kühlmann, "Neo-Latin"], which operated on a discrete track separate from the vernacular culture. While some German humanists contributed to both traditions, the literary products in German and those in Latin had divergent aims. It is impossible to estimate how many Germans contributed to Latin literature in the fifteenth and sixteenth centuries, since the types of writing were manifold, ranging from pedagogy to poetry. Selections have been gathered in recent editions,[88] though these represent only the tip of the iceberg. Consequently, in 1617, when the twenty-year-old Opitz composed his Latin-language appeal for poetry to be written in German — *Aristarchus sive de contemptu linguae teutonicae* (Aristarchus; or, On Contempt for the German Language) — he could rely on established formal models. All that was lacking was a German poetics that explained the rules and collected samples for emulation. Opitz himself supplied it in 1624 with his *Buch von der Deutschen Poeterey* (Book of German Poetics), with models primarily from French and Dutch, but also from Neo-Latin. Commentators have sometimes referred to his poetics and the subsequent rapid spread of its principles as "revolutionary." But that is to forget the vital fountain from which it drew. In truth, the *Poeterey*, while ingenious, was a conservative summary of available models.

Initial poetic attempts tended toward strict imitation, and few lived up to expectations. Opitz's own *Teutsche Poemata*, composed just prior to the publication of the *Poeterey*, was released without his approval by an overly eager Zincgref [Verweyen]. Horrified by its lack of readiness, Opitz undertook revisions — these related not only to elements of style but also to implications about confessional politics — and republished the collection in 1625 under the slightly altered title *Deutsche Poemata*. Within a few years, however, other German poets had begun to find their own voices and to push back against some of the classical prescriptions of Opitz's poetics. The lyrics of the young Leipzig poet Paul Fleming seem to spring directly from personal experiences; the

Silesian lawyer Andreas Gryphius (1616–64) fills the classical sonnet with theological and existential meditations; the combinational imagination of the exiled Austrian Protestant Catharina Regina von Greiffenberg (1633–94) stretches the traditional linguistic bounds of German poetry; the eccentric Quirinus Kuhlmann (1651–89), before his death in Moscow by burning, loaded his poems with messianic language punctuated with exclamations and incantations that threaten the very idea of form. Harsdörffer's Nuremberg colleague Johann Klaj (1616–56), one of the most gifted, if unheralded, poets of the century, invented a dithyrambic form, neither drama nor epic nor lyric, for public performance, accompanied by music, called *Redeoratorium* (declamatory oratorio), which enjoyed a sensational but brief life.[89]

In keeping with Horace's axiom "ut pictura poesis" (poetry is like a picture), baroque writers cultivated a highly imagistic aesthetics. It is especially on display in the emblematic genre [Daly], which has applications in many other forms (figured poetry, staged tableaux, epideictic narrative,[90] among others). The related acoustic practice of *Klangmalerei* (sound painting), associated especially with Nuremberg, was related to deeper theological speculations about the divine voice in creation. Contemporary German language specialists promoted the thesis that German was coeval with Hebrew, hence an original tongue [Born]. Baroque experimental forms were too great in number for overview here. They included oddities like poems cut and scattered to be found and reconstructed, riddle epigrams, numerological puzzles, echo poems, and countless other ephemera. The language of the so-called Second Silesian School overturned traditional norms in its reach back to the elaborate styles of Italian concettism and Spanish "Gongorism."[91] Critics of this movement use the term *Schwulst* (bombast) to characterize what they consider its inflationary rhetoric, especially the penchant for compounding figures, such as congeries and repetitive naming. The Breslau patrician Christian Hofmann von Hofmannswaldau (1616–79) turns Petrarchist imagery [Hoffmeister] — itself a scandal to readers who thought of poetry in moralistic terms — toward an erotic flirtation with death:

> Es wird der bleiche tod mit seiner kalten hand
> Dir endlich mit der zeit umb deine brüste streichen /
> Der liebliche corall der lippen wird verbleichen;
> Der schultern warmer schnee wird werden kalter sand /
> Der augen süsser blitz / die kräffte deiner hand /
> Für welchen solches fällt / die werden zeitlich weichen.

[Pale Death with his cold hand will eventually in time stroke you about your breasts. The lovely coral of your lips will pale; the warm snow of your shoulders will turn into cold sand. The sweet flash of your eyes, the powers of your hand — for whomever such gestures are made — these will weaken in time.]

The seventeenth-century debate, reminiscent of the one that swirled around Celtis, about whether to allow non-Christian elements in poetry or on stage was answered in individual ways:[92] in Nuremberg, Sigmund von Birken (1626–81) evicted the traditional mythological figures of pastoral eclogue and replaced them with Christian ones; conversely, Lohenstein's poems and historical dramas revel in Roman, Egyptian, and Turkish exoticism.

The practice of writing poems for special occasions (*Gelegenheitsdichtung*), whether in recognition of achievements within the republic of letters itself or to celebrate events in the life of a patron, city, or country, was common throughout Europe in the seventeenth century, as it had been in the sixteenth.[93] Cultivated in antiquity as a convivial style, it represented in the sixteenth century the largest corpus of Neo-Latin poetry (some 100,000 individual publications) and constituted the very "nerve center of early modern poetic and scholarly communication" [Kühlmann, "Neo-Latin"]. In his *Poeterey* Opitz warns against its potential abuse of the poetic calling: it should remain an amateur practice, lest poets be reduced in the public mind to mere hacks for hire. Despite the precaution, seventeenth-century German poets produced such poems in quantities that matched their earlier Neo-Latin counterparts. The occasional poem, which is by nature a social construct involving a triangular relationship between the poet, the occasion, and the addressee, has become a key genre for investigating the social role of poets in early modernity.

The spread of the Opitzian literary reform was hampered by the old want of a national political and cultural center as well as that of a standard German dialect; nevertheless, and in spite of the war's impediments on every side, the process moved forward. The reconstruction of the routes this process followed through Germany's many urban and courtly institutions has shed new light on cultural contexts. The most interesting concerned the demographics of the religious and social affiliations. That the reform was primarily a Protestant affair may seem obvious enough — but not "Protestant" in its original meaning of the combined evangelical fronts.[94] The confessional motor of the seventeenth-century reform was Calvinist, usually called Reformed. Furthermore, most of the reform's early patrons belonged to the nobility — as explained in the second part of this introduction, the phenomenon of noble patronage was one of the principles in the origins and genesis of the republic of letters — most of whom had little higher education, by contrast with the writers themselves, who were mostly university-trained *poetae doctae*. Good reasons existed for a man with political ambitions to stop short of the ultimate academic degree. There was always the sense, of course, that humanist education stood in the way of or was superfluous to actual political practice, and this sense only sharpened in the seventeenth century into a philosophical and pedagogical pragmatism. In some places already in the sixteenth century, moreover, *doctores* were legally barred from sitting on the innermost governing bodies. This was famously the case in Nuremberg.[95]

The significance of confessional affiliation was not adequately appreciated until the "discovery" of confessionalization in the 1980s.[96] Opitz himself makes an interesting case study [Verweyen]. In 1619, not long after having composed *Aristarchus*, Opitz moved to Heidelberg, the seat of the Calvinist court of Elector Palatine Friedrich V, where he matriculated at the university and became employed as a tutor in the home of the electoral privy counselor G. M. Lingelsheim (1556–1636). Lingelsheim's was one of the most active literary homes in Germany, and he himself had long been deeply involved in confessional politics in the Palatinate and across Europe.[97] It was in these circumstances that Opitz worked out the principles of his poetics and composed many of his early poems. The links fostered in Heidelberg between the ideas of nation and literature seemed to hinge on the political success of Friedrich, who was elected king of Bohemia to protect the interests of the Protestant Union after war broke out in 1618. After Friedrich's defeat in 1620, imperial forces occupied Heidelberg, and the political aspirations of the Reformed faith had to be recalculated. Confessional and aesthetic affinities quickly became apparent around Germany, most impressively in the Fruchtbringende Gesellschaft, whose largely aristocratic membership was mainly Calvinist-Reformed, as we saw earlier. The Fruchtbringende Gesellschaft rose rapidly to intellectual and cultural preeminence in Germany and influenced the founding of many more language and literary societies (*Sprachgesellschaften*). Among the most important were the Kürbishütte (1620s), the Aufrichtige Tannengesellschaft (Honorable Society of the Pines, 1633 in Strasbourg), the Deutschgesinnete Genossenschaft (Germanophile Brotherhood, 1642 in Hamburg), and the Pegnesischer Blumenorden (Flower Order on the Pegnitz, 1644 in Nuremberg).[98] The cultivation of the humanist values of friendship, peace, and humanity was not intended in the first place to serve spiritual reformation. It was practiced rather for the sake of the German language, though the reformed language was in turn to serve as the conduit to a general cultural renewal. This aspiration is voiced repeatedly in the correspondence and fiction of the literary societies.

It has been suggested that the war helped the German language "grow up," rather like the boy hero Simplicissimus in Grimmelshausen's (1621/2–1676) famous postwar novel *Der Abenteurliche Simplicissimus Teutsch* (The Adventurous Simplicissimus German, 1669). Simplicissimus (or, Simplicius) began life as an ignorant peasant but matured linguistically as he acquired the many idioms of the social situations forced upon him over the course of the war. One encounters the metaphors of war over and over in seventeenth-century German literature.[99]

In response to the perpetual state of war, a rich literature of consolation arose in Germany. Sometimes the themes of war and consolation exist side by side within a single work, as in a captivating moment in Book 1 of Grimmelshausen's novel. Simplicissimus has just fled an attack on the family farm by marauding soldiers only to become lost in the woods. Having fallen asleep in mortal fear, he wakes to the sweet voice of a hermit singing a song of consolation: "Komm Trost der Nacht, o Nachtigall" (Come, Consolation of Night, O Nightingale). Consolation literature may be classified as secular or spiritual, depending on the themes of the individual work or episode. Spiritual consolation belongs to the larger movement of religious literature and therefore adduces mainly biblical and spiritual themes and images. Secular types draw especially on the principles of Neo-Stoic philosophy.[100] Fleming's often anthologized sonnet "An sich" (To

Oneself), for example, encourages the reader to dare to refuse to be defeated, however daunting the odds may seem:[101]

> Sey dennoch unverzagt. Gieb dennoch unverlohren.
> Weich keinem Glücke nicht. Steh' höher als der Neid.

> [Be nevertheless undaunted. Act nevertheless undefeated. Yield not to any chance. Stand higher than envy.]

An indication outside of the realm of fiction of the importance of consolation was the hope expressed by Harsdörffer in 1643, in volume 3 of the *Frauenzimmer Gesprächspiele* (Playful Colloquies for the Ladies), that Boethius's *De consolatione philosophiae* would soon find a German translator.

Hymnody was one of the most innovative types of spiritual poetry in the Baroque. It derives mainly from two sixteenth-century sources: the Spanish mystical tradition of Teresa of Avila and Juan de la Cruz, and the sixteenth-century Lutheran hymn (*Kirchenlied*) repertoire. An early attempt in 1572 in Heidelberg by Paul Melissus Schede (1539–1602) to Germanize the French Huguenot Psalter turned out oddly for two reasons: he kept too close to the French versification rather than, as Opitz later insisted, using regular alternation of stressed and unstressed syllables; and, as he himself admitted, he aimed at too lofty a style for what is essentially a modest genre. A superior version by the Prussian humanist Ambrosius Lobwasser (1515–85) appeared the following year and was authorized by Elector Friedrich III. The Lutheran hymn, unlike almost all other reform genres, had its roots in indigenous culture but proved adaptable to baroque formal sensitivities. The Berlin pastor Paul Gerhardt (1607–76), following in the tradition of the late-humanist Lutheran hymnists Philipp Nicolai (1556–1608) and Johannes Heermann (1585–1647), wrote hymns of surpassing beauty. His best-known hymn, "O Haupt voll Blut und Wunden" (1656, in English-language hymnals as "O Sacred Head Now Wounded"), borrowed music composed in 1601 by Hanns Hassler. It is integrated into J. S. Bach's *Matthäus-Passion* (1727, 1736) as a repeating chorale.

Other writers specialized in spiritual lyrics more suited for reading than for singing. Klaj's declamatory oratorio has been mentioned, as have the religious sonnets of Greiffenberg and Gryphius. The Sulzbach polyhistor Christian Knorr von Rosenroth (1636–89) cultivated a synesthetic language that resonates with imagery from mysticism, alchemy, and kabala that was, for all that, quite singable. His "Abends-Andacht" (Evening Devotion) of 1684 continues to be anthologized in hymnbooks. The Catholic tradition was adapted by Friedrich Spee von Langenfeld (1591–1635) to portray affecting expressions of love: Jesus as the tender shepherd, or the soul as Christ's beloved. In the epigrams of the Catholic convert Johannes Scheffler (a.k.a. Angelus Silesius, the Silesian Angel, 1624–77), human and divine realms of thought and experience often converge startlingly: "Ich weiß das ohne mich GOtt nicht ein Nu kan leben" (I know that without me GOd cannot exist even one moment).

Italian spectacles (masque, carnival, ballet, opera) dominated the German stage for most of the seventeenth century. Performances of Italian opera are recorded in some of the larger German halls, such as Salzburg, Vienna, Innsbruck, and Prague, even prior to 1620. The first German-language opera, a production of Ottavio Rinuccini's *Dafne*, translated by Opitz and set to music (now lost) by Heinrich Schütz (1585–1672), was mounted in 1627. By the end of the century many more German operas were finding performances, especially on courtly stages in leading centers like Bayreuth, Braunschweig-Wolfenbüttel, Lüneburg, and Weissenfels; a bourgeois opera house was founded by Hanseatic merchants in Hamburg in 1678. For most of the century, however, German secular theater was handicapped by a shortage of stages; only small venues were available at most universities, schools, and courts. Perhaps in part for that reason, many German plays seem to have been conceived of only for reading (*Lesedramen*). Opitz's early translations of ancient tragedies, Seneca's *Trojan Women* (as *Die Trojerinnen*, 1625) and Sophocles' *Antigone* (1636), were no doubt intended to serve as models of translation.[102] To modern readers, many of these sometimes staggeringly erudite plays, documented in appendices that sometimes exceed the length of the dramas themselves, may be of more historical than literary interest. For example, Gryphius's *Ermordete Majestät, oder Carolus Stuardus* (Regicide, or Charles Stuart), written shortly after the execution of Charles I in 1649, is revealing of the German philosophy of sovereignty. However wrong Charles may have been for violating English royal custom vis-à-vis Parliament, Gryphius maintained an unwavering Lutheran loyalty to the principle of *Obrigkeit* (secular authority) and a correlative disdain for the rebellious Roundheads. Curiously, a scant ten years later Gryphius offered up a decidedly anti-Stuart view in the eponymous *Papinianus* (1659), which features a republican hero in the mold of the great Florentine civic humanists Coluccio Salutati and Leonardo Bruni. The late twentieth century found in the intriguing plots and psychological complications of Lohenstein's dramas reasons for a scholarly revival [Alexander].

Nevertheless, the major plays of Gryphius and Lohenstein and Johann Christian Hallmann (ca. 1640–ca. 1714) were in demand in theatrical-minded cities having stages large enough to accommodate considerable logistical demands. This was notably the case in Breslau (the German name for Wroclaw), home to two renowned schools, the Maria-Magdalena-Gymnasium and the Elisabeth-Gymnasium, both of which boasted excellent stages and active performance schedules, especially in the years between about 1643 and 1671. Lohenstein and Hallmann wrote a number of their dramas expressly for the Breslau stage and appeared as actors on occasion.[103] Despite a reactionary trend in the 1680s and 1690s against the theater — led by certain Pietist, orthodox Lutheran, and Calvinist moral fundamentalists — the theatrical tradition in Breslau continued into the early eighteenth century under the direction of the school rector Christian Gryphius (1649–1706), who produced several of the martyr- and tyrant-dramas of his father, Andreas Gryphius, on the stage of the Maria-Magdalena-Gymnasium.[104]

Whereas religious drama in sixteenth-century Germany and Switzerland had been primarily the domain of the Protestants (biblical drama, Reformation drama), in the seventeenth century it became the chief weapon in the literary arsenal of the Jesuits and the Counter-Reformation. Magnificent stages represented the three tiers of the universe — heaven, earth, and hell — and overwhelmed the senses and the will. It is reported that following one performance in Munich of Jakob Bidermann's *Cenodoxus* (1602), a play about a too-proud humanist whose learning and manners avail him nothing but damnation, several audience members, including a nobleman, were moved to take vows of celibacy and enter a monastery.

The novel, "the last major genre to be created in early modernity" [Garber], was imported into Germany through translation, since none of the forms was indigenous to Germany (*Prosaekloge*, "prose eclogue," represents a certain exception, as we shall see). Notwithstanding its immense popularity in other European national literatures of refinement and the fact of its authentic roots in antiquity (Hellenistic romance, Menippean satire), the novel receives no discussion in the *Buch von der Deutschen Poeterey*. As he did for the drama, however, Opitz produced translations of well-known European novels, most notably John Barclay's *Argenis* (1626–31, from Latin),[105] though later German writers of courtly novels followed these models only loosely [Solbach]. In their search for workable models, German writers of the first reform generation turned repeatedly to translations of successful European novels and epics ("novels" in verse). Thus, translation became one of the major occupations of the *Sprachgesellschaften*. Diederich von dem Werder (1584–1657), a diplomat and member of the Fruchtbringende Gesellschaft, in translating Torquato Tasso's *Gerusalemme Liberata* (as *Das Erlösete Jerusalem*, 1626) and Ludovico Ariosto's *Orlando Furioso* (1632–36), hoped to inspire a German epic poem of comparable sophistication. The Spanish pastoral novel *Diana* by Jorge de Montemayor was introduced into Germany in 1619 through the partial translation of Hans Ludwig von Kuffstein (1582–1656), an Austrian diplomat; it was left for Harsdörffer to complete, a generation later, in 1646. Harsdörffer's recommendation of Boethius was taken up by the Nuremberg physician Johann Hellwig (1609–74) and published in 1660.[106] This list of German translations of ancient and contemporary European novels could be extended indefinitely. But lest the impression remain that this activity was the pastime of dilettantes, let us recall that the German concept of imitation, *Nachahmung*, connoted emulation, a certain going-beyond the original. In Harsdörffer's formulation of the principle, the original can and should be "besser gemacht" (improved upon) if the poet is capable of "sinnreiche Erfindung" (ingenuity).[107] Harsdörffer mentions three strategies by which an original work can be improved in the German language: by enhancing rhetorical color, by bringing moral clarity to bear on the story, and by integrating authentic German themes and motifs.

As a result of this preliminary search for models, three distinct novelistic forms came to be practiced in seventeenth-century Germany: picaresque, pastoral, and courtly. Having evolved in sixteenth-century Spain from the models

Lazarillo de Tormes and *Don Quixote* as a knightly travesty of the medieval epic in the high courtly style, the picaresque novel (German, *Schelmenroman*) was imported by an anonymous translator into Germany in the second decade of the seventeenth century. However, we may trace the real origins of the German picaresque novel to the translation by the Bavarian chancery officer Ägidius Albertinus (ca. 1560–1620) of Mateo Alemán's *Gusman de Alfarache* (as *Der Landstörtzer* [The Vagrant, or Runagate], 1615). The eyewitness fiction of an anti-hero narrator, combined with an adventurous linear structure, proved to be the ideal vehicle for a realistic, if not real,[108] portrayal of war and human comedy. Christian Reuter's (1665–ca. 1712) *Schelmuffsky* (1696)[109] and some of the novels of Johann Beer (1655–1700), such as *Teutsche Winter-Nächte* (German Winter Nights, 1682),[110] can still be read with pleasure.

Grimmelshausen's *Simplicissimus*, however, ranges above not only the other German picaresque novels but all German novels of the seventeenth century and stands shoulder to shoulder with the greatest novels of the century in all of Europe.[111] It is one of those ironies of reception history that, in its own time, this novel, written by a modestly educated burgher in the language of the people — it delights in realistic attention to local detail, scenic description, and mastery of dialects — was disparaged and then ignored as inconsequential by the *cognoscente*. That notwithstanding, its general popularity prompted six editions (not to mention a spate of pirated versions) over the following six years before the author's death.[112] Scholars have concocted various theories to explain the work's underlying intention and effectiveness. One that riveted the attention of many scholars in the 1960s and 1970s sought to demonstrate that it is structured around astrological principles.[113] However that may be, *Simplicissimus* remains one of Germany's great contributions to world literature.

The German pastoral novel was assembled from multiple European traditions: southern (Italian and Spanish), exemplified by Jacopo Sannazaro's *Arcadia* and Montemayor's *Diana*; English, exemplified by Sidney's *Arcadia*; and French, exemplified by Honoré d'Urfé's *L'Astrée*. Plots typically revolve around the social misfortunes of the landed aristocracy in the wake of the economic crisis, the so-called *Kipper und Wipper* period between about 1620 and 1626, in which rural property values plunged and noble privileges vanished.[114] *Die verwüstete und verödete Schäferey* (The Devastated and Desolate Pastoral, anon., 1642) and Johann Thomas's (1624–80) *Damon und Lisille* (1663) are two of the literary responses to this time of crisis [Hoffmeister].

A second pastoral type, prose eclogue,[115] arose in Germany about midway through the Thirty Years' War. It was an invention of Opitz — exemplified in his *Schäferey von der Nimpfen Hercinie* (Pastoral of the Nymph Hercinie, 1630) — which alternated in equal measure prose narration (pastoral novel) and versified passages (eclogue), to which he added a substantial middle panegyrical section in verse dedicated to his patron. It was brought to maturity by the so-called *Schäferdichter* (shepherd poets) in Nuremberg in the 1640s. Until the literary sociological scholarship of the 1960s discovered its critical potential, the prose eclogue had been largely dismissed, owing to the playful nature of the conversations and poetic experiments that constitute most of the

action, as a type of baroque trivial literature.[116] Its expansive tripartite structure, consisting of an opening walk through nature, a middle panegyric, and a
closing walk through nature, allows ample opportunity for eclectic observations — on nature, morality, industry, history, customs — that often contain
implicit social criticism.[117] The great scholar of modern utopia Ernst Bloch
observed that the counterworld of Arcadia, by virtue of its qualities of
Freundlichkeit, Friedlichkeit, Menschlichkeit (friendliness, peacefulness, humanity), precisely the qualities that the real world lacks, constitutes a negative criticism.[118] This negative potential makes prose eclogue one of the best examples
in early modern German literature of dialogical narrative.

The sensationally popular sixteenth-century courtly romance *Amadís de
Gaula*, first published in a Portuguese version in 1508 and subsequently translated, adapted, and broadened in Spanish, French, German, and other languages by the end of the century, was the general model for the
seventeenth-century German courtly novel (or novel of state). Opitz's translation of Barclay's *Argenis* helped to establish the literary representation of absolutist culture with its trappings of power and courtly manners, including a
highly stylized type of love. Philipp von Zesen's (1619–89) translation in 1645
of Madeleine de Scudéry's (1607–1701) widely read French novel *Ibrahim
Bassa* (1641) superseded the Barclay-Opitz model. Inexplicably, Zesen did not
include in his translation Scudéry's introduction, widely considered to be the
best theoretical discussion of the courtly novel of the century. It was Scudéry
who drew the historical connection to the Greek romance (Heliodorus's
Aithiopika), which enhanced the appeal of noble lovers and their adventures in
exotic lands. The cast of characters sometimes reached into the hundreds, and
plots were proportionately complicated. As a result of new information gathered from unpublished manuscripts and other archival research in the second
half of the twentieth century, Lohenstein's *Arminius* (1689–90)[119] and Duke
Anton Ulrich's *Octavia* (1677–79, 1703–4, 1712–14) are now appreciated as
milestones in the literary representation of political theory.[120] With these two
works, Lohenstein and Anton Ulrich transcended the role of writers of adventurous entertainment and attained to the stature of political visionaries.
Lohenstein wrote *Arminius* (as explained above, Arminius was the Germanic
tribal leader praised by Tacitus for his victory over Roman forces in the first
century A.D.) in the wake of Louis XIV's hegemonic advances on German territory and his revocation of the Edict of Nantes in 1685; the latter action effectively returned France to a policy of religious intolerance.[121] Against this state
of affairs *Arminius* presents an alternative of a unified Germany under a great
emperor. Similarly, Anton Ulrich seems to have been negotiating his way
through the never-completed *Octavia* toward a grand solution to the confessional conflicts that had so long beset Germany and Europe.

Thus, at the end of the early modern period twin visions of national unity
and religious peace arose and looked confidently across the threshold of Old
Europe into modernity. It was a vision that inspired the elderly Kant to speculations about a permanent peace: "As the times required for equal steps of progress
become, we hope, shorter and shorter, perpetual peace is a problem which,

gradually working out its own solution, steadily approaches its goal."[122] Hocke may have been overly sanguine about the Baroque's search for stability: there would be no real stability either in the Baroque or any time soon in Europe. What remains of that search is the same thing that remained around 1700 of the idea expressed some 400 years earlier by Dante — and repeated time and again throughout the early modern period — of the possibility of political unity, religious concord, and the renewal of ancient greatness in the modern world.

Notes

[1] 15 February 1824. In *Gespräche mit Goethe in den letzten Jahren seines Lebens* (Berlin: Deutsche Buchgemeinschaft, 1984). Translation: *Conversations with Eckermann (1823–1832)*, trans. John Oxenford (San Francisco: North Point, 1984), 31.

[2] This is the question that motivates the study by Klaus Garber, "Begin with Goethe? Forgotten Traditions at the Threshold of the Modern Age," trans. Karl F. Otto Jr., in *Imperiled Heritage: Tradition, History, and Utopia in Early Modern German Literature*, ed. Max Reinhart, Studies in European Cultural Transition 5 (Aldershot: Ashgate, 2000), 209 51.

[3] See, for example, the standard work by Peter Kriedte, *Peasants, Landlords and Merchant Capitalists: Europe and the World Economy 1500–1800* (Cambridge: Cambridge UP, 1983).

[4] See Rondo Cameron, "A New View of European Industrialization," *The Economic History Review* N.S. 38, no. 1 (1985): 1–23. For literature, however, the year 1750 is more commonly taken as the turning point to modernity, marked by the publication of Klopstock's *Der Messias* (1748).

[5] See Georg G. Iggers and James M. Powell, eds., *Leopold von Ranke and the Shaping of the Historical Discipline* (Syracuse: Syracuse UP, 1990), and Georg G. Iggers, *The German Conception of History: The National Tradition of Historical Thought from Herder to the Present*, rev. ed. (Middletown, CT: Wesleyan UP, 1983). The most recent summary of this narrative has been drawn in a too-little-known paper by Thomas A. Brady Jr., *The Protestant Reformation in German History*, Occasional Paper No. 22 (Washington, DC: German Historical Institute, 1997).

[6] Named after the journal *Annales d'histoire économique et sociale*, founded in 1929 by Marc Bloch and Lucien Lebvre. This "school" rejected the former dominant political historiography in favor of an interdisciplinary one emphasizing geography and sociology and viewing history from a perspective of the *longue durée*.

[7] Besides Klaus Garber's chapter in the present volume see also his discussion in his preface, trans. Michael T. Jones and Max Reinhart (as well as the observations in the editor's introduction), in Garber, *Imperiled Heritage*, ix–xv (esp. xi–xii) and xvi–xxx.

[8] The *Annales* historians recognized certain factors, constituting *mentalité*, beyond the formal ones (events, genre, motifs, structure, and so on) that humans bring to experience, say, of literature, that have their own power to shape meaning. These include values and beliefs. Sometimes "culture" is used in the broad sense for this force.

[9] "In the Middle Ages both sides of human consciousness [. . .] lay dreaming or half awake beneath a common veil. The veil was woven of faith, illusion and childish

prepossession, through which the world and history were seen clad in strange hues. [. . .] In Italy this veil first melted into air; an *objective* treatment and consideration of the state and of all the things of this world became possible. The *subjective* side at the same time asserted itself with corresponding emphasis; man became a spiritual *individual*, and recognised himself as such." Jacob Burckhardt, *The Civilisation of the Renaissance in Italy: An Essay* (1860), trans. S. G. C. Middlemore (London: The Folio Society, 2004), 103.

[10] On Heinrich von Treitschke's views see Jan Herman Brinks, "Luther and the German State," *The Heythrop Journal* 39, no. 1 (1998): 1–17.

[11] Heinrich Wölfflin, *Renaissance und Barock: eine Untersuchung über Wesen und Entstehung des Barockstils in Italien* (Munich: Ackermann, 1888). National Socialism would exploit such categories to "discover" the "manly Goth."

[12] Klaus Garber argues that the first scholar to have made this case convincingly was Konrad Burdach (1859–1936), who related the Renaissance back to the reformist (protohumanist) theology of the Middle Ages. See "Versunkene Monumentalität: Das Werk Konrad Burdachs," in *Kulturwissenschaftler des 20. Jahrhunderts: Ihr Werk im Blick auf das Europa der Frühen Neuzeit*, ed. Garber, with Sabine Kleymann (Munich: Fink, 2002), 109–57. See also the classic revision of the Renaissance by Wallace K. Ferguson, *The Renaissance in Historical Thought* (Cambridge, MA: Riverside, 1948).

[13] This view was held most notably by Georg Gervinus. See Peter Hohendahl, "Gervinus als Historiker des Barockzeitalters," in *Europäische Barock-Rezeption*, ed. Klaus Garber, Wolfenbütteler Arbeiten zur Barockforschung 20 (Wiesbaden: Harrassowitz, 1991), 561–76, here 562, note 2.

[14] This position was espoused by spokesmen of the so-called "konservative Revolution" of the early twentieth century, such as Hugo von Hofmannsthal and Rudolf Borchardt.

[15] Thomas A. Brady Jr., Heiko A. Oberman, and James D. Tracy, eds., *Handbook of European History, 1400–1600* (Leiden: Brill, 1994–95), 1:xxi. The Motley reference regards his discussion of Luther in *Democracy: The Climax of Political Progress and the Destiny of Advanced Races: An Essay*, 2nd ed. (Glasgow, 1869), 23.

[16] See Wilfried Barner, *Barockrhetorik: Untersuchungen zu ihren geschichtlichen Grundlagen* (1970), 2nd ed. (Tübingen: Niemeyer, 2002).

[17] Burckhardt, *Cicerone: eine Anleitung zum Genuß der Kunstwerke Italiens* (Basel: Schweighauser, 1855).

[18] For the central terms of this accord see "Der Augsburger Religionsfriede," in *Deutsche Geschichte in Quellen und Darstellung*, vol. 3, *Reformationszeit 1495–1555*, ed. Ulrich Höpf (Stuttgart: Reclam, 2001), 471–84.

[19] "The Peasant War spawned strict supervision and state control which modern research tends to associate with 'confessionalization,' a development today relegated to the later-half of the century." "Introduction: The Unsettling Settlements," in Brady, Oberman, and Tracy, eds., *Handbook of European History, 1400–1600*, 2:xviii.

[20] See, among the many studies, Robert M. Kingdon, "International Calvinism," in Brady, Oberman, and Tracy, eds., *Handbook of European History, 1400–1600*, 2:249–82; W. Fred Graham, ed., *Later Calvinism: International Perspectives*, Sixteenth Century Essays & Studies 22 (Kirksville, MO: Sixteenth Century Journal Publications, 1994); and Menna Prestwich, ed., *International Calvinism: 1541–1715* (Oxford: Clarendon, 1985).

[21] This thought may be compared with Stephen Greenblatt's notion of social energy in *Shakespearean Negotiations: The Circulation of Social Energy in Renaissance England,*

New Historicism: Studies in Cultural Poetics, series no. 4 (Berkeley: U of California P, 1988), though among German early modernists the belief still prevails that texts had more authorial stability than this notion may seem to imply.

[22] Heiko A. Oberman, *The Dawn of the Reformation: Essays in Late Medieval and Early Reformation Thought* (Edinburgh: T. & T. Clark, 1986).

[23] Andreas Solbach, in the opening of his chapter in this volume, speaks of the "vitality" of the German tradition in the transmission of medieval forms — "whether anecdotes, short tales, or novelistic forms" — into the early modern period. (Henceforth, references to chapters in this volume will be indicated simply by the name of the author in square brackets; e.g., as here: [Garber]).

[24] "Je stereotyper ein Text das Gattungshafte wiederholt, desto geringer ist sein Kunstcharakter und desto geringer ist auch sein Grad an Geschichtlichkeit." Hans Robert Jauss, "Theorie der Gattungen und Literatur des Mittelalters," in *Alterität und Modernität der mittelalterlichen Literatur: Gesammelte Aufsätze 1956–1976* (Munich: Fink, 1977), 339.

[25] See especially Wilhelm Kühlmann, "Kombinatorisches Schreiben — 'Intertextualität' als Konzept frühneuzeitlicher Erfolgsautoren (Rollenhagen, Moscherosch)," in *Intertextualität in der Frühen Neuzeit: Studien zu ihren theoretischen und praktischen Perspektiven*, ed. Kühlmann and Wolfgang Neuber (Frankfurt am Main: Lang, 1994), 111–39.

[26] See Heinz Schilling, "Der Gesellschaftsvergleich in der Frühneuzeit-Forschung — ein Erfahrungsbericht und einige (methodisch-theoretische) Schlussfolgerungen," in Hartmut Kaelbe and Jürgen Schriewer, eds., *Vergleich und Transfer: Komparatistik in den Sozial-, Geschichts- und Kulturwissenschaften* (Frankfurt am Main: Campus, 2003), 283ff.

[27] Much excellent research on this subject has been done — especially that of Klaus Conermann, such as his edition *Fruchtbringende Gesellschaft: Der Fruchtbringenden Gesellschaft Geöffneter Erzschrein, das Köthener Gesellschaftsbuch Fürst Ludwigs I. von Anhalt-Köthen 1617–1650*, 3 vols. (Weinheim: VCH, 1985) — without this question having been clarified. More recent research continues to suggest how sensitive the issue was, but still without being fully able to explain why. See Max Reinhart, "Battle of the Tapestries: A War-Time Debate in Anhalt-Köthen (Georg Philipp Harsdörffer's *Peristromata Turcica* and *Aulaea Romana*, 1641–1642)," *Daphnis* 27, nos. 2–3 (1998): 291–333.

[28] Research on this question has not moved beyond the options posed a quarter-century ago by Werner Schneiders, "Gottesreich und gelehrte Gesellschaft: Zwei politische Modelle bei G. W. Leibniz," in *Università, Accademie e Società scientifiche in Italia e in Germania dal Cinquecento al Settecento*, ed. Laetitia Boehm and Ezio Raimondi (Bologna: Il Mulino, 1981), 395–419, and Klaus Garber, "Zentraleuropäischer Calvinismus und deutsche 'Barock'-Literatur: Zu den konfessionspolitischen Ursprüngen der deutschen Nationalliteratur," in *Die reformierte Konfessionalisierung in Deutschland — Das Problem der "Zweiten Reformation,"* ed. Heinz Schilling (Gütersloh: Mohn, 1986), 317–48.

[29] Gombrich, *A Little History of the World* (1936), trans. Caroline Mustill (New Haven: Yale UP, 2005), 163.

[30] To take only the topic of the early modern family see especially studies by Steven Ozment, such as *Ancestors: The Loving Family in Old Europe* (Cambridge: Harvard UP, 2001), and *Flesh and Spirit: Private Life in Early Modern Germany* (New York: Viking, 1999). See also the volume in honor of Ozment edited by Mark R. Forster and

Benjamin J. Kaplan, *Piety and Family in Early Modern Europe* (Aldershot: Ashgate, 2005).

[31] Stolleis, "Einleitung," in *Staat und Staatsräson in der frühen Neuzeit: Studien zur Geschichte des öffentlichen Rechts*, suhrkamp taschenbuch wissenschaft 878 (Frankfurt am Main: Suhrkamp, 1990), 9.

[32] "[D]ie Urheber sprechen aus einer sozialen Lage [. . .] heraus; sie sprechen in eine Lage [. . .] hinein, die für eine ganz spezifische [. . .] Gesellschaft [. . .] von Menschen charakteristisch ist." Elias, "Thomas Morus' Staatskritik: Mit Überlegungen zur Bestimmung des Begriffs Utopie," in *Utopieforschung*, ed. Wilhelm Voßkamp, suhrkamp taschenbuch 1159 (Frankfurt am Main: Suhrkamp, 1985), 2:101.

[33] On *Verwilderung*, "barbarization," see Karlheinz Stierle, "Die Verwilderung des Romans als Ursprung seiner Möglichkeit," in *Literatur in der Gesellschaft des Spätmittelalters*, ed. Hans Ulrich Gumbrecht (Heidelberg: Winter, 1980), 253–313.

[34] The most important treatise on church politics was *Defensor pacis* (Defender of Peace), written in 1324 by the rector of the University of Paris, Marsilius of Padua. Marsilius blamed the clergy for claiming too great authority in temporal affairs. This abuse was to be corrected, in his view, by greater participation of laity, formed as councils, in ecclesiastical decision-making.

[35] See George Huppert, *After the Black Death: A Social History of Early Modern Europe* (Bloomington: Indiana UP, 1986).

[36] Citing Bernhard Burchert's *Die Anfänge des Prosaromans in Deutschland: Die Prosaerzählungen Elisabeths von Nassau-Saarbrücken* (Frankfurt am Main: Lang, 1987), Solbach emphasizes the role of prose in this appeal to the new bourgeoisie: "Some scholars believe that Elisabeth embraced the new literary form of expression in order to convey to her peers — and specifically to her son, Johann III — that the rise of a potent urban bourgeoisie made it historically necessary to shift from a confrontational (top-down) to a cooperative (horizontal) type of politics based on a shared form of communication."

[37] "There is a pervasive misconception that late medieval religion had become lax and the medieval church tolerant to a fault of human weakness, a conclusion often drawn in contrast to Protestantism. Only the religiously indifferent, unbelieving, and/or reclusive could have found them to be such." Steven Ozment, *The Age of Reform 1250–1550: An Intellectual and Religious History of Late Medieval and Reformation Europe* (New Haven: Yale UP, 1980), 216. See also John Van Engen, "The Church in the Fifteenth Century," in Brady, Oberman, and Tracy, eds., *Handbook of European History, 1400–1600*, 1:305–30.

[38] See Steven E. Ozment, *Homo spiritualis: A Comparative Study of the Anthropology of Johannes Tauler, Jean Gerson and Martin Luther (1509–16) in the Context of Their Theological Thought* (Leiden: Brill, 1969).

[39] See Erika Rummel, "Voices of Reform from Hus to Erasmus," in Brady, Oberman, and Tracy, eds., *Handbook of European History, 1400–1600*, 2:61–92.

[40] See Helmut Kreuzer, ed., *Verschriftlichung* (Stuttgart: Metzler, 1997), and Jan-Dirk Müller, *"Aufführung" und "Schrift" in Mittelalter und früher Neuzeit* (Stuttgart: Metzler, 1996).

[41] Pascal, *German Literature in the 16th and 17th Centuries: Renaissance — Reformation — Baroque* (New York: Barnes & Noble, 1968), 10.

[42] Research into this subject began in the former GDR with a collection of studies on the social history of what we now call early modern Europe: Robert Weimann, Werner Lenk, and J. J. Slomka, eds., *Renaissanceliteratur und frühbürgerliche Revolution:*

Studien zu den sozial- und ideologiegeschichtlichen Grundlagen europäischer Nationalliteraturen (Berlin: Aufbau, 1976). More recently see Klaus Garber, "The Republic of Letters and the Absolutist State: Nine Theses," trans. Max Reinhart, in Garber, *Imperiled Heritage*, 41–53.

[43] See Iring Fetscher and Herfried Münkler, eds., *Pipers Handbuch der Politischen Ideen*, vol. 2 (Munich: Piper, 1990).

[44] The word *Humanismus* was coined in Germany in the early nineteenth century.

[45] Dante had made his plans known to compose his *Divina Commedia* in Italian, for which he was reproached by the grammarian Giovanni, who insisted that the vernacular should be reserved only for humble speech.

[46] This extremely interesting topic is vividly presented in two sources: Werner Bahner, "Dantes theoretische Bemühungen um die Emanzipation der italienischen Literatursprache," in *Formen, Ideen, Prozesse in den Literaturen der romanischen Völker* (Berlin: Akademie, 1977), and Konrad Krautter, *Die Renaissance der Bukolik in der lateinischen Literatur des 14. Jahrhunderts: Von Dante bis Petrarca* (Munich: Fink, 1983). See also Klaus Garber, "Utopia and the Green World: Critique and Anticipation in Pastoral Poetry," trans. James F. Ehrman, in Garber, *Imperiled Heritage*, 73–116, here 82–83.

[47] For an introduction specific to early modern Germany see Volker Sinemus, *Poetik und Rhetorik im frühmodernen deutschen Staat: Sozialgeschichtliche Bedingungen des Normenwandels im 17. Jahrhundert* (Göttingen: Vandenhoeck & Ruprecht, 1978); Klaus Bleeck and Jörn Garber, "Nobilitas: Standes- und Privilegienlegitimation in deutschen Adelstheorien des 16. und 17. Jahrhunderts," in *Hof, Staat und Gesellschaft in der Literatur des 17. Jahrhunderts*, ed. Elger Blühm et al. (Amsterdam: Rodopi, 1982), 49–114; and Klaus Garber, "Zur Statuskonkurrenz von Adel und gelehrtem Bürgertum im theoretischen Schrifttum des 17. Jahrhunderts: Veit Ludwig von Seckendorffs *Teutscher Fürstenstaat* und die deutsche 'Barockliteratur,'" ibid., 115–43.

[48] See Brandon Bradshaw, "Transalpine Humanism," in *The Cambridge History of Political Thought*, ed. J. H. Burns (Cambridge: Cambridge UP, 1991), 95–131.

[49] See Hans Baron, *The Crisis of the Early Italian Renaissance: Civic Humanism and Republican Liberty in an Age of Classicism and Tyranny* (1955), rev. ed. (Princeton: Princeton UP, 1966).

[50] See Frank Baron, "Peter Luder," in *German Writers of the Renaissance and Reformation, 1280–1580*, ed. Max Reinhart and James Hardin, vol. 179 of *Dictionary of Literary Biography* (Detroit: Gale Research, 1997), 129–34, here 130.

[51] See Gerald Strauss, "Ideas of *Reformatio* and *Renovatio* from the Middle Ages to the Reformation," in Brady, Oberman, and Tracy, eds., *Handbook of European History, 1400–1600*, 2:1–30.

[52] Klaus Garber, "Sozietäten, Akademien, Sprachgesellschaften," in *Europäische Enzyklopädie zu Philosophie und Wissenschaften*, ed. Hans Jörg Sandkühler (Hamburg: Meiner, 1990), 366–84, here 366.

[53] Celtis, "Ad Ioannem Vigilium," in *Libri Odarum quatuor*, ll. 48–55. Quoted from Hedwig Heger, ed., *Spätmittelalter, Humanismus, Reformation: Texte und Zeugnisse*, vol. II/2 of *Die Deutsche Literatur: Texte und Zeugnisse* (Munich: Beck, 1978), 2:29–33, here 31–32.

[54] Dach, "Perstet amicitiae semper venerabile Faedus!," in *Gedichte des Barock*, comp. and ed. Ulrich Maché and Volker Meid, Universal-Bibliothek 9975 (Stuttgart: Reclam, 1980), 86–87.

[55] *Deutsche Gegenreformation und deutsches Barock: Die deutsche Literatur im Zeitraum des 17. Jahrhunderts* (1935), 3rd ed. (Stuttgart: Metzler, 1964), 43.

[56] See Max Reinhart, "Welt und Gegenwelt im Nürnberg des 17. Jahrhunderts: Ein einleitendes Wort zur sozialkritischen Funktion der Prosaekloge im Pegnesischen Blumenorden," in *Pegnesischer Blumenorden in Nürnberg: Festschrift zum 350jährigen Jubiläum*, ed. Werner Kügel (Nuremberg: Tümmel, 1994), 1–6. For more on the genre of prose eclogue see the "Late Humanism and Baroque" section below.

[57] See Klaus Garber, "Paris, Capital of European Late Humanism: Jacques Auguste de Thou and the Cabinet Dupuy," trans. Joe G. Delap, in Garber, *Imperiled Heritage*, 54–72.

[58] See Conermann, *Fruchtbringende Gesellschaft*, 2:31.

[59] See Karl F. Otto, *Die Sprachgesellschaften*, Sammlung Metzler 109 (Stuttgart: Metzler, 1972).

[60] Max Reinhart, "Poets and Politics: The Transgressive Turn of History in Seventeenth-Century Nürnberg," *Daphnis* 20, no. 1 (1991): 199–229, describes one such confrontation between the intellectual estate and the ruling patriciate. This article built on the little-known study by Ferdinand Elsener, "Die Doktorwürde in einem 'Consilium' der Tübinger Juristenfakultät des 18. Jahrhunderts: ein Beitrag zur Geschichte der Stände im 'Imperium Romano-Germanicum,' " in his *Mélanges Philippe Meylan: Recueil de travaux publiés par la Faculté de droit* (Lausanne: Impr. Centrale, 1963), 2:25–40.

[61] See Eckhard Bernstein, *Die Literatur des deutschen Frühhumanismus*, Sammlung Metzler 168 (Stuttgart: Metzler, 1978).

[62] See Lewis Spitz, *The Religious Renaissance of the German Humanists* (Cambridge: Harvard UP, 1963).

[63] An excellent introduction is Heinz Otto Burger, *Renaissance, Humanismus, Reformation: Deutsche Literatur im europäischen Kontext* (Bad Homburg: Gehlen, 1969).

[64] See for instance the large *Katalog der fürstlich Stolberg-Stolberg'schen Leichenpredigten-Sammlung*, vols. I–IV/2, ed. Friedrich Wecken, Bibliographie familiengeschichtlicher Quellen 2 (Leipzig: Degener, 1927–28). Most of the individually printed works are available in Wolfenbüttel, Germany, at the Herzog-August-Bibliothek.

[65] See Joseph Leo Koerner, *The Moment of Self-Portraiture in German Renaissance Art* (Chicago: U of Chicago P, 1993).

[66] See Frank Borchardt, *German Antiquity in Renaissance Myth* (Baltimore: Johns Hopkins UP, 1971).

[67] See Donald R. Kelly, "*Tacitus Noster*: The *Germania* in the Renaissance and Reformation," in *Tacitus and the Tacitean Tradition*, ed. T. J. Luce and A. J. Woodman (Princeton: Princeton UP, 1993), 152–67. For the later period of humanism see Michael Stolleis, "Public Law and Patriotism in the Holy Roman Empire," in *Infinite Boundaries: Order, Disorder, and Reorder in Early Modern German Culture*, ed. Max Reinhart, Sixteenth Century Essays & Studies 40 (Kirksville, MO: Sixteenth Century Journal Publishers, 1998), 11–33.

[68] Celtis, *Oratio in gymnasio in Ingelstadio publice recitata*, in *Selections from Conrad Celtis 1459–1508*, trans. and ed. Leonard Forster (Cambridge: Cambridge UP, 1948), 36–64, here 60.

[69] Hutten of course wrote in Latin. The German comes from a translation edition by Martin Treu, *Arminius*, in *Ulrich von Hutten: Die Schule des Tyrannen: Lateinische Schriften* (Darmstadt: Wissenschaftliche Buchgesellschaft, 1997), 191–206, here 193.

[70] Heinz Scheible, "Melanchthons Bildungsprogramm," in *Lebenslehren und Weltentwürfe im Übergang vom Mittelalter zur Neuzeit: Politik, Bildung, Naturkunde, Theologie*, ed. Hartmut Boockmann, Bernd Moeller, and Karl Stackmann (Göttingen: Vandenhoeck & Ruprecht, 1989), 233–48.

[71] Translation edition (Luther's text is drastically abbreviated): *Erasmus — Luther: Discourse on Free Will*, trans. and ed. Ernst F. Winter (New York: Continuum, 2000).

[72] See Walter M. Gordon, *Humanist Play and Belief: The Seriocomic Art of Desiderius Erasmus*, Erasmus Studies 9 (Toronto: U of Toronto P, 1990).

[73] See Erika Rummel, *The Confessionalization of Humanism in Reformation Germany* (New York: Oxford UP, 2000), and most recently Ute Lotz-Heumann and Matthias Pohlig, "Confessionalization and Literature in the Empire, 1555–1700, *Central European History* 40 (2007): 35–61.

[74] Hessus, "In Martinvm Lvthervm elegiarvm libellus: De eius in urbem Erphurdiam ingressu, Elegia prima," in *Humanistische Lyrik des 16. Jahrhunderts*, comp. and ed. Wilhelm Kühlmann, Robert Seidel, and Hermann Wiegand, Bibliothek der Frühen Neuzeit 5 (Frankfurt am Main: Deutscher Klassiker Verlag, 1997), 252.

[75] Sachs, *Die wittembergisch Nachtigall, die man ietzt höret überall*, in *Hans Sachsens Gedichte [und] ausgewählte Werke* (Leipzig: Insel, 1911), 1:8–24, here 22.

[76] Garber, "Sozietäten, Akademien, Sprachgesellschaften," 377a.

[77] See Geoffrey Parker, "Germany Before the War," in *The Thirty Years' War* (London: Routledge, 1984), 12–24.

[78] See Elisabeth G. Gleason, "Catholic Reformation, Counterreformation and Papal Reform in the Sixteenth Century," in Brady, Oberman, and Tracy, eds., *Handbook of European History, 1400–1600*, 2:317–45.

[79] Jeffrey K. Jue, "Protestant Irenicism and the Millenium: Mede and the Hartlib Circle," in *Heaven upon Earth*, Archives internationales d'histoire des idées 194 (Dordrecht: Springer, 2006), 65–85. An extreme devotion to the thought of Erasmus developed as early as the 1520s and 1530s in Spain, a movement known as *Erasmianismo*, which continued to be vital until around 1600. The possible connections between Spanish Erasmianism and northern irenicism have not been well traced.

[80] See Heinz Schilling, ed., *Die reformierte Konfessionalisierung in Deutschland: Das Problem der "Zweiten Reformation"* (Gütersloh: Mohn, 1986).

[81] See Günter Brinkmann, "*Das Irenicum* des David Pareus in theologiegeschichtlicher Sicht" (Ph.D. diss., University of Marburg, 1971).

[82] Bernegger, *Tuba pacis* (1621). See the published dissertation by Waltraud Foitzik, *"Tuba pacis": Matthias Bernegger und der Friedensgedanke des 17. Jahrhunderts* (Ph.D. diss., University of Münster, 1955).

[83] Rist (with Ernst Stapel), *Irenaromachia Das ist Eine newe Tragico-comaedia von Fried und Krieg* (1630).

[84] Translated by Willard R. Trask as *European Literature and the Latin Middle Ages* (1953), 7th ed. (Princeton: Princeton UP, 1990).

[85] Edited by Curt Grützmacher and published by Rowohlt (Reinbek bei Hamburg); new edition 1991.

[86] The year 1572 has sometimes been taken by literary historians as the Baroque's *terminus a quo*. The watershed event of that year was the publication of Paul Melissus Schede's German translation of the French Huguenot Psalter. This work will receive comment later in this introduction.

[87] Erich Trunz, "Der deutsche Späthumanismus um 1600 als Standeskultur" (1931), in *Deutsche Barockforschung*, ed. Richard Alewyn, 2nd ed. (Cologne: Kiepenheuer & Witsch, 1966), 147–81.

[88] Most importantly, Kühlmann et al., eds., *Humanistische Lyrik*; still useful but currently out of print, *Lateinische Gedichte deutscher Humanisten*, 2nd ed., comp. and ed. Harry C. Schnur, Universal-Bibliothek 8739 (Stuttgart: Reclam, 1978).

[89] See Conrad Wiedemann, *Johann Klaj und seine Redeoratorien: Untersuchungen zur Dichtung eines deutschen Barockmanieristen* (Nuremberg: Carl, 1966).

[90] The classical example is *Aeneid* 1.157–79.

[91] "Gongorism," an extravagant style, *estilo culto*, named after the Spanish baroque lyric poet Luis de Góngora y Argota (1561–1627).

[92] See Joachim Dyck, *Athen und Jerusalem: Die Tradition der argumentativen Verknüpfung von Bibel und Poesie im 17. und 18. Jahrhundert* (Munich: Beck, 1977).

[93] See Wulf Segebrecht, *Das Gelegenheitsgedicht: ein Beitrag zur Geschichte und Poetik der deutschen Lyrik* (Stuttgart: Metzler, 1977), and Klaus Garber, ed., *Handbuch des personalen Gelegenheitsschrifttums in europäischen Bibliotheken und Archiven* (Hildesheim: Olms-Weidmann, 2001–).

[94] The Catholic majority at the Diet of Speyer in 1529 lumped all parties who continued to support the evangelical movement into the "protesting estates," and anyone who left the Catholic fold was considered a "protestant."

[95] See Gerald Strauss, *Nuremberg in the Sixteenth Century* (New York: Wiley, 1966).

[96] Two of the first discussions were Wolfgang Reinhard, "Zwang zur Konfessionalisierung? Prologomena zu einer Theorie des konfessionellen Zeitalters," *Zeitschrift für historische Forschung* 10 (1983): 268–77, and Heinz Schilling, "Die Konfessionalisierung im Reich: Religiöser und gesellschaftlicher Wandel in Deutschland zwischen 1555 und 1620," *Historische Zeitschrift* 246 (1988): 1–45. The first major study of its implications for literature was Garber, "Zentraleuropäischer Calvinismus und deutsche 'Barock'-Literatur."

[97] Axel E. Walter, *Späthumanismus und Konfessionspolitik: Die europäische Gelehrtenrepublik um 1600 im Spiegel der Korrespondenzen Georg Michael Lingelsheims*, Frühe Neuzeit 95 (Tübingen: Niemeyer, 2004).

[98] To begin with the vast scholarship see Otto, *Die Sprachgesellschaften*; Martin Bircher and Ferdinand van Ingen, eds., *Sprachgesellschaften, Sozietäten, Dichtergruppen*, Wolfenbütteler Arbeiten zur Barockforschung 7 (Hamburg: Hauswedell, 1978); Sebastian Neumeister and Conrad Wiedemann, eds., *Res Publica Litteraria: Die Institutionen der Gelehrsamkeit in der frühen Neuzeit*, 2 vols., Wolfenbütteler Arbeiten zur Barockforschung 14 (Wiesbaden: Harrassowitz, 1987); and Klaus Garber, ed., *Europäische Sozietätsbewegung und demokratische Tradition: die europäischen Akademien der Frühen Neuzeit zwischen Frührenaissance und Spätaufklärung*, 2 vols., Frühe Neuzeit 27 (Tübingen: Niemeyer, 1996).

[99] See especially Marianne Beyer-Fröhlich, *Selbstzeugnisse aus dem Dreissigjährigen Krieg und dem Barock* (Darmstadt: Wissenschaftliche Buchgesellschaft, 1970).

[100] The classic formulation of this philosophy at the time was found in Justus Lipsius's *De constantia* (1584), soon thereafter translated into German by Andreas Viritius as *Von der Beständigkeit* (1599).

[101] The attitude of Fleming's poem is singularly reflected in certain songs by Wolf Biermann written in the former East Germany: for example, in "Trotz alledem" and, especially, "Ermutigung," which begins: "Du, laß dich nicht verhärten / In dieser harten Zeit" (You, don't let yourself be hardened in this hard time).

[102] See Richard Alewyn, *Vorbarocker Klassizismus und griechische Tragödie: Analyse der Antigone-Übersetzung des Martin Opitz* (1926; repr., Darmstadt: Wissenschaftliche Buchgesellschaft, 1962).

[103] See Roswitha Schieb, *Literarischer Reiseführer Breslau: Sieben Stadtspaziergänge* (Potsdam: Deutsches Kulturforum Östliches Europa, 2004).

[104] See James Hardin, "Authorship as Job Requirement: Seventeenth-Century School Drama and Christian Gryphius," in *The Professions of Authorship: Essays in Honor of Matthew J. Bruccoli*, ed. Richard Layman and Joel Myerson (Columbia, SC: U of South Carolina P, 1996).

[105] Opitz also published "an improved translation" (Pascal, *German Literature*, 131) of Sir Philip Sidney's *Arcadia* in 1629. He worked from the German translation by Valentinus Theocritus von Hirschberg, who himself seems to have worked from the original English and a French translation. See the title page of the 1643 edition in Curt von Faber du Faur, *German Baroque Literature: A Catalogue of the Collection in the Yale University Library* (New Haven: Yale UP, 1958), 474, no. 214a.

[106] Hellwig titled his translation *Christlich vernünftiges Bedenken*, a rather curious formulation that means something like "Wise Christian Meditation." Knorr von Rosenroth found it "unverständlich" (unintelligible) and produced his own translation, which was admired by Johann Christoph Gottsched.

[107] Harsdörffer, *Poetischer Trichter* (1650; repr., Darmstadt: Wissenschaftliche Buchgesellschaft, 1975), 1:13.

[108] Research has shown that Grimmelshausen borrowed from published accounts of the war, as well as from pre-war topological compendia, such as the Italian *Piazza Universale* of Tommaso Garzoni and the French *Théâtre du monde* of Pierre Boaystuau. See Dieter Breuer, "Krieg und Frieden in Grimmelshausens *Simplicissimus Teutsch*," *Der Deutschunterricht* 37, no. 5 (1985): 79–101, and Max Reinhart, "Unexpected Returns: Some Literary Uses of Erasmus' *Adagia* in 17th-Century Germany," *Erasmus of Rotterdam Society Yearbook* 19 (1999): 47–60.

[109] Translated by Wayne Wonderley as *Christian Reuter's* Schelmuffsky (Chapel Hill: U of North Carolina P, 1962).

[110] Translated by John R. Russell as *German Winter Nights* (Columbia, SC: Camden House, 1998).

[111] Two of the best starting points on this question are George Schulz-Behrend, Introduction, *The Adventures of Simplicius Simplicissimus*, 2nd, rev. ed. (Columbia, SC: Camden House, 1993), vii–xxiv, and Dieter Breuer, "Simplicianischer Zyklus," part 3 of *Grimmelshausen-Handbuch* (Munich: Fink, 1999), 27–114.

[112] The last edition to appear, following three posthumous editions, was in 1713. After that, as literary taste (*Geschmack*) in Germany moved still further from vernacular

realism, Grimmelshausen's work rapidly became obscure. Like so many other early modern works rejected by the new rationality of the early eighteenth century, *Simplicissimus* was rediscovered at the beginning of the nineteenth century by the Romantics.

[113] See especially Helmut Rehder, "Planetenkinder: Some Problems of Character Portrayal in Literature," *The Graduate Journal, The University of Texas* 3 (1968): 69–97, and Günther Weydt, "Planetensymbolik im barocken Roman," part 1, "Die astrologische Struktur des Romans," part 4 of *Nachahmung und Schöpfung im Barock: Studien zu Grimmelshausen* (Bern: Francke, 1968). This theory was roundly criticized by Blake Lee Spahr. See especially his "Grimmelshausen's *Simplicissimus*: Astrological Structure?" *Argenis* 1 (1977): 7–29.

[114] Winfried Stadtmüller, "Münzwesen und Preispolitik im 17. Jahrhundert," in *Deutsche Geschichte*, vol. 7, *Dreißigjähriger Krieg und Absolutismus 1618–1740*, ed. Heinrich Pleticha (Gütersloh: Lexikothek, 1984), 140–52. Establishing the weight of the money determined its worth: a coin was placed on a scale, called a *Wipper* (see-saw), by a *Kipper* (tipper). The *Wipper* "tipped" (German, *kippen*) if the coin's weight determined it was of full value.

[115] The term was coined in the 1960s by Klaus Garber to convey both the prosimetric form and the two European pastoral traditions that make up prose eclogue, and by the 1970s had become generally accepted. See his "Nachwort," in *Pegnesisches Schäfergedicht 1644–1645*, Deutsche Neudrucke, Reihe Barock 8 (Tübingen: Niemeyer, 1966), 3*–27*.

[116] Its reevaluation goes back to the groundbreaking work of Klaus Garber, *Der locus amoenus und der locus terribilis: Bild und Funktion der Natur in der deutschen Schäfer- und Landlebendichtung des 17. Jahrhunderts* (Cologne: Böhlau, 1974).

[117] As an introduction to the structure, style, and purpose of prose eclogue see Max Reinhart, "*Die Nymphe Noris* as Literary Artifact," in *Johann Hellwig's "Die Nymphe Noris" (1650): A Critical Edition*, ed. Reinhart (Columbia, SC: Camden House, 1994), xxviii–xli. Klaus Garber has written extensively on the genre. See especially "Vergil und das *Pegnesische Schäfergedicht:* Zum historischen Gehalt pastoraler Dichtung," in *Deutsche Barockliteratur und europäische Kultur*, ed. Martin Bircher and Eberhard Mannack (Hamburg: Hauswedell, 1977), 168–203; "Martin Opitz' *Schäferei von der Nympfe Hercinie:* Ursprung der Prosaekloge und des Schäferromans in Deutschland," *Daphnis* 11 (1982): 547–603; and "Nuremberg, Arcadia on the Pegnitz: The Self-Stylization of an Urban Sodality," trans. Karl F. Otto Jr., Michael Swisher, and Max Reinhart, in Garber, *Imperiled Heritage*, 117–208.

[118] Bloch, "Arkadien und Utopien," in *Gesellschaft, Recht und Politik*, ed. Heinz Maus, Soziologische Texte 35 (Neuwied: Luchterhand, 1968), 39–44.

[119] Among the recent studies on *Arminius* see Thomas Borgstedt, *Reichsidee und Liebesethik: Eine Rekonstruktion des Lohensteinschen Arminiusromans* (Tübingen: Niemeyer, 1992), and Cornelia Plume, *Heroinen der Geschlechterordnung: Weiblichkeitsprojektionen im epischen und dramatischen Werk Daniel Caspers von Lohenstein und die Querelle des femmes* (Stuttgart: Metzler, 1996).

[120] As a starting place see Giles Reid Hoyt, *The Development of Anton Ulrich's Narrative Prose on the Basis of Surviving "Octavia" Manuscripts and Prints* (Bonn: Bouvier, 1977); more recently, Stephan Kraft, *Geschlossenheit und Offenheit der* Römischen Octavia *von Herzog Anton Ulrich: "der roman macht ahn die ewigkeit gedencken, den er nimbt kein endt"* (Würzburg: Königshausen, 2004).

[121] The Edict of Nantes was signed in 1598 by Henry IV to guarantee all citizens, Catholic and Protestant (including Huguenots), the free exercise of religion.

[122] *Zum ewigen Frieden* (1795), in *Kant's Werke*, ed. Königlich Preußische Akademie der Wissenschaften (Berlin: de Gruyter, 1923), 8:343–86, here 386. The passage was translated by Peter Rosenbaum. See Klaus Garber, "Prophecy, Love, and Law: Visions of Peace from Isaiah to Kant (and beyond)," in Garber, *Imperiled Heritage*, 1–18, here 15–16.

Part I:

Transitions

Frühe Neuzeit — Early Modernity: Reflections on a New Category of Literary History

Klaus Garber

The Rise of a Macroepoch in the Cultural Sciences

*F*RÜHE NEUZEIT AS A HISTORICAL CATEGORY did not yet exist for our great teachers in the early twentieth century. The primary challenge they set for themselves, especially in the extraordinarily productive decade of the 1920s, was to restore the concept of the baroque to its proper meaning.[1] An eighteenth-century term from art history meant as a contrastive stylistic concept to *Renaissance*,[2] *baroque* was further distorted in the nineteenth century by purveyors of a romantic nationalism, who sought to invest it with distinctively Germanic qualities. This issue turned into a cardinal problem of the discipline of German literary studies (*Literaturwissenschaft*) and stirred deep feelings related to national identity and modernity. By contrast, it found little resonance among scholars of other European literatures, for whom the Baroque represented only one cultural epoch among others without exceptional significance for the larger questions of identity. Nor did the concept resonate as a term designating a period within the discipline of history (*Geschichtswissenschaft*). In the 1940s historians introduced *Frühe Neuzeit* as a unitary concept for apprehending the development of Europe between the late Middle Ages and the Enlightenment.[3] *Literaturwissenschaft* did not begin to organize the relevant subperiods (Renaissance, Reformation, Baroque) under this rubric until about the last third of the century.[4] Although it has become the accepted period term for scholarship in the field, "early modernity" has not been applied, until the present undertaking, as a category within the writing of a complete history of German literature.

We may begin by considering the temporal and structural boundaries of early modern literature. Simply to make the macroepoch coterminous with the outer temporal boundaries of the epochs that gave us our previous nomenclatures (Renaissance, Reformation, Baroque) and to make its problems synonymous with those with which scholarship in these epochs has been traditionally concerned would yield an all too narrow view. To presume, on the other hand, to absorb the entire interpretive history of those combined individual periods would be overwhelming, since that history contains nothing less than the phenomena that gave birth to the modern world. To attempt either kind of cultural history of early modernity would be an adventurous enterprise in any event, motivated by the seductions of a grandiose experiment but vulnerable to the fatal danger of either under- or overreaching.[5] It is therefore imperative at the outset of this groundbreaking volume briefly to set forth for the first time, as a heuristic for German literary history, the general contours of the early modern period as they have emerged in scholarship since about the 1960s. This will entail some review of the historical and critical thinking that effected the paradigm change as well as some reflections on its implications for research in the field of German literary history between about 1350 and about 1750, that is, between the late Middle Ages and the Enlightenment; or, framed another way: between Reformation and Revolution.[6]

In the wake of the Reformation the dissolution of Christendom as *una societas christiana* represents a watershed in European history. The counterpart of this confessional upheaval was the movement of bourgeois revolutions of the late eighteenth century, culminating in the French Revolution, which produced similarly profound social and cultural changes. Efforts to understand the history between Reformation and Revolution were well underway by 1800, concentrated initially on major figures and events at the beginning and end of the period but soon broadening to include relevant movements, groups, and tendencies. The volatile debates of the nineteenth and twentieth centuries about the origins and nature of modern history — understood as encompassing the preceding three to six centuries and framed in large binary terms, such as regression and progression, authoritarianism and democracy — were symptomatic of Europe's search for its intellectual identity.[7] Historians sought to appropriate the apparent lessons of the past to uses in the present. In the following synopsis we will look at a few of the issues and figures pertinent to a culturally based literary history of early modernity; most had become controversial already in the sixteenth and seventeenth centuries, though they grew in intensity over the following two centuries.

One of the first controversies concerned the reform movements within the church, especially the Lutheran reform, which soon overran its theological bounds to spill into larger ideological and social questions, among them the distribution of wealth and power and which authorities should have this responsibility. This question of authority had been evolving since the Carolingian renaissance[8] around the concept of the *renovatio* of classical antiquity. That is, what nation and which institutions, secular or ecclesiastical, should appropriate and control the ancient heritage, and which forms should it take politically and culturally? The struggle that ensued overturned the mental and material foundations of medieval life. Nineteenth-century idealism and liberalism (also called modernism) interpreted the postmedieval tendencies as "progressive," encouraging the fullest possible development of the modern personality.[9] Propagated by the educated bourgeoisie and by labor movements alike, this liberalism, or modernism, had its roots in the teleological optimism of the Enlightenment concerning the social and intellectual progress of the human species, and it held in force until the second half of the twentieth century. The liberal model found powerful voices in the historians Karl Friedrich Eichhorn, Jules Michelet, Max Weber, and Ernst Troeltsch, to name only a few of the most prominent theoreticians.[10] Conservative opposition, expressed in manifestoes like *Die Christenheit oder Europa* (Christendom or Europe, 1799, published 1826) by Friedrich von Hardenberg (Novalis, 1772–1801) or "Der Adel und die Revolution" (The Nobility and the Revolution, 1807) by Josef von Eichendorff (1788–1857), objected that the old order had in fact remained essentially intact under the universal aegis of Christendom.[11] The radiance of this revisionist interpretation increased as the attractions of idealism and liberalism faded over the course of the century.[12] As the twentieth century proceeded and devastating social and human tragedies further eroded liberalism's positions and betrayed the shortcomings of enlightened bourgeois innovations,[13] the conservative response only gained in strength. Once again, around 1900, a nostalgic vision of an Old Europe dominated by an aristocratic elite seized the imagination of many. By the eve of the First World War the conservative version of early modern history was attracting a range of literary minds in Germany that included the dramatist Hugo von Hofmannsthal and the poet/translator Rudolf Borchardt.[14]

Between these liberal and conservative fronts, however, other thinkers, almost from the beginning, called attention to questions neglected by the extremes. In the spirit of the Renaissance, and as a rebuke of ascendant rationalism, the Neapolitan philosopher Giambattista Vico (1668–1744), in his *Scienza nuova* of 1725, rejected the clear and distinct ideas of Cartesian logic in favor of seeing poetic creativity and imagination as unitary properties (body and soul) of the human. In Germany, Johann Gottfried Herder (1744–1803) repudiated the modeling of the modern mind on Greco-Roman values and the Latin language, even as he remained thoroughly a creature of the Enlightenment, ever insisting, as in his *Ideen zur Philosophie der Geschichte der Menschheit* (Ideas for the Philosophy of the History of Mankind, 1784–91), that all classes should receive an education. Herder mistrusted religion in its organized form — his published regret that Luther did not establish a national church had nothing to do with organized religion[15] — and diagnosed confessionalism as a pestilence. His views were inspired in part by certain sixteenth- and seventeenth-century religious dissenters who obeyed, not secular or even ecclesiastical authorities, but only the dictates of the Holy Spirit. Such dissenters included Sebastian Franck (1499–1542), Jakob Böhme (1575–1624), and Johann Valentin Andreae (1586–1642). Later intellectuals fall into this middle category as well. One of the most important was Konrad Burdach (1859–1936), whose balanced conceptualization helped to lay the foundation for our specialized study of early modernity. As we shall see, Burdach staunchly opposed the strictly liberal, "modernistic," appropriation of the Renaissance. He showed instead how intimately the Renaissance meshed with the reformist theology of the late Middle Ages, finding in its universalizing and humanizing motifs the very impulses for national consolidation that had begun in early Renaissance Italy. This thesis built a bridge to the following generation of intellectuals, including Hofmannsthal, who likewise discerned that the period we are calling early modernity contained immense, but historically explicable, cultural and ideological complexities.

A number of German-Jewish intellectuals were also important predecessors of early modern German scholarship. Leaving aside the renowned Jewish names of the nineteenth century — Heinrich Heine, Ludwig Börne, Karl Marx — whose work contributed indirectly to the discovery of the new macroepoch, certain figures of the twentieth century are exemplary. Until the National-Socialist racial laws of 1933, these scholars worked in Germany or other German-speaking countries, enhancing with their bold ideas the nation's reputation for innovative thought for one last time. Compelled to emigrate — many of them to the United States — they left behind a lasting intellectual deficit. Engineering a comprehensive methodology, they took into consideration evidence from all cultural spheres. The philosophies of Ernst Cassirer and Hannah Arendt; the critical social theories of Max Horkheimer and Franz Borkenau; the sociologies of Karl Mannheim and Norbert Elias; the art criticism of Erwin Panofsky and Raymond Klibansky, of Fritz Saxl and Edgar Wind; the literary studies of Walter Benjamin and Erich Auerbach, Arnold Hirsch and Richard Alewyn — all were driven by the ambition to discover the complex origins of modernity and the historical processes leading to it. The revolutionary cultural-historical research of the 1960s and its subsequent impact on the field of early modernity would have been inconceivable without their preliminary work.

Clearly, the rapid acceptance of the idea of early modernity in the cultural sciences owed much to political circumstances. The crises experienced by western democracies some twenty years after the Second World War had a profound impact on the university. The radical tides that swept through the institutional structures opened up new avenues of research and methodology, especially that of interdisciplinarity. This coincided with the rediscovery of the traditions of liberalism and radical democratic thought, but also of socialism and communism. As different as the theories and political intentions of these philosophies were, they shared an interest in the structural origins of bourgeois society and its culture — and these structures (early capitalism, mass communications, educated officialdom, and so on) were discovered in early modernity. The most fruitful impulses for early modern scholarship came out of the social research in the school of critical theory. Horkheimer's contributions on the dialectics of middle-class liberalism in the *Zeitschrift für Sozialforschung* (Journal for Social Research, 1930s), Benjamin's "Thesen zum Begriff der Geschichte" (Theses on the Concept of History, 1939), or Jürgen Habermas's *Strukturwandel der Öffentlichkeit* (Structural Transformation of the Public Sphere, 1961) are three prominent examples. These influences significantly changed the direction of research in political science, sociology, and philosophy, but also in art and literary history over the following generation.

Those heady times are long gone, and future scholars must assess their ultimate value to scholarship. Since then, however, early modernity has become one of the most productive fields of research and theory in the humanities and social sciences. Among other achievements, it has led to the rediscovery of vast areas of knowledge that had vanished with the academic departmentalization of knowledge in the early nineteenth century. As we now can appreciate, the compilations of universal knowledge (*Litterärgeschichten*) of the eighteenth and early nineteenth century — so despised in the later nineteenth and early twentieth century — in fact provided indispensable bibliographical data about the early modern archives of knowledge. Today, the archeological exploration of early modern informational systems makes use of precisely those curious hermetic inventories; indeed, together with the identification of texts in need of editorial elucidation, these neglected data represent one of the field's most active research components. To borrow a metaphor from the bibliographer Gerhard Dünnhaupt, only "the tip of the iceberg" has yet been uncovered with respect to this fundamental research.[16] We now realize that all early modern forms of cultural expression rested on assumptions of universal, Latin-based knowledge.[17]

Early modern texts demand interdisciplinary approaches to fathom their combinational structures.[18] In this spirit, cooperative research teams from various disciplines have formed over the past twenty years. The Universities of Vienna, Augsburg, Frankfurt, and Osnabrück led the way in founding institutes for early modern literary and cultural studies; in the United States, the interdisciplinary society for early modern research, Frühe Neuzeit Interdisziplinär (FNI), has its headquarters at Duke University.[19] Several other centers have developed specializations in the transitional epoch between the late Middle Ages and early modernity. Essential research tools are still needed, however: dictionaries, lexicons, handbooks, manuscript inventories, bibliographies, editions.[20] Other desiderata include a yearbook for early modern studies and additional university teaching chairs, to ensure that research in this field remains vital.

Early Modernity and Literary Studies: Questioning Epochal Nomenclatures

The temporal boundaries of early modernity remain somewhat variable. Opinions divide over whether the *terminus ad quem* should reach into the eighteenth century, or how far; a few scholars maintain the extreme view that it should extend deep into the nineteenth century to include Germany's belated connections to the bourgeois revolutions in Western Europe. All of this reminds us that debates over nomenclature can illuminate central problems of the disciplines. As noted above, the name first took hold within *Geschichtswissenschaft* as a kind of shorthand for the Reformation in its widest sense, that is, of embracing the entire age of confessionalization. In literary studies the curriculum traditionally had been ordered into "older" and "newer" literature, and narrowly defined boundaries often aroused self-defeating disputes. In was not until about 1980 that universities in Germany began to create professorships for early modern literature. Since then, these chairs have generally exploited existing resources and structures to construct the early modern component: either combining areas of medieval literature and early modern literature (as at the University of Munich) or combining periods from approximately 1500 to 1750 (as at the University of Osnabrück).[21] Another reason for the delay in accepting the macroepoch in literary studies is that literary movements — not to mention those in art and music — are driven not only by historical but by stylistic changes as well, and periods therefore often bear the names of those styles (classical, baroque, sentimental, romantic). In literature, art, and music, the term "early modern" therefore had to compete with canonically valued stylistic period terms.[22]

Ultimately overriding reasons, however, have led to adopting early modernity as a macroepochal term to replace, or at least embrace, the traditional divisions. Above all, its scope is advantageous for grasping the structures and stature of the period's art, music, and literature. These disciplines benefit uniquely from analysis within a capacious frame that does not force developmental phases into overly restrictive or static divisions such as to imply that one is somehow antithetical to or supplants another. Early modernity holds a series, or network, of epochal subcategories in a relatively value-neutral equilibrium. Comprehended within this megastructure each subcategory may possess singular claims to time, place, or style without demanding hermeneutic autonomy. Renaissance and Humanism, Mannerism and Baroque, Enlightenment and Rococo, Sentimentality and Storm and Stress — these common pairings remain useful as terms for successive epochs of the arts and literature. However, their character changes when regarded within the process of early modernity, since the larger context places them in a context of phenomena and spheres of activity outside their traditional purview. No sensible person would question the validity of the venerable category *Renaissance*, of course. Viewed as part of early modernity, however, it loses its claim to historical originality, as something distinct from all that had gone before.[23] The Renaissance can now be related meaningfully to the culture of the late Middle Ages. Indeed, this focus has resulted in one of the most fruitful currents of research today and is showing us how to discern the avenues of transition by which the structures of the late Middle Ages evolved into those of the early modern period.[24] Put another way, the new historical category of early modernity has opened a fresh chapter in the search for the sources of modernity.

It is now plausible to reconstruct literature's evolution over some four hundred years as a process of unfolding in coherent phases. As interpreters of this process, early modern literary historians serve as mediators between apparent extremes and as synthesizers of the differences. Long-term processes, identifiable within the category of early modernity as historical arcs that take in culturally related regions and points in time, now become visible and help us to discern the proper beginnings, ends, and contexts. For instance, we may now comprehend the social revolutions of the late eighteenth century as the completion of epochal processes that began to appear some three hundred years earlier as another kind of revolution. The early modern megastructure must be understood as permeable, elastic, and flexible, both with respect to the epochs and regions it embraces as well as to the specific qualities of artistic and literary traditions it contains.

The European Horizon of Early Modern Literature: A Historical Sketch

The European-wide field of orientation is hardly a distinctive feature of early modern literature alone. The ancient and medieval literatures thrived on active interchanges, giving and taking across national borders. During the Age of Hellenism, Greek literature was transmitted to Rome by way of Alexandria; the medieval religious and courtly literatures spoke a common conceptual language shaped in France and Germany; later authors continued to draw on a common store of formal traditions reaching back to Homer and the Old Testament. The history of European literature is one of incessant adaptation and rewriting. If we know only one national literature, we know none. Vergil is incomprehensible without knowledge of Homer, Dante without knowledge of Vergil, Goethe without knowledge of Dante. Early modern European literature comprised a single entity even as it subsumed many discrete forms and negotiated constant reciprocity among its national and ethnic cultures. As early modernity drew to its conclusion toward the end of the eighteenth century, its greatest writers, Goethe above all, foresaw the advent of world literature and speculated on its implications.[25]

A crucial structural force within early modernity was *nationalization*, which swept the continent and set its stamp on the various literatures. National identity and national literature developed together.[26] The competition for poetic laurels that began in the early Renaissance in Italy took on a decidedly nationalistic tone with the rise of the nation-states. Cultural documents across early modern Europe reveal the shared dignity of political greatness and cultural prestige. This reciprocity held true even in instances where author and patron were motivated individually by self-interest. The idea of the nation joined them. The overarching ideology was that a nation must discover its own cultural sources and have its own linguistic and literary traditions if it is to understand itself and be understood by others. Never has faith in the interdependence of politics and the arts been as deeply seated or as elegantly stated as in early modernity.

Humanists took the lead in transmitting these ideas. As the guardians of tradition, they controlled the primary instrument of maintaining it: competence in ancient languages. All were conversant in Latin; many knew Greek, some knew Hebrew, a few knew Arabic. Mainstream early modern literature was by and for the learned. That was so to an unprecedented degree if only because the inventory of traditions had grown immensely over the centuries. Early modern literature thrived on rediscovering and making available lost or neglected cultural ideas, artifacts, and texts, especially from antiquity but including the major Christian traditions and the church fathers (Jerome,

Augustine, Origen, Chrysostom). Humanists felt called upon in the first place to restore Greek, Hellenist, and Roman writers to their rightful places; they carried out this mission by preparing critical editions and commentaries, by emulating them in their own works, and by harmonizing them with Christian thought.[27] That common foundation established *a priori* the European implications of early modern texts.

One research component of literary historical research in early modernity examines how this common European literature formed into the various cultural and national contexts and their unique reception of these texts. This happened over the lengthy maturation process of the individual national literatures, each of which contributed specific forms and styles to the whole. Given its special affinity for and proximity to the traditions of ancient Greece and Rome, Italy had prominence in the formation of Europe's literary culture. Its wealthy and sophisticated urban and courtly infrastructures provided ideal political and social circumstances for rediscovering and appropriating the classical literary heritage. In Italy's small territories and communes a veritable republic of humanist scholars fostered the culture of antiquity. They received generous support from the dominant urban social classes and the princely courts, diverse social spheres that each had its respective interest in restoring the ancient cultural treasures. Classical literature, especially in its Roman, specifically Augustan phase with Vergil and Horace, aroused fierce pride in all rising European nation-states. This was perhaps particularly true in Italy and in Germany, given the similarly acute political crises in the recent history of both countries.[28] Not surprisingly, therefore, intimate cultural relations formed between these two nations as early as the mid-fourteenth century. At the court of Emperor Charles IV (r. 1355–78) in Prague, discussions between Germans and Italians ranged from epistolary style to political revolution. The dramatic story of these meetings in Prague between the humanist Petrarch, his political ally the revolutionary Roman tribune Cola di Rienzi, Emperor Charles, and his chancellor Johann von Neumarkt, has been recounted elsewhere.[29] The evocation in these exchanges of Rome's former grandeur and its possible *renovatio* under German auspices inspired statesmen and humanists north of the Alps and evolved into a separate nationalist ideology in Renaissance and Reformation Germany.[30]

The subsequent emergence of the individual European literatures encompassed the whole of Europe. Its full history has yet to be written. Even Ernst Robert Curtius's monumental *Europäische Literatur und Lateinisches Mittelalter* (1948),[31] a breathtaking survey of the shared literary identity of Europe, concerns mainly western Europe and therefore offers only a partial appreciation of the vastness of the actual development. States and territories throughout Europe adopted the literary forms and ideas of classical antiquity in their own "national" rhythms and patterns, each taking part in the complex and shifting ideological and stylistic interchanges.

Of all the revolutionary movements and crises in the early modern period, *confessionalization* produced the deepest splits and alliances — ideological, political, and cultural.[32] The departure of the Protestant states and territories from the Catholic community and, following the Peace of Augsburg (1555),[33] the proliferation of independent territories, each with its own policies relating to cultural expression and organization, had lasting influence on the shaping of literary traditions, especially in the north and west of Europe.[34] Confessional exclusionary policies caused quasi-independent "national" literatures to form, which in turn reinforced the sense of political autonomy of the new territories. The ones that continued to adhere to the old faith brought forth, thanks in part to revitalized religious orders, particularly important achievements in drama and theater.[35] Still, for all of these territorial and confessional differences, the linguistic *koine* of old Europe's educated elite provided a unifying force and barrier to particularization. Transcending vernacular and confessional linguistic boundaries, Latin remained the undisputed medium of education, communication, and literature until the eighteenth century.[36] Its mastery was prerequisite to taking part in the intellectual and literary life of the age within the *respublica litteraria*. In the witty intellectuality of Neo-Latin, writers between Renaissance and Enlightenment expressed a unity amid diversity that was strikingly different from the monastic and clerical expression of spirituality in the Middle Ages.[37]

A further underpinning of the homogeneity and stability of the literature of early modern Europe was its constitution according to genres. Early modern writers adopted and perpetuated the classical formal repertoire — ideas and images from pagan antiquity of course had to be made morally and theologically harmonious with the Christian world of letters. Poets often boasted of surpassing the ancients, a competitive but essentially playful gesture of the early modern culture of emulation. The ability to connect with this tradition reflected one's cultural sophistication and agility. This playful competition has been passed down as the so-called *querelle des anciens contre les modernes*. In their renewal of the classical genres the architects of the *via moderna* sought to close ranks with their great predecessors to gain greater prestige for their own efforts, whether in Latin or the vernacular.[38] Writers from Dante to Goethe engaged in this practice, as scholarship in early modern rhetoric and poetics has demonstrated.[39] Clearly, the literature of early modern Europe must be appreciated in its combined practices of *imitatio, aemulatio*, and *innovatio*. Even minor poets could be feted as poets laureate in a learned world steeped in the generic conventions of ancient and modern intertextuality. The literary community knew well who the true innovators were: their names appear regularly in prefaces, manuals of poetics, and correspondence.

The first prominent vernacular poet at the threshold of early modernity was Dante (1265–1321), whose *Divina commedia* (1307–21), despite its medieval philosophical difficulties, provided a model for poetry in the *volgare*. Dante also composed treatises on the superiority of the new national languages over Latin.[40] It was Petrarch (1304–74) and Boccaccio (1313–75), however, who made the native literary idiom accessible to national poets. Petrarch's collection of 366 sonnets to the beloved Laura, the *Canzoniere* (concluded shortly before his death), perhaps the most celebrated work of the early modern period, and Boccaccio's novellas, most notably in *Il Decamerone* (completed 1353), but also in *Comedia delle Ninfe fiorentine* (called *Amato*, 1341–42) and *Elegia di*

Madonna Fiammetta (1343–44), inspired emulation throughout Europe. Still, both poets continued to compose in Latin. The eclogue, the epistle, the treatise, the mythological genealogy, the heroic panegyric — all these they revived in the spirit of the ancients. Short forms were preferred, though Petrarch did experiment with the epic (his unfinished *Africa*). Many later humanist writers sought to master the epic genre of Homer and Vergil, but few were successful. Comic epics such as Matteo Boiardo's (1434–94) *Orlando innamorato* (1495) and its sequel by Ludovico Ariosto (1474–1533), *Orlando furioso* (1516), have proven the most durable over the centuries.

The last major genre to be created in early modernity, the novel, provoked aesthetic and philosophical debates over the questions of originality and imitative quality. Though writers produced many imitations of the Hellenistic romance (such as *Pyramus and Thisbe*), the greatest literary achievement of early modern Europe was the novel. Three types of novel dominated the practice: courtly, picaresque, and pastoral. The leading national literatures in Europe (Italy was the exception) discovered the greatest part of their literary mission in the novel: Spain, with the *novela sentimental*, such as Diego de San Pedro's *Cárcel de amor* (1492), or the picaresque *Lazarillo de Tormes* (1554); France, with the satirical *Gargantua et Pantagruel* (1532–52) of Rabelais; and England, with works like Philip Sidney's verse-and-prose pastoral *Arcadia* (1590). In the genre of the novel, the early modern potential for innovation within the framework adapted from antiquity is vividly evident.

Early Modern German Literature in European Context: Some Structural Considerations

Early modern writing in the German-speaking lands shared features with the other European literatures while revealing specific indigenous traits. This may be illustrated by recalling its place within the two great contexts that framed all European literature: the genre traditions extending from the late Middle Ages, and the forces of the Reformation and subsequent confessionalization.

Medieval genre traditions. — These traditions survived well into the sixteenth century with extraordinary tenacity. In their final phase, they especially affected the literary culture of the cities, mainly in the flourishing communes of southern and southwestern Germany.[41] Many medieval manuscripts were commissioned by members of the wealthy urban elites in these geographical regions. This reception occurred across diverse regional languages and dialects. The familiar distinction between High and Low German is only the most evident instance of the wide range of linguistic differences that existed during this transitional period. Attempts to establish critical norms and standards for the written language began in earnest only in the seventeenth century and succeeded only gradually, with printed texts continuing to reflect regional practices, including the peculiarities of the typesetters, until the time of the Enlightenment.[42] Until then, standardizing attempts by individual authors and the so-called *Sprachgesellschaften* (language societies) had limited general effect. While they did provide models and theoretical impulses, only the rise of the great printing and publishing concerns in the eighteenth century created the modern production methods that would turn standardization into national practice. The delay in standardization allowed traditional medieval literary forms to continue to flourish despite the simultaneous arrival of innovations from Italy and elsewhere in Europe. The resulting formal syncretism, together with the great variety of audiences it created, is perhaps the most conspicuous phenomenon of the late-medieval-to-early-modern transition. It may be in this regard, in fact, that the usefulness of the category early modernity shows to its best advantage: it simultaneously comprehends, synchronically and diachronically, heterogeneous regulatory systems of literature without privileging the value of certain phenomena and reducing them to oversimplified period terms. Early modernity is not a literary epoch in which old and new can be cleanly distinguished; one cannot reconstruct an innovation-by-innovation evolution or assign "regressive" and "progressive" tendencies to a given phase. We must understand early modernity in the broadest scope of its multifarious forms and styles and themes if we are to perceive the many other complexities of influence and interchange occurring simultaneously.

Early modern German literature manifests a dual linguistic structure: the medieval genres were fostered mostly in German (*Volksbuch*, sermon, song) — one indication of the continued vitality of native literary conditions — and the humanistic genres mostly in Latin (elegy, epistle, school drama, and so on). This duality must be appreciated comparatively and in European context. Competence in Latin was required to participate in humanism's literary endeavors as a writer or reader; lacking this competence, one remained outside the *respublica litteraria*. A stubborn but misguided notion thus arose in literary history that a learned elite dominated the early modern literary scene to the exclusion of commoners. This is wrong, as many individual cases illustrate, since even a commoner could, though education, rise to the ranks of the learned; it is also patently misleading given that literacy was rare across the entire social spectrum. If audiences were to receive ideas as literature at all, they often required oral and visual mediation, whether in the form of songs, dramas, sermons, or broadsheets. The critical pairings "speech versus writing" and "writing versus image" have proven to be useful paradigms for investigating the degrees of *literarization* of early modern social orders and have helped to overturn received assumptions.[43] We now know, for example, that authors of *volkstümlich*, or popular, texts were often more learned than previously thought. Indeed, many scholars now doubt the validity of the commonly made distinction between "popular literature" (mostly in German) and "learned literature" (mostly in Latin). These two types of literature were, in fact, practiced within a single, dual-linguistic cultural system — yet another argument against casting apparent dichotomies in early modern Europe in binary terms. A more judicious approach is to assess how forces balanced, or related to, each other within the neutralizing contexts of the *longue durée* between the late Middle Ages and the Enlightenment.[44]

Reformation. — The movement of the Reformation was the most important influence on literary developments in the early modern period.[45] In the Reformation's extended history, confessionalization (sometimes called "the long Reformation") led to fundamental rethinking about the place of language and literature in culture. This was so not only for its universally recognized contributions to reviving the German language, including linguistic standardization, and making it a suitable vehicle for many forms of literary expression. It is also central to understanding humanism properly, that is, within its wider cultural and political perspectives.[46] Indeed, as pointed out earlier, the Reformation and confessionalization comprised the great watershed in the evolution of modern German literature, a protracted event, as it were, with permanent consequences.[47] Even the Enlightenment did not reverse its forces; it continued to influence literary life throughout the nineteenth century and even well into the twentieth.

A host of smaller and larger doctrinal and philosophical disagreements within the ranks of the early reformers themselves eventually grew into the schismatic forces of confessionalization. To enumerate them all would take us far beyond the limits of this sketch. One of the first and in some ways the most decisive of these battles arose from the exchange in 1524–25 between Erasmus and Luther over the question of free will: to what degree, if at all, is the individual Christian able to participate in the act, or process, of salvation?[48] Erasmus thought: to a limited but significant degree; Luther thought: not at all. For many evangelicals and humanists this fundamental philosophical difference marked a parting of the ways. But even less essential arguments in the early years of the Reformation between Luther and others, including his associate in Wittenberg, Philipp Melanchthon (1497–1560), generated divisions over the following decades that had significant literary consequences. The humanist *nobilitas literaria* felt more of a kinship, both intellectually and behaviorally, with the supremely learned Erasmus or the judicious Melanchthon than with the mercurial and uncompromising Luther. It was mainly Melanchthon, moreover, who designed the Latin-based pedagogical system and instituted humanist studies at the universities, developments that guaranteed employment and influence for humanists over the succeeding generations. What began as academic quarrels ostensibly over *adiaphora* (indifferent things) — for example, whether Christ was actually present in body or only in spirit in the bread and wine of the Lord's Supper — between Luther and Huldrych Zwingli (1484–1531) soon led to a schism in the evangelical community. The Reformed Church in Zurich, founded by Zwingli and incorporating the teachings of John Calvin (1509–64), grew into a powerful ecclesiopolitical movement that attracted large numbers of intellectuals across Europe for about a hundred years. At its zenith around 1600 the great Calvinist centers in the Upper Palatinate (especially at the Heidelberg court) encouraged the adoption and refinement, in distinctive German forms, of the Neo-Latin humanist culture.[49] The boundary between Protestant and Catholic territories established at the end of the Thirty Years' War by the Peace of Westphalia (1648) — from which the Calvinists were excluded! — only confirmed the depths of the confessional divisions of the sixteenth century. A history of early modern German literature must give serious attention to the cultural and political implications of these confessional divisions.

This fundamental bifurcation in Germany obtained until the later eighteenth century, when first attempts were made to establish the northeastern variety of Protestantism as the norm for the intellectual culture of the nation as a whole.[50] Johann Christoph Gottsched (1700–1766), a professor of rhetoric and philosophy in Leipzig, was the leading literary authority in this movement.[51] Still, however, the world of German letters continued to struggle to overcome the trammels of confessional and regional traditions. More than any other figure, Herder devoted himself to this task; his efforts and those of other opponents of particularization represented first steps in the consolidation of a national literary culture in Germany.[52] A budding national theater, plans for a national academy, limits on censorship, and the new disciplines of journalism and criticism were some of the more obvious signs that the boundaries of confessionalism were being overcome in at least some quarters.

In the country at large, however, these efforts proved only marginally effective. The bastions of the various confessions remained unmoved and Germany's territorial and social landscapes unrepaired. The popular notion that modern German literature was driven by some centrally inspired aim of achieving glorious classical stature was the fanciful invention of nineteenth-century nationalism. Even the "classical" Weimar of Goethe and Schiller has become subject to debate.[53] During the era of the French Revolution, the final phase of European early modernity, German literature reflected the tenacity of the old political struggles, now being conducted with unprecedented vehemence.[54] Today we can hardly take seriously the harmonizing, teleological accounts from the nineteenth century that viewed history from on high, willfully ignoring the destructiveness of those battles. Georg Gottfried Gervinus (1805–71) and other literary historians of his generation exhausted this vein of historicist interpretation.[55] Lesser minds, some of them spurred by *völkisch*, or racist, presumptions, degraded German literary historiography to the point of celebrating only "essentially Germanic" qualities, discrediting and rejecting all influences from abroad, especially from the hated *welsch*, or Romance, cultures.

Regions of Practice — Phases of Development

Despite the continuing vitality of medieval themes and forms, the new Italian styles began to be received very early in Germany and were decisive in shaping intellectual and cultural trends. Burdach traced these connections and their implications in his monumental *Vom Mittelalter zur Reformation* (19 vols., 1893–1939), as well as in many monographs. He was concerned above all to show which forms the Italian Renaissance had taken in Germany and how they developed. Burdach endured harsh criticism for asking these questions at all.[56] Some nativist critics expressed their disapproval in chauvinistic, occasionally *völkisch* language — all the more reason at last to grant his ambitious project the attention it deserves.

Among other things, Burdach discovered that the gateway for the great intellectual innovations in early modern Germany was the court of the Luxemburg emperors in Prague.[57] Charles IV's chancellor, Johann von Neumarkt (ca. 1310–80), hoping to reinvigorate the chancery use of classical Latin, engaged in lively correspondence with Petrarch about the new *ars bene dicendi et scribendi*. He himself composed a beautifully rendered translation of the pseudo-Augustine *Buch der Liebkosung* (Book of Adoration, 1355). Situated on the periphery of the German language area, Bohemia remained, as to both religion and the arts, a place where experimentation was encouraged. Two major periods of cultural efflorescence are associated with Bohemia:[58] The first began with the reforms at the court of Charles IV and lasted until the Hussite Wars (1420–34). The second arose a century later along with Calvinism, which found particular favor among the Bohemian nobility under Emperor Rudolf II. Around 1600, Prague had the reputation of being a cultural crucible and a primary locus of intellectual exchanges in Central Europe.[59] Early humanists were concerned in the first place with securing proper forms and styles. The first great formal and stylistic achievement of Bohemian humanism was a gem of stylistic elegance in German prose, *Der Ackermann aus Böhmen* (The Plowman from Bohemia, 1400/1) by Johannes von Tepl (ca. 1350–1414/15), a notary and rector of the Latin school in Saaz. The Bohemian culture that produced so fine a work stands at the beginning of early modernity, not far behind the first achievements in Italy's own literary renaissance.[60]

After about 1400, however, humanistic studies generally became concentrated in major cities, mainly in the German southwest: Strasbourg, Basel, Ulm, Augsburg, and Nuremberg were the cradles of the early humanist movement and centers for the incipient printing trades.[61] A prosperous urban patrician class supported the *studia humanitatis* through patronage, receiving in return printed dedications, poetic tributes, and commemorative dramatic scenes. The cities, especially the free imperial cities with jurisdiction over surrounding territories, had an urgent need for officials trained in the law. Not surprisingly, during European humanism's early phases, lawyers especially, some of them high civic officials (notable example: the Florentine chancellor Coluccio Salutati, 1331–1406), and other private men of wealth (such as Petrarch) were the first to propagate and support the new ideas and styles. We have only recently become fully aware of how far northward the early humanism of the cities reached, extending its influence through social connections and networks as far as Vilnius, Riga, and Reval by way of Rostock, Danzig, and Königsberg.[62] This created a solid foundation for the development of German literature and culture in the early modern period. No other region provided early humanism such a variety of opportunities to flourish as did the German-speaking towns and cities of Central Europe in the late fourteenth and fifteenth centuries.

However, humanism also remained firmly associated with the courts of Germany's territorial rulers.[63] This too reflected the Italian heritage.

Humanism in Italy, as later in the transalpine lands, could not have consolidated as a movement without princely protection. In these courtly circumstances, humanist writers brought unprecedented prestige to the courts and ruling dynasties — the revival of poetic studies in Italy reintroduced the panegyrical genres that had been practiced so effectively in Imperial Rome — and received privileges in return. This penetration of humanism into the courts comprises a fascinating chapter in early modern German literary history, not least because a number of the most cultivated principalities were ruled by women of strong character and intelligence, many of whom took an active role within the humanist culture of refinement.[64] Indeed, women regents were in the vanguard of courtly patronage of humanists throughout Europe.[65] Among the outstanding centers were the small courts of Mechthild of the Palatinate (1418–82) in Rottenburg on the Neckar and of Eleonore of Austria (1433–80). As the humanist movement developed, however, the principal writers gravitated toward the major centers of political power, often establishing intellectual societies there — in Vienna, Munich, and Heidelberg, later Kassel, Dresden, and Prague. Bishoprics in Mainz, Würzburg, and Bamberg, but as far away as Breslau in Silesia, attracted concentrations of humanists as well.[66] Again, we are reminded that the old Holy Roman Empire, thanks to its decentralized structure and countless princely seats, offered ample opportunity for ideas to flourish.[67] Although there were no true capital cities in greater Germany (even Vienna could not play that role), exchanges and learned communication among courtly centers enabled a broad sharing of humanist ideas and encouraged their practical application.

The third main concentration of early humanist activity (in addition to Bohemia and the territorial courts) was centered in the universities and gymnasia in the cities, though its institutionalization met with initial resistance where medieval academic structures still prevailed or where curricula were controlled by religious orders. It is rewarding to study individual cases in this struggle to renew courses of study in the *Artes* faculties in particular. Some places, most prominently Heidelberg, saw the implementation of comprehensive reforms;[68] others, such as Cologne, with its Dominican faculty, stubbornly retained the old ways. Widespread educational reforms took place only in the postconfessionalization era, as we shall see.[69] And everywhere — and this was most symptomatic of how they organized themselves — humanists founded learned societies outside the structures of the courts, universities, and schools, an initiative that testifies both to the need to secure a home for the new studies free from institutional and traditional strictures as well as to the new movement's bid for social approval and moral support.[70] North of the Alps no individual did more than Conrad Celtis (1459–1508) to spread the new learning through founding and promoting learned societies, literally in the four geographical regions of greater Germania.[71] This tradition remained vital throughout the early modern period and deep into the eighteenth century.

With the Reformation, however, the influence of one man in particular came to dominate German social and intellectual life. The national encounter with Luther, the *Gottesmann*, inscribed itself deeply in the cultural identity of the German people. Debates continue over whether he caused greater good or greater harm. However that may be, he affected German culture more profoundly than any personality before Goethe. Post-Reformation literature everywhere bears the marks of his influence.[72] This is so not only because of the genres he created: congregational hymns and the hymnal, the German Bible and the Great and Little Catechisms, the unique Lutheran sermon, the pronouncements from his table talks and elsewhere on the worldly and spiritual matters that guided Protestant Germany in a thousand facets of practical life. Most significantly, Luther gave Germans the power to use their own language in all matters, private and public. The resonance of his work among the German people — even the illiterate could hear it read aloud in churches, on street corners, in public buildings — sealed this empowerment. Inspired by his example, literary creativity in the native language exploded over the following decades, not only in the genres just enumerated, but also in biblical and comedic dialogues and dramas; in spiritual and secular song; and in the private realm of letters, diaries, and biographies. This turn to personal forms of expression, indeed, testified both to a general intensification of feeling as well as to a rising confidence in the authenticity of individual faith. All of this activity extends far beyond the limits of what is literary in the strict sense, of course, since Luther's mission aimed at overturning all circumstances of life. In short, Luther's contribution remains a milestone in the history of European private and public culture, but especially in Germany.

The Lutheran upheaval altered the structures of humanistic studies, and by no means entirely negatively. Thanks primarily to Melanchthon, the utility of a humanistic education secured for its graduates a definitive place in the schools and universities.[73] In the Protestant lands this had incalculable consequences for literature in terms of its functions, its inventory of forms, and the nature and size of its audiences. Melanchthon's pedagogical agenda established Latin as the basis of education in the secondary schools and made the ancient languages and their texts central to the curriculum. Because the substance of Greek and Roman culture was integral to the school disciplines of rhetoric and poetics, it was transmitted with lasting effect to successive generations. By the second half of the sixteenth century, Greek and Latin studies had become firmly institutionalized. Poetry in Latin, but also in Greek, flourished in the schools, especially through the cultivation of *casualcarmina*, occasional poems, to celebrate the special occasions of an individual's life or of the academic community, in keeping with the convivial styles and practices of antiquity.[74] Over time most cities between Strasbourg and Reval, the Rhine and the Oder, boasted a thriving community of poets within the school and university milieu; a few poets managed to gain entrance to princely courts, which gave them somewhat wider influence. By about 1600 the practice of writing in Latin was sufficiently vigorous and widespread to constitute a cultural matrix.[75] If efforts did not generally transcend the conventional, we should not underestimate their combined impact on literary styles and critical standards for the next century. Writers skilled in Latin, whatever their social function — academic, bureaucratic, legal, scientific, or literary — kept the coinage inherited from ancient Rome in circulation. During this period of Late Humanism, Latin was practiced with greater vitality than ever again.

However, anyone alert to happenings abroad could see that writing of the kind that aspired to ancient standards was no longer being done exclusively in Latin. With Luther, Germany had taken the lead in the reform of religious life, but the literary product of the Reformation primarily served confessional purposes and was formally limited to the pertinent genres for evangelical needs, such as polemic, tract, sermon, biblical drama, and devotional meditation. Now, a century later, Germany stood as the last important European nation to produce a humanistically based vernacular poetry.[76] The obverse of Luther's movement became evident: a nation had immersed itself in the struggle for the true faith; bitter conflicts had eventuated between Lutherans and Catholics and, with still greater invective, between their various wings and factions. While this disputatious culture inspired the use of German in the media of propaganda and polemics, it did nothing to develop the aesthetic standards of form in the vein of classical antiquity or contemporary writing in Italy and France, England and the Netherlands, even in Poland and Hungary. In those lands, writers had long before adapted their native languages and poetic practices to classical criteria. At the threshold to the seventeenth century, vernacular German trailed far behind.

This cultural deficit motivated the new generation of poets to undertake a radical reform of German literature. The movement's leader, Martin Opitz (1597–1639), raised the challenge, to create a vernacular literature equal to the best European writing, in a Latin treatise of 1617, *Aristarchus sive de contemptu linguae Teutonicae* (Aristarchus; or, On the Contempt for the German Language). This was exactly one century after Luther had set the Reformation in motion with the posting of his *Ninety-Five Theses*. Opitz recognized that German in the colloquial manner practiced by Luther, as effective as it was for the reformer's purposes, could not match the formal sophistication of the leading European languages. Setting this as his goal, Opitz adopted a Latinate infrastructure of forms and styles that had been perfected over the Latin centuries and absorbed in the sixteenth century by the national literatures with which German was to compete. Opitz himself provided the rationale and European models for emulation in his *Buch von der Deutschen Poeterey* (Book of German Poetics, 1624).[77] Its great attention to rules and details, followed meticulously by most seventeenth-century German poets, though not by all, was unjustly ridiculed as pedantic by later detractors.

The reform took hold most successfully in regions where humanism had put down roots: in the Palatinate and the upper Rhine, with Heidelberg and Strasbourg as cornerstones in the west; and in Bohemia, Silesia, and Lusatia to the east, especially in Prague, Breslau, and Görlitz, as well as at certain princely courts. Most of the major reform locales were deeply influenced both by their rich humanist traditions and by the cultural and intellectual life of Calvinism.[78] Calvinism's theological positions and its encouragement of social activism militated far more effectively than orthodox Lutheranism against the powerfully organized Catholic Counter-Reformation.[79] Recent textual evidence has shown how persistently the Opitzian reforms spread even during the Thirty Years' War, despite its brutalities and depravations, and how literary culture took hold across the broad linguistic landscape of German-speaking Europe, especially in the north and east between the Baltic and Transylvania.[80] The old concept of "baroque literature," which located the main cultural influences in the Catholic South, is decidedly unhelpful in this regard. Just as in the rest of Europe, the German vernacular gradually adopted the structuring values of classical humanism, and with them at last, an educational and literary undertaking could begin on a grand scale.

At the outset of these reflections we acknowledged our debt to the early twentieth-century interpreters of the structures of what we now call early modern literature and culture, to Richard Alewyn (1902–79) above all, for showing how best to understand the concept of the baroque.[81] In his *Vorbarocker Klassizismus* (1926) Alewyn made it clear that the term *barock* was unsuited to describing Opitz's reforms, since they were essentially classical — Alewyn speaks of "pre-baroque" — and predicated on humanist principles. Alewyn showed that the Baroque period had courtly origins and that this courtly culture had unfolded within the Catholic sphere of sixteenth- and seventeenth-century Romance Europe. Theater, opera, ballet and dance, processionals, and festive pageants were the authentic courtly genres. The culture of *das Wort* (the word), of literature, was only minimally present in these forms, he argued, as compared with the more strictly literary forms shaped by the traditions of humanism. Alewyn thus explained how *baroque* and *pre-baroque* could be practiced simultaneously. To be sure, special circumstances obtained for Germany, where a European-style courtly culture did not emerge until the second half of the seventeenth century. Again, a delay had to be accounted for; and so it was that the paradoxical claim came about that courtly culture in Germany reached its height in the Age of Enlightenment. A history of early modern German literature over the *longue durée* refutes the ahistoricity of this canonical representation.

That Gottsched, one century after the literary reformer Opitz and two centuries after the literary reformer Celtis, felt the need to undertake basic reforms all over again testifies to how skeptically cultural experts still pondered the status of German literature. This was to become one of the defining problems of the eighteenth century. Gottsched, the great strategist and early arbiter of native culture, still could discern no clear lines of a national literary development. That was due in part to his bias against what he considered the "unnatural" conventions of German literary style in the second half of the seventeenth century, especially in the works of the poets of Nuremberg and Silesia: its overwrought, or mannerist, artistry; its nonnative qualities; its unseemly courtly elements. To Gottsched's taste, they violated the proprieties of Opitz, Paul Fleming (1609–40), Simon Dach (1605–59), and others he considered authentically German. To appreciate his point of view we must recall the extreme conventionality of contemporary courtly culture.[82] Gottsched was by no means anticourtly; he was criticizing rather the failed opportunities of the courts to promote what was inherently German instead of imitating Romance habits. What fueled his desire to gain access to the powerful courtly centers was the hope of cleansing German culture of the foreign strain and restoring a literary culture of *das Wort*.

An Observation on the End of the Early Modern Period

As a scholar of the Baroque, Alewyn was uniquely qualified to recognize the eighteenth century's peculiarities. He located the end of the period we are calling early modernity in the phenomenon of *Empfindsamkeit* (sentimentality) as exemplified in the work of Friedrich Gottlieb Klopstock (1724–1803), the celebrated author of the epic poem *Der Messias* (1748), which ushered in a stunningly fervent poetic style.[83] Alewyn was suggesting, astutely but pragmatically, that the literary culture of the early modern period drew to its close as writers began to abolish the aesthetic presupposition of necessary conformity to generic conventions within intertextual frames of reference,[84] and as they came to understand art as an individual expression of the self, or genius, or soul. While it is true that early modern writers had spoken in similar terms, modern writers of the new sentimentality set about abandoning the received rhetorical criteria for measuring poetic effectiveness. *Originality* became the new touchstone: a great, unique work of genius requires a great, unique genius who alone commands the vision and the powers to produce a monument of originality. Both the production of a work of art as well as the work itself belong within a poetic process deemed divine, indeed, Promethean. In the humanist era, poetic creation amounted to an act of reinvention from a cornucopia of topics (some of the most important are found in Curtius's book); now understood as an act of creation, it is exalted as sublime. For Alewyn, Klopstock was the first European writer to embody this ethos. Soon it would be associated with the name of Germany's greatest poet, Goethe.

Even Germany's *Klassik*, the flowering of the arts inspired by Goethe and Schiller at Weimar, was a late arrival on the European cultural stage.[85] Italians revere their three great Florentine poets, Dante, Petrarch, and Boccaccio, for having founded the literary language of the nation and brought it to its early perfection already in the *trecento*. Sixteenth-century Spain produced the *siglo de oro*, exemplified in Lope de Vega and Calderón, Cervantes and Gracián. England celebrates the Elizabethan Age of Shakespeare and Spenser as a high point in its literary achievements. France's mid-seventeenth century with Corneille, Racine, and Molière is memorialized as the Classical Age in the nation's literary memory. Poland can claim Jan Kochanowski (1530–84) as its greatest poet before the nineteenth century. For reasons that we have suggested, the extraordinary length of time required for a literature in German to evolve to these standards set Germany apart among its European neighbors.

It may have been this very delay that motivated, after the founding of the Reich in 1871, the furious commitment to reevaluating and rewriting

Germany's literary history, above all that of the *Klassik*, but also especially that of the *Barock*. It did much to affect the attitudes of literary scholarship and to shape theoretical writings, all of which, to one degree or another and often mistakenly, were said to go back to Goethe. The post Goethean fixation on a pseudotheological aesthetics of creativity, on personal experience and confession, and on individual style played out to the disadvantage of early modern literature. How essentially different early modern culture was from its modern assumptions did not become apparent again until late-twentieth-century comparative studies at last demolished the ahistorical views about the Age of Goethe.[86] Our continuing investigations into the knowledge-based foundations and their intertextual networks throughout Europe between the late Middle Ages and the Enlightenment reaffirm that the historical category of *Frühe Neuzeit* deserves to have a productive role in future scholarship.

Translated by Michael M. Metzger and Max Reinhart

Notes

[1] In 1940, one literary historian summed up these efforts as the search for "das eigentliche Barock" (the authentic Baroque): Erich Trunz, "Entstehung und Ergebnisse der neuen Barockforschung," repr. in *Deutsche Barockforschung*, ed. Richard Alewyn, 2nd ed. (Cologne: Kiepenheuer & Witsch, 1966), 449–58, here 449.

[2] See especially August Buck, ed., *Renaissance — Reformation: Gegensätze und Gemeinsamkeiten* (Wiesbaden: Harrassowitz, 1986); it is summarized briefly by Max Reinhart, "Baroque," in *Encyclopedia of German Literature*, ed. Matthias Konzett (Chicago: Fitzroy Dearborn, 2000), 1:70–74, here 70.

[3] This began as an extension of medieval research, as the titles suggest. For example, Fritz Wuessing, *Die Geschichte der aussendeutschen Länder vom Mittelalter zur frühen Neuzeit* (Berlin: Schulz, 1948), or Werner Goez, *Translatio imperii: ein Beitrag zur Geschichte des Geschichtsdenkens und der politischen Theorien im Mittelalter und in der frühen Neuzeit* (Frankfurt am Main: Killian, 1954). Historical studies of *frühneuzeitlich* culture began with the *Handbuch der Kulturgeschichte* (Frankfurt am Main: Athenaion-Verlag, 1977); the German series *Zeitalter deutscher Kultur* included Ernst Walter Zeeden's *Deutsche Kultur in der frühen Neuzeit* in 1968. By the late 1960s historians had begun to produce first summaries and introductions to the period: for example, Ernst Walder, "Zur Geschichte und Problematik des Epochenbegriffs 'Neuzeit' und zum Problem der Periodisierung der Europäischen Geschichte," in *Festgabe Hans von Greyerz zum sechzigsten Geburtstag* (Bern: Lang, 1967), 21–47, or Ilja Mieck, *Europäische Geschichte der frühen Neuzeit: eine Einführung* (Stuttgart: Kohlhammer, 1970). As late as the mid-1970s historians were still concerned with elucidating "epochal" qualities: for example, Johannes Kunisch, *Über den Epochencharakter der frühen Neuzeit* (Stuttgart: Klett, 1974). For an overview of scholarship see Nada Boskovska Leimgruber, ed., *Die Frühe Neuzeit in der Geschichtswissenschaft: Forschungstendenzen und Forschungserträge* (Paderborn: Schöningh, 1997).

[4] In literary history the earliest use of "frühe Neuzeit" began, as in the historical sciences, as an extension of medieval studies, as reflected in the title of the first text anthology by

Wolfgang Stammler, *Texte des späten Mittelalters und der frühen Neuzeit* (Berlin: Schmidt, 1956). Independent use of the concept may be traced to the founding of what remains the major scholarly journal for early modern studies, founded by Hans-Gert Roloff: *Daphnis: Zeitschrift für mittlere deutsche Literatur und Kultur der frühen Neuzeit*, which issued its first number in 1972 (*mittlere* "middle" intends in principle the same historical range: 1350/1400–1700/1750). Monographs in "early modern" literature did not begin to appear regularly for several more years, however. A similar genesis obtained for art history: earliest programmatic titles include Gottfried Boehm, *Studien zur Perspektivität: Philosophie und Kunst in der frühen Neuzeit* (Heidelberg: Winter, 1969). The term began to be adopted for music history only much later, in the 1990s, and has gradually found an auxiliary place alongside the traditional period terms: for example, Rob C. Wegman, *The Crisis of Music in Early Modern Europe, 1470–1530* (New York: Routledge, 2005). In the present volume see the chapter "Music in Early Modern Germany" by Steven Saunders.

[5] A recent publishing project seeks to apprehend the cultural history of early modern Europe in terms of "cultural exchange." Each of its four volumes has a particular focus (vol. 1, religion; vol. 2, cities; vol. 3, correspondence; vol. 4, European identities): *Cultural Exchange in Early Modern Europe*, gen. ed., Robert Muchembled, assoc. ed., William Monter (New York: Cambridge UP, 2007).

[6] "Reformation" here in the broadest sense as an "age of reform." Compare Steven Ozment's similar, though less extensive, conceptualization in *The Age of Reform 1250–1550: An Intellectual and Religious History of Late Medieval and Reformation Europe* (New Haven: Yale UP, 1980).

[7] These debates will be well known to many readers and are too numerous to enumerate here. For readers unfamiliar with them, the following may serve as a point of departure: for the nineteenth century, David Blackbourn and Geoff Eley, *The Peculiarities of German History: Bourgeois Society and Politics in Nineteenth-Century Germany* (Oxford: Oxford UP, 1984); for the twentieth century, Edward Ross Dickinson, "Biopolitics, Fascism, Democracy: Some Reflections on Our Discourse about 'Modernity,'" *Central European History* 37 (2004): 1–48. More generally see also Ingo R. Stoehr, *German Literature of the Twentieth Century: From Aestheticism to Postmodernism*, Camden House History of German Literature, vol. 10 (Rochester: Boydell & Brewer, 2001).

[8] A classic introduction to this topic is Percy Ernst Schramm, *Kaiser, Rom und Renovatio: Studien zur Geschichte des römischen Erneuerungsgedankens vom Ende des Karolingischen Reiches bis zum Investiturstreit* (1929; repr. Darmstadt: Wissenschaftliche Buchgesellschaft, 1992).

[9] For an introduction see James C. Sheehan, *German Liberalism in the Nineteenth Century* (U of Chicago P, 1978); also Leonard Krieger, *The German Idea of Freedom: The History of a Political Tradition* (Chicago: U of Chicago P, 1972).

[10] Eichhorn (1781–1854), lawyer and scholar of constitutional law; Michelet (1798–1874), French historian of vast erudition; Weber (1864–1920), economic and social historian, most noted for his book *The Protestant Ethic and the Spirit of Capitalism*; Troeltsch (1865–1923), philosopher of religious history, especially remembered for his book *The Social Teachings of the Christian Church.*

[11] Among the many studies on this subject see the recent collection of essays *Der europäische Adel im Ancien Régime: Von der Krise der ständischen Monarchien bis zur Revolution (ca. 1600–1789)*, ed. Ronald G. Asch (Cologne: Böhlau, 2001).

[12] The failure of idealism as a moral and social force was the subject of a celebrated postwar essay by Hajo Holborn, "Der deutsche Idealismus in sozialgeschichtlicher Beleuchtung," *Historische Zeitschrift* 174 (1952): 359–85. This is the subject of recent observations by Gerhard A. Ritter, "Meinecke's Protégés: German Émigré Historians Between Two Worlds," *Bulletin of the German Historical Institute* 39 (2006): 23–38, here 27–28; Ritter provides other pertinent references on nineteenth-century liberalism as well (esp. p. 32).

[13] This was most famously expressed in the 1944 collection of essays by Theodor W. Adorno and Max Horkheimer, *Dialektik der Aufklärung: Philosophische Fragmente* (Frankfurt am Main: Fischer, 1969).

[14] Both men have been regarded as part of the so-called "konservative Revolution," a term coined by Hofmannsthal, a third-generation Catholic and cofounder of the Salzburg Festival, in a 1927 speech in Munich, though some critics' further associations of them with later National Socialism are unfortunate. Borchardt called for a "creative restoration" of ancient, medieval, Reformational, and Weimar Classical values as an antidote to the destructive forces of modernism (including naturalism and the obfuscation of traditional forms).

[15] See Michael Embach, *Das Lutherbild Johann Gottfried Herders* (Frankfurt am Main: Lang, 1987); also Lowell Anthony Cook, "Luther, Herder, and Ranke: The Reformation's Impact on German Idealist Historiography" (Ph.D. diss., North Texas State University, 1983), University Microfilms International: 83-27018.

[16] Dünnhaupt, "Der barocke Eisberg: Überlegungen zur Erfassung des Schrifttums des 17. Jahrhunderts," *Aus dem Antiquariat* 10 (1980): 441–46.

[17] See Richard van Dülmen and Sina Rauschenbach, eds., *Macht des Wissens: Die Entstehung der modernen Wissensgesellschaft* (Cologne: Böhlau, 2003), and Wolfgang Detel and Claus Zittel, eds., *Wissensideale und Wissenskulturen in der frühen Neuzeit* (Berlin: Akademie, 2002).

[18] This research was summarized most recently in Helmut Puff and Christoph Wild, eds., *Zwischen den Disziplinen: Perspektiven der Frühneuzeitforschung* (Göttingen: Wallstein, 2003).

[19] The U.S. society was inspired by the Osnabrück model, Interdisziplinäres Institut für Kulturgeschichte der Frühen Neuzeit. See the preface (p. xi) to the volume of selected papers from FNI's first triennial: *Infinite Boundaries: Order, Disorder, and Reorder in Early Modern German Culture*, ed. Max Reinhart, Sixteenth Century Essays & Studies 40 (Kirksville, MO: Sixteenth Century Journal Publishers, 1998). FNI limits its scope to German studies but extends to all relevant disciplines; Osnabrück embraces all of Europe.

[20] Since the literature and culture of early modernity was European in scope, proposals are being made to the European Union to establish a major research institute for basic work of this kind.

[21] The establishment of interdisciplinary institutes for early modern studies at a number of universities has effected certain other changes as well, the most important of which are research and teaching across national borders. In Germany, this is being encouraged through cooperation between the two fields most preferred by students in the humanities, *Germanistik* and *Geschichtswissenschaft*.

[22] See Barbara Mahlmann-Bauer, ed., *Scientiae et Artes: Die Vermittlung alten und neuen Wissens in Literatur, Kunst und Musik* (Wiesbaden: Harrassowitz, 2004).

[23] The same may be argued for Weimar Classicism. See Klaus Garber, "Begin with Goethe? Forgotten Traditions at the Threshold of the Modern Age," trans. Karl F. Otto Jr., in *Imperiled Heritage: Tradition, History, and Utopia in Early Modern German Literature*, ed. Max Reinhart (Aldershot: Ashgate, 2000), 209–51.

[24] Among the growing number of studies on this topic see Dorothea Klein, "Wann endet das Spätmittelalter in der Geschichte der deutschen Literatur?" in *Forschungen zur deutschen Literatur des Spätmittelalters: Festschrift für Johannes Janota*, ed. Horst Brunner and Werner Williams-Krapp (Tübingen: Niemeyer, 2003), 299–316, and Walter Haug, ed., *Mittelalter und Frühe Neuzeit: Übergänge, Umbrüche und Neuansätze* (Tübingen: Niemeyer, 1999). In the present volume see the chapter by Graeme Dunphy.

[25] Among the many publications on Goethe's concept of world literature see Horst Steinmetz, "Weltliteratur: Umriß eines literaturgeschichtlichen Konzepts," *Arcadia* 20 (1985): 2–19; Fawzi Boubia, "Goethes Theorie der Alterität und die Idee der Weltliteratur: Ein Beitrag zur neueren Kulturdebatte," in *Gegenwart als kulturelles Erbe: Ein Beitrag zur Kulturwissenschaft deutschsprachiger Länder*, ed. Bernd Thum (Munich: Iudicium, 1985), 269–301; and Klaus Manger, ed., *Goethe und die Weltliteratur* (Heidelberg: Winter, 2003).

[26] See Klaus Garber, ed., with Winfried Siebers, *Nation und Literatur im Europa der Frühen Neuzeit: Akten des 1. Internationalen Osnabrücker Kongresses zur Kulturgeschichte der Frühen Neuzeit* (Tübingen: Niemeyer, 1989), and Herfried Münkler, Hans Grünberger, and Katrin Mayer, eds., *Nationenbildung: Die Nationalisierung Europas im Diskurs humanistischer Intellektueller: Italien und Deutschland* (Berlin: Akademie, 1998).

[27] On the humanists' return to the ancient sources and their editorial activities see the chapter by Erika Rummel in this volume.

[28] In Germany the demise of the Hohenstaufen dynasty in the mid-thirteenth century ushered in a period of instability in the empire that did not begin to be corrected until the accession of Charles IV. In Italy the oft-remarked "calamitous fourteenth century" was very real, marked by a nearly chaotic level of political confusion as despotism (*signoria*) and tyranny threatened to replace consensus.

[29] See especially Konrad Burdach, *Rienzo und die geistige Wandlung seiner Zeit*, vol. 2 of *Vom Mittelalter zur Reformation: Forschung zur Geschichte der deutschen Bildung* (Berlin: Weidmann, 1928); Paul Piur, *Cola di Rienzo: Darstellung seines Lebens und seines Geistes* (Vienna: Seidel, 1931); Heinz Otto Burger, "Neue Laienbildung und neue Laienfrömmigkeit im 14. Jahrhundert," in *Renaissance, Humanismus, Reformation: Deutsche Literatur im europäischen Kontext* (Bad Homburg: Gehlen, 1969), 15–44, esp. 15–31; and most recently Klaus Garber, " 'Your arts shall be: to impose the ways of peace' — Tolerance, Liberty, and the Nation in the Literature and Deeds of Humanism," trans. Westfälisches Landesmuseum für Kunst und Kulturgeschichte, Münster, and Michael Swisher, in Garber, *Imperiled Heritage*, 19–40, here 24–29.

[30] See Donald R. Kelley, "*Tacitus noster*: The *Germania* in the Renaissance and Reformation," in *Tacitus and the Tacitean Tradition*, ed. T. J. Lude and A. J. Woodman (Princeton: Princeton UP, 1993), 152–67.

[31] *European Literature and the Latin Middle Ages*, trans. Willard R. Trask (1953; repr. Princeton: Princeton UP, 1991).

[32] Briefly, *confessionalization* defines the process following the Peace of Augsburg (1555) by which church and state fused into absolutist territories, each state having

exclusionary rights to choose its own religion, or confession; by the same token, the confession exercised its own political will upon the state. This process is explained at greater length in Scott Dixon's chapter in the present volume, together with pertinent references to scholarship. As a first reference, however, see Heinz Schilling, "Die Konfessionalisierung im Reich: Religiöser und gesellschaftlicher Wandel in Deutschland zwischen 1555 und 1620," *Historische Zeitschrift* 246 (1988): 1–45.

[33] The concordat formula *cuius regio eius religio* (whose territory, his religion) coined around this event meant that each territory had the right to choose which confession would be practiced there, to the exclusion, or near exclusion, of all others.

[34] See Klaus Garber, "Zentraleuropäischer Calvinismus und deutsche 'Barock'-Literatur: Zu den konfessionspolitischen Ursprüngen der deutschen Nationalliteratur," in *Die reformierte Konfessionalisierung in Deutschland — Das Problem der "Zweiten Reformation,"* ed. Heinz Schilling (Gütersloh: Mohn, 1986), 317–48.

[35] See in this volume the chapter on Neo-Latin literature by Wilhelm Kühlmann.

[36] From the vast scholarship on this subject see Manfred Fuhrmann: *Latein und Europe: Geschichte des gelehrten Unterrichts in Deutschland von Karl dem Grossen bis Wilhelm II.* (Cologne: Dumont, 2001); Bodo Guthmüller, ed., *Latein und Nationalsprachen in der Renaissance* (Wiesbaden: Harrassowitz, 1998); and Wilhelm Kühlmann, "Nationalliteratur und Latinität: Zum Problem der Zweisprachigkeit in der früh-neuzeitlichen Literaturbewegung Deutschlands," in *Nation und Literatur im Europa der Frühen Neuzeit*, ed. Klaus Garber (Tübingen: Niemeyer, 1989), 1:164–206.

[37] In the vacuum left by the decline of Latin-based culture, a vernacular imitation arose in the nineteenth century that, despite ostensible similarities such as cultural and patriotic vocabulary, would develop virulently nationalistic tendencies.

[38] See Guthmüller, ed., *Latein und Nationalsprachen in der Renaissance.*

[39] Early modern scholarship on this subject is summarized in the chapter by Joachim Knape in this volume.

[40] The story of Dante's controversial efforts on behalf of the *lingua volgata* is told, among other places, in Werner Bahner, "Dantes theoretische Bemühungen um die Emanzipation der italienischen Literatursprache," in part 1 of *Formen, Ideen, Prozesse in den Literaturen der romanischen Völker* (Berlin: Akademie, 1977), and in Konrad Krautter, *Die Renaissance der Bukolik in der lateinischen Literatur des 14. Jahrhunderts: Von Dante bis Petrarca* (Munich: Fink, 1983). See also Klaus Garber, "Utopia and the Green World: Critique and Anticipation in Pastoral Poetry," trans. James F. Ehrmann, in *Imperiled Heritage*, 73–116, esp. 82–83.

[41] See Klaus Garber, ed., with Stefan Anders and Thomas Elsmann, *Stadt und Literatur im deutschen Sprachraum der Frühen Neuzeit*, 2 vols. (Tübingen: Niemeyer, 1998); Nikolaus Henkel and Nigel F. Palmer, eds., *Latein und Volkssprache im deutschen Mittelalter 1100–1500* (Tübingen: Niemeyer, 1992); and Bernd Moeller, Hans Patze, and Karl Stackmann, eds., *Studien zum städtischen Bildungswesen des späten Mittelalters und der frühen Neuzeit* (Göttingen: Vandenhoeck & Ruprecht, 1983).

[42] On the standardization of German see the chapter by Renate Born in this volume.

[43] See, for example, Werner Röcke and Ursula Schaefer, eds., *Mündlichkeit, Schriftlichkeit, Weltbildwandel: Literarische Kommunikation und Deutungsschemata von Wirklichkeit in der Literatur des Mittelalters und der Frühen Neuzeit* (Tübingen: Narr, 1996), and Jan-Dirk Müller, ed., *"Aufführung" und "Schrift" in Mittelalter und früher Neuzeit* (Stuttgart: Metzler, 1996).

44 The term *longue durée* is most closely associated with the name of Fernand Braudel, a second-generation member of the French school of historiography known as the *Annales*, which favored viewing history in long-term structures rather than, as traditionally, as narrowly defined periods or events.

45 Richard van Dülmen, "Reformation und Neuzeit: Ein Versuch," *Zeitschrift für Historische Forschung* 14 (1987): 1–25, provides an excellent introduction to this subject.

46 See Erika Rummel, *The Confessionalization of Humanism in Reformation Germany* (Oxford: Oxford UP, 2000); Rummel also offers a brief summary of this problem in her chapter in the present volume.

47 See Kaspar von Greyerz et al., eds., *Interkonfessionalität — Transkonfessionalität — binnenkonfessionelle Pluralität: Neue Forschungen zur Konfessionalisierungsthese* (Gütersloh: Mohn, 2003).

48 The two texts are gathered in English translation (Luther's is condensed) in *Erasmus — Luther: Discourse on Free Will*, trans. and ed. Ernst F. Winter (New York: Continuum, 2000). The utter implications of the humanist/evangelical exchange have never been more incisively formulated than in Heiko A. Obermann, *Luther: Man Between God and the Devil* (1982), trans. Eileen Walliser-Schwarzbart (New York: Doubleday, 1989), 211–25.

49 See most recently Axel E. Walter, *Späthumanismus und Konfessionspolitik: Die europäische Gelehrtenrepublik um 1600 im Spiegel der Korrespondenzen Georg Michael Lingelsheims* (Tübingen: Niemeyer, 2004).

50 See Jans Rohls and Gunther Wenz, eds., *Protestantismus und deutsche Literatur* (Göttingen: Vandenhoeck & Ruprecht, 2004), and Nicholas Hope, *German and Scandinavian Protestantism, 1700–1918* (Oxford: Oxford UP, 1999).

51 See Katherine Goodman, "Gottsched's Literary Reforms: The Beginning of Modern German Literature," in *German Literature of the Eighteenth Century: The Enlightenment and Sensibility*, ed. Barbara Becker-Cantarino, Camden House History of German Literature, vol. 5 (Rochester: Boydell & Brewer, 2005), 55–76; further, Gunter E. Grimm, "Gottscheds 'Critische Dichtkunst' und die Vernunft-Poesie der Frühaufklärung," in *Literatur und Gelehrtentum in Deutschland* (Tübingen: Niemeyer, 1983), 620ff., and Garber, "Begin with Goethe?," esp. 213–16.

52 In works such as *Fragmente über die neuere deutsche Literatur* (1766–67) and *Abhandlung über den Ursprung der Sprache* (1772) the implications for a national literary culture arise from Herder's primary historical concern with the elements of a broadly shared German culture through achieving a national language and political independence. Of the many studies on this subject see most recently Wulf Koepke, "Herder and the Sturm und Drang," in *Literature of the Sturm und Drang*, ed. David Hill, Camden House History of German Literature, vol. 6 (Rochester: Boydell & Brewer, 2003), 69–93.

53 Gerhart Hoffmeister, *A Reassessment of Weimar Classicism* (Lewiston, NY: Mellon, 1996). Further, see W. Daniel Wilson, *Das Goethe-Tabu: Protest und Menschenrechte im klassischen Weimar* (Munich: Deutscher Taschenbuch Verlag, 1999), and "The Political Context of Weimar Classicism," in *The Literature of Weimar Classicism*, ed. Simon Richter, Camden House History of German Literature, vol. 7 (Rochester: Boydell & Brewer, 2005), 347–68.

54 As a point of departure see Thomas P. Saine, *Black Bread — White Bread: German Intellectuals and the French Revolution* (Columbia, SC: Camden House, 1988).

[55] Peter Hohendahl, "Gervinus als Historiker des Barockzeitalters," in *Europäische Barock-Rezeption*, ed. Klaus Garber (Wiesbaden: Harrassowitz, 1991), 561–76.

[56] Among Burdach's critics who did not share his interdisciplinary embrace of cultural history, including iconography and the history of ideas, were Paul Joachimsen, Karl Brandi, and Gerhard Ritter. The groundwork for a reassessment of Burdach has been laid by Klaus Garber in "Versunkene Monumentalität: Das Werk Konrad Burdachs," in *Kulturwissenschaftler des 20. Jahrhunderts: Ihr Werk im Blick auf das Europa der Frühen Neuzeit*, ed. Garber, with Sabine Kleymann (Munich: Fink, 2002), 109–57; see also Garber's article on Burdach in the *Literaturlexikon: Autoren und Werke deutscher Sprache*, ed. Walther Killy (Gütersloh: Bertelsmann Lexikon, 1989), 2:325–26.

[57] A useful introduction to Prague humanism is still S. Harrison Thomson, "Learning at the Court of Charles IV," *Speculum* 25, no. 1 (1950): 1–29.

[58] A standard introduction to this topic is Hans Bernd Harder, *Studien zum Humanismus in den böhmischen Ländern* (Cologne: Böhlau, 1988); and *Später Humanismus in der Krone Böhmen: 1570–1620* (Dresden: Dresden UP, 1998).

[59] See R. J. W. Evans, *Rudolf II and His World: A Study in Intellectual History 1576–1612* (Oxford: Clarendon, 1993; corrected paperback edition: London: Thames and Hudson, 1997).

[60] For a discussion of *Der Ackermann aus Böhmen* see in this volume the chapter by Graeme Dunphy.

[61] Paul Gerhard Schmidt, ed., *Humanismus im deutschen Südwesten: Biographische Profile* (Sigmaringen: Thorbecke, 1993). In the present volume see also the chapter by Erika Rummel and that by Stephan Füssel.

[62] Klaus Garber, *Das alte Buch im alten Europa: Auf Spurensuche in den Schatzhäusern des alten Kontinents* (Munich: Fink, 2006); also Garber, Manfred Komorowski, and Axel E. Walter, eds., *Kulturgeschichte Ostpreussens in der Frühen Neuzeit* (Tübingen: Niemeyer, 2001).

[63] See August Buck, ed., *Höfischer Humanismus* (Weinheim: Acta humaniora, 1989). In the present volume see the chapter by Helen Watanabe-O'Kelly.

[64] On the subject of early modern women writers see the chapter by Anna Carrdus in the present volume.

[65] See Sharon L. Jansen, *The Monstrous Regiment of Women: Female Rulers in Early Modern Europe* (New York: Palgrave McMillan, 2002), and Lisa Hopkins, *Women Who Would Be Kings: Female Rulers in the Sixteenth Century* (London: Vision, 1991).

[66] The scholarship on this subject is now vast. For an introduction see Sebastian Neumeister and Conrad Wiedemann, eds., *Res Publica Litteraria: Die Institutionen der Gelehrsamkeit in der Frühen Neuzeit* (Wiesbaden: Harrassowitz, 1987), and Werner M. Bauer, "Humanistische Bildungszentren," in *Von der Handschrift zum Buchdruck: Spätmittelalter — Reformation — Humanismus 1320–1572*, ed. Ingrid Bennewitz and Ulrich Müller, vol. 2 of *Deutsche Literatur: Eine Sozialgeschichte* (Reinbek bei Hamburg: Rowohlt, 1991), 274–86.

[67] See Hans Erich Bödeker and Ernst Hinrichs, eds., *Alteuropa — Ancien Régime — Frühe Neuzeit: Probleme und Methoden der Forschung* (Stuttgart-Bad Cannstatt: Frommann-Holzboog, 1991).

[68] Walter, *Späthumanismus*, esp. Teil 1.

[69] See the chapter by Wilhelm Kühlmann on education in this volume.

[70] For an introduction to early modern intellectual societies, including a sketch of their historical traditions beginning with Plato, see Klaus Garber, "Sozietäten, Akademien, Sprachgesellschaften," in *Europäische Enzyklopädie zu Philosophie und Wissenschaften*, ed. Hans Jörg Sandkühler (Hamburg: Meiner, 1990), 4:366–84.

[71] See Jörg Robert, *Konrad Celtis und das Projekt der deutschen Dichtung* (Tübingen: Niemeyer, 2003).

[72] There is no better introduction to this subject than Marian Szyrocki, *Martin Luther und seine Bedeutung für die deutsche Sprache und Literatur* (Wroclaw: Wydawnictwo Uniwersytetu Wroclawskiego, 1985). An excellent if little known publication (in pamphlet form) on the "grand narrative" of Reformation history is Thomas A. Brady Jr., *The Protestant Reformation in German History*, Occasional Paper No. 22 (Washington, DC: German Historical Institute, 1997).

[73] As an introduction see Gerhard Arnhardt and Gert-Bodo Reinert, *Philipp Melanchthon: Architekt des neuzeitlich-christlichen deutschen Schulsystems* (Donauwörth: Auer, 2001).

[74] The standard work on the genre of the occasional poem is Wulf Segebrecht, *Das Gelegenheitsgedicht: ein Beitrag zur Geschichte und Poetik der deutschen Lyrik* (Stuttgart: Metzler, 1977).

[75] Erich Trunz, "Der deutsche Späthumanismus um 1600 als Standeskultur" (1931), in Alewyn, ed., *Deutsche Barockforschung*, 147–81.

[76] See in this volume the chapter by Peter Hess, part III: "Representative Culture: Vernacular Learned Poetry in the Humanist Tradition."

[77] On personal circumstances surrounding the writing of this poetics and his first book of collected verse see in this volume the chapter by Theodor Verweyen.

[78] See Garber, "Zentraleuropäischer Calvinismus," and Walter, *Späthumanismus*.

[79] Among recent studies on this subject see André Biéler, *Calvin's Social and Economic Thought*, trans. James Greig, ed. Edward Dommen (Geneva: World Alliance of Reformed Churches, 2006); also Patrick Collinson, "Calvin and Calvinism," in *The Reformation: A History* (New York: Modern Library, 2004), 87–102.

[80] Klaus Garber and Martin Klöker, eds., *Kulturgeschichte der baltischen Länder in der Frühen Neuzeit: Mit einem Ausblick in die Moderne* (Tübingen: Niemeyer, 2003), and Garber, *Das alte Buch*; see also Thomas Haye, ed., *Humanismus im Norden: Frühneuzeitliche Rezeption antiker Kultur und Literatur an Nord- und Ostsee* (Amsterdam: Rodopi, 2000), and Edmund Kotarski, ed., with Malgorzata Chojnacka, *Literatur und Institutionen der literarischen Kommunikation in nordeuropäischen Städten im Zeitraum vom 16. bis zum 18. Jahrhundert* (Gdansk: Wydawnictwo Uniwersytetu Gdanskiego, 1996).

[81] Among his many monographs and articles specifically on the Baroque see this cross-section: *Vorbarocker Klassizismus und griechische Tragödie: Analyse der Antigone-Übersetzung des Martin Opitz* (1926; repr. Darmstadt: Wissenschaftliche Buchgesellschaft, 1962); review of "Karl Viëtor: *Probleme der deutschen Barockliteratur* (1928)," in Alewyn, ed., *Deutsche Barockforschung*, 421–26; "Formen des Barock," *Corona* 10 (1943): 678–90; and "Goethe und das Barock," in *Goethe und die Tradition*, ed. Hans Reiss (Frankfurt am Main: Athenäum, 1972), 130–37. On implications for early modernity in Alewyn see Max Reinhart, "Der Detektiv in der Geschichte: Richard Alewyn und das Problem der Frühen Neuzeit," *Daphnis* 34, nos. 3–4 (2005): 381–428.

[82] Jörg Jochen Berns and Thomas Rahn, eds., *Zeremoniell als höfische Ästhetik in Spätmittelalter und Früher Neuzeit* (Tübingen: Niemeyer, 1995).

[83] See the collected papers from the 2002 colloquium in Osnabrück: *Das Projekt Empfindsamkeit und der Ursprung der Moderne: Richard Alewyns Sentimentalismusforschungen und ihr epochaler Kontext*, ed. Klaus Garber and Ute Széll (Munich: Fink, 2005).

[84] See Wilhelm Kühlmann and Wolfgang Neuber, eds., *Intertextualität in der frühen Neuzeit: Studien zu ihren theoretischen und praktischen Perspektiven* (Frankfurt am Main: Lang, 1994).

[85] Garber, "Begin with Goethe?"

[86] The patterns of literary developments during the eighteenth century are extremely complex and have long caused uncertainty about appropriate terminology. Beginning in West Germany in the 1960s, Werner Krauss and his followers began to clarify matters through comparative investigations into previously ignored aspects of the German Enlightenment from its inception until the revolutionary era. For example, see Krauss, *Perspektiven und Probleme: Zur französischen und deutschen Aufklärung und andere Aufsätze* (Neuwied, Berlin-West: Luchterhand, 1965). Heuristic approaches sought to explain the developmental logic driving texts with different themes, styles, and forms, each with its explicit purpose and appearing simultaneously or in close succession; how they related to each other historically; and how they might be interpreted as evidence of a literary practice of enlightenment that was becoming increasingly radical. Some studies suggested that the Rococo as a literary phenomenon accorded well with the spirit of the Enlightenment, which aimed to promote humanity's free exercise of all of its powers. It could be demonstrated that this leitmotif, grounded in enlightened anthropological thought, ran all the way through the eighteenth century and encouraged a climate of critical opinion regarding *Empfindsamkeit*, the culture of feeling and sensibility. Its practical orientation, based on enhancing empathy and sympathy, was in no way at odds with the way the Enlightenment characteristically made moral values of Christian virtues. Moreover, the social criticism in documents of the Storm and Stress could be read as a sign of rebellion — in the best spirit of the Enlightenment — against petrified and inhumane political institutions. This revolutionary impetus, rooted in ideas of natural law and critical of prevailing systems, especially in France, corresponded to a prerevolutionary disposition within broad sectors of German literary production of the 1770s and '80s, which was undeniably in tune with ideas expressed by the enlightened avant-gardes of Europe.

German Literature of the Middle Period: Working with the Sources

Hans-Gert Roloff

In memoriam Victor Lange et Herbert Penzl

Middle German Literature

IN THE HISTORY OF GERMAN LITERATURE the middle period (*Mittlere Literatur*) came to be regarded not only as independent of medieval literature, on the one hand, and modern literature, on the other, but as having fundamental significance for the subsequent evolution of German literature after the eighteenth century. Middle German literature includes the period from the end of the fourteenth to the middle of the eighteenth century, approximately 1400 to 1750. The term *Frühe Neuzeit* (early modern period) has become the designation of choice for cultural historians of the middle period, and in this essay both terms — middle and early modern — will be used interchangeably.[1]

The period of middle German literature thus covers some 350 years. Texts have been transmitted to us in abundance in all their variety, but most have yet to be edited, annotated, and properly understood. The intensive textual criticism of the last forty years has made clear that the terminology traditionally used for the historical evaluation of these texts was entirely unsuited to a systematic description of the multifaceted phenomena and problems of this massive body of literature. The individual texts defy the traditional categories that derived not from literature but from the realms of politics, philosophy, religion, and art. The basic error in traditional methodology was that it failed to view literature — which is a humanly constructed world of textuality — as an independent historical achievement (*Geschichtsleistung*), and instead as a handmaiden to abstract ideologies.

However, when these texts are systematized according to their own literary criteria and reception, an entirely different perspective arises, because texts (and their authors) communicate in reaction to problems, ideas, events, forms, and the like, and produce human discourses that introduce us to the existential problems of people at particular times in history. The middle period is rich in human questions about the right way of living, about values, dangers, the need for change, about criticism and affirmation of old and new authorities. The real purpose of a literary history oriented toward human values is to discover and interpret these issues. Recent research on early modern Germany has demonstrated gratifying signs of progress toward making this literature comprehensible in its human component, whether in the form of carefully documented biographies, interpretive monographs, or comprehensive editions with extensive commentaries.

The fact that research began to focus intensively on middle German literature only in the second half of the twentieth century has to do with the sharp increase in sociohistorical method in literary studies and the concomitant distancing from the narrower poetic aesthetics. With this development the dictum — traditional since the positivism of Wilhelm Scherer (1841–86) — that the literature between Middle Ages and Enlightenment was aesthetically inferior, collapsed. The related idea of a widened concept of literature opened up the early modern fountainhead of literary sources, which portray the problematic nature of human experience with greater intensity and immediacy than the other historical disciplines. This led rapidly to the fundamental realization that literary-historical research and the adequate historical understanding of texts cannot occur without interdisciplinary cooperation.

The 350-year period of German literature between medieval and modern — "German" understood in the linguistic and geographical sense as the territory in which German was the national language of communication, parallel, of course, to Neo-Latin, which provided access to the European intellectual world — reveals a series of structural commonalities that permit us to speak, in spite of the myriad of themes and forms, of a discrete historical *block*. Within this block it is clear that the seventeenth century consciously looks back to the views and events of the fifteenth and sixteenth centuries. The turns of century at 1500 and 1600 — the so-called thresholds to the Reformation and to the Baroque — could not interrupt the vital outpouring of literature. At least four basic historical features are constitutive of middle German literature:

1. The evolution and standardization of language. Early New High German began to develop in the fourteenth century and emerged in the eighteenth in the standard New High German. Parallel to this development, Neo-Latin emerged from medieval Middle Latin as a result of exposure to the literature of Roman antiquity as the language of scholarly, scientific, and technical discourses (medicine, pharmacy, philosophy, law). This German-Latin bilingualism was taken for granted in the middle period; an author's decision to use one or the other language depended on the communication intention of the given situation. Indeed, both languages influenced each other, particularly in structure: on the one hand a certain Latinism made itself felt in German, while on the other a certain German influence prevented Neo-Latin from becoming a mere imitation of the ancient idiom. The reasons for Latin's equality in literary communication were, first, its ability to integrate crucial German concerns into the European discourse, and second, cultural-political pride in claiming European intellectual superiority in Germany via *translatio imperii* (transfer of rule). German literature in Neo-Latin assumed a high intellectual priority in the

middle period. It was therefore a serious error of older German literary-historical scholarship, under the influence of a nationalistic vision, largely to ignore this rich body of Neo-Latin literature in favor of literature written in "the Protestant dialect" (Jakob Grimm) of Early New High German — and all this, despite statistical proof that books published in Latin, well into the seventeenth century, were far more numerous than those in the national vernacular.

2. The influence of literature, culture, mentality, and the sociopolitical sphere. The reception of the *studia humanitatis* occurred, to be sure, on terrain that had already been prepared literarily and culturally to assure that the "new" aspects of Roman antiquity transmitted through literature would serve to produce intellectual innovation. The amalgamation between "old" and "new" in early modern German literature has only recently begun to be appreciated in its proper historical perspective. Although Latin-Roman influences had an immense effect on middle German literature, they were rejected in the philosophical upheaval of the eighteenth century in favor of an idealized culture of Greek antiquity: Rome versus Athens, Latin versus Greek, Horace versus Pindar, Vergil versus Homer.

3. The turn to rhetorics and poetics, first to those of antiquity, then to native conceptions that modulated classical principles to fit contemporary needs. Two insights formed the basis for this active mode of reception: writing (including poetic composition), is, like speaking, learnable and teachable; and all written expression obeys the principles of communication and aims to persuade the reader to one's own cause. Without consideration of this communication system one cannot approach early modern German literature with understanding. Rhetoric, which was commonly taught as a technical subject, was the real writing school of these centuries. The literary theories of communication that gradually developed from applied rhetorics gave authors the possibilities they needed to create the wealth of formal innovations that eventually guaranteed this literature its unique position in the history of German literature.

4. Middle German literature as a sophisticated experimental laboratory. This produced both new literary forms and new instruments of literary distribution: copying of manuscripts, printing, theater, and official oratory. From the fifteenth century on we encounter new genres and other small literary forms that over the centuries had gradually become established forms: epic long and short forms, a wide breadth of theatrical text forms, and an abundance of German and Latin lyrical forms. We also find other important forms of specifically literary communication: letters, tracts, sermons, biographies, historiographical writings, travel reports, chronicles, commentaries, orations, and so on. The 350 years of middle German literature constitute one of the most creative periods in the entire western history of literary form.

In addition to these four features we may also observe that middle German literature was anchored deeply in the social, political, and religious problems of the time. Indeed, neither before nor after has literature been integrated with history to such a degree, making pragmatic use of its sophisticated strategies of communication to teach, admonish, enlighten — in short, to win the public for a given cause over a long period of time in which struggles raged over changing political, religious, social, economic, and other power structures.

Middle German literature comprises the most recent research area of Germanic studies; cultivated only since the last third of the twentieth century, it has subsequently become a model of modern research strategies, notwithstanding the aversion it has aroused in some quarters because of its solidly historical methodology. Any attempt to search out the formal origins of modern and current literature must lead back to the fifteenth and early sixteenth century. Here the beginnings of the genres drama, novel, novella, short story, biography, and technical writing began; here too the primary avenues of literary distribution began to thrive: printing and theater. It was in this period that printed literature was discovered to be a commodity requiring production, distribution, and consumption. The early years of middle German literature were thus full of literary innovations.

Early Source Scholarship

To understand early modern German literature correctly, one must start with basic research: consulting the bibliographical compilations of the literature that has been handed down to us in manuscript and print and determining where they are preserved (archives, libraries, and other repositories). Establishing comprehensive lists of manuscripts and prints for the fifteenth, sixteenth, and seventeenth centuries remains a philological desideratum that will require future generations for completion. The production of lexicons is a related activity. Lexicons mine information about known and unknown authors and their works and provide contextual and historical information. For the middle German period one should begin with the biographical and bibliographical lexicon *Die deutsche Literatur*.[2]

The work of basic research continues with the process of making new texts accessible in critical editions and commentaries. This is a huge area for future research, and one of immense significance, for the extent to which well-planned and well-executed editions exist determines both what sources are available as well as the literary picture we have of a given period. Access to source texts is the precondition not only for interpretation but also for interdisciplinary evaluation and cooperation. Older literary scholarship failed badly in this respect, with the result that literary histories as late as the twentieth century offered inaccurate views of the actual textual realities in middle German literature, thus preventing meaningful discussion. The literary historical coverage of middle German literature provided by earlier source scholarship is replete with gaps that mislead and even distort the picture. There are a few important exceptions, such as the authoritative volumes by Richard Newald, Hans Rupprich, and Hedwig Heger in the renowned De Boor/Newald series,

Geschichte der deutschen Literatur.[3] It was with these volumes that the newer early modern philology can be said to have begun. These excellent volumes made full use of what trustworthy editions of primary texts existed, and in doing so demonstrated how intimately literary history and editorial source research are bound together.

But even these solidly philological works provided little help beyond manifold positivisitic data (titles, dates, etc.). Certain other monographs from this earlier period on neglected authors have turned out to be disappointingly unreliable, given that they were not based on critical editions and often substituted unverifiable opinions, conceptions, and judgments; still others projected subjective aesthetic or ideological biases. Nineteenth- and early-twentieth-century scholarship indeed largely ignored early modern German literature or rejected it on the alleged ground that it did not meet the intellectual and aesthetic standards and values of Weimar Classicism. Certain interest was shown, for nationalistic reasons, in allegedly nativist figures such as the Nuremberger Hans Sachs and others from Alsace and Silesia. Few scholars were interested in or were qualified to deal with the Neo-Latin literature; one may say in fact that the bilingualism of middle German literature, a unique and determinative feature of the early modern period, was a major reason for its being ignored by Germanists. To be sure, texts of modern literature are incomparably easier to access than those of the middle period; and the relatively small corpus of German medieval texts are firmly in the hands of the medieval philologists. But for early modern German literature the situation is precarious.

We realize today that the total production of early modern literary texts was made available in the nineteenth and twentieth centuries only selectively, and was guided mainly by other disciplines, especially church history. Consequently, vast thematic areas are still waiting for analysis and historical-critical editions. The earlier editions that exist do not so much represent *examples* of early modern works as they do only *selections* meant to demonstrate their place in a presumed literary-evolutionary process toward the telos of modernity. This very selectivity, however, has grossly distorted both the texts themselves and the larger truth about production. This unsystematic selection arose mainly from doctoral dissertations.

Alongside several readers and anthologies, such as Karl Goedeke's *Elf Bücher deutscher Dichtung* (1849), complete texts and larger works were published chiefly in series. They included Johann Scheible's twelve-volume *Das Kloster, weltlich und geistlich: Meist aus der ältern deutschen Volks-, Wunder-, Curiositäten-, und vorzugsweise komischen Literatur* (The Cloister, Secular and Spiritual: Mostly from the Older German Folk, Miracle, Curiosity, and Comic Literature, 1845–49) and *Schatzgräber* (Treasure Seeker, 1846–48, 5 vols.); Hermann Kurz's *Deutsche Bibliothek* (1862–68); *Kürschners Deutsche National-Litteratur* (1882–99); and the short-lived *Lateinische Litteraturdenkmäler des 15. und 16. Jahrhunderts* (1891–1912). The majority of middle German editions appeared in the series *Bibliothek des Litterarischen Vereins Stuttgart* (BLVS), beginning in 1842, which continues into the present and has published over 300 volumes, and the reprint series founded by Wilhelm Braune, *Hallesche Neudrucke deutscher Literaturwerke des 16. und 17. Jahrhunderts* (1876–1957; continued as *Neudrucke deutscher Literaturwerke*, 1961 to the present). In addition to single works, the BLVS also published editions of major writers of the late medieval period and of the middle period: *Fastnachtsspiele* (Shrovetide plays), Hans Sachs, Jörg Wickram, Jakob Ayrer, Paul Fleming, Hans Jakob Christoffel von Grimmelshausen, Andreas Gryphius, Simon Dach, and others.[4] The *Hallesche Neudrucke*, which made an effort to bring out a varied series consisting largely of individual texts of the sixteenth and seventeenth centuries, published as its first volume Opitz's epoch-making *Buch von der Deutschen Poeterey*. Edmund Goetze's editions of Sachs's *Fastnachtspiele* and *Fabeln und Schwänke* (Fables and Jests) plus the writings of Johann Eberlin von Günzburg appeared in the series in piecemeal fashion, though with continuous pagination. The series had the great merit, by virtue of its exemplary variety of texts, of demonstrating the colorful nature of the literature of these two centuries. In keeping with its times, to be sure, it too favored an agenda emphasizing the German-national aspect and did not produce any works in Neo-Latin. The editorial quality of the individual works is variable but consistent with philological practices of the nineteenth and early twentieth century. With certain exceptions, however, they remain useful. Their chief fault is the lack of commentaries — considered redundant at the time since they were intended for use only by experts in the field.

In this overview of earlier editions treating early modern German literature it is notable that, other than those few in the BLVS, hardly any extensive "work" editions (*Werkeditionen*) of individual authors were undertaken. The large editions of Martin Luther, Philipp Melanchthon, and Huldrych Zwingli were made by theologians, with some help from Germanists in the case of Luther. Two exceptions may be regarded as models by modern editorial standards: Eduard Böcking's seven-volume Hutten edition (1859–70) and the five-volume Aventinus edition (1881–86).[5] It is surprising that, until the second half of the twentieth century, no comprehensive critical edition of Erasmus was undertaken, meaning that scholars had to be content with the early-eighteenth-century edition by Jean Leclerq (1703–6, 11 vols.). P. S. Allen's magisterial edition of Erasmus's letters in twelve volumes (Oxford, 1906–58) remained unmatched on the Continent until much later.

Even in the first half of the twentieth century, in spite of the innovative research on baroque literature, little motivation was shown for discovering, editing, and writing adequate commentary on the works of middle German literature. The BLVS and the *Hallesche Neudrucke* did continue to bring out new works. An acceptable edition of the writings of the Franciscan satirist Thomas Murner appeared in the years between 1918 and 1931 (9 vols.), although, again as a product of the contemporary mentality, it included only his German-language writings and crassly ignored his many Latin texts.[6] Heinz Kindermann's monumental collection, *Deutsche Literatur: Sammlung literarischer Kunst- und Kulturdenkmäler in Entwicklungsreihen*, which began to appear in the 1920s and was stopped only by the Second World War, provided new texts, including Neo-Latin works, in middle literature and continues to be useful to modern scholars for its expert introductions to the individual volumes. The original plan of the series for the period 1400–1750 included the following series: *Meistersinger* (4 vols.), Humanism and Renaissance (6 vols.), Reformation (7 vols.), *Volksbücher* and *Schwankbücher* (chapbooks and jest books, 7 vols.), Baroque (28 vols.) — altogether some fifty-two volumes. Twenty-five actually appeared, five of which cover the baroque tradition of southern Germany.

Modern Source Scholarship

The nineteenth and earlier twentieth century made a large number of individual texts accessible, but few complete editions of particular authors or genres. Although these editions facilitated the extraction of much positivistic information (as noted above for the De Boor/Newald series), they were much less useful for literary-historical analysis. Research was thus held hostage, as it were, to the ideological exploitation of texts qua superstructural documents. With the profound reorientation of *Literaturwissenschaft* after about 1960 toward the view of texts as conveyers of unique forms of literary expression within particular historical contexts, it became clear that the older method of source scholarship was an inadequate instrument for the new demands of historical research. The methodological acknowledgement of the causal nexus between literature and history was the prime motivation for the modern science of source scholarship.

Modern research on German literature and culture between 1400 and 1750 began in earnest in the 1970s and by the 1980s had begun to yield significant results. The subsequent eruption of critical editions — many of them undertaken as corrections to previous ones — gave rise to new areas of early modern scholarship and established the science of critical editions as a new field of research. One insight that drove the production of critical editions was that interpretive monographs, important as they are, cannot replace the primary works themselves: each generation reads texts differently and therefore runs the risk of falling into its own ideological traps if the sources — the genuine representations of the historical time of the texts — are not available for objective verification. An example may suffice. The distinguished scholar of late medieval *Erbauungsliteratur* (literature of edification), the Berlin philologist Wieland Schmidt, after long and patient research, published an exemplary study in 1938 on the manuscript transmission of Otto von Passau's *Die Vierundzwanzig Alten* (1480), a text that existed in some 150 manuscripts and prints. Schmidt's laudable intention was to make this mass of material comprehensible; but he did not actually edit the work itself, since he considered it of inferior quality, notwithstanding the great popularity it had enjoyed in its own time. In failing to do so, he thereby obfuscated the salient fact that precisely its popularity provided valuable historical evidence about the mentality of its recipients. Modern source scholarship, by seeking to work from the historical situation of the text, hopes to avoid such limiting personal judgments based on taste or ideology.

Producing such editions is now a central activity of early modern scholarship. Marketing considerations require, however, that most appear in series, meaning that they are subject to the structural principles of the particular series.[7] This is by no means universally the case, however, such as for the comprehensive new critical editions of Melanchthon, Johann Valentin Andreae, Martin Bucer, Heinrich Bullinger, and Sigmund von Birken. Besides the BLVS and the *Hallesche Neudrucke*, which continue their programs, many new series have come into existence, though some only briefly. Among the major series still active are the following: the *Ausgaben Deutscher Literatur des XV. bis XVIII. Jahrhunderts* (ADL), which commenced in 1967 and has brought out 170 volumes to date, including complete editions of Geiler von Kaysersberg, Alexander Seitz, Johannes Adelphus, Jörg Wickram, Thomas Naogeorg, Wolfhart Spangenberg, Daniel Czepko, Johann Rist, Philipp von Zesen, Johann Christian Hallmann, Christian Weise, Wolfgang Caspar Printz, Johannes Riemer, and Johann Christoph Gottsched. ADL has also published a number of non-series editions, including the *Sprichwörtersammlungen* (Collections of Aphorisms) of Johann Agricola; the *Sämtliche Dramen* of Sixt Birck; *Teufelbücher* (Devil Books); and *Spieltexte der Wanderbühnen* (Plays by the Itinerate Players). The *Berliner Ausgaben* series has published editions of Johann Reuchlin, Johann Fischart, Sebastian Franck, Nicodemus Frischlin, and Friedrich Nicolai since the early 1990s. The series *Mittlere Deutsche Literatur in Neu- und Nachdrucken* has brought out the corpus of the *Geistliche Spiele* (Spiritual Plays) of the Tyrolean *Sterzinger Spielarchiv* and — in addition to individual editions — the critical edition of the complete works of Johann Beer. The extensive series *Nachdrucke Deutscher Literatur des 17. Jahrhunderts* (Bern) publishes important individual texts of the seventeenth century in facsimile with critical commentaries. The *Bibliothek Deutscher Klassiker*, whose ambitious and comprehensive program included twenty-four early modern volumes, was abruptly discontinued recently. The volumes that were published, however, are of the highest editorial quality, especially for their exhaustive commentaries. Of the early modern volumes actually published, several of the texts already existed in other philologically acceptable editions (Gryphius and Grimmelshausen, among others) — the curse and blessing of such inclusive series that attempt to market more to a general than to a specialized readership. One more recent series should be mentioned, since it promises to fill in a notable lacuna in the area of middle German literature, if only sufficient numbers of scholars participate and if the series remains financially solvent: the program of TRANSLATIO is to publish both complete editions and reception literature. The very significant area of reception literature, including translation, has been almost completely overlooked, in spite of its enormous impact on the early modern evolution of German literature and culture. The main sources, of course, were ancient Greek and Roman literature, Renaissance literature of the Romance countries, and Neo-Latin literature.

These initiatives to discover and edit source materials have also led to innovations in editorial practice that answer the unique demands of middle German literature, which are distinctively different from those for medieval literature. For the fifteenth century, most texts were handwritten and transmitted in that form, usually as an *apograph* (copy, transcript); autographs, manuscripts in the hand of the author, were rare, and are found mostly as personal letters, often preserved among authors' literary remains (*Nachlässe*) in archives and libraries. In the sixteenth and seventeenth centuries, transmittal via manuscript continued to be practiced in certain circles, particularly in those, such as the courtly sphere, that had little interest in publicity. Other manuscripts remained unpublished because they were considered merely functional (*Gebrauchsliteratur*), such as written-out versions of Jesuit dramas.

In general, however, after the invention of movable type, texts increasingly were transmitted in printed form and could be marketed in all parts of Germany. With only rare exceptions among printed works, the preprint manuscripts have not been transmitted. Since very few authors had or took the opportunity in the early modern production process to read proofs during the typesetting, the final form of the printed work reflects in language, orthography, and structure the practices of the printer. The modern editor is in effect forced to accept the *editio princeps* as the provisionally authoritative text. A normalization of the various versions for the sake of effecting an early modern German linguistic standard, or *Kunstsprache* — Karl Lachmann employed a standardized orthography in his nineteenth-century editions of medieval manuscripts — is unacceptable, given the extraordinary irregularities in early modern dialectal, grammatical, and orthographical forms. As analyses of autographs have shown, orthographical license is attributable less to printers' arbitrariness than to authors' whimsy. Thus, "corrections" or modernizations of the text being edited must be avoided, absent some convincing philological reason. But since, as practice has shown, the printed texts of the sixteenth and seventeenth centuries are by no means free of error, it is inadvisable simply to provide the editions in facsimile; only expert philological and linguistic judgment can establish the final form of the edition. The number of printed works that lend themselves to facsimile reproduction is quite small. Some texts were printed repeatedly, which testifies to the enthusiasm and curiosity of the reading public for this literature. From printing to printing one regularly finds textual variants (*Lesarten*) that show, first, that nearly every subsequent issue was newly typeset, and second, that their reception evolved in ways that reflect the changes in social, educational, linguistic, and literary conditions, though scholars may differ in exactly how they define and evaluate these phenomena.

A particularly gratifying development in source scholarship is the new conception of the commentary: greater emphasis is now placed on broad historical developments and intellectual and cultural contexts rather than on narrower work-internal issues. This approach makes the distant world of middle German literature more accessible to the general reader. Doubtless the most important advance coming from this new conception of early modern literary history, however, is the inclusion of Neo-Latin literature. Every new edition of such texts from the fifteenth to the seventeenth century fills in one more space in the literary map of the period. The fact that in recent years it has become customary to provide a parallel translation of the Latin texts will be helpful in the integration of these heretofore largely neglected materials into literary history.

The question is often raised whether it is now possible to write a general literary history of the middle period. The answer must be a qualified "yes." The state of source scholarship has advanced greatly over the past generation; but much remains to be done. Whatever history we may attempt must of necessity be only a snapshot of the whole. That is true of any period of literary history, but especially of the middle period. Literary history is continuously modified and enriched by new discoveries and evaluations. The more exhaustively the creations of the past are documented and made accessible to new generations the more structurally refined will become our picture of literary history — not only in its harmony, but in its vital contradictions as well.[8]

Translated by James Hardin

Notes

[1] My concept of the middle German period is outlined in detail in *Das Berliner Modell der mittleren deutschen Literatur*, ed. Christiane Caemmerer, Chloe 33 (Amsterdam: Rodopi, 2000), 469–94.

[2] *Die deutsche Literatur: Biographisches und bibliographisches Lexikon*, ed. Hans-Gert Roloff, Reihe 2, *Die deutsche Literatur zwischen 1450 und 1620* (Stuttgart: Frommann-Holzboog, 1983–), Reihe 3, *Die deutsche Literatur zwischen 1620 und 1720* (1987–), and *Literaturlexikon: Autoren und Werke deutscher Sprache*, ed. Walther Killy, 15 vols. (Gütersloh: Bertelsmann Lexikon Verlag, 1988–93). See also the earlier lexicon founded and edited by Wilhelm Kosch, *Deutsches Literatur-Lexikon: Biographisches und bibliographisches Handbuch* (1927–30), 2nd ed., 4 vols. (1949–58), 3rd ed., 16 vols., ed. Bruno Berger and Heinz Rupp (Munich: Francke [later Saur], 1968–96).

[3] *Geschichte der deutschen Literatur von den Anfängen bis zur Gegenwart*, founded by Helmut de Boor and Richard Newald, 12 vols. (Munich: Beck, 1949–94). Hans Rupprich, *Vom späten Mittelalter bis zum Barock*, vol. 4, part 1, *Das ausgehende Mittelalter, Humanismus und Renaissance 1370–1520*, 2nd ed., ed. Hedwig Heger (Munich: Beck, 1994); Rupprich, part 2, *Das Zeitalter der Reformation 1520–1570* (1973); Richard Newald, vol. 5, *Vom Späthumanismus zur Empfindsamkeit 1570–1750*, 6th ed. (1967).

[4] The series was also open to medieval works and included culturally interesting texts such as Endres Tucher's *Baumeisterbuch von Nürnberg* (1862), or the Nuremberg *Polizeiordnungen* (1861).

[5] Hutten edition: *Opera quae reperiri potuerunt omnia*, 5 vols. plus 2 indices (Leipzig: Teubner, 1859–70; repr., Aalen: Zeller, 1963–66). Aventinus edition: *Johannes Turmair's genannt Aventinus Sämmtliche Werke*, 5 vols., individual vols. ed. Siegmund Riezler and Matthias Lexer (Munich: Kaiser, Königliche Akademie der Wissenschaften, 1881–86).

[6] *Thomas Murners Deutsche Schriften mit den Holzschnitten der Erstdrucke*, 9 vols., ed. Gustav Bebermeyer, Eduard Fuchs, Paul Merker, et al. (Berlin: de Gruyter, 1918–31).

[7] Recently, it has become much more difficult to obtain copies or microfilms, much less the original works, due to new restrictions by lending libraries. Often now, for example, books cannot be sent to university departments or institutes; or microfilming is refused because of possible damage to the original works; or copying fees are prohibitive. Such hindrances to access thus makes the creation of reliable critical editions all the more urgent.

[8] Special thanks to Professor James Hardin, who is himself a specialist in middle German literature, for soliciting and translating this article.

Literary Transitions, 1300–1500: From Late Medieval to Early Modern

Graeme Dunphy

A Period of Flux?

A POPULAR IF UNINFORMED MANNER of speaking refers to the medieval period as "the dark ages." If there is a dark age in the literary history of Germany, however, it is the one that follows: the fourteenth and early fifteenth century, the time between the Middle High German *Blütezeit* and the full blossoming of the Renaissance. It may be called a dark age, not because literary production waned in these decades, but because nineteenth-century aesthetics and twentieth-century university curricula allowed the achievements of that time to fade into obscurity.[1] If we compare the high medieval writings of Walther von der Vogelweide or Wolfram von Eschenbach with the Reformation writings of Martin Luther or Ulrich von Hutten, the cultural gulf that opens up before us seems enormous, leaving the impression that the intervening years were ones of rapid transition. But when we acknowledge that a full three centuries lie between these two familiar landmarks, we realize that the rate of change was doubtless no faster than in any other literary epoch. If the period from the mid-thirteenth century to the end of the fifteenth may be called a transition, it is because the early thirteenth and early sixteenth centuries are established coordinates in the discipline of literary history. There are good reasons for this: the *Blütezeit* produced Middle High German poetics of particular genius, the Reformation intellectual exchanges of an extremely high caliber. If we define the former as medieval and the latter as early modern, it can be useful to see the gradual dawning of modernism as the years "between." But it is important to recognize that all such constructs are arbitrary.

What characterizes the literature of the transition? In the late medieval period the forms and aspirations of literary endeavor stood in clear continuity with those of the High Middle Ages; but they were also rapidly expanding in scope, with many innovations that would become important for the Renaissance and the Reformation. The bulk of chirographic[2] production continued to be written in Latin, but the German language was quickly gaining ground. The student approaching the period for the first time will be struck by obvious linguistic developments.[3] Diphthongization (*hût* > *Haut*) set in from the late thirteenth century, though the monophthongization that filled the gap left by the splitting of the long vowels (*huot* > *Hut*) had yet to occur. The lengthening of short vowels, the disappearance of the preterit singular grade of ablaut, and various other forms of leveling also fell in these centuries. Late Middle High German had become Early New High German. However, for literary historians the transition from late medieval to early modern is above all defined by the emergence of intellectual, social, political, and aesthetic developments that lie at the heart of our conception of modernity. In particular, the evolution of new types of writing was driven by changes in the milieus that fostered literature, the rise of new literate classes of society, the spread of printing, and a redefinition of the role of writing. A decisive development of the fifteenth century was the importation to Germany of Italian humanism, for which reason the phrase "Northern Renaissance" has been used to sum up the spirit of the age. Equally, several new forms of religious awakening can be characterized as typically late medieval. Bringing all these elements under a common denominator we may say that the intellectual life of the centuries of transition showed a great openness to new ideas — an openness that stands in contrast both to the more rigid cognitive hierarchies of the High Middle Ages and to the entrenched positions of the Reformation.[4] The resulting diversification of German literature reveals itself in the new forms of writing pioneered by new classes of writers for ever-widening circles of readers. We shall observe this increased diversity in the traditional centers of literary production, the court and the cloister, but even more so in the new literary world of the cities. And we shall see the parallel rise of Jewish literary awareness as belonging in the same broad context.

Courtly Life in Transition

What we call the Middle High German *Blütezeit* (1170–1230) was the zenith of a specifically courtly literature at a time when the great courts were able to provide a level of patronage unknown elsewhere in society. This tradition of poetics sponsored by powerful princes continued throughout the later Middle Ages and well into the early modern period, though it represented an ever-diminishing proportion of the total output of new writing in German. Geographically speaking, courtly patronage of literature continued to spread, northward and eastward; where thirteenth-century German literature had been practiced most actively, in the Austrian and Bavarian courts and to a lesser extent in the Rhineland, we now find courts such as at Prague or Braunschweig becoming literary centers. In the first instance it was the old forms of courtly literature that were promulgated. The courts in this period were, after all, probably the most conservative part of society; at a time when the urban societies and even the peasantry were looking for new ways to define themselves, the nobility wanted to maintain the identity it had enjoyed in the age of chivalry. The main concern of the great territorial princes, whose status was enhanced by the increased privileges granted by the Golden Bull of Charles IV (1356), was to consolidate their power in the face of the rise of urban society. Meanwhile the lower nobility was losing power to the great nobles above them and the cities below them. More than ever, courtly literature celebrated a world view rooted in an idealized past; and as the discrepancy between this ideal and the realities of courtly life widened, nostalgic calls for restoration of the good old days became more urgent. In view of this conservatism it is no surprise that we seldom find radically new perspectives, or that the "post-classical" courtly novel — everything after Konrad von Würzburg (ca. 1230–87) — turned into an epigonal, tired imitation of the romance of the golden age.

Nevertheless, certain courtly novels of the fourteenth and fifteenth centuries became highly successful. At the beginning of the period of transition Johann von Würzburg[5] wrote an extremely well-received novel, *Wilhelm von Österreich* (1314). Its popularity is attested by the survival of seventeen manuscripts, ten of which are complete, and by the reception of the protagonists Wilhelm and Aglye as ideal lovers in the anonymous mid-fourteenth-century novel *Friedrich von Schwaben*. Johann records that his *Wilhelm von Österreich* was commissioned by the dukes Friedrich and Leopold of Austria — a poignant example of literature serving the purposes of princely legitimacy, in that the eponymous hero, though fictitious, is cast as the patrons' forebear. The novel tells of the love of young Wilhelm of Austria for the "heathen" princess Aglye, which is frustrated when her father betroths her to King Walwan of Phrygia. Walwan is in conflict with Melchinor of Marocco, and Wilhelm joins his expeditions, excelling in all kinds of adventures. In essence a typical *Minne* (love) and *Aventiure* (adventure) romance, *Wilhelm von Österreich* contains much that is traditionally courtly, combining the familiar chivalric concerns with the heightened late medieval interest in the Orient. However, in terms of characterization Johann's novel represents a step in the direction of modern perspective. In contrast to earlier heroes, such as Erec or Parzival, whose quest was ultimately fulfilled by locating themselves correctly within society, Wilhelm is individualistic: he seeks his identity within himself and cannot come to rest.[6] This explains why the novel does not have the expected happy ending. Ultimately, Wilhelm and Aglye marry, but he is killed treacherously with a poisoned spear while hunting a unicorn, and she dies of grief, leaving their son Friedrich the throne of Austria. He dies not because, like Tristan or Schionatulander, he has been denied the object of his quest, but because it was granted him and he was not content.

One remarkable courtly novelist of the fifteenth century was Elisabeth von Nassau-Saarbrücken (ca. 1393–1456).[7] Born princess of Lorraine, she governed her principality as regent for over a decade (1429–42) during the minority of her sons. Her four romances, *Herpin*, *Sibille* (ca. 1437, published 1514), *Loher und Maller* (before 1437), and *Huge Scheppel* (1437, published as *Hug Schapler*, 1500), are adaptations of French works, and all are historically anchored, a feature that generally characterizes the later courtly novel in contrast to the classical courtly novel. In Elisabeth's case, the claim of historical truth seems to be particularly strong, underlined by her use of the generic tag "warhaftige cronik" (true chronicle), and it is in this context that we may understand why she was one of the first in German to use prose for the writing of a romance: by the fifteenth century the modern view was gaining ground that prose is more suitable than verse for a strictly factual report.

Despite the author's claims, however, *Huge Scheppel* is a fictional account of the tenth-century Hugh Capet, King of France and progenitor of the Capetian dynasty.[8] The historical Hugh was a grandson of Robert I of France and on his mother's side a nephew of Emperor Otto the Great; in the novel, Huge is the offspring of a nobleman and a butcher's daughter, an inauspicious match that should have condemned the boy to his mother's rank. But Huge is not content with this and declares: "Jch hab wol ein ander besser meynung von mir. Metzlen oder kouffmanschatz zů triben hab ich keynen můt/oder ouch ochsen oder schwyn ab zů thůn. Ich hab vil ein hübscher hantwerk gelernet" (I have indeed a better opinion of myself. I have no desire to pursue butchery or the merchant's treasures, nor to slaughter oxen or swine. I have learned a far more courtly trade). Thus he seeks out the life of a knight, and by a series of adventures culminating in a royal marriage he attains the French throne. This rags-to-riches story offends the order of chivalric fiction, in which a young Parzival, Tristan, or Lancelot may appear to come from nowhere and succeed through personal merit, only to be revealed in the end to have impeccable parentage; the illusion of the self-made man ultimately confirms rather than undermines the doctrine that one must be born to high estate. The upward mobility of Huge, however, radically challenges this doctrine, and it is surprising to find an author of Elisabeth's rank feeling comfortable with such material. One explanation may be that she herself, like the Huge of the novel, lived through a turbulent period and succeeded in maintaining the stability of her realm by sustaining an alliance with the now powerful urban upper classes. This alliance of noble and patrician worlds lies behind the figure of Huge, and indeed, although the romance was written for the entertainment of the court, it became immensely popular in the literate circles of the cities as well. Besides this, Elisabeth clearly intended her hero to be a role model for her sons, making the work something of a *Fürstenspiegel* (mirror of princes), which teaches the right manner of courtly conduct: young Huge may be a ruffian, but as a king he embodies wisdom and prudence.

Another female author from the highest courtly circles was Eleonore of Scotland (1433–80), also known as Eleonore von Österreich or Eleonore Stuart. A daughter of James I of Scotland, she married Siegmund of Tirol in 1448, and similarly to Elisabeth of Nassau-Saarbrücken she became actively involved in governing the principality during the years of her husband's absence. Though her authorship has been called into question,[9] it seems certain that the prose novel *Pontus und Sidonia* (1463), another adaptation from the French, was at least written under her patronage at the court of Innsbruck. It tells how Pontus, prince of Galicia, flees to Brittany when his father's kingdom falls to the armies of the sultan. Arriving incognito he proves himself as a knight and wins the love of the princess Sidonia. In subsequent adventures he wins back his father's kingdom, and the couple become ideal rulers of their joint realms. The plot is nostalgic for traditional courtly values, and like Elisabeth's novels, it may be seen as a mirror of princes. Written shortly after the fall of Constantinople, it highlights the perceived threat of the rising power of Islam, a theme that became increasingly urgent in European literature until the Turkish expansion was contained a century later with the Battle of Lepanto (1571).

In the later fifteenth century a center of literary activity emerged at the court of the Electoral Palatinate in Heidelberg under the reigns of Friedrich der Siegreiche (the Victorious, 1449–76) and Philipp der Aufrichtige (the Honest, 1476–1508); it was inspired in no small part by Friedrich's learned sister Mechthild.[10] The best known of the Heidelberg romancers was Johannes von Soest, whose *Die Kinder von Limburg* (The Children of Limburg, ca. 1480) is a curious blend of Arthurian epic, Tristan romance, *chanson de geste*, and *Antikeroman* (the courtly romance tradition drawing on classical Greek and Roman material), possibly a deliberate synthesis of the familiar strands of courtly fiction. One focus of this group of writers was the rewriting in German of Middle Dutch romances (most of these were themselves translated from French), and Johannes's novel is a fine example. Another is the anonymous *Ogier von Dänemark* (1479), which is particularly interesting for its political implications. Ogier's life is threatened by the vindictiveness of Charles the Great, but he succeeds in establishing his place in the feudal society when it becomes clear that Charles needs him in the fight against the Saracens. In the end Charles holds Ogier's spurs, thus inverting the classical symbol of the acknowledgement of a feudal superior. *Ogier von Dänemark* is often bracketed with the thirteenth-century romances *Gerart van Rossiliun* and *Reinolt von Montelban* under the heading *Empörerepen* (*empören*, "to rebel"), in which the hero is an upstart vassal in conflict with his overlord. In the original French context these may have had their place in the resentments of lower nobility in their little courts far from the eyes of the king. In Germany the background was the independence that the great lords claimed with respect to the emperor, especially in the century after the Golden Bull reinforced princely autonomy. The purpose of such a tale is not to undermine the feudal system but to set limits to its imperial dimension.

Turning to lyrics, we find in the fourteenth century the last phase of the traditional Middle High German genres of *Minnesang* and *Sangspruchdichtung* (aphoristic poetry), which lost vitality as the focus of interest switched to the new urban idiom of *Meistersang* (also called *Meistergesang*, "master song"). Nevertheless, *Minnesang* in the traditional mould is found well into the period of transition.[11] Here the literary giant of the late thirteenth and early fourteenth century is the Meissen poet Heinrich Frauenlob (ca. 1250–1318).[12] His work covers the full range of courtly lyrics as we know them from the poets of the previous generation, including courtly love songs, political *Sangsprüche*, and a series of formally more complex songs, known as *Leiche*, on the Trinity and the Virgin; many of his melodies have also survived. In his portrait in the *Manessische Handschrift* (the famous Manessa Codex, or Heidelberg Manuscript C, begun during his lifetime), he seems to be conducting a choir of nine singers and players, which suggests the performance of a *Leich*, as only these extended religious pieces would have been performed by an ensemble. The cognomen *Frauenlob* (praise of Our Lady) probably referred originally to this praise of the Virgin, though later tradition links it to his dispute with the poet Regenbogen about the relative merits of the terms *wîp* (woman) and *vrouwe* (lady). This *wîp/vrouwe* controversy in fact constituted one of the most fascinating episodes in his career.[13] In the Manessa Codex one group of songs is ascribed alternately to Frauenlob and to "Regenbog," forming a dialogue in which the Regenbogen stanzas argue for *wîp*, the Frauenlob verses for *vrouwe*. Behind this arrangement lies a romantic notion of singers' joust, though it is doubtful whether these songs were sung as a contest in quite this form. At any rate, the argument develops with challenge and counter-challenge, until the final piece in the set wins the debate for Frauenlob by producing telling etymologies for the two words: *vrouwe* receives an honorable etymology, from the joy (*vrô*) and pain (*wê*) of love, but for *wîp* the poet invents the story of an unpleasant king:

> Vrankriche, ich nenne dich durch Wippeon den künic.
> des mut was rünic.
> er hiez der kindel varen,
> die da meidel waren,
> unz sie verlurn der blumen lust mit der meide jaren;
> so was im lieb ir stolzer lib unz das sie wurden swanger.   (V, 104, 1–6)
>
> [France, I mention you because of King Wippeon. He was fickle. He ordered the children — the girls in that country — to be spied out, until they lost the flower of joy along with their maiden years. Then he rejoiced in their fine figures until they became pregnant.]

If they became pregnant they were banished; but as long as they were neither virgins nor mothers, he took pleasure in them. These in-between women (*mittenkünne, mittel-sie*) were named *wîp* after the lecherous pedophile Wippeon. Can a word with such origins stand beside the noble *vrouwe*, asks the poet? As it happens, Frauenlob was not so far from the truth with his fictitious etymologies, though he could not have known it. Modern linguistics derives *vrouwe* from Germanic **frawan, *frōwō* (lord, or lady) from an Indo-European root **per* (first, chief); *wîp* on the other hand is thought to go back to IE **ghwibh-* (pudenda). And indeed, the subsequent semantic development in modern German, which makes *Frau* the standard term and *Weib* derogatory, would seem to answer Frauenlob's plea.

After Frauenlob, *Sangspruch* went into a sharp decline, though in the later fourteenth century, Heinrich von Mügeln, and in the fifteenth, Muskatblüt and Michel Beheim, were still producing gnomic works for the courts.[14] *Minnesang*, however, was to have one last blossom, as the outstanding singer of the early fifteenth century, the South Tyrolean Oswald von Wolkenstein (1376–1445), at least fleetingly reversed the trend.[15] Unusual for a poet of this period, Oswald's biography can be reconstructed in detail, thanks in part to frequent autobiographical references in his poems, which testify to a particularly strong authorial self-awareness. His corpus of some 133 songs reveals a highly innovative poet. His love songs are firmly rooted in the *Minne* tradition, yet he goes new ways in introducing melodies and poetic techniques from Italian, French, and Flemish contemporaries. The thematic breadth of his range of songs is astounding: travel, war, marriage, spring, dawn; songs of the Virgin, repentance, and the city; songs full of social critique and autobiography. How far his technique exceeded that of earlier courtly lyricists can be seen from the opening of one of the travel songs:

> Durch Barbarei, Arabia,
> durch Hermani in Persia,
> durch Tartari in Suria,
> durch Romani in Türggia,
> Ibernia,
> der sprüng han ich vergessen.   (Song 44, I, 1–6)

[Through Berberland, Arabia, through Armenia to Persia, through Tartarland to Syria, through Byzantium to Turkey, Georgia, such hops I've long forgotten.]

The short lines and cataloguing effect lend the poem a momentum that suggests the excitement of the journey. Many of Oswald's travel songs have such lists of places, though it is unlikely that he actually visited them all. A conflict of the estates appears in song 25, "Ain burger und ain hofman," a disputation between a knight and a burgher, about which is best fitted to win the love of a young woman; interestingly, the knight comes off rather badly. Oswald was imprisoned twice in his life, and he introduced the new form of prisoner's song to his colorful *oeuvre*. In one song the image of the prisoner is fed back into the love poem:

> Gevangen und gefüret
> ward ich ainst als ain dieb
> mit sailen zü gesnüret;
> das schüff meins herzen lieb,
> von der ich hab erworben
> mein aigen leiden swër.
> wer si noch ainst gestorben!
> noch ist si mir gevër.   (Song 23, III, 9–16)

[Once I was captured and led away like a thief, bound up by ropes. It was the love in my heart that did this, a love that has caused me great suffering. If only this love had died! But still it haunts me.]

Oswald is also noteworthy for his mastery of the relationship between text and music; his melodies, like Frauenlob's, which have been recorded, were often set in polyphony and quite sophisticated, if imitative.[16] This was without doubt the acme of the late medieval lyric. Oswald was exceptional, however, and possibly out of step with the prevailing mood, for after his death his poetry was all but forgotten until modern scholarship rediscovered it. With him died the tradition of the courtly troubadour.

However, if the old forms of courtly literature suffered neglect, the four-teenth century did produce a number of new, specifically courtly forms, which focused on the characteristics that distinguished the nobility from the other classes of society. One was the chessbook, a peculiar form that turned the game into a didactic allegory of the feudal order. The *Schachzabelbuch* (Chessboard Book, 1337) of Konrad von Ammenhausen (b. 1280/90) is the best known of this series of mostly anonymous German verse and prose reworkings of a Latin tract by the Italian Dominican Jacobus de Cessolis (fl. 1288–1322), which takes the chessboard as the starting point for an extended metaphorical exploration of the divinely appointed social structure. King and queen (*chünig, chünigin*) head the dignitaries, aided by bishop (*alde*), knight (*ritter*), and rook (*roch*) leading an army of pawns (*venden*).[17] The knights are the easiest of the middle-ranking pieces to locate in the feudal order; in the prose version of the text we read:

> Der ritter auf dem schachtzabel sol sitzen auf ainem ross, mit allem har-nasch vnd gantzem wappen getzyert vnd angelegt vnd also geschykcht, das er hab ainen helm auf seinem hawpt vnd ain sper in der rechten hant vnd bedecktt in ainem schilt, vnd in der lenken hant ein swert vnd an dem leib ain pantzir, vnd vor ain prustplech, vnd mit armgerät vnd mit paingerät angelegt, vnd sporn an seinen füessen vnd plechhantschuech an seinen henten, vnd vnder im ain pfard, das tzw streit getzogen sey vnd mit einer pfell wedekcht.[18]

> [The knight on the chessboard is to sit on a steed, adorned with full armor and weapons, and to be crafted with a helmet on his head and a lance in his right hand, covered by a shield, and in his left hand a sword and on his body a coat of mail and on his chest a hauberk, and wearing arm and leg protection and spurs on his feet and metal gloves on his hands, and under him a horse that is trained for battle and covered in silk cloth.]

As the pieces were differently shaped from today's, the modern reader is grate-ful that the text takes time to describe exactly what each one looked like. We thus have the full image of the knight as we know him from battle scenes in courtly novels, mounted on his steed with all the requisite accoutrements, and the text goes on to discuss the virtues he must possess and the tasks with which he is charged. The rook represents the king's deputy and is depicted holding a symbolic rod. The piece called a bishop in English is in Middle High German known simply as the elder, which the text allegorizes as a judge, and the figure on the board can be identified by the open book he is holding. This means that the ecclesiastical princes are not represented on the chessboard at all: the ori-gins of chess lie in the Islamic world, and it was not until the sixteenth century that the English language Christianized the game by upgrading the Middle English archer to a bishop; German never did so. At the bottom of the structure, of course, are the pawns. Where modern German speaks of the *Bauer* (peas-ant), medieval *vende* (like English pawn) means "foot-soldier."[19] However, since medieval warfare made more use of armed peasants and townspeople than of professional soldiers, the text is free to identify each of the eight pawns as representing a different group of agricultural or urban trades. Despite the

Dominican affiliation of Jacobus, chessbooks were fundamentally courtly in their interest and sought to strengthen feudal power structures by developing idealized models of each estate of secular society.

Another interesting form coming to prominence in the fifteenth century, but not achieving high fashion until the mid-sixteenth, was the *Hauschronik* (housebook), the chronicle of a noble family designed to demonstrate its antiquity and grandeur.[20] At a time when humanism was demanding that scholarship pay rigorous attention to sources and distinguish *res factae* from *res fictae*, the housebook became popular among ruling houses — especially those of the lower ranks of the nobility that had recently enjoyed some rise in fortune — to underpin their legitimacy with elaborately embellished accounts of the origins of their bloodlines. In the attempt to meet the expectations of both patrons and peers, humanistically trained historians had to juggle contradictory demands. The *Hauschronik* thus became a hybrid form. Occupying a position between the late medieval chronicle and early modern historiography it integrates elements of mythology, travel literature, biography, genealogy, objective history, and blatant fiction. An early example is the *Schaumburgische Chronik* by Hermann von Lerbeck (fl. 1380), a Dominican theologian working in the service of the dukes Bernhard and Otto von Schaumburg. It runs from 1030 to 1407 and draws on the local history of Minden as well as the history of Hermann's own order but concentrates principally on the successes of the family. The two best-known housebooks, the *Truchsessenchronik* and the *Zimmerische Chronik*, are both sixteenth-century.

As a postscript to this survey of the late medieval courts we must also take note of the bishops' courts, which obviously stand apart from the secular courts and yet are closer in their thinking to the courtly world than to the monasteries. Bishops, after all, were often scions of ruling houses. The best-known writer at a bishop's court in this period was Heinrich Wittenwiler (ca. 1395–1426), whose *Ring* is a comic-didactic verse satire, probably written in the first decade of the fifteenth century.[21] Wittenwiler was presumably engaged in the service of the bishop of Constance, to whom he would later become *Hofmeister*. In the prologue to the *Ring* he explains that, since pedagogy is usually boring, he has chosen to communicate through the medium of an entertaining tale. The ring of the title is an allusion to the cycle of the world, and he wishes above all to inculcate good manners and right conduct in the world, though he is equally concerned with literary style. In the manuscript, colored marginal stripes identify in green those passages that satirize peasant boorishness and in red those that can serve as stylistic models for young writers; simply put, green is for comic relief, red for the serious or sententious.

The *Ring* tells how the peasant lad Bertschi Triefnas of Lappenhausen sets out to win the love of the unspeakably ugly Mätzli Rüerenzumph. The first green passage in the work describes her virtues in terms perhaps meant to invoke Wolfram's depiction of Cundrie:

> Ir wängel rosenlecht sam äschen,
> Ir prüstel chlein sam smirtäschen.

> Die augen lauchten sam der nebel,
> Der aten smacht ir als der swebel. (ll. 89–92)

[Her cheeks were as rosy as ashes, her breasts as delicate as sacks of fat. Her eyes glowed like fog, her breath was scented like sulfur.]

He first woos her in a peasant tournament that parodies the knightly joust, then by singing on her rooftop; and when this results in disaster and Mätzli is locked in her room by her father, he turns to love letters. Unfortunately, neither of them can read. Bertschi seeks the help of the clerk Nabelreiber, and Mätzli turns to the apothecary Chrippenchra, who however takes advantage of her and leaves her pregnant. The young woman is now as keen as her suitor to marry, but the parents' objections must be overcome. Bertschi's family debates the pros and cons of marriage, while Mätzli's requires the groom to undergo an examination to prove his fitness for family life. When these obstacles have been surmounted, the wedding takes place and, despite the unpalatable fare, degenerates into an orgy of gluttony and drunkenness ending in a brawl between the Lappenhausen locals and the Nissingen neighbors. While the happy couple enjoy their wedding night, the two villages go to war, supported by witches, giants, and dwarfs, the only allies they can find. After lengthy campaigns, Lappenhausen is defeated through treachery and razed to the ground; all the inhabitants (including Mätzli) are slaughtered, with the sole exception of Bertschi, who retreats to the Black Forest to live as a hermit.

The basic plot comes from a short *Schwank* (farce) known as *Von Metzen hochzit* (On Metze's Wedding) and is expanded to some 9,700 lines. As the names of the protagonists suggest, the entire tale is a parody of crude peasant mores. However, Wittenwiler's point is not that peasants in particular are to be condemned for such behavior, but that all who behave in this way are peasants. Thus the courtly sneering at the rural poor is harnessed for the instruction of the reader on all questions concerning, "wie ein man sich halten schol / an sel und leib und gen der welt" (how a man should conduct himself in his soul and body, and in his dealings with the world). Wittenwiler builds into the narrative all kinds of didactic material. For example, Mätzli's father examines Bertschi on his knowledge of religion, health, and managing a household, as well as on general questions of virtue and right conduct. While the element of preaching clearly stands in the forefront, with many dogmas of the church carefully documented, Wittenwiler's clerical and courtly audiences obviously set equal store by the finer points of culinary sophistication, for the hero also has to proclaim in demonstration of his learning: "Chäs nach flaisch und nuss zuo fischen / Geb man uns ze allen tischen!" (At every meal let us be given cheese after the meat, and nuts with the fish!).

Monasticism and New Spiritualities

Medieval European literature was dominated by the church, and despite the explosion of secular literature from the twelfth century onward the traditional forms of religious writing continued to be produced in vast quantities throughout the later Middle Ages, principally in the monasteries. It is estimated that 75% of all late medieval German manuscripts contain spiritual texts.[22] Most were written in Latin, but German-language texts increased proportionately in response to changes in the educational demographics of German society. Biblical texts gradually became available in the vernacular, first as freely related verse narratives, such as Lutwin's *Eva und Adam* (fourteenth c.),[23] then as prose in the tradition of the *Historienbibeln*,[24] and from the mid-fourteenth century as more disciplined prose translations. The Augsburg Bible of 1350 contains the first complete New Testament in German; the Wenzel Bible of 1389 added the Old Testament; in 1452–55 the Latin Gutenberg Bible became the first book to be printed with movable type in the Christian West; the Mentel Bible, the first printed German translation, was produced by Johannes Mentel in Strasbourg in 1466; it was followed by the Cologne Bible of 1478–79 and others. The language of Mentel's Bible is archaic, suggesting that he took the text from an early-fourteenth-century manuscript that may predate the 1350 Augsburg text.[25] Meanwhile the *Biblia pauperum* (Paupers' Bible) tradition flourished in the fourteenth century, presenting the Bible in opulent painted manuscripts in which illustrations of scenes from the two testaments appear in parallel showing typological relationships; thus a scene from a Gospel would be flanked by one *ante legem* and one *sub lege*[26] to illustrate the integrated nature of God's plan of salvation. Some of the large colorful manuscripts with eight roundels on a page were entirely textless, but others, such as those printed as blockbooks,[27] had some commentary. Because of the great costs of production, this was clearly not, as the name might suggest, a Bible intended for the poor; the *pauperes* have been interpreted as the uneducated wealthy, but that too is problematic, for the visual program of these works is intellectually demanding. Alongside the Bible the most sought-after vernacular religious texts were legends, that is, biographies of saints, which began to be collected in vast legendaries, such as the various translations of the *Legenda aurea* (Golden Legend, ca. 1260) of Jacobus de Voragine (ca. 1229–98).[28] There were also books of discipline, meditative texts, various forms of expository works, and a new fashion for histories of the foundation of monasteries.

In the late Middle Ages, Europe experienced a series of religious renewals, whose origins reached back to the Cluniac reforms of the eleventh century and whose influences reached forward to the Reformation of the sixteenth; from the late thirteenth century they gave rise to uniquely late medieval forms of spirituality. The most important was mysticism.[29] Christian mysticism was summed up in the phrase *cognitio Dei experimentalis* (knowing God by experience), a paraphrase of St. Bonaventura's statement, "Optimus enim modus cognoscendi Deum est per experimentum dulcedinis" (The best way to know God is by experiencing his sweetness); similar formulations occur in Thomas Aquinas. Mysticism denotes an intense personal experience in which the believer has a sense of being taken up into oneness with God (*unio mystica*); it is commonly portrayed as a love relationship — with the Almighty, with Jesus, with the Holy Spirit — and may be drastically erotic.[30] Knowledge of self and of God are achieved through self-denial, spiritual exercises, and ecstatic trances. Mysticism held a particular appeal to certain women, who found in its practice an area of religious life that often inspired literary expressions of their special relationship with God. As *religiosae mulieres* (religious women) they were able to participate on an equal basis with men, though many pursued their spiritual enlightenment under the guidance of a male confessor. The great founders of German mysticism were David von Augsburg (ca. 1200–1272), Hadewijch of Brabant (fl. ca. 1240–50), Mechthild von Magdeburg (ca. 1207–ca. 1282), Meister Eckhart (ca. 1260–ca. 1328), Johannes Tauler (ca. 1300–1361), and Heinrich Seuse (ca. 1295–1366). Although their dates give the impression that the golden age of mysticism lay between the mid-thirteenth and the mid-fourteenth centuries, the movement commanded an undiminished popular following in the later fourteenth century too. At the same time, a new wave of piety known as the Devotio Moderna was emerging from the Low Countries, inspired above all by the teaching of Geert Groote (1340–84). Geert's influence is visible in the asceticism of the most original fifteenth-century writer on spirituality, Thomas à Kempis (1379–1471). Like mysticism, Devotio Moderna stressed experience — better to feel contrition than to be able to define it, as Thomas wrote in the first chapter of his *Imitatio Christi* (ca. 1418) — but it remained wary of visionary rapture; the aim was still closeness to God, but no longer conceived as mystic union.

Thomas was a member of the Augustinian Order, which like the Benedictine Order had exerted decisive influence on German culture through-out the Middle Ages. Though these older orders remained influential, their preference continued to be for writing mainly in Latin. The upsurge of vernacular religious writing was driven by new institutions and by the spiritual awakening of the laity. The Teutonic Order (1190), the Franciscans (1210), and the Dominicans (1215) came into existence during the Middle High German *Blütezeit* but had a significant impact on German literature only later. To these orders we must add the enormously influential lay movement begun in the late twelfth century, the Beguines. It is in these settings that we will find the literary fruits of the new spiritualities.[31]

The Teutonic Order (members may have the letters OT = *Ordo Teutonicus* after their names) was originally established in the Holy Land by Hanseatic crusaders as a medical brotherhood in imitation of the Templars and Hospitallers. In 1198 it was raised to the status of a knightly order comparable to the Maltese Order, and as such it was a religiously based organization of lay people trained in arms for the defense of Christendom. A papal *exemptio* freed it from the jurisdiction of local civil and ecclesiastical authorities, allowing it to take military action almost autonomously. Led by a *Hochmeister* (Grand Master) and organized in provinces, it grew rapidly in the following century and by 1300 had more than 300 *Kommenden* (command posts). In 1224 it turned its force against the "heathen" Prussians and in the ensuing wars not only subdued and Christianized the populations of the eastern Baltic but also established there a Teutonic Order state with its residence at

Königsberg. This territorial entity endured for 300 years and provides part of the historical background to the German-speaking East Prussia of modern times. The Teutonic Knights were eventually dislodged from the Baltic by the rise of Poland in the sixteenth century. A second main concentration was the province of Austria, where the order became involved in the Turkish wars.[32]

The literature of the Teutonic Order, which is substantial, was at its most productive in the fourteenth and fifteenth centuries.[33] Recent scholarship has questioned whether all of it was actually written, or commissioned, by members of the order or merely used by them; for instance, in some of the religious literature they may simply have appropriated existing works. However that may be, the writings found their place in the life of the order and have come down to us as a comprehensive corpus testifying to the literary awareness of the community. The importance of the order for literature has often been underestimated; but the huge volume of knights who passed through its doors in the course of these centuries made it a formidable force in the shaping of early modern German society and culture.

The cult of the Virgin was particularly important for the religiosity of the Teutonic Order; members were sometimes called *Marienritter* (Knights of Mary). A series of works produced by the order are dedicated to her life, foremost among them Bruder Philipp's *Marienleben* (Life of Mary, early fourteenth c.), a particularly fine poem.[34] Philipp himself was a Carthusian, but a dedication in his prologue declares he is writing for "den brüdern von dem deutschen hůs" (the brothers of the German Order). St. Martina was also the subject of a number of pious legends originating in the order, and Luder von Braunschweig (1275–1335) wrote a celebrated life of St. Barbara. More generally, the Teutonic Knights' interest in inspirational saints is seen in their two great legendaries, the *Väterbuch* (Book of the Church Fathers) and the *Passional*, apparently both by the same late-thirteenth-century poet. The focus of these works on the *miles Christi* (soldier of Christ) and on conversion is characteristic of the Teutonic Order.

The extent to which the order contributed to the tradition of the biblical epic may seem surprising. Throughout the first half of the fourteenth century an apparently systematic attempt was made to render the most useful parts of the Bible into German. Besides the *Historia der alden ê* (History of the Old Covenant), which covers longer stretches of biblical history, a series of works reproduce individual books of the Bible: Judith, Esther, Job, the Maccabees, the Book of Acts, and the Apocalypse. The *Hiob-Paraphrase* (Paraphrase of Job) may serve as an example of the method. Each verse receives paraphrase and commentary, so that text and exegesis flow together and the interpretations of the poet appear to fall in the mouth of Job himself.[35] The biblical epics are generally anonymous, a possible exception being the *Makkabäer*, tentatively ascribed to Luder von Braunschweig, and there is some question whether the composition of certain of the biblical epics predates their adoption by the order. Among other religious writings to emerge from the Teutonic Order is a curious text by Tilo von Kulm entitled *Von siben ingesigeln* (1331), in just over 6,000 lines of rhyming couplets.[36] In allusion to

Revelation 5 and 6, the seven seals of the title are seven theological wonders, sealed to readers lacking insight: the incarnation of Christ, his baptism, passion, resurrection, ascension, the outpouring of the Holy Spirit, and the Last Judgment. *Von siben ingesigeln* is not a narrative account of these events but seeks rather to "unseal" their mystery. The Teutonic Order is not usually known for contemplative writings, but this work is an exception in its sense of inner reflection.

The order also produced a smaller corpus of secular writings. One category beginning in the early fourteenth century was historiography, which chronicled the order's activities and the regions implicated in its military campaigns. Foremost among these were histories of Prussia: Nikolaus von Jeroschin's (d. ca. 1345) *Kronike von Pruzinlant*; Peter von Dusburg's *Cronica terre Prussie*; the *ältere* and *jüngere Livländische Reimchronik*; and the *ältere* and *jüngere Hochmeisterchronik.*[37] Other text types include a chessbook — a form that transferred readily from the court to the knightly order — and a life of Marco Polo — perhaps the prototype of the German-language travel report,[38] whose observations about the non-Christian East made it of obvious interest to this order of crusaders.

The second influential order to appear in this period was founded in Italy by Francis of Assisi (1182–1226). The Franciscans, also known as Friars Minor (OFM = *Ordo Fratrum Minorum*) or in England as Grey Friars, were a mendicant order committed to extreme poverty, hence their popular name in German: *Barfüsser* (The Barefoot Order). The Italian Thomas of Celano (ca. 1190–1260), a confidant of Francis and his earliest biographer (ca. 1230), was among the first group of Franciscans sent north of the Alps to establish provinces in Germany. The order was popular because of its simple spirituality and service to the poor, and spread rapidly. Important German Franciscans of the early period were Lamprecht von Regensburg, who wrote a *Sanct Francisken Leben* (Life of St. Francis) around 1238; David von Augsburg, the first German mystic; and David's pupil, the prolific preacher Berthold von Regensburg (ca. 1220–72). By the beginning of our transition centuries, then, the order was well established and already had a literary tradition.[39]

In the fourteenth and fifteenth centuries the Franciscans were less productive in literary output than other orders, perhaps because their principal calling led them away from the scriptorium. Nevertheless, a complete inventory of Franciscan writings would be extensive. An important center of Franciscan activity developed in Erfurt, and it is notable that this convent had a role in the biographies of many Franciscan authors of the late Middle Ages.[40] Usually, their work took the form of sermons in German or Latin. Since medieval preachers did not carry scripts into the pulpit, manuscripts of written sermons must have been intended as textbooks or sourcebooks for younger members of the order. Among the notable sermon writers were Berthold of Wiesbaden, Erasmus Schaltdorfer (both fourteenth century), and Hermann Etzen (fifteenth).

In the fifteenth century the Franciscan Order was troubled by an internal conflict. A laxness in observance of the rule led to a reform movement that reached Germany around 1420, beginning in Cologne, and over the course of the century spread to include the majority of German Franciscans. The Observants, as they were called, insisted on absolute poverty, while the part of the order known as Conventuals permitted property. In 1517 the two groups finally split, the Observants becoming the modern Franciscans, while the Conventuals took the name Minorites. These tensions lie behind the *Chronica Ordinis Minorum Observantium* (Chronicle of the Order of Minor Observants) of Nikolaus Glasberger (d. 1508), which was begun in 1506 and continued by another hand after the author's death. The principal early chronicle of the Franciscans in Germany, it catalogues the observant monasteries and supports their cause. It is in the same context that we must read Bruder Heinrich's *Lob der Armut* (Praise of Poverty), an open letter testifying to his strict adherence to the observant lifestyle.

The most prolific Franciscan writer in late medieval Germany was Marquard von Lindau (ca. 1320–92), who wrote mainly in Latin. *De reparatione hominis* (On the Renewal of Mankind, ca. 1421–26) expounds salvation history in thirty chapters. Marquard also produced a number of important works in German: most notably his elucidation of the Decalogue, a collection of sermons, and tractates on the Book of Job and the Eucharist.[41] The *Dekalogerklärung*, or *Buch der Zehn Gebote* (Decalogue Elucidation, or Book of the Ten Commandments), is a comprehensive guide to Christian living based on scholastic thinking but with strong elements of mysticism and the cult of the Virgin. Formally the text is presented as a dialogue in which a teacher (*der meister*) responds to questions from a student (*der iünger*) with lengthy expositions on each of the commandments. When, for example, the student asks, "Sag mir fůrbas von dem dritten gebot als dů mir von den andern gesagt hast von seinen synnen vnd materien etc." (Tell me about the third commandment as you told me of the others, about its sense and meaning, etc.), the teacher begins to expound on the holiness of Sunday, beginning with the days of creation.[42] We are obliged, he explains, to abstain not only from work but also from trade and legal proceedings, "es wer dann v̂mb fried oder v̂mb gehôrsame oder von notdurft oder das vil guts dovon kôm douon got gelobt wůrd" (unless it be a matter of maintaining the peace, or of obedience, or of urgent necessity, or if much good would come of it, through which God would be praised). The Sabbath begins at vespers, but this varies from place to place, and we should respect local customs. Question: Is it permissible to dance or feast on a Sunday? Answer: Distinctions have to be made, for this is more reprehensible in a cleric than in a layman. All this seems quite legalistic, as an exposition of ancient laws must inevitably be; but soon the discussion moves on to the ways in which Mary kept the commandments, and positive examples take the place of prohibitions: how Mary prepared her prayers, how she listened to the sermon, with what piety she lay down to sleep, and — entirely in the spirit of mysticism — the six stages of her contemplation.

A number of other Franciscan writers of this period are worthy of note, though few were widely known outside the order. Otto von Passau was a religious didactic writer of the second half of the fourteenth century. His most influential work, *Die vierundzwanzig Alten oder der goldene Thron der min-nenden Seele* (The Twenty-Four Elders, or the Golden Throne of the Loving Soul, 1418), contains instructions for the Christian life. Friedrich von Saarburg wrote a poem in rhyming couplets on the antichrist.[43] The majority of the best authors wrote in Latin, however. Doubtless the most important Franciscan historian of the fourteenth century was Johannes von Wintertur (ca. 1302–after 1348), whose chronicle was planned to account for world history but never got beyond the years 1190–1348. Rudolf von Biberach (ca. 1270–1326), a mystic theologian, wrote *De septem itineribus aeternitatis* (On the Seven Journeys of Eternity), which describes the ascent of the soul to God in seven stages; Johannes von Erfurt (fl. ca. 1300) was known for his theological, philosophical, and juridical manuals. However, none of these equaled the status of Marquard von Lindau, and few were widely known outside the order. It was only in the sixteenth century, with Thomas Murner, that the Franciscans again produced a writer with great appeal to a secular readership.

The Dominicans, the third new order, were also known as Predicants, or Order of Preachers (OP = *Ordo Praedicatorum*), or in England as Black Friars. Like the Franciscans, on whom to some extent they were modeled, the Dominicans were a mendicant order, but their focus on preaching made them a more aggressive force. Founded by the Spaniard Dominic of Calaruega (ca. 1170–1221), their origins lay in the Albigensian controversy, which had lasting implications for their understanding of their mission.[44] It motivated them, for example, to high intellectual aspirations in order to be armed for disputations against heresy. Like the Franciscans, they drew many of their neophytes from the cities, but with the difference that their recruitment targeted well-educated people from the upper burgher classes. Many Dominicans had a university education, and the order produced great scholars, foremost among them Albertus Magnus (1193–1280), an authority on everything from biblical exegesis to zoology, and his pupil, the most gifted systematic theologian of the late Middle Ages, Thomas Aquinas (1224–74). The darker side of the order's history was its advocacy of the forceful suppression of deviance. As early as 1227 the Dominican Konrad von Marburg was placed in charge of the German Inquisition, which he pursued with extreme cruelty. This facet of the order left a literary testament in the form of the *Hexenhammer* (The Witches' Hammer, 1487) by the Dominican friar Heinrich Kramer (Institoris, 1430–1505), the most notorious treatise on witch hunting of the fifteenth century.[45]

The Dominican Order struggled against perceived pagan tendencies in humanism, and their most powerful response to this competing source of learning was to produce kerygmatics — works on the exposition and preaching of the gospel — of the highest quality. Jakob von Soest (ca. 1360–after 1438) was a scholar of broad distinction whose writings include theological, homiletic, historical, and legal texts. His work on preaching technique may be regarded as his main contribution to the life of the order: *Distinctiones longiores pro arte praedicandi* (Longer Book of Distinctions on the Art of Preaching,[46] ca. 1400) is an alphabetically arranged encyclopedia of the sermon genre, with explanatory lemmata on themes, biblical characters, points of doctrine, and theoretical problems. The amassing of comprehensive collections of alphabetically organized information was characteristic of the scholars of this period, though the use of alphabetical order was still far less common that it would become. Johannes Herolt (before 1390–1468) deserves mention as another respected author of preaching aids.

Dominican scholarship produced a number of significant historians in addition to Jakob von Soest. Hermann Korner (1365–1458) must have spent most of his life working on his *Chronica novella*, as he revised it repeatedly in both Latin and German, prose and verse. In essence a compilation of the works of earlier historians, but with personal critique of the events recorded, this chronicle runs from the foundation of Rome down through the sequence of emperors, but focuses particularly on Korner's home town of Lübeck. Hermann von Lerbeck's *Schaumbergische Chronik* was mentioned above; on behalf of his order he also composed ecclesiastical chronicles of Minden.

The Dominicans made a particularly strong contribution to German mysticism, with Meister Eckhart, Heinrich Seuse, and Johannes Tauler all standing in this tradition. The first and greatest was the creative theologian Meister Eckhart.[47] Eckhart himself never speaks of visionary experiences or emotional catharses, but he laid the philosophical foundation on which many subsequent mystics built their ideas. Eckhart's was more of an intellectual mysticism. He is best known for his German works, particularly his sermons and his *Buoch der goetlichen troestunge* (Book of Divine Consolations, ca. 1314), generally known as the *Trostbüchlein* (Little Book of Consolation), a short, sophisticated work that couches complex spiritual ideas in a dense prose style. It is impossible to understand Eckhart's German correctly without an awareness of certain key ideas that he expounds fully only in his Latin works, and this is no doubt one reason why his intentions have often been confused. Eckhart's mystical teachings take as their starting point the distinction between the temporal and the eternal, whereby only God the Eternal really *is*, while his creatures receive *being* as long as the Creator allows it to flow to them out of himself. Eckhart describes this process by analogy with a mirror, which receives an image though it produces none. The incarnation of the divine logos is thus a divine self-projection into time, and this — like everything in Eckhart's metaphysics — has two aspects: as an act of God it is eternal, but as an event in history it is rooted in time. The same two aspects lie at the root of his understanding of the human soul, whose vital spark, the *scintilla animae*, or *Seelenfünklein*, is both eternal and transitory; it is one with God and thus uncreated, yet at the same time divinely created and bound by the dimensions of this world. This paradox provides the metaphysical basis for Eckhartian mysticism; it became one of the principal complaints in turning the ecclesiastical establishment against him.

Fourteenth-century mysticism had formidable opponents on the conservative side of the church. In 1326 Eckhart became a *cause célèbre* in the political wrangling when the archbishop of Cologne instigated heresy proceedings against him through the Inquisition. It was unusual for this instrument to be used against a leading theologian working within a major order, and since the Dominicans defended him — papal representative Nikolaus von Strassburg OP declared Eckhart's writings to be free of error — the Franciscans were asked to lead the prosecution. A series of theses, mostly from the *Trostbüchlein*, were adduced as evidence of unorthodoxy, and the defendant's rebuttal focused on the spirit of his intentions rather than the letter of the disputed theses. Ultimately, he appealed to the pope but lost his case, though the verdict of heresy did not fall until 1329, the year after his death.

This institutional disapproval did little to dampen the enthusiasm of those to whom he was a beacon of mystic enlightenment. Most of his Latin writings were translated into German in the subsequent decades, but his popularity went far beyond the reception of his works. The *Eckhart-Legenden*, actually sermon illustrations containing anecdotes of his wisdom, reflect that popularity. Examples are *Meister Eckharts Tochter* (Daughter) or *Meister Eckhart und der nackte Knabe* (and the Naked Boy). In the former, a "daughter" knocks at the monastery door asking for the master and declaring that she is neither virgin nor married nor widow, neither woman nor man; the solution to the riddle is that she exists in a transcendental state of enlightenment, and Eckhart declares her to be the "aller lütersten menschen" (most enlightened person) he has ever met. The latter story tells how God appears in the form of a poor boy and engages Eckhart in a philosophical dialogue on the nature of divinity and revelation.

Eckhart's younger contemporary, Johannes Tauler, was deeply affected by the master's preaching. Tauler's own sermons are contained in over 200 manuscripts. They explore the *transformatio* or *deificatio* of the believer, which can occur in that divine *scintilla animae*, whereby God perfects the human soul by resolving it to himself. Tauler's influence was enormous, and it is telling that he was valued equally in the sixteenth century by the reformers and by the Jesuits. The other great original thinker to follow in Eckhart's wake was Heinrich Seuse, who as a young man received pastoral counseling from his mentor. Seuse's German writings are classics of mysticism. These include an autobiography, *Vita* (ca. 1362–66), a relatively new form in this period that lent itself to mystic explorations. This book concentrates on his sufferings, likened to Job's, and includes a running analogy with a knightly career: he is raised to spiritual knighthood and wounded in spiritual jousts, but in his tribulations he is comforted by visions, in one of which Meister Eckhart appears.

The Dominicans were keen to bind the new movement of female spirituality into their institution, and thus set up convents of nuns under their auspices.[48] The *cura monualium*, the pastoral care of women by the brethren, was in fact an obligation placed on both the Franciscans and the Dominicans by the church authorities to bring these women under the discipline of their organizations. For the monks this responsibility was not always welcome, but they pursued it with diligence; indeed, this may be the main reason why a highly intellectual order like the Dominicans produced vernacular literature at all. It has been asserted that Eckhart wrote in German only when he was writing for the nuns. *Yolanda von Vianden*, a 6,000-line verse account by the Trier

Dominican Hermann von Veldenz, straddles the genres of courtly romance and biography. It tells of the childhood of Yolanda (1231–83), a daughter of the Luxembourg nobility, who rejected her parents' plans for an advantageous marriage and instead entered the Dominican convent at Marienthal. Hermann's manuscript was spectacularly rediscovered in 1999.

Of this lively tradition of Dominican women who tended toward mysticism, Margareta Ebner (ca. 1291–1351), a Swabian and close correspondent of Tauler, is known for her *Offenbarungen* (Revelations), a kind of inner autobiography. Among her correspondents was Heinrich von Nördlingen, whose letters survive as testimony to his almost hagiographical reverence for her. Christine Ebner (1277–1356), no relation, was also a confidant of Heinrich — a good example of how mystics moved in tight circles. Encouraged by her confessor Konrad von Füssen, she too wrote autobiographical revelations and composed the *Engelthaler Schwesternbuch* (Book of the Engelthal Sisters), a collection of accounts of the experiences of the nuns in her convent. A similar work is the *Chronik* of Anna von Munzingen (fl. 1316–27), a collection of lives of female mystics in southern German Dominican convents. Adelheid Langmann (1306–75) was a member of the convent at Engelthal, but a generation younger. Her own *Offenbarungen* were influenced by Christine Ebner but are less pointedly autobiographical. They chart the stages of the gradual elevation of a soul to God, climaxing in an erotic allegory in which *Spes* (Hope) and *Caritas* (Love) lead the enraptured soul to the marriage bed, where it experiences the *Unio* with Christ.

Any account of new spiritualities in late medieval Germany would be incomplete without some account of the lay movement of women who chose reclusive lives and often found their spiritual homes in mysticism. The Beguines, an independent movement, developed from the twelfth century onward, starting in the Netherlands and spreading rapidly to the cities of the Rhineland and southern Germany. The most famous Beguines were the great mystics of the thirteenth century, Mechthild von Magdeburg (for part of her career she was also a Cistercian) and the Brabantine visionary Hadewijch. Their male counterparts were called Béghards, but the lay movement had a special appeal for women. The persona of the *religiosa mulier* allowed a Beguine to achieve social acceptance as a spiritual authority without disappearing from the world. The women lived austerely, but they remained free of vows or hierarchy or any common rule. Although they practiced chastity, they could at any time return to normal life and marry, and they were permitted to hold property. However, the Beguines were under the scrutiny of the church establishment. In 1310 a French Beguine, Margareta Porete, was burned at the stake for her mystical writings, and a bull of 1312 declared that a dangerously heretical spirit of freedom was at large in the German Beguine and Béghard circles. By the mid-fourteenth century, the movement was in decline.[49]

Their numbers and visibility give the Beguines significance as the most obvious users of lay religious literature. The lay mystic was a natural recipient, for example, of a work like *Christus und die minnende Seele* (Christ and the

Loving Soul; anon.),[50] which presents the way to the *unio mystica* in pictures
and verse, using the image of the lover from the Song of Solomon to depict
the love affair of the soul with Christ. Both its simple style of presentation and
the fact of its appearance in print imply a primary readership among the laity,
an assumption supported by the fact that one of the best manuscripts was commissioned by a patrician woman, Margarethe Ehinger of Constance.[51]

Similarly, the macaronic Christmas carol *In dulci iubilo*, which is still sung
today, had its origin in a fourteenth-century mystic community, probably lay.
The manuscript testimony suggests that, already in the earliest stages, it existed
in at least two versions, one Upper German and the other Dutch, which corresponds to the geographical distribution of the main groups of Beguines at
the time. The Upper German version has exactly the strophic structure of the
modern German and English carols, but the Middle Dutch text has two extra
lines; the texts vary from four to seven strophes. The mixture of languages creates a sense of fun; this and the accompanying bouncy rhythm conjure up a
feeling of Christmas joy. Typical features of mysticism here include the ecstatic feeling and the image — in the first strophe of the Dutch version — of
hearts soaring up to God. The nineteenth-century poet Hoffmann von
Fallersleben first published the historical lyrics (German version, left; Dutch,
right):[52]

In dulci iubilo	In dulci iubilo
nu singet und seit fro!	singhet ende weset vro!
alle unser wonne	al onse hertenwonne
leit in praesepio,	leit in presepio,
sie leuchtet vor die sonne	dat lichtet als die sonne
matris in gremio,	in matris gremio.
que est a et o.	ergo merito,
que est a et o.	ergo merito,
	des sullen alle herten
	sweven in gaudio.

[German: In sweet rejoicing now sing and be merry! All our joy lies in a
manger. It shines more than the sun in the bosom of the mother, and is
alpha and omega.]

[Dutch: In sweet rejoicing sing and be merry! All the joy of our hearts
lies in a manger. It shines like the sun in the bosom of the mother; therefore, to our benefit all hearts should soar in joy.]

Literature in the Cities

The most important contextual development between medieval and early
modern German literature was the emergence of an entirely new literary
milieu. The cities, not even on the literary landscape in the early thirteenth
century, had by the sixteenth century replaced the courts as the centers of
innovative writing. In the fourteenth and fifteenth centuries many of the most

significant authors belonged to the new urban intellectual world: Johannes von Tepl, Hans Rosenplüt, Heinrich Kaufringer, Thüring von Ringoltingen, Hans Folz, Sebastian Brant.[53] The southern German cities led in printing from the beginning, and one characteristic of urban literature is that it was intended for a far broader reading public than ever before. The spread of literacy to the urban populations began in earnest with the formation of new schools in the thirteenth century; in 1348 the first German-speaking university was founded in Prague, followed by Vienna, Heidelberg, Cologne, and Erfurt, and in the fifteenth century by a further eleven. Always, universities were located in cities. One factor driving this upsurge in urban erudition was a recognition of the usefulness of reading and writing skills for trade; but we should not underestimate the extent to which education and culture were ends in themselves for social classes with a new-found self-confidence and aspirations to a ranking hitherto barred to them.

The new cities represented an anomaly in the feudal thinking of the medieval courtly world, which with its pyramid structure of service and land tenure was fundamentally rural in conception. Even in the earlier Middle Ages city populations had enjoyed freedoms unknown to the peasantry, and city walls had as much to do with marking the boundaries of these privileges as with practical defensive purposes. While the cities too had clear power structures, in which for example patricians defined their identity in contradistinction to artisans, the potential for upward mobility within the ranking system of a city was far greater than on the land. The medieval cities mostly came under the direct rule of feudally appointed overlords, the dukes of Vienna, for example, or the bishops of Cologne; but as early as the beginning of the Middle High German period the citizenry was enjoying some degree of self-government in many cities. The transition to the early modern period was characterized by a striving for greater urban independence. Usually this meant persuading the feudal superior not to intervene in municipal affairs, but fuller legal independence was possible by attaining the status of imperial free city (*freie Reichsstadt*), as Regensburg did in 1285. In the north, the foundation of the Hanseatic League in 1160 was partly a question of the emancipation of the cities, as it was again in the south with the rise of the Swiss Confederation in the fourteenth century. The emergence of the term *stat* in place of *burg* must be seen in the context of the city becoming something more than merely the seat of a nobleman.[54]

One of the new literary forms of this period, the town (or city) chronicle (*Stadtchronik*), was often dedicated to this struggle.[55] The *Zerbster Ratschronik*, commissioned 1451, charts the history of Zerbst, near Magdeburg, from 1259 to 1445.[56] The first century is covered cursorily, recording documents granting trade prerogatives to the city, cited by incipit[57] and briefly described; but the bulk of the chronicle is a narrative account of the city's assertions of prerogatives against the dukes of Anhalt from the late fourteenth century onward. The activities of the mayor Peter Becker, who represented the city before the emperor, are recorded sympathetically. The purpose of the *Zerbster Ratschronik* was to provide a pool of information from which the interests of the city could be defended, and a docket in the manuscript warns that it should be shown only to trusted collaborators: "sal nyemant lesen, er sie denn met eyden der stadt verwandt!" (no one shall read it unless he is bound to the city by oath!).

The literary classes of urban society had an ambivalent view of the courtly world. On the one hand, the older, higher estate was resented, and some began to question the principle of the inherent superiority of the nobility. One of the first patrician writers, the Viennese Jans der Enikel, has such a program in mind in his *Weltchronik* (World Chronicle, ca. 1272). He first rehearses the old interpretation of the Noah story, that servitude comes from the curse of the renegade Ham and that the noble lines descend from the righteous brothers Shem and Japheth; but then Jans abruptly challenges this view:

> doch hân ich dick vernomen,
> daz wir von Evâ sîn bekomen
> und von Adâmen
> und von ir beider sâmen,
> herren unde knehte. (ll. 3121–25)[58]

[yet I have often heard that we are all descended from Eve and from Adam and from their offspring, masters and servants alike.]

The argument has an egalitarian ring, but Jans, a member of one of the city's elite families, is not thinking of the rights of all social groupings alike. Rather, the jibe is directed upward, toward the tension between the Viennese patriciate and the Viennese court. This rebelliousness against authorities above or outside the city allowed urban literature to go in different directions.

On the other hand, the leading patrician circles styled themselves as a new urban aristocracy, as *Ritterbürger* or *Stadtadel* (urban nobility), and in maintaining their preeminence within the cities they drew on precisely those concepts of nobility that troubled them at the court. It would therefore be a mistake to imagine that the urban centers of literary production rejected chivalric ideals. Their writings consciously seek continuities with the courtly traditions of the *Blütezeit*. Such a desire may have prompted Ulrich von Rappoltstein, the *Domherr* (lit., cathedral director) in Strasbourg, to commission the *Rappoltsteiner Parzifal* (1331–36).[59] This vast work — a team effort, written mainly by two goldsmiths, Philipp Colin and Claus Wisse, but also with a Jewish collaborator, Samson Pine — is in fact a compilation of Wolfram's *Parzival* (all sixteen books), a 36,000-line translation of Chrétien's *Perceval* (including the French continuations), and a collection of *Minnesang*. The result is rambling and inconsistent, as its philosophy (as in other urban compilatory works of this period — witness the chronicles of Heinrich von München) is to accumulate rather than to distil. The *Rappoltsteiner Parzival* was written in verse, but many urban versions of courtly romances were prose reductions, as for example an anonymous *Tristrant und Isalde* (printed 1488); Ulrich Fuetrer (d. 1496), a church painter from Landshut, produced both a prose and a strophic version of the Lancelot story. Thus, the narrative forms of courtly literature found their urban reworkings, and from the fifteenth century they were often printed for a wider audience.

Thüring von Ringoltingen's (ca. 1415–83) genealogical novel *Melusine* (1456, printed 1474),[60] offers an instructive example of the literature of the urban nobility. A relatively close reworking of the fourteenth-century French courtly romance by Couldrette, it is given a fresh dynamic in the context of Thüring's status among the elite of the city of Bern.[61] Reymund, son of an impoverished nobleman of Poitou, marries the mysterious Melusine, who had promised him prosperity when he encountered her by a spring. As a condition for the marriage, she sets one taboo: Reymund must never seek her out on a Saturday. They have ten sons, who are all, except the two youngest, marked by some facial disfigurement, be it a birthmark, an extra eye, or a boar's tooth. The eldest sons, Urien and Gyot, go to war, and the novel takes a lengthy digression on their exploits and successes, in which we see a reflection of the contemporary fear of Turkish expansion. At home, Reymund's brother misses Melusine at court on Saturdays and plants in her husband's mind a suspicion of misconduct. Reymund spies on his wife and discovers her in the bath, her lower body transformed into a serpent's winding tail. This is her curse, to be altered one day per week. Reymund regrets his disloyalty and keeps the secret until his son Goffroy, in a fury that his brother Freymund has joined a religious order, burns down the monastery, killing all the monks. In a voice loud enough for the members of the court to hear him, Reymund rages against Goffroy and his "demonic" mother. Thus exposed, Melusine must leave the courtly world. Goffroy later finds the tomb of his grandparents and discovers the secret of Melusine's curse, a parallel breach of trust in the previous generation: Melusine's father had broken a taboo laid on him by her mother, in retribution for which Melusine and her sisters killed him. Through this deed she earned the curse that could be removed only through marriage to a man who would keep the clause of their contract. Unfortunately, Reymund fails her, and her chance is lost; but Goffroy makes good his own failings, rebuilding the monastery and finally succeeding to his father's title.

As a symbol, the serpent's tail is multiapplicable. The fact that no harm comes of Reymund's initial breach of trust — Melusine knows he has spied on her and ignores it because she also knows he has told no one — suggests that it is not the taboo itself that matters but rather the public consequences of exposure. The novel is therefore a study in the social damage done when skeletons are allowed out of closets. Melusine's secret could speak to readers of various potential scandals that might lead to the social ruin of a dynasty. A pivotal question concerns Melusine's origins. If her parents are human and she herself a normal woman cursed for her sin, then the message of the novel relates to fall and redemption. However, if her mother is a water sprite, as is more likely, then the supernatural element does not originate from Melusine's patricide but from her matrilineal prehistory, and the difficulty with her socialization lies not in her personal failing but in her genealogy. The focus on lineage implies that for Thüring the stigma was above all the disgrace of having parentage below the social ranking to which a family aspired. When Reymund invites his feudal

mein schall vil mer dann tausent mal· Ich nun gesegen
dich got mein allerliebster trost vñ hort in meines her=
tzen grunde Gesegen eüch got alles volck/Gesegen dich
got dz schloß lusine so rein vñ so schön·dz ich gemacht
vñ selbs gestifft hab· Gesegẽ dich got du süsses seitẽspil
Gesegen dich got aller preiß diser welt/gesegẽ dich got
alles dz einer frauẽ wol gevallen mag· gesegẽ dich got
mein allerliebster freünt·d mein hertz gantz hat besessẽ·
❡ wie Mlusina Reymund gesegnet vñ alles volck vñ
schied weinende vñ schreiende hinweg·

o nun Mlusina dise wort alle volbrächt·do
thett sy aor in allen einen sprung·vñ sprang
gegen einem venster vñ schoß also zü de ven
steraus vñ wz zü stund eines augeplickes vnd der gürtel

Melusine flies away after jumping from the castle.
Courtesy of Bayerische Staatsbibliothek, Munich.

superior to the wedding, the latter replies with the question, "wer oder von
wannen ist die frawe die du da nimest. Acht das du nit mißfahrest von welcher
gegent / oder was geschlächtes. Auch sag mir / ob sÿ fast wol und
Hochgeboren seÿ" (Who or from where is the woman you are marrying? Take
care that you are not misled about her country or family. And tell me if she is
of high and noble birth). Reymund is forced to admit that he does not know,
"wer oder von wannen sÿ seÿ / oder was ir wesen seÿ" (who or from where
she is or what her essence is), except insofar as her "stand und gestalt" (rank
and nature) are obvious for all to see. This thematic linking of Melusine's

Wesen, her monstrous nature, with her *Geschlecht*, or *Stand*, her bloodline, is programmatic: we might say that *Wesen* is a metaphor for *Stand*. In this case, the novel is grappling with the problem of the integration into high society of a family whose origins are inferior. Although for Melusine herself success comes too late, her progeny is able to establish itself and break the stranglehold of its history.[62]

The story has direct relevance to Thüring's own socialization. His family had soared to the heights of Bernese society; his father, Rudolf, served several terms as mayor. They belonged to a cartel of eight ruling families, the so-called *Berner Twingherrengeschlechter*,[63] who laid claim to urban nobility. This elite group signaled its status through a dress code, which exacerbated tensions with other groupings in the city. In a celebrated case known as the *Twingherrenstreit* (1469–71), twenty-two members of this circle, among them Thüring, were convicted of breaching a ban on such sartorial symbols. Thüring was actually born with the surname Zigerli (quark-maker), which bore shades of the agrarian world of the Niedersimmertal, whence the family had moved to Bern as wine merchants in 1350.[64] In 1439 Rudolf changed the family's name to obliterate the memory of its mercantile origins, and the young Thüring assisted him with the archival research, producing the documentation necessary for a claim of genealogical succession to the now extinct line of von Ringoltingens. Thüring's requisitioning of the genre of the courtly romance may have been a strategic move: the family could compensate for their ancestral deficits through cultural competence. However, if the serpent's tail represents a failure of lineage, then Melusine becomes an allegory of the author's own family history, her ultimately successful struggle for class assimilation reflecting the genealogical self-invention that both Thüring and his primary readership practiced with such great creativity and dedication.

The growth of the modern city required a bureaucratic apparatus, which in turn led to the rise of an administrative class that by virtue of its education and social contacts was well placed to make a significant contribution to urban literature. The prominence of incumbents of the high civil office of *Stadtschreiber* (city clerk, director of the city chancery, responsible for official correspondence), especially among the authors of the fifteenth and sixteenth centuries, provides ample testimony to this.[65] This urban executive could be recruited from the ruling circles of the cities, but equally it provided an excellent career opportunity for young men of middle-ranking families. Johannes von Tepl (ca. 1350–1415) was apparently such a man. He was notary of the Bohemian city of Saaz by 1383, presumably having moved there from his northern Bohemian hometown of Tepl. He was also a teacher and held other public offices. Of his writings, only the *Ackermann aus Böhmen* (The Plowman of Bohemia, 1400/1) survives.[66]

The *Ackermann* is a disputation between a bereaved "plowman" and the personified figure of Death. It is organized in thirty-three prose chapters (a spiritually significant number) averaging barely 200 words each. Each chapter is a speech, assigned alternately to the plowman and Death, until in the final chapter God speaks. There is no framework narrative, and only a postscript, in which the author's voice is heard, falls outside the direct speech of the litigants. At the beginning of the third chapter, the agricultural metaphor is explained: "Ich bins genant ein ackerman, von vogelwat ist mein pflug" (I am called a plowman, my plow is of a bird's attire), that is, he "plows" with a quill; the plaintiff is by profession a writer. The plowman laments the passing of Margaretha, his wife and the mother of his children. An acrostic in the post-script reads IOHANNES-MA, and the name Margaretha is introduced at the letter M, which suggests that the lamenting plowman may be identical with the author Johannes. Such a biographical interpretation is appealing, as the work appears more poignant if we believe it to be a cry from the heart; but it is equally possible that the drama of bereavement is merely a narrative prerequisite for the debate.

The literary power of the *Ackermann* owes much to the new chancery German style cultivated at Charles IV's Prague court by Johann von Neumarkt (d. 1380).[67] Based on the rhetorical forms of trecento Italian humanists, most notably the elegant epistolary style of Petrarch,[68] with whom Neumarkt exchanged letters regularly, German chancery style was full of formulaic, rhythmical devices. Johannes's admiring imitation of this characteristic is obvious from the very first sentence of the *Ackermann*, a bitter tirade against Death, with its double- and triple-repetitions and variations that enhance the effect of the outrage of the newly widowed plaintiff: "Grimmige tilger aller lande, schedlicher echter aller werlte, freissamer mörder aller guten leute, ir Tod, euch sei verfluchet!" (Cruel scourge of all nations, destructive purger of the world, terrible murderer of all good people, you, Death, be cursed!). Death answers in a tone of bewilderment, calling him "son" and challenging him to prove that he has been wronged. At this the plowman complains, "ir habt mir den zwelften buchstaben, meiner freuden hort, aus dem alphabet gar freissamlich enzücket" (you have most terribly plucked the twelfth letter [that is, M], my entire joy, out of my alphabet). He speaks of his former joy, but now "mein anker haftet ninder" (my anchor finds nothing to grip). In the ensuing exchange it is striking how reasonable Death is. While the plowman again and again rages bitterly about his loss — she was his "beloved," his "guiding star," his "sun," his "honorable falcon," his "hen with her chickens" — and curses his adversary in furious emotional tirades, Death patiently explains to him the way of the world. He describes the intolerable crush there would be in the world, and the terrible consequences that would follow, if all the animals and people born since creation were still alive; the mosquitoes would be unbearable! He argues that it would not be better to wait until people are so sick of life that they desire death, for that is not honorable. And things are not that bad: after all, there are other women, and in any case, is a man not better off without a wife, marriage being only a sequence of trials? Death repeatedly takes the pragmatic approach: since decay is the way of all flesh, it is wise to accept what one cannot change. Besides, who is this plowman to question a primeval force? In a mocking variant of God's answer to Job in the Bible, Death pretends to remember how the plowman was present at all the great events in history, when Moses was promised the land or Alexander defeated Darius — the implication being that since Death really was there, only an upstart plowman can challenge him. This reaches its ironic climax when he pretends to recall the plowman's appearance before the heavenly council to advise God when Eve took the forbidden fruit — and then the anticlimax, with the final mocking words of praise, "du bist zumale ein kluger esel!" (you are indeed a clever ass!).

The plowman may call on God to testify against Death, but Death insists he is doing the work of God, and like God, who makes his sun shine on the good and the evil alike (an allusion to Matt. 5:45), he treats all with equal force. In a key passage in chapter 16, Death declares himself God's reaper, created in Paradise when Eve fell, and pictured on a fresco from noble antiquity:

> Du fragest, wer wir sein. Wir sein Gotes handgezeuge, herre Tod, ein rechte würkender meder. [. . .] Du fragest, was wir sein. Wir sein nichts und sein doch etwas. Deshalben nichts, wan wir weder leben weder wesen, noch gestalt noch understand haben, nicht geist sein, nicht sichtig sein, nicht greiflich sein; deshalben etwas, wan wir sein des lebens ende, des wesens ende, des nichtwesens anfang, ein mittel zwischen in beiden. [. . .] Du fragest, wie wir sein. Unbescheidenlich sein wir, wan unser figure zu Rome in einem tempel an einer wand gemalet was als ein man sitzend auf einem ochsen, dem die augen verbunden waren. Der selbe man furte ein hauen in seiner rechten hand und ein schaufel in der linken hand; damit facht er auf dem ochsen. Gegen im slug, warf und streit ein michel menige volkes. [. . .] In unser bedeutnüß bestreit der und begrub sie alle.

> [You ask *who* we are. We are God's tool, Lord Death, a most effective reaper. You ask *what* we are. We are nothing, and yet something indeed. Nothing, because we have neither life nor being nor form nor foundation, are not spirit, not visible, not tangible; something, because we are the end of life, the end of being, the beginning of nonbeing, a midpoint between the two. You ask what we are *like*. We are ruthless, for our image was painted on a wall in a temple in Rome in the form of a man sitting on an ox, his eyes bound. The same man held a hoe in his right hand and a shovel in his left, and with these he drove the ox forward. A large crowd of people beat him, threw things at him and argued with him. In our parable he overcame them and buried them all.]

And yet Death is not entirely right. The plowman's arguments gradually become more sober and rational while Death's become more subjective and disparaging. When Death denigrates humanity (chap. 24) and the plowman argues that people are "Gotes aller hübschestes werk" (God's finest work, chap. 25), it appears as if the indignant mortal has won a round. In the end, God reprimands Death for ignoring the source of his power, the plowman for refusing the sway of mortality. God, the ultimate judge, concludes the debate with a final statement that balances the domains of man and Death: "klager, habe ere, Tod, habe sige" (Plaintiff, I award you honor; Death, I award you victory, chap. 33). In the epilogue the narrator is a model of Christian patience; the plowman has learned, has given up his complaint, and praises God, committing his late wife into the hands of the Eternal.

Sebastian Brant (1457–1521), the preeminent literary figure of the closing decades of the fifteenth century, was by descent a representative of the lower-to-middle echelons of city life: his parents ran the inn Zum Goldenen Löwen in Strasbourg.[69] At the same time, he represents urban intellectuality at its highest. In 1475 he enrolled at the recently founded University of Basel, where he studied humanities and law and became a lecturer even before completing his doctoral exams. He remained in Basel teaching, writing, publishing, and practicing law, for a quarter of a century before returning to his native city in 1500 and assuming the position of *Stadtschreiber*. University education as a path to authorial success was a new dynamic at the dawn of the early modern period and was typically urban. Even Brant's name is urban in conception. Most of the authors so far examined in this chapter have a name and a sobriquet, such as Johannes von Tepl, who may be referred to simply as "Johannes," but never as "Tepl," and is properly listed alphabetically under "J"; with the surname "Brant" we encounter the modern convention of nomenclature, which in Germany was an innovation of the artisan class.

Brant's *oeuvre* in German and Latin is strikingly diverse, including legal discourses, religious, political, and historical tracts and poems, and moral-didactic exhortations of various kinds. Many of these are short works that appeared as single-sheet pamphlets, so-called *Flugblätter* (broadsheets), which were so popular in the early days of printing. In his political writings he displays his loyalty to the empire and his hopes that the election of Maximilian I will lead to a Germany more united under a strengthened imperial sway; it is said to have been this stance that forced his return to Strasbourg after Basel joined the Swiss Confederation in 1499. Other pieces describe natural catastrophes, astronomical occurrences, and prodigies. His Latin eulogy on Petrarch is one of his finest poems. The intended readership varied considerably. While the Latin poems targeted the poet's academic contemporaries, possibly his students, the more popular topics were published in the vernacular for a wider reception. Single-sheet pamphlets may be thought of as the predecessors of newspapers, and one can imagine them being read aloud and thus reaching even the least literate of the city's residents. The aim was invariably to educate.

These diverse interests flow together in the work with which Brant's name is most closely associated, the *Narrenschiff* (Ship of Fools, 1494).[70] The genre of moralistic social satire on the theme of the fool was already coming into vogue when Brant appeared on the literary scene, but his *Narrenschiff* raised it to respectability. The Latin version, *Stultifera navis* (1497), translated by Brant's student Jacob Locher (1471–1528),[71] achieved international acclaim. The success of Brant's work lay above all in the manner in which it resonated with the mood of the day. All human eccentricities are catalogued and characterized in rhyming couplets. Each of the 112 short chapters addresses a different vice, from amiable silliness to wanton sinfulness. With biting wit Brant attacks the immoral and the irreligious, the boorish, ungrateful, envious, or vain; adulterers, flatterers, gamblers, dancers, and singers; parents who set their children a bad example, children who will not take a telling. Sometimes the butt of his jibe is a source of minor irritation, like people who take their dogs with them when they go to church; sometimes it is a serious threat to the social order, like Hans Böhme, the "bag-piper of Nickelshausen," who instigated the peasants' revolt of 1476. The evidence of folly is categorized finely, but the ultimate verdict is undifferentiating: all belong on board. The ship of fools was a popular image long before Brant adopted it: the ship going nowhere because of its crew's incompetence; the ship that encompasses the fools of the world, who despite their variety are in reality all "in the same boat"; the sinking ship full of exultant passengers ignorant of their impending destruction; or as Brant put it, the ship bound for the Land of Fools, Narragonia. The exact interpretation of the allegorical vessel need not be consistent or clear; it is enough that the ship can appear on the title page, crammed with figures in jesters' caps, an absurd visual image of human foolishness.

The visual presentation of the work was clearly foremost in Brant's mind as he wrote, and there can be little doubt that the relationship of text and image provides one key to the book's success. Each chapter is introduced by a woodcut, superscripted by a sententious three-line rhyme, and under this stand the title and the expository poem; the relationship between text and image was carefully planned and brilliantly executed — probably by the young Albrecht Dürer himself.[72] The chapters are always precisely thirty-four or ninety-four lines in length, calculated to fill exactly two or four pages respectively, with the result that the woodcut always appears on the right-hand side. A few woodcuts are used more than once in the work, such as the famous picture of the wheel of fortune in chapters 37 and 56, a frugality encouraged by the considerable expense involved in hand-carving the pictures; but one is never left with the impression that images have been recycled clumsily, as is often the case in prints of this period. On the contrary, the detail in which text and image echo each other testifies to careful planning. Every image contains at least one fool in his distinctive cap, and the humorous caricature of the theme carries the reader into the subsequent text. "Von zů vil sorg" (On Worrying too much, no. 24) shows the fool with the world literally on his shoulders; "Von nachtes hofyeren" (On Nighttime Courting, no. 62) depicts a woman, undressed for bed, emptying a chamber-pot over the unwelcome singers below her window; "Von alten narren" (On Old Fools, no. 5) plays with two different German idioms, showing an old man both with one foot in the grave and with the "Schindmesser im Arsch" (the butcher's knife in his arse).

In the prologue Brant declares that the book is a *Narrenspiegel* (mirror of fools), in which fools should see themselves and learn. Though the success of the book derives in part from the way it pokes fun in all directions, its humor is challenging rather than vindictive. A combination of parody and preaching seeks to bring the fool back onto the way of salvation. The key to salvation, however, is learning. This is underlined by the patterns of biblical citation: Brant's most frequented portion of scripture is the Old Testament wisdom literature, followed by the books of the Law. The volume opens with the *Büchernarr* (Fool for Books), the would-be scholar who does not truly understand his books, and it returns frequently to the theme of useful and useless

Wie wol jch vff der grüßen gan
Vnd das schyntmesser jm ars ßan
Mag jcß myn narrßeyt doch nit lan

haintz Nar

Von alten narren.
Myn narrßeyt loßt micß nit sin gryf
Jcß ßyn fast alt / docß gantz vnwyf
Eyn ßößes kynt von ßundert jor
Den jungen trag icß die schellen vor

Von alten Narren, illlustration from chapter 5 of Sebastian Brant's Das
Narrenschiff, *Courtesy of Bayerische Staatsbibliothek, Munich.*

learning. In part, Brant is making fun of academia, for there are many side-
swipes at the culture of students, disturbing the peace, for example, by singing
below the window of their beloved, but mainly it serves to indicate the true
purpose of learning. For folly's opposite is wisdom, and one achieves wisdom
through judicious and informed self-reflection. The optimistic humanist

assumption is that the sin and corruption that flow from folly (an intellectual failing) can be cured through education.

The principal contribution of the early cities to German lyric poetry is associated with the distinctive figure of the *Meistersinger* (also called *Meistersänger*, "master singer").[73] *Meistersang* has been seen as an urban attempt to usurp *Minnesang* (love song), a view encouraged by the singers' identification of Frauenlob, Heinrich von Mügeln, and other late-courtly troubadours, as their founders. However, the idea of a historical continuum is problematic, and the immediate precursors were probably traveling urban singers rather than courtly ones.[74] In contrast to the peripatetic *Minnesänger*, the *Meistersinger* were settled and organized in guilds like other urban trades; their meetings, or concerts, were known as *Singschulen*.[75] With the business-like efficiency of the urban classes, these "singing schools" established rules to make poetry and music teachable techniques; their codification was published in a tablet called the *Tabulatur* (tablature). Strict regulations were also enforced for the conduct of their closed meetings. Adam Puschmann first elucidated the principles in 1571 in his *Gründlicher Bericht des deutschen Meistergesanges* (Thorough Report on the German Master Song); the first history of *Meistersang* was composed by Cyriacus Spangenberg (1528–1604) and published in Strasbourg in 1598. But one of our best sources for this subculture was written much later, in 1697, by Johann Christoph Wagenseil (1633–1705):[76] *Buch von der Meistersinger holdseligen Kunst* (Book of the Mastersingers' Lovely Art), from which Richard Wagner drew much of the material for his opera *Die Meistersinger von Nürnberg*. Wagenseil reveals rituals and methods, reproduces the most important *Töne* (tones, melodies; each song used a specific *Ton*) in musical notation, offers a full-page woodcut of a master presiding in his finery, and reflects the great erudition with which the *Meistersinger* approached their art.

In the early period, that is, in the first half of the fifteenth century, Mainz was the leading center of *Meistersang*, followed by Nuremberg; later Augsburg, Strasbourg, Colmar, Freiburg, and Ulm became famed for their *Singschulen*. The leading singer of the late fifteenth century was Hans Folz (ca. 1435–1513), who expanded the repertoire, though he now seems to have been less of a reformer than was once assumed.[77] A barber from Worms, Folz settled in Nuremberg, where he joined the singers' guild and became a leading practitioner. His literary activity was far broader than simply *Meistersang*; like his great successor in Nuremberg, Hans Sachs (1494–1576), he also excelled as a dramatist and produced historical, political, and alchemistic tracts, as well as one disturbingly anti-Semitic piece, *Jüdischer Wucher* (Jewish Usury, 1491). However, it seems to have been for his *Meisterlieder* (master songs) that he was most prized by his contemporaries. The bulk of these treat of religious themes, but Folz breaks with tradition, for example by making a *Meisterlied* out of a misogynous *Schwank*: a man dies, he tells us, and his apparently distraught wife accompanies the bier to the cemetery. The pallbearers wish to rest beneath a certain tree, but the widow objects, remembering that her first husband, in being carried to his grave, was mysteriously brought back to life while the procession rested under this same tree. She would not wish this to happen again, she explains with feigned altruism, because his soul is at rest, and her grief is not reason enough to disturb his sleep. A week later she has remarried. Folz concludes:

> Das peispel merckt, ir jungen gseln,
> Hie von der weiber liste,
> Sie wein und lachen wan sie weln,
> Des yn nümer gepriste,
> Wan sie hant kurczen mut und lange cleider.
> Das clagt vil mancher leider.
> Es sind nit newe mer,
> Spricht Hanß Folcz barwirer.　(20, 63–70)

[Note well this example of female deceit, you young journeymen.[78] They weep and laugh when they will; this never fails them, for they are short in brains but long in clothes. Many a man has cause to rue this. There is nothing new about that, says Hans Folz the barber.]

The *Meistersang* tradition continued to blossom into the sixteenth century, reaching its golden age with Sachs, through whom it entered the service of the Reformation. After this it stagnated somewhat but survived for a further three centuries: the last German *Singschule*, in Memmingen, shut its doors in 1875.

The New Jewish Vernacular

From the tenth century onward Germany — אשכנז (*Ashkenaz*)[79] — had developed its own discrete brand of Judaism with distinctive customs and rituals, and a number of German cities became centers of international Jewish scholarship, foremost among them Mainz, Vienna, and Regensburg.[80] The visible presence of this community resulted in the frequent appearance of the Jew as a stock figure in, for example, the courtly novel, usually with a hostile overtone.[81] However, a host of Jewish motifs in Middle High German texts testify as well to a positive intellectual exchange.[82] Thus, the Jews left their mark on early German literature, but not as authors. Notwithstanding the celebrated case of the late-thirteenth-century Jewish *Minnesänger* Süsskind von Trimberg (ca. 1230–ca. 1300), whose *Sangsprüche* are transmitted in the Manessa Codex,[83] or of Samson Pine (fl. 1336), mentioned earlier in connection with the *Rappoltsteiner Parzival*, Jews did not contribute greatly to mainstream German literature until well into the modern period. However, bearing in mind that each of the various groupings of late medieval society produced a different literature for its own consumption, it is, in any case, problematic to apply the concept of mainstream to the literature of that time. Like urban, monastic, and courtly authors, Jews wrote mostly for a readership in their own communities, and this meant that they wrote in Hebrew. For the Jews of medieval Europe, Hebrew enjoyed a similar status to that of Latin for Christians: as the language of religion and scholarship, but with the difference that the average Jew commanded a far greater competence in the sacred language than the average Christian. It was no doubt for this reason that the Jewish communities turned later to the common language as a literary medium.[84]

Jewish vernacular works began to appear from the beginning of the fourteenth century. In its earliest phase the Judeo-German that later became the Yiddish language was a variety of Middle High German with a significant number of distinctive lexemes, mostly taken from Hebrew. It was written in Hebrew characters, the consonants *aleph*, *yod*, *waw*, and *ayin* being pressed into service as vowels. Later, as Yiddish came to be spoken across large parts of eastern Europe and to acquire a stronger Slavic influence, its kinship with German became less immediate; but in the late medieval period, writers in Old Yiddish perceived their language as טויטש (*tuitsh*), that is, *Deutsch*.[85]

In a manner similar to the first Christian excursions into vernacular writing in Old High German, the Judeo-German chirographic tradition began with glosses on the Bible and other Hebrew religious works and with inserts and asides in sacred manuscripts.[86] Probably the earliest example of the latter is a single rhyming couplet in a *machsor* (prayer book) datable to 1272–73, in which the scribe blesses the user with the wish:

> gut ták ím betáge
> se wǽr dis máchasór in béss hakenéssess tráge!

[May he be granted a good day who carries this machsor into the synagogue.]

In the years that followed, prayers and religious verse appeared, such as the macaronic pieces and Hebrew poems with German versions collected by the late-fifteenth-century Menahem ben Naphtali Oldendorf. By the sixteenth century, Yiddish had acquired sufficient respectability to allow interpretive translations of scripture; the paraphrase on the Book of Job (1557) by Avroham ben Schemuel Pikartei is reminiscent of the comparable work by the Teutonic Order. The use of written Jewish vernacular for secular purposes began slightly later than for sacred, and it too developed through phases broadly parallel to those earlier experienced by German Christian literature, beginning with small-scale functional writings, such as private letters or snippets of medical lore that sometimes have the character of charms. Although the earliest surviving examples of these are from the fifteenth century (the oldest known letter in Yiddish is dated 1478), the regular migrations of European Jewish populations in the face of pogroms and expulsions, combined with their lack of enduring institutions such as monastic or courtly libraries, mean that a great deal must have been lost. Functional writing in Judeo-German therefore probably began as early as the late thirteenth century.

The earliest monument of Judeo-German narrative literature are the verse narratives collected in the Cambridge Codex, which may date back as far as the early fourteenth century.[87] Dated 1382, the manuscript was partly written by one Isak der Schreiber. It was discovered in the archives of the Ezra Synagogue in Fostat, Cairo, in 1896;[88] that it reached Egypt is testimony to the great mobility of medieval Jewish communities. It contains six narrative poems: the closing lines of a poem about Moses, *Gan Eden* (The Garden of Eden), *Awroham owinu* (Abraham our Father), *Josef ha-zadik* (Joseph the Righteous), the *Lion Fable*, and *Dukus Horant*.[89] Although the texts are Judeo-German, the titles (only two of which are in the manuscript) are Hebrew. *Dukus* is a borrowing into Hebrew of Latin *dux* "leader," in the medieval sense of duke. Most of these poems contain biblical narrative, but the *Lion Fable* is secular. *Dukus Horant* stands on its own as a Jewish adaptation of a German heroic epic and has received the most scholarly attention of all the works in proto-Yiddish. It is composed in strophes of four lines, the first pair being the long two-part lines familiar from Germanic heroic poetry (though distichal verse, albeit unrhymed, is also typical in Hebrew), the second pair being short lines. The opening strophe, transcribed and transliterated, gives a flavor of the style and language:[90]

עש וש אין טוצן ריכן   איין קוניק וויט ארקנט

איין דעגן אלזא קונא   איטנא וש ער גננט

ער וש מילדא און שונא

ער טרוק דער אירן קרונא

's uus 'in tužn rikn	'iin quniq uuit 'rqnt
'iin d'gn 'lz' qun'	'itn' uus 'r gnnt.
'r uus mild' 'un šun'	
'r truq der 'irn qrun'	

[There was in the German lands a famous king, a most valiant hero; Etene was his name. He was generous and fair, and bore the crown of honor.]

If we now translate this into a normalized Middle High German, it becomes obvious that the two are very similar:

Ez waz in tiutschen rîchen	ein kunic wît erkant,
ein degen alsô kuone	Etene waz er genant.
Er waz milde unde schône,	
er truoc der êren krône.	

Whether these two forms of language are different at all depends on how the script is interpreted, and it has been argued that *Dukus Horant* is nothing more than standard Middle High German in Hebrew characters. However, the modern consensus is that the language of the poem does already have a distinctively Jewish tone.

The poem tells the story of Etene, a young German king, whose hegemony extends to Denmark, Spain, Italy, France, and Hungary. Etene is advised by his confidant, Duke Horant, to seek a wife. At a council of his vassals, the Greek princess Hilde is proposed as his wife, though the ferocity of her father, King Hagen, is a cause for concern. Accompanied by his brother Morunk, three giants who recognize Etene as their feudal superior, and 200 knights,

Horant embarks on a journey to Greece to win the bride on his king's behalf. Arriving at a vast eastern port (presumably Constantinople) Horant first seeks contact in patrician circles, eventually finding quarters in the home of one of the richest merchants in town. After twenty-eight days, the Whitsun festivities furnish Horant with the opportunity to catch the eye of the princess. Later that same evening Horant sings in the courtyard of his merchant host, and now his true gift is revealed: the birds fall silent, the animals come out of the woods, and even the wild boar — for Jewish listeners the epitome of the uncivilized — ceases to roll in the mud. From the palace roof, Hilde hears and is captivated. A meeting is arranged and Horant presents Etene's suit. When he promises to sing for her in Germany, Hilde agrees to abscond after the festival. During the festivities Horant's men kill a lion, while Horant acquits himself well in a joust. Both incidents attract Hagen's attention; Horant offers to become Hagen's vassal and promises to return the next day. At this point the manuscript breaks off. Obviously, the tale must end with a successful conclusion to Horant's quest. Presumably, his ruse initially will be successful, allowing him to smuggle Hilde from the city; presumably, Hagen will come after him, since a military confrontation involving the knights, the giants, and ultimately Horant's own prowess is a necessary ingredient, given the rules of the heroic epic; and presumably, this battle will end with Hagen submitting to the feudal supremacy of Etene. Two loose ends may be significant: Hilde gives Horant a ring with a magic stone that may be instrumental in Horant's ruse; and Horant has his horses shod with golden shoes fixed only with a single nail, so that they periodically fall off, a strategy aimed at winning the affection of the impoverished townspeople: perhaps their support is later valuable to him.

The work has been referred to as the "Jewish *Kudrun*," since several characters share names and attributes with those of the Middle High German *Kudrun* epic,[91] and the parallels come particularly close in the sections where Hilde is wooed at Hagen's court, in Ireland. A parallel has also been suggested with another epic, *König Rother*; it too has a bridal quest, and in this case the particular similarity to *Dukus Horant* lies in the locations, the German King Rother seeking to woo the princess of Constantinople. What these analogies indicate is not any direct intertextual relationship but rather a shared oral tradition finding an independent literary expression in both Jewish and Christian milieus.[92] This most likely represents a Jewish tradition of oral performance consisting of both indigenous Jewish material and tales from the majority Christian community sung in a vernacular that at the time still had only a slight Jewish coloring. It may point to the presence in the Jewish community of professional peripatetic singers who practiced oral performance poetry for the entertainment of their peers. Earlier scholarship spoke of the Jewish *spilman*, though the word is unfortunate, both because it forces Jewish culture into Christian terms and because the concept of the *spilman* is in any case an inaccurate way of describing what was going on in German oral tradition. An intriguing suggestion is that these singers might have been the cantors of the synagogues. Cantors certainly had the necessary performance skills as well as a natural place in the limelight. Against this conjecture is the fact that some Jewish religious authorities spoke out against secular songs.

The *Dukus Horant* manuscript is the earliest surviving witness to this tradition, but it clearly was no isolated curiosity. Another early Judeo-German retelling of a courtly novel, *Widuwilt*, also known as *Kinig Artus Hof* (King Arthur's Court), is an adaptation of the late-thirteenth-century Middle High German romance *Wigalois* by Wirnt von Gravenberg.[93] The first poet in this tradition whose name is recorded became active toward the end of the fifteenth century: Elia Levita Bachur (1469–1549), author of the *Bovo-Buch* and *Paris un Viene*. In the centuries that followed, the range of Judeo-German and Old Yiddish literature broadened immensely. Thus, by the time mainstream modern German literature was flourishing in the Baroque period, Yiddish too had become a fully-fledged literary idiom.

Notes

[1] This neglect has been partly rectified by a surge of interest in recent decades. Particularly useful orientations are Thomas Cramer, *Geschichte der deutschen Literatur im späten Mittelalter*, vol. 3 of *Geschichte der deutschen Literatur im Mittelalter* (Munich: DTV, 1990); Wolfgang Spiewok, *Geschichte der deutschen Literatur des Spätmittelalters*, 3 vols. (Greifswald: Reineke, 1997–99); and Johannes Janota, *Vom späten Mittelalter zum Beginn der Neuzeit*, vol. 3/1 of *Geschichte der deutschen Literatur von den Anfängen bis zum Beginn der Neuzeit* (Tübingen: Niemeyer, 2004). Helmut de Boor and Richard Newald, *Geschichte der deutschen Literatur*, parts 3/1 (5th ed., 1997), 3/2 (1986), and 4/1 (2nd ed., 1994) (Munich: Beck) also give thorough coverage. The element of transition is highlighted in Werner Röcke and Marina Münkler, eds., *Die Literatur im Übergang vom Mittelalter zur Neuzeit* (Munich: Hanser, 2004). See also Wolfgang Harms and Peter Johnson, eds., *Deutsche Literatur des späten Mittelalters* (Berlin: Schmidt, 1975); Walter Haug, Timothy R. Jackson, and Johannes Janota, eds., *Zur deutschen Literatur und Sprache des 14. Jahrhunderts* (Heidelberg: Winter, 1983); and Horst Brunner and Werner Williams-Krapp, eds., *Forschungen zur deutschen Literatur des Spätmittelalters* (Tübingen: Niemeyer, 2003). On the novel see Walter Haug and Burghart Wachinger, eds., *Positionen des Romans im späten Mittelalter* (Tübingen: Niemeyer, 1991). On historical writing: Hans Patze, ed., *Geschichtsschreibung und Geschichtsbewußtsein im späten Mittelalter* (Sigmaringen: Thorbecke, 1987). For career biographies on individual authors see Max Reinhart and James Hardin, eds., *German Writers of the Renaissance and Reformation 1280–1580*, vol. 179 of *Dictionary of Literary Biography* (Detroit: Gale, 1997). Henceforth cited as Reinhart and Hardin, eds., *DLB 179*.

[2] "Chirographic" refers to handwritten documents and may be contrasted with "typographic"; see R. Graeme Dunphy, "Orality," in *Early Germanic Literature and Culture*, ed. Brian Murdoch and Malcolm Read, vol. 1 of *Camden House History of German Literature* (Rochester: Boydell & Brewer, 2004), 103–18. The Camden House series will hereafter be cited as *CHHGL*.

[3] See in this volume the chapter by Renate Born.

[4] See Dorothea Klein, "Wann endet das Spätmittelalter?," in Brunner and Williams-Krapp, eds., *Forschungen*, 299–316.

[5] Ernst Regel, ed., *Johanns von Würzburg Wilhelm von Österreich* (1906; repr., Zürich: Weidmann, 1970).

[6] This interpretation is expounded in Gisela Vollmann-Profe, "Johann von Würzburg, 'Wilhelm von Österreich,' " in Haug and Wachinger, eds., *Positionen des Romans,* 123–35.

[7] Wolfgang Haubrichs, ed., *Zwischen Deutschland und Frankreich: Elisabeth von Lothringen, Gräfin von Nassau-Saarbrücken* (St. Ingbert: Röhrig, 2002).

[8] Edition: Jan-Dirk Müller, ed., *Romane des 15. und 16. Jahrhunderts: Nach den Erstdrucken mit sämtlichen Holzschnitten* (Frankfurt am Main: Deutscher Klassiker Verlag, 1990). Also Hermann Urtel, ed., *Der Huge Scheppel der Gräfin Elisabeth von Nassau-Saarbrücken nach der Handschrift der Hamburger Stadtbibliothek* (Hamburg: Gräfe, 1905).

[9] Reinhard Hahn, *"Von frantzosischer zungen in teütsch": Das literarische Leben am Innsbrucker Hof des späteren 15. Jahrhunderts und der Prosaroman "Pontus und Sidonia"* (Frankfurt am Main: Lang, 1990).

[10] See Martina Backes, *Das literarische Leben am kurpfälzischen Hof zu Heidelberg im 15. Jahrhundert: Ein Beitrag zur Gönnerforschung des Spätmittelalters* (Tübingen: Niemeyer, 1992). Also Richard Benz, *Heidelberg: Schicksal und Geist* (Sigmaringen: Thorbecke, 1961), esp. 63–81.

[11] See Will Hasty, *"Minnesang* — The Medieval German Love Lyrics," in *German Literature of the High Middle Ages,* vol. 3 of *CHHGL* (2006), 141–59.

[12] Not to be confused with an earlier *Minnesinger,* the margrave Heinrich von Meissen, Margrave Heinrich III (1218–88), also called Heinrich der Erlauchte. The works of both appear, clearly distinguished, in the Heidelberg manuscript C. The standard edition of Frauenlob is Karl Stackmann and Karl Bertau, eds., *Frauenlob (Heinrich von Meissen): Leichs, Sangsprüche, Lieder* (Göttingen: Vandenhoek & Ruprecht, 1981).

[13] See Burghart Wachinger, *Sängerkrieg: Untersuchungen zur Spruchdichtung des 13. Jahrhunderts* (Munich: Beck, 1973), chap. 10.

[14] On gnomic (moralizing or didactic) poetry see Nigel Harris, "Didactic Poetry," in Hasty, ed., *CHHGL 3,* 123–40.

[15] Karl Kurt Klein, ed., *Die Lieder Oswalds von Wolkenstein* (Tübingen: Niemeyer, 1962). See also Albrecht Classen, "Oswald von Wolkenstein," in Reinhart and Hardin, eds., *DLB 179,* 198–205.

[16] The melodies are in the appendix to Klein, ed., *Die Lieder Oswalds.* See also Elke Maria Loenertz, *Text und Musik bei Oswald von Wolkenstein* (Frankfurt am Main: Lang, 2003). Biography: Alan Robertshaw, *Oswald von Wolkenstein: The Myth and the Man* (Göppingen: Kümmerle, 1977). As Steven Saunders points out in "Music in Early Modern Germany" in the present volume, Oswald often only reworked French or Italian antecedents.

[17] The MHG terms for the chess pieces differ from those used in modern German: *König, Dame, Läufer, Springer, Turm,* and *Bauer.*

[18] Gerard F. Schmidt, ed., *Das Schachzabelbuch des Jacobus de Cessolis, O.P. in mittelhochdeutscher Prosa-Übersetzung* (Berlin: Schmidt, 1961), 48. The last word, *wedekcht,* is a regional variant of *bedeckt.*

[19] *Pawn* is French, from Latin *pedo, -onis* (a person on foot); *vende* comes from the IE *pend-* (to go, to find one's way), and so is actually most closely related to *finden,* but again implies "walking."

[20] See Gerhard Wolf, *Von der Chronik zum Weltbuch: Sinn und Anspruch südwestdeutscher Hauschroniken am Ausgang des Mittelalters* (Berlin: de Gruyter, 2002).

[21] Edition: Bernhard Sowinski, ed., *Heinrich Wittenwiler, Der Ring* (Stuttgart: Helfant, 1988). English translation by George Fenwick Jones, *Wittenwiler's "Ring" and the Anonymous Scots Poem "Colkel-bie Sow": Two Comic-Didactic Works from the Fifteenth Century* (Chapel Hill: U of North Carolina P, 1956). For his career biography see Albrecht Classen, "Heinrich Wittenwiler," in Reinhart and Hardin, eds., *DLB* 179, 326–31.

[22] Dorothea Klein, "Spätmittelalter," in Brunner and Williams-Krapp, eds., *Forschungen*, 306.

[23] Mary-Bess Halford, *Lutwin's Eva und Adam: Study — Text — Translation* (Göppingen: Kümmerle, 1984). For an introduction to the biblical epic see Brian Murdoch, *The Medieval Popular Bible: Expansions of Genesis in the Middle Ages* (Cambridge: Brewer, 2003); on its earlier history, Dieter Kartschoke, *Bibeldichtung: Studien zur Geschichte der epischen Bibelparaphrase von Juvencus bis Otfrid von Weißenburg* (Munich: Fink, 1975).

[24] The *Historienbibeln* contain selected episodes from the historical books of the Bible freely rewritten in the vernacular. In the absence of a satisfactory edition the most reliable texts are to be found in H. F. L. Theodor Merzdorf, *Die deutschen Historienbibeln des Mittelalters* (1870; repr., Hildesheim: Olms, 1963), though Merzdorf's presentation of only two basic texts is a serious over-simplification of this vast and complex tradition. See also Ute von Bloh, *Die illustrierten Historienbibeln: Text und Bild in Prolog und Schöpfungsgeschichte der deutschsprachigen Historienbibeln des Spätmittelalters* (Frankfurt am Main: Lang, 1991–92).

[25] For an introduction to Bible translations see Geoffrey W. H. Lampe, ed., *The Cambridge History of the Bible*, vol. 2, *The West from the Fathers to the Reformation* (Cambridge: Cambridge UP, 1969), esp. W. B. Lockwood, "Vernacular Scripture in Germany and the Low Countries before 1500," 415–36. Sample texts for comparative study in Joseph Kehrein, *Zur Geschichte der Deutschen Bibelübersetzung vor Luther* (1851; repr., Walluf: Sändig, 1972).

[26] Medieval biblical interpretation distinguishes three phases: *ante legem* (before the law) refers to everything before Moses; *sub lege* (under the law) is the remainder of the Old Testament; and *sub gratia* (under grace) is the dispensation beginning with the birth of Jesus. The exegetical discipline of typology drew parallels between these, so that, for example, Abraham's sacrifice of Isaac (*ante legem*) speaks of God's sacrifice of Jesus (*sub gratia*); Isaac is a type of Christ, and the two might appear in parallel in the illustration program.

[27] Blockbooks were the first, rather crude, book illustrations in Europe, printed from engraved wooden blocks, one block per page. The *Biblia pauperum* is the most renowned example.

[28] With respect to literature prior to Luther the term *legend* connoted a biography of a saint. Though vernacular legends appeared in OHG times, the compilation of legendaries began in the thirteenth century. Jacobus de Voragine's Latin legendary dates from ca. 1267. The first German-language legendary is a fourteenth-century translation, the *Elsässische Legenda Aurea* (1350). Text: Ulla Williams and Werner Williams-Krapp, eds., *Die 'Elsässische Legenda Aurea,'* vol 1, *Das Normalcorpus* (Tübingen: Niemeyer, 1980). See also Williams-Krapp, *Die deutschen und niederländischen Legendare des Mittelalters: Studien zu ihrer Überlieferungs-, Text- und Wirkungsgeschichte* (Tübingen: Niemeyer, 1986). Edith Feistner, *Historische Typologie*

der deutschen Heiligenlegende des Mittelalters von der Mitte des 12. Jahrhunderts bis zur Reformation (Wiesbaden: Reichert, 1995).

[29] On mysticism see Kurt Ruh, *Geschichte der abendländischen Mystik*, 4 vols. (Munich: Beck, 1990–99), esp. vol. 2, *Frauenmystik und Franziskanische Mystik der Frühzeit* (1993), and vol. 3, *Die Mystik des deutschen Predigerordens und ihre Grundlegung durch die Scholastik* (1996); also Bernard McGinn, *The Presence of God: A History of Western Christian Mysticism* (New York: Herder, 1998), esp. vol. 3, *The Flowering of Mysticism 1200–1350*; Peter Dinzelbacher, *Christliche Mystik im Abendland: Ihre Geschichte von den Anfängen bis zum Ende des Mittelalters* (Paderborn: Schöningh, 1994); Uta Störmer-Caysa, *Entrückte Welten: Einführung in die mittelalterliche Mystik* (Leipzig: Reclam, 1998).

[30] On mystic experience as a love affair see Hildegard Elisabeth Keller, *My Secret Is Mine: Studies on Religion and Eros in the German Middle Ages* (Louvain: Peeters, 2000); Caroline Walker Bynum, *Fragmentation and Redemption: Essays on Gender and the Human Body in Medieval Religion* (New York: Zone Books, 1991). On the element of secrecy — hiding one's particular state of grace from the other nuns — see Keller, "Absonderungen: Mystische Texte als literarische Inszenierung von Geheimnis," in Walter Haug and Wolfram Schneider-Lastin, eds., *Deutsche Mystik im abendländischen Zusammenhang: Neu erschlossene Texte, neue methodische Ansätze, neue theoretische Konzepte* (Tübingen: Niemeyer, 2000), 195–221.

[31] See Herbert Grundmann, *Religiöse Bewegungen im Mittelalter* (Darmstadt: Wissenschaftliche Buchgesellschaft, 1970); Arno Angenendt, *Geschichte der Religiosität im Mittelalter*, 2nd ed. (Darmstadt: Wissenschaftliche Buchgesellschaft, 2000).

[32] Today it survives mainly in Austria as a charitable organization. On the history of the Teutonic Order see Hartmut Boockmann, *Der deutsche Orden: Zwölf Kapitel aus seiner Geschichte* (Munich: Beck, 1981); Marian Biskup and Gerard Labuda, *Die Geschichte des deutschen Ordens in Preußen: Wirtschaft — Gesellschaft — Staat — Ideologie* (Osnabrück: Fibre, 2000); also the many volumes in the series *Quellen und Studien zur Geschichte des deutschen Ordens*, gen. ed., Udo Arnold (Marburg: Elwert).

[33] The most useful overview of Teutonic Order literature, though not always reflecting current opinions, remains Karl Helm and Walther Ziesemer, *Die Literatur des Deutschen Ritterordens* (Giessen: Schmitz, 1951). A more recent study focusing on reading (as opposed to writing) in the order is Arno Mentzel-Reuters, *Arma spiritualia: Bibliotheken, Bücher und Bildung im Deutschen Orden* (Wiesbaden: Harrassowitz, 2003). At the turn of the twentieth century the series *Deutsche Texte des Mittelalters* (Berlin: Weidmann) produced a subordinated series of editions entitled *Dichtungen des Deutschen Ordens*.

[34] Edition: Heinrich Rückert, ed., *Bruder Philipp des Carthäusers Marienleben* (1853; repr., Amsterdam: Rodopi, 1966).

[35] See Graeme Dunphy, "Rabengefieder, Elefantengezisch: Naturdeutung in der 'Mitteldeutsche Hiobparaphase,' " in *Natur und Kultur in der deutschen Literatur des Mittelalters*, ed. Alan Robertshaw and Gerhard Wolf (Tübingen: Niemeyer, 1999), 91–102.

[36] Karl Kochendörffer, *Tilos von Kulm Gedicht von siben Ingesigeln* (Berlin: Weidmann, 1907).

[37] The main historical works of the Teutonic Order are contained in the series *Scriptores rerum Prussicarum: Die Geschichtsquellen der preussischen Vorzeit*, vols. 1–5, ed. Max Töppen Hirsch, et al. (1861–74; repr., Frankfurt am Main: Minerva, 1965); vol. 6, ed.

Walther Hubatsch (1968). Also Nicolaus von Jeroschin, *Deutschordenschronik* (1854), ed. Franz Pfeiffer (Hildesheim: Olms, 1966). See Hartmut Boockmann, "Die Geschichtsschreibung des Deutschen Ordens: Gattungsfragen und 'Gebrauchssituationen,' " in Patze, ed., *Geschichtsschreibung*, 447–69.

[38] On the genre of the travel report see in this volume the chapter by Wolfgang Neuber, especially the section "Cosmography and Apodemics." Neuber explains that the genre's first fully formed German travel report was the *Wahrhaftige Historia*, written in 1557 by Hans Staden.

[39] The starting point for any study of Franciscan literature is the anthology *Franziskanisches Schrifttum im deutschen Mittelalter*, ed. Kurt Ruh, vol. 1 (Munich: Beck, 1965), vol. 2 (Munich: Artemis, 1985).

[40] See Ludger Meier, OFM, *Die Barfüsserschule zu Erfurt* (Münster: Aschendorffsche Verlagsbuchhandlung, 1958).

[41] Jacobus Willem van Maeren, ed., *Marquard von Lindau OFM, Das Buch der Zehn Gebote (Venedig 1483): Textausgabe mit Einleitung und Glossar* (Amsterdam: Rodopi, 1984); Rüdiger Blumrich, ed., *Marquard von Lindau, Deutsche Predigten: Untersuchungen und Edition* (Tübingen: Niemeyer, 1994); Eckart Greifstein, *Der Hiob-Traktat des Marquard von Lindau: Überlieferung, Untersuchung und kritische Textausgabe* (Munich: Artemis, 1979).

[42] Marquard, *Buch der Zehn Gebote*, 23. The passage in Exod. 20 from which the Ten Commandments are taken can be divided up in various ways. Where a Protestant reading takes "no other gods" and "no idols" separately as the first two commandments, medieval practice saw these as a single commandment and divided "coveting" into "coveting neighbor's property" (no. 9) and "coveting neighbor's wife" (no. 10). Thus the commandment about the Sabbath was no. 3 in medieval lists, but no. 4 in many modern representations.

[43] Ute Schwab, ed., *Der Endkrist des Friedrich von Saarburg und die anderen Inedita des Cod. Vind. 2886* (Naples: Istituto Universitario Orientale, 1964); W. Röll, "Die Antichrist-Rede Friedrichs von Saarburg," *Zeitschrift für deutsches Altertum* 96 (1967): 278–320.

[44] The Albigensians, or Cathars, of southern France followed a dualistic religion akin to Gnosticism. Dominic had been involved in a mission to convert them and was a supporter of the brutal Albigensian crusade that led to the crushing of the Provençal civilization (1209–29). The Dominicans were founded (1215) and received papal approval (1216) in the context of this conflict, and from the beginning were a driving force in the Spanish and French Inquisitions.

[45] Kramer was the sole author of this work; in earlier research another inquisitor, Jakob Sprenger, was wrongly assumed to have been his collaborator. The two did work together on other witch-finding missions, however, as Gerhild Scholz Williams explains in the present volume in "Demonologies: Writing about Magic and Witchcraft": "The papal bull *Summis desiderantes affectibus,* issued in December of that year by Innocent VIII, authorized two inquisitors, the Dominican friars Heinrich Kramer (Institoris) and Jakob Sprenger (1436–95), to identify, imprison, and prosecute the witches allegedly plaguing southwestern Germany and parts of present-day Austria."

[46] "Longer" because about five years earlier he had written a *Distinctiones breviores pro sermonibus* (Short Book of Distinctions for Sermons, ca. 1395).

[47] A new edition of Eckhart's complete works was begun in 1958, with various volume editors, under the title *Meister Eckhart, Die deutschen und lateinischen Werke* (Stuttgart: Kohlhammer). Reliable partial editions: *Meister Eckhart, Werke I: Predigten*, and *Werke*

II: Traktate: Lateinische Werke, trans. Josef Quint, ed. Niklaus Largier (Frankfurt am Main: Deutscher Klassiker Verlag, 1993). Among the many single-volume general introductions to Eckhart see esp. Bernard McGinn, *The Mystical Thought of Meister Eckhart: The Man from Whom God Hid Nothing* (New York: Crossroad, 2001), and Kurt Ruh, *Meister Eckhart: Theologe, Prediger, Mystiker* (Munich: Beck, 1985).

[48] See for example Hieronymus Wilms, *Geschichte der deutschen Dominikanerinnen* (Dulmen: Laumann, 1920); Anette Hettinger and Amalie Fößel, *Klosterfrauen, Beginen, Ketzerinnen: Religiöse Lebensformen von Frauen im Mittelalter* (Idstein: Schulz-Kirchner, 2000); Susanne Bürkle, *Literatur im Kloster: Historische Funktion und rhetorische Legitimation frauenmystischer Texte des 14. Jahrhunderts* (Tübingen: Francke, 1999); Ursula Peters, *Religiöse Erfahrungen als literarisches Faktum: Zur Vorgeschichte und Genese frauenmystischer Texte des 13. und 14. Jahrhunderts* (Tübingen: Niemeyer, 1988).

[49] The most useful starting place for literature on the Beguines is Frank-Michael Reichstein, *Das Beginenwesen in Deutschland* (Berlin: Köster, 2001), which has an extensive bibliography. On Mechthild see Frank Tobin, *Mechthild von Magdeburg: A Medieval Mystic in Modern Eyes* (Columbia, SC: Camden House, 1995); Elizabeth A. Andersen, *Mechthild of Magdeburg: Selections from The Flowing Light of the Godhead* (Cambridge: Brewer, 2003).

[50] It is difficult to say confidently by or for whom it was composed. We know this tract from fifteenth-century prints, but it is likely to go back to a fourteenth-century manuscript version.

[51] See Keller, *My Secret,* chaps. 4 and 5.

[52] A. H. Hoffmann von Fallersleben, *In dulci jubilo, nun singet und seid froh: Ein Beitrag zur Geschichte der deutschen Poesie,* 2nd ed. (1861; repr. as an appendix to Fallersleben's *Geschichte des deutschen Kirchenliedes bis auf Luthers Zeit,* Hildesheim: Olms, 1965), 46–50. Fallersleben, an enthusiastic collector of German antiquities, takes the credit for the rediscovery of the OHG *de Heinrico.*

[53] The standard work on the urban literature of at least the earlier part of the transitional period is Ursula Peters, *Literatur in der Stadt: Studien zu den sozialen Voraussetzungen und kulturellen Organisationsformen städtischer Literatur im 13. und 14. Jahrhundert* (Tübingen: Niemeyer, 1983). See also Heinz Schilling, *Die Stadt in der frühen Neuzeit* (Munich: Oldenbourg, 1993).

[54] *Burg* is derived by ablaut from the same root as *Berg,* meaning a (fortified) high place: IE *b^herg^h-* (high; *Burg* from the zero grade), hence its modern meaning of "castle"; however, parallel to English *borough,* it applied in OHG and MHG also to a walled city, the sense retained in modern *Bürger* (citizen). MHG *stat,* from the same root as *stehen,* means "place" (as in *Werkstatt*), as indeed does English *stead* (literal meaning in *homestead,* metaphorically in both languages: *anstatt/instead* = "in place of"); already in OHG *stat* could mean "place of settlement," but in the legal sense of "city" it replaced *burg* from the twelfth century onward; the distinction in spelling (*Stadt/Statt*) emerged only between the sixteenth and eighteenth centuries. We may surmise that the impulse causing *stat* to supplant *burg* as "city," and indeed leading English *borough* as "fortification" to be replaced by the French loan-word *castle,* was that sociological changes forced a distinction not required in earlier centuries.

[55] See the thirty-seven-volume series *Chroniken der deutschen Städte vom 14. bis ins 16. Jahrhundert* (1862–1968; repr., Göttingen: Vandenhoeck & Ruprecht, 1961–69).

[56] Hermann Wäschke, ed., *Die Zerbster Ratschronik* (Dessau: Dünnhaupt, 1907). Frank Kreissler, "Peter Becker (um 1385–1455): Ratmann und Bürgermeister in Zerbst," in

Mitteldeutsche Lebensbilder: Menschen im spätern Mittelalter, ed. Werner Freitag (Cologne: Böhlau, 2002), 137–56.

[57] In medieval library catalogues and bibliographical lists many works were identified not by author and title but by their *incipit,* the first few words of the text.

[58] Philipp Strauch, ed., *Jansen Enikels Werke,* Monumenta Gemaniae Historica, deutsche Chroniken II (1891–1900; repr., Munich: Monumenta Gemaniae Historica, 1980). Graeme Dunphy, ed., *History as Literature: German World Chronicles of the Thirteenth Century in Verse* (Kalamazoo, MI: Western Michigan UP, 2003). On this passage, Dunphy, *Daz was ein michel wunder: The Presentation of Old Testament Material in Jans Enikel's Weltchronik* (Göppingen: Kümmerle, 1998), 120–22.

[59] Edition: Karl Schorbach, ed., *Parzifal von Claus Wisse und Philipp Colin* (Strasbourg: Trübner, 1888). See Dorothee Wittmann-Klemm, *Studien zum 'Rappoltsteiner Parzifal'* (Göppingen: Kümmerle, 1977); Sonja Emmerling, "Geld und Liebe: Zum Prolog des 'Rappoltsteiner Parzifal,' " in Brunner and Williams-Krapp, eds., "Forschungen," 31–49.

[60] Cited from Jan-Dirk Müller, ed., *Romane des 15. und 16. Jahrhunderts: Nach den Erstdrucken mit sämtlichen Holzschnitten* (Frankfurt am Main: Deutscher Klassiker Verlag, 1990). Other editions: Karin Schneider, ed., *Thüring von Ringoltingen, Melusine: Nach den Handschriften kritisch herausgegeben* (Berlin: Schmidt, 1958); Hans-Gert Roloff, ed., *Thüring von Ringoltingen, Melusine,* rev. ed. (Stuttgart: Reclam, 1991).

[61] This is validated by the most recent research. My interpretation of Melusine substantially follows Hildegard Elisabeth Keller, "Berner Samstagsgeheimnisse: Die Vertikale als Erzählformel in der *Melusine," Paul und Braunes Beiträge zur Geschichte der deutschen Sprache und Literatur* 124 (2005): 208–39.

[62] Keller, "Berner Samstagsgeheimnisse," has usefully employed the tag "verticality" as a means of conceptualizing this parallel: the verticality of Melusine's body, of the social hierarchy, and of the family tree as popularized in the symbolic art of the fifteenth century.

[63] Twingherr (*twingen = zwingen,* "force") is a specifically Swiss word for the *Stadtadel,* highlighting the power they had within the city.

[64] On the etymology of *Zigerli* see Keller, "Berner Samstagsgeheimnisse."

[65] On the *Stadtschreiber* see Peters, *Literatur in der Stadt,* chap. 4, "Die Bedeutung städtischer Beamter für das literarische Leben ihrer Stadt," esp. 225–68.

[66] Johannes von Tepl, *Der Ackermann,* ed. Willy Krogmann (Wiesbaden: Brockhaus, 1978); Johannes von Tepl, *Der Ackermann und der Tod,* ed. Christian Kiening (Stuttgart: Reclam, 2000); Gerhard Hahn, *Der Ackermann aus Böhmen des Johannes von Tepl* (Darmstadt: Wissenschaftliche Buchgesellschaft, 1984); Anne Winston-Allen, "Johannes von Tepl," in Reinhart and Hardin, eds., *DLB* 179, 287–92; and Kiening, *Schwierige Modernität: Der Ackerman des Johannes von Tepl und die Ambiguität historischen Wandels* (Tübingen: Niemeyer, 1998). The *Ackermann* has been translated into English as *The Plowman from Bohemia,* trans. Alexander and Elizabeth Henderson (New York: Unger, 1966). The translations of the quotations that follow, however, are primarily those of the author of the present article.

[67] In the epilogue Johannes directly includes a number of passages from Neumarkt's translation of the pseudo-Augustinian *Soliloquia animae ad deum* (The Soul's Soliloquy to God).

[68] See Heinz Otto Burger, *Renaissance, Humanismus, Reformation: Deutsche Literatur im europäischen Kontext* (Berlin: Gehlen, 1969), 15–31 and 45–53.

[69] Recent literature includes: Vera Sack: *Sebastian Brant als politischer Publizist: Zwei Flugblatt-Satiren aus den Folgejahren des sogenannten Reformreichstags von 1495* (Freiburg i.B.: Stadtarchiv, 1997); Silke Mausolf-Kiralp, *Die "traditio" der Ausgaben des Narrenschiffs von Sebastian Brant mit besonderer Berücksichtigung der Straßburger Editionen* (Aachen: Shaker, 1997); Cordula Peper, *"zu nutz und heylsamer ler": Das "Narrenschiff" von Sebastian Brant (1494): Untersuchung der Zusammenhänge zwischen Text und Bild* (Leutesdorf, Krautsgasse 1: Peper, 2000); Thomas Wilhelmi, *Sebastian Brant: Forschungen zu seinem Leben, zum "Narrenschiff" und zum übrigen Werk* (Basel: Schwabe, 2002). A full bibliography of Brant scholarship to 1985: Joachim Knape, *Sebastian-Brant-Bibliographie* (Tübingen: Niemeyer, 1990); see also Wilhelmi, *Sebastian Brant Bibliographie* (Bern: Lang, 1990).

[70] Cited from Manfred Lemmer, ed., *Sebastian Brant, Das Narrenschiff: Nach der Erstausgabe (Basel 1594) mit den Zusätzen der Ausgaben von 1495 und 1499 sowie den Holzschnitten der deutschen Originalausgabe*, 3rd ed. (Tübingen: Niemeyer, 1986). The Reclam edition by H. A. Junghans modernizes the language, altering the text freely to keep the rhyme.

[71] Edition: *Die "Stultifera Navis": Jakob Lochers Übertragung von Sebastian Brants "Narrenschiff,"* 2 vols., ed. Nina Hartl (Münster: Waxmann, 2001).

[72] Albrecht Dürer, who at the time was learning his vocation as a journeyman, probably designed many of the woodcuts for Brant's great project. John Van Cleve, "Sebastian Brant," in Reinhart and Hardin, eds., *DLB* 179, 19a, claims that Dürer in fact led the effort.

[73] See in this volume, the chapter by Peter Hess.

[74] On continuities see Michael Baldzuhn, *Vom Sangspruch zum Meisterlied: Untersuchungen zu einem literarischen Traditionszusammenhang auf der Grundlage der Kolmarer Liederhandschrift* (Tübingen: Niemeyer, 2002).

[75] Though literature on the *Meistersinger* frequently refers to the guilds themselves as *Singschulen*, the singers in fact only used this word to mean a meeting, or a concert, of the guild, held on Sundays.

[76] Photographic reprint with commentary by Horst Brunner (Göppingen: Kümmerle, 1975). Note that the title of Wagner's opera uses the form *Meistersinger* rather than *Meistersänger*, influenced no doubt by Wagenseil.

[77] The older literature goes back to August L. Mayer, ed., *Die Meisterlieder des Hans Folz* (1908; repr., Hildesheim: Weidmann, 1970). More recent assessments include Rüdiger Krohn, "Hans Folz," in *Deutsche Dichter der frühen Neuzeit (1450–1600): Ihr Leben und Werk*, ed. Stephan Füssel (Berlin: Schmidt, 1993), 111–24, and Joe G. Delap, "Hans Folz," in Reinhart and Hardin, eds., *DLB* 179, 63–69.

[78] *Junger Geselle* (young journeyman) may already have the modern sense of *Junggeselle* (bachelor) here; the two are in any case synonymous in a social class that regarded marriage, accreditation as a master craftsman, and attainment of adulthood as a single transition. See Michael Mitterauer, *A History of Youth*, trans. Graeme Dunphy (Oxford: Blackwell, 1992).

[79] According to Genesis 10:3, Ashkenaz was a son of Gomer, one of the Japhethite (traditionally understood to mean European) nations; the *Targumim* (early medieval Aramaic translations) of this verse identified Gomer with Germania. The geographical

boundaries of Jewish cultural areas did not follow the political or linguistic boundaries of Christian society. The Ashkenazi area stretched farther west, covering most of northern France, while the Jews of southern France belonged to the (Spanish) Sephardic Jewry.

[80] On Jewish life in this period see Dan Cohn-Sherbok, *Atlas of Jewish History* (London: Routledge, 1994); Michael Toch, *Die Juden im mittelalerlichen Reich* (Munich: Oldenbourg, 1998); Klaus Geissler, *Die Juden in Deutschland und Bayern bis zur Mitte des vierzehnten Jahrhunderts* (Munich: Beck, 1976); Siegfried Wittmer, *Jüdisches Leben in Regensburg vom frühen Mittelalter bis 1519* (Regensburg: Universitätsverlag, 2001); Klaus Lohrman, *Die Wiener Juden im Mittelalter* (Berlin: Philo, 2000); Thérèse and Mendel Metzger, *La vie juive au moyen âge illustrée par les manuscrits hébraïques énluminés du XIIIe au XVIe siècle* (Freiburg: Office du Livre, 1982).

[81] On Jews in early German literature see Helmut Birkhan, "Die Juden in der deutschen Literatur des Mittelalters," in *Die Juden in ihrer mittelalterlichen Umwelt,* ed. Birkhan (Bern: Lang, 1992); Edith Wenzel, *Do worden die Judden alle geschant: Rolle und Funktion der Juden in spätmittelalterlichen Spielen* (Munich: Fink, 1992); Andrew Colin Gow, *The Red Jews: Antisemitism in an Apocalyptic Age 1200–1600* (Leiden: Brill, 1995); Hans-Martin Kirn, *Das Bild vom Juden im Deutschland des frühen 16. Jahrhunderts, dargestellt an den Schriften des Johannes Pfefferkorns* (Tübingen: Mohr, 1989).

[82] On German-Jewish relations see the seven articles under the collective title "Grenzen und Grenzüberschreitungen: Kulturelle Kontakte zwischen Juden und Christen im Mittelalter," *Aschkenaz: Zeitschrift für Geschichte und Kultur der Juden* 14 (2004): 1–162. Also R. Po-Chia Hsia and Hartmut Lehmann, *In and Out of the Ghetto: Jewish-Gentile Relations in Late Medieval and Early Modern Germany* (Cambridge: Cambridge UP, 1995), and Achim Jaeger, "'Ghetto' oder 'Symbiose'? Überlegungen zur Rezeption höfischer und populärer volkssprachlichen Literatur in jüdischen Kontexten," in *Ein jüdischer Artusritter: Studien zum jüdisch-deutschen 'Widuwilt' ('Artushof') und zum 'Wigalois' des Wirnt von Gravenberc* (Tübingen: Niemeyer, 2000), 117–66.

[83] Dietrich Gerhardt, *Süßkind von Trimberg: Berichtigungen zu einer Erinnerung* (Bern: Lang, 1997).

[84] For an orientation in early Yiddish literature see Sol Liptzin, *A History of Yiddish Literature* (Middle Village, NY: Jonathan David Publishers, 1972); also Helmut Dinse, *Die Entwicklung des jiddischen Schrifttums im deutschsprachigen Gebiete* (Stuttgart: Metzler, 1974).

[85] The precise definitions of the terms *Judeo-German* and *Old Yiddish* remain controversial, but it is advisable to use the former when referring to the fourteenth and fifteenth centuries, the latter from the early sixteenth. *Judeo-German* implies a unique coloring to the German language, whereas *Old Yiddish* implies a distinct language. See Edith Wenzel, "Alt-Jiddisch oder Mittelhochdeutsch?," *Aschkenas: Zeitschrift für Geschichte und Kultur der Juden* 14 (2004): 31–50. On the language generally see David Katz, ed., *Origins of the Yiddish Language* (Oxford: Pergamon, 1987); Bettina Simon, *Jiddische Sprachgeschichte* (Frankfurt am Main: Athenäum, 1988); and Max Weinreich, *History of the Yiddish Language* (Chicago: U of Chicago P, 1980).

[86] On the equivalent developments in OHG see the relevant chapters in Brian Murdoch, ed., *German Literature of the Early Middle Ages,* vol. 2 of *CHHGL* (2004).

[87] The Cambridge Codex is located in Cambridge University Library, CY,T.-S.10.K.22.

[88] As Jewish law forbids the destruction of documents containing the name of God, old books no longer fit for ritual use were "retired" to a *genisa* (archive).

[89] Edition: Lajb Fuks, *The Oldest Known Literary Documents of Yiddish Literature (c. 1382)*, 2 vols. (Leiden: Brill, 1957). Vol. 1 has photographic reproductions on the left hand pages and a transcription in Hebrew square characters on the right; vol. 2 has a transliteration into the Latin alphabet on the left, and a (rather inadequate) translation into modern German on the right. The most thorough linguistic analysis of the codex as a whole remains Heikki J. Hakkarainen, *Studien zum Cambridger Codex* T.S.10.K.22, vol. 1, *Annales Universitatis Turkuensis* B104 (Turku: Turun Yliopisto, 1967), vols. 2 and 3 as *Annales Academiae Scientiarum Fennicae*, B174 (Helsinki: Annales Academiae Scientiarum Fennicae, 1971) and B 182 (1973). Edition for *Dukus Horant*, with a thorough linguistic analysis, P. F. Ganz, F. Norman, and W. Schwarz, eds., *Dukus Horant* (Tübingen: Niemeyer, 1964). Literature: Manfred Caliebe, *Dukus Horant: Studien zu seiner literarischen Tradition* (Berlin: Schmidt, 1973); Friedrich Mader, *Die "Dukus-Horant"-Forschung: Bericht und Kritik* (Osnabrück: Biblio, 1979); Gabriele Strauch, *Dukus Horant: Wanderer zwischen zwei Welten* (Amsterdam: Rudopi, 1990). On *Josef ha-zadik* see James Marchand and Frederic Tubach, "Der keusche Josef," *Zeitschrift für deutsche Philologie* 81 (1962): 30–52.

[90] Yiddish transcription follows Fuks; my transliteration follows the usual English system for Hebrew, but representing *yod* with *i* and *waw* with *u*, since these are vowels in Judeo-German. *Aleph* (transliterated with a comma pointing left) and *ayin* (comma pointing right) both mostly correspond to *e*. For comparison, Fuks, Hakkarainen, and Ganz et al. all have transcriptions using different systems.

[91] On *Kudrun* see William H. Jackson, "Court Literature and Violence in the High Middle Ages," in Hasty, ed., *CHHGL* 3, 268; bibliography, 313–14.

[92] On oral performance poetry see Dunphy, "Orality." An alternative theory, that the writer of *Dukus Horant* had a MHG written source, cannot be entirely discounted, but another work in the same manuscript has an acrostic that only works in the Hebrew alphabet; so clearly the writer sees himself as more than a copyist.

[93] Edition: Sigmund A. Wolf, ed., *Ritter Widuwilt: Die westjiddische Fassung des Wigalois des Wirnt von Gravenberc: Nach dem jiddischen Druck von 1699 besorgt* (Bochum: Brockmeyer, 1974). The most recent discussions are Jaeger, *Ein jüdischer Artusritter*, and Neil Thomas, *Wirnt von Gravenberg's "Wigalois": Intertextuality and Interpretation* (Woodbridge, UK: D. S. Brewer, 2005).

The Evolution of Modern Standard German

Renate Born

IN MODERN WESTERN SOCIETIES, where standard languages are considered the most prestigious forms of linguistic expression, dialects tend to be derided as inferior — substandard — forms of speech. Few who disdain dialectal varieties, however, realize that the standard European languages themselves have been in existence for only a relatively short time — in the case of Modern Standard German no more than three centuries. Before the first comprehensive German grammar was published in the seventeenth century, manuscripts and printed works exhibited regional linguistic features and varied considerably in spelling, grammar, sentence structure, and vocabulary. On this evidence, the language historian can determine with reasonable certainty where a text written between the fourteenth and early seventeenth centuries was written or printed. From a linguistic perspective, the hallmark of the early modern German period was the gradual reduction of regional variation in the written language. Over the fourteenth and fifteenth centuries written versions of local dialects were replaced with regional writing languages, which in turn yielded two major competitors in the sixteenth century.[1] The standardization of German in the seventeenth century was a deliberate act of language planning undertaken by grammarians and literary scholars to create a form of the language free of regional linguistic characteristics — a *Kunstsprache* (artificial language, or language of the arts) that could be acquired only formally in an educational institution. This early form of literary German was the prerequisite for the emergence of a national German literature in the eighteenth century and set the linguistic stage for the classicism of Lessing, Goethe, and Schiller.

Modern Standard German arrived belatedly, a phenomenon attributable to the splintered political landscape of the early modern period. The area now comprising Germany and Austria was then part of the Holy Roman Empire, a multilingual and multicultural conglomerate of territorial states governed by princes set on increasing their individual dynastic powers. Their relentless struggles prevented the formation of a national political and cultural center of gravity comparable to London or Paris. Politically divided into more than 300 independent principalities, duchies, and counties, Germany had no national capital city with writing conventions sufficiently prestigious to be adopted by writers and printers in the provinces. Had it been otherwise, greater efforts would doubtless have been made toward linguistic regularization. The confessional and political discord in the wake of the Reformation erected an additional cultural barrier between Protestant territories in central and northern Germany and Catholic territories in the south. At a time when the English and French considered themselves citizens of nation-states, Germans could claim only regional identities as Bavarians, Hessians, Saxons, or Swabians, or as citizens of free imperial cities (Nurembergers, Augsburgers, Strasbourgers).

Linguistic factors likewise prevented earlier adoption of a homogenous written language. Northern Germany had its own Middle Low German (*Mittelniederdeutsch*), the language of the Hanseatic League, the powerful economic alliance of free imperial cities that dominated commerce in northern Europe under the leadership of the city of Lübeck. Southeastern Germany and Austria had Common German (*gemeines Deutsch*), a regional variant that was regularized orthographically in the late fifteenth century during the rule of Maximilian I (r. 1508–19).[2] As the language of the imperial chancery in Vienna and its Augsburg printers, Common German enjoyed great prestige until the early seventeenth century. But Middle Low German and Common German were mutually unintelligible; neither could bridge the linguistic gap between north and south and serve as the basis for a national standard language.

This intermediary role would fall to Eastern Central German (*Ostmitteldeutsch*), the writing language popularized during and after the Reformation by Luther's translation of the Bible. Johann Gutenberg's invention of printing with movable type ensured the rapid and wide distribution of Luther's Bible, and the "Lutheran" linguistic variety of Eastern Central German soon gained sufficiently in status to replace the Middle Low German writing language in northern Germany. During the Counter-Reformation in Catholic Austria and Bavaria, however, Eastern Central German was associated with religious heresy and rejected. The linguistic division between the south and the rest of Germany would remain in effect for two and a half centuries.

In the seventeenth century the majority of the grammarians who gathered in language societies (*Sprachgesellschaften*) and embarked on an ambitious program of linguistic standardization were Protestants from northern or central Germany. They were united in their repudiation of Common German and in their determination to create a linguistic medium of sufficient prestige to be capable of replacing French as the language of polite society and Latin as the language of science and scholarship. In the eighteenth century this new Standard German became the language of the German Enlightenment, associated with scientific innovation, technical progress, and literary accomplishment. Still, Austria clung to the southern variety of the written language until after the death of Empress Maria Theresa in 1780, when her son and successor decreed that Modern Standard German be implemented in the schools and public arena; Bavaria soon followed suit.[3] In Switzerland, Standard German was adopted gradually. The indigenous Alemannic writing language competed with the German version for more than two centuries.[4]

Temporal Boundaries: The Beginning and End of Early Modern German

Modern scholars of German language history agree that Early Modern German (*Frühneuhochdeutsch*) constitutes an autonomous linguistic period rather than merely a transitional stage between Middle High German and Modern Standard German. Whereas historians have traditionally viewed the Reformation as the dividing line between the medieval age and the beginning of the modern era, German language scholars do not unanimously accept this view. One problem has to do with establishing the beginning of Early Modern German, which is impossible on linguistic grounds alone, given that the changes separating it from Middle High German spread only slowly from their areas of origin to other writing regions. The vowel shifts, for example, are not reflected in all southern and central German texts until the sixteenth century, by which time the language was clearly no longer Middle High German. However, determining the end point of the early modern period (and the beginning of modern German) presents equally thorny difficulties for the language historian. Such a determination involves analysis and assessment both of the contemporary codification of often contradictory grammatical rules into a normative grammar and of the subsequent effort to adopt this form of the language in the greater German-speaking area.

The first comprehensive grammar, *Ausführliche Arbeit von der Teutschen HaubtSprache* (A Thorough Study of the German Principal Language, 1663), of Georg Justus Schottelius (1612–76) uses as its primary model the Latin grammars, which focused on orthography, the inflectional system, and word formation.[5] Accordingly, the syntactic rules governing sentence structure and word order receive only cursory treatment.[6] This work demonstrates that the language of the seventeenth century was still a distant predecessor of Modern Standard German. Sentence structure and word order remained flexible until Johann Christoph Adelung (1732–1806) codified syntactic rules in his *Umständliches Lehrgebäude der deutschen Sprache* (Comprehensive School Grammar of German) in 1782.[7]

Historical linguistics offers three major theories of what constituted the early modern German language period. Wilhelm Scherer (1841–86) argued that Early Modern German represents a transitional stage, extending from the middle of the fourteenth to the middle of the seventeenth century, between Middle High German and modern German, the span between the new vernacular writing language at the Prague court of Charles IV (r. 1346–78) and the end of the Thirty Years' War (1648).[8] Hugo Moser (1909–89) saw late medieval German extending from 1250, when German began to replace Latin as the language of law, to the eve of the Reformation. In this view Early Modern German covers roughly the first century (1520–1620) of the Age of Absolutism, or approximately the period between Luther's translation of the New Testament and the beginning of the Thirty Years' War (1618).[9] As noted above, more recent scholarship considers the early modern language period to have been an independent rather than a transitional stage. Peter von Polenz stresses that the invention of printing, with the concomitant increase in literacy rates among urban populations, was the most significant social factor separating Early Modern German from Middle High German.[10] Borrowing a designation first employed by scholars in the former German Democratic Republic (with reference to the Peasants' War of 1524–25), Polenz calls the linguistic stage between the early fifteenth and seventeenth centuries "Deutsch in der frühbürgerlichen Zeit" (German of the early bourgeois period). It was at this time that powerful urban patricians and merchants, whose sons were being educated in the newly established universities, shaped the language to their commercial, administrative, and literary needs. This development was terminated by the devastation of cities and interruption of commerce in the Thirty Years' War; in a word, the war brought to an end the economic and cultural dominance of the very social class that had shaped Early Modern German as a medium of written communication.

Contexts: The Decline of Feudalism and the Flowering of Early Modern City Culture

Feudalism was based on a rigid tripartite division into social classes, or estates: clergy, nobility, and peasantry. Cities were small, and their burgher inhabitants did not constitute a separate estate in the feudal world. The economy was based largely on agriculture and the limited production of goods for immediate consumption. Since barter was the prevailing mode of payment, little money was in circulation. Political, economic, and military power lay in the hands of nobles who owned much of the land and were responsible for military defense. The decline of the feudal system was the direct effect of economic change and technical innovation. As money and commerce rather than birth and land ownership became the basis of the new economic system, a gradual transfer of economic power occurred from the castles in the countryside to the cities, where merchants and artisans were better equipped to acquire wealth through commerce. These new hubs of economic activity attracted serfs, formerly tied to the land by feudal laws, who could gain their legal freedom by living in a city for a year and a day. Urban populations exploded from an average of 2,500 in the first half of the thirteenth century to, in some cases, in excess of 20,000 by the end of the fourteenth. By 1500, approximately one-third of all Germans resided in cities.

The introduction of gunpowder and the development of artillery made the armies of mounted and armored knights technically obsolete, further diminishing the elevated social position the nobles had enjoyed in the medieval social order. Cities could now defend themselves, and those located along major trade routes, rivers, or the sea — in the south and west, Augsburg, Nuremberg, Regensburg, Strasbourg, Cologne, and Frankfurt; in the north, Hamburg, Lübeck, Bremen, and Rostock — were transformed into centers of marvelous wealth, which they put on display by constructing huge cathedrals, fancy guild houses, and stately private homes. Some cities formed alliances for the mutual protection of their merchants from rogue knights — the proverbial robber barons, or highway robbers — pirates on the high seas, and territorial lords who exacted egregious tolls and duties at their borders. The Rhenish cities united in a protective confederation in 1254 and again in 1381, the Swabian cities in 1376. The Hanseatic League, which dominated trade in northern Europe, established branch offices in the Netherlands, England, Norway, Sweden, Russia, and Belgium. Under the leadership of the city of Lübeck, the League had sufficient financial resources to acquire a fleet of armed ships, muster an army, and defeat the king of Denmark, who had disputed its trade monopoly, in 1370. In the fourteenth and fifteenth centuries, Middle Low German, the language of this urban confederation, served as an international medium of communication, a *lingua franca*, in its Baltico-Scandinavian sphere of influence.

This early form of capitalism created a fourth estate, an urban middle class with its own concerns and aspirations. These patricians and burghers were practical men, not devoted to the ideological code of knighthood, and bent on acquiring money rather than honor or land, traveling more often on business than for pleasure. Between the fourteenth and early seventeenth centuries, merchants expanded trade relationships to the Orient, India, and the Americas. Official contracts became their economic bedrock. Few merchants had expertise in Latin; the majority recorded their transactions in the vernacular (the Middle High German poetic language of the feudal aristocracy lacked the practical vocabulary necessary for business). Initially, written versions of local urban dialects replaced Latin in business books, letters, and legal contracts.

The flowering of city culture occurred at a time when the rulers of the large German territorial states were gaining power at the expense of the centralizing force of the Holy Roman Empire. Emperor Charles IV, who spoke German only haltingly and had little interest in Germany, granted territorial princes unprecedented privileges in the *Goldene Bulle* (Golden Bull) of 1356 that would harden political divisions for centuries to come. The princes gained absolute judicial power and the right of primogeniture within the boundaries of their territories. In return, the princely electors agreed that all German emperors would henceforth be Habsburg. These political divisions slowed developments toward a standardized language, ensuring that German would lag behind France and England as a national language by at least a century and a half.

The Linguistic Boundaries of Early Modern German

Until the eleventh century the regions east of the Elbe and Saale rivers were populated entirely by Slavic-speaking peoples. For the next 300 years a steady stream of peasants and city dwellers migrated from the more densely populated western

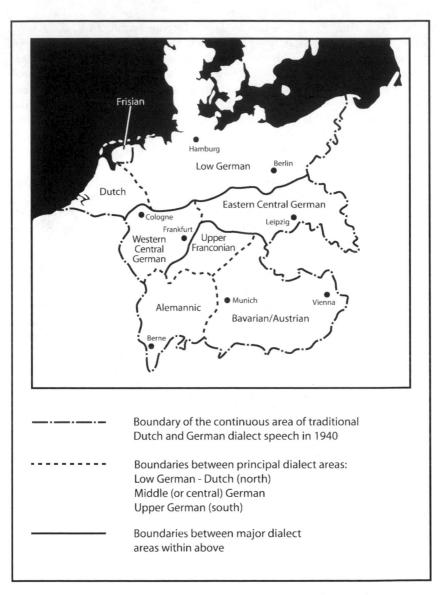

Frisian

Hamburg

Low German   Berlin

Dutch

Cologne   Eastern Central German

Frankfurt   Leipzig

Western
Central   Upper
German   Franconian

Alemannic   Munich   Vienna

Bavarian/Austrian

Berne

— ▪ — ▪ — ▪ —   Boundary of the continuous area of traditional
Dutch and German dialect speech in 1940

- - - - - - - - - -   Boundaries between principal dialect areas:
Low German - Dutch (north)
Middle (or central) German
Upper German (south)

————————   Boundaries between major dialect
areas within above

Map of German dialects before 1945. Adapted from Barbour and Stevenson,
Variation in German *(Cambridge: Cambridge UP, 1990), 76.*

and southern parts of Germany and the Netherlands to the relatively sparsely populated eastern territories in search of land for farming and other economic opportunities in newly established German towns. The plague reduced the German population by approximately one-third and, with the sudden demand for artisans and laborers in western cities and towns and a surplus of arable land, put an end to the migrations. "Colonial" eastern German dialects in Upper Saxony, Silesia, eastern Prussia, Brandenburg, Pomerania, and Mecklenburg are (or were) the linguistic products of the migrations, which came into being when people from different parts of Germany speaking different dialects settled together in an area. The Silesian and Upper Saxon speech patterns would become the most prestigious forms of the vernacular in the seventeenth and eighteenth centuries. By the middle of the fourteenth century the linguistic boundary between French and German in the west, which fluctuated in earlier centuries, had become firmly established. For the next 600 years the geographic area where German was the dominant language would remain essentially unchanged. Only at the end of World War II, when the ethnic German population was expelled from much of the territory acquired during the Middle Ages, did the line demarcated by the Oder and Neisse rivers become the linguistic boundary between German and the Slavic languages of eastern Europe.[11]

The Rise of the Vernacular and the Shift from Latin to German

Over the course of the fourteenth century, European vernaculars gradually replaced Latin in legal documents issued by the chanceries as well as in business and personal communications. The explosive growth of written legal documentation accompanying the introduction of Roman law necessitated a correspondingly large bureaucracy of notaries and scribes. Whereas oral agreements had been sufficient in German common law, the new legal code required written contracts, property deeds, wills, and charters. The church, whose prerogative in the Middle Ages was education, could not meet these new demands, and secular universities were established in part to serve administrative needs. Regularization of vernacular spelling conventions fell to the chanceries, especially the imperial chancery, since its documents had to be comprehensible in all German-speaking lands. Imperial documents thus reflect the changes in the vowel system that separated Early Modern German from Middle High German as early as the mid-fourteenth century.

During the transition from Latin to the vernacular for legal and business matters, written versions of local dialects were used initially. These were replaced gradually, through imitation and consensus, by regional writing languages having fewer idiosyncratic linguistic features, to ensure comprehension outside the immediate area of document production. In the fifteenth century these included Eastern Central German, Eastern Upper German (Common German), Southwestern German, and Middle Low German (the medium of written communication of the Hanseatic League and its Scandinavian trading partners). By the sixteenth century two varieties of written German had become predominant: Eastern Central German — soon to be popularized by Luther's translation of the Bible — in Protestant northern and central Germany, and Common German, which was based on the linguistic conventions embraced by the Catholic imperial chancery in Vienna. Since both varieties enjoyed equal prestige, the earliest grammars, so-called *Kanzlei- und Titelbüchlin* (Chancery and Title Manuals), encouraged writers to follow the "good German usage" of either Luther or the imperial chanceries. As long as the large urban centers and imperial cities served as economic and cultural hubs, linguistic diversity was generally accepted. Gradual regularization happened for practical rather than ideological reasons.

After the application of papermaking technology to printing (Gutenberg printed most of his books on paper), which made the production of books and pamphlets affordable for the urban middle classes, German became the language of popular literature as well. Chronicles, devotional writings, travel reports, cookbooks, instructional manuals, and many other types of prose works were published in ever-increasing numbers. Reading became a leisure activity for people wealthy enough to have free time. It was enhanced by the Italian invention of reading glasses, which had been introduced into Germany in the early fourteenth century; the first manufacturers of reading glasses established themselves in Frankfurt in 1450 and in Nuremberg in 1478. The rising numbers of literate women, mostly from upper-middle-class homes with servants, also helped to expand the market for vernacular publications.[12]

Notwithstanding the German linguistic inroads in the domains of law, business, and popular entertainment, Latin continued to be the standard medium for intellectual discourse in the arts and sciences. Luther wrote in German mainly for the common people and in Latin for scholars. His *Tischreden* (Table Talks), conversational opinions delivered informally to students and colleagues in his own home over dinner, are mainly in German, with Latin added here and there.[13] The predominance of Latin in the academy was not seriously questioned until the seventeenth century, when some educational reformers began to use German in lecture halls. As late as 1663, when he published his German grammar, Schottelius felt obliged to include extensive grammar annotations in Latin, lest scholarly readers be offended. Although German became one of the primary biblical and theological languages with Luther's translation of the Bible, it still lacked linguistic prestige in the eyes of the Latin-educated elite. The literature of vernacular poets, even great ones like Hans Sachs (1494–1576), was scorned by this elite as suitable only for public entertainment.

Education

The fourteenth-century system of Latin schools run by monastic clerics was incapable of providing the numbers of lawyers, administrators, and scribes needed by the chanceries to handle the surge in written documents. Lacking universities at home, young Germans traveled to Spain or Italy to become qualified for these positions. The first German university was not founded until 1348, in Prague, by Charles IV; others followed in rapid succession — Vienna in 1365, Heidelberg in 1386, Cologne in 1388, Erfurt in 1389[14] — established by territorial rulers anxious to provide their own centers of academic training. Most students were sons of urban patricians; some came from commoner (merchant and artisan) stock. Socially upward mobility based on merit alone became possible for gifted youths.

In the modern era, the language in which the education of the young is conducted is the linguistic variety that enjoys the highest social prestige. It serves as the official linguistic medium of the state in the domains of law, education, religion, the arts, and the sciences. It has a substantial body of literature, is codified in grammars, and is transmitted to children in formal educational institutions. Mastery of the standard variety is a prerequisite for social advancement. At the beginning of the early modern period only Latin could claim this status. By the middle of the seventeenth century, however, scholars had standardized and enhanced the vernacular to the extent that it could begin to replace Latin as the medium of scholarly discourse and higher education. The supplanting of one language of instruction by another has always happened in response to massive social changes and needs. When language shift occurs in only some institutions of learning, the result is a two-tiered system with distinct languages of instruction and individual objectives, indicative that society has changed in a way that has brought educational value systems into collision. In the early modern period the linguistic needs of a prosperous merchant class, for which German was the primary language of business, law, and literature, conflicted with the educational policies of the humanist establishment, which prohibited the use of German in its Latin schools on pain of corporal punishment or expulsion.

The academic view of the vernacular as a vulgar tongue useful only for colloquial communications reflected the Renaissance view of a world divided between the realms of the divine and the secular. Only the divinely inspired languages of Latin, Greek, and Hebrew were deemed suitable for written expression. The primary objective of a Latin humanist education was attainment of wisdom, virtue, and eloquence. Patricians and burghers wished, on the other hand, for their sons to be educated in the prestige language for an entirely practical end: advancement into the professions or civil administration. Whereas skills in written German were required of chancery clerks and notaries, the Latin schools provided no formal training in German, assuming that pupils would learn to write in their native tongue as a natural by-product of studying the classical language. The vernacular began to invade the domain of education only with the advent of the opposite theory, which asserted that German translations of Latin school grammars could facilitate acquisition of the classical language — this despite the reality that instruction was conducted by the method of total immersion from the age of seven. The earliest of these German translations were published in the late fifteenth and early sixteenth century.[15]

Merchants and artisans found themselves thus confronted with an educational establishment unresponsive to their needs. Since only the wealthiest patricians and burghers could afford to hire private tutors, city councils sought to remedy this deficit by licensing *Schreib- und Rechenschulen* (writing and reckoning schools) and paying the tuition for needy students with public funds. Much of the curriculum in the boys' schools addressed the copying of German documents and letters, though the German language itself was not yet taught as a subject. These new German schools proved so popular that enrollments in the Latin schools began to drop, which in turn threatened their economic viability. As a compromise solution, unlicensed *Winkelschulen* (private German schools) were declared illegal and licensed schools were barred from teaching Latin, thereby reducing the competition over students with higher aspirations. Prior to the Reformation, vernacular education — also provided to girls in separate schools — was restricted to the cities, where pragmatic councils realized the economic and social benefits of literate citizens and workers.

While the Protestant reformers and advocates of educational reform used the vernacular when it suited their purposes, they questioned neither the Renaissance theory of the separation between divine and secular languages nor the supremacy of Latin. Luther himself, who appreciated to what degree the success of the Reformation as a popular movement depended on writings in German and the increased literacy of the general population, considered such materials suitable mainly for commoners, however. He was dismayed by the negative effect of the vernacular trend on student enrollments at Latin schools, which were designed to prepare young men for the priesthood and monastic orders, occupations that no longer existed for Protestants. He was similarly horrified in the early 1520s that one of the unintended consequences of broader literacy was contributing to the peasant uprisings, which were being encouraged by *Flugblätter* (broadsides) in the language of the folk.

Luther and his humanist colleague Philipp Melanchthon (1497–1560) therefore advocated a state-sponsored educational system in two tiers: vernacular instruction for the urban and rural masses, and classical Latin education for the sons of the patrician and upper middle classes. In the German schools, children of both sexes were to be taught fear of God, obedience to secular authority, and adherence to a uniform set of religious, moral, and social values. Literacy could also have practical value for the body politic: reading, writing, and arithmetic would make for more productive artisans and laborers, not to mention preparing homemakers in the art of managing a Christian household. To reverse the perceived moral decline among young people, Luther and Melanchthon recommended a uniform curriculum based on religious doctrine, supported teacher certification, and insisted on regular visitations by experts to ensure both doctrinal compliance and adherence to the curriculum. They also encouraged patricians and wealthy burghers to continue sending their sons to Latin schools. In time, this institution, which produced an educated urban middle class firmly rooted in the Protestant ethic, would become a mechanism of social change.

At the beginning of the seventeenth century the educational reformer Wolfgang Ratke (1571–1635) made the revolutionary proposal to make German the primary medium of instruction in all school subjects, including foreign languages.[16] This view was later shared by the eminent philosopher and mathematician Gottfried Wilhelm Leibniz (1646–1716). Indeed, Leibniz and certain other scholars entertained an even more radical notion: German should become the language of instruction in the universities. All that was lacking was the development of a German vocabulary in the fields of law, medicine, and philosophy. Thus, it was the newly educated upper middle class — the *Bildungsbürgertum* — that supplied the writers, poets, scientists, preachers, doctors, and lawyers who would ultimately determine the linguistic shape of Modern Standard German. In the seventeenth and eighteenth centuries, mastery of this variety of German separated this social class from the nobility on the one hand and the lower strata of society on the other. In the nineteenth century the *Bildungsbürgertum* at last displaced the nobility as the major sponsor of artistic and cultural endeavors.

Regional Writing Languages

Modern dialects, which vary widely in pronunciation and vocabulary, are restricted to oral communication between relatives, friends, and members of the local community. From Schleswig-Holstein in the north, to the South Tyrol in northern Italy, we can trace a geographical continuum of comprehensibility: dialects in contiguous areas are mutually intelligible, whereas northern German dialects and those spoken near the southern language boundary separating German from adjacent languages are not. Thus, Swiss German is understood by speakers of Swabian dialects but is virtually incomprehensible to central and northern Germans. Similarly, the northern Low German dialects are extremely difficult to understand for Austrians, Swiss, and southern Germans. *Stadtsprachen* (city vernaculars), which emerged in the nineteenth century when speakers of varying rural dialects flocked to urban centers in search of economic opportunities, have fewer strongly dialectal features than their rural counterparts. Regional colloquial varieties, such as Swabian, Bavarian, or Upper Saxon, are closer to the standard language than either the rural or the urban dialects but still retain a sufficient number of regional linguistic features to identify the geographic origin of a speaker. In Germany (but not in Austria and Switzerland, which have their own linguistic national identities), the ideal form of the *Schriftsprache* (standard written language) taught in the schools and codified in the *Duden Rechtschreibung* (Duden Orthography), the lexicon that is the final arbiter of correct German usage, is devoid of regionalisms.[17]

This spectrum of contemporary German corresponds to the development of the written language over time. The earliest German document languages were written versions of dialects differing considerably in spelling, grammar, and word choice. During the fifteenth century, regional writing languages emerged to ensure that documents, letters, and other manuscripts were comprehensible over larger areas. By the beginning of the sixteenth century, four central and southern German regional writing languages existed: Eastern Central German in Thuringia, Upper Saxony, and Silesia; Eastern Upper German (Common German) in Bavaria, Austria, and eastern Franconia;

Western Central German in Hessia and the regions along the Rhine and Moselle rivers; and Western Upper German in Wurttemberg, Swabia, Alsace, and Switzerland. The following orthographic comparison shows that Eastern Central German spelling was somewhat closer to modern German norms than that of its competitors:[18]

Modern German	Eastern Central	Eastern Upper	Western Central	Western Upper
frei "free"	frey	frey	frei / frey	frei / frey
heim "home"	heim / haim	heim / haim	heem / heim	heim / haim
Haus "house"	haus	haws	haus / haws	huß / haus
gut "good"	gut	guet	gut	gut
zu "to"	zu	zuo	zu	zu
König "king"	könig	khünig / chunig	könig	künig
Acker "field"	acker	ackher	acker	acker / ackher
Stadt "city"	stadt	schdadt / stadt	schdadt / stadt	schdadt / stadt

Although all regional writing languages were considered equally acceptable and linguistic variation was tolerated as long as it did not impede comprehension, by the middle of the sixteenth century only two of these regional variants were serious contenders for national language status: the Eastern Central German variety publicized by Luther's translation of the Bible, and the Austro-Bavarian Common German. At the beginning of the seventeenth century the remaining linguistic differences had been reduced to minor variations in spelling, inflection, and vocabulary.

Printing Languages

The revolutionary effect of the invention of the printing press on mass communication was no less profound than that of the invention of the personal computer at the end of the twentieth century.[19] Books, pamphlets, and other written materials could now be produced inexpensively and disseminated rapidly and widely. Greater numbers of people could afford them, and censoring authorities had less time to react to perhaps unwelcome ideas and information. The early printers produced for local markets and initially used written versions of dialects as their printing medium. These earliest printers' languages were therefore less regularized than the regional varieties, though the desire to sell to larger markets soon convinced printers to eliminate blatant local dialectal features. Certain Swiss printers, for instance, replaced indigenous long vowels with German diphthongized equivalents: *haus* "house," *deutsch* "German," *Schweiz* "Switzerland" rather than *hus, dütsch, Schwitz*. By the early sixteenth century, eight regional printers' languages had emerged in urban centers of printing: Southeastern German in Munich, Vienna, and Ingoldstadt; Swabian in Augsburg, Ulm, and Tübingen; Upper Rhenish in Strasbourg and Basel; Swiss German in Zurich and Bern; Western Central German in Cologne, Mainz, Worms, and Frankfurt; Eastern Central German in Wittenberg, Leipzig, Erfurt, and Jena; and Low German in Cologne, Magdeburg, and Rostock.[20] The Reformation was a financial boon to the printing business. Between 1518 and 1524, German-language book printings soared from 150 to 990.[21]

Many of the early printers were university educated and imposed their own linguistic conventions on manuscripts or reprints. Luther complained of the practices of some of them in his introduction to the last edition of his Old Testament in 1545: "Vnd ist mir offt wiederfaren, das ich der Nachdruecker druck gelesen, also verfelscht gefunden, das ich meine eigene Arbeit, an vielen Orten nicht gekennet"[22] (And it happened to me often that I read the reprinters' text and found it so falsified that in many places I did not recognize my own work). Since business was risky and failure common, many printers moved frequently from one location to another, earning them the name *Wanderdrucker* (traveling printers). They adapted their language to local customs while retaining certain of their own linguistic conventions, with the result that their books often contain a mixture of styles. The reading public appears to have accepted the diversity. Still, printers realized that dialectal differences would limit marketability and therefore, when a book was intended for broader distribution, appended glossaries of regional terms. The increasing awareness of regional linguistic variation in the early sixteenth century probably motivated the publication of the first writing manuals and handbooks on orthography; these in turn contributed to the notion of "good" German writing practices.

Chancery Languages[23]

Working under the direction of a chancellor (*Kanzler*), notaries and scribes in their various jurisdictions (local, territorial, imperial) produced massive quantities of legal contracts, registers, city chronicles, financial records, and other official documents. By the middle of the fourteenth century, 90% of all documents were issued in German, and the spelling conventions, vocabulary, and grammatical systems of the most powerful chanceries (*Kanzleien*) were being imitated elsewhere. Luther acknowledged the linguistic authority of both the Upper Saxon state chancery and Maximilian's imperial chancery, treating them essentially as variations of a single language. A century later Martin Opitz (1597–1639), in chapter 7 of his epochal *Buch von der Deutschen Poeterey*

(Book of German Poetics, 1624), praised the German chanceries as "die rechten lehrerinn der reinen sprache" (the proper teachers of the pure language).[24] Modern Standard German owes its complex sentence structure to the chancery style promoted by the grammarians of the seventeenth and early eighteenth centuries.

In the late nineteenth century, Konrad Burdach (1859–1936) described the court and chancery of Charles IV as the "cradle" of modern German, where Renaissance scholars under the auspices of his chancellor Johann von Neumarkt (ca. 1310–80) cultivated vernacular humanist writing on the model of the Italian humanist Petrarch. The first great work of Early Modern German prose, *Der Ackermann aus Böhmen* (The Plowman from Bohemia), written around 1400 in the elegant Prague chancery style by Johannes von Tepl (ca. 1350–1414/15),[25] reflects the linguistic changes separating it from Middle High German at a time when other chancery languages had not yet incorporated them. Burdach attempted to establish a direct link between the humanist chancery style and Modern Standard German by referencing two events: the transference of this form of the language from Prague to Vienna when the Habsburg dynasty succeeded the Luxemburg dynasty as emperors, and its adoption in the adjacent state of Upper Saxony where Luther was born and educated. In so doing he neatly accounted for Luther's assertion that the Saxon chancery language and that of the imperial chancery in Vienna were one and the same.

This elitist theory of language evolution was challenged by the dialectologist Theodor Frings (1886–1968), who argued that the spoken language of the people, rather than the literary chancery style, formed the basis of Modern Standard German.[26] Frings hypothesized that Luther's Eastern Central variety was based on the mixed dialect from the areas east of the Elbe and Saale, where migrants from all German dialect regions had settled. As the dialectal differences — they initially would have impeded communication — were gradually leveled out, a colonial linguistic compromise emerged that had fewer strongly dialectal features than the older western and southern German dialects. Frings concluded that this new dialect was the linguistic basis for the written chancery and business style used in cities between Meissen in the east and Eisenach in the west and later popularized by Luther's Bible.

Newer research reveals a more complicated process than either Burdach or Frings imagined.[27] We now know that the earliest German documents were written versions of dialects that later coalesced into regional writing languages. In the fifteenth and sixteenth centuries, scribal practices were regularized in the Eastern Central chancery language of the Saxon Wettin dynasty, as well as in Common German, the language of the imperial chancery and the southeastern business community. Eastern Central German was used in what are now the states of Thuringia, Saxony, and Saxon-Anhalt; Common German in the region between Vienna in the east, Nuremberg in the north, and Augsburg and Regensburg in the west. The linguistic conventions of the imperial chancery language also affected the urban business and administrative language in Nuremberg and Regensburg, where the imperial diet convened, and in Augsburg, where the imperial documents were printed. At a time when the economy was dominated by powerful merchant dynasties, most notably the Fugger family of Augsburg, these linguistic conventions were adopted into the business language of the urban patriciate in the entire region. The widely used Common German also influenced the scribal practices of the Wettin chancery and the business language of Upper Saxony. In western and south-western Germany regional features survived longer because the area was divided into numerous smaller political entities, where linguistic regularization seemed less necessary than in the larger states.

The competition between orthographic variants and word forms was eventually resolved in favor of those preferred by the chancery with the high-est prestige, widest geographical distribution, and highest frequency of use. One example concerns the unstressed prefixes *be-, er-, ent-, ver-, zer-* that are added to basic verbs to create derived verb forms, such as *gehen* "go" resulting in *be-gehen* "commit," *er-gehen* "stroll" or "happen," *ent-gehen* "escape." In the fourteenth and fifteenth centuries these prefixes still had the older ortho-graphic variants *bi-, ir-, int-, unt-, ont-, vir-, vor-, zur-*, which were eliminated first in the southeastern and southwestern writing and printing centers of Vienna, Augsburg, and Zurich; by the sixteenth century they had disappeared almost everywhere.[28]

The Linguistic Structure of Early Modern German

As the sixteenth century progressed, Protestant printers and writers increas-ingly adopted the new "Lutheran" Eastern Central German whereas their Catholic counterparts opted for the relatively standardized Common German. The gradual leveling of regional linguistic differences was motivated by the practical concern that printed materials be comprehensible outside the area of production; linguistic variation was accepted only as long as it did not impede communication. Common German and Eastern Central German enjoyed equal status, so that the authors of writing manuals and handbooks could counsel young scribes to imitate both writing convention models, that of Luther's Bible and that of the imperial chancery in Vienna and its Augsburg printers, without fear of contradiction. The concept of a single standard vari-ety had not yet arisen, precisely because German was still thought of primarily as a language for practical purposes and popular literature. Linguistic diglossia — the condition where two languages are employed in strictly separate areas of use — was no less accepted now than it had been during the Renaissance. Intellectual and scientific discourse was conducted exclusively in Latin, popu-lar discourse in German.

We shall now turn to the major differences between Eastern German and Common German, the two dominant writing varieties in early modern Germany, and to the salient linguistic changes separating Middle High German from Early Modern German and their incorporation into the regional writing languages.

Orthography

The most significant differences between Middle High German and Early Modern German are in the vowel system. The monophthongization of Middle High German diphthongs (two adjacent vowels of different height and degree of rounding) and the diphthongization of Middle High German monophthongs (long vowels) were ultimately graphically represented in the writing languages of all regions, even if the dialect was not affected. The monophthongization is thought to have begun in the twelfth century in the western central German dialects near the border of what are now the Netherlands and Belgium. It spread gradually to the south and east but never reached the Bavarian and Alemannic (Swiss, Swabian, Alsatian) dialects of the south. The Middle High German diphthongs *ie, ue, üe* changed to the modern German long monophthongs *i, u, ü*, so that *liep* "dear," *fuez* "foot," and *füeze* "feet" came to be pronounced as in modern German *lieb, Fuß, Füße*. In the case of *ie* the modern German spelling continues to reflect the Middle High German diphthongal pronunciation.

The diphthongization of long monophthongs, which originated in the thirteenth century in southeastern Austria, had affected the entire Bavarian dialect region by the end of that century and subsequently spread to the central German dialects as well. This change in the vowel system converted the Middle High German monophthongs *î, û, iu*, in such words as *mîn* "my," *hûs* "house," *liute* "people" into diphthongs pronounced *ai, au*, and *oi*, as in modern German *mein, Haus, Leute*. The new diphthongs spread in a northeasterly direction and by the sixteenth century were orthographically represented in all German writing languages except Middle Low German. This vowel shift never reached spoken Alemannic (including Swiss German) or the Low German dialects at the extreme southwestern and northern edges of the German-speaking area. Consequently, the dialectal designations for the spoken language of Switzerland and the Low German dialects are *Schwitzerdütsch* (Swiss German) and *Plattdütsch* (Flat German), rather than *Schweizerdeutsch* and *Plattdeutsch*.

The spelling of the Early Modern German diphthong *ai* is one of the more obvious features differentiating Common German and Eastern Central German, and the consistent representation of this diphthong is a good indicator for the regional origin of a text: *Kaiser ~ Kayser* "emperor" point to southern Germany and Austria, *Keiser ~ Keyser* to central Germany. Both geographic variants survive in modern German orthography, as in the designations of the rivers *Main* and *Rhein*, where the diphthongs are pronounced identically but spelled differently. The form of a common family name also indicates where the family resided originally: *Meier ~ Meyer* point to a central or northern German derivation, *Maier ~ Mayer* to a southern.

Other vocalic changes, for example the rounding of Middle High German unrounded vowels and the derounding of rounded vowels, were reflected only sporadically and inconsistently in individual words rather than in the entire vocabulary. Modern German words with unrounded vowels could be spelled in Early Modern German with rounded vowels and vice versa: *Kissen* "pillow" as *küssen*, *Nerz* "mink" as *nörz*, *Löffel* "spoon" as *leffel*, and *ohne* "without" as *âne*. This inconsistency owes to the lack of the rounded vowels *ü* and *ö* in many central and southern German or Austrian dialects, which replace them with their unrounded counterparts *i* and *e*; other dialects substitute rounded *ü* for unrounded *i*. Thus, the spoken language is the likely source for the Early Modern German orthographic variation between rounded and unrounded vowels.

Reflecting dialectal differences, the orthographic representation of the consonants also varied in Early Modern German texts. Bavarian, Alemannic, and Franconian dialects do not distinguish between word-initial voiced and voiceless consonants, so that such word pairs as *Paar* "pair" and *Bar* "bar," *Torf* "peat" and *Dorf* "village," *kriechen* "crawl" and *Griechen* "Greeks" are pronounced identically with voiceless but weakened initial consonants. This Central German consonant weakening is reflected orthographically in the fifteenth and sixteenth centuries. In southern texts the equivalents of modern German *badet* "bathes," *Abt* "abbot," *bist du* "are you" often were *padat*, *apt*, *pistu*. In the case of the word for "German," *deutsch*, the Common German spelling variant *teutsch* was favored by many writers regardless of their regional origin, probably because it occurred frequently in documents issued by the imperial chancery. The preferred form until the eighteenth century, it appears in the title of two works that will be discussed later in this essay, Schottelius's grammar *Ausführliche Arbeit von der Teutschen HaubtSprache* and Harsdörffer's *Der Teutsche Secretarius*.

In Eastern Central German dialects, such as Upper Saxon, the opposite phenomenon occurs: the voiceless consonants *p*, *t*, *k* are replaced by their voiced equivalents *b*, *d*, *g*, so that *packen* "pack" and *backen* "bake," *Tier* "animal" and *dir* "you," *Karten* "cards" and *Garten* "garden" are pronounced identically with voiced consonants. In the early modern period, Eastern Central German writing conventions reflect this dialectal consonant merger especially frequently in the case of *d* and *t*: *Tochter* "daughter," *Tag* "day," *trinken* "drink" appear as *dochter*, *dag*, *drinken*. In this respect Modern Standard German orthography represents a compromise or mixture of writing conventions: Common German *Papst* "pope" and *Tochter* "daughter," but Eastern Central German *Bach* "brook" and *Griechen* "Greeks." In spoken German all voiced consonants become voiceless at the end of a word. This rule of word-final devoicing means that such word pairs as *Bund* "federation" and *bunt* "colorful" or *Rat* "senator" and *Rad* "wheel" are pronounced identically as *bunt* and *Rat*. Early Modern German texts tend to reflect this phonological rule, since words such as *Geld* "money," *Land* "land," *Leib* "body" were frequently spelled *gelt*, *lant*, *leip*.

Another notable feature distinguishing Common German and Eastern Central German is the use of doubled or trebled voiceless consonants. For the modern reader this clustering of consonants adds to the archaic quality of the southern writing language when compared to the more contemporary appearance of Eastern Central German. Luther's early texts, which reflect considerable southern influence, exhibit double consonants more frequently than his later works. This can be illustrated by comparing the phrase "and lead us not into temptation" from the first and last editions of the Lord's Prayer: *vnnd fure vnns nitt ynn versuchung* (1522), *vnd nit für vns in versuochung* (1534).[29]

In central and southern German dialects, word-initial Middle High German *s* changed to *sh* (spelled *sch*) before the consonants *l*, *m*, *n*, and *v* (written *w*), altering the pronunciation of such words as *slange* "snake," *sne* "snow," *swarz* "black" to *Schlange, Schnee, schwarz*. In the written language, however, the older forms persisted until the sixteenth century. In some central German dialects, intervocalic *b* is pronounced as *v*, a feature that also appears in Early Modern German documents until the sixteenth century: *farwe* "color," *lewen* "life," *arweiten* "work" rather than *Farbe, leben, arbeiten*.[30]

Inflection

Just as the inflectional systems of modern German dialects can differ significantly from the standard language, Early Modern German texts exhibit considerable regional variation. Beginning in the thirteenth century, word-final unstressed *-e* was deleted in southern German dialects, a feature reflected in Common German so that *Die lieb frau* "the good woman," *der gut mann* "the good man," *ich sag* "I say" are the rule rather than *die liebe Frau, der gute Mann, ich sage*. Because of its linguistic prestige the simplified inflectional system appeared in other writing regions as well. Luther frequently omitted word-final *-e* in his early writings; the full verbal and adjectival paradigms are more characteristic of his later work. Seventeenth-century grammarians disparaged the practice in Common German of omitting final *-e* as unsystematic and erroneous. Early Modern German noun plural forms also manifest competing variants, such as *bilde ~ bilder* "pictures," *menner ~ mannen* "men," *brüdere ~ brüdern* "brothers" well into the late seventeenth century.[31]

Prepositional case government was variable as well and is frequently different in modern German. For example, the preposition *für* (often written *fur*) was also used in the semantic context of modern German *vor*. In this case it tended to be followed by a dative rather than an accusative object (as with modern German *für*). An example occurs in Luther's translation of the sentence from the Twenty-third Psalm "You prepare before me a table in the presence of my enemies": *Du bereitest fur mir einen Tisch gegen meine Feinde*. As in the modern Austro-Bavarian dialects, *gegen* frequently governed the dative rather than the accusative case: *daz sie gegen dem kung waren* "that they were against the king."

Verb forms also varied between writing regions as well as in individual writing practice. The usual *-st* ending of second person singular present of auxiliary verbs could be replaced with *-t* in Early Modern German: *du solt/darft/willt* and *du sollst/darfst/willst* "you shall/may/will" could alternate freely in the same text. Since the fourteenth century the number of irregular strong German verbs has decreased steadily and regular weak verbs have increased proportionally. Early Modern German verb forms were so variable that writers and printers appear to have improvised. Irregular verbs could be regular, regular verbs could be irregular, and the forms of irregular verbs themselves were highly idiosyncratic — a consequence of the lack of reference grammars and formal instruction in German as well as grammatical change in the spoken language.

Beginning in the fifteenth century all southern and certain central German dialects lost the simple past tense and replaced it with the present perfect, a phenomenon that continues to be observable today. In the written language, on the other hand, probably under the influence of Latin grammar, writers began distinguishing semantically between the simple past and the present perfect tenses. In regions where simple past tense forms were no longer used in the spoken language, early modern authors had to acquire such irregular verb forms for the sole purpose of writing. The vowel distinction between the singular and plural forms of the simple past tense in certain verb classes, which was not leveled out until the eighteenth century, represented an additional complication: *er half ~ sie hulfen* "he/they helped," *er schwor ~ sie schwuren* "he/they swore," *es schwall ~ sie schwollen* "it/they swelled." Accordingly, certain strong verb conjugations could have four different vowels: *sie sterben* "they die," *er starb* "he died," *sie sturben* "they died," *er ist gestorben* "he has died." Remnants of these extinct past tense forms survive today as archaic subjunctives or as nouns derived from verbs: *hülfe* "would help," *Hubschrauber* "helicopter," both from *heben* "lift"; *Schwall* "surge" from *schwellen* "swell." Some Early Modern German regular verbs, now irregular, were then regular, for example *vermeidete* "avoided" rather than *vermied*; but more frequently, the reverse was the case so that such past tense forms as *er roch sich* "he avenged himself" or *er friehe* "he married" have the modern equivalents *er rächte sich, er freite.* Mixed-class verb forms were also numerous: *sie schankte ~ schunkte* "she donated," *er begunnte* "he began," *er tochte* "he was of use," rather than *sie schenkte, er begann, er taugte.*[32] Compared to modern German, the Middle High German tense system was uncomplicated, consisting only of the present and simple past tenses along with a rudimentary past perfect tense. The present perfect tense did not yet exist. By the middle of the fifteenth century, however, present and past perfect tenses formed with the auxiliary verbs *haben* and *sein* were reflected in the written language.

The Modern Standard German system of verbal tenses and the passive voice began to emerge from two conditions as German replaced Latin as the medium of written communication and as writers sought to express the precise distinctions of tense and voice in their native language. As in modern colloquial German, where the future tense with the auxiliary verb *werden* rarely occurs, the early modern present tense included the notion of futurity; and the combination of the auxiliary verb *werden* with an infinitive or present participle form of the main verb tended to signify the onset of an action. Luther's sentences *Moses aber ward zittern* and *da ward das gantze Heer lauffendt* indicate that Moses was beginning to tremble and that the whole army was beginning to run. Well into the sixteenth century, *wollen* rather than *werden* could be used in combination with an infinitive to indicate a future action, as in

Luther's question *Wie will dirs gehen?* "How will you do? How are you?" As in many modern German dialects, in Early Modern German the verb *tun* "do" could function as a modal auxiliary to add emphasis to the action expressed by the main verb: *tue mir ein brieflein schreiben* "do write me a letter."[33]

In modern colloquial German, especially in the south, speakers prefer the analytic subjunctive construction, consisting of *würde* and an infinitive of the main verb, to the synthetic subjunctive forms of the main verbs, which are considered stilted or even archaic. *Katrin würde ja gerne schon heute fahren* "Katrin would really like to leave today" is generally preferred to *Katrin führe ja gerne schon heute*. By contrast, in written Standard German the *würde*-form of the subjunctive is generally considered to be stylistically inferior. The emergence of the *würde*-construction in the sixteenth century, after the simple past tense had been lost in southern German dialects, may mean that there was a causal relationship between these developments, since the synthetic subjunctive forms of irregular strong verbs are based on their simple past tense forms: *er kam* "he came" ~ *er käme* "he would come," *er schlug* "he beat" ~ *er schlüge* "he would beat." When speakers no longer had recourse to the simple past tense forms, the *würde*-construction may have become more prevalent because it reduced the memory load — the number of grammaticalized forms to be retained by the speaker. The use of the analytic subjunctive increased in the sixteenth century when the style of writing was relatively close to the spoken language, but decreased in the seventeenth century when language scholars promoted a literary language modeled on the legal chancery style.

Negation

In Middle High German, negation could be achieved by simply prefixing the particle *en-* to the verb and adding an optional *niht*, so that modern German *er weiß es nicht* "he doesn't know it" corresponds to Middle High German *er enweiz es* or *er enweiz es niht*.[34] This particle survived into the fourteenth and fifteenth centuries. When the freestanding negative *niht/nit/nyt* was applied serially, it conveyed the meaning of *neither . . . nor*, as in the example: *nit ein blat, nit ein stro, nit ein har* "neither a leaf, nor a straw, nor a hair." In the early printing period the Common German negative form *nit* predominated but was subsequently replaced by Eastern Central German *nicht*. The position of the negative particle *nicht* also differs from modern German norms since it can occupy the final position in declarative sentences, presumably for poetic reasons: *Sie bauen auf den Schein des schnöden Wesens nicht*, literally: "They build upon the appearance of mean being not." At the end of the fifteenth century and in the first decades of the sixteenth the archaic negative particle *en-* still accounted for approximately 11% of all negations; it had become rare in Luther's Eastern Central German, however.

Double negatives were grammatical in Middle High German. This is still the case in the modern Austro-Bavarian dialect, where the statement *I hob ka Göld ned* "I ain't got no money," for example, corresponds to Standard

German *Ich habe kein Geld*. In Early Modern German, as well, when an intensified negation was desired, the double negative could be recommended, as
Schottelius says: "Wenn zusammengesetzet werden zwey Verneinungswörter,
alsdenn verneinen sie in Teutscher Sprache noch härter" (When two negative
words are placed together, they make the negative sense even stronger in
German). Sentences such as *Gerechter Leute Licht Verleschet nimmer nicht* "The
light of the just is not never extinguished" or *Seyd stille/ als sonst keiner nicht*
"Keep still as not no other" are adduced frequently in his work.[35] Double
(occasionally even triple) negatives abound in Luther's texts: for example, *aber
nie keiner ist . . . gebeten worden* (but never nobody was asked). Only at the
beginning of the eighteenth century did they begin to be viewed as illogical
and therefore ungrammatical.

Sentence Structure

Two characteristics distinguish modern German sentence structure from English
and other Germanic languages: in main clauses the sentence frame or bracket
consisting of the conjugated and non-conjugated parts of the predicate encloses
all other sentence constituents; in dependent clauses, all verb forms are clustered
at the end, with the conjugated verb occupying final position. In the statement
*Mein Mann ist heute morgen mit einem Kollegen zu einer Konferenz nach
Hamburg gefahren*, literally: "My husband has this morning with a colleague to
a conference in Hamburg driven," all the pertinent information is wedged
between the auxiliary and main verbs; in the dependent clause (*ich bezweifele*),
daß dieses Problem jemals gelöst werden wird, literally: "I doubt that this problem
ever solved be will," the conjugated verb form is in final position. Since neither
rule was obligatory until the grammarians of the eighteenth century made them
so, early modern writers could exercise considerable syntactic flexibility and still
be regarded as writing in good style. Although the use of fully framed main
clauses increased over time, partially framed sentences — where some elements
are placed after the second part of the predicate — as well as entirely unframed
constructions — where the predicate is completed before the other constituents
are added — were common.[36] *Sydonie was gangen inn ir cleyderkamer* "Sydonie
had gone to her dressing room" is unframed whereas *sie hetten da zu viel birs
getruncken nach der kindtöffe*, literally: "they had too much beer drunk after the
christening," is partially framed, because the prepositional phrase follows the second part of the predicate. Optional sentence constituents, especially prepositional phrases, could still be placed after the sentence frame. However, fully
framed main clauses were preferred, already in the first decades of the sixteenth
century, to the unframed equivalent in all writing regions and all types of texts:
Evlenspiegel wolt kein handtwerck lernen, literally: "Eulenspiegel wanted no craft
to learn," rather than *Evlenspiegel wolt lernen kein handtwerck*. Nevertheless,
writers continued well into the eighteenth century to use partially framed sentences as a literary device to give emphasis, express emotions, reflect the colloquial language of the people, or convey a sense of the archaic.[37]

Modern Standard German sentence structure is more complex than the colloquial language, because it is not the result of a natural linguistic evolution but a product of the efforts of normative grammarians to create a linguistic style — including extensive use of subordinate clauses — far removed from the language of the common people. Between 1500 and 1550, when the spoken language served as a model for writing, sentences were still comparatively short, though dependent clauses were used more frequently than before. Between 1550 and 1700, however, the practice of embedding subordinate clause structures into main clauses became more prevalent and resulted in lengthy sentences, especially in certain text genres. Those intended for the public, such as fables, narratives, travel reports, and farces, were closer to the spoken language and tended toward short dependent clauses or toward paratactic constructions, in which main clauses are linked with other main clauses simply through coordinating conjunctions. By contrast, legal, theological, and scholarly writings exhibited extensive use of hypotactic constructions, in which complex dependent clauses are employed. At the end of the seventeenth century, sentences in theological treatises contained on average eighty-eight word forms. In a certain ordinance issued by the Leipzig city council, one sentence consisted of fourteen clauses containing a total of 275 word forms.[38] Written Modern Standard German clearly owes its complex sentence structure to the chancery style of the second half of the sixteenth and first half of the seventeenth century, when language scholars considered it exemplary of good writing. Many writers, especially of the later baroque, reveled in lengthy, intricately constructed sentences; the grammarians of the eighteenth century formulated the syntactic rules of Modern Standard German and thereby codified the complex style in reference grammars.

Martin Luther's Linguistic Influence

Because the specialized vocabulary and complex syntactic structure of chancery language made it unsuitable for his purposes, Luther looked to the vernacular for linguistic guidance in translating the Bible. Thus, he avoids Latin loan words and includes numerous proverbs and folk metaphors. As he explains in his *Sendbrief vom Dolmetschen* (Treatise on the Art of Translation, 1530), the language of the common people — the man in the market place, the housewife, the children playing in the streets — will serve as the basis for his prose style. He vigorously defends this belief against the objection that a free translation into the vernacular obscures and falsifies the sacred text. Luther's experience as a preacher of popular sermons galvanized his ability to render complex theological topics in an accessible style.[39]

However, it was the grammarians of the seventeenth century who, in their program to create a national language, guaranteed Luther's primary place in the history of the standardization of German. They quote liberally from his opinions on language and regularly adduce passages from his Bible in their grammars, though in a modernized form. The great linguistic achievement of

Luther's Bible is that it established a dominant writing language; he explains its origins in the *Sendbrief*:

> Ich rede nach der sächsischen Canzeley, welcher nachfolgen alle Fürsten und Könige in Deutschland; alle Reichsstädte, Fürsten-Höfe schreiben nach der sächsischen und unseres Fürsten Canzeley, darum ists auch die gemeinste deutsche Sprache. Kaiser Maximilian, und Kürfürst Friedrich, Herzog zu Sachsen, haben im römischen Reich die deutschen Sprachen also in eine gewisse Sprache gezogen.[40]

> [I speak the language of the Saxon chancery, which is used by all princes and kings in Germany. All imperial cities, all princely courts write like the Saxon chancery of our ruler. Therefore, it is the most commonly used German language. Emperor Maximilian and Elector Friedrich, Duke of Saxony, have merged the German languages in the Roman Empire into one particular language.]

As of the eve of the Reformation, a considerable degree of linguistic adjustment and cross-fertilization had already occurred between Common German and Eastern Central German. The gradual leveling of orthographic differences between the writing regions may have been facilitated both through exchanges of official documents and correspondence as well as by trade relations.[41] Luther's assertion that Common German and Eastern Central German were essentially one language appears to the modern reader to ignore their obvious linguistic differences. However, it is probable that Luther, who grew up and lived most of his life near the transition zone between Eastern Central German and Low German, thought the differences inconsequential in comparison to the deep linguistic gap that separated his own language from Middle Low German. The latter was virtually incomprehensible to southern readers, because it was more closely related to Dutch than to other German writing languages.

The Upper Saxon chancery language, with its admixture of Common German elements, provided Luther with the linguistic foundation upon which to build his biblical language.[42] Many of his word choices survive in modern German. They include Common German *durst* "thirst," *wurtzel* "root," *herrschen* "rule," *gehen* "go," *gewesen* "been," and *oder* "or," instead of Eastern Central German *dorst, wortzel, hirrschen, gahn, gewest, adder*. In other instances, the choice of his native forms resulted in modern German *brennen* "burn," *Sonne* "sun," *kommen* "come," *König* "king," rather than Common German *brinnen, sunne, kummen, kuenig*. In yet others, he began with originally Common German (and now modern) German variants, only to replace them with his native forms: *kaufen* "buy," *tauffen* "baptize," *jude* "jew," which later became *keuffen, teuffen, juede*. Further changes occurred after Luther's time, of course, such as *helle* "hell," *schweren* "swear," *du solt* "thou shalt," which became modern German *Hölle, schwören, du sollst*. Regional lexical variants, such as northern German *Kohl* "cabbage," *Kloß* "dumpling," *Fleischer* "butcher," and their southern synonyms *Kraut, Knödel, Metzger*, were as abundant in the regional writing languages of the sixteenth century as they are in the modern dialects. For this reason, the early editions of the Bible included glossaries of regional synonyms for the benefit of readers in other areas of Germany. Since these were no longer included in the final edition, it can be assumed that the need for them diminished as the public grew familiar with Luther's lexical choices.

Luther used the rules of German word formation, such as compounding and addition of prefixes and suffixes, in creating new vocabulary. Many of his neologisms still survive, for example *Feuereifer* "fiery zeal," *Ebenbild* "image" or "likeness," *Machtwort* "powerful word," *friedfertig* "peaceful," *wetterwendisch* "changeable," *gastfrei* "hospitable"; others do not, such as *Afterrede* "false testimony" or "gossip," *erzbös* "very evil." Luther redefined the meaning of many existing words to reflect the Protestant ethic or to create religious connotations. *Arbeit* "work," which formerly denoted physical toil, turned into a virtuous activity; *Beruf* "calling" was extended to include the secular meaning "chosen work" or "office"; the secular terms *Gemeinde* "community" or "congregation," *fromm* "good" or "pious," *gerecht* "just" were semantically broadened to embrace religious connotations. The high regard of the Protestant grammarians of the seventeenth and eighteenth centuries for the language of Luther's Bible led to the popularization of many of his lexical choices and their inclusion in the first modern German dictionary, Adelung's *Grammatisch-kritisches Wörterbuch der hochdeutschen Mundart, mit beständiger Vergleichung der übrigen Mundarten, besonders aber der Oberdeutschen* (1774–86) (Grammatical-critical Dictionary of the High German Dialect with Continuous Comparison with the Other Dialects, but especially Upper German). They were subsequently incorporated into Modern Standard German.

Initially, Luther's language exhibited more regional features and orthographic inconsistencies than the official document language of professional chancery scribes. Over time, however, it moved closer to what became Modern Standard German norms. The graphemes representing the vowels *i* and *u*, for example, at first could appear respectively as *i, y, j* and *u, w, v*; in later printings, consonantal graphemes such as *jn* "him," *bleyben* "stay," *vnd* "and," *ewer* "your," *haws* "house," tended to be replaced with modern German vowels: *ihn, bleiben, und, euer, Haus*. Unnecessarily complex consonant clusters — a characteristic feature of Common German — such as in *krankch* "sick" and *czeitenn* "times," appear frequently in Luther's early works, only to be simplified later on. Since Common German orthography reflected the dialectal phonological rule of Central German consonant weakening, which neutralizes the distinction between voiced and voiceless consonant pairs (for example, $p \sim b$ and $t \sim d$), the younger Luther frequently opted for the southern spelling variant; the older Luther changed it in the direction of what became modern German: *purg* "fortress" > *burg*, *seistu* "you are" > *seist du*. In other instances, Luther's orthography reflects the pronunciation of his Upper Saxon dialect, in which the distinction between voiced *b, d, g* and voiceless *p, t, k* is neutralized in favor of the voiced variant, as in the spelling of the word for pope: early *Bab(e)st* gives way later to Common German (and modern) *Papst*.

The Common German system of inflection was simpler than Modern Standard German, word-final -*e* being omitted in the verbal, nominal, and adjectival paradigms. Early Luther tended to omit the suffix, writing *ich sag* "I say" or *das Neu Testament* "the New Testament," but opted increasingly for fully inflected forms: *ich sage, das Neue Testament.* Between 1522 and 1545, fully inflected forms increased from 66% to 81% in Eastern Central German editions of his Bible.[43] As in the modern Austro-Bavarian dialects, the Common German past participle prefix *ge-* was omitted under certain phonological conditions — again more often in the early editions: *kumen* "has come" becomes *gekumen* in later versions. The Common German negative form *nit* predominates in his early printings, the Eastern Central German *nicht* in his later ones. As mentioned above, double negatives appear consistently in Luther's texts.

Word order and sentence structure likewise increasingly approximated Modern Standard German norms. Luther gradually distinguished more clearly between main and subordinate clauses, and he replaced simple main clauses conjoined by coordinating conjunctions with subordinate clauses having the inflected verb in final position. In the first edition of the New Testament, obligatory objects frequently appear after the sentence frame formed by two-part predicates: *unnd sie wird geperen eyen son* "and she will bear a son." The last edition of his Bible manifests the modern order of syntactic elements: *und sie wird einen Son geberen.*[44]

In time, Luther's style became both more concise and more literary. This may be illustrated by two passages from the Twenty-third Psalm: "Er lesst mich weyden da viel Gras steht" (He lets me graze where there is a lot of grass) in the first edition of the New Testament becomes the more poetic "Er weidet mich auf einer grünen Awen" (He lets me graze in a green meadow) in the last edition, published in 1546. Similarly, "zum wasser das mich erkulet" (to the water that cools me) changes to the more concise "zum frischen Wasser" (to fresh water).[45]

In preliterate or semiliterate societies, proverbs play an important role in reinforcing community standards of behavior, accounting for the vagaries of life, and helping to educate young people. Luther's Bible is a treasure trove of German folk wisdom.[46] His sermons and table talks are replete with pithy formulations of his coinage, many of which eventually achieved proverbial status, such as "Wer anderen eine Grube gräbt, fällt selbst hinein" (He who digs a pit for someone else, himself falls into it).[47]

In his polemics against theological adversaries, especially the pope and the Catholic clerical establishment, Luther's rhetorical style is by modern standards quite crude. Derogatory designations like *Papstesel* "ass of a pope," *Eselskoepff* "ass's heads," *diese Esel* "these asses," *Hurentreiber* "pimps" appear frequently. His pungent language, far from being considered offensive at the time, reflects the discourse of the age of *Grobianismus* (coarseness). In 1530, his Wittenberg colleague Erasmus Alberus spoke for many of his fellow humanists in hailing Luther as the German Cicero: "Dr Martinus ist der rechte man, der wol verdeütschen kan, er ist ein rechter Teutscher Cicero. Er hat uns . . . auch die Teutsche Sprache reformiert, und kein Schreiber auff erden, der es ihm nach thun kann"[48] (Dr. Martin is the right man who can translate well into German. He is a veritable German Cicero. He has also reformed the German language for us, and there is no writer in the whole world who can match him).

Although Luther was hardly the creator of Modern Standard German, as once proposed, the influence of his biblical language on modern German should not be underestimated. The language scholars and teachers of the sixteenth, seventeenth, and eighteenth centuries rightly acknowledged him as an authority on linguistic style and quoted him extensively, even as the language of his Bible was adapted with each reprinting to reflect the continuing evolution of German. His straightforward manner, made forceful by avoiding foreign loan words and writing in relatively simple sentence structures, left a powerful imprint on subsequent German style from the Storm and Stress to Berthold Brecht.

The significance of the printing press in disseminating his explosive message to a mass audience in so short a time bears repeating here. Since Luther became a national celebrity in a matter of weeks after he posted his *Ninety-Five Theses* against the sale of indulgences in 1517, neither church nor emperor could react fast enough to stem the tide of the new religion. Without printing, the reformer might well have suffered the fate of earlier heretics whose ideas were successfully contained by the clerical and secular establishments. Luther's call for Bible study in the homes of his followers ensured that the demand for his translation would continue without interruption. In the quarter of a century between 1522 (the year the German New Testament was published) and 1546 (the year of his death), 260 partial or complete reprints of his Bible and ninety Low German editions were published. It has been estimated that at the time of Luther's death half a million partial or complete copies of the Bible were in circulation among a total population of twelve to fifteen million people, of whom only a small percentage were fully literate.[49]

Chancery Manuals, Title Booklets, and Early German Grammars

Some of the early humanist elite considered German to be a barbaric language lacking the systematic uniformity of the classical languages; some even expressed repugnance at being obliged to write lyrics in the vernacular for their German lovers.[50] The first German grammars, published in the late fifteenth and early sixteenth centuries, were translations of Latin grammars for Latin schools, where speaking German was prohibited. But the great volume of documents now emanating from the chanceries and the general explosion of Reformation writings revealed an urgent need for manuals specific to German writing style. The authors of these vernacular chancery manuals and handbooks were trained in Latin and thus tended to impose the structure of Latin grammar on the vernacular. The initial focus was on spelling conventions, rules of punctuation, petitioning style, legal documents, and epistolary form (both official and personal). They contained important sections on the terms of address to be used in correspondence and on how to use the elaborate system of titles characteristic of highly stratified societies.[51] The manuals typically dealt with grammar only to explain the parts of speech or, occasionally, word formation with prefixes. The first German writing handbook, the *Schryfftspiegel* (Mirror of Writing), was printed in Cologne and probably written in 1527 in the northern city of Braunschweig.[52] Written anonymously by one or more authors, its purpose was to facilitate letter writing; it includes rules of spelling, punctuation, and the correct use of titles. Its rules for capitalization are closer to modern English than to modern German: only the first word in each sentence, the names of princes, persons, cities, and geographic designations are to be capitalized; capitals may also be used for emphasis.

The second German grammar was *Ein Canzley- und Titel buechlin* (A Chancery and Title Booklet) by Fabian Frangk, published together with his *Orthographia*, in Wittenberg in 1531. Frangk, who had studied at the university in Frankfurt on the Oder, became tutor to the younger son of the elector of Brandenburg, Margrave Johann of Küstrin, who would later charge him to establish a German school in Frankfurt on the Oder. In addition to spelling rules, the manual includes forms of address, instructions for writing letters, and sample letters that the reader may adapt to individual use. Frangk's objective was to reduce regional dialectal features and avoid their "errors" in the written language. He advises, "vieler Land sprachen mit jren missbreuchen zewissen/ damit man das vnrecht moeg meidenn"[53] (to know the languages of many regions with their errors, so that one may avoid bad usage). Frangk permits space-saving abbreviations, such as for word-final -*n*, gives instructions on how to mark long and short vowels, and warns against the excessive consonant clusters in Common German. His handbook does not cover the grammatical rules of German.

A third major early work on German usage and grammar, *Handbuechlin gruntlichs berichts* (Handbook with Thorough Information) by Johann Elias Meichssner, was published in Tübingen in 1538 (numerous reprints followed, the last in 1588). Meichssner began his career as a city scribe in Stuttgart and rose to become secretary to Margrave Ernst of Baden; he later served as chancery and legal secretary of the state of Baden. The title page claims that the book will be the reference work for *all* secretaries, notaries, and scribes working at imperial, territorial, or urban chanceries. Meichssner especially wants to reach the younger generation, whom he criticizes for poor spelling habits. Orthographic rules, the parts of speech with their inflectional endings, and principles of German word formation with prefixes complete the book. The first German reference work to include the term *grammar* in the title was Valentin Ickelsamer's *Teütsche Grammatica* of 1535. The German grammars of Laurentius Albertus (1573), Albertus Olearius (Öhlinger, 1573), and Johannes Clajus (1578) were written in Latin.

In the seventeenth century the focus of grammarians shifted from orthography to the regularization of the systems of inflection and to the principles of word formation. Because Latin is highly inflected, the function of its parts of speech readily identifiable, and its word order relatively unrestricted, grammars did not include rules for ordering syntactic elements in the sentence. Firmly wedded to this Latin model, German grammars before the seventeenth century neglected German word order and clause structure. The first German grammar to include exhaustive paradigms as well as instruction in syntax was Ratke's *Allgemeine Sprachlehr* (Common Grammar) of 1619. Grammatical rules are illustrated with quotations from Luther's Bible. The fact that Ratke's tends to capitalize most if not all nouns in his text, whereas Luther, Frangk, and Meichssner adhere to the older orthographic conventions (similar to the rules of modern English), suggests that capitalization had become more topical in the second half of the sixteenth century. The modern German rule that all nouns be capitalized appears to have originated in the Baroque, when an ornamental style of writing and printing became fashionable. Ratke's grammar was soon forgotten, but his rational recommendations for educational reform — among others, that teachers be trained not only in their subject matter but also in a methodology appropriate for young children and that German be the primary language of instruction — were widely, if unevenly, implemented.[54] Still, Latin would remain the preferred language of higher education for another century.

Georg Philipp Harsdörffer

Known as *der Spielende* (the Playful One) in Germany's leading intellectual society, the Fruchtbringende Gesellschaft (Fruitbringing Society) in Anhalt-Köthen, near Weimar, and founder of the Pegnesischer Blumenorden (Flower Order on the Pegnitz) in Nuremberg,[55] Georg Philipp Harsdörffer (1607–58) was one of the most influential advocates of German in the seventeenth century. He intended *Der Teutsche Sekretarius* (The German Secretary, 2 vols., 1655 and 1659) as a reference tool for chancery as well as private use. A combination grammar, chancery manual, and commentary on the state of the German language, it includes an extensive collection of sample letters and model responses for petitioning higher authorities or for composing official and personal letters to superiors, friends, women, and the bereaved; model forms for legal and inheritance matters; lists of Italian business terms with German glosses; and a concise dictionary. A typical example of Hardsdörffer's method is the entry for *Rabe* "raven," which combines instruction in spelling, semantics, and grammar: "Rabe männliches Geschlechtes. der Rabe mit dem einfachen a und mit dem e zuletzte ist der bekannt diebische Vogel"[56] (Raven, masculine gender. The *Rabe* with a single *a* and final *e* is the well-known thieving bird). The *Sekretarius* also contains orthographical rules; pronouncements on morality; observations on nature; reflections on the low status of the German language; chastisement of soldiers and courtiers for their misuse of

French and Italian, and of scholars for their sole reliance on Latin; and disdain
for lawyers who put on intellectual airs by tossing about Latin loan words in
court proceedings. Harsdörffer often employs the method of question and
answer: Why do we have no German scientific and scholarly vocabulary?
Because our teachers are ignorant and our scholars too lazy to devise native
equivalents for foreign words. Why does the public use so many foreign words?
Because foreign troops occupy German soil — and it must have an end.
Indeed, it is our patriotic duty not to use foreign words unnecessarily:
"Warumb dann solten wir neugierige Teutschen uns entblöden unsre Sprache
ohne Noht mit frembden Flickwörtern zu beflecken, mit ausländischen
Anstriche zu beschminken mit dem Französisch-Welsch-Lateinischen
Bettlersmantel zu verhüllen, da wir uns doch sonsten der Lumpen unserer
Bekleidung schämen?" (Why should we curious Germans be so stupid as to
soil our language unnecessarily with foreign patch words, to cover it with a foreign coat of paint, to hide it under a French-Italian-Latin beggar's coat, even
though we are otherwise ashamed of ragged clothing?)[57]

Although Harsdörffer advocates replacing loan words with their native
counterparts and eliminating superfluous "foreign invaders," he nevertheless
approves of retaining well-integrated loan words that have achieved "German
citizenship." For most, he offers German lexical replacements: *Bittschrift* "petition" for *Supplication*; *ansuchen* and *anmahnen* "to petition" for *solicitieren*.
Harsdörffer doubts that regional variation can be eliminated from the written
language, given the dialectal differences in the spoken language; people are,
after all, as attracted to their own language as birds to their own tunes. He
quotes the saying, "Und singet ein jeder Vogel wie ihm der Schnabel gewach-
sen ist" (Every bird sings according to how its beak is shaped). To illustrate the
effect of dialectal differences on poetry, he adduces the sentence, "Wann die
schwarze Kuh brüllt, es im Tale widerschillt" (When the black cow bellows, it
echoes in the hollows), in which *brüllt* and *schillt* would rhyme in Silesian
dialect, where *ü* is replaced by *i*, but not in the Upper Saxon dialect of Meissen.
Unlike many of his peers in the language societies, Harsdörffer tolerates
regional linguistic variation as long as it is modeled on "guter Gebrauch" (good
usage), by which he means the spoken language of courtiers and polite society.
In his view, orthography should be based on logical principles advocated by
grammarians and on the writing conventions of prestigious chanceries. He considers it illogical, for example, to interchange the consonants *j* and *v* with the
vowels *i* and *u*: vowels and consonants must be kept strictly separate. If there is
no logical reason for a certain orthographic convention, the dialect (*Mundart*)
should serve as a guide. Harsdörffer adamantly advises against crude language
and the common expressions of the *Pöbel*, or lower classes.

Georg Justus Schottelius

German scholars of the seventeenth century sought to devise a standardized
variety of the language as structurally and lexically complex and functional as

the other European languages, including Latin.[58] Schottelius, the first gram-marian to devote himself exclusively to the study of German, created a German linguistic terminology, though he was careful to provide Latin equivalents for readers unfamiliar with the vernacular terms.[59] He insists that the new German be based not on colloquial practice but on theoretical rules established by trained grammarians; but he also considers usage to be a valid criterion. Where actual usage conflicts with a *Hauptgesetz*, or principal grammatical rule, how-ever, the rule is to take precedence. Schottelius observes that Cicero and Vergil paid little heed to the spoken language of the people in the cabbage markets of Rome or in peasant cottages. He goes a step beyond Harsdörffer in reject-ing regional linguistic features outright, arguing that they would lead to gram-matical uncertainty and destabilize the language. In reminding that common speech is acquired naturally, whereas elevated language is obtained only through diligent study, he anticipates the formal distinction modern linguists make between *Hochdeutsch* (Standard German) and *Umgangssprache* (collo-quial speech). Schottelius likens the state of contemporary German to a thorny bush and rebukes scholars, scientists, and the upper classes for the contempt they show for their native language, since their snobbery only reinforces the perception of the vernacular as the poor medium of artisans and peasants. In response to the objection that German cannot function as the medium of the arts and sciences because it lacks an adequate terminology, he holds up the example of the Dutch, who have created a sophisticated aesthetic vocabulary. Indeed, as he sees it, the native processes of German word formation — the creation of new vocabulary through compounding of nouns or by adding pre-fixes and suffixes to existing *Stammwörter* (basic words) — make German an especially promising linguistic medium for future scholarly discourse.

In arguing that German is sufficiently ancient and prestigious to replace Latin in academia, Schottelius reiterates a typical pre-Enlightenment narrative of the German language that does not distinguish between biblical and lin-guistic history: he accepts as scientific fact that Adam and all humankind spoke a universal language before the Babylonian dispersion. In this view, what he calls the *Ertzprache* (protolanguage) is the direct ancestor of German, and German is the ancestor of all modern European languages. Schottelius points to the phonetic similarity between the German verb *babbeln* "babble" and the name *Babylon* as proof of his thesis. During the migrations following the dis-persion, so Schottelius, the German people were led to Europe by Ashkenaz, Noah's grandson (son of Gomer; 1 Chron. 1:6), who became the father of the German people. He cites the designation for eastern European Jews, *Askenazi*, as further evidence for this illustrious racio-linguistic descent from Ashkenaz.

Because the genetic relationships between the Indo-European family of languages had not yet been discovered, Schottelius's generation could hardly have distinguished between the Celtic and Germanic peoples and languages; the ancient Germans, it was believed, were the original *Hauptgeschlecht* (chief race), the tribe that assumed the name *Celtic* upon arrival in Europe. Their ancient Germanic-Celtic tongue was thought to have spread to other regions of Europe through subsequent intra-European migrations, during which it formed into the many dialectal ancestors of the modern European languages. Schottelius believed that Celtic, Romance, Slavic, and the Germanic languages descended from this ancient Germanic protolanguage. To support his theory he worked out the same method nineteenth-century philologists would apply to their own theory of the genetic relationship between the languages of Europe and Asia. This theory rests on the analysis of cognates, the shared vocabulary of multiple related languages. *Alemania,* the term for Germany in some Romance languages, provided Schottelius with additional linguistic evidence that German was the original language of Europe. When the Germanic tribes united in A.D. 358 to fight the Roman army, he says, they called their elite warriors *allerley Männer* (selected men), and claims that this term was later shortened to *Aleman* and applied to the German people in general. He adduces the Roman historian Tacitus's account (in his *Germania*) of the Germanic tribes in the first century A.D. in explaining the origin of the term *Germanier,* the Latin-based designation for the ancient Germanic tribesmen. Schottelius interprets it as having derived from a blended loan compound consisting of French *guerre* and German *man,* hence *Ger-man* "war-man," known also by the synonyms *Kriegsheld* "battle hero" and *Kriegsknecht* "battle servant."

Having established German as the European mother language, Schottelius documents, by an etymology of the term *deutsch,* German's place among the divine languages, Latin, Greek, and Hebrew. The chief god of the ancient Egyptians was called *Teut,* that of the Greeks *Zeus,* and that of the Romans *Deus*: the adjective *Teutisch* or *Teutsch* as applied to German can therefore only have the meaning "divine language." Schottelius also compares the lexical purity of German favorably to the "mixed" vocabulary of French, which he deems to have been corrupted with Latin and Greek loan words — he of course did not know that French descended directly from Latin. French, he observes, lacks the large stock of *Stammwörter* that enable German to remain "pure"; indeed, the ancient French vocabulary was so limited that the people were forced to adorn their language with "foreign feathers." And yet, notwithstanding the antiquity, sacredness, purity, and beauty of German, Schottelius concedes that it cannot take its place among the languages of Europe as a medium for written and oral academic discourse until its linguistic rules have been codified in a grammar and a scientific vocabulary created and compiled in a dictionary. His *Ausführliche Arbeit von der Teutschen HaubtSprache* was the first step in this direction, but the realization of his goal would still take more than a century.

Not only did Schottelius compose the first comprehensive grammatical description of German, he also created a German grammatical terminology: for example, *Nennwort* "noun," *Zeitwort* "verb," *Zeitwandlung* "tense," *benennendes Geschlechtwort* "definite article." In the nominal paradigm, Schottelius applies the analogical principle and requires that plural forms be marked with a suffix: *die Bürgere* "the burghers," *die Vormündere* "the guardians," *die Himmele* "the heavens," and so forth (none of which have endings in Modern Standard German). He does not permit forms without plural suffixes, and chastises printers who adhere to this (Common German) convention. He also

marks the genitive and dative singular case forms of feminine nouns ending in
-*e* with the suffix -*n*: *bei der Schantzen* "near the entrenchment" (modern
German *bei der Schantze*). The analogical principle leads him to supply the
genitive and dative plural case forms of the definite article with an additional
syllable: *derer guten Männer* "of the good men" (for modern German *der
guten Männer*).

In the verbal category, the forms of irregular verbs are highly variable,
unlike Modern Standard German.[60] Many verbs that were irregular for
Schottelius are now regular and vice versa: *jug* rather than *jagte* "hunted" and
preisete for *pries* "praised"; some of his verb forms no longer exist: *es schmalz*
instead of *es schmolz* "it melted." He often lists verbs with competing forms,
none of which survive in modern German: *sie sturben* ~ *storben* for *sie starben*
"they died."

The adjective paradigm in Schottelius also differs to some degree from
modern German. Both the so-called weak and strong suffixes (the strong endings are those that tend to tell the reader or listener something about the case
and/or gender of the modified noun) are permitted after the masculine definite article: *der starke(r) Adler* "the strong eagle," but Schottelius considers
the strong suffix -*er* to be more virile and poetically more pleasing then the
weak form -*e*, which he claims has a feminine character. In the genitive case,
unpreceded adjectives, which require the weak suffix -*en* in modern German,
take the strong suffix -*es* in Schottelius: *er ist vornehmes Geschlechtes* "he is of
high birth," *voll süsses Weins sein* "be drunk with sweet wine."

Although prepositional case government largely anticipates modern
German norms, there are certain differences. As in some modern German
dialects, *ausser* and *bei* are assigned to the class of prepositions that govern
either the (stative) dative or the (dynamic) accusative case, depending on the
nature of the verb. Thus, Schottelius contrasts the dynamic accusative *bei das
Buche setzen* "sit down next to the book" and the stative dative *bei dem Buch
stehen* "stand next to the book." The preposition *über* appears to govern the
dative case in most instances where modern German requires the accusative:
ich will mich über dir allein Erlüsten und fröhlich sein "I want to rejoice and be
glad about you." As in modern Bavarian dialects, *gegen* always governs the
dative rather than the accusative case: *gegen mir* "against me."

The reason for presenting German with six rather than four cases may have
been the belief in the inherent superiority of morphologically complex languages
— as would be held by the German philologists of the nineteenth century who
established the genetic relationships between the languages of Europe and Asia.
Since Schottelius was determined to elevate German to the same high degree of
linguistic prestige as Latin, he may have feared that presenting the language with
only a four-case system would jeopardize his program among his peers, the
majority of whom believed that a complex inflectional system was proof of a distinguished, even sacred linguistic ancestry.

Schottelius was the first grammarian to include an analysis of German sentence structure. In accordance with the baroque style of his age, he found elaborate sentences with extended nominal premodifiers to be stylistically more

pleasing than the relative clauses that they can replace. Hence, such phrases as *die hohe vor Augen schwebende Noht und Gefahr des Türkischen Einbrechens*, literally: "the before our eyes wafting worry and danger of the Turkish invasion" is preferred to the semantic equivalent *die hohe Noht und Gefahr/ welche jetzund vor Augen schwebet* "the great worry and danger that wafts before our eyes."

Syntactic rules governing verb position in main and dependent clauses did not become obligatory until the eighteenth century. Thus, for Schottelius, semantically optional elements (for example, prepositional phrases) in main clauses containing two-part predicates commonly follow the second part of the predicate: *und wird ausgeübet durch die Erfahrung* "and is done by experience." In dependent clauses the inflected verb tends to precede the uninflected members of the predicate rather than occupy the absolute final position:[61] *Wie sie recht in deutscher Sprache müssen und können genant werden*, literally: "How they in the German language must and can named be." Occasionally, however, the position of the verbs is like modern German: *damit der Leser . . . zugleich mit den teutschen Worten das Teutsche begreiffen und behalten könne*, literally: "so that the reader equally with the German words German to understand and retain be able."[62]

To Schottelius, German word formation — the compounding of nouns, and derivation by means of prefixes and suffixes — is the greatest asset to the language scholar engaged in the creation of a German scientific and scholarly vocabulary. Hence, he provides the grammatical meaning of the most productive suffixes, including *-bar, -e, -haft, -ig, -keit, -sal, -sam*. Since *-sal* and *-tum* were more productive in the seventeenth century than they are today, many of the cited examples evolved differently in Modern Standard German: *Armsal* "poverty," *Kummersal* "worry," *Weistuhm* "wisdom," *Weetuhm* "pain," and others.[63] His section on the formation of compound nouns is primarily a dictionary with Latin glosses for the German compounds, such as *Schuldherr* "creditor," and contains references to other written works, including the Luther Bible.

Schottelius's *Ausführliche Arbeit von der Teutschen HaubtSprache* was the first universally accepted normative grammar of German. It served as a point of reference for the grammarians of the Enlightenment until the end of the eighteenth century, when Adelung published the first comprehensive grammar of Modern Standard German and finished compiling the dictionary his predecessor had envisioned more than a century earlier.

Foreign Influences in Early Modern German

Borrowing — the importation of foreign words from one language into another — takes place when a speech community adopts foreign vocabulary to fill real or perceived lexical gaps in the native language. If, for instance, the intellectual elite considers another country to be technically more advanced or culturally superior, it will import the new technology and patterns of behavior, together with the vocabulary; individuals who master the foreign expressions will gain linguistic prestige. The choice of loan words depends on the intellectual and social climate among the elites as well as on the practical needs of occupations and professions. Once accepted, the lexical material becomes integrated into the native phonological and grammatical systems and is no longer perceived as foreign. An example of phonological integration is the French loan word *Balkon* "balcony," pronounced in German with a native final consonant rather than with the French nasalized vowel. The noun *Thema* "topic" has two competing plural forms, the original Greek *Themata*, now considered archaic, and the newer, grammatically integrated *Themen*, which has taken on the native German plural suffix *-en*. A second method of integrating foreign lexical material, employed extensively in the early modern period in Germany, is loan translation or loan formation, whereby the meaning of a loan word is conveyed with existing native vocabulary either literally or figuratively. To take a modern example: the German word *Computer* is a loan word from American English, whereas *Rechner* "main-frame computer" is a loan translation involving the verb stem *rechn-* "calculate" and the nominalizing suffix *-er*. A third method blends native and foreign elements, as in *Kohlenhydrat* "carbohydrate," where a German noun (*Kohl*) is combined with a Greek element. In the early modern period, German vocabulary was enlarged considerably through these processes.

When humanist scholars rediscovered ancient Roman and Greek culture, the Latin of Cicero, Ovid, Horace, and Vergil replaced medieval Latin as the prestige language for intellectuals, and Latin words were borrowed extensively in areas — especially law and medicine, but also administration and politics, higher education, and publishing and printing — where German vocabulary was inadequate or lacking. The Modern Standard German vocabulary in these areas is replete with Latin and Greek loan words imported during the early modern period to fill lexical gaps, including the following:[64]

> Law: *Akte, Argument, Arrest, Familie, legal, Prozeß* "trial."
> Administration and politics: *Monarch, Polizei, Rebell, Regent, Residenz, Tumult.*
> Higher education: *Bibliothek* "library," *Dekan* "dean," *Disziplin, Examen, Fakultät, Professor.*
> Publishing and printing: *Autor, Edition, Faksimile, Format, Korrektur, Orthographie.*
> Medicine: *Anatomie, Apotheke, Arterie, Chirurg* "surgeon," *Diät, Epidemie, Infektion, Nerv.*

Mastery of the classical stock of loan words became a requirement for membership in the emerging educated upper middle class. Although ancient Greek also enjoyed social prestige and was viewed as one of the sacred languages, far fewer scholars were fluent in Greek than in Latin. Consequently, as of the beginning of the sixteenth century, only about 17% of new loan words were of Greek origin, compared to approximately 80% of Latin origin. Over the next century the percentage of Latin loans decreased steadily except for the two decades between 1520 and 1540, when the confessional debates were conducted primarily in Latin or in a mixture of Latin and German. By the middle of the seventeenth century, Latin loan words constituted no more than 45% of new lexical imports.[65] The common practice, especially in the sixteenth century, among scholars in the arts and sciences of changing their family names from German to Latin or Greek to enhance their status in the intellectual community testifies to the prestige the classical languages enjoyed as the vehicles of intellectual discourse. Name changes could be accomplished by simply translating the entire German name into Latin: *Weber* ~ *Textor*, *Bauer* ~ *Agricola*, *Hundt* ~ *Canisius*, or by adding a Latin ending to a German family name: *Ratke* ~ *Raticus*, *Schottel* ~ *Schottelius*, *Claj* ~ *Claius*.

The transition to baroque culture around 1600 was accompanied by a shift to French as the primary source of new loan words: in the first eight decades of the sixteenth century, French had provided only between 7% and 10% of new loans, but by the middle of the seventeenth century, French-based loan translations and formations accounted for approximately 40%. They include *rival* ~ *Nebenbuhler*, *façon de parler* ~ *Redensart* "manner of speaking," *bel esprit* ~ *Schöngeist*, *hommes d'affaires* ~ *Geschäftsmann* "business man," *passion* ~ *Leidenschaft*.[66] German territorial rulers began to reshape their *Residenzen* architecturally, politically, and culturally in the French courtly image during the reigns of Louis XIII (r. 1610–43) and, particularly, of his successor Louis XIV (r. 1643–1715); the urban upper middle class adopted the lifestyle and manners of the courtiers. Key areas of technical vocabulary included:

> Military: *Admiral, Armee, Artellerie, Kanone, Kapitän, Munition, Offizier, Regiment, Soldat.*
> Civil and political administration: *Gouverneur, kontrollieren, Patent, Pension, Rebell, revoltieren.*
> Economics and transportation: *Adresse, Artikel, Etikette, Finanzen, Paket* "package."
> Society: *Courage, delikat, Diskretion, Konversation, korrekt, Respekt, Rivale.*
> Arts, crafts, and architecture: *Farce, Furnier* "veneer," *Klavier* "piano," *Park, Pavillion, Poesie, violett.*

Proportionally as Germany borrowed vocabulary from foreign cultures, the indigenous culture and language suffered in prestige, being denigrated as inelegant, even crude. For example, the French pronunciation of the German consonant *r* is thought to have originated in seventeenth-century polite society. It was at first pronounced, as in Spanish or Italian, with the tip of the tongue briefly flapping against the gums above the incisors producing the so-called "rolled *r*" (alveolar *r*). In Parisian society, however, *r* was pronounced with vibration of the fleshy lobe at the end of the soft palate. It is likely that the throaty (uvular) pronunciation was introduced into German by aristocratic bilinguals either because they found it more elegant or because they were more fluent in French than in German and therefore spoke with a French accent. This fashionable *r* was adopted by the upper middle class in the cities, and it is still the preferred standard pronunciation in Germany, though not in Austria or Switzerland.

French remained the preferred language of high society and the upper middle classes well into the eighteenth century. The educator Christian Thomasius (1655–1728) commented at the end of the seventeenth century that French had become so common that in many places even cobblers, tailors, children, and servants spoke it well.[67] When Voltaire visited Potsdam at the personal invitation of Friedrich the Great in 1750, he quipped that everyone spoke French and that German was used only for talking to soldiers and horses.[68]

Other languages also supplied significant quantities of loan words to German in the early modern period. Between the fourteenth and the seventeenth centuries, Italian business practices, including the system of double entry bookkeeping, spread throughout Europe, and numerous Italian loan words were incorporated into German. In fact, after Latin and French, Italian provided the third-largest contingent of loan words, the majority of which were borrowed during the fifteenth and sixteenth centuries when Italian culture dominated Europe. Examples from important areas include the following:

> Banking and commerce: *Bank*, *bankerott* "bankrupt," *brutto* "gross," *Giro-Konto* "checking account," *Kredit*, *Procura* "power of attorney," *Prozent* "percent," *Saldo* "balance."
>
> Music: *allegro*, *Alt* "alto," *Bass*, *Tenor*, *Spinett* "harpsichord," *Partitur* "musical score," *Oper*.
>
> Lifestyle: *Bankett*, *Marzipan*, *Matratze* "mattress," *Pantoffel* "slipper," *Porzellan*, *Salat*, *Stiefel* "boot," *Stuck* "stucco," *Torte*.

In spite of Germany's geographic proximity to the Slavic countries, only a handful of Slavic loan words became part of the general German vocabulary, probably because Slavic languages were not considered prestigious. Some of the most frequently used are *Grippe* "influenza," *Droschke* "horse drawn cab," *Grenze* "border," *Halunke* "scoundrel," *Knute* "lash," *Peitsche* "whip," *Schmetterling* "butterfly," *Tolpatsch* "clumsy person," *Zobel* "sable." Yiddish contributed a number of colorful words to colloquial German, including *Gauner* "rogue," *betucht* "wealthy," *mies* "bad," *Pleite* "bankruptcy," *foppen* "to tease," *blechen* "to pay," *schachern* "to bargain," *Schmus* "meaningless talk," *Schlamassel* "difficult situation."[69]

Whereas vocabulary transfers readily from one language to another, grammar and word order are more resistant. An example is modern German dependent clause syntax, which requires, as noted earlier, that the entire predicate be moved to the end of the clause and the inflected verb occupy the final position. This peculiar word order is thought to have originated in the legal language of the chanceries in the early modern period, though modern language historians are divided over the reason for it. One faction considers it to be an inherently German tendency; the other — based on observations of bilingual individuals, who tend to inject words or entire phrases from one language into the other unless each of the languages is used in strictly separate domains (areas of usage) — attributes it to Latin influence.[70] For the scribes and notaries in the chanceries, German and Latin were clearly not restricted to separate domains: both languages were used in written documentation, so that individuals had to shift from Latin to German and back again as they went about their tasks. This situation is clearly conducive to language mixing, and it is therefore theoretically possible that the word order in a Latin dependent clause like *quod dictum est*, literally: "what said is," could have been transferred to German by bilingual chancery scribes, translating the phrase as *was gesagt ist* rather than *was ist gesagt*. It is further possible that the syntactic rule originated in the Latin-influenced chancery style and then was popularized through the German glosses in the grammars studied in the Latin schools — the training grounds for future writers, scholars, and administrators.[71] Exposure to the chancery style certainly affected verb placement in dependent clauses in letters, diaries, and other documents, as is evident in fourteenth- and fifteenth-century Nuremberg, when the final position of the inflected auxiliary verb increased through exposure to the language of the city chancery.[72] University-educated administrators fluent in Latin demonstrated the highest incidence of the modern word order, followed by educated merchants having either Latin or German school training. The writings of artisans, students, and nuns had lower rates of modern word order than those of the merchants, but higher rates than those of secular women educated in women's schools with no Latin and little exposure to chancery style. Since chancery style was considered exemplary, the new word order may have been copied by other writers and in this way eventually become codified in grammars.

Occupational Jargons

The vocabulary of modern German has also been enriched by occupational jargons (*Fachsprachen*) from the early modern period. In most instances an originally restricted meaning was connotatively extended to more general contexts when it was no longer used exclusively for the original specialized purposes.[73] The language of the hunter was the source of designations for the body and organ parts of certain wild animals: *Lauscher* "ear of deer," *Löffel* "ear of a rabbit," *Schweiß* "blood," *Fallstrick*, originally a snare made of rope used to trap animals, generalized to mean "pitfall"; *Pranke*, the forepaw of large predators, extended to refer to a very large human hand; *bärbeißig* "bear biting" describing a hunting dog eager for the bear hunt, modified to refer to a grumpy or quarrelsome person; *unbändig* "unbindable" for a dog that would not train, now meaning simply huge or excessive, as in the expression *eine unbändige Freude erfaßte sie* "she was seized by a great joy." Common expressions, such as *auf die Sprünge helfen* "to help (someone) get started," *auf falscher Fährte sein* "be on the wrong track," or *ins Gehege kommen* "get in (someone's) way," all derive from early modern hunting.

The mining of coal and iron ore was professionalized in the early modern period, and a number of words from this activity survive in modern German, often with altered meanings. *Ausbeute*, once the output of a mine, now refers to general profit; *Belegschaft*, originally a crew of miners, now the total staff of an organization or business; *Fundgrube*, a productive mining pit, now a rich source of any kind; *Raubbau*, unregulated mining activity, now implying the ruthless exploitation of any natural resource; *reichhaltig*, describing a rich vein of ore or coal, now general abundance; *Stichprobe*, a probe to test the quality of the refined metal, now a random sample or spot check. Many terms from seafaring have come from Middle Low German and, in some cases, Dutch: *bugsieren* "take in tow," *Flagge* "flag," *Kurs* "course," *Lotse* "pilot," *Matrose* "seaman," *Wrack* "wreck." The secret language of thieves, *Rotwelsch*, was designed to prevent comprehension by the uninitiated. Most of these words have disappeared, but a few, including *schwänzen* "be absent without an excuse," *Schmiere stehen* "stand lookout during the commission of a crime," or *Stromer* "vagrant," survive in colloquial slang.

Cultural Patriotism, Language Cleansing, and the Status of German

The humanists distinguished between the sacred languages (Latin, Greek, and Hebrew), which were suitable for religious and intellectual discourse, and profane vernacular languages, which were not. German humanists, however, were particularly concerned with using different languages for distinct domains: Latin as the universal medium of intellectual discourse, German for formally unlearned audiences. Accordingly, they saw no value in teaching German as a subject in the Latin schools, much less in embarking on a program of linguistic standardization that would reduce regional variation in the written vernacular. Neither the invention of printing nor the Protestant Reformation, which increased the number of vernacular publications drastically, measurably affected this pattern of linguistic diglossia. Luther's translation of the Bible into German, therefore, strikingly disrupted the familiar domain distribution, for it elevated German from a common, pragmatic language to a medium suitable for sacred and literary texts. Latin's undisputed position was further undercut by the invasions of international troops during the Thirty Years' War, which created ill will in Germany toward all things foreign and galvanized feelings of national identity. With the Peace of Westphalia (1648), German territorial lords demanded and received greater independence from the multinational and multicultural Holy Roman Empire. German grammarians demanded no less autonomy for the German language.

For the language planners of the Baroque, a national standard language was an absolute prerequisite for a national German literature; Ratke insisted that a unified German nation-state governed by a single ruler would be impossible by any other means.[74] The movement for standardization was led by an elite of central and northern German scholars and their aristocratic patrons set on creating a *Kunstsprache* cleansed in three respects: of all but essential foreign words, of the earthy expressions indigenous to the literature of the sixteenth century, and of regional dialectal features. Schottelius's membership name in the *Fruchtbringende Gesellschaft, der Suchende* (the Searcher), symbolized his determination to establish an ideal variety of German having a systematic body of grammatical rules to be mastered by all who strove for social advancement through education.[75] This language eventually became the pride of the new *Bildungsbürgertum*, which would produce the majority of German scholars, lawyers, administrators, physicians, professors, and clergymen. Such a program could have succeeded only in the absolutist intellectual climate of the seventeenth century; it would have failed in the more democratic sixteenth, which tolerated linguistic diversity.

Controversy arose over whether the new standard German should be based on educated usage (*der gute Gebrauch*) or on the analogical principle, whereby existing inflectional and derivational patterns are extended to similar linguistic environments to regularize the language grammatically. The disagreement between proponents of analogy and good usage reflected a larger dispute among language scholars. One faction proposed that the educated Eastern Central German speech of Upper Saxony (Meissen), which enjoyed prestige in central and northern Germany, should become the universal linguistic standard. The other insisted on an idealized linguistic medium superimposed on all regional varieties of German. Schottelius vacillated between the two, finally accepting both good usage and analogy as guidelines in formalizing his grammatical rules.

Before German could ultimately replace Latin as the language of scholarly discourse in all academic areas, of course, the cultural obstacle of German's low esteem — an issue of continuing concern throughout the early modern period — had to be overcome and an adequate German scientific vocabulary created — a goal that would not be accomplished until the Age of Enlightenment. Both of these aspirations depended on the crucial preliminary step of cleansing the German language of foreign influence.[76] Already in the fifteenth century, Niklas von Wyle (1415–79), a scribe and translator in the city of Esslingen, castigated poets for using words from multiple languages in their poetry, comparing their work to the appearance of young men who wore the fashions of multiple countries.[77] In the following century, Sebastian Franck (1499–1542), a radical spiritualist, chastised his countrymen for having adopted foreign speech, manners, and fashion to such an extent that Germans were now recognizable as such only by their "national vices" of foolishness, laziness, drinking, and brawling. A generation later the grammarian Laurentius Albertus (1540–83) criticized the profusion of foreign words not only in elevated discourse but in colloquial speech as well. In the early seventeenth century, Opitz, in the sixth chapter of his *Poetery*, on the invention and ornamentation of words, finds it "zum hefftigsten vnsauber / wenn allerley Lateinische / Frantzösische / Spanische vnnd Welsche wörter in den text vnserer rede geflickt werden" (extremely corrupting when Latin, French, Spanish, and Italian words are patched into the text of our speech). A few years later, in his treatise *Sprach- Sitten- und Tugendverderber* (Spoilers of Language, Customs, and Morals, 1643), the Swabian physician and poet Christoph

Schorer (1618–71) decried the deleterious effects of linguistic and cultural borrowing on German society. Young men, he said, spoil the German language in showering French compliments on young women as a way of enhancing their own sexual attractiveness; indeed, they spoil German womanhood in preferring fashionable French-speaking girls to their plain-spoken German sisters. As for Francophile young women, Schorer predicts for them as well that ornamenting their speech with fashionable French words will breed French vices. Then, instead of remaining at home and doing housework as decent German girls should, they will gad about in mixed company, take leisurely walks with their girlfriends, and seek out weddings as venues for gossip. Worse yet, they will neglect Bible reading for newspapers and love songs — abhorrent activities for future German wives and mothers.

Leibniz, who personally admired French culture, feared that Germany was on the verge, however, of losing its identity to France through slavish imitation:

> Anitzo scheinet es, dass bey uns das Übel ärger worden, und hat der Mischmasch abscheulich überhand genommen, also daß der Prediger auff der Cantzel, der Sachverwalter auf der Cantzley, der Bürgersmann im Schreiben und Reden, mit erbärmlichen Frantzösischen sein Teutsches verderbet [. . .] haben solche Frantz-Gesinnte viele Jahre über Teutschland regieret, und solches fast, wo nicht der Frantzösischen Herrschaft [. . .] doch der Frantzösischen Mode und Sprache unterwürfig gemacht.[78]

> [It seems these days that the bad habit has become worse, and the mixing has become so excessive that the preacher in the pulpit, the administrator in the chancery, and the burgher in his writings and speech spoil their German with miserable French; such Francophiles have ruled over Germany for many years. If they have not made Germany politically subservient to France, they have all but succeeded in making Germany subservient to French fashion and the French language.]

Furthermore, he asked, why have the reforms of the language societies not yet unseated Latin as the language of the *Hauptmaterien*, the primary corpora of knowledge? Only by Germanizing the entire intellectual culture with a refined vernacular can Germany hope to stand shoulder to shoulder with other European nations.[79] As a starting place, the German vocabulary must be enlarged with loan words from related Germanic languages — English, Dutch, Scandinavian. By the nineteenth century, Leibniz's claim that the Germanic languages and cultures were inherently superior to the Romance languages and cultures had become firmly entrenched in the newly established academic discipline of historical linguistics.[80]

Language scholars debated the judicious limits of linguistic purification. A minority faction argued for the wholesale replacement of foreign words. Philipp von Zesen (1619–89) was an extreme advocate of this position, and in his zeal to rid German of foreign terms he created hundreds of often strange neologisms, few of which have survived. Among his more bizarre Germanizations were *Grohs-erz-vater* "grand-arch-father" for *Papst* "pope," *Jungfernzwinger* "virgin kennel" for *Nonnenkloster* "nunnery," and *Gesichtserker* "facial bay" for *Nase* "nose." The majority, including Harsdörffer and Schottelius, took the moderate view allowing two categories of foreign words to remain: words of foreign origin now common enough to have gained "German citizenship," and terms for objects or concepts not native to Germany. As the Ratke disciple Christian Gueintz (1592–1650) pointed out in *Die Deutsche Rechtschreibung* (German Orthography, printed 1645), the Germans could not properly name something they had not invented. Opitz (chapter 6) advocated retaining foreign expressions with exceptional connotations, such as the French verb *petrarquiser* "to speak erotically like Petrarch,"[81] but translating into German those referring to common actions, such as *approchiren* "approach" or *dubitiren* "doubt." Where semantically similar German words existed, they were simply accepted as equivalent for the foreign term. Lacking a native lexical equivalent, a German word was to be created; thus, *Schuldherr* "debt master" for Latin *creditor*.

In spite of these and other efforts of baroque language scholars and their successors in the next century to cleanse the German language of foreign elements, the fashion of interspersing vernacular discourse with foreign, especially French, loan words continued in polite society. This changed only when German nationalism emerged as a popular movement during the Napoleonic Wars. Linguistic purification became official German policy after the Franco-Prussian War (1870–71). With the establishment of the German Reich in 1871, military, postal, and railway designations in French began to be translated back into German.

Conclusion

This account of the historical development of modern German shows that the beginning of the early modern period was characterized by the emergence of the vernacular as a medium of written discourse for the patrician and upper middle classes in the economically powerful urban centers of commerce. The chanceries of the larger territorial states were instrumental in transforming what had initially been written versions of local dialects into regional writing languages with fewer dialectal features to ensure comprehension beyond the immediate area where a text was produced. The invention of printing, the Reformation, and rising literacy rates caused an explosive growth in printed works of all text types, which led to further reduction in linguistic diversity. By the time Luther began publishing his theological views, two equally prestigious but competing varieties of written German had emerged: the Common German of the imperial chancery and the southern cities, and the Eastern Central German of Saxony and its chancery. Luther chose the latter in translating the Bible into German. The Protestant grammarians of the seventeenth century, who vilified Common German, enhanced the prestige of Luther's biblical language as they strove to create a national language with sufficient prestige to replace Latin, as the medium of academics, and French, as the preferred language of society. This lofty goal would be achieved only at the end of the eighteenth century. Its success was signaled by Austria's and Bavaria's abandonment at last of their traditional writing conventions and by their official adoption of Modern Standard German.

Notes

[1] "Writing language" translates German *Schreibsprache*, which designates the written version of a regional vernacular in the early modern period. German linguists use the term *Schriftsprache* "written language" exclusively to refer to the written form of modern standard German.

[2] The designation *gemeines Deutsch* (Common German, or commonly used German), is no longer employed as a technical term by German linguists. For purposes of the present essay, however, it will be useful as a term of convenience to refer to the southern Austro-Bavarian variety of written Early Modern German.

[3] Peter Wiesinger, "Die sprachlichen Verhältnisse und der Weg zur allgemeinen Deutschen Schriftsprache in Österreich im 18. und frühen 19. Jahrhundert," in *Sprachgeschichte des Neuhochdeutschen*, ed. Andreas Gardt, Klaus J. Mattheier, and Oskar Reichmann (Tübingen: Niemeyer, 1995), 319–67. Ingo Reiffenstein, " 'Oberdeutsch' und 'Hochdeutsch' in Bayern im 18. Jahrhundert," ibid., 307–17.

[4] Stefan Sonderegger, "Frühneuhochdeutsch in der Schweiz: Versuch einer Standortbestimmung," in *Die Vielfalt des Deutschen: Festschrift für Werner Besch*, ed. Klaus J. Mattheier et al. (Frankfurt am Main: Lang, 1993), 11–36.

[5] Schottelius, *Ausführliche Arbeit von der Teutschen HaubtSprache* (1663), 2 vols., 2nd ed., ed. Wolfgang Hecht (Tübingen: Niemeyer, 1995).

[6] Latin is quite free in its word order, since the grammatical relations between the parts of speech in heavily inflected languages are clear, regardless of the position of a part of speech in the sentence.

[7] Johann Christoph Adelung, *Umständliches Lehrgebäude der deutschen Sprache*, 2 vols. (1782; repr., Hildesheim: Olms, 1971).

[8] Wilhelm Scherer, *Zur Geschichte der deutschen Sprache* (Weidmann: Berlin, 1878), 11–13.

[9] Hugo Moser, "Probleme der Periodisierung des Deutschen," in *Periodisierung: Die zeitliche Gliederung der deutschen Sprachgeschichte*, ed. Thorsten Roelcke (Frankfurt: Lang, 2001), 111–23.

[10] Peter von Polenz, *Deutsche Sprachgeschichte vom Spätmittelalter bis zur Gegenwart*, 2nd ed. (Berlin: de Gruyter, 2000), 1:99–101.

[11] As a result, the Eastern Prussian, Silesian, and Pomeranian dialects no longer exist.

[12] Polenz, *Sprachgeschichte*, 119.

[13] They were collected and published posthumously by one of his students, Johannes Aurifaber (1519–75), in 1566. A convenient, selected, edition is *Tischreden*, ed. Kurt Aland, Universal-Bibliothek 1222 (Stuttgart: Reclam, 1981).

[14] Polenz, *Sprachgeschichte*, 126. In the fourteenth century the ruling class in this Czech city spoke German since the court of Charles IV was located there.

[15] Erika Ising, *Die Herausbildung der Grammatik der Volkssprachen in Mittel- und Osteuropa: Studien über den Einfluß der lateinischen Elementargrammatik*

des Aelius Donatus De octo partibus oriationis ars minor (Berlin: Akademie-Verlag, 1970). Ising includes the two earliest translations of the Roman grammarian Aelius Donatus.

[16] Erika Ising, *Wolfgang Ratkes Schriften zur deutschen Grammatik (1612–1630)* (Berlin: Akademie-Verlag, 1959). For more on Ratke see the chapter on education by Wilhelm Kühlmann in this volume.

[17] After the Orthographic Conference in Berlin in 1876 Konrad Duden (1829–1911) published the results in the dictionary *Vollständiges orthographisches Wörterbuch der deutschen Sprache*. One year after the second Orthographic Conference in Berlin in 1901 a revised edition was published, which established modern standard German spelling conventions. They remained essentially unchanged until the recent (and controversial) orthographic reforms. Theodor Siebs (1882–1941) published the manual on standard German stage pronunciation, the *Deutsche Bühnenaussprache* (Stage Pronunciation) in 1898, based on the northern German pronunciation conventions. This work soon became the basis for "good" spoken standard German.

[18] The data were extracted from Ilpo T. Piirainen, "Die Diagliederung des Frühneuhochdeutschen," in *Sprachgeschichte: Ein Handbuch zur Geschichte der deutschen Sprache und ihrer Erforschung*, ed. Werner Besch, Oskar Reichmann, and Stefan Sonderegger (Berlin: de Gruyter, 1985), 2:1368–78.

[19] On the invention and importance of the printing press for early modern Germany see the chapter by Stephan Füssel in this volume.

[20] Polenz, *Sprachgeschichte*, 172.

[21] Frédéric Hartweg, "Die Rolle des Buchdrucks für die frühneuhochdeutsche Sprachgeschichte," in Besch et al., eds., *Sprachgeschichte*, 2:1420.

[22] Ibid., 1424.

[23] Hans Moser, "Die Kanzleisprachen," in Besch et al., eds., *Sprachgeschichte*, 2:1398–1407.

[24] Martin Opitz, *Buch von der Deutschen Poeterey (1624)*, ed. Cornelius Sommer, Universal-Bibliothek 8397 (Stuttgart: Reclam, 1970), 46.

[25] Gerhard Philipp, *Einführung ins Frühneuhochdeutsche: Sprachgeschichte — Grammatik — Texte* (Heidelberg: Quelle & Meyer, 1980), 269. On the *Ackermann* see the chapter by Graeme Dunphy in this volume.

[26] Theodor Frings, *Grundlegung einer Geschichte der deutschen Sprache*, 3rd ed. (Halle/Saale: Niemeyer, 1957), 42.

[27] Polenz, *Sprachgeschichte*, 161–67.

[28] Hugo Stopp, *Vokalismus der Nebensilben II*, vol. 1, 2 of *Grammatik des Frühneuhochdeutschen* (Heidelberg: Winter, 1973).

[29] Philipp, *Einführung ins Frühneuhochdeutsche*, 184.

[30] Ibid., 45 and 49.

[31] Ibid., 79–80.

[32] Mixed class verbs are inflected like regular (weak) verbs but, like the irregular (strong) verbs, also have a different stem vowel in preterite and past participle forms: for example, *rennen* "run" *rannte* "ran."

[33] See Polenz, *Sprachgeschichte*, 189, and Philipp, *Einführung ins Frühneuhochdeutsche*, 119–28.

[34] On negation see Franz Josef Pensel, "Die Satznegation," in *Zur Ausbildung der Norm in der deutschen Literatursprache (1470–1730)*, part 1, *Auf der syntaktischen Ebene: der Einfachsatz*, ed. Gerhard Kettmann and Joachim Schildt (Berlin: Akademie, 1976), 219–340.

[35] Schottelius, *Ausführliche Arbeit*, 1:776.

[36] With respect to the sentence frame see Joachim Schildt, "Zur Ausbildung des Satzrahmens," in Kettmann and Schildt, eds., *Zur Ausbildung der Norm der deutschen Literatursprache*, 235–384.

[37] Wladimir G. Admoni, *Historische Syntax des Deutschen* (Tübingen: Niemeyer, 1990), 215.

[38] Ibid., 199.

[39] Polenz, *Sprachgeschichte*, 229.

[40] Luther, *Sendbrief vom Dolmetschen*, ed. Ernst Kähler, Universal-Bibliothek 1578 (Stuttgart: Reclam, 1962).

[41] Commerce in northern Europe was dominated by the Hanseatic League, and one of the major European trade routes connecting the Baltic ports with those of the Mediterranean linked the territory of the Wettin dynasty with urban economic centers of the southeast. Business contacts and the ensuing exchanges of letters, legal contracts, and other agreements might have contributed to the adoption of southern linguistic features into the official and business language of Upper Saxony.

[42] The sources for the following description of Luther's language are Heinrich Bach, "Wo liegt die entscheidende Wirkung der 'Luthersprache' in der Entwicklung der deutschen Standardsprache?" (1984), in *Luthers Deutsch: Sprachliche Leistung und Wirkung*, ed. Herbert Wolf (Frankfurt am Main: Lang, 1996), 126–35, and Polenz, *Sprachgeschichte*, 229–51.

[43] Werner Besch, "Sprachliche Änderungen in Lutherbibeldrucken des 16. bis 18. Jahrhunderts," in Wolf, ed., *Luthers Deutsch*, 265. The precise figures are 64.8% and 80.8%.

[44] Polenz, *Sprachgeschichte*, 235.

[45] Werner Besch, *Die Rolle Luthers in der deutschen Sprachgeschichte* (Heidelberg: Winter, 1999), 28.

[46] Proverbs were popular among the educated European elites until the seventeenth century, when many collections were published. Schottelius, for example, includes a large selection in the second volume of his grammar (1112–50). For a discussion on the role of proverbs in early modern Europe see James Obelkevich, "Proverbs and Social History," in *The Social History of Language*, ed. Peter Burke and Roy Porter (Cambridge: Cambridge UP, 1987), 43–72.

[47] Polenz, *Sprachgeschichte*, 234.

[48] Rudolf Betzinger and Gerhard Kettmann," Zu Luthers Stellung im Sprachschaffen seiner Zeit" (1983), in Wolf, ed., *Luthers Deutsch*, 202.

[49] Besch, *Die Rolle Luthers*, 27.

[50] Joachim Knape, "Humanismus, Reformation, deutsche Sprache und Nation," in *Nation und Sprache: Die Diskussion ihres Verhältnisses in Geschichte und Gegenwart*, ed. Andreas Gardt (Berlin: de Gruyter, 2000), 104.

[51] The cultivation of proper titles was inculcated through *Titellehre* (doctrine of titles). On this and other early modern rhetorical doctrines see the chapter by Joachim Knape in this volume.

[52] Source for the information on the *Schryfftspiegel*, Meichssner, and Frangk is Ursula Götz, *Die Anfänge der Grammatikschreibung des Deutschen in den Formularbüchern des frühen 16. Jahrhunderts* (Heidelberg: Winter, 1992).

[53] Ibid., 109.

[54] Ising, *Wolfgang Ratkes Schriften*, 99.

[55] On these and other early modern language and literary societies see the chapter by Max Reinhart in this volume.

[56] Harsdörffer, *Der Teutsche Secretarius: Titular und Formularbuch* (Hildesheim: Olms, 1971), 1:517.

[57] Ibid, 1:4.

[58] Andreas Gardt, *Geschichte der Sprachwissenschaft in Deutschland: Vom Mittelalter bis ins 20. Jahrhundert* (Berlin: de Gruyter, 1999), 128.

[59] Schottelius, *Ausführliche Arbeit*, 1:8.

[60] For purposes of this essay the category "irregular" verbs includes all verbs that mark tense changes with vowel alternations. This includes the traditional "strong" verbs with past participle forms ending in the suffix *-en*, for example er *singt, sang, hat gesungen* (he sings, sang, has sung) as well as "mixed" verbs, which are inflected like regular "weak" verbs but also show vowel changes: er *bringt, brachte, hat gebracht* (he brings, brought, has brought).

[61] Schottelius, *Ethica: Die Sittenkunst oder Wollebenskunst* (1669; repr., ed. Jörg Jochen Berns, Bern: Francke, 1980), a3–a8.

[62] Schottelius, *Ethica*, a8.

[63] Schottelius, *Ausführliche Arbeit*, 1:377.

[64] See Polenz, *Sprachgeschichte*, 210–28.

[65] In his chapter in this volume on education, Kühlmann speaks of the "pragmatization of educational theory" in the seventeenth century.

[66] Adolf Bach, *Geschichte der deutschen Sprache* (Heidelberg: Quelle & Meyer, 1965), 312.

[67] William Jervis Jones, *Sprachhelden und Sprachverderber: Dokumente zur Erforschung des Fremdwortpurismus im Deutschen (1478–1750)* (Berlin: de Gruyter, 1995), 582. Jones reprints Thomasius's Leipzig lecture of 1687, "Welcher Gestalt man denen Frantzosen in gemeinem Leben und Wandel nachahmen solle?"

[68] Ibid., 313–14.

[69] Polenz, *Sprachgeschichte*, 227; Bach, *Geschichte der deutschen Sprache*, 317.

[70] The case for Latin can be made on the basis of modern studies of bilingualism, which have found that fully bilingual individuals tend to transfer words, phrases, and even patterns of word order from one language to another. Transfer is less likely if the languages are used in separate domains that do not overlap. When Latin was still used exclusively in the domain of legal documentation, there could be no transfer of Latin word order patterns since German was never used as a legal language.

[71] The two earliest German translations of Latin grammars were written in the late fifteenth and early sixteenth century by the notary Conrad Bücklin and by the humanist poet Glareanus (see Ising, *Die Herausbildung der Grammatik*, which includes two translations of this Latin grammar). Bücklin tends to translate Latin *significans* as *was betüten ist* "which means"; the humanist poet Glareanus tends, more simply, to leave out the auxiliary.

[72] Robert Ebert, "Social and Stylistic Variation in the Order of Auxiliary and Non-Finite Verbs in Dependent Clauses in Early New High German," *Beiträge zur Geschichte der deutschen Sprache und Literatur* 103 (1981): 204–37.

[73] Bach, *Geschichte der deutschen Sprache*, 241–44; Polenz, *Sprachgeschichte*, 201. See also John T. Waterman, *A History of the German Language*, 2nd ed. (Seattle: U of Washington P), 120–27.

[74] Wolfgang Huber, *Kulturpatriotismus und Sprachbewußtsein: Studien zur deutschen Philologie des 17. Jahrhunderts* (Frankfurt am Main: Lang, 1984), 248–50.

[75] Markus Hundt, *Spracharbeit im 17. Jahrhundert: Studien zu Georg Philipp Harsdörffer, Justus Georg Schottelius und Christian Gueintz* (Berlin: de Gruyter, 2000), 122.

[76] On linguistic cleansing see Jones, *Sprachhelden und Sprachverderber*, 1–49. Schorer's *Sittenverderber* is reproduced in Jones, 304–42.

[77] See the chapter by John L. Flood in this volume.

[78] Leibniz, *Unvorgreiffliche Gedancken, betreffend die Ausübung und Verbesserung der Teutschen Sprache*, in Jones, *Sprachhelden und Sprachverderber*, 545–69, here 550–51. Leibniz's seminal work on the connection between language and national culture is *Ermahnung an die Teutschen, ihren Verstand und Sprache besser zu üben* (Exhortation to the Germans to Make Improved Use of Their Reason and Language, 1697), conceived as a prolegomenon to the founding of a German national intellectual center. Three years later, the Prussian Academy of Sciences was founded in Berlin.

[79] On Leibniz's role as an instigator of German cultural independence see Klaus Garber, "Begin with Goethe? Forgotten Traditions at the Threshold of the Modern Age," in *Imperiled Heritage: Tradition, History, and Utopia in Early Modern German Literature*, trans. Karl F. Otto Jr., ed. Max Reinhart (Aldershot, UK: Ashgate, 2000), sect. 2, "Leibniz and the 'German-Minded Society,' " 228–37.

[80] Jones, *Sprachhelden und Sprachverderber*, 563.

[81] On *petrarquiser* and early modern erotic poetry see the chapter by Gerhart Hoffmeister in this volume.

Part II

Formations

Education in Early Modern Germany

Wilhelm Kühlmann

German Humanism as a Pedagogical Movement

Connections — Impulses — Ideals

IN ITS AGENDA, THE LOGIC OF ITS DEVELOPMENT, and its literary expression, European Renaissance Humanism was a movement for pedagogical reform, whose goal was to improve the cultural and social life of humanity (*humanitas*). The German word for education, *Bildung*, has its origins in theology and contains elements of religious mysticism;[1] we must keep these connotations at a distance when considering early modern educational theory and practice. The Renaissance model for the improvement of the self, mediated through the symbolic language of literature — a conception of humanity, therefore, as manifest in speech and behavior — more closely resembles the English conception of education than the myth of *Bildung* in German idealism. What pioneers like Petrarch (1304–74) and Leonardo Bruni (ca. 1370–1444) represented, how humanistic studies (*studia humanitatis*) were designed, and what determined educational practice at the schools of northern Italy all derived from a fundamental anthropological distinction between the primal, quasi-bestial nature of man and the highest qualities deemed worthy of man. One could acquire these qualities through the cultivation of independent thinking and a new social personality. Humanism was at first committed almost solely to inculcating the elementary tools for using language effectively. The modern training in reason (*ratio*) and oratory (*oratio*) developed in yoke with the theory that each individual can achieve human perfection only through knowledge (*eruditio*) and that the project of civilizing society requires the consensus and discourse of its educated members.

As the result of active Italian-German cultural exchanges, early modern pedagogy in Germany bore the stamp of a naturalized Italian humanism. Since the fourteenth and fifteenth centuries, wealthy students had been traveling to Italy to study law and medicine; by the seventeenth century less affluent young people as well, serving as travel companions and tutors, could acquaint themselves firsthand with Italian cultural centers and universities. Biographical documents, such as the letters of the Nuremberg patrician Willibald Pirckheimer (1470–1530),[2] reveal that students took intense interest, beyond their formal studies, in the newly printed works of ancient Roman and Greek authors. Quite beyond the standard pedagogical treatises by Italian humanists, students also copied poetry in Latin by contemporary authors, and some acquired first editions of these works. Early humanism in Germany received significant impulses from scholarly conversations with Italian delegations at the Councils of Constance (1414–18) and Basel (1431–39). Employed in the entourages of the Holy Roman emperors and sometimes of the territorial princes, Italian officials and diplomats — most notably Enea Silvio (Aeneas Silvius) Piccolomini (1405–64; Pope Pius II after 1458) — wrote works that aroused German imperial patriotism, discussed the conflicts of life at court, and championed new literary models in exemplary "Letters on Education."[3]

Early humanism's success was the result of far-reaching processes of intellectual and social reorientation. Independent of traditional restrictions on social mobility and competing with the clergy's monopoly in education, a new intellectual elite skilled in speaking and writing, attuned to an increasingly competent reading public after the invention of the printing press, and occupying key posts in territorial administrations rose by virtue of its technological expertise. Language served not only for simple communication but also to demonstrate competence, rank, and power, not to mention aesthetic sophistication and intellectual worthiness. Education became essential to social advancement and provided a sense of cultural achievement that called into question hereditary aristocracy's social privileges and claims on political power.

Education in early modern Germany was decidedly academic, that is, it was practiced almost exclusively within the institutions of the preparatory schools and universities. Its reforms, aimed primarily at revisions of the traditional liberal arts (*artes liberales*) and pedagogy, less at major structural changes, brought about reconstituted curricula and methodologies of grammar, rhetoric, and poetics, as well as moral philosophy and historiography.[4] Humanism consolidated the sense of identity that arose from newly defined qualifications; this identity expressed itself symbolically in academic degrees and socially in the privileged status of being formally educated. What humanists had in common was primarily a command of elegant Latin modeled on that of classical antiquity, the language of the sciences and arts that unified Europe. Dissociation from the lay culture of colloquial languages did not impede the rich growth of literature in translation, however, nor did it adversely affect the spiritual work of pastors among the common people.

A bitter anti-academic resentment festered, however, within the radical wing of the German Reformation and traumatized the disciples of serious literature (*bonae litterae*). This opposition, which carried the banner of Christian simplicity (*simplicitas*), was of little consequence in the sixteenth century but gathered momentum in the seventeenth by valorizing an approach to education geared to practical success in life. It emphasized skills that were basic for understanding politics, behaving appropriately at court, and calculating one's chances for social advancement. Under the influence of conversational literature, or literature of dialogues, another type of practical literature that streamed in from Italy and France, Christian humanists by the later sixteenth century felt pressured to bring their ideals of Christian education, so-called *litterata pietas*, into some conformity with the new pragmatism. For a society of the educated — shaped by the needs of the newly prosperous bourgeoisie and the courtly aristocracy — to evolve, the goals of humanist education had to be commensurate with those of courtly pragmatism; a vernacular literary culture with high aspirations also had to be cultivated. Middle-class practicality and princely mercantilism alike questioned the emphasis humanist schools had placed on languages, grammar, and rhetoric. Demands for change emerged in an endless stream of reform projects to make education more responsive to actual needs. Initial attempts were unimpressive. Even the cognitive model of the experimental sciences, grounded in mathematics and mechanics and focusing on achieving accurate perceptions, failed as late as the early Enlightenment to undercut the dominance of traditional humanist schooling.

The humanism adopted in the schools offered far more than a vague general education or a mere passing on of techniques of communication. Hearkening back to the "authentic" sources of classical antiquity, scholarly educators exposed complexes of meanings, values, and modes of living that seemed at first alien to Christian modernity.[5] The appropriation of the Roman and Greek heritage signified, on the one hand, an intellectual challenge and, on the other, the fascinating possibility that individuals might learn to express, in discourses of another time and place, their own problems and situations, indeed the entire complex of subjective actions and behaviors. Classical popular philosophy, which emphasized the virtues and the quest for the highest good (*summum bonum*), was often self-contradictory, manifesting at once empirical skepticism and Platonic idealism, Epicurean pleasure and Stoic constraint,[6] personal responsibility and the spectrum of social theories. This was reflected in the growing number of modern fields of action and knowledge that had been too little respected in the ecclesiastically supervised educational institutions. Classical antiquity had not defined man in terms simply of a metaphysical need for salvation; the tension between the Fall and God's grace was made problematic only later by Christianity. Humanism's affinity with classical antiquity lay in the shared conception of the nature of the subjective individual. Caught between the glories and the perils of linguistic, rational, and emotional modes of self-expression and the moral postulate of autonomous action, the human being was the great and endlessly fascinating mystery of this new era. Among the dominant themes of Italian humanism were the human desire for happiness, the structure of the human emotional life, the achievement of personal worthiness, and the contingencies of experience. The humanists were not deceived, however, about the degree to which the resolution to these questions depended on the play of fate and fortune (*fatum* and *fortuna*), that is, to what extent the individual will was subject to determinative forces, and never lost sight of the collective nature of the conduct of life (*ratio vivendi*).

The "Discovery of the World and of Man," as Jacob Burckhardt summarized the achievement of the Renaissance,[7] took place within a conception of language liberated from that of being merely the medium of elementary communication. This language had broken free of Scholasticism's audacious attempt to reconcile Holy Writ with Aristotelian philosophy through a logically regulated inventory of concepts. For humanism, rhetoric as *ars bene dicendi,* the art of speaking well, concerned the motives of the will and the emotional temper of the distinctive, individual self amid life's myriad circumstances and choices. Humanist pedagogy thus centered on rhetoric, for it was precisely the *copia verborum,* that abundance of words, as Cicero and Quintilian had emphasized, that brought forth the knowledge of everything worth knowing.

Reformers within the Catholic Church shared humanism's concentration on linguistic mastery and the symbolic power of rhetorical and poetic eloquence and on how this reflected human morality as well. Humanists recognized no conflict between being educated in humane letters and practicing a religiosity of scripturally based good works; they defended this position vigorously over the objections of academic scholastics by citing no lesser authorities than the church fathers. To be sure, pagan literature was no more generally acceptable now than it had been in Christian late antiquity; early modern educators regularly faced opposition to their attempts to introduce classical texts, thus creating a polarity characterized as "Athens vs. Jerusalem."[8] Sixteenth-century Christian humanism operated under constant threats from zealots and repeatedly had to do obeisance before the orthodoxy of the state church. Balancing the needs and goals of private individuals with the obligations and norms of cities and states, humanist educators insisted that reading, writing, and speaking, that poetry, prose, and science — all subsumed in the larger concept of literature — are indispensable to humane intercourse. Humanism's project of civilizing humankind initiated the process of modern enlightenment; properly regarded, the modern conception of culture has enjoyed legitimacy only since the European Renaissance.

The Literature of Education in the Sixteenth and Seventeenth Centuries: A Survey

We can treat the vast early modern literature on the theory and practice of education only selectively, pointing out exemplary texts and significant issues and trends. These include not only works of academic humanism but also documents whose historical value is not yet fully understood, particularly writings meant for oral delivery, such as sermons and academic speeches of various kinds. Teachers, professors, and clergy were the chief producers of these works, but other specialists, including writers on practical issues and urban or princely officials, also contributed their share. It is useful to classify these texts, many of them by authors all but forgotten today, according to types and functions, bearing in mind that mixed or transitional genres often fall outside strict categories.

1. Discourses on learning and instruction in general, usually having a strong protreptic, or didactic, emphasis, as well as apologetic or polemical tendencies. Academic declamatory writings and orations constituted the bulk of this type of text. While their implications sometimes reached far beyond the classroom, they typically announce series of lectures or mark the occasion of curricular or extracurricular ceremonies (*actus publici*) at schools

and universities. Audiences included the student body, parents and colleagues, and patrons within the church, city, or state.[9] Pedagogical arguments often extend to discussions of human nature or cultural life. Justification for a particular area of study, for example from the *trivium* (grammar, rhetoric, and poetics), might be expressed in axiomatic treatises, forewords to textbooks, prefaces to the reader, or dedications, often marshaling an impressive range of didactic strategies. Texts of this type sometimes emerged from epistolary correspondence into formal essays.

2. Texts on learning theory and on instruction in specific subjects, including treatises on designing private tutorials (*Hofmeisterliteratur*) and the education of princes.[10] Themes include the aims and methods of acquiring knowledge and accounting for the efficacy of both *ratio vivendi* and *ratio studii* (method of study). They may consider the psychology of learning, the proper conduct and economy of everyday life, the motivation and guidance of individual talents, learning environment, and external social factors.

3. Encyclopedic textbooks, often in the medieval tradition of writing for the liberal arts.[11] These include manuals and guides specific to the area of instruction (grammar, prosody, rhetoric, logic) and writings on mnemonic techniques to refresh knowledge.[12] Dramatic performances, intensively cultivated at humanistic schools (NL),[13] served to improve the command of spoken Latin and confidence in moving before an audience. The themes and didactic functions of school dramas show affinities with oration (*declamatio*) but also with student colloquies (*Schülergespräche*).[14] Because humanist teaching drew on specific authors, critical text editions were encouraged,[15] as were commentaries and paraphrase books, some bearing the evidence of their origins as oral interpretive lectures.[16] In explaining words and facts in the context of the grammatical, logical, and rhetorical analysis of a work, commentaries usually emphasize the text's relevance to historical context or moral values. A great variety of books appeared on the subject of achieving mastery in schools and private instruction alike: lexicons and encyclopedias, *Schatzkammern* (treasure chests of knowledge), anthologies and readers, bibliographic guides, and compendiums of elementary learning.[17] Some essays aimed to entertain by imitating antiquity's tradition of assembling "colorful" miscellanies.[18]

4. Ecclesiastical and political (territorial and city) regulations on instruction. Melanchthon's *Unterricht der Visitatoren* (Instructions for School Inspectors, 1528) established the format as minutely detailed school regulations.[19] Melanchthon's disciples Valentin Trotzendorf (1490–1556) in Silesia[20] and the renowned Strasbourg rector Johann Sturm (1507–89)[21] each developed specialized versions that became influential models in their own right. Under the supervision of city *scholarchs* (directors of educational academies) regulations governed pedagogical goals, curricula, selection and use of texts, duties of students and teachers, scheduling of classes, examinations, and discipline. The secular government thus wielded its authority to standardize education and keep it free of undesirable developments, such as the unauthorized founding of private schools.

5. Other extraordinarily rich varieties of writing at the margins of the academic disciplines. These texts related to specific groups, social classes, functions, and professions:

- Travel guides for scholars and aristocrats preparing for their Grand Tour (*peregrinatio academica*).[22]
- Medical or pharmaceutical treatises (*regimina sanitatis*), which, in the tradition of ancient and medieval treatises (especially the *Regimen sanitatis Salernitanum*), constitute a subgenre for advice on hygiene and healthy living (dietetics).[23] Special therapies, such as the medical or psychotheological treatment of melancholia,[24] sometimes include magical formulas and prescriptions from the occult sciences.[25]
- Various genres within the spectrum of moral philosophy (*philosophia moralis*),[26] including treatises on the social order, the education of princes, and the art of governing;[27] handbooks based on French, Italian, or Spanish sources for the *Politicus* (elite of courtly officials);[28] and the *Hausbuch*, a practical household manual for issues and answers related to medicine or agriculture.[29] A related discourse critical of courtly life arose (it would last well into the eighteenth century) that can be morally prescriptive though not hostile to the system as such.[30]
- Textual types from Italy, Spain, and France on correct deportment and courtly elegance, including manuals of courtly life (*Hofschulen*), guides to polite behavior and conviviality, books of proper compliments, instructions in sociable conversation (even discourses in the vernacular on the conduct of ordinary communication[31]), and descriptions of courtly ceremony.[32] Georg Philipp Harsdörffer (1607–58) and Kaspar Stieler (1632–1707) introduced or brought up to date handbooks from the medieval tradition of the arts of speaking (*artes dictaminis*) with respect to chancery and secretarial practices. Theoretical manuals on letter writing on the model of Cicero and Pliny gradually drifted in the seventeenth century toward the colloquial and *galant*.[33]
- Texts on the education of women. Those by Erasmus and the distinguished Spanish humanist Juan Luis Vives (1492–1540) are decidedly emancipationist, supporting the ideal of the learned woman (*femina docta*).[34] Interest in gender-related questions increased in the seventeenth century, especially in the context of home schooling and marriage theory, with its focus on women's roles as homemakers and mothers.[35]
- Handbooks on practical eloquence and the cultivation of poetry in the colloquial language — a large category.[36] In the seventeenth century, following the lead of Martin Opitz (1597–1639), these handbooks frequently appeal to humanism's cultural patriotism under reference to central concepts of Renaissance literary theories.
- Last wills and testaments of fathers to their families or rulers to their heirs. These texts contain legacies of instruction in ethical and practical matters of life.[37]

6. Works of religious edification and sermons.[38] The writings in this large body of literature — it is impossible to overestimate the typological variety of this ecclesiastical literature — include a great variety of forms and serve many functions: proselytizing, instruction in the articles of faith, discussion of social ethics, or private devotional practice. This category embraces catechisms,[39] collections of occasional poetry and anthems (sometimes complemented by song sermons), theological polemics on the Bible, especially the Psalms and Psalm paraphrases (NL), anthologies of prayers and devotions, exegetical texts, and sermons relating to official occasions or specific groups.[40] Manuals for the training of clergy (sermons, homily collections)[41] are complemented by others that offer spiritual, often casuistic (case-based reasoning), guidance to laity and households. Johann Arndt's (1555–1621) *Vier Bücher vom Wahren Christentum* (Four Books of True Christianity, 1610) were enormously influential and were reprinted regularly into the nineteenth century.[42] Guided by Spiritualist and Paracelsian ideas, Arndt's writings were paradigmatic for later Pietism and its vast literature.[43] Catholicism is represented by hagiography, devotional practices on the sacraments, and guides (such as confessional manuals) to moral scrupulousness. Texts reminiscent of medieval mysticism (Bernard of Clairvaux, Johann Tauler) echoed impulses from Spain and France and influenced orthodox and anti-orthodox Protestant writers alike.[44] Theology as the guiding science of the age and piety (*pietas*) as the definitive norm of individual conscience and behavior affected the entire educational domain, not only with respect to curricular choices but to special events as well, such as deciding which dramas to perform in the schools.

7. Reformist theories in education and methods, particularly in the seventeenth century. These reforms generated a specifically critical vein of literature, such as satires and utopias.

Education and Piety: Humanism before the Reformation

His friends and admirers regarded him as something of a savior; and even modern historians agree that, north of the Alps, one man stood out in the quest for educational renewal: the Frisian, Rodolfus Agricola (Roelof Huysman, 1444–85). Agricola possessed a rare combination of strengths: elegant Latin, skills in Greek literature and the Hebrew language, outstanding musical talent, an appreciation for the flourishing art of painting, aesthetic sophistication, and courtly poise gained at the court at Ferrara. *De laude philosophiae et reliquarum artium oratio* (Oration in Praise of Philosophy and the Other Arts, between 1474–79) has its roots in the traditional Stoic triad of logic, ethics, and knowledge of nature, but Agricola avowed that philosophy must convey and guarantee freedom of intellect and pleasure of human knowledge. Philosophy's nearly limitless claims find harmony with a moral discipline that controls harmful passions. Thus philosophy — to Cicero it was "dux vitae" (life's guide) — signifies humane autonomy as a reflection of joyous self-apprehension.

In Agricola's oration questions about learning and conduct enhance the unprecedented, primal sense of being alive. In the rise to moral perfection of the individual nature and in the intellectual mobilization of its powers, personal identity is expressed in a single-word sentence: "Vivo" (I am alive).[45]

Agricola's *De formando studio* (On the Design of Studying, 1484), composed as a letter to a friend, is of historic significance. Going back to Quintilian by way of Battista Guarini the Younger (1434–1513), whom he had met in Italy, Agricola considers how to choose a field of study and succeed at it. Inclinations and talents are important, but two qualities take precedence: accurate judgment and appropriate verbal expression. Agricola stresses that knowledge of nature and the objective world (*rerum notitia*), together with the cultivation of one's native language, guarantee precise communication. His program of reading recommends historians, poets, and orators; focuses on examples of virtue and courage (*exempla virtutis*); and includes within the consideration of moral discipline the promise of salvation enshrined in the Scriptures, the *sacrae litterae*. Understanding a text and fruitfully using what one learns from it are complementary actions, the practical consummation of the education of the self. Agricola thereby anticipates his most important work, *De inventione dialectica libri tres* (On Dialectical Invention: Three Books, completed 1476–79, published posthumously 1515), which was widely reprinted well into the following century.[46] *Inventio* means for Agricola the finding of all experiences relating to any phenomenon and of all arguments arising from any problem, thereby combining the traditions of Aristotelian categorization and the topical methodology of Cicero and Boethius. In grasping factual matters through formal concepts (either by definitions or in terms of what is essential, similar, or related), an empirical domain of everything knowable about a subject is established by logical operations, which is to say, *dialectically*. This finding procedure benefits above all the orator and the quest for plausible arguments, not so much to determine what is true but what is socially probable under the given circumstances. By integrating the elements of classical rhetoric into his educational program with the help of the anthropological theory of the passions, Agricola achieves a synthesis of medieval scholastic traditions and the expectations of the modern, philosophically trained orator (in Cicero's term, the *orator sapiens*).

The itinerary of Agricola's life, including the locations of his influence, links the major stations of the educational reform that had begun within the church. In Heidelberg in 1484–85 the circle of scholars around Agricola included the Benedictine Johannes Trithemius (1462–1516), a typical representative of monastic humanism.[47] This early group anticipated the later humanistic sodalities founded in Heidelberg, Augsburg, and Vienna by the poet Conrad Celtis (1459–1508; NL). The informally organized cultural elite reflected the ideals of the academies of Florence and Rome in seeking financial patronage, intellectual exchanges, and even national recognition.

One of Agricola's friends was Alexander Hegius (ca. 1433–98), rector of the capital school in the Dutch town of Deventer. Hegius followed the Devotio Moderna, a religious movement borne in part by groups of laity but organized too in the cloisters of the congregation of Windesheim.[48] It had affinity with humanism insofar as it rejected scholastic intellectualism and sought to penetrate to the inner truths of the Bible and the church fathers through discerning reading. These Brothers of the Common Life maintained boarding schools that admitted, for the honor of God, underprivileged students, among others. They rejected worldly temptations and embraced the ascetic ideals propounded by Thomas à Kempis (Haemerken, "of Kempen," 1379/80–1471) in his renowned *De imitatione Christi* (1420–41), which, through Ignatius of Loyola, would shape the spiritual exercises of the Jesuits in the next century. The ideas on education both of the devout Brothers and of Christian humanism emphasized daily discipline. The Devotio Moderna set strict limits on the degree to which Italian culture had influence in Germany. Hegius also did away with obsolete textbooks, had works by the ancients printed, cultivated instruction in the elegant use of Latin, and combated the speculative grammar of the scholastic modalists, Christian grammarians active in the thirteenth and fourteenth centuries. With his friend Rudolf von Langen (1483–1519),[49] dean of the Cathedral at Münster, he definitively influenced the schools of northern Germany, the Rhineland, and elsewhere. Quite different personalities, such as the Gotha canon Mutianus Rufus (Conrad Muth, 1471–1526) and the Westphalian Hermann Buschius (von dem Busche, 1486–1534; NL), began their careers under Hegius. After many years in Italy Mutianus became the intellectual father of the young humanists at Erfurt. He did not publish books; his influence proceeded mainly from his letters, many of them daringly critical of accepted religious practices.[50] Buschius had visited Rome, Bologna, and other cities before coming to the defense of the modernized *artes* against religious critics in his *Vallum humanitatis* (Rampart of Humanity, 1518), citing as authorities St. Jerome and St. Augustine, as well as the great names of the Renaissance culture of Florence.

Hegius also trained Ludwig Dringenberg (1410–77), rector at Schlettstadt (Sélestat).[51] It was Dringenberg who imparted to the "patriarch of German education," Jakob Wimpfeling (1450–1528),[52] the conception of an educational reform still faithful to the church. A professor and later rector in Heidelberg, and for a time a preacher at the cathedral in Speyer, Wimpfeling adopted the causes of the Paris theologian and educational reformer Jean Gerson (1363–1429) and the Strasbourg preacher Johann Geiler von Kaisersberg (1445–1510), both critics of the church and the social order. A patriotic supporter of the empire, not unlike many humanists,[53] Wimpfeling hoped that by changing the thinking of the elite leadership, the secular clergy, and the nobility, he might halt the decay within the *respublica Christiana*. He would replace illiterate rulers and uneducated holders of sinecures who neglected their pastoral duties with well-trained, morally upright persons. Wimpfeling sought to advance their education through his textbooks and editions of "classical" early Christian works. With respect to correct Latin, to be sure, he recommended the *Elegantiae linguae latinae* of the great Italian humanist Lorenzo Valla (ca. 1406–57). Wimpfeling's *Isidoneus germanicus* (Guide to German, 1497), *Agatharchia* (1498; a manual for rulers), and

Diatribes (1514, aimed mainly at the clergy), are arranged topically within a compilation of pedagogical texts called *Adolescentia* (Youth, 1500).[54] The mosaic form of this book, in which the writer embeds his own ideas on education in various authoritative texts, suited a syncretistic appropriation of traditional sources. Wimpfeling reconciled ideas of the renowned Italian teacher Guarino da Verona, Enea Silvio Piccolomini, and the scholar of Greek and Latin Francesco Filelfo, but also of the Carmelite Battista Mantovan, "the Christian Vergil," with the strictures of a disciplined Christian life. One of his models for this was the medieval work *Tractatus de ordine vitae et morum institutione* (Tractate on Instruction in the Order of Life and Customs) of Pseudo-Bernard (Jean, l'Homme de Dieu). Ultimately, only pedantic categories of good and bad behavior came of this attempt. Wimpfeling had a particular interest in adolescent psychology and insisted that young people be inculcated with precepts of *vita honesta*, which involved a web of moral-social duties toward parents, friends, and persons in authority; they should also be guided by virtues of noble conduct, especially the control of passions. For Wimpfeling, "pius et bene morigeratus adolescens" (pious and obedient youth) embodied the *integritas* necessary to combat the world's general public and private moral failings.

Similar ideas occurred regularly in the learned dialogues and dramas in the period of Early Humanism (NL). The six comic scenes of Wimpfeling's *Stylpho* (1480, published 1494), set in Heidelberg, contrast an intellectually lazy candidate for a priestly benefice, who relies in vain on social connections and ends up herding swine, with an "amator scientiarum" (lover of knowledge), who studies law and rises to the rank of bishop. Ignorance of Latin is symptomatic of moral weakness and, as in other school plays that imitate the Roman dramatist Terence (ca. 190–158 B.C.), it is employed to satiric effect. Terence's dramas provide heartening or cautionary examples of how disciplined study, success in learning, and worldly ambition are causally linked. The *Comoedia de optimo studio iuvenum* (Comedy on the Best Education for Young People, 1504) by Heinrich Bebel (1472–1518; NL) of Tübingen employs a popular comedic theme of the sixteenth century. Another work in this vein is *Studentes* (1549, many later reprints) by the Pomeranian Christoph Stymmelius (Stummel, 1525–88), which compares life in the freer atmosphere of the universities with the work ethic of the middle classes. Such "comedies of manners" depicted milieu graphically. A favorite topic was the parable of the prodigal son, which Luther himself had recommended as an ideal subject for biblical drama. The stories of Rebecca and Susanna, often staged by post-Reformation school playwrights, such as Nikodemus Frischlin (1547–90; NL), were not only popular but also useful as vehicles of instruction for proper conduct in marriage, virtuous statecraft, and the duties of officials.

Wimpfeling's literary efforts paralleled those of certain northern German humanists, especially the Dutch scholar Johannes Murmellius (Roermond, 1480–1517), who lived and worked in Münster and Alkmaar. Murmellius published educational handbooks and guides typical of the time, edited ancient and early Christian authors, and wrote skillful moral elegies (*elegiae morales*).

Inspired by Wimpfeling's *Adolescentia* he compiled works of contemporary Italian and German authors into a *Scoparius in barbariei propugnatores et osores humanitatis* (Defender [literally, Sweeper] of Barbarian Enemies and Haters of the Humanities, 1517).[55] Wimpfeling, however, represents far more forcefully than Murmellius the restrictiveness of fundamentalist Christian cultural policies; indeed, he anticipates the moralistic censorship in schools that will become pronounced in the post-Reformation period. To combat the alleged obscenities of the heathen poets (particularly Catullus, Ovid, Juvenal, and Martial), Wimpfeling recommends "Christian poets," who are to guide "Christian pupils" and "Christian teachers" in a "Christian way."

Debates raged over works not easily morally domesticated; others about how to understand ancient myths. These controversies endured into the seventeenth century as signs of a fundamental conflict between humanists and scholastic theologians. The new poets insisted on the right to discuss all areas of knowledge, even to protest or support secular ideas, and to reject the teachings of academic scholasticism. As outsiders, however, their assertions often were disparaged, even within the arts faculties; their paltry salaries reflected their low status and kept them on the move from university to university in search of lectureships. Prominent examples are Peter Luder (1415–72; in Heidelbert, Erfurt, and Leipzig),[56] Hermann von dem Busche, and Ulrich von Hutten (1488–1523). Since the humanistic subjects they taught were not integral to academic examinations, enrollments were small. Bebel enjoyed an exceptional situation in Tübingen, where the *litterae humaniores* coexisted without rivalry with the traditional disciplines. The so-called "Battle over Reuchlin," however, in which representatives of Catholic universities confronted a phalanx of determined young intellectuals, became spectacularly intense. Johann Reuchlin (1455–1522), a celebrated Hebrew scholar, opposed the destruction (by burning) of Jewish sacred books, a stance that earned him the enmity of the Dominican theologians at Cologne and put him on the defendant's dock at the Vatican. The highly publicized affair polarized the ideological frontlines, cast doubt on the church's claim to cultural authority, and, in the *Epistolae obscurorum virorum* (Letters of Obscure Men [literally, Men in the Dark], 1515–17; NL), written by Crotus Rubeanus (1480–ca. 1545) and (especially) Hutten, inspired an incomparable exercise in mimetic satire. The "obscure" men (monks and scholastic theologians) write in an incompetent, and often hilarious, Latin even as they reveal that they are living lives of gluttony and sexual excess. This devastating satirizing of their lack of modern education served as a general intellectual and moral critique of theological authorities.

Erasmus of Rotterdam[57]

It is hardly possible to treat adequately in so brief a forum the relevance of the contribution of Erasmus of Rotterdam (ca. 1467–1536) to the history of education. He was the leading figure of European humanism:[58] philologist, rhetorician, critical theorist, translator, collector, editor, and commentator; theologian, champion of an ethical *philosophia Christi*, and pioneering advocate of free will (*liberum arbitrium*); satirist, skeptic, critic of church and culture. What united the divergent facets of his personality, achievements, causes, and visions was his desire that human society be educated. We may attempt to identify three integrative principles as a shorthand summary of his significance:

1. The individual and society are interconnected. Erasmus had to ignore his own doubts about the nature of man in promoting education as the means to humane civilization. In his *Laus Stultitiae* (Praise of Folly, 1511) he dons the mask of Folly (Latin *Stultitia*, Greek *Moria*) to confront, more profoundly than any other Renaissance author, the human necessity of creating illusions. Illusions constitute our essential network of self-deceptions; life's little white lies spring from the heart of egoism; only omnipresent folly enables one to live at peace with oneself and to associate with others in marriage, friendship, and communal life. Erasmus is not concerned with sin or the catechism of salvation, least of all with traditional theology, but rather with human culture and society, the keys to his conception of education through humane letters. Insofar as man is of a "bestial" nature, and however well culture and education may rehabilitate him, a certain reservation lingers like a ground bass: some religious underpinning — Erasmus conceives of it as *pietas* — must support the project of civilization. It is that reservation, expressed with all irony, which is the great and constant message of Folly across the entire spectrum of social relations. Before education can ever hope to begin, however, one is faced with the fundamental problem simply of being at all able to tolerate, even bear (*ferre*) oneself and others. This is the primal recognition that the inner life of the self depends for its survival on stable social relationships. Individual identity and social order coexist in a state of precarious but necessary equilibrium. This depends on tolerance, a quality that is the opposite of rigid, fanatical enthusiasm for possessing truth.

2. Education in humane letters must embrace a conception of virtue grounded in reciprocal benevolence among men (*mutua benevolentia*). To this end Erasmus invented a literary vehicle that allowed him to speak freely through an assumed voice, as in *Laus Stultitiae*. *Querela Pacis* (Complaint of Peace, 1517), is another such work. A highly political declaration read throughout Europe at least as late as Kant, *Querela Pacis* established the notion of a human culture of communication rooted in humane learning and the mastery of languages. In his *Antibarbari* of 1493, in response to the trauma of his own school days, Erasmus had already protested the rejection of language and intellect by mystics and the devout. The ancients as well as the modern Italians understood the concept *barbarism* as a dark foil that helped to illuminate new ideas.[59] Erasmus's pedagogical texts, whether addressed to students or teachers, courtiers or the middle classes, rulers or political leaders (as guides to princely conduct and proper government), endlessly reiterate their ultimate goal: to educate society.[60] Speaking through the voice of Peace at this particular historical moment,[61] Erasmus formulates his essential conception

of *humanitas*.[62] On the one hand he opposes it to Machiavellian power politics and on the other to unholy aggressions in the private sphere. *Humanitas* requires a cooperative attitude; it may derive less from innate qualities (biology) than from "disciplinarum ac virtutum semina,"[63] the seeds of discipline and virtue. We must cultivate a predisposition toward intellect and morality that demonstrates, as a kind of second nature, the natural dignity of the human being as species. But what is, in fact, a second "nature" that reveals itself in habits; and what is its real relationship to human behavior? In the midst of these musings Erasmus issues a statement that appears to suggest that philosophy and theology are superior to humane letters, when in fact he is actually denying their influence on normal human behavior: "Bonae litterae reddunt homines, Philosophia plusquam homines, Theologia reddit divos" (Humane letters restore men, philosophy makes them more than men, theology restores the gods). Erasmus always shows high regard in his treatises and letters for "litterae humanae, litterae humaniores, politiores, elegantiores; studia humaniora" (humane letters and more humane, more polite, and more elegant letters: humanistic studies). In the *Antibarbari*, which allies *eruditio* and *pietas* (learning and piety), he affirms the humanizing effect of literature, how it sensitizes the emotions and promotes civilization by overcoming class boundaries. This idea inhabits his entire *oeuvre*, not least in connection with the education of princes: "Maturescunt eruditione ingenia, reddunturque tum molliora, tum mitiora" (They will develop intellectually and will receive in return things gentler, milder).[64]

3. The integration of humane letters, virtue, and piety is essential to *philosophia Christi*. North of the Alps the purpose, or *telos*, of human nature and the educability of the human being continued to be addressed basically — this only intensified with Luther — within the discourse of theology, the epoch's leading science. Erasmus had wrested from skepticism one certainty: Christ is the promise that the life of individuals and society can change for the better. The moral rigor that he urged upon rulers in his guide for Christian princes, *Institutio principis christiani* (1516),[65] had its roots in this religiosity, as did the biting pacifism with which he repeatedly condemned Europe's bloody dynastic struggles. Not all debate in the theological code, however, actually intended a theological goal. In his debate with Luther over the question of free will, for instance, Erasmus reached regularly into the arsenal of Scholasticism to frame certain mundane philosophical arguments. On the question of free will, he returned to the old battleground between the Pelagians (proponents of free will) and Augustinians (defenders of the doctrine of necessity). Ultimately, he was contending as a cultural anthropologist to retain a last preserve of human autonomy, one, namely, in which salvation was at least partly the work of education and morality. Erasmus saw himself trapped between two unacceptable principles: on the one hand, Luther's *sola scriptura* and *sola fides*, which he viewed as superstitious and dogmatic relics of the old church, and on the other, a self-glorifying, quasi neo-pagan humanism obsessed with

style (he ridicules this in his *Ciceronianus*, 1528).[66] His view of theology as *philosophia Christi* placed unique stress on the cultural remnants of original Christianity that were accessible to reason and therefore credible; he believed with equal conviction in the intellectual culture of (pagan) antiquity. *Literae, virtus*, and *pietas* constitute a new trinity, setting us free in this life and guiding us to a tranquil mind and the joy of a pure conscience. His break with tradition did not lie in a decision to ignore religion and espouse a worldly philosophy but rather in his view that Christian and ancient philosophical teachings are mutually supportable. Luther seized on the essential difference that separated him from Erasmus and defamed his adversary, with typical hyperbole. In his *Tischreden* (Table Talks, published posthumously in 1566) he calls Erasmus "ein Feind aller Religion und ein sonderlicher Feind und Widersacher Christi, ein vollkommen Conterfeit und Ebenbild des Epicuri und Luciani" (an enemy to all religion and a particular foe and opponent of Christ, a perfect counterfeit and image of Epicurus and Lucian).[67]

Indeed, the concord between Christian ethos and humanistic learning in Erasmus included an appeal to "holy Socrates"[68] as well as a certain dehistoricizing of Christ as prefiguration of love, integrity, patience, and purity — Christ as personified moral textbook.[69] The agreement between moral Christian living and humanistic learning propounded by the *philosophia Christi*[70] tended to divest Christ of his historicity in favor of an allegorical reading.[71] Both Lutheran and Catholic adversaries of Erasmus noted with disapproval this lowering of the metaphysics of Christian salvation to the level of practical morality. Luther accused Erasmus of "godlessness" and "Epicureanism," anticipating the threats to humanism's cultural agenda in the post-Reformation era. Erasmus's transposition of metaphysics to ethics went hand in hand with his distinct lack of participation in the bitter dogmatic fights raging about him: on the church and its functions, on the nature of Christ, on salvation, predestination, the sacraments. Erasmus demolished traditional differentiations between learning from revelation and learning from the observation of the natural world by relating knowledge and faith to a single ethical goal and measuring both by a single criterion: social utility. Through his study of the church fathers — more Jerome than Augustine[72] — he discovered in the history of antiquity what awaited the modern world: the emergence of multiple competing ideologies, power centers, authorities, domains of experience, explanatory systems, and subjective ethical codes. Most of these had been rife since Petrarch and the Florentine civic humanists Coluccio Salutati (1331–1406) and Leonardo Bruni, among others, in their various quests for a *ratio vivendi* for this present life, without need of a transcendental rationale. Especially the Italian humanists Lorenzo Valla and Pico della Mirandola (1463–94), but also Hegius and Agricola, inspired Erasmus's return to classical antiquity, which for him represented the ultimate integration of the complex associations of ideas, values, and ways of life that were considered by many of his contemporaries to be alien to Christianity. Language, given exemplary form in literature, expresses the complex, even turbulent inner life of man, who must accommodate himself to whatever are the prevailing rules of conduct and proper discourse. Language makes sense of it all: "lingua humanae mentis interpres" (language as interpreter of human mind).[73] Meaning arises, however, not only through language but also with the aid of the civilizing influence of society on human conduct.

We now turn to certain lines of Erasmian argument about education, specifically as related to methods, practices, and purposes of educating young people. From Erasmus's early works, many of which come from his life as a teacher and tutor, to later treatises like *De lingua* (1525), pedagogy is a regular concern. These works by no means are specifically Christian in philosophy. They include the widely read *De civilitate morum puerilium* (On the Civility of Youthful Morals, 1530; cited hereafter as *Civilitas*), which has been called a standard document of western conduct.[74] It expands on the earlier treatises *De ratione studii* (On the Method of Study, 1512) and *De pueris statim ac liberaliter instituendis* (On the Progressive and Liberal Instruction of Youth, 1529).[75] *De ratione* and *De pueris* belong to the first of the nine *ordines* (classes) that Erasmus established as the model for all subsequent complete editions of his works.[76] This first class consists of works "quae spectant ad institutionem literarum" (that treat of instruction in literature); these will be joined by works of the fourth class, "quae faciunt ad morum institutionem" (which constitute moral education), and the fifth, "quae instituunt ad pietatem" (which teach piety). In his *Civilitas*, which takes the form of a letter to young Henry of Burgundy (later Emperor Charles V), Erasmus describes how his pedagogical works relate to each other as phases of a process of adolescent education. The civility of conduct and physical appearance, while stressing aesthetic, external, and sensuous aspects, paradoxically represents a quality of the inward being, the well-ordered mind: "Bene compositus pueri animus undique relucet" (The well-ordered mind of the youth shines everywhere). This is also true of the *cultus* (custom, culture) of clothing, "ex hac quoque licet habitum animi conjicere" (from which one is likewise able to judge one's habit of mind). This methodically arranged curriculum also stipulates rules for mutually agreeable social relationships and addresses techniques for living well in society, which involve the internalization of cognitive, verbal, and physical behaviors. Semantically and functionally congruent with the precepts of civil elegance are notions associated with polished and effective rhetoric (*decorum* and *elegantia*) — thus the lexical analogy between *animus compositus* and *oratio composita* (well-ordered mind and well-ordered speech).

Although Erasmus directs his precepts to a young courtly nobleman, he insists that they have general applicability. A person's behavior and appearance must agree: there must be a studied harmony between a person's crude nature — the organs, functions, reactions, and symptoms of the body — and his cultivated appearance: "decet autem ut homo totus sit compositus animo, corpore, gestibus, ac vestitu" (it is proper that man be completely integrated in mind, body, gestures, and clothing).

The conscious cultivation of one's appearance was not yet expressly motivated in the sixteenth century — as it would be in the seventeenth — by *prudentia civilis* (social prudence, or good sense), calculated to enhance one's chances for success; rather it was guided by the cardinal virtue of *modestia*, which can be traced to the ethical Aristotelian avoidance of aberrations and extremes. Sociable behavior remained linked to an ethos determined *a priori* by the quest for the nature and possibilities of humanity, not by its social functions. Nathan Chytraeus (Kochhafe, 1543–98), professor in Rostock and later school rector in Bremen, who translated Giovanni della Casa's (1503–56) guide to conversation, *Il Galateo* (ca. 1555), into Latin and German, would later ask, "an studium bonorum morum deceat Christianum" (whether the study of refined habits becomes a Christian). For Erasmus the question clearly needs no more debate.[77] He both affirms and rejects the class-specific character of his *Civilitas*, for "nobility" means "nobility through education." This treatise is a necessary complement to his writings on the *ratio studii*. It is not speaking about an individual's moral culture as defined by the ideal of *humanitas* in the *Querela Pacis*; rather the governing principle of grace (*gratia*) comes into play here. Grace combines outward charm and social acceptance, indeed esteem, a quality that may be wanting even in "probi et eruditi homines" (honest and learned men), which may even point to a troubling deficit in such persons' fitness for life, unrelated to educational attainment or moral integrity. A semantic seed is contained in the concept of grace, which, reinforced with Platonic ideas, will grow into that vast corpus of French, Italian, and Spanish handbooks and compendia of proper etiquette and polite conversation (NL);[78] renowned for their maxims on *l'art de plaire* (the art of pleasing), they derived in the first place from Erasmus's *Civilitas*.

Erasmus's purpose was not to write a *Hofschule*, a handbook for courtiers. Nevertheless, he presents a systematic and detailed field of characteristics (his modern counterpart would surely be Pierre Bourdieu[79]) that differentiate the social instincts and even the appearance of a person educated in the spirit of humanism and morality from the brutal grossness of thought and action of those whom he calls "the others." The others — this includes one's own coarser inclinations, or alter ego — are not characterized primarily by social status; proper manners arise from a congruence of *natura* and *ratio*. While Erasmus insists that noble ancestry obligates a person to behave well, he also gives students of modest birth the chance to compensate for their chance disadvantages by striving after *morum elegantia* (elegance of habits). In describing how to correct wrong habits he blends advice on *urbanitas* in manners with injunctions to show respect for persons of higher rank. His *Civilitas* follows Cicero's *De officio* in harmonizing the categories of *honestum* and *decorum*, rejecting the traditional espousal of general virtues in favor of empirical advice on right and wrong behavior in concrete situations. As the century wore on, and then especially in the seventeenth century, this idea of purposeful life-formation through aesthetic precepts — beyond what occurs *ex more*, out of old social custom — was gradually reduced and stripped of Erasmian precepts. It was embellished instead with details of ceremony and ritual, conventions of cultivated conversation, stratagems of courtly politics, and social "accommodation" and became merely a behavioral code for the middle and upper classes. According to the sociologist Norbert Elias the German middle classes took most seriously Erasmus's exhortation that a nation must undergo the process of civilization.[80] One sees this in the grossness of life at the minor German territorial courts until well into the seventeenth century. In this light it would be misguided to read Erasmus's letter as though it were concerned chiefly with life at court, or to interpret it as reflecting older precepts of religious or monastic education.[81]

Across Europe, a trail of adaptations, editions, and translations of the *Civilitas* leads through the era of confessional struggles to the seventeenth century's updated guides to polite conversation.[82] As early as the 1530s many German schools adopted it along with several other books, in particular: *Praecepta vitae puerilis* (Principles for Youth, 1528?) by the Melanchthon pupil Joachim Camerarius (Liebhard, 1500–1574), *Aphorismi institutionis puerorum* (Aphorisms on the Education of Boys, 1519) by the botanist Otto Brunfels (1488–1534), and *Christiana studiosae juventutis institutio* (Christian Education for Young Students, 1526) by Christoph Hegendorff (1500–1540), who had a hand in the reorganization of the University of Rostock in the post-Reformation years.[83] The new treatments expanded on many of Erasmus's ideas and transposed them into sometimes very different contexts. The theologian David Chytraeus (Kochhafe, 1531–1600), for instance, published his *Regula vitae* (Rules for Life) in Wittenberg in 1562, which rigorously subordinated faith, piety, education, and morality to the Ten Commandments. Guides to proper conversation and manners, beginning with della Casa's aforementioned *Il Galateo*, and especially *La civil conversazione* by Stefano Guazzo (1530–96), were addressed chiefly to adults, supplying what Erasmus had not: rules for conducting conversations and guidelines for people of different backgrounds for getting along with each other at court and in respectable society. German scholars knew Latin versions of della Casa's and Guazzo's conversation books, often called *politica*, and responded with commentaries, dissertations, and synopses.[84] A teaching chair for a *professor morum* (professor of ethics) was not established until the seventeenth century, however, at Beuthen in Silesia. Its occupant, Caspar Dornavius (Dornau, 1577–1632), young Martin Opitz's most important teacher, entitled his inaugural speech *Charidemus* (1617);[85] in it he transforms the sober categories of conduct into an aesthetics of living a sociable and orderly life. Dornau bases his arguments on the utility of *civilis prudentia* and on a conception of harmonious beauty derived from Neo-Platonism, which, as *concordia discors*, represents the harmony between nature and the cosmos as well as that between the social hierarchy and the "world theater" of society. The presence of Erasmus's *Civilitas* is often obvious here, but his main ideas are now applied to radically altered social circumstances and philosophical expectations. A systematic discussion of the proper domains of laws and morality and their differences from social convention would not occur until later in the seventeenth century, with Christian Thomasius (1655–1728), a legal scholar and educational reformer at the universities in Leipzig and Halle.

Erasmus regarded humanistic education under the aegis of *litterae humanae* as the only hope for overcoming man's natural bondage to the passions, which he saw as antithetical to *eruditio*. Erasmus was a theologian only insofar as he was also a pedagogue. The New Testament, which he had published as a critical edition in 1516 in the original Greek with a new Latin translation — prerequisite for Luther's German translation — was sacred to him; for Erasmus, Christianity's claim to moral authority lay entirely in the imitation of Christ, the truest argument against the worldly-wise skepticism he mocks in *Laus Stultitiae*. The "folly of the cross" mentioned at the end, echoing St. Paul, has nothing to do, however, with Luther's metaphysics of suffering and theology of the cross. Erasmus the philologist, in contrast to Luther, doubted that the Scriptures alone (*sola scriptura*) could give guidance in faith and right conduct. On the other hand he regarded Catholic "ceremonials," as he called them (fasting, pilgrimages, veneration of relics), as vestiges of Jewish practices; they should not be done away with all at once, but their only value was to support the weak in faith. Erasmus avoided wherever possible basic theological questions that were too often merely sources of contention (the Trinity, salvation, predestination, etc.). His renowned disputes with Luther, half forced on him but which he nevertheless accepted as an obligation, revealed an abyss between a theocratic ideology he feared could retheologize public life and the rights of the individual to be informed and educated. Erasmus struggled to confirm the stature of the human being as autonomous subject with free will, for only on that ground could he legitimize the humanist ideal of the educated individual, which he took as the irreducible prerequisite for a civilized humanity.

Unlike most humanists Erasmus did not teach much in later life. His works, however, some of which were later censored, continued to serve the educated as a common ground. For *Colloquia familiaria* (Familiar Conversations, 1522), originally conceived as dialogues between students, Erasmus borrowed the form from similar works by the Latin school director Paul Niavis (Schneevogel, 1460–1514),[86] the Leipzig rector Petrus Mosellanus (Schade, 1493–1524),[87] and Christoph Hegendorff.[88] The frequently reprinted *Colloquia familiaria* offers a colorfully satiric panorama of many of the age's social and ethical questions, including morality and religious observance, married life, politics, clerical ignorance, and the privileges of the nobility. Whether in this or in his advice on interpreting Scripture or in his ideal of the true theologian, set forth in notes to his scholarly edition of the Bible, Erasmus always sought the restoration of Christianity in its most original and authentic form. Like Lorenzo Valla, he extended ultimate authority for determining the meaning of biblical texts to secular philologists, thus opening the door to critical historical scrutiny of the scriptural bases of Christian teachings, an intellectual liberation that would also eventuate in unintended negative consequences.

As noted, Erasmus preferred to avoid religious controversies. Some of his most ardent followers, however, came from the ranks of the dissidents, or spiritualists, who decried all orthodoxies. At their head was Sebastian Franck

(1500–1543),[89] who translated numerous works by Erasmus, sometimes adapting them to fit his vision of an invisible and universal church of the spirit. Franck resisted both Luther's assertion that the Bible alone should govern the faith as well as the claims of the orthodox *Mauerkirchen* (churches of walls) that they alone could dispense truth and divine mediation. He applied Christianity to transforming inward experience into moral practice in the world. In this he anticipated the Paracelsist Valentin Weigel (1533–88).[90] Many of Erasmus's ideas proved to be adaptable by the dissidents in their struggle against what they perceived to be the socially irrelevant dogmas of the territorial churches and the embittered, and equally irrelevant, polemics of so many mainline theologians.[91]

Humanistic Pedagogy and the Cultural Politics of the Confessions

Humanists were often personally victimized by the Reformation's shattering social changes (elimination of church sinecures, etc.), some of which threatened to end learned studies altogether. Luther's polemics against late medieval Aristotelianism, together with his return to the authority of the Bible and his imperial-patriotic opposition to the pope and the curia, however, did bring about a fragile alliance with the leaders of the humanist movement. In his missive *An die Ratherren aller Städte deutsches Landes, daß sie christliche Schulen aufrichten und erhalten sollen* (To the Councilors of All Cities in Germany, that They Are to Institute and Maintain Schools, 1524),[92] Luther classified educational policy as an important function of secular government, along with religious and cultural policies. Opposing the radical religiosity of spiritual and revolutionary wings of Protestantism, which he accused of being undisciplined and doctrinally unreliable, Luther demanded that preachers receive solid philological training in the ancient languages and their literatures.

It was Melanchthon (NL), the so-called *praeceptor Germaniae* (teacher of Germany), who consolidated the humanistic educational model and reformed the universities' arts faculties.[93] The unity of *eruditio* and *pietas* that he cherished required that all subject areas be established upon biblically sound precepts; he was able thereby to guarantee the curricular place of Renaissance letters, along with related humanistic educational goals and methods. In prefaces to books and in academic orations, beginning with his inaugural lecture at Wittenberg, *De corrigendis adolescentiae studiis* (On the Reform of Youth Education, 1518),[94] Melanchthon repeatedly emphasizes the encyclopedic interconnectedness of philology, moral philosophy, history, and the natural sciences. Against the protest of professors of philosophy and the applied sciences, he insists on systematic instruction in languages and eloquence according to classical rhetorical theory. Rhetorical analysis of exemplary authors like Cicero will uphold the universal status of the ancient *orator sapiens* as authoritative, though now with a particular view to the necessary connection between knowledge of the world and linguistic expertise. To Melanchthon, words are "signs of things." Language is therefore, quite beyond being the ground for basic communication, the key to accessing universal knowledge. Until the close of the seventeenth century, theology, jurisprudence, and other disciplines continued to adapt their discourses and organizational principles to the topic-oriented methods devised by Erasmus and Melanchthon for excerpting and retrieving data. *Topoi* (Latin *loci*) in this sense no longer merely provided handy compartments for arguments but now, as *loci communes* (commonplaces), became concepts that structured and guided knowledge of every kind. Humanist scholars were henceforth obliged to categorize the fruits of their reading in these categories. A system of rubrics evolved under which one could arrange and sort vast bodies of information according to degrees of significance and abstraction. This *memoriae subsidium*, or aid to remembering, gave early modern scholarship its polyhistoric character and its unique culture of writing.[95]

We can measure Melanchthon's epochal importance only in part by his numerous textbooks (frequently reprinted and intensively used) and editions, his orations and lectures, and his far-reaching reorganization of schools and universities. His significance also owes to the unique position he occupied as a mediator at the sensitive boundary between the claims of theology and philosophy to authority and power. By reserving for theology everything relating to salvation, he created, once more following Aristotle, a domain for a non-religious psychology and a system of ethics basic not only to everyday life but to political and social actions as well. These norms held over the course of the century in published interpretations of literary and historical texts.

Proceeding accordingly to an essentially Aristotelian theory of the passions derived from human experience, Melanchthon predicates his conception of virtue on the cultivation of a practical attitude that becomes second nature and makes the emotionally chaotic human will obedient to right reason. Natural reason (*naturalis ratio*), though dimmed by the fall from grace, still points the way to Christian dignity, namely, the original state of man as the image of God. The Ten Commandments are thus interpretable as natural laws of morality. Cautiously reconciling the positions of Luther and Erasmus, Melanchthon concedes freedom of choice in human actions coupled, however, with moral responsibility and clearly expressed cultural values. Life in society and the duties of rulers he grounds in a design for civilizing humanity that guarantees the rational ordering of "outward" actions and conditions as the product of the acquired human ability to differentiate both spontaneously and retrospectively between *honestum* and *turpe*, the morally good and the morally depraved.

Melanchthon's pedagogical ideas served rectors well in various territories, notably Trotzendorf in Silesia, Sturm in Strasbourg, and Michael Neander (1520–95) in Ilfeld/Harz.[96] In accordance with the ideal of *sapiens atque eloquens pietas* (wise and eloquent piety) Sturm developed a curriculum organized into six — later nine, then ten — classes, which linked the schedule of readings of classical authors to students' acquisition of writing and verbal skills. Prototypically for all secondary education following the Reformation, Sturm insisted upon the cultivation of correct and elegant Latin even in everyday life at the school, and he stressed the significance of the triad of *ars*, *usus*, and *imitatio* (art, practice, and imitation). Grammar, logic, and rhetoric conveyed the teaching principles (*praecepta*) at work in reading the "best" authors as models (*exempla*) and learning to write in their styles. Students attempted, according to the principle of *aemulatio*, to rival the skills of the ancient authors and create literary works of their own. The purpose was to discover the potential for nobility and ingenuity in modern poetry so that, eventually, dependence on the old models would disappear. Sturm and Melanchthon alike wanted also to apply the rules of rhetoric to preaching as a way of improving on the *Volksrede* (informal "talk to the people") of traditional sermons.

The imitative method established canons of carefully selected authors, such as the one devised by Sturm in his six-volume *Volumina poetica* (Poetic Volumes, or Rolls, beginning 1565). Ever since Petrarch, Cicero was held up as the exemplary author: every nuance of stylistic modulation was visible in his works; he embodied the unity of eloquence and philosophy, of personal enlightenment and public efficacy. Sturm regarded Cicero as a bulwark against the constant threat of barbarism. German humanists thus participated in the broader European debate on Ciceronianism, which was concerned — sometimes to an exaggerated degree, as Erasmus saw, with dismay — with the relationship of modern culture to antiquity. In his satirical dialogue *Ciceronianus* Erasmus rejects classical Latin as the canonical model, arguing that it diminished linguistic vitality to the point where language could lose its historical capacity to adapt and develop in response to new circumstances. Furthermore, casting Christian terms in the idiom of antiquity was anachronistic and illusory; similarly, the use of ancient models for modern politics could be dangerously misleading.[97] For Erasmus, to emulate Cicero in the true spirit meant to act as Cicero himself would have acted under modern prevailing conditions. Toward the end of the century, under the aegis of Neo-Stoicism and Taciteanism,[98] humanists approached the modernization of classical ideas pragmatically, comparing the structure of a state to that of a well-made oration or comparing Rome under Augustus to a modern territorial principality.

The controversy over principles of style and conceptual models raged among the Jesuits as well (NL). Well established in Germany by the 1560s, the Society of Jesus dominated higher education in the Catholic territories until its dissolution in 1773. Curricula and pedagogy, codified internationally in the *Ratio studiorum* of 1599, grounded in rhetoric and the universality of Latin, aimed at the training of an intellectual elite of future leaders to propagate the faith and promote the post-Tridentine reformist goals of the Counter-Reformation.[99] A culture of piety guided the individual but was equally useful in meeting the intellectual challenges of princely politics. Jesuit secondary schools differed from those of the Protestant humanists mainly in their tighter organization of classes and examinations and in their scrupulous appraisals of how students performed in disputations, orations, and ceremonies.

Aristotle's theory of the drama was first adapted in Jesuit poetics, notably by the Augsburg Jesuit Jacobus Pontanus (1542–1626) and the Cologne professor Jacob Masen (1606–81). With an intensity rare among Lutherans, the Jesuits regularly presented ancient and modern dramas in their schools

(NL). Using examples from history or the Bible, which they enhanced with technologically sophisticated visual and acoustic effects, the Jesuits treated in their dramas not only current political problems and sensational examples of defending the faith (in *Märtyrerdramen*, dramas of martyrdom) but also troubling secular or heretical political theories (Neo-Stoicism, Machiavellianism).

Jesuit theatrical practice, embedded in the order's school system, aimed both to abet the education of the entire person and to demonstrate the Catholic version of Christian humanism. Supervised by their priests, congregations assigned to schools and universities directed the emotional and intellectual powers of their students into the service of Christianity, emphasizing asceticism, the Holy Sacraments, and the veneration of Mary. Religious pamphlets from Spain and France aided instruction of young nonprofessionals both at school and in extracurricular devotions; German Jesuit devotional works included the *Güldenes Tugend-Buch* (Golden Book of Virtue, 1649) by Friedrich Spee von Langenfeld (1591–1635), renowned for his defense of the accused in witchcraft trials.[100] Many of these devotional works grew out of their authors' pastoral care in communities of religious women. To many Protestants, the general attractiveness of the Jesuit schools, which offered not only rigorous and effective education but did so free of tuition, made them a threat to the viability of their own schools.

New Pedagogical Approaches of the Seventeenth Century

Reformed Orthodoxy — Pietism — Pansophism

Developments in the natural sciences and the accompanying explosion of knowledge, together with the growing dissatisfaction of the rising middle classes with the Latin gymnasia, led to calls for pedagogical reform. Among the many complaints was that a "practical atheism" had invaded both private and public life. This anxiety arose in part from a creeping sense that Lutheranism had been retreating over the past half century into inconsequential ceremonics and endless academic haggling over theology and was losing influence against Calvinism's stern regulation of churches or against Counter-Reformation assaults on Protestant culture. Johann Valentin Andreae (1586–1654; NL), a theologian in Württemberg, transformed Arndt's call for a kind of piety useful for daily life (*praxis pietatis*) into an aggressive criticism of the church, schools, and territorial states.[101] As coauthor of three works on Rosicrucian thought, including the *Fama fraternitatis* (Fraternal Fame, 1614), Andreae initiated a debate on reform that spread throughout the Holy Roman Empire. His plan to rally reform-minded Lutherans to restore society's Christian identity included a philosophy of nature derived from ideas of Weigel and Paracelsus (1493–1541). Rosicrucianism, a theosophical form of Christianity readily absorbed into Andreae's proposed *societas christiana*, expected to see the wisdom of antiquity restored in a chiliastic period of historical fulfillment; God would become visible in the world and the world in God. That implied a mystical turning away from the language-centered learning of academic humanism, which Andreae satirized in his dialogical *Menippus* (1617). Melanchthon's system of schooling, to which Andreae owed so much, was felt to be complicit in the church's erroneous conformity to worldly politics.

What discontented intellectuals had discussed among themselves and often satirized in fiction was reflected as a positive model in Andreae's *Respublicae Christianopolitanae descriptio* (Description of the Republic of a Christian State, 1619), commonly known as *Christianopolis,* his utopian design of an ideal city republic. In the name of a rebirth of Christianity out of the forfeited purity of the Lutheran Reformation, Andreae — influenced in part by Tommaso Campanella's utopian *Civitas solis* (City of the Sun, 1623), which he had read before 1619 in manuscript form — proposed a community regulated down to the smallest detail. The lecture halls and laboratories of scholars and scientists are integrated with the workshops of artisans in a well-ordered manufacturing economy. The message of the gospel, together with the idea of the "construction of a Christian life," gives overriding purpose to all intellectual endeavors: not in the service of unchecked *curiositas* but of an aggressive, quasi-theocratic, regulatory system meant to remedy the shortcomings of experiential science through moral integrity and the rational organization of labor and governance. In short, it mirrored the Heavenly Jerusalem as ultimate judge of this-worldly reality. By grounding his state in *conscientia, ratio,* and *veritas* (conscience, reason, and truth), Andreae obligated its citizens to lives of self-discipline, self-examination, and moral probity. These qualities are implied in the subtitle of his chief pedagogical work, *Theophilus* (1622): "über die Heiligung der christlichen Religion, die maßvollere Ordnung des Lebens und die vernunftgemäßere Lehre der Wissenschaft" (On the Sanctification of the Christian Religion, a More Moderate Way of Living, and an Approach to the Sciences More Suited to Reason).[102] Here as elsewhere Andreae combines respect for the natural sciences with skeptical mistrust of human reason unchecked by commitment to God and moral discipline. Education of the young should also bring about renewal and improvement of the realities of social and political life. In strict adherence to the Bible, pagan elements of humanist literary training are banished, practical subjects such as physics and mathematics upgraded, and Latin reduced in importance to a language of instruction only, no longer to be learned for its own sake.

Reputable theologians of the so-called Reformed orthodoxy in Strasbourg, Nuremberg, and elsewhere shared Andreae's desire to create a fresh start for the Reformation. Important followers also came later from the ranks of the Pietists. Philipp Jakob Spener (1635–1705) rehabilitated lay religiosity, insisted on the "Heiligung" (sanctification) of individual lives, and sought to replace theological quarrels with a "Besserung der Kirche" (betterment of the church) through gatherings of "wahre Christen" (true Christians). *Pia desideria oder Hertzliches Verlangen Nach Gottgefälliger Besserung der wahren Evangelischen Kirchen* (Pious Desires or Heartfelt Longing for Devout

Betterment of the True Evangelical Church, 1675),[103] his manifesto, was supplemented by works that called attention to deficiencies in the pastoral care and education of the people. In Halle, August Hermann Francke (1663–1727) worked to remedy pedagogical and organizational weaknesses.[104] His rationally integrated school system included an orphanage, workshops, a publishing house (soon to become renowned), and education for girls. What he accomplished there was, in many respects, the realization of Andreae's Christian state.

While Thomasius and, still later, Johann Gottfried Herder (1744–1803) continued to feel the impact of Andreae's ideas, among his most avid contemporary readers was the Moravian Johann Amos Comenius (Jan Komensky, 1592–1670),[105] whose pedagogical works included manuals for teachers and parents, textbooks for younger and older students, and proclamations on current cultural matters. Based on his personal experiences as a teacher, they also propagated his theory of a revived *philosophia christiana*, which, inspired by Platonism, envisioned blessed domestic and communal harmony. Comenius developed his ideas on pansophism, as harmony of morality and science, under the influence of the encyclopedic thought of the Calvinist Johann Alsted (1588–1638) of Herborn. Alsted's work inspired Comenius to try to integrate the methodical principles of *sensus, ratio,* and *divina revelatio* with the ultimate aim of creating a moral-intellectual force capable of putting a halt to the "scientiarum laceratio" (mortal combat among the sciences) and of overcoming the progressive differentiation among the separate branches of knowledge. Humanity's partnership in the divine plan of creation and the confidence that the "lux veritatis" (light of truth) would blaze anew in history's final days demanded a radical change in the lives of men. Only his Christian conviction that the end of the world would bring about a pansophist synthesis of knowledge allowed Comenius to hope that intellectual, political, and religious struggles might end in an *orbis christianus* and peace prevail at last. This hope became his cause. As the most significant figure of the Moravian Brotherhood, a religious minority persecuted and expelled by the Habsburgs but devoted to peace and reconciliation, Comenius was skeptical of Cartesianism's strictly rational epistemology. He likewise rejected limits set by theologians:

> Sed hoc volumus, ut in concinnando Pansophico opere, omnes, qui de pietate, moribus, scientiis & artibus commentati sunt (posthabito respectu, Christianus an Mahumetanus, Judaeus an Ethnicus, & cuicunque etiam inter illos addictus sectae quis fuerit [. . .] omnes, inquam, ut admittantur, & audiantur, quid boni ferant.[106]

> [We intend that, in the harmony of pansophism, everyone who has presented something regarding religion, the sciences, or the arts, be he Christian, Moslem, Jew, or pagan and regardless of sect, that everyone, I say, be admitted and heard for whatever good he might contribute.]

The reception of pansophism was particularly enthusiastic in the Netherlands and among English Puritan circles. Comenius regarded as his enterprise's crowning achievement the seven-volume *De rerum humanarum emendatione consultatio catholica* (Catholic Inquiry on Change in the Lives of Men), which began to appear in 1645, though only parts of it saw publication during his lifetime. Pansophism was incorporated into a comprehensive educational plan known as *Panpaedia*, which aimed at improving morality and politics, to create an all-encompassing philosophy of ascending steps. It ultimately anticipated, as a visionary postulate resembling that of the Rosicrucians, humanity's fulfillment of Creation in a general reformation of the world leading to a new dawn of enlightenment and peace.

In the subtitle to his *Didactica magna* (Great Treatise on Didactics, 1657) Comenius summarizes the aims of seventeenth-century reformers of adolescent education: for the sake of success in this life and the next, boys and girls alike are to be instructed, as quickly, pleasantly, and thoroughly as possible, in the sciences; taught proper behavior; and filled with piety. Comenius has in mind the evidence of natural science in proposing a curriculum responsive to the actual needs and experiences of young minds, including life outside of school, both in order to make teaching and learning easier and to provide a basis for compulsory universal education. Ideas of earlier humanists appear too, notably those of Juan Luis Vives, who emphasized regimen, conduct, and efficiency of institutional organization, as well as making serious provision for the education of young women. But the concept of nature, quite beyond its methodological implications for education, also had for Comenius genuine value within the theology of Creation, for it was an implicit challenge to the artificial relationship between word and matter that had become standard in traditional approaches to education. Before we can learn about things through language and thought, Comenius believed, we must verify their existence by observing them in the visible world. In young people learning does not occur through the names of things but through the divinely ordained arrangement of the world itself, from the cosmos of things to be named, and thus from fundamental acts of perception. Comenius was convinced that both spheres, words and things, belonged to the operation of human reason, the one not taking precedence over the other.[107]

In several of the texts comprising his *Opera didactica omnia* (Complete Didactic Works, 1657–58) Comenius calls for reforms in the teaching of Latin and the *trivium*; for the benefit of ordinary people, however, he urges the schools to offer a general education in the mother tongue. The idea of education as a basic human right began thus to gain ground. Comenius believed that the education imparted to an individual affects the welfare of the entire nation, for each person learns to partake of the divine order that radiates in our knowledge of the universe. Pre-school training figured in his general curriculum as well, and Comenius belongs among the pioneering figures in early-childhood pedagogy. His *Informatorium der Mutterschul* (Manual for Mothers' Schools, 1633) addresses parents and insists on the importance of play, that children learn from each other, and that opportunities should be provided for creative activities and for working on their own. More than a century later the noted educators Johann Pestalozzi (1746–1827) and Friedrich Fröbel (1782–1852) would take up these ideas. Comenius's *Orbis sensualium pictus* (Theater of the

Visible World, 1658), which claims to be a "brief representation of the entire world and all of language," was widely hailed in his lifetime and was still renowned during the life of Goethe. God's goodness, the world of nature, humanity's historical and everyday activities, and biblical narratives: all of these combine within an allusive, unifying matrix of illustrations, concepts, and explanations in both Latin and the vernacular. The purpose of this "theater" is to encourage sensual perception of the world and to take pleasure in the art of naming and describing it. In stressing *realia* and in reviving the use of colloquial languages Comenius's achievements reflected general changes taking place in the world.

National Literatures — Vernacular Language — Reality-Based Pedagogy

During the first third of the seventeenth century, objections multiplied to the dominance of Latin and the claim of academically trained scholars to exclusive authority over literary discourses. The quality and quantity of literature in German compared unfavorably with the national literatures in the Netherlands, France, Italy, and Spain. Poetry in Latin circulated only within the class of learned academics, while poetry in German, such as that of the obsolescent schools of *Meistersinger*, did not meet the humanists' standards for formal elegance and linguistic purity. Martin Opitz (NL), praised as the father of German poetry, aspired to make young German poets capable of competing in the international literary arena by establishing a common aesthetic standard for literary quality, an aim previously thwarted by religious narrow-mindedness, cultural isolation, and the monopolistic claims of scholars over such matters.[108] Opitz's prescriptions for technical innovations and strict definitions of literary genres are only marginal to his real significance, however. His motivating concern was to restore the social prestige of learned poets so that they would be entrusted with significant social and intellectual roles; the first act was to liberate them from the reputation of being hired hacks. Poets must therefore be educated both intellectually and socially to assume responsibilities suited to a culturally sophisticated society; as members of the academic intelligentsia they must be able to prove themselves, especially at princely courts, equally as versed as aristocrats in the ways of the world. Opitz wished to demonstrate that the quality, seriousness, and elegance of writing in German not only avoided cheap popularity, triviality, or crudeness, but that it could rise to the expectations of an elevated public. He did not limit his struggle to free German literature of its provincialism to the mere composition of poetic manuals, proclamations, or narrow rules. He modeled his principles by personal example through his distinguished translations and original compositions. These works set the standard in German poetry for more than a century.

Opitz received his early education at the Gymnasium Schönaichianum at Beuthen, founded by Georg von Schönaich in 1616 with the goal of giving young people a superlative preparation for university study. Beuthen operated according to the principles and methods of Melanchthon. Perceptible seventeenth-century shifts in emphasis, however, reflected the program's flexible accommodation to the real-life demands of administrative careers at court and in the ever-expanding bureaucracy; the intelligentsia, increasingly dependent on these positions, could hardly afford any longer to ignore their demands. The impulses for reform at the Schönaichianum were especially embodied in Caspar Dornavius, a physician who had received his doctorate in medicine at Basel in 1604.[109] Dornavius maintained close contacts with the Bohemian nobility and traveled extensively in France, England, and the Netherlands before becoming rector of the school at Görlitz, whence he received his call to Beuthen as professor of ethics, with a mandate to emphasize the personal skills needed for gaining access to elevated social positions. It was amply clear by now that social success had an aesthetic dimension and depended on a command of manners, cultural competence, and the harmony of speech and bearing.

In 1617 in his inaugural address in Latin, Dornau spoke "de morum pul chritudine, necessitate, utilitate ad civilem conversationem" (on the beauty, necessity, and utility of moral behavior for social life). This significant pedagogical document proclaims that through the doctrine of decorum, or proper manners, a person may learn how to offer, in appearance, behavior, movements, and speech, an image of perfect harmony; in a word, the skills essential to carry out the roles expected by society. The controlling principle of this discipline is *prudentia*, proper social and political behavior, not least in keeping one's passions in check (*dominari affectibus*), which is indispensable for meeting courtly standards of etiquette. The discipline of propriety, of rejecting boorish directness in word and action, involved the mastery of elegant speech through the concise poetic rules that Opitz laid down a few years later. Social harmony is a form of beauty, for beauty is the manifestation of perfect order, the proper gradation of low and high, of greater and less moral value; order is the prerequisite for a stable and just constitution of society. The struggle of "everyone against everyone" and the mentality of "might makes right" that overwhelmed Europe during the wars of religion are antithetical to beauty. In praising beauty Dornau seeks to make aesthetic considerations congruent with politics and morality, concluding: "Nihil hoc universum, nisi pulchritudo est; pulchritudo est, quidquid in rerum natura consequi vides fastigium felicitatis suae, ad quam ab Opifice in prima creatione destinatum fuit"[110] (All of this is nothing but beauty; beauty is whatever one sees in nature reaching the pinnacle of its fortune, the goal of its existence, which was ordained for it at the very start of Creation by the divine Master of the World).

In a brief treatise, originally delivered as an oration under Dornau's supervision, the twenty-year-old Opitz published his manifesto on the new poetry: *Aristarchus sive de contemptu linguae Teutonicae* (Aristarchus, or Of Contempt for the German Language, 1617).[111] Naturally, the speaker first lays down the doctrine of humanism's cultural patriotism, in keeping with Tacitus's *Germania*: the myth of a free Germania, unsullied by moral decay, opposes the idealization of ancient Rome or the Italian claim to cultural and political supremacy. The German language has been preserved uncontaminated and unfalsified since ancient times, and this purity reflects the "fides et candor" (trueness and simplicity) of the Germans. One may need to receive instruction from the Italians and the French, but it is of utmost importance to cultivate one's own language, not to esteem the native substance less than the foreign.

Opitz suggests a complex of associations between German poetry, aristocratic dignity, and the ancient majesty of the empire; between patronage by the wealthy, aesthetic taste, and an alliance of intellect and power. In an age in which many aristocrats were drawn to the French language and culture Opitz asserts that the ruling elites have a responsibility to their own German culture. Whoever scorns the German language and literature scorns himself, contributes to Germany's political downfall, extends the past century's decline in the quality of poetry, and makes of the German nation a laughingstock for foreigners.

Opitz put his ideas into practice in the *Buch von der Deutschen Poeterey* (Book of German Poetics, 1624), which establishes rules and models not only for the poet but also for any educated person wishing to write. Particular emphasis falls on the theory of genres and the theory of stylistic elegance. Seventeenth-century readers should be educated in aesthetics as well, and writing and critical skills need much improvement. First, however, Opitz strives to correct entrenched prejudices, asserting that poetry is a "vorneme Wissenschaft" (worthy science) founded on knowledge and competence in many areas and therefore capable of doing justice to even the most exalted subjects, including theology. Because poetry affects human feelings, it has a civilizing mission: to contribute to a better life for people in a well-ordered society. A poet pursuing this goal may ignore the reproaches of the uninformed, that he is immoral or lying; but he must do more than clothe the truth in elegant phrases. Poetry is a product of the thinking mind, which discovers the hidden relationships within the world and formulates ingenious inventions that challenge the reader's intellect.

Opitz's promotion of literature in the German language did not mean that he rejected poetry and learning in Latin (NL). On the contrary, writers with high aspirations must command the skills endowed by humanist poetics and rhetoric. However, one no longer writes only for other scholars, but for worldly men and women as well who have the sophistication to appreciate it. Opitz's poetics inspired many other writers during the seventeenth century to compose similar manuals. Augustus Buchner (1591–1661), a professor of rhetoric and poetics at Wittenberg,[112] taught augmented versions of the new poetic rules in two major works: *Kurzer Wegweiser zur deutschen Dichtkunst* (A Brief Guide to Poetry in German, 1663) and *Anleitung zur Deutschen Poeterey* (Introduction to German Poetry, 1665). Philipp von Zesen (1619–81),[113] who strove to reform the German spelling system and rid the vocabulary of foreign loanwords, and Georg Philipp Harsdörffer,[114] first president of Nuremberg's Pegnesischer Blumenorden (Flower Order on the Pegnitz), one of Germany's most progressive intellectual societies, were among the leading lights who led German literature to heightened formal artistry, cultural self-awareness, and poetic creativity. In Harsdörffer's *Poetischer Trichter* (Funnel for Poetics, 1647–53)[115] — the title of which offered a proverbial image of pouring knowledge into a pupil's head — older humanist ideas about content and structure are everywhere in evidence. However, together with a taste for the allegorical constructions of texts and images in emblematic poetry,[116] interest arose too in the homegrown qualities of the German language no longer measurable by classical standards. Following the lead of the great treatises on the German language, especially the *Ausführliche Arbeit von der Teutschen HaubtSprache* (A Thorough Treatise on the German Language, 1663) by Justus Georg Schottelius (1612–76),[117] Germans began to regard their native tongue as a grammatical system in its own right, accessible to reason and having the power to combine art and nature. The autonomy of the native idiom and the idea of a primal connection in German between instinctively uttered sounds in a "natural language" and their meaning functioned as a cultural analogue to a general rise in national self-awareness.[118]

Harsdörffer also published didactic works that present religious, scientific, and cultural topics in a pleasing and informal style.[119] His eight volumes of *Frauenzimmer Gesprächspiele* (Conversational Games for Ladies, 1641–49)[120] transpose the literary forms of French and Italian salon culture to Germany. Dialogue among friends in a relaxed social setting appears as a style of instruction. His use of a literary medium within the current discussion about methods implies a rejection of scholastic didactic systems. The repeated mention of the great English empirical scientist Francis Bacon (1561–1626) is indicative of Harsdörffer's practical interest in new methods of communicating knowledge. Thus, "playing games" in dialogue becomes an act of emancipation: "weil der Verstand dardurch alles Zwanges fürgeschriebener Lehren entbunden / sich in seiner eingeschaffnen Freyheit befindet nachzusinnen" (because reason is thereby freed of all prescribed ideas and achieves its inborn freedom to reflect).[121] Harsdörffer is not so much concerned with autonomous *raison*, in the Cartesian sense, as with liberation from the vogue for encyclopedism, or learning only from books; he is looking to embrace new realities and experiences.

In the *Frauenzimmer Gesprächspiele* women appear as autonomous partners with men in a cultivated society, entitled to participate and to be equally respected. Even in this stiff, schematic form the pattern of the *bonne compagnie* is emerging: a group of private persons with strong cultural interests assembles, as in the French salons, at home, one which exists at an independent distance from both the academic and courtly spheres. The notions of taste cultivated by the succeeding *galant* epoch (ca. 1680–1730) will take for granted this fundamental change in the expectations of the functionality of literature and learning. To the congenial world of polite society, which had adapted the rules of political *prudentia* and the rhetorical tactics of social decorum to the private sphere, the old republic of letters had the musty smell of a solely masculine, self-absorbed, exclusivist culture:

Wann aber solches *entretien* nicht *a la moderne accomodirt* ist / so werden gewiß die Damen einen schlechten *gusto* darvon haben / und viel lieber *Cavalliers discuriren* hören / als *scholaren*. Der Herr *perdonire* meiner *libertet* im Reden / ich will mich *candidè expectoriren*: Die *tratementi* der Gespräch-Spiel sind nicht wenig mit der Schulfüxerey *parfumiret*, und bringen viel *res sur le tapis*, welche unter den *Philosophis* besser als unter den Damen können *agitiret* werden.[122]

[But if such a treatise is not in keeping with the style *à la moderne*, it will provide the ladies only with a poor *gusto*, so that they will rather hear *Cavalliers* speak than *scholares*. *Pardon* the *liberté* of my discourse, I wish to express myself *candidè*. The *tratementi* of the *Gespräch-Spiele* are strongly *parfumé* with schoolmasters' pedantry, and they bring many *res sur le tapis*, which would be better discussed among the *philosophes* than by ladies.]

Harsdörffer's parodic German-French-Latin medley illustrates that what he calls a "verständige Gesprächübung" (exercise in sensible conversation) must go beyond addressing only learned men. It is time, rather, to step down from the presumed heights of academic jargon to the mother tongue, which non-formally trained women too can understand and use in a literary manner.

Breaching the language barrier between humanism and scholasticism also signified that the nonacademic laity would begin to influence matters of taste. Traditional scholarly benchmarks — the canon, the emulative ideal of imitating or surpassing models, a defined referential horizon, and the dominance of theory — would be gradually absorbed into a notion that all humans are capable, by using their natural reason, of exercising appropriate critical judgment. For *Weibspersonen* (women) to be included among readers of literature in modern languages not only signified their liberation from the ghetto of pious, edifying pamphletry, but at last acknowledged their intellectual abilities, already obvious enough in the rational operation of their households. A female member of the group points this out:

Solte man nun auch des Lesens der ergetzlichen Lustgedichte uns berauben / würden wir gewiß aller Weltlichen Händel / Wolredenheit / Höflichkeit / und Gemüths-Belustigung entnommen / unsere angeborne Einfalt noch in viel grössern Schimpff und Spott setzt [sic] / da uns doch zu Regierung deß Hauswesens nicht weniger Verstand / so durch das Lesen ausgeschärffet wird / vonnöhten als denen / welchen Land und Leute zu beherrschen obliget.[123]

[If we were to be deprived of reading pleasant poetry we would be removed from the world's affairs, its eloquence, its manners, and its entertainments, and our native simplicity would be condemned and ridiculed, even though governing our households demands no less reason, which reading can enhance, than is needed to govern a country and its people.]

Harsdörffer was often accused by so-called *Schulfüchse* (school foxes, that is, old-fashioned teachers) of having a contempt for Latin and thus of being unscientific. Quite to the contrary, he had a high regard for the communicative and scientific qualities of scholarly discourse, and certainly Latin, as his early Latin writings demonstrate.[124] Because terminology in the German language still needed to be developed by scholars, Harsdörffer did not aim his criticism at the auxiliary vocabulary of the sciences but at the undisciplined use of the language in law courts and government activities, in sociable gatherings, and in the belles lettres. Like other representatives of the seventeenth-century language and literature societies, he condemned the indiscriminate mixing of German with other tongues, but certainly not the learning and proper use of foreign languages. Contaminating German with Latin was as bad as writing *à la mode*, including French words everywhere. Both vices met with his patriotic revulsion, as they detracted from what he most wanted to achieve, namely, the unity of the nation, symbolized in its language and culture, for only this could guarantee economic and scientific progress. The efforts of Harsdörffer and his allies on behalf of the German language shared a purpose with the French Academy and the general European movement for *umanesimo volgare* (humanism in the language of the people): to make manifest the distinctiveness and merits of the language shared by all the people of a powerful, unified state. The small size and relative weakness of the German middle classes, however, which had abandoned the protected culture of the Latin republic of letters and now wished to assume responsibility and gain public acknowledgment at least in the cultural sphere, made this a difficult venture.

Toward the end of the Baroque era modernized theories of education gained ground that were to fulfill the exploitative needs of political utility. Students should master eloquence free of *Schwulst* (bombast) and florid pomp and should cultivate instead the rules of refined courtly conversation and etiquette; they should think of poetry as a *galant* diversion for idle hours. Christian Weise (1642–1708) built upon this utilitarian rationale in a voluminous corpus of Latin and German rhetorics, poetics, school dramas — more than sixty, some dealing with current events — and "political" novels that instructed readers in the ways of the world. As a private tutor, teacher at the Gymnasium in Weissenfels, and rector in Zittau since 1678, Weise adapted the traditional school curriculum to provide what members of the courtly nobility and aspiring bureaucrats alike needed for their careers.[125] This meant rejecting florid speech and useless disputations. Following the model of the elitist *Ritterakademien* (schools for young nobles),[126] mathematics and physics, political administration and law received increased attention; students were even encouraged to read "newspapers."[127]

All of the authors mentioned in this section were concerned with education for practical life. Comenius especially admired the ambitious reforms of Wolfgang Ratichius (Ratke, 1571–1635),[128] who declared himself a "Didaktiker," focusing on pedagogical theory and methods. On 7 April 1635, at the Imperial Diet assembled at Frankfurt am Main, Ratichius presented a *memorandum* that advocated universal educational reform (free of the chiliastic elements in Comenius) as an urgent priority for the nation. His opening three points define its aims and intellectual framework:

Wolfg. Ratichius weiß mit Göttlicher hülffe zu Dienst vnd Wolfahrt der gantzen Christenheit Anleitung zu geben.

1. Wie die Ebraische, Grechische, Lateinische vnd Andere sprachen mehr, Jn gahr kürtzer Zeit, so wol bey Alten Alß Jungen Leichtlich zu lernen vnd fortzupflantzen sein.

2. Wie nicht Allein Jn hochteutscher, sondern Auch in Allen Andern Sprachen ein Schule Anzurichten, darinnen Alle Künste vnd Faculteten außführlich können gelernet vnd propagirt werden.

3. Wie Im Gantzen Reich, ein einträchtige Sprach, ein einträchtige Regierung, vnd Endlich Auch ein einträchtige Religion, bequemlich ein zuführen, und friedlich zuerhalten sey vnd mit Göttlicher hülffe zu.[129]

[Wolfgang Ratichius knows, with God's help, how to guide all Christendom to well-being.

1. How Hebrew, Greek, Latin, and other languages may quickly be learned and then taught by young and old.

2. How schools may be established, not only for German but also for all other languages, in which all skills and subjects may be learned and propagated comprehensively.

3. How throughout the empire a unified language, a unified government, and a unified religion may be conveniently instituted and preserved in peace with God's help.]

The details and the resonance of proclamations of reform such as this one ultimately depended on political and economic considerations. Because the traditional humanist school left the middle classes — craftsmen, shopkeepers, merchants — without educational institutions of their own, their attention turned to the flourishing economies of countries like the Netherlands, making them acutely aware of the backwardness threatening Germany. Ratichius did not plan to do away with Latin and Greek, but he did insist that German be the preferred language of instruction and that it be, within limits, taught as an independent subject. In their formal evaluation of Ratichius's plan, Christoph Helwig (1581–1617), professor of Hebrew and Greek in Giessen, and Joachim Jungius (1587–1657), professor of natural sciences in Hamburg, stressed that achieving the practical capabilities needed for prosperity was interdependent with teaching in the native language:

Zu dem ist es auch die lautere warheit / dz alle Kunst vnd Wissenschaften / als Vernunfftkunst / Sitten- vnd Regierkunst / Maß- Wesen- Naturkündigung / Artzeney- Figur- Gewicht- Stern-Baw- Befestkunst / oder wie sie Nahmen haben mögen / viel leichter / bequemer / richtiger vollkömlicher vnd außführlicher in Teutscher Sprach können gelehret vnd fortgepflanzet werden. [. . .] Dadurch dann nicht allein die Teutsche Sprach vnd Nation mercklich gebessert und erhaben / sondern auch die Künste vnnd Wissenschafften selbst mit newen Erfindungen / Auffmerckungen / Bewehrungen Erörterungen vnsäglich können gemehret / gegründet / befestiget und erkleret werden. Dann [. . .] muß vngleich mer besserung erfolgen / wenn eine solche weitleufftige Nation mit gesampten fleiß in Künsten arbeiten würd.[130]

[Furthermore, it is the simple truth that all such arts and sciences as philosophy, morals and politics, geometry, taxonomy, natural science, medicine, sculpture, statics, astronomy, architecture, and fortification, or any other, can be taught and propagated more correctly, more perfectly, and more comprehensively in German. That would not only truly improve and ennoble the German language and nation, but the arts and sciences would be immeasurably nourished, supported, strengthened, and enlightened by new inventions, treatises, applications, and discussions. Then a still greater improvement must occur if such a large nation expects to exercise thoroughly all of its skills.]

Like Comenius, though in a more pragmatic context, Ratichius set forth a plan for "Allunterweisung" (the literal German word for "encyclopedia," meaning "instruction in every topic") and described seven branches of an educational design that recognized the arts of speaking and comprehending as well as an early metatheory of didactics, or instructional methodology. By insisting, especially for the needs of the higher faculties of theology and law, that a specifically German terminology be created, Ratichius was pointing out a shortcoming that could, for the moment, be corrected only through isolated efforts in German, such as Schottelius's *Ethik* (1669). To remedy matters in respect to loanwords and loan translations in grammatical terminology, Ratichius himself published *Allgemeine Sprachlehr* (General Manual of Language, 1619). Some of his expressions — *Ausrufungszeichen* (exclamation mark), *einsilbig* (monosyllabic), *Vorwort* (pronoun), *Wortbedeutung* (a word's meaning) — are still current today.

In the years that followed, Ratichius's criticisms continued to be effective, for example, for the widely traveled social satirist Johann Balthasar Schupp (1610–61), professor in Marburg and later pastor in Hamburg.[131] Although Schupp acknowledged the value of Latin, he also polemicized against its "Tyrannei" in schools when it provided no apparent advantage over colloquial German for the common people. Schupp argues in terms of causes and effects within society; he openly identifies as oppression the fact that certain professions are open only to people who have acquired some Latin. He often reflects on how European nations have cultivated their own vernaculars and that this has benefited ordinary people. He scolds contemporary German "halbgelehrte Tiere" (half-learned beasts) as poor substitutes for the veritable "ReligionsWerck" (literally, work of religion, i.e., the Reformation) of the previous century, but also the well-conducted schools presently flourishing in other countries,

daß in allen Wissenschafften / auch unter den gemeinen Handwerckern / die allergeschickteste gefunden werden / das der so mit jhnen umbgehet / sich schämen muß / zu gedencken daß er studiret habe. Wenn aber die

Handgewerbe wol floriren und im Schwange gehen / so muß denn auch das gemeine Wesen in gutem Auffnehmen seyn / und das Geld von andern Orten herbey gebracht werden. (538)

[such that, in all occupations, among common artisans too, we find the most skillful people, so that when a (German) who has studied encounters them, he feels ashamed (for his own country). When the crafts are flourishing and prosperous, society in general is at peace, and money from elsewhere flows in.]

Schupp betrays his middle-class outlook in the way he stresses the essentially economic aspects of princely rule; he does not criticize the court's monopoly on power so much as its inability or lack of will to conduct its affairs according to the solid mercantile principle of profit and loss. He valued conditions in the Netherlands, where he had traveled as a young man and which became for him a significant intellectual and social point of reference. Although Schupp discusses practical aspects of society and the state in his critique, his opposition to the sophistic narrow-mindedness of the humanist tradition is by no means an attack on the political system. In his *Salomo Oder Regenten-Spiegel* (Solomon, or a Mirror for Regents, 1657), written as a manual for rulers and a treatise on the state in the tradition of Dietrich Reinkingk's (1590–1664) *Biblische Policey* (Biblical Governance, 1653), the undiluted vehemence of rigorously Bible-driven Christian orthodoxy confronts the "Pedanterey" of academic "Politik."

For the time being, however, such advances had little effect on the daily routine of most scholarly institutions. Ratichius's situation was somewhat exceptional. Having found a patron in Prince Ludwig of Anhalt-Köthen, the head of the Fruchtbringende Gesellschaft, Germany's foremost intellectual society, he was able to implement some of his experiments in Köthen and in the Weimar School Regulations of 1619 and to have his works published by the court printer at Köthen.[132] The stigma of failure could only be relieved in such places where a distinguished schoolmaster or university professor was able to put ideas of pedagogical reform into practice. This applies to Christian Weise to a certain degree and conspicuously so to Erhard Weigel (1625–99), professor of mathematics at Jena, who borrowed certain of Comenius's ideas.[133] Weigel is best known, however, for bringing to the forefront instruction in mathematics and natural sciences (including technological instruction) as a patriotic cause of enhancing the common good.

Thus, the modernizing pedagogy of the Baroque period increasingly reflected needs of the middle classes, though these needs would find no fulfillment for still another century. Neither Ratichius's nor Comenius's ideas had any significance in the next century for the enlightened reorganization of academic faculties. Rather, following the lead of Christian Thomasius, it was the theory of *criticism*, guided by reason, that initiated scrutiny of both personal and social *Vorurteile* (prejudices), including blind traditionalism and political confessionalism.[134]

Translated by Michael M. Metzger

Notes

Key to frequently cited works in the endnotes

ASD = *Opera omnia Desiderii Erasmi Roterodami, recognita et adnotatione critica instructa notisque illustrata.* Amsterdam: North Holland, 1969–.

Barockrhetorik = Wilfried Barner. *Barockrhetorik: Untersuchungen zu ihren geschichtlichen Grundlagen.* Tübingen: Niemeyer, 1970.

CE = *Contemporaries of Erasmus: A Biographical Register of the Renaissance and Reformation.* 3 vols. Ed. Peter G. Bietenholz and Thomas B. Deutscher. Toronto: U of Toronto P, 1985–87.

Clericus = *Desiderii Erasmi Roterodami Opera in decem tomos distincta.* 11 vols. Ed. Ioannes Clericus. Leiden, 1703–6; reprint, Hildesheim: Ohms, 1961–62.

Dichter 17 = *Deutsche Dichter des 17. Jahrhunderts: Ihr Leben und Werk.* Ed. Harald Steinhagen and Benno von Wiese. Berlin: Schmidt, 1984.

DLB 179 = *Dictionary of Literary Biography.* Vol. 179: *German Writers of the Renaissance and Reformation, 1280–1580.* Ed. Max Reinhart and James Hardin. Detroit: Gale Research, 1997.

Dünnhaupt = *Personalbibliographien zu den Drucken des Barock.* 6 vols. Ed. Gerhard Dünnhaupt. Stuttgart: Hiersemann, 1990–93.

EE = *Opus epistolarum Desiderii Erasmi Roterodami.* Ed. P. S. Allen. 12 vols. Oxford: Clarendon, 1906–58.

Glaser = *Deutsche Literatur: Eine Sozialgeschichte.* Ed. Horst Albert Glaser. Vol. 2: *Von der Handschrift zum Buchdruck: Spätmittelalter — Reformation — Humanismus 1320–1572.* Reinbek b. Hamburg: Rowohlt, 1991; Vol. 3: *Zwischen Gegenreformation und Frühaufklärung: Späthumanismus, Barock 1572–1740.* 1985.

GuF = Wilhelm Kühlmann. *Gelehrtenrepublik und Fürstenstaat: Entwicklung und Kritik des deutschen Späthumanismus in der Literatur des Barockzeitalters.* Tübingen: Niemeyer, 1982.

HWR = *Historisches Wörterbuch der Rhetorik.* 6 vols. Ed. Gert Ueding. Tübingen: Niemeyer, 1992–.

LL = *Literatur-Lexikon: Autoren und Werke deutscher Sprache.* Ed. Walther Killy. Gütersloh: Bertelsmann Lexikon, 1988–.

LuG = Gunter E. Grimm. *Literatur und Gelehrtentum in Deutschland: Untersuchungen zum Wandel ihres Verhältnisses vom Humanismus bis zur Frühaufklärung.* Tübingen: Niemeyer, 1983.

Philosophie 17 = *Die Philosophie des 17. Jahrhunderts.* Vols. 4/1 and 4/2: *Das Heilige Römische Reich Deutscher Nation: Nord- und Ostmitteleuropa.* Ed. Helmut Holzhey and Wilhelm Schmidt-Biggemann, with Vilem Mudroch. Basel: Schwabe, 2001.

RL = *Reallexikon der deutschen Literaturwissenschaft.* 3 vols. Ed. Klaus Weimar, with Harald Fricke, Klaus Grubmüller, and Jan-Dirk Müller. Berlin: de Gruyter, 1997–.

TRE = *Theologische Realenzyklopädie.* 35 vols. Ed. Gerhard Krause and Gerhard Müller. Berlin: de Gruyter, 1977–.

VD = *Verzeichnis der im deutschen Sprachbereich erschienenen Drucke des 16. Jahrhunderts.* To date: Abteilung 1, 22 vols.; Abteilung 2, 3 vols. Ed. Irmgard Bezzel and Bayerische Staatsbibliothek, Munich, with Herzog August Bibliothek, Wolfenbüttel. Stuttgart: Hiersemann, 1983–2002.

Verfasserlexikon = Die deutsche Literatur des Mittellalters: Verfasserlexikon. 2nd ed. Ed. Kurt Ruh et al. 11 vols. Berlin: de Gruyter, 1978–2004.

WA = *Martin Luthers Werke: Kritische Gesamtausgabe* (Weimarer Ausgabe). Weimar: Böhlau, 1883–.

Welzig = *Erasmus von Rotterdam: Ausgewählte Schriften, Lateinisch und deutsch.* Ed. Werner Welzig. 8 vols. Darmstadt: Wissenschaftliche Buchgesellschaft, 1967–80.

[1] Günther Dohmen, *Bildung und Schule: Die Entstehung des deutschen Bildungsbegriffs und die Entwicklung seines Verhältnisses zur Schule*, 2 vols. (Weinheim: Beltz, 1964–65); Ernst Lichtenstein, *Zur Entwicklung des Bildungsbegriffs von Meister Eckhart bis Hegel* (Heidelberg: Quelle & Meyer, 1966); Hans Weil, *Die Entstehung des deutschen Bildungsprinzips*, 2nd ed. (Bonn: Bouvier, 1967); Georg Bollenbeck, *Bildung und Kultur: Glanz und Elend eines deutschen Deutungsmusters*, 2nd ed. (Frankfurt am Main: Insel, 1994). With respect to the entire range and depth of this theme see *Handbuch der deutschen Bildungsgeschichte*, vol. 1, *15. bis 17. Jahrhundert*, ed. Notker Hammerstein (Munich: Beck, 1996), esp. the following contributions: August Buck on "italienischer Humanismus," Hammerstein on "historische und bildungsgeschichtliche Physiognomie des konfessionellen Zeitalters," Paul Münch on "Lebensformen, Lebenswelten und Umgangserziehung," Klaus Arnold on "Familie-Kindheit-Jugend," Arno Seifert on "höhere Schulwesen, Universitäten und Gymnasien," and Wilhelm Kühlmann, "Pädagogische Konzeptionen," which is basic to the present discussion. Among the available studies that overlap in part with mine: Eugenio Garin, *Geschichte und Dokumente der abendländischen Pädagogik*, comp. and ed. Eckhardt Keßler, vol. 2, *Humanismus*, vol. 3, *Von der Reformation bis John Locke* (Reinbek b. Hamburg: Rowohlt, 1966–67); Theodor Ballauff and Klaus Schaller, *Pädagogik: Eine Geschichte der Bildung und Erziehung*, 3 vols. (Freiburg i.B.: Alber, 1969–73); Ernst Lichtenstein, "Bildung," in *Historisches Wörterbuch der Philosophie*, ed. Joachim Ritter (Darmstadt: Wissenschaftliche Buchgesellschaft, 1971), 1:921–37; Wolfgang Reinhard, ed., *Humanismus im Bildungswesen des 15. und 16. Jahrhunderts* (Weinheim: Acta Humaniora, 1984); Fritz-Peter Hager, "Bildung," in *Der Neue Pauly: Enzyklopädie der Antike*, ed. Hubert Cancik (Stuttgart: Metzler, 1999), 13:505–15. For the older scholarship see Karl Adolf Schmid, ed., *Enzyklopädie des gesamten Erziehungs- und Unterrichtswesens*, 10 vols., 2nd ed. (Gotha: Besser, 1876–87); Friedrich Paulsen, *Geschichte des gelehrten Unterrichts auf den deutschen Schulen und Universitäten vom Ausgang des Mittelalters bis zur Gegenwart*, 2 vols., 2nd ed. (Leipzig, 1896).

[2] See Emil Reicke, ed., *Willibald Pirckheimers Briefwechsel*, vol. 1 (Munich: Beck, 1940), esp. the first letters with the father's behavioral rules (29ff.) and list of books to be acquired. On Pirckheimer (including his translations of pedagogical writings), Niklas Holzberg, *Willibald Pirckheimer: Griechischer Humanismus in Deutschland* (Munich: Fink, 1981); on the German-Italian exchange, Agostino Sottili, "Ehemalige Studenten italienischer Renaissance-Universitäten: ihre Karriere und soziale Rollen," in *Gelehrte im Reich: Zur Sozial- und Wirkungsgeschichte akademischer Eliten des 14. bis 16.*

Jahrhunderts, Beiheft 18 of *Zeitschrift für historische Forschung,* ed. Rainer Christoph Schwinges (Berlin: Duncker & Humblot, 1996), 41–74.

[3] On Piccolomini see Franz Josef Worstbrock, in *Verfasserlexikon* 7:634–69; also Paul Weinert, in LL 9:157–60.

[4] August Buck, "Die studia humanitatis und ihre Methode," in *Die humanistische Tradition in der Romania* (Bad Homburg: Gehlen, 1968), 133–49; Buck, ed., *Zu Begriff und Problem der Renaissance* (Darmstadt: Wissenschaftliche Buchgesellschaft, 1969); Buck, "Der Wissenschaftsbegriff des Renaissance-Humanismus," in *400 Jahre Bibliothek zu Wolfenbüttel* (Frankfurt am Main: Klostermann, 1973), 45–63; Buck, *Studien zu Humanismus und Renaissance* (Wiesbaden: Harrassowitz, 1991). Still standard are the many studies by Paul Oskar Kristeller, including *The Renaissance Philosophy of Man* (Chicago: U of Chicago P, 1956), *Renaissance Philosophy and the Mediaeval Tradition* (Latrobe, PA: Archabbey, 1966), and *Renaissance Concepts of Man, and Other Essays* (New York: Harper and Row, 1972). On Italian humanism see esp. Gregor Müller, *Mensch und Bildung im italienischen Renaissance-Humanismus* (Baden-Baden: Koerner, 1984). Also of importance: William Harrison Woodward, *Studies in Education during the Age of Renaissance 1400–1600* (1906; repr., New York: Teachers College P, 1967); Charles G. Nauert, Jr., "The Humanist Challenge to Medieval German Literature," *Daphnis* 15 (1986): 277–306; Charles Trinkaus, *The Scope of Renaissance Humanism* (Ann Arbor: U of Michigan P, 1988); Albert Rabil Jr., ed., *Renaissance Humanism: Foundations, Forms and Legacy,* 3 vols. (Philadelphia: U of Pennsylvania P, 1988), here esp. vol. 3, *Humanism and the Disciplines,* and Hans-Ulrich Musolff, *Erziehung und Bildung in der Renaissance: Von Vergerio bis Montaigne* (Cologne: Böhlau, 1997). On the post-Reformation period see Gerald Strauss, *Luther's House of Learning: Indoctrination of the Young in the German Reformation* (Baltimore: Johns Hopkins UP, 1978).

[5] On the humanistic turn to the sources see in this volume the chapter by Erika Rummel.

[6] The eudaemonic question regarding human purpose and life's highest purpose implies further the dichotomy between the Stoic control of the emotions on the one hand and the conception on the other of a kind of happiness rooted in pleasure and satisfaction (*voluptas*). In Italy it had been raised by Lorenzo Valla in *De voluptate* (1431) and in northern Europe by Erasmus in many of his writings. On these conflicts, and including references to earlier scholarship see Claudia Schmitz, *Rebellion und Bändigung der Lust: Dialogische Inszenierung konkurrierender Konzepte vom glücklichen Leben (1460–1540)* (Tübingen: Niemeyer, 2004).

[7] This is the title of part 4 of *Die Kultur der Renaissance in Italien* (1860).

[8] In this regard, Wilhelm Kühlmann, "Poeten und Puritaner: Christliche und pagane Poesie im deutschen Humanismus," *Pirckheimer-Jahrbuch* 8 (1993): 149–80; also Joachim Dyck, *Athen und Jerusalem: Die Tradition der argumentativen Verknüpfung von Bibel und Poesie im 17. und 18. Jahrhundert* (Munich: Beck, 1977), and Dyck, *Ticht-Kunst: Deutsche Barockpoetik und rhetorische Tradition,* 3rd ed. (Tübingen: Niemeyer, 1991), esp. "Christliche Literaturtheorie," 135–73; also August Buck, "Der Rückgriff des Renaissancehumanismus auf die Patristik," in *Festschrift, Walter von Wartburg,* ed. Kurt Baldinger (Tübingen: Niemeyer, 1968), 153–75. For an outstanding reception study see Luzi Schucan, *Das Nachleben von Basilius Magnus "Ad Adolescentes": Ein Beitrag zur Geschichte des christlichen Humanismus* (Geneva: Droz, 1973).

[9] On this question see *Barockrhetorik,* 258–366. For a discussion of academic declamatory literature see GuF; on scholarly writing, LuG.

[10] Paradigmatic works are Konrad Heresbach, *De educandis erudiendisque principum liberis* (Frankfurt am Main, 1570); Reinhard Lorichius, *Paedagogia Principum: Das ist: Ein [. . .] Tractatlein / wie [. . .] man der hohen Potentaten [. . .] Kinder vorstehen soll* (Frankfurt am Main, 1595); Georg Engelhard Löhneyss, *Aulico Politica: Darin gehandelt wird 1: Von Erziehung und Information Junger Herren* (Remlingen, 1622). On the education of princes, Wilhelm Münch, *Gedanken über Fürstenerziehung aus alter und neuer Zeit* (Munich: Beck, 1909); Hans Heim, *Fürstenerziehung im 16. Jahrhundert: Beiträge zur Geschichte ihrer Theorie* (Paderborn, 1918); Jörg Jochen Müller, "Fürstenerziehung im 17. Jahrhundert: Am Beispiel Anton Ulrichs von Braunschweig und Lüneburg," in *Stadt — Schule — Universität — Buchwesen und die deutsche Literatur im 17. Jahrhundert*, ed. Albrecht Schöne (Munich: Beck, 1976), 243–60; Ludwig Fertig, *Der Hofmeister: Ein Beitrag zur Geschichte des Lehrerstandes und der bürgerlichen Intelligenz* (Stuttgart: Metzler, 1979); Notker Hammerstein, "Fürstenerziehung der Frühen Neuzeit am Beispiel Hessen-Homburg," in *Bad Homburg v. d. H.*, ed. Erich Gunkel (Bad Homburg: Grasberg, 1983), 133–90; Hammerstein, "'Großer fürtrefflicher Leute Kinder': Fürstenerziehung zwischen Humanismus und Reformation," in *Renaissance — Reformation: Gegensätze und Gemeinsamkeiten*, ed. August Buck (Wiesbaden: Harrassowitz, 1984), 265–86; Laetitia Böhm, "Konservatismus und Modernität in der Regentenerziehung an deutschen Höfen im 15. und 16. Jahrhundert," in Reinhard, ed., *Humanismus im Bildungswesen*, 61–94 (see note 1).

[11] For the early period see esp. Hans Rupprich, *Die deutsche Literatur vom Späten Mittelalter bis zum Barock*, part 1, *Das ausgehende Mittelalter, Humanismus und Renaissance 1370–1520*, 2nd ed., revised by Hedwig Heger (Munich: Beck, 1994), esp. 435–60 and 652–99; Volkhard Wels, *Triviale Künste: Die humanistische Reform der grammatischen, dialektischen und rhetorischen Ausbildung an der Wende zum 16. Jahrhundert* (Berlin: Weidler, 2000).

[12] This is summarized and further developed in Jörg Jochen Berns and Wolfgang Neuber, eds., *Seelenmaschinen: Gattungstraditionen, Funktionen und Leistungsgrenzen der Mnemotechniken vom späten Mittelalter bis zum Beginn der Moderne* (Vienna: Böhlau, 2000).

[13] This topic and others identified by the abbreviation "NL" will be found treated in a different context, namely, in the companion chapter by Kühlmann in this volume "Neo-Latin Literature in Early Modern Germany." On German-language drama see also in this volume the chapter by John Alexander.

[14] Alois Bömer, *Die lateinischen Schülergespräche der Humanisten*, 2 vols. (Berlin: Harrwitz, 1897–99); Gerhard Streckenbach, *Stiltheorie und Rhetorik der Römer im Spiegel der humanistischen Schülergespräche* (Göttingen: Gratia, 1979).

[15] On humanists as editors and on early modern text editions see in this volume the chapter by Rummel and that by Roloff.

[16] See esp. Jürgen Leonhardt, "Exegetische Vorlesungen in Erfurt 1500–1520," in *Humanismus in Erfurt*, ed. Gerlinde Huber-Rebenich and Walther Ludwig (Rudolstadt: Hain, 2002), 91–108; for the entire country, Nikolaus Henkel, *Deutsche Übersetzungen lateinischer Schultexte: Ihre Verbreitung und Funktion im Mittelater und in der frühen Neuzeit* (Munich: Artemis, 1988). On the subject of lectures in the period of early humanism see Ludwig Bertalot, "Humanistische Vorlesungsankündigungen in Deutschland im 15. Jahrhundert," in his *Studien zum italienischen und deutschen Humanismus*, ed. Paul Oskar Kristeller (Rome: Edizioni di Storia e Letteratura, 1975), 1:219–49.

[17] See esp. Helmut Zedelmaier, *Bibliotheca universalis und Bibliotheca selecta: Das Problem der Ordnung des gelehrten Wissens in der frühen Neuzeit* (Cologne: Böhlau, 1992); Joseph Freedman, "Encyclopedic Philosophical Writings in Central Europe During the High and Late Renaissance (ca. 1500–1700)," *Archiv für Begriffsgeschichte* 37 (1994): 212–56; Franz M. Eybl, ed., *Enyzklopädien der frühen Neuzeit: Beiträge zu Ihrer Erforschung* (Tübingen: Niemeyer, 1995); Udo Friedrich, "Grenzen des Ordo im enzyklopädischen Schrifttum des 16. Jahrhunderts," in *Die Enzyklopädie im Wandel vom Hochmittelalter bis zur frühen Neuzeit*, ed. Christel Meier (Munich: Fink, 2002), 391–408 and 576–79; Gilbert Heß, "Konstanz und Beweglichkeit in frühneuzeitlichen Florilegien und Enyzklopädien," in *Autorität der Form — Autorisierung — Konstitutionelle Autorität*, ed. Wulf Oesterreicher et al. (Münster: Lit, 2003), 75–84; in the same volume, Martin Schierbaum, "Vorbildhaftigkeit — Konkurrenz — Kontinuität: Probleme der Antikerezeption in den Bibliographien und Eyzklopädien der frühen Neuzeit," 85–104.

[18] Wilhelm Kühlmann, "Lektüre für den Bürger: Eigenart und Vermittlungsfunktion der polyhistorischen Reihenwerke Martin Zeillers," in *Literatur und Volk im 17. Jahrhundert*, ed. Wolfgang Brückner et al. (Wiesbaden: Harrassowitz, 1985), 917–34; Kühlmann, "Polyhistorie jenseits der Systeme: Zur funktionellen Pragmatik und publizistischen Typologie frühneuzeitlicher 'Buntschriftstellerei,'" in *Erschließung und Speicherung von Wissen in der Frühen Neuzeit*, ed. Frank Grunert and Fritz Vollhardt (in press).

[19] Still useful in this regard, Reinhold Vormbaum, ed., *Evangelische Schulordnungen*, 2 vols. (Gütersloh, 1860–63); also Paulsen, *Geschichte des gelehrten Unterrichts* (see note 1).

[20] On Trotzendorf see Jörg Köhler, in LL 11:428.

[21] On Sturm's *oeuvre* and the scholarship on it see Heinz Holeczek, in LL 11:272–73; also the older work by Walther Sohm, *Die Schule Johann Sturms und die Kirche Straßburgs* (Munich: Oldenbourg, 1912); most important, Anton Schindling, *Humanistische Hochschule und Freie Reichsstadt: Gymnasium und Akademie in Straßburg 1538–1621* (Wiesbaden: Steiner, 1977).

[22] Justin Stagl, *Apodemiken: Eine räsonnierte Bibliographie der reisetheoretischen Literatur des 16., 17. und 18. Jahrhunderts* (Paderborn: Schöningh, 1983); additional scholarship inventoried by Wolfgang Neuber, "Der Arzt und das Reisen: Zum Anleitungsverhältnis von Regimen und Apodemik," in *Heilkunde und Krankheitserfahrung in der frühen Neuzeit*, ed. Udo Benzenhöfer and Wilhelm Kühlmann (Tübingen: Niemeyer, 1992), 94–113.

[23] See esp. Gundolf Keil, "Organisationsformen medizinischen Wissens," in *Wissensorganisierende und wissensvermittelnde Literatur im Mittelalter: Perspektiven ihrer Erforschung*, ed. Norbert Richard Wolf (Wiesbaden: Reichert, 1985). An overview of the early modern period on this subject remains to be written. Meanwhile see Werner Friedrich Kümmel, "Der *Homo litteratus* und die Kunst, gesund zu leben: Zur Entfaltung eines Zweiges der Diätetik im Humanismus," in *Humanismus und Medizin*, ed. Rudolf Schmitz and Gundolf Keil (Weinheim: Acta Humaniora, 1984), 67–86; for an analogous example from poetry, Harry Vredeveld, "Helius Eobanus Hessus' *Bonae Valetudinis Conservandae Rationes Aliquot*: An Inquiry into its Sources," *Janus* 72 (1975): 83–112; finally, the exhibition catalogue compiled by Joachim Telle, *Pharmazie und der gemeine Mann*, 2nd ed. (Weinheim: Acta Humaniora, 1988).

[24] References to scholarship are included in the collection of sources compiled by Johann Anselm Steiger, *Melancholie, Diätetik und Trost: Konzepte der Melancholie-Therapie im 16. und 17. Jahrhundert* (Heidelberg: Manutius, 1996).

25 For an introduction to this wide terrain see Will-Erich Peuckert, *Gabalia: Ein Versuch zur Geschichte der magia naturalis im 16. bis 18. Jahrhundert* (Berlin: Schmidt, 1967).

26 Moral philosophy included the subcategories ethics, economics, and politics. On political writings and related genres see GuF 43–66 and 319–71; Peter Jochen Winters, *Die Politik des Johannes Althusius und ihre zeitgenösischen Quellen: Zur Grundlage der politischen Wissenschaft im 16. und beginnenden 17. Jahrhundert* (Freiburg i.B.: Rombach, 1963); Horst Dreitzel, *Protestantischer Aristotelismus und absoluter Staat: Die "Politica" des Henning Arnisaeus (ca. 1575–1636)* (Wiesbaden: Steiner, 1970); for the broadest view, Michael Stolleis, *Geschichte des öffentlichen Rechts in Deutschland*, vol. 1, *Reichspublizistik und Policeywissenschaft* (Munich: Beck, 1988). On the important subcategory of prudent-political reception of antiquity see Kühlmann, "Geschichte als Gegenwart: Formen der politischen Reflexion im deutschen Tacitismus des 17. Jahrhunderts," in *Literatur im Elsaß von Fischart bis Moscherosch: Gesammelte Studien*, ed. Kühlmann and Walter E. Schäfer (Tübingen: Niemeyer, 2001), 41–60.

27 In addition to Stolleis, *Geschichte des öffentlichen Rechts* (see note 26), see Bruno Singer, *Die Fürstenspiegel in Deutschland im Zeitalter des Humanismus und der Reformation* (Munich: Fink, 1981); Hans-Otto Mühleisen and Theo Stammen, eds., *Politische Tugendlehre und Regierungskunst: Studien zum Fürstenspiegel in der Frühen Neuzeit* (Tübingen: Niemeyer, 1990); on the entire complex of courtly literature, August Buck, ed., *Höfischer Humanismus* (Weinheim: Acta Humaniora, 1989); in the same volume, with respect to the "contact zones" between the court and representatives of the *studia humanitatis*, Jan Dirk Müller, "Der siegreiche Fürst im Entwurf des Gelehrten: Zu den Anfängen des höfischen Humanismus," 17–50, and Wilhelm Kühlmann, "Edelmann — Höfling — Humanist: Zur Behandlung epochaler Rollenprobleme in Ulrich von Huttens Dialog *Aula* und in seinem Brief an Willibald Pirckheimer," 161–82.

28 A specialized study on this textual type remains to be written. For the present state of research, particularly as it relates to Christian Weise, see the following: Dietmar Till, "Politicus," in HWR 6:1422–45; Gotthardt Frühsorge, *Der politische Körper: Zum Begriff des Politischen im 17. Jahrhundert und in den Romanen Christian Weises* (Stuttgart: Metzler, 1974); GuF references the older studies of Gerhard Oestreich; *Barockrhetorik*; and finally Karl-Heinz Mulagk, *Phänomene des politischen Menschen im 17. Jahrhundert* (Berlin: Schmidt, 1973), and Stolleis, *Geschichte des öffentlichen Rechts* (see note 26).

29 Otto Brunner, "Das 'ganze Haus' und die alteuropäische Ökonomik," in his *Neue Wege der Verfassungs- und Sozialgeschichte*, 3rd ed. (Göttingen: Vandenhoeck & Ruprecht, 1980); Julius Hoffmann, *Die "Hausväterliteratur" und die Predigten über den christlichen Hausstand* (Weinheim: Beltz, 1959); Gotthard Frühsorge, "Die Gattung der Oeconomica als Spiegel des adeligen Lebens," in *Arte et Marte*, ed. Dieter Lohmeier (Neumünster: Wachholtz, 1978), 213–35; also Frühsorge, "Die Begründung der 'väterlichen Gesellschaft' in der oeconomia christiana: Zur Rolle des Vaters in der Hausväterliteratur des 16. und 18. Jahrhunderts," in *Das Vaterbild im Abendland*, ed. Hubertus Tellenbach (Stuttgart: Kohlhammer, 1978), 1:110–23.

30 See Helmuth Kiesel, *"Bei Hof, bei Höll": Untersuchungen zur literarischen Hofkritik von Sebastian Brant bis Friedrich Schiller* (Tübingen: Niemeyer, 1979).

31 Ralf Georg Bogner, *Die Bezähmung der Zunge: Literatur und Disziplinierung der Alltagskommunikation in der frühen Neuzeit* (Tübingen: Niemeyer, 1997).

32 Till, "Politicus," 146–80 (see note 28); Georg Braungart and Friedmann Harzer, "Höfische Rhetorik," in HWR 3:1454–76; Karl Borinski, *Balthasar Gracian und die*

Hofliteratur in Deutschland (1894; repr., Tübingen: Niemeyer, 1971); Claus Uhlig, "Moral und Politik in der europäischen Hoferziehung," in *Literatur als Kritik des Lebens*, ed. Rudolf Haas (Heidelberg: Quelle & Meyer, 1975), 25–51; Manfred Beetz, *Frühmoderne Höflichkeit: Komplimentierkunst und Gesellschaftsrituale im alt-deutschen Sprachraum* (Stuttgart: Metzler, 1990); Klaus Conermann, "Der Stil des Hofmanns: Zur Genese sprachlicher und literarischer Formen aus der höfisch-politischen Verhaltenskunst," in *Europäische Hofkultur*, ed. August Buck (Hamburg: Hauswedell, 1979), 1:45–56; Georg Braungart, *Hofberedsamkeit: Studien zur Praxis höfisch-politischer Rede im deutschen Territorialabsolutismus* (Tübingen: Niemeyer, 1988); Ursula Geitner, *Die Sprache der Verstellung: Studien zum rhetorischen und anthropologischen Wissen im 17. und 18. Jahrhundert* (Tübingen: Niemeyer, 1992); Jörg Jochen Berns and Thomas Rahn, eds., *Zeremoniell als höfische Ästhetik in Spätmittelalter und Früher Neuzeit* (Tübingen: Niemeyer, 1995). On the culture of conviviality (*Geselligkeit*) see the discussion below on Harsdörffer, as well as Wolfgang Adam, ed., *Geselligkeit und Gesellschaft im Barockzeitalter* (Wiesbaden: Harrassowitz, 1997).

[33] The standard work on nonacademic rhetoric (including a rich bibliography): Dietmar Till, *Transformationen der Rhetorik: Untersuchungen zum Wandel der Rhetoriktheorie im 17. und 18. Jahrhundert* (Tübingen: Niemeyer, 2004), specifically on the epistle, 197–258; Franz-Josef Worstbrock, ed., *Der Brief im Zeitalter der Renaissance* (Weinheim: Acta Humaniora, 1983); also the articles "Brief" and "Briefsteller," in HWR 2:60–76 and 76–86.

[34] See Barbara Becker-Cantarino, "Die 'gelehrte Frau' und die Institutionen und Organisationsformen der Gelehrsamkeit," in *Res publica litteraria: Die Institutionen der Gelehrsamkeit in der frühen Neuzeit*, ed. Sebastian Neumeister and Conrad Wiedemann (Wiesbaden: Harrassowitz, 1987), 2:559–76; Becker-Cantarino, *Der lange Weg zur Mündigkeit: Frau und Literatur (1550–1800)* (Stuttgart: Metzler, 1987); Paul Gerhard Schmidt, ed., *Die Frau in der Renaissance* (Wiesbaden: Harrassowitz, 1994); Wilhelm Ruhmer, *Pädagogische Theorien über Frauenbildung im Zeitalter der Renaissance* (Bonn: Ludwig, 1915). See also in the present volume the chapter by Anna Carrdus.

[35] See Rüdiger Schnell, ed., *Geschlechterbeziehungen und Textfunktionen — Studien zu Eheschriften der Frühen Neuzeit* (Tübingen: Niemeyer, 1998), including an introductory survey of scholarship; Schnell, *Frauendiskurs, Männerdiskurs, Ehediskurs: Textsorten und Geschlechterkonzepte in Mittelalter und Früher Neuzeit* (Frankfurt am Main: Campus, 1998); Schnell, *Sexualität und Emotionalität in der vormodernen Ehe* (Cologne: Böhlau, 2002); Pia Holenstein, *Der Ehediskurs der Renaissance in Fischarts "Geschichtklitterung"* (Bern: Lang, 1991).

[36] See the concise survey in this volume by Joachim Knape; also Bernhard Asmuth, in HWR 6:1339–54. On the early phase of vernacular rhetoric, Erich Kleinschmidt, "Humanismus und urbane Zivilisation: Friedrich Riedrer (um 1450–1510) und sein 'Spiegel der waren Rhetoric,'" *Zeitschrift für deutsches Altertum und deutsche Literatur* 112 (1983): 269–313; and Heinz Entner, "Zum Dichtungsbegriff des deutschen Humanismus," in *Grundpositionen der deutschen Literatur im 16. Jahrhundert* (Berlin: Aufbau, 1972), 331–480. Further, Volker Sinemus, *Poetik und Rhetorik im frühmodernen Staat: Sozialgeschichtliche Bedingungen des Normenwandels im 17. Jahrhunderts* (Göttingen: Vandenhoeck & Ruprecht, 1978); Entner, "Der Weg zum 'Buch von der deutschen Poeterey,'" in *Studien zur deutschen Literatur im 17. Jahrhundert* (Berlin: Aufbau, 1984), 111–44; for a systematic and detailed study, Bruno Markwardt, *Geschichte der deutschen Poetik*, vol. 1, *Barock und Frühaufklärung*, 3rd ed. (Berlin: de

Gruyter, 1964). The most comprehensive studies of the vast scholarship on the German history of rhetoric are *Barockrhetorik* and Till, "Politicus" (see note 28).

[37] Representative works would be *Politisches Testament* of Melchior von Osse, on which see Stolleis, *Geschichte des öffentlichen Rechts* (see note 26), and Johann Michael Moscherosch's *Insomnis cura Parentum: Vermächtnusz Oder / Schuldige Vorsorge eines Treuen Vaters* (1653, 1678). On Moscherosch see Wilhelm Kühlmann and Walter E. Schäfer, *Frühbarocke Stadtkultur am Oberrhein: Studien zum literarischen Werdegang J. M. Moscheroschs (1601–1669)* (Berlin: Schmidt, 1983), esp. 161–88, which deals with Reformed orthodoxy in Strasbourg.

[38] Susanne Schedl and Dietz Rüdiger Moser, "Erbauungsliteratur," in RL 1:484–88; Dieter Gutzen and Martin Ottmers, "Christliche Rhetorik," and Ottmers, "Erbauungsliteratur," in HWR 2:208–22 and 1347–56; Hans-Henrik Krummmacher, "Überlegungen zur literarischen Eigenart und Bedeutung der protestantischen Erbauungsliteratur im frühen 17. Jahrhundert," *Rhetorik* 5 (1986): 97–113; Krummacher, "Lehr- und trostreiche Lieder: Johann Rists geistliche Dichtung und die Predigt- und Erbauungsliteratur des 16. und 17. Jahrhunderts," in *Vox Sermo Res: Festschrift Uwe Ruberg*, ed. Wolfgang Haubrichs et al. (Stuttgart: Hirzel, 2001), 143–68. Overviews of sermon literature may be found in Johann B. Schneyer, *Geschichte der katholischen Predigt* (Freiburg: Seelsorge, 1969); Urs Herzog, *Geistliche Wohlredenheit: Geschichte der katholischen Barockpredigt* (Munich: Beck, 1991); Werner Welzig, ed., *Predigten der Barockzeit: Texte und Kommentar* (Vienna: Verlag der österreichischen Akademie der Wissenschaften, 1995); Welzig, ed., *Katalog deutschsprachiger katholischer Predigtsammlungen*, 2 vols. (Vienna: Verlag der österreichischen Akademie der Wissenschaften, 1984, 1987); Gottfried Bitter and Albrecht Beutel, "Predigt," in TRE 27:262–312.

[39] See particularly Christoph Moufang, *Katholische Katechismen des 16. Jahrhunderts* (Mainz, 1881); Josef Hofinger, *Geschichte des Katechismus in Österreich von Canisius bis zur Gegenwart* (Innsbruck: Rauch, 1937); Ernst Wilhelm Kohls, *Catechismus: Die evangelischen Katechismen von Ravensburg 1546–1733* (Stuttgart: Kohlhammer, 1963); Kohls, *Evangelische Katechismen der Reformationszeit* (Gütersloh: Gütersloher Verlags-Haus Mohn, 1971); Wolfram Metzger, *Beispielkatechese der Gegenreformation* (Würzburg: Bayerische Blätter für Volkskunde, 1982).

[40] Wolfgang Sommer, *Gottesfurcht und Fürstenherrschaft: Studien zum Obrigkeitsverständnis Johann Arndts und lutherischer Hofprediger zur Zeit der altprotestantischen Orthodoxie* (Göttingen: Vandenhoeck & Ruprecht, 1988).

[41] Comprehensive article by Johann Anselm Steiger, "Seelsorge I," in TRE 31:7–31.

[42] An excellent English translation edition is *Johann Arndt: True Christianity*, trans. and ed. Peter Erb, with a preface by Heiko A. Oberman, The Classics of Western Spirituality (New York: Paulist Press, 1979).

[43] Summarized in Martin Brecht, ed., *Der Pietismus vom siebzehnten bis zum frühen achtzehnten Jahrhundert* (Göttingen: Vandenhoeck & Ruprecht, 1993). On Arndt see Martin Schmidt, in TRE 4:121–29 (includes older scholarship); Edmund Weber, *Johann Arndts "Vier Bücher vom Wahren Christentum" als Beitrag zur protestantischen Irenik des 17. Jahrhunderts: Eine quellenkritische Untersuchung*, 3rd ed. (Hildesheim: Gerstenberg, 1978); Johannes Wallmann, "Herzog August zu Braunschweig und Lüneburg als Gestalt der Kirchengeschichte: Unter besonderer Berücksichtigung seines Verhältnisses zu Johann Arndt," *Pietismus und Neuzeit* 6 (1980): 9–32; Wallmann, "Johann Arndt und die protestantische Frömmigkeit: Zur Rezeption der mittelalterlichen Mystik im

Luthertum," in *Theologie und Frömmigkeit im Zeitalter des Barock: Gesammelte Aufsätze* (Tübingen: Mohr, 1995), 1–19; Hans Schneider, "Johann Arndts 'verschollene' Frühschriften," *Pietismus und Neuzeit* 21 (1995): 29–68; Ferdinand van Ingen, "Die Wiederaufnahme der Devotio Moderna bei Johann Arndt und Philipp von Zesen," in *Religion und Religiosität im Zeitalter des Barock*, ed. Barbara Becker-Cantarino et al. (Wiesbaden: Harrassowitz, 1995), 467–75; Hans Schneider, "Johann Arndts *Vier Bücher von wahrem Christentum*: Offene Fragen der Quellen- und Redaktionskritik," in *Pietas in der Lutherischen Orthodoxie*, ed. Udo Sträter (Wittenberg: Drei-Kastanien, 1998), 61–77; Schneider, "Johann Arndt und die Mystik," in *Zur Rezeption mystischer Traditionen im Protestantismus des 16. bis 19. Jahrhunderts*, ed. Dietrich Meyer and Udo Sträter (Cologne: Rheinland, 2002), 59–90.

[44] Scholars are only beginning to assess the significance of these works. We must exclude from consideration here the breadth and depth of this cultural sector, just as we must the reception in Germany, starting in the seventeenth century, of devotional texts from England.

[45] See C. G. van Leijenhorst, in CE 1:15–17; Fokke Akkerman and A. J. Vanderjagt, eds., *Rodolphus Agricola Phrisius 1444–1485* (Leiden: Brill, 1988), 159–84. An excellent edition of the letters is now available: *Rudolph Agricola: Letters*, ed. and trans. Adrie van der Laan and Fokke Akkerman (Assen: Royal van Gorcum 2002).

[46] Critical edition: *De inventione dialectica libri tres: Drei Bücher über die Inventio dialectica: Auf der Grundlage der Edition von Alardus von Amsterdam (1539)*, ed. and trans. Lothar Mundt (Tübingen: Niemeyer, 1992).

[47] For a revealing look at Trithemius's library see in this volume the chapter by Jill Bepler.

[48] On Hegius see C. G. van Leijenhorst, in CE 2:173; Franz Josef Worstbrock, in *Verfasserlexikon* 3:572–77; E. Brouette, in TRE 8:605–9. On Devotio Moderna see R. Mokrosch, "Verhältnis zu Humanismus und Reformation," in TRE 8:609–16; Albert Hyma, *The Christian Renaissance: A History of the "Devotio Moderna,"* 2nd ed. (Hamden, CT: Archon, 1965); R. R. Post, *The Modern Devotion* (Leiden: Brill, 1968); Georgette Epiney-Burgard, "Die Wege der Bildung in der Devotio Moderna," in *Lebenslehren und Weltentwürfe im Übergang vom Mittelalter zur Neuzeit*, ed. Harmut Bookmann et al. (Göttingen: Vandenhoeck & Ruprecht, 1989), 181–99; also Paul Mestwerdt, *Die Anfänge des Erasmus: Humanismus und "Devotio Moderna"* (1917; repr., New York: Johnson, 1971).

[49] On von Langen see Wilhelm Kühlmann, in LL 7:144, and Robert Stupperich, in CE 2:290–91.

[50] On Mutian see Eckhard Bernstein, in LL 8:319–20, and Erich Kleineidam, in CE 2:473. Also Lewis W. Spitz, "Mutian," in *The Religious Renaissance of the German Humanists* (Cambridge: Harvard UP, 1963); Fritz Halbauer, *Mutianus Rufus und seine geistesgeschichtliche Stellung* (Leipzig: Teubner, 1929); Fidel Rädle, "Mutians Briefwechsel und der Erfurter Humanismus," in Huber-Rebenich and Ludwig, eds., *Humanismus in Erfurt*, 111–29 (see note 16).

[51] On Dringenberg see Franz Josef Worstbrock, in *Verfasserlexikon* 2:235–37; Francis Rapp, "Die Lateinschule von Schlettstadt," in *Studien zum städtischen Bildungswesen des späten Mittelalters und der frühen Neuzeit*, ed. Bernd Moeller et al. (Göttingen: Vandenhoeck & Ruprecht, 1983), 215–34.

[52] See Otto Herding and Dieter Mertens, eds., *Briefwechsel: Kritische Ausgabe mit Einleitung und Kommentar*, 2 vols. (Munich: Fink, 1990).

[53] On humanist patriotism, esp. in conjunction with public law, see Michael Stolleis, "Public Law and Patriotism in the Holy Roman Empire," in *Infinite Boundaries: Order, Disorder, and Reorder in Early Modern German Culture*, ed. Max Reinhart (Kirksville, MO: Thomas Jefferson UP, 1998), 11–33.

[54] Critical edition: *Jakob Wimpfelings Adolescentia*, ed. Otto Herding, with Franz Josef Worstbrock (Munich: Fink, 1965).

[55] On Murmellius see C. G. van Leijenhorst, in CE 2:470–71. Editions: Dietrich Reichling, ed., *Ausgewählte Gedichte: Urtext und metrische Übersetzung* (Freiburg i.B., 1881); Alois Böhmer, ed., *De magistri et discipulorum officiis Epigrammatum liber* (Münster, 1892), *Enchiridion Scholasticorum* (1892); *Elegiarum moralium libri quattuor* (1893), *Pappa Puerorum* (1894); *Scoparius in barbariei propugnatores* (1895); on *Scoparius*, James V. Mehl, "Johannes Murmellius' *Scoparius* (1517–18): Another German Defense of Humanistic Study," in *Acta Conventus Neo-Latini Torontonensis*, ed. Alexander Dalzell et al. (Binghamton, NY: Center for Medieval and Early Renaissance Studies, 1991), 471–80.

[56] On Peter Luder see Frank Baron, in DLB 179, 129–34.

[57] Relevant editions here: Clericus; Welzig; ASD; EE; *Ausgewählte pädagogische Schriften des Desiderius Erasmus*, ed. Dietrich Reichling (includes pedagogical writings by Johannes Ludovicus Vives) (Freiburg i.Br., 1896); *Ausgewählte pädagogische Schriften*, ed. Anton J. Gail (Paderborn: Schöningh, 1963).

[58] On his life see in this volume the chapter by Laurel Carrington. On Erasmus within the history of education, Cornelis Augustijn, *Erasmus von Rotterdam: Leben, Werk und Wirkung*, trans. (from Dutch) Marga E. Baumer (Munich: Beck, 1986); Roland H. Bainton, *Erasmus of Christendom* (New York: Scribner, 1969); Franz Bierlaire, "Erasmus at School: The *De Civilitate Morum Puerilium Libellus*," in *Essays on the Works of Erasmus*, ed. Richard L. DeMolen (New Haven: Yale UP, 1978), 239–51; Jacques Chomarat, ed., *Actes du Colloque international Erasme* (1986; Geneva: Droz, 1990); Léon E. Halkin, *Erasmus von Rotterdam: Eine Biographie*, 2nd ed., trans. (from French) Enrico Heinemann (Zürich: Benziger, 1992); Dietrich Harth, *Philologie und praktische Philosophie: Untersuchungen zum Sprach- und Traditionsverständnis des Erasmus von Rotterdam* (Munich: Fink, 1970); Dilwyn Knox, "Erasmus' *De Civilitate* and the Religious Origins of Civility in Protestant Europe," *Archiv für Reformationsgeschichte* 86 (1995): 7–55; Jan-Dirk Müller, "Warum Cicero? Erasmus' 'Ciceronianus' und das Problem der Autorität," *Scientia Poetica* 3 (1999): 20–46; Richard J. Schoeck, *Erasmus of Europe: The Prince of Humanists*, 2 vols. (Edinburgh: Edinburgh UP, 1990–93); William Harrison Woodward, *Desiderius Erasmus: Concerning the Aim and Method of Education* (1904; repr., New York: Franklin, 1971).

[59] On the complex history of this work's transmission and printing see the introduction to the edition by Kazimierz Kumanecki, in ASD 1:1:7–32.

[60] See in particular Rädle, "Erasmus als Lehrer," in Bookman et al., *Lebenslehren*, 214–15 (see note 48), in connection with Holeczek, "Erasmus von Rotterdam": "Erasmus hat vielleicht wie kein anderer unter seinen Zeitgenossen, auch nach seinem eigenen Selbstverständnis für die Unterweisung der Menschen gewirkt." Erasmus was indeed essentially a teacher of teachers. See Halkin, *Erasmus von Rotterdam*, 31–41 (see note 58). His exemplary letter in 1497 to his young charge Christian Northoff is found in EE 1:172–74. The concept of *mutua benevolentia*, which will be a key to the idea of *humanitas* in *Querela Pacis*, is already present here.

[61] Erasmus wrote *Querela Pacis* in response to an invitation, either directly from the young duke of Burgundy (later Emperor Charles V) or indirectly from the chancellor Jean Le Sauvage, to an international peace conference planned for Cambrai in 1517. The conference never took place, but Erasmus completed his work; Leo Jud translated it into German in 1521. See Alois M. Haas and Urs Herzog, eds., introduction to *"Ein Klag des Frydens": Leo Juds Übersetzung der Querela Pacis von 1521* (Zurich: Füssli, 1969), 52–55; Roland Bainton, "The *Querela Pacis* of Erasmus: Classical and Christian Sources," *Archiv für Reformationsgeschichte* 42 (1951): 32–48; most recently, Klaus Garber, "The Erasmian Legacy of Conciliation," part 1 of " 'Your arts shall be: to impose the ways of peace' — Tolerance, Liberty, and the Nation in the Literature and Deeds of Humanism," trans. Westfälisches Landesmuseum für Kunst und Kulturgeschichte and Max Reinhart, in Garber, *Imperiled Heritage: Tradition, History, and Utopia in Early Modern German Literature*, ed. Reinhart (Aldershot: Ashgate, 2000), 19–24.

[62] The older studies by Otto Schottenloher, *Erasmus im Ringen um die humanistische Bildungsform* (Münster: Aschendorff, 1933), and Rudolf Pfeiffer, *Humanitas Erasmiana* (Leipzig: Teubner, 1931), remain standard.

[63] This and the following quotations from *Querela Pacis* are taken from Welzig 5:366 and 372.

[64] Quotation from *Antibarbari* after Mattheeussen, " 'Religio' und 'Litterae' im Menschenideal des Erasmus," in *Scrinium Erasmianum*, ed. Joseph Coppens (Leiden: Brill, 1969), 1:351–74, here 372; here too, comprehensive references to Erasmus's relationship to the Devotio Moderna.

[65] Ferdinand Geldner, *Die Staatsauffassung und Fürstenlehre des Erasmus von Rotterdam* (Berlin: Ebering, 1930); Otto Herding, "Isokrates, Erasmus und die *Institutio Principis Christiani*," in *Dauer und Wandel der Geschichte*, ed. Rudolf Vierhaus (Münster: Aschendorff, 1966), 101–43; Eberhard von Koerber, *Die Staatstheorie des Erasmus von Rotterdam* (Berlin: Duncker & Humblot, 1967).

[66] See most recently Müller, "Warum Cicero?" (see note 58). According to Müller the partners in the dialogue arrive at a point, "at which the humanistic educational program becomes a vehicle for the renewal of the ancient rhetorical art toward the ultimate goal of completely reforming life. [. . .] This is a symptom of a crisis in which the new authorities can no longer hold their own with the old authorities, and as a consequence the humanistic attempt at a total transformation of the world fails in terms of its own premises, and the discovery of the ideal in a historical culture leads to the historicization of cultural ideals in general" (trans. M. Metzger).

[67] Thus it is in Luthers *Tischreden*, WA 6:252, no. 6887.

[68] One of the dialogue partners quips thus in the colloquium *Convivium religiosum* ("Das geistliche Gastmahl"), in Welzig 6:87.

[69] In the *Enchiridion militis Christiani* (Welzig 1:168): "Christum vero esse puta non vocem inanem, sed nihil aliud quam caritatem, simplicitatem, patientiam, puritatem, breviter quicquid ille docuit."

[70] See the passage from the *Paraclesis*, in Welzig 3:22: "Quid autem aliud est Christi philosophia, quam ipse renascentiam vocat, quam instauratio bene conditae naturae?"

[71] *Enchiridion*, in Welzig 1:168. On the *Enchiridion* see Alfons Auer, *Die vollkommene Frömmigkeit des Christen nach dem "Enchiridion militis Christiani" des Erasmus von Rotterdam* (Düsseldorf: Patmos, 1954), and Robert Stupperich, "Das *Enchiridion*

militis christiani des Erasmus von Rotterdam nach seiner Entstehung, seinem Sinn und Charakter," *Archiv für Reformationsgeschichte* 69 (1978): 5–22.

[72] Rädle, "Erasmus als Lehrer," 221–27 (see note 60).

[73] Quoted in Erasmus's *Lingua* (Clericus 4:660B); also, in the broader context of Erasmus's linguistic thought (interrelationship of *verbum, sermo, cogitatio,* and of speaking vs. writing), see Harth, *Philologie und praktische Philosophie,* here 66 (see note 58).

[74] Elias, *Über den Prozeß der Zivilisation: Soziogenetische und psychogenetische Untersuchungen,* 2nd ed. (Frankfurt am Main: Suhrkamp, 1977), 1:65–76, notes 312–16; translated into English as *The Civilizing Process.* The theses of Elias are discussed by Bogner, *Die Bezähmung der Zunge,* esp. 47–53 (see note 31). There is no critical edition of *De civilitate morum puerilium;* nor is there a recent German translation. For now see the excellent Italian edition by Rosa, *Il Galateo dei Ragazzi,* which includes the pertinent literature from the Middle Ages and the Italian humanists. For the present I am using Clericus 1:1033–44.

[75] Both works are in the critical edition of Jean-Claude Margolin, in ASD 1:2,1ff. and 79ff.; Margolin also has an individual edition of *De pueris instituendis* with extensive commentary and glosseries (Geneva: Droz, 1966). His Index rerum documents that the concept *civilitas* does not occur in the earlier work of Erasmus.

[76] First in the well-known letter to Johannes Botzheim of 30 January 1523; cf. Rädle, "Erasmus als Lehrer," 218 (see note 60).

[77] See the reprint of the German translation of 1597: *Galateus: Das Büchlein von erbarn / höflichen und holdseligen Sitten,* trans. Nathan Chytraeus, ed. Klaus Ley (Tübingen: Niemeyer, 1984). Latin translations had been available since 1579.

[78] See Beetz, *Frühmoderne Höflichkeit* (see note 32), and Emilio Bonfatti, *La "Civil Conversazione" in Germania* (Udine: Del Bianco, 1979).

[79] French sociologist (1930–2002) who put education and, in a particularly aggressive way, the role of general cultural factors at the center of his analysis.

[80] Elias (1897–1990) is known as a "process sociologist" as a result of his studies of civilization as a process.

[81] Erasmus's precepts on decorous personal behavior (facial expressions, gestures, movements) shared certain ideas from medieval treatises, such as Hugo of St. Victor's *De institutione novitiorum,* but clearly rejected others, such as the norms of ascetic *verecundia* (shyness, modesty) or mortification of the flesh (*mortificatio*). There are many source references and quotations in Knox, "Erasmus' *De Civilitate*" (see note 58); on linguistic discipline in the older literature on order and behavior see Bogner," *Die Bezähmung der Zunge,* 54–69 (see note 31).

[82] In the year of its publication *De civilitate* was reprinted more than ten times; the first German translations appeared in Augsburg (1523) and Strasbourg (1532); a German translation was published in Hamburg as late as 1673. VD lists 114 printings (E 2186–2300). *Civilitas* here signifies the quintessence of "polite and decorous manners." Joannes Plouvier rendered the treatise into Latin verse, "Elegiaco carmine" (Augsburg, n.d.).

[83] Knox, "Erasmus, *De Civilitate,*" esp. 10ff. and 24ff. (see note 58), pursues the tracks of its reception in the schools; detailed analysis of lesson plans in Bierlaire, "Erasmus at School" (see note 58). We find evidence of the book's influence in Friedrich Dedekind's (NL) verse satire on table manners (1549), translated by Caspar Scheidt (1551), and thus merged with older types of guides to proper manners. Influences on della Casa's

Galateo require confirmation; what is clear is that Nathan Chytraeus was familiar with *De civilitate*, given that he was its German editor and translator.

[84] In addition to Chytraeus's work on della Casa there is another valuable Latin edition, accompanied by dissertations: *Stephani Guazzi De civili conversatione dissertationes politicae enucleatae* (Leipzig, 1673).

[85] Charidemus was a respected Athenian general of the fourth century B.C. GuF 141–48 analyzes the speech and its most important quotations. On the life and work of Dornau see Robert Seidel, *Späthumanismus in Schlesien: Caspar Dornau (1577–1631): Leben und Werk* (Tübingen: Niemeyer, 1994), 265–306 for the doctrine of decorum.

[86] On Niavis see my article in LL 8:383–84.

[87] On Mosellanus and his *Paedologia* (reprinted into the eighteenth century; 1906 Berlin edition by Hermann Michel) see Stefan Rhein, in LL 8:235–36; Michael Erbe, in CE 2:466–47.

[88] Among other things Hegendorff published *Dialogi pueriles* (Leipzig, 1519) and *Christianae studiosae juventutis institutio* (Hagenau, 1526; Paris, 1529, etc.); see my article in LL 5:103; also C. G. van Leijenhorst, in CE 1:171–73; Franz Bierlaire, "Les *Dialogi pueriles* de Christophe Hegendorff," in *Acta Conventus Neo-Latini Turonensis*, ed. Jean-Claude Margolin (Paris: Libr. Philos. Vrin, 1980), 389–401.

[89] On Franck see Christoph Dejung, in LL 3:467–69; Jan-Dirk Müller, ed., *Sebastian Franck (1499–1542)* (Wiesbaden: Harrassowitz, 1993); Wilhelm Kühlmann, "Auslegungsinteresse und Auslegungsverfahren in der Sprichwortsammlung Sebastian Francks (1541)," in *Literarische Kleinstformen*, ed. Walter Haug and Burghart Wachinger (Tübingen: Niemeyer, 1994), 117–31.

[90] On Weigel see Siegfried Wollgast, in LL 12:192–93; critical edition: Horst Pfefferl, ed., *Sämtliche Schriften*, 4 vols. to date: nos. 3, 4, 7, 8 (Stuttgart-Bad Cannstatt: Frommann-Holzboog, 1996–2002); see also Weigel's *Ausgewählte Werke*, ed. Siegfried Wollgast (Stuttgart-Bad Cannstatt: Frommann-Holzboog, 1978). Studies: Wollgast, *Philosophie in Deutschland zwischen Reformation und Aufklärung 1550–1650* (Berlin: Akademie, 1988), 499–600; and *Philosophie 17*, 4/1:18–23.

[91] On borrowings (both attributed and unattributed) of Erasmus's *Adagia* in the wake of the confessional struggles see Max Reinhart, "Unexpected Returns: Some Literary Uses of Erasmus' *Adagia* in Seventeenth-Century Germany," *Erasmus of Rotterdam Society Yearbook* 19 (1999): 47–60.

[92] WA 15, 2753. On school sermon as genre see A. Schnitzlein "Die sog. Schulpredigten des 16., 17. und 18. Jahrhunderts," *Zeitschrift für Geschichte der Erziehung und des Unterrichts* 5 (1915): 25–54.

[93] Study edition of selected writings in Latin and German: Günter R. Schmidt, ed., *Glaube und Bildung: Texte zum christlichen Humanismus* (Stuttgart: Reclam, 1989).

[94] Printed, together with other important speeches (including the 1523 *Encomion eloquentiae*), in *Melanchthons Werke in Auswahl*, vol. 3, *Humanistische Schriften*, 2nd ed., ed. Richard Nürnberger (Gütersloh: Bertelsmann, 1969), 29–42. See also Heinz Scheible, "Melanchthons Bildungsprogramm," in Bookmann, ed., *Lebenslehren*, 233–48 (see note 48).

[95] See Wilhelm Kühlmann and Wilhelm Schmidt-Biggmann, "Topik," in RL 3:646–49, and Peter Hess, "Topos," in RL 3:649–52; also Helmut Zedelmaier and Martin Mulsow, eds., *Die Praktiken der Gelehrsamkeit in der Frühen Neuzeit* (Tübingen: Niemeyer, 2001).

[96] On Neander see Heinz Scheible, in LL 8:340.

[97] Welzig 7:206: "Maximae vero res hodie per consilium quod arcanum vocant confici-untur; ad id vix tres homines adhibentur, illiterati fere."

[98] Tacitus wrote a detailed and admiring history of contemporary Germans. His *Germania* was rediscovered in manuscript form in the 1420s and became a canonical document in the cultural wars between Germanists and Romanists of the late fifteenth and sixteenth century. Of particular importance were the Germanic virtues noted by Tacitus, which in the hands of Celtis, Wimpfeling, and other humanist patriots, were turned against the putative decadence of Italian culture. See esp. Donald R. Kelley, "*Tacitus noster:* The *Germania* in the Renaissance and Reformation," in *Tacitus and the Tacitean Tradition*, ed. T. J. Lude and A. J. Woodman (Princeton: Princeton UP, 1993), 152–67.

[99] For a measured discussion of the history of scholarship on the often acrimonious debate over Catholic reform or antireform in the later sixteenth century see John W. O'Malley, *Trent and All That: Renaming Catholicism in the Early Modern Era* (Cambridge: Harvard UP, 2000).

[100] Critical edition: Theo G. M. van Orschot, ed., *Güldenes Tugend-Buch* (Bern: Francke, 1968); on Spee see esp. Martina Eicheldinger, *Friedrich Spee — Seelsorger und poeta doctus* (Tübingen: Niemeyer, 1991).

[101] G. H. Turnbull, "Johann Valentin Andreaes' Societas christiana: A. Model of Christian Society," *Zeitschrift für deutsche Philologie* 74 (1955): 151–85; Donald R. Dickson, "Johannes Saubert, Johann Valentin Andreae and the *Unio Christiana*," *German Life & Letters* 49, no. 1 (1996): 18–31; Brecht, ed., *Der Pietismus*, 151–65 (see note 43).

[102] Bilingual edition: Richard van Dülmen, ed., *Theophilus: lateinisch und deutsch* (Stuttgart: Calwer, 1973).

[103] On Spener see Brecht, ed., *Der Pietismus*, 281–390 (see note 43); Brecht, *Ausgewählte Aufsätze*, vol. 2, *Pietismus* (Stuttgart: Calwer, 1997); Johannes Wallmann, *Philipp Jacob Spener und die Anfänge des Pietismus*, 2nd ed. (Tübingen: Mohr, 1986). For an in-depth discussion of Pietism in its broadest contours see Dietrich Blaufuss, ed., *Pietismus-Forschungen* (Frankfurt am Main: Lang, 1986); specifically there, Rüdiger Mack, "Pädagogik bei Philipp Jacob Spener," 53–116. Also by Blaufuss, *Korrespondierender Pietismus: Ausgewählte Beiträge*, ed. Wolfgang Sommer and Gerhard Philipp Wolf (Leipzig: Evangelische Verlags-Anstalt, 2003). Finally, Klaus Garber, "Arnold and the Church of the Spirit," part 1 of "Begin with Goethe? Forgotten Traditions at the Threshold of the Modern Age," in Garber, *Imperiled Heritage*, 209–51, here 220–27 (see note 61).

[104] On Francke see Brecht, ed., *Der Pietismus*, 440–540 (see note 43).

[105] On Comenius see *Philosophie 17*, 4/1, 166–80; Hans Scheuerl and Henning Schröer, in TRE 8:162–69; Klaus Schaller, *Die Pädagogik des Johann Amos Comenius und die Anfänge des pädagogischen Realismus im 17. Jahrhundert*, 2nd ed. (Heidelberg: Quelle & Meyer, 1967); Schaller, *Die "Pampaedia" des Johann Amos Comenius: Eine Einführung in sein pädagogisches Hauptwerk*, 4th ed. (Heidelberg: Quelle & Meyer, 1967); Mila Blekastad, *Comenius: Versuch eines Umrisses von Leben, Werk und Schicksal* (Oslo: Universitt-Forl., 1969); Franz Hofmann, *Jan Amos Comenius: Lehrer der Nationen* (Cologne: Pahl-Rugenstein, 1976); Gerhard Michel, *Die Welt als Schule: Ratke, Comenius und die didaktische Bewegung* (Hannover: Schroedel, 1978).

[106] *Opera didactica omnia* (Amsterdam, 1657; repr., Prague: Academia Scientiarum Bohemoslovenica, 1957), 1:428–29.

[107] *Das Labyrinth der Welt und andere Schriften*, ed. Ilse Seehase (Frankfurt am Main: Röderberg, 1985), 89.

[108] See in this volume the chapter by Theodor Verweyen. From the wealth of Opitz studies see esp. Entner, "Der Weg zum 'Buch von der deutschen Poeterey'" (see note 36); Sinemus, *Poetik und Rhetorik* (see note 9); Dünnhaupt 4:3005–74; GuF 255–67; LuG 115–223; Klaus Garber, "Martin Opitz," in *Dichter 17*, 116–84; Rolf Baur, *Didaktik der Barockpoetik: Die deutschsprachigen Poetiken von Opitz bis Gottsched als Lehrbücher der "Poetery"* (Heidelberg: Winter, 1982); Kühlmann, *Martin Opitz: Deutsche Literatur und deutsche Nation*, 2nd ed. (Heidelberg: Manutius, 2001); *Thomas Borgstedt und Walter Schmitz*, eds., *Martin Opitz: Nachahmungspoetik und Lebenswelt* (Tübingen: Niemeyer, 2002).

[109] On Dornau see Seidel, *Späthumanismus in Schlesien* (see note 85).

[110] This text is dealt with in detail in GuF 136–51 (Latin text, 144, note 15).

[111] The standard Opitz edition is *Gesammelte Werke: Kritische Ausgabe*, ed. George Schulz-Behrend, 4 vols. to date (Stuttgart: Hiersemann, 1968–90). A useful study edition, which contains both the *Poeterey* and *Aristarchus* (the latter in both original Latin and German translation, 51–75) is *Martin Opitz: "Buch von der Deutschen Poetery" (1624)*, ed. Herbert Jaumann (Stuttgart: Reclam, 2002).

[112] Dünnhaupt 2:855–910; Kühlmann, in LL 2:281–82.

[113] Dünnhaupt 6:427–31; Ferdinand van Ingen, in *Dichter 17*, 497–516; Herbert Blume, in LL 12:483–86.

[114] Dünnhaupt 3:1969–2031; Irmgard Böttcher, in LL 5:25–26; GuF 382–93; Jean-Daniel Krebs, *Georg Philipp Harsdörffer (1607–1658): Poétique et Poésie*, 2 vols. (Bern: Lang, 1983); Italo Michele Battafarano, ed., *Georg Philipp Harsdörffer: Ein deutscher Dichter und europäischer Gelehrter* (Bern: Lang, 1991). Of the vast literature on Harsdörffer and the circle of poets of the Pegnesischer Blumenorden see from recent scholarship esp. Irmgard Böttcher, "Der Nürnberger Georg Philipp Harsdörffer," in *Dichter 17*, 289–346; John Roger Paas, ed., *der Franken Rom: Nürnbergs Blütezeit in der zweiten Hälfte des 17. Jahrhunderts* (Wiesbaden: Harrassowitz, 1995); Peter Hess, "Georg Philipp Harsdörffer," in DLB 179, 145–60; Max Reinhart, "Battle of the Tapestries: A War-Time Debate in Anhalt-Köthen (Georg Philipp Harsdörffer's *Peristromata Turcica* and *Aulaea Romana*, 1641–1642)," *Daphnis 27*, nos. 2–3 (1998): 291–333; Klaus Garber, "Nuremberg, Arcadia on the Pegnitz: The Self-Stylization of an Urban Sodality," trans. Karl F. Otto Jr., Michael Swisher, and Max Reinhart, in Garber, *Imperiled Heritage*, 117–208 (see note 61); Reinhart, ed. and trans., *Georg Philipp Harsdörffer: Lamentation for France and Other Polemics on War and Peace: The Latin Pamphlets of 1641–1642* (New York: Lang, forthcoming).

[115] See Peter A. Hess, *Poetik ohne Trichter: Harsdörffers Dicht- und Reimkunst* (Stuttgart: Heinz, 1986).

[116] See in this volume the chapter by Peter M. Daly. Also Jean-Daniel Krebs, "G. Ph. Harsdörffers geistliche Embleme zwischen katholisch-jesuitischen Einflüssen und protestantischen Reformbestrebungen," in van Ingen and Moore, eds., *Religion und Religiosität*, 539–52 (see note 43).

[117] Dünnhaupt 5:3824–46; Volker Meid, in LL 10:376–78; Jörg-Jochen Berns, in *Dichter 17*, 415–34; Andreas Gardt, *Sprachreflexion in Barock und Frühaufklärung: Entwürfe von Böhme bis Leibniz* (Berlin: de Gruyter, 1994); Wolfgang Huber, *Kulturpatriotismus und Sprachbewußtsein* (Frankfurt am Main: Lang, 1984). In 1669

Schottelius also published a German-language ethics: *Ethica: Die Sittenkunst oder Wollebenskunst*, ed. Jörg Jochen Berns (Bern: Francke, 1980); Berns's afterword offers a history of the German-language scholarship on the subject "Schulphilosophie und Verdeutschungsinteresse" as well as an index of sixteenth- and seventeenth-century German-language textbooks on logic and ethics.

[118] On the linguistic development of German see in this volume the chapter by Renate Born.

[119] In addition to the famous multivolume *Frauenzimmer Gesprächspiele* these include *Nathan und Jotham: das ist: geistliche und weltliche Lehrgedichte*, 2 vols. (1659; repr., ed. Guillaume van Gemert, Frankfurt am Main: Keip, 1991); *Hertz-bewegliche Sonntagsandachten*, 2 vols. (Nürnberg, 1649–52); *Mathematisch-Philosophische Erquickstunden*, 3 vols. (1636–53; repr., ed. Jörg Jochen Berns, Frankfurt am Main: Keip, 1991).

[120] *Frauenzimmer Gesprächspiele*, 8 vols. (1641–49; repr., ed. Irmgard Böttcher, Tübingen: Niemeyer, 1968–69). See esp. Rosmarie Zeller, *Spiel und Konversation im Barock: Untersuchungen zu Harsdörffers "Gesprächspielen"* (Berlin: de Gruyter, 1974). Zeller, "Die Rolle der Frau in Gesprächspiel und Konversation," in Adam, ed., *Geselligkeit*, 531–41 (see note 32). Among the most important manuals for polite conversation is Harsdörffer's *Ars apophthegmatica: Das ist: Kunstquellen Denckwürdiger Lehrsprüche und Ergötzlicher Hofrede*, 2 vols. (1655–56; repr., ed. Georg Braungart, Frankfurt am Main: Keip, 1990). Daly in this volume examines in detail how Harsdörffer expresses his understanding of the emblem in the *Frauenzimmer Gesprächspiele*.

[121] Harsdörffer, "Zuschrift," *Frauenzimmer Gesprächspiele* 8:9.

[122] Harsdörffer, *Frauenzimmer Gesprächspiele* 2:53–54.

[123] Harsdörffer, *Frauenzimmer Gesprächspiele* 1:281–82.

[124] See, for example, Max Reinhart, " 'The younger Harsdörffer': Widening the View," part I of "Battle of the Tapestries," 291–296 (see note 114).

[125] On Weise see Dünnhaupt 6:4179–250; Uwe-K. Ketelsen, in LL 12:212–14; Wilfried Barner, in *Dichter 17*, 690–725. Fundamental to Weise, Frühsorge, *Der politische Körper* (see note 28); *Barockrhetorik* 190–220, LuG 314–46; also Peter Behncke and Hans-Gert Roloff, eds., *Christian Weise: Dichter-Gelehrter-Pädagoge: Jahrbuch für Internationale Germanistik* 37 (1994); in that same volume see for bibliography Benedikt Sommer, "Christian Weise — Verzeichnis der Forschungsliteratur," 361–73; further see Andreas Keller et al., "Beiträge zur Christian Weise-Bibliographie," *Daphnis* 24 (1995): 645–708 (= the Weise mss. in the Christian-Weise-Bibliothek in Zittau). Standard edition: *Sämtliche Werke*, ed. John D. Lindberg, continued by Hans-Gert Roloff (Berlin: de Gruyter, 1971–). On education and the evolution of poetological conventions, Hans Arno Horn, *Christian Weise als Erneuerer des deutschen Gymnasiums im Zeitalter des Barock: Der Politicus als Bildungsideal* (Weinheim: Beltz, 1966); Konradin Zeller, *Pädagogik und Drama: Untersuchungen zur Schulcomödie Christian Weises* (Tübingen: Niemeyer, 1980).

[126] See esp. Norbert Conrads, *Ritterakademien der Frühen Neuzeit: Bildung als Standesprivileg im 16. und 17. Jahrhundert* (Göttingen: Vandenhoeck & Ruprecht, 1982); Klaus Bleek, *Adelserziehung auf deutschen Ritterakademien: Die Lüneburger Adelsschulen 1665–1880*, 2 vols. (Frankfurt am Main: Lang, 1977).

[127] Newspapers at this time in Germany were closer to the broadsheet, or news pamphlet, and tended to emphasize sensational events. The best ones, such as those

printed in Amsterdam, did report international news quite thoroughly, usually in sets under name headings of cities.

[128] The most recent account, with new sources and complete bibliography including the older studies, is Uwe Kordes, *Wolfgang Ratke (Ratichius, 1571–1635): Gesellschaft, Religiosität und Gelehrsamkeit im frühen 17. Jahrhundert* (Heidelberg: Winter, 1999); see also Gerhard Michel, in *Philosophie 17*, 4/1, 150–57; also Michel, "Wolfgang Ratke: Die Muttersprache in Schule, Staat und Wissenschaft," in Schöne, *Staát*, 185–97 (see note 10).

[129] Quoted from Erika Ising, ed., *Wolfgang Ratkes Schriften zur deutschen Grammatik (1612–1630)* (Berlin: Akademie, 1959), 101.

[130] *Kurtzer Bericht von der Didactica, oder LehrKunst Wolfgangi Ratichii* (Frankfurt am Main, 1613; Magdeburg, 1614); quoted here from Michel, "Wolfgang Ratke," 190 (see note 128).

[131] On Schupp see Dünnhaupt 5:3847–94; Herbert Jaumann, in LL 10:435–36; GuF 151–61 and 393–98; Hildegarde E. Wichert, *Johann Balthasar Schupp and the Baroque Satire in Germany* (New York: King's Crown, 1952); Stefan Trappen, *Grimmelshausen und die menippeische Satire: Eine Studie zu den historischen Voraussetzungen der Prosasatire im Barock* (Tübingen: Niemeyer, 1994), 168–88; Klaus Schaller, "Muttersprache und realistische Bildung," in Schöne, *Staát*, 198–209 (see note 10).

[132] See Gerhard Dünnhaupt "Die Fürstliche Druckerei zu Köthen," *Archiv für Geschichte des Buchwesens* 20 (1979): 895–950.

[133] On Weigel see Herbert Jaumann, in LL 12:190–92; Edmund Spiess, *Erhard Weigel: Ein Lebensbild aus der Universitäts- und Gelehrtengeschichte des 17. Jahrhunderts* (Leipzig, 1881).

[134] On Thomasius see Walther Gose, in LL 11:346–48; Werner Schneiders, *Naturrecht und Liebesethik: Zur Geschichte der praktischen Philosophie im Hinblick auf Christian Thomasius* (Hildesheim: Olms, 1971); GuF 423–54; LuG 346–425; most recently, Fritz Vollhardt, ed., *Christian Thomasius (1655–1728): Neue Forschungen im Kontext der Frühaufklärung* (Tübingen: Niemeyer, 1997); Klaus Garber, "Thomasius and the Christian Egalitarian State," part 3 of "Begin with Goethe?," in Garber, *Imperiled Heritage*, 237–45 (see note 61); Manfred Beetz and Herbert Jaumann, eds., *Thomasius im literarischen Feld: Neue Beiträge zur Erforschung seines Werkes im historischen Kontext* (Tübingen: Niemeyer, 2003).

The Reformation Movement in Germany

C. Scott Dixon

The Rise of the Reformation Movement

REFLECTING ON EVENTS A FEW YEARS after the rise of the Reformation, the Dominican monk Johann Lindner held Elector Friedrich the Wise (1463–1525) to blame for developments in Germany, for in his opinion it was the University of Wittenberg, founded by Friedrich in 1502, that had served as the seedbed for the growth of the new faith.[1] In suggesting this Lindner drew attention to an important fact about the origins of the Reformation in Germany: it was a creation of the university. It was the university — its teachers, its forums, its networks, its institutions, its cultural matrix, and its ideas — that provided the context for the rise of the movement. And it was the unique conditions of the University of Wittenberg in particular, this small and seemingly insignificant institution on the banks of the Elbe, that made possible a type of laboratory, or *Experimentierfeld*, for the evolution of a new faith.[2] For those caught up in the early stages of the Reformation, Friedrich the Wise among them, it was not just the figure of Martin Luther that dominated the movement but the entire like-minded community of scholars and clergymen in Wittenberg.[3] In his preface to St. Augustine's *De spiritu et litera*, for instance, Andreas Rudolph Bodenstein von Karlstadt (ca. 1477–1541), Luther's faculty colleague, congratulated Wittenberg students that years of collaborative preaching and reading had led to the rediscovery of the "true faith" at their university.[4] Johann Lang (1488–1548) thought in similar terms, as did Johannes Dölsch (1485–1523) and Nikolaus von Amsdorf (1483–1565), all university colleagues and all devoted supporters of Luther. Indeed, even Luther himself spoke of "theologia nostra" (our theology) after his emergence as the leader of the movement, and he continued to think of the university as the birthplace of the faith. As he reminded the Franciscans of Jüterbog on 15 May 1519, his teachings had already been the subject of debates, lectures, readings, sermons, and disputations for over three years, and in that time they had not yet been revealed as mistaken or erroneous.[5] In its origins the Reformation was the creation of university culture in Wittenberg.

The context of development changed, however, during the period between Luther's distribution of the *Disputatio pro declaratione virtutis indulgentiarum* (Disputation on the Declaration Concerning the Power of Indulgences), better known as the *Ninety-Five Theses*, on 31 October 1517, the traditional starting point of the Reformation, and the disputation in Leipzig during June and July of 1519, the first staged defense of evangelical theology. Ideas and events breached the walls of Wittenberg, and the movement became a national event. This was no accident of history. Both Karlstadt and Luther had made deliberate attempts to reach a broader audience. In April of 1517 Karlstadt wrote a number of theses against scholastic theology and made efforts to publicize the Wittenberg reforms: a few months later Luther followed suit with *Contra scholasticam theologiam*, an attempt to broaden the dialogue. He sent copies to Johann Lang in Erfurt, for instance, with the request that Lang distribute them at the university, lest the Erfurters think that he was content to remain in Wittenberg, as he put it, mumbling away in a corner.[6] The Wittenbergers thought much the same about the program of university reform they were developing: it was realized *in situ* but imagined on a national scale and thus directed at the other institutions of Germany. But in the end it was the *Ninety-Five Theses* that did the most to take the faith beyond the town, for with this document the Wittenberg reformers entered into a direct dialogue with the Catholic Church on themes of fundamental theological importance.[7] Among the Catholics, Johannes Tetzel (ca. 1465–1519), the Dominican indulgence peddler who had been the object of Luther's criticism, complained loudly to his employer, Cardinal Albrecht of Mainz; Johannes Eck (1486–1543), Ingolstadt professor and one of Germany's premier theologians, followed with a list of critical comments; soon thereafter even the papal theologians entered the fray, the first being Sylvester Prierias (1456–1523), master of the sacred palace, who in 1518 quickly drafted a *Dialogus* defending the pope's power and condemning many of Luther's theses on indulgences. The debate had begun.

After the posting of the *Ninety-Five Theses* the Wittenberg movement turned into the Luther affair (*causa Lutheri*). Although Luther still often spoke of "our theology," even after his meeting in Augsburg in 1518 with the papal legate Cardinal Cajetan (1469–1534), by this stage he was seen as the inspirational leader. Luther had done much to fashion his own fame. Within the university he used every means available to get his ideas across — lectures, sermons, disputations, and a flood of German and Latin writings, including topics of debate and personal letters. Following the spread of his theses against Scholasticism and indulgences in 1517 he began to tailor his works for a wider public, preparing both the *Resolutiones* (1518) and *Eynn Sermon von dem Ablasz unnd Gnade* (A Sermon on Indulgences and Grace, 1518), for example, to ensure that there would be no misunderstanding about his position in the indulgence debate. He also emerged as a public figure spreading his theological insights in lectures and disputations, impressing many onlookers with his powerful presence and skills as a debater. Years after Luther's death the evangelical clergyman Martin Frecht (1494–1556) would remember the Heidelberg disputation of 26 April 1518 as the birthplace of the Reformation, for that is where Luther, speaking before Frecht and a gathering of fellow Augustinians, including a host of future reformers, first presented his theology to the world beyond Wittenberg.[8] Luther's appearance in 1519 at the disputation in Leipzig, where he came face to face with Eck, made an even greater impression on the growing community of supporters, because Luther used every means at his disposal to sway public opinion, from the works he published in advance of the debate, to his insistence that the proceedings be recorded by notaries (so that his words might be preserved for all to see), to his gestures in the lecture hall.[9] All of this had an effect. By the end of the debate Eck had no doubt that it was Luther alone who was responsible for the rise of the *nova doctrina*, while Philipp Melanchthon (1497–1560) expressed his wonder at Luther's performance ("his pure and Christian spirit"), thus anticipating the general cast of mind that turned Luther into a celebrity and his reform movement into one of the most important developments of the age.[10]

The theological ideas at the heart of the Reformation in Germany evolved in a similar way, first as part of a general intellectual stirring and then finding form and definition in the works of Luther. Of course, evangelical theology was more than just the creation of a reformer or a group of reformers in Wittenberg, no matter how instrumental Luther and his followers may have been. Historians have long since identified the complex fusion of novel insights and medieval continuities that made up the corpus of Reformation thought.[11] This is not the place to offer a genealogy of this development, but a few words on the key beliefs will help to place the movement in context.

For all evangelical reformers the leading idea was to effect a renewal of theology, which meant in the first instance returning to the source of the faith, Scripture, and reading it afresh. Complex scholastic commentaries were devalued or rejected outright in favor of a return to the original texts in the original languages.[12] It was this hermeneutic shift[13] — this move away from reliance on secondary glossaries to the pure Word of God — that served as a foundation for the evangelical faith. Once "the Word" had been encountered in its purity, the process of reinterpretation began. Luther's early lectures on the Psalms (1513–15) and the epistles of Paul (1515–16), for instance, inspired him to develop a new understanding of sin, reformulate the distinctions between human and divine justification, and reject the medieval notion of works' righteousness in favor of a new theology of humility. In later years Luther would synthesize these and similar theological insights under the rubric of a single principle of evangelical thought: *sola fide*, justification through faith alone. As he makes explicit in his reforming tract *Von der Freyheyt eynisz Christen menschen* (On the Freedom of a Christian Man, 1520), faith alone is the fulcrum of the Christian life:

> Hierauß leychtlich zu mercken ist, warumb der glaub szo vill vormag, und das keyne gutte werck yhm gleych seyn mugen, Den keyn gut werck hanget an dem gottlichen wort, wie der glaub, kan auch nit yn der seelen seyn, sondern alleyn das wort und glaube regiren yn der seelen. Wie das wort ist, szo wirt auch die seele von yhm, gleych als das eyssen wirt gluttrodt wie das fewr auß der voreynigung mit dem fewr. Alszo sehen wir, das an dem glaubenn eyn Christen mensch gnug hatt, darff keynis wercks, das er frum sey: darff er den keynis wercks mehr, szo ist er gewißlich empunden von allen gepotten und gesetzen: ist er empunden, szo ist er gewißlich frey. Das ist die Christlich freiheit, der eynige glaub, der do macht, nit das wir müszsig gahn oder übell thun mugen, sondern das wir keynis wercks bedurffen zur frumkeyt und seligkeyt zu erlangen.[14]

[From what has been said it is easy to see from what source faith derives such great power and why a good work or all good works together cannot equal it. No good work can rely upon the Word of God or live in the soul, for faith alone and the Word of God rule in the soul. Just as the heated iron glows like fire because of the union of fire with it, so the Word imparts its qualities to the soul. It is clear, then, that a Christian has all that he needs in faith and needs no works to justify him; and if he has no need of works, he has no need of the law; and if he has no need of the law, surely he is free from the law. This is that Christian liberty, our faith, which does not induce us to live in idleness or wickedness but makes the law and works unnecessary for any man's righteousness and salvation.]

With Luther's idea of justification — which holds (1) that salvation is an unconditional gift of God, (2) that righteousness is a state beyond ourselves by which the sinner is placed in a new relationship with the divine, and (3) that faith "is the means whereby man is led from his moral subjective existence into the final validity of the righteousness of Christ, in which he is preserved for salvation" — the medieval theology of justification and its associated cycle of salvation (with many of the sacraments in tow) was undone.[15] In medieval Catholic theology, justification was conditional: it occurred in stages, with the sinner moving along a gradual path toward salvation and back again to a state of sin. The Reformation principle of justification replaced this medieval cycle by the unconditional, and instantaneous, state of righteousness. God becomes the active element in the quest for salvation, the sinner passive; Scripture becomes the sole standard of religious truth and the Word of God the only route to salvation; faith, not works, is necessary for justification; and religion becomes a concern of the worshiping community, no longer the preserve of a sacerdotal elite. It was this idea of faith alone that sat at the heart of evangelical theology, and it represented a fundamentally new relationship between the Christian believer and the divine.[16]

Theology mattered, but in the beginning the Luther affair was not a dispute about justification and righteousness; it was not perceived or expressed in the terms that would later define it. The Catholic authorities wrote against Luther because he challenged the principles of papal supremacy, but it was less an issue of doctrine than of authority.[17] When the Catholic controversialists took up their pens after the posting of the theses, for instance, there was no consensus about how indulgences should be understood or how Luther had violated medieval teaching. Each chose a different theme: Eck took offence at the challenge to canon law, Konrad Wimpina (1460–1531) defended the sacrament of penance, Prierias came to the defense of the supremacy of Rome. Only one concern was held in common, and that was the issue of authority, for that is what represented the most immediate threat. As Tetzel remarked, Luther's doubts about the opinions of the Catholic Church would encourage people to question the authority of Rome.[18] Beyond that, however, few people, even those at the center of the debate, could appreciate how profound the division actually was. Church authorities underestimated the threat posed by Luther and his teachings. In reaction to the *Ninety-Five Theses* Albrecht of

Brandenburg (1490–1545), Archbishop of Mainz, passed on a copy to the University of Mainz with a request for advice and forwarded another to Rome, but otherwise did nothing and simply awaited the judgment of the papal theologians.[19] In Rome many viewed it as yet another dispute between the monastic orders, and one best resolved with an appeal to authority. There was a tacit admission that doctrinal matters were involved but no understanding of the theological issues at stake, and certainly no sense that it was a debate that would go beyond Saxony and undermine the Catholic Church.[20]

Only after the meeting in Heidelberg in April of 1518 did the curia step up its efforts against Luther, partly in reaction to growing warnings, and partly in response to the new works that rolled off the presses of Wittenberg. There was now little doubt, as Prierias would assert, that the German professor held and taught opinions considered heretical by the Catholic Church. Consequently, a legal process against Luther began in Rome in the summer of 1518. Political affairs more or less suspended proceedings the following year, but by early January 1520 the papacy pronounced Luther an enemy of the faith and on 15 June 1520 published *Exsurge Domine*, the bull threatening excommunication, declaring Luther a heretic and forbidding the faithful to read, preach, publish, or defend his opinions. The following year Emperor Charles V endorsed the excommunication with the publication of the Edict of Worms (26 May 1521), thus placing Luther under the imperial ban while repeating the demand to avoid Luther's works.[21]

Battle lines had been drawn, and yet it was not this juxtaposition of extremes that gave the Reformation its early momentum as an intellectual movement. To a large extent the Reformation evolved as part of a "constructive misunderstanding," a misreading by many humanists in Germany who viewed Luther as a fellow crusader against Scholasticism and the Luther affair as one in a series of conflicts between the forerunners of the new learning and the aged custodians of the old.[22] There were good reasons for this association. Since its foundation, Wittenberg had been one of the leading centers of humanism in Germany. Its reform program was the most progressive of its kind in the empire, aiming to reduce the influence of scholastic theology and increase the profile of the *studia humanitatis*. Luther himself owed a considerable debt to the humanist learning he acquired while at Erfurt (indeed, his reading of Paul would have been impossible without the hermeneutical skills it provided), and throughout his career he acknowledged the importance of languages for the understanding of Scripture. Little wonder the humanists at first considered Luther one of their own: he shared the same interest in language, the same urge to return to the original languages of the Scriptures, the same low opinion of Scholasticism, and the same desire to preserve the distance between philosophy and theology.[23] He also touched on the same nerves: the sense of German nationalism, the mood of expectation, the anticlericalism, and the apocalyptic belief that the end of time was at hand — pervasive in the late medieval age. Luther was lumped together with the champions of humanist reform and his persecution at the hands of the papal theologians viewed as part of the same battle for academic freedom. Catholic opponents largely agreed. Hieronymus Aleander (1480–1542), papal nuncio at the Diet of Worms, referred to Erasmus as "the director of the Lutheran tragedy," while Johannes Cochlaeus (1479–1552), Luther's first biographer, remained convinced that those most attracted to the evangelical movement were the highly educated young people, those who had been raised on a diet of rhetoric and philology and schooled by the works of Erasmus.[24] This marriage between the humanists and the evangelicals would not hold for long, especially after Luther and Erasmus parted company over the issue of free will,[25] but it was an important vehicle for the faith in the early days.

By the time Luther made his famous appearance before Emperor Charles V at the Diet of Worms, on 17 April 1521, the Luther affair had become the principal concern of the German Nation, even if it had minor billing on the imperial agenda. Events had moved far beyond the University of Wittenberg, and Luther had become an international figure. What began as an exercise in exegesis and the reform of university curriculum had developed into a national event, with as many hidden consequences for the German lands as there were passions for the cause. Humanists and theologians were joined in support of evangelical ideas by princes and knights, councilors and city secretaries, parish priests and monks — all with an interest in common, if different outcomes in mind. The appearance in Worms was supremely important because it revealed the sheer scale of support in Germany and the complex of interests that underlay it. Of course, there was a momentum already in place, and to a great extent the Reformation, especially in its political dimensions, must be seen as a continuation of medieval developments. For Friedrich the Wise, as for many other authorities in the empire, the "Luther affair" was yet another manifestation of the *gravamina* (grievances) against the papacy that had rankled Germans for so long.[26] Catholics, however, saw it differently, as did the reformer himself, but by the time Luther appeared in Worms it was too late to stamp any one imprimatur on the movement, and it was certainly too late to rein it in.[27] By this time, as the papal officials remarked, Luther had become the hero of the German people, and his journey to Worms nothing less than a triumphal procession. When he arrived in the city thousands of supporters came to greet him, one of whom, as Aleander described it, was a priest who embraced Luther and touched his habit three times "as if he had had a relic of the greatest saint in his hands."[28] Luther had become the figurehead for a national movement.

Message and Media

Historians have often termed the Reformation a media event, usually placing particular stress on the importance of the printed word.[29] It is a fitting description, and a fair judgment as well, for the Reformation was the first period in European history during which issues of such fundamental importance became a matter for such widespread speculation, just as it was the first time that so many different forms of expression were mobilized to give voice and meaning to personal opinion. In all of this the published text was paramount; without the press there would not have been a Reformation movement on this scale.

And the corollary is true as well: without the rise of the Reformation the printing press would not so quickly have become one of the foremost technologies of the age. But the printed word was not the only method or the only medium that was used. Evangelical ideas were communicated in a wide variety of ways. Urban reformers lectured in town halls and preached from pulpits, many taking to open fields and village greens when the churches were closed; reform-minded artists reworked the iconography of Catholic Europe, filling the churches with objects and imagery more in tune with their ideas of faith, justification, and righteousness; evangelical supporters gathered in groups to effect religious change and make their opinions known — through public displays and collective action, through the inversion of ritual and the reworking of religious rites, through open dialogue and snatches of conversation in church yards, street corners, and village inns.[30] To call the Reformation a media event thus captures much of its essence, both in terms of its form and dynamic as well as its animating spirit. It also reveals something of the depth of support, for this was a media revolution generated and sustained by public interest.[31]

At the beginning, the belief that religious truth could be revealed by way of public dialogue was a widespread conviction. According to the Wittenberg reformers truth was not the product of *ex cathedra* pronouncements or the subtleties of human thought; truth emerged as part of a cooperative undertaking, a consensual search for certainty, in which the dialogue served only to mediate, not to manipulate, the Word of God.[32] This conviction was first revealed during the debate in Leipzig, where Luther became convinced that Eck's reliance on his own powers of reason and his reluctance to engage in debate meant he could not probe the depths of religious truth. Luther likened him to a spider on the water, just sitting on the surface of things.[33] The evangelical reformers, in contrast, thought they were in a quest for deeper certainties, and they believed that the more subject one was to the thought of man the more distant one was from the Word of God. The only certain source of religious knowledge was Scripture. Consequently, all the reformers placed great importance on the power of the Word, that is the Holy Scripture. It was in effect the third sacrament — besides baptism and Holy Communion — of the Reformation, and many preachers believed that it had a power of its own to persuade and convert, just as they believed that the faithful had the native ability to understand it. The Swiss reformer Huldrych Zwingli (1484–1531) insisted in *Von Klarheit und Gewissheit des Wortes Gottes* (On the Clarity and Certainty of the Word of God, 1522) and elsewhere that even the most humble of believers, with persistence and a pure heart, could discover the truth of the faith in the Scriptures. He drew on his own experience to make the point:

> Ich hab wol als vil zûgenommen in minen jungen tagen in menschlicher leer, als etlich mines alters, und als ich vor ietz siben oder acht jar vergangen mich hûb gantz an die heyligen gschrifft lassen, wolt mir die philosophy und theology der zanggeren ümmerdar inwerffen. Do kam ich zum letsten dahin, das ich gedacht — doch mit gschrifft und wort gottes ingfûrt —, du mûst das alles lassen liggen und die meinung gottes luter

uß sinem eignen einvaltigen wort lernen. Do hůb ich an got ze bitten umb sin liecht, und fieng mir an die geschrifft vil lichter werden — wiewol ich sy bloß laß, — denn hette ich vil comment und ußleger gelesen. Sehen ir, das ist ie ein gwüs zeichen, das got stürt, denn nach kleine mines verstands hett ich dahin nienen kummen mögen. Ietz verstond ir, min meinung nit uß übernemmen sunder us hinwerffen min kummen.[34]

[When I was younger, I gave myself overmuch to human teaching, like others of my day, and when about seven or eight years ago I undertook to devote myself entirely to the Scriptures I was always prevented by philosophy and theology. But eventually I came to the point where led by the Word and spirit of God I saw the need to set aside all these things and to learn the doctrine of God direct from his own Word. Then I began to ask God for light and the Scriptures became far clearer to me — even though I read nothing else — than if I had studied many commentators and expositors. Note that that is always a sure sign of God's leading, for I could never have reached that point by the feebleness of my own understanding. You may see then that my interpretation does not derive from the overestimation of myself, but the subjection.]

For men like Zwingli religious understanding was not the preserve of a clerical elite; it was the common property of the worshiping community, and it was now free for all men to acquire in the flood of texts that washed over the German lands.[35]

Print was essential for the rise of the Reformation movement. Although Luther hedged some reservations about the printing trade later in life, in the beginning he viewed it as God's own gift to the German people to carry forth the gospel.[36] And it proved a fateful conjunction of technology and ideas: both benefited from the association. Although relatively recent, the printing trade by the start of the sixteenth century seemed to have reached its natural limitations. The technology had developed considerably over its first fifty years, and a network of exchange was in place, with centers of printing and publishing in the larger cities (including Augsburg, Nuremberg, Basel, Cologne, Leipzig, and Erfurt) joined together by a trade route of book fairs. But books still remained expensive objects written with a narrow readership, primarily the humanists, in mind. Sales declined or stagnated, and public interest was limited. For instance, for all its resonance in correspondence of the day, and for all its centrality in the debates that prepared the ground for the Luther affair, the importance of Johannes Reuchlin's *De rudimentis hebraicis* (The Rudiments of the Hebrew Language, 1506) was not reflected in its sales. Even at the Frankfurt book fair it was difficult to move.[37]

With the rise of the Reformation movement, however, the printing and publishing industries were radically transformed within the space of a few years. The number of books increased multifold, publishing houses in Germany proliferated, and the printed text vaulted onto the market as one of the central commodities of the age. It had been a technology lying in wait; the Reformation set it in motion. In Augsburg, for example, primarily through the publication of works by Luther, the industry's profits increased sixfold between 1517 and

1525. Other centers of the trade experienced a similar increase, while some locations, Wittenberg being the obvious example, were more or less created by the movement. From the very beginning the press served as a handmaid for the faith. The very nature of the movement was mirrored in the character of the published texts, from the theses and disputations of the initial confrontation, the sermons, pamphlets, and works of devotion as the theology evolved, to the catechisms and the church orders of the established church. Of course, tensions arose. As early as 1524 the reformer Eberlin von Günzburg (1470–1533) was remarking on how the desire for profit often eclipsed all other concerns.[38] But overall, the printed word proved both a faithful and a critically important collaborator in the emergence of the Reformation. The partnership was evident at the outset, indeed, as with the publication of the *Acta Augustana* (1518), Luther's edited and annotated account of his Augsburg meeting with Cardinal Cajetan. History was written almost as quickly as it was made, and it was written with a plot already in mind. As the reformers believed that they were agents acting out the divine will, they tended to view events against the backdrop of the master, that is, evangelical, narrative. God spoke to his people through a text, and it was only natural that his people should use the same medium to extend the dialogue. Kept within reason it is not too farfetched to suggest that the Reformation itself was a creation of the printed word, as deliberate, self-conscious, and "authored" as any text of the age.[39]

By far the most successful author of the Reformation was Luther. A recent synthesis of the confessional age has referred to his works as the *Urmedium* (primal medium) of the movement, a term meant in this instance to capture the functional as much as the theological importance of his publications.[40] Luther's was a powerful voice in more than one medium. He made use of all means of expression available, from sermons and disputations to broadsheets and public gestures. Luther did not believe he had to make a choice between the "medieval" and the "modern" when it came to spreading the word. Correspondence, for instance, remained his favorite mode of expression, and he was quick to admonish others when they underestimated the importance he attached to letter writing.[41] But Luther's lasting fame was primarily a creation of the printed word; he was in effect, along with other luminaries, such as Erasmus, one of the first literary celebrities of the modern age. The sheer range of his publications was enormous: by 1519 there were over 250,000 copies of his works in circulation; by 1521, at the time of the meeting in Worms, up to 500,000 individual texts in his name had been sold; by 1525 there were over 2,000 editions of his works, and historians calculate the number of copies to have run in the millions. During the early years of the movement it was enough for the Wittenberg publishers to print M. L. A. (Martin Luther Augustinian) or simply M. L. on the title page for the reading public to know which author was meant.[42] A large part of Luther's success was due to his ability to write profoundly in a wide range of different genres, from the Latin theses, commentaries, resolutions, and theological tracts to the German works for a broader readership, including the pastoral and devotional works, the sermons, catechisms, and pamphlets.

His greatest literary creation, however, was his translation of the Bible,[43] a work that enabled him to give full rein to his powers as a writer and a linguist, and a work that provided Luther with another textual platform for the launch of his theological ideas. Catholic controversialists pointed out that it was not a dispassionate or transparent reading of Holy Writ. On the contrary, they argued that the translation had been shaped by the evangelical doctrine of justification, thus allowing Luther to present his idea of Christ "pure and simply" within the context of a textual field that, even with *sola scriptura* as a hermeneutical guide, could not fail but to lead the reader in a direction that favored Luther's reading of Scripture.[44]

In strictly quantitative terms no form of publication was as important for the Reformation as the *Flugschrift*, or pamphlet. As pamphlets were small, lightweight, and relatively cheap, they soon proved to be the most popular means of disseminating the evangelical message. No other medium could spread ideas so quickly while reaching so far. Yet the essential value of the pamphlet literature was that it was a spur to dialogue; it provided a textual forum for the massive outpouring of ideas and opinions that characterized the early Reformation. There had been no precedent in German history for literature of this kind, and therefore pamphlets assumed many literary forms, from sermons, epistles, songs, and prayers to plays, poems, and set-piece dialogues. Moreover, the pamphlet also proved to be the ideal medium for the formation of public opinion, for the narrative was often couched in the style of a debate. Thus, the reader, or the hearer, could play witness to the logic of conversion by following a staged encounter between the principles of evangelical theology, often personified in simple and virtuous laymen (the "good Lutheran peasants"), and the teachings of the Catholic Church, often little more than caricatures of perceived abuses — depraved monks, money-grubbing priests, hair-splitting theologians, predatory bishops, and satanic popes.[45]

In the early years of the Reformation the diversity of voices and the range of topics were immense. Some authors, clergymen in particular, made use of the pamphlet medium to elucidate the general principles of Lutheran thought. Others picked up on a specific theme and gave it voice: Haug Marschalck (1491–1535), captain of imperial troops, incensed by the aggressive reaction of the Catholic authorities, wrote a defense of Luther and the gospel; Pamphilus Gengenbach (ca. 1480–1525), a printer in Basel, published his vision of a Christian utopia based on the principles of evangelical thought; Hans Füssli (1477–1538), Swiss bell founder, wrote on the reputed errors of Rome; and Lazarus Spengler (1479–1534), secretary to the city council of Nuremberg, wrote the first public defense of Luther to come from the desk of a layman, claiming that true religion could only be found in the Word of God and that the teachings of the Catholic clergy had reduced Scripture to a secondary authority.[46] Ulrich von Hutten (1488–1523), man of letters and Imperial Knight, waged a war of words against Rome in the name of German nationalism and gave thanks that he lived in an age when so many people spoke their minds in the German tongue. Luther himself did much to stir the passions of his countrymen, and never more effectively than in his manifesto of reform, *An den Christlichen Adel deutscher Nation* (Address to the Christian Nobility of the German Nation, 1520), a work that called on the German Nation to awake to the state of affairs:

> die not und beschwerung, die alle stend der Christenheit, zuvor deutsche landt, druckt, nit allein mich, szondern yderman bewegt hat, viel mal zuschreyen und hulff begeren, hat mich auch itzt zwungen zuschreyen unnd ruffen, ob got yemand den geyst geben wolt, seine hand zureychen der elenden Nation. Es ist offt durch Concilia etwas furgewant, aber durch etlicher menschen list behendiglich vorhyndert und ymmer erger worden, wilcher tuck und boszheit ich itzt, gott helff mir, durchleuchten gedenck, auff das sie erkant hynfurt nit mehr so hynderlich und schedlich sein mochten. Got hat uns ein jungs edlisz blut zum heubt geben [Charles V], damit viel hertzen zu groser guter hoffnung erweckt, daneben wil sichs zymen, das unser datzu thun, und der zeit und gnade nutzlich brauchen.[47]

> [All classes in Christendom, particularly in Germany, are now oppressed by distress and affliction, and this has stirred not only me but everyman to cry out anxiously for help. It has compelled me to beg and pray that God will endow someone with his spirit to bring aid to this unhappy nation. Proposals have often been made at councils, but have been cunningly deferred by the guile of certain men, and matters have gone from bad to worse. Their artifices and wickedness I intend with God's help to lay bare in order that, once shown up, they may never again present such hindrances or be so harmful. God has given us a young man of noble ancestry to be our head (Charles V) and so has raised high hopes in many hearts. In these circumstances, it is fitting for us to do all we can to make good use of the present time and of God's gracious gift to us.]

Pamphlets were also an effective medium for visual propaganda. Many were furnished with woodcuts, either in the form of a single-leaf illustration (a title page, for instance) or a series of images to accompany the written text.[48] Protestant artists reworked the visual traditions of medieval Europe, drawing on the stock of images and allusions in the world of popular culture and popular belief to make religious themes visual and transparent.

More direct methods of indoctrination developed as well, codes and symbols with specific theological meanings, making it possible for artists and authors to exploit the woodcut image as a method of teaching the basics about the faith.[49] The first master of the Protestant image was the Wittenberg artist Lucas Cranach the Elder (1472–1553). Soon after a relatively unsuccessful collaboration with Karlstadt, Cranach began to produce a series of works, mostly woodcuts, but paintings as well, devised as visual renderings of evangelical thought. The first, *Passional Christi und Antichristi* (1521), conceived in cooperation with Luther and Melanchthon, consists of a chain of woodcuts juxtaposing the life of Christ with the perceived failings of the papacy. It is a sequence of cosmic extremes and moral contrasts (probity versus depravity, compassion versus cruelty, poverty versus wealth), and it invites the viewer to draw the obvious conclusions. More sophisticated, at least in its attempts to relate the subtleties of evangelical thought, was Cranach's rendering of *Gesetz und Evangelium* (The Law and the Gospel, 1529). Taking his cue from Melanchthon's *Loci communes* (1521), a work of systematic theology, Cranach uses symbols, characters, and narratives from the Old and the New Testaments to relate the distinction between law and gospel. Thus on the left of the image: the depiction of the sinner subject to the law, pursued by Death and the devil, confronted by Moses (Decalogue in hand) and the prophets, with images of the Fall in the background and Christ as judge above. On the right of the image: the sinner under the gospel, supplicatory before the crucified Christ, the risen lamb triumphant over Death and the devil, with images of the shepherds and the Visitation in the background.[50] In later years this type of Protestant imagery filtered down into the churches, as altar and pulpit scenes, and on fonts and walls as portraits and epitaphs. For without the visual, as Luther realized, it is not possible to understand the word.[51]

For all of the evangelical reformers the nature of the medium was less significant than the message it revealed. Whether the faith was broadcast in text, image, or sermon was secondary in importance when set against the basic need to spread the Word of God. As the Lutheran superintendent of Eisleben, Georg Major (1502–74), once remarked, all men have been mandated to spread the Word of God by any means possible, not just through the spoken word, but through writings, paintings, plastic arts, music, and song.[52] This was the sentiment behind yet another collaboration between the Reformation and the media, and one that may serve as a final example of the process at work: Protestant theater.[53] Historians can learn much from this type of staged performance, for even though it was an indirect or ephemeral way to spread the Word, it was nevertheless a fertile setting for the elaboration of religious ideas.

In Bern, for instance, there was a long tradition of religious drama, and resident playwrights such as Niklaus Manuel (ca. 1484–1530) and Hans von Rüte (died 1558) reworked the stock of themes and created a few of their own in an effort to advance the cause of evangelical reform. Manuel's early run of anticlerical plays — such as *Von Papsts und Christi Gegensatz* (The Difference between the Pope and Christ) and *Vom Papst und seiner Priesterschaft* (The Pope and His Priests), which were published together in 1524, or *Der Ablaßkrämer* (The Indulgence Merchant) of the following year — are clear testimony to his interest in the movement, at times shrugging off the satire and speaking in plain terms about papal corruption and the pope as antichrist. Later works by Rüte, staged after the Reformation had been introduced in the city, were less belligerent and in their readings of biblical history more sophisticated in theological understanding.[54] Drama could thus serve as an effective method for the teaching of the faith, as the Strasbourg reformer Martin Bucer (1491–1551) believed.[55] Reservations about the theater remained, however; many reformers could not dissociate this type of drama from the sacerdotal masques of the medieval age. Others, Luther included, thought that the stage might prove a useful ally in the spread of God's Word, but only if the viewer could go beyond the surface performance and grasp the deeper themes. He used the image of the crucified Christ to make the point, advising the faithful to look further than the scenes of suffering and behold the very heart of Christ (by which Luther meant the spirit of love that bears so many burdens and takes on so many sins), for this would lead to affection, trust, and ultimately a strengthening of faith.[56] Luther was thus expecting the same thing from a theater audience as he was from the faithful in a church or the solitary reader confronted by a text: to see beyond the medium to the religious message inside.

Contexts of Reform

With the publication of the Edict of Worms, Luther and his teachings were outlawed in the Holy Roman Empire. Despite this condemnation, evangelical ideas continued to spread. Hidden away in the small Saxon town of Wittenberg, Luther and the other reformers inundated the German lands with their correspondence and their printed works. And it was a two-way flow: sympathetic students and clergymen made the trek to Wittenberg to study at the side of the famous reformers; after having spent some time at the source they then returned home as ambassadors of the faith.[57] A similar process occurred within Zurich's area of influence, as the Swiss reformer Huldrych Zwingli gathered followers and pulled neighboring cities into the gravity of his teachings. Much of southern Germany turned to Zwingli rather than to Luther in the early years of reform, including the cities of Strasbourg, Constance, Augsburg, Ulm, Esslingen, and Biberach.[58]

Once the Reformation had been planted in a town or a city the message could be spread anew, with the radius of influence reaching into the outlying parishes. The most influential setting for the Reformation was the free imperial city. These urban centers not only served as locations of agitation but were also public models of evangelical reform. Many large territorial cities became Lutheran as well, especially in the north of Germany, and even in some of the bishoprics the faith took root. Events in the principalities are more difficult to characterize, as it was not possible for a territorial ruler to contain or to direct the early movement, but no doubt most territories, even the most airtight Catholic duchies, experienced the spread of the evangelical message to some degree. In Albertine Saxony, for instance, despite the best efforts of Luther's archnemesis Duke Georg (1471–1539), the movement took hold in the parishes: in Kölleda, where a monk preached evangelical sermons; in Thamsbrück, where anti-Catholic pamphlets were readily sold; in Zörbig, where four parishioners were expelled for their refusal to accept communion in one kind; in Döbeln, where an evangelical clergyman preached to a growing band of supporters; and in Dresden, where Hieronymus Emser (1477–1527), one of the Catholic controversialists who first wrote against Luther, had the windows of his house smashed in by evangelical sympathizers. Duke Georg took steps to suppress the movement, but largely in vain.[59]

As the evangelical movement spread beyond Wittenberg and Zurich it could no longer be orchestrated or controlled by a single reformer. Inspirational figures remained, but the Reformation fragmented as it began to draw its essential energy from the local settings. Moreover, as the message found a growing audience, it was no longer possible to limit its reach. Parishioners of all social categories became followers of the movement. The sheer extent and variety of interest is what makes it so difficult for historians to speak of a single Reformation movement. Clearly, the theological principles held in common by the early reformers imparted a sense of unity. Yet it is equally true that different reformers interpreted the gospel in different ways, and this necessarily gave rise to heterogeneity.[60] It is a difficult question to answer with any satisfaction, partly because it skirts a central concern. In dealing with the Reformation as a historical phenomenon, the main issue is not so much *what* was preached and printed as *how* the message was actually understood. With this question in mind, two basic features of evangelical understanding stand out. First, many of the earliest supporters articulated their convictions in the language of anticlericalism. Attacking the Catholic clergy and the Catholic Church in both word and deed made it possible for the parishioners to contextualize and familiarize their religious ideas, for there were obvious (and numerous) points of contact between the themes of evangelical teaching and traditional religious culture.[61] Second, all followers of the movement, regardless of social standing, expressed a desire for the Word of God. The demand to hear the gospel preached clear and pure was universal, whether in the urban communes or the hamlets and villages of rural Germany. In Alsace, for instance, the peasants made repeated demands for the preaching of the gospel, as this was the "light of truth" and the only means of salvation. Further north in the parishes of Ansbach the peasant communities made similar requests, speaking of the need to be "educated and instructed in the Word of God."[62] This was the second general feature of the movement, this relentless demand for the Word of God. Once combined with the tendency to search for points of contact in the social and political order, it could have a revolutionary effect.

The power of the word to effect radical social change first became apparent in the German countryside. The evangelical peasant had been around in the pamphlet literature for years, but the good Lutheran peasant of these tracts was little more than a caricature, a paragon of simple folk. In reality, the evangelical peasant was much less deferential and much more critical than the reformers imagined. The rural parishioners were quick to embrace the faith, but it was accepted on their terms, in accordance with their notions of local religion. Throughout the parishes of southern Germany and Switzerland peasant grievances, supplications, and manifestoes made repeated demands that reform be implemented at the level of the rural parish.[63] This was the peasant notion of reformation, a reading of the evangelical message that translated its theological principles into social and political norms. (Luther considered it a pretext to distort the Word of God for earthly advantage, a deliberate perversion of law and gospel.) When rural parishioners first expressed their interest in the faith, requests for a communal church came to the surface, all derived from Scripture and all with practical consequences for local religion. The parishioners demanded the unrestricted preaching of the gospel; they demanded the right to appoint and dismiss the pastor, the right to supervise his income, as well as the right to judge his teaching; and they demanded that the gospel serve as a guide for social relations, that people should live in a state of brotherly love.[64] It was a vision of the worshiping community rooted in the gospel and realized in the parish, a tropological reading of the evangelical message, and for a short time it proved revolutionary.

Throughout the year 1524, as the wave of preaching and publishing reached its peak and as the visions of reform became more and more radical, the rural movement could no longer be contained, and it passed over to revolution. The subject population took to the field in a series of extended sieges and regional battles that historians have termed the Peasants' War of 1525, a wave of unrest that swept through most of the German lands, including Alsace, Franconia, Thuringia, Upper Swabia, Switzerland, and the Tyrol. In voicing their demands the same approach to the faith was in evidence, the same complete trust in the gospel and demand for "godly justice," only now the social and political horizons had broadened and the visions had become extreme. There was a conflation of religious expectations with age-old social and political grievances. Peasant bands drew directly from Scripture in order to demand the lifting of fees and dues, access to the waters and the forest of the demesne lands, the elimination of tithes, and at the most extreme, the end of servitude and feudalism. Manifestoes circulated, allegedly written to represent the views of the bands of rebel peasants, demanding the root-and-branch reform of church and state in accordance with the principles of godly justice and foretelling the rise of Christ's Kingdom on earth.[65]

The most prominent evangelical clergyman to take up arms with the peasants was Thomas Müntzer (ca. 1489–1525). Once a follower of Luther and the Wittenberg reformers, Müntzer began to develop his own understanding of the faith while serving as a preacher in the Saxon towns of Zwickau, Allstedt, and Mühlhausen. Ultimately Müntzer's activity led to unrest and he was forced to move on to Prague, where he published the *Prager Manifest* (1521), the first explicit declaration of his reforming ideas. In this work Müntzer declared true religion to be a matter of the spirit. He ridiculed the dead letter of Scripture and spoke of a mystical union between the true believers, termed "die Auserwählten" (the elect) and God, a union that could only be effected through fear and suffering for the faith. He also made a complete break with Wittenberg, later going so far as to attack Luther in print, calling him "das geistlose sanfftlebende Fleysch zu Wittenberg" (that spiritless soft-living flesh in Wittenberg). Over time Müntzer's preaching became more aggressive and intolerant, his theology more mystical and internal, and his visions more revolutionary. In his so-called *Fürstenpredigt* (Sermon to the Princes, 1524), a public lecture held before the princes of Saxony, Müntzer spoke of the deceit of the clergy, the decline of the church, the downfall of earthly kingdoms, and the coming reign of Christ. He also admonished the princes to prepare for the coming struggle between the godless and the elect. Once the princes failed to respond, however, he turned to the peasants. Müntzer returned to Mühlhausen, and it was there, together with the former

Cistercian Heinrich Pfeiffer (d. 1525), that he realized his theology of revolution. In April 1525 he formed the *Ewiger Bund Gottes* (Eternal League of God), a military association of true believers convened in order to defeat the godless. The intention was clear: once victorious, the League would bring down the mighty, give power to the poor in spirit, and overthrow the false clergy and their godless followers. In his *Manifest an die Verschworenen des Allstedter Bundes* (Manifesto to the Conspirators of the Allstedt League) of the same year Müntzer called the Allstedters to violence in the colorful vernacular for which he is famous:

> Dran, dran, dyeweyl das feuer hayß ist. Lasset euer schwerth nit kalt werden, lasset nit vorlehmen! Schmidet pinkepanke auf den anbossen Nymroths, werfet ihne den thorm zu boden! [. . .] Dran, dran, weyl ir tag habt, gott gehet euch vor, volget, volget![66]

> [On, on, while the fire is hot! Don't let your swords grow cold, don't let yourselves grow weary! Pound your weapons bang bang bang on Nimrod's anvils! Throw down their tower to the ground! On, on, while it is yet day! God goes before you. Follow, follow!]

But in the end the peasant army was no match for the combined military strength of the princes. Müntzer was captured, tortured, and executed, his body left on public display as a warning against the dangers of disobedience and false belief.[67]

Müntzer was representative of the strain of evangelical thought that modern historians have termed the "radical Reformation." The radicals first took root in Saxony, but they soon spread throughout the empire, and cognate strains also developed in the lands of southern Germany and Switzerland, where Zwingli, no less than Luther, faced growing opposition from within his own ranks. The radical reformers did not agree among themselves; there was no core theology or canon of faith, and no single figure united the later Anabaptist communities. Nevertheless, four basic features were held in common, and we may take these as representative of the tradition as a whole.[68] First, in both Germany and Switzerland the radical reformers adopted an extremely literal approach to Scripture. The radical reformers went beyond the Lutherans and Zwinglians in their unadulterated reliance on the Word of God. The most famous literal reading of Scripture (Matt. 7:14) was the rejection of infant baptism, a corollary to the conviction that faith must precede admittance to the worshiping community. Not all of the radical reformers made this distinction in print, but in a very short time the rite of adult baptism (or rebaptism, which is the meaning of the term Anabaptism) became the distinguishing mark of the radical tradition. Second, many of the radical reformers sanctioned an aggressive anticlericalism. The Catholic priesthood was the main target, but, in time, the radicals began to direct their published attacks against mainstream evangelical reformers as well. The third feature of the movement was its exclusiveness. Its communities sought separation. For the radicals there could be no dialogue with the existing churches, only the hope that the true believers might ultimately find their way into the fold. In Saxony, as we have seen, Müntzer thought in terms of the exclusive community, envisioning a final battle between his army of the Eternal League and the godless on earth. This was an extreme vision of separation, but all radical communities necessarily broke with the broader *corpus Christianum* to some degree. Finally, the radical Reformation was colored by the language of mysticism, spiritualism, and apocalypticism. It owed much to medieval spirituality. The leaders of the movement rejected traditional interpretations, subjected the gospel to an intensely personal reading, and used vague, poetic language to express their revelations. This approach reached its apogee in the thought of the Spiritualists, thinkers such as Kaspar von Schwenkfeld (1489–1561) and Sebastian Franck (1499–1542), who believed that only the spirit could determine religious truth.

Emperor Charles V had issued the Edict of Worms precisely with a view to preventing the type of unrest that later surfaced during the early phase of the radical Reformation and the Peasants' War. The mandate had not only been directed at the theological dangers posed by Luther's teaching but at its perceived threat to the social and political fabric as well. Once issued, however, the edict had little impact. Many estates challenged its legality, since it had been passed by a rump diet, and some actually worked to have it repealed, including the princes of Saxony, Brandenburg, and Hesse. Even those who did not voice opposition did little to enforce it, justifying their lack of compliance in terms similar to those offered by the city council of Nuremberg, which claimed that it was beyond its power to suppress the movement now that the *gemeiner Mann* (common man) showed such interest in the faith.[69] Charles took up residence in Spain in 1522 and remained there until late 1529. Given his absence from the German lands and that his regency council could not agree on a response to events in the North, no effective political opposition existed to the spread of the early Reformation. Some princes moved to contain the movement, in particular Duke Georg of Saxony; but many if not most of the estates were noncommittal, preferring to wait until the emperor negotiated a settlement (most hope was placed in a church council in the German lands) while allowing for the spread of reform in their principalities. Those waiting for a swift political solution were waiting in vain. Despite the rising need to find a way out of the growing difficulties, the series of diets held in Nuremberg between 1522 and 1524 did not find a solution. On the contrary, at the opening of the third diet the emperor simply reissued the Edict of Worms and commanded "that every ruler make sure that his subjects live according to His Majesty's edicts," but this did little more than increase political tensions.[70]

In the end the problems raised by the evangelical movement were not addressed until the Diet of Speyer, a year after the end of the revolution, when the diet published its recess on 27 August 1526. Even then the solution was ambiguous and provisional, but it granted just enough political leeway to release reforming energies. The recess ordered the estates to pursue a policy in religious affairs "as [they] hope and trust to answer to God and his Imperial Majesty."[71] Although intended as a stopgap interdict against further innovation, the evangelical estates interpreted the wording in a positive sense and viewed it as the political endorsement of their right to reform the territorial church, a right formulated in the phrase *ius reformandi*. Against the actual intentions of the emperor and his imperial officials, the recess provided the evangelical estates with legal and political legitimacy for the spread of the faith. Speyer thus set the stage for the introduction of Lutheranism in Germany, and from this point forward the Reformation was ingrained in the dynamic of political relations.

The first political and institutional context of development for the Reformation was the city. On the surface, the city was a natural environment for the movement, for it had the churches and preachers, the printers and booksellers, and the complex landscape of human relations that infused the word with such social energy. But there was a deeper affinity as well. Urban rulers, drawing on the notion of the common good (*Gemeinnutz*), were able to integrate religious developments into patterns of governance. The Reformation effected a communalization, or domestication, of the urban church. The clergy fell subject to secular rule, the council increased its control over clerical appointment, the ecclesiastical structure merged with the organs of civic governance, the legal immunity of the church was abolished, and religion and piety were more closely allied with urban values. And while this institutional transformation occurred the evangelical message itself provided the authorities with powerful ideological legitimacy, for not only did it offer a blueprint for the new church, it also sanctified the entire undertaking. There had long been a tendency to think of the city, or commune, as a type of sacral corporation, with each member of the union contributing to the salvation of the whole. The evangelical message, with its emphasis on the importance of the worshiping community and brotherly love, revived this vision.

Thus, from the beginning the Reformation was bound up with the broad framework of urban relations, and it evolved as a social and political event with social and political consequences.[72] Perhaps the most dramatic examples of this linkage occurred during the Reformation in the Hanseatic cities in the north (Dortmund, Stralsund, Münster, Paderborn, Soest, Osnabrück, Lübeck). In these cities the Reformation took shape as a conflict between principles of communal rule, led by the guilds and the influential burghers who supported the Reformation, and the oligarchic city councilors, those Catholic members of the ruling elite who defended tradition and were associated with a closed patriarchy. The Reformation had revolutionary potential here and could bring about, as in Lübeck, a usurpation of rule and thus a change of the governing elite. But events did not have to be that dramatic to influence the structures of rule. Even in the large free imperial cities, where the implementation of the Reformation was effectively controlled by the city council, the change of religion could influence the constitution of governance and the profile of the ruling elite.[73]

The political dynamic can be illustrated by events in the free imperial city of Nuremberg, where the evangelical movement forced the ruling elite to moderate between the demands of the urban commune and the Catholic empire. Nuremberg's only effective (and constitutional) overlord was the emperor. Consequently, as soon as the Luther affair became an issue, Charles V himself advised the city to suppress the movement. But his counsel came too late. The message spread, resulting in popular and widespread agitation in favor of religious reform. Throughout the early 1520s, in an effort to maintain public order, the city council was forced to intervene. Preachers were told to leave off incendiary sermons, restrictions were placed on the printing of books, and the posting of anticlerical placards and pamphlets in the public squares was forbidden. And yet these measures could not put an end to public sympathy or the strength of support, especially as both Andreas Osiander (1498–1552) and Dominicus Schleupner (d. 1547) preached in favor of the new faith in the two parish churches.[74] Once the emperor learned of the state of affairs in Nuremberg he ordered the city council, under a veiled threat of force (and a more direct caution that he might rescind Nuremberg's imperial privileges), to put an end to the movement. The council was faced with a political dilemma. Approval of the movement was, in essence, a form of rebellion; but refusal to compromise with the commune could be, in effect, political suicide, for the peasants were gathering in strength and there was no certainty that the city's inhabitants would remain calm. Moreover, the idea of a reform of the urban church sat well with city magistrates such as Lazarus Spengler, for civic notions of communal governance were easily associated with the evangelical ideal of brotherly love. For men like Spengler order in the secular world followed order in the world of religion.[75] In the face of this dilemma the council adopted the most appropriate political solution. It made a show of obeying the imperial requests — including censorship and control of public preaching — while at the same time allowing for religious observance strictly according to Scripture. When reprimanded by the imperial authorities for allowing this contradictory state of affairs, the council referred to the strength of support for the movement among the parishioners and its inability to act.[76] The threat presented by the commune, at least in the eyes of the ruling elite, posed a greater political risk than the disapproving, but distant, imperial government. Nuremberg became a Lutheran city, a gradual process of religious change that gathered pace after the introduction of the evangelical service in 1525.

By the time the Reformation had been consolidated in Nuremberg the momentum in the empire had begun to shift. Up to this point the cities had been the social and political framework for the evolution of the faith; by the late 1520s, however, the German territories emerged as the crucial setting. There were two reasons for this: First, the evangelical cities had never been able to effect a common policy. There had been no wider sense of religious solidarity (a problem compounded by the tensions between the followers of Zwingli and Luther), and thus most of the major urban communes, weakened by the consequences of the Peasants' War, had turned in on themselves. Second, once the dust from the revolution had settled it was clear that the German princes had emerged from the war as the dominant political force in the empire. This had never really been in doubt, but now it was a manifest truth, and it had important implications for the fate of the Reformation, for it meant that if the movement were to survive it would have to be absorbed into princely politics.[77] This is exactly what happened. Landgrave Philipp of Hesse (1504–67) was the first to act, but it was the electors of Saxony, guided by the reformers Luther and Melanchthon, who provided the blueprint for the princely Reformation. The process and the timetable varied from territory to territory, but in general all the Lutheran rulers took similar steps to fashion a Reformation church, beginning with the toleration of the preaching of the Word "clear and pure," the appointment of evangelical clergymen, the change of the religious service, the publication of confessional statements (church orders, visitation orders, catechisms), and the construction of the territorial church — which in the Lutheran variant meant the establishment of regular visitations, marriage courts and consistories, and a range of new officials, starting at the level of the parish with the Protestant clergyman and reaching to the superintendents at the upper echelons of government. Lutheran Reformations of this kind first occurred in the lands of Saxony (1522–28), Hesse (1526–32), Brandenburg-Ansbach-Kulmbach (1528–33), Braunschweig-Lüneburg (1526–27), Anhalt (1526), and Mansfeld (1525–26), and others would follow in Württemberg (1534), Brandenburg (1540), and Albertine Saxony (1539). Later in the century territorial Reformations of Reformed (or Calvinist) Protestantism — sometimes known under the rubric "Second Reformation" — would intensify the process, as the German lands experienced the onset of religious division and the rise of the confessional powers.[78]

In the end, the only natural context of development for the Protestant church in Germany was the princely territory. The relationship itself was rooted in the principles of Lutheran thought. Luther's idea of the priesthood of all believers eliminated the distinctions between the spiritual and the temporal in the sphere of ecclesiastical rule, thus making the church an earthly institution, and it was only natural that responsibility for the supervision of the church would fall to the German prince. Moreover, given Luther's doctrine of the Two Kingdoms (that there were two distinct spheres of rule, the rule of the church and that of the state), there was no necessary tension or contradiction in suggesting that the rule of Christian society, including the rule over the earthly church, belonged to the secular arm. Other reformers would build on this doctrine, Melanchthon and the Swabian reformer Johannes Brenz (1499–1570) in particular, both of whom believed that the secular lords had been entrusted by God to rule over and protect the community of Christians. Tensions and ambiguities certainly remained, and the relationship between church and state continued to produce conflict throughout the century of Reformation, especially when Protestant clergymen started to base their theories of ecclesiology on the principle that the prince had to correspond to their notions of a "Christian" ruler in order to govern legitimately.[79] But in the beginning the notion of the princely Reformation was widely supported by the Protestant reformers, and as a consequence, in both the practice of rule and the theoretical dimensions of sovereignty, little distinction was made between the secular and the spiritual spheres of authority. The Reformation church took shape as a territorial church.

In German historiography this process of fusing church and state is referred to as *confessionalization*.[80] Religious reform, both the Catholic and the Protestant variety, had an ordering function in the broader framework of historical change. There was a structural link between politics and religion that affected the entire social system.[81] The result of this process was the rise of the confessional state, a political territory that derived both an awareness of public identity and a sense of ideological purpose from a canon of religious thought. By the end of the sixteenth century, large Protestant territories such as Brandenburg, Saxony, and Württemberg, as well as large Catholic territories like Bavaria, had evolved into powerful and sophisticated sovereign states, with systems of governance that made little or no distinction between the secular and the spiritual, notions of nationality rooted in the symbols, ritual, and language of religion, and a philosophy of rule that sought its final justification in works of theology. Over time the sense of religious identity would filter down to the subject populace. The people of Germany would begin to think of themselves in confessional terms, as Lutherans and Calvinists and Catholics, and the idea of a German Nation joined by a common faith would become a distant memory.

Notes

[1] Maria Grossmann, *Humanism in Wittenberg 1485–1517*, Bibliotheca Humanistica et Reformatorica 11 (Nieuwkoop: de Graaf, 1975), 17, note 30.

[2] Fundamental for the analysis that follows: Jens-Martin Kruse, *Universitätstheologie und Kirchenreform: Die Anfänge der Reformation in Wittenberg 1516–1522*, Veröffentlichungen des Instituts für Europäische Geschichte Mainz 187 (Mainz: von Zabern, 2002); Ulinka Rublack, *Die Reformation in Europa* (Frankfurt am Main: Fischer, 2003), 23–91, from which the term *Experimentierfeld* is taken. My thanks to Ulinka Rublack for letting me see a copy of this chapter in advance of publication. See the similar observations about the importance of the university for the Reformation in Thomas Kaufmann, "The Clergy and the Theological Culture of the Age: The Education of Lutheran Pastors in the Sixteenth and Seventeenth Centuries," in *The Protestant Clergy of Early Modern Europe*, ed. C. Scott Dixon and Luise Schorn-Schütte (Basingstoke: Palgrave, 2003), 120–36.

[3] Wilhelm Borth, *Die Luthersache (Causa Lutheri) 1517–1524: Die Anfänge der Reformation als Frage von Politik und Recht*, Historische Studien 414 (Lübeck: Matthiesen, 1970), 62, 67–68, 88–94.

[4] Kruse, *Universitätstheologie*, 2.

[5] Kruse, *Universitätstheologie*, 1.

[6] Kruse, *Universitätstheologie*, 104.

[7] Heiko A. Oberman, "Wittenbergs Zweifrontenkrieg gegen Prierias und Eck: Hintergrund und Entscheidungen des Jahres 1518," *Archiv für Reformationsgeschichte* 80 (1969): 331–58, here 333.

[8] Karl-Heinz Zur Mühlen, "Die Heidelberger Disputation Martin Luthers vom 26. April 1518," in *Reformatorisches Profil: Studien zum Weg Martin Luthers und der Reformation*, ed. Johannes Brosseder and Athina Lexutt (Göttingen: Vandenhoeck &

Ruprecht, 1995), 187. Included among the future reformers present in Heidelberg were Johannes Brenz, Martin Bucer, Theobald Billican, Hieronymus Ebener, and Erhard Schnepf.

[9] On Luther as a charismatic figure and his importance for the making of the German Reformation see Rublack, *Reformation in Europa*, 23ff.

[10] Martin Brecht, *Martin Luther: His Road to Reformation 1483–1521*, trans. James L. Schaaf (Minneapolis: Fortress, 1985), 324. On the rise of Luther's celebrity see Bernd Moeller, "Das Berühmtwerden Luthers," *Zeitschrift für historische Forschung* 15 (1988): 65–92; Thomas Fuchs, "Martin Luther: Führungsgestalt in der Reformation der Reformatoren," in *Luther in seiner Zeit*, ed. Martin Greschat and Günther Lottes (Stuttgart: Kohlhammer, 1997), 69–87.

[11] Alister McGrath, *The Intellectual Origins of the European Reformation* (Oxford: Blackwell, 1987); Euan Cameron, *The European Reformation* (Oxford: Clarendon, 1991), 1–198; Heiko A. Oberman, *The Dawn of the Reformation* (Edinburgh: T&T Clark, 1992).

[12] For a focused study of the humanists' methodological return to the sources see the chapter by Erika Rummel in this volume.

[13] Hermeneutics is the theory and practice of interpretation. It was developed during the Reformation as a discipline particularly concerned with biblical-textual criticism.

[14] "Von der Freyheyt eynisz Christen menschen," in *D. Martin Luthers Werke: Kritische Gesammtausgabe* (Weimar: Böhlau, 1897), 7:24–25. (Hereafter: *D. Martin Luthers Werke.*) Translation taken from John Dillenberger, ed., *Martin Luther: Selections from his Writings* (New York: Doubleday, 1962), 58–59. The *sola fide* doctrine was explicitly written into Article 4 of the Augsburg Confession of 1530.

[15] Berndt Hamm, "What was the Reformation Doctrine of Justification?" in *The German Reformation: The Essential Readings*, ed. C. Scott Dixon (Oxford: Blackwell, 1999), 79.

[16] Berndt Hamm, "Einheit und Vielfalt der Reformation — oder: was die Reformation zur Reformation macht," in Berndt Hamm, Bernd Moeller, and Dorothea Wendebourg, *Reformationstheorien: Ein kirchenhistorischer Disput über Einheit und Vielfalt der Reformation* (Göttingen: Vandenhoeck & Ruprecht, 1995), 57–127; Bernhard Lohse, *Luthers Theologie in ihrer historischen Entwicklung und in ihrem systematischen Zusammenhang* (Göttingen: Vandenhoeck & Ruprecht, 1995).

[17] Jaroslav Pelikan, *Reformation of Church and Dogma (1300–1700)* (Chicago: U of Chicago P, 1984), 262: "the problem of authority had disturbed the church more than the doctrine of justification."

[18] David V. N. Bagchi, *Luther's Earliest Opponents: Catholic Controversialists, 1518–1525* (Minneapolis: Fortress, 1991), 33–34.

[19] Borth, *Die Luthersache*, 31.

[20] As suggested in the instructions sent by Pope Leo X to Gabriel Venatus, protomagister of the Augustinian Hermits. See Zur Mühlen, "Die Heidelberger Disputation," 175.

[21] Brecht, *Martin Luther*, 391–94 and 474.

[22] Bernd Moeller, *Imperial Cities and the Reformation*, trans. H. C. Erik Midelfort and Mark U. Edwards Jr. (Durham, NC: Labyrinth, 1972), 29.

[23] Scholasticism, capitalized, was a medieval school, or method, that sought answers to theological questions by dialectical reasoning. Insofar as this method had seemed to the

humanists, and Luther, to have degenerated into pedantry and lost sight of real values, "scholasticism" began to acquire the connotation of mere hairsplitting. Leif Grane, *Martinus Noster: Luther in the German Reform Movement, 1518–1521,* Veröffentlichungen des Instituts für Europäische Geschichte Mainz 155 (Mainz: von Zabern, 1994), 1–58.

[24] Erika Rummel, *The Confessionalization of Humanism in Reformation Germany* (Oxford: Oxford UP, 2000), 16, 27–28.

[25] The texts of the controversy are readily available in English in *Erasmus — Luther: Discourse on Free Will,* trans. and ed. Ernst F. Winter (New York: Continuum, 2000).

[26] Borth, *Die Luthersache,* 77.

[27] Nevertheless, there was still room for negotiation. See Bernd Moeller, "Luthers Bücher auf dem Wormser Reichstag von 1521," in Moeller, *Luther-Rezeption: Kirchenhistorische Aufsätze zur Reformationsgeschichte,* ed. Johannes Schilling (Göttingen: Vandenhoeck & Ruprecht, 2001), 121–40.

[28] Heiko A. Oberman, *Luther: Man between God and the Devil,* trans. Eileen Walliser-Schwarzbart (London: Fontana, 1989), 199.

[29] Berndt Hamm, "Die Reformation als Medienereignis," *Jahrbuch für biblische Theologie* 11 (1996): 137–66; Mark U. Edwards Jr., *Printing, Propaganda, and Martin Luther* (London: U of California P, 1994), 21: "the West's first large-scale media campaign."

[30] On the modes of dissemination see R. W. Scribner and C. Scott Dixon, *The German Reformation,* 2nd ed. (Basingstoke: Palgrave Macmillan, 2003), 17–24, 73–76.

[31] Rainer Wohlfeil, "Reformatorische Öffentlichkeit, Literatur und Laienbildung im Spätmittelalter und in der Reformationszeit," in *Literatur und Laienbildung im Spätmittelalter und in der Reformationszeit,* ed. Ludger Grenzmann and Karl Stackmann, Germanistische Symposien-Berichtsbände 5 (Stuttgart: Metzler, 1984), 41–54.

[32] Thomas Fuchs, *Konfession und Gespräch: Typologie und Funktion der Religionsgespräche in der Reformationszeit,* Norm und Struktur 4 (Cologne: Böhlau, 1995), 155–87.

[33] Kruse, *Universitätstheologie,* 214.

[34] "Von clarheit und gwüsse oder krafft des wort gottes," in *Huldreich Zwinglis Sämtliche Werke* (Berlin, 1905), 1:379–80. Translation taken from G. W. Bromiley, *Zwingli and Bullinger* (Philadelphia: Westminster, 1953), 90–91.

[35] Arnold Snyder, "Word and Power in Reformation Zurich," *Archiv für Reformationsgeschichte* 8 (1990): 269; Norbert Schindler, "Die Prinzipien des Hörensagens: Predigt und Publikum in der Frühen Neuzeit," *Historische Anthropologie: Kultur — Gesellschaft — Alltag* 3 (1993): 360–72.

[36] Scribner and Dixon, *German Reformation,* 19.

[37] Reinhard Wittmann, *Geschichte des deutschen Buchhandels,* 2nd ed. (Munich: Beck, 1990), 48.

[38] Wittmann, *Geschichte des deutschen Buchhandels,* 56: "Sieh dir an, wie bedenkenlos sich die Drucker auf die Bücher stürzen, ohne darauf Rücksicht zu nehmen, ob eine Sache böse oder gut, geziemend oder ärgererregend sei. Sie nehmen Schandbücher, Buhlbücher, Spottlieder und was ihnen in die Hand kommt und gewinnbringend scheint, zum Drucke an — wodurch der Leser Geld geraubt, Sinn und Herz verwüstet und Zeit vergeudet wird."

[39] Johannes Burckhardt, *Das Reformationsjahrhundert: Deutsche Geschichte zwischen Medienrevolution und Institutionsbildung 1517–1617* (Stuttgart: Kohlhammer, 2002), 30–48.

[40] Wolfgang Reinhard, *Probleme deutscher Geschichte 1495–1806: Reichsreform und Reformation 1495–1555*, Gebhardt Handbuch deutscher Geschichte 9 (Stuttgart: Kohlhammer, 2001), 279.

[41] Horst Wenzel, "Luthers Briefe im Medienwechsel von der Manuskriptkultur zum Buchdruck," in *Die deutsche Reformation zwischen Spätmittelalter und Früher Neuzeit*, ed. Thomas A. Brady Jr., Schriften des Historischen Kollegs 50 (Munich: Oldenbourg, 2001), 203–29.

[42] Reinhard, *Probleme*, 279; Burckhardt, *Reformationsjahrhundert*, 29.

[43] For a more detailed analysis of Luther as biblical translator and his importance for the development of a standardized German see in this volume the chapter by Renate Born.

[44] Edwards, *Printing, Propaganda*, 122: "It suffices to note that Luther chose to translate crucial passages in a way not only consistent with his theological program but in a way that tended to reinforce the points he wanted the reader to take away from the text"; see also Burckhardt, *Reformationsjahrhundert*, 47–53.

[45] Jürgen Kampe, *Problem "Reformationsdialog": Untersuchungen zu einer Gattung im reformatorischen Medienwettstreit*, Beiträge zur Dialogforschung 14 (Tübingen: Niemeyer, 1997), 164–227; Alejandro Zorzin, "Einige Beobachtungen zu den zwischen 1518 und 1526 im deutschen Sprachbereich veröffentlichten Dialogflugschriften," *Archiv für Reformationsgeschichte* 88 (1997): 77–117, here 78, note 6.

[46] Miriam Usher Chrisman, *Conflicting Visions of Reform: German Lay Propaganda Pamphlets, 1519–1530* (Atlantic Highlands, NJ: Humanities Press, 1996), 70–72, 114, 126–27, 156–60, 209; Bernd Moeller and Karl Stackmann, *Städtische Predigt der Frühzeit der Reformation: Eine Untersuchung deutscher Flugschriften der Jahre 1522 bis 1529*, Abhandlungen der Akademie der Wissenschaft in Göttingen, Philologisch-Historische Klasse 3/220 (Göttingen: Vandenhoeck & Ruprecht, 1996), 301ff.; Martin Arnold, *Handwerker als theologische Schriftsteller: Studien zu Flugschriften der frühen Reformation (1523–1525)*, Göttinger theologische Arbeiten 42 (Göttingen: Vandenhoeck & Ruprecht, 1990).

[47] *An den Christlichen Adel deutscher Nation von des Christlichen standes besserung*, in *D. Martin Luthers Werke* (1888), 6:405. Translation taken from Dillenberger, ed., *Martin Luther*, 405.

[48] The language of Reformation and early modern art is the subject of the chapter by Jeffrey Chipps Smith in this volume.

[49] R. W. Scribner, *For the Sake of Simple Folk: Popular Propaganda for the German Reformation* (Oxford: Clarendon, 1994), passim.

[50] Christoph Weimer, "Luther und Cranach: Das Rechtfertigungsthema in Wort und Bild," *Luther* 74 (2003): 22–38; Frank Büttner, "'Argumentatio' in Bildern der Reformationszeit: Ein Beitrag zur Bestimmung argumentativer Strukturen in der Bildkunst," *Zeitschrift für Kunstgeschichte* (1994): 23–44.

[51] Siegfried Müller, "Repräsentationen des Luthertums — Disziplinierung und konfessionelle Kultur in Bildern: Ein Problemaufriß anhand von regionalen Beispielen," *Zeitschrift für historische Forschung* 29 (2002): 217.

[52] Glenn Ehrstine, *Theatre, Culture, and Community in Reformation Bern, 1523–1555*, Studies in Medieval and Reformation Thought 85 (Leiden: Brill, 2002), 4–5.

[53] For a full account see the chapter in this volume by John Alexander.

[54] Ehrstine, *Theatre*, 79–200.

[55] See the chapter in this volume by Laurel Carrington.

[56] Ehrstine, *Theatre*, 25.

[57] Rudolf Mau, *Evangelische Bewegung und frühe Reformation 1521 bis 1532*, Kirchengeschichte in Einzeldarstellungen 2/5 (Leipzig: Evangelische Verlagsanstalt, 2000), 90–91.

[58] Gottfried W. Locher, *Die Zwinglische Reformation im Rahmen der europäischen Kirchengeschichte* (Göttingen: Vandenhoeck & Ruprecht, 1979), 452–501.

[59] Günther Wartenberg, *Landesherrschaft und Reformation: Moritz von Sachsen und die albertinische Kirchenpolitik bis 1546*, Quellen und Forschungen zur Reformationsgeschichte 55 (Gütersloh: Mohn, 1988), 27–61.

[60] For the debate about the unity and plurality of the evangelical movement see the discussion and the literature cited in Kruse, *Universitätstheologie*, 12ff.

[61] Hans-Jürgen Goertz, *Antiklerikalismus und Reformation: Sozialgeschichtliche Untersuchungen* (Göttingen: Vandenhoeck & Ruprecht, 1995), 1–24.

[62] Franziska Conrad, *Reformation in der bäuerlichen Gesellschaft: Zur Rezeption reformatorischer Theologie im Elsass*, Veröffentlichungen des Instituts für Europäische Geschichte Mainz 116 (Stuttgart: Steiner, 1984), 96; C. Scott Dixon, *The Reformation and Rural Society: The Parishes of Brandenburg-Ansbach-Kulmbach, 1528–1603* (Cambridge: Cambridge UP, 1996), 37.

[63] Peter Blickle, *Communal Reformation: The Quest for Salvation in Sixteenth-Century Germany*, trans. Thomas Dunlap (Atlantic Highlands, NJ: Humanities Press, 1992); Conrad, *Reformation in der bäuerlichen Gesellschaft*, 97–99; C. Scott Dixon, *The Reformation in Germany* (Oxford: Blackwell, 2002), 77–87.

[64] Blickle, *Communal Reformation*, 12–53.

[65] Dixon, *Reformation in Germany*, 87–96; Peter Blickle, *Der Bauernkrieg: Die Revolution des gemeinen Mannes* (Munich: Beck, 1998); Richard van Dülmen, *Reformation als Revolution: Soziale Bewegung und religiöser Radikalismus in der deutschen Reformation* (Frankfurt am Main: Fischer, 1987), 11–58; James M. Stayer, *The German Peasants' War and Anabaptist Community of Goods*, McGill-Queen's Studies in the History of Religion 6 (Montreal: McGill-Queen's UP, 1991), 45–92.

[66] "An die Allstedter," in *Blütezeit des Humanismus und Reformation*, vol. 2/2 of *Spätmittelalter — Humanismus — Reformation: Texte und Zeugnisse*, ed. Hedwig Heger (Munich: Beck, 1978), 363–65, here 365.

[67] Tom Scott, *Thomas Müntzer: Theology and Revolution in the German Reformation* (Basingstoke: Macmillan, 1989); Hans-Jürgen Goertz, *Thomas Müntzer: Mystiker, Apokalyptiker, Revolutionär* (Munich: Beck, 1989).

[68] The analysis is based on Hans-Jürgen Goertz, *The Anabaptists*, trans. Trevor Johnson (London: Routledge, 1996), passim.

[69] "[D]as die gemein zue Nurmberg zue dem Wort Gottes gantz begirig worden ist, also das in eines erbern raths macht dieser zeit nit steet, auch inen keins wegs muglich ist, dise furgenomene neuerung mit einichem gewalt und zuvor on erkantnus eins christlichen conciliums irer geimen zu benemen und mit ernst abzuschaffen." Cited in Heinrich Richard Schmidt, *Reichsstädte, Reich und Reformation: Korporative*

Religionspolitik, 1521–1529/30, Veröffentlichungen des Instituts für Europäische Geschichte Mainz 122 (Stuttgart: Steiner, 1986), 163.

[70] Thomas A. Brady Jr., *Turning Swiss: Cities and Empire 1450–1550* (Cambridge: Cambridge UP, 1985), 168.

[71] Dixon, *Reformation in Germany,* 121.

[72] Peter Blickle, *Die Reformation im Reich,* 2nd ed. (Stuttgart: Ulmer, 1992), 81–105; Moeller, *Imperial Cities,* 54–89; Berndt Hamm, *Bürgertum und Glaube: Konturen der städtischen Reformation* (Göttingen: Vandenhoeck & Ruprecht, 1996).

[73] On the political dynamic effected by the Reformation see C. Scott Dixon, "Die Reformation und das Schicksal der Eliten in Deutschland im Zeitalter der Konfessionalisierung," in *Geburt oder Leistung? Elitenbildung im deutsch-britischen Vergleich,* ed. Franz Bosbach, Keith Robbins, and Karina Urbach, Prinz-Albert-Studien 21 (Munich: Saur, 2003), 43–53.

[74] Gunter Zimmermann, *Prediger der Freiheit: Andreas Osiander und der Nürnberger Rat 1522–1548,* Mannheimer Historische Forschungen 15 (Mannheim: Palatium, 1999), 19–56.

[75] Hamm, *Bürgertum und Glaube,* 156.

[76] Schmidt, *Reichsstädte,* 163.

[77] On the rise and fall of the urban front see Brady, *Turning Swiss.*

[78] C. Scott Dixon, "The Princely Reformation in Germany," in *The Reformation World,* ed. Andrew Pettegree (London: Routledge, 2000), 146–68; Eike Wolgast, "Formen landesfürstlicher Reformationen in Deutschland: Kursachsen — Württemberg — Brandenburg — Kurpfalz," in *Die dänische Reformation vor ihrem internationalen Hintergrund,* ed. Leif Grane and Kai Hørby, Forschungen zur Kirchen- und Dogmengeschichte 46 (Göttingen: Vandenhoeck & Ruprecht, 1990), 57–90; Eike Wolgast, "Die deutschen Territorialfürsten und die frühe Reformation," in *Die frühe Reformation in Deutschland als Umbruch,* ed. Stephen E. Buckwalter and Bernd Moeller, Schriften des Vereins für Reformationsgeschichte 199 (Gütersloh: Gütersloher Verlagshaus, 1998), 407–34.

[79] Luise Schorn-Schütte, *Evangelische Geistlichkeit in der Frühneuzeit: Deren Anteil an der Entfaltung frühmoderner Staatlichkeit und Gesellschaft,* Quellen und Forschungen zur Reformationsgeschichte 62 (Gütersloh: Gütersloher Verlagshaus, 1996), 390–416.

[80] Fundamental for the original conceptualization of the idea: Wolfgang Reinhard, "Zwang zur Konfessionalisierung? Prologomena zu einer Theorie des konfessionellen Zeitalters," *Zeitschrift für historische Forschung* 10 (1983): 268–77; Heinz Schilling, "Die Konfessionalisierung im Reich: Religiöser und gesellschaftlicher Wandel in Deutschland zwischen 1555 und 1620," *Historische Zeitschrift* 246 (1988): 1–45. The literature on confessionalization is now legion. For a synthesis of recent research see Heinrich Richard Schmidt, *Konfessionalisierung im 16. Jahrhundert,* Enzyklopädie deutscher Geschichte 12 (Munich: Oldenbourg, 1992); Stefan Ehrenpreis and Ute Lotz-Heumann, *Reformation und konfessionelles Zeitalter,* Kontroversen um die Geschichte (Darmstadt: Wissenschaftliche Buchgesellschaft, 2002), 62–81.

[81] This is stated succinctly in Schilling, "Konfessionalisierung," 5; see also Ehrenpreis and Lotz-Heumann, *Reformation und konfessionelles Zeitalter,* 64–65.

Lyoner Totentanz. *(Lyon: Matthias Huß, 1499). The first known depiction of a printing press (showing setting cases, inking balls, and adjacent bookbindery). From Stephan Füssel,* Gutenberg und seine Wirkung *(Frankfurt am Main: Insel, 1999).*

Early Modern German Printing

Stephan Füssel

D IE LITERARISCHEN STUDIEN BLÜHEN, eine Menge Bücher steht um billiges Geld auch den Minderbemittelten zur Verfügung; bei so bequemer Möglichkeit des Zugangs zur Welt der Bücher sieht sich jedermann geradezu verlockt, höherer Bildung teilhaftig zu werden" (Literary studies are blossoming, a host of books is available for so little money that even those of modest means have access to them; with the comfortable possibility of such easy access to the world of books, everyone is virtually seduced to partake in higher education). So euphorically did the Bavarian ducal historiographer Johannes Turmair (1477–1534), also known as Aventinus, describe the cultural situation in his 1525 *Annales ducum Boiariae* (translated into German as *Bayerische Chronik*, 1533) owing to the invention of printing.[1] This glorification of the art of printing is a much-used literary topos, however, and not to be taken literally, coming as it does some seventy-five years after the actual invention; it had become a commonplace already before 1500 to praise the printing of books as a decisive step in the evolution of the community of educated peoples. Thus the German "arch-humanist," Conrad Celtis (1459–1508), writes in one of his odes that it is thanks to a certain son of the city of Mainz that the Germans no longer can be ridiculed by the Italians as intellectually lazy. The *translatio artium* (literally, "transfer of the arts") was the highest objective of the German humanists, for it was the process by which they could access the intellectual greatness of antiquity.[2] It had once been transferred from Greece to Rome, in the time of Cicero, Horace, Ovid, and Vergil; Johannes Gutenberg had made it possible for the ancient learning to be transferred across the Alps to Germania, as Celtis writes in Ode 3, 9 ("Laudat Germanum inventorem artis impressoriae"):

> Qui sculpsit solidas aere citus notas,
> Et versis docuit scribere litteris,
> Quo nasci vtilius non poterat magis
>   Cunctis (credite) saeculis.
> Iam tandem Italici non poterunt viri
> Germanos stolida carpere inertia,
> Cum nostris videant crescere ab artibus
>   Romanis saecula litteris. (ll. 9–16)

[In a brief time he poured solid molds from bronze and instructed how to print with movable type. It seems to me that nothing more useful could ever have been invented in all the centuries! No longer will the Italians be able to accuse the Germans of dumb laziness, for now they can see that our technological skill is overtaking all the centuries of Roman literature.]

The technology of the printing press made several things possible:

- The preparation of texts by authors from antiquity for anthologies and editions.
- The transfer of knowledge as a goal of education, made possible with affordable and philologically accurate editions in convenient form.
- A solid base for university teaching and research.
- The preservation of international and national manuscript treasures.

The printing press did not simply fall from the sky, of course, but was a consequence of technologies that had been in existence for decades before Gutenberg, who ingeniously combined them into a single effective instrument. Another powerful cultural development had also been underway since the thirteenth century that contributed to this revolution in communications: the process of *Verschriftlichung*, of turning all communication into written form.[3] Not only clerics but laity as well had been using written forms more and more, both in Latin and in the vernacular, for literary and technical publications. The rise of the cities in the thirteenth and fourteenth centuries, together with the development of international banking and marketing, led to an increasing need for written information and to the necessity of contracts in written form. The early modern state rose on written culture, as did the early modern church, which had begun the practice centuries before. Magnificent parchment manuscripts gave way to simpler, cheaper manuscripts during the fourteenth century as paper was imported from Spain, France, and Italy; since 1390 it was purchased from the paper mill of Ulman Stromer (1329–1407) in Nuremberg. This use of paper as writing material was essential for the later mass production, which would not have been possible on limited, expensive quantities of animal skin. The emergence of universities in the twelfth century had professionalized the copying of texts. For daily use, "writing rooms," which prepared texts to keep on hand, had become common. In Italy it was the office of Vespasiano de Bisticci (1421–98), the scribe and book dealer of the Medici family in Florence; in Alsace, in Hagenau, Diebold Lauber (fl. 1427–71) took orders for copying devotional literature, historiography, and epics in the vernacular.

In addition to paper, the *Holzmodeldruck* (wood pattern press), which had been developed in East Asia in the eighth century and arrived in Europe via the Silk Road, was also available. Pictures and shorter written texts in wood began to be made in the German-speaking lands around 1420. One of the earliest (1423) depicts a St. Christopher. This so-called *Buxheim St. Christopher*[4] includes a written blessing:

> Christofori faciem die quacumq[ue] tueris
> Illa nempe die morte mala non morieris.

[If you look upon the face of Christopher any day, On that day you will surely not die an unlucky death.]

Playing cards and depictions of saints were the preferred topics of these early woodcut printings, which, in the course of the century, also included lengthier texts — among others the Lord's Prayer and the Song of Songs — and could be used for religious instruction, such as in the *ars moriendi* (art of dying). The time was ripe, so to speak, for an invention that could answer the demand for a larger variety of literary and informational texts.

Apart from the sermon, instruction in the church had been limited to the centuries' old tradition of illustrating biblical and theological themes in church windows, on bronze doors, in sculptured alabaster, in cycles of frescoes, or in *Tafelbilder* (pictures painted on wood surfaces). This tradition expanded at the beginning of the fifteenth century, when the chancellor of the University of Paris, Jean Gerson (1363–1429), a tireless reformer of religious life, proposed that "tables of text" be hung in churches in order to help remediate the general spiritual ignorance among the common people. Cardinal Nicolas of Cusa (Cusanus, 1401–64) took up this challenge in the German-speaking lands. On visits to German dioceses he had observed that even the most important prayers were known neither to the laity nor to the clergy. His solution was to have woodcut tables containing the Lord's Prayer installed in churches. In May 1451 Cusa took part in the Fourteenth General Chapter of the Benedictines in Mainz, where the topic under discussion was monastic reform, including the monastery libraries and their importance for the monastic community. Already in *De concordantia catholica* (1434), which he wrote while attending the Council of Basel (1431–48), he had indicated his support for the compulsory use of correct textual editions of missals for the entire area served by the Catholic Church. Only a reliable, standardized text, he felt, could guarantee a uniform celebration of the liturgy. It is possible that Cusa had heard that one Johannes Gensfleisch was working in Mainz in this very year on a certain technique for mechanical reproduction — one that would prove to be the basis for the spread of knowledge and education of generations to follow.

Johannes Gutenberg and His Bible

Gutenberg's date of birth is uncertain. Certain inheritance documents of 1420 indicate that he has reached his majority, meaning that he must have been born about 1400. His father was a patrician and seems to have been involved in cloth manufacture; he belonged to the minters' guild and was for a time an accountant for the city. One can only speculate about his son's early years. Given his competence in Latin and technical expertise, we can assume that Johannes attended a monastery school and a university. Together with his father and siblings he had to leave Mainz early in life, when in August 1411 the conflict between the patricians and the guilds suddenly turned dangerous.

At the beginning of the fifteenth century, Mainz had about 6,000 inhabitants. Its new constitution gave the guilds a weightier political voice vis-à-vis the patriciate. In the ensuing conflict, members of various families had to leave the city. The Gensfleisch family probably went to the other side of the Rhine, to Eltville, where his mother had inherited a house and where there was certainty of a good education. Grammar and rhetoric from the texts of the grammarian Aelius Donatus (fl. 350 A.D.) and readings of the canonical Latin writers were taught in the community school. One "Johannes de Alta Villa" registered there in summer semester 1418. The following year he matriculated at the University of Erfurt[5] — a possession of the archbishopric of Mainz — and received his baccalaureate degree in winter semester 1419–20. According to the curriculum of the faculty of arts, in which the *septem artes liberales* were taught (grammar, rhetoric, dialectics, astronomy, mathematics, arithmetic, and music), the first examination was possible only after three semesters of study. There followed the study of Latin grammar, Greek and Latin philosophy, and basic courses in the natural sciences. Gutenberg's father died in autumn 1419. Nothing is known of Gutenberg's whereabouts during the 1420s.

The next record locates him in Strasbourg in 1434, a cosmopolitan city of some 25,000 inhabitants on the upper Rhine, and a prominent center for artisans and trade. Strasbourg was home to one of Europe's most important church builders' guilds — in the 1430s the guild completed the first of two planned Gothic towers on the cathedral — and was renowned for bell-making and the production of paper. Trade flourished with southern France and northern Italy, as well as with Augsburg, Nuremberg, and Prague. Gutenberg resided outside the city gates near the Benedictine Monastery of St. Arbogast. Judicial records, which reference his financial dealings, reflect an entrepreneurial merchant and inventor.[6] In 1437 he appears as a master craftsman: a citizen, Andreas Dritzehn, had turned to Gutenberg to learn "Polieren von Edelsteinen" (the polishing of precious stones), that is, the crafting of coins and goldsmithing.

The records further indicate that Gutenberg cofounded a financial society — one of the new ideas recently introduced to Strasbourg by bankers from northern Italy — as a means of procuring advance financing for a certain new technical process. After the death of one of the cofounders, a legal struggle ensued over the payment of interest, and a number of accounts by witnesses to these events shed light on Gutenberg's activities at this time. As of 1438 he ran a business producing pilgrimage souvenirs for the annual exhibition of relics in Aachen, one of the most important pilgrimage sites since the twelfth century. Aachen claimed to possess four "great relics": a dress belonging to the Virgin Mary, the diapers of the Christ Child, the loincloth worn by Jesus at his crucifixion, and the towel used in the beheading of John the Baptist. As many as 15,000 pilgrims, mostly from Central Europe, Poland, Hungary, and Slovenia, journeyed to Aachen for the Great Indulgence in July. In 1440, when Gutenberg's consortium was selling so-called "Pilgrim Mirrors" (souvenirs with an integrated mirror for "catching" the efficacy of the blessings), Duke Philipp the Good of Burgundy and his retinue visited Aachen. Since mass production of pilgrimage souvenirs was not subject to guild control, their sale was allowed to any entrepreneur in Aachen. Gutenberg's "Pilgrim Mirrors" were manufactured in great quantities from an alloy of lead and tin.

The participants in Gutenberg's venture had also signed a second contract stating that he would teach them "alle sin künste vnd aventur" (all his arts and experiments). During the early modern period the phrase "künste vnd aventur" was commonly applied to the skills and entrepreneurial undertakings of exceptionally gifted artisans. The fact that the members of the group obligated themselves not to make the inventions public right away made good business sense. Certain technical terms from the trial records imply a wooden press and the making of "Formen" to be melted down; a certain goldsmith testifies that he has been paid more than 100 gulden to make everything having to do with printing. It is likely that the "Formen" were actually *literae formatae*, individual letters made from metal. Such experiments as the mixing of lead, and the decision to have a wooden press made, suggest initial steps in the development of the printing press. One member of the society, Andreas Heilman, together with his brother Nikolaus, owned a paper mill outside the city gates. To turn a paper press into a book press was both possible and logical, and to involve a paper dealer for the production of books was nothing less than ingenious.

Yet another step toward his great invention may have come from the making of bells in Strasbourg. Blessings and dates could be added by pouring individual forms on the lower rim of the body of the bell. The bells were produced from bronze alloyed with 20–25% tin. Gutenberg's partners occupied high positions in the city government and were respected merchants and artisans. Hans Friedel von Seckingen, who appeared as a witness in the trial, belonged to one of the city's most important financial concerns.[7] The Seckingen family was involved in the metal business and traded in brass; owned wholesale and retail businesses; and maintained financial interests in Venice, Milan, and Basel, as well as Nuremberg and Frankfurt. Seckingen himself had a fascination for technical innovations and was involved in erecting the first windmill in upper Germany in 1440.

In 1448 Gutenberg was again in Mainz seeking financing for experiments. In 1449 he borrowed 800 gulden at 6% from Johann Fust and in 1453 another 800 gulden for a collaborative "enterprise for books." Considering that a fine burgher house could be purchased for about 500 gulden in 1450, Gutenberg's investments at this time amounted to the modern equivalent of a million dollars. In the years between 1450 and 1454 he perfected the technology and began printing broadsheets, letters of indulgence, and other smaller works; two and a half years of this time were dedicated to what would be called the "Gutenberg Bible."

His invention was as simple as it was ingenious: essentially, the text was simply broken down into its smallest component parts, the twenty-six letters of the Latin alphabet. The reorganization of the individual letters could produce, time and again, a text that made sense. For centuries, texts had been duplicated by hand or by cutting the entire text into wood; now one had only to cut the individual letters of the alphabet to make as many new texts as one wanted to print. Instead of transferring the ink onto paper by rubbing pieces of wood together, as had been done in East Asia for over 700 years, Gutenberg used the physical laws of the *Spindelpresse* (paper or wine press) in order to transfer the "ink" from colored type to the dampened paper by applying an intense amount of pressure evenly.

Many steps were necessary, however, in order to develop the process. Goldsmiths cut a precise punch (the *Patrize*) for every letter, in deep relief and in mirror image, on the tip of a steel bar or cube. This was then struck with a hammer into softened copper such that a deeply sunken letter, in actual image (the *Matrize*, "matrix") resulted, which then had to be correctly positioned into the casting instrument. This hand mould was fundamentally different from the experimental metal letter casting in East Asia, which cast letters into "lost forms," as a rule into wet sand. Since Gutenberg was able to use these matrices again and again, an unlimited number of symmetrically similar, peripherally straight printed letters remained, theoretically, at the printer's disposal. The exact composition of the alloy can be reconstructed from later analyses: more than 80% lead, about 9% tin, 6% antimony, and 1% each of copper and iron. The composition had the advantage of cooling quickly, and thus it was immediately available for reuse. The first pictorial representation of a printer's workshop (taken from an incunabulum printed in Lyon in 1499) shows a compartmentalized case that stored the individual letters according to use. The individual letters were gathered up into a composing stick (originally from wood, later from metal), in which the individual lines could be justified using so-called blind metal spacing (below the printing height), which evened out the spacing between the letters or words. The individual lines were then put together in a galley, probably a stable wooden tray, either in a column or as a complete page. The whole page, the exact area of type, was then justified. Next, the set type was inked using a semicircular leather ball and laid into the press. The paper to be printed was then dampened so it would take the impression from the ink and positioned on a number of pins or needles within a hinged tympan (thus the so-called "punctures"). The frisket (for holding the typesetting) and the cover with the paper were then pushed under the platen (printing plate), which was maneuvered onto the paper with a firm amount of pressure. This so-called *Schöndruck*, or first printing, was followed by the printing of the verso, whereby the punctures allowed the page to be fixed so that the printed area on both sides of the page were exactly on top of one another. Sheets of varying (not normalized) sizes were printed at first. First, the recto was printed — later, forms allowing for two, four, or eight pages to be printed simultaneously — then the verso, and folded. The pages were so printed that, when folded, they appeared in the correct order.

For the first prints only the black print was done by the press itself; all decorative elements — ornamental initials, colored column titles, illustrations, rubrications (red letters and drawings) — were done later by hand. Since they were always decorated manually, many early prints are reminiscent of manuscripts. None of the forty-nine extant Gutenberg Bibles looks like any of the others; each has been rubricated and illuminated differently. The four complete copies on parchment are located in the Library of Congress in Washington, the British Museum in London, the Bibliothèque Nationale in Paris, and the Staats- und Universitätsbibliothek in Göttingen. The copy in

Göttingen was designated "Memory of the World Heritage" in the year 2000.[8]

Besides creating the twenty-six basic letters in both capital and small forms, Gutenberg took great pains to apply the characteristics of good manuscripts to the printed page, beginning with the double-column style and right justification, so-called block printing. To this end, he cut and poured a total of 290 different letters: forty-seven capitals, sixty-three small letters, ninety-two letters with shortening signs (abbreviations), eighty-three combinations of letters (ligatures), and five commas. Ligatures joined in a single unit of type pairs of letters often occuring together and lending themselves graphically to combination in order to save space and enhance the aesthetic appearance of the page. Examples are the ligatures still sometimes used today fi and fl and others for the letter combinations ff, ll, and st. Abbreviations taken from Latin manuscript usage — for example, for the prefixes *pro, prae, per;* for case endings *um, am, as,* or for double consonants *mm, nn* — were similarly economical. By using these techniques the compositor was able to set a perfect line. To allow several typesetters to work simultaneously on the Gutenberg Bible, about 100,000 individual types (letters) or combinations thereof had to have been cast. Such technological sophistication allowed the possibility of reproducing the manuscript in all of its details and actually exceeding it with regard to accuracy. Since the abbreviations used made sense only in Latin, it is apparent that the typeface of the so-called B 42 — the Gutenberg 42-line Bible — was first developed for Latin texts. It is obvious here that typesetters had to have a considerable command of Latin.

Between 1452 and 1454 Gutenberg printed the 1,282 pages of the Latin Bible.[9] He chose for that work St. Jerome's fourth-century Vulgate, the standard text for all theological works and religious instruction during the entire Middle Ages. Gutenberg probably took one of the manuscript Bibles available in Mainz as a sample and simply set it to print. That copy has never been found; presumably, it was "used up" by the various typesetters who copied from it. Gutenberg imitated the manuscript in all aspects: the columnar division, the block format, the missal-type letter (*textura,* "woven letters"). The large missal letters he used were modeled on the letters in the mass books so that they would be legible in the less illuminated areas of the church. In his initial experiments Gutenberg tried to assume the work of the rubricators, printing the chapter headings in red ink. Apparently, many problems resulted from using two colors and trying to get the print into the precise spaces, because a slow-down occurred, making it necessary for him to turn to professional rubricators for further coloring, just as would have been done in the manuscript era. On the last leaf of both volumes of the Gutenberg Bible in the Bibliothèque Nationale a handwritten note indicates that Heinrich Cremer, the vicar of St. Stephan's in Mainz, had finished rubricating, illuminating, and binding these copies by 15 and 24 August 1456, respectively.

An important source for the early history of printing is a letter from the learned secretary to Emperor Friedrich III, Enea Silvio Piccolomini (1405–64), the later Pope Pius II, written to Cardinal Juan de Carvajal. Reporting from the Reichstag in Frankfurt in October 1454,[10] Enea Silvio says he has found an amazing man, a "vir mirabilis," a book dealer who has shown him various unbound sheets of a Latin Bible printed absolutely clearly and correctly, legible even without the assistance of eyeglasses. He has been able to ascertain that all copies had been sold in advance of the printing — by one report 158 copies, by another 180. These data suggest that Gutenberg's printing business was brisk. However, they may be deceptive, given the delayed method of payment standard for the time, typically six to twelve months after it was due; it may also have been that delays occurred in finishing the work. At any rate, we know that Gutenberg was not in a position, as of fall 1455, to repay his creditors. One of them, Johann Fust (ca. 1400–1466), therefore retained possession of the remaining Bibles and printing machines, and had put the rights to the printing process itself in his own name. Together with his son-in-law, Gutenberg's former chief journeyman, Peter Schöffer (1430–1502), Fust continued to run the printing shop as "Fust and Schöffer," the leading printshop in fifteenth-century Mainz.[11]

It is likely that Gutenberg worked as a printer (and, in effect, publisher) for the rest of his life. His whereabouts may be followed by observing the locations of his various prints, as in Eltville on the Rhine, where in 1465 he was made "Hofmann" by Prince Elector of Mainz, Adolf of Nassau.[12] However, he is not mentioned in any of the colophons in those prints, and one can only speculate about his actual responsibilities. But it is probable that he continued to print small items, at least — calendars, grammars, broadsheets, certificates of indulgence — in a private workshop. The certificates of indulgence made a particularly lucrative business in early modern Europe, with typical print runs of 2,000 to 2,500; some ran into the tens of thousands and, in one instance in Santiago di Compostella, a printing of 192,000 copies. On this standardized form (as a rule, thirty-one lines per page) the recipient simply entered name and date by hand. For the year 1455 Gutenberg printed the German translation of a widely circulated calendar with the popular *Türkenrede* (Speech Concerning the Turks) of Enea Silvio, who had delivered it on 15 October 1454 at the Imperial Diet in Frankfurt. In this speech, all social estates within Christendom were challenged to oppose the Ottoman Empire, which had conquered Constantinople just two years earlier. Gutenberg died on 3 February 1468.

The Spread of the Art of Printing

Knowledge of the art of printing spread rapidly in Europe. As early as 1460 a printshop was opened in Bamberg by Albrecht Pfister (d. 1466). In 1461 Pfister printed the Swiss Ulrich Boner's collection of fables from 1349, *Der Edelstein* (The Jewel), for which he obviously used type materials from Gutenberg's shop (these had probably been taken by traveling journeymen). There is evidence that the eminent typographer Johannes Mentelin (ca. 1410–78) was at work in Strasbourg in this year. The printing shop at the cloister Santa Scholastica in Subiaco near Rome, established in 1465, is particularly interesting to book historians. It had the support of the Roman Curia and was dedicated especially to printing texts from Roman antiquity that were then in demand by humanists. Among the most important texts were works by Cicero and Augustine, as well as the collected works of Lactantius, one of the revered church fathers.[13] The printers were German guest workers, Konrad Sweynheim (d. 1477) and Arnold Pannartz (d. 1477). In 1468 the bishop in Aleria, Andrea del Bussi, the first Vatican librarian, praised the German invention of the printing press and identified Cusa as its great promoter.[14] During the era of the incunabula (Latin *incunabulum*, "cradle," designating the printing period before 1500), Rome remained the center of printing in Italy, though some forty other printing centers have also been documented. About twenty-five of them used German typographers.

Venice was the second most active early printing center in Italy, specializing, as did most Italian shops, in classical Latin authors and law. In 1468 Johann von Speyer obtained from the city council a five-year monopoly on printing of books. The French engraver and typographer Nicolaus Jenson (1420–80), from Sommevoir near Troyes, arrived in Venice after having first been sent by the mint master of Charles VII of France to Mainz in 1458 to learn the new technology. Beginning in 1470, Jenson printed classical Roman authors and church fathers in an exceptionally elegant antiqua (or Roman) typeface, later known as "Venetian old style," that is still in use today. He operated his printing shop in Fondace dei Tedeschi as a commercial enterprise with two German merchants. The most famous of the early printers in Venice, and probably all of Italy, was Aldus Manutius (1459–1515), who founded a printing shop in 1490 with the express aim of publishing Roman and Greek authors. Toward the end of the fifteenth century, bookmaking in Germany began to be influenced in turn by journeymen and master tradesmen returning from Italy.

Humanism contributed greatly to the spread of the art of printing and was a major beneficiary of it.[15] Just as Vergil announced in his *Georgica* the transfer of the Greek Muses and their arts in Italy, we have seen that Celtis now invites the Muses of poetry and science across the Alps into Germania. During the incunabulum period the most frequently printed texts from antiquity were the works of Cicero; half of the known 316 editions — his letters and rhetorical works were especially celebrated as new ideals for art and style — came from the great Italian centers of printing in Rome, Venice, Milan, and Parma. From the Roman poets one finds eighty editions of Ovid, whose verses were among the favorite readings in schools. The comedies of Terence, available in the German Empire as early as 1470, were widely disseminated. Editions of Horace and Vergil were also printed in the workshop of Johannes Grüninger (d. 1522). Those of Vergil were particularly numerous; indeed, they had circulated widely already in the manuscript era. After some fifty generations had repeatedly copied his texts by hand, the first printed edition of his works appeared in 1469 in Rome. From that point to the present, there has scarcely been a year in which no Vergil edition has appeared. Between the years 1469 and 1500 alone some eighty-one printings were made. The humanists were sustained by their belief in the general educability of mankind and that the availability of texts would enhance and expedite the process. This utopian idea of education stimulated a massive promotion of Latin-based education, not only because of the language's logical and formal advantages, but especially because, as the renowned Italian humanist Lorenzo Valla (ca. 1406–57) claimed, through the very act of learning the language students would simultaneously acquire the knowledge contained in the ancient texts.[16] The humanists therefore viewed printing as a gift that could further their own educational goals.

The universities immediately seized on the potential of printing for conveying knowledge. The first print shop in France was established at the Sorbonne in 1470. Three German journeyman printers, Ulrich Gehring from Constance, Michael Friburger from Colmar, and Martin Crantz from Strasbourg, were commissioned to print classical and humanistic texts. Other important French university cities soon followed Paris's lead: Lyon in 1473, Albi in 1475, Toulouse in 1476.

Thus, in less than a decade after Gutenberg's death his technology had spread to most European countries; within fifty years about 1,000 print shops were active in some 350 cities across the continent. Between 1450 and 1500 they published an estimated 30,000 titles with a total circulation of nearly ten million volumes. It was boasted, as in this chapter's opening quotation, that any person of modest means now had access to the necessary resources of a higher education.[17] The possibilities associated with the printing of books supported the educational movement of the late Middle Ages, institutionalized by the emerging universities of the fourteenth and fifteenth centuries; promoted the spread of Renaissance and humanistic ideas; and created the prerequisites for the reform of the Roman Church and the popularization of the tenets of belief in the vernacular.

What is fascinating about the early history of printing is this interaction between the history of technology and the history of ideas. The new medium did not suddenly replace the old one but at first simply took over previous contents in externally similar forms: early prints mimicked manuscripts in their division into pages, their selection of writings, and in their format. Furthermore, the same grammars and textbooks were chosen for distribution in the printed medium as had proven their value through the centuries in manuscript form. Only gradually were the revolutionary possibilities of the new medium recognized. Beginning about 1480 a title page was put at the front of the book and formats were developed that were easier to use. Epic poetry in verse — the external sign that it was publicly read aloud — was no longer printed; instead, a literature consisting of novels in prose for private reading was developed in the form of "pocket books." The first nonfiction literature made medical and scientific knowledge available, including prints of European and world maps, calendars, and almanacs.

The Workshop of Fust and Schöffer

Since the partners Fust and Schöffer applied a printer's imprint and printer's mark, one can readily identify their products, all of which exemplify mastery of the art of printing, improving even on Gutenberg's own work with regard to the decorative elements of metal cut and red printing. On 14 August 1457 they brought out their first deluxe edition, the *Psalterium Moguntinum* (Hessian Psalter), printed on parchment. It contains, for the first time in the history of printing, a colophon and a printer's device.[18] This new method is designated with the Latin terms *Ars imprimendi ac caracterizandi*. In classical Latin, *imprimere* refers to an impressing action. Suetonius employs the verb in speaking of a coin or a ring with a picture pressed onto it; Vergil speaks in the *Aeneid* of a jug or ewer on which pictures have been imprinted; Tacitus mentions wooden sticks in which signs have been printed or scratched. This new word for printing books is reinforced by the use of another verb, *caractericare*, which derives from Greek and means much the same thing (to incise, engrave, sink a hole into, or imprint). In the coining process, the die used in the striking of coins is called *character*; the same word is later applied to what has actually been minted or molded. Whereas *imprimere* relates to the printing process itself, *caractericare* indicates the phase of the actual making of the letters. In the French noun *imprimerie* (printshop) the classical term has been retained, as it has in the English word *print* (both noun and verb). The word *impressum* remains a legally binding printer's mark, and *imprimatur* (let it be printed) an official permission to print.

In working on the *Psalter*, Fust and Schöffer took Gutenberg's basic idea, that books should improve on manuscripts, to a new level of quality. Although the B 42 had contained only a few lines of red printing on the first pages, here red printing is employed throughout the book, the publishers having assumed the work of rubricators, by inserting red uncial letters, and of illuminators, by doing metal cut initials in red and blue. Initial letters are in three different sizes, in each case made with metal printing plates; presumably, the ornamentation of these initial letters was cut into a block of wood in an embossed manner the same height as the letter such that it could be pressed, in a precolored condition, into the press. The process was more or less as follows: first, a completely justified page with all the types and decorative elements was composed, locked up, and inked in black; then the printer took out all the colored parts, colored them separately, colored the text black, and justified the printed page again after all parts had been reinserted — a tedious process indeed, but one that offered the best guarantee of maintaining the register and decreasing the possibility of overlapping letters. A few garbled Lombard initials indicate that those letters got mixed up when they were replaced into the rest of the text, which was otherwise complete. This first multicolor work in the history of printing was extraordinary in several other ways as well: the printers worked with a large Psalter font (ca. 39 point) from 210 individual letters and with a smaller Psalter font (ca. 32 point) from 185 individual letters; they had a total of fifty-three decorative uncial letters and 228 colored initial letters in three different sizes. The design of the letters and the ornamental elements, the casting, and the typesetting must have been time-consuming, with preparations reaching back to 1453–54, when Gutenberg was still working with Fust and Schöffer.

All ten extant copies, each consisting of 340 folio pages, are printed on parchment, which suggests their special place in the liturgy. The psalms, canticles, hymns, antiphons, and responses are arranged as they would be in the breviary, which contained the canonical hours and songs of the religious day. Since the Psalter followed the organization of the breviary in use in Mainz, we can see that it was meant for use only in the diocese of Mainz; the hymnal too was clearly specific to Mainz. In the same year, a second edition with only 246 pages appeared, which was also permitted to be sold outside the diocese; and in 1459 a revised edition appeared, the *Psalterium Benedictum*, reworked according to the guidelines of the Congregation of Benedictines in Bursfeld. Since the size of the paper used for this edition is larger, the individual pages are more harmonious and probably more representative of the will of the Benedictine monastery, which may have commissioned it.

In addition to this Psalter type, the studio of Fust and Schöffer employed a small but easily legible set of Gothic-Roman characters for the Latin texts. It was first used, on 6 October 1459, for the *Rationale divinorum officiorum* (an eight-book compendium of laws, ceremonies, and explications of Roman Catholic worship and practice) of Guillelmus Durandus (1237–96), one of the most important liturgical writers of the Middle Ages. The same font was used to set two works of canon law: in 1460 the *Constitutiones* of Pope Clement V and in 1465 the *Liber sextus* of Pope Boniface VIII. In 1462 Fust and Schöffer printed an excellent Bible of forty-eight lines per page, the so-called B 48, for which the type was set from newly cut Gothic-Roman letters. The use of a smaller point type suggests that these Bibles were intended for personal reading rather than for religious services or for reading aloud or teaching.

After Fust's death in 1466 Schöffer became the sole heir of both the printing house and the publishing house. Around 1470 he began to include pictures in his books; in 1484 and 1485 he introduced two richly illustrated books onto the market: a plant book and a guide to herbal medicine. The modern herbology derived from the philological work of the earliest humanists, who had edited the ancient Latin texts on the subject, including numerous translations from the Greek. The writings of Theophrastus, a student of Aristotle and the founder of botany, had only recently been rediscovered. They contain theological, philosophical, medical, folkloric, and natural scientific interpretations and transmit medical knowledge known to antiquity. In 1484 Schöffer marketed a Latin *Herbarius* in his Psalter type, a simple compilation of basic instructions about medicinal herbs for a wide range of interests. It was illustrated with 150 woodcuts, mostly showing the outlines of plants; hatching technique was only seldom used, and most extant copies were richly painted. The depiction of plants is quite stiff, suggesting that the plants were drawn using pressed plants as models. In March 1485, Schöffer produced a popular version of this work in German with the title *Gart der Gesundheit* (Garden of Health). Some 378 new woodcuts illustrate the 720 pages in large format. The author, Johannes Wonnecke of Kaub, a physician in Frankfurt around 1500, offers a comprehensive account of what was known in the fifteenth century about medicinal plants. In the first part he describes the pharmacological properties of plants, animals, and inorganic materials; in the second part he provides systematic information about laxatives, aromatic substances, fruits, seeds, roots, stones, and animals. An index lists 313 illnesses according to catchwords, with practical references to the curative plants. At the end of the 1486 edition of Justinian's *Institutiones* printed in Peter Schöffer's shop, there is a poem in which the poet claims that Schöffer has outdone "both Johanneses" as an expert in the cutting of type ("sculpendi lege sagetius"). It would appear that after the deaths of Johannes Fust (1466) and Gutenberg (1468) the high honor of master printer was conferred on Schöffer. The abbot Johannes Trithemius supports this assumption in his *Annales Hirsaugiensis* (1515) when he states that it was Schöffer who had refined the process of casting type.

Vernacular Publication in the Fifteenth Century

Less than 15% of the incunabula appeared in the vernacular, although the percentage rose steadily. Entertaining novels, herbal books, and advice and other didactic writings on living were published in German. The circulation of narrative literature in German had already begun during the late Middle Ages, but reception conditions became increasingly favorable in the early fifteenth century as a readership arose outside of exclusively clerical and noble circles. The new readers consisted of urban artisans, merchants, officials, and courtly personnel. Evidence of the rise of German reading in the late medieval period may be found in the manuscript collections themselves, which are heavily vernacular. The manuscript workshop of Diebold Lauber in Hagenau in Alsace, with five copyists and sixteen illustrators, was perhaps the most productive shop of the entire century. Its publishing repertoire consisted of thirty-eight titles, including Conrad von Megenberg's *Buch der Natur*, the legal texts *Schwabenspiegel* and *Belial*, Wolfram von Eschenbach's *Parzival* and Gottfried von Strassburg's *Tristan* (courtly epics), a *Sterbebüchlein* (Little Book on Death and Dying), prayer books, the Ten Commandments, and the *Legende der Heiligen Drei Koenige* (Legend of the Three Saintly Kings).

In Strasbourg in 1477, Mentelin printed Wolfram's works and Gottfried's *Tristan*. Günther Zainer (d. 1478) acquired his skills in Mentelin's print shop and brought the new technology along with the successful program of titles back to his hometown of Augsburg. Augsburg subsequently, in the 1470s and 1480s, became a center for the printing of German-language prose novels in the shops of Johann Bämler (1425–1506), Anton Sorg (ca. 1430–93), and Johann Schönsperger the Elder (fl. 1481–1524). Sorg printed the *Alexander* novel nine times from 1472, Petrarch's novella *Griseldis* (also nine times), *Tristrant* in 1484, and Johann von Würzburg's *Wilhelm von Österreich* (1314) in 1491. Beginning in 1483 Schönsperger produced four editions of the novel *Pontus and Sidonia*, said to have been translated by Eleonore von Österreich (1433–80).[19] Some of these texts appeared in pirated editions in Strasbourg, among other places; for example, the *Troja* (Troy) novel in 1489, which had first been printed with Bämler, Sorg, and Schönsperger. In addition to German literature of the late Middle Ages, popular Italian works of the fifteenth century and earlier (such as Boccaccio's version of the story *Florio and Biancefora*), were disseminated in German translation. Novels based on French tales also enjoyed great popularity, especially the *Melusine* (1456) of Thüring von Ringoltingen (ca. 1415–83) and the collection of didactic tales known as *Ritter von Turn*, in the translation of Marquard vom Stein (1425–95).

The early nineteenth century called these texts *Volksbücher* (chapbooks), though many literary historians now prefer the term *Prosaromane* (prose novels).[20] The contemporary designation was *historia* — novelistic narratives with a core of historical factuality[21] — a genre that combined the presumed truthful content of popular historiography with a didactic intention. As in the practice of historiography, sources are cited, such as eyewitness reports (as in Johannes Hartlieb's *Alexander des Grossen Historie*), allegedly biographical data, or bibliographical references from posthumous works (as in *Eulenspiegel* or *Doktor Faustus*). One type of *historia* warns about the frailty of earthly fortune, as in *Melusine*; a precept in *Fortunatus* reads "Weisheit statt Reichtum" (wisdom rather than riches). Concrete indications of place, date, or distance contribute to the believability. The stereotypical depiction of emotions in the narratives is reflected in the woodcuts: a box with a heart is offered as a symbol of love; departure and welcoming are represented on a city wall or along the seashore. The Augsburg prints contain especially fine illustrations that support the narration. Once they were used, the wooden blocks were often sold to another printer to be reshaped and deployed in new projects. Typically, if a story had ended with a moralistic reminder: "Hye endet sich das Buch und Histori, wie die reiche, köstlich und mächtig Stadt Troya wart zerstört durch die Verhängnuß Gottes. Zu einem Exempel der ganzen Welt" (Here ends the book and story about how the rich, magnificent, and powerful city of Troy was destroyed by the wrath of God. As an example for the whole world), it would be refocused, emphasizing its entertainment potential: "Hiernach folget die Histori von Herrn Tristrand und der schönen Isolden von Irlande, welche Histori einer Vorrede wohl würdig wäre, und doch unnütz, denn die Lesenden und Zuhörenden lange Vorreden verdriessen" (Here follows the story of Tristan and the beautiful Isolde from Ireland, which story is well worth an introduction, and yet useless, because readers and listeners are annoyed by long introductions).[22]

Besides these fictional narratives, didactic fables and other instructional works were also popular prose texts in German among the new urban reading public; they included herbaria, medical advice books, and encyclopedias. The most widely known early modern encyclopedia, whether in Latin or German, was the *Nürnberger Weltchronik* (Nuremberg Chronicle of the World) commissioned by a consortium of humanists and published in 1493 by the Nuremberg physician Hartmann Schedel (1440–1514) in the large publishing house of Anton Koberger (ca. 1445–1513).[23] Approximately 1,400 copies of the Latin version and 700–800 of the German edition were printed. Its more than 1,800 magnificent woodcuts were made from 680 wood blocks. Some, obviously, were used several times, such as those of the cities of Mainz, Naples, Aquilea, Bologna, and Lyon. In keeping with the medieval *laus urbis* (praise of city) tradition, the towns typically appear well protected behind high walls, situated on a river for commerce, and near a mountain for good climate. A few, like Regensburg or Nuremberg, are depicted in large format and are highly valued even today because of their extraordinary attention to detail.

Schedel divides his chronicle into seven sections, in keeping with the biblical story of creation, and simply strings them together in additive fashion. One of the books articulates his organizational principle: "Colligite fragmenta, ne pereant" (Gather the fragments, so that nothing goes to waste), words taken from the biblical miracle of the feeding of the multitude. The encyclopedia offers a compendium of contemporary knowledge, theologically shaped, to be sure, yet open to experiences of the present. Manifold references are made throughout the sixteenth century to this chronicle, even in other historical and geographical descriptions of the world, most notably in Sebastian Münster's famous *Cosmographia*, printed in Basel in 1550, or in fictional travel reports.[24] Records from Koberger's international businesses indicate that copies of Schedel's encyclopedia were sold in Florence, Venice, Bologna, Milan, Lyon, Basel, and Paris, as well as in Graz, Vienna, Budapest, Breslau, Kraków, and Danzig, among other places. Gutenberg's invention is described and praised for how it has disseminated knowledge and for its renown as one of the greatest achievements in human progress:

> Kunst der truckerey hat sich erstlich in teütschem lannd in der statt Mayntz amm Rhein gelegen im iar Christi M.cccc.xl ereignet. vnnd fürdan schier in alle örter der werlt außgespreüßt. dardurch die kostpern schertze schrifftlicher kunst vnd weißheit so in den alten büechern langzeit als der werlt vnbekant in dem grabe der vnwissenheit verborgen gelegen sind herfür an das liecht gelangt haben. [. . .] Und so nw die erfinder yezuzeiten handwercklicher kunst nit wenig lobs wirdig sind. wer kan denn außsprechen mit was lob. preyse. eren vnd rům die teütschen zeer heben seyen die auß irer erleüchten synnreichen schicklichkeit ertrachtet vnd erfunden haben. Die kunst der truckerey durch die der lang verschloßen prunn vnaußsprechlicher weißheit menschlicher vnnd auch götlicher kunst in die gemayne außgelaytet wirdt.[25]

> [The art of printing first occurred on German territory in the city of Mainz on the Rhine in the year of our Lord 1440, and from there it spread throughout to all places in the world. Thereby came to light the most wonderful treasures of written art and wisdom, which had lain buried in the tomb of oblivion, unknown to the world. And so now the inventors of this craft of printing of books are worthy of not a little praise. Who can truly say with what praise, awards, honor, and fame we should laud the Germans, who invented this printing press from their enlightened, perspicacious skillfulness! Through it the long-locked fountain of inexpressible knowledge of both the human and the divine art will be available to common people.]

Specialist Books

It is of great interest in the history of learning that the printing of books made specialist literature available not only in Latin for theoretical education at the university but also in impressively large print runs in German for the continuing education of the urban public.[26] The Augsburg city physician, Bartholomäus Metlinger (ca. 1440–92), published a *Kinderbüchlein* (Little Children's Book) in 1473 with Zainer, which became a popular reference book (more than thirty editions by 1571), dedicated to parents, on the care of infants and rearing of children. Metlinger had studied medicine in Padua and learned the anatomic order of illustrations of illness from the acclaimed scholar of pediatrics Paolo Bagellardi (d. ca. 1493). Hieronymus Brunschwig (ca. 1450–1512) also focused on the practical side of medicine in *Dies ist das Buch der chirurgia* (This Is the Book of Surgery, 1492; 2nd ed. 1497), the first medical textbook in German. It is filled with graphic illustrations meant for physicians, medical students, and other caregivers. Brunschwig found in Grüninger a publisher experienced in the use of large-format woodcut illustrations of high quality. In 1513 the publishing house of Martin Flach (fl. 1491–1513) in Strasbourg printed a book of advice for midwives by the Worms city physician Eucharius Rösslin (ca. 1470–1526): *Der swangeren frauwen und hebammen Rosegarten* (Rose Garden of Pregnant Women and Midwives). Physicians themselves rarely assisted at births, leaving this activity almost solely in the hands of midwives, so-called "weise Frauen" (wise women). Rösslin's book served a crucial social need by applying scholarly medical theory to lay practice in a language understandable to readers untrained in Latin. It proved to be a tremendous success — more than 100 printings appeared over the following decades.

Mathematics, both theoretical and applied, was another important area of specialist printing. *Rechenung auff der linihen* (Calculating on the Abacus, 1518) by Adam Riese (1492–1559) enjoyed some 108 editions; the *Geometria deutsch* (1487 or 1488) of the Regensburg master architect Matthäus Roritzer (1440–95) related specifically to architecture. Doubtless the most famous works of applied mathematics, however, were in the area of the fine arts: Albrecht Dürer's *Underweyssung der messung* (Manual of Measurement, 1525) and *Vier Bücher von menschlicher Proportion* (Four Books on Human Proportion, 1528) systematized the doctrine of the human body both verbally and pictorially in a comprehensible fashion.

The humanists' return to the classical texts of antiquity and their new curiosity about the empirical world stimulated a climate conducive to creative research, especially in the universities. Simultaneously, the new political influence of the urban elites and their access to the universities brought about a publishing boom for specialist texts in the vernacular. The invention of the printing press offered the possibility of satisfying these educational needs with books in relative large editions and affordable prices. This tendency would increase spectacularly during the century of the Reformation.

Reformation and the Printing of the Book

"Doctor Martinus Luther sprach: Die Druckerey ist *summum et postremum donum*, durch welches Gott die Sache des Evangelii fort treibet. Es ist die letzte Flamme vor dem Auslöschen der Welt" (The printing press is *summum et postremum donum* [the greatest and ultimate gift] through which God continues to spread the word of the gospel. It is the last flame before the end of the world).[27] This euphoric statement was placed at the end of the 1566 edition of Luther's *Tischreden* (Table Talks, 1566) by his disciple Johannes Aurifaber (1519–75); it attests to the important role of the printing press for the spread of the Reformation and, above all, of the Holy Scriptures. The Latin phrase also reminds us of the literary bilingualism in the fifteenth and sixteenth centuries — though by the end of the second decade of the new century German was rapidly catching up with Latin as a printing language: between 1518 and 1526 almost three times as many texts were printed in German as had been in the first two decades. It is a commonplace in early modern research that without the printing press the Reformation could not have succeeded as quickly as it did, if at all.[28] As the Reformation spread, so did the print shops. Book historians argue that the Reformation was second only to humanism among the major themes disseminated by the printing press.

Given Luther's seminal doctrine that God announces his message of salvation to all people through the gospel, it followed that he would encourage access to the Bible through translation and liturgical reform.[29] Luther's German translation of the Bible, however, was by no means the first; at least eighteen versions had been printed previously, several of them in rather large numbers of copies.[30] During the course of the incunabula period ninety-four Vulgate editions appeared, twenty-two of which were directly modeled on the Gutenberg Bible. The first complete Bible in German was published in 1466 by Mentelin in Strasbourg, based on a translation that had originated in Bavaria nearly a century earlier; however, because the German of Mentelin's Bible followed the Vulgate closely, it could be understood well only by readers with a good command of Latin grammar. Nevertheless, it was reprinted thirteen times before 1518. In the second and third editions, printed respectively in 1470 in Strasbourg by Heinrich Eggestein (ca. 1420–ca. 1488) and in 1475 in Augsburg by Jodokus Pflanzmann (fl. 1465–94), unidiomatic and archaic words were replaced. Finally, Zainer's fourth edition in 1475 attempted a linguistic modernization on the basis of the original Latin. In a publisher's ad from 1476 — one of the first printed book dealer ads — Zainer advertises it aggressively: "Das Buch der teutschen Bibel mit figuren mit grössten fleiß corrigiert und gerechtgemacht. Also dz alle frembde teutsch und unverstenliche wort, so in den erstgedruckten kleinen bibeln gewesen, gantz ausgethan, und nach dem latein gesetzt und gemacht seind" (The book of the German Bible, with illustrations, corrected and made right with great diligence. Such that all unusual German words that are not understandable, which were in the first printed small Bibles, have been removed and now revised according to the Latin original).[31]

In addition to modernizing the text itself, Zainer added illustrations for the first time in a German language Bible: seventy-three pictorial initials, one at the beginning of each book of the Bible. Narrative woodcuts were then incorporated in further translations. They were meant not only to stimulate the reading of the Bible but also to assist in the understanding of the written word. Two Low German Bibles by Bartholomäus von Unkel (d. ca. 1484) and Heinrich Quentell (1440–1501), at the behest of a consortium of publishers in Cologne, followed Zainer's lead in 1478–79. One of the partners, Koberger, subsequently acquired the wooden blocks and had 109 of them colored in his print shop and incorporated into his Nuremberg Bible of 1483. He too subjected the text to a complete revision. Two richly illustrated editions of the Bible also appeared in the Augsburg print shop of Schönsperger. Two additional Low German editions — one in 1494 in Lübeck and the other in 1522 in Halberstadt — again demonstrate that the general standardizing tendency of printers' language had not yet led to a common written language in German as of the turn of the century.

The unprecedented success of Luther's Bible, however, owed both to the sovereign value he gave to the Bible for the religious life of all believers and to his extraordinary translation itself.[32] What set his translation apart from all earlier ones was, in the first place, his humanistic turn to the original Greek and Hebrew texts; the previous translations had relied solely on the Latin Vulgate.[33] Luther also emancipated German from Latin style by translating, not word for word, but rather meaning for meaning, much as Heinrich Steinhöwel (1411/12–1478) had recommended in his prose translations.[34] In *Sendbrief vom Dolmetschen* (Treatise on the Art of Translation, 1530), Luther attacks the "Buchstabilisten" (literalists):

> Denn man muss nicht die buchstaben in der lateinischen sprachen fragen, wie man soll Deutsch reden, wie diese Esel thun, sondern man muss die Mutter im Hause, die Kinder auf der Gassen, den gemeinen Mann auf dem Marckt darumb fragen, und den selbigen auf das Maul sehen, wie sie reden, und darnach dolmetzschen, so verstehen sie es denn und mercken, dass man deutsch mit jhnen redet.[35]

> [For one ought not to ask the letters in the Latin language how one is to say something in German, as these asses do, but rather one ought to ask the mothers at home, the children on the streets, the common man at the market place, and look them in the mouth and listen to how they talk, and then translate in that way. Then they will understand it and see that one is speaking German with them.]

He describes his painstaking search for just the right German word to convey the Bible's precise meaning and not falsify it. The biblical work itself, he avows, is its own best interpreter; accordingly, one is obliged to look at comparable texts when problems arise in translating. Individual verses, moreover, must be considered within the context of the entire Bible — thus Luther's famous hermeneutic, his circular, detailed method of interpretation, which proceeds from the specific to the whole, from the letter to the spirit. As the quotation above implies, his style is always oriented toward the spoken word, hence his introduction of "flavoring particles" — he calls them "Würzworte," such as *allein, doch, eben, nur, nun, schon* — that not only provide for rhythm, resonance, and repetition, but also bring out the homiletic character of the translation.

Luther began with the New Testament. It is important to observe — and it does not diminish the brilliance of his personal accomplishment — that Luther regularly sought the support of other scholars, particularly his younger colleague at Wittenberg, Philipp Melanchthon (1497–1560), a professor of Hebrew and Greek. It was common for humanists to collaborate on projects, though a single name may ultimately stand on the title page. Luther and Melanchthon together revised the translation in summer 1522 during Luther's stay at the Wartburg under the protection of Duke Friedrich the Wise. Luther's primary reference work was the second edition of the original Greek text that had appeared in the publishing house of Johann Froben (1460–1527) in Basel together with the revised Latin translation and notes by Erasmus of Rotterdam. Luther's accomplishment was not limited to his superb command of language: his interpretive notes, introductory prologues, marginal glosses that mediate between the Old and the New Testament, and explanations of words and topics are all authoritative and assure the translation its place in intellectual history.

Luther's New Testament translation was published in folio format in the Wittenberg print shop of Melchior Lotter (fl. 1491–1536, at first in Leipzig) in an edition of 3,000 copies in time for the fall book fair in Leipzig. The cost of this *September-Testament* was about one gulden, comparable to two months' wages for a school teacher or the price for a calf. Lotter began immediate work on a second, revised edition, and on 19 December 1522 the *Dezember-Testament* was finished. It includes hundreds of improvements in word choice and syntax and the addition of parallel texts. In 1523, twelve complete but unauthorized editions appeared in Augsburg, Basel, Grimma, and Leipzig. Fourteen authorized editions and sixty-six reprints came out in 1523–24. It was his concern about falsification of the text — not about potential losses of honoraria — that caused Luther to include, as of 1524, a protective marking or trademark in his authorized editions.

Even as the New Testament was being printed, Luther began to translate the Old Testament, for which he again returned to the original language texts. The project dragged on for over twelve years, owing both to the much larger amount of text and to the difficulty of translating from the Hebrew. Separate inexpensive printings of individual books of the Old Testament were put on sale as early as 1523. An edition published by Christian Döring (d. 1533) and Lucas Cranach the Elder (1472–1553) in Wittenberg included, in the second half of the Old Testament, an escutcheon with the Lamb of God holding a flag with the so-called *Luther-Rose* (a cross with a red heart enclosed in a rose blossom): this was to indicate that the print had been authorized by Luther. The first *Vollbibel* (complete Bible) did not appear until 1534 in Wittenberg in the publishing house of Hans Lufft (1495–1584).[36] This edition received the

equivalent of a permanent copyright from Prince Elector Johann Friedrich of
Saxony, so that the publisher Döring had to work out a separate contract with
the printer Lufft, the most important printer of Luther's works as late as the
1560s. Döring's financial difficulties led to a consortium of publishers taking
over the project of the complete edition, a fact that may explain why the edition lacks a unified editorial reworking (it lacks even unified pagination).
Illustrations were provided by an artist using the monogram "MS" — 117 narrative images and ten pictorial initials. A bound copy of this complete Bible
cost two gulden and eight groschen, which was about five times the cost of a
copy of the New Testament. Despite the high price, the first edition of 3,000
copies quickly sold out, and minimally altered reprints were published in
Wittenberg in 1535, 1536, and 1539. The revisions undertaken in the years
between 1539 and 1541 show Luther's continued attention to the texts. The
final authorized edition, produced by Lufft in 1545, bears the title *Biblia: das
ist: die gantze Heilige Schrifft: deudsch: Auffs new zugericht* (Bible: That Is: The
Complete Holy Scriptures: German: Newly Revised). It soon acquired canonical authority and, contrary to Luther's express wishes, remained largely unim-
proved for centuries. From 1521 until Luther's death in 1546 about 300 High
German editions of the Bible appeared, with the total number of copies reaching more than half a million — an astonishing figure given that the book market was still a recent phenomenon (just two generations earlier Gutenberg had
printed a mere 180 copies of the Bible) and that less than 10% of the population was literate. Approximately one-third of the German-language book production in the first half of the sixteenth century can be accounted for by
Luther's writings alone.

Luther contributed decisively to the standardization of the German language, particularly to the standardization of the written language.[37] That influence was due to several factors: the widespread distribution of his works,
especially his Bible; his general avoidance of dialectal expressions; and his use of
the language of eastern central Germany, which was understandable to readers
in large areas of the remainder of that country. Additionally, his own neologisms,
idioms, and metaphors all abetted the development of a distinct new German
style. Some 7,000 neologisms are attributable to Luther, including many compound words, such as *Feuereifer* (burning enthusiasm), *Herzenslust* (heart's
desire), or *Denkzettel* (literally a "think note," that is, memo). Among the many
popular idioms he coined are "seine Hände in Unschuld waschen" (to wash
one's hands in innocence), "der Dorn im Auge" (the thorn in one's eye), and
"im Dunkeln tappen" (to grope in the dark). While much has been made of
Luther's "folksy" language, more recent research has demonstrated that he was
equally concerned with creating a sacred language in the elevated mold of classical rhetoric and the stylistic dignity of the original biblical texts.[38] Luther's
influence on German language and style cannot be fully appreciated apart from
his other writings as well: the theological tracts, the catechisms, hymns, sermons,
and disputations, not to mention the propagandistic *Flugschriften*.

Although the Catholic Church had made use of the book printing
technology from the beginning and had encouraged the early spread of the

technology, it simultaneously limited the possibility of the technology's effectiveness by issuing edicts of censure. In 1475 it forbade translations of the Bible into German and the issuing of theological tracts in German, arguing that they were "nicht förderlich" (not suitable) for "den gemeinen man" (the common man); and in swift response to Luther's spate of reformational writings in 1520, the Church had the *Bulla contra errores Martini Lutheri* (Bull against the Errors of Martin Luther) printed in Rome and publicly circulated. Official ecclesiastical writings, which heretofore had been distributed only via a limited number of manuscript copies, now became topics of public debate. In the 1520s the "old" church in Germany turned to its loyal printers and publishers in an effort to compete with the influence of Luther's Bible translation. Duke Georg of Saxony (1471–1539), who in 1522 had issued a territorial ban on the Luther Bible,[39] commissioned the anti-Luther theologian Hieronymus Emser (1477–1527) to create a *Neues Testament*; it was published in Dresden by Wolfgang Stöckel (ca. 1473–1540). Emser based his translation intimately on Luther's *September-Testament* and various older German-language Bibles, as well as on the original Greek. For illustrations he used woodcuts — purchased from Cranach! — out of the *Dezember-Testament* itself. In his afterword, returning to the notion prevalent in the fifteenth century, he recommends against lay reading of the Bible: "Darum so bekömmere sich nun eyn itzlicher Ley [. . .] mehr umb eyn gut Gottselig Leben, dann vmb die Schrifft, die alleyn den Gelahrten befohlen ist"[40] (Therefore let every lay person be more concerned with living a pious life than with reading the Bible, which is recommended solely to the educated).

More successful was the *Biblia beider alt und newen Testamenten* (Bible Containing both the Old and New Testaments) of the Dominican theologian in Mainz, Johannes Dietenberger (ca. 1475–1537), which appeared in Cologne and Mainz in 1534, furnished with an imperial privilege, shortly before Luther's complete edition. Dietenberger used Luther's translation, both directly and indirectly (he also followed Emser closely), as well as older German translations. He provides summaries of the individual books of the Bible and places translation variants and explanations in the margin, among which he notes the "falsifications" of Luther's interpretations. Dietenberger's Bible went through forty-six editions by 1776. Yet another Bible, the so-called *Mainzer Bibel*, which was produced by theologians in Mainz on the basis of Dietenberger's version, found widespread use in the Catholic areas of Germany in the seventeenth and eighteenth centuries.

All of these Bible translations, though especially Luther's, influenced the style and form of German literature and education in the succeeding centuries. Since the Bible was commonly the only book in a house, it frequently served the secondary purpose of teaching reading. In a sermon in Strasbourg in 1624 about proper Christian readings, the rhetorician and theologian Johann Conrad Dannhauer (1603–66) condemns the reading of novels and recommends Luther instead: "Hinweg mit Amadis, Schäfereien, Eulenspiegel, Gärtengesellschaft, Rollwagen und dergleichen heillosen Bücher mehr — das Teutsch lernt sich besser in der Bibel und den Büchern Lutheri" (Away with

Amadis, bucolics, *Eulenspiegel*, the garden salons, *Rollwagen*, and all such unholy writings — German can be better learned in the Bible and the books of Luther).

In addition to the Bible, *Flugschriften* flooded the market — unbound brochures of sixteen to sixty-four pages containing theses, disputations, sermons, or other polemical writings of a currently topical nature. The *Flugblatt*, a smaller variant (single-page leaflets or "broadsheets," or "broadsides"), usually decorated with provocative woodcuts that made propaganda more compelling, was often printed in runs reaching into the millions. Topics varied widely — warnings about counterfeit money, sensational reports on astronomical phenomena, such as the plunging of a comet to earth, or attacks on the Catholic Church; a flood in 1524 was reported on hundreds of broadsheets throughout Central Europe. The genre was one of the most important "weapons" in the confessional battles, forcing printers themselves to confront the issues directly and inspiring basic changes in the way both printing and marketing were done.

During the first thirty years of the sixteenth century, about 11,000 broadsheets were printed. In 1524 alone, more than twenty-four printings by eighteen printers in fifteen different cities were made of a single provocative broadsheet, the incendiary *Zwölf Artikel der Bauernschaft* (Twelve Articles of the Peasantry) of the revolutionary peasants.[41] In 1517 and 1518, the first two years of the Reformation, Nuremberg, Augsburg, Strasbourg, and Basel were the dominant confessional and printing cities; after that they were joined by Wittenberg and Leipzig. The printers distributed these publications on their own, assisted by bookbinders, shopkeepers, and traveling salesmen who also had other "Newe Zeitungen" (news) for sale at the markets and fairs. The various communities remained in close contact and sent each other the newest *Flugschriften*, which would be read aloud and discussed. Between 1520 and 1526 approximately 11,000 individual brochures were printed, most in runs of about a thousand, yielding around 11,000,000 copies. This number corresponds roughly to the population at that time. Given that less than 10% of the population was literate, this means that approximately twenty brochures were in circulation per literate citizen. Hans Joachim Köhler has calculated an equivalent selling price of one to two cents per printed sheet, approximately one-third of a journeyman's daily wages.[42]

Hymnal and Catechism

Just as Luther's printed sermons carried his message to communities beyond the space in which liturgical services were held, he also used the genre of the church hymn to popularize the basic tenets of his faith. Thirty-six hymns are ascribable to Luther; twenty-four appeared in a single year, in 1523,[43] expedited by the urgency of reforming the German-language worship service, but doubtless owing also to the strategy of communicating special news rapidly via broadsheets. So it was that Luther's first well-known hymn, "Ein neues Lied wir heben an" (We Begin a New Song, 1523), was inspired by a "news item": the execution, carried out by the Inquisition in the Netherlands, of two Augustinian monks who had converted to the evangelical faith. The hymn is a kind of rhymed journalism of the sort that had been practiced for over a century in a type of inflammatory folk song; even Emperor Maximilian I (1459–1519) had exploited it in his presentation in public.[44] Luther's hymns, which were widely distributed in single leaf, often took positions on confessional issues and consequently assumed a significance well beyond the liturgy itself.

His second important song, "Nun freut euch, lieben Christen gmein" (Now Rejoice, Dear Christians, Together), likewise springs from the joy over Christ's act of salvation. Luther's seven *Psalmlieder* (Psalm Songs) return to the venerable ecclesiastical hymn tradition, but actualize it with references to the specific situation within the evangelical communities. This is illustrated in his famous hymn "Ein' feste Burg ist unser Gott" (A Mighty Fortress Is Our God). Because Luther was so adept at bringing biblical stories into whatever he wrote, including his hymns, and given his penchant for borrowing melodies for his hymns from popular songs, the Lutheran hymn achieved great popularity. Many were transmitted on broadsheets printed in runs of 500 to 800 copies and therefore reached many communities, where they were read aloud and sung. Their familiar formulations, popular melodies, and pleasing rhymes aided easy memorization.

Numerous songs that had appeared as individual prints were rearranged in multiple voices for boys' choir and appeared in the Wittenberg *Gesangbüchlein* (1524) before being made available in 1526 to the church community as a whole. The actual history of the hymnal begins with an edition of *Geistliche Lieder* (Spiritual Songs) printed by Joseph Klug in Wittenberg in 1529 (the earliest extant edition is the second, from 1533; improved edition, 1535). It contains a didactic preface by Luther; later, woodcut illustrations were added and the songs ordered in the definitive manner familiar to evangelicals. The hymnal made it possible for congregants to participate actively in the liturgy, unlike the former Latin rite, which had been murmured by the celebrant with his back to the congregation. Sermon song, broadsheet, and folksong combined in the Lutheran hymn into an indivisible symbiosis.

Der Kleine Katechismus (The Small Catechism, 1529) became popular in the same manner, as a question-and-answer game that transmitted the basic tenets of the faith. The first version was distributed in early 1529 as a broadsheet; it appeared in May as a "pocket book" in small format with illustrative woodcuts, an elucidation of the Ten Commandments, and an appendix with answers to fundamental questions. These first editions were likely intended for the catechists' repetitions during the liturgy and devotional services; subsequent editions, which numbered in the hundreds of thousands, were meant for the faithful themselves and, later, for children. Besides the commandments, the Apostles' Creed and the Lord's Prayer were explicated in detail; the pregnant formulations served Christians for centuries as an orientation toward Christian values. *Der Grosse Katechismus*, or *Deudsch Catechismus* (The Large, or German, Catechism,

1529), offered, beyond simple responses, a great number of scriptural references and cross-references meant to establish a firmer basis of belief as well as to provide preachers with further textual and explanatory material.

Related to the catechism, the didactic Lutheran broadsheet in the traditional (Latin) dialogue form proved to be particularly popular and useful in spreading the ideas of the Reformation. For example, in 1524 the shoemaker poet from Nuremberg, Hans Sachs (1494–1576), an ardent supporter of the Reformation, created a broadsheet scene between a canon and a shoemaker, "darin das Wort Gottes und ein recht christlich Wesen verfochten wird" (in which the word of God and the essence of a true Christian are defended). The dialogue betrays the true, superficial, character of the canon, whereas it shows the cobbler Hans to be a genuine believer, firmly grounded in the Bible. Sachs is dealing here with the three critical questions that Luther himself had addressed four years earlier in his brochure *An den christlichen Adel deutscher Nation* (To the Christian Nobility of the German Nation, 1520): the claims of the pope to have sole authority in interpreting the Bible, to call councils, and to secure the dominance of ecclesiastical over secular powers. In another illustrative poem by Sachs, "Ein neuer Spruch, wie die Geistlichkeydt und etlich Handwercker ueber den Luther clagen" (A New Lesson: How the Clergy and Some Artisans Argue over Luther), readers or listeners can choose between "godless" arguments and those of Luther. It concludes with Christ's pronouncement in favor of Luther.

German-Language Bestsellers at Book Fairs in the Sixteenth Century

Gutenberg's technical invention underwent no essential changes before about 1800. Certain wooden parts of the press were replaced with metal ones, of course, but the basic principles of the invention with regard to setting and printing of type remained unaltered. The book itself changed considerably over this time, however, in its structural features — smaller format, addition of title page,[45] table of contents, indices, notes or footnotes, pagination and marginal notes, more complex woodcuts, use of copper plates — and was marketed and distributed with ever greater sophistication. Around 1530 the book fair (*Buchmesse*) at Frankfurt established itself as one of the major European trading centers for books; Frankfurt's central location on the Main and Rhine made it easy to attract publishers and authors from Paris, Rome, Geneva, or Antwerp, particularly given the continuing role of Latin as the *lingua franca*. The renowned French publisher Henri Estienne proclaimed in 1574 that Frankfurt had become the new Athens.[46] Leading intellectual societies organized their annual meetings around the event, and the fair figured in publication calendars. Correspondence within the republic of letters by midcentury makes frequent mention of the need for books to be finished in time for the spring or fall fair.

In 1564 an Augsburg book dealer, Georg Willer, published the *Messneuigkeiten*, the first privately compiled catalogue of the Frankfurt Book Fair. It lists a large portion of the books on sale and offers an instructive look into the fair's organization and importance. Willer's catalogue is divided according to the four university faculties — Theology, Law, Medicine, and Philosophy — but also indexes belles-lettres. Such bibliographical helps were necessary given the immense upsurge in the sixteenth century in the number of printed books. The *Verzeichnis der Drucke des 16. Jahrhunderts* (Index of Printed Books of the Sixteenth Century) lists nearly 160,000 titles, though to appreciate this number one must be aware that in the last quarter of the century three times as many books were printed as in all previous years. The actual number of copies printed in the sixteenth century in German-speaking lands may have run to 140 million. The outbreak of the Thirty Years' War in 1618 caused a significant decline in the annual production of books; only around the middle of the eighteenth century did production again reach previous levels.

The phenomenon of large-volume book dealers came about in the sixteenth century. One was Michael Harder, of Frankfurt, whose *Mess-Memorial* (Book Fair Record) from the year 1569 shows that during a single Easter fair he sold 6,000 books,[47] among them a number of prose novels, including *Melusine* and *Schöne Magelone*, and the famous collection of farces *Schimpf und Ernst* (Mischief and Morality, 1522) by Johannes Pauli (ca. 1450–1530/33). He also offered many specialist works for sale, ranging from books on home remedies to arithmetic to cuisine. The printer publishers, especially those in Frankfurt, weighted their catalogues to sure-sale titles — knightly tales from the Middle Ages, romantic novels, and travel reports; comical tales and farces attracted buyers perennially, especially translations from Italian or Latin. One of the most popular was the *Liber facetiarum* (Book of Farces, 1508–12) of Heinrich Bebel (ca. 1472–1518), a professor of rhetoric in Tübingen, who began translating farces into German in 1588; the collection was copied repeatedly.

Midcentury in Strasbourg saw the publication of Jörg Wickram's (ca. 1505–ca. 1561) *Rollwagenbüchlein* (Carriage Booklet, 1555), a popular collection of sixty-seven morally educative tales, expanded and reprinted at least seventeen times by 1613. Similar works followed by Jacob Frey (1520–62), a city scribe, with *Fröhlich Gesprächen, Schimpfreden und Speiwerk* (Merry Conversations, Farces, and Pranks, 1577), and Hans Wilhelm Kirchhof (1525–1605), a soldier and adventurer, with *Wendunmuth* (1563–1603), a multivolume collection of farcical stories. Tales that had been published during the age of the incunabula were sometimes reprinted, as in the didactic collection translated from the French by the Swabian nobleman Marquard vom Stein as *Der Ritter vom Thurn* (The Knight from Thurn). Printed in Basel in 1493, it was reprinted more than 100 times before 1682; in 1553 the historian Cyriacus Spangenberg counted it among the most widely read books of the age.[48]

This farcical literature was related to certain other genres that flourished in the sixteenth century, notably the emerging novel and the travel report, narrative forms that combined fictional imagination, geographical exploration, and utopian fancy.[49] Often — whether in the *enfant terrible* hero of *Eulenspiegel* (1510) or the foolish-but-wise citizens of the *Lalebuch* (The Lale Folk, 1597; published the following year as the *Schildbürger*, Citizens of Schilda) — it turns a critical, if humorous, eye on society. The anonymous author of the *Historia von D. Johann Fausten*[50] (1587) exploits various strains of oral and written traditions, in this case taking the legend of a man who conjures the devil, and adding the phenomenon of encyclopedic knowledge and the form of the theological tract. The *Faust* chapbook, or prose novel, which was repeatedly printed, first appeared in the house of the Frankfurt printer publisher, Johann Spiess (ca. 1550–1623), whose success may be measured by the fact that, beginning in 1586, he produced on average twenty new publications annually for about twenty years, including a great deal of popular fiction.

There were two other particularly successful publishers besides Spiess in Frankfurt: Sigmund Feyerabend (1528–90) and his distant cousin Johann Feyerabend (1550–99). The Feyerabends published numerous illustrated volumes, among them Boccaccio's *De claris mulieribus* (On Famous Women), Georg Rüxner's *Turnierbuch* (Tournament Book, 1566), and *Eygentliche Beschreibung Aller Stände auff Erden* (Exact Description of All Ranks on Earth, 1568; translated as *The Book of Trades*, 1973) with woodcuts by Jost Amman and verses by Hans Sachs. Their best-known printings, however, were volumes of prose narratives, including the *Theatrum diabolorum* (Theater of Devils, 1569–88) and a German translation (1569–76) of thirteen volumes of the extraordinarily popular Romance serial novel, the *Amadís de Gaula*.[51] The success of the Feyerabend enterprise owed not only to a judicious selection of material, but especially to commercial acumen, apparent in the clever advertisements for the collections. For example, the *Buch der Liebe* (Book of Love, 1587) — "enthaltend herrliche schöne Historien allerlei seltene und neue Exempel daraus manniglich zu vernehmen, beide was recht, ehrliche dagegen was auch unordentliche buhlerische Lieb sei" (containing wonderful stories, rare and never before told, from which can be learned not only what is right and honorable but also what is improper in matters of love) — is an anthology of individually successful titles. Feyerabend simply gave them a provocative collective title and advertised that the collection would be "allen hohen Standspersonen, der Liebenden vom Adel, züchtigen Frauen und Jungfrauen, auch jedermann in gemein sowohl zu lesen lieblich und kurzweilig" (endearing and entertaining for all persons of higher classes, for noble lovers, for virtuous women and young ladies, indeed for everyone in general to read).

Conclusion

Although the fifteenth century is justifiably admired for developing printed works of high quality, the most successful titles were still mainly those from the manuscript era, and the number of copies sold did not exceed what a relatively constant number of educated readers could support. During the sixteenth century the quantity and distribution of printed books increased immensely. A *Gebrauchsliteratur* (functional literature, writing for a particular purpose) took hold, more simply written and mostly in the vernacular, spurred on both by the educational goals of the Reformation as well as by the social and theological agitation stirred up by the subsequent confessional battles. The quantity of specialist and fictional writings in the vernacular reached unprecedented heights during the second half of the century, due in particular to the marketing skills of publishers and book dealers; their entrepreneurial strategies, especially at the book fair in Frankfurt, resulted in massive sales. Success on the book market was certainly a by-product of improved education in the schools, which stimulated interest in reading of all kinds. By 1600, publishers had developed catalogues of great variety for an ever-expanding reading public, ranging from historical chronicles in large format to novels in small format. Fictional and empirical travel reports were extremely popular. The most famous, *Cosmographia, Das ist Beschreibung der gantzen Welt* (Cosmography: Description of the Entire World) of the cartographer Sebastian Münster (1488–1552) appeared between 1541 and 1650 in forty-six printings and in eight different languages. It was superceded only in the seventeenth century by the grand topographical works of the Frankfurt publisher Matthaeus Merian (1593–1650), who produced the richly illustrated and extensively annotated *Theatrum europaeum* — a work of some 20,000 pages.

Newspapers in a more or less modern sense — public organs appearing at regular intervals and distributed widely — are inventions of the seventeenth century. The periodic press, beginning in 1609 with the appearance of two German weeklies, one by Johann Carolus in Strasbourg, the other by Lucas Schulte in Wolfenbüttel, became the primary source of news and henceforth a controlling element for public political awareness. The modern scholarly journal, conceived as a platform for enlightened discussion, arose during the last third of the seventeenth century, and by 1730 a wide range of journalistic opinion was provoking thought throughout intellectual Europe. The new forum of learned debate in the first half of the eighteenth century may be seen as a harbinger of the Enlightenment.

Translated by Karl F. Otto Jr.

Notes

1 Johannes Aventinus, *Baierische Chronik*, ed. Georg Leidinger, 2nd ed. (Munich: Diederichs, 1988); original German modernized.

2 See Stephan Füssel, " 'Barbarus sermo fugiat . . .': Das Verhältnis der Humanisten zur Volkssprache," *Pirckheimer-Jahrbuch* 1 (1985): 71–110.

3 Joachim Knape refers to this historical development as "scriptorality" in his chapter in this volume. See also Helmut Kreuzer, ed., *Verschriftlichung* (Stuttgart: Metzler, 1997), and Jan-Dirk Müller, ed., *"Aufführung" und "Schrift" in Mittelalter und früher Neuzeit* (Stuttgart: Metzler, 1996).

[4] The colored leaf is preserved in the John Rylands Library at the University of Manchester. The artifact is discussed by Jeffrey Chipps Smith in this volume.

[5] Stadtarchiv Erfurt, Universitätsmatrikel, Signatur I-16XB XIII -46, Bd. 1, Fol. 51 verso.

[6] The sources are documented in Karl Schorbach, "Die urkundlichen Nachrichten über Johann Gutenberg," in *Festschrift zum fünfhundertjährigen Geburtstage von Johann Gutenberg*, ed. Otto Hartwig (Leipzig: Harrassowitz, 1900), 133–256.

[7] Wolfgang von Stromer, "Hans Friedel von Seckingen, der Bankier der Straßburger Gutenberg-Gesellschaften," *Gutenberg-Jahrbuch* (1983): 45–48.

[8] A digital version is available at: www.gutenbergdigital.de.

[9] See Severin Corsten, "Die Drucklegung der 42-zeiligen Bibel: Technische und chronologische Probleme," in *Gutenbergs zweiundvierzigzeilige Bibel: Faksimile-Ausgabe nach dem Exemplar der Staatsbibliothek preußischer Kulturbesitz Berlin*, ed. Wieland Schmidt (Munich: Idion, 1979), 33–68.

[10] Translated into German by Stephan Füssel, *Johannes Gutenberg*, 3rd ed. (Reinbek b. Hamburg: Rowohlt, 1999), 138.

[11] Peter Schöffer from Gernsheim on the Rhine is documented in 1449 as a cleric and calligrapher at the University of Paris. In the statement of the notary public Helmasperger in the legal proceedings of Fust vs. Gutenberg he is designated as Peter Gerinssheim, a cleric of the city and bishop of Mainz.

[12] Hans Widmann, *Eltvilles Anteil am Frühdruck: Tatsachen und Probleme* (Eltville: Burgverein, 1970).

[13] Arnold Esch, "Deutsche Frühdrucker in Rom in den Registern Papst Paul II.," *Gutenberg-Jahrbuch* (1993): 44–52.

[14] "Deutschland ist in der Tat wert, geehrt und durch alle Jahrhunderte hoch gepriesen zu werden als Erfinderin der segensreichen Kunst. Das ist auch der Grund dafür, dass die stets rühmenswerte und des Himmelreiches würdige Seele des Nikolaus von Kues, des Kardinals zu *Sanct Peter ad Vincula*, den heißen Wunsch hatte, dass diese heilige Kunst, die man damals in Deutschland entstehen sah, auch in Rom heimisch werde." Esch, "Deutsche Frühdrucker," 51.

[15] Stephan Füssel, " 'Dem Buchdrucker aber sage er Dank . . .': Zur wechselseitigen Bereicherung von Buchdruckerkunst und Humanismus," in *Artibus: Kulturwissenschaft und deutsche Philologie des Mittelalters und der Frühen Neuzeit*, ed. Stephan Füssel, Gert Hübner, and Joachim Knape (Wiesbaden: Harrassowitz, 1994), 167–78.

[16] Laurentius Valla, *Opera omnia*, ed. Eugenio Garin (Torino: Bottega d'Erasmo, 1962), 1:249. See Hanna-Barbara Gerl-Falkovitz, *Rhetorik als Philosophie: Lorenzo Valla* (Munich: Fink, 1974).

[17] Füssel, *Gutenberg*, 139.

[18] Otto Mazal, *Der Mainzer Psalter von 1457* (Dietikon-Zürich: Stocker, 1969).

[19] A German-language prose novel would have been unthinkable without the translations by two women of high nobility from Germany and Austria: Elisabeth von Nassau-Saarbrücken (1393–1456) and Eleonore von Österreich. Both were significant political figures, and both were intensively engaged with French and Latin literature. The translation of *Pontus and Sidonia*, which was written around 1400 in France, is thought to have been translated by Eleonore. On Eleonore and the early prose novel see the chapter in this volume by Graeme Dunphy.

[20] Hans Joachim Kreutzer, *Der Mythos vom Volksbuch* (Stuttgart: Metzler, 1977). See also the research summary on prose novel by Jan-Dirk Müller, "Volksbuch/Prosaroman im 15./16. Jahrhundert — Perspektiven der Forschung," *Internationales Archiv für Sozialgeschichte der deutschen Literatur*, Sonderheft: *Forschungsreferate* (1985): 1–128.

[21] Joachim Knape, *"Historie" in Mittelalter und Früher Neuzeit* (Baden-Baden: Koerner, 1984).

[22] *Tristan* edition of 1484.

[23] Hartmann Schedel, *Chronicle of the World (1493): The Complete and Annotated Nuremberg Chronicle of 1493*, ed. Stephan Füssel (Cologne: Taschen, 2001); Christoph Reske, *The Production of Schedel's Nuremberg Chronicle* (Wiesbaden: Harrassowitz, 2000).

[24] On the travel report see in this volume the chapter by Wolfgang Neuber.

[25] Schedel, *Die Schedelsche Weltchronik*, afterword by Rudolf Pörtner, 3rd ed. (Dortmund: Harenberg Kommunikation, 1985), CCLII[v].

[26] Ute Schneider, "Das Buch als Wissensvermittler in der Frühen Neuzeit," in *Kommunikation und Medien in der Frühen Neuzeit*, ed. Johannes Burkhardt (Munich: Oldenbourg, 2005), 63–78.

[27] No. 1038 in the Weimar edition of the *Tischreden*.

[28] See, for example, Johannes Burckhardt, *Das Reformationsjahrhundert: Deutsche Geschichte zwischen Medienrevolution und Institutionenbildung 1517–1617* (Stuttgart: Kohlhammer, 2002).

[29] Gerhard Hahn, "Literatur und Konfessionalisierung," in *Die Literatur am Übergang von Mittelalter zur Neuzeit*, ed. Werner Röcke and Martina Münkler (Munich: Hanser, 2004), 242–62, here 243.

[30] Walter Eichenberger and Henning Wendland, *Deutsche Bibeln vor Luther: Die Buchkunst der achtzehn deutschen Bibeln von 1466 bis 1522*, 2nd ed. (Hamburg: Wittig, 1983); see also Heimo Reinitzer, *Biblia deutsch: Luthers Bibelübersetzung und ihre Tradition*, exhibition catalogue (Wolfenbüttel: Herzog August Bibliothek, 1983), 63–86.

[31] In the Staats- und Universitätsbibliothek Göttingen, Sign.: 4° Hll I, 7304 Inc.

[32] Stephan Füssel, "Luther und die Biblia Deutsch," in *Von der Handschrift zum Buchdruck: Spätmittelalter, Reformation, Humanismus*, vol. 2 of *Deutsche Literatur: Eine Sozialgeschichte*, ed. Ingrid Bennewitz and Ulrich Müller (Reinbek b. Hamburg: Rowohlt, 1991), 329–42.

[33] On the humanists' return to the ancient sources see the chapter in this volume by Erika Rummel.

[34] Discussed in this volume in the chapter by John L. Flood.

[35] This work is available in a modernized German edition in: *An den christlichen Adel deutscher Nation. Von der Freiheit eines Christenmenschen. Sendbrief vom Dolmetschen*, ed. Ernst Kähler, Universal-Bibliothek 1578 (Stuttgart: Reclam, 1975), 151–73, here 159.

[36] See the commentary in *The Book of Books: The Luther Bible of 1534: A Cultural-Historical Introduction*, ed. and comm. Stephan Füssel (Cologne: Taschen, 2003).

[37] For an analysis of Luther's role in the standardization of Early Modern German see the chapter in this volume by Renate Born (section: "Martin Luther's Linguistic Influence").

[38] Herbert Wolf, "Zum Stand der sprachlichen Lutherforschung," *Zeitschrift für deutsche Philologie* 106, Sonderheft: *Frühneuhochdeutsch*, ed. Werner Besch and Klaus-Peter Wegera (1987): 246–72.

[39] This mandate may be found in *Hertzog Georgen von Sachsen Mandat an die Vnterthanen, das New Testament durch D.M.L. verdeudscht, zu vberantworten. Anno MD.XXII.*, Herzog August Bibliothek Wolfenbüttel, Sign.: 269 Theol. 2°.

[40] *Das naw testament nach lawt der Christlichen kirchen bewerten text, corrigirt vnd widerumb zu recht gebracht*, folio 195 verso, 196 recto; in the Herzog August Bibliothek Wolfenbüttel, Sign.: Bibel-S. 4° 269.

[41] Peter Blickle, *Der Bauernkrieg* (Munich: Beck, 1998).

[42] Hans Joachim Köhler, ed., *Flugschriften als Massenmedien der Reformationszeit* (Stuttgart: Klett-Cotta, 1981), 342.

[43] Gerhard Hahn, "Literatur und Konfessionalisierung," in Röcke and Münkler, eds., *Die Literatur am Übergang*, 253–56. On Luther as a hymn writer see the chapter in this volume by Steven Saunders (section: "The Chorale and Music in the Early Reformation Church").

[44] Stephan Füssel, "Maximilian I.," in *Deutsche Dichter der Frühen Neuzeit*, ed. Füssel (Berlin: Schmidt, 1993), 200–216. On *Publizistik* see Michael Stolleis, "Public Law and Patriotism in the Holy Roman Empire," in *Infinite Boundaries: Order, Disorder, and Reorder in Early Modern German Culture*, ed. Max Reinhart (Kirksville, MO: Thomas Jefferson UP, 1998), 11–33.

[45] Margaret M. Smith, *The Title-Page: Its Early Development 1460–1510* (London: The British Library & Oak Knoll Press, 2000).

[46] Hans Widmann, ed., *Der deutsche Buchhandel in Urkunden und Quellen* (Hamburg: Hauswedell, 1965), 1:36.

[47] See Ernst Kelcher and Richard Paul Wülcker, eds., *Mess-Memorial des Frankfurter Buchhändlers Michael Harder* (Frankfurt am Main: Baer, 1873).

[48] Paul Heitz and François Ritter, eds., *Versuch einer Zusammenstellung der deutschen Volksbücher des 15. und 16. Jahrhunderts nebst deren späteren Ausgaben und Literatur* (1924; repr., Baden-Baden: Heitz, 1964), 193.

[49] An exemplary and accessible edition is *Fortunatus: Studienausgabe nach der Editio Princeps 1509*, ed. Hans-Gert Roloff, Universal-Bibliothek 7721 (Stuttgart: Reclam, 1981).

[50] *Historia von D. Johann Fausten: Kritische Ausgabe*, rev. ed., ed. Stephan Füssel and Hans Joachim Kreutzer, Universal-Bibliothek 1516 (Stuttgart: Reclam, 2006).

[51] During the sixteenth and seventeenth centuries the *Amadis* novel, first published in Spain in 1508, went through more than 600 editions in Spanish, Italian, French, and German versions, eventually comprising twenty-four volumes in the German version.

Poetics and Rhetorics in Early Modern Germany

Joachim Knape

F ROM ANTIQUITY ON, REFLECTION ON MEANS of communication — on texts in general and poetic texts in particular — brought about two distinct genres of theoretical texts: rhetorics and poetics. Theoretical knowledge was systematized in these two genres for instructional purposes, and its practical applications were debated down to the eighteenth century. At the center of this discussion stood the communicator (or, text producer), armed with procedural options and obligations and with the text as his primary instrument of communication. Thus, poeto-rhetorical theory always derived its rules from and reflected the prevailing practice.[1]

This development began in the fourth century B.C. with Aristotle's *Rhetoric* and *Poetics*, which he based on the public communicative practices of the Greek *polis* in politics, theater, and poetic performance. In the Roman tradition, rhetorics[2] reflected the practice of law in the forum (*genus iudiciale*), political counsel (*genus deliberativum*), and communal decisions regarding issues of praise and blame (*genus demonstrativum*). These comprise the three main speech situations, or cases (*genera causarum*). The most important theoreticians of rhetoric were Cicero and Quintilian, along with the now unknown author (presumed in the Middle Ages to have been Cicero) of the rhetorics addressed to *Herennium*. As for poetics, aside from the monumental *Ars poetica* of Horace, Roman literature did not have a particularly rich theoretical tradition. The Hellenistic poetics *On the Sublime* by Pseudo-Longinus (first century A.D.) was rediscovered only in the seventeenth century in France and England; it became a key work for modern aesthetics.

The classical theoretical works from antiquity were available in the Middle Ages and Renaissance.[3] Their use in communication and textual theory, however, remained the exclusive domain of scholars who had little interest in vernacular texts and whose theories reflected the hermetic Latin discourse of classroom exercises. Certain poetics and rhetorics written in the twelfth and thirteenth centuries, however, became particularly influential; these included Galfridus de Vinosalvo's *Poetria nova* (ca. 1210) — so named to contrast with the "old poetics" of Horace's *Ars poetica* — which was transmitted in hundreds of manuscripts into the fifteenth century. It is a kind of textual grammar with rules and techniques for formulating Latin verse and prose. The only poeto-rhetorics by a German from this period was the *Laborintus* (Labor Within, before 1250), written by the grammarian Eberhard the German, who was educated in Paris and Orléans.

The development of poeto-rhetorical theories in early modern Germany will be the subject in this chapter in two parts. Part 1 reviews the state of German source materials between the thirteenth and seventeenth centuries. Part 2 attempts a unified theory of early modern German-language poetics and rhetorics.

Source Materials in Germany to 1600

The rhetorics and poetics of the fifteenth century had two major goals:[4] to make classical knowledge of these areas known in a pure form (epistemology), establish Latin-language sources (linguistics) for contemporary scholarship, and bring the pertinent genre and text models up to the sophistication of classical Latinity (textuality); and to establish classical antiquity as the single standard for all discourses.[5] Nearly all German humanists in the fifteenth, sixteenth, and seventeenth centuries adhered to and promoted this standard. In Germany after the invention of the printing press, Latin rhetorics and poetics continued to be published regularly, though with somewhat different contents and purposes than before.

Latin Rhetorics

The classical system of rhetoric concerned the competence and effectiveness of the orator and led to expertise in four component areas: speech situations, stages of text production, parts of prose speech, and stylistics, especially rhetorical figures. Humanists dedicated monographs and comprehensive systematic studies alike to these concerns. Primers on stylistics (*elocutio*) facilitated the acquisition of a Neo-Latin prose style comparable to that of classical Latinity. This demanded mastery of elegance, synonyms, vocabulary — Erasmus's *De duplici copia verborum ac rerum* (The Double Treasury of Words and Things, 1512) was the standard source book — and sentence construction (*compositio*). The fifty principles of textual stylistics outlined by Albrecht von Eyb (1420–75) in his *Praecepta artis rhetoricae* (Principles of the Art of Rhetoric, 1457) were considered indispensable.[6] The *Ars oratoria* (printed ca. 1485) of Peter Luder (ca. 1415–72),[7] adapted and elaborated the three speech situations: judicial speech (*genus iudicale*), deliberative political speech (*genus deliberativum*), and epideictic speech for special occasions (*genus demonstrativum*); examples accompanied the theoretical presentation of each genre. Systematic *officia* rhetorics (*officia*, "offices") followed, such as the *Epithoma rhetorices graphicum* (Perfect Summary of Rhetorics, 1496) of Jacob Locher (1471–1528) or the *Margarita philosophica* (Philosophical Pearl, 1503) of Gregor Reisch (ca. 1470–1525), and brought back the classical five-stage scheme of speech production to the center of attention.[8] This scheme begins with the cognitive operations of the orator: discovery or invention (*inventio*) and arrangement (*dispositio*); proceeds to the semiotic: manner and style (*elocutio*); and concludes with the performative: memorization (*memoria*) and performance (*actio*). This ancient system remained, with variations, the core of humanistic rhetorics throughout the early modern period, as reflected in the *Rhetorica contractae* (Condensed Rhetorics, 1621) of Gerhard Johannes Vossius (1577–1649)[9] or *De arte rhetorica* (On the Art of Rhetoric, 1569) of the Jesuit Cyprianus Suárez (1524–93).[10] The theory of the parts of a speech was integrated into this rhetorical system. In 1492 Conrad Celtis (1459–1508) expanded the system to include epistolary theory, modeling his *Epitome in utramque Ciceronis rhetoricam* (Summary of Both of Cicero's Rhetorics)[11] on the Hispano-Italian Jacobus Publicius's recent *Oratoriae artis epitoma* (Summary of the Art of Oratory, 1482).[12] Epistolary theory, an offshoot from the tradition of *ars dictaminis* (art of formulating), became one of the most significant humanistic enterprises.[13]

Latin rhetorical theory in Germany developed steadily over the fifteenth and sixteenth centuries and achieved a comprehensive and highly differentiated form in the seventeenth century.[14] To the humanists of the Renaissance, rhetoric always implied writing. Prose writing has special importance in Philipp Melanchthon's (1497–1560) *Elementa rhetorices* (1531)[15] and occupies a central position in the *Praecepta rhetoricae inventionis* (1556) of his pupil David Chytraeus (1530–1600). Melanchthon's innovation consisted of placing alongside the political, legal, and demonstrative genres of speech a fourth: the didactic (*genus didascalicum* or *didacticum*), which he understood as the scientific or informative genre. He also paid great attention to *elocutio*, the theory of style and formulation, with its vast corpus of rhetorical figures.[16] The Frenchman Pierre de La Ramée (Petrus Ramus, 1515–72), indeed, in *Rhetoricae distinctiones in Quintilianum* (1549),[17] reduced the whole system of rhetoric to *elocutio* (especially figuration) and performance. The *Rhetorica* (1548) of his pupil Omer Talon (Audomarus Talaeus, ca. 1510–62) was one of the most frequently reprinted rhetorics in seventeenth-century Germany;[18] Ramist influence lies behind the twofold systems of the *Institutiones rhetoricae* (1613) of Conrad Dieterich (1575–1639) and the *Teutsche rhetorica* (1634) of Johann Matthäus Meyfart (1590–1642).[19]

Latin Poetics

Rhetorics and poetics represent a theoretical division of labor, reflecting the premise that all varieties of texts are heteronomous (functional, not autonomous) and that they have communicative goals. Their ancient theoretical sources were largely identical in the late Middle Ages and the early modern period. Whether they were writers of rhetorics or poetics, all relied on Quintilian's authority. Joachim von Watt (Vadianus, 1484–1551), the author of *De poetica et carminis ratione* (Of Poetics and the Structure of Poetry, 1518), is one notable example.[20] The theory of rhetoric specifically focuses on communicative cases calling for practical prose texts, and it elucidates the stages of production and performance (including prose style, figuration, and syntax). The regular appearance of chapters on metrics (*numerus*) in the *compositio* part owes to the relatedness of metrics to prose rhythm and clauses, as described in part two of Vossius's *Commentaria rhetorica* (1630). Metrics falls under stylistics and figuration (*elocutio*), which constitute an intersection between rhetorics and poetics.

The theory of poetics concentrates specifically on aesthetically constructed texts that may be subsumed essentially under the forms known today as epic, drama, and lyric.[21] The following groupings of Latin poetics produced in Germany can be distinguished down to the end of the sixteenth century according to general content:

1. *Metrics*, in which the prosody and structure of Latin verses and other poetic forms are presented and sometimes supplemented with stylistic illustrations and references: Luder's lectures of 1462 on meter; Jakob Wimpfeling's *De arte metrificandi* (1484); Celtis's *Ars versificandi et carminum* (The Art of Versification and of Poems, 1486); Laurentius Corvinus's *Structura carminum* (1496); Jacob Magdalius's *Stichologia* (The Art of Making Verses, 1503); Heinrich Bebel's *Ars versificandi* (1506); Ulrich von Hutten's *De arte versificatoria* (1511); Johannes Murmellius's *Versificatorie artis rudimenta* (ca. 1511); Eobanus Hessus's *Scribendorum versuum ratio* (Method of Writing Verse, 1526); Jacobus Micyllus's *De re metrica* (1539); and Johannes Claius's *Prosodiae libri tres* (1570) and *Grammatica germanicae linguae* (1578).[22]

2. *Poetic elegantiae*, in which elegant text passages and compositional models are collected: Eyb's *Margarita poetica* (Poetic Pearl, 1472); Hermannus Torrentinus's *Elucidarius carminum* (Explanation of Poems, 1501); Georg Fabricius's *Elegantiae poeticae ex Ovidio, Tibullo, Propertio elegiacis* (Elegant Expressions from the Elegiacists Ovid, Tibullus, and Propertius, 1549); *Elegantiarum ex Plauto et Terentio libri ii* (Two Books of Elegant Expressions by Plautus and Terence, 1554); *Elegantiarum puerilium ex Ciceronis epistolis libri tres* (Three Books of Elegant Expressions for the Youth from Cicero's Letters, 1554); and Johann Buchler's *Officina poetica* (Poetic Laboratory, 1605).[23] Torrentinus says in his *Praefatio* that he means to provide the essential elements for the kind of elegant poetry being demanded today. He also includes in his editorial apparatus a glossary of definitions relating to mythology, such as who Apollo was, or Antigone.

3. *Genre poetics and drama commentaries*: Joachim Camerarius's *Commentatio explicationum omnium tragoediarum Sophoclis* (Preparation for the Explications of All the Tragedies of Sophocles, 1556); Melanchthon's *Epistola de legendis tragoediis et comoediis* (Letter on Reading Tragedies and Comedies, 1545); Micyllus's *De tragoedia et eius partibus* (On Tragedy and its Parts, 1562); and Daniel Heinsius's *De tragoediae constitutione* (On the Structure of Tragedy, 1611).

4. *Commentaries on the poetics of Aristotle and Horace*: Jodocus Willich's *Commentaria in artem poeticam Horatii* (Commentaries on the Poetic Art of Horace, 1545); Veit Amerbach's *Commentaria in artem poeticam Horatii* (1547); Johannes Sturm's *Commentarii in artem poeticam Horatii* (1576); Johannes Schosser's *Disputatio de tragoedia ex primo libro Aristotelis* (Disputation on Tragedy from the First Book of Aristotle, 1569); and Heinsius's *De tragoediae constitutione*.

5. *Apologies for poetry*: Thomas Murner's *De augustiniana hieronymianaque reformatione poetarum* (About the Reform of Poetry according to Augustine and Jerome, 1509); Bonifacius Helfricht's *Declamatio in laudem poeticae* (Declamation in Praise of Poetry, 1548); Zacharias Orth's *Oratio de arte poetica* (1558); Johannes Caselius's *Pro arte poetarum oratio* (1569);[24] and Gregor Bersmann's *De dignitate atque praestantia poetices* (On the Dignity and Nobility of Poetry, 1575).

6. *Universal poetics* deal in a summary fashion with authors, genres, themes, and forms, as well as with the role of poetry in society: Vadianus's *De poetica*;[25] Fabricius's *De re poetica libri iiii* (1556–72); and Jacob Pontanus's *Poeticarum institutionum libri iii* (1594).

German Rhetorics and Poetics in Germany to 1700

German Rhetorics

German-language rhetorics of the Old High German period — the first vernacular rhetorics in Europe — is represented only by Notker Teutonicus in St. Gallen.[26] No independent German rhetorics from the Middle High German period have been transmitted. In 1472, during the transition to the Early New High German period, a single short verse treatment appeared in German as a component of moral didactic literature, *Die Räte von der Rede* (Advice for Speaking), a translation of the *Doctrina dicendi et tacendi* (Doctrine of Speaking and Keeping Silent, 1245) of Albertanus Brixiensis (ca. 1190–after 1250).[27] German rhetorics began to appear as early as the first half of the fifteenth century, long before the grammars, dialectics, and poetics of the sixteenth century.[28] Thus, rhetorics became the gateway to German literature within the trivium, the first three, language-based, disciplines among the seven *artes liberales*. Few German rhetorics were produced during the sixteenth or first half of the seventeenth century. This changed markedly after the Thirty Years' War (1618–48), when a rich and varied literature of rhetorical theory began to appear.[29] The majority of German baroque rhetoricians did not deal with the entire system of the classical five stages of production, however, but only with specific areas of everyday rhetoric. With respect to the development of German rhetorics from the fifteenth to the end of the seventeenth century, five groupings emerge:

1. *Epistolary rhetorics*.[30] The earliest German rhetorics dealt especially with epistolary communication in the vernacular, a distinct form of practical communication that had been responding since the fourteenth century to the rise of a universal German administrative language and to the penetration of writing into all areas of daily life. A number of handwritten rhetorics containing the rudiments of epistolary theory in German predate the advent of printing.[31] The *Formulare und Tütsche rhetorica* (Formulary and German Rhetorics) of 1478 was one of the first printed epistolary rhetorics. Epistolary, notarial, and chancery rhetorics occupy the greatest part of Friedrich Riederer's (ca. 1450–ca. 1508) systematic *Spiegel der*

waren Rhetoric (Mirror of True Rhetoric, 1493).[32] German rhetorical works most often printed down to the eighteenth century concerned the composition of epistles and other written forms relevant for chanceries; together they made up about one-sixth of the entire production of rhetorical literature.[33] The trend culminated in Kaspar Stieler's 4,000-page *Teutsche Sekretariat-Kunst* (German Art of the Secretary) of 1673/74. Of increasing significance — a sign of the modern, highly regulated activity of communication and of increasing social stratification — was *Titellehre*, a guide to recognizing proper social ranks and using correct conventions of address accordingly.[34]

2. *Stylistics.* German stylistics, first written within the framework of epistolary theory, compiled rules and examples for figural stylization, relating both to figures of speech as well as to the structuring of rhetorical elements. The first of these was the *Figurenlehre* (Doctrine of Figuration, 1478) of the Esslingen chancery director Niklas von Wyle (ca. 1415–79).[35] In his *Spiegel*, Riederer produced an impressive German adaptation of Eyb's fifty Latin *praecepta*.[36] Independent treatises on German figuration and stylistics were published rarely; most were targeted for inclusion in larger works. Meyfart's *Teutsche rhetorica* is an example of a pure study of figural stylistics. Caspar Goldtwurm's (1524–49) *Schemata rhetorica* (Rhetorical Figures, 1545) became a standard resource work also for Protestant homiletics.

3. *Rhetorics of composition and model speeches.* This grouping, for which the most significant are Christian Weise's (1642–1708) *Politischer Redner* (Political Orator, 1677) and Johann Riemer's *Lustige Rhetorica* (Cheerful Rhetorics, 1681), includes instructions for composing specific kinds of texts as well as collections of model speeches for all occasions. Other important examples include the anonymous *Schatzkammer schöner zierlicher Orationen* (Treasury of Well-made Orations, 1597), Johann Rudolf Sattler's *Instructio oratoris* (The Orator's Instruction, 1618), and Balthasar Kindermann's *Der Deutsche Redner* (The German Orator, 1660).[37]

4. *Conversational and behavioral rhetorics.* A rich literature on courtly behavior and ordinary polite conversation evolved during the Baroque, since mastery of highly regulated communicative rituals (whether at princely courts or public venues) had become necessary for the practitioner's reputation and social standing. Albertanus's *Die Räte von der Rede*, which concerned the conditions and standards of proper communicative behavior, was not only the first but also one of the most successful rhetorics of the early modern period. Some 105 manuscripts were made of the original Latin version alone; thirty-eight printed editions were published between 1471 and 1546 as well as several German translations, in addition to the standard one of 1472.[38] Translations of well-known Italian works on the culture of courtly conversation began to appear in the mid-sixteenth century and had a great impact in Germany.[39] Among the most influential were Baldassare Castiglione's *Il Cortegiano* (1528), translated by Laurenz

Kratzer as *Hofman* (Courtier, 1566); Giovanni della Casa's *Galateus* (1558), translated by Nathan Chytraeus as *Das Büchlein von erbarn, höflichen und holdseligen Sitten* (The Little Book of Honorable, Polite, and Charming Manners, 1597); and Stefano Guazzo's *La civil conversatione* (1574), translated by Nicolaus Rucker as *Von dem bürgerlichen Wandel und zierlichen Sitten* (About Civil Behavior and Polite Manners, 1599). Original works followed somewhat later, including Gutthäter Dobratzky's *Wol-qualificirter Hofe-Mann* (The Cultivated Courtier, 1664) and August Bohse's *Der getreue Hoffmeister* (The Loyal Courtly Teacher, 1706), which described proper *conduite* in social situations.[40] An early primer on behavior for Protestant ministers was written by Niels Hemmingsen: *Pastor, hoch-nothwendige Unterrichtung* (The Pastor's Indispensable Instruction, 1562).[41]

The literature on *Komplimentierkunst* (the art of compliment) treated the different ritualized forms — verbal and nonverbal, written and oral — of courteous behavior (congratulations, recommendations, reverences, felicitations, condolences).[42] These included Johann Georg Greflinger's *Complementir-Büchlein* (A Manual for Making Compliments, 1645), Georg Philipp Harsdörffer's *Poetischer Trichter* (The Poet's Funnel, 1647–53), and Julius Bernhard von Rohr's *Einleitung zur Ceremonial-Wissenschaft der grossen Herren* (Guide to the Ceremonial Science of Ruling Men, 1728). In order to hold one's own in conversation and correspondence, a great amount of factual knowledge was necessary; Weise indeed regarded factual knowledge as the key to rhetorical competence. These knowledge-based works, especially prominent during the Baroque, included sayings and other suitable formulas for effective communication. Notable are the *Alamodische Damen Sprichwörter* (A la Mode Ladies' Sayings, 1648), Harsdörffer's *Frauenzimmer Gesprächspiele* (Playful Colloquies for the Ladies, 1641–49), and Johann Adam Weber's *Hundert Quellen der Unterredungs-Kunst* (One Hundred Sources of the Art of Conversation, 1676).

5. *Systematic officia rhetorics.* The five-stage system of production and performance was not only maintained in the reprints of the classic texts but also formed the explicit foundation for many German works by rhetorics, including Riederer's *Spiegel*, Wolfgang Ratke's *Allgemeine RednerLehr* (Universal Instruction for Orators, 1619), Riemer's *Lustige Rhetorica*, Weise's *Gelehrter Redner* (The Learned Orator, 1692), and Johann Christoph Gottsched's (1700–1766) *Ausführliche Redekunst* (Comprehensive Rhetorics, 1736).

German Poetics

The German-language theory of poetics evolved only gradually over the centuries. During the Middle High German *Blütezeit*, poetic works were sometimes interrupted by digressions that commented, either positively or negatively, on practices of fellow poets (that of Gottfried von Strassburg in his

254 👻 EARLY MODERN GERMAN LITERATURE 1350–1700

Tristan und Isolde is a famous example).[43] Only toward the end of this period did poetological reflection become an independent enterprise in the German vernacular. Five groupings of German poetics may be distinguished between the late thirteenth century and the end of the Baroque:

1. *Prologue poetics.* Excursive poetological discussions were inserted in the prologues of works by three poets around the turn of the fourteenth century, beginning with Konrad von Würzburg (ca. 1230–87) in his prologues to *Partonopier und Meliur* (1277) and the *Trojanischer Krieg* (before 1287). Konrad wrote in the literary tradition of noble courtly conventions; but given the rise of urban culture, with its accompanying changes in communicative environment, he was obliged to rethink poetological principles. By contrast, Heinrich von Hesler's *Apokalypse* (before 1312) and Nikolaus von Jeroschin's (d. ca. 1345) *Deutschordenschronik* (Chronicle of the Teutonic Order, 1331–41) belonged intimately to the sphere of communication of the Teutonic Order.[44] Hesler as well as Jeroschin were devoted to the metric principles of German didactic poetry and developed a body of paradigmatic rules for its practice by the order. Hesler considers both the subject matter (*materie*) as a whole as well as the meaning (*sin*) of the particular text.[45]

2. *Meistersinger tablatures and Schulkünste* (arts of the "schools" for singers) relate to a precisely defined area of communication, prescribing solid norms for the urban circles of poets and singers first established in German towns in the fifteenth century.[46] The *Merker* ("marker," that is, judge), shielded from the audience, applied these norms in noting the mistakes of the singers. The rules were specific to hermetic groups — in Nuremberg songs were subject to a ban on publication — and texts were recorded in handwritten form for internal documentation. The approximately sixty *Schulkünste*, mostly in verse, and the few extant *Tabulaturen* (tablets containing the codified rules), comprise the sources for our knowledge of the rules of the *Meistersinger*: the *Nürnberger Schulzettel* (Nuremberg Tablature, 1540), the *Colmarer Gemerkbuch* (Colmar Tablature, 1549) of Jörg Wickram, the *Steyrer Tabulatur* (1562) of Lorenz Wessel of Essen, the *Iglauer Tabulatur* (1571), the *Breslauer Tabulatur* (1598), and the *Memminger Tabulatur* (1660).[47]

3. *Meistersinger ordinances* supplemented the purely technical tablatures. In these ordinances, *Meistersinger* behavior was legally codified by the city authorities. Among the few extant texts are the *Freiburger Artikel der Singer* (Freiburg Singer Articles, 1513), the *Strassburger Meistersingererlasse* (Strasbourg Meistersinger Records, 1598 and 1633), the *Augsburger Meistersingerordnung* (Augsburg Meistersinger Ordinance, 1611), and the *Iglauer Schulordnung* (Iglau School Ordinance, 1615).

4. *Histories of the Meistersinger* began to be written toward the end of the sixteenth century, a development that coincided with the decline of the actual practice. The most important of these are Adam Puschmann's *Gründlicher Bericht des deutschen Meistergesanges* (Thorough Report on the German

Master Song, 1571), Cyriacus Spangenberg's *Von der Edlen und Hochberümbten Kunst der Musica* (On the Noble and Renowned Art of Music, 1598), and Johann Christoph Wagenseil's *Buch von der Meistersinger holdseligen Kunst* (Book of the Meistersingers' Charming Art, 1697).[48]

5. *Poetics of the Baroque. Meistersinger* poetics were discontinued in the first half of the seventeenth century. The hiatus owed in part to the cultural catastrophe of the Thirty Years' War, but also to the new theory of German poetry propounded in the *Buch von der Deutschen Poeterey* (Book of German Poetics, 1624) by Martin Opitz (1597–1639), which burst the confines of urban-based, artisan-driven *Meistergesang*. Opitz and his colleagues considered *Meistergesang* hopelessly antiquated, and they distanced themselves from its theoretical discourse. After Opitz, the standards established in Neo-Latin literature by Celtis, Wimpfeling, Bebel, Vadianus, and others, also became normative for German literature.[49] German poetics thus sprang from two sources: classical rhetorics and humanistic poetics. The traditional principles of poetics now appeared in the form of a reformed German language. Theorists insisted that modern vernacular poets were due the same respect as their Latin-language counterparts and that the German language should be acknowledged alongside the other national languages of Europe. The purpose of German poetics was in the first place to refine the German language to a degree that made it competitive with them.[50]

A wave of German poetics arose about twenty years into the war. The continuity of baroque poetological theory may be discerned in the following chronological list of influential works: Philipp von Zesen's *Deutscher Helicon* (German Helicon, 1641), Johann Peter Titz's *Von der Kunst Hochdeutsche Verse und Lieder zu machen* (On the Art of Composing High German Verses and Songs, 1642), Johann Klaj's *Lobrede der Teutschen Poeterey* (In Praise of German Poetry, 1645), Martin Rinckart's *Von Teutschen Versen, Fusstritten und vornehmsten Reim-Arten* (On German Verses, Meters, and Primary Rhyme Patterns, 1645), Johann Rist's *Poetischer Schauplatz* (The Stage of Poetry, 1646), Harsdörffer's *Poetischer Trichter* (1647), Justus Georg Schottel's *Teutsche Vers- oder Reimkunst* (The Art of German Verse or Rhyme, 1656), Zesen's *Deutsch-lateinische Leiter* (German-Latin Guide, 1656), Kindermann's *Der deutsche Poet* (The German Poet, 1664), August Buchner's *Anleitung zur Deutschen Poeterey* (Introduction to German Poetry, 1665), Sigmund von Birken's *Teutsche Rede-bind- und Dicht-Kunst* (German Art of Versification and Poetry, 1679), Daniel Georg Morhof's *Unterricht von der Teutschen Sprache und Poesie* (Instruction in German Language and Poetry, 1682), Stieler's *Die Dichtkunst des Spahten* (Poetical Treatise of the Late One, 1685), and Weise's *Curiöser Gedanken von Deutschen Versen* (Curious Thoughts on German Verses, 1691). Gottsched's *Versuch einer Critischen Dichtkunst* (Attempt at a Critical Theory of Poetry, 1730) and *Ausführliche Redekunst* represent the simultaneous conclusion of baroque poetics and the beginning of a new aesthetic trend.

Toward a Unified Theory of
Early Modern German Poetics and Rhetorics

Theoretical Positions to 1700

Three years before the end of the Thirty Years' War, Johann Klaj (1616–56) writes at the beginning of his *Lobrede der Teutschen Poeterey*: "Unser durch die blutigen Mordwaffen ausgemergeltes Teutschland / ruffet uns / seinen Hetzgeliebten / zu: Redet / Redet / Redet, daß ich gelehrter absterbe" (Our Germany, gutted by the bloody weapons of murder, calls to us, her beloved ones: Speak, speak, speak, that I might die more learned). This is an emphatic avowal that, even in times of war, vernacular German has the power to communicate knowledge that validates its humanity.[51] As of 1645, the two theories concerning human speech, namely, rhetorics and poetics, were still understood as integrally related theories of communicative action and text production.[52] Although historically, as explained at the beginning of this chapter, they derived from distinct traditions,[53] focusing on one of them leads to ignoring their essential unity. It is as wrong to think of early modern poetics as a latecomer in rhetorical theory as it is to think of rhetorics as a mere handmaiden to poetics.[54] Their themes complement one another and overlap only at specific points (especially in the theories of form and figuration).[55] Both genres would yet undergo significant transformation in the eighteenth century in the process of philosophical change.[56]

Grammar books also played a role in the standardization of High German.[57] According to Schottel's *Ausführliche Arbeit von der Teutschen HaubtSprache* (A Thorough Study of the German Principal Language, 1663), German had evolved into a linguistic vehicle of efficient use "in den Abschieden / in den Catzleyen / Gerichten und Trükkereyen" (in its imperial diets, in its ministries, courts, and printing offices). The goal now, he maintains, should be to find a universal, binding code of communication, "communis Germaniae Mercurius" (like the god Mercury, suitable for the whole of Germany; chap. 2.1).

Even before the fifteenth century, rhetoric was regarded as the source both for the fundamentals of communication in general as well as for the prose forms of practical written communication in particular. Poetry, on the other hand, was considered the source for the theory of the written production of aesthetic texts; poetic texts were also expected to follow general rhetorical principles. Practitioners of aesthetic communication in the seventeenth century followed developments in both rhetorics and poetics; books concerning either theoretical area stood side by side in libraries. The ancient Greek representatives of rhetoric and poetry, the orator Demosthenes and the poet Homer, enjoy equal status in Opitz's *Poeterey*: "Das ist Demosthenes. Welcher ob er zwar als der vornemeste redner in hohe ehren gehalten worden, ist doch der rhum nicht geringer denn Homerus erlanget" (That is Demosthenes, who, though it was as the greatest orator that he was so highly esteemed, has gained no less fame than Homer; chap. 8).

Many of the theoretical questions of modern (sociological) communications, particularly with respect to media, would arise, of course, only after the early modern period. But interest was occasionally expressed in the special problem of performance (writing vs. speech) — rhetorics and poetics were, after all, simultaneously theories about how to formulate texts (production) and how to apply them (performance) and certainly were not intended as guides for textual analysis in the sense of modern literary criticism. This is not to suggest, however, that rhetorics and poetics did not implicitly provide analytical paradigms useful for classroom instruction or that in individual cases literary-historical and literary-critical perspectives did not begin to manifest themselves. Morhof's *Unterricht* and Albrecht Christian Rotth's *Vollständige Deutsche Poesie* (Complete German Poetics, 1688) provide strong evidence of this.[58]

We may now turn to three topics, or problems, related to the dynamics of communication that were of particular interest to German rhetorics and poetics of the late Middle Ages and the early modern period:

1. *Communicative interaction* primarily has to do with the active communicator (orator or poet) but also with the partners in communication (audience), forms of social interaction (settings and *genera causarum*), and rules of interaction (*aptum* and *decorum*).

2. *Communicative performance* concerns what is communicatively acceptable in society, what social purpose is served by the communicative forms treated in rhetorics and poetics, and what kind of communicative performances they should generate (the role of literature in general, individual text genres, etc.).

3. *Text as communicative instrument* deals with theories of textual construction and the employment of texts in communicative interaction. What are the possible kinds of texts (genres), techniques of construction (structuring), and principles of construction (form criteria, aesthetics)?

Communicative Interaction: *Orator* and *Poeta*

As early as the fifteenth century, Sebastian Brant (1457–1521), the renowned author of the European bestseller *Das Narrenschiff* (The Ship of Fools, 1494), was responding to the potential offered by the printing press by making adjustments in his communicative role.[59] In theoretical circles, questions about the social functions of the *orator* and the *poeta* were receiving vigorous attention, as were related questions about changing goals, rules, boundaries, pertinent skills, and forms of interaction. In *Die Räte von der Rede*, Albertanus contemplates the relationships of interactive partners (senders and receivers) and the complex conditions of communication for every utterance in every social context. As sender, or speaker, the communicator must decide how to express his relationship with the addressee verbally and how to regard his communication partner; he is always conscious of which rhetorical strategies will achieve the specifically intended meaning and motivation.

Ancient theory separated the spheres of interaction between orator and poet. The orator was responsible for practical communication in the public sphere (decisions about the *genera causarum*). Albertanus addresses four communicative cases: sermon, letter, messenger report, and court defense. The poet, on the other hand, as Julius Caesar Scaliger (1484–1558) points out in the first volume of his renowned *Poetices libri septem* (Seven Books of Poetics, 1561), is responsible for aestheticized forms of communication, that is, for specialized genres and forms of poetry. Brant exploits the possibilities of the recently invented printing press for composing and distributing "journalistic" texts, thereby putting himself in the tradition of the German minstrel, who performed tasks of practical communication in aesthetic form. This tradition of occasional poetry (*Gelegenheitsdichtung*, Latin *casualcarmina*) and occasional poet (*Gelegenheitsdichter*) continues into the sixteenth century, notwithstanding the distinct preference of the Reformation for prose.

The sudden appearance of German-language rhetorics in the fifteenth century was one answer to the new developments in communicative demands. *Scriptorality* — the written, or textual, alternative to *orality*, the traditional performance-based conceptualization of rhetorics and poetics (this extended to texts in musical compositions as well) — advanced rapidly to become the assumed norm of performance in all relevant areas, including epistolary rhetorics,[60] and remained so for the next two centuries. As a consequence, the orator came to be treated as a "writer" in fifteenth- and sixteenth-century rhetorical theory.[61] Riederer's *Spiegel der waren Rhetoric* is the most important testament to this historico-cultural development. Riederer systematically distinguishes the person (or institution) sending the communication from the expert who actually writes the communication. In the early modern period, writers capable of epistolary communication were still important to agencies (both individuals and institutions) that depended on the epistle in social transactions. Riederer therefore had good reason to include an expansive theory of the writer at the beginning of his rhetorics — one of the most original texts in early modern rhetorical theory.[62] In addition to other ancient and humanistic works, Riederer adduces the authority of Cicero's *De oratore*, in which the orator as public communicator is central to rhetorical theory. In emulating Cicero, Riederer discerns an analogy between modern and ancient instruments of communication: the modern writer with his chancery epistle corresponds to the ancient orator with his oral speech. Riederer is speaking of the professional *Schreiber*, "als der fürsten vnd cantzelschriber, der Stett, rat und gerichtschriber, notarien, vnd ander, die sich der practic übend vnd neerend" (as princely and chancery writers, municipal writers, council and court writers, notaries, and others who carry out and cultivate the practice; lxii). Compared to private individuals who engage in writing, these experts possess a higher level of competence with regard to "tütscher wort, vnd die ze ordnen vnd formlich zu verfügen" (German words and the ability to order and shape them). Riederer constructs a graduated typology ranging from schooled and experienced writers to those who are still learning. This entails acquaintance with law: only well-trained writers in this "kunst vnnd gestalt der Rhetoric" (art and form of rhetoric) can guarantee that their compositions are legally sound. Riederer finds this confirmed in Cicero's *De oratore*, book 1, which, among other things, talks about the necessity of the orator's knowledge of law.

Orality as the primary condition of rhetorical communication naturally had its place in the various Latin and German rhetorical systematics (especially Riederer's *Spiegel* and Goldtwurm's *Schemata rhetorica*) until about 1600. Monological oral speech itself, however, became a discrete theoretical subject in Germany only after German-language rhetorics were established. Specialized literature on the classical monological speech arose only after 1566, with the translations of Italian conversational classics; these were followed in the early seventeenth century with works on courtly speech and occasional speech, most notably Sattler's *Instructio oratoris* and his *Werbungsbüchlein* (Little Book of Courtship, 1611), the first two independent German rhetorics to deal explicitly and primarily with the speaker.[63]

After 1600, German rhetorics expanded to include discussions of the orally performing speaker, particularly with respect to the communicative conditions of baroque courtly culture and bourgeois occasional speech (*Kasualrede*). Meyfart's *Teutsche Rhetorica* includes the various speech acts of the military commander, of whom rhetorical competence is expected. He then turns to the speech of the diplomat, who at court wishes to cull the favor of the prince and his councilors. Princely court hearings are included as well, for a well-constructed speech can move the prince as judge to lean toward one of the parties. In his treatment of the office of preaching (*Predigtamt*), for which elegance is also essential, Meyfart names typical speech acts that a clergyman should master: "Tröstungen / Warnungen / Vermahnungen / Widerlegungen / Unterrichtungen" (consolations, warnings, admonitions, refutations, instructions; 35). He also stresses that any social class can be made to appear more positively by expert use of rhetorical ornamentation: "Die WohlRedenheit gleisset wie ein Hyacinth an den Bürgern / grünet wie ein Smaragd an den Edlen / pranget wie ein Jaspis an den Fürsten" (Eloquence gleams like a hyacinth on the citizenry, radiates green like an emerald on the nobles, and shines like a jasper on princes).

We now turn to the theory of the special communicative role of the poet, known in poetics as *poetology* (literally, the theory of the poet).[64] Konrad von Würzburg speaks of the functional role of the poet and about the literary-communicative conditions of interaction; in the prologue to *Partenopier und Meliur* he observes that poets constitute a distinct social institution, or tradition, or communicator class of *Meister*: "In Wort und Melodie haben die Meister so Treffliches geschaffen, daß man sich an ihren herrlichen Werken ein vorzügliches Beispiel nehmen kann" (The *Meister* have created such wonderful things in word and melody that their splendid works may serve as excellent examples).[65] The art of poetry had attained a significant degree of self-confidence with respect to its technical possibilities, but Konrad complains about those poets who, for all their ambition, lack genuine talent and consequently — since common people lack powers of discrimination and will buy anything, good or bad, on the market — impede the careers of truly gifted poets. In the prologue to the *Trojanischer Krieg* he expresses this complaint through the allegory of the nightingale, which ignores the necessities of life, "denn sie findet ihr Lied so schön und so lieblich, daß sie sich zu Tode singt.

Ein wahrer Dichter soll sich daran ein Beispiel nehmen und nicht auf seine Kunst verzichten, weil man nicht nach ihr verlangt und sich nicht um sie kümmert" (for she finds her song so beautiful and lovely that she sings herself to death. A true poet should learn from this and not neglect his art, because one dare not desire it and then ignore it). With these words the poet is given the opportunity to choose between taking part in a communicative interaction or rejecting it. Thus a position of poetic self-referentiality has been attained even before 1300, asserting the liberty to cancel the expected communicative contract; indeed, the poet may step out of any rhetorical interaction. This had been unthinkable only a few decades earlier for Gottfried von Strassburg.[66]

This tendency toward a socially distinct role for the poet evolved into a hermeticism, or esotericism, in the *Meistersinger* schools — private, guild-like associations that sprang up in many German cities in the fifteenth and sixteenth centuries. The Freiburg Articles of 1513 describe a fraternal community with strict rules for membership; it is a kind of mythical brotherhood with common privileges that were believed to have been pledged by Emperor Otto in Mainz.[67] As with the trades, external guests in these singing communities were given special status. Quasi-religious regulations gave the brotherhoods an aura of piety that restricted public access. The *Colmarer Ordnung der Meistersingerschule* (Colmar Meistersinger School Ordinance) of 1549 states that only "Doctores, Priester, Edelüt vnd alle Radtsuerwandte sampt vnsern bruodernn vnd schwestern einen freyen zuogang zuo vns habenn" (doctors, priests, nobility, and all members of the city government, as well as our brothers and sisters, have free access to us). The proscription of publications of *Meistergesang*, expounded in paragraph 35 of the Nuremberg Tablature, relates to this general retreat from social communicative contexts: the group will give public performances only a few times per year.

The esoterica of the brotherhoods included strict regulations, even threats of punishment extending to behavior outside the singing school itself. The Iglau School Ordinance prescribes exact rituals, including seating orders, gestures, and attire. Singers are expected to behave in a seemly fashion in inns and are not to sing on the streets at night; disreputable persons are to be turned away from the performances. The singing group must be mindful of its actions and view itself as an institution. Thus, all important matters were recorded and kept in an archive. The goal of the group's activities was to optimize technical skills to the level of *Meisterschaft* (mastery). The inversion of this idea was the ambitious but unskilled *Gelegenheitssinger* (occasional singer) described in the Colmar Ordinance: he lacks all skill and travels from pub to pub; he is to be expelled. The internal instrument for judging performance and ranking skill levels was the publicly staged singing competition, in which prizes were awarded as the judge deemed fit. Not surprisingly, the songs contain an abundance of the motifs of challenge, competition, and excellence.[68]

The theoreticians of the Baroque — foremost among them Martin Opitz — rejected the sixteenth-century ideal of the guild poet-singer who mastered the technical skills of versification and submitted to group discipline. In chapter 1 of his *Poeterey* Opitz emphatically denies a purely technical view of poetry:

"bin ich doch solcher gedancken keines weges, das ich vermeine, man könne iemanden durch gewisse regeln vnd gesetze zu einem Poeten machen" (I am in no way of the opinion that someone can be made into a poet through particular rules and laws). In chapter 3 he repudiates the expectation that a poet should be on call with some conventional verses for any social event. Such a pragmatic understanding of the work of poets, he says, is degrading:[69] "Es wird kein buch, keine hochzeit, kein begräbnüß ohn vns gemacht; vnd gleichsam als niemand köndte alleine sterben, gehen vnsere gedichte zuegleich mit jhnen vnter" (No book, no wedding, no funeral is carried out without us; and it is as if no one can die alone without our poems being buried with them). The poetry of the true poet escapes this fate by refusing to be bound to concrete, practical situations. Opitz saw as one of his primary challenges the depragmatizing of poetry: to create, beyond function, a certain autonomous space for poetry as an aesthetic form of verbal interaction, granting its performance the status of a unique communicative event — an appropriation of the Renaissance ideal of the autonomy of the arts. For Opitz, the arts should be far more than ornamentation to social communicative life.

Baroque poetics thus generally presumed a more open sphere of communication in both writing and oral performance than had previously been the case. All narrow restrictions on communication were dismissed, at least in theory. Opitz's *Poeterey* is motivated by high seriousness of purpose, assuming a national perspective in which German poetry is of proprietary interest to all Germans in cultural competition with other nations. It is by no means true of Germany, he writes in chapter 3, "das es nicht eben dergleichen zue der Poesie tüchtige *ingenia* können tragen, als jergendt ein anderer ort vnter der Sonnen" (that its industrious gifts cannot contribute to good poetry just as much as any other country under the sun).

The printing press had long since created new conditions for the distribution and performance of literature.[70] Printing and the culture of scriptorality were now presumed conditions for poetry and drama; still, oral performance in specific, ritualistic contexts — though these were no longer determinants in the poetic process — remained common, and the poet continued to be understood essentially, as in the Latin theoretical literature, as orator-poet. Withdrawal from the social communicative context is never intended, not even when Opitz seems to give preference to the solitary poet over the public orator. The *poeta doctus* lives in and is active within the communicative world; he devotes himself to reclusive study because it is essential to the poetic process, but ultimately he does what he does for the sake of society.

The poet was regularly identified in German-language poetics, as in the *Poet* (1665) of August Buchner (1591–1661), by the technical term *orator*, just as in the Latin-language poetics, such as Vadianus's *De poetica*.[71] Scaliger's *Poetices*, which the German Baroque accepted as a primary authority, justifies the poetic art in an introductory chapter. This apologia offers nothing essentially new to the traditional understanding of the poetic process in which poetry is conceptualized as a kind of rhetoric and the poet as a particularly eloquent and subtle speaker.[72] Still, the Renaissance conception of inspired poetry gave the seventeenth-century German orator-poet a unique fashioning, lifting, by force of its inner, depragmatizing logic, the communicative activity of the poet above the merely practical forms of mundane human interaction.[73]

Opitz too draws a distinction between the ambitious dilettante and the true poet: "Doch muß ich gleichwohl bekennen, das auch an verachtung der Poeterey die jenigen nicht wenig schuldt tragen, welche ohn allen danck Poeten sein wollen, vnd [. . .] ihre vnwissenscheit vnter dem Lorbeerkrantze verdecken" (And I must also observe that there are certain others guilty of bearing scorn for poetry, namely those who wish to be poets without deserving it and veil their ignorance behind the laurel wreath; chap. 3). What distinguishes them is not the mechanical art of rhyme and singing but rather divine inspiration and natural talent: the work of real poets comes (he recalls Plato here) from nature and divine inspiration. Opitz does not exaggerate this side of the ancient rhetorical opposition of talent and learned technique (*natura* and *ars*),[74] since this would be to ignore the indispensability of "vbung" (exercise) and "fleiss" (hard work). However, while granting the usefulness of technique, *furor poeticus* is not given to imitation:[75] "ein Poete kan nicht schreiben wenn er wil, sondern wenn er kan" (a poet cannot write when he wants but when he is able). This certainty is expanded by Opitz's successors.[76] In 1645 Klaj writes in his *Lobrede der Teutschen Poeterey*:

> Gleichwie aber das Eisen von Magnet zwar gezogen wird / kein Mensch aber weis die stumme Krafft: Also wird die Dicht- und Reimkunst nicht durch Menschliche Wirkungen / sondern durch sonderbare Himmels-gnade eingegossen: sie wird nicht von dem Meister / sondern aus den süssen Vorgeschwätze und Gesäussel der Ammen / erlernent: nicht in den Schulen aus dem Münde der Lehrer gefasset / sondern aus den Mütterlichen Milchbrünlein eingesogen [. . .]: Ein König und Poet die werden nur geboren.[77]

> [Just as iron is attracted to a magnet, but no man understands its silent power, the art of poetry and rhyme is infused not by human strategies but by special divine grace; not learned from the master but rather from the sweet babblings and murmurings of wet-nurses; not comprehended in schools from the mouths of teachers but rather sucked in through the motherly fountains of milk: A king and a poet are only born.]

Buchner says in his *Poet* (12–13) that the poet is a "Macher über alle Macher / oder Meister über alle Meister" (doer above all doers, or master above all masters), compelled to do justice to the "Hoheit diser Kunst" (majesty of this art) through diligent study and daily practice. The gradual liberation and expansion of the concept of the poet is also apparent when Opitz, adducing Horace in contrast to the narrow moral rules of *Meistersinger* doctrine, allows a degree of personal license with respect to temperament, appetite for wine, or penchant for erotic libertinage. Still, this license by no means releases the poet from social obligation.

Communicative Performance

In *Teutsche Rhetorica* (1634) Meyfart defines rhetoric as follows:

> ein Kunst von einem vorgesetzten Ding zierlich zureden / vnd künstlich zuverreden. Es heisset aber zierlich reden / nicht mit lustigem Gethön die Ohren füllen / sondern mit weisen / scharffen vnd druchdringenden Machtsprüchen: auch mit außerlesenen / zu der Sach dienlichen vnd heilsamen Worten reden. (59–60)

> [an art of speaking gracefully on a given topic and persuading artfully. To speak gracefully does not mean to fill the ears with sweet-sounding expressions, however, but rather with meaningful, incisive, emphatic formulations: with well-chosen words as well, which are useful and salutary to the topic.]

Both classical conceptions of rhetoric are alluded to here: as the art of formulating well (*ars bene dicendi*) and as the art of persuading (*ars persuadendi*). Meyfart's contemporaries certainly would have accepted his definition for all forms of communication, both practical and poetic.[78]

No doubt existed in the early modern period that poetry was a communicative act.[79] Opitz avows in chapter 8 that poetry reaches its social, indeed historical purpose, only insofar as it can continue over time to persuade and move worthy individuals.

> Welches denn der grösseste lohn ist, den die Poeten zue gewarten haben; daß sie [. . .] von grossen vnd verständigen Männern getragen [. . .] in die bibliotheken einverleibet, öffentlich verkauffet vnd von jederman gerhümet werden. Hierzue kömpt die hoffnung vieler künfftiger zeiten, in welchen sie fort für fort grünen, vnd ein ewiges gedächtniß in den hertzen der nachkommenen verlassen.

> [The greatest reward that can await poets is when they are recited by great and understanding men, incorporated into libraries, publicly sold, and praised by all. There is also the hope for a long future in which they continue to bear fruit and leave a lasting memory in the hearts of generations to come.]

This passage reflects the fundamentally rhetorical orientation of early modern poetics. While Opitz's *Poeterey* initiated the depragmatizing tendency in writing poetry, it is important not to construe this as his wish to prescribe for aesthetic texts a free, playful character. Depragmatization rather means that poetry should deal primarily with universal topics that transcend specific occasions and that are not exhausted in casuistic or situational pursuits. In principle the heteronomy (or, functionality) of poetic expression is never in doubt; the ideology of artistic autonomy would arise only in the future[80] — in any case, Opitz refutes it emphatically: "So ist auch ferner nichts närrischer, als wann sie meinen, die Poeterey bestehe bloß in jhr selber; die doch alle andere künste vnd wissenschafften in sich helt" (There is nothing more foolish than thinking that the art of poetry consists only in itself, when in fact it contains within itself all other arts and sciences; chap. 3).

Theoreticians between Konrad von Würzburg and Buchner generally shared this opinion. All subscribed to the two principles famously articulated by Horace in verses 333–34 of his *Ars poetica*: good poetry must simultaneously be useful (*prodesse*) and delightful (*delectare*). Both principles were seminal in the textual theories of Cicero and Quintilian: a text should persuade (*persuadere*); its content should profitably instruct (*docere*) or even prove (*probare*); it should also arouse (*movere*) and affect the senses (*flectere, delectare*). Thus Opitz: "Dienet also dieses alles zue vberredung vnd unterricht auch ergetzung der Leute; welches der Poeterey vornemster Zweck ist" (All this then serves to convince and instruct, but also to delight, which is the loftiest goal of poetry; chap. 3). Aesthetic pleasure provides the difference-making elements missing in purely prosaic and expository texts: "wie alles mit lust vnd anmutigkeit geschrieben wird, so wird es auch nachmals von jederman mit dergleichen lust vnd anmutigkeit gelesen" (what is written with joy and grace will later be read by everyone with the very same joy and grace; chap. 8).

In Konrad's prologue to *Partenopier und Meliur* an allegory of blossoms and fruit connects sensual, aesthetic form and intellectual content, a precept of literary theory as late as the eighteenth century.[81] By following its own, autonomous aesthetic law, art leads the audience to specific communicational targets in a rhetorically persuasive manner. The listener should be so charmed by the artistic offering that instruction occurs naturally. This means imparting three things: sensual delight (*delectare*); lessons on life, especially on principles of aristocratic behavior for the individual as well as for the nation (the *docere* of ethics); and expressiveness (the *docere* of rhetorics).[82]

The *Meistersinger* essentially shared this view. An extant placard from the official ratification of the Freiburg Articles states the purpose of *Meistergesang* and the concept of the *Meistersinger* as learned poet: *Meistergesang* promotes the spiritual and moral virtues of the members of its fraternity; the traditional seven liberal arts constitute its foundation; poetry and the sciences are inseparably connected.[83] The "göttliche Kunst" (divine art) of the masters of the liberal arts is to be anchored in the "ungelerte Leien" (uneducated laity) — something that priests cannot achieve with their sermons but that *Meistersinger* accomplish "mit übersüßisten Gedichten ze singen in den zwölf meisterlichen Tönen" (with incomparably sweet poetry sung in the twelve master melodies). The texts of the songs incorporate the teachings of the liberal arts and apply them performatively. They follow the rules of logic and grammar and are metrically based on the mathematical rules of the *ars metrica*, or *Arismetrica*. In all cases they function according to the *ars rhetorica*, "die Rede in zierlicher Ordnung ze behalten nach Tulio und sinen Nachfolgern" (to keep the composing of speech in an artistic order according to Tullius [Cicero] and his successors). Likewise, songs and melodies obey the rules of *ars musica*. On the authority of all of these arts, the *Meistersinger* sought to rejuvenate the prestige of the poetic arts.

Of much greater importance than this rejuvenation of art, however, especially after the Reformation, was the goal of praising God in song as a form of worship or religious proclamation. It would be hyperbolical to claim to discover in *Meistergesang* an afterlife for the concept of the *poeta theologicus*; still, established religious and biblical themes do run throughout the official singing exercises. The Freiburg Articles assure a close connection with religious cultic practices (singing in church, predominance of religious themes in songs, concerts in monasteries). Indeed, the Freiburg city government attempted to establish the fraternity in such a way, "daß dennocht Gott der allmächtig dardurch gelobt, die Selen getrost, und die Menschen zu Ziten so sie dem Gesang zuhorten, von Gotslästerung, auch vom Spil und anderer weltlichen Ueppigkeit gezogen wurden" (that God Almighty thereby be praised, souls comforted, and hearers of the songs turned away from blasphemy, gambling, and other worldly excess). The Colmar Ordinance had similarly strict formal regulations against offensive language in the singing schools. As a rule, only biblical themes were permitted; in the guild room after official performances, swearing was forbidden; nor could idle stories about God or the mother of Jesus be told or sung, though respectable stories — such as from Roman history — were acceptable after dinner. The Nuremberg Tablature permits the performance of non-religious songs (school exercises, fables, farces) only before the regular singing school.

For modern baroque poetics, poetry became *prima philosophia* as understood by Petrarch in his *Epistolae familiares* (X,4), and the concept of the *poeta philosophus* was now dominant, notwithstanding Opitz's excursus in chapter 2 on theology as the origin of poetry. Opitz strongly denies that poets wish to make themselves agreeable only through "ergetzung" (*delectare*) rather than equally through "vnterrichtung" (*docere*). On the contrary, poetry is "die erste Philosophie, eine erzieherin des lebens von jugend auff, welche die art der sitten, der bewegungen des gemütes vnd alles thuns vnd lassen lehrte" (the first philosophy, an educator of life from youth forward, which teaches the cultivation of manners, the animation of the mind, and all that should be done or left undone). Buchner subscribes to the same premise in his *Poet*, that wisdom and virtue are and have always been the chief goals of poets.

Text as Communicative Instrument

Rhetorics and poetics deal with communicative processes in the world, with communicative interaction, and with the various roles assumed by people in communication. Both genres have an extrinsic perspective, directed toward the external contexts of interaction and effectiveness. And because they simultaneously deal with the most important communicative tool, the text, the genres also have an intrinsic perspective, focused on the internal structures of texts as well as the rules and procedures of text production.

The classical five-part rhetorical system operated within a broader three-stage scheme of text production: the planning stage (*intellectio*); the heuristic stage, with its preparatory cognitive processes (*inventio, dispositio*); and the stage of formulation (*elocutio*). Memory and performance (*memoria, actio/pronuntiatio*) completed the process. The theory of rhetoric thereby offered a production and performance model for all semiotic areas, including poetry, the sister discipline of rhetoric; the model was also partially assimilated in early theories of music and art.[84] Of primary importance for poetics were the author's initial production tasks (*officia*). Opitz recognized this connection to rhetorical systematics in Pierre de Ronsard's *Abrégé de l'art poétique français* (1565), which he claimed, in his fifth chapter, as his major poetological source.[85] Finally, Opitz focuses on the theory of textual genres, an expected part of all poetics.

This intrinsic perspective had been cultivated since Aristotle, particularly by Horace, as a systemic self-reflection on facts specific to the work of the poet; hence, the theory of poetics should be called *poeseology* (the theory of making poems).[86] As we observed in Konrad's prologue to *Partenopier und Meliur*, the logic of poetry was already independent by that time; literary tradition had created its own norms. High-courtly formalism represented the ideal standard, mastery of which was self-evident and in need of no external authority.[87] The intrinsic focus on the technical aspects of poetic text production only intensified with *Meistergesang*. The artisan ideal of perfection, achievable through technical mastery, extended to the creation of precisely defined textual structures. *Meistergesang* characteristically evinced blindness for what a later time would take to be the special qualities of a work of art; it had virtually no vocabulary by which aesthetic ideas might be formulated.[88] Indeed, as Karl Stackmann has noted, *Meistergesang* had no term for *beauty*. If "art" is ascribable to *Meistergesang* at all, it is to the quality of the *correct*, of conformity to general normative values.[89]

This aesthetic blindness was overcome in the seventeenth century. Technical aspects of text production found new contexts, particularly under the demands of modern education, which elevated humanistic eloquence to the reigning stylistic ideal. The highest form of eloquence, and the new touchstone of elite education, was the metered and rhymed poem, rendered with painstaking imitation of the hallowed models. Birthdays, weddings, name days, the assumption of office — every occasion required an honorific poem, the requisite implements of which were canonized in poetics, now considered an *ars* in its own right alongside the traditional trivium.[90]

Genre

Classical rhetoric dealt explicitly only with prose speech (Greek *logos*, Latin *oratio*).[91] Rules were developed for the discovery of topics (contents) and tectonics (sections), and were related to the three situational cases of rhetorical invention. In the seventeenth century this genre system was reduced in some aspects but expanded in others, adding new rationalizations, or *Kasuistik* (casuistry). During the course of the Thirty Years' War it became clear that the era of great political speeches at courts and provincial diets was gone for good.[92] The political function of speeches became increasingly a matter of ceremony — paying homage, honoring ambassadorial service, providing ornamentation for commemorative events.[93]

Gottsched's *Ausführliche Redekunst* later drew from this development pertinent consequences for a new theory of genre. Taking modern texts as his point of departure, he rejects the ancient rhetorical tripartite scheme of text production, arguing that radical changes in modes of governing have rendered obsolete both the *rathschlagende* (deliberative) and *gerichtliche* (judicial) genres; thus he subsumes modern speech production almost exclusively under the *erweisende* (epideictic) genre of *genus demonstrativum*. Otherwise, however, he retains the general rules of rhetoric and the validity of the specific genres of antiquity. In the "Besondern Teil" (Special Section) of his *Redekunst* he identifies the most important modern rhetorical genres: 1. "grosse Lobreden oder sogenannte Panegyricis" (great encomia, or so-called panegyrics); 2. "Trauerreden oder Parentationen" (funeral speeches, or *parentationes*); 3. school speeches; 4. university speeches; 5. "Hof- und Staatsreden" (court and state speeches); 6. "Standreden, Personalien und Trostschriften" (eulogies, life sketches, and consolations); 7. "Verlobungs- Trauungs- und Strohkranzreden" (speeches at engagements, weddings, and wedding roasts); and 8. sermons. Several introductory sections also deal with the subjects of translation and imitation of classical speech models. Gottsched's intent is not to diminish the question of genre but to update it. He also wishes to establish a common set of rules for all modes of speech:

> Wir läugnen es nicht, daß es nicht heute zu Tage allerley Arten von Reden geben sollte, davon die Alten nichts gewußt haben: Z.E. unsere Predigten, unsere Huldigungs- und Landtagsreden u.s.w. Allein ungeachtet wir von diesen Arten, in dem zweyten Theile unserer Redekunst, ins besondere handeln werden: so ändern doch dieselben in den allgemeinen Regeln der Redekunst nichts. Denn gesetzt, daß wir alle heutigen Reden, auch in drey Gattungen eintheilen wollten; nämlich lobende, lehrende und complimentirende Reden [. . .]: so würde doch auch diese Abtheilung in den Hauptbegriffen der Beredsamkeit nichts ändern. (126)

> [We cannot deny that there are many kinds of speeches today of which the ancients knew nothing, such as our sermons, our homages, orations at provincial diets, etc. We shall deal specifically with these genres in the second section of our *Redekunst*, though they change nothing in the general rules of rhetoric. Assuming that we did wish to divide the various kinds of modern speech into three types, namely, speeches that praise, instruct, and compliment, such an ordering of the main concepts of rhetoric would not change a thing.]

Some two hundred years before Gottsched, text genre theory for practical written communication, which had been developing since the fifteenth century, was summed up by Alexander Huge (ca. 1460–1529) on the title page of his epistolary rhetorics, *Rethorica unnd Formularium teütsch* (German Rhetorics and Formulary, 1528). It is apparent that German writing-rhetorics dealt with many formulaic text genres:

> vilerley Episteln, Supplicationes, gerichtlicher proceß mit vor vnd nachgenden anhengen, früntlichen vnd vnfründtlichen schrifften, anlässen, verträgen, außsprüchen, tagsatzungen, geleitten, klagen, vrteiln, verkündungen, gewälten, kundtschafften, manrechten, vidimus, Appellationen, Commissionen, Rotweilischen vnd Westfälischen schrifften, vrfehden,

Testamenten, Gemechten, übergabungen, Widem, pfründ, Stifftungen, Patrimonien, Presentationen, kauff, gült vnd leigeding, hinderlegungen, schadloß, manungen, quittantzen, schuld, eestewr, heyrats vnd verzei-hungen, vogteybrieffen.

[various kinds of epistles, supplications, court trials with pre- and post-trial attachments, amicable and inimical texts, occasions, contracts, decla-rations, hearings, escorts, complaints, judgments, proclamations, restraints, notices, letters of dunning, attestations, appellations, commis-sions, writings for the court of Rottweil or the courts of Westphalia, oaths of truce, testaments, accords, transfers, dowries, benefices, endowments, patrimonies, presentations, purchases, payment and loan contracts, escrows, indemnities, appeals, receipts, debts, marriage taxes, certificates of marriage, pardons, and jurisdictions.]

Christian Weise's critique of such rigid formulaicism shows just how much the discipline had changed by the late seventeenth century. The school rector maintains that the ancient system of the *genera causarum* has lost its relevance, and he gives instructions for the composition of texts in actual demand in schools, churches, and politics.[94] For Weise the *cheria*, that is, "a pregnant sen-tence borrowed from some other author, and worked out by certain rules" (*OED*), becomes the primary model for text composition. In all instances, aca-demic training must proceed according to rational methods derived from core philosophical principles, suitable for being put into good textual form by the learned and prudent orator.

Poetics is concerned with completely different kinds of texts: generally speaking, for all verse genres, or standardized verse texts. Opitz looked primar-ily to Neo-Latin literature and reclaimed these models for German. His first interest lies in the subject matter (*res*) of texts and their inner structures (*inven-tio* and *dispositio*). He specifically addresses the genres of heroic epos, tragedy, comedy, satire, epigram, eclogue, elegy, echo, hymns, and sylvan and lyrical poetry (including the ode). Some two decades later, in his *Poetischer Trichter*, Harsdörffer deals expansively with plays but ignores these smaller, lyrical gen-res.[95] From our modern perspective, it is astonishing just how many contem-porary genres were *not* discussed in seventeenth-century poetics.[96]

Modes of Speaking

Genres were organized not only according to content but often also by con-ventional modes of speaking — to use modern parlance, according to formal structures that obey specific "overcode" rules. Early German rhetorics usually treated questions of genre in a lengthy chapter on elocution containing the rich arsenal of rhetorical figures.[97] In this area, rhetorics and poetics were brought into a close relationship, and a number of poetics, such as Stieler's *Dichtkunst des Spahten*, expanded the chapter to extraordinary length.[98] Opitz dedicates chapter 6 of his *Poeterey* to formulation and stylistics, focusing on the language-use principles of *elegantz*, *composition*, and *dignitet* from the third rhetorical stage of production and encompassing word choice, usage (including archaisms, neologisms, and barbarisms), sentence structure, and rhetorical figures.[99] Rhetorical suitability (*aptum, decorum*) occupied the highest regulative principle for stylistic decisions.[100] All poetics included a chapter on the *licentia poetica*, on the poet's limited freedoms within the rhetorical regulative system.[101]

Also unique to poetics was the chapter on metrics and versification; it overlapped only minimally with the *numerus* (metrics) chapter of rhetorics, which dealt with clause construction in prose texts. Opitz handles this issue in his decisive chapter 7 on meter and strophic form, the technical core of his poetics, where he sets out his rule for German accentuating verse.[102] Verse technique was central to poetics as early as the prologue poetics of the Teutonic Order. Heinrich von Hesler and Nikolaus von Jeroschin were the first theorists after Otfried (ninth c.) to deal explicitly and extensively with German verse. Hesler calls for purity of rhyme and aesthetic unity of the individual verse, which is to have four accents just as it did among the ancient masters. Hesler deals with unaccented syllables and anacrusis as well as abbreviations, inclination,[103] elision, and syncope. Hesler and Jeroschin recommend the same classical means for balancing and providing metrical rhythm in order to avoid too much brevity or too great length in their verses.[104]

At this early time, the demands of scriptorality and orality were similar. Konrad conjoins the techniques of spoken text and song (*rede unde sanc*), applying the performative verbs *sagen*, or *sprechen*, and *singen*, often in the double-form: *sagen und singen*, meant to achieve the elaborate effect of "edele doene und edeliu worte" (noble melodies and noble words).[105] Albertanus's Latin theory of the same period was based in classical orality, of course, and focused on performance principles. Preformulated written texts obviously played no part in his thinking, for he specifies neither concrete structures of text formulation nor rules for written preformulation. *Meistergesang* of the fifteenth and sixteenth centuries also presumed the oral and situational conditions of performance and communication of poetic texts: thus its strictly codified guild rules, which evince the same tendency toward extreme regulation of the forms of textual communication stipulated in contemporary rhetorics for writing.[106] It has been argued that the very establishment of the schools, with their apparatus of regulations and tablatures, was proof of the artificial, normative character of *Meistergesang*, which distanced itself aesthetically from conventional poetry.[107] In this view, the *Merker*, as art referee, supervised and evaluated these regulations as an expression of aesthetic quality in the various skill areas: purity of rhyme, metrical and musical exactness, diction, and content. Four observations obtain with respect to the art of rhyme in *Meistergesang*: the bulk of regulations consisted of rules for rhyming; rhyming mistakes were especially egregious transgressions; skill at rhyming was the most important artistic quality; and instruction in artistic rhyming was the indispensable component of a masterful poetics. While all of this applied in the first place to sung texts, the *Meistergesang* tablatures likewise addressed the linguistic side of the songs in a detailed manner.

It would appear that the older scholarly assumption — based on the erroneous claim that no related theories of German poetry, or even versification, existed in Germany — that Opitz had no previous exposure to German-language theoretical influences must be modified.[108] For one thing, *Meistergesang* theory served Opitz effectively at least as a negative foil; for another, the new rudiments of a theory of verse and prosody had already been formulated in the *Prosodiae* (1570) and *Grammatica germanicae linguae* (1578) of Johannes Claius (1535–92). Claius in fact developed a theory of German syllabic accent, having worked it out through a comparison with the prosody of the classical languages.[109] Opitz consulted this theory in composing his *Poeterey*.

Poetic Fiction and Narrativity

In following the humanist differentiation — taken from the *Nichomachean Ethics* of Aristotle — between *poiesis* (textual construction), especially of fictions, and *praxis* (communicative intervention), baroque poetics honed a new conception of the poet and poetry (as the poet's own work).[110] There had been no place for a theory of fiction in the older German poetics. Even in the Latin poetics the question of fiction presented special difficulties in sixteenth-century Germany.[111] *Meistergesang*'s simplistic solution was to restrict subject matter to biblical themes. This changed with Opitz's *Poeterey*. Going back to the Greeks, specifically the ninth chapter of Aristotle's *Poetics*, Opitz took the concepts of mimesis and fantasy as his points of departure. According to Aristotle, poetry should only simulate natural relationships in order to demonstrate the potentialities of reality. In Opitz's formulation in chapter 3: "die ganze Poeterey [bestehe] im nachäffen der Natur" (the whole of poetry consists in the imitation of nature), which means that the poet should not so much describe things as they are, "als wie sie etwan sein köndten oder solten" (but as they could or should be). But the depiction of potential realities requires employment of the imagination — this is the new conception of the poet as master not only of *diction* but of *fiction* as well (to borrow Gérard Genette's terms).[112] The old rhetorical doctrine of *inventio* thus regains importance in poetic theory:

> Die worte vnd Syllaben in gewisse gesetze zue dringen, vnd verse zue schreiben, ist das allerwenigste was in einem Poeten zue suchen ist. Er muß *euphantasiotós*, von sinnreichen einfällen vnd erfindungen sein, muß ein grosses vnverzagtes gemüte haben, muß hohe sachen bey sich erdencken können, soll anders seine rede eine art kriegen, vnd von der erden empor steigen. (Chapter 3)
>
> [Setting words and syllables according to certain principles and writing verses accordingly is the very least to be expected of a poet. He must possess *euphantasiotós* (Quintilian 6.2.30), imaginative and inventive ideas, must be of an undaunted spirit, and must be able to conceive of lofty things if his speeches are to be exceptional and rise above the earth.]

In his *Poet*, Buchner expands on these ideas in terms of the Aristotelian concepts of *mythos* (Latin *fabula*), *mimesis* (depiction, as semiotic simulation of reality), and *mimetes* or *poietes* (simulator, or maker of textures). A precursor of Buchner, the Jesuit Pontanus (*Poeticae institutiones*, Teaching in Poetics, 1594), for whom the *fabulosa fictio* (fictional story) was nothing less than the formative soul of the poetic work,[113] saw the poet engaged as simulator and maker in the activity of representing human actions. Pontanus uses *imitari* (to imitate) and *fingere* (to fabricate) synonymously, in keeping with the Aristotelian understanding of *mimesis* as "depiction," as interpreted in late-sixteenth-century Italian poetics; Latin *fingere* is likewise employed as "to depict." Even when the focal concern of depicting is the simulation of the sensually evident (*procreando*), as opposed to purely informative reporting (*narrando*), and even though it seems that poets create works out of nothing (*e nihilo*), the problem of fiction remains unsolved. For *fingere* (German *fingieren*) is meaningful only in making visible something that is universal, and this cannot be accomplished through imitation of what is historically accidental or individual. Pontanus elaborates on this relationship in connection with the epos.

The new emphasis on the poet as no longer merely versifier but as producer and depicter of semiotic and artistic realities reflects a theoretical turn toward Aristotle's *Poetics*. Aristotle's rhetorical theory concerns questions of human intellectual guidance, for which, in his nineteenth chapter, he adduces the concept *diánoia* (intellect, mind); his poetic theory concentrates on the production of simulative representations or semiotic depiction (*mimesis*). According to Buchner (26) such results obtain especially in the process of fabricating narration; the poet gets his name, after all, from the Greek word for "to make." In practice this means that he has to produce either a new work or one based on an existing one, striving mimetically "gleich einem mahler" (like a painter), who depicts something "das mans erkennen kann" (that one can recognize). The poet is not to argue dialectically like a philosopher, dissecting, dividing, and distinguishing, but should rather portray an object as a semiotic image, as "sein äusserlich wesen und der Augenschein" (its outward being and as it appears to the eye) — a work, that is, that serves the act of viewing. Poetic production consists of "thun und wircken" (doing and effecting). "To make" (*schaffen*) reality in a work is not the same as finding reality through "inquiry" (*erkundigen*), as the scholar does: *erkundigen* reflects the "verborgene Natur" (hidden nature) of the scholar, which motivates the investigation of causes and qualities.

In this narrative process the poet finds his true calling. Opitz had already dealt with the epos; the prose novel and other forms of narrative prose texts would not become poetological subjects until the second half of the century.[114] Until then they will be treated only generally under the rubric of *historia* and categorized according to classical rhetorical theory (Cicero, *De oratore* 2.36; Vossius, *Commentaria rhetorica* 2.4.3).[115] Just as Vadianus in *De poetica et carminis ratione*, Buchner in his *Poet* views the fable as the ideal narrative form and uses it as a basis for elaborating the new conception of German poetry.[116] Buchner argues that ancient poets had created the fable for instruction in divine things, a form more enigmatic than some but clearer than others (such as the riddle), thus existing in the middle ground between knowledge and uncertainty. In its literary form its truth was readily believable, though it simultaneously gave rise to doubt, "weil Sie so wunderliche und seltzame Sachen erzehlete" (because it dealt with such fantastic and strange things; 8). But this was precisely the intention, for it spurred people to think more deeply about things. In the course of its development it evolved to the extent,

> daß endlich die Fabel nicht nur ein Stück Ihrer Wercke / sondern das Werck selbst worden / [. . .] / und zufoderst diejenigen für Poeten gehalten / die eine Fabel fein künst- und zierlich abhandelten. Die aber solches nicht thaten / die wurden etwa Sänger oder Versmacher geheissen. [. . .] Hier hat nun der Poet seinem Nahmen ein Genüge gethan / und sich desselben allerdings fähig und würdig gemacht / indem Er nicht allein die in Warheit wesende Sachen / herrlicher fast / als Sie für sich beschaffen / sondern auch diejenigen / so niemals gewesen/ gleich als wären Sie / fürzustellen / und / so zu reden / von neuen zu schaffen gewußt. [. . .] Aus welchem allen erscheinet / wie hoch und herrlich die Poeten anfangs gehalten / ja Gott selbsten gleich geachtet worden seyn. (9–11)

> [that the fable was no longer just a part of their poetic works but became the work itself. And first and foremost those who could fashion a fable in an accomplished and graceful manner were considered the real poets, while those who did not were called singers or versifiers. In this way the poet lived up to his name and showed himself capable and worthy of it by not only presenting things that actually existed before (and doing so almost more splendidly than in their original form), but also by conceiving of new ones that had never existed, indeed in such a manner as if they had, and as though he were now recreating them afresh. All this explains why poets at first were held in high, even god-like esteem.]

Both Opitz and Buchner contributed to the development of an elementary narrativity that anticipates Genette's theoretical discourse of *histoire*.[117] Opitz explains in chapter 5 that the narrative verse epos need not be as precise as historiographical writings, though one must handle the narrative freedom "mit solcher ordnung, als wann sich eines auff das andere selber allso gebe, vnnd vngesucht in das buch keme" (in such an order as if one thing moved naturally to the next and thus entered the book effortlessly). The narrative epos form has, like fiction, broad license to deal with "allerley fabeln, historien, Kriegskünste, schlachten rathschläge, sturm, wetter, vnd was sonsten zue erweckung der verwunderung in den gemütern von nöthen ist" (all kinds of made-up stories, histories, information on wars and battles, reports about storms and weather, and whatever else might awaken amazement in people's minds). For Buchner narration becomes, on the one hand, the mimetic form par excellence (hence his use of the mirror metaphor), and, on the other, a free space for pictorial, that is, poetic, "making" in its most original sense:

> Also wenn Er von weltlichen Händeln / und die in der Menschen Leben vorlauffen / zu schreiben gesinnet / damit wir daraus / als in einem Spiegel / zu sehen haben / was etwa in unserm Leben krumm und unrecht / so erzehlet Er nur den blossen Verlauff / nach denen umbständen / als sie hergegangen sind / hergehen sollen oder können / in einer sonderbahren Ordnung und Art / durch welche Er von den

Geschichtschreibern unterschieden wird / denen Er sonst fast gleich kommt. Denn die Historici ebener massen den blossen Verlauf der Geschichte erzehlen / das andere aber des vernünfftigen Lesers Urtheil und Nachsinnnen anheim stellen. (*Poet*, 28–29)

[When therefore he determines to write about events in the world and in the lives of individuals, as if we were looking into a mirror and viewing what is twisted and wrong in our lives, he simply relates the pure course of the story line according to the circumstances as they occurred, or should or could occur, in a specific order and manner. In doing so, he distinguishes himself from the historiographers, with whom he is otherwise nearly identical. For historiographers must likewise relate the simple course of events and leave everything else to the judgment and reflection of the intelligent reader.]

Summary

One of the great epistemic achievements of Renaissance Humanism was the development of a modern theory of communication. From the fifteenth century on, ancient sources concerning communication assumed new importance in scholarly discourse under the organizational genres of rhetorics and poetics. Two publication dates mark this development: 1430, the first major humanistic general rhetorics in Latin, by the Byzantine Georgios Trapezuntios,[118] then teaching in Rome; and 1508, the first printed Greek edition of Aristotle's *Poetics*. The independent turn to the European vernacular languages ran parallel to this development. In Germany two other publication dates mark the beginning of vernacular humanism: 1493, the first major humanistic general rhetorics in German, Riederer's *Spiegel der waren Rhetoric*; and 1624, Opitz's *Buch von der Deutschen Poeterey*. The temporal distance between these two works is significant. The rhetorical theory of the fifteenth century arose out of the classical rhetorical tradition and was adapted relatively early for the new practical, vernacular written forms of communication (especially letter writing); this was not the case for poetic theory. Down to the early seventeenth century, German sources, especially *Meistergesang*, betrayed their theoretical indebtedness to the indigenous German tradition. But *Meistergesang* theory, essentially a reductionist and regulated continuation of the doctrine of medieval *Minnesang* and *Sangspruch*, was rejected in Germany in the late Renaissance in favor of simultaneously renewing the ancient paradigm and developing a unique structure for German language and literature. Using the model of Latin and French treatises, Opitz treated German literature as a purely theoretical problem. There now arose in Germany a rich literature in the sister areas of rhetorics and poetics, as a result of which a new understanding of the communicator (whether as *orator* or *poet*) and the possibilities for social interaction came about, together with an intensified and greatly differentiated arsenal of text models for every kind of communication. This theoretical development ended around 1750. The baroque codifications and its taxonomies of occasional poetry could not answer the new demands for the authenticity of personal experience and its correlative deregulation of authority. In the eyes of Goethe's contemporaries, all forms and conditions of communication had to give way to the postulates of naturalness, sensibility, and originality. For rhetorics and poetics this signified an epochal transformation.

Translated by Michael Swisher

Notes

[1] See Martin Opitz, "Vorrede," *Buch von der Deutschen Poeterei* [*sic*], 1624 (repr. of first ed.), 7th ed., ed. Henrik Becker (Halle/Saale: Niemeyer, 1962).

[2] The metaconcept *rhetorics*, like *poetics*, has both a singular and a plural usage and denotes a systematic view of *rhetoric*, the art or technique of persuasion.

[3] Paul Klopsch, *Einführung in die Dichtungslehren des lateinischen Mittelalters* (Darmstadt: Wissenschaftliche Buchgesellschaft, 1980).

[4] For an overview of sources see Wilfried Barner, *Barockrhetorik: Untersuchungen zu ihren geschichtlichen Grundlagen* (Tübingen: Niemeyer, 1970); Dieter Breuer and Günther Kopsch, "Rhetoriklehrbücher des 16. bis 20. Jahrhunderts: Eine Bibliographie," in *Rhetorik: Beiträge zu Ihrer Geschichte in Deutschland vom 16. bis 20. Jahrhundert*, ed. Helmut Schanze (Frankfurt am Main: Athenäum 1974), 217–92; James J. Murphy, comp., *Renaissance Rhetoric: A Short Title Catalogue of Works on Rhetorical Theory from the Beginning of Printing to A.D. 1700* (New York: Garland, 1981); Adam Skura, *Katalog druków XV–XVIII w. z zakresu poetyki i retoryki* (Wrocław: Wydawnictwo U, 1987); Joachim Knape, "Barock," *Historisches Wörterbuch der Rhetorik* (hereafter: *HWR*) (Tübingen: Niemeyer, 1992), cols. 1285–332; Knape, "Elocutio," *HWR* (1994), cols. 1022–83; Murphy and Martin Davies, "Rhetorical Incunabula: A Short-Title Catalogue of Texts Printed to the Year 1500," *Rhetorica* 15 (1997): 355–470.

[5] Joachim Knape, "Humanismus," in *Literaturwissenschaftliches Lexikon: Grundbegriffe der Germanistik*, ed. Horst Brunner and Rainer Moritz (Berlin: Schmidt, 1997), 144–46.

[6] Knape, "Elocutio," 1047–49. See in this volume the chapter by John L. Flood.

[7] See Frank Baron, "Peter Luder," in *German Writers of the Renaissance and Reformation, 1280–1580*, vol. 179 of *Dictionary of Literary Biography*, ed. Max Reinhart and James Hardin (Detroit: Gale, 1997), 129–34.

[8] See Joachim Knape, *Allgemeine Rhetorik: Stationen der Theoriegeschichte* (Stuttgart: Reclam, 2000).

[9] Barner, *Barockrhetorik*, 265ff.; C. S. M. Rademaker, *Life and Works of Gerardus Joannes Vossius (1577–1649)* (Assen: von Gorcum, 1981); Ralph Häfner, *Götter im Exil: Frühneuzeitliches Dichtungsverständnis im Spannungsfeld christlicher Apologetik und philologischer Kritik* (Tübingen: Niemeyer, 2003).

[10] Barbara Bauer, *Jesuitische "ars rhetorica" im Zeitalter der Glaubenskämpfe* (Frankfurt am Main: Lang, 1986).

[11] The second is the *Ad Herennium*, ascribed to Cicero.

[12] Franz Josef Worstbrock, "Die Brieflehre des Konrad Celtis: Textgeschichte und Autorschaft," in *Philologie als Kulturwissenschaft: Studien zur Literatur und Geschichte*

des Mittelalters, ed. Ludger Grenzmann, Hubert Herkommer, and Dieter Wuttke (Göttingen: Vandenhoeck & Ruprecht, 1987), 242–69.

[13] Kurt Smolak, ed., Erasmus von Rotterdam: *De conscribendis epistolis / Anleitung zum Briefeschreiben*, vol. 8 of *Erasmus: Ausgewählte Schriften* (Darmstadt: Wissenschaftliche Buchgesellschaft, 1980).

[14] For more on the genres of rhetoric in Germany during the baroque period see Knape, "Barock," 1289ff.

[15] Knape, "Elocutio," 1052–54.

[16] Joachim Knape, *Philipp Melanchthons Rhetorik* (Tübingen: Niemeyer, 1993), 30 and 40.

[17] See Knape, *Allgemeine Rhetorik*, 237–59.

[18] Knape, "Barock," 1287.

[19] Knape, "Barock," 1290.

[20] Karl Stackmann: "Quaedam Poetica: Die meisterliche Dichtung Deutschlands im zeitgenössischen Verständnis," in *Literatur, Musik und Kunst im Übergang vom Mittelalter zur Neuzeit*, ed. Hartmut Boockmann (Göttingen: Vandenhoeck & Ruprecht, 1995), 132–61, here 139 and 149.

[21] The novel as such is of course not yet explicitly mentioned. See overviews in Heinz Entner, "Zum Dichtungsbegriff des deutschen Humanismus," in *Grundpositionen der deutschen Literatur im 16. Jahrhundert*, ed. Ingeborg Spriewald, Werner Lenk, and Heinz Entner (Berlin: Aufbau, 1976), 330–98; Gunter E. Grimm, *Literatur und Gelehrtentum in Deutschland: Untersuchungen zum Wandel ihres Verhältnisses vom Humanismus bis zur Frühaufklärung* (Tübingen: Niemeyer, 1983), 80–94; Bernhard Asmuth, "Anfänge der Poetik im deutschen Sprachraum: Mit einem Hinweis auf die von Celtis eröffnete Lebendigkeit des Schreibens," in *Renaissance-Poetik/Renaissance Poetics*, ed. Heinrich F. Plett (Berlin: de Gruyter, 1994), 94–113. For an introduction to poetics see Werner Jung, *Kleine Geschichte der Poetik* (Hamburg: Junius, 1997).

[22] Entner, "Zum Dichtungsbegriff"; Hermann Wiegmann, *Geschichte der Poetik: Ein Abriß* (Stuttgart: Metzler, 1977), 39–49; Reiner Schmidt, *Deutsche Ars Poetica: Zur Konstituierung einer deutschen Poetik aus humanistischem Geist im 17. Jahrhundert* (Meisenheim am Glan: Hain, 1980), 63ff.; Franz Josef Worstbrock, "Die 'Ars versificandi et carminum' des Konrad Celtis: Ein Lehrbuch eines deutschen Humanisten," in *Studien zum städtischen Bildungswesen des späten Mittelalters und der frühen Neuzeit* (Göttingen: Vandenhoeck & Ruprecht, 1983), 462–98; Heinz Entner, "Der Weg zum Buch von der Deutschen Poeterey," in *Studien zur deutschen Literatur im 17. Jahrhundert*, ed. Entner (Berlin: Aufbau, 1984), 82–84; Asmuth, "Anfänge der Poetik"; Jörg Robert: *Konrad Celtis und das Projekt der deutschen Dichtung* (Tübingen: Niemeyer, 2003).

[23] Knape, "Elocutio," 1047.

[24] Entner, "Zum Dichtungsbegriff," 388.

[25] Entner, "Zum Dichtungsbegriff," 368 and 383; Stackmann, "Quaedam Poetica."

[26] Knape, *Allgemeine Rhetorik*, 175–206.

[27] Reproduction in J. Knight Bostock, *Albertanus Brixiensis in Germany* (Oxford: Clarendon, 1924), 79–115.

[28] Joachim Knape and Bernhard Roll, eds., *Rhetorica deutsch: Rhetorikschriften des 15. Jahrhunderts* (Wiesbaden: Harrassowitz, 2002).

[29] Some writers indeed began to enjoy impressive publication numbers. See Knape, "Barock," 1289.

[30] Paul Joachimsen, "Aus der Vorgeschichte des 'Formulare und deutsche Rhetorica'" (1893), *Gesammelte Aufsätze: Beiträge zu Renaissance, Humanismus und Reformation*, ed. Notker Hammerstein (Aalen: Scientia, 1970), 23–120; Dietmar Till, *Transformationen der Rhetorik: Untersuchungen zum Wandel der Rhetoriktheorie im 17. und 18. Jahrhundert* (Tübingen: Niemeyer, 2004), 197–98; texts in Knape and Roll, eds., *Rhetorica deutsch*, and Jürgen Fröhlich, *Bernhard Hirschvelders Briefrhetorik (Cgm 3607): Untersuchung und Edition* (Frankfurt am Main: Lang, 2003); bibliography in Reinhard Nickisch, *Die Stilprinzipien in den deutschen Briefstellern des 17. und 18. Jahrhunderts: mit einer Bibliographie zur Briefschreiblehre (1474–1800)* (Göttingen: Vandenhoeck & Ruprecht, 1969).

[31] From 1420: Clm 6009, 170^r–178^v; from 1427: Cgm655,444^{ra}–480rb.

[32] Knape, *Allgemeine Rhetorik*, 207–36.

[33] Knape, "Barock," 1295.

[34] Joachim Knape, ed., "Niklas von Wyle: Unterweisung," in Knape and Roll, eds., *Rhetorica deutsch*, 185–203, here 189.

[35] See in this volume the chapter by John L. Flood.

[36] Knape, *Allgemeine Rhetorik*, 218–22.

[37] Georg Braungart, *Hofberedsamkeit: Studien zur Praxis höfisch-politischer Rede im deutschen Territorialabsolutismus* (Tübingen: Niemeyer, 1988), 50ff.; Till, *Transformationen der Rhetorik*, 111ff.

[38] Angus Graham, "Who Read Albertanus? Insights From the Manuscript Transmission," in *Albertano da Brescia: Alle origini del Razionalismo economico, dell'Umanesimo civile, della Grande Europa*, ed. Franco Spinelli (Brescia, 1996), 69–82; Joachim Knape, ed., "Albertanus Brixiensis: *Die Räte von der Rede*," in Knape and Roll, eds., *Rhetorica deutsch*, 235–52; here also for a discussion of the translation of 1472, 235ff.

[39] Emilio Bonfatti, "Verhaltenslehrbücher und Verhaltensideale," *Zwischen Gegenreformation und Frühaufklärung: Späthumanismus, Barock, 1572–1740*, ed. Harald Steinhagen, vol. 3 of *Deutsche Literatur: Eine Sozialgeschichte* (Reinbek: Rowohlt, 1985), 74–87; Karl-Heinz Göttert, "Konversation," *HWR* 4 (1998), cols. 1322–33.

[40] For further sources see Knape, "Barock," 1296.

[41] Knape, "Barock," 1297.

[42] Manfred Beetz, *Frühmoderne Höflichkeit: Komplimentierkunst und Gesellschaftsrituale im altdeutschen Sprachraum* (Stuttgart: Metzler, 1990); Dietmar Till, "Komplimentierkunst," *HWR* 4 (1998), cols. 1211–32.

[43] At ll. 4589–823. Wolfram von Eschenbach is the only poet he criticizes. All the others (Hartmann von Aue, Bligger von Steinach, Veldeke) he praises and wishes to imitate. On the general subject see Günther Schweickle, ed., *Dichter über Dichter in mittelhochdeutscher Literatur* (Tübingen: Niemeyer, 1970).

[44] See in this volume the chapter by Graeme Dunphy.

[45] Carl von Kraus, "Die metrischen Regeln bei Heinrich von Hesler und Nikolaus Jeroschin," *Festschrift Max H. Jellinek* (Vienna: Österreichischer Bundesverlag für Unterricht, Wissenschaft und Kunst, 1928), 57.

46 See in this volume the chapter by Peter Hess.

47 Bert Nagel, *Meistergesang* (Stuttgart: Metzler, 1971), 63–76.

48 See Horst Brunner, afterword, *Johann Christoph Wagenseil: Buch von der Meister-Singer Holdseligen Kunst (Aus: De civitate Norimbergensi commentatio)*, ed. Brunner (Göppingen: Kümmerle, 1975).

49 Entner, "Zum Dichtungsbegriff"; Worstbrock, "Brieflehre"; Asmuth, "Anfänge der Poetik"; Stackmann, "Quaedam Poetica."

50 Joachim Dyck, *Ticht-Kunst: Deutsche Barockpoetik und rhetorische Tradition*, 3rd ed. (Tübingen: Niemeyer, 1991), 14.

51 Conrad Wiedemann, "Engel, Geist und Feuer: Zum Dichterselbstverständnis bei Johann Klaj, Catharina von Greiffenberg und Quirinus Kuhlmann," *Literatur und Geistesgeschichte: Festgabe für Heinz Otto Burger*, ed. Reinhold Grimm and Wiedemann (Berlin: Schmidt, 1968), 85–109.

52 Wilfried Barner, "Spielräume: Was Poetik und Rhetorik nicht lehren," *Künste und Natur in Diskursen der Frühen Neuzeit*, ed. Hartmut Laufhütte (Wiesbaden: Harrassowitz, 2000), 1:33–67. Barner remarks that they accompany the early modern period as a kind of ideal *Doppelgänger* (33).

53 Dietmar Till, "Affirmation und Subversion: Zum Verhältnis von 'rhetorischen' und 'platonischen' Elementen in der frühneuzeitlichen Poetik," *Zeitsprünge: Forschungen zur Frühen Neuzeit* 4, no. 3 (2000): 181–210, here 182.

54 See Dyck, *Ticht-Kunst*, 7: "eine späte Blüte am weitverzweigten Baum der rhetorischen Theorie"; ibid. 25.

55 Dietmar Till: "Poetik (A.)," *HWR* 6 (2003), cols. 1304–7, here 1306.

56 Till, *Transformationen der Rhetorik*.

57 Joachim Knape, "Humanismus, Reformation, deutsche Sprache und Nation," *Nation und Sprache: Die Diskussion ihres Verhältnisses in Geschichte und Gegenwart*, ed. Andreas Gardt (Berlin: de Gruyter, 2000), 103–38. See in this volume the chapter by Renate Born.

58 Renate Hildebrandt-Günther, *Antike Rhetorik und deutsche literarische Theorie im 17. Jahrhundert* (Marburg: Elwert, 1966), 54ff.; Dyck, *Ticht-Kunst*, 10–12; Glenn Most, "Rhetorik und Hermeneutik: Zur Konstitution der Neuzeitlichkeit," *Antike und Abendland* 30 (1984): 62–79; Klaus Petrus, *Genese und Analyse: Logik, Rhetorik und Hermeneutik im 17. und 18. Jahrhundert* (Berlin: de Gruyter, 1997), 77ff.

59 Joachim Knape, "Autorpräsenz: Sebastian Brants Selbstinszenierung in der Oratorrolle im Traum-Gedicht von 1502," *Self Fashioning / Personen (selbst)darstellung*, ed. Rudolf Suntrup and Jan R. Veenstra (Frankfurt am Main: Lang, 2003), 79–108.

60 Joachim Knape, ed., "Briefrhetoriken," in Knape and Roll, eds., *Rhetorica deutsch*, 38–182.

61 Joachim Knape, introduction, in Knape and Roll, eds., *Rhetorica deutsch*, 11–36.

62 It is supplemented by a typology of patronage. Knape, *Allgemeine Rhetorik*, 231.

63 Braungart, *Hofberedsamkeit*, 52; Till, *Transformationen der Rhetorik*, 111ff.

64 Barner, "Spielräume," 34–35.

65 Modern High German version here and in subsequent Konrad quotations taken from Walter Haug, *Literaturtheorie im deutschen Mittelalter von den Anfängen bis zum Ende des 13. Jahrhunderts*, 2nd ed. (Darmstadt: Wissenschaftliche Buchgesellschaft, 1992); in English translation as *Vernacular Literary Theory in the Middle Ages: the German*

Tradition, 800–1300 in its European Context, trans. Joanna M. Catling (Cambridge: Cambridge UP, 1997).

[66] On the *contratto communicazionale* see Livio Rossetti, *Strategie macro-retoriche: la "formattazione" dell'evento communicazionale* (Palermo: Univ. Facoltà di lettere e filosofia, 1994), 31–36. With respect to Gottfried see Haug, *Literaturtheorie im deutschen Mittelalter*, 361.

[67] *Colmarer Ordnung der Meistersingerschule* (1549), 404, note 2. It is available in full in *Alsatia* 10 (1873–74): 97–110. The poet Frauenlob, one of the twelve old masters of *Meistergesang* responsible for the creation of its tradition, is buried in the cloister of the Mainz cathedral. See Stackmann, "Quaedam Poetica," 146.

[68] Stackmann, "Quaedam Poetica," 147.

[69] Rudolf Drux, *Martin Opitz und sein poetisches Regelsystem* (Bonn: Bouvier, 1976); Wulf Segebrecht, *Das Gelegenheitsgedicht: Ein Beitrag zur Geschichte und Poetik der deutschen Lyrik* (Stuttgart: Metzler, 1977), 202–3; Till, "Affirmation und Subversion," 198ff.

[70] See in this volume the chapter by Stephan Füssel.

[71] Stackmann, "Quaedam Poetica," 149.

[72] Thus the standard exempla upon which Scaliger bases his argumentation; Dyck, *Ticht-Kunst*, 14.

[73] Christoph J. Steppich, *Numine afflatur: Die Inspiration des Dichters im Denken der Renaissance* (Wiesbaden: Harrassowitz, 2002).

[74] Florian Neumann, "Natura-ars-Dialektik," *HWR* 6 (2003), cols. 139–71; Till, *Transformationen der Rhetorik*, 77ff.

[75] Entner, "Zum Dichtungsbegriff," 383f.

[76] Wiedemann, "Engel, Geist und Feuer"; Theodor Verweyen, "Dichtungstheorie und Dichtungsverständnis bei den Nürnbergern," in *"Der Franken Rom": Nürnbergs Blütezeit in der zweiten Hälfte des 17. Jahrhunderts*, ed. John Roger Paas (Wiesbaden: Harrassowitz, 1995), 178–95; Till, *Transformationen der Rhetorik*, 67.

[77] *Lobrede*, 20. On the principle of *poeta nascitur, orator fit* see Till, "Affirmation und Subversion," 201ff.

[78] Barner, *Barockrhetorik*, 74ff.

[79] Dyck, *Ticht-Kunst*, 25–39.

[80] It is postulated indeed as autarchy in the *l'art pour l'art* ideology of the eighteenth- and nineteenth-century *Kunstperiode*. See Stackmann, "Quaedam Poetica," 149.

[81] "[D]ie schönen und makellosen Blüten, die eine Dichtung zunächst trägt und die dann zu Früchten werden, das ist das unterhaltende Vergnügen, das wie die Blütenpracht des Mai über das Herz kommt und den, der sie sieht, erfreut. [. . .] Was verstehe ich nun unter der Frucht, die auf die Blüte des Gedichts folgt? Es sind der nützliche kluge Rat und die vortreffliche Beispielhaftigkeit, was beides mit dem Gewicht der Lehre diejenigen besser macht, die willens sind, auf das zu achten, was man ihnen in Wort und Sang vorträgt." [The beautiful, unblemished blossoms that poetry bears and that become fruit are the pleasure that comes over the heart like the splendor of blossoms in May and gives joy to whoever sees it. What do I mean by the fruit that follows the blossom of the poem? It is the useful wise counsel and the superb exemplarity that, combined with the weight of instruction, improve the person who pays attention to what is presented in word and song.]

[82] Haug, *Literaturtheorie im deutschen Mittelalter*, 352ff.

[83] The following two paragraphs are indebted to Stackmann, "Quaedam Poetica," 115–53.

[84] Joachim Knape, "Rhetorizität und Semiotik: Kategorietransfer zwischen Rhetorik und Kunsttheorie der Frühen Neuzeit," in *Intertextualität in der Frühen Neuzeit: Studien zu ihren theoretischen und praktischen Perspektiven*, ed. Wilhelm Kühlmann and Wolfgang Neuber (Frankfurt am Main: Lang, 1994), 507–32.

[85] Entner, "Der Weg," 34–35.

[86] Barner, "Spielräume," 34–35.

[87] Haug, *Literaturtheorie im deutschen Mittelalter*, 355.

[88] This point is well demonstrated in the art of the German Renaissance. See Christopher Wood, "Germany's Blind Renaissance," in *Infinite Boundaries: Order, Disorder, and Reorder in Early Modern German Culture*, ed. Max Reinhart (Kirksville, MO: Thomas Jefferson UP, 1998), 225–44.

[89] Stackmann, "Quaedam Poetica," 151–52.

[90] Dyck, *Ticht-Kunst*, 13.

[91] Joachim Knape, "Rede," *Reallexikon der deutschen Literaturwissenschaft* (2003), 3:233–35.

[92] Braungart, *Hofberedsamkeit*, 49.

[93] See examples of this in Till, *Transformationen der Rhetorik*, 111–12.

[94] Till, *Transformationen der Rhetorik*, 127–28. In this volume in the chapter "Education in Early Modern Germany" (section: "New Pedagogical Approaches of the Seventeenth Century"), Wilhelm Kühlmann discusses analogous changes in German education in the seventeenth century.

[95] Bernhard Asmuth, "Poetik (Frühe Neuzeit: Deutschland)," *HWR* 6 (2003), cols. 1339–54, here 1342.

[96] Barner, "Spielräume."

[97] For an overview of the figures see Joachim Knape and Armin Sieber, *Rhetorik-Vokabular zur zweisprachigen Terminologie in älteren deutschen Rhetoriken* (Wiesbaden: Harrassowitz, 1998), 89–136.

[98] Asmuth, "Poetik," 1343.

[99] Knape, "Elocutio," 1025–32.

[100] Barner, *Barockrhetorik*, 150–51.

[101] Barner, "Spielräume," 55.

[102] Erich Trunz, "Die Entwicklung des barocken Langverses," *Euphorion* 39 (1938): 427–68; Christian Wagenknecht, *Weckherlin und Opitz: Zur Metrik der deutschen Renaissancepoesie* (Munich: Beck, 1971). Unlike Greek and Latin, which determine the accent by syllable length, German verse, according to Opitz, is to reflect natural word accent.

[103] *Inclination*: "the throwing of the accent on an enclitic upon the last syllable of the word to which it is attached" (*OED*). Kraus, "Die metrischen Regeln," 60–61.

[104] "Beide wägen, d.i. rhythmisieren ihre Verse auf die gleiche Weise mit den Mitteln der älteren Kunst, und beide gewinnen einen äußeren Behelf, ihre Verse zu messen und dadurch vor zu großer Kürze oder Länge zu bewahren, in der Zählung der Silben eines jeden Verses, die an ein bestimmtes Maß gebunden sind. Aber dieses Maß ist nur nach

unten das gleiche, nämlich sechs Silben, während nach oben Jeroschin nur neun, Hesler dagegen noch zehn Silben zuläßt." Kraus, "Die metrischen Regeln," 73–74.

[105] See Haug, *Literaturtheorie im deutschen Mittelalter*, 352–53.

[106] Knape, introduction, 22–23.

[107] This and the remainder of this paragraph is based on Bert Nagel, *Meistergesang* (Stuttgart: Metzler, 1971), 52.

[108] Entner, "Der Weg," 20.

[109] Schmidt, *Deutsche Ars Poetica*, 100–107; Entner, "Der Weg," 21 and 82–84.

[110] Entner, "Der Weg," 379; Philipp Rippel, "Nachwort," *Niccolò Machiavelli: Il principe/Der Fürst*, trans. and ed. Rippel (Stuttgart: Reclam, 1986), 240; Georg Braungart, "*Praxis* und *poesis*: zwei konkurrierende Textmodelle im 17. Jahrhundert," in *Rhetorik zwischen den Wissenschaften: Geschichte, System, Praxis als Probleme des "Historischen Wörterbuchs der Rhetorik,"* ed. Gert Ueding (Tübingen: Niemeyer, 1991), 87–98.

[111] Entner, "Zum Dichtungsbegriff," 354ff., and Entner, "Der Weg."

[112] Gerard Genette, *Fiktion und Diktion*, trans. Heinz Jatho (Munich: Fink, 1992).

[113] The analysis in the remainder of this paragraph derives largely from Entner, "Zum Dichtungsbegriff," 379ff.

[114] Barner, "Spielräume," 57–58.

[115] Joachim Knape, *"Historie" in Mittelalter und früher Neuzeit: Begriffs- und gattungsgeschichtliche Untersuchungen im interdisziplinären Kontext* (Baden-Baden: Koerner, 1984), 397–98; Joachim Knape, "Narratio," *HWR* 6 (2003), cols. 98–106.

[116] Entner, "Zum Dichtungsbegriff," 378–79.

[117] Knape, "Narratio."

[118] John Monfasani, *George of Trebizond: A Biography and a Study of His Rhetoric and Logic* (Leiden: Brill, 1976).

Neo-Latin Literature in Early Modern Germany

Wilhelm Kühlmann

Premises and Dimensions

REACHING BACK TO ANTIQUITY AND REJECTING "barbarian" medieval Latin, Neo-Latin literature represents the third and final phase of the Latin culture of Old Europe. Supplanting the Latin that once served as the medium of scholastic-dialectical discourse, the new literary-rhetorical Latin, Neo-Latin, cultivated especially for its stylistic elegance, became the vehicle of a general education from the middle of the fifteenth century to well into the eighteenth. Mastery of Neo-Latin fundamentally affected the very conditions, the *habitus*, of reasoning in language, especially in the moral, political, and anthropological discourses, and guaranteed access to the modern academic culture of knowledge. In the higher disciplines of theology and law, as well as in the natural sciences, the terminological precision and international usefulness of Neo-Latin ensured that it would flourish for at least another century; only toward the end of the seventeenth century did the number of German-language publications begin to equal that of Latin-language titles.[1] The affinity of Neo-Latin for the intellectual pluralism of classical Latin, and its new stylistic taste modeled on the great classical rhetoricians, made its practitioners natural antagonists of scholastic theologians, who continued to think and write in the allegedly more ponderous categories of medieval church Latin. Despite efforts to harmonize the two traditions, a secular view predominated in Neo-Latin culture: the reflexive activity of the modern subject reveals itself in diverse mental attitudes, moral positions, political models, and literary forms. Notwithstanding the massive changes in social and philosophical conditions and assumptions that gave rise to early modern Europe, the production and reception of Neo-Latin literature that accompanied that development constitutes an overarching cultural-historical unity. Coherent traditions bind the varieties of styles, forms, and purposes of Neo-Latin literature practiced between the mid-fifteenth and early eighteenth centuries.

Even prior to the Reformation, oral and written command of Latin had been the key to acquiring knowledge. In the sixteenth and seventeenth centuries, however, it became instrumental in training a new class of experts to meet the technological and governing needs of modern society. The new education was driven equally by a moral vision contained in literature. Good literature, according to Erasmus of Rotterdam (1466 or 1469–1536), transforms people into genuine human beings: "bonae litterae reddunt homines."[2] This theory raised the value of the disciplines that constituted the new *studia humanitatis*: grammar, rhetoric, poetry, history, and moral philosophy, and led to pedagogical reforms in schools and universities across Europe. The "messengers" of this reform were the new phenomena of (reprintable) textbooks, editions, and anthologies, most of them adapted directly or indirectly from Italian models. Works by Alexander Hegius (Heek, ca. 1439–98),[3] Rudolf Agricola (1444–85), Peter Luder (ca. 1415–72),[4] Jacob Wimpfeling (1450–1528), Conrad Celtis (Bickel, 1459–1508), Jacob Locher (1471–1528), Heinrich Bebel (ca. 1472–1518), Johannes Murmellius (Roermond, 1480–1517), and Hermann von dem Busche (1468–1534)[5] competed for the attention of students, aristocrats, and territorial lords. These early humanists attacked as foes all who defended monastic piety against the secular literary culture or otherwise defended the conventional scholastic canon. The preface to Busche's eight-volume *Vallum humanitatis* (Rampart of Humanity, 1518) aims at winning over an aristocracy suspicious of education and at overcoming theological objections to the proposed unification of linguistic, behavioral, and factual knowledge. Under thesis-like headings — reminiscent of the scholastic method of posing *quaestiones* but now emphatically historical and empirical — examples from as early as ancient Greek are adduced to urge the adoption of classical precepts and poetry. Busche's inclusion of relevant patristic literature (mainly Augustine, Basil, Ambrose, and Jerome) helps to justify bringing pagan authors into the Neo-Latin curriculum. In part, humanists argued for the implementation of the *studia humaniora* by demonstrating their utility, especially for biblical exegesis and preaching. In book 8 Busche contrasts Germany's backwardness with the civilized state of literature he had witnessed on his journey through Italy. He portrays papal Rome and Renaissance Florence with equal enthusiasm, admiring both as centers of advanced educational patronage.

To be sure, Neo-Latin literature abounds in local, regional, and national topics. However, it served above all as the universal language of communication for the *respublica litteraria*; across academic Europe, scholars and students were able to move about freely and familiarly. Access to the literature of antiquity, with all its stylistic models, themes, and motifs, meant that humanists had a rich world of allusions and the elements of compositional imitation at their fingertips. The rhetorical and poetic *praecepta* and the stylistic and typological *exempla* learned in the schools constituted the building blocks of *imitatio*, though the ultimate goal was *aemulatio*, the emulation of the canonical models achievable by a sort of friendly competition with them.[6] The rise of German national culture owed much to these aspirations, for by these standards a nation could measure its educational progress against that of its neighbors. Some historians of the nineteenth century, echoing Herder in the eighteenth, argued that the humanists' pursuit of a Latin literary language signified a lack of patriotism; in fact, it signified a cultural ambition that ran parallel to and decisively influenced developments in the vernacular.[7] Far from suppressing the rise of a German vernacular literature, Neo-Latin inspired and made it possible. Neo-Latin symbolized the linguistic continuity of the Holy Roman Empire that included Germanic culture in all its dialectical and orthographical variants. In the seventeenth century, Martin Opitz (1597–1639) would derive his principles for a reform of vernacular poetics, elucidated in his *Buch von der Deutschen Poeterey* (1624), from Latin antiquity and its heritage in modern Romance and Dutch literary practice.[8]

Philipp Melanchthon (1497–1560),[9] professor of Greek in Wittenberg since 1519 and Luther's close associate, guided the post-Reformation alliance between biblical Christianity and humanistic *litterata pietas* (learned piety) and helped in this way to ensure the continued dominance of Latin literary and scholarly discourse into modern Europe. Melanchthon's pedagogical reforms had far-reaching consequences for the Protestant school system as late as the eighteenth century.[10] His astonishing literary productiveness encompassed all subjects of the trivium and quadrivium and provided new models for the selection of canon, the adaptation of themes, and the Christian moral assimilation of pagan authors. His inaugural address at Wittenberg, *De corrigendis adolescentiae studiis* (On the Reform of Youth Education),[11] drew on the cultural precepts of the Italian Renaissance and expanded the program of the *artes liberales* to an ideal of universal education in the service of evangelicalism and the Protestant state. The goals of this return to classical roots combined linguistic and logical competence (through mastery of dialectic and rhetoric) with factual knowledge, gave enhanced attention to ancient Greek authors, and affirmed sound moral principles of behavior, not only on religious but on historical and natural scientific grounds as well.[12] By introducing *declamationes* alongside the traditional scholastic *disputationes* Melanchthon turned the mastery of practical rhetoric, on the models of Cicero and Quintilian, into an academic standard and contributed at least indirectly to the flowering of school drama, which evolved in part from the staging of *orationes fictae* (invented speeches).

Melanchthon wrote in a wide variety of academic forms, beginning with his lectures. Often based on student notes taken from his classes, these were typically author commentaries, accompanied by annotations and recommendations; occasionally they were published under names other than his own, such as his commentary on Ovid's *Metamorphoses* (1554) attributed to the Königsberg scholar Georg Sabinus, Melanchthon's son-in-law.[13] They typically focus on the rhetorical explication of texts and on tracing moral rules by comparing the *hypothesis* of a specific case with the normative *thesis*.[14] Melanchthon's Greek and Latin grammars, logics, dialectics — for example, the *Erotema dialectices* (Inquiry on Dialectics, 1547) — and rhetorics — for example, the *Elementorum rhetorices libri duo* (Two Books on the Elements of Rhetoric, 1531) — were widely disseminated.[15] *De inventione dialectica* (On Dialectical Invention, printed 1515) by Rudolf Agricola, about whom more will be said below, motivated Melanchthon's fusion of the Aristotelian logical categories with the doctrine of invention and the question of status (the situation of the case), as derived from Cicero and Quintilian.[16] He introduced a category of didactic rhetoric (*genus didaktikon*) as a means of advancing skills in spiritual eloquence, though in general he understood rhetoric less as a system of oratory than as a guide to textual hermeneutics. The *Ethicae doctrinae elementa* (1550), an exegesis of Aristotelian ethics, derives moral rules for daily life, harmonizes elementary understanding of natural law with the Decalogue, and establishes the boundaries between ethics (or gospel) and theology (or law).[17] The latter led inevitably to conflicts with Gnesio- (strict) Lutherans and inspired a camp of moderate theologians calling themselves Philippists in acknowledgement of Melanchthon's example. A theologically grounded psychology, or anthropology, rests at the center of his *Liber de anima* (Book on the Mind, 1553), which combines principles from the Greek physician Galen (second century A.D.) with the modern anatomical theory of Andreas Vesalius (1514–64), elucidated in *De humani corporis fabrica* (On the Structure of the Human Body, 1543). Similarly, Melanchthon's *Initia doctrinae physicae* (Introduction to Physics, 1549) rests on a natural science having both empirical and cosmological features.

Many of Melanchthon's writings were not published in his lifetime: lectures and university addresses, chrestomathies and textbooks, commentaries and preambles. They cover in thematic scope nearly all of antiquity (the taboo zones of Epicurean materialism are conspicuously absent). Nor can Melanchthon's significance be properly assessed apart from the secondary impact made by the vast circle of his students,[18] not to mention the importance of his travels throughout the Protestant territories as school inspector on behalf of the reorganization of German education.

As the language of culture, Neo-Latin was generally more dominant in the Habsburg Catholic territories, particularly in Bavaria, than in the Protestant lands.[19] The fastidiously organized Catholic educational offensive began with a decree at the Council of Trent in 1563 and was largely the work of the Jesuits; these auspices guaranteed its pure Catholic character and international usage. The terms of the reform are articulated in the *Ratio studiorum* (Program of Studies) of 1599.[20] The modernized literary and theater culture of the Jesuits was supported by a broad network of schools, seminaries, and universities, some recently founded, some taken over from Protestants.[21] The Jesuit Gymnasium, which held considerable attraction for Protestants as well, was structured in five years of "classes" in grammar, humanities, and rhetoric, leading in turn to a three-year study of Aristotelian logic, natural philosophy, and metaphysics. To ensure new generations of recruits for the order, a four-year curriculum of theological studies was added. It retained not only the study of the major authors of antiquity — cleansed of all "obscenity," to be sure, particularly in the cases of Ovid, Horace, and Martial — but also the traditional combination of elementary doctrine and practical exercises. This strict curriculum led in the Catholic lands to a blossoming of Christian literature, often bellicose in tone but genuinely humanistic in character,[22] inculcated through internationally adopted anthologies, such as Antonio Possevino's (1533–1611) *Biblioteca selecta* (especially the new edition in two volumes, 1607) and Jacobus Pontanus's (1542–1626) *Progymnasmata latinitatis* (1588–94), which enjoyed twenty-two printings through 1752.[23] Dialectic and rhetoric were taught from renowned textbooks, such as *De arte rhetorica* (1569) by the Spaniard Cypriano Suárez or *De eloquentia sacra et humana* (1636) by the Frenchman Nicolas Caussinus. In Germany the Rhenish Jesuit historian and dramatist Jacob Masen (1606–81) covered all aspects of literary didactics, notably in his *Palaestra eloquentiae ligatae* (Guide to Poetry, 1657). Masen keyed much of his theory to his own work, especially his dramas (his theory of drama will be discussed below). He also produced a compendium of new emblems, the *Speculum imaginum veritatis occultae* (Mirror of Hidden Truth, 1650).[24] Emblematics came in many Latin-language collections, including the *Iconologia* (1593) of Cesare Ripa or the *Emblemata* (1565) of the Hungarian physician Johannes Sambucus; Protestants preferred the politically accented *Emblematum ethico-politicorum centuria* (One Hundred Ethical-Political Emblemata, 1619) of Opitz's friend, the Palatine scholar Julius Wilhelm Zincgref (1591–1635).[25] Rhetorical and poetic exercises and model speeches were likewise anthologized in international editions. These massive undertakings sometimes addressed controversial issues as well, such as confessional politics, methods of governing, Platonism versus Aristotelianism, moral rigorism versus pragmatic probabilism, or stylistic debates, especially between proponents of Ciceronian (elegant, balanced) and Lipsian (effective, striking) styles.[26] Using the tradition of commentaries on Aristotle's *Poetics* as a model, Jesuits devised a modern theory of drama embracing martyr plays and political didactic plays within the context of the current reception of Seneca and Tacitus. The opulent Catholic theater, sometimes state-subsidized, as in Bavaria, retained the traditions of the older school drama but modernized them and brought stage technologies up to date. The suspension of the Jesuit Order in 1773 interrupted the tradition of literary Latin and contributed to its final decline.

Forms, Themes, Representatives

The Genre Spectrum of Neo-Latin Lyric and Verse Poetry

Humanist poetics, like the poetics of antiquity, developed no comprehensive genre categories for verse forms. According to classifications of late antiquity, lyric poetry belongs to the *genus commune*, which allows the poet to speak through his own person or through fictitious characters.[27] Biographical material, including intimate and private matters, could be exploited within the broad range of life's reflective and emotional experiences; our modern sensibilities for subjective, lyrical inwardness, must not blind us to the rhetorically distanced and distinctly social character of early modern poetry. Horace and the elegiacists treated lesser lyric poetry mostly as dialogue, a form of social communication having specific addressees, occasions, and situations and calculated to achieve predictable effects within well-defined communicative contexts.[28] The ode, hymn, and dithyramb associated with Horace (after the mid-sixteenth century Pindar and Anacreon became the chief models) constituted the narrower radius of musical, or singable forms. Widespread adaptations of the Psalter since that of Helius Eobanus Hessus (Koch, 1488–1540),[29] as well as devotional poetry (*poemata sacra*), were often understood as musical, or lyrical poetry, sometimes with reference to authorities from Christian late antiquity, such as the fourth-century Christian poet Prudentius.[30] Elegiac verse — written in distichs (hexameter and pentameter) — was ubiquitous. Often interpreted etymologically in relation to funeral hymns and dirges (Greek *eleos* "pity"), the elegy soon acquired the reputation, as Murmellius said, of being suitable for every subject.[31] Special traditions developed of the versified Horatian epistle and of the historical and allegorical figures from Ovid's *Heroides*.[32]

Because of his *Heroidum Christianarum epistolae* (Letters of Christian Heroines, 1514), Hessus is considered the founder of the *heroid* genre in Germany (Luther called him the "rex poetarum," king of poets). He later revised the cycle to meet the demands of the Reformation's biblical rigorism, and thereby modernized, that is, Christianized, an ancient genre: Helen writes to Constantine, Monica to Augustine,[33] Mary to the beloved disciple John, Mary Magdalene to the resurrected Christ. The compelling character of this form, a kind of dramatic portrait, owes to its rhetorical inventiveness and psychological insight.

Another genre, the fictitious verse epistle, which sometimes made explicit references to contemporary history, was extraordinarily popular from the sixteenth through the eighteenth century. The Königsberg professor Georg Sabinus (Schüler, 1508–60)[34] sometimes turned the verse epistle to political exhortation, as when allegorical Germania writes to the emperor. The Jesuits, most notably Jacob Bidermann (1578–1639), censor of the order in Rome, exploited within this genre the entire historical, biblical, and legendary traditions of edification.[35] Bidermann's *Heroum et Heroidum epistolae* (Letters of Heroes and Heroines, 1633–34) were often reprinted and used as textbooks; he rarely touched the erotic elegies of classical Roman authors, of course, given the obscenity taboos. Ovid's erotic poetry was condemned by Christian zealots as lascivious;[36] Luther vilified the *Amorum libri IV* (1542) of Simon Lemnius (Mardagant, 1511–50) as obscene and did what he could to hinder the young Wittenberg poet's career.[37] In spite of clerical opposition, however, the inventory of Catullan themes and forms found many practitioners in Germany, especially Celtis, Locher, and Petrus Lotichius (Lotze) Secundus (1528–60). Catullus's kiss poems as adapted in the *Basia* cycle of the young Flemish poet Johannes Secundus (Everaerts, 1511–36), as well as in the *Rubella seu suavorium Liber* (Rubella, or Book of Pleasures, 1631) by Paul Fleming (1609–40), an early adherent of Opitz, inspired broad resonance.[38]

Stimulated by Romance precedents, especially as practiced by the renowned French poetic society, the Pléiade, erotic poetry in late-sixteenth-century Germany was often fused with Petrarchist motifs.[39] The outstanding example was the widely traveled Palatine counselor and librarian Paul Melissus Schede (1539–1602).[40] Schede's main work, *Schediasmata* (1586), a kind of "who's who" of the European scholarly world, was inspired by the Horatian ode and the richly metaphorical Pindaric ode. It contains poems to Queen

Elizabeth I, the French poet Pierre de Ronsard, the Flemish composer
Orlando di Lasso, and many others. Early baroque Neo-Latinists, such as the
Wittenberg rector Friedrich Taubmann (1565–1613) and his disciple, the
uncommonly prolific polyhistor Caspar von Barth (1587–1658) rejected classicistic moderation in favor of elaborate mannerist techniques or the gesture of
the carefree, nonheroic life championed by the Neo-Anacreontic movement.[41]
Barth's extraordinarily versatile lyric production encompasses historical
prosopopoeia, satires, odes, elegies, iambic verse, and collections of barbed
epigrams, which audaciously combine archaisms with neologisms. His imaginative use of Anacreon differs markedly in style from the older, biographical,
Anacreonticorum odae (Odes of Anacreontic Poets, 1570) of the Catholic
Johannes Aurpach (1531–82).[42]

> In ElysI viretis
> Fui, Neaera, campi.
> . . . .
> Regnum est piorum amantum
> Illic, Neaera; solum.
> Et amabiles Poetae
> Modimperant Choreis
> Anacreonte saltu.[43]

[I was in the Elysian Fields, Neaera. There alone is the kingdom of true
lovers, Neaera. And loving shepherds lead the dancers to the rhythm of
Anacreon.]

Gelegenheitsdichtung (occasional poetry, Latin *casualcarmina*), an immense
poetic category and cultural resource preserved in more than 100,000 individual imprints, comprises the largest corpus of Neo-Latin poetry and represents the nerve center of early modern poetic and scholarly communication.[44]
In the hands of connoisseurs and dilettantes, the famous and the unknown,
occasional poetry celebrates the special moments of life in aesthetically inflated
terms according to conventional rules: wedding (*epithalamion*), death
(*epicedium*),[45] birthday (*genethliacon*), jubilee, academic graduation, book
publication, even the start of a journey (*propemptikon*). Occasional writers (and
that included all writers) served the culture of memory, strengthened categories of values and meanings, and reinforced social consensus as to what was
morally appropriate, from intimate discourse to representational praise (panegyric). Occasional poems reveal much about society and are useful in helping
to define the *caesurae* between social and historical epochs. Enduring examples
are Hessus's memorials to Desiderius Erasmus, Albrecht Dürer, Ulrich von
Hutten, and Willibald Pirckheimer, or the memorial poems by various writers
on the death of Melanchthon.[46] The purpose of ruler or clientele panegyric
(the latter addressed to noble or wealthy benefactors) was not only to cull
patronage but also to remind of the responsibilities that accompany social privilege. The point often has less to do with flattery than with instructing through
praise (*laudando praecipere*). Thus, literature as oration and poem may fulfill

a public function. Many poems dedicated to princes and emperors express fervent imperial patriotism, sometimes written on the occasion of imperial diets, which transcend confessional differences and exhort to freedom and unity, as in the face of perceived Turkish threats.[47]

The eclogue was adopted in Germany in cyclical groupings on the model of Petrarch's *Bucolicum carmen* (Bucolic Poem, 1346–49); the *Eclogae* (1498) of Baptista Mantuanus (Spagnoli)[48] were also widely appreciated by German humanists. The first important German practitioner was Eobanus Hessus (*Bucolicon*, 1509; expanded 1528).[49] Standing in the ancient tradition of the idylls of Theocritus — these were translated into Latin by Hessus as *Bucolicorum idyllia* (Bucolic Idylls) in 1528 — and the *Eclogae* of Vergil, the eclogue was unsurpassed as a vehicle of enciphered events and personal portrayals. Hessus portrays the Erfurt circle of humanists in pastoral clothing;[50] Euricius Cordus (Eberwein, 1486–1535), one of his Erfurt colleagues, portrays in his *Bucolica* (1514) an unusually realistic view of the actual working life and hardships of the peasant, probably as a way of representing the difficulties he personally encountered on his career path from his native Hessia.[51] The bucolic cycles of Joachim Camerarius (Kammermeister, 1500–1574), Lemnius, and Johannes Bocerus (Boedeker, 1526–65)[52] were imitated and emulated in individual pieces or smaller groupings by many other poets, among them Melanchthon's disciple, the poet laureate Johannes Stigelius (Stigel, 1515–62). All employ an allegorical code in the conversations between fictitious shepherds: to comment on contemporary events, such as the Peasants' War (1524–25);[53] to depict current sociocultural conflicts and experiences; to praise or instruct a sovereign;[54] or to memorialize loved ones or famous persons. The goal was ultimately to cultivate a fictional realm for experimentation; to present a masque of pastoral voices responding to specific occasions or conflicts, such as current controversies within Protestant circles.

This occasion-based writing anticipates the advent of the occasional poetry that became ubiquitous in German in the seventeenth century. Christian baroque writers extrapolated a type of pastoral poetry inspired by the allegedly messianic motifs in Vergil's fourth eclogue — "At tibi prima, puer [. . .]" (But for thee, child) — whereby the figure of Christ is projected onto the shepherd Daphnis (Vergil was actually addressing the young emperor Octavian). Some dramatists wrote pastoral nativity plays in Latin. *Carminus, sive Messias in praesepi, Ecloga* (Carminus, or Messiah in a Manger: Eclogue) by Georg Calaminus (Roericht, 1547–95), a Silesian living in Strasbourg, appeared in 1576.[55]

The epigram too, whose great thematic variety was codified by Euricius Cordus in extensive collections, often served as occasional poetry.[56] Traditionally related to satire, the epigram was well suited to criticism of current events or conditions, as demonstrated in Ulrich von Hutten's (1488–1523) *Epistola fictitia* (Fictive Letter, 1516) dedicated to Emperor Maximilian I.[57] Some used it to assail personal enemies, perhaps reducing them to caricatures, as Luther did to Lemnius in trying to have him expelled from the University of Wittenberg.[58] Late in the sixteenth century the epigram became especially pointed, sharp-witted, and marked by brevity — a style called *argute* — as practiced by the Roman epigrammatist Martial and prescribed by the theoretician Julius Caesar Scaliger (1484–1558);[59] sometimes it served simply as a collective term for any short poetry of simpler style. A type of gnomic (moralizing or didactic) poetry, much in evidence in the *Anthologia Graeca* (an epigrammatic collection from the ancient and Byzantine eras, widely known in early modern Europe), the epigram combined easily with other media to create applied forms, such as inscriptions for gravestones. Bidermann's three-volume collection of spiritual epigrams (*Epigrammatum libri tres*, 1620) was reprinted throughout Europe well into the eighteenth century.[60]

By contrast, cycles of verse satire (inspired by Horace, Juvenal, and Persius) were uncommon in Germany. The Latin translation by Jacob Locher (1471–1528) of Sebastian Brant's *Narrenschiff* (1494) as *Stultifera navis* (Ship of Fools, 1497) became a European bestseller.[61] In his *Satyrarum libri quinque* (Five Books of Satires, 1555) Thomas Naogeorgus, or Naogeorg (Kirchmair, 1508/9–1553), known chiefly as a writer of Latin-language Reformation dramas,[62] including *Hieremias* (1551) and *Judas Iscariotes* (1552), occasionally slips into the role of Old Testament prophet to rail against decadent school and church systems or the belligerent confessionalism emanating from Wittenberg.[63] In the seventeenth century the Jesuit Jacob Balde (1604–68), who was the master of almost all textual forms, satirized errors in science, most memorably in his lampooning of medical quacks in *Medicinae gloria per satyras XXII asserta* (The Glory of Medicine, Stated in Twenty-two Satires, 1651).[64] This and an array of traditional topics of satire are the backdrop for Balde's positive opinion of the new anatomy of Vesalius. In *Vesalii anatomici praestantissimi laus: Contra atheos* (Praise of the Distinguished Anatomy of Vesalius: Against the Atheists) Balde derides would-be atheists.

Another kind of panegyric, also based on an Italian model, was the *laus urbis* (praise of city). Early-sixteenth-century German versions include Murmellius's praise of Münster and Busche's celebrations of Cologne and Leipzig. The *laus urbis* was expanded by Hessus in 1532 into an ambitious cycle in hexameters in honor of Nuremberg: *Urbs Noriberga illustrata* (Illustrated City of Nuremberg)[65] consists not only of epic excurses and antiquarian reminiscences but also of detailed descriptions of local landscapes and buildings; it also memorializes the accomplishments of leading urban enterprises, such as the constitution and the orderly administration, defense and welfare, trade, economy and transportation, even the exemplary care of churches and schools. Many German cities were honored in the sixteenth and seventeenth centuries with their own *laudes urbis*. The genre functioned as a key element in the intellectual alliance between urban and scholarly cultures.

The *hodoeporicon* (poetic travelogue) was also practiced by many German writers; uniquely, it had no direct Italian model and evolved beyond mere imitation of Horace or Ovid or the minor poet Rutilus Namatianus (5th c. B.C.).[66] Employing a variety of forms, including the Horatian ode, the elegy, and the hexameter poem, German Neo-Latinists used this genre to invigorate their travel experiences with descriptions of landscapes and cultural phenomena encountered along the way. A favorite topic was the *peregrinatio academica* (academic journey, or Grand Tour) to Italy, as exemplified in the *Hodeoporicon itineris Italici* (Italian Journey, printed 1544) of Sabinus. Remembrances of the birthplaces of humanistic culture overlap confessional and national boundaries. Older medieval commonplaces about national characteristics, as in epic travelogues of Turkey, in which the Turks are portrayed as barbarians, are often overlaid with images from antiquity. *Hodoeporica* sometimes converged with the blossoming genres of landscape description and biography and contributed to the later German poetic discovery of *Heimat* (homeland).

Panegyric verse, which not only praised the addressee but simultaneously related historical events and gave voice to behavioral norms, developed among its many variants an epic verse form, dynastic panegyric, that has only recently become a subject of research. Following the model of Vergil (and certain poets from late antiquity, particularly Claudian Claudianus), Ricardo Bartholini (ca. 1470–1529), having moved from Italy to Germany, presents the genealogy, history, and legacy of the House of Habsburg in *Austriados libri duodecim* (Twelve Books on the Habsburgs, 1516).[67] Habsburg panegyric prevailed throughout the century in a variety of forms, including a rare type of historical epos, in the *Bohemais* and the *Gotiberis* (both 1587) by the Palatine superintendent Pantaleon Candidus (Weiss, 1540–1608).[68]

Territorial epic and epyllion (love narrative) combined elements of history and geography.[69] Contemporary themes and events — the Reformation, elevation to knighthood, the Peasants' War, the Anabaptists — found poetic expression in various forms. Hessus's *In Martinum Lutherum elegarium libellus* (Little Book of Elegies for Martin Luther, 1521) breathes the revolutionary spirit of the Reformation. His elegy "Bellum servile Germaniae" (German Peasants' War), contained in a cycle entitled *De tumultibus horum temporum querela* (Complaint About the Unrest in Our Day, 1528), laments the violent excesses of the peasants and ultimately their threat to the new faith:

> Heu afflicta fides, heu magni prodita Christi
> Religio, quo te deplorem carmine? nullae
> Sufficiunt lachrymae, non si mihi lumina totus
> Irriget Oceanus, fontesque hoc flumine manent
> Perpetui. [. . .] (HL 260, ll. 40–43)

[O, oppressed faith; O betrayed religion of mighty Christ! In what sort of song shall I bewail you? Tears cannot suffice, not even if the entire ocean washed over my eyes and fountains fed it perpetually.]

Euricius Cordus expresses much the same anti-insurgent sentiment in his *Antilutheromastix* (Hostage of the Enemies of Luther, ca. 1525). Cordus condemns Thomas Müntzer (ca. 1489–1525), the radical social theologian and leader in the Peasants' War of 1525, as "hortator scelerum" (instigator of evils) and associates him with the dark powers of the underworld, as described by Vergil and Claudian.[70] About 1540 one Fabricius Bolandus treats the

Anabaptist movement in Münster; the Wittenberg professor of theology Johann Forster (1576–1613) deals with the Schmalkaldic War (1546–47); and the prolific observer Caspar Ens (1569–ca. 1642)[71] writes on the free peasant republic of Dithmarschen (western Holstein) from the perspective of the king of Denmark, Frederick II, to whom it was granted in 1559. *Ludus Martius sive Bellicus* (War Play, or Bellicus, 1526) is an interesting but little-known historical play about the Peasants' War by the otherwise unsung writer Hermannus Schottenius Hessus, a professor in Cologne.[72]

Among the Neo-Latin works by Italian poets of the "golden age" of Pope Leo X, the Vergilian religious epics of the Spanish-Italian poet Jacopo Sannazaro, *De partu virginis* (On the Virgin Birth, 1527), and the Italian poet Marcus Hieronymus Vida, *Christias* (1535), enjoyed fame across Europe, whereas in Germany Neo-Latin biblical epics remained obscure. This field reaches forward to the early Latin works of Andreas Gryphius (1616–64), who wrote two *Herodes* epics and a three-volume epic about the Mount of Olives (*Olivetum libri tres*, 1646).[73] Somewhat earlier, Bidermann had composed in three books an epic on Herod's massacre of the innocents (*Herodiados libri tres*, 1622); before that the Württemberg dramatist Nicodcmus Frischlin (1547–90) had written *Hebraeis* (1599), a grand epic on ancient Israel conceptualized as a Christian counterpart to Vergil's *Aeneid*. The particular attraction of the sixteenth century to biography was realized in various small epics, such as one by Calaminus on the celebrated Strasbourg physician and philologist Johann Winter von Andernach (Vesalius was his most famous pupil). Calaminus lived the last part of his life in Linz and — largely on the merits of his epic drama *Rudolphottocarus* (1594), which reaches deep into the history and native character of Austria — is considered a precursor of the great nineteenth-century Austrian dramatist Franz Grillparzer. His voluminous *oeuvre* shares features with the Neo-Latin literary practices of Bohemia and Upper Austria.[74] Writers from this school included the love poet Christoph von Schallenberg (1561–97).[75]

Didactic epic poetry was practiced less commonly in Germany than in the Romance countries, though no less effectively. Among its well-worked topics, found even in elegies and versified tractates, were nature, dietetics, and praise of the disciplines.[76] From about the last third of the sixteenth century the conflict between academic medicine and Paracelsian reformism often played out in the medium of verse.[77] A productive editor and former student of Melanchthon, Vincentius Opsopoeus (Koch, d. 1539),[78] moved into the area of behavioral instruction with his Ovidian, facetious didactic work *De arte bibendi libri tres* (Three Books on the Art of Drinking, 1536). Friedrich Dedekind (1524–98), a theologian noted principally for his secular writings, achieved extraordinary success with *Grobianus: De morum simpicitate libri duo* (Grobian: Two Books on the Simplicity of Morals, published 1549; numerous translations and more than twenty editions by 1700), which inspired the concept of the "Grobian Age."[79] In the tradition of literature on table manners, Dedekind gives Grobianus (literally "crudeness"), a figure borrowed from Brant's *Narrenschiff*, advice on socially acceptable behavior; but it is inverted so that what is recommended is, ironically, unacceptable behavior.

The social-didactic criticism exploited by Dedekind may also be found among certain fables scattered about Neo-Latin verse and prose.[80]

The full depth of Neo-Latin literature in Germany becomes visible only after the generation of the early humanistic itinerant teachers, namely, in the literary life of the great cities and territories. Around schools and universities, sometimes also with courtly support, literary circles had begun to appear as early as the mid-fifteenth century. At first, their memberships were made up largely of friends and school contacts.[81] Sketches of a few of the most important personalities from this movement follow.

The Franconian peasant's son Conrad Celtis stands as the founder of Neo-Latin literature in Germany and is the pivotal figure of the epochal turn to humanist studies, Germany's "arch-humanist."[82] His *Ars versificandi et carminum* (The Art of Versification and of Poems, 1486) represents a German cultural-historical analogy to the political concept of *translatio imperii* (transfer of empire, i.e., from the Roman Empire to the respective modern one).[83] In the ode "Ad Apollinem," which has been called the "manifesto of German Neo-Latin literature,"[84] he proclaims that the time has come for the god of poetry to give up his seat among the Italians and come to Germany:

> Linque delectos Helicona, Pindum et,
> Ac veni in nostras vocitatus oras
>   Carmine grato.

[Leave your beloved Helicon and Pindus and come to our land invoked by the poetry you love].

His poetic coronation by Emperor Friedrich III in Nuremberg in 1487 — the first German to be so feted[85] — symbolized a turn to an alliance of power and intellect in a national program of rejuvenation to rival the Romance lands. Celtis elevated poetry to a literary philosophy that revealed the thematic universality of the world and established the ground for a campaign against the "foeda barbaries" (repulsive barbarism), as he calls it in his famous *Oratio in gymnasio in Ingelstadio publice recitata* (Public Oration Delivered in the University of Ingolstadt) of 1492.[86]

Journeys to Rome and Kraków intensified his interest in nature and the natural sciences, especially astronomy; in Florence he acquired an intimate knowledge of Neo-Platonism and the culture of the intellectual societies. These credentials helped to open the door to a professorship in Vienna in 1497 following brief stints in Heidelberg (1495) and elsewhere; at the University of Vienna he was appointed director of the new Collegium poetarum et mathematicorum.[87] Wherever Celtis took up residence he organized literati and patrons into *sodalitates* (sodalities) devoted to German cultural and patriotic ideals.[88] His renowned edition of the *Germania* (1498/1500) of the Roman historian Tacitus (ca. A.D. 55–ca. 117) represented, well beyond the sixteenth century, the symbiosis of imperial universalism and a Germanic ideology critical of modern cultural and political failings. It appealed to a national consciousness that took special patriotic pleasure in Germany's geographical wonders.[89]

Influenced by Flavio Biondo's *Italia illustrata* (1482) Celtis planned a comprehensive poetic description of Germany, to be named *Germania illustrata*. He never completed it, but a similarly conceived poem cycle, *Germania generalis*,[90] emerged from his efforts to expand the Tacitus edition and helped to shape his conception of the *Quattuor libri Amorum*. The *Amores* appeared in 1502 in Nuremberg and included a programmatic, allegorical woodcut of Philosophia by Dürer.[91] Employing a strategy of quasi-biographical role-playing, Celtis looks back at his ten years of wandering and symbolizes Germany by the four points of the compass and the landscapes between the Weichsel and the Rhine, the Baltic and the Danube. Eschewing the narrow moralism of the early Christian humanists on the Upper Rhine (Brant and Wimpfeling)[92] and in Rhine-Westphalia (Murmellius), Celtis places in the middle of each book a fictitious love affair: with the Polish Hasilina in the East (Kraków), the Regensburger Elsula in the South, the Rhenish Ursula in the West, and the Lübecker Barbara in the North. He celebrates Eros, the world-ordering principle of Neo-Platonism,[93] as omnipresent and omnipotent, and weaves exotic descriptions into the fabric of the travelogue throughout: a journey to Thule in the extreme north, a descent into the Polish salt mines, a dangerous hunt for bison. Celtis is as much philosopher as poet. The grace and intellectual order of the poetic symbol-world reflect the inner law of the life force manifested in all phenomena and confirm the place of man as knowing being in the cosmos. He adapts the love elegy of antiquity to assert an independent literary claim for the processing of tensions between philosophical reflection, erotic metaphysics, and historical discontent. Aggressive satire, even obscenity, and always the Tacitean ideal of Germanic *simplicitas* transform the criticism of German decadence into an anti-Italian and anticlerical polemic, culminating in the elegy to his southern lover "Ad Elsulam," which expresses the hope of a blessed reign for Emperor Maximilian I. A closing elegy to German youth appeals to the historical dignity of the German *poeta vates* (poetic bards), who will live forever among the great poets of antiquity. Much as Hessus is concerned in his renowned Ovidian elegy "Ad Posteritatem," which concludes his *Heroides*, with how he will be remembered by posterity, Celtis's closing elegy is driven by an intensely personal consciousness of achievement.[94]

A collection of Celtis's odes and epodes, published posthumously in Strasbourg in 1513, initiated a period of Horatian imitations by German poets that lasted through the Jesuit practice of the seventeenth century.[95] The collection itself is modeled on Roman precedent in its inventory of themes and its dialogical form; Celtis takes pains to invent a modern version of each of the ancient strophic forms. Philosophical meditations on life, justifications for the new learning, poetic inquiries into the *causae latentes* of the cosmos — all of these themes unfold either as poetic conversations with the various addressees or as homage to celebrated personalities, such as the distinguished Hebraicist and dramatist Johannes Reuchlin (1455–1522). Celtis's sense of patriotic mission, delivered with particular fervor in the final poem of the epodes, "Ad poetas Germanos," regularly accompanies the eroticism of the *Amores*. His reminiscence "De nocte et osculo Hasilinae" (On the Night and Hasilina's

Kiss)[96] is graphic but not voyeuristic, expressing unapologetically the pleasure of indulging the psycho-physical appetites of human nature. His uncensored use of mythology provoked conservative contemporaries, who declared eight of his odes to heathen gods, despite their allegorization, to be unacceptably offensive.

Celtis died before the Reformation began. Other authors, especially Hutten, tried to galvanize the tentative alliance between humanist and theological reformers. Luther was celebrated early on in an entirely undogmatic fashion, most notably in Hessus's elegies.

Like the epigrammatist Cordus, Hessus belonged to an elite group around the Gotha canon Conrad Mutianus Rufus (Muth, 1470–1526), an association that blossomed into a prolific and elegant correspondence. The cult of the Muses and an ancient lifestyle (the ideal of *beata tranquillitas*) were of far greater interest to the humanists than theological controversies. Still, Neo-Latin poetry provided a way to express the personal problems in the daily life of a scholar. For example, the elegy of Jacob Micyllus (1503–58) on the death of his wife in 1548 is a gripping account of physical suffering; and many other of his descriptions, such as his journey from Wittenberg to Frankfurt via Erfurt in 1526, or the burning of Heidelberg Castle in 1527, exemplify a realistic type of literature in verse.[97]

Contemporaries of Petrus Lotichius Secundus, a devoted disciple of Micyllus,[98] saw in his work the pinnacle of post-Reformation humanistic poetry. If *Erlebnisdichtung*, the poetry of experience,[99] can be said to have existed prior to the eighteenth century, then surely — within the poetological boundaries of imitation, of course — it is exemplified in the life and work of Lotichius. Lotichius was born in the Hessian town of Schlüchtern in 1528 and died as a professor of medicine in Heidelberg in 1560.[100] As Celtis had in the *Amores*, Lotichius placed his own life in the center of his first three books of *Elegiae* (1551, 1553, 1556). The first book is full of complaints about the Schmalkaldic War, which Lotichius experienced firsthand. Some of his poems belong to a lyrical genre known as *de se aegrotante* (on sickness).[101] Originating with Tibullus and Ovid, this genre was widely practiced in Europe and is extraordinarily useful to cultural historians for how it conveys subtle shifts in anthropological discourse. In one addressed to Micyllus, Lotichius bemoans having been deprived of his studies for the life of a soldier:

> Nobis nulla quies, nec cum se condit in vndas,
> Nec cum Sol versis mane recurrit equis.
> Quam miserum est rigido cum milite ducere vitam,
> Qui putat armata cuncta licere manu?

[We know no peace, neither when the sun hides itself in the waves, nor when it returns with its redirected horses in the morning. How miserable it is to lead a common life with the hard soldier, who thinks that everything is for the taking by an armored hand.]

Another Lotichius poem of this type, on the siege of Magdeburg (1550–51), was quoted on many memorial occasions well into the seventeenth century.

Lotichius's longing for peace and his loyalty to his poetic calling, even in time of war, show how determined he was to live above the vagaries of mundane politics. In one particularly moving poem Lotichius describes the rescue of two soldiers from captivity, after which they and an imperial officer share a common memory of the great Italian poet Sannazaro. Lotichius never tires of expressing his personal gratitude for the inspiration of Italian humanistic poetry. The second and third books of the *Elegiae* are dominated by experiences related to his studies in southern France (Montpellier, Avignon, Toulouse) and in Italy (Padua, Venice). His visualization of the rich southern landscape stands in contrast to the stark images of his homeland. Erotic encounters, to which he gives subtle psychological nuances, betray the influence of the Roman love elegy.

Lotichius is also noted as a talented writer of poems of friendship and mourning. His memorial to a dolphin, "Ad deos maris in funere delphini" (To the God of the Sea on the Death of a Dolphin), is a highly stylized poem comparable to the work of Sabinus or Stigelius.[102]

Within Lotichius's narrower circle of friends in the Palatinate the physician Johannes Posthius (1537–99) produced a large corpus of lyrical works based on his international travels.[103] Sabinus and Stigelius represent the Latin poetic practice in Wittenberg, associated most closely with the humanism of Melanchthon, a tradition that lasted into the seventeenth century. Stigelius and Johannes Major (1533–1600),[104] among others, were involved in the dogmatic controversies within Protestantism that arose in the mid-1550s; Major is particularly associated with the controversy over good works and justification. The death of Melanchthon affected the literary world deeply and stimulated, among other things, a great interest in spiritual poetry. Deserving special mention in this regard are Georg Fabricius (1516–71)[105] and Adam Siber (1516–84), both headmasters; the Rostock professor Nathan Chytraeus (1543–98); the Leipzig physician and rector Andreas Ellinger (1526–82); and the Zerbst philologist Gregor Bersmann (1538–1611), a Calvinist. Their topics range from the simple to the elevated, from devotional prayers to the triumph of Christ. Bible paraphrases abound, as do Protestant reworkings of traditional Christian hymns, such as the "Veni redemptor gentium."[106] Reliance on ancient models, as in the Horatian poetry of Fabricius, brought about a kind of Christian parody and led in extreme cases to the Christianization of entire corpora of ancient poetry — hence such titles as *Horatus christianus, Catullus christianus, Martialis christianus.*

The poetic innovations of fin-de-siècle humanism were inspired by two stirring events at midcentury: the publication in 1554 by the French scholar and printer Henri Estienne (1528–98) of the *Anacreonta*, a collection of sixty odes ascribed incorrectly to the ancient Greek poet Anacreon — now known as (Pseudo-) Anacreon; and his publication in 1560 of fragments of Sapphic odes, *Carminum poetarum novem.* The rediscovery of the formal possibilities of the low and high styles motivated countless adaptations and imitations, especially by the poet-philologists of the French Pléiade and the Dutch Neo-Latinists. German late humanists fell entirely under their spell. The

Anacreontic lyric — set in a playfully erotic Elysium of aesthetic grace remote from the realm of virtuous society — was especially cultivated by the Wittenberg school. Taubmann and Barth wrote with sovereign disregard for the pedantic classicism of school humanism, blasting away at the conventions that regulated the formal repertoire. Their work and that of the greatest German poet of the time, Paul Melissus Schede, discussed above, anticipated the poetic styles of the Baroque. Schede's Protestant-themed works represent the last great German national poetry in Latin. Schede's wide travels brought him into intimate contact with the poets of the Pléiade, with whom he compared his work, and he insisted that he was the equal of his three renowned German predecessors: Celtis, Hutten, and Lotichius. To his contemporaries he was indeed the *poeta princeps*. Elisabeth I of England held him in the same high esteem.

After Schede and Barth the best Latin poetry in the Protestant regions was that of Opitz's friend during his early Heidelberg years Balthasar Venator (1594–1664), the Regensburg scholar Johannes Prasch (1637–90), the Tübingen professor for poetics Christoph Kaldenbach (1613–98), and the Halle professor of philosophy Christian Adolph Klotz (1738–71).[107] General readers, however, were increasingly drawn to poetry in the vernacular over Latin. Despite this trend, a surprising number of Latin translations of vernacular works from the eighteenth century appeared (for example, Pope and Klopstock), as well as many anthologies of recent poetry in Latin by German poets, such as the two-volume *Recentiora Poetarum Germanorum Carmina Latina Selectiora* (1751).

Theory and practice in Jesuit literature had a different character. The work of the Alsatian Jacob Balde, who held various important offices in Bavaria (Munich, Neuburg an der Donau), enjoyed Europe-wide success that crossed confessional boundaries.[108] After having fallen into obscurity he was rediscovered in the mid-eighteenth century by Herder, who proclaimed him an extraordinary German patriot and poet with incomparable skills as a critical observer of the Thirty Years' War.[109] Balde's main works, often reprinted, are the *Lyricorum libri iv, Epodon liber unus* (Four Books of Odes, One Book of Epodes, 1643; corrected and enlarged, 1645) and the *Sylvarum libri VII* (Seven Books of *Sylvae*, 1643; expanded to nine books, 1646). Influenced by the work of the Polish monk Mathias Casimir Sarbiewski (1595–1640), these poems, along with his satires, also betray their debt to Horace, who was himself the "poeta Proteus."[110] Balde himself was widely known as "der deutsche Horaz." Paradoxical conjunctions of contemporaneity and antiquity, Christian faith and pagan-modernist *ratio vivendi*, asceticism and zest for life, epicurism and *vanitas*, utopia and *melancholia* are dealt with, especially in Balde's odes, with linguistic and intellectual daring; many conservative critics and censors felt threatened by their ironies and paradoxes. Balde emulated ancient poets as a spur to his own imagination: "Q. Horatium Flaccum imitari se nonnumquam non imitando" (To imitate Horace Flaccus means sometimes not to imitate), he remarks in *Sylva* 5. Balde's imaginative, concettist, combinations aim to achieve a "modern" liberation; the poet, he avows, is "nauta sui" (his own captain).

His stunningly original treatise *De studio poetico* (1658), which challenged writers to mine their powers of creativity, shook school humanism to the core.[111] Didactic, edifying, and panegyric goals are secondary to Balde, who considered himself a linguistic and conceptual artist, even when he gave the appearance of being merely the good monk at work on his pious and esoteric Marian poetry.[112] He had gained much more than knowledge of poetic forms from Horace: above all, he discovered how to assert the poetic self in times of political crisis. Thus, in Balde's Horatian poems the Roman civil war becomes the foil for the Thirty Years' War; on another occasion (*Sylvae*, book 3) the Tacitean patriotism of Celtis paves the way for a satirical criticism of modern decadence.[113] Criticism of current events, often interlaced with asceticism and an awareness of modern science and the fine arts,[114] is especially typical of his later work; mangled and reduced by church censors, it has been transmitted in only a single volume, *Urania Victrix* (Urania the Victor, 1663), a wreath of elegies structured as a fictitious correspondence.[115] This conscious variation on Ovid, combined with components of the Jesuit *heroides*, reflects the struggle between human sensuality and heaven-directed piety; but at a more profound level it presents a panorama of modern worldliness, against which the voice of piety can only struggle to compete.

German Jesuit poetry has been generally neglected by scholars. Certainly the works of the great poets Pontano and Bidermann deserve much more attention. But so do many other Jesuit works as well, including allegorical cycles of elegies like the *Deliciae Veris* (Joys of Spring, 1638) and the *Deliciae Aestatis* (Joys of Summer, 1644) of the Bavarian historian Johannes Bisselius (Bissel, 1601–82), which intersperses historical and spiritual excurses among verses dedicated to spring and summer;[116] or subsequent collections like *Poesis lyrica* (1659) of the Austrian Nicolaus von Avancini (1611–86; he was also a dramatist), or the *Lyricorum libri III* (Three Books of Odes, 1674) of the little-known Adam Widl (1639–1710), who acknowledges his indebtedness to Balde.[117] Of less historical importance was the literature of the Benedictines. Only Simon Rettenpacher (1634–1706), a dramatist, epigrammatist, and satirist wrote at a comparable level of sophistication.[118]

Neo-Latin Drama[119]

The Italian rediscovery of the comedies of Plautus and Terence and the tragedies of Seneca sparked the revival of drama in Renaissance Europe. Since Plautus often provoked ethical controversy, German Neo-Latinists turned primarily to the plays of Terence, which they disseminated in editions and commentaries; Melanchthon recommended the comedies in various of his prologue poems. Terence adapted readily to social and pedagogical purposes. His family stories, full of memorable character types, corresponded more closely to the urban world of the public than did Seneca's court dramas with their high pathos.[120] The new political issues that arose in the German territories toward the end of the sixteenth century, however, motivated the turn to tragedy and the political play, and thus to Seneca as leading authority. Practitioners largely ignored the formal division between tragedy and comedy found in Aristotle and created hybrid forms that survived through the later Jesuit theater. School drama continued to dominate both Protestant and Catholic stages. Until the advent of the great tragedies of the late seventeenth century, therefore, most of the personnel — actors, playwrights, directors — were neither professionals nor lay performers but students and teachers. Latin academic theater depended largely on translations and thrived particularly in cities with an active theater culture, such as Strasbourg and Augsburg, but also at court residences, such as Munich and Tübingen. Composition and staging of dramatic texts were integrated into the academic curriculum; performances represented the high point of festivities in the presence of local worthies. Student actors had to learn not only a cultivated workaday Latin but also control of body language and the value of societal norms, all of which enhanced their awareness of the roles they would eventually assume as the social elite. Whereas the commentaries of Aristotle were widely read in Italy, the Germans looked primarily to Cicero, as transmitted by Donatus, for an understanding of comedy: "Comoediam esse imitationem vitae; speculum consuetudinis, imaginem veritatis" (Comedy is the imitation of life, the mirror of life's customs, and the image of the truth).[121]

Early attempts by Heinrich Bebel in Tübingen,[122] Jacob Wimpfeling in Heidelberg (*Stylpho*, performed 1480, printed 1494),[123] Johannes Kerckmeister in Münster (*Codrus*, 1485),[124] and Johannes Reuchlin in Heidelberg (*Henno*, 1497),[125] represented the demands and opportunities of the humanistic new learning by staging conflicts between serious and lazy students and academics.[126] Reuchlin's *Henno* imitates the characters of *commedia dell'arte* — an improvisational style with colorful comic scenes based on stock situations, such as adultery, old age, theft. The new dramaturgy of the humanistic stage is operative here: five acts, prologue, chorus, and versification. The two-dimensional *Simultanbühne* (simultaneous stage) and the linear *Stationendrama* (station play) inherited from medieval biblical and mystery plays passed through a transitional *Reliefbühne* (relief stage) on the way to acquiring a complex form featuring scenically organized plot development and a structure of suspense. Morally and psychologically contoured figures, and heroes in real social contexts and conflicts, began to emerge. While religious folk plays continued to be staged here and there in Catholic regions, the illusionist *Raumbühne* (spatial stage), with its sequential scenes, eventually dominated, culminating at last in the Jesuits' opera-like productions that involved sophisticated use of stage machines.[127] Within the ambit of the imperial court and influenced by the Italians, a number of patriotic festival plays appeared, including *Ludus Dianae* (The Play of Diana, 1501) by Celtis in Nuremberg and *Tragoedia de Turcis* (Tragedy of the Turks, 1498) by Locher in Strasbourg. The abbot of the Vienna Scottish Cloister, Benedictus Chelidonius (Benedikt Schwalbe, ca. 1460–1521), who had also been a member of Dürer's circle in Nuremberg, takes on the struggle between sin and virtue in his allegorical drama *Voluptatis cum Virtute disceptatio* (The Contest between Pleasure and Virtue, 1515).[128]

Two Dutch writers, Guilielmus Gnapheus and Georg Macropedius, drew directly from the forms and language of Roman comedies to bring seminal reformational issues to the stage. Gnapheus (Willem van de Voldersgraft, 1492–1568),[129] who served a lengthy term as headmaster in Elbing and Königsberg, influenced — as a kind of *Terentius christianus* — many later *Prodigus* (Prodigal Son) dramas with his *Acolastus sive de filio prodigo* (Acolastus, or the Prodigal Son). First published in Antwerp in 1529, *Acolastus* went through some forty editions and numerous translations in the sixteenth century. In the *Prodigus* dramas a life of sin (disobedience, sloth, self-indulgence, sexuality, card playing) is contrasted with an exemplary life (piety, patriarchal work ethic) in realistic, colorful scenes (tavern, pig sty, brothel) involving moralistic character types (parasites, dandies, courtesans). Gnapheus also influenced a type of milieu play that depicts student life. One prominent example was *Studentes: Comoedia de vita studiosorum* (Students: A Comedy from the Life of Students, 1549) by the Lutheran theologian Christophorus Stymmelius (Stummel, 1525–88).[130] Macropedius (Joris van Lanckvelt, 1487–1558) wrote farcical school and Bible dramas. His Everyman play *Hecastus* premiered in Utrecht in 1538 (printed in Cologne, 1539); among its translations is one by Hans Sachs. *Hecastus* drew the ire of Macropedius's fellow orthodox Catholics with its emphasis on the themes of repentance and belief, which they associated with Protestantism.[131]

Luther had given his enthusiastic sanction for writing plays based on Bible stories as a way of spreading the gospel and teaching evangelical moral and social values. Encouraged by his support, writers of biblical plays transformed the stage into a moral institution concerned not least with problems of social discipline. The socially didactic theater of the sixteenth century was populated everywhere with biblical figures (Esther, Joseph, Judith, Tobias, Lazarus). Newer research, especially on the *Joseph* drama, has followed the lines of reception of didactic theater — its impact, interpretative tendencies, dramaturgical conceptions — deep into Jesuit terrain.[132] Sixtus Birck (1501–54), a headmaster in Basel and Augsburg, was a prodigious writer of biblical dramas. His two *Susanna* plays, one in German (1532), one in Latin (1537), made the story of Susanna one of the most popular socially critical dramatic topics of sixteenth-century school theater: a virtuous wife resists sexual seduction by men who misuse the power of their authority.[133] Naogeorg brought Protestant drama to its high point.[134] An early zealous adherent of Luther, he later fell out with him and was accused by Wittenberg dogmatists of being a follower of Luther's hated Swiss opponent, the reformer Huldrych Zwingli (1484–1531). Naogeorg was familiar with Aristophanes, translated the works of Sophocles into Latin verse,[135] and created a militant style through a symbiosis of the older forms of world theater and the passion play. In *Pammachius* (1538; numerous German translations) he depicts the antichrist from a Protestant perspective and conceptualizes the struggle for the true faith as a force driving world history. *Mercator seu Iudicium* (The Merchant, or the Judgment, 1540), a Reformation comedy in the spirit of the comedic dramatist Aristophanes, takes aim at the Catholic doctrine of good works. The Everyman theme is adapted here into the story of a tradesman who finds no surcease through good works from his burden of conscience; he is at last freed — by vomiting and nose-blowing — from his former enslavement to pilgrimages, almsgiving, fasting, and absolutions.

National and confessional motifs overlap in the epic, lyric, and dramatic works of Nicodemus Frischlin (mentioned above as author of the biblical epic *Hebraeis*). His teaching and writing in Tübingen often brought him into conflict with the university; on at least one occasion, a socially critical oration in 1580 on the virtues of the simple rural life in Vergil, he provoked the ire of the local nobility as well.[136] With the occasional backing of the Württemberg court in Stuttgart and the assistance of his brother Jacob, who translated several of his works into German, Frischlin distinguished himself as the most significant dramatist of the later sixteenth century.[137] His *Rebecca* (1576) and *Susanna* (1578)[138] stand in the tradition of Bible drama; *Hildegardis Magna* (performed in 1579) borrows a story from the Age of Charlemagne to give instruction to marriage partners, including rulers and their consorts.[139] *Priscianus vapulans* (The Beaten Priscian, published posthumously in 1592) was first performed in 1578 at the centennial celebration of the University of Tübingen.[140] Priscian represents the humanist program of studies. In a burlesque staging with borrowings from Aristophanes (translated by Frischlin into Latin), the dramatist puts himself into the action as a grammarian harassed by academic barbarians in the higher faculties. He enlists the collaboration of Erasmus and Melanchthon to defeat his opponents. The comedy *Julius redivivus* (Julius Brought Back to Life, 1585),[141] an extraordinary historico-cultural statement in context of the rising *Querelle des anciens et des modernes*, seeks to reassure his contemporaries about the progress of German civilization. Inspired by Lucian and Hutten, Frischlin brings the Germanic hero Arminius to the stage; leads Caesar and Cicero from the netherworld into the light of flourishing German cities, where they marvel over the new German inventions of gun powder, artillery, and the printing press; and has Eobanus Hessus introduce Cicero to eminent German poets and scholars, thus dispelling once and for all the odium of German barbarism.

As a playwright, Frischlin deals with confessional struggles only in *Phasma* (The Vision, published posthumously in 1592), first performed in 1580 on the fiftieth anniversary of the *Confessio Augustana*.[142] Writing in the sensitive ecclesiopolitical context of the adoption of orthodox Lutheran articles of faith, Frischlin stages his opinions in typically heavy-handed fashion. Wrapped in a heroic aura, his Luther dispatches all of his major opponents: Zwingli, the papal legate Tommaso Campeggio, and two of the radical reformers, the Wittenberg iconoclast (destroyer of church art) Andreas Karlstadt and, according to Luther, the crypto-Anabaptist Kaspar von Schwenkfeld. The play's vitality owes mainly to the vigorous disputation scenes, but elements of the world-judgment play also enliven it. The devil, instigator of dissention within Protestant ranks, drags the sectarians into hell and inspires the Catholic Council of Trent. In various episodes, especially in the conversations among peasants, Frischlin casts light on the destructive effects of confessional and political fighting on common people. In an adaptation of Vergil's first eclogue, the peasant woman Thestylis reports that her husband Meliboeus has joined the Anabaptists and hopes to emigrate to Moravia. Frischlin's orthodox opponents accused him of Calvinist tendencies and prevented the play's publication until after his death. Frischlin spent the last years of his life in prison for having delivered a speech too critical of the feudal aristocracy. Attempting to escape from the cliffs of the mountain stronghold Hohenurach, he fell to his death. Liberal poets and scholars of the eighteenth and nineteenth centuries celebrated the memory of this critical intellectual. The Storm and Stress poet Friedrich Daniel Schubart (1739–91) wrote of Frischlin: "Als Römer schriebst du; aber deine Seele / Voll Vaterland, liebt Deutschen Biederton" (You wrote as a Roman; but your soul, full of Fatherland, loves German simplicity).

Latin school theater, which was adapted only haltingly into German, was practiced as late as the eighteenth century in some Protestant regions. Most of Frischlin's works were published in Strasbourg. It was there that the renowned educator Johann Sturm (1507–89), with the encouragement of the magistrate, founded an academic Gymnasium that became the leading center for late humanist school theater. Between 1583 and 1621 at least twenty-five dramas by contemporary German and foreign authors, as well as Seneca and Sophocles, were staged in the Strasbourg Gymnasium.[143] The local audience was familiar not only with the *Poetics* of Aristotle but modern theorists as well, Scaliger above all, and was appreciative of the new works by Daniel Heinsius (1580–1655) and other Dutch dramatists.[144] Strasbourg playwrights wrote with this audience in mind and provided suitable stage effects. Some ventured to adapt classical models of state's politics: they included a *Julius Cäsar*, a *Chariklia* (based on Heliodorus's *Aithiopika*), and a *Moyses*, all by the local professor of poetry Caspar Brülow (1528–1627). Brülow's successor Johann Paul Crusius (1588–1629), wrote an eponymous *Croesus* (1611) about the Lydian king whom Herodotus had pronounced an example of overweening pride.[145] Dramaturgically concentrated word dramas with small casts were exceptions to the general rule of early baroque classicism. Among these were the so-called "tragedies" (printed after 1608) of the Altdorf professor Michael Virdung (1575–1637) and, especially, the dramatic works of Theodor Rhodius (1575–1625),[146] a preacher living in the Palatinate. Rhodius's historical drama *Colignius* — printed in Oppenheim in 1614 and not performed in Lutheran Strasbourg — concerns the horrors of the St. Bartholomew's Day Massacre of 1572. It was influenced by Heinsius's *Auriacus sive libertas saucia* (Auriacus [Orange], or Wounded Liberty, 1602), which dealt with the murder of William of Orange. Rhodius contemporizes the provocative story of the Huguenot leader Coligny by dedicating it to the Calvinist elector, Friedrich V of the Palatinate.

After 1621 school drama receded in Strasbourg. It enjoyed a final flourishing in Württemberg in the work of the Tübingen professor Hermann Flayder (1596–1640),[147] who treated material from German sagas in *Imma portatrix* (Imma the Bearer, 1625), *Ludovicus bigamus* (Ludwig the Twice-married, 1625), and *Moria rediviva* (The Fool Brought Back to Life, 1627), which reprises the obsolescent motif of the fool in humanist satire. Formally and thematically significant plays were rare. One of the better examples is

Turbo (1616) by the Lutheran theologian Johann Valentin Andreae (1586–1654), a burlesque about the student Turbo whose doubts about the world and the sciences motivate his journey to France in search of firsthand knowledge.[148]

Jesuit theater in Germany, which included many plays by foreign authors, was fueled for more than 200 years by massive, opera-like productions, mainly in Latin. Some 120–150 dramas per year over a span of many decades are estimated to have been performed in the schools of German-speaking territories. Although the Jesuits continued to write in Latin, their plays had wide influence, owing to the universality of Catholic culture, the educational mission of the order, and the sacred reputation and expressivity of the language itself. To assist non-Latin-speaking audiences, plot lines were sketched and information about the sources and the cast was provided in dual-language programs called *Periochen*.[149] At folk festivals lavish accoutrements and allegorical, or emblematic, figures helped to orient and involve the audience. The authoritative handbooks by J.-M. Valentin[150] and the monumental commentary edition by Elida Maria Szarota[151] of some 600 *Periochen* between 1597 and 1765 give an impression of the scope of the dissemination, thematic depths, conceptual complexities, and general vitality of Jesuit drama and theater life. Almost every Gymnasium had a resident *pater comicus*, who wrote original plays or adapted those of others. Few of these plays were ever printed — mainly those of Bidermann, Masen, Avancini, Jacob Gretser, and, later, Franciscus Lang (1654–1725) — and then sometimes only fragmentarily as examples within poetological discussions.[152] Most, including Catholic versions of the Faust material, such as the *Theophilus* dramas (1621–22) by Georg Bernardt (1595–1660), have remained in manuscript form in various archives. The plays generally served only the religious schools and were performed at academic festivals by students for audiences of students. The Jesuits did, however, participate actively in spectacular political and courtly productions in hopes of reaching the wider public. *Triumphus Divi Michaelis Archangeli* (Triumph of St. Michael the Archangel) was first performed in 1597 on the occasion of the consecration of St. Michael's Church in Munich; the Viennese *Ludi Caesarei* (Caesar Plays) by Avancini were performed before the emperor.[153] To advance the political interests of the church, exemplary Christian rulers, such as Emperor Constantine, were often made the central characters.

In its essential qualities, Jesuit school drama conformed to the older repertoire (Macropedius, biblical dramas). But it also promoted the causes of the Counter-Reformation as a representation of Catholic piety (veneration of Mary and the saints, repetition of the catechism).[154] It also offered a Catholic version of world theater by drawing on ancient legendary traditions in addition to occidental sacred and profane history and by providing graphic models demonstrating how to master worldly conflicts and ultimately to achieve salvation.[155] The multimedia theater grew out of this mix of tragedy and comedy in a decidedly non-Aristotelian manner.[156] Great political events involving the dynamics of sin, repentance, and conversion, exemplified in the rise and fall of powerful figures or antinomic martyrs and tyrants (Thomas More, Mary

Stuart), are examined in disputation scenes and reinforced by the prototypically modern gesture of illustration and instruction. Target audiences were mainly the governing aristocratic elites and the educated bourgeoisie, whose sons, as student actors, rehearsed their later responsibilities in dramatic roles. Classicistic limitations were introduced only later (division of comedy and tragedy; observance of the unities of place, time, and action). Indeed, it was Jesuit theoreticians, such as Masen, who returned to the Aristotelian theory of drama, including the idea of catharsis. They tailored it, according to modern theories of the human emotions, to a new kind of drama that interpreted truths not only historically but also allegorically and spiritually and elevated the saint to poetic hero.

Among the few Jesuit dramas translated for contemporary audiences was Bidermann's *Cenodoxus*. Written in Latin in 1602, it was translated into German in 1635 by Joachim Meichel (1590–1637), privy secretary to the Bavarian elector.[157] Bidermann had achieved success as a playwright in Augsburg, Munich, and Dillingen and would repeat his success in Rome after 1619. Borrowing episodes from burlesque comedy and introducing the legend of Bruno, a pious Carthusian monk, *Cenodoxus* caused an immediate spiritual stir: one lead actor left to join the Jesuit Order, and several noblemen, in imitation of Bruno, submitted to Ignatian discipline.[158] Bidermann stages a contrast between the two most powerful but latent tensions of the age, as the Jesuits perceived them: true Christian humility and religious indifference, the latter allegedly full of humanistic self-righteousness and fadish Neo-Stoicism.[159] The guardian angel of the great Parisian scholar Cenodoxus (Greek *ceno* "empty" + *doxus* "learning") tries in vain to make the doctor see his hypocrisy. In Meichel's German translation:

> Dem Menschen kan man zwar vorliegen /
> Gott aber läst sich nit betriegen.
> Sih / wie offt steht die Hoffart da?
> Superbia, Superbia:
> . . . .
> Sichstus wol? (Act 3, sc. 2, ll. 85–93)

[One can of course deceive man, but God cannot be deceived. Behold! How often do we find Pride before us? Pride, pride: Do you not see it?]

Bidermann spares no dramatic technique, from allegorical personification of Vice and Conscience to the staging of heaven and hell, for the sake of expanding the Bruno legend both anthropologically as world theater and metaphysically as cosmic drama as well. Among his other dramatic works (including a *Belisar* and a *Joseph*), the comedy *Philemon Martyr* (after 1602), which stages the transformation of a hedonistic comedian into a pious martyr, enjoyed special success.

Jacob Gretser (1562–1625), a Graecist and theologian in Ingolstadt, was well known for his three-volume *Regnum humanitatis* (Kingdom of Humanity, 1587–90), which defended the foundations of Jesuit humanism. A prolific writer, Gretser's printed works number well over 200; the *Opera omnia* in seventeen volumes appeared in Regensburg only much later (1734–41).[160] He also wrote cautionary dramas on the theme of conversion, using the experiences of St. Paul and St. Augustine as illustrations.[161] Gretser's play *Udo* (1587), about the Magdeburg archbishop of that name who ends up in hell, warns against the seductions of courtly life. Jesuit theater repeatedly assumed the function of a *Fürstenspiegel* (mirror of princes), focusing on justice while being careful not to criticize monarchy.

Jacob Masen's *Rusticus imperans* (The Shepherd King, printed after 1657 as an appendix to his *Palaestra eloquentiae ligatae*, mentioned above) is a dramatization of the older tradition of the peasant as king for a day. In the form of a play within a play and against a burlesque background, it warns of the dangerous ambitions and emotions of mere subjects.[162]

The great authors of baroque tragedy, such as Andreas Gryphius and Daniel Caspar von Lohenstein (1635–83), acquired many of their techniques from the Latin dramas of Jesuit practitioners.[163] Late Jesuit drama, which extended into the eighteenth century, assimilated the dominate themes of the age, including the new patriotism. Jesuit dramatists turned increasingly to the vernacular and showed a preference for the more popular forms, especially *Singspiel*, a small comic opera in German with spoken dialogue. The enlightened revision of the Christian worldview, Lessing's criticism of martyr drama and the concept of pity, and the middle-class appropriation of Neo-Aristotelianism all contributed to the gradual diminution of Jesuit influence. Certain late plays reflect a culture on the wane, at a time when the Jesuits themselves were becoming a historical theme.[164]

A Sketch of Neo-Latin Writings in Prose[165]

The voluminous repertoire of early modern Latin prose consists largely of academic qualifying papers (dissertations, declamations), textbooks, commentaries based on university lectures, and pedagogical writings. As noted above, much of Melanchthon's literary reputation rests on his massive output of just such small genres. The dissemination of knowledge through prose was complemented by a literature of tracts and speeches on current issues, some of which turned out to be of epochal significance. One such work was Opitz's *Aristarchus sive de contemptu linguae Teutonicae* (Aristarchus or, On the Contempt for the German Language, 1617), which he first delivered as a school oration.[166] One of the major controversies in the period of Late Humanism had been raised in Erasmus's attack a century before, in his *Ciceronianus* of 1528, on the widespread slavish imitation of Ciceronian style;[167] it concerned questions related to the new stylistic canon and continued to be debated deep into the seventeenth century. Erasmus challenged the assumption that a purist, classicistic model, Ciceronianism, could adapt to the changes occurring in social conditions and tastes. Another controversy concerned the legitimacy of the stylistic plurality that arose toward the end of the sixteenth century; still another had to do with the assimilation of pagan authors of the imperial era and late antiquity, inspired by a new appreciation for idiomatic archaism, neologism, laconism, and *argute* mannerism. Others concerned suitable subject matter, the role of the author in society, or the position of literature within philosophical and scientific discourse. It is worth repeating that all of these controversies could be possible only within a tradition of writing in which Latin was still alive.

The European republic of letters was held together by intensive personal correspondence in Latin. Sometimes authors collected their own letters, sometimes those of others, usually intending to have them printed or at least to preserve them in private archives. The letter was a prose art form, its rules codified in rhetorical manuals. It applied a private conversational style to treatise-like discussions involving critical observations and commentaries on intellectual life.[168] The great epistolary collection of the Greifswald Germanist Alexander Reifferscheid, *Briefe G. M. Lingelsheims, M. Berneggers und ihrer Freunde* (1889),[169] which helped to establish Late Humanism as a discrete epoch for scholarship, represents a continuation of the tradition of letter writing that began in the earlier sixteenth century with Erasmus, Celtis, Conrad Peutinger, Beatus Rhenanus, Mutianus Rufus, Johannes Cuspinian, and many others. Several older and newer collections of correspondence are indispensable to the scholarship of Late Humanism.[170]

It hardly needs mentioning that the writings of the early modern scientists were written in Latin. Among the most influential were Georg Agricola's (1494–1555) *De re metallica* (On Metallurgy, 1530), Nicolaus Copernicus's (1473–1543) *De revolutionibus orbium coelestium* (On the Orbits of the Heavenly Bodies, 1543), and Johann Kepler's (1571–1630) *Mysterium cosmographicum* (1596), as well as his later books on the laws of the universe. Some of the most important Jesuit writings are those of the Würzburg mathematician and physicist Caspar Schott (1608–66) and the Hessian polymath Athanasius Kircher (1602–80).[171] Schott wrote an influential work on hydraulics called *Mechanica hydraulico-pneumatica* (1657); Kircher, who lived in Rome, is renowned for a work on hieroglyphics called *Oedipus Aegyptiacus* (1652). The Göttingen professor of mathematics Carl Friedrich Gauss (1777–1855) composed his number theory in Latin, *Disquisitiones arithmeticae* (1801); Alexander Gottlieb Baumgarten (1714–62), the founder of modern aesthetic theory, wrote his groundbreaking work in Latin, the two-volume *Aesthetica* (1750–58). Even the champions of Paracelsian hermeticism, who about 1560 became fierce opponents of the academic educational system, wrote their tracts and manifestoes in Latin in order to reach an international audience.[172] The physician Michael Maier (1568–1622), best known for his allegorical alchemical illustrations and poetic elucidations *Atalanta fugiens* (1617), spoke for a subculture outside the orthodox monopoly of church and state.[173] Parallel to the textbook and tractate literature, polyhistorical compendiums in Latin, above all the renowned seven-volume *Encyclopaedia* (1630) of Johann Heinrich Alsted (1588–1638), contributed to the dissemination of universal knowledge.[174] So-called *Buntschriftstellerei*, which gathered disparate anecdotal materials into instructive and entertaining conversations, all in a lively essayistic form, was an early encyclopedic genre. The protagonist of enlightened rationalism, Christian Wolff (1659–1754), published mainly in Latin as late as the mid-eighteenth century.

Political and legal writings by political theorists, such as Johannes Althusius (1557–1638) and Samuel Pufendorf (1632–94), constituted an especially influential corpus of Latin literature.[175] Smaller specialized writings — usually having an aphoristic or essayistic style in the manner cultivated along the upper Rhine in imitation of Tacitus; most were targeted at regents, courtiers, and the general sphere of officialdom.[176] In Tacitus's finely drawn historical characters, especially the emperor Tiberius, late humanist scholars discovered classical prefigurations of the modern Machiavellian politics of power and courtly dissimulation, and elaborated on the apparent historical similarities according to the topos of *similitudo temporum* (similarity of the times). The dominant Neo-Stoic thought in the age of confessionalization integrated readily with modern political pragmatism. This is paradigmatic in two works of the Dutch scholar Justus Lipsius (1547–1606): *De constantia* (On Constancy, 1584; translated into German as *Von der Bestendigkeit* by Andreas Viritius, 1599) and *Manuductio ad stoicam philosophiam* (Introduction to Stoic Philosophy, 1604).[177] The Lipsian elitist ethical system combined within the conception of *constantia* — often later reflected in the heroic images of baroque tragedy — the reality of private fate (*fortuna*) with a consciousness of personal duty that necessitates disciplining the individual's emotions to the authority of the absolute state.

In Strasbourg, Jakob Wimpfeling's *Germania* (1502), a pro-German call for unity, peace, and prosperity, was countered by the *Germania nova* (1502) of a young Franciscan controversialist, Thomas Murner (1475–1537), who objected to Wimpfeling's depiction of Alsatian history. His attack prompted Wimpfeling, himself never one to avoid controversy, to respond with *Epithoma rerum Germanicorum* (Summary of German Affairs, 1505). The first published work to focus in its entirety on German history, it represents the beginning of Latin-language national historiography. The legal and historical writings, organized in the form of table talks, by the Augsburg city scribe Conrad Peutinger (1465–1547), were likewise composed in Latin.[178] The traditional methodology of the *Annales ducum Boiariae* (Annals of the Dukes of Bavaria, 1519–21), which simply compiled facts, was reworked in its German translation (begun 1522) by Celtis's disciple Johannes Aventinus (Turmair, 1477–1534),[179] ducal historiographer and tutor to the prince of Bavaria, into an interpretational narrative in the manner of modern historiography. A decade later the methodology was further refined into a masterpiece, *Rerum Germanicarum libri III* (Three Volumes of German Affairs, 1531), by Beatus Rhenanus (1485–1547),[180] philologist, editor, and biographer of Erasmus. The Reformation history *De statu religionis Carolo V. Casesare commentarii* (Commentaries on the State of Religion during the Reign of Charles V, 1555) by Johannes Sleidanus (Johann Philippi aus Schleiden, 1506–66)[181] remained a standard work in European historiography into the nineteenth century. Sleidanus's compendium of universal history, *De quattuor summis imperiis* (On the Four Great Empires, 1556), went into sixty-six editions by 1701.

Specialized areas of interest included an international literature on the Turks; Catholic prose histories, such as the widely circulated *Bavaria sancta* (3 vols., 1615–27) by Matthäus Rader, SJ; and regional historiography.[182] Most autobiographical writings remained unpublished, though a good number of biographies, often written as remembrances and eulogies, began to appear in the sixteenth century in voluminous collections.[183]

Ulrich von Hutten, one of the greatest early humanist Latin stylists, made the patriotic decision in 1520, hoping to better serve the cause of Luther's Reformation, to begin writing in German. His first effort was a stinging pamphlet, *Clag und vormanung gegen dem übermaessigen vnchristlichen gewalt des Bapsts zu Rom und der vngeistlichen geistlichen* (Complaint and Warning Against the Presumptuous Unchristian Power of the Pope in Rome and the Unspiritual Spiritual Estate). This in no way, however, signified a general turning away from Latin as a literary instrument. Latin prose dialogue remained highly effective even after 1520 — the "wonder year" for German-language printing with Luther's first major writings on the new faith — for humanistic as well as reformist purposes. One example is Pirckheimer's satire *Eccius dedolatus* (Eck Planed Down, 1520), a brilliant send-up of the scholastic thought processes of Luther's early opponent Johann Eck, with many allusions to classical Latin and Greek authors, especially Aristophanes.[184] Well into the seventeenth century, writers like Johann Balthasar Schupp (1610–61), senior pastor at the Jakobikirche in Hamburg, cultivated prose satire in the Menippean tradition inspired by Lucian and practiced with such effectiveness by Hutten.[185] Prose satire embraced several genres, among them the ironic encomium, as in Pirckheimer's *Apologia seu Podagrae laus* (Apologia in Praise of the Gout, 1522), and was anthologized in such collections as the *Amphitheatrum sapientiae Socraticae ioco-seriae* (Ampitheater of Socratic Wisdom, both Humorous and Serious, 1619) by the professor of ethics at the Schönaichian school in Bèuthen, Caspar Dornau (1577–1631).[186]

The most sensational publication event of the Reformation was the *Epistolae Obscurorum virorum* (Letters of Obscure Men, 1516; enlarged edition, 1517, with a second book of letters).[187] The work served as a kind of manifesto in support of Reuchlin's cause of defending and cultivating Hebrew books and scholarship. A merciless satire on the coarse style of Middle, or Church Latin practiced by Reuchlin's opponents, mainly the Dominican theologians in Cologne, the work accuses them both of linguistic barbarism as well as cultural benightedness (for failure to appreciate the new learning) and gross behavior (sexual improprieties, drunkenness). Most of the letters are by Hutten but with significant contributions by friends of his, especially Crotus Rubeanus (Johannes Jäger, 1480–1545), a rector of the University of Erfurt. The letters are composed in mimic satire (parody), in the voices of Reuchlin's opponents, who are thus made to mock themselves, revealing their intellectual pretensions and moral corruption. The discourse is generally prose, but verse insertions are added for humorous effect. In volume 2, one obscure man reminisces to another about the good old days in Cologne, "quando habuimus bona convivia, / Et viximus in hilaritate, et non curavimus de gravitate" (where we reveled to our hearts' content and lived in bliss without cares or concern). Lately, he has been traveling to various German universities on behalf of the theologians to speak out against Reuchlin. He has written a poem about it in which he complains, among other things, of having been mistreated along the way by poets friendly to Reuchlin:

> Etiam sciatis, quod composui rithmice non attendens quantitates et pedes, quia videtur mihi, quod sonat melius sic. Etiam ego non didici illam poetriam, nec curo. [. . .]
>
>> Christe Deus omnipotens, in quem sperat omne ens,
>> Qui es Deus deorum per omnia saecula saeculorum,
>> Tu velis mihi esse propitius, quando tribulat me inimicus.
>> Mitte unum diabolum, qui ducat ad patibulum
>> Poetas et iuristas, qui dederunt mihi vexas.
>> Praesertim in Saxonia. [. . .][188]

> [Note that I've composed it in rhythm but without regard for syllable length or meter, since I think it sounds better like that. Anyway, I never did learn that poetic stuff, since it just doesn't interest me.
>
>> Almighty Christ the Lord, in whom every being has hope,
>> You who are God of gods forever and ever,
>> Be gracious to me when my enemy troubles me.
>> Send one of the devils to lead to the gallows
>> The poets and lawyers that vexed me.
>> Especially in Saxony.]

The *Utopia* (1516) of the English royal adviser Thomas More inspired the earliest German utopias, which were written in Latin: *Eudaemonensium respublica* (Republic of Happiness, 1555) by Caspar Stiblin (fl. 1555–62), also known for his Latin translations of Euripides, and *Respublicae Christianopolitanae descriptio* (Description of the Republic of a Christian State, 1619) by Andreae.[189] The *Christianopolis*, as it was called, is a geometrically ordered theocracy, a center for a Christianity of good works, in which scholars and workers unite in a kind of well-ordered and pious manufactory. Andreae, whose writings reanimated the spirit of Württembergian Lutheranism and whose influence was felt as late as Herder, was also one of the guiding lights of Rosicrucianism, a utopian brotherhood that flourished in seventeenth-century Europe; its struggle for survival is documented in hundreds of Latin publications, many by Andreae himself.[190] His interests included bold treatises and prospectuses for social projects; the drama *Turbo*;[191] autobiography; and a collection of exceptionally relevant satires under the title *Menippus sive dialogorum satyricorum centuria* (Menippus, or One Hundred Satirical Dialogues, 1617), a revealing anatomy of his times. Few other works of the seventeenth century demonstrate such affinity with the heterodox sociocritical streams of the sixteenth century while simultaneously manifesting openness to the empirical sciences and the new technologies, or *artes mechanicae*.

Much of the edifying literature of Late Humanism was composed in Latin and then translated into German. The collected works of the Bavarian Jesuit Jeremias Drexel (1581–1638),[192] four massive volumes in more than 160 Latin editions and more than forty German editions, were also reprinted abroad and soon translated into German; in Munich alone more than 170,000 copies of Drexel's works had been printed by 1642. Conversely, some Italian and Spanish texts, including novels, made their way to German readers initially in Latin translations by Caspar Ens and Caspar von Barth. One of the great defenses of those accused of witchcraft was the Jesuit Friedrich Spee's (1591–1635) *Cautio criminalis* (Precautions in Criminal Matters, 1631).[193]

A literature of entertainment in Latin prose spread during the sixteenth century. Farcical writings — witty short stories inspired by the *Facetiae* (1474) of the Italian humanist Poggio Bracciolini — enjoyed great popularity in Germany. Outstanding examples are the *Facetiae Latinae et Germanicae* (1486) by Augustin Tünger (1455–after 1486), a procurator at the bishopric of Constance, and the *Facetiae* (1508–12) of Heinrich Bebel, a professor of poetics in Tübingen. Many were included in collections of farces assembled by Frischlin and in others by the Hessian lawyer Otho Melander (*Jocoseria*, 1600). John Barclay invented the modern Latin-language novel with his *Argenis* (1621, translated into German by Opitz in 1626), a *Staatsroman* (novel of state).[194] While Latin was universally employed as the preeminent linguistic instrument for academic and scientific discourses, it seems to have been less well suited to the genre of the novel, for which the vernacular was generally preferred. The relative success of novels of state by the Jesuits Adam Contzen (1571–1635), particularly his *Abissimi Regis historia* (History of the Abyssianian King, 1628), and Bidermann, particularly his *Utopia* (1640; last printing 1762), as well as the satirically tinged prose narratives of Bisselius, mentioned above (*Icaria*, 1637; *Argonauticum Americanorum*, 1647),[195] only proved this general rule.

Eighteenth-century satires, notably *De Charlataneria eruditorum* (On the Vanity of Scholars, 1715) by the Leipzig polymath Johann Burchard Mencke (1674–1732), were symptomatic of the diminishing capacity of the class-conscious Latin republic of letters to defend itself against the growing criticism of socially useless pedantry.[196] By the end of the seventeenth century, modern historians, such as the Wolfenbüttel librarian Jacob Burckhard (1681–1752), in *De linguae Latinae in Germania per XVII saecula fatis* (On the Fate of the Latin Language in Germany through Seventeen Centuries, 1713),[197] were looking back on history and the phases of Latin language and literature with a critical eye. The nationalistic paradigm of the German Reformation constructed in the nineteenth century took a dim view of Neo-Latin literature. Encouraged, however, by Georg Ellinger and other twentieth-century pioneers,[198] the state of research in Neo-Latin literature took a decidedly positive turn in a period of only a few decades — and this despite sharp reductions everywhere in Latin instruction.

Translated by Michael Swisher

Notes

Key to frequently cited works in the endnotes

DLB 164 = *Dictionary of Literary Biography*. Vol. 164: *German Baroque Writers, 1580–1660*. Ed. James Hardin. Detroit: Gale Research, 1996.

DLB 179 = *Dictionary of Literary Biography*. Vol. 179: *German Writers of the Renaissance and Reformation, 1280–1580*. Ed. Max Reinhart and James Hardin. Detroit: Gale Research, 1997.

Dünnhaupt = *Personalbibliographien zu den Drucken des Barock*. 6 vols. Ed. Gerhard Dünnhaupt. Stuttgart: Hiersemann, 1990–93.

Füssel (1993) = Stephan Füssel. Deutsche Dichter der frühen Neuzeit (1450–1600): Ihr Leben und Werk. Berlin: Schmidt, 1993.

GL = *Germania latina — Latinitas teutonia: Politik, Wissenschaft, humanistische Kultur vom späten Mittelalter bis in unsere Zeit*. 2 vols. Ed. Eckhard Keßler und Heinrich C. Kuhn. Munich: Fink, 2003.

HDS = *Humanismus im deutschen Südwesten: Biographische Profile*. 2nd ed. Ed. Paul Gerhard Schmidt. Stuttgart: Thorbecke, 2000.

HL = *Humanistische Lyrik des 16. Jahrhunderts: Lateinisch und deutsch*. Trans. and ed. Wilhelm Kühlmann, Robert Seidel, and Hermann Wiegand; with C. Bodamer, L. Claren, J. Huber, V. Probst, W. Schibel, and W. Straube. Bibliothek deutscher Klassiker 146. Bibliothek der Frühen Neuzeit, vol. 5. Frankfurt am Main: Deutscher Klassiker Verlag, 1997.

LL = *Literatur-Lexikon: Autoren und Werke deutscher Sprache*. Ed. Walther Killy. 14 vols. Ed. Volker Meid. Gütersloh: Bertelsmann, 1988–93. Vol. 1, 1988; 2–4, 1989; 5–8, 1990; 9–11, 1991; 12–13, 1992; 14, 1993.

Parnassus Palatinus = *Parnassus Palatinus: Humanistische Dichtung in Heidelberg und der alten Kurpfalz. Lateinisch und deutsch*. Ed. W. Kühlmann und Hermann Wiegand. Heidelberg: Manutius, 1989.

RL = *Reallexikon: Reallexikon der deutschen Literaturwissenschaft*. 3 vols. Ed. Klaus Weimar (vol. 1), Harald Fricke (vol. 2), Jan-Dirk Müller (vol. 3). Berlin: de Gruyter, 1997–2003.

Roloff (1965) = Hans-Gert Roloff. " 'Neulateinische Dichtung' und 'Neulateinisches Drama.' " In *Reallexikon der deutschen Literaturgeschichte*. 2nd ed. Berlin de Gruyter, 1965. 2:621–44 and 645–78.

Rupprich (1973) = Hans Rupprich. *Das Zeitalter der Reformation 1520–1570*, part 2 of *Die deutsche Literatur vom späten Mittelalter bis zum Barock*. Geschichte der deutschen Literatur, IV/1. Munich: Beck, 1973.

Trillitzsch = Winfried Trillitzsch. *Der deutsche Renaissance-Humanismus: Abriß und Auswahl*. Leipzig: Reclam, 1981.

[1] Overview: Jozef Ijsewijn, *Companion to Neo–Latin Studies,* part 1, *History and Diffusion of Neo-Latin Literature,* 2nd ed. (Leuven: Leuven UP, 1990); part 2, Ijsewijn with Dirk Sacré, *Literary, Linguistic, Philological and Editorial Questions,* 1998, supplies literature on individual countries and territories as well as on genres and larger questions of reception. See also Walther Ludwig, "Die neuzeitliche lateinische Literatur seit der Renaissance," in *Einleitung in die lateinische Philologie,* ed. Fritz Graf (Stuttgart: Teubner, 1997), 323–56; Heinz Hoffmann, "Neulateinische Literatur: Aufgaben und Perspektiven," *Neulateinisches Jahrbuch* 2 (2000): 57–98; Laetitia Boehm, "Latinitas — Ferment europäischer Kultur: Überlegungen zur Dominanz des Latein im germanisch-deutschen Sprachraum Alteuropas," in GL 21–70; Walther Ludwig, "Latein im Leben: Funktionen der lateinischen Sprache in der frühen Neuzeit," in GL 73–106. On German-Latin coexistence: Wilhelm Kühlmann, "Nationalliteratur und Latinität: Zum Problem der Zweisprachigkeit in der frühneuzeitlichen Literaturbewegung Deutschlands," in *Nation und Literatur im Europa der Frühen Neuzeit,* ed. Klaus Garber (Tübingen: Niemeyer, 1989), 1:164–206; Stephan Füssel, "Barbarus sermo fugiat . . ." "Über das Verhältnis der Humanisten zur Volkssprache," *Pirckheimer–Jahrbuch* 1 (1985): 71–110. On the tradition up to the early nineteenth century, Robert Seidel, "Die 'tote Sprache' und das Originalgenie: Poetologische und literatursoziologische Transformationsprozesse in der Geschichte der deutschen neulateinischen Lyrik," in *Lateinische Lyrik der Frühen Neuzeit: Poetische Kleinformen und ihre Funktionen zwischen Renaissance und Aufklärung* ed. Beate Czapla, Ralf Georg Czapla, and Robert Seidel (Tübingen: Niemeyer, 2003), 422–48. On the European context, *Latein und Nationalsprachen in der Renaissance,* ed. Bodo Guthmüller (Wiesbaden: Harrassowitz, 1998); Kühlmann and Hermann Wiegand, "'Humanismus' and 'Neulateinische Literatur,'" in LL 13, 421–26, and LL 14, 150–58. In general, Hans-Gert Roloff, "'Neulateinische Dichtung' und 'Neulateinisches Drama,'" in *Reallexikon der deutschen Literaturwissenschaft,* 3rd ed., ed. Harald Fricke (Berlin: de Gruyter, 2000), 2:621–44 and 645–78, and Rupprich (1973).

[2] In *Querela Pacis,* in *Ausgewählte Schriften: Lateinisch und Deutsch,* trans. and com. Gertraud Christian, ed. Werner Welzig (Darmstadt: Wissenschaftliche Buchgesellschaft, 1967), 5:372.

[3] For Hegius see esp. LL 5, 104–5; for other authors mentioned here as well see *Das ausgehende Mittelalter, Humanismus und Renaissance 1370–1520* (Hans Rupprich), 2nd ed., revised by Hedwig Heger, part 1 of *Die deutsche Literatur vom Späten Mittelalter bis zum Barock* (Munich: Beck, 1994); Eckhard Bernstein, *Die Literatur des deutschen Frühhumanismus* (Stuttgart: Metzler, 1978). Especially for pedagogical writings see Erich Meuthen, "Charakter und Tendenzen des deutschen Humanismus," in *Säkulare Aspekte der Reformationszeit,* ed. Heinz Angermeier (Vienna: Oldenbourg, 1983), 216–66.

[4] On Luder see B. Coppel, in LL 7, 362–63; Frank Baron, in Füssel (1993), 83–95; Rudolf Ketterman, in HDS 13–34; Frank Baron, in DBL 179, 129–34; excerpts of his lecture announcements in Trillitzsch 149–52; Veit Probst and Wolfgang Metzger, "Zur Sozialgeschichte des deutschen Frühhumanismus: Peter Luders Karriereversuch in Heidelberg 1456–1460," *Pirckheimer Jahrbuch* 18 (2003): 545–85.

[5] On Hermann von dem Busche: Wilhelm Kühlmann, in LL 2, 335–36; James V. Mehl, "Hermann von dem Busche's *Vallum humanitatis* (1518): A German Defense of the Renaissance Studia Humanitatis," *Renaissance Quarterly* 42 (1989): 480–506.

[6] Nikola Kaminski, "Imitatio," in *Historisches Wörterbuch der Rhetorik,* ed. Gert Ueding (Tübingen: Niemeyer, 1998), 4: para. 3–4, cols. 257–75, and Barbara Bauer,

"Aemulatio," in ibid. (1992), 1: para. 3, cols. 164–77. On the full context of educational practice in early modern Germany see the seminal works by Wilfried Barner, *Barockrhetorik: Untersuchungen zu ihren geschichtlichen Grundlagen* (Tübingen: Niemeyer, 1970), and Joachim Dyck, *Ticht-Kunst: Deutsche Barockpoetik und rhetorische Tradition*, 3rd ed. (Tübingen: Niemeyer, 1991). Also Heinz Entner, "Der Dichtungsbegriff des deutschen Humanismus," in *Grundpositionen der deutschen Literatur im 16. Jahrhundert* (Weimar: Aufbau, 1972), 330–479, and Gunter E. Grimm, *Literatur und Gelehrtentum in Deutschland: Untersuchungen zum Wandel ihres Verhältnisses vom Humanismus bis zur Frühaufklärung* (Tübingen: Niemeyer, 1983).

[7] German national identification blended gradually with the Renaissance and Latin traditions. See Günter Hess, "Deutsche Literaturgeschichte und neulateinische Literatur," in *Acta Conventus Neo-Latini Amstelodamensis*, ed. Pierre Tuynman (Munich: Fink, 1979), 493–538.

[8] An annotated dual-language edition of Opitz's complete Latin works is currently being compiled in Germany under the title *Opitius Latinus*. The most recent comprehensive account of modern research on Opitz: Julian Paulus and Robert Seidel, *Opitz-Bibliographie 1800–2002* (Heidelberg: Palatina, 2003). On Opitz's place in late humanism and on the historical transition to baroque literature, Kühlmann, *Gelehrtenrepublik und Fürstenstaat: Entwicklung und Kritik des deutschen Späthumanismus in der Literatur des Barockzeitalters* (Tübingen: Niemeyer, 1982); Manfred P. Fleischer, ed., *The Harvest of Humanism in Central Europe* (St. Louis: Concordia Publishing House, 1992); Notker Hammerstein und Gerrit Walther, eds., *Späthumanismus: Studien über das Ende einer kulturhistorischen Epoche* (Göttingen: Wallstein, 2000); Ralph Häfner, *Götter im Exil: Frühneuzeitliches Dichtungsverständnis im Spannungsfeld christlicher Apologetik und philologischer Kritik (ca. 1590–1736)* (Tübingen: Niemeyer, 2003); Klaus Garber, "Späthumanistische Verheißungen im Spannungsfeld von Latinität und nationalem Aufbruch," in GL 107–42. New impulses in Opitz research: Kühlmann, "Martin Opitz in Paris (1630) — Zu Text, Praetext und Kontext eines lateinischen Gedichtes an Cornelius Grotius," in *Martin Opitz (1597–1639): Nachahmungspoetik und Lebenswelt* (Tübingen: Niemeyer, 2002), 191–221; Stefanie Arend, "Zu Topik und Faktur von Martin Opitzens Panegyricus auf Ludwig Camerarius," in Czapla, et al., eds., *Lateinische Lyrik*, 330–55 (see note 1); Kühlmann, "Von Heidelberg zurück nach Schlesien — Opitz' frühe Lebensstationen im Spiegel seiner lateinischen Lyrik," in *Regionaler Kulturraum und intellektuelle Kommunikation vom Humanismus bis ins Zeitalter des Internet: Festschrift für Klaus Garber*, ed. Axel E. Walther (Amsterdam: Rodopi, 2005), 413–30.

[9] Introductions to Melanchthon: Heinz Scheible, in LL 8, 8–92; Scheible, *Melanchthon: Eine Biographie* (Munich: Beck, 1997); Derk Visser, in DLB 179, 166–77; Scheible, in HDS 221–38; Barbara Bauer, in Füssel (1993), 428–63; Manfred P. Fleischer, "Melanchthon as Praeceptor of Late-Humanist Poetry," in *Sixteenth Century Journal* 20 (1989): 559–80; Michael Beyer, ed., *Humanismus und Wittenberger Reformation* (Leipzig: Evangelische Verlags-Anstalt, 1997), esp. Stefan Rhein on "Melanchthon und der italienische Humanismus," 367–88. Two essay collections deal with evangelical humanism and Melanchthon: Walther Ludwig, ed., *Die Musen im Reformationszeitalter* (Leipzig: Evangelische Verlags-Anstalt, 1999), and Günther Wartenberg, ed., *Werk und Rezeption Philipp Melanchthons in Universität und Schule bis ins 18. Jahrhundert* (Leipzig: Evangelische Verlags-Anstalt, 1999). Selections from his lyrical output: HL 339–57.

[10] Overview: Jürgen Leonhardt, ed., *Melanchthon und das Lehrbuch des 16. Jahrhunderts* (Rostock: Universität, Philosophische Fakultät, 1997).

[11] In Robert Stupperich, ed., *Melanchthons Werke in Auswahl*, vol. 3 of *Humanistische Schriften*, 2nd ed., ed. Richard Nürnberger (Gütersloh: Mohn, 1969), 29–42. On Melanchthon as orator see Horst Koehn, *Philipp Melanchthons Reden: Verzeichnis der im 16. Jahrhundert erschienenen Drucke* (Frankfurt am Main: Buchhändler Vereinigung, 1985).

[12] Günther Frank and Stefan Rhein, eds., *Melanchthon und die Naturwissenschaften seiner Zeit* (Sigmaringen: Thorbecke, 1998).

[13] On Melanchthon's approach to poetic texts see Heinz Hofmann, "Melanchthon als Interpret antiker Dichtung," *Neulateinisches Jahrbuch* 1 (1999): 99–127.

[14] Kühlmann, *Gelehrtenrepublik*, 113–18 (see note 8).

[15] See the dual language edition by Joachim Knape, *Philipp Melanchthons "Rhetorik"* (Tübingen: Niemeyer, 1993); also Olaf Berwald, *Philipp Melanchthons Sicht der Rhetorik* (Wiesbaden: Harrassowitz, 1994), and Carl Joachim Classen, "Neue Elemente in einer alten Disziplin," in GL 325–74.

[16] See in this volume the chapter by Joachim Knape. These complicated influences are investigated in detail by Lothar Mundt, "Rudolf Agricolas *De inventione dialectica* — Konzeption, Wirkung, historische Bedeutung," in *Rudolf Agricola, 1444–1485: Protagonist des nordeuropäischen Humanismus*, ed. Kühlmann, et al. (Bern: Lang, 1994). Further on Agricola see Fokke Akkermann, in LL 1, 63–77.

[17] Melanchthon and natural law: Merio Scattola, *Das Naturrecht vor dem Naturrecht: Zur Geschichte des "ius naturae" im 16. Jahrhundert* (Tübingen: Niemeyer, 1999), esp. 29–54.

[18] Heinz Scheible, ed., *Melanchthon in seinen Schülern* (Wiesbaden: Harrassowitz, 1997), and Udo Sträter, ed., *Melanchthonbild und Melanchthonrezeption in der Lutherischen Orthodoxie und im Pietismus* (Wittenberg: Drei-Kastanien, 1999).

[19] On the Catholic cultural sphere see Dieter Breuer, *Oberdeutsche Literatur (1565–1650): Deutsche Literaturgeschichte und Territorialgeschichte in frühabsolutistischer Zeit* (Munich: Beck, 1979); Reinhold Baumstark, ed., *Rom in Bayern: Kunst und Spiritualität der ersten Jesuiten* (Munich: Hirmer, 1997). For an overview of Bavarian Jesuit culture in texts, pictures, and architecture see the editions: *Trophaea Bavarica: Bayerische Siegszeichen*, ed. Günter Hess et al. (1597; facsimile repr., Regensburg: Schnell + Steiner, 1997); *Triumphus Divi Michaelis Archangeli Bavarici: Triumph des Heiligen Michael*, trans. and ed. Barbara Bauer and Jürgen Leonhardt (Regensburg: Schnell + Steiner, 2000). Related studies: Jeffrey Chipps Smith, "The Jesuit Church of St. Michael's in Munich: The Story of an Angel with a Mission," in *Infinite Boundaries: Order, Disorder, and Reorder in Early Modern German Culture*, ed. Max Reinhart (Kirksville, MO: Thomas Jefferson UP, 1998), 147–69; Smith, *Sensuous Worship: Jesuits and the Art of the Early Catholic Reformation in Germany* (Princeton: Princeton UP, 2002), 57–101; and Ulrich Schlegelmilch, *Descriptio Templi: Architektur und Fest in der lateinischen Dichtung des konfessionellen Zeitalters* (Regensburg: Schnell + Steiner, 2003).

[20] Miquel Batllori SJ, "Der Beitrag der 'ratio studiorum' für die Bildung des modernen katholischen Bewußtseins," in *Ignatianisch: Eigenart und Methode der Gesellschaft Jesu*, ed. Michael Sievernich SJ and Günter Switek SJ (Freiburg: Herder, 1990), 314–22.

[21] Karl Erlinghagen, *Katholische Bildung im Barock* (Hannover: Schroedel, 1972); Karl Hengst, *Jesuiten an Universitäten und Jesuitenuniversitäten: Zur Geschichte der*

Universitäten in der Oberdeutschen und Rheinischen Provinz der Gesellschaft Jesu im Zeitalter der konfessionellen Auseinandersetzungen (Paderborn: Schöningh, 1981). Among the most important histories of Jesuit schools and universities, Harald Dickerhof, "Die katholische Gelehrtenschule des konfessionellen Zeitalters," in *Die katholische Konfessionalisierung*, ed. Wolfgang Reinhard and Heinz Schilling (Münster: Aschendorff, 1995).

[22] For the theory and practice of Jesuit rhetoric, poetics, and emblematics as well as textbooks and authors see Barbara Bauer, *Jesuitische "ars rhetorica" im Zeitalter der Glaubenskämpfe* (Frankfurt am Main: Lang, 1986).

[23] Franz Günter Sieveke, in LL 9, 204–6, and Paul Richard Blum, in Füssel (1993), 626–35. On Platonism in Pontano's work, Barbara Bauer, "Jakob Pontanus SJ, ein oberdeutscher Lipsius: Ein Augsburger Schulmann zwischen Renaissancegelehrsamkeit und jesuitischer Dichtungstradition," *Zeitschrift für bayerische Landesgeschichte* 47 (1984): 77–120.

[24] Masen's other works on this subject: *Palaestra oratoria; Palaestra eloquentiae ligatae; Palaestra styli Romani; Exercitationes oratoriae; Ars nova argutiarum; Familiarium argutiarum fontes*. See Dünnhaupt 4, 2673–964, and Franz Günter Sieveke, in LL 7, 509–11. On emblematics see in this volume the chapter by Peter M. Daly.

[25] The standard edition is *Julius Wilhelm Zincgref: Emblemata ethico-politica*, ed. Dieter Mertens and Theodor Verweyen, 2 vols. (Tübingen: Niemeyer, 1993). For more on Zincgref see in this volume the chapter by Theodor Verweyen. On Joachim Camerarius, *Symbola et Emblemata* (1590–1604), ed. Wolfgang Harms and Ulla Britta Kuechen (Graz: Akademische Druck- und Verlags-Anstalt, 1988); Jonathan P. Clark, "Julius Wilhelm Zincgref," in DLB 164, 379–83. On emblematics in Jesuit practice see Peter M. Daly, ed., *Emblematik und Kunst der Jesuiten in Bayern: Einfluß und Wirkung* (Turnhout: Brepols, 2000).

[26] "Lipsian" so named to characterize the style of the Dutch Neo-Stoic political theorist Justus Lipsius (discussed below). For context see Kühlmann, *Gelehrtenrepublik*, 189–266 (see note 8).

[27] On genre see Stefan Trappen, *Gattungspoetik: Studien zur Poetik des 16. bis 19. Jahrhunderts und zur Geschichte der triadischen Gattungslehre* (Heidelberg: Winter, 2001).

[28] On the rhetorical and poetological framework of early modern writing see in this volume the chapter by Joachim Knape.

[29] Gerlinde Huber-Rebenich, "Der lateinische Psalter des Eobanus Hessus und das Ideal der *docta pietas*," in Ludwig, ed., *Die Musen im Reformationszeitalter*, 289–303 (see note 9), and Anja Stewing, "Die Psalterübertragung des Eobanus Hessus," in *Humanismus in Erfurt*, ed. Gerlinde Huber-Rebenich and Walther Ludwig (Rudolstadt: Hain, 2002), 195–212. For Psalter adaptations, Johannes A. Gaertner, "Latin Translation of the Psalms 1520–1620," *Harvard Theological Review* 49 (1956): 271–305; Inka Bach and Helmut Galle, *Deutsche Psalmendichtungen vom 16. bis zum 20. Jahrhundert: Untersuchungen zur Geschichte einer lyrischen Gattung* (Berlin: de Gruyter, 1989). Edition: *Dichtungen der Jahre 1528–1537*, vol. 3 of *Dichtungen: Lateinisch und Deutsch*, trans. and ed. Harry Vredeveld (Bern: Lang, 1990). Introduction to Hessus, Vredeveld, "Eobanus Hessus," in DLB 179, 97–110. The first vita of Hessus, written by Joachim Camerarius: *Narratio de Helio Eobano Hesso: Lateinisch und deutsch*, trans. Georg Burkard, ed. Burkard und Kühlmann (Heidelberg: Manutius, 2003).

[30] On Neo-Latin devotional poetry: Walther Ludwig, *Christliche Dichtung des 16. Jahrhunderts: Die "Poemata sacra" des Georg Fabricius* (Göttingen: Vandenhoeck & Ruprecht, 2001); with reference to the reception of Prudentius in Neo-Latin, Kühlmann, "Poeten und Puritaner: Christliche und pagane Poesie im deutschen Humanismus — mit einem Exkurs zur Prudentius-Rezeption in Deutschland," *Pirckheimer-Jahrbuch* 8 (1993): 149–80.

[31] On Murmellius see Kühlmann, in LL 8, 301–2.

[32] On the tradition of genres up to the early nineteenth century, including the Jesuits, see Heinrich Dörrie, *Der heroische Brief: Bestandsaufnahme, Geschichte, Kritik einer humanistisch-barocken Literaturgattung* (Berlin: de Gruyter, 1968).

[33] Edition: *Heroidum Libri tres*, ed. Harry Vredeveld (Ph.D. diss., Princeton U, 1970). Also Vredeveld, "Der heroische Brief der 'Maria Magdalena Iesu Christo' aus den *Heroidum libri tres* des Helius Eobanus Hessus (1488–1540)," *Daphnis* 6 (1977): 65–90. Selections: HL 319–27.

[34] On Sabinus see Reinhard Düchting, in LL 10, 88–96; HL 500–539; Jerzy Starnawski, *Die Beziehungen des Humanisten Georg Sabinus (1508–1560) zu Polen*, in GL 469–82; Kühlmann and Waldemar Straube, "Zur Historie und Pragmatik humanistischer Lyrik im alten Preußen: Von Konrad Celtis über Eobanus Hessus zu Georg Sabinus," in *Kulturgeschichte Ostpreußens in der Frühen Neuzeit*, ed. Klaus Garber (Tübingen: Niemeyer, 2001), 657–736.

[35] Kühlmann, "Religiöse Affektmodellierung: Die heroische Versepistel als Typus der jesuitischen Erbauungsliteratur in Deutschland," in *Aedificatio: Erbauung im interkulturellen Kontext in der Frühen Neuzeit*, ed. Andreas Solbach (Tübingen: Niemeyer, 2004). Bidermann's works: Dünnhaupt 1, 550–81, and Franz Günter Sieveke, in LL 1, 494–96. More generally on Bidermann, Jean-Marie Valentin, "Die Jesuitendichter Bidermann und Avancini," in *Deutsche Dichter des 17. Jahrhunderts: Ihr Leben und Werk*, ed. Harald Steinhagen and Benno von Wiese (Berlin: Schmidt, 1984), 385–414; Thomas W. Best, *Jacob Bidermann* (Boston: Twayne Publishers, 1975). His dramatic works will be discussed below.

[36] This opposition and the development of the elegy genre in Europe, as well as newer, Platonized forms of Eros, are discussed in Jörg Robert, "'Amabit sapiens, cruciabitur autem stultus'": Neuplatonische Poetik der Elegie und Pluralisierung des erotischen Diskurses," in Czapla et al., eds., *Lateinische Lyrik*, 11–73 (see note 1).

[37] On Lemnius see Hans-Jürgen Bachorski, in LL 7, 219–20, and HL 547–69 (further on Lemnius below). Bilingual editions of Lemnius: *Amorum Libri IV — Liebeselegien in vier Büchern*, trans. and ed. Lothar Mundt (Bern: Lang, 1988), and *Bucolica: Fünf Eklogen*, trans. and ed. Lothar Mundt (Tübingen: Niemeyer, 1996).

[38] Edition: Johannes Nicolai Secundus, *Basia*, ed. Georg Ellinger (Berlin: Weidmann, 1899). On the tradition see Nicolas James Perella, *The Kiss Sacred and Profane: An Interpretative History of Kiss Symbolism* (Berkeley: U of California P, 1969). On Fleming's Latin poetry see Hans Pyritz, *Paul Flemings Liebeslyrik: Zur Geschichte des Petrarkismus* (Göttingen: Vandenhoeck & Ruprecht, 1963); Beate Czapla, "Erlebnispoesie oder erlebte Poesie? Paul Flemings Suavia und die Tradition des zyklusbildenden Kußgedichtes," in Czapla et al., eds., *Lateinische Lyrik*, 356–97 (see note 1).

[39] See in this volume the chapter by Gerhart Hoffmeister.

[40] On Schede see *Parnassus Palatinus* 82–105 and 289–91; Eckart Schäfer, in LL (1991), 167–69; David Price, in DLB 179, 260–64; Schäfer, in HL 753–862, in HDS

239–64, and in Füssel (1993), 545–60. Kühlmann, "Humanistische Geniedichtung in Deutschland: Zu Paul Schede Melissus' *Ad Genium suum* (1574–75)," in James Hardin and Jörg Jungmayr, eds., *"der Buchstab tödt — der Geist macht lebendig" : Festschrift zum 60. Geburtstag von Hans-Gert Roloff* (Bern: Lang, 1992), 1:117–30.

[41] There had been a revival of interest in the themes of wine, friendship, feasting, love, and nature of the Greek poet Anacreon (6th c. B.C.). See Kühlmann, " 'Amor liberalis': Ästhetischer Lebensentwurf und Christianisierung der neulateinischen Anakreontik in der Ära des europäischen Späthumanismus," in *Das Ende der Renaissance: Europäische Kultur um 1600*, ed. August Buck and Tibor Klaniczay (Wiesbaden: Harrassowitz, 1987), 165–86. On Taubmann, Dünnhaupt 6, 4004–28, and Hermann Wiegand, in LL 11, 310. On Barth, Dünnhaupt 1, 401–21; Kühlmann, in LL 1, 321–22, and *Gelehrtenrepublik*, 255–63 (see note 8). Selections: HL 863–904. On the manneristic development of style see Karl Otto Conrady, *Lateinische Dichtungstradition und deutsche Lyrik des 17. Jahrhunderts* (Bonn: Bouvier, 1962).

[42] On Aurpach see Hans Pörnbacher, in LL 1, 257; selections: HL 653–78.

[43] In HL 876.

[44] The standard study: Wulf Segebrecht, *Das Gelegenheitsgedicht: Ein Beitrag zur Geschichte und Poetik der deutschen Lyrik* (Stuttgart: Metzler, 1977). See also Wolfgang Adam, *Poetische und kritische Wälder: Untersuchungen zu Geschichte und Formen des Schreibens 'bei Gelegenheit'* (Heidelberg: Winter, 1988). Its geographical scope is considered by Klaus Garber, ed., introduction, in *Stadt und Literatur im deutschen Sprachraum der frühen Neuzeit* (Tübingen: Niemeyer, 1988). With respect to the mass of occasional themes see the continuing series of funeral sermons, *Katalog der Leichenpredigten und sonstiger Trauerschriften in Bibliotheken, Archiven und Museen*, ed. Rudolf Lenz (Stuttgart: Steiner, 1979–2005). The most recent major bibliographical project on occasional poetry is a collection on microforms, *Handbuch des personalen Gelegenheitsschrifttums in europäischen Bibliotheken und Archiven*, ed. Klaus Garber (Hildesheim: Olms Neue Medien, 2001–).

[45] Standard work: Hans-Henrik Krummacher, "Das barocke Epicedium: Rhetorische Tradition und deutsche Gelegenheitsdichtung im 17. Jahrhundert," *Jahrbuch der deutschen Schillergesellschaft* 18 (1974): 89–147; see also Ingeborg Gräßer, *Die Epicedien-Dichtung des Eobanus Hessus: Lyrische Totenklage zur Zeit des Humanismus und der Reformation* (Frankfurt am Main: Lang, 1994).

[46] HL offers examples for Dürer (274–84) and Hutten (284–90). An especially interesting case is Johannes Kepler's obituary for Tycho Brahe, *In obitum Tychonis Brahe*, ed. Hans Wieland (Munich: Bayerische Akademie der Wissenschaften, 1972).

[47] Humanist imperial patriotism is the subject of Michael Stolleis, "Public Law and Patriotism in the Holy Roman Empire," in Reinhart, ed., *Infinite Boundaries*, 11–33 (see note 19), and Kühlmann, "Reichspatriotismus und humanistische Dichtung," in *Frieden und Krieg in der Frühen Neuzeit: die europäische Staatenordnung und die außereuropäische Welt*, ed. Ronald G. Asch et al. (Munich: Fink, 2001), 375–93; Kühlmann, "Der Poet und das Reich: Politische, kontextuelle und ästhetische Dimensionen der humanistischen Türkenlyrik in Deutschland," in *Europa und die Türken in der Renaissance*, ed. Bodo Guthmüller and Kühlmann (Tübingen: Niemeyer, 2000), 139–248; and in ibid., *Europa*, 65–78, Dieter Mertens, *"Claromontani passagii exemplum"*: Papst Urban II. und der erste Kreuzzug in der Türkenkriegspropaganda des Renaissance-Humanismus," deals with the oratorical practices and publishing.

[48] Harry Vredeveld, "Pastoral Inverted: Baptista Mantuanus' Satiric Eclogues and their Influence on the *Bucolicon* und *Bucolicon Idyllia* of Eobanus Hessus," *Daphnis* 14 (1985): 461–96.

[49] Mundt, *Bucolica* reviews Latin bucolic poetry in Germany. See also Mundt, "Die sizilischen Musen in Wittenberg: Zur religiösen Funktionalisierung der neulateinischen Bukolik im deutschen Protestantismus des 16. Jahrhundert," in Ludwig, *Die Musen*, 265–88 (see note 9). For European practice, Leonard W. Grant, *Neo-Latin Literature and the Pastoral* (Chapel Hill: U of North Carolina P, 1965); further see Margarete Stracke, *Die lateinische Ekloge des Humanismus* (Gerbrunn bei Würzburg: Lehmann, 1981).

[50] On Hessus and the Erfurt Circle see Heger, ed., *Das ausgehende Mittelalter*, 619–25 (see note 3); Harry Vredeveld, in LL 5, 282–85; selections in HL 247–337; see also Walther Ludwig, "Eobanus Hessus in Erfurt: Ein Beitrag zum Verhältnis von Humanismus und Protestantismus," *Mittellateinisches Jahrbuch* 33 (1998): 155–70.

[51] He was the youngest of thirteen children, hence *cordus* (late-comer). See Peter Dilg, in LL 2, 460–61; Jozef Ijsewijn, "Euricius Cordus als Epigrammatiker," in Hardin and Jungmayr, eds., "*der Buchstab tödt*," 2:1047–65 (see note 40); Eckart Schäfer, "Euricius Cordus: Vergil in Hessen," in *Candide Iudex*, ed. Anna Elissa Radke (Stuttgart: Steiner, 1998), 283–313. Selections: HL 221–45. On the eclogues and the technique of enciphering, Gisela Mönck: "Der hessische Humanist Euricius Cordus und die Erstausgabe seines *Bucolicon* von 1514," *Daphnis* 14 (1985): 65–98, and Armgard Müller: *Das Bucolicon des Euricius Cordus und die Tradition der Gattung* (Trier: WVT, 1997).

[52] Johannes Bocer, *Sämtliche Eklogen*, trans. and ed. Lothar Mundt (Tübingen: Niemeyer, 1999).

[53] On the eclogue and the Peasants' War see Eckart Schäfer, "Bukolik und Bauernkrieg: Joachim Camerarius als Dichter," in *Joachim Camerarius (1500–1574): Beiträge zur Geschichte des Humanismus im Zeitalter der Reformation*, ed. Frank Baron (Munich: Fink, 1978), 121–51. More generally, Schäfer, "Der deutsche Bauernkrieg in der neulateinischen Literatur," *Daphnis* 9 (1980): 1–31; Joachim Hamm, *Servilia bella: Bilder vom deutschen Bauernkrieg in neulateinischen Dichtungen des 16. Jahrhunderts* (Wiesbaden: Reichert, 2001).

[54] As a comparison see the eclogue *Iolas* written for Charles V by Johannes Stigelius in HL 584–95.

[55] On German Christmas literature in the Neo-Latin tradition see Martin Keler, *Johann Klajs Weihnachtsdichtung: Das "Freudengedichte" von 1650* (Berlin: Schmidt, 1971).

[56] Cordus's witty, often biting epigrams appear in two (1517) and then in three (1520) posthumous complete editions in thirteen books of *Opera Poetica*. For further literature on the development of the genre and its typology see Hermann Wiegand, in LL 13, 220–23, and Peter Hess, *Epigramm* (Stuttgart: Metzler, 1989).

[57] On Hutten and the epigram see Barbara Könneker, in LL 6, 27–30. This subject will be discussed further in the section "A Sketch of Neo-Latin Writings in Prose" below. Epigram selections in HL 174–201. The Latin epigrams of Andreas Gryphius are available in *Lateinische Kleinepik: Epigrammatik und Kasualdichtung*, trans. and ed. Beate Czapla and Ralf Georg Czapla (Berlin: Weidler, 2001).

[58] A dual-language edition of these epigrams, Lothar Mundt, trans. and ed., *Lemnius und Luther: Studien und Texte zur Geschichte und Nachwirkung ihres Konflikts (1538–39)* (Bern: Lang, 1983).

[59] The Italian Scaliger, one of the major poetic authorities of late humanism, moved to France in mid-life. On the *argute* tradition of the epigram see Kühlmann, *Gelehrtenrepublik*, 228–34 (see note 8). Further, Manfred Beetz, *Rhetorische Logik: Prämissen der deutschen Lyrik im Übergang vom 17. zum 18. Jahrhunderts* (Tübingen: Niemeyer, 1980).

[60] See the pioneering study by Günter Hess, "Die Kunst der Imagination: Jacob Bidermanns Epigramme im ikonographischen System der Gegenreformation," in *Text und Bild, Bild und Text*, ed. Wolfgang Harms (Stuttgart: Metzler, 1990), 183–96. For a view of the overlapping of tradition and genre see Manuel Baumbach, "Der Heilige Meinrad und die Protestanten: Jacob Bidermanns politisch-religiöse Dichtung am Beispiel der Meinradvita," in Czapla et al., eds., *Lateinische Lyrik*, 304–29 (see note 1).

[61] On Locher's translation, Nina Hartl, *Die "Stultifera navis": Jacob Lochers Übertragung von Sebastian Brants "Narrenschiff,"* 2 vols. (Münster: Waxmann, 2001); on Locher, Kühlmann, in LL 12, 317–18, and Bernhard Coppel, in HDS 151–78. For the larger field of fool's literature, Günter Hess, *Deutsch-lateinische Narrenzunft: Studien zum Verhältnis von Volkssprache und Latinität in der satirischen Literatur des 16. Jahrhunderts* (Munich: Beck, 1971).

[62] Naogeorg as satirist: Rupprich (1973), 360–61. Further, Hans-Gert Roloff, in LL 12, 330–32; Franz Günter Sieveke, in Füssel (1993), 477–93; selections: HL 679–91; also Roloff, "Thomas Naogeorgs Satiren," *Daphnis* 9 (1980): 743–62.

[63] On the meaning of *confessionalism* and the related process of *confessionalization* see, among other places in this volume, the chapter by Scott Dixon, the section: "Contexts of Reform."

[64] On Balde as satirist see Doris Behrens, "Jakob Baldes Auffassung von der Satire," in *Jacob Balde und seine Zeit*, ed. Jean Marie Valentin (Bern: Lang, 1986), 109–26; Hermann Wiegand: " 'Ad vestras, medici, supplex prosternitur aras': Zu Jacob Baldes Medizinersatiren," in *Heilkunde und Krankheitserfahrung in der frühen Neuzeit: Studien am Grenzrain von Literaturgeschichte und Medizingeschichte*, ed. Udo Benzenhöfer und Kühlmann (Tübingen: Niemeyer, 1992), 247–69.

[65] Edition: Vredeveld, *Dichtungen* 3, 183–267 (see note 29). On *laus urbis*: Hermann Goldbrunner, "*Laudatio urbis*: Zu neueren Untersuchungen über das humanistische Städtelob," *Quellen und Forschungen aus italienischen Archiven und Bibliotheken* 63 (1983): 313–28. On prose forms, Walther Ludwig, "Die Darstellung südwestdeutscher Städte in der lateinischen Literatur des 15. bis 17. Jahrhunderts," in *Stadt und Repräsentation*, ed. Bernhard Kirchgässner and Hans-Peter Behr (Sigmaringen: Thorbecke, 1995), 41–76; Nikolaus Thurn, "Deutsche neulateinische Städtelobgedichte: Ein Vergleich ausgewählter Beispiele des 16. Jahrhunderts," *Neulateinisches Jahrbuch* 4 (2002): 253–70.

[66] See in this volume the chapter by Wolfgang Neuber. Also Hermann Wiegand, *Hodoeporica: Studien zur neulateinischen Reisedichtung des deutschen Kulturraums im 16. Jahrhundert* (Baden-Baden: Koerner, 1984); Beate Czapla, "Neulateinische Lehrdichtung zwischen der literarischen Tradition von Hesiod bis Manilius und der neuzeitlichen *Ars Apodemica* am Beispiel von Bernhardus Mollerus *Rhenus* und Cyriacus Lentulus' *Europa*," *Neulateinisches Jahrbuch* 1 (1999): 21–48.

[67] Stephan Füssel, *Riccardus Bartholinus: Humanistische Panegyrik am Hofe Kaiser Maximilians I.* (Baden-Baden: Koerner, 1987). With respect to genre: Siegmar Döpp, "Claudian und die lateinische Epik zwischen 1300 und 1600," *Res publica litterarum* 12 (1989): 39–50. On borrowing Claudian in early modern Germany see Max Reinhart,

"Battle of the Tapestries: A War-Time Debate in Anhalt-Köthen: Georg Philipp Harsdörffer's *Peristromata Turcica* and *Aulaea Romana*, 1641–1642," *Daphnis* 27, nos. 2–3 (1998): 291–333, and Reinhart, "Text and Simultext: Borrowing Claudian in Seventeenth-Century Germany," *German Life and Letters*, N.S. 52, no. 3 (1999): 281–96.

[68] On Latin forms of Habsburg panegyric, including the *Austrias* epos, see Franz Römer und Elisabeth Klecker, "Poetische Habsburg-Panegyrik in lateinischer Sprache: Bestände der österreichischen Nationalbibliothek als Grundlage eines Forschungsprojektes," *biblos* 43, nos. 3–4 (1994): 133–98; Römer, "Klassische Bildung im Dienst habsburgischer Propaganda: Lateinische Panegyrik in der Donaumonarchie," *International Journal of the Classical Tradition* 5 (1998): 195–203. On Candidus see Kühlmann, in LL 2, 354.

[69] See Rupprich (1973), 209–10. With respect to regional considerations: Hermann Wiegand: "Johann Seckerwitz als neulateinischer Dichter," in *Pommern in der Frühen Neuzeit: Literatur und Kultur in Stadt und Region*, ed. Kühlmann and Horst Langer (Tübingen: Niemeyer, 1994), 125–44.

[70] Selections: Hessus in HL 248–73; Cordus in HL 221–45. On Müntzer see in this volume the chapter by Scott Dixon.

[71] On Ens and his extensive journalistic work and on the Latin translations from Italian and Spanish see Kühlmann, in LL 3, 266.

[72] Hermann Schottenius Hessus, *Ludus Martius sive Bellicus: Mars- oder Kriegsspiel*, trans. and ed. Hans-Gert Roloff (Bern: Lang, 1990).

[73] Andreas Gryphius, *Herodes: Lateinische Epik*, trans. and ed. Ralf Georg Czapla (Berlin: Weidler, 1999); see Ralf Georg Czapla: "Epos oder Dramen? Gattungstheoretische Überlegungen zu Andreas Gryphius' lateinischer Bibeldichtung," *Jahrbuch für Internationale Germanistik* 32, no. 2 (2000): 82–104.

[74] On Calaminus see Kühlmann, in LL 2, 343. Edition: *Georg Calaminus: Sämtliche Werke (lateinisch/deutsch)*, 4 vols., ed. Robert Hinterndorfer (Vienna: Ed. Praesens, 1998). The vast Latin literature of Bohemia and Moravia, including many important German authors, is catalogued, with bibliographies, in *Enchiridion renatae poesis [sic] Latinae in Bohemia et Moravia cultae*, 5 vols., comp. Antonio Truhlár and Carolo Hrdina; continued by Josef Hejnic and Jan Martinek (Prague: Akademie, 1966–82). For the equally rich Latin literature of Silesia see Manfred P. Fleischer, *Späthumanismus in Schlesien* (Munich: Delp, 1984).

[75] Schallenberg, an important representative of the German love poetry inspired by Italy, wrote Latin poetry mainly in his youth. See Gert Hübner, "Christoph von Schallenberg und die deutsche Liebeslyrik am Ende des 16. Jahrhunderts," *Daphnis* 31 (2002): 127–86.

[76] On praise-of-discipline literature see Kühlmann, "Lehrdichtung," in Fricke, ed., *Reallexikon*, 2:393–97 (see note 1); Harry Vredeveld, "Helius Eobanus Hessus' *Bonae Valetudinis Conservandae Rationes Aliquot*," *Janus* 72 (1985): 83–112; Barbara Bauer, "Philipp Melanchthons Gedichte astronomischen Inhalts im Kontext der natur- und himmelskundlichen Lehrbücher," in Frank and Rhein, eds., *Philipp Melanchthon*, 137–82 (see note 12).

[77] On the Italian models for alchemistic didactic poetry see Kühlmann, "Alchemie und späthumanistische Formkultur: Der Straßburger Dichter Nicolaus Furichius (1602–1633), ein Freund Moscheroschs," in Kühlmann and Walter E. Schäfer, *Literatur im Elsaß von Fischart bis Moscherosch* (Tübingen: Niemeyer, 2001), 175–200.

320 ¥ EARLY MODERN GERMAN LITERATURE 1350–1700

[78] On Opsopoeus see Kühlmann, in LL 8, 510–11.

[79] Barbara Könneker, trans. and ed., *Grobianus: de morum simplicitate* (Darmstadt: Wissenschaftliche Buchgesellschaft, 1979); also Könneker, in LL 3, 11–12.

[80] Adalbert Elschenbroich, "Sammeln und Umgestalten aesopischer Fabeln bei den Neulateinern des 16. Jahrhunderts," *Daphnis* 14 (1985): 12–63; Elschenbroich, *Die deutsche und lateinische Fabel in der Frühen Neuzeit*, 2 vols. (Tübingen: Niemeyer, 1990).

[81] For the European networking and regional contexts of the early modern intellectual societies see Klaus Garber and Heinz Wismann, eds., *Europäische Sozietätsbewegung und demokratische Tradition: Die europäischen Akademien der Frühen Neuzeit*, 2 vols. (Tübingen: Niemeyer, 1996); Kühlmann, "Das humanistische Westfalen: Zur Bewußtseinsgeschichte von Regionalität in der Frühen Neuzeit," in *Region-Literatur-Kultur: Regionalliteraturforschung heute*, ed. Martina Wagner-Egelhaaf (Bielefeld: Aisthesis, 2001), 121–31.

[82] Lewis W. Spitz, *Conrad Celtis: The German Arch-Humanist* (Cambridge: Harvard UP, 1957). On the question of epoch, Wilfried Barner, "Über das Negieren von Traditionen: Zur Typologie literaturprogrammatischer Epochenwenden in Deutschland," in *Epochenschwelle und Epochenbewußtsein*, ed. Reinhart Herzog and Reinhart Kosellek (Munich: Fink, 1987), 3–51. Editions and studies up to the late 1980s: Dieter Wuttke, in LL 2, 394–400; also Wuttke, in Füssel (1993), 173–99; updated in HL 920–1019 (selections, 11–137). From the massive bibliography see as an introduction Franz-Josef Worstbrock "Konrad Celtis: Zur Konstitution des humanistischen Dichters in Deutschland," in *Literatur, Musik und Kunst im Übergang vom Mittelalter zur Neuzeit*, ed. Hartmut Bookmann (Göttingen: Vandenhoeck & Ruprecht, 1995), 9–35; David Price, "Conrad Celtis," in DLB 179, 23–33; and Jörg Robert, *Konrad Celtis und das Projekt der deutschen Dichtung: Studien zur humanistischen Konstitution von Poetik, Philosophie, Nation und Ich* (Tübingen: Niemeyer, 2003). On Celtis reception see Günter Hess, "Selektive Rezeption: Conrad Celtis im literarischen Bewußtsein des 16. und 17. Jahrhunderts," in *Kleinstformen in der Literatur*, ed. Walter Haug and Burghart Wachinger (Tübingen: Niemeyer, 1994), 247–90.

[83] Franz Josef Worstbrock, "Die *Ars versificandi et carminum* des Konrad Celtis," in *Studien zum städtischen Bildungswesen des späten Mittelalters und der frühen Neuzeit*, ed. Bernd Moeller, Hans Patze, and Karl Stackmann (Göttingen: Vandenhoeck & Ruprecht, 1983), 462–98.

[84] In *Selections from Conrad Celtis 1459–1508*, trans. and ed. Leonard Forster (Cambridge: Cambridge UP, 1948), 20–21.

[85] On the political function of the numerous poetic coronations see Dieter Mertens, " 'Bebelius . . . patriam Sueviam . . . restituit': Der *poeta laureatus* zwischen Reich und Territorium," *Zeitschrift für württembergische Landesgeschichte* 42 (1983): 146–73; Alois Schmidt, " 'Poeta et Orator a Caesare laureatus': Die Dichterkrönungen Kaiser Maximilians I.," *Historisches Jahrbuch* 109 (1989): 56–108.

[86] Forster, *Selections*, 36–65, here 42–43 (see note 84).

[87] Helmuth Grössing, *Humanistische Naturwissenschaft: Zur Geschichte der Wiener mathematischen Schulen des 15. und 16. Jahrhunderts* (Baden-Baden: Koerner, 1983).

[88] On the Heidelberg sodality: Kühlmann, "Vom humanistischen Contubernium zur Heidelberger Sodalitas Litteraria Rhenana," in Kühlmann, ed. *Rudolf Agricola*, 387–412 (see note 16); Hermann Wiegand, " 'Phoebea sodalitas nostra': Die Sodalitas litteraria Rhenana: Probleme, Fakten und Plausibilitäten," *Pirckheimer-Jahrbuch* 12 (1997): 187–209.

[89] Ludwig Krapf, *Germanenmythus und Reichsidee: Frühhumanistische Rezeptionsweisen der taciteischen "Germania"* (Tübingen: Niemeyer, 1979). Further on the patriotic Tacitus reception see Kühlmann, "Nationalliteratur," 201–3 (see note 1), and Donald R. Kelley, "*Tacitus Noster*: The *Germania* in the Renaissance and Reformation," in *Tacitus and the Tacitean Tradition*, ed. T. J. Luce and A. J. Woodman (Princeton: Princeton UP, 1993), 152–67.

[90] Gernot Michael Müller, *Die "Germania generalis" des Conrad Celtis: Studien mit Edition, Übersetzung und Kommentar* (Tübingen: Niemeyer, 2001).

[91] See the exhibition catalogue *Amor als Topograph: 500 Jahre "Amores" des Conrad Celtis: Ein Manifest des deutschen Humanismus*, ed. Claudia Wiener et al. (Schweinfurt: Bibliothek Otto Schäfer, 2002). An interdisciplinary perspective: Dieter Wuttke, *Der Humanismus als integrative Kraft: Die Philosophia des deutschen "Erzhumanisten" Conrad Celtis: Eine ikonologische Studie zu programmatischer Graphik Dürers und Burgkmairs* (Nürnberg: Carl, 1985).

[92] See Thomas Wilhelmi, ed., *Sebastian Brant: Kleine Texte*, 3 vols. (Stuttgart-Bad Cannstatt: Frommann-Holzboog, 1998). On Brant's collected works other than the *Narrenschiff* see Joachim Knape, *Dichtung, Recht und Freiheit: Studien zu Leben und Werk Sebastian Brants, 1457–1521* (Baden-Baden: Koerner, 1992). On Wimpfeling's religious poetry, Susann El Kholi, "Jakob Wimpfelings *De nuntio angelico*: Versuch einer Analyse und Interpretation," *Jahrbuch für Internationale Germanistik* 34, no. 2 (2002): 25–46.

[93] See in this volume the chapter by Gerhart Hoffmeister.

[94] On the importance of Ovid for the autobiographical self–awareness of German poets see Karl Enekel, "Autobiographisches Ethos und Ovid-Überbietung: Die Dichterautobiographie des Eobanus Hessus," *Neulateinisches Jahrbuch* 2 (2000): 25–38; Jörg Robert: " 'Exulis haec vox est': Ovids Exildichtungen in der Lyrik des 16. Jahrhunderts," *Euphorion* N.F. 52 (2002): 437–61.

[95] See Eckart Schäfer, *Deutscher Horaz: Conrad Celtis — Georg Fabricius — Paul Melissus — Jacob Balde* (Wiesbaden: Steiner, 1976); more recently Ulrike Auhagen, Eckard Lefèvre, and Eckart Schäfer, eds., *Horaz und Celtis* (Tübingen: Niemeyer, 2000).

[96] On the literary mystification of the Hasilina figure see Ursula Hess, "Erfundene Wahrheit: Autobiographie und literarische Rolle bei Conrad Celtis," in *Bildungsexklusivität und volkssprachliche Literatur: Literatur vor Lessing — nur für Experten?* ed. Klaus Grubmüller et al. (Tübingen: Niemeyer, 1986), 136–47.

[97] For more on Micyllus with a selection of his poetry see *Parnassus Palatinus*, 16–35, 278–80, and HL 359–93.

[98] See his elegy on the death of Micyllus, addressed to Melanchthon, in HL 484–92.

[99] So-called *Erlebnisdichtung* (poetry of actual experience) that shapes and is shaped by the individual has traditionally been considered in literary history not to have existed until the Age of Sentimentalism.

[100] Twenty-one Lotichius editions appeared between 1551 and 1842. On Lotichius see Bernhard Coppel, in LL 7, 352–65, and in Füssel (1993), 529–44; selections: HL 395–498; also Stephen Zon, *Petrus Lotichius Secundus: Neo-Latin Poet* (Berne: Lang, 1983).

[101] Kühlmann, "Selbstverständigung im Leiden: Zur Bewältigung von Krankheitserfahrungen im versgebundenen Schrifttum der Frühen Neuzeit," in Benzenhöfer and Kühlmann, eds., *Heilkunde*, 1–29 (see note 64). On the mythology

reception in autobiographical fiction, Ralf Georg Czapla, "Pagane Frömmigkeit und lyrische Erlebnisfiktion: Präsenz und Funktion des antiken Mythos in Petrus Lotichius' Secundus Elegie *Ad Lunam*," in *Renaissancekultur und antike Mythologie*, ed. Bodo Guthmüller and Kühlmann (Tübingen: Niemeyer, 1999), 149–66. Following selection in HL 396–400, ll. 33–36.

[102] On Stigelius see Reinhard Düchting, in LL 11, 205–6; selections: HL 571–606; also Stefan Rhein, "Johannes Stigel (1515–1562): Dichtung im Umkreis Melanchthons," in Scheible, ed., *Melanchthon in seinen Schülern*, 31–50 (see note 18); Bärbel Schäfer, "Johann Stigels antirömische Epigramme," ibid., 51–68.

[103] On Posthius see Hermann Wiegand, LL 9, 219; *Parnassus Palatinus*, 72–81 and 286–88; selections: HL 707–51; also Klaus Karrer, Johannes Posthius *(1537–1597)*: *Verzeichnis der Briefe und Werke mit Regesten und Posthius-Biographie* (Wiesbaden: Harrassowitz, 1993).

[104] Major selections: HL 541–45.

[105] Fabricius selections: HL 607–51.

[106] An exemplary study of the adaptation of this song is Artur Göser, *Kirche und Lied: Der Hymnus "Veni redemptor gentium" bei Müntzer und Luther* (Würzburg: Königshausen & Neumann, 1995).

[107] On Venator: *Gesammelte Schriften*, trans. and ed. Georg Burkard and Johannes Schöndorf, 2 vols. (Heidelberg: Manutius, 2001). On Prasch: Dünnhaupt 5, 3194–230; Herbert Jaumann, in LL 9, 223–24; on Kaldenbach: Dünnhaupt 3, 2214–57; Ulrich Maché, in LL 6, 191–99; on Klotz: Günter Häntzschel, in LL 6, 401.

[108] On Balde see Kühlmann, LL 1, 296–98; Dünnhaupt 1, 378–400; George C. Schoolfield, "Jacob Balde," in DLB 164, 29–44. Reception bibliography in the appendix of Georg Westermeyer, *Jacob Balde (1604–1668): sein Leben und seine Werke* (1868), ed. Hans Pörnbacher und Wilfried Stroh (Amsterdam: Rodopi, 1998). Edition: *Jacob Balde S.J.: Opera Poetica Omnia: Neudruck der Ausgabe München 1729*, 8 vols., ed. Kühlmann and Hermann Wiegand (Frankfurt am Main: Lang, 1990). On the international resonance of Balde and other Jesuit writers see Kühlmann, "'Ornamenta Germaniae': Zur Bedeutung des Neulateinischen für die ausländische Rezeption der deutschen Barockliteratur," in *Studien zur europäischen Rezeption deutscher Barockliteratur*, ed. Leonard Forster (Wiesbaden: Harrassowitz, 1983), 13–36.

[109] Overview by Jürgen Galle, *Die lateinische Lyrik Jacob Baldes und die Geschichte ihrer Übertragungen* (Münster: Aschendorff, 1973); Wilfried Barner, "Das europäische 17. Jahrhundert bei Lessing und Herder," in *Europäische Barock-Rezeption*, ed. Klaus Garber (Wiesbaden: Harrassowitz, 1991), 397–417, and Barbara Bauer, "Intertextualität und das rhetorische System der Frühen Neuzeit," in *Intertextualität in der Frühen Neuzeit*, ed. Kühlmann and Wolfgang Neuber (Frankfurt am Main: Lang, 1994), 31–61.

[110] On Balde's imitation of Horace see Schäfer, *Deutscher Horaz*, 109–231 (see note 95); and 113–26 on the impact of Sarbiewski.

[111] Breuer, *Oberdeutsche Literatur*, 218–76. Balde encountered censorship in his relationship with the elector Maximilian of Bavaria; see Breuer, *Geschichte der literarischen Zensur in Deutschland* (Heidelberg: Quelle & Meyer, 1982), 58–64.

[112] Urs Herzog, *Divina Poesis: Studie zu Jacob Baldes geistlicher Odendichtung* (Tübingen: Niemeyer, 1976); also Spolia Vetustatis, "Die Verwandlung der heidnisch-antiken Tradition," in *Jakob Baldes marianischen Wallfahrten: Parthenia, Silvae II, Nr. 3 (1643)*, trans. and ed. Andreas Heider (Munich: Utz, 1999).

[113] Wilhelm Kühlmann, "Alamode-Satire und jesuitischer Reichspatriotismus: Zu einem Gedichtzyklus in den *Sylvae* (1643) des Elsässers Jacob Balde S.J.," *Simpliciana* 22 (2000): 201–26.

[114] Gisbert Kranz, "Zu Jacob Baldes Bildgedichten," *Archiv für Kulturgeschichte* 60 (1978): 305–25; Günter Hess, "Triumph und Vanitas: Jacob Baldes Ode zu Peter Candids Hochaltarbild in der Münchener Frauenkirche," in *Monachium Sacrum* (Munich: Deutscher Kunstverlag, 1994), 233–46.

[115] *Urania Victrix: Die siegreiche Urania: Liber I–II*, trans. and ed. Lutz Claren et al. (Tübingen: Niemeyer, 2003).

[116] On Bisselius see Franz Günter Sieveke, in LL 1, 523–24; with regard specifically to his lyrics see Hermann Wiegand, "Marianische Liebeskunst: Zu den Anfängen der Lateinischen Lyrik des Johannes Bisselius S.J. (1601–1682)," in *Acta Conventus Neo-Latini Guelpherbytani*, ed. Stella P. Revard et al. (Binghamton: State U Center for Medieval and Early Renaissance Studies, 1988), 383–93; Kühlmann: "'Parvus eram': Zur literarischen Rekonstruktion frühneuzeitlicher Welterfahrung in den 'Deliciae Veris' des deutschen Jesuiten Johannes Bisselius," in *Zwischen Renaissance und Aufklärung*, ed. Klaus Garber and Winfried Neumann (Amsterdam: Rodopi, 1988), 163–77.

[117] On Widl see Hermann Wiegand, in LL 12, 293.

[118] On Rettenbacher, Dünnhaupt 5, 3305–8; Franz Günter Sieveke, in LL 9, 396–97.

[119] For the history of early modern plays in the vernacular see in this volume the chapter by John Alexander.

[120] Otto Francke, *Terenz und die lateinische Schulcomoedie in Deutschland* (1877; repr., Leipzig: Zentralantiquariat der DDR, 1972); Frank Baron, "Plautus und die deutschen Frühhumanisten," in *Studia Humanitatis*, ed. Eginhard Hora and Eckhard Keßler (Munich: Fink, 1973), 89–101. On Melanchthon and school comedy see Robert Seidel, "Praeceptor comoedorum: Philipp Melanchthons Schultheaterpädagogik im Spiegel seiner Prologgedichte zur Aufführung römischer Komödien," in Günther Wartenberg, ed., *Werk und Rezeption Melanchthons*, 99–122 (see note 9). Little work has been done on the German reception of Seneca since Paul Stachel, *Seneca und das deutsche Renaissancedrama: Studien zur Literatur- und Stilgeschichte des 16. und 17. Jahrhunderts* (Berlin: Mayer & Müller, 1907).

[121] Aelius Donatus (fl. 350 A.D.), grammarian and commentator on Cicero, Vergil, and many others. This understanding of comedy prevailed throughout the Renaissance and is repeated in various forms deep into the seventeenth century.

[122] On Bebel see Helmut Kiesel, in LL 7, 360–62; Klaus Graf, in Füssel (1993), 281–95; HDS 179–94; selections: HL 203–20. Edition of *Comoedia de optima studio iuvenum* (1504), trans. and ed. Wilfried Barner et al. (Stuttgart: Reclam, 1982). On the social function of his poetry see Dieter Mertens, "Bebels Einstand," in *Aus südwestdeutscher Geschichte*, ed. Wolfgang Schmierer et al. (Stuttgart: Kohlhammer, 1994), 307–24. Selection of Bebel's *facetiae* in Trillitzsch 361–70.

[123] *Stylpho*, trans. and ed. Harry C. Schnur (Stuttgart: Reclam, 1971). On Wimpfeling see Dieter Mertens, in LL 12, 341–42; HDS 35–58; excerpts of the pedagogical and historical writings in Trillitzsch 184–94, 401–11.

[124] *Codrus: ein neulateinisches Drama*, ed. Lothar Mundt (Berlin: de Gruyter, 1969).

[125] *Henno*, trans. and ed. Harry C. Schnur (Stuttgart: Reclam, 1995). On the state of Reuchlin research see Manfred Krebs, ed., *Johannes Reuchlin (1455–1522)*, 2nd ed., ed.

Hermann Kling and Stefan Rhein (Sigmaringen: Thorbecke, 1994); on his life and works, David Price, "Johannes Reuchlin," in DLB 179, 231–40. On Reuchlin and school comedy see also Jane O. Newman, "Textuality versus Performativity in Neo-Latin Drama: Johannes Reuchlin's *Henno,*" *Theater Journal* 38 (1986): 259–74.

[126] Overview, Roloff, " 'Neulateinische Dichtung' " (see note 1); Wolfgang F. Michael, *Das deutsche Drama der Reformationszeit* (Bern: Lang, 1984), and Michael, *Ein Forschungsbericht: Das deutsche Drama der Reformationszeit* (Bern: Lang, 1989); also James A. Parente Jr., *Religious Drama and the Humanist Tradition: Christian Theater in Germany and the Netherlands 1500–1680* (Leiden: Brill, 1987). A voluminous compilation of European titles in Leicester Bradner, "The Latin Drama of the Renaissance (1340–1640)," *Studies in the Renaissance* 4 (1957): 31–70.

[127] On the history of the stage and theater see Manfred Brauneck, *Die Welt als Bühne: Geschichte des europäischen Theaters* (Stuttgart: Metzler, 1993), 1:513–53, 2:358–412.

[128] On Chelidonius see Stephan Füssel, in LL 2, 404.

[129] On Gnaphieus see Kühlmann, in LL 4, 180–81; Fidel Rädle: "Acolastus – der Verlorene Sohn: Zwei lateinische Bibeldramen des 16. Jahrhunderts," in *Gattungsinnovation und Motivstruktur,* ed. Theodor Wolpers (Göttingen: Vandenhoeck & Ruprecht, 1992), part 2:15–34.

[130] On Stymmelius, Kühlmann, in LL 11, 277.

[131] On Macropedius, Fidel Rädle, in LL 7, 419–20; Thomas W. Best, *Macropedius* (New York: Twayne Publishers, 1972).

[132] Jean Lebeau, *Salvator Mundi: L`Exemple de Joseph dans le théâtre allemand au XVIe siècle,* 2 vols. (Nieuwkoop: de Graaf, 1977); Ruprecht Wimmer, *Jesuitentheater: Didaktik und Fest: Das Exemplum des ägyptischen Joseph auf den Bühnen der Gesellschaft Jesu* (Frankfurt am Main: Klostermann, 1982).

[133] Edition: *Sämtliche Dramen,* ed. Manfred Brauneck, 3 vols. (Berlin: de Gruyter, 1969–80). On Birck see Elke Ukena-Best, in LL 1, 514–16; Paul F. Casey, *The Susanna Theme in German Literature* (Bonn: Grundmann, 1976).

[134] Naogeorg's dramatic operas in *Thomas Naogeorg: Sämtliche Werke,* 4 vols., ed. Hans-Gert Roloff (Berlin: de Gruyter, 1975–87). Further studies by Roloff: "Thomas Naogeorgs 'Judas,' ein Drama der Reformationszeit," *Archiv für das Studium der neueren Sprachen und Literaturen* 208 (1972): 81–107; "Naogeorg und das Problem von Humanismus und Reformation," in *L' Humanisme Allemand* (Munich: Fink, 1979), 455–75; "Heilsgeschichte, Weltgeschehen und aktuelle Polemik: Thomas Naogeorgs 'Tragoedia nova Pammachius,' " *Daphnis* 9 (1980): 743–67.

[135] On the reception of Sophocles see Anastasia Daskarolis, *Die Wiedergeburt des Sophokles aus dem Geist des Humanismus: Studien zur Sophokles-Rezeption in Deutschland vom Beginn des 16. bis zur Mitte des 17. Jahrhunderts* (Tübingen: Niemeyer, 2000).

[136] On Frischlin see Adelbert Elschenbroich, in LL 4, 37–39; Richard E. Schade, in Füssel (1993), 613–25; Kühlmann, in HDS 265–88; Wilfried Barner, "Nicodemus Frischlins 'satirische Freiheit,' " in *Pioniere, Schulen, Pluralismus: Studien zu Geschichte und Theorie der Literaturwissenschaft,* ed. Barner (Tübingen: Niemeyer, 1997), 47–68; David Price, *The Political Dramaturgy of Nicodemus Frischlin: Essays on Humanist Drama in Germany* (Chapel Hill: U of North Carolina P, 1990). Research report in *Nikodemus Frischlin: Poetische und prosaische Praxis unter den Bedingungen des konfessionellen Zeitalters,* ed. Sabine Holtz and Dieter Mertens (Stuttgart-Bad Cannstatt: Frommann-Holzboog, 1999).

[137] Günter Hess, "Deutsch und Latein bei Frischlin Imitatio und Abweichung," in Holtz and Mertens, eds., *Nicodemus Frischlin*, 471–93 (see note 136).

[138] David Price, "Die (Ohn-)Macht des Wortes: Humanistische Gesellschaftskritik in Frischlins *Susanna*," in Holtz and Mertens, eds., *Nicodemus Frischlin*, 543–61 (see note 136); Lothar Mundt, "Fürs Gymnasium und für tugendliebende Jungfrauen: Zu fünf zeitgenössischen Übersetzungen von Frischlins *Rebecca*," in Guthmüller, ed., *Latein und Nationalsprachen*, 259–85 (see note 1).

[139] Nicola Kaminski, "Dekonstruktive Stimmenvielfalt: Zur polyphonen Imitatio-Konzeption in Frischlins Komödien *Hildegardis Magna* und *Helvetiogermani*," *Daphnis* 24 (1995): 79–133.

[140] In comparison with the two-part, thematically similar *Regnum humanitatis* (discussed below) by Jacob Gretser see Bauer, Jesuitische *"ars rhetorica*," 1–15 (see note 22).

[141] Edition with the translation by Frischlin's brother: Richard E. Schade, ed. (Stuttgart: Reclam, 1983); Wilfried Barner, "Vorspiel der Querelle: Neuzeitlichkeitsbewußtsein in Nicodemus Frischlins *Julius Redivivus*," in *Festschrift für Walter Haug und Burghart Wachinger*, ed. Johannes Janota et al. (Tübingen: Niemeyer, 1992), 2:843–92; Schade, "Nicodemus Frischlin und der Stuttgarter Hof: Zur Aufführung von *Julius redivivus*," in *Europäische Hofkultur im 16. und 17. Jahrhundert*, ed. August Buck and Conrad Wiedemann (Hamburg: Hauswedell, 1981), 2:335–44.

[142] Adalbert Elschenbroich, "Imitatio und Disputatio in Nikodemus Frischlins Religionskomödie *Phasma*," in *Stadt-Schule-Universität-Buchwesen und die deutsche Literatur im 17. Jahrhundert*, ed. Albrecht Schöne (Munich: Beck, 1976), 179–95; Richard E. Schade, "Komödie und Konfession: Eine Dokumentation zu Frischlins *Phasma* (1592)," *Euphorion* 83 (1992): 284–318; Fidel Rädle, "Frischlin und die Konfessionspolemik im lateinischen Drama des 16. Jahrhunderts," in Holtz and Mertens, eds., *Nicodemus Frischlin*, 495–523 (see note 136).

[143] James A. Parente Jr., *"Tragoedia politica*: Strasbourg School Drama and the Early Modern State, 1583–1621," *Colloquia Germanica* 29 (1996): 1–11.

[144] Overview by Otto v. Tetzlaff, "Neulateinische Dramen der Niederlande in ihrer Einwirkung auf die deutsche Literatur des sechzehnten Jahrhunderts," *Amsterdamer Beiträge zur älteren Germanistik* 1 (1972): 111–92.

[145] On Brülow see Dünnhaupt 2, 839–54; Kühlmann, in LL 2, 256–57. On Crusius see Kühlmann, in LL 2, 484.

[146] On Virdung and his tragedies *Saulus*, *Brutus* and *Thrasea* see Markus Mollitor, in LL 12, 35. On Rhodius see *Parnassus Palatinus* 170–83, 288–89; Kühlmann: "Zur literarischen Lebensform im deutschen Späthumanismus: Der pfälzische Dramatiker Theodor Rhodius (ca. 1575–1625) in seiner Lyrik und in seinen Briefen," *Daphnis* 17, no. 4 (1988): 671–749. On Rhodius's dramas, Hans-Gert Roloff, "Klassizismus im deutschen Drama um 1600: Beobachtungen an der *Tragoedia Colignius* des Theodor Rhodius," in *Festschrift für Joseph P. Strelka*, ed. Karl Konrad Polheim (Bern: Lang, 1987), 23–35.

[147] Kühlmann, in LL 3, 409–10.

[148] For more on Andreae see below. The German translation of *Turbo* is by Wilhelm Süß (Tübingen: Laupp, 1907).

[149] On the relationship between Latin and German see Barbara Bauer, "Deutsch und Latein in den Schulen der Jesuiten," in Guthmüller, ed., *Latein und Nationalsprachen*, 227–57 (see note 1); Fidel Rädle, "Lateinisches Theater für das Volk: Zum Problem des frühen Jesuitendramas," in *Zwischen Festtag und Alltag: Zehn Beiträge zum Thema*

"Mündlichkeit" und "Schriftlichkeit," ed. Wolfgang Raible (Tübingen: Narr, 1988), 133–47.

[150] *Le Théâtre des Jésuites dans les Pays de Langue Allemande: Répertoire chronologique des Piéces representées et des Documents conservés (1555–1773),* 2 vols. (Stuttgart: Hiersemann, 1983–84); *Le Théâtre des Jésuites dans les pays de langue allemande (1554–1680): Salut des âmes et ordre des cités,* 3 vols. (Bern: Lang, 1978); "Jesuiten-Literatur als gegenreformatorische Propaganda," in *Zwischen Gegenreformation und Frühaufklärung: Späthumanismus, Barock, 1572–1740,* ed. Harald Steinhagen (Reinbek b. Hamburg: Rowohlt, 1985), 172–205.

[151] *Das Jesuitendrama im deutschen Sprachgebiet: Eine Periochen-Edition: Texte und Kommentare,* 4 vols. (Munich: Fink, 1979–87); "Versuche einer neuen Periodisierung des Jesuitendramas: Das Jesuitendrama der oberdeutschen Ordensprovinz," *Daphnis* 3 (1974): 158–77; "Das Jesuitendrama als Vorläufer der modernen Massenmedien," *Daphnis* 4 (1975): 129–43.

[152] For Masen see below. On Pontano as dramatist see Joseph Bielmann, "Die Dramentheorie und Dramendichtung des Jakobus Pontanus S.J. (1542–1626)," *Literaturwissenschaftliches Jahrbuch* 3 (1928): 45–85. On Father Lang see Franz Günter Sieveke, in LL 7, 133, and Barbara Bauer, "Das Bild als Argument: Emblematische Kulisse in den Bühnenmeditationen Franciscus Langs," *Archiv für Kulturgeschichte* 64 (1982): 79–170.

[153] *Nicolaus Avancini S.J.: Pietas victrix – Der Sieg der Pietas,* trans. and ed. Lothar Mundt and Ulrich Seelbach (Tübingen: Niemeyer, 2002); Dünnhaupt 1, 357–77.

[154] Fidel Rädle, "Gegenreformatorischer Humanismus: Die Schul- und Theaterkultur der Jesuiten," in Hammerstein and Walther, eds., *Späthumanismus,* 128–47 (see note 8).

[155] With respect to world theater see Fidel Rädle, "Gottes ernstgemeintes Spiel: Überlegungen zum welttheatralischen Charakter des Jesuitendramas," in *Theatrum Mundi: Götter, Gott und Spielleiter im Drama von der Antike bis zur Gegenwart,* ed. Franz Link and Günther Niggl (Berlin: Duncker & Humblot, 1981), 135–59.

[156] The differences and peculiarities are described by Barbara Bauer, "Multimediales Theater: Ansätze einer Poetik der Synästhesie bei den Jesuiten," in *Renaissance-Poetik,* ed. Heinrich Plett (Berlin: de Gruyter, 1994), 197–238; Peter Sprengel, "Der Spieler-Zuschauer im Jesuitentheater: Beobachtungen an frühen oberdeutschen Ordensdramen," *Daphnis* 16 (1987): 47–106.

[157] Editions: *Ludi theatrales, 1666,* ed. Rolf Tarot, 2 vols. (Tübingen: Niemeyer, 1967); *Cenodoxus,* trans. Joachim Meichel, ed. Rolf Tarot (Stuttgart: Reclam, 1981). See Peter-Paul Lenhard, *Religiöse Weltanschauung und Didaktik im Jesuitendrama: Interpretationen zu den Schauspielen Jacob Bidermanns* (Frankfurt am Main: Lang, 1976).

[158] See the analysis of theater and social history by Günter Hess, "Spectator — Lector — Actor: Zum Publikum von Jacob Bidermanns *Cenodoxus,*" with materials on the literary and sociohistorical contexts by Ursula Hess, *Internationales Archiv für Sozialgeschichte der deutschen Literatur* 1 (1976): 30–106.

[159] Barbara Bauer, "Apathie des stoischen Weisen oder Ekstase der christlichen Braut? Jesuitische Stoakritik und Jacob Baldes *Jephthias,*" in *Res Publica Litteraria: Die Institutionen der Gelehrsamkeit in der frühen Neuzeit,* ed. Sebastian Neumeister and Conrad Wiedemann (Wiesbaden: Harrassowitz, 1987), 2:453–74.

[160] On Gretser, Dünnhaupt 3, 1759–824; Franz Günter Sieveke, in LL 4, 342–43. On the *Regnum humanitatis* see Eugene J. Devlin, "The *Regnum humanitatis* Trilogy: A Humanist Manifesto, *Comparative Drama* 26, no. 1 (1992).

[161] *Augustinus conversus*, trans. and ed. Dorothea Weber (Vienna: Österreichische Akademie der Wissenschaften, 2000).

[162] Thomas W. Best, "Time in Jacob Masen's *Rusticus imperans*," *Humanistica Lovaniensia* 27 (1978): 287–94, and "On Psychology and Allegory in J. Masen's *Rusticus imperans*," *Mittellateinisches Jahrbuch* 13 (1978): 247–52; Kühlmann, "Macht auf Widerruf: Der Bauer als Herrscher bei Jacob Masen SJ und Christian Weise," in *Christian Weise: Dichter– Gelehrter – Pädagoge*, ed. Peter Behnke and Hans-Gert Roloff (Bern: Lang, 1994), 245–60; English translation, Michael C. Halbig, trans. and ed., *The Jesuit Theater of Jacob Masen* (New York: Lang, 1987).

[163] James A. Parente Jr., "Andreas Gryphius and the Jesuit Theater," *Daphnis* 13 (1984): 525–51.

[164] In one play, for instance, the renowned poet Jacob Balde occupies the stage as a dramatic hero. See Günter Hess, "*Fracta Cithara* oder Die zerbrochene Laute: Zur Allegorisierung der Bekehrungsgeschichte Jacob Baldes im 18. Jahrhundert," in *Formen und Funktionen der Allegorie*, ed. Walter Haug (Stuttgart: Metzler, 1980), 605–31.

[165] On German vernacular prose see in this volume the chapter by Andreas Solbach.

[166] Facsimile reprint in *Martin Opitz: Jugendschriften vor 1619*, ed. Jörg Ulrich Fechner (Stuttgart: Reclam, 1970). German translation in the afterword to *Martin Opitz: Buch von der Deutschen Poeterey (1624)*, ed. Herbert Jaumann (Stuttgart: Reclam, 2002).

[167] Kühlmann, *Gelehrtenrepublik*, 189–253 (see note 8). For a discussion that ranges into the baroque period see Dietmar Till, *Transformationen der Rhetorik: Untersuchungen zum Wandel der Rhetoriktheorie im 17. und 18. Jahrhundert* (Tübingen: Niemeyer, 2004), 181–96. On Erasmus, Jan-Dirk Müller, "Erasmus' *Ciceronianus* und das Problem der Autorität," *Scientia poetica* 3 (1999): 20–46.

[168] See in this volume the chapter by Joachim Knape. Research catalogued and expanded by Till, *Transformationen*, 197–259 (see note 167). See also Hans-Henrik Krummacher, ed., *Briefe deutscher Barockautoren: Probleme ihrer Erfassung und Erschließung* (Hamburg: Hauswedell, 1978); Franz Joseph Worstbrock, ed., *Der Brief im Zeitalter der Renaissance* (Weinheim: Acta Humaniora, 1983).

[169] This great collection is volume 1 of Reifferscheid's larger project, *Quellen zur Geschichte des geistigen Lebens in Deutschland während des siebenzehnten Jahrhunderts: Nach Handschriften herausgegeben und erläutert* (Heilbronn: Henninger, 1889). A companion to Reifferscheid in context of Palatine late humanism: Axel E. Walter, *Späthumanismus und Konfessionspolitik: Die europäische Gelehrtenrepublik um 1600 im Spiegel der Korrespondenzen Georg Michael Lingelsheims* (Tübingen: Niemeyer, 2004).

[170] The starting place is the vast Amerbach correspondence at the University of Basel, where editions of letters have been appearing since 1942. For the historical place of the Amerbach printers in Basel see in this volume the chapter by Erika Rummel. Other important editions: Pirckheimer (since 1940), Melanchthon (since 1977), Reuchlin (since 1999), Wimpfeling (1990), and Rudolf Agricola (2002). — Pirckheimer: as of 2004, six volumes with C. H. Beck publishers in Munich under the title *Willibald Pirckheimers Briefwechsel*. Melanchthon: as of 2005, twelve volumes with Fromann-Holzboog publishers in Stuttgart-Bad Cannstatt under the title *Melanchthons Briefwechsel: kritische und kommentierte Gesamtausgabe*. Reuchlin: as of 2004, two volumes with Fromann-Holzboog publishers in Stuttgart-Bad Cannstatt under the title *Briefwechsel: Johannes Reuchlin*, trans. Adelbert Weh, ed. Manfred Fuhrmann. Wimpfeling: *Jacobi Wimpfelingi opera selecta*, 3 vols., ed. and com. Otto Herding and

Dieter Mertens (Munich: Fink, 1990). Agricola: *Letters: Rudolf Agricola*, trans. and ed. Adrie van der Laan and Fokke Akkerman (Assen: Royal van Gorcum, 2002).

[171] On Agricola see Lothar Suhling, in LL 1, 60–62. On Schott see Dünnhaupt 5, 3810–23, and Franz Günter Sieveke, in LL 10, 375. On Kircher see Dünnhaupt 3, 2326–49; Franz Günter Sieveke, in LL 6, 330–33; Thomas Leinkauf, *Mundus combinatus: Studien zur Struktur der barocken Universalwissenschaft am Beispiel Athanasius Kirchers SJ (1602–1680)* (Berlin: Akademie, 1993).

[172] Kühlmann, "Der vermaledeite Prometheus: Die antiparacelsistische Lyrik des Andreas Libavius und ihr historischer Kontext," *Scientia poetica* 4 (2000): 30–61.

[173] Erik Leibenguth, ed., *Hermetische Poesie des Frühbarock: Die "Cantilenae intellectuales" Michael Maiers* (Tübingen: Niemeyer, 2002).

[174] Overview in Franz M. Eybl et al., eds., *Enzyklopädien der Frühen Neuzeit: Beiträge zu ihrer Erforschung* (Tübingen: Niemeyer, 1995); also Helmut Zedelmaier, *Bibliotheca Universalis und Bibliotheca Selecta: Das Problem der Ordnung des gelehrten Wissens in der Frühen Neuzeit* (Cologne: Böhlau, 1992). The encyclopedia of Alsted is available in reprint: *Encyclopaedia: Faksimileneudruck der Ausgabe Herborn 1630*, 4 vols. (Stuttgart-Bad Cannstatt: Frommann-Holzboog, 1990). On the scholarly culture see Helmut Zedelmaier and Martin Mulsow, eds., *Die Praktiken der Gelehrsamkeit in der Frühen Neuzeit* (Tübingen: Niemeyer, 2001).

[175] Overview, Kühlmann, *Gelehrtenrepublik*, 434–66 (see note 8). See also Horst Dreitzel, *Protestantischer Aristotelismus und absoluter Staat: Die Politica des Henning Arnisaeus (ca. 1575–1636)* (Wiesbaden: Steiner, 1970), and Michael Stolleis, *Reichspublizistik und Policeywissenschaft 1600–1800*, vol. 1 of *Geschichte des öffentlichen Rechts in Deutschland* (Munich: Beck, 1988).

[176] Kühlmann, "Formen der politischen Reflexion im deutschen 'Tacitismus' des 17. Jahrhunderts," in Kühlmann and Schäfer, eds., *Literatur im Elsaß*, 41–60 (see note 77).

[177] Scholarship on Lipsius is vast. For an introduction see *The World of Justus Lipsius: A Contribution towards His Intellectual Biography*, ed. Marc Laureys et al. (Turnhout: Brepols, 1998), and Jan Papy, "Justus Lipsius and the German Republic of Letters: Latin Philology as a Means of Intellectual Exchange and Influence," in GL 523–38.

[178] On Peutinger, Hartmut Kugler, in LL 9, 136–37.

[179] On Aventinus, Hans Pörnbacher, in LL 1, 263–64.

[180] On Beatus Rhenanus, Hubert Meyer, in LL 9, 415–16.

[181] On Sleidanus, Gustav Adolf Benrath, in LL 11, 53–54.

[182] See Franz Brendle et al., eds., *Deutsche Landesgeschichtsschreibung im Zeichen des Humanismus* (Stuttgart: Steiner, 2001).

[183] August Buck, ed., *Biographie und Autobiographie in der Renaissance* (Wiesbaden: Harrassowitz, 1983); Walter Berschin, ed., *Biographie zwischen Renaissance und Barock* (Heidelberg: Mattes, 1993); James Michael Weiss, "The Harvest of German Humanism: Melchior Adam's Collective Biographies as Cultural History," in Fleischer, *Harvest of Humanism*, 341–50 (see note 8).

[184] See Niklas Holzberg, trans. and ed., *Eckius dedolatus: Der enteckte Eck* (Stuttgart: Reclam, 1983).

[185] Menippean satire frequently blended verse and prose and lent itself particularly to parody. Menippus of Gadara (fl. 290 B.C.), a Syrian Cynic philosopher, first practiced the style, hence the name; Varro (116–27 B.C.) adapted it into Latin. Examples of

Hutten's imitative adaptations from Lucian, in German translation, in *Die Schule des Tyrannen: Lateinische Schriften*, trans. and ed. Martin Treu (Darmstadt: Wissenschaftliche Buchgesellschaft, 1996).

[186] Edition by Robert Seidel (Goldbach: Keip, 1995). On Dornau's seminal role in Saxon late humanism see Seidel, *Späthumanismus in Schlesien: Caspar Dornau* (Tübingen: Niemeyer, 1994).

[187] See Ute Mennecke-Haustein, in LL 3, 270–72; historical context in James H. Overfield, *Humanism and Scholasticism in Late Medieval Germany* (Princteon: Princeton UP, 1984).

[188] In *Die Deutsche Literatur: Texte und Zeugnisse*, vol. II/2: *Spätmittelalter — Humanismus — Reformation: Blüte des Humanismus und Reformation*, ed. Hedwig Heger (Munich: Beck, 1978), 161–62.

[189] Jörg-Jochen Berns, "Caspar Stiblins Macaria-Utopie und die utopische Satiretradition des Oberrheins," *Simpliciana* 2 (2000): 129–44. On Andrea's utopian work see Wilhelm Vosskamp, "Von der Staats- zur Bildungsutopie: Johann Valentin Andreaes Christianopolis," in *Innovation und Originalität*, ed. Walter Haug and Burghart Wachinger (Tübingen: Niemeyer, 1993), 196–205. For a general view of early utopias, Walter Berschin, "Neulateinische Utopien im Alten Reich (1555–1741)," in GL 693–704. Dual-language edition of the *Christianopolis*, trans. and ed. Richard van Dülmen (Stuttgart: Reclam, 1982).

[190] See Donald R. Dickson, "Johann Valentin Andreae's Utopian Brotherhoods," *Renaissance Quarterly* 49 (1996): 760–802, and Dickson, *The Tessera of Antilla: Utopian Brotherhoods and Secret Societies in the Early Seventeenth Century* (Leiden: Brill, 1998). On Andreae scholarship, Dünnhaupt 1, 255–93; Kühlmann, in LL 1, 170–72.

[191] *Turbo* is briefly discussed in the present volume by Kühlmann, "Education in Early Modern Germany."

[192] On Drexel see Dünnhaupt 2, 1368–418; Barbara Bauer, in LL 3, 112–13; Karl Pörnbacher, *Jeremias Drexel: Leben und Werk eines Barockpredigers* (Munich: Seitz, 1965).

[193] On Spee and the reception of the *Cautio criminalis* see Franz Günter Sieveke, in LL 11, 91–93; G. Richard Dimler, "Friedrich Spee von Langenfeld," in DLB 164, 316–20; Kühlmann, "Das Werk Friedrich Spees im Horizont der deutschen Aufklärung," *Spee-Jahrbuch* 9 (2002): 29–54.

[194] See Susanne Siegl-Mocavini, *John Barclays "Argenis" und ihr staatstheoretischer Kontext: Untersuchungen zum politischen Denken der Frühen Neuzeit* (Tübingen: Niemeyer, 1999).

[195] On Contzen see LL 2, 457–59. On Bisselius' *Icaria*: Hermann Wiegand, "Die Oberpfalz im konfessionellen Umbruch: Eine jesuitische Reisesatire aus dem Jahr 1632," in *Der Pfälzer Löwe in Bayern*, ed. Hans-Jürgen Becker (Regensburg: Universitätsverlag, 1997), 130–56; on the *Argonauticum*: Harold C. Hill, "Johann Bissel's *Argonauticon Americanorum* (1647): A Reexamination," *Modern Language Notes* 85 (1970): 652–62.

[196] Kühlmann, *Gelehrtenrepublik*, 423–54 (see note 8).

[197] Walther Ludwig, "De linguae Latinae in Germania fatis: Jacob Burckhardt und der neuzeitliche Gebrauch der lateinischen Sprache," *Neulateinisches Jahrbuch* 5 (2003): 185–218.

[198] Ellinger, *Geschichte der neulateinischen Literatur Deutschlands im 16. Jahrhundert*, 3 vols. (1933; repr., Berlin: de Gruyter, 1969).

Ad fontes: German Humanists as Editors and Translators

Erika Rummel

The Italian Origins of the Movement

RENAISSANCE HUMANISTS USED THE SLOGAN *Ad fontes* (to the sources) to promote the use of classical Greek and Latin sources.[1] The humanistic movement grew out of an admiration for classical civilization and the desire to revive and emulate classical authors. It was, moreover, part of a larger movement to study the remains of Greek and Roman culture and to appropriate or recreate its style. The endeavor of collecting the vestiges of the past — particularly on the history of Rome — began in Italy in the fourteenth century. Petrarch, the archetypal figure of the Renaissance humanist, discovered Cicero's *Pro Archia* and his letters to Atticus and attempted to reconstruct the first three decades of Livy (the most prominent source for the early history of Rome) from extant manuscripts. Indeed, the hunt for classical manuscripts was a lifelong pursuit for Petrarch, as it was for other humanists of the fourteenth and fifteenth centuries: Giovanni Boccaccio, Coluccio Salutati, Poggio Bracciolini, Angelo Poliziano, and Lorenzo Valla, to name the most prominent representatives of the drive to collect the literary sources of the past.

Humanists recognized that the texts they unearthed were often corrupt and the meaning and context of many passages obscure to Renaissance readers. They therefore embarked on the task of editing, translating, and annotating the texts to open them up to a larger readership. In the course of collating and emending texts they developed methods of dating manuscripts on the basis of script and established the first principles of textual criticism: among others, verifying historical usage, preferring the older over the later source, and lending greater credibility to the more difficult reading than to the more obvious one. In this way a historical and text-critical methodology emerged that led to a better understanding of the process of textual transmission and to a sharper discrimination between what was original and what was derivative. The scholarly scrutiny of classical texts resulted in commentaries and annotations that surpassed traditional philological considerations by reflecting not only on the grammatical but also on the historical aspects of the text, thus providing a more sophisticated appreciation of the author's meaning. More important still was the gradual change that evolved in the general approach to texts, leading humanists to replace medieval with classical authorities and, more radically, to value experience and observation over tradition and authority.

The New Learning North of the Alps

Developments in Germany lagged behind those in Italy, so that Desiderius Erasmus (ca. 1466–1536) could write in 1523:

> Repullulascere quidem coeperant apud Italos bonae literae, sed ob typographorum artem aut nondum repertam aut paucissimis cognitam nihil ad nos librorum perferebatur, et altissima quiete regnabant ubique qui literas docebant illiteratissimas. Rodolphus Agricola primus omnium aurulam quandam melioris literaturae nobis invexit ex Italia.[2]

> [The humanities had begun to put forth fresh shoots among the Italians; but because the printer's art was either not yet invented or known to very few, nothing in the way of books came through to us, and unbroken slumber graced the universal reign of those who taught ignorance in place of knowledge. Rudolf Agricola was the first to bring us a breath of more humane learning out of Italy.]

Erasmus mentions two factors responsible for propelling the humanistic movement north of the Alps: traveling scholars and the art of printing. The princely courts that hosted learned diplomats like Johann von Neumarkt (ca. 1310–80) and Enea Silvio Piccolomini (1405–64; later Pope Pius II); monasteries like that of the Cistercians of Adwert near Groningen or the Benedictine community led by the learned abbot Johannes Trithemius of Sponheim (1462–1516);[3] and, in the sixteenth century, the shops of Basel printers like Johann Amerbach (d. 1513) and his younger colleague Johann Froben (1460–1527) functioned as meeting places for itinerant humanists and promoted a wide exchange of ideas. In a letter to Neumarkt, Petrarch paid tribute to him as the first northern transmitter of Italian learning, remarking that, although Neumarkt had been born far from Rome, he nevertheless possessed Roman eloquence. Because of writers like Neumarkt, Petrarch went on to say with an excess of flattery, Germany's repute was now equal to Italy's.[4]

It took another century, however, until the humanistic movement took root in Germany. Rudolf Agricola (born Huisman, 1444–85) was among the earliest German travelers to introduce Italian humanism to a northern readership. Agricola entered the service of Duke Ercole I d'Este in Ferrara in 1475, perfecting his Latin and acquiring a knowledge of Greek during his stay there. He also imbibed the humanistic distaste for the scholastic translations and interpretations of Aristotle, and attempted in his *De inventione dialectica* (printed 1515) to give a humanistic direction to dialectical studies.[5] Upon returning to Germany Agricola moved to Heidelberg, where he took up the study of Hebrew and in time became the central figure of a fledgling humanistic circle at the university. His life's work combines several features typical of German humanism as it developed in the sixteenth century: the obligatory pilgrimage to Italy, the cradle of the New Learning; an interest in pedagogics, formulated in his curriculum proposal *De formando studio* (On Designing a Curriculum, 1484); the copying and annotating of ancient manuscripts (Seneca, Tacitus, Pliny); and translations of ancient Greek texts (Isocrates, Aphthonius).

Many of Agricola's works were published and disseminated posthumously. It was only after the invention and commercialization of the printing press that humanism penetrated German culture. Until then it had been confined to a relatively small number of scholars who discussed and compared their work in circles defined by personal and professional friendships. Conrad Celtis (1459–1508), the German "archhumanist" (as the nineteenth-century theologian David Friedrich Strauss called him), could declare enthusiastically that, due to the powerful impact of printing, Greek and Latin sources were now available to all students of classical civilization.[6]

Northern humanism developed its own, distinctive characteristics, which included a strong interest in the application of philological, historical, and philosophical aspects of the New Learning to the practical pursuit of a Christian life. This development inspired a wealth of editions, translations, and commentaries of patristic and biblical texts. Erasmus is regarded as the principal representative of this northern variant of what came to be called Christian humanism. The application of philological skills to sacred texts led to sharp controversies between humanists and professional theologians, who had so far held a monopoly on that field. The tension was especially pronounced at northern universities, where faculties of theology were powerful and stood in direct competition with teachers of the humanities; in Italy, theology continued to be taught largely at the houses of religious orders. The Reformation movement in Germany exacerbated the situation. Humanists and reformers were for a time seen as cohorts of the same party because of an initial confusion over the respective agenda of each group. Here again, the north was more affected than the Italian peninsula, where the Catholic Church remained dominant and the evangelical movement was largely suppressed. In the following, I shall discuss the contributions of German humanists under three headings: humanists and the classics; biblical humanism; and the confessionalization of humanism.

German Humanists and the Classics

Although an effort to restore pure Latinity to its place of honor was well under way in the second half of the fifteenth century, knowledge of Greek was still a relatively rare skill north of the Alps. Complaints about the scarcity of Greek texts and the lack of Greek teachers are commonplace in the correspondence of German humanists. Lectures in Greek were instituted at German universities only in the second decade of the century; knowledge of Hebrew was equally rare, so that the first generation of German humanists was largely autodidact in both languages. In 1497 the Alsatian humanist Jacob Wimpfeling

(1450–1528) could provide only a short list of Germans who knew or could teach Greek: Rudolf Agricola; Johann von Dalberg, Bishop of Worms;[7] Johannes Trithemius; Johann Reuchlin; and Conrad Celtis.[8] Twenty years later Greek studies had made such inroads that Johann Reuchlin (1455–1522) could proclaim them an essential element in a well-rounded education: "Deinde accessit graecarum literarum studium, sine quibus nemo sat politus censeri potest" (Then came the study of Greek letters, without which no one can be judged a polished man).[9] Erasmus, who had published the first Greek grammar in Latin (*Grammatica institutio*, a translation of Theodore of Gaza's Greek textbook) and the *editio princeps* of the Greek New Testament (1516), was instrumental in fostering the study of Greek. Language studies were also enthusiastically promoted by young lecturers like Petrus Mosellanus (Peter Schade, 1493–1524) and Philipp Melanchthon (Schwarzerd, 1497–1560), hired in 1518 at Leipzig and Wittenberg respectively. In the 1520s Erasmus was content to report that demand for his translations from the Greek was on the decline, because readers were now able to go to the original text.[10]

Reuchlin,[11] in addition to promoting the study of Greek, may be regarded as the father of Hebrew studies in Germany. He obtained B.A. and M.A. degrees at the University of Basel, studied law in Poitiers, and embarked on a successful legal and diplomatic career in the service of Count Eberhard of Württemberg. Reuchlin began his Hebrew studies when traveling in Italy on diplomatic missions and later was instrumental in introducing the study of Hebrew at universities in Germany, publishing a widely used elementary grammar, *De rudimentis Hebraicis* (1506); a Latin dictionary he had compiled in 1475, *Vocabularius breviloquus* (Short Dictionary), was similarly popular. He was one of the first German humanists to master all three biblical languages, and he published Latin translations of classical and patristic works, among them texts by Athanasius, Demosthenes, Hippocrates, and Homer. Although he continued to teach at the University of Tübingen until his death, his old age was marred by a drawn-out controversy over the use of Hebrew literature. When an imperial commission was established in 1510 to discuss the confiscation of Hebrew books, Reuchlin was the lone dissenting voice among a group of university professors who supported the culling of Hebrew sources to facilitate the conversion of Jews. He was subsequently accused and condemned of Judaism and of authoring heretical tracts. After a series of appeals and counter-appeals his conviction was upheld, but he was let off with a fine.

Although the trial was a personal tragedy for Reuchlin, it contributed greatly to the consolidation of German humanism. It galvanized humanists, who saw the controversy between Reuchlin and his opponents, the Dominican theologians of Cologne, as an instance of the humanist-scholastic debate, that is, a struggle over cultural values rather than orthodoxy. They cast Reuchlin in the role of the scholar recalling students to the sources (in this case, Hebrew) and the scholastic theologians as boors hostile to a discipline of which they were ignorant. The Reuchlin affair was also caught in the undertow of the Reformation debate. Luther's trial went forward at the Diet of Worms in 1521, just as Reuchlin's case went through the final instance at the papal court in Rome. This unfortunate conjunction of events no doubt determined the outcome of Reuchlin's trial.[12]

The religious debate that characterized the next thirty years until the de facto acknowledgement of the schism in the Peace of Augsburg (1555)[13] drove some humanists to abandon the study of sacred texts as too controversial. The Alsatian humanist Beatus Rhenanus (Bild, 1485–1547)[14] is a typical example of the scholar who yielded that territory to theologians for the sake of peace. A pioneer of textual and historical criticism, Beatus studied at Paris, then settled in Basel, where he became a corrector for the Froben press. He began his career working on Christian historians[15] — contemporaries and near contemporaries of Beatus — and the early Latin Father Tertullian. Caught up in the religious controversies that enveloped Basel on the eve of its shift to Protestantism he decided in 1527 to return to his native Sélestat in order to refocus his studies on secular texts. He had already edited the works of the Roman historian Velleius Paterculus (1520) and written annotations on Pliny's *Naturalis Historia* (1526); his masterpiece, however, was the *Rerum Germanicarum libri tres* (Three Books of Germanic Affairs, 1531), a critical, source-based account of German history. His brilliant editions of the Roman historians Tacitus (1533) and Livy (1535), which set a new standard of historical criticism and became a model of manuscript-based research, established his reputation as a scholar. Analyzing the script, interpreting the meaning in accordance with the usage of the writer's time, and producing a historical synthesis, Beatus successfully combined classical philology with textual criticism and historiography. Although he built on text-critical skills and procedures initiated in fifteenth-century Italy, he brought to them a new level of accuracy and sophistication.

Religious strife also affected the careers of two other humanists, Willibald Pirckheimer of Nuremberg and Conrad Peutinger of Augsburg. Pirckheimer (1470–1530)[16] acquired a taste for the New Learning while studying law in Italy. Friendship linked him with Erasmus and his circle and with the artist and fellow Nuremberger Albrecht Dürer (1471–1528). During his lengthy tenure (1496–1523) on Nuremberg's *Stadtrat* (city council) he was instrumental in instituting schools, among them a short-lived school of poetry. He was a collector of books and manuscripts and published an edition of St. Fulgentius (1520) based on a manuscript in the library of Johannes Trithemius. He learned Greek, and from 1513 on produced Latin translations from Plutarch's *Moralia* (1513) as well as of Lucian's dialogues (1517), Aristophanes' *Plutus* (unpublished), Theophrast's *Characteres* (together with the *editio princeps* of the text in 1527), Xenophon's *Hellenica* (1532), and Ptolemy's *Geographia* (1525). He resigned his seat on the city council in 1523 after being named a follower of Luther in the papal bull of excommunication and therefore subject to the same church penalty. A lengthy appeal eventually cleared Pirckheimer of the charge, but his acquittal came, ironically, only as the city formally embraced Lutheranism (1525). In the meantime, Pirckheimer had become increasingly disenchanted with the radicalism of the reformers. The dissolution of monasteries affected him personally, moreover, since several of his sisters and daughters had taken vows.[17] The ensuing legal challenges embittered his old age.

Conrad Peutinger (1465–1547)[18] was likewise obliged to sacrifice his career to his beliefs. After studying in Basel and traveling in Italy, where he met such humanist luminaries as Ermolao Barbaro, Giovanni Pico della Mirandola, and Angelo Poliziano, he returned to Augsburg and became the city's chief clerk, among whose duties was to represent Augsburg at several imperial diets. When the city accepted Protestantism in 1534, Peutinger was forced to resign his office; like Pirckheimer in Nuremberg, he turned to humanistic studies full time. He was joined in his efforts by his scholarly wife, Margarethe Welser (1481–1552).[19] He learned Greek in order to be able to consult source texts, but he was primarily interested in Latin epigraphy and published a noted collection of Roman inscriptions, *Romanae vetustatis fragmenta in Augusta Vindelicorum et eius diocesi* (Fragments of Roman Inscriptions in Augsburg and its Diocese, 1505). Peutinger was the leading figure among a small number of German scholars — including the Schedel cousins, Hermann (1410–85) and Hartmann (1440–1514), and Jacob Questenburg (1460s–ca. 1524) — who were devoted collectors of inscriptions; Hartmann Schedel's personal library, which incorporated items inherited from his older cousin, contained some 370 manuscripts and 670 printed books. The most significant item in Peutinger's extensive collection of artifacts, coins, manuscripts, and books was a map — known to scholarship as the *Tabula Peutingeriana* (Peutinger Table) — of military roads from the late Roman empire. He facilitated the publication of manuscripts that had a bearing on German history, such as the *Chronica* of Burchard of Ursberg, which he discovered in 1496 (it was edited by Johann Mader in 1515), and Paulus Diaconus's *Historia Langobardorum* (History of the Langobards, 1515), but he died before completing work on his own edition of Macrobius's *De somnio Scipionis* (On the Dream of Scipio).

Whereas Beatus Rhenanus, Pirckheimer, and Peutinger were men of independent wealth, Hermann Buschius (von dem Busche, 1468–1534) earned his living as a teacher of the humanities and served the humanistic cause by making the products of his pedagogical work available to a larger public. An itinerant scholar and Neo-Latin poet who was first introduced to the New Learning by Agricola in Heidelberg, his Italian journey brought him into association with the circles of Pomponius Leto in Rome and the elder Filippo Beroaldo in Bologna. After returning to Germany he matriculated at Cologne in 1495 with the intention of studying law, but was soon on the road again, supporting himself with temporary teaching appointments in half a dozen cities in northern Germany. In 1502 he taught rhetoric and poetry at Wittenberg, then transferred to Leipzig, where he obtained a B.A. in law in 1503. By 1507 he was again in Cologne, but he found himself *persona non grata* because of his support for Reuchlin.[20] After serving briefly as rector of the Latin school in Wessel he resumed his ambulatory life.

Although Buschius is known primarily for his poetry and his comprehensive defense of the New Learning, *Vallum humanitatis* (Rampart of Humanity,

1518), he was also active as an editor and translator of the classics. In most cases his publications were meant to serve as textbooks and were no doubt prepared for the use of his own students. In 1505 he put together a collection entitled *Spicilegium XXXV illustrium philosophorum auctoritates utilesque sententias continens* (Collection of Thirty-Five Illustrious Philosophers, Containing Authoritative and Useful Thoughts). It was comprised of a selection of passages, translated into Latin, from Diogenes of Laertes' *Lives of Eminent Philosophers*. Another collection, entitled *Flora* (published 1508), contained passages in praise of the city of Cologne drawn from modern and ancient sources, among them Caesar, Strabo, Ammianus Marcellinus, and Sextus Aurelius Victor. The following year Buschius published a commentary on the *Ars grammatica* of Donatus — the chief authority on grammar in the Middle Ages — together with passages drawn from Priscian and Servius. He prefaced the collection with an appeal for a reform of grammatical studies, that is, for a departure from medieval texts and the introduction of classical sources. In 1517 Buschius published an anthology of Cicero's letters for class use, *Breviores Ciceronis Epistolae* (Shorter Letters of Cicero), followed in 1522 by a commentary on satires by Persius. Buschius's editions speak to the pedagogical interests of the Renaissance humanists, many of whose source collections and commentaries were prepared as teaching aids and aimed at making the classics accessible to young students.

Petrus Mosellanus,[21] like Buschius, put his experience as a teacher to good use. His literary output was remarkable, considering his short lifespan (he died in his twenties after years of ill health). He wrote the opening speech, *De ratione disputandi, praesertim in re theologica* (On the Method of Disputing, Especially in Matters of Theology, 1518), for the Leipzig Disputation — made famous as the occasion of Luther's defense of evangelical theology against Johannes Eck. He also composed a popular textbook on rhetoric and several pedagogical tracts as well as editions and commentaries on a number of classical writers — Aristophanes, Isocrates, Lucian, Aulus Gellius, Quintilian — and patristic (Gregory of Nazianzenus, among others) writers. An oration in praise of language studies earned him the wrath of the theologians because he urged them to acquire language skills in order to avoid mistakes in interpreting scripture. The oration, which followed in the wake of a similar curriculum proposal for theology students by Erasmus, *Ratio verae theologiae* (The Method of True Theology, 1518), prompted the Louvain theologian Jacques Masson to reply with a eulogy of Scholasticism and a sharp rebuke for what he saw as the pretensions of the humanists to knowledge in theology.

The work of German humanist editors and translators was not confined to the field of literature; they also extended the call *Ad fontes* to jurisprudence, music, and astronomy. Ulrich Zasius (1461–1535) of Constance spent most of his career as town clerk in Freiburg im Breisgau, where he took up the formal study of law, received his doctorate in 1501 and began lecturing at the university. He was deeply engaged in the study of Roman law and played an important role in its interpretation north of the Alps. As the city's legal adviser he revised its statutes according to Roman law in his *Freiburger Neuen*

Stadtrecht (The New Freiburg City Laws, 1520), which described current practices and compared them with relevant Roman statutes. His annotations, in which he attempts to reconstruct the thought of pre-Justinian jurists as collected in the *Digest*, appeared in 1526 under the title *Intellectus singulares et novi* (Singular and New Interpretations). Zasius was renowned as much for the purity of his Latin as for his scholarship. His interest in the Latin language prompted him to write critical notes on Valla's *Elegantiae* (1518) and a commentary on the *Rhetorica ad Herennium* (1537; attributed at the time to Cicero). His son, the jurist and imperial vice-chancellor Johann Ulrich Zasius (d. 1570), saw the definitive edition of his father's *Intellectus* through the press in 1541 and was himself the author of *Catalogus legum antiquarum* (Catalog of Ancient Laws, 1551).[22]

The Swiss Henricus Glareanus (Heinrich Loriti, 1488–1563)[23] made his name primarily as a musicologist. He studied at Cologne, was crowned *poeta laureatus* in 1512, then moved to Basel in 1514, where he taught and worked as a corrector for the Froben press. His scholarly output attests to his versatility. He was interested in history, geography, and music and collaborated on editions of the historians Tacitus, Livy, Dionysius of Halicarnassus, Caesar, Valerius Maximus, Curtius Rufus, and Suetonius, and of the poets Horace and Ovid, as well as of numerous other Greek and Roman classics. In preparation for his own lectures he wrote scholia — learned commentaries — on Donatus's grammar and on the vocabulary of Homer. In 1510 he published a world map — based on the *Cosmographia* (1507) of the cartographer Martin Waldseemüller (1470–1522) — which showed the eastern coast line of the American continent with some accuracy; in 1527 he completed a description of Asia, Africa, and Europe entitled *De geographia*. In his *Descriptio Helvetiae* (Description of Switzerland, 1514) he offers not only a geographical description of Switzerland but also gives expression to his cultural aspirations and his desire to see his native region become part of the humanistic world. His reputation rests, however, on his books on musical theory: *Isagoge in musicen* (Introduction to Music, 1516) and *Dodecachordon* (The Twelve-Stringed Lyre, 1547), which form an important contribution to Renaissance musicology. The *Dodecachordon*, inspired by the idea of a synthesis between Christian religion and classical erudition, and by the need for its renewal after their corruption in the "dark" Middle Ages, manifests the humanistic roots of Glareanus's learning.

In the field of astronomy Johannes Regiomontanus (Johann Müller, 1436–76)[24] holds the crown among German humanists. He was a student of Georg von Peuerbach (1423–61), who helped lay the groundwork for Copernicus's discoveries. It was Peuerbach who directed Regiomontanus's interest to the source texts; in 1457 Regiomontanus joined him as a colleague on the faculty of the University of Vienna. After travels in Italy, where he acquired a knowledge of Greek from the highly learned Cardinal Bessarion (besides his astonishing linguistic accomplishments, Bessarion's private library contained some 800 Greek manuscripts), Regiomontanus began to collect classical manuscripts. He also wrote a commentary on Ptolemy's *Almagest*

BRVNO ET BASILIVS AMORBACHII
CANDIDO LECTORI. S. D.

Sceptsi, quos Aristotelis & Theophrasti libros, a Neleo, iure hæreditatis acceperãt, timore regũ Attalicorũ, q tum unde/ eunq comparatis libris bibliothecã Pergami instituebant, in hypogæum quoddã abdiderunt. Hos partim tineis, partim humiditate labefactos, Apelicon Theius, magno redemptos precio, restituere conatus, scriptura nõ recte suppleta, publica uit erroribus plenos. Sed ab inclinatione imperij citra, longe sævior pestis in optimos quosq scriptores, & e sacris authori bus in Hieronymũ præcipue debacchata est. Nam laudi cedere debuit Apeliconi, quod in operib* Aristotelicis reponere sit adnixus, quæ deesse comperiebat. At quibus tandẽ crucibus digni censeantur, qui cum in alijs authoribus, tum in Hie ronymo maxime, nõ modo emaculare mẽdas, quæ uel temporis uitio, uel inscitia librariorum inoleuerant: sed his quæ re ctissime se habebãt, suas impẽras inan* admoliri, polluere, adulterare, omnia deniq nullo nec pudore nec iudicio interuerte re sunt ausi. Verũ de his in prioribus Tomis ab E R A S M O nostro satis multa dicta sunt: quare nos istis omissis de instituti operis ratione breuiter differemus. Ioannes Amorbachius parens noster cũ quatuor doctorũ (ut uocant) omnia monumẽta suis typis procudere destinasset, & iam Ambrosiũ & Aurelĩũ Augustinũ haud infeliciter absoluisset, Hierony/ mus restabat. Ad huius castigationẽ cũ exemplaria, ductu humanissimi, doctissimiq parrũ Gregorij Reischij Chartusiĩ, ex innumeris bibliothecis comparauisset & ex omni Germania uiros undeciĩq doctissimos acciuit, nam eo planissime erat animo erga restituendos sacros illos ac ueteres Christianæ religionis authores, ut huius rei studio, nec rei pecuniariæ, nec ætati iam ingrauescenti parceret. Inter hos itaq quos accersijt, Ioannes Reuchlinus in hebraicis nonnulla reposuit. Conon Norimbergensis in græcis & latinis multa castigauit. Sed longe plurimũ momenti attulit E R A S M V S ille R O/ T E R O D A M V S, qui si nobis in tempore contigisset, uel unus ad omnia fuerat suffecturus, uir præter eruditionem uariam, minimeq uulgarem, diligẽtia infatigabili, prorsusq adamantina, iudicio exactissimo, & in diuinãdo cũ res postu/ lat, mira quadam solertia. Is quatuor primos Tomos in se recepit, in quos addidit & scholia, ne post hac facile deprauari possent. Nos in hebraicis alicubi commodauimus operã, quod in his sine nobis nostet iudicare. Porro pater cum in hoc nos ante uelut instruxisset trium linguaru qualicunq peritia, Latinæ, Græcæ, & Hebraicæ, quod sine horum præsidio, nihil agi poterat in hoc negocio, tam egregio operi tandem immoriens, hanc prouinciam uelut hæreditariam nobis delegauit, futurum sperans, ut si uerus illa theologia reuiuisceret, minus ualeret spinosum istud sophistarũ & frigidum theologorum genus, & Christianos haberemus magis ingenuos & germanos. Abeunt enim studia in uitam, & tales euadimus, quales quotidie legimus. Enimuero cum iuxta Isocratem non modo paternarum facultatum, sed & paternorum amicorum, τρὶν ἐντοὺς παῖδας ἅμα τῆς οὐσίας... καὶ τῆς φιλίας τῆς πατρικῆς κληρονόμους...atq adeo studiorũ successionẽ ca/ pesere deceat, nos omissis optimis simul ac suauissimis studijs, annos aliquor in hunc laborẽ insumpsimus, & nonnulla optimæ ætatis portionẽ Hieronymo impendimus, ijs quidẽ laboribus, qui cuius adolescenti senium conciliare possent. Primũ, quantũ difficultatis habuerit ueteri uolumini uix legibilũ collatio, quorũ nobis ingens copia fuit, omnibus fere Germaniæ bibliothecis, exemplaria suggerentibus, si nosse poterit, qui in ea re aliquãdo sunt uersati. Nec tota res ab exem pluribus pēdebat, sæpenumero inter se pugnantib*, sæpissime corruptis, iudicio opus erat ad delectũ, nonnunq & diuina tione, quæ quidẽ in re magis religione opus fuit q temeritate. Atq in alijs quidẽ reb* uoluptas, sensum laboris adimit, aut certe mitigat: hac nihil nisi labor, & semp eodẽ tenore recurrẽs molestior. Adde qd nullus labor molestior, q emẽdare talcis authores, ex quo minus gratiæ redit ad eum qui suscipit. Verũ hoc heroicũ est, etiam gratis bene mereri de genere morta lium. Sic deus cum nullius egeat, nec ab ullo gratiam repetat, tamẽ omnibus benefacit. Et rex bonus consimili est animo. Quamq castigatis authorib* magnã laudi qdã cõsecuti sunt, Aristarchus notus quod Homeri obelis & asteriscis distin xerit. Hermolaus nõ minus clarus est q ipse Plinĩ. Libris medicorũ qd corruptius? In qbus restituẽdis, egregiã nauauit operã & nauat Guliehm* Copus, Basileis urbis immortale decus. Iuris peritorũ libris qd deprauati? In his nõ infeliciter rẽ aggressus Budeus, Galliæ suæ primũ honestamẽtũ. Nec hoc inferior Zasius, q in Pandectas uolumnia pari studio cõmẽ tarios meditat. Deniq quid superetat Aristotelis? Hic adhiuit Theodorus & Argyropylus, & Leonardus Aretinus. Sic enim prohdolor in omnibus disciplinis, bonorũ authorũ monumenta, per indoctũ quorundã audaciã, & audacẽ inscitiã impune corrupta sunt, ut nisi in tempore succurrissent docti, plane de his fuerit actum. Quod si nõ omnia restituta sunt in opere tamẽ immenso, minime mirũ uideri debet, si quidem nec Hercules suffecit aduersus hydram & cãcrũ duo monstra. Nos ergo qui parũ esse poteramus aduersus tot milia portentorũ primũ iuuenes, deinde mediocri doctrina? Certe magis adlaborari nõ potuit, & plæraq omnia restituta sunt, ut opinamur. Si uero neutiq reprehendũdũ, si quid discrepat a ueteri gustu, aut si qd parũ assequaris. Alioquin magis arguẽdus ipse Hieronymi*, quod Græca & Hebræa admiscuerit, nobis danda uenia, si quod ille scripsit, nos restituimus. Nam si pulchrũ fuit illi scribere, nobis honestum erit restituisse. Q uin potius hæc debet nos ad studiũ earum linguarũ inhortari, sine quibus diuinæ litteræ cognosci non possunt. Porro auẽ hic quintus Tomus, commentarios habet diui Hieronymi in maiores prophetas, ut uocant, tum insignes, ut hic de eo di ci possit, quod ille de Origene Canticũ candicorũ interpretante dixit, in cæteris uicit omnes, in his propheturũ cõmentarijs seipsum. Nam iam diuitino studio maturuerat eruditio. Et certe uetus testamentum a Græcis pene neglectum uidetur, quod nouo græce scripto, magis fauerẽt, ut Hieronymus duos Cherubim ex æquo coniunxit, & abyssũ abysso copu/ lauit. Quod superest quandoquidẽ syncera fide sudeuimus in restituendo Hieronymo, uestrũ est o lectores, grato acci pere animo & dare operam, ne post hac deprauetur quod emendatum est. Nos sane non contenti collatione latinorum codicum tametsi uetustissimorũ, Hebræa quoq consuluimus uolumina, sicubi hærebamus, uelut in hebraicis nomini/ bus, in locis hebraicis, in dictionibus deprauatis. Sed & locos citationum magna cura adnotauimus, non ut in cæteris ubi sepius fallitur lector q adiuuat. Præterea quoties æditio septuaginta ab Hebraica ueritate discrepat, interuallo medio distinximus, suo utramq titulo prænotantes. Vbi uero conueniunt perpetuo uersuum contextu, sumũ utramq complexi. Bene uale lector & fruere, & cum in his spiritalibus opibus uersaberis, fac faueas inclytæ ciuita ti Basileæ, quæ prima thesaurum hunc orbi protulit, faucas officinæ Frobenianæ, in qua la/ bor hic defudatus est. Deniq nobis, quorum immensa pecunia, tamen nulla pecunia æstimandis sudoribus res peracta est. Nam tametsi totam pene rem paternam in hoc opere periclitati sumus, tamen ætatis ac studij intermissi maior nobis uidef sumptus.

Iterum uale. Basileæ Nonis Maijs.

Anno a Christo nato.

· M. D. XVI.

Hieronymi opera *v* (Basel: Froben, 1516), *title-page verso. Preface to the reader by Bruno and Basilius Amerbach. The Beinecke Rare Book and Manuscript Library, Yale University. Reprinted from* Collected Works of Erasmus, *vol. 61,* Patristic Scholarship: The Edition of St. Jerome, *trans. and ed. James F. Brady and John C. Olin (Toronto: U of Toronto P, 1992), 232.*

based on Peuerbach's emendation and translation of the Greek text. Although neither Peuerbach nor Regiomontanus departed from the Ptolemaic system, the commentary on the *Almagest* influenced Copernicus. After some years in the service of Matthias Corvinus of Hungary and as lecturer at the newly founded University of Pressburg, Regiomontanus moved to Nuremberg and established his own printing press, where he produced critical editions of mathematical and astronomical texts. His notes for a planned edition of Ptolemy's *Geographia* were appended in 1525 to Pirckheimer's translation.

No discussion of humanists as editors and translators is complete without acknowledging the role played by their publishers. The most prominent representatives and earliest promoters of German humanism were the Basel printers Amerbach and Froben. A steady stream of classical and patristic editions issued from their shops; indeed, they became social and intellectual centers for visiting humanists as well as clearing houses for information. Trithemius, Jacob Wimpfeling, Sebastian Brant (1457–1521),[25] Reuchlin, and Erasmus were among the scholars who collaborated with the Basel printers; other scholarly contributors and correctors included Beatus Rhenanus, Glareanus, Conrad Pellicanus (Kürschner, 1478–1556), and Sigismund Gelenius (Zikmund Hrubý z Jelení, 1497–1554).[26] Although they published many standard scholastic texts, they made their lasting reputation as publishers of first editions of the *Opera omnia* of Basil, Augustine, and Jerome; the first Greek text of the New Testament; and numerous Greek and Roman classics.

A scholar in his own right, Amerbach[27] had international connections and agents in Paris and London. His sons, Bruno, Basil, and Boniface, were schooled in Latin and Greek and worked as editors in their father's firm. Boniface (1495–1562), the most scholarly of the brothers, studied law under Zasius at Freiburg, then completed his studies under the famous Italian jurist and epigrammatist Andrea Alciati at Avignon. A practicing lawyer and professor of law at the University of Basel, Boniface Amerbach was an avid collector of books and manuscripts. Although he produced no major work himself, his collection of legal opinions and manuscripts on history, art, geography, and archeology give ample proof of his humanistic learning, and his voluminous correspondence with humanistic friends attests to his role as a promoter of the New Learning. His brother Bruno (1484–1519) was more actively involved in the practicalities of running the family business. An energetic collaborator, he was the driving force behind the firm's humanistic publishing program.

After the elder Amerbach's death the firm merged with the Froben press, which remained a leading publishing concern throughout the sixteenth century. Its founder, Johann Froben, was a craftsman and designer rather than a scholar, and produced some 500 editions over the thirty-five year span of his career. He was responsible for hiring the services of first-rate artists like Urs Graf (ca. 1485–1528) — Graf was one of the first to exploit the new technique of white-line engraving, in which letters appear in white against a black background — and Hans Holbein the Younger (1497–1543) for supplying woodcut frontispieces and other typographical ornaments. He was also an important distributor of Aldine publications,[28] making his firm a gateway of Italian

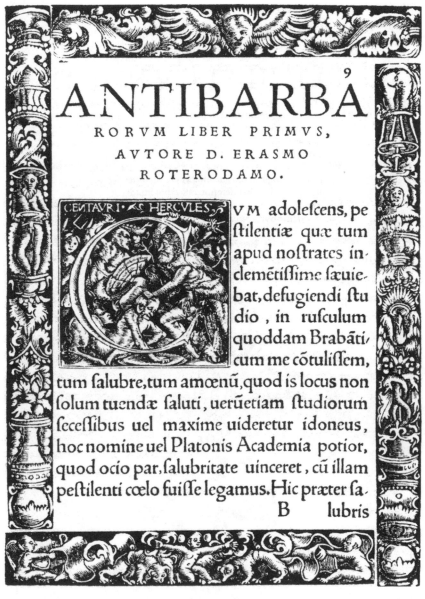

ANTIBARBÁ

RORVM LIBER PRIMVS,
AVTORE D. ERASMO
ROTERODAMO.

VM adolefcens, pe
ftilentiæ quæ tum
apud noftrates in-
clemétiffime fæuie-
bat, defugiendi ftu
dio, in rufculum
quoddam Brabāti,
cum me cótuliffem,
tum falubre, tum amœnū, quod is locus non
folum tuendæ faluti, uerūetiam ftudiorum
feceffibus uel maxime uideretur idoneus,
hoc nomine uel Platonis Academia potior,
quod ocio par, falubritate uinceret, cū illam
peftilenti cœlo fuiffe legamus. Hic præter fa-

    B   lubris

The title page to the first edition of the Antibarbari *(Basel: Froben, May 1520), with decorative border by Hans Holbein. From volume 23 of Erasmus's* Collected Works *(1978), 4. Reproduced courtesy of the Beinecke Library, Yale University.*

IOANNES FROBENIVS LECTORI   S.   D.

EN DAMVS

C· PLINII SECVNDI DI

VINVM OPVS CVI TITVLVS, HISTORIA MVNDF,
multo quàm antehac unqtam prodijt emaculatius: idép primum ex annota
tionibus eruditorum hominum, præfertim Hermolai Barbari: deinde
ex collatione exemplariorum, quæ hactenus opera doctorum no/
bis quàm fieri potuit emendatiffime funt excufa: poftremo ex
fide uetuftiffimorum codicum, ex quibus non pauca reftitui
mus, quæ alioqui nemo, quamlibet eruditus, uel depre
hendit, uel deprehendere poterat. Abfit inuidia di
cto. Vicimus fuperiores omneis. Si quis hanc pal
mam nobis eripuerit, non illi quidé inuide
bimus, fed ftudijs publicis gratulabi/
mur. Bene uale lector, & fruere
Αγαδῆ τύχη.
Additus eft index, in quo nihil defideres.

Bafileæ apud Io. Frobenium, Menfe
Martio. An. M · D · XXV ·

humanism as well. Erasmus, who made Froben his principal publisher, was instrumental in shaping the humanistic direction of the printer's output. The typographical style of the press was renowned and thought by some to surpass even that of the famed Aldine press in clarity and design.

Biblical Humanism[29]

The first Italian humanists focused on literary sources, but by the fifteenth century they had begun to apply their philological skills to sacred texts. Among the pioneers of Italian biblical humanism were Gianozzo Manetti, Aurelio Brandolini, and Lorenzo Valla. Valla's collation of gospel manuscripts had a significant influence on German biblical scholarship. It was Erasmus who discovered a manuscript of Valla's annotations in an abbey near Louvain and published it in 1505 under the title *In Latinam Novi Testamenti Interpretationem ex Collatione Graecorum Exemplarium Adnotationes* (Notes on the Latin Translation of the New Testament, Based on a Collation of Greek Manuscripts). When Italian humanists turned their attention to the biblical texts, they found themselves in conflict with professional theologians, who regarded Holy Writ as their exclusive domain. Three issues were at stake in the controversies ensuing between the two parties: the qualifications necessary to edit, translate, or comment on the biblical text; the authority of the received Latin text; and the extent to which the writing of biblical authors was guided by divine inspiration. As to the first, the theologians insisted on an academic degree in theology from a recognized university, fearing that humanist dilettantes would introduce erroneous and heretical interpretations. The humanists, by contrast, claimed that they were solely concerned with textual problems, ignoring the fact that textual changes often affected the meaning and thus the exegesis of a passage. The second issue of controversy was the reluctance of the theologians to contemplate changes in the Vulgate text, whether or not such changes affected the meaning. Since both St. Jerome, who was widely regarded as the translator of the Vulgate, and the authors of the original text were credited with divine inspiration, the text was presumed to be flawless. Humanists sharply questioned the authorship of Jerome in view of the discrepancies between the Vulgate and biblical quotations in his other works. They furthermore pointed out mistakes in biblical manuscripts circulating in their time. Their claims that the Latin had been corrupted in transmission or that the translation was wrong or misleading were met with howls of protest and accusations of blasphemy. Humanists, however, insisted that divine inspiration extended only to doctrinally significant passages and to content, not to grammar and style.

At the end of the fifteenth century, humanists outside of Italy began to apply the New Learning to the biblical texts and met with objections similar to those confronted by Manetti, Brandolini, and Valla. Antonio Nebrija (the first grammarian of the Spanish language), Jacques Lefèvre (the French philosopher and biblical scholar), and Erasmus all found themselves involved

C calypfi ciuitas magni regis extruitur. O eremus familiarius deo gaudens.Quid agis frater
✗ in fæculo:qui maior es mundo? Quâdiu te tectorum umbræ premunt? quamdiu fumofarum   A
urbium carcer includit? Crede mihi,nefcio quid plus lucis afpicio.Libet farcina corporis abie/
cta,ad purum ætheris euolare fulgore.Paupertatem times? Sed beatos Chriftus pauperes ap
pellat.Labore terreris? At nemo athleta fine fudore coronat. De cibo cogitas? fed fides famé
non timet. Super nudam metuis humû exefa ieiuniis membra collidere? fed dñs tecum iacet.
Squalidi capitis horret inculta cæfaries? fed caput tuum Chriftus eft.Infinita eremi uaftitas te
terret? fed tu paradifum mente deambula.Quotiefcunq; illuc cogitatione confcenderis:toties
in eremo non eris. Scabra fine balneis attrahitur cutis:fed qui in Chrifto femel lotus eft: non
illi necefle eft iterû lauare.Et ut breuiter ad cuncta audias Apoftolû refpondente:Nô funt(in
quit)condignæ pafliones huius fæculi ad fuperuenturam gloriâ,quæ reuelabitur in nobis.De/
✗ licatus es frater,fi & hic uis gaudere cû fæculo:& poftea regnare cû Chrifto.Veniet ueniet illa
dies,qua corruptiuû hoc & mortale,incorruptioné induat & immortalitaté.Beatus feruus qué
dñs inuenerit uigilantem.Tunc ad uocem tubæ pauebit terra cum populis,& tu gaudebis. Iu
dicaturo dño, lugubre mundus immugiet: tribus ad tribû pectora feriét. Potentiffimi quon/
dam reges,nudo latere palpitabunt.Exhibebitur cum prole fua Venus.Tunc ignitus Iuppiter
adducetur:& cum fuis ftultus Plato difcipulis. Ariftotelis arguméta nô proderunt.Tunc tu ru
fticanus & pauper exultabis,& ridebis:& dices:Ecce crucifixus meus:ecce iudex:q obuolutus pâ
nis in prefepio uagiit.Hic eft ille operarii & queftuariæ filius:hic qui matris geftatus finu,ho/
miné deus fugit in Aegyptû: hic ueftitus coccino:hic fentibus coronatus:hic magus dæmoniû
habés & Samarites.Cerne manus Iudæe quas fixeras:cerne latus Romane quod foderas:Vi
dete corpus an idem fit:quod dicebatis dam nocte fuftulifle difcipulos.Dilectio tua me com
D pulit:ut hæc tibi frater dicerem:ut his tum interefle côtingat,pro quibus nunc labor durus eft.

ARGVMENTVM ERASMI ROTERODAMI THEOLOGI IN EPISTOLAM PRAECEDENTEM.
B

Vm diuus Hieronymus,Eremû adiffet:Heliodorum fodalem chariffimum:qui fe officii
causa fuerat profecutus, ut alibi teftatur, conatus eft apud fe retinere:quod cum nô pof
tuiffet efficere:litteris ad illû datis,hortatur ad folitariæ uitæ focietaté. Refellens fingula:
quæ eû uel ab Eremo deterrere:uel in urbibus remorari poffent.Oftendensq; qj non fit tu
tû epifcopi munus fufcipere:& qj non facile tueri fufceptû. Deinde uelut in peroratione:
eremiticæ uitæ felicitaté decantat:ac fupremi iudicii terrorem ob oculos ponit.Huius epiftolæ nomina
tim mentioné facit in Catalogo operû fuorû,& exhortatoriam uocat.Scripfit autem admodum adolef
cens ac pene puer,quéadmodû in proxima teftatur epiftola,illud addés,fefe in hac calentibus adhuc
rhetorû ftudiis, p illius ætatis ratiôe,fcholaftico flore lufiffe. Proinde fcatet,metaphoris,allegoriis,etiâ
fabulofis:epiphonematis,dilemmatis,ac reliquis id genus orationis ornamétis.Conatus artis ciufmodi
eft,ut tyroné, fed fummæ fpei tyroné poffis agnofcere. Cæterum argumenti genus προτρεπτικόν eft,de
quo paulo poft dicemus.

SCHOLIA

Vanto amore.) Hic locus ufq; ad illum : Nolo priftinarum, procemii loco eft , Comple
ctitur autem & propofitione & narrationem,admifcens nonnihil & de affectibus. La
chrymis interlitas.) id eft , paffim deletas, a lino, unde & litura,deletio fcripturæ. Pri
ftinarum neceffitudinum.) Quidam codices habebant, neceffitatum, Vterq; fenfus qua
drat, Si neceffitudinû legis,intellige de affectibus amicorum,quos effet relicturus:Si ne
ceffitatum,de his accipe uitæ cômodis, quibus carent in Eremo uerfantes. Quâdi & neceffitudine pro
neceffitate legimus, Verû magis placet,ut de affectibus accipiatur. Affatim) ,i.abunde Vallû & fof
fa) Vocabula funt militaria.Nam his duabus rebus muniuntur caftra,uallo , hoc eft trabibus ac palis cô
geftis,& foffa. Sub pellibus.) ~~Confule~~ ... ~~Abimat.~~ ... Pelles appellat tentoria,quæ quondâ e pellibus confi
ciebantur. Solent milites rigéte bruma in hyberna fe recipere,hoc eft in oppidum aliquod cômodius.
Duriffimum autem erat & hyemem fub pellibus non fub tectis agere, quod tamen erat aliquoties mi/
liti faciundum. Caput opertum linteo.) Olim linteorû ufus & barbaricum habebatur, & parû uiro
dignû,ut abunde teftatur Plinius. Affuetum tunicæ.) Tunica delicatior erat ueftis,& in ocio agen
tium. Sagum erat militaris,& hoc durior lorica. Exafperat capulus.) Capulus hoc loco éa gladii pars
eft,qua tenetur. Recordare tyrocinii.) Apte cômonefacit,olim fufcepti facramenti,Si quidem fere
fit,ut Chriftiani,quoniam pueri baptiçantur,non admodû meminerint,quid in baptifmo iurauerint ni
fi nouum aliquod uotû accefferit.Cû non poffit aliud fanctius aut religiofius effe uotum,qj id quod,in

Hieronymi opera *i* (Basel: Froben, 1516), f2 verso, *showing Jerome's text and
Erasmus's annotations. Centre for Reformation and Renaissance Studies,
Victoria University, University of Toronto. Reprinted from* Collected Works of
Erasmus, *vol. 61,* Patristic Scholarship: The Edition of St. Jerome, *trans. and
ed. James F. Brady and John C. Olin (Toronto: U of Toronto P, 1992), 116.*

in such controversies and at length caught in the web of the Inquisition. The Reformation movement introduced further problems for the biblical humanists, since the Lutheran principle of *sola scriptura* (by Scripture alone) seemed to be derived from the *ad fontes* regimen of the humanists. More generally the views of reformers like Melanchthon, Johannes Oecolampadius (Husschin, 1482–1531), and Wolfgang Capito (Köpfel, ca. 1478–1541) appeared to be informed by their humanistic education. Erasmus, who remained a Catholic, was nevertheless labeled as Luther's inspirational source. The widely circulating quip "Erasmus laid the egg and Luther hatched it"[30] gave expression to the perception, current as a popular opinion in the 1520s at any rate, that humanism was closely linked with the nascent Reformation.

Erasmus was no doubt the most influential and widely read biblical humanist of his time.[31] His intellectual preeminence, high profile, and international connections made him a lightning rod for the enemies of humanism and involved him in many controversies.[32] Erasmus studied in Paris, taught at Cambridge, traveled in Italy, and resided for extended periods in Louvain, Basel, and Freiburg. He was an experienced scholar and, as an ordained priest and member of the Augustinian order, spoke with the authority of an ecclesiastic. Although he had not received formal academic training in theology, he was awarded a doctorate in theology *per saltum* (without fulfilling the regular requirements) by the University of Turin in 1506. The degree, however, became a bone of contention when Erasmus engaged in biblical studies. While he considered the degree an adequate reflection of his qualifications, traditional scholastic doctors scoffed and denied that it had academic value. In their eyes Erasmus remained an interloper, one of the *humanistae theologizantes* (theologizing humanists).[33]

Erasmus began his editorial career with work on secular classical authors, producing, among others, translations of Euripides, Plutarch, and Lucian, though he regarded this work merely as preliminary to the more important task of editing and translating theological texts. In his prefatory letter to the Euripides translations (1506) he described them as exercises affording him practice, "citra sacrarum scripturarum iniuriam solius ingenii periculo peccaretur" (but any mistake I made would be at the cost of my intellectual reputation alone, causing no harm to Holy Writ). Later, reflecting on his long career as editor and translator of literary texts, he explained that he studied the classics in order to prepare himself for the more important work on the biblical text. They were merely *progymnasmata* (preliminary exercises). "Si negem me favere politioribus literis, plane mentiar; sed tamen ita faveo ut velim eas servire gloriae Christi" (I would obviously be lying if I denied my interest in *belles lettres*, but my interest is such that I want to see them serve the glory of Christ).[34] The discovery of Valla's annotations on the New Testament came as an inspiration to Erasmus and confirmed his belief that the Vulgate text was corrupt and in need of emendation. For a decade he collected and collated biblical manuscripts. The result was a bilingual edition of the New Testament (1516) containing the *editio princeps* of the Greek text, the slightly revised Vulgate, and annotations to explain editorial decisions. Additional research, often carried out in response to the attacks of theologians claiming that his changes were unjustified and injurious to the orthodox faith, led to four revised editions (1519, 1522, 1527, 1535). The number and size of the annotations increased with each edition, offering a wide array of proof texts from classical and patristic sources. Erasmus also began a series of commentaries on the Psalms as well as paraphrases — or, running commentaries, as he described them — on the New Testament and was responsible for or contributed to editions and translations of numerous patristic texts. These included the monumental *Opera* of Jerome and Augustine as well as individual texts of the Greek fathers Origen, Chrysostom, and Theophylactus.

Erasmus came under attack by a series of Catholic theologians and was investigated both by the Spanish Inquisition (1527, investigation prorogued indefinitely) and by the University of Paris (censures published in 1531). Erasmus had demonstrated a number of truisms that were unpalatable to the theologians: that orthodoxy based on historical arguments was a slippery concept; that the beliefs and practices of the church were by no means uniform; and that the disagreements of the church fathers had been resolved only by the fiat of modern theologians and the authority of the church. Unlike the reformers, however, Erasmus accepted the teaching authority of the church and insisted that he was a loyal follower of the Catholic Church. Yet his finely nuanced approach to doctrinal problems and his reluctance to give unqualified support to the pronouncements of the theologians — of whatever stripe — earned him the suspicion of both religious camps and a reputation for being a hypocrite and fence-sitter.

Like Erasmus, his younger contemporary Melanchthon[35] engaged in both secular and biblical humanism and earned his place in history as a reformer of the educational system as well as a reformer of the church. Melanchthon was a great-nephew of Reuchlin, who promoted his education and career until the young man's support for the Lutherans led to a falling-out between the two men. Melanchthon received his B.A. from the University of Heidelberg in 1511 and his M.A. from the University of Tübingen in 1514. Engaged in teaching at the University of Wittenberg from the age of twenty-one he produced a slate of textbooks, including a popular *Institutiones graecae grammaticae* (1518) and a widely used Latin grammar and syntax (1526),[36] both of which demonstrate the characteristically humanistic commitment to language studies. He also edited or wrote commentaries on many of the Roman classics used in the humanistic curriculum, such as Cicero, Ovid, Vergil, and Terence; the edition of Terence (1516) contains a programmatic oration on the importance of the liberal arts. He also wrote commentaries on Greek classics, among them works by Aristophanes, Demosthenes, Euripides, Lucian, and Thucydides. After Luther died, in 1546, his followers looked to Melanchthon for leadership, which involved him more than ever in theological issues. This engagement led in turn to expositions on Old Testament books, on the Gospels of Matthew and John, and on several Pauline epistles. Yet Melanchthon never abandoned the humanities for theology. Rather, he combined the two disciplines, insisting on the importance of training in the classical languages and literature as the basis for a proper understanding of theology, and clarifying — in an essay, known as the *Encomium eloquentiae* (In Praise of Eloquence, 1521) — the relationship between secular and sacred studies. His extraordinary promotion of learning earned him the title *praeceptor Germaniae*, teacher of Germany.

By contrast, Wolfgang Capito of Haguenau in Alsace may serve as an example of a man whose transformation from humanist to reformer led to a curtailment of his sphere of activities. Educated at Ingolstadt and Freiburg (doctorate in theology, 1515), Capito was one of the first Christian Hebraists; his Hebrew grammar, *Hebraicarum institutionum libri duo* (Two Books of Instruction in the Hebrew Language, short version 1516, longer version 1518) was generally considered superior to Reuchlin's as a pedagogical tool. From 1515 he preached in Basel and taught at the university, where, as a protégé of Erasmus, he was regarded as a promising humanist. During this time he published a translation of works by Chrysostom, helped prepare the index to Froben's edition of Jerome's works, and — in an unpublished effort that reflected his wide reading in classical and patristic texts — wrote a commentary on Paul's Epistle to the Romans. Sympathetic to the Lutheran reform, Capito entered the service of Elector Albert of Brandenburg, Archbishop of Mainz, in 1520 and played a significant role in persuading the elector to adopt a lenient attitude toward the reformers. When his relationship with Luther became known through the unauthorized publication of their correspondence, he left Albert's service and became a citizen in Strasbourg (1523). The following year he married and, together with Martin Bucer (Butzer, 1491–1551), promoted the Reformation in Alsace.[37] At this juncture he seems to have laid his philological studies aside and concentrated on theology instead. Significantly, most of his subsequent writings were published in German rather than Latin, the *lingua franca* of the humanists, and were devoted exclusively to theological questions: commentaries on Habakkuk (1526), Hosea (1527), Jeremiah (1533), and Ezekiel (1534).

A similar development — the neglect of humanistic/philological in favor of theological studies — can be witnessed in Capito's friend Johannes Oecolampadius, the chief reformer of Basel. Like Capito, Oecolampadius had been a member of the humanistic circle at the Froben press, working as a corrector for the printer. In the 1520s he began to concentrate on doctrinal questions even as he continued to edit and translate certain patristic texts (for example, exegetical and homiletic works of Chrysostom) that played an important role in the shaping of the Lutheran creed. It is significant, however, that Oecolampadius, who had undertaken his academic pilgrimage to Italy as a young man and was there imbued with the Latin-based New Learning, began lecturing in German in the 1520s. As in Capito's case, the switch to the vernacular had programmatic significance: it implied that he was distancing himself from classical scholarship and turning to pastoral concerns.

Pellicanus, another of Capito's friends and the author of the first Hebrew grammar for Christian readers, *De modo intelligendi Hebraeum* (On Understanding Hebrew, 1504), was also part of the humanist circle in Basel and acknowledged the intellectual influence of Erasmus. Pellicanus, however, had put his skill in the classical languages into the service of religion from the beginning. He published a multilingual edition of the Psalter, made significant contributions to the Zurich translation of the Bible, and wrote a commentary on the entire Bible (*Commentaria Bibliorum*, 1532–39).

The Confessionalization of Humanism

Capito and his friends typify the development in the Reformation at midcentury: the consolidation of successes and strengthening of organizational structure, which in turn prompted a further movement toward confessionalization. The effort to establish doctrinal formulations and to differentiate between regional groups had a profound impact on the relationship between humanism and the Reformation.[38] Humanism was perceived by many in the sixteenth century as the intellectual underpinning of the Reformation, an idea that made its imprint on modern historiography as well, as reflected in Berndt Moeller's famous quip "Ohne Humanismus keine Reformation" (Without Humanism, no Reformation).[39] Although the relationship between the two movements is too complex to be summed up in this epigrammatic form, one may state unequivocally that reformers trained in the humanities applied the New Learning toward the purpose of confessionalization. They selected elements suitable for advancing their aims, notably humanistic philology and historical investigation; they subscribed to the humanistic call *Ad fontes*, which meant in their specific sphere of interest a return to the biblical and patristic sources. Conversely, they rejected humanistic skepticism as adverse to their goal of creating unwavering belief and unquestioning acceptance of the confessionally defined creed. The "hijacking" of humanism by the reformers was perhaps to be expected. Many humanists saw it as their mission to make the classics relevant, to provide a modern context for their interpretation. Humanist editors regularly employed the topos *coincidentia temporum* (showing that different eras shared the same concerns) in book prefaces. They drew comparisons between historical and contemporary conditions and encouraged readers to apply classical precepts to modern problems.[40] They aimed at being topical and invited representatives of other disciplines to apply the lessons of antiquity to their own field, hoping at last that scholars from all fields would become citizens of a single scholarly community and share their insights accordingly, "ut utraque res alteri sit tum ornamento tum usui futura" (so that we should see each discipline bring ornament and benefit to the other), as Erasmus wrote.[41] One might say that the reformers, in appropriating humanistic features and adapting them to their own purposes, did indeed accept this invitation.

Not everyone was content with the perceived link created by this merging of methods. Fearing for the progress of literary studies, were they to be drawn into the maelstrom of religious controversies, Erasmus denounced the association of humanism with the Reformation as a conspiracy.[42] In his view, Catholic theologians were casting around for a scapegoat, and reformers were trying to capitalize on the popularity of humanism with the younger generation. The outspoken poet laureate Ulrich von Hutten (1488–1523) admitted the strategic advantage of linking humanism with the Reformation and urged Erasmus to be discreet in his criticism of Luther, suggesting that a victory for the Reformation would be tantamount to a victory for humanism.[43] Luther himself was wont to draw analogies between his own case and the persecution of high-profile humanists such as della Mirandola, Reuchlin, and Erasmus.[44] He clearly wanted to establish a pedigree that would place himself within a historical lineup suggestive of a close connection between humanism and the Reformation. Erasmus, for his part, rejected this course of action, warning fellow humanists that Luther had no good claim on membership in the humanist Republic of Letters; indeed, excepting only the learned Melanchthon, Erasmus spoke disdainfully of the reformers' questionable commitment to education and the New Learning.[45]

The fact remains, however, that the reformers were as zealous in promoting language studies during the second half of the century as the humanists had been in the first, even if they did so for different reasons. While earlier humanists had been interested in languages as the medium of access to the treasure house of classical antiquity, the reformers saw languages as necessary tools to provide access to the original biblical texts and, consequently, to a better understanding of God's Word. They also used philological and historical arguments gleaned from earlier humanist writings — for example, Valla's exposure of the forged Donation of Constantine, or Erasmus's emendation of the Vulgate's "poenitentiam agite" (do penance) to "poenitemini" (repent) — in order to bolster their own doctrinal positions on the powers of the pope and on the sacrament of penance. In a sense, therefore, the Bible editions and the philological and historical arguments in the commentaries of the German reformers do indeed represent a continuation and further development of the humanistic appeal for a return to the sources.

The continued religious strife and its political fallout in the seventeenth century ultimately contributed to a decline of German classical scholarship and brought about the shift from the centers of learning in Germany to those in the Netherlands, particularly in Antwerp, the home of the Plantin press, and Leiden, where a university was founded in 1575. The new institution boasted a slate of distinguished philologists: Justus Lipsius (1547–1606), the eminent political philosopher; Joseph Justus Scaliger (1540–1609), the renowned scholar of the French Renaissance; Daniel Heinsius (1580–1655), whose Latin tragedies were translated and imitated in seventeenth-century Germany; and Gerhard Johannes Vossius (1577–1649), one of Europe's leading scholars of rhetoric. This stellar faculty gave Leiden international standing. By the seventeenth century, German philology had passed its zenith; but not before its representatives had succeeded in building an infrastructure for humanism and entrenching the study of classical languages at the universities — an achievement that would bear renewed fruit in the Age of Enlightenment.

Notes

[1] On this subject see R. R. Bolgar, *The Classical Heritage and Its Beneficiaries* (Cambridge: Cambridge UP, 1954); A. C. Dionisotti, Anthony Grafton, and Jill Kraye, eds., *The Uses of Greek and Latin: Historical Essays* (London: Warburg Institute, 1988); Anthony Grafton, *Commerce with the Classics: Ancient Books and Renaissance Readers* (Ann Arbor: U of Michigan P, 1997); Grafton, "Quatrocento Humanism and Classical Scholarship," *Renaissance Humanism: Foundations, Forms, and Legacy*, ed. Albert Rabil, Jr. (Philadelphia: U of Pennsylvania P, 1988), 3:23–66; Jill Kraye, ed., *The Cambridge Companion to Renaissance Humanism* (New York: Cambridge UP, 1996); Rudolf Pfeiffer, *History of Classical Scholarship from 1300–1850* (Oxford: Clarendon, 1976); L. D. Reynolds and N. G. Wilson, *Scribes and Scholars: A Guide to the Transmission of Greek and Latin Literature*, 3rd ed. (Oxford: Clarendon, 1991); Ingrid D. Rowland, *The Culture of the High Renaissance: Ancients and Moderns in Sixteenth-Century Rome* (Cambridge: Cambridge UP, 1998); N. G. Wilson, *From Byzantium to Italy: Greek Studies in the Italian Renaissance* (Baltimore: Duckworth, 1992).

[2] *Collected Works of Erasmus* (Toronto: U of Toronto P, 1974–), Ep. 1341A: 31–36 (edition cited hereafter as CWE). For a concise account of German humanism and recent literature on the subject see Noel L. Brann, "Humanism in Germany," in Rabil, ed., *Renaissance Humanism*, 2:123–55. Brann quotes, in translation, similar complaints by the poet Conrad Celtis: "There is no institution for the youth among the Germans dedicated to obliterating our ignorance.[. . .] I have sought to recover (if I may put it so) all the juice of Ciceronian eloquence" (133–34).

[3] Trithemius learned Greek and Hebrew in Heidelberg. He entered the Cistercian Order and was elected abbot of Sponheim in 1483. An avid book collector, he kept in contact with German humanists, among them Conrad Celtis and Alexander Hegius (von Heek, 1433–98), a former pupil of Rudolf Agricola and a teacher of Erasmus at Deventer.

[4] Quoted by Hans Rupprich, *Die Frühzeit des Humanismus und der Renaissance in Deutschland* (1938; repr., Darmstadt: Wissenschaftliche Buchgesellschaft, 1964), 83.

[5] That is, training in the art of disputation, based on the rules of logic, rather than rhetoric.

[6] Brann, "Humanism in Germany," 2:140.

[7] Dalberg (1455–1502), chancellor of the University of Heidelberg, was the owner of a rich collection of manuscripts that became a mother lode for German printers in the sixteenth century.

[8] Quoted by Merrick Whitcomb, comp., *A Literary Sourcebook of the Renaissance*, rev. ed. (Philadelphia: U of Pennsylvania P, 1903), 142–43.

[9] Ludwig Geiger, ed., *Johann Reuchlins Briefwechsel* (1875; repr., Hildesheim: Olms, 1962), 283.

[10] CWE Ep. 1341A: 240–44.

[11] On Reuchlin see the classic account of Ludwig Geiger, *Johann Reuchlin: Sein Leben und seine Werke* (1871; repr., Nieuwkoop: de Graaf, 1964); James Overfield, *Humanism and Scholasticism in Late Medieval Germany* (Princeton: Princeton UP, 1984); David Price, "Johannes Reuchlin," in *German Writers of the Renaissance and the Reformation*, vol. 179 of *Dictionary of Literary Biography*, ed. Max Reinhart and James Hardin (Detroit: Gail Research, 1997), 231–40; and Erika Rummel, *The Case of Johann*

Reuchlin: Religious and Social Controversy in 16th Century Germany (Toronto: U of Toronto P, 2002).

[12] See also the section below, "The Confessionalization of Humanism."

[13] It left the choice of confession up to the regional ruler, according to the principle *cuius regio, eius religio* (whoever controls the territory also controls the religion).

[14] For a general account of Beatus's textual work see John F. D'Amico, *Theory and Practice in Renaissance Textual Criticism: Beatus Rhenanus between Conjecture and History* (Berkeley: U of California P, 1988).

[15] These included Pomponio Leto (Julius Pomponius Laetus, 1428–98; work: *Compendium historiae romanae*), Baptista Mantuanus (Spagnoli, 1448–1516; work: *De fortuna Francisci Marchionis Mantuae*), Andrea Alciati (1492–1550; work: *Annotationes* [on Tacitus]).

[16] On Pirckheimer see Niklas Holzberg, *Willibald Pirckheimer: Griechischer Humanismus in Deutschland* (Munich: Fink, 1981), and Willehad Paul Eckert and Christoph von Imhoff, *Willibald Pirckheimer, Dürers Freund, im Spiegel seines Lebens, seiner Werke und seiner Umwelt* (Cologne: Wienand, 1971), which contains selected writings in a German translation.

[17] For a discussion of the work of his renowned sister Clara see elsewhere in this volume the chapter by Anna Carrdus, "Women's Writing in the Context of Their Lives, 1520 to 1720."

[18] On Peutinger see H. Lutz, *Conrad Peutinger: Beiträge zu einer politischen Biographie*, Abhandlungen zur Geschichte der Stadt Augsburg 9 (Augsburg: Wissner, 1958), and Konrad Miller, ed., *Die Peutingersche Tafel* (Stuttgart: Brockhaus, 1962).

[19] Compare the letter she enclosed in one of her husband's to Erasmus discussing variant readings in the New Testament (CWE, Ep. 1247).

[20] He was a contributor to the *Epistolae obscurorum virorum* (Letters of Obscure Men, 1515), which lampoons Reuchlin's scholastic critics.

[21] In spite of Mosellanus's significant pedagogical writings no recent biography exists; but see the biographical entry in Peter G. Bietenholz and Thomas B. Deutscher, eds., *Contemporaries of Erasmus: A Biographical Register of the Renaissance and Reformation* (Toronto: U of Toronto P, 1986), and Oswald G. Schmidt, *Petrus Mosellanus: Ein Beitrag zur Geschichte des Humanismus in Sachsen* (Leipzig: Fleischer, 1867). On Mosellanus's controversy with the Louvain theologian Jacques Masson see Erika Rummel, *The Humanist-Scholastic Debate in the Renaissance and Reformation* (Cambridge: Harvard UP, 1996), 92–93, 115–18.

[22] On Zasius senior see Steven Rowan, *Ulrich Zasius: A Jurist in the German Renaissance, 1461–1535*, Ius commune, Sonderhefte: Studien zur europäischen Rechtsgeschichte, no. 31 (Frankfurt am Main: Klostermann, 1987), and Guido Kisch, *Erasmus und die Jurisprudenz seiner Zeit*, Basler Studien zur Rechtswissenschaft 56 (Basel: Helbing & Lichtenhahn, 1960).

[23] The best biography, though now antiquated, is still Otto Fridolin Fritzsche, *Glarean, sein Leben und seine Schriften* (Frauenfeld: Huber, 1890).

[24] On Regiomontanus see Ernst Zinner, *Regiomontanus: His Life and Work*, trans. Ezra Brown, Studies in the History and Philosophy of Mathematics 1 (1968; repr., Amsterdam: Elsevier Science & Technology Books, 1990).

[25] Wimpfeling studied canon law and theology and taught at Heidelberg. In 1501 he retired to a monastery in Strasbourg and entered his most productive phase as a writer

of literary, historical, and theological works. He was one of the leading figures in the Strasbourg literary society. Brant taught literature and law in Basel from 1483. Known best for his satirical *Narrenschiff* (Ship of Fools, 1494), he also published legal texts and, together with Jacob Locher (1471–1528), planned an edition of the complete plays of Terence, of which six appeared in 1503.

[26] Gelenius of Prague traveled in Italy, where he was introduced to the New Learning and acquired a knowledge of Greek. In 1524 he settled in Basel and, attaching himself to the Froben press, devoted his life to editing and translating the classics. Declining a position at Nuremberg he collaborated instead with Froben and was involved in many of his humanistic publications: the Greek editions of Aristophanes and Josephus and the Latin editions of Pliny and Seneca. He also produced translations of Arrian and Appian (the latter published posthumously) and a lexicon, in which he described what he saw as linguistic affinities between Greek, Latin, German, and Slavonic languages.

[27] On the Amerbachs see Hans R. Guggisberg, *Basel in the Sixteenth Century: Aspects of the City Republic Before, During, and After the Reformation* (St. Louis: Center for Reformation Research, 1982); Friedrich Luchsinger, *Der Basler Buchdruck als Vermittler italienischen Geistes, 1470–1529*, Basler Beiträge zur Geschichtswissenschaft 45 (Basel: Helbing & Lichtenhahn, 1953); Barbara Halporn, *Johann Amerbach's Correspondence: Early Printing in Its Social Context* (Ann Arbor: U of Michigan P, 2000).

[28] The Venetian printer Aldo Manuzio (d. 1515) was the principal publisher of humanistic scholarship in Italy.

[29] For a general account see Jerry H. Bentley, *Humanists and Holy Writ: New Testament Scholarship in the Renaissance* (Princeton: Princeton UP, 1983).

[30] "Ego peperi ovum, Lutherus exclusit"; cited by Erasmus, in *Opus epistolarum Desiderii Erasmi Roterodami*, ed. P. S. Allen, et al. (Oxford: Clarendon, 1906–58), Ep. 1528: 11. (Edition cited hereafter as Allen.)

[31] On Erasmus's career as editor and translator see Erika Rummel, *Erasmus as a Translator of the Classics*, Erasmus Studies 7 (Toronto: U of Toronto P, 1985), and *Erasmus's Annotations on the New Testament: From Philologist to Theologian*, Erasmus Studies 8 (Toronto: U of Toronto P, 1986). For a recent and comprehensive account of his life and career see Cornelius Augustijn, *Erasmus: His Life, Work, and Influence*, trans. J. C. Grayson, Erasmus Studies 10 (Toronto: U of Toronto P, 1986).

[32] Today Erasmus is claimed by the Dutch by virtue of his birthplace, Rotterdam, but in the sixteenth century he was widely regarded as German by virtue of being born in the territory of the Habsburgs and being a councilor to Charles V. It is not unusual therefore to see him addressed in the letters of his humanist friends as "ornament of Germany"; but when he was asked to pronounce himself a German, Erasmus hedged, responding that both France and Germany had claims on him, but that he preferred to see himself as a citizen of the world. His inclusion in this study, then, follows the general perception rather than his own sentiments. Compare Erasmus's discussion of his nationality at CWE, Ep. 1147: 33–50.

[33] The term was coined by Natalis Beda in his *Annotationes* (Paris, 1526): sig. aa1 verso.

[34] CWE, Epp. 188: 12–14; 164: 48–52.

[35] On Melanchthon as a humanist see the classic study by Karl Hartfelder, *Philipp Melanchthon als Praeceptor Germaniae* (1889; repr., Nieuwkoop: de Graaf, 1972); on his work as biblical humanist see Timothy J. Wengert, *Philip Melanchthon's Annotationes in Johannem in Relation to Its Predecessors and Contemporaries*, Travaux

d'humanisme et Renaissance 220 (Geneva: Droz, 1987); the most recent comprehensive account of his life and career is Heinz Scheible, *Philipp Melanchthon: Eine Biographie* (Munich: Beck, 1997).

[36] The title of this work varies. In 1526 it is *Grammatica Latina*; in 1532 it is *Grammatica Latina et Syntaxis*; from the 1540s on it is generally *Grammatices Latinae elementa*.

[37] On Bucer and his relationship to Erasmus see elsewhere in this volume the chapter by Laurel Carrington, "Parallel Lives: Desiderius Erasmus and Martin Bucer."

[38] On this subject see Erika Rummel, *The Confessionalization of Humanism* (New York: Oxford UP, 2000); Hans-Christoph Rublack, *Die Lutherische Konfessionalisierung in Deutschland*, Schriften des Vereins für Reformationsgeschichte 197 (Gütersloh: Gütersloher Verlagshaus, 1992); Heinz Schilling, *Religion, Political Culture, and the Emergence of Early Modern Society* (Leiden: Brill, 1992), and his summary and bibliography on the subject of "Confessional Europe" in *Handbook of European History, 1400–1600*, ed. Thomas A. Brady, Jr., Heiko A. Oberman, and James D. Tracy (Leiden: Brill, 1995), 2:641–81.

[39] Berndt Moeller, "Die deutschen Humanisten und die Anfänge der Reformation," *Zeitschrift für Kirchengeschichte* 70 (1959): 59.

[40] When Pirckheimer edited Lucian's *Piscator* he drew parallels between the pseudo-philosophers criticized by the ancient Greek author and the scholastic "pseudo-theologians" of his own day (*Epistola apologetica*, prefixed to the 1517 edition). Erasmus did likewise in his translation of Lucian's *Convivium* (CWE, Ep. 550: 9–12).

[41] CWE, Ep. 1062: 65–87.

[42] He uses the term "conjurare" at Allen, Ep. 1167: 67.

[43] CWE, Ep. 1161: 18–47.

[44] *D. Martin Luthers Werke: Kritische Gesamtausgabe* (Weimar: Böhlau, 1883–), 1:574; 6:184–85.

[45] Allen, Ep. 2615: 427–29.

Part III

Forms

Early Modern German Drama, 1400–1700

John Alexander

D URING THE TRANSITION FROM THE MEDIEVAL FEUDAL STATE to the age of monocentric absolutism, thinking continued to be dominated by a Christian theology whose validity, in spite of doctrinal differences during the Reformation, was to remain largely unquestioned until after the Thirty Years' War (1618–48). As justification for a society with extremely rigid class and gender distinctions, this theology provided a metaphysical framework that is either explicitly present, as in the religious plays, or implied, as in the carnival plays (*Fastnachtspiele*) and *Meistersinger* plays; this condition also holds true for other works where the playwright is focused more on secular issues or a non-Christian setting, and includes not only German-language drama but also the Latin corpus, which was intended for a smaller, elite audience. No matter the audience, however, the plays were regarded as an effective means of complementing and reinforcing the conservative teachings of the church and the state on religion, social roles, and politics, the ultimate goal being a reaffirmation of the status quo.[1] This message continued to be conveyed by medieval dramatic forms (biblical, allegorical, carnival) and figures (fool, martyr, tyrant), which are found throughout the period. Their authors ranged from humanists, who reintroduced the external structures of classical drama (such as the division into acts and scenes) late in the fifteenth century, to Catholic and Protestant school dramatists.

It was not until Martin Opitz (1597–1639) published his pioneering theoretical *Buch von der Deutschen Poeterey* (Book of German Poetics) in 1624 that plays in the vernacular, written for the most part within a strongly Lutheran environment in Silesia, became part of the European mainstream by drawing on the theoretical and practical expertise of the Greeks, the Romans, the Jesuits, the English Players, the Dutch, and the Italians. The addition of music to dramatic texts led to the creation of opera in Italy in 1594 and provided a model for Opitz and other German librettists and composers throughout the seventeenth century.

Opposition from the clergy to performances, especially in Calvinist Switzerland, was directed at certain forms and practices in particular: carnival plays, because of their pagan origins and content; romantic comedies, because of their secular topics; coarse or obscene language; performance violations of Holy Days; and the allegedly immoral conduct of the itinerant players. Outside

Switzerland, however, drama remained throughout the early modern period an important didactic tool and a major source of entertainment.

Late Medieval Religious Plays

The Easter plays, which had their genesis in church liturgy, were written and performed in either Latin or German. They culminated in the late fourteenth century with the *Innsbrucker Osterspiel* (Innsbruck Easter Play) before being superseded by the passion plays around the middle of the fifteenth century.[2] A craze for the theater, fueled by passion plays — these reached their own apogee around 1500 — continued throughout the early modern period. Passion plays and, to a lesser extent, Easter plays, were performed well into the nineteenth century, primarily in the Catholic areas of the German-speaking world. Because religion played such an important role in the life of the community and the individual, the introduction of the vernacular, which marked the transition from liturgical to folk play, became a means of attracting and keeping the largest possible audience; plays written in German (though often containing Latin songs) were already commonplace by 1450.

By reinforcing the message of the church sermons with a visual reenactment of Christ's crucifixion and the proclamation of the resurrection, the priests hoped to reinvigorate or to renew the faith of the spectators, at the same time reminding them of their duties as Christians. Such a performance itself was seen as an act of faith, bringing redemption to the community, and was not intended, by the priests at least, as an attempt to escape divine retribution for sinful behavior. The *Großes Frankfurter Passionsspiel* (Great Frankfurt Passion Play, 1493) was based on the earliest known German passion play and in turn served as a model and source for many similar plays that were often little more than religious sermons in dramatic form. These include the Alsfeld (performed 1501) and the Augsburg plays (late fifteenth century), the first printed passion play by the Augsburg *Meistersinger* Sebastian Wild from 1566, and the *Oberammergauer Passionsspiel* (performed 1634, printed 1662).

The plays often consist of nothing more than an arbitrary number of biblical scenes that have been recast as dialogue. The emphasis is on the message; consequently the figures, as part of the effort to reinforce proper comportment, represent either model Christian attitudes or their opposite. It is therefore no surprise that such plays are populated with victorious priests and any number of highly imaginative scenes, such as those in which devil figures manipulate terror-stricken members of the public into a life of remorse and atonement. These spectators included Jews, who were encouraged in the play to convert to Christianity; on occasion they were even demonized in virulently anti-Semitic works, such as the *Fritzlarer Passionsspiel* (Fritzlar Passion Play) and the *Egerer Passionsspiel* (Eger Passion Play), both dating from around 1460. It was not uncommon to find devils and other allegorical figures satirizing human weaknesses, and actors frequently addressing the spectators directly. Because of the lack of a real antagonist and because the content was known by the audience in advance, there could be little dramatic tension. And because the plays themselves were regarded as communal property, often being the work of multiple collaborators, they and the message were modified over time, depending on the interests and whims of the particular adapters.

The use of familiar surroundings and music, together with references to the present, allowed the spectators to identify with the staged production, which often added secular scenes in order to compete with simultaneous shows in the market place. It is clear that such techniques could evoke feelings of empathy, admiration, joy, fear, and consolation in a form of Christian catharsis or purgation of sinful feelings. But because the plays end with the triumph of Christ and the restoration of divine order in which the devils have their part to play, the Aristotelian concept of tragedy, in which pity and fear are induced to lead to a cleansing of such feelings, does not apply to early modern drama. It was, moreover, common practice to maintain the metaphysical framework by holding a religious service in the church both before and after the performance. But in the fourteenth and fifteenth centuries, when religious plays dominated the stage this emphasis on communal involvement resulted in such massive numbers of actors and spectators that a move from the church to the market place became necessary. The market place itself was divided into the three interrelated venues of heaven, earth, and hell in accordance with the prevalent theological view of history. After long preparation a play with as many as 300 or even 400 roles was performed over a period of one to three days; the crucial roles were assumed by the priests and later by prominent citizens.

Although the Reformation put an end to the performances of these plays in Protestant areas, they did continue to be popular, particularly in Bavaria and other Catholic areas. They were so closely intertwined with the festivals of the common people that they had become a part of these very customs, and no differentiation was made between actors and spectators, producers and recipients. A prime example is the *Luzerner Passionsspiel* (Lucerne Passion Play, 1583), which was performed in the Swiss city of the same name where the Jesuits had established a school in 1577 and where the city clerk, Renward Cysat (1545–1614), directed Easter plays in the market place with large acting casts and thousands of spectators. To entertain the audience between acts or to underscore the action Cysat made effective use of liturgical music. A more famous example is the *Oberammergauer Passionsspiel*, which originated with an oath made in 1633 to perform the play regularly henceforth if the town should be saved from the plague — then at its deadliest. It was performed in the village cemetery until 1930 under the auspices of the Benedictine Order in Ettal and of the Augustinians in Rottenbuch.[3] The tendency toward popularization had already been indicated in the switch from Latin to German and in the moving of the place of performance to the market square. There was also a tendency toward realism, as in the depiction of Pope Jutta, an early proponent of gender equality, in Dietrich Schernberg's *Spiel von Frau Jutten* (Play of Jutta, ca. 1490), and also of Theophilus who, like Faust, makes a pact with the devil. This time, however, both negative models are "saved" through the intercession of the Virgin Mary, thus leaving the traditional metaphysical framework intact. The inclusion of realistic scenes, such as Mary and Mary Magdalene buying ointments for Christ in the market place (Mark 16:1) from a charlatan merchant — often accompanied by a witty servant, Rubin — introduced a comic element rarely found in the passion plays.[4]

Shrovetide or Carnival Plays

These predominantly short plays, reminiscent of earlier secular plays centered around the exploits of a knight named Neidhart noted for taking advantage of peasants, were performed as part of the pre-Lenten celebrations known as Mardi Gras or Carnival. Although their origins remain shrouded in mystery, they have been connected with ancient Germanic fertility rites and even with cultic performances because of their heavy emphasis on basic human drives; the vitalistic sense of humor in carnival plays can be both scatological and sexual.

Of the texts extant today most *Fastnachtspiele* were written in the city of Nuremberg during the period 1440–1605 by Hans Rosenplüt (ca. 1400–1460), Hans Folz (1435/40–1513), Hans Sachs (1494–1576), Peter Probst (d. 1576), and Jacob Ayrer (1543/44–1605). Others were performed in places such as Lübeck (seventy-three titles known, only one text preserved), in Basel by Pamphilus Gengenbach (ca. 1480–1525), in Berne by Niklaus Manuel (ca. 1484–1530), and in Sterzing by Vigil Raber (d. 1552). These middle-class authors aimed their satirical barbs both at members of the aristocracy who abused their positions to satiate their appetites as well as at crude, simple-minded peasants. Tyrannical wives and weak husbands were likewise often made the butt of cruel but humorous tricks or jokes perpetrated by their spouses or rivals.[5] Also popular were allegorical plays depicting antagonisms in love affairs, or religious and social conflicts, between Shrove Tuesday and Lent; others exposed the chicanery of charlatans in the marketplaces. Although few of these works dealt with serious topics, isolated instances can be found of more polemical plays warning against the dangers posed by the Turks, the Jews, or in particular the pope.

The connection with the pre-Lenten celebrations can best be seen in the early Nuremberg plays in which the director or leader of the troupe, by way of a prologue, greets the audience, announces the content, and apologizes for anything in the performance that might offend. In the epilogue he expresses gratitude to the audience for its attention, doubtless in hope of a gratuity or donation. Performances took place in private houses, taverns, and guild rooms, with little attempt to maintain dramatic illusion. With an average of some 300 to 400 lines of verse and between two and twelve roles, most were one-act plays that could be performed in approximately twenty minutes, although the more serious plays could last an hour. More often than not the reward was free drinks.

Two structural types are discernible in the initial stages of the Shrovetide plays, with a few combining features of both. In Rosenplüt's revue forms, for example, each actor in turn steps forward to explain something, such as the significance of education for a good love life, or to describe a comic event from his life; pertinent gestures and facial expressions underscore the content. When these juxtaposed monologues were replaced by dialogues, however, the story could be acted out, resulting in the second structural type, whereby the closed plot revolved around a central figure or motif. The early Nuremberg plays of Hans Folz, for example, display simple linear plots involving court scenes, marital strife, and bartering.

The master of this subgenre was Hans Sachs. By ridiculing human weaknesses in a humorous way he imparted, in the tradition of Folz, moral values to his audience. Sachs thus created a new type of carnival comedy largely eschewing obscenity; employing genuinely comic elements, realistic situations, and character types; and in the later plays cultivating the more sophisticated closed plot of humanist drama. He also strove for clarity by introducing the *dramatis personae* list,[6] reducing the number of roles to between three and six, simplifying the conflicts, and better motivating the action.

Humanist Drama

As the medieval period waned, a great new movement started in Italy. It was known as the Renaissance because it sought, against the wishes of the church, to revive interest in the pagan Greek and Roman cultures of classical antiquity. This new focus was catalyzed by the rediscovery of Latin drama and theoretical manuscripts around the middle of the fifteenth century, including, in Mainz in 1433, Aelius Donatus's (fourth century A.D.) commentary on the Roman comedy writer Terence (ca. 195–59 B.C.), and Nicolaus von Cues's (1401–64) finding, probably in Fulda, of twelve comedies of Plautus (ca. 254–184 B.C.). This led in turn to university lectures, beginning in Vienna in 1455, as well as to extensive commentaries and published editions by Dutch and German scholars — the Strasbourg edition of Terence around 1670 represents the start of a long line of such scholarly works. By the beginning of the next century Terence had been integrated into the humanist curriculum as a model of linguistic clarity and burgher morality. In Vienna, Erfurt, Breslau, Rostock, Mainz, and Zwickau his plays, in particular *The Eunuch* and *Hecyra* (The Mother-in-Law), were performed before enthusiastic audiences, as were those of Plautus, *Aulularia* (The Pot of Gold) being his most popular. The German translation of Plautus's *Menaechmi* and *Bacchides* by Albrecht von Eyb (1420–75) around 1474; that of Terence's *Eunuch* by Hans Neidhart (ca. 1430–after 1502) in 1486; the publication of Seneca's (ca. 4 B.C.–A.D. 65) Latin tragedies in Italy in 1484; and the reprinting of two of Seneca's tragedies by Conrad Celtis (1459–1508) in 1487 and three by Jacob Locher (1471–1528) in 1520, provided further models for both German and Neo-Latin school plays.

The rediscovery of the Roman manuscripts led in turn to a revival of interest in Italy of Greek drama manuscripts. In 1498 the nine comedies of

Aristophanes (ca. 445–ca. 388 B.C.) were published, followed in 1502 by an edition of the plays of Sophocles (ca. 497–405 B.C.), and two years later by the tragedies of Euripides (480–406 B.C.). Because so few scholars could read let alone understand Greek, most plays were translated into Latin almost immediately; performances in the original language, such as the one in Zwickau in 1517, were rare indeed.

In addition to the classical plays and mythology, early Italian Renaissance comedies by authors of whom little is known, such as Leonardo della Serrata's *Poliscena* (ca. 1433), provided models for greater dramatic tension in the early German humanist plays. With this exception, the Germans showed no real concern for the internal dynamics of comedy and tragedy, which were defined theoretically in terms of dramatic ending and social class; nobility appeared only in tragedy, common people only in comedy. However, the external structure was appropriated: the plays were typically divided into five acts, which were in turn subdivided into scenes, with choruses occurring frequently between acts.

The early German humanists did not restrict themselves to classical and Italian plays but turned also, when composing their highly didactic dramas, to indigenous narrative works and the medieval allegorical tradition. Scholars such as Johann Tröster (*De remedio amoris* [A Cure for Love, 1454]) and Hermann Knuyt van Slyterhoven (*Scornetta*, 1497) composed what amounted to little more than dramatized dialogues, though they did reveal new themes (especially love) within the new form.

Much more successful were those Latin plays that satirized the old learning of medieval scholasticism and sought to propagate the value of the humanistic new learning in classical Latin and Greek. In *Stylpho* (1480), the first Latin humanistic drama to be published in Germany, Jacob Wimpfeling (1450–1528) uses six scenes to treat the question: Under what circumstances are ecclesiastical benefices or sinecures justifiable? Wimpfeling excoriates corruption within the papacy and the lack of educational qualifications by proponents of the older learning. In contrast to Stylpho, who is better suited for a career as a village swineherd, Vincentius is rewarded with a bishopric for his diligence in mastering classical Latin. This encomium of the new erudition is also reflected in Johannes Kerckmeister's (ca. 1450–ca. 1500) *Codrus* (1485), Heinrich Bebel's (ca. 1472–1518) *Comoedia de optimo studio iuvenum* (Play on the Best Kind of Study for Young Men, 1501), and Joseph Grünpeck's (1473–1540) allegorical *Festspiel* (festival play) *Virtus et Fallacicaptrix* (Battle of Virtue and Dame Fortune, 1497), the first German humanistic play to incorporate the highly popular court scene from the Shrovetide plays.

In his comedy *Scenica Progymnasmata* (Teaching by Drama, 1498), better known as *Henno*, Johann Reuchlin (1455–1522) presents a sophisticated dramatic work inspired by Terence and Italian farce that satirizes cunning peasants and immoral lawyers.[7] The dramatic action continues to be framed by a prologue and an epilogue. The prologue serves a number of functions, which include greeting the audience, apologizing in advance for any offensive situations or language, warning the spectators not to confuse the fictional plot with reality, and focusing attention on the message — much as the figure of the precursor does in the *Wiener Osterspiel* (Viennese Easter Play, 1472). *Henno* was the first play to be divided into both acts and scenes, with a chorus to demarcate the end of the act. It was an immensely popular work that was republished thirty-one times between 1498 and 1531 and translated into German by five different authors between 1502 and 1558.

Jacob Locher (1471–1528), a notably versatile playwright, often dealt with contemporary political events, as in *Historia de rege Franciae* (History of the King of France [Charles VIII], performed 1495) and *Tragedia de Turcis et Suldano* (Tragedy of the Turks and the Sultan, 1497). In a mythological and allegorical piece entitled *Iudicium Paridis de pomo aureo* (The Judgment of Paris and the Golden Apple, 1502), based on Fabius Planciades Fulgentius's (fifth century A.D.) *Mythologiarum tres libri*, Locher depicts three different lifestyles: Diana represents the active life, Pallas the contemplative, and Venus the epicurean. Paris's choice of Venus as the most beautiful goddess and his subsequent elopement with Helen, the wife of Menelaus, precipitates the Trojan War and shows how the self-indulgence of a single individual can bring about the destruction of a powerful city-state. The ultimate victor, as selected by the students in the play, is Pallas. Locher has perhaps incorporated a folk element into the serious plot by providing an intermezzo with a peasant dance. Indicative of his range, Locher also wrote a farce that elaborates on the ending of Plautus's *Asinaria* (The Comedy of Asses) entitled *Ludricum drama Plautino more fictum de sene amatore, filio corrupto et dotata muliere* (Farce in the Plautine Manner about an Old Man in Love, a Dissolute Son and a Rich Woman, 1502). It is thematically related to Christoph Hegendorff's (1500–1540) *Comoedia nova de sene amatore* (New Comedy about an Old Man in Love, 1521), which was itself inspired by the study of Plautus, but concluded with a chorus written in German.

Of the other noteworthy plays from this period most are allegorical and mythological festival plays. Conrad Celtis wrote two such dramas in praise of the military prowess of Emperor Maximilian I (1459–1519) and intended primarily as tools for teaching young noblemen the art of rhetoric: *Ludus Dianae* (Diana's Play, 1501) and *Rhapsodia, laudes et victoria de Boemannis* (Rhapsody, Praise, and Victory over the Bohemians, 1502). Benedictus Chelidonius's (ca. 1460–1521) *Voluptatis cum Virtute disceptatio* (Debate of Pleasure and Virtue, 1515), with choral music, and Joachim von Watt's (Vadianus, 1484–1551) satire on theologians, *Gallus pugnans* (The Cockfight, 1514), deserve mention as well.

Reformation Drama

Encouraged by humanists such as Celtis and Philipp Melanchthon (1497–1560) or by leading religious figures, especially Martin Luther, teachers and preachers, predominantly in Saxony, created a school drama based on the external form of humanist drama but intended for the spread of reformed Christian values in a sectarian guise. Their plays were usually performed by students or burghers before an urban middle-class audience. Lutherans were also quick to capitalize on the use of the vernacular already present in the medieval religious plays in order to spread their own faith, especially since Luther had rejected the passion plays and proclaimed the biblical stories of Judith and Tobias to be particularly suitable for performance. As a result, dramatists tended to draw heavily on the Bible (including the apocryphal books) for their content, but they did turn increasingly to historical subjects in the second half of the sixteenth century.

The initial Catholic response, prior to the advent of the powerful Neo-Latin Jesuit plays in the latter half of the sixteenth century, was remarkably mild. Johannes Aal (ca. 1500–1551), for one, contented himself with a play in 1549 on John the Baptist as a prefiguration of Christ. Aal combines the lengthy medieval religious play with the external form and genre classifications of humanism. The contrast between scenes depicting the luxurious and intrigue-filled court of Herod, on the one hand, and the scenes of John in the wilderness, on the other, effectively conveys the true spiritual nature of the old faith.

A good early example of Protestant biblical drama is Sixt Birck's (1501–54) *Susanna* (1532), which fused the Swiss medieval religious tradition (folksy, coarse, many roles) with the external dramatic structure of Seneca's tragedies. This realistic milieu, where the importance of marriage and family is opposed to the celibacy of the Catholic clergy, reappeared three years later in the treatment of the same subject matter by Paul Rebhun (ca. 1500–1546). Rebhun was also the first German dramatist to replace rhymed doggerel with metrical improvements that anticipate Opitz's reform in the seventeenth century. His *Susanna* (1535) adheres to the classical divisions into acts and scenes with a chorus after each act to underscore the message of the plot.

In addition to the pious and obedient female protagonist of the Susanna type, masculinized female figures also appear with regularity throughout the early modern period. The heroic and beautiful Judith, who cut off the head of the Assyrian general Holofernes in order to save her people, was able, by virtue of her chastity, to transgress gender norms in committing an act of homicide for a divine cause.[8] Joachim Greff (1510–52), the first German dramatist to base an entire drama (*Jacob*, 1534) on the structural model of Terence, also wrote a Judith play (1536) in which he appeals to the audience to trust God for ultimate victory over the papacy. Greff's turn to polemics is consonant with his desire to use drama — especially accompanied by music — as a tool in propagating the teachings of Luther. The extraordinarily popular drama of Johannes Chryseus (fl. 1540s) entitled *Hoffteufel* (Court Devils, 1545) resorted to a still sharper degree of polemic. Chryseus was inspired by Thomas Naogeorg's (1511–63) biting Neo-Latin play *Pammachius* (The Destroyer of All, i.e., the Pope, 1538), which started the trend in devil plays that would last for more than thirty years. In depicting the figure of Daniel as a sincere Protestant leader maligned by the papacy, Chryseus criticizes the influence of the pope on the emperor and the decline of justice within the Holy Roman Empire. That God will reward the faithful and punish the papists is his consoling message.

The propagation of Lutheran values through drama did not depend exclusively on Old Testament stories. Two of the most popular dramatic subjects were the New Testament parable of the Prodigal Son and the medieval theme of Everyman. Guilielmus Gnapheus's (Willem van de Voldersgraft, 1493–1568) *Acolastus, sive de filio prodigo comoedia* (Acolastus, a Play about the Prodigal Son, 1529), was the first biblical drama written specifically for a school production. Gnapheus himself, who is credited for the subsequent profound influence in Germany of Dutch humanist theater, was extolled as the "new Terence," and his Neo-Latin play enjoyed success throughout Europe. In its German translation in 1530 by Georg Binder (d. 1545) the main figure is intended to be emulated by both Catholics and Protestants alike.

Hans Sachs, the founder and leading exponent of the *Meistersinger* stage, was more strongly influenced by humanism than by biblical themes. Until 1536 he wrote plays based on classical sources — Aristophanes, Plautus, Terence, Ovid — or taken from humanistic sources (Boccaccio) before turning his attention to Protestant school drama and later to German legend. In keeping with his primary interest in religion, morality, and pedagogy, Sachs praised conjugal love. He also stressed the element of plot, though his approximately 100 plays published between 1550 and 1560 can in general hardly be called "dramatic." Although Sachs divided his plays into "comedies" and "tragedies," depending on the ending, and although he was the first German writer to use the terms *actus* and *tragoedia* (in *Lucretia*, 1527), he concerned himself in his earlier works more with epistemological content than with form, as is strikingly evident in his dramas containing as many as ten acts. In the later plays, however, he occasionally used the prologue as the exposition, and the epilogue — rather than using a chorus after each act — to reformulate or recapitulate the main lessons of the plot. His figures are typically fixed types, who play out their roles without experiencing the conflicts or undergoing the development necessary for producing dramatic tension.

Toward the end of the sixteenth century other dramatists also turned to German legend and history as a source of material. In *Fraw Wendelgart* (1579) Nicodemus Frischlin (1547–90) deals with the legend of a daughter of Emperor Heinrich I, who, on the news of her husband's death, withdraws from the world to serve the poor, only to rediscover him among the beggars she is feeding. Skillfully woven into the main plot — like many of Frischlin's plays, it centers around marital fidelity — is a contrastive comic subplot derived from the Shrovetide plays and other satirical literature of the Reformation. The satirical element occurs similarly in a masterful funeral oration at the end of *Der Reiche Mann und der arme Lazarus* (The Rich Man and Poor Lazarus, 1590), a five-act adaptation of the biblical story, with 100 character roles, written by Georg Rollenhagen (1542–1609). In an opulent banquet scene in the third act a variety of contemporary social types appear, including the dandy, the mercenary soldier, the fool, and the parasite. The issues presented by Rollenhagen are topical and domestic, yet they manage to avoid the dogmaticism or polemicism common to so much contemporary satire.

Although the late medieval religious plays had declined in importance by 1570, they continued to flourish in Catholic territories, where they were produced by a number of religious societies, including the Rosicrucians. Passion plays in particular remained popular in the Catholic rural areas, whereas in the Protestant urban centers the biblical plays that had dominated the school stages gradually disappeared, though not before some notable successes were mounted in the early seventeenth century. One was Caspar Brülow's (1585–1627) highly popular school drama *Moyses* (staged 1621, translated into German and published by Johann Merck, 1641), the purpose of which was to strengthen the faith of the Lutherans in Strasbourg and even to gain converts from a nearby Jesuit school. Notwithstanding the biblical content of this play, it was written as an allegory to satirize the Catholic leadership as well as the veneration of saints and reliquaries.

Seventeenth-Century Tragedy: A New Beginning

During the Thirty Years' War a new form of high German drama appeared: baroque tragedy. Older dramatic traditions were now largely eschewed as authors looked both toward classical antiquity as well as to current trends in European drama to produce original works of art that would equal those of neighboring cultures.

In his groundbreaking work *Buch von der Deutschen Poeterey* Opitz introduced a major reform of the German literary language, rejecting the cruder urban idiom of the sixteenth century and recommending refined practices modeled on the more advanced European vernaculars. As the chief theoretician of this reform movement, he relied heavily on the *Poetices libri septem* (Seven Books of Poetics, 1561) of the Italian humanist Julius Caesar Scaliger (1484–1558) and strongly advocated the translation of plays from classical and European literatures. For Opitz these foreign models were treasure troves of fresh subject material, themes, motifs, genres, stylistic forms, and figures of speech. The first model he provided was *Die Trojanerinnen* in 1625, a translation of Seneca's *Trojan Women*. What attracted him to this work was the portrayal of atrocities so reminiscent of his own times, in which wars, political and social disorder, diseases, and natural catastrophes aggravated the sense of extreme crisis. He found a solution in Seneca: the moral superiority of the Trojan women, who faced their Greek persecutors without flinching. Opitz wanted this courage to be expressed as a combination of Christian and Neo-Stoic values, as described by the Dutch political philosopher Justus Lipsius (1547–1606) in *De constantia* (On Steadfastness, 1584), a work based on Seneca's moral teachings.

Opitz offers his audience consolation in this ideal of unwavering *constantia*, a virtue that can withstand the corrupting world of courtly intrigue and inure the spectators to repeated acts of violence as a means of coping with reality:

Solche Beständigkeit aber wird vns durch beschawung der Mißligkeit des Menschlichen Lebens in den Tragedien zu föderst eingepflantzet: dann in dem wir grosser Leute / gantzer Städte vnd Länder eussersten Vntergang zum offtern schawen vnd betrachten / tragen wir zwar / wie es sich gebühret/ erbarmen mit jhnen / können auch nochmals aus wehmuth die Thränen kaum zu rück halten; wir lernen aber daneben auch aus der stetigen besichtigung so vielen Creutzes vnd Vbels das andern begegnet ist / das vnserige / welches vns begegnen möchte / weniger fürchten vnd besser erdulden.[9]

[This constancy is implanted in us by contemplating the misery of the human condition in the tragedy, for by observing over and over again the extreme fate of famous people, of whole cities and countries we, as is proper, sympathize with them and can scarcely suppress the tears that our sadness brings, and by inuring ourselves to the hardships and evil that befall others we are better prepared to handle the fate that awaits us and not to fear it.]

The inculcation of Christian-Stoic ethics and Lutheran political beliefs by means of the persuasive tool of rhetoric was an important function of the humanist schools, whose mission included the training of future politicians and administrators.[10] In combining these diverse goals drama proved to be an effective pedagogical tool.

Johann Rist (1607–67), a pastor in Wedel, near Hamburg, was aware of Opitz's normative poetics but chose to ignore its injunctions, in part because they restricted the depiction of conflicts between the ruling and lower classes. To portray this kind of social conflict would violate Opitz's rule for keeping the various dramatic genres separated. In *Perseus* (1634), his only surviving tragedy, Rist follows the practices of the immensely popular English Players (Englische Komödianten) — they decided to tour the continent because of adverse social and political circumstances in England, but also for the sake of adventure and financial gain — by writing in prose, by adding comic interludes in Low German rather than adhering to the strict separation of the comic and the tragic, and by staging atrocities (in this case, the murder of Demetrius at the behest of his brother Perseus, a Machiavellian tyrant). Although this didactic play does illustrate the *vanitas* theme of the fall of the mighty, Demetrius lacks the Christian-Stoic features that would lend the martyrs of post-war Silesian tragedy an enhanced ethical dimension. Nevertheless, the work served as a model for the anonymously published allegorical play *Ratio Status* (Reason of State, 1668), which examines the dire political consequences for a country when ethics are ignored in favor of Machiavellian politics. Rist also published three allegorical dramas in the same vein as *Perseus*, the most important of which is *Irenaromachia* (Peace and War, 1630; co-authored with Ernst Stapel), in which the Thirty Years' War is interpreted in the traditional theological manner as divine retribution for the abandonment of moral values, including patriotism. Because the Peace of Westphalia (1648) heralded the restoration of these values, however, all three plays ended on an optimistic note.

Silesian Tragedy

Andreas Gryphius (1616–64), a Silesian attorney, is generally considered to be Germany's most distinguished author of the seventeenth century. He was the first major dramatist to follow Opitz's recommendations, as he demonstrated in his four historical tragedies published shortly after the cessation of hostilities in 1648: *Leo Armenius: Oder Fürsten-Mord* (Leo Armenius, or Regicide, 1650), *Catharina von Georgien: Oder Bewehrete Beständigkeit* (Catharina of Georgia, or The Triumph of Constancy, 1657), *Ermordete Majestät: Oder Carolus Stuardus König von Groß Britannien* (Murdered Majesty, or Charles Stuart, King of Great Britain, 1657–63), and *Großmüttiger Rechts-Gelehrter: Oder Sterbender Aemilius Paulus Papinianus* (The Noble-Minded Jurist, or The Death of Aemilius Paulus Papinianus, 1659). All four reveal a strong interest in secular matters. In *Cardenio und Celinde: Oder Unglücklich Verliebte* (Cardenio and Celinde, or the Unfortunate Lovers, 1657), however, a romantic tragedy set in an urban middle-class milieu, Gryphius shows the mystical relationship of the individual to God rather than the lofty world of politics, thereby asserting his independence from the Opitzian strictures on content and social class.[11]

These plays, which would provide a benchmark for German tragedy well into the eighteenth century, may seem to have arisen from a vacuum, though this was hardly the case. Like Opitz, Gryphius had begun his career as a dramatist, probably already as a student in the 1630s. His first work, a translation of the martyr drama *Felicitas* by the Jesuit Nicolas Caussinus (1583–1651), was called in German *Die Beständige Mutter: Oder Die Heilige Felicitas* (The Steadfast Mother, or St. Felicitas, 1635). In this gloomy work Gryphius found most of the ingredients for his own martyr plays: Roman (read: Catholic) decadence, the martyr-tyrant constellation, Christian-Stoic values, a theological interpretation of history, monological and stichomythic forms, and effective stage effects involving ghosts, magicians, and allegorical figures. He omitted all specifically Catholic concepts while retaining a Catholic protagonist, whose silhouette would later serve as a model for the more fleshed-out martyr figure of Catharina of Georgia.

Although Jesuit drama provided Gryphius with themes and stage technique, he turned to the Dutch for structure, particularly the use of the chorus. He had studied for six years (1638–44) at Leiden, then the foremost university in Europe, where he became acquainted with the theoretical work of the tragedian Daniel Heinsius (1580–1655) as well as with the Stoic philosophy of Seneca. It was probably during this time or shortly thereafter that he started translating Joost van den Vondel's (1587–1679) *De Gebroeders* (1640), printed posthumously in 1698 as *Die Sieben Brüder: Oder Die Gibeoniter* (The Seven Brothers, or the Gibeonites). His reasons for undertaking this work of translation may be ascribed to his strong affinity for the religious and political views of Vondel, many of whose plays, in particular *Palamedes oft Vermoorde Onnozelheit* (Palamedes, or Innocence Murdered, 1625), influenced Gryphius's tragedies both as to content and form.

Deeply affected by the war and sustained by his deep Lutheran faith, Gryphius maintained a moral posture in all his literary endeavors. This is most obvious in his depiction of politics. In contemporary terms, the fall from power was best illustrated by the examples of rulers and highly placed statesmen who became victims of political plots or circumstances: assassination (Leo Armenius), civil strife (Charles Stuart), war and torture (Catharina of Georgia), or tyranny (Papinian). If these rulers, divinely appointed symbols of justice and morality, could be murdered under the pretext of legality or in the name of religion, then chaos would have replaced order. Gryphius's belief in the divine right of kings and their absolute power was unbending. He was so offended by the glorification of tyrannicide in a Jesuit performance of Joseph Simons's (1593–1671) *Leo Armenus* (1646) that he rewrote the material from his own perspective, under the slightly modified title *Leo Armenius oder Fürstenmord* (1650). For Gryphius, regicide was tantamount to deicide, a satanic act that not only destroyed the individual monarch — who alone could guarantee peace and order — but the divine principle itself. The assassination or execution of the legitimate ruler of the state therefore threatened not only the social, but the cosmic fabric as well.

To pound home this point Gryphius often resorts to shock effects, such as reporting in detail or even staging the torture and executions of protagonists who, by refusing to carry out a royal mandate (Papinian) or to abjure their Christian faith (Catharina refuses to bend to Islam), challenge a tyrannical government.[12] Both Papinian and Catharina act in conformity with their conscience and their idea of justice, thereby asserting a morally superior rectitude over political necessity.[13] Even the absolute ruler is subject to a conscience that is of divine provenience. No matter how clever the tyrant's political arguments may be, for Gryphius they remain specious;[14] for whoever acts against his or her better judgment will suffer mental anguish many times worse than the physical torment of the victims.

Terrifying deeds and other affronts to human dignity, perpetrated by antagonists who abuse their power by seeking primary satisfaction of their personal needs and desires, make for vivid examples of *vanitas mundi*. Ultimately, the efforts of tyrants prove futile, and they are overcome by protagonists like Catharina who adhere to Christian-Stoic values, especially to that of *constantia*:

> Wir gehn durchs Finsternüß zu Gott der Licht von Licht.
> . . . .
> Creutz/ Messer/ Zang vnd Herd
> Sind Staffeln zu der Ehr'. (IV, ll. 331, 352–53)

[We pass through the darkness to God, the Light of all Light. (. . .) Cross, dagger, tongs, and fire are but rungs to eternal honor.]

In contrasting the destructiveness of the physical world with the indestructibility of the spirit Gryphius recreated a dualistic model that would be used by many future dramatists.

Gryphius underscores the moral authority of his protagonists by adding, either directly or by way of analogy, a mythical dimension: identification with

Christ. To do so he typically deviates from the empirical facts, notwithstanding his provision of an elaborate footnote apparatus that avows historical
authenticity.[15] Leo Armenius dies on Christ's very cross on 24 December;
Charles Stuart's beheading takes place at precisely 3:00 P.M. in obvious post-
figuration of the crucifixion.[16] It may be historically accurate that Charles's
decollation was principally occasioned by political ineptitude and not religious
belief, but for the Silesian playwright the deeper significance of history is
embedded in theology.[17] For Gryphius, the maintenance of the status
quo through theological argument is the *sine qua non* for social and cosmic
stability; and yet all his protagonists, with the exception of King David (in the
translation of Vondel's *De Gebroeders*, where Providence provides a *deus-
ex-machina* solution), are simultaneously political failures and extraordinary
examples of personal courage and moral integrity. This does not mean, however, that they are morally perfect. On rare occasions Gryphius will permit the
ruler to use dubious means, though only in the interest of preserving order in
the divinely sanctioned state.[18]

Gryphius's idealized models demonstrate resistance to the pressures to
convert from the true faith. How great this need was can be seen in *Catharina
von Georgien*. Elida Maria Szarota has gone so far as to interpret it as a political allegory of the post-Westphalian Peace conflict between the powerful
Habsburg Empire (represented by Persia) and Gryphius's Protestant homeland of Silesia (represented by Georgia).[19]

The Silesian lawyer Daniel Casper von Lohenstein (1635–83), extolled by
his contemporaries as "the German Seneca," began to receive due recognition
for his outstanding accomplishments as a writer of tragedies only in the 1960s.
From his older countryman Gryphius he learned the effective use for drama
not only of the six-foot alexandrine verse (with its natural caesura between feet
three and four, it lent itself to an effective thesis/antithesis presentation of
ideas) but also of strategies of emblematic representation (such as staged
tableaux with interpretational dialogue).[20] Lohenstein had a unique interest,
however, in the exotic historical settings of Turkey, Rome, and Northern
Africa, as his titles suggest: *Ibrahim Bassa* (1650) and *Ibrahim Sultan* (1673);
Agrippina (1665) and *Epicharis* (1665); *Cleopatra* (1661; revised 1680) and
Sophonisbe (1669; revised 1680). His focus on the politics of pagan times and
his general disregard for a Christian perspective initially led some scholars to
believe that Lohenstein, in diametrical opposition to Gryphius, had written a
secularized corpus that presaged the Age of Enlightenment. However, by
1970 scholarly opinion concluded that Lohenstein too had a teleological view
of history as a divinely guided process, in which Rome — or its successors, the
Habsburg emperors of the Holy Roman Empire — would ultimately prevail.[21]
Anyone opposed to this divinely sanctioned plan — and that included the non-
Christian Turkish and African nations — could either become political converts, like Masinissa (in *Sophonisbe*), or suffer the consequences.

Lohenstein's figures and constellations of figures are more intricate than
those in the less nuanced tragedies of Gryphius, due primarily to his fascination
for the subtle interrelationships of human passions and rational actions in

politics. This interest is reflected in his *Staats-Kluger Catholischer Ferdinand* (Ferdinand, the Catholic Statesman, 1672), a translation of Baltasar Gracián's political drama *El Político Don Fernando el Católico* (1640). Rulers of the Augustan type represent a new political ideal: pragmatic politicians not easily swayed by emotion, and concerned about the ends rather than the means. This new model, which first becomes apparent in *Cleopatra*, implies that political success is predicated not only on the ability to control one's own emotions but also on a willingness to manipulate the political ambitions of others. Antony is a political failure in both respects. Notwithstanding the essential abandonment in his dramas of a theological theory of government in favor of a pragmatics of action, an ethical dimension is always implied in Lohenstein.[22]

Augustus and Scipio are at once idealized models and prefigurations of the Habsburg emperors Charles V and Leopold I.[23] As such they are indications of Lohenstein's support for Habsburg absolutism, especially as the Habsburgs constituted the last bastion of defense against the Turks. The Turks had seemed to threaten the existence of Christendom until they were finally defeated when the siege of Vienna was raised in 1683 — a defeat that Lohenstein had wishfully predicted a decade earlier in his last tragedy, *Ibrahim Sultan*. The laudatory tone in his plays, particularly in those dedicated to the emperor, as well as the avoidance of overt religious polemicism, bespoke Lohenstein's desire to see a reconciliation between Protestant Silesia and the Catholic Viennese court. However, Lohenstein's dual function as a representative of Breslau at the Habsburg court and as imperial counselor gave rise to ambivalent attitudes. On the one hand, he was unwilling to condone tyrannicide in all cases; on the other, he avoided definitive support of republicanism, an equivocation found especially in the Turkish plays. Despots like Suleiman the Magnificent in *Ibrahim Bassa* are ruled by their emotions and can be manipulated by ambitious advisors into committing judicial murder. Political expedience wins over legality. The court that Lohenstein knew so well is presented as a hotbed of intrigue and murder. No Christian-Stoic apotheosis occurs at the end, only the pagan victim's primal cry for vengeance and the madness of the tyrant. To the Christian mind this constituted a form of spiritual death foreshadowing the everlasting torments of hell.

Lohenstein's ambivalence toward the court is further exemplified in the Roman tragedies, *Epicharis* and *Agrippina*. Here the focus is no longer on vacillating tyrants dominated by their passions but on powerful women; Agrippina, for one, will use any means, including her sexuality and even incest, in order to survive.[24] The passions are now associated with the protagonists rather than with the antagonists, as was the case in Gryphius. Catharina of Georgia, for example, was a passive victim who used her Christian-Stoic values to cope with adversity; Lohenstein's Epicharis, on the other hand, is an energetic political activist who seeks through direct action to impose her will on the current government. Because her aims are in direct conflict with the divine plan — as such, they are examples of hubris — she is doomed to fail, however magnificently. With the collapse of the conspiracy against Nero, Epicharis is subjected to brutal torture, but she remains impervious to all pain until she is in a position to commit suicide. Her steadfast courage is not, as Catharina's was, inspired by divine grace but is rather an expression of free will. Her suicide, therefore, is both a moral and a political act. By overcoming pain and the fear of death, both of which the tyrant relies on for social control, Epicharis hopes that her execution will inspire others to political action. She is not a martyr in the Gryphian sense, but an admirable republican facing up to insurmountable odds.[25]

In Gryphius's tragedies an emblematic structure prevails, as suggested by his double titles. The name of the protagonist serves as the *pictura* (picture), and the principle involved serves as the *subscriptio* (significance); this is uniquely evident in the relationship of act to chorus (*Reyen*), in which the latter interprets the preceding action.[26] In the case of Lohenstein this strict emblematic structure does not always apply. If anything, the choruses — now containing elements from ballet and opera — offer an analogy to the plot and leave the interpretation to the audience.

Johann Christian Hallmann (ca. 1640–1704), like his two predecessors an upper middle-class Silesian, published five tragedies for performance on the school stage in Breslau: *Verführter Fürst: Oder Entseelter Theodoricus* (The Seduced Prince, or the Deceased Theodoricus, 1667), *Die Beleidigte Schönheit: Oder Sterbende Mariamne* (Beauty Outraged, or the Death of Mariamne, 1670), *Die Himmlische Liebe: Oder Die beständige Märterin Sophia* (Heavenly Love, or the Steadfast Martyr Sophia, 1671), *Die Sterbende Unschuld: Oder Die Durchlauchtigste Catharina Königin in Engelland* (The Death of Innocence, or Her Majesty, Catherine, Queen of England, 1684), and *Die Unüberwindliche Keuschheit: Oder Die großmüthige Prinzessin Liberata* (Invincible Chastity, or the Noble-Minded Princess Liberata, 1700). Hallmann's most successful play, *Mariamne*, is a biblical drama that emulates the martyr-tyrant constellation and emblematic structure of Gryphius, though here, as in Lohenstein, the political component is upgraded when the intriguer is given a role of central importance. However, Hallmann's original aesthetic intentions, which combine serious ethical content with a crescendo of theatrical and operatic effects borrowed from Italian opera and the itinerant players, are quite different from those of his better known countrymen. While the addition of special effects is clearly a concession to the public, it also marks a switch in emphasis and signals the collapse of the dramatic structure of high baroque tragedy.[27]

August Adolf von Haugwitz (1647–1706), a Lutheran nobleman from the Lausitz, a Saxon territory since 1635, falls somewhat outside of the Silesian School. His *Schuldige Unschuld: oder Maria Stuarda* (Guilt and Innocence, or Mary Stuart, 1683) was intended as an alternative to the *Maria Stuart* (1672) of the Dresden lawyer and playwright Christoph Kormart (1644–1701), as well as to Jesuit plays on the same topic,[28] and represents an attempt to revitalize a moribund Silesian tragedy.[29] Insofar as the protagonist views her execution as a political act that will benefit the Catholic Church,[30] she is closer to Epicharis than to any of the Gryphian martyr figures, even though Haugwitz does revert to the aesthetics and language of Gryphius.[31] Haugwitz also published the drama *Soliman* (1684), which follows the structure of baroque tragedy for four acts, only then in the final act to allow the potential tyrant to develop into a model ruler. The breakdown of the dualism typical of Gryphian tragedy and the adherence to the three dramatic unities (place, time, and action) anticipate the drama of the approaching Age of Enlightenment.

Saxon Tragedy

Almost all of the aforementioned dramatists hailed from Silesia. Although economically stable throughout the first half of the Thirty Years' War, Silesia served as a flashpoint in the conflict between Catholics and Lutherans. Because there was no university in Protestant Silesia, the secondary schools in the capital city of Breslau — one Jesuit and two Protestant — became the center of intellectual life, but also of social tensions. The plays of Gryphius, Lohenstein, and Hallmann were written expressly for the two Lutheran schools, the Elisabeth Gymnasium and the Magdalena Gymnasium, and were performed many times on their stages. Students in their final year were given the opportunity to display their skills in public speaking and acting before an audience of parents, friends, and well-wishers. The emphasis in the plays on morality and absolutism was intended to convince parents — a major source of donations for salaries, production costs, and recruitment — that their offspring had received a politically useful education.

Written for the most part in Saxony, the school tragedies hark back to the school plays of the humanists, the reformers, and the Jesuits. Most authors were Lutheran schoolteachers and clerics who saw in drama a vehicle for the teaching of rhetoric, politics, ethics, morality, and theology to future civil servants in need of polished social and speaking skills as well as moral instruction appropriate to their function as advisors to local rulers. This pedagogical gain came at a certain aesthetic expense: the sprawling increase in speaking roles required to accommodate as many students as possible resulted in an episodic structure having many superfluous scenes. This development was accompanied by an enhanced pragmatism as playwrights began to select subjects from recent history (Louis XIV, Ancre, Biron, Masaniello) through which to demonstrate ideal conservative Lutheran positions with respect to regicide, rebellion, and other forms of resistance to those in power; preference was generally expressed for an enlightened form of absolutism. The depiction of all social classes, the mixture of the comic and the tragic, the use of prose and everyday speech patterns, and the emphasis on satire doubtless owe much to the influence of the English Players and earlier folk traditions in this final stage of the school drama tradition.

Johann Sebastian Mitternacht (1613–79) produced some fifteen plays for the school stage in Gera but published only two: *Trauer-Spiel: Der Unglückseelige Soldat und Vorwitzige Barbirer* (Tragedy of the Unfortunate Soldier and the Curious Barber-Surgeon, 1662) and *Politica Dramatica: Das ist die edle Regimentierkunst* (Political Drama, or the Noble Art of Governing,

1667). *Trauer-Spiel* demonstrates an extremely conservative opposition to the new empiricism in the natural sciences, particularly in the way it equates rebellion with vivisection.[32] In *Politica Dramatica* Mitternacht adopts a more moderate stance in seeking to impress visually upon his students that the removal of any ruler, no matter how tyrannical, will result in anarchy. As a political pragmatist and an early proponent of the separation of church and state, Mitternacht did not favor a return to a feudal state but the establishment of an enlightened form of absolutism that would encourage both parties to cultivate a mutually beneficial self-interest.[33]

Christian Zeidler (1643–1707) was heavily influenced by Mitternacht. *Paedia Dramatica: Oder die Gute und Böse Kinder-Zucht* (Teaching through Drama, or the Right and Wrong Way to Raise Children, 1675) expresses a strong faith in traditional methods of education while at the same time criticizing the court for its Machiavellian ways. Nevertheless, Zeidler was a strong supporter of the monarchy in *Monarchia optima reipublica forma* (Monarchy as the Best Form of Government, 1679), his version of Mitternacht's *Politica Dramatica*; in cases where the ruler acted against the laws of the land, however, resistance by the subjects is condoned.

Johann Riemer's (1648–1714) political views were similar to those of Mitternacht and Zeidler. A Lutheran who believed in the divine right of kings and who advocated a strict separation of church and state,[34] Riemer wrote seven prose plays for the Weissenfels school stage, including *Von der erlöseten Germania* (Germany Redeemed, 1679), *Von hohen Vermählungen* (Marriages in High Places, 1679), and *Von Staats-Eiffer* (Political Ambition, 1681). *Von der erlöseten Germania* contrasts the Machiavellian policies of the French king, Louis XIV, unfavorably with the ethical actions of the Habsburg emperor, Leopold I, who is depicted in idealized terms as a constitutional rather than an absolute monarch. In the other two dramas, which focus on the person and execution of Mary Stuart, Riemer attempts to do justice to both parties before ultimately condemning the act of regicide.

More prolific than either Mitternacht or Riemer, Christian Weise (1642–1708), a school principal in Weissenfels and later in Zittau, wrote and directed for the school each year a trilogy that included a biblical play, a comedy, and a tragedy. As was typical of the school play, he wrote in a large number of roles in order to accommodate as many students as possible — a practice that necessarily relegated the aesthetic structure to secondary importance. Of his plays, four can definitely be labeled "tragedies": *Der Tochter-Mord: Welchen Jephtha unter dem Vorwande eines Opfers begangen hat* (Filiacide, which Jephtha Committed under the Guise of Religious Sacrifice, 1679), *Der gestürtzte Marggraff von Ancre* (The Fall of the Margrave of Ancre, 1681), *Trauerspiel von dem neapolitanischen Haupt-Rebellen Masaniello* (Tragedy of the Neapolitan Rebel Leader Masaniello, 1683), and *Der Fall des Frantzösischen Marschalls von Biron* (The Fall of Field Marshal Biron of France, 1693). Written in didactic prose, and taking Rist rather than the Silesians as his model, Weise's plays bear all the markings of a conservative revival of the traditional school drama, though modified by the addition of carnivalesque elements.[35]

These interests are especially reflected in Weise's best-known tragedy, *Masaniello*, an eponymous story about a fisherman who led an unsuccessful uprising in Naples in the late 1640s. Although Weise sympathizes with the demands of the rebels and wishes to see certain members of the aristocracy held responsible for their corrupt taxation policies, he still shares the traditionally negative Lutheran attitude toward rebellion. For this reason he uses the fool to depict Masaniello as the "Lord of Misrule," a tyrant who has inverted the social hierarchy. It is left to Cardinal Philomarini, a figure reminiscent of the successful rulers in the tragedies of Lohenstein, to use whatever means necessary to quell the rebellion and restore order to the state.

Seventeenth-Century Comedy

Modern scholars have focused their attention on the tragedies of Gryphius and Lohenstein and largely ignored the comedies. In general, the comedies have been deemed inferior, perhaps in part because of their popular success; according to Opitz, tragedy was to be restricted to a portrayal of the serious sphere of government and members of the ruling aristocratic class. In the seventeenth century, however, tragedy shared with comedy a common goal: the depiction and amelioration of human foibles. It is also true that comedy was valued by both dramatists and theoreticians and that Gryphius wrote and translated as many comedies as tragedies. The classical structure of exposition, peripetia (turning point), and catastrophe were replaced in Gryphius by a structural principle based on parallels and contrasts.[36]

Many poetic handbooks of the seventeenth century, beginning with Opitz's *Buch von der Deutschen Poeterey*, attempted to define comedy. Opitz recommends figures representing the common people and their everyday activities:

> Die Comedie bestehet in schlechtem wesen vnnd personen: redet von hochzeiten / gastgeboten / spielen / betrug vnd schalckheit der knechte / ruhmrätigen Landtsknechten / buhlersachen / leichtfertigkeit der jugend / geitze des alters / kupplerey vnd solchen sachen / die täglich vnter gemeinen Leuten vorlauffen.[37]

> [Comedy concerns itself with crude topics and persons: it deals with marriages, banquets, games, the deception and roguery of knaves, boastful mercenaries, love affairs, the frivolities of youth, the miserliness of old people, fornication, and such matters as occur among common people.]

This catalog of topics, motifs, and figures, along with many comic situations, is taken directly from the comedies of the Roman dramatists Plautus and Terence. Rediscovered and translated into German in the late fifteenth century, they were often performed in the schools.

In addition to the Roman models, and to a lesser extent the Greek comedy writer Aristophanes, other foreign influences also made inroads into German drama during the second half of the sixteenth century, most notably the Italian *commedia dell'arte* and the English Players. *Commedia dell'arte* was a theatrical style based on improvisation; it was staged with great success at various European courts, particularly in Paris. In Germany, however, no play in this style was performed until 1568, and *commedia dell'arte* did not achieve wide popularity until after the Thirty Years' War. In addition to a set number of plots, many stock comic figures, often taken from the Roman tradition, found their way into German comedy: the harlequin, the chambermaid Columbina, the distrustful father Pantalone, the *miles gloriosus* (boastful soldier), the doctor, and the comic servant, or *zanni*. The three most popular of these comic types in German from the late sixteenth until the eighteenth century were the harlequin, which was conflated with the older German figure of the Hanswurst and often served to satirize the actions of the protagonist; the doctor, a parody of those intellectuals still mired in medieval scholasticism; and the boastful soldier, who appeared in the leading role in both *Von Vincentio Ladislao* (Vincentius Ladislaus, 1594), by Duke Heinrich Julius von Braunschweig (1564–1613), and *Horribilicribrifax* (The Horrible Sieve-maker, 1663), by Gryphius. Because of language constraints, the Italian troupes kept for the most part to the courts and did not have the same direct effect on the German stage and drama as the English Players, who had a profound influence on German theater from their first appearance in Dresden in 1586 until around the time of the restoration of the English monarchy (1660).[38] A few of the players remained as actors in Germany through the end of the century. The English Players owed their initial success in Germany to their professional acting, dancing, singing, and acrobatic skills, as well as to their ability to engage aspiring German actors.

The German troupes that emerged during and after the Thirty Years' War found both a model and a rich source of plays in the English Players, who brought with them scripts for Shakespeare, Marlowe, Thomas Kyd, and Philip Massinger, among others. The plays were translated into German prose and published anonymously in collections. Among the most important collections were the *Englische Comedien und Tragedien* (English Comedies and Tragedies, 1620 and 1624), *Liebeskampf* (Battle of the Sexes, 1630), and *Schaubühne englischer und französischer Comedien* (French and English Comedies on Stage, 1670). From Manfred Brauneck's reprint of these collections it is apparent that the most popular topic was romantic love, including the battle of the sexes; that tragic and comic elements were inextricably intertwined; that the higher and lower classes coexisted in the same drama; and that the plays were geared primarily toward entertaining the public, who provided the wherewithal for the troupes to survive. Much emphasis was placed on both the beloved figure of the Pickelhering — appearing either as a clown or a fool in almost all plays — and on special effects, including the staging of garish torture and execution scenes.[39]

Two of the earliest and most important German comedies in the manner of the English Players were Heinrich Julius's *Von Vincentio Ladislao* and Ludwig Hollonius's (ca. 1570–1621) *Somnium vitae humanae* (Life is a Dream, 1605). Heinrich Julius's comic effects derive from his title figure's inability, as a representative of the late feudal period, to adapt to the new absolutism. In *Somnium vitae humanae*, Hollonius adapts the age-old technique of social role-reversal, whereby a peasant becomes king for a day, a theme later treated by the Jesuit dramatist Jacob Masen (1606–81) in his immensely popular comedy *Rusticus imperans* (The Peasant Emperor, 1654). Perhaps because of the intervening war, the plays of Heinrich Julius and Hollonius did not much influence later baroque comedy.

Toward the end of the Thirty Years' War, however, two comedies by the indefatigable Gryphius, *Absurda Comica Oder Herr Peter Squentz* (Absurd Comedy; or Mr. Peter Squentz, 1658) and *Horribilicribrifax*, reinvigorated the tradition.[40] A third — actually a romantic double-comedy from 1660 — *Verlibtes Gespenst* (Ghost in Love) and *Die gelibte Dornrose* (The Beloved Briar Rose), violated the Opitzian insistence on the strict separation of social classes. The name Peter Squentz was taken from the Shakespearean character Peter Quince in *Midsummer Night's Dream*, but the play itself was based probably on an adaptation, now lost, of Shakespeare by Daniel Schwenter (1585–1636), a professor of mathematics and Oriental languages at the University of Altdorf. Gryphius rejects the supernatural element in Shakespeare. *Peter Squentz* deals with the farcical situation of crude village artisans attempting to stage Ovid's *Pyramus and Thisbe*, providing Gryphius the occasion to lampoon outmoded *Meistersinger* practices oblivious to the new aesthetic theories based on classical and European models. Their amateurish literalism, which confuses the differences between comedy and tragedy, produces often hilarious effects; in the end the villagers are rewarded not for their efforts but for their mistakes. Gryphius was doubtless aware of the offense his play would cause to the powerful artisan guilds, and his decision to publish the play anonymously may well have owed to his fear of their political retaliation.[41]

Social pretensions are also mercilessly caricatured in *Horribilicribrifax*, a play that deals with the reintegration of soldiers into civilian life after the Thirty Years' War.[42] The title figure, a *miles gloriosus* from the Plautine tradition, encounters his double in another vain braggart, an ex-officer with the bizarre and unpronounceable name of Daradadiridatumtarides; one character loads his speech with Italian phrases, the other with French, each equally clumsily. The two are obviously allegorical representations of the two main parties in the recently ended war.[43] Their political and social ambitions match those of the pseudoscholar Sempronius and are eventually unmasked by their own foibles and the actions of the comic servants. In addition to these antimodels Gryphius provides positive figures in Palladius, a young patrician whose religious conversion owes to divine grace, and Sophia, a chaste but poor young noblewoman, whose conduct remains exemplary. This play reinforces Gryphius's ideal of an ethically based absolutism.[44]

If the doubling of the main character in *Horribilicribrifax*, an idea taken from the *commedia dell'arte*, was innovative for German comedy, then the same was true for the two interlinked comedies *Verlibtes Gespenst* and *Die gelibte Dornrose*. This single work combines a romantic comedy set in a middle-class milieu and written in alexandrine verse (*Gespenst*) with a similar play

(*Dornrose*) composed in a Silesian dialect and set in a coarse peasant environment. While each comedy has its own plot, both conclude with a common chorus. Because of the comic contrast between the normative romantic comedy and the rural play, it is possible that the second play was based originally on comic interludes that were developed into a separate work.[45] The thematic bond that unites the two comedies is love. This represents an enhanced status for the peasant play inasmuch as love acquires an ethical or spiritual, even a metaphysical dimension (a foretaste of eternal bliss) when apotheosized in the final chorus. Before they have attained insight into love as the real meaning of life, however, the lovers in both plays must be able to discern between apparent and true values. On the social plane the love that results in marriage symbolizes the restoration of social harmony, just as the nuptials of the duke of Liegnitz and Brieg in Glogau in 1660 — the play was performed on this occasion — point to the peace hoped for through dynastic politics. The emphasis on social order in this comedy stands in stark contrast to Gryphian tragedies, which focus more on life after death. However, the ending is reminiscent of his other comedies, in that not all turns out well. The marriage of Matz Aschwedell to Salome hardly offers a satisfactory solution, given their differences in age and social status, suggesting rather a world still out of joint, plagued by wars, famine, and pestilence.

In his comedies as in his tragedies Gryphius tried desperately, if not always successfully, to reestablish order and meaning to a chaotic world by exposing violence, crudity, pretentiousness, and overindulgence for what they are. Like most of his contemporaries he favored social criticism over the romantic comedy so popular on the itinerant stage, and as a conservative moral and political thinker he was quick to use verbal satire and slapstick to mock those who would disrupt the status quo by disregarding basic Christian morality and the social codes that guarantee order and security.

The early prose comedies written for the school stage by the Zittau principal Christian Weise were predominantly satirical in nature. By 1688, however, when *Die Unvergnügte Seele* (The Discontented Soul) was published, his work demonstrated a clear predilection for romantic plots within a middle-class milieu. This new setting and the new emphasis on realism has led many scholars to conclude that Weise's later comedies represent a transitional phase to the Age of Enlightenment. This assumption is clearly wrong, however. Weise's primary interest, in embracing all social classes and mixing the tragic with the comic, was to revive the earlier school plays.[46]

Like Lohenstein, Weise was a careful observer of the empirical world, especially the dichotomy between ethics and reality, though for him this concern had a metaphysical link. Weise's early comedies attempted to bridge this gap by hurling satirical barbs, not merely at generic foibles, but specifically at Catholic clergy and certain other identifiable individuals, even literary elements that he considered crude or outdated. The figure of Machiavelli in *Bäuerischer Machiavellus* (Machiavelli as Peasant, 1679) justifies his own behavior by pointing out that what he has observed at court can also be found in other social classes. This includes, in his opinion, the peasants living in Querlequitsch (a malapropism for *Quirlequetsche*, the sense of which might be expressed as the "bull-headed inhabitants of Podunk"), whose reactions to a public advertisement for the position of Pickelhering are nothing short of hilarious. The inverse is also true: aristocratic politicians can act like peasants. Given Weise's Lutheran belief in the divine right of kings, it would appear that he is attacking social evils and unethical behavior rather than a particular class or political system — an interpretation borne out by the conclusion of the drama, when the allegorical figure of Virtue emerges as the unambiguous winner.

Christian Reuter (1665–ca. 1712), best remembered for his satirical novel *Schelmuffsky* (1696), also wrote three satirical comedies lambasting the pretentious, upwardly mobile middle class and the inadequacies of the nobility: *L'Honnête Femme: Oder die Ehrliche Frau zu Plissine* (The Honest Woman of Plissine, 1695), *Der ehrlichen Frau Schlampampe Krankheit und Tod* (The Illness and Death of Honest Mrs. Slovenly, 1696), and *Graf Ehrenfried* (Count Peacewithhonor, 1700). The first two plays were transparently based on real events in Leipzig and intended as revenge against a landlady who had evicted him; Reuter was sued for slander and lost. Perhaps because of the personal aspects attending these plays, little attention has been paid to the aesthetic structure of these realistic middle-class vignettes, with their extraordinarily humorous characterizations of individuals.

The Mixed Genres

Mixed dramatic genres in the early modern period combined, both in theory and especially in practice, the elements of comedy and tragedy and fell into three main categories: plays that use both tragic and comic elements; plays in which the upper and lower classes appear together; and serious plays with aristocratic figures that have a happy ending. Genre designations included *Tragikomödie* (tragicomedy), *Komikotragödie* (comicotragedy), *Schäferspiel* (pastoral play), and *Allegorie* (allegory). Opitz deemed inappropriate the mixing of the social classes in a given genre. Consequently, this type of comedy, although popular on the stage of the itinerant troupes and later with Gryphius and Kaspar Stieler (1632–1707), was generally ignored in German theoretical works of the seventeenth century.

Tragicomedy can be traced back to a joke in Plautus's comedy *Amphitryon*, in which the gods mingle with the common people,[47] but refers more directly to the romantic comedy of the Italian Renaissance, with its aristocratic figures, love plot, potentially disastrous passions, and happy ending. In Germany the designation *Tragikomödie* first appeared in 1501 in the title to the Latin play *Tragicomoedia de iherosolomitana profectione illustrissimi principis pomerani* (Tragicomedy on the Departure for Jerusalem of the Most Illustrious Duke of Pomerania) by Johann von Kitzscher (d. 1521), a courtly adviser to the Pomeranian duke, Bogeslaw X.[48] Tragicomedy is romantic comedy set in the upper classes and occasionally combines tragedy with a happy ending. As such it concerns itself with the qualities of the model ruler and holds up a mirror to the ruling class. The Nuremberg poet and dramatist Sigmund von Birken (1626–81) labeled it *Heldenspiel* (heroic play) and dealt with it theoretically as a separate genre that arouses moderate rather than strong emotions. In *Ernelinde* (1665) Stieler seeks to influence the behavior of rulers by postulating an enlightened form of monarchy in which the king acts morally and in the interests of his subjects rather than following his personal drives and interests.

Between 1665 and 1667, during his tenure as secretary at the court of Count Albrecht Anton von Schwarzburg-Rudolstadt, Stieler published six romantic comedy plays anonymously and for various festivities. They included *Der vermeinte Printz* (The Prince Presumptive, 1665), *Die erfreuete Unschuld* (Innocence Overjoyed, 1666), and *Der betrogene Betrug* (Deception Deceived, 1667). Stieler was the first significant German author to devote himself exclusively to writing romantic comedy in aristocratic settings. He regarded the form as an innovative genre and gave it the name *Heldenspiel*, believing it would induce in the audience moderate emotional reactions similar to those produced by the pastoral plays. It has been said that Stieler's heroic play was in reality a romantic comedy concealed by a pastoral ambience.[49] Beneath this guise, however, one finds a courtly society living out its romantic fantasies in a rural setting. Of the many figures Stieler borrowed from the *commedia dell'arte* none had greater impact than the new figure of the clown Scaramutza, who is more worldly-wise, more sophisticated in the ways of the court, than earlier comic figures. His sharp insights and constructive criticism of his fellow actors and the audience identify him closely with the Pickelhering.

The concept of comicotragedy was synonymous with tragicomedy in the sixteenth century and appeared on the title pages to the biblical dramas of Sixt Birck and Hieronymus Ziegler (1514–62), a Catholic professor in Munich. An attempt to differentiate the two genres, however, can be found among the Jesuits as early as 1540 and extended to the writings of the Nuremberg critic Magnus Daniel Omeis (1646–1708). Comicotragedy, according to these theoreticians, denotes a tragedy set in the lower classes and may, as is the case of the Jesuit Masen, even have a middle-class citizen as protagonist.[50] In the seventeenth century this was to remain only a hypothetical possibility, yet it did point toward the middle-class tragedy of the eighteenth century and, beyond that, to the tragedies with proletarian protagonists of the nineteenth century.

In pastoral drama, a creation of the Italian Renaissance, aristocratic figures from classical mythology, the *Idylls* of Theocritus, the *Eclogues* of Vergil, and the Late Greek romantic novel are commingled. By 1619 most of the better-known Italian pastoral works, including Torquato Tasso's *Aminta* (1573), Giovanni Battista Guarini's *Il Pastor Fido* (1589), and Ottavio Rinuccini's *Dafne* (1594) had been translated into German. The German translations extended to works of other Italian-influenced national literatures as well, such as the French pastoral plays of Nicolas de Montreux, Antoine de Montchrétien, Jean Mairet, and Thomas Corneille; German stage renditions were also made of Sir Philip Sidney's novel *Arcadia* by Heinrich Schaeve (1650) and of Jacob Cats's *Aspasia* (1656). The latter, translated anonymously in 1672, is a work of particular interest, in that the pastoral form is used to point out the dangers of absolutism.[51] Guarini's *Il Pastor Fido* was the most popular pastoral drama in all of Europe, given its eminent theatricality and advocacy of Christian-Stoic values, in particular its ethical view of human love. Most German pastoral plays took Guarini as a formal model as well, copying the large number of romantic couples (usually four to seven), the numerous plots, the entanglements, figures, and bucolic settings. Worthy of mention among the German pastoral dramas are Heinrich Elmenhorst's (1632–1704) *Rosetta* (1653), Wilhelm Cronpusch's (1644–85) *Jauchzender Cupido* (Jubilant Cupid, 1669), and two plays by Hallmann, *Urania* (1666) and *Adonis und Rosibella* (1673). This genre, which arose concomitantly with absolutism and reflects the social structures of this new political order, could be shockingly erotic, one of the reasons it did not find resonance with elite dramatists in German-speaking areas. In *Adonis und Rosibella* the figure of the ruler, who appears in pastoral costume, embodies perfect virtue and is lauded as an ideal monarch. Those who reject love or lack the proper ethical perspective are made to see the error of their ways before being reunited with their partners and reintegrated into society. Love in its middle-class moral guise conquers all. The pastoral plays also depict the private life of the aristocracy, in which potentially harmful passions are neutralized by reason and self-control.[52]

Some versions of pastoral drama, less generically strict but more popular, employed ethical, spiritual, or political allegory. The love of the human soul for Christ is illustrated in such religious plays as Georg Philipp Harsdörffer's (1607–58) *Seelewig* (The Soul Eternal, 1644) and Stieler's *Basilene* (1667); Simon Dach's (1605–59) *Cleomedes* (performed 1635; published 1696) deals with the Polish-Swedish conflict, and Birken's *Margenis* (1651) the Thirty Years' War. Allegory was also used to satirize contemporary literature. In the interludes to two of his plays, *Das Friedewünschende Teutschland* (Germany Longing for Peace, 1647) and *Das Friedejauchzende Teutschland* (Germany Rejoicing in Peace, 1653), Rist mocks the stylistic idiosyncrasies — extraordinarily complex syntax, extreme preciosity — of his Hamburg contemporary Philipp von Zesen (1619–89). Even more popular were Heinrich Tolle's (1629–79) three allegorical school dramas, which illustrate moral principles: *Kundegis* (The Desire for True Knowledge, 1670) deals with the victory of philosophy over the senses, *Wahrgilt* (Truth Prevails, 1672) with that of science over medieval scholasticism, and *Willbald* (The Temptations of the Human Will, 1673) with that of virtue over lust.

Seventeenth-Century Opera

Another new genre that became increasingly popular in aristocratic circles was the opera form created in Italy at the end of the sixteenth century by Ottavio Rinuccini and Jacopo Peri with *Dafne* (1594), a *dramma per musica*.[53] *Dafne* served as a basis for the first German opera of the same name (1627), the result of collaboration between Opitz and the composer Heinrich Schütz

(1585–1672). This pioneering work, however, lacks arias, and the verse is not sufficiently supple to capture the natural rhythms of the Italian recitative.[54] The faults were replicated in Opitz's second operatic attempt, *Judith* (1635), which he adapted from the libretto by a contemporary Italian poet, Andrea Salvadori. In his preface to the opera Opitz draws a parallel between the historical situation described in the Bible and the current war raging across central and eastern Europe that pitted Catholic against Protestant. His yearning for the restoration of order anticipates later baroque topics, especially that of *vanitas* (the idea that all terrestrial matters are transitory and worthless in respect to the soul and eternal salvation), but also of political and religious freedom.

Many further experiments were made with the new genre. These included August Buchner (1591–1661) and Schütz's *Die Bußfertige Magdalena* (The Repentant Magdalene, 1635), Dach and Heinrich Albert's (1604–51) *Cleomedes* (1635), Daniel Czepko's (1605–60) *Pierie* (1636), Harsdörffer and Sigmund Theophil Staden's (1607–55) *Seelewig*, and *Kampf und Sieg* (Battle and Victory, 1645), with music by the Magdeburg vicar Georg Weber (fl. 1645–52). However, a verse form suitable for recitative was not invented until about 1653. In that year Kaspar Ziegler (1621–90) published *Von den Madrigalen* (On Madrigals), a theoretical work that recommended iambic madrigalic verse, a random rhyming pattern, and enjambement.[55] In addition, Duke Anton Ulrich von Braunschweig (1633–1714) was able to separate the aria more clearly from recitative, eventually achieving true operatic alternation in *Orpheus* (1659).[56] David Elias Heidenreich (1638–88) established the two short strophes as the standard pattern for arias, as well as the *endecasillabo* (eleven syllables) line as a form corresponding to tragic stichomythia. His twenty librettos between 1665 and 1679, including *Liebe kröhnt Eintracht* (Love Crowns Harmony, 1669), represent the coming-of-age of German opera.

Because of its strong emotive power and obligatory happy ending, opera gained rapidly in popularity and was performed during celebrations at the German courts and in the cities. When Dresden turned to Italian opera around 1680, its position as the focal point of German-language opera was assumed by Hamburg, which would dominate the scene for the next 100 years. The two most influential librettists for the new opera house were both Hamburg lawyers: Christian Heinrich Postel (1658–1705) and Barthold Feind (1678–1721), who used a variety of literary sources (Italian, French, Greek, Roman); the musical scores were written by the highly talented composer Reinhard Keiser (1674–1739). Postel in particular is credited with helping to create an original German operatic text through his creative application of allegorical language; his use of alliteration at the beginning and ending of a duet, which enhanced dramatic tension; and his addition of the comic clown to satirize contemporary issues. In *Die Wunderbahr-errettete Iphigenia* (The Miraculous Rescue of Iphigenia, 1699), an opera that features a heroic female figure in the tradition of Lohenstein, Postel flawlessly integrates an amorous subplot into the main action. Although love is the main theme, it always has a moral component. Feind, for his part, was more gifted in the area of psychological motivation, both of individuals and of plot. The sophisticated pace of the action is particularly effective in two operas published in 1705, *Oktavia* and *Lucretia*.

One of the other innovative theatrical forms of the seventeenth century was the so-called *Redeoratorium* (declamatory oratorio) created by Johann Klaj (1616–56) in Nuremberg. Declamatory oratorio mixes prose texts from the New Testament with poetic narrations and declaimed commentaries, in contrast to choruses that are sung. A good example among Klaj's six declamatory oratorios is *Herodes der Kindermörder* (Herod the Infanticide, 1645), an adaptation of Daniel Heinsius's tragedy *Herodes infanticida* (1632). Klaj's version, a recitation of nearly two hours, including instrumental interludes, not only uses the martyr-tyrant format of baroque tragedy and the religious setting of the "slaughter of the innocents," but also provides political commentary in pleading for an end to the war.[57] A climactic moment describes a feverish Herod experiencing a nightmare after having decided to put the children to death. His wife Mariamne, whom he had also had murdered, speaks in irregular lines and rhythms that bespeak his terror:[58]

> Ach! mein liebes Ehgemahl
> Wilstu mich umarmen?
> Ach! ihr Geister aus der Qwal
> Ubet doch erbarmen.
> Lauter Ungemach,
> Uberfält mich, Ach, Ach, Ach, Ach!

[Alas, my dearest wedded mate, art thou come to hold me? Alas, thou ghosts of hate, in mercy do enfold me. Miserable distress befalls me, alas, alas, alas, alas!]

Criticism of Theater and Drama

The humanists' attempts to revive classical drama, combined with Luther's recommendation to stage certain biblical stories, such as those of Judith, Susanna, and Tobias, resulted in a largely positive attitude toward drama and the theater during the first half of the sixteenth century. In Zurich, Huldrych Zwingli (1484–1531) composed the musical interludes for a production of Aristophanes' *Pluto*, and his successor, Heinrich Bullinger (1504–75), published his own *Lucretia* drama (1533), a political work that uses a Roman setting to help stage the foundation of a Swiss republic. John Calvin himself (1509–64) on occasion defended the theater against orthodox fanatics, and his successor in Geneva, Théodore de Bèze (1519–1605), sought to establish a new tradition of Calvinist biblical drama with the publication of *Abraham sacrifiant* (Abraham and Isaac, 1550).

This initial support for theater stemmed from the Protestant view that the arts belonged to the moral and theological *adiaphora* (middle, or indifferent, things) and that performances could therefore be permitted. Beginning around the middle of the sixteenth century, however, and continuing through the seventeenth, Protestant theologians mounted a virulent opposition to the theater. Their primary authority was an ultraconservative work by the third-century Roman theologian Tertullian entitled *De spectaculis* (On Plays), which sought to ban plays because they were pagan and thus inspired by the devil. The Catholic Church shared this position with respect to classical drama and all other plays and practices that did not reflect its own ideology, and even banned dramatic performances outright on holy days. On the other hand, perhaps fearing competition from the itinerant players to whom it sometimes refused last rites, the church did not oppose the theater in principle; during the Counter-Reformation it wholeheartedly embraced Jesuit and Benedictine drama as an instrument of *propaganda fidei* (the propagation of faith). From 1540 on these new, eminently theatrical plays, ancillary to theology and written in Latin for Catholic schools, greatly enriched the theater, including drama in the German-speaking world.

However, in the second half of the sixteenth century in Switzerland, as well as in the Baltic and North Sea cities where they constituted at least a strong vocal minority, Calvinists became far less tolerant of all forms of secular entertainment, including dancing, songs, and plays, especially the pre-Christian comedies of the Roman dramatists Plautus and Terence. The important political theorists Jean Bodin (1530–96) and Johannes Althusius (1557–1638) held actors to be dissolute and the theater itself little more than a den of iniquity that led only to sin and the forfeiture of salvation.

This position was not shared by all Calvinist rulers, especially not those having close connections with the English court. Moritz, Landgrave of Hesse-Kassel (1572–1632), an avid fan of the theater and the professional English Players, erected the first freestanding theater on German soil, the so-called Ottoneum. Friedrich V, Elector of the Palatinate (1596–1632), was ever ready to welcome the itinerant troupes to Heidelberg. Around the middle of the seventeenth century, Calvinist dramatists began to translate renowned French plays into German or even to write their own plays. The Strasbourg Calvinist Isaac Clauss (1613–after 1662) published a German translation of Pierre Corneille's *Le Cid* (1637) in 1655; *Carle von Burgund* (Charles of Burgundy), written by Josua Wetter (1622–56) of St. Gall in 1653, was performed locally by some eighty students.

Such support of the theater was, however, not the norm. During the early seventeenth century, Johann Jacob Breitinger (1575–1645), a fanatical Calvinist preacher, published anonymously his pamphlet *Bedencken von Comoedien oder Spilen* (Reservations about Comedies or Plays, 1624), which found great resonance among orthodox Calvinist clergy and led almost immediately to the prohibition of public performances in Geneva and Zurich. This prohibition would last for well over a century. Fully aware of Luther's support of the theater as well as of the tolerance of plays by prominent members of his own confession — some of whom wrote plays themselves — Breitinger nevertheless followed Tertullian, Bodin, and Althusius in inveighing against all theatrical forms. He expressed forceful opposition to what he saw as the hedonism of actors, the immorality of secular comedies with love themes, and the bawdiness of the Pickelhering. Breitinger adhered to the Platonic notion, adopted by many fathers of the church, that the depiction of vice or violence causes its imitation among actors and audience; indeed, because he believed that metaphysical entities, such as devils, could literally partake of the action on stage, any natural calamity that occurred during a performance became a sign of divine anger. Ironically, Breitinger also criticized drama as frivolous, worthless fiction, a sinful attempt to reenact God's creation. Another Calvinist, Gotthard Heidegger (1666–1711), recurred to these opinions in his *Mythoscopia romantica* (1698), where he advances the belief that the genre of the novel derived from such comedies and pastoral plays.

The Pietists in Frankfurt am Main likewise objected to the dissolute behavior of actors, a grievous condition thought to have been exacerbated by the appearance of actresses and female singers on the German stage since 1653. While Philipp Jacob Spener (1635–1705) was offended by lewd actions in the comedies, he nevertheless saw fit to praise Gryphius's tragedy *Catharina von Georgien*. This ambivalent attitude toward the theater was not shared by the later Pietist theologians in Halle an der Saale: they banned drama in 1698 and two years later extended the ban to all public performances.

In agreement with those Calvinists and Pietists who did not believe that plays or operas belonged to the *adiaphora*, the Lutheran preacher Anton Reiser (1628–86) initiated a vociferous attack against the recently consecrated Hamburg Opera House in his *Theatromania* (1681). Quoting liberally from the patristic tradition Reiser lambasted the theater as the work of the devil himself. He was unable to prevail against the city council and broader-minded theologians, however, perhaps because some opera libretti were written by eminent city councilmen, such as Lucas von Bostel (1649–1716), or by lawyers, such as the aforementioned Christian Heinrich Postel.

Reception of Early Modern Drama

The 1612–16 Kempten edition of Hans Sachs's works and the influence that they exerted on the Shrovetide plays of the Nuremberg lawyer-playwright Jacob Ayrer, in particular, indicates that Sachs remained popular well into the seventeenth century. Although the arrival of the English Players at the end of the sixteenth century, followed by the adoption of a new theater aesthetic, had made the Sachsian model largely obsolete by the end of the first quarter of the seventeenth century, his tragedy *Lorenzo und Lisabetha* (1546) could still be staged as late as 1646 at the Dresden court. For Opitz he was irrelevant; and for the Gryphius of *Peter Squentz*, Sachsian drama, with its unsophisticated handling of the stage, became the subject matter of comedy.

However, the arbiter of literary taste in the first half of the eighteenth century, Johann Christoph Gottsched (1700–1766), looked favorably on the Shrovetide plays in his history of German drama, entitled *Nöthiger Vorrat* (Necessary Supplies, 1757). The rehabilitation of Sachs's reputation in elite literary circles, along with that of the rhymed doggerel that he was thought to have invented, was due, however, not to Gottsched but to Johann Wolfgang von Goethe. In 1776 the young Goethe paid him respectful homage in the poem "Hans Sachsens poetische Sendung" (Hans Sachs's Poetic Mission), and in the following year he produced Sachs's carnival play *Das Narrenschneiden* (On Playing the Fool, 1561), though with little critical success.

Although the Sachsian Shrovetide play could not be revived in later times as a serious subgenre, it proved to be a popular target in the literary farces of leading dramatists of the Storm and Stress movement, such as Jakob Michael Reinhold Lenz (1751–92) and Friedrich Maximilian Klinger (1752–1831), and of Romanticism, such as August Wilhelm Schlegel (1767–1845) and Ludwig Tieck (1773–1853). Some twenty plays dealing primarily with Sachs's early married life, including one published in 1829 by the Austrian court theater director Johann Ludwig Deinhardtstein (1794–1859), were highly successful. Of course, the most famous work to thematize Sachs, one that has influenced our picture of him down to the present day, was Richard Wagner's (1813–83) opera *Die Meistersinger von Nürnberg* (1862). It was not until the end of the nineteenth century, however, that his texts found their way into critical scholarly editions. Depending on the political bent of the editors, Sachs was portrayed either as a German patriot or as a representative of the working class. Interest in Sachs — and the sixteenth century in general — began to wane around 1920 and did not revive until 1966, with Eckehard Catholy's now standard monograph on carnival plays.[59]

The reception of Gryphius and Lohenstein followed a similar path. Each was apotheosized during his own lifetime as a German "Euripides," "Sophocles," or "Seneca," and then as late as the mid-eighteenth century in the epic poem *Messias* (Messiah, 1748) by Johann Gottlieb Klopstock (1724–1803). Their tragedies in particular proved to be a reservoir of figures, scenes, motifs, and sayings for Hallmann,[60] Haugwitz, Kormart, Riemer, and a host of now largely forgotten seventeenth- and early eighteenth-century authors of martyr and tyrant plays. These included the Jesuit dramatist Franz Neumayr (1697–1765), who adapted *Papinianus* for the stage in 1733.

Toward the end of the seventeenth century a strong reaction set in against the florid poetic language of Lohenstein, leading Weise to offer in its place a realistic, down-to-earth prose style. Weise's school plays, along with Gryphius's *Peter Squentz* and Stieler's *Der vermeinte Printz*, continued to be performed into the next century, even if they did not enjoy the same degree of popularity as the interludes in peasant dialect populating Rist's dramas.

The attractive figure of the clown or fool, ever present in the performances of the itinerant troupes and school plays, found renewed popularity within a decade after the end of the Thirty Years' War. Indeed it dominated the stage until Gottsched, who believed that it had an adverse affect on the unity of the plot and was little more than a concession to popular taste, banned it in 1737. Nevertheless, Gottsched owed much to Silesian drama. In his tragedy *Sterbender Cato* (The Death of Cato, 1732) he borrowed the subgenre of the martyr drama, the verse form, the style, and the concept of tragedy employed by Gryphius in *Leo Armenius*. Gottsched praised *Leo Armenius*, in particular, and was generally approving of the comedies of Gryphius, though he disparaged the use of supernatural elements and emblematic form. He also criticized Silesian tragedy for its courtly setting and attempted to modernize it by creating a mixed protagonist (a hero with a flaw) from the middle classes, even as his ultimate goal remained a rapprochement between the middle class and the aristocracy.

Lohenstein, regarded as a viable model until around 1730, was subjected thereafter to simultaneous attacks by Gottsched and the Swiss critics Johann Jakob Bodmer (1698–1783) and Johann Jakob Breitinger (1701–76). At issue were his euphuistic style, his disregard of the classical rules for drama, his allegedly inconsistent characterization of Sophonisbe, and his erudite footnotes — all of which added up, in the opinion of his detractors, to poor taste (*Geschmack*). Despite an attempt by the popular Swiss novelist Heinrich Zschokke (1771–1848) to salvage Lohenstein's reputation at the end of the eighteenth century, his works continued to be identified with bad style and tastelessness until rehabilitated in the 1950s.[61] Weise's school dramas were likewise considered defective for ignoring Aristotelian precepts and for employing prose rather than verse. Gottsched's praise, however, of the prose translation of Corneille's *Le Cid* by the Calvinist Clauss, because of its retention of the structure of the French original, suggests that form was even more important to him than style.

From Gottsched until the end of the eighteenth century, Silesian drama attracted little interest. Nevertheless, there were exceptions. Johann Elias Schlegel (1719–49) published an essay on Shakespeare and Gryphius in 1741 in which he lauded the characterizations in *Leo Armenius*; Johann Gottfried Herder (1744–1803) considered writing a history of Jesuit drama; and the eminent critic Gotthold Ephraim Lessing (1729–81), in a letter of 14 July 1773 to his brother Karl, praised Weise's *Masaniello* for its characterizations. Despite reservations about its pedantry, Lessing enthusiastically compared some passages from the tragedy to similar ones in Shakespeare. Two years later Goethe was inspired by the anonymous comedy *Des Harlekins Hochzeitsschmaus* (The Harlequin's Wedding Banquet, after 1695) to publish his own version, entitled *Hanswursts Hochzeit oder der Lauf der Welt* (The Clown's Marriage, or the Way of the World, 1775); in *Wilhelm Meisters Lehrjahre* (Wilhelm Meister's Apprenticeship, 1795–96) he mentions that Friedrich has read the works of Gryphius;[62] in his *Italienische Reise* (Italian Journey) dated September 4, 1786, Goethe also expresses appreciation for the creativity of the Jesuit dramaturges.[63] Goethe's friend Friedrich Schiller (1759–1805) devoted much attention to the sixteenth and seventeenth centuries, both as a historian — among other things he wrote a notable history of the Thirty Years' War — and as a dramatist. His fascination with powerful but enigmatic historical personalities resulted in a number of great plays on early modern subjects, including *Don Carlos* (1787), *Maria Stuart* (1801), and the trilogy *Wallenstein* (1800), considered by many to be the greatest tragedy in the German language. Schiller was also the first to point out the antithetical structure of alexandrine verse as expressive of the contradictions of the Baroque, an age for which he felt great affinity.[64]

The Romantic critics were kinder to Gryphius and Rist. Achim von Arnim (1781–1831) appropriated parts of Gryphius's *Cardenio und Celinde* for his play *Halle und Jerusalem* (1811)[65] and even considered reprinting it. Rist's *Das Friedewünschende Teutschland*, a patriotic call for German unity, was republished by contemporary Germany's greatest actor, August Wilhelm Iffland (1759–1814) in 1806 during the Napoleonic occupation,[66] and it continued to appear in one guise or another during further periods of political instability as late as 1915.[67] The favorite baroque play of literary historians through the first third of the nineteenth century was Gryphius's *Die gelibte Dornrose*, though Tieck did not reprint it along with *Peter Squentz*, *Horribilicribrifax*, and *Cardenio und Celinde* in his *Deutsches Theater* (German Theater) of 1817. Although today its Silesian dialect makes it virtually indecipherable, *Dornrose* is thought to have served as an inspiration and source for Gerhart Hauptmann's (1862–1946) social tragedy *Die Weber* (1892). *Horribilicribrifax* similarly inspired Hauptmann's historical play *Florian Geyer* (1896).

Interest in Gryphius's comedies continued into the twentieth century. Between the years 1900 and 1932 *Die gelibte Dornrose* was adapted eight times for the stage, *Peter Squentz* twice, and *Horribilicribrifax* once.[68] Arno Holz (1863–1929), whose later work has a distinctly baroque affectation, was particularly enamored of the language in *Horribilicribrifax*, which reappears in his work *Die Blechschmiede* (The Tin Smith) of 1924.[69] Herbert Eulenberg (1876–1949), one of the writers of the early twentieth century who looked to the distant past for their dramatic themes, also included a scene from *Horribilicribrifax*, along with several carnival plays by Sachs, in his *Schattenbilder: Eine Fibel für Kulturbedürftige in Deutschland* (Silhouettes: A Primer for the Culturally Challenged in Germany), a popular work that was published sixteen times between 1909 and 1913.[70]

Franz Werfel's (1890–1945) *Die Troerinnen* (The Trojan Women, 1915), an adaptation of Euripides' play, represented the dawn of a new literary epoch: Expressionism (in 1625, Optiz's translation of Seneca's play on this same theme had similarly opened up a new epoch in German literature).[71] In the 1920s two influential scholarly works on German baroque drama appeared: Willi Flemming's *Andreas Gryphius und die Bühne* (1921) argued persuasively that the plays of Gryphius were not simply works to be read but to be performed,[72] and in 1925 Walter Benjamin (1892–1940) established the parameters that separate seventeenth-century tragedy — understood specifically as *Trauerspiel* (tragic drama) — from its classical counterpart.[73] Reprints and adaptations of numerous baroque tragedies continued to appear throughout the twentieth century.[74]

While Marieluise Fleisser (1901–1974) seems to have written her *Karl Stuart* (1946) without knowledge of the play by Gryphius,[75] the East German writer Günther Deicke (born 1922), in an anthology of poetry published in 1953 entitled *Deutschland, es werden deine Mauern nicht mehr voll Jammer stehen: Gedichte* (Germany, Your Walls Will No Longer Resound with Grief: Poems), focused on the folksy comedy *Die gelibte Dornrose*.[76] The East German dramatist Heiner Müller (1929–95) demonstrated in *Die Bauern*

(The Peasants, 1964) that he was fully conversant with the central baroque motifs of *vanitas mundi* (vanity of the world), tyranny (portrayed by Müller as capitalists), and allegorical-emblematic structures.

Notwithstanding Theodor Adorno's (1908–69) admonition that analogies tend to dissipate when one analyses them more closely,[77] attempts have been made to link by analogy the work of Bertolt Brecht (1898–1956) with the seventeenth-century tradition. The alleged commonalities rest on certain techniques and goals (including the figure of the nontragic protagonist), the exemplary nature of the drama, and particularly the episodic or didactic structures, such as the emblematic form. The Christian metaphysical ideology of early modern drama, however, has — despite Marxist studies of works such as Weise's *Masaniello* — resisted identification with a philosophy of materialism.

The works of Gryphius have not always been received in a positive light. In *Das Treffen in Telgte* (1979), the Nobel Prize winning novelist Günter Grass (b. 1927) employs a fictitious version of the playwright in lambasting the rhetoric of *Leo Armenius* and other baroque plays.[78] This opinion was not shared by the Austrian writer Thomas Bernhard (1931–89), whose interest was piqued not only by baroque stylistic devices (antithesis, hyperbolism, neologism) but also by themes (the fall of the mighty, appearance versus reality) and figures such as the tyrant (albeit in a middle-class setting) and the intriguer.[79] An even greater fascination for Lohenstein was shown by the director Hubert Fichte (1935–86), who saw in the tragedies models of racial, gender, and sexual equality,[80] and who devoted much of the last ten years of his life to holding lectures on this topic and staging adaptations of the plays.

Both the professional as well as amateur stage have regularly engaged in productions of early modern drama: the *Oberammergau Easter Play* is still performed every ten years, and schools and universities stage Hans Sachs's *Fastnachtspiele* and Gryphius's *Peter Squentz* with some frequency. The Jesuit drama *Cenodoxus*, written by Jacob Bidermann (1578–1639) in 1602, was performed regularly in the 1635 translation by Joachim Meichel (1590–1637) between 1932 and 1975; Bidermann's *Philemon Martyr* in 1958 and 1973; *Leo Armenius* in 1968 and 1974; *Papinianus* in 1967; *Masaniello* in 1976; *Epicharis* in 1977–78; *Agrippina* in 1977 and 1991; *Ibrahim Bassa* in 1979; and *Sophonisbe* in 1985. For the most part these productions were experimental in nature and failed to generate much audience enthusiasm.

Notes

[1] Sarah Colvin, *The Rhetorical Feminine: Gender and Orient on the German Stage, 1647–1742* (Oxford: Clarendon, 1999), 286.

[2] Rolf Steinbach, *Die deutschen Oster- und Passionsspiele des Mittelalters: Versuch einer Darstellung und Wesensbestimmung nebst einer Bibliographie zum deutschen geistlichen Spiel des Mittelalters* (Cologne: Böhlau, 1970), 20.

[3] The oldest extant text, based on two Augsburg passion plays, was revised in 1674 to accommodate the *Weilheimer Passionsspiel* (Weilheim Passion Play), and various additions including music, allegorical figures, operatic features, and alexandrine verse appeared in the text. Nevertheless, Ferdinand Rosner (1709–78) retained the old rhymed doggerel of the sixteenth century in his definitive version from 1750.

[4] It provided the basis for *Ipocras*, a *Fastnachtspiel* or Shrovetide play by Vigil Raber (d. 1552).

[5] Leif Søndergaard, "Combat between the Genders: Farcical Elements in the German *Fastnachtspiel*," *Ludus: Medieval and Early Renaissance Theatre and Drama* 6 (2002): 169–87; Helen Watanabe-O'Kelly, "Das weibliche Publikum und die soziale Funktion des deutschen Dramas im 16. Jahrhundert," in *"Verbergendes Enthüllen": Zu Theorie und Kunst dichterischen Verkleidens*, ed. Wolfram Malte Fues and Wolfram Mauser (Würzburg: Königshausen & Neumann, 1995), 67–75.

[6] Barbara Könneker, *Hans Sachs* (Stuttgart: Metzler, 1971), 52.

[7] Hans-Gert Roloff, "Sozialkritik und Komödie: Reuchlin als Komödienautor," in *Kleine Schriften zur Literatur des 16. Jahrhunderts*, ed. Christiane Caemmerer et al. (Amsterdam: Rodopi, 2003), 131.

[8] Gabrijela Mecky Zaragoza, "Virgo and Virago: zwei neuzeitliche Judith-Figuren im Vergleich," *Daphnis* 31 (2002): 126.

[9] Martin Opitz, "Vorrede 'An den Leser'," in *Weltliche Poemata* (1644), ed. Erich Trunz (Tübingen: Niemeyer, 1967), 1:315.

[10] For a discussion of the significance of rhetoric in the school system, in public life, and in drama see Wilfried Barner, *Barockrhetorik: Untersuchungen zu ihren geschichtlichen Grundlagen* (Tübingen: Niemeyer, 1970). On the importance of legal structures and forensic rhetoric in seventeenth-century tragedy see Adalbert Wichert, *Literatur, Rhetorik und Jurisprudenz im 17. Jahrhundert: Daniel Casper von Lohenstein und sein Werk: Eine exemplarische Studie* (Tübingen: Niemeyer, 1991).

[11] Nicola Kaminski, *Andreas Gryphius* (Stuttgart: Reclam, 1998), 124.

[12] For Peter Brenner, "Der Tod des Märtyrers: 'Macht' und 'Moral' in den Trauerspielen von Andreas Gryphius," *Deutsche Vierteljahrsschrift für Literaturwissenschaft und Geistesgeschichte* 62 (1988): 246–65, the main conflict in *Papinianus* is a secular one centered on the growing interest in the rights of the individual vis-à-vis those of the state.

[13] For the Lutheran concept of the conscience and its important role in *Papinianus* see Andreas Solbach, "Amtsethik und lutherischer Gewissensbegriff in Andreas Gryphius' *Papinianus*," *Daphnis* 28 (1999): 668–72.

[14] Ralf Georg Bogner, "Die Not der Lüge: Konfessionelle Differenzen in der Bewertung der unwahren Rede am Beispiel von Andreas Gryphius' Trauerspiel 'Catharina von Georgien,'" *Daphnis* 28 (1999): 595–611, reveals that the contemporary debate on the definition and permissibility of certain forms of lies is mirrored in the conflict between Chach Abas (Jesuit position on mental reservations) and Catharina (Lutheran justification of the lie for the greater good in exceptional circumstances).

[15] The focus on salvation history in the tragedies of Gryphius is well described in James Parente's *Religious Drama and the Humanist Tradition: Christian Theatre in Germany and in the Netherlands, 1500–1680* (Leiden: Brill, 1987), 186–98.

[16] Albrecht Schöne's *Säkularisation als sprachbildende Kraft: Studien zur Dichtung deutscher Pfarrersöhne* (Göttingen: Vandenhoeck & Ruprecht, 1958), 52–72.

[17] Jean-Louis Raffy, "Die *Civitas Dei* in Gryphius' Trauerspielen," *Daphnis* 28 (1999): 729–60, examines the Augustinian two-state theory as reflected in the tragedies and demonstrates that Gryphius was a very conservative Lutheran whose ultimate goal was the revival of an ethically based Christian politics.

[18] Bogner, "Die Not der Lüge," 610.

[19] Elida Maria Szarota, *Geschichte, Politik und Gesellschaft im deutschen Drama des 17. Jahrhunderts* (Bern: Francke, 1976), 68.

[20] For an account of the emblematic uses see in this volume the chapter by Peter M. Daly, "The Emblem and Emblematic Forms in Early Modern Germany."

[21] Gerhard Spellerberg, *Verhängnis und Geschichte: Untersuchungen zu den Trauerspielen und dem "Arminius"-Roman Daniel Caspers von Lohenstein* (Bad Homburg: Gehlen, 1970), 115.

[22] Judith P. Aikin, *The Mission of Rome in the Dramas of Daniel Casper von Lohenstein: Historical Tragedy as Prophecy and Polemic* (Stuttgart: Akademischer Verlag Heinz, 1976), 14–15.

[23] Bettina Müsch, *Der politische Mensch im Welttheater des Daniel Casper von Lohenstein: eine Deutung seines Dramenwerkes* (Frankfurt am Main: Lang, 1992), 125.

[24] For an examination of the strong female figures in terms of the formation of gender identity and intertextuality see Jane O. Newman, *The Intervention of Philology: Gender, Learning, and Power in Lohenstein's Roman Plays* (Chapel Hill: U of North Carolina P, 2000). This work also treats the negative portrayal of other races, the role of female rulers in Silesia, and the possibility of resistance to the power of the Habsburg court.

[25] Sarah Colvin, " 'Die Wollust ist die Cirz': Daniel Casper von Lohenstein and the Notion of Witchcraft," *Daphnis* 28 (1999): 279, points out that it is not the masculinized Epicharis but rather the effeminate Lord of Misrule, Nero, who is the ultimate anti-ideal for both schoolboy actors and audience.

[26] Albrecht Schöne, *Emblematik und Drama im Zeitalter des Barock*, 3rd ed. (Munich: Beck, 1993), 169–70.

[27] Schöne, *Emblematik und Drama*, 174.

[28] Szarota, *Geschichte, Politik und Gesellschaft*, 81.

[29] Pierre Béhar, "Nachwort," in *August Adolph von Haugwitz: Prodromus poeticus, oder: Poetischer Vortrab: 1684*, ed. Béhar (Tübingen: Niemeyer, 1984), 83*.

[30] See Robert R. Heitner's introduction to his edition of Haugwitz's *Schuldige Unschuld oder Maria Stuarda* (Bern: Lang, 1974), 37.

[31] By the same token, however, Haugwitz rejects all forms of orthodoxy. See Pierre Béhar, "Drama in the Empire," in *Spectaculum Europaeum*, ed. Béhar and Helen Watanabe-O'Kelly (Wiesbaden: Harrassowitz, 1999), 273.

[32] Norbert Sorg, *Restauration und Rebellion — Die deutschen Dramen Johann Sebastian Mitternachts: Ein Beitrag zur Geschichte des protestantischen Schuldramas im 17. Jahrhundert* (Freiburg i.B.: Hochschulverlag, 1980), 265.

[33] Klaus Reichelt, *Barockdrama und Absolutismus: Studien zum deutschen Drama zwischen 1650 und 1700* (Bern: Lang, 1981), 259.

[34] Helmut Krause, *Feder contra Degen: Zur literarischen Vermittlung des bürgerlichen Weltbildes im Werk Johannes Riemer* (Berlin: Hofgarten, 1979), 206.

[35] Peter-Henning Haischer, "Zur Bedeutung von Parodie und Karneval in Christian Weises *Zittauisch Theatrum*," *Daphnis* 28 (1999): 321.

[36] Jolanda Lötscher, *Andreae Gryphii Horribilicribrifax Teutsch: Formanalyse und Interpretation eines deutschen Lustspiels des 17. Jahrhunderts im soziokulturellen und dichtungstheoretischen Kontext* (Bern: Lang, 1994), 92.

[37] Opitz, *Buch von der Deutschen Poeterey*, ed. Cornelius Sommer (Stuttgart: Reclam), 27.

[38] For more on the English Players at the German courts see in this volume the chapter by Helen Watanabe-O'Kelly.

[39] Manfred Brauneck and Alfred Noe, eds., *Spieltexte der Wanderbühne*, 4 vols. (Berlin: de Gruyter, 1970–75).

[40] Lötscher, *Horribilicribrifax*, 70.

[41] While his authorship has been questioned, there no longer seems to be any doubt that Gryphius actually wrote the play, perhaps as a comic epilogue to *Cardenio und Celinde*. See Gerhard Dünnhaupt and Karl-Heinz Habersetzer's "Nachwort" in their edition of *Herr Peter Squentz* (Stuttgart: Reclam, 1983), 70.

[42] Susan L. Clark, " 'Ihr verstehet mich nicht recht': Use and Abuse of Language in 'Horribilicribrifax,' " in *"Der Buchstab tödt — der Geist macht lebendig": Festschrift zum 60. Geburtstag von Hans-Gert Roloff*, ed. James Hardin and Jörg Jungmayr (Berlin: Lang, 1992), 2:842.

[43] Walter Hinck, "Gryphius und die italienische Komödie: Untersuchungen zum 'Horribilicribrifax,' " *Germanisch-romanische Monatsschrift* 44 (1963): 124.

[44] Helmuth Kiesel, "Höfische Gewalt im Lustspiel des Andreas Gryphius: Bemerkungen zum 'Horribilicribrifax' im Vergleich zu deutschen Lucretia- und Virginia-Dramen," in *Andreas Gryphius*, ed. Heinz Ludwig Arnold, 2nd ed. (Munich: Text + Kritik, 1980), 74–77.

[45] Eberhard Mannack, "Andreas Gryphius' Lustspiele — ihre Herkunft, ihre Motive und ihre Entwicklung," *Euphorion* 58 (1954): 90.

[46] Haischer, "Parodie und Karneval," 321.

[47] Karl S. Guthke, "Das Problem der gemischten Dramengattung in der deutschen Poetik und Praxis vom Mittelalter bis zum Barock," *Zeitschrift für deutsche Philologie* 80 (1961): 346.

[48] Guthke, "Das Problem der gemischten Dramengattung," 347.

[49] Judith P. Aikin, *Scaramutza in Germany: The Dramatic Works of Caspar Stieler* (University Park: The Pennsylvania State UP, 1989), 97.

[50] Masen and Stieler also wrote allegorical plays on moral and religious themes. Masen's *Androfilo* (Son of Andros, i.e., God, 1648) deals with the victory of Christ over the courtier Andromiso (Enemy of Andros, i.e., Satan), whereas Stieler's *Willmuth* (The Will, 1680) depicts the right and wrong choices of an initially willful prince.

[51] Klaus Garber, *Der locus amoenus und der locus terribilis: Bild und Funktion der Natur in der deutschen Schäfer- und Landlebendichtung des 17. Jahrhunderts* (Cologne: Böhlau, 1974), 238.

[52] Conrad Wiedemann, "Heroisch — Schäferlich — Geistlich: Zu einem möglichen Systemzusammenhang barocker Rollenhaltung," *Dokumente des Internationalen Arbeitskreises für Barockliteratur* 3 (1977), 109. Hallmann's two pastoral plays were parodied in his own lifetime. For further information on Jacob Reich's *Der unbeglückte*

Schäffer Corydon (1686) see Christiane Caemmerer, *Siegender Cupido oder Triumphierende Keuschheit: Deutsche Schäferspiele des 17. Jahrhunderts dargestellt in einzelnen Darstellungen* (Stuttgart-Bad Cannstatt: Frommann-Holzboog, 1998), 458–62.

[53] For a general overview of music in this period, and specifically of German opera, see in this volume the chapter by Steven Saunders.

[54] Judith P. Aikin, *A Language for German Opera: the Development of Forms and Formulas for Recitative and Aria in Seventeenth-Century German Libretti* (Wiesbaden: Harrassowitz, 2002), 49 and 61.

[55] Aikin, *A Language for German Opera*, 176–81.

[56] Aikin, *A Language for German Opera*, 247, 252–57.

[57] Judith P. Aikin, *German Baroque Drama* (Boston: Twayne, 1982), 138–39.

[58] The following quotation and translation is from Max Reinhart, "Johann Klaj (Klajus)," in *German Baroque Writers, 1580–1660*, vol. 164 of *Dictionary of Literary Bibliography*, ed. James Hardin (Detroit: Gale Research, 1996), 200.

[59] Eckehard Catholy, *Fastnachtspiel* (Stuttgart: Metzler, 1966).

[60] Although Hallmann's works had little impact on the further development of German drama, his translation of Beregan's Italian opera *L'Eraclio* (Hercules, 1684) was nevertheless adapted by Heinrich Anselm von Ziegler und Klipphausen (1663–97), who then appended it to his novel *Asiatische Banise* (Banise of Asia, 1689).

[61] Daniel Casper von Lohenstein, *Sämtliche Trauerspiele: Historisch-kritische Gesamtausgabe*, ed. Klaus Günther Just, 3 vols. (Stuttgart: Hiersemann, 1953–57).

[62] Johann Wolfgang von Goethe, *Wilhelm Meisters Lehrjahre*, in *Werke*, ed. Erich Trunz (Hamburg: Wegner, 1964), 7:558.

[63] Johann Wolfgang von Goethe, *Italienische Reise*, in *Goethes sämtliche Werke*, ed. Karl Goedeke (Stuttgart: Cotta, n.d.), 22:12.

[64] Albrecht Schöne, *Das Zeitalter des Barock: Texte und Zeugnisse*, 2nd ed. (Munich: Beck, 1968), ix.

[65] Roger Paulin, *Gryphius' Cardenio und Celinde und Arnims Halle und Jerusalem: Eine vergleichende Untersuchung* (Tübingen: Niemeyer, 1968), 174, points out that von Arnim took over only those elements that dovetailed with his conservative agenda.

[66] August Wilhelm Iffland, ed. *"Das Friedewünschende Teutschland" in einem Schauspiele vorgestellt und beschrieben* (1806).

[67] Heinrich Stümcke, *Das Friedewünschende Teutschland: Ein Schauspiel aus dem Dreißigjährigen Kriege: In neuer Fassung* (Gotha: Perthes, 1915).

[68] The information in this paragraph is taken from Eberhard Mannack, "Andreas Gryphius," in *Barock in der Moderne* (Frankfurt am Main: Lang, 1991), 59–61.

[69] Arno Holz, *Die Blechschmiede*, vols. 3–4 of *Das Werk: Monumentalausgabe in 12 Bänden* (Berlin: Dietz, 1924).

[70] Herbert Eulenberg, *Schattenbilder* (Berlin: Cassirer, 1909).

[71] Walter Benjamin, *Ursprung des deutschen Trauerspiels* (Frankfurt am Main: Suhrkamp, 1963), 41.

[72] Willi Flemming, *Andreas Gryphius und die Bühne* (Halle: Niemeyer, 1921).

[73] Benjamin, *Ursprung des deutschen Trauerspiels*, 41.

[74] I am thinking here primarily of Rolf Tarot's 1967 reprint of Jacob Bidermann's Latin plays as *Ludi Theatrales* as well as the stage adaptations in German of *Cenodoxus* by Herbert Rommel (1932), Heinrich Bachmann (1932), Joseph Gregor (1934 and 1956), Stephan Schaller (1953), Artur Müller (1954), Dieter Forte (1972), and J. A. Müller (1975), and of *Philemon Martyr* by Bernd von Heiseler (1958) and Luise Rinser (1973). In the aftermath of the First and Second World Wars many of the dramatic and operatic works of Rist, Gryphius, Lohenstein, Anton Ulrich, Hallmann, Haugwitz, Weise, and others were reprinted.

[75] Mannack, "Lustspiele," 66.

[76] Günther Deicke, *Deutschland* (Berlin: Aufbau, 1953).

[77] Theodor Adorno, "Der mißbrauchte Barock," in *Ohne Leitbild: Parva aesthetica* (Frankfurt am Main: Suhrkamp, 1967), 136.

[78] Günter Grass, *Das Treffen in Telgte* (Darmstadt: Luchterhand, 1979).

[79] Burghart Damerau, "Barockes in Thomas Bernhards Theaterstücken," in *"Ach, Neigung zur Fülle . . .": Zur Rezeption 'barocker' Literatur im Nachkriegsdeutschland*, ed. Christiane Caemmerer and Walter Delabar (Würzburg: Königshausen & Neumann, 2001), 157–61.

[80] Michael Fisch, "'Der halb-geschmeckten Lust mehr reiffe Früchte': Hubert Fichtes Rezeption des literarischen und musikalischen Barocks, vornehmlich des Werkes von Daniel Casper von Lohenstein," in Caemmerer and Delebar, eds., *Ach, Neigung zur Fülle*, 36.

Poetry in Germany, 1450–1700

Peter Hess

TWO DISTINCT LITERARY TRADITIONS REPRESENTING two strands of cultural advancement marked the development of early modern German poetry: a vernacular, or "popular," culture transmitted in pragmatic secular and religious forms and inspired by the Reformation; and an international humanist culture rooted in classical traditions, communicated mainly in Latin but eventually developing a vernacular learned culture as well.[1] In Germany, many learned poets wrote both in Latin and German, Latin being dominant up to the late sixteenth century and German in the seventeenth. It is impossible to establish absolute temporal boundaries for early modern German poetry: the late medieval song tradition remained vital well into the sixteenth century, while the gallant and political poetry of the eighteenth century had distinct beginnings before 1700.

The development of poetry in early modern Germany was affected by profound changes in politics, society, economy, religion, and science; the renewed interest in classical antiquity and the rise of humanism; the cataclysm of the Protestant Reformation and subsequent confessional strife; the devastation of the Thirty Years' War; and the rise of the absolutist territorial state. One of the most significant extrinsic factors was the invention of movable type, with the ensuing proliferation of printed books. In the subsequent shift from an oral to a written culture, new patterns of distribution and dissemination as well as new poetic forms arose. While the late medieval song tradition declined in the sixteenth century, the evolving print culture supported media such as the broadsheet and poetry collections as well as new genres such as the emblem, the sonnet, and the pattern poem.

Poetry as a generic term had a different meaning to the early modern poet and reader. Hybrid and mixed forms were common. The modern triad of poetic, epic, and dramatic literature originated in Italian Renaissance poetics (Giovanni Giorgio Trissino, *Poetica*, 1529) and was not yet definitively established in German poetics until the eighteenth century.[2] Of the three basic forms, *lyric* did not yet exist as a generic concept until toward the middle of the eighteenth century.[3] This notion informed the Goethean "Naturformen der Dichtung" (natural poetic forms),[4] which in turn shaped conceptions of lyric poetry in twentieth-century literary scholarship, particularly in Germany.[5] Emil Staiger's vastly influential definition of lyric as describing a mood, an emotion, or a personal experience and as being quintessentially personal and subjective (so-called *Erlebnisdichtung*) was patterned after his reading of the poetry of the Storm and Stress, classicism, and romanticism.[6] It is not useful, however, for the understanding of early modern poetry.

Humanist poetics discussed genres, but in an unsystematic way that lacked a reliable typology and did not prescribe consistent generic features. As late as 1624, in his *Buch von der Deutschen Poeterey* (Book of German Poetics), Martin Opitz (1597–1639) listed tragedy, satire, eclogue, echo, and other forms side by side. For Opitz, a *Geticht* (*Gedicht*, "poem") meant any poetic text in verse form, including *Schäfergedicht* (pastoral poem), *Heldengedicht* (heroic epic), drama, and all sorts of didactic texts. The ability to sing a poetic text was considered significant, since song was associated with the origins of poetry; for that reason, early modern poetics sometimes classified poems as *odes*. Boundaries between poetic, didactic, and narrative forms were fluid, and no technical distinction obtained between fictional and nonfictional texts. Further complicating the issue for the modern reader, early modern poetry evolved from a formally and generically undifferentiated, subservient system of communication into a more tightly organized and formalized one, which grew increasingly independent of religion, politics, the arts, and natural science.[7]

Poets wrote for social, moral, or religious ends, conscious of the purpose, function, and general communicative situation. Early modern poetics recognized no qualitative distinction between poems celebrating social occasions and poems recounting subjective experiences. Horace's injunction, in verses 333–34 of his *Ars poetica*, that good poetry must fulfill both functions of *prodesse* and *delectare* (being useful and being entertaining) was still seminal for early modern poetry. Put in modern terms, poetry always had a social field of reference. Our definition of early modern German poetry needs therefore to be as inclusive as possible, and must include a group of texts that exhibit a specific bundle of textual features: poetry is oral or written speech in verse where the line as a unit offers an additional opportunity to pause. In contrast to drama, poetry is not role-playing and is not devised for scenic performance, even though poetry can be performative in character. Texts that are narrative, whether in prose or in verse, are not included. Metric patterns and rhyme schemes are typically present. Poetic expression tends to be concise and to create a sense of immediacy.

Access to early modern poetic texts is still limited today. Many poetic texts were never printed, particularly songs prior to the Reformation that were part of the late medieval oral tradition. Of those that were printed, many appeared on broadsheets, in pamphlets, or other ephemera printed for specific occasions. Others served as dedicatory poems in books by other authors; still others were inserted into anthologies containing texts representing numerous genres, either by the same or by a different author. Cataloguing, reprinting, or making them otherwise accessible (such as CD-ROM and online) is one of the most important activities of specialists of early modern German literature.

This chapter is divided into three main parts, corresponding to the major contexts and traditions within which literature was produced. The first part deals with the continuous vernacular song tradition extending from the late Middle Ages.[8] As they were rooted in social status and class identities, the various forms will be identified primarily in terms of social settings, such as courtly, urban, or liturgical, rather than content categories, such as religious, political, didactic, or love song. The second part — very brief, because it is the focus of an extended discussion elsewhere in this volume[9] — addresses Neo-Latin poetry as it relates directly to the vernacular tradition. The third and longest part will examine the literature in the German vernacular that evolved out of the literary norms and traditions re-established by Neo-Latin humanist culture. Focal points are the relationships with classical culture, Neo-Latin literature, the other European vernacular traditions, inner-German literary movements, and regional traditions. Opitz's reform gave this poetry its form and shape, and confessionalization provided its thematic frame. Our discussion therefore will distinguish between cultural strands and be confessionally and regionally differentiated.

I. Vernacular Poetry in the Oral Performance Tradition

In spite of the rapid advances of print culture, the oral tradition in poetry remained alive well into the sixteenth century, owing in part to continued widespread illiteracy, even in cities. This was equally true for early modern song culture. Although an increasing number of songs were printed on broadsides, in pamphlets, and in collections, oral transmission remained essential; local dissemination happened largely through oral performance in streets, inns, and homes. Given the dominance of the oral tradition, the actual quantity of sung poetry of the period is impossible to calculate.

Poetry in the oral performance tradition falls into two groups: sung (*Lied, Sangverslyrik*) and spoken (*Spruch, Spruchlyrik*). Yet, this modern generic terminology, which was developed only in the nineteenth century, is neither congruent with textual evidence nor theoretically well grounded. Spoken verse forms usually were not strophic. Strophic song was common in the fifteenth and sixteenth centuries in the forms of single-leaf prints, pamphlets, and song collections, both in manuscript and print. Some songs may be grouped according to their representation of traditional values identified as medieval, such as the seven deadly sins. Others having an urban context, such as *Meisterlieder*, may be classified as humanist in the sense of creating and supporting a secularized vernacular culture with which artisans could identify. Still others are of a particular didactic type that reflects a moral philosophy related to but beyond late medieval theology.

Early modern song, with its numerous forms, represents a continuous tradition from the Middle Ages well into the seventeenth century.[10] Great numbers of song texts, mostly by urban writers, fall outside defined forms and can be located only loosely between the courtly song tradition and *Meistergesang* (also called *Meistersang*, "master song").[11] While we can identify specific traditions within the song literature, many of the songs, or *Lieder*, defy easy categorization.

Text and music formed a symbiotic unit, and tensions between the rhythmic patterns of language and music were common. There are several reasons for these basic taxonomic difficulties: we are acquainted with only few of the authors; we have little knowledge about audiences or the functions of specific kinds of songs; and musical settings were notated in rudimentary fashion (and many of these are not extant).

Courtly Poetry

Minnesang (courtly love poetry) began to decline in the fourteenth century and splintered into several song traditions (these will be discussed below). Remnants of courtly poetry survived into the sixteenth century,[12] by which time a new ethos of love, based on consensual attitudes, had largely supplanted the impersonal love ethos. Post-medieval love poetry lamented reciprocal sorrow over departure or separation, bemoaned circumstances detrimental to the fulfillment of mutual love, expressed affection in the context of a specific occasion, or celebrated affective and ethical aspects of the relationship.[13]

At the courts of the rising territorial states, advisers, diplomats, and other nobility sometimes engaged in literary activities, including the composing of songs. Eberhard von Cersne (fl. early fifteenth century), for instance, is known for *Der mynnen regeln* (*Der Minne Regel*, Rules of Courtly Love, ca. 1404), a didactic tract with an appendix of twenty songs that illustrate the rules. Hugo von Montfort (1357–1423) wrote didactic songs on religious and moralistic themes. Other noble poets in this tradition include Hermann von Sachsenheim (1366/69–1458), Hans Heselloher (fl. 1451–83), and Count Heinrich von Württemberg (1448–1519). Of each, only a handful of songs survive. A related form practiced at territorial courts is *Sangspruch*, that is, didactic, gnomic, religious, or political song,[14] modeled on the late medieval poets Frauenlob (Heinrich von Meissen, ca. 1250–1318) and Heinrich von Mügeln (fl. ca. 1350–80). Muskatblüt (ca. 1390–after 1458), long active at the court in Mainz, practiced mostly traditional *Spruch* themes, such as morality, wisdom, religion, and the praise of women; 104 songs are attributed to him. Michael Beheim (1416/21–1474/78) left 452 songs, which he collected himself, as well as three historical chronicles in strophic form. Among his works are a number of political songs, each adapted to the respective patron and audience. Both poets were in residence at princely courts during parts of their lives, but their association with cities is indicative of the growing significance of cities in the late Middle Ages as the new centers of administration and diplomacy.

Oswald von Wolkenstein (1376/77–1445) was the most original courtly poet of the late Middle Ages, making frequent and creative use of vivid imagery and metaphors, of word-based figures and onomatopoeia, and of neologisms. Of his songs, 132 are extant, most with musical settings. Many testify directly to his life as nobleman, landowner, warrior, and diplomat, though we have to assume that he embellished facts poetically to suit his purpose. Oswald covers the whole range of late medieval lyric genres: devotional and didactic songs, love songs, dawn songs, pastourelles, crusade songs, and political songs, among others. In Oswald, courtly poetry reached a last high point. Yet, the poetic subject asserts itself in a novel way, and the degree of autobiographical reference in his works is highly unusual.

Meistergesang

These late courtly forms continued to be practiced regularly during the period of transition to the urban poetic forms of the fifteenth century.[15] Itinerant poets often performed in both courtly and urban contexts, thereby enhancing cultural transfer. Increasingly, however, poets settled permanently in cities and contributed to the gradual urbanization of literary culture. Many names have been lost to history, and it is impossible to classify these disparate individuals as a homogeneous group.

It is unclear when and why these urban poets, who began to call themselves *Meister* (masters), decided to organize into guilds and to codify their art in rules and bylaws. The poetry served ethical and religious instruction and conferred secular knowledge; its didactic authority was demonstrated by claims to artfulness. Their complex stanza structures were evidence of the competence of the author, and the poetological attention to technical precision suggests the existence of loosely organized groups or joint performances by the late fourteenth century. The only poet known to us representing early forms of *Meistergesang* is Jörg Schiller (documented in Augsburg 1453–62), whose melodies were popular in the late fifteenth century. Schiller's eleven signed songs deal with urban topics. The largest and most significant collection of early *Meistergesang* was compiled in Speyer by Nestler von Speyer. His *Kolmarer Liederhandschrift* (Colmar Song Manuscript, ca. 1460) contains some 950 songs, using more than 100 melodies. It is unclear why this large collection was compiled; there is no known patron and no known local society. In 1546 the novelist Jörg Wickram (ca. 1505–ca. 1561) became a citizen of Colmar and purchased the manuscript as a model for his new *Meistersingerschule*.[16]

In several cities, most notably Nuremberg and Augsburg, *Meistergesang* societies were established around 1450, though lack of documentation before the early sixteenth century makes it difficult to determine what circumstances prevailed and how the societies were institutionalized. *Meistergesang* societies are known later in a number of other western and southern German cities, including Mainz, Worms, Speyer, Strasbourg, Ulm, Freiburg im Breisgau, and Munich. Although some societies existed until the eighteenth and even nineteenth centuries, their cultural significance declined rapidly in the second half of the sixteenth century. The purpose of these strictly organized societies was the regulated production, performance, reception, and critique of songs. Also referred to as *Singschulen* (singing schools), they established firm poetic rules and codified them in a tablet called the *Tabulatur*. The pedagogical system of *Meistergesang* mimicked the educational scheme of the guilds. The *Schüler* (student) was the novice; the *Schulfreund* (friend of the school) knew the rules; the *Singer* could perform several melodies; the *Dichter* (poet) wrote new poems to existing melodies; and the *Meister* composed new *Töne* (melodies). The singing schools organized public performances, which were often set up as competitions, complete with a jury of *Merker* (markers, or judges) and prizes.

Meistergesang is relatively well documented. About 16,000 master songs are known to us today (most of them collected in private manuscripts), as well as some 380 named authors.[17] Most manuscripts are undated, unattributed, and say little about context and use of the song. The printing of master songs was forbidden; the form remained firmly anchored in the oral tradition. It was thus the last performance art in the late medieval sense. However, many authors, notably Hans Sachs (discussed below), subverted this precept by publishing similar versions in the form of a *Spruch*, or spoken poem.

Meistergesang was written for one voice only and performed without instrumental accompaniment. The persistent adherence to this monophonic performance practice began to be seen as anachronistic and led to the final decline of the genre after 1550. The stanzas, always odd in number, follow the medieval tripartite bar form: two identical stanzas known as *Stollen* constitute the opening *Aufgesang*, followed by a differently structured concluding *Abgesang*. Stanzas ordinarily have twenty to thirty lines — but can have as few as five and as many as 100. Each poem uses a specific *Ton*. Sachs indicates in the song's headline the name of the melody to be used. As other authors reused melodies, specific stanza forms and metric schemes became associated with them; eventually, each was given a specific name for easy identification. The meter of choice was *strenger Knittelvers*, or doggerel, a verse with four stresses and eight or nine syllables, although a larger number of unstressed syllables was possible. Linguistic and metric accents did not have to coincide, theoretically, though in practice most poems have a distinct iambic feel. Complicated rhyme schemes were common and taken as a mark of mastery.

The fact that urban artisans wrote and composed songs is unique in the history of German literature. Poetry was taught like a craft, and its mastery enhanced the social prestige of the poet. This practice accounts for the aesthetic problem of *Meistergesang*: artistic rules were to be observed meticulously, while at the same time the poet was under pressure to display inspiration and demonstrate his ability to find his own form.[18] The formal schooling did not require knowledge of humanist forms and their traditions, but the master nevertheless was expected to be able to read Latin and later also to be able to quote the Luther Bible accurately. However, the art of *Meistergesang* consisted in more than mere dilettantish delight. By conveying educational contents, they represented an attempt to allow the nonacademic urban middle classes to participate in a worldly education program rooted in the traditional *septem artes liberales* (seven liberal arts) and to acquire a contemporary knowledge base.

Religious, spiritual, and devotional topics dominated — songs about the Virgin Mary, the Trinity, legends of saints (mainly before 1520) — but not biblical themes. After the Reformation, songs focused increasingly on the text of the Bible and its interpretation. Worldly themes include history, astronomy, and nature, ethical and moral norms, love and marriage, and rules and practices of *Meistergesang* itself. This self-conscious concern of the genre soon resulted in the creation of a founding myth, which located the origin of the art in the thirteenth and fourteenth centuries and recognized the twelve old masters as models. Among them were Walther von der Vogelweide, Konrad von

Würzburg, Frauenlob, and Heinrich von Mügeln. The *Kolmarer Liederhandschrift* was thought to be around 600 years old, which explains the esteem in which it was held. Pioneering literary histories focused on *Meistergesang*, thus illuminating the central social role of this genre in sixteenth-century urban society as well as reflecting the desire to preserve a literary form in decline. Notable works are Adam Puschmann's (1532–1600) *Gründlicher Bericht des deutschen Meistersanges* (Thorough Report on the German Master Song, 1571) and Johann Christoph Wagenseil's (1633–1705) *Buch von der Meistersinger holdseligen Kunst* (Book of the Mastersingers' Lovely Art, 1697). Wagenseil's book was published as an appendix to a history of the city of Nuremberg, which served as the principal source for later admirers of the *Meistergesang* tradition, such as E. T. A. Hoffmann and Richard Wagner. Early representatives of *Meistergesang* in Nuremberg were Fritz Kettner (fl. 1392–1430), Konrad Nachtigall (ca. 1410–1484/85), Hans Folz (ca. 1435/40–1513), and Hans Sachs's teacher Lienhard Nunnenbeck (d. 1518/27). Folz with his nearly 100 songs was the most prolific in the group. Significantly, a number of his songs rejected exclusive reliance on the melodies of the old masters and urged the composition of new ones.

The Nuremberg shoemaker Hans Sachs (1494–1576) was by far the most significant *Meistersinger* and one of the most prolific writers in German literary history. He became familiar with *Meistergesang* during his apprenticeship (1509–11) and wrote his first song in 1514 while a journeyman. Sachs found his own voice once he had committed to the cause of the Lutheran church reform, a decision signaled by his master song "Die Wittenbergisch Nachtigall Die man yetz hôret vberall" (The Nightingale from Wittenberg, Whom One Now Hears Everywhere), published in 1523 in the form of a *Spruchgedicht*. His intense engagement with reformational issues is evident from his ownership of forty original writings by Luther and supporters as early as 1522 as well as from a string of publications in support of Luther in subsequent years. In this poem the nightingale is Luther, the messenger of Christ; at its conclusion the papacy is equated with Babylon:[19]

> Darumb jr Christen wûe jr seyt
> Kert wider auß des Babstes wyste
> Zû vnserm hyrten Jesu Christe
> Der selbig ist ein gûtter hyrt
> Hat seyn lieb mit dem todt probyrt
> Durch den wir alle seyn erlost
> Der ist vnser ayniger trost
> Vnd vnser aynige hoffnung
> Gerechtigkait vnd sâligung
> All die glauben in seynen namen
> Wer das beger der sreche Amen.

[Therefore, you Christians, wherever you are, turn away from the pope's desert and toward our shepherd Jesus Christ, who himself is a good shepherd. He proved his love by giving his life, through whom we all are absolved. He is our only consolation and our only hope, justice, and salvation. All those who believe in his name, whoever desires this, shall say Amen.]

The fact that a simple shoemaker should become involved in confessional disputes was provocative. In 1527 the Nuremberg city council condemned his antipapal polemics and prohibited the printing of his works. Sachs then returned largely to secular topics and introduced drama to the Nuremberg *Meistersinger* society in 1527; he wrote some 120 plays for this stage, many of which were never performed. Sachs's use of *Meistergesang* in the service of the Reformation permanently altered the genre. Marian songs and others about saints disappeared completely in favor of songs that explicate passages from Luther's German Bible. Sachs introduced a new range of secular topics, including literary and historical plots from works of antiquity, such as Ovid's *Metamorphoses* and the legend of Troy, and the Middle Ages, such as courtly epics and Boccaccio's *Decamerone*. His pre-eminence seemed unchallenged; he often served as mediator in conflicts in his school. All together, Sachs wrote more than 6,200 individual works. In his poem "Summa all meiner gedicht" (Sum of All My Poems, 1567) he recapitulated his literary *oeuvre*. He elsewhere carefully recorded them in thirty-three folio volumes, sixteen of which contain 4,275 master songs using 275 different melodies, thirteen his own.[20] He reworked many of the songs as *Sprüche* for print. He also collected the songs of other poets in various manuscripts.

As of 1558, the Nuremberg society still had 250 members; even after Sachs ceased to write songs in 1567 the society flourished, if less brilliantly. Noteworthy are Jörg Schechner (ca. 1500–1572); Adam Puschmann; Georg Hager (1552–1634), who wrote some 1,000 songs and seventeen melodies; Benedict von Watt (1569–1616); Hans Deisinger (1572–1617); Ambrosius Metzger (1573–1632), who wrote 3,000 songs and 340 melodies, among them a cycle of 155 songs on Ovid's *Metamorphoseses*; and Hans Winter (1591–1627). The last public event of the society took place in 1774.

While other societies played important roles in the artistic lives of their respective cities, few achieved the prominence of Nuremberg, and none equaled the Nuremberg poets for sheer productivity. Among the most significant urban poets elsewhere were Johannes Spreng (1524–1601) in Augsburg, Cyriacus Spangenberg (1528–1604) in Strasbourg, and Valentin Voigt (1487–after 1558) in Magdeburg. Other poets also wrote songs in the *Meistergesang* tradition without being part of its institutions. One was the blind Nuremberg poet Jörg Graff (1475/80–1542), a former mercenary who made his living performing songs. In spite of its significance for the dissemination of the Reformation, the rule-driven *Meistergesang* eventually went into decline because of its own rigidity.

Volkslied

The *Meistergesang* is the only song form that constitutes a separate genre. This owes both to its distinctive generic features and social function as well as to the comparatively large amount of scholarship on the subject. The distinction between secular and religious song is modern; in the early modern period, secular and religious issues formed a broad continuum. In spite of its important propagandistic role during the Reformation, the *Volkslied* (song, popular song) remains inadequately researched.

The *Volkslied* is a simple strophic form with rhymed verses organized either in stanzas or in the more complex bar form. In its basic monophonic form it could be performed informally without great effort, and it could be passed down easily, both orally and as part of a written record. The term *Volkslied* commonly applies to this type of song, although songs that are clearly religious or political usually fall under separate headings. It is problematic, however, to the degree that it evokes the romantic notion of the anonymous masses creating songs out of some collective spirit; the anonymity of most authors has contributed to this myth of collective authorship. Most popular songs doubtless were authored by literate representatives of the rising urban middle class — in some cases even by noblemen — whose identities simply have not come down to us. *Volkslied* was of course constantly subject to reworking, which further obfuscated authorship. Nor was it the domain of a specific social group. The terms *gemeiner Mann* (common man) and *Volk* could refer to "simple folk," which Robert Scribner has usefully characterized as "wayfaring folk, journeymen," or "the plebeian lower strata."[21] It could also connote peasants, the urban lower classes, or artisans; or it could imply the illiterate from the point of view of the learned, subjects from the point of view of the governing class, or commoners from the point of view of nobility, bureaucracy, or clergy.[22] We know little about the place of songs in daily life. Doubtless, some were sung in the streets, as the term *Gassenhauer* (simple, popular street song) implies. Drinking songs and songs associated with festivities presumably were sung at the corresponding social events.[23] Love songs also were part of community life, performed at social events, though whether as individual performances with instrumental accompaniment, as at the court, is not certain.

The oral nature of the popular song tradition poses a methodological problem. Song was disseminated and received primarily through oral performance — nearly impossible to research and reconstruct — while our perception of song is shaped by the written record in the form of songbooks, pamphlets, and broadsides, most of them collected and edited in large anthologies in the second half of the nineteenth century. Furthermore, what we know about the lives and music of ordinary people comes from scholarly mediators. We also need to keep in mind that music was part of daily civic and religious life and that folksong was a universal part of a German culture whose practice was not limited to the lower, less educated classes. Folksongs adapted as polyphonic compositions had meaning for the upper classes as well.[24]

Song collections proliferated from the second half of the fifteenth to the late sixteenth century.[25] Many survive in manuscript form, while some were printed as well. Collections were compiled both randomly and systematically; some represent a cross-section of various genres, while others were added to unsystematically.[26] Some collections indicate which melodies are to be used with the songs. Musically more complex polyphonic settings, such as those in the *Lochamer Liederbuch* (Locham Song Book), written between 1451 and 1453, started to appear in the fifteenth century. These collections were usually commissioned and compiled by citizens for specific occasions within urban life.

Pre-Reformation songs fall into five broad thematic groups: (1) love songs in the tradition of courtly *Minnesang* but "urbanized" such that the courtly motif of unattainable love is transformed into disappointed love; (2) drinking and social songs, including student songs, in which performer and audience interact playfully; (3) narrative songs, including ballads, which report and retell remarkable events, but also anecdotes, tales, and jokes; (4) songs containing games and riddles; and (5) songs about occupations, particularly that of the journeyman.

The theme of the Reformation itself, which remained a major topic in popular song through the sixteenth century, brought about a second wave of song production. Popular song was the most direct way to reach the vast audience of average Germans lacking the education to read pamphlets but having opportunity to hear songs in public places. The hybrid genre of the broadsheet, which relied on both printed word and image and was accessible to the literate and illiterate alike, was an ideal medium for publishing songs. The view often espoused, that the printing press singularly enabled the success of the Reformation, must be modified to embrace the role of song: illiteracy was too widespread for the dissemination and discussion of Reformation ideas based on print media alone.

Three categories of monophonic Reformation songs may be distinguished:[27] (1) prayers, musical sermons, biblical stories, and translations of psalms, all written by the educated and religious elite; (2) newsworthy events of the Reformation, such as battles or imperial diets, told in ballad-like songs whose length suggests that they were written by educated authors: Luther's "Ein newes lied wir heben an" (A New Song We Raise, 1523), occasioned by the execution of two Augustinian monks in Brussels, was a prototype; (3) short and simple satirical and polemical songs, most of which were composed by scholars, preachers, and theologians.

Most songs of the Reformation are contrafacta, new texts set to extant melodies to serve new purposes.[28] As most Germans could not read musical notation, a contrafactum solved the problem by using a familiar, usually secular, tune. Printers simply indicated the *Ton*. Memorization and transmissibility of a new lyric were likewise facilitated in this way. Protestant propagandists often used parodic contrafacta of traditional Catholic devotional music to mock the old faith, as in the song "Ain Doctor in dem Sachsser land" (A Doctor in the Land of the Saxons, ca. 1525). These songs demonstrate that the modern distinction between sacred and secular contradicts sixteenth-century practice. The sacred was considered part of everyday life. Confessional polemics mixed naturally with the fears of war, illness, hunger, inflation, disorder, marvelous celestial events, or the Turks. An example is Martin Luther's "Ein Kinderlied/ zu singen/ wider die zween Ertzfeinde Christi vnd seiner heiligen Kirchen/ den Bapst vnd Türcken/ etc." (A Children's Song to Sing

against the Two Archenemies of Christ and His Holy Church, the Pope and
the Turk, etc.) of 1543:[29]

> Erhalt vns Herr bey deinem Wort/
> Vnd steur des Bapsts vnd Türcken Mord
> Die Jhesum Christum deinen Son/
> Wolten stürtzen von deinem Thron.

[Safeguard us, Lord, with your word, and avert the murder by the pope
and by the Turk who both wanted to topple Jesus Christ, your son, from
your throne.]

The first stanza of this simple song, which later found inclusion in Lutheran
hymnals, equates the threats posed by the pope and by the Turks. Songs
traditionally categorized as political frequently dealt with conflicts surrounding the Reformation, such as the Peasants' Revolt, the persecution of the
Anabaptists, the Schmalkaldic Wars, or the Augsburg Interim (1548) of
Charles V. Obvious exceptions are liturgical or other songs that serve a specific
religious function. These include procession or pilgrimage songs (discussed
below).

Liturgical Songs and Church Hymns

Religious topics were omnipresent in the late medieval song literature, and virtually all known authors wrote secular as well as religious and devotional songs.
Prayers, hymns, greetings to Mary, requests for favors, lamentations of sins,
Christmas and Easter songs, and songs on spiritual awakening were common
even among authors whose main work was secular, such as Oswald von
Wolkenstein, Hugo von Montfort, or the *Meistersinger*. We may group religious songs, depending on function, into liturgical songs (part of worship but
not of the Mass), and devotional songs practiced in the private realm. Before
the Reformation, the congregation only rarely took part in liturgical singing
and never during the actual Mass, which explains why there are no German
translations of Latin liturgical texts. German-language congregational songs
were not intended for the liturgy but rather for feast day celebrations, such as
Christmas and Easter, and for pilgrimages.[30]

Based on social function, songs may be described as either congregational
or communal. Congregational song tended to be simple, socially inclusive, and
often without artistic aspiration. A large number were contrafacta. Communal
song, on the other hand, was restricted to certain social and institutional
groups, such as *Meistergesang* or songs written for performance at courts
(court airs). These songs usually are artistic but not liturgical, and the high
degree of mastery required served as a tool of social exclusion. The present discussion will focus on congregational song.[31]

The most prolific author of religious song before the Reformation was the
theologian Heinrich Laufenberg (ca. 1390–1460). His 120 religious songs
mostly used melodies adapted from secular songs. Other important authors are

Anthonius von Lambsheim (d. 1458) and Ludwig Moser (1442–1510). The *Hohenfurter Liederbuch* (Hohenfurt Song Book, mid-fifteenth century) with its eighty-one German and two Latin songs in paired rhyme was the outstanding collection of religious songs of the time. Forty-nine of the songs constitute a continuous narration of the life of Christ.

The place of vernacular song during worship changed dramatically in the early phase of the Reformation, when in many cities church service in the vernacular was introduced. Thomas Müntzer (1490–1525) published his *Deutsch Kirchenamt* (German Church Order), which included German translations of ten Latin hymns, in Allstedt in 1523; Martin Bucer (1491–1551) followed his example in Strasbourg in 1524. As Mass was already being held in German in cities like Basel, Strasbourg, and Nuremberg, Martin Luther (1483–1546) established a definite form for it in 1523 in his *Formula missae et communionis* (Rules of Mass and Communion) and included communal singing in German. He wrote twenty-four of his own thirty-six songs from the middle of 1523 to the middle of 1524, setting off a wave of song production, since worship in the vernacular required the replacement of the old Latin hymns.[32] The earliest vernacular songs focused on faith and attacked traditional theology, though without directly assailing the pope. Luther understood that hymns in the vernacular served the proclamation of the glory of God and obeyed the biblical demand to praise the Lord in song. The ascent of vernacular hymns in liturgy thus went hand in hand with the elevation of the spoken word as a vehicle of the expression of faith. Furthermore, the new emphasis on song indicates that the propagation of the Word of God was not limited to church worship.

Early in the Reformation, congregational singing became a sign of solidarity among Lutherans and a source of identity for the neonate Lutheran community. Although limited use of vernacular songs became permissible in German Catholic churches, as Sebastian Brant's (1457–1521) pioneering German translations of Catholic Latin hymns disseminated on signed broadsides in the 1490s demonstrate,[33] the singing of German chorales was one of the distinctive characteristics that set the Lutheran community apart. Lutheran hymns played an important role in the success of the Reformation, helping to transform both society and piety.[34] Most of Luther's own hymns were translations, adaptations, or expanded versions, based on older Latin hymns by the Monk of Salzburg, Heinrich Laufenberg, Jan Hus, and others.[35] Some were based on psalmic or other biblical sources. One of the most famous is "Ein feste burg ist vnser Gott" (1528):[36]

> Ein feste burg ist vnser Gott
> Ein gute wehr vnd waffen /
> Er hilfft vns frey aus aller not /
> die vns jtzt hat betroffen /
> Der alt bůse feind /
> mit ernst ers jtzt meint /
> gros macht vnd viel list /

> sein grausam rüstung ist /
> auff erd ist nicht seins gleichen.

[A mighty fortress is our God, a trusty shield and weapon. He helps us free from every need that has afflicted us. The old evil foe now is resolved with seriousness, great force, and much cunning. His dreadful arms have no match on earth.]

Among other notable Luther songs based on older German versions was "Christ lag in Todesbanden" (Christ Lay in Death's Strong Bands, 1524). He also wrote original songs, of course, such as the Christmas song "Vom Himmel hoch da komm ich her" (From Heaven Above to Earth I Come, 1533/35). Luther also advanced the development of hymnals, the most important being his own Wittenberg hymnals of 1524 and 1529. Valentin Babst (also Bapst, d. 1556) published the hymnal *Geystliche Lieder* (Religious Songs, 1545) — equally renowned as a beautiful printing — in Leipzig in 1545; it includes Luther's *Begräbnisgesänge* (Funerary Songs) of 1542.[37]

Elsewhere in Germany, Hans Sachs wrote thirteen songs based on psalms in Nuremberg in 1526; Burkhard Waldis (ca. 1490–1555) published German psalm versifications in Riga in 1553; Sigmund Hemmel's (d. 1564) psalms were published in Tübingen posthumously in 1569. Among the many other important authors of songs in the Lutheran tradition were Lazarus Spengler (1479–1534), Paul Speratus (1484–1551), Ambrosius Blaurer (1492–1564), Justus Jonas (1493–1555), Johann Walter (1496–1570, Luther's principal musical adviser), Erasmus Alberus (ca. 1500–1553), Paulus Eber (1511–69), and Elisabeth Cruciger (ca. 1500–1535, the first female author of church hymns). Cruciger's "Herr Christ der einig Gottes Sohn" (Lord Christ the Only Son of God, 1524) is still sung today.[38]

Religious dissidents, such as the Bohemian Brethren, also used songs to spread their message and to build community.[39] Michael Weisse's (ca. 1488–1534) *Ein New Geseng buchlen* (A New Song Book, 1531), with its 157 songs, was the most voluminous German-language hymnal at the time of its publication, and Weisse generally is considered the most significant song author of the Reformation beyond Luther. Other poets in the dissident tradition are Adam Reissner (1496–1575), Valentin Triller (ca. 1493–1573), and Daniel Sudermann (1550–1631). Numerous songs in Anabaptist hymnals describe the martyrdom of their brethren, many of whom were song authors themselves.[40] Beginning in 1535, members of the Moravian group, led by Jakob Huter (or Hutter, ca. 1500–1536), established a prolific song tradition that continued well beyond the seventeenth century.[41]

Toward the middle of the sixteenth century, devotion and edification evolved as dominant themes in religious song. Songs by Georg Niege (1525–89), Nikolaus Selnecker (1530–92), Ludwig Helmbold (1532–98), Philipp Nicolai (1556–1608), Martin Böhme (1557–1622), and Valerius Herberger (1562–1627) became more personal and spiritualized, lacking the fire and anger of songs from the Reformation's formative years of struggle.

Around 1600, motifs from the mystical traditions began to appear in devotional song.[42]

Other reformers, especially in Switzerland, such as Ulrich Zwingli (1484–1531) and Jean Calvin (1509–64), supported vernacular church songs as well, although the iconoclast Zwingli did not tolerate music in the worship service and Calvin approved only of monophonic church hymns based on biblical texts. In 1539, during his Strasbourg exile, Calvin compiled a collection of psalm translations set to music entitled *Aulcuns pseaulmes et cantiques* (Some Psalms and Songs), commonly known as the *Geneva Psalter*.[43] It contains thirteen French translations by Clément Marot (1495–1544) and nine that are presumably Calvin's own. A later complete version of the *Geneva Psalter* (1562) included forty-nine psalm translations by Marot and 101 by Théodore de Bèze (1519–1605); it was translated into German, beginning with a partial version in 1572 by Paul Melissus Schede (1539–1602)[44] and then in a complete and more successful version in 1573 by Ambrosius Lobwasser (1515–85).[45] Lobwasser's translation appeared in more than sixty editions and established the foundation of Reformed (Calvinist) hymnals until the early eighteenth century. It is possible to view these psalm translations into German as the beginning of German art poetry (*Kunstlyrik*), although the impact of the new aesthetic on the production of hymns was not felt until after the Opitzian verse reform of 1624 (discussed below).

In response to the success of Protestant religious song, Catholic theologians — among them Georg Witzel (1501–73), an outspoken opponent of Luther and admirer of Erasmus — started to support congregational singing in German before and after sermons as well as during processions and pilgrimages, though never during Mass. The first Catholic hymnal to reflect this attitude was *Ein new Gesangbüchlein Geystlicher Lieder* (A New Song Book of Spiritual Songs, 1537) by the Dominican Michael Vehe (1485–1539). Many Catholic songs followed Lutheran patterns, and some Lutheran songs were included in Catholic hymnals without change. Johann Leisentritt's (1527–86) *Geistliche Lieder und Psalmen* (Spiritual Songs and Psalms, 1567), the second important Catholic hymnal of the period, has sixty-six songs by Protestant authors, including four by Luther himself. Other collections were published by Witzel, Adam Walasser (d. 1581), Caspar Ulenberg (1549–1617), and Johann Haym von Themar (d. 1593).

Historical and Political Poetry

Poetry that focused on historical and political events was not generically uniform, extending even to songs, as well as to spoken rhymed verse in paired or alternating rhymes. These texts shared a common function, however, in their publicizing of historical or current political events while taking a polemical stance. This kind of poetry, usually anonymous, is often called *Ereignisdichtung* (poetry on historical and political events).[46] Many of the songs are fashioned after courtly song (*Hofton*), as evidenced by their poetic quality.[47] Songs that focus specifically on current or recent political events — called *Zeitungslieder* (news songs) — or on well-known political figures are commonly categorized as political or historical song. Carrying on a late medieval tradition, they recount political events or battles in a partisan fashion. Ulrich von Hutten's (1488–1523) "Ich habs gewagt mit sinnen" (I Ventured It with Forethought, 1521) is the most significant example. Often, these songs dealt with conflicts within or between cities. Political song was thus primarily a tool to inform or to manipulate the masses. Secondarily, it could function didactically, whether to portray a historical event as *exemplum* or to present current events that stirred the imagination, such as great discoveries, catastrophes, celestial events, or miracles.[48]

Most historical or political songs, particularly those concerned with legitimacy, were handed down in chronicles. The Swiss songs collected by the Basel scholar Aegidius Tschudi (1505–72) in the *Chronicon Helveticum* (Swiss Chronicle, before 1556) became famous. Other themes include the Peasants' Revolt of 1524–25, battles against the Hussites and the Turks, and issues or events with political significance for the Reformation, such as indulgences, imperial diets, and religious wars. These songs remain poorly researched, because literary scholars have generally disparaged their aesthetic value and historians have recognized little worth in them as source material.

Spoken Poetry

All types of oral performance poetry discussed so far, with the exception of certain forms of political poetry, are singable. However, one category, *Spruchdichtung*, or *Sprechverslyrik* (spoken verse), was usually recited without musical settings. Spoken verse is not strophic, and it is most often rhymed in pairs. Spoken poetry marked the transition to print as medium of dissemination: music as mnemotechnical and as performance-enhancing device was not available to fulfill that function. Inversely, poetry after the arrival of the printing press no longer was dependent on a musical setting to be disseminated but rather could rely on a wide range of media, from broadside to book. Typically didactic in character, it also could be narrative in form; late-sixteenth-century authors like Cyriacus Spangenberg (1528–1604) turned it to devotional ends. In literary history it has generally been classified as *Gelegenheitsdichtung* (occasional poetry), which may be a reason it is not well researched.

While most oral performance poetry was written to be sung rather than spoken, the distinction between the two forms was not always obvious. Some songs lent themselves readily to being spoken, and others existed only in spoken versions. *Meistergesang*, for example, by its own rules could not be printed and thus had to be an oral performance genre. Many songs in that tradition, particularly those by Hans Sachs, also exist in a slightly altered nonstrophic version specifically conceived for print. Sachs wrote some 1,500 nonstrophic poems in paired rhyme.

Rhymed speeches (*Reimreden*) flourished as early as the fourteenth century.[49] They typically contain between eighty and 200 verses but sometimes as few as twenty and as many as 600. Shorter forms, often only four lines in the practice of Hans Rosenplüt (ca. 1400–ca. 1460), are sometimes referred to as *priamel*. While spoken poems were mostly didactic in character, they also could be panegyric, devotional, or assume an epic character, such as the rhymed chronicles of the second half of the fifteenth century. Historical events, such as the Swabian War (1499) or the Peasants' Revolt, gave rise to rhymed (but not strophic) chronicles; these were likely conceived for print.

City panegyric (*Städtelob, laus urbis*), which became especially popular in the sixteenth century, arose from the emerging humanistic urban print culture. The *laus urbis* describes law, order, and peace in the politically independent imperial city. The city represents a space for the development of the human potential in the absence of aristocratic control, in contrast to the countryside governed by nobility. Poems of this type exist in both German and Latin.[50] The earliest German example is the "Spruch von Nürnberg" (Encomium to Nuremberg, 1447) by the artisan Rosenplüt. Johannes von Soest's (1448–1506) "Wy men wol ein stat regyrn sol" (How One Should Govern a City Well, 1495), which was written for the city council in Worms, promoted the values of community and political union. He describes the city as a *civium unitas*, or *burgerlich vereynung* (bourgeois union), thus introducing bourgeoisie as an idealized ideological concept. Sachs's "Lobspruch der Stadt Nürnberg" (Encomium to the City of Nuremberg, 1530) draws an analogy between the architectural order in the layout of his city to its social order, which guarantees the city's future:[51]

> Geschmück vnd zier gemeiner Stat
> Eynigkeyt der gemein vnd Rat
> Ordnung der Burgerlichen stend
> Ein weiß fürsichtig Regiment

[Adornment and grace of our common city, harmony in the community and the council, order among the ranks of the citizens, a wise and careful government.]

Important Neo-Latin examples that followed the vernacular model are the panegyrical poems to the cities of Münster (1503) by Johannes Murmellius (1480–1517), Leipzig (1521) by Hermann von dem Busche (1468–1534), and Nuremberg (1532) by Eobanus Hessus (1488–1540).[52]

The late fifteenth century saw the emergence of hybrid literary forms clearly indebted to a late medieval didactic verse tradition but firmly embedded in the emerging humanist book culture. The main example is Sebastian Brant's *Narrenschiff* (Ship of Fools, 1494), a collection of 113 didactic poems with allegorical woodcuts, which furnish a secularized moral philosophy in the vernacular for politically autonomous urban merchants and artisans. The *Narrenschiff* marks the emergence of a commercial book culture that allowed for the dissemination of information and values beyond the control of the church.

The study of poetry in the oral performance tradition shows considerable continuity in forms and themes in late medieval and early modern poetry, despite gradual change in many areas, such as the urbanization of the production of poetry. The increasing influence of humanist thought is clear, though most of these songwriters probably did not use Latin in their writings. The fact that a simple shoemaker like Hans Sachs could involve himself in Reformation polemics with his printed poems illustrates the shift to a secularized, written literary culture. While this literature was not usually philosophical in nature, it did address moral issues in a secularized context in the form of didactic poetry, detached from religious discourse. Starting around 1520, Reformation themes took on a dominant role, both in church hymns and in political songs. The song tradition, both secular and sacred, continued deep into the seventeenth century,[53] but it became increasingly part of the rising learned culture of the book and therefore lost most features of the earlier oral tradition.

II. Humanist Culture: Neo-Latin Poetry

For humanists, the Latin language was the proper medium for literary expression and learned exchange. Humanist rhetoric and poetics, which derived from classical models, promoted a Latin-based education program and demanded formidable Latin proficiency. This program also led to a late blossoming of a written literary culture in Latin that coincided with the advent of the printing press and remained a dominant force in European learned culture from the fifteenth well into the eighteenth century. This new Latin-based culture, conscious of its superiority to vernacular cultures and socially exclusive, was inaccessible to the uneducated masses.[54] Neo-Latin literature did not connect directly to the vernacular cultures and literary traditions, with the exception of certain areas of religious poetry. Nevertheless, some humanists, such as Hutten, also wrote poetry in German. Inversely, many German-language poets of the seventeenth century wrote extensively in Latin — Caspar von Barth (1587–1658), Johann Lauremberg (1590–1658), Jacob Balde (1604–68), Daniel Czepko (1605–60), Paul Fleming (1609–40), Christoph Kaldenbach (1613–98), and Johannes Prasch (1637–90), to mention only a few. The Neo-Latin culture gave impetus to the creation of literary vernaculars in the sixteenth century, although serious efforts to create a German literary language did not take shape until early in the following century.

The subject of this section is discussed in detail elsewhere in this volume, in Wilhelm Kühlmann's chapter "Neo-Latin Literature in Early Modern Germany." Nevertheless, it is important to bear in mind here that it created a common cultural system that served as the foundation for the learned vernacular literatures emerging in most European cultures in the sixteenth and early seventeenth centuries. Conrad Celtis (1459–1508), in his *Ars versificandi et carminum* (1486), created this national literary program, though in the Latin language.[55] However, other Neo-Latin writers, particularly from the Netherlands, were influential in Germany as well, notably Julius Caesar Scaliger (1484–1558) and Daniel Heinsius (1580–1655).

Learned literature, whether in Latin or in a national language, was practiced by a new, highly educated urban elite, known in literary history as the *nobilitas literaria*, which drew its identity from humanistic studies. Celtis's coronation as *poeta laureatus* by Emperor Friedrich III in 1487 was indicative of this new nexus of literary accomplishment and political power. Humanist poetics instructed learned poets in several major areas that would carry over into vernacular poetics, including the rules of classical metrics, classical verse and stanza forms, and poetic genres. Another effect was an increasingly relaxed relationship with classical mythology. Finally, Neo-Latin literature generated new literary forms, most notably the emblem, which was pioneered by the Italian Andrea Alciati (1492–1550) and practiced widely in Germany by Mathias Holtzwart (ca. 1540–after 1589), Gabriel Rollenhagen (1583–1619), and Julius Wilhelm Zincgref (1591–1635), among many others.[56]

III. Representative Culture: Vernacular Learned Poetry in the Humanist Tradition

German poetry of the later early modern period, specifically the seventeenth century, may be distinguished by five unique historical characteristics, or categories:

1. Occasionality:[57] Early modern poets did not recognize an essential difference between poetry occasioned by external (social) occurrences and that stimulated by individual experience, and no stigma attached to it before the Age of Goethe, perhaps with certain exceptions, such as commissioned or paid work. Logau famously referred to occasional poems as "Töchter freyer Eile" (daughters of leisure).[58] Occasions included all significant events in the lives of the cultural elites — baptisms, birthdays, weddings, funerals, journeys, treaties. Panegyrical poems (*encomia*) praised rulers, high-ranking persons, benefactors, and patrons, as well as public or private events. Authors seized the occasions to display their erudition and personal merit (the Renaissance ideal of true nobility), whether for social prestige, competition for a position in the growing state administrations, or financial reward.

2. Didacticism: Didactic elements permeated nearly all of secular as well as religious poetry. Humanist poetics perpetuated Horace's dictum that poetry be both enjoyable (the category of *delectare*) and morally useful (the category of *prodesse*).[59] Early modern poetry was expected to cover specific topics, ranging from table manners to history to natural science, often in an eclectic and playful manner. Because occasionality and didacticism are ubiquitous in learned poetry of the seventeenth century, they are central for its understanding, but for the same reason they are unsuitable as a basis for its taxonomy.

3. Religion: Religious poetry, a vast category, was predominantly Lutheran but also significantly Calvinist. Luther regarded the spoken and written word — in sermons, hymns, and religious tracts — as central for the expression of faith, while the Catholic side relied on multisensory religious rituals and magnificent church architecture. Given that religious poetry is often simultaneously didactic and occasional in character, it is difficult to

categorize. Only two groups of poetry with religious content have distinct functions and purposes and therefore will be discussed in separate sections below: liturgical song, including devotional poetry, still had a performative role in the seventeenth century, though it relied increasingly on dissemination in printed form; and mystical poetry, which addressed a learned audience, was always written and was intended to be read rather than performed.

4. Relationality: Neo-Platonic natural philosophy saw nature as a physical manifestation of God's will; thus permeated by divine spirit, nature's parts stood in analogy to each other and could be mediated by language. Representation and reality, sign and meaning were inherently linked, making analogy, comparison, simile, parable, word speculation, and etymology powerful tools of poetic invention. The process of analogy informed such genres as pattern poems, echo poems, emblems, and contrafacta. This is in evidence in the playful, sometimes cabbalistic, techniques of acrostic, anagram, chronogram, and gematria[60] in poetry based on riddles, witty questions, numbers, and dialogues, or in rhetorical figures.[61] The resulting imagery has a visual dimension,[62] which helps to explain the phenomenal rise of the genre of the emblem.[63] The fourfold method, developed in the Middle Ages as an exegetical method in the belief that the Bible had four corresponding levels of meaning (literal-historical, allegorical-typological, moral-tropological, mystical-anagogical), was often applied in the early modern period to secular texts as well.[64] Florilegia, such as Christoph Lehmann's *Florilegium Politicum* (Political Collection of Flowers, 1639), and poetic dictionaries, such as the appendix to the third volume (1653) of Georg Philipp Harsdörffer's (1607–58) *Poetischer Trichter* (Poetic Funnel, 1647–53), served poets as lexica and thesauruses — one of the reasons early modern poetry can sound formulaic or overly ornate.

5. Representation and self-representation:[65] Urban poets found themselves obliged to adapt to the demands of rising courtly absolutism that increasingly dominated German society politically and promoted a culture of representation.[66] Literary success could mean ennoblement (Opitz, Czepko, Zesen, and Lohenstein, to name only a few cases). Rhetoric and poetics, which formed the backbone of the school and university curricula, gave practical instruction in the strategies of self-representation (*ethos*) and in achieving proper and optimal emotional effect (*pathos*). Poetic dedications in books — to city councils, territorial princes, noble patrons — comprise a particularly revealing genre for the rise of representative culture. On a material level, these dedications reflect the financial and material dependence of poets on benefactors; they also indicate a far-reaching ideological congruence between poets and sovereigns, who represented the best hope for a peaceful order in times of political, social, and cultural uncertainty.[67] Poetry did not simply serve society as a moral institution; it mirrored society in all its public and private events, and ultimately celebrated it.

Transitions: Beginnings of a Learned Literature in German

The movement to emulate Neo-Latin poetry as a learned, artistically ambitious poetry in the German vernacular began in the early sixteenth century. The literary production arising from it remained small, however, in comparison to both popular song and Neo-Latin poetry itself.[68] Among the most important early attempts were Hutten's "Ich habs gewagt mit sinnen" and Zwingli's poems in remembrance of his recovery from the plague in 1519.[69] Certain church hymns of the time also reflect the trend toward learnedness. The movement gained momentum in the last third of the sixteenth century as German poetry came under the influence of the Romance literatures. The earliest experiments dealt with imported meters (*vers commun*, alexandrine) and forms (sonnet) unsuited for singing.[70] An important contribution toward the evolution of a more artful poetry in the vernacular were the aforementioned translations by Lobwasser of the 1562 *Geneva Psalter* as well as a later version of the same text by Philipp von Winnenberg (1538–1600). Konrad Gesner (1516–65) experimented with hexameter in "Es macht alleinig der glaub die gleubige sälig" (It Is Faith Alone that Saves Believers, 1555).[71] Balthasar Froe's (fl. 1570) "Auff einem Fluss sag ich ein Nimph trawt sehre" (On a River I Saw a Nymph Who Was Mourning, 1572) was the first German poem to employ the alexandrine, though without fixed alternating meter. Tobias Hübner (1577–1636) further refined the German alexandrine under influence of Pléiade rules of versification, which fixed the number of syllables and regulated use of caesura and rhyme; he did not carry it out to the degree of regularity later recommended by Opitz, however.[72] "Zů dem Bastardischen Christenthumb" (On the Bastardly Christianity, 1556) by Christoff Wirsung (1500–1571) was the first sonnet to be composed in German,[73] and Johann Fischart's (1546/47–90) *Etlich Sonett* (Several Sonnets, 1575) is the first known cycle of German sonnets. The seven sonnets take the side of the Huguenots in a polemic against Catherine de'Medici's role in the St. Bartholomew's Day massacre of 1572. The powerful queen mother is likened to a hen in the first sonnet, which concludes with the following tercets:[74]

> Wann die Henn wil die Hanen führen:
> Da muß sie die gewiß verführen:
> Dann es ist wider die Natur
> Daß das schwächer das stärcker führt
> Das vnzierlichst das zierlichst ziert:
> Welch vngleicheit dient zur auffruhr.

[When the hen wants to lead the roosters, it has to seduce them for sure, for it is against nature that the weaker leads the stronger, which ungracefully adorns the graceful: Such inequality serves to promote unrest.]

Fischart laments the backlash that female regency is claimed to cause. While Fischart uses the French sonnet form to comment on French politics, the verse still is conventional doggerel: each line contains eight or nine syllables, but the four stresses are relatively freely distributed.

Antonio Scandello (1517–80), who was active at the Dresden court, introduced Italian song forms to Germany in his *Canzoni Napolitane* (Neapolitan Songs, 1556) and in several subsequent German collections, including *Nawe und schöne deudsche Liedlein* (New and Beautiful German Songs, 1568). Orlando de Lassus (di Lasso, 1532–94), at the court of the Wittelsbach in Munich, and Jacob Regnart (1540–99), at the Habsburg courts in Vienna and Prague, developed a more cosmopolitan Italianate song in Germany with the introduction of additional genres, such as *canzone*, *villanella*, madrigal, and *canzonetta*.[75] Romance verse, meter, and stanza forms boosted a more sophisticated practice of polyphonic song in the Italian style and moved toward alternation of stressed and unstressed syllables, later championed by Opitz. This wave of Italian influence also introduced the Petrarchan love poem to Germany and enabled the representation of personal feelings in vernacular poetry.[76] Important authors included Regnart, Christoph von Schallenberg (1561–97), Hans Leo Hassler (1564–1612), and Johann Hermann Schein (1586–1630).[77]

In the last decade of the sixteenth century and in the early seventeenth century, poets of the Heidelberg circle around Schede and Zincgref initiated a decided effort to introduce the poetic reforms of the Pléiade, which was led by Pierre de Ronsard (1524–85) and Joachim du Bellay (1522–60), into German literature.[78] This was accompanied by a consciousness of new literary beginnings.[79] Theobald Hock's (1573–ca. 1624) poetry, published in his collection *Schönes Blumenfeld* (Beautiful Meadow of Flowers, 1601), anticipated many of Opitz's reforms.[80] Georg Rodolf Weckherlin's (1584–1653) collection *Oden und Gesänge* (Odes and Songs, 1618–19) represented the first attempt at a learned German poetry oriented on Renaissance metrics.[81] Shortly thereafter, in 1624, Zincgref's friend Opitz designed a literary program based on the humanist tradition and Pléiade ideals that would revolutionize German poetry, and published it in a slender volume called *Buch von der Deutschen Poeterey*.[82]

Opitz and the Emergence of a National Literary Program

Opitz's reform, which imported a formal literary culture from Romance countries after German popular poetry had ceased to be innovative in the second half of the sixteenth century,[83] completed the merger of the vernacular and Neo-Latin literary traditions in Germany.[84] The literary conventions introduced by Opitz are oriented almost exclusively on the Neo-Latin tradition or on French, Italian, and Dutch models, which likewise were informed by the Neo-Latin tradition.[85] The Neo-Latin poetry of the sixteenth century offered the paradigm for Opitz's vernacular middle poetic style,[86] which features clarity of expression, grammatical correctness, mastery of rhetoric, understanding of German verse and meter, and literacy in the Neo-Latin culture and the classical tradition. Not only the writer but also the reader now was expected to command these essentials of literary education. Removed from the sphere of popular culture, the new vernacular poetry was to be the privileged domain of a learned few; thus, a lasting cleavage opened between learned and non-learned audiences.[87] While popular song continued to be practiced throughout the seventeenth century, even flourishing briefly between 1630 and 1660,[88] its cultural significance was minimal.

Buch von der Deutschen Poeterey was the first influential modern poetic handbook in German for a specifically German reader.[89] Its main emphases were the technical aspects of prosody and rhetoric, though Opitz harbored no illusion that poetic handbooks actually made poets. His most important metrical innovation was based on the insight that, for German, natural word stress mattered rather than syllable length, as in Latin and Greek and as prescribed by classical metrics. This led him to prescribe alternating meter, a demand that by the 1630s would be rejected by his contemporaries to allow dactylic verse. For the first time in German poetics, meter and rhythm were kept distinct from one another, thereby reducing the influence of *Knittelvers*, which had long dominated popular verse. Opitz's preference for iambic meter led him to promote alexandrine and *vers commun* as the two verse types most appropriate for German poetry. In his view, the alexandrine was the German equivalent of the classical hexameter and thus the appropriate medium to express refined thought and emotion. Its caesura after the third stressed syllable (that is, precisely in the middle of the line) could be used to effect antithesis, with a rising first half and a falling second half of the verse. Poetry had to be rhymed, and rhymes had to be pure, uncolored by dialect. For that reason, the use of a cultivated, standardized literary language was crucial, as were specific stylistic requirements — adornment, purity, clarity, tone, and appropriateness of poetic expression.[90]

Opitz's quest for a literary language, which he first proclaimed in *Aristarchus sive de contemptu linguae Teutonicae* (Aristarchus; or, On the Contempt for the German Language, 1617), promoted a national cultural program that could compete with the French and Dutch models. He had studied Ronsard, and he had personally met Daniel Heinsius and Gerhard Vossius (1577–1649) in Leiden in 1620, having fled there from Heidelberg after the outbreak of the Thirty Years' War. This vision was already driving the agenda of Germany's leading language and literary society, the Fruchtbringende Gesellschaft (Fruitbringing Society, founded 1617), and would be further developed by Philipp von Zesen (1619–89) in Hamburg, Harsdörffer in Nuremberg, and the grammarians Christian Gueintz (1592–1650) and Justus Georg Schottelius (1612–76). Opitz thus stood at the beginning of a national literature that drew on classical, Neo-Latin, and contemporary vernacular models but that aspired to become independent of, and even surpass, all of them.

Opitz defined a poem, *Geticht*, as any text written in verse, and emphasized its affinity to music (hence it was often called an *Ode*), no doubt an allusion to the Greek origins of poetry accompanied on the lyre. This conception owed to the enormously influential theorist Julius Caesar Scaliger, who thought of lyric as related to all sung verse: odes, idylls, paeans, and celebratory compositions of various kinds.[91] Opitz thus did not conceptualize poetry as a discrete category within poetics but shared Scaliger's Aristotelian view — explained in *Poetices libri septem* (1561), which was authoritative until the time of Gottsched in the mid-eighteenth century — that textual forms develop either out of objects (*res*) or out of the descriptive strategies used to represent them (*verba*). This explains why Opitz talks about different genres in two separate chapters of the *Poeterey*.[92] In chapter 5, on the organization of texts — the *dispositio* was traditionally the locus to discuss genres — he discusses various groups of poetic texts, mostly distinguished by content: epic, tragedy, comedy, satire, epigram, eclogue, elegy, echo, and panegyric. Each addresses a specific function. In chapter 7, on prosody, which relates to verbalization (*elocutio*), he discusses the sonnet, Pindaric ode, quatrain, and again the epigram. Here, formal elements define the communication of meaning. Both epigram and sonnet, for instance, focus on closure; thus, the pointed ending, or conceit, is a unique formal feature that allows the poet to convey his message.

Most of Opitz's poetic works, both secular and religious, reflect the precepts established here, starting with the ample poetic illustrations and model poems in the *Poeterey*. These sample poems also served to rectify his own poetic record: his poetics may have been written hastily in response to the unauthorized edition of his *Teutsche Poemata* (German Poems) published by Zincgref in 1624. Zincgref included poems from as early as 1620, which Opitz did not consider ready for print.[93] A year later, therefore, Opitz published a revised edition as *Acht Bücher deutscher Poematum* (Eight Books of German Poems), which thoroughly incorporated his precepts.[94] His collected works, the *Geistliche Poemata* (Religious Poems, 1638) and *Weltliche Poemata* (Secular Poems, 1644), set the standard for the remainder of the seventeenth century.

Trostgedichte in Widerwertigkeit deß Krieges (Poems of Consolation in the Adversity of War), the peak of Opitz's poetic accomplishments, were originally written during his exile in Denmark in 1620–21, but not published until 1633. A set of four extensive poems of great political and moral gravity, they are a demonstration of a major poet at work. They open with the following lines:[95]

> DEß schweren Krieges Last / den Teutschland jetzt empfindet /
> Vnd daß Gott nicht vmbsonst so hefftig angezündet
> den Eyffer seiner Macht / auch wo in solcher Pein
> Trost her zuholen ist / sol mein Gedichte seyn.

[The heavy burden of war that Germany now endures; and so that God did not in vain so powerfully ignite the eagerness of his might; also where consolation can be found in such pain — all of this shall be my poem.]

The first book describes the devastation of the land, the disruption of natural order, and the loss of virtue. The other three books offer consolation, conveyed through the good offices of the poet. According to Opitz, humans can find solace by practicing virtue, spurning human desires, rejecting the vanity of the world, and stoically relying on divine providence. The fourth book likens life to a journey on heavy seas and ends in this prayer:

> Gib vns den Muht der Noht vnd Tod verachten kan /
> Bind' vns mit deiner Hand starck an den Himmel an /

Auff daß wir nicht vergehn / gib vns in diesem Schmertzen
Ein frewdiges Gemüht vnd Königliche Hertzen /
Damit wir wider Grimm / Gewalt vnd Vberlast
Mit kräfftiger Gedult vnd Hoffnung seyn gefaßt. (407)

[Give us the courage that can despise misery and death. Bind us firmly
with your hand to heaven so that we not perish. In these sorrows give us
a joyous spirit and royal hearts so that we are prepared for horror, violence, and hardship with strong patience and hope.]

Opitz's impact on the literary scene of his time was far-reaching. At his death
in 1639, many poets composed epicedia in his memory, and panegyrical
poems to him appeared throughout the century. Opitzian poetic notions prevailed until Klopstock's groundbreaking *Messias* appeared in 1748, which
rejected both alternating meter and rhyme as fundamentals of poetry. In
German literary history, Opitz continues to enjoy the reputation as the
"Vater der deutschen Dichtung" (father of German poetry).[96] To be sure,
Opitz was never without his critics. For example, August Buchner
(1591–1661) and Zesen disapproved of his exclusion of dactylic verse.
Buchner introduced it in his lectures at Wittenberg University around 1638,
and most baroque poets after Zesen, who promoted it in his *Deutscher
Helikon* (German Helicon) in 1640, put it to regular use. Johann Rist
(1607–67), Harsdörffer, Andreas Gryphius (1616–64), and Andreas
Tscherning (1611–59) accused him of serving conflicting political and confessional masters, which implied deficient faith, or at least hypocrisy. Others
questioned his poetic skills, his lack of originality, or his use of dialectal
expressions in violation of his own rules.[97]

Genres: Differentiation in Form and Function

Genre definitions and boundaries were unclear throughout the seventeenth
century. Opitz defined some genres by content, others by form. This dual
genre system was theoretically problematic, as the two types occupied different places in the rhetorical system: the content-based genre in *inventio* and the
form-based genre in *elocutio*. A given text might therefore belong to two different genres, one in each category. Inversely, a genre designation defined
either form or content, but typically not both. As the century progressed,
genre definitions gradually stabilized and poetry evolved into a relatively differentiated subsystem of literary production. No clear concept of the lyric
existed, however.

In his seminal *Ausführliche Arbeit Von der Teutschen HaubtSprache*
(A Thorough Study of the German Principal Language, 1663), Schottelius outlines a genre theory in three parts, according to derivation from meter, stanza
form, or content matter.[98] The section on meter discusses trochaic, iambic,
dactylic, and anapestic poetry, as well as new verse forms, including Sapphic
ode and elegy. Over the following twenty-three chapters, he considers genres
of poems derived from stanza forms, among them the heroic poem, elegy
(again), sonnet, echo poem, pattern poem, anagram, sestina, Pindaric ode,

epigram, and riddle. The wealth of forms is evidence of how far efforts had advanced to create a German literary tradition and of the degree to which the quality of German poetry had evolved. Schottelius offers only a sketch of genres identified by content: tragic, comic, tragicomic, or deliberative (expressing praise or criticism); each of the four groups may include genres that are not formally connected. Texts dealing with matters neither tragic nor comic may be emblems, tragicomedies, or riddle poems. Each genre, in other words, may fall into any of the three categories. Poets also were at liberty to vary existing genres or to devise their own forms. In what follows, I will discuss only five frequently used forms with established generic identities: epigram, ode, madrigal, sestina, and sonnet.

Epigram: The epigram was the only major genre of classical origin, originating with Martial, Catullus, and the poets of the *Anthologia Graeca*. The classical epigram employed hexameter and pentameter; initially, the German epigram mostly used what Opitz took to be its equivalent, the alexandrine. Brevity was its most important quality, in the sense of linguistic economy rather than numeric limit, although the couplet was its most common form; the epigram enhanced the quality of brevity by stressing only a single thought, object, or person.[99] Epigrams also featured a pointed, often witty ending (*argutia*). The satirical epigram, while exemplary for theory, was in fact less common than other types: most common was the gnomic (moralizing or didactic) epigram, followed by the satirical, playful-conceited, and panegyrical-hymnlike types.[100] Many epigrams, particularly of the gnomic and panegyrical types, were religious in character.[101]

In the schools, epigram composition belonged to the study of rhetoric, and almost all poets of the time tried their hand at the genre.[102] Lobwasser's *Deutsche Epigrammata*, published posthumously in 1611, was the first collection of epigrams in German, at least in name: most of the epigrams in the collection remained indebted to the tradition of the *Spruch*. On the other hand, the epigrams of both Weckherlin and Opitz derive from humanist models and thus stand in a long generic tradition in German literature. The most important collection is Friedrich von Logau's (1604–55) *Salomons von Golaw Deutscher Sinn-Getichte Drey Tausend* (Three Thousand German Epigrams by Salomon von Golaw, 1654), which contains 3,560 epigrams modeled after Martial, John Owen ("the English Martial," 1564–1622), and other Neo-Latin authors. Logau broke the dominance of the alexandrine by using a variety of verse forms: very short lines, dactylic verse, or even trochaic verse with eight feet. The majority of his epigrams are couplets. To his longest epigram (196 lines) he added the witty marginal note, "Epigramma est brevis Satyra; Satyra, est longum Epigramma" (The epigram is a short satire; the satire is a long epigram).[103] Logau wrote about whatever occupied his mind: war and peace, religious and devotional issues, contemplative and intellectual concerns, love and lust, social mores and conditions, occupations, character types, moral issues, and the epigram itself. The chronogram "Das Jahr 1640" (The Year 1640) is playful even as it addresses the serious issue of war and peace (the "numerical" letters add up to 1640):

GIeb / gIeb / O gIeb Vns FrIeD / O FrIeDe gIeb Vns / Gott!
FrIeD Ist Vns Ia so nVtz aLs etWa LIebes Brot. (1,4,73)

[Give, give, o give us peace, o peace give us, God! Peace is as useful to us
as precious bread.]

Epigrams also figure prominently in the mystical works of Logau's contemporaries
Daniel Czepko and Johannes Scheffler (Angelus Silesius, 1624–77); both
authors will be discussed later in this chapter. The epigram enjoyed a revival
late in the century: like Logau, Johannes Grob (1643–97) and Christian
Wernicke (1661–1725) wrote epigrams almost exclusively. In 1698, Johann
Gottlieb Meister (1665–99) published the first tract on the epigram in
German, which confirmed traditional epigram theory, including Opitz's definition of the epigram as a satiric genre. Meister refuted the French opinion
that German culture lacked *bel esprit*, as Dominique Bouhours (1628–1702),
a Jesuit, had claimed in 1671 in *Les Entretiens d'Ariste et d'Eugène*. According
to Meister, the German epigram proved that German wit and spirit equaled
that of the French.[104]

Ode: The continuity of song tradition precluded distinct formal features,
though this did not prevent innovation. A poetic text intended to be set to
music and sung could also be read without music. Until 1660, simple strophic
song dominated; thereafter, more complex forms, such as aria and cantata,
became common.[105] Song was a principal genre for the Königsberg circle
around Simon Dach (1605–59) and the composer Heinrich Albert (1604–51)
and for the Leipzig group around Christian Brehme (1613–67), Gottfried
Finckelthaus (1614–48), and Georg Greflinger (1620–77). Other important
writers of song include Rist, Zesen, and David Schirmer (1623–87). In his collection *Die Geharnschte Venus* (The Armored Venus, 1660), Caspar Stieler
(1632–1707) shows a deep understanding of musical settings, and in later
works he contributed substantially to the continuo *Lied* and opera.[106] While
songs could be published in any collection of poetry, a number of songbooks
contain both lyrics and musical notation. One of the most important is
Schirmer's *Singende Rosen* (Singing Roses, 1654), with melodies by Philipp
Stolle (1614–75); another is Heinrich Albert's *Arien* (8 vols., 1638–50). Most
songbooks, including Finckelthaus's *Deutsche Gesänge* (1640), also include
other genres; some contain no musical notations.[107]

The German ode of the seventeenth century alludes to the classical tradition in name only. For Opitz and others the ode was synonymous with
artistic rather than popular song, meaning that it was free in form and content. Weckherlin's *Oden und Gesänge* followed Pléiade models. For
Schottelius, the ode was a song or poem of any form, using any rhythm and
verse. Mandatory rhyming and the awkwardness in adapting classical prosody
rendered a direct borrowing into German of the classical forms of the ode
nearly impossible. The Pindaric ode, following Ronsard's model, had three
parts but was otherwise formally free, as Opitz illustrates in chapter 7 of his
Poeterey. It was typically used in German for festive celebrations, whether
worldly or spiritual. The Sapphic ode was the only form in which a German

ode used the classical stanza structure of three identical verses and a fourth abbreviated one.

Madrigal: The madrigal was one of the Italianate forms that entered German poetry in the late sixteenth century. In its original sense, the name referred to poetic texts written for polyphonic secular song. Hassler and Schein pioneered its development in Germany. The madrigal typically is limited to one stanza of five to sixteen lines, often of varying length, some unrhymed. Its brevity and propensity for a pointed ending made the madrigal text increasingly independent of the musical setting, so that it became more closely associated with the epigram. This is particularly true for the emerging standard form: three tercets and two couplets (abb cdd eff gg hh). Caspar Ziegler (1621–90), in his *Von den Madrigalen* (1653), the most important theoretical text on the madrigal, discusses only the pointed, epigrammatic form, though always insisting that it be singable.[108]

Sestina: The sestina, of Provençal origin, was a favorite genre of Petrarch, Dante, and the poets of the Pléiade. It consists of six sestets and a closing tercet. The same six ending words rotate through all six stanzas (123456, 612345, etc.). The tercet, referred to as *envoy*, contains all six recurrent words. In German poetry, Opitz, Weckherlin, Gryphius, and Hans Assmann von Abschatz (1646–99) made greatest use of the genre.[109]

Sonnet: The sonnet was the signature genre of the seventeenth century.[110] Of Italian origin and popularized by Petrarch, it dominated European Renaissance poetry. In Germany, the sonnet was not practiced seriously until the early seventeenth century, although Wirsung and Fischart, among others, experimented with it in the preceding century.[111] Ronsard was the primary model: his rhyme pattern (abba abba ccd eed) was divided into two quatrains and two tercets, usually with a break in sense and feeling occurring between the expository octave and the tercets, which tended to lead to a pointed ending in the fourteenth line and to add an epigrammatic effect to the conclusion. Alexandrine and *vers commun* were the most common verse forms in the German sonnet — indeed, the only ones recommended by Opitz. The first sonnet cycles contained one hundred each: *Trawr- und Treu-Gedichten* (Poems of Grief and Faith, 1630) by Johannes Plavius (b. ca. 1600) and *Krieg vnd Sieg Christi* (War and Victory of Christ, 1631) by Diederich von dem Werder (1584–1657).[112] The first master of the form and its most prolific practitioner was Paul Fleming; many of his more than 350 sonnets are love poems in the Petrarchan tradition. Zesen opened the sonnet to other verse forms, including dactylic and short trochaic verse. He even prefaced his *Deutscher Helicon* with a "Dactylisch Sonnet" dedicated to Buchner.

Gryphius was the most accomplished German master of the sonnet form. His *Sonnete* (1637), the first of several collections known as "Lissa" sonnets,[113] written at the peak of the Thirty Years' War, reiterate the themes of war, destruction, suffering, loss of faith, and apocalypse, but simultaneously exude confidence in an eternal life that positively inverts this transitory world. Most of Gryphius's sonnets are profoundly moral and spiritual; only rarely, in contrast to Fleming, are they lighthearted, though Gryphius, like Fleming, tends to build toward a pointed ending in the fourteenth line. The *Geistliche Sonnette/ Lieder und Gedichte* (Religious Sonnets, Songs, and Poems, 1662) of Catharina Regina von Greiffenberg (1637–94), an Austrian Protestant exile in Nuremberg, contains 250 sonnets, followed by additional songs and epigrams. Many of her sonnets end in rhymed couplets and thus give the illusion of consisting of three quatrains. Greiffenberg prefers spiritual and devotional themes and often achieves mystical expressiveness. Quirinus Kuhlmann (1651–89) experiments with meter in his early mystical sonnets, while Christian Hofmann von Hofmannswaldau (1616–79) explores daring imagery and exuberant metaphorical language. Christian Gryphius (1649–1706), the son of Andreas, was the last poet to write large numbers of sonnets; among them is the first in German without rhyme: "Ungereimtes Sonnet" (Unrhymed Sonnet). Later poets, such as Johann Burkhard Menke (Philander von der Linde, 1674–1732) or Johann Christian Günther (1695–1723), wrote few sonnets; indeed, their experimentation with genre norms suggests that the sonnet form was by now obsolescent.

Though we may associate particular poets with specific poetic genres, early modern poets usually did not focus on a single genre. Seventeenth-century collections typically contained a variety of genres arranged, garden-like, into many different kinds of plants; dramas and short epics, for instance, coexisted in a given collection without tension. The imprecision in the definition of forms and the possibility of creating new forms allowed writers to address a broad range of topics and themes: occasional, devotional, religious, didactic, philosophical, pastoral, amatory, among others. It bears repeating that early modern poetry defies narrow classification, since many poems belong to more than one of the categories mentioned above. Only two categories of poetry, therefore, will be discussed as such later in the chapter: liturgical and devotional, and mystical.

Regional Traditions

Confessional boundaries formed a literary line of demarcation well into the eighteenth century: a Protestant literary landscape flourished in northern, eastern, and central Germany, while in the south and west a Catholic literature more modest in scale subsisted. Given the lack of an imperial cultural center, regionalism was a powerful force in early modern Germany. Most of the more than 300 largely sovereign states had their own courts, though it is also true that common courtly norms enforced a certain degree of uniformity of literary expression.[114] The free imperial cities, such as Nuremberg, Hamburg, and Strasbourg, and university towns, such as Leipzig, continued to operate as regional cultural hubs in their own right, and many of them boasted literary and language societies (*Sprachgesellschaften*), a fact that further encouraged regional literary movements.

Silesia, with the free city of Breslau at its center, constituted the major regional literary center. Its many principalities and cities supported a class of educated public servants who were exposed to humanist and Calvinist ideas at external German universities like Heidelberg and Strasbourg, but abroad as well at Orléans, Paris, Leiden, and elsewhere. Given the many intellectual, religious, and national influences, the older Silesians remained a diverse group, ranging from Opitz, Logau, Tscherning, and Gryphius to the hymnist Matthäus Apelles von Löwenstern (1594–1648), Opitz's disciple and biographer Christoph Köler (Colerus, 1602–58), and the lyricist Johann Peter Titz (1619–89). A number of these poets studied in or visited Strasbourg, where they were introduced to the Neo-Stoic ideas of the Dutch political theorist Justus Lipsius (1547–1606) through Matthias Bernegger (1582–1640), a professor at the university.[115] The later Silesian poets tended toward mannerist practices, a style known in older baroque scholarship as the Second Silesian School, of which the most significant poet was Hofmannswaldau. Other important Silesian poets included Wencel Scherffer von Scherfferstein (1603–74), Christoph Kaldenbach, Daniel Casper von Lohenstein (1635–83), Christian Knorr von Rosenroth (1636–89), Heinrich Mühlpfort (1639–81), Hans Assmann von Abschatz, and Benjamin Neukirch (1665–1729). Three of the most remarkable mystics, Czepko, Scheffler, and Kuhlmann, were Silesians as well.

The free imperial city of Nuremberg was a second important literary center, home to the Pegnesischer Blumenorden (Order of Flowers on the Pegnitz), founded in 1644 by Harsdörffer, the author of the *Poetischer Trichter*, which formulated its poetological program. The members of the group experimented with language and sounds (*Klangmalerei*, "sound painting"). They practiced pastoral poetry, which, in their view, originated in the Old Testament (with the shepherd-king David, singer of the psalms). The perceived pre-classical, implicitly Christian roots of the genre helped them build the argument that its use proved the superiority of German literature over classical models.[116] In that vein, Sigmund von Birken's (1626–81) sonnet "Der Norische Parnaß" (The Nuremberg Parnassus, 1677) suggests erecting a Christian temple of the Muses near Nuremberg. The most important local members, besides Harsdörffer and Birken, were Johann Klaj (1616–56), a master of dactylic verse and an unusual genre of spoken oratorio (*Redeoratorium*), and Johann Hellwig (1609–74), an eminent physician and author of a major pastoral work; Rist and Schottelius were active corresponding members. The pastor Johann Michael Dilherr (1604–69) served as religious and literary mentor of the group, though he never formally joined.[117] Starting in 1659, Greiffenberg was involved with the Nuremberg group, particularly with Birken. (Her spiritual poetry will be discussed below.)

Saxony was a relatively diverse literary center. Leipzig attracted intellectual exchange because of its university and business fairs — especially its renowned book fair — while the Dresden court served as a focal point of an emerging courtly culture.[118] An early courtly poet from the neighboring principality of Anhalt, Diederich von dem Werder, authored devotional poetry and important translations of Italian chivalric epics. Most of the Leipzig poets of the 1630s and 1640s were followers of Opitz, Fleming being the most important. Many cultivated love poetry or witty parodies; Brehme and Finckelthaus were known especially for their drinking and student songs. Later Leipzig poets, such as

Zacharias Lund (1608–67) in Schleswig and Greflinger, who moved to Hamburg in 1646, began to look beyond Opitz to the authority of Buchner in Wittenberg. Buchner further systematized and refined Opitz's approach and dedicated much of his writing to metrics, rhyme, ornamentation, and purity of poetic language, as well as issues of phonology and word formation, which affect versification. Buchner also issued a more generous license for experimentation, particularly in his advocacy of the dactyl, which profoundly altered the nature of learned German verse. Schirmer, who was active at the Dresden court after 1650 and who developed a less experimental style that borrowed from Opitz's Petrarchist language, influenced the styles of Ziegler, Justus Sieber (1628–95), and Johann Georg Schoch (1627–90).[119]

The literary scene in Hamburg was a forum for an open rivalry between Rist and Zesen. Rist founded the Elbschwanorden (Order of the Swans of the Elbe) in 1660 and introduced the Opitzian reform to the Low German area; he was important in establishing the literary culture in Hamburg. Zesen, who was close to Buchner and Harsdörffer, was inspired by the Strasbourg Aufrichtige Tannengesellschaft (Honorable Society of the Pines), which had been founded in 1633 by Jesaias Rompler von Löwenhalt (1605–ca. 1676). In 1642, Zesen organized a circle of friends into the Deutschgesinnte Genossenschaft (German-Minded Society), which was more open to literary experimentation than the Rist circle.

In the Königsberg circle, secular song was particularly cultivated, and many songbooks were published there. Besides Dach, who was the leading personality of the group, the key figures were Robert Roberthin (1600–1648), Kaldenbach, and the composer Albert. The Königsberg poets often met in the *Kürbishütte* (pumpkin cabin) in Albert's garden (the pumpkin thus became their emblematic plant); its razing in 1641 to make way for a road occasioned a great outpouring of poetic lamentation.[120] The literary topos of the *locus amoenus* (pleasance), with its requisites of bird song, brook, and meadow, where poetry and friendship could mingle in a pastoral idyll, was a lived reality in Königsberg.[121] Many of Dach's songs were set to music by Albert and published in his *Arien*, mentioned above. Dach is also noted for his large number of occasional poems. The Low German spoken in the region provided Dach with the language for some of his popular songs, such as "Anke van Tharaw." The Königsberg circle also engaged in intellectual exchange with poets in Danzig, which became home to Plavius and Titz, among others.[122] Opitz lived in both cities late in life; he died in Danzig.

Styles and Movements

Opitz's influence was felt throughout the seventeenth century, and many writers remained loyal to the Opitzian program well beyond his death in 1639. Anna Ovena Hoyers (1584–1655) was among the very few poets who ignored his reforms during his lifetime. Her *Geistliche und Weltliche Poemata* (Religious and Secular Poems, 1650), for example, employ mostly doggerel verse. By the time of Opitz's death, in 1639, however, younger poets had begun to experiment in non-Opitzian ways with poetic forms and literary language.

Logau, for one, pushed the boundaries by taking on a range of political, social, and philosophical issues. On the other hand, he continued to practice epigrammatic form in a conventional manner.

Masters of the Convention

Paul Fleming. Paul Fleming was a unique figure in many ways. He was not active in the network of *Sprachgesellschaften,* and his close associations were limited to his teachers Johann Hermann Schein and Adam Olearius (1599–1671) and to the poets he met as a student at the University of Leipzig. Fleming spent most of his productive years abroad: from 1633 to 1639 he traveled to Russia and Persia as part of a diplomatic mission on behalf of Friedrich III, Duke of Holstein-Gottorf, with longer stays in Reval (now Tallinn, Estonia).[123] His poetry is more personal than that of his contemporaries, which has led many scholars, mistakenly, to rely on it for biographical information. Fleming wrote only poetry, but his work touches on a great variety of themes and moods.[124] As a follower of Opitz, he strictly adhered to alternating meter, both in short and long verse, and mastered the stanza and verse forms recently introduced into German literature. His preferred genres were the sonnet, ode, song, epigram, and longer poems in paired rhyme.[125] His *Teütsche Poemata* (German Poems), edited and published posthumously by Olearius in 1646, are organized by genres: "poetische Wälder" (poetic forests, nonstrophic poems), odes (strophic poems or songs), epigrams, and sonnets. The sections fall into three broad functional categories: spiritual and devotional, occasional (felicitations, funerals, weddings), and amatory. Only some of his occasional poetry and small collections of poems in Latin in the humanist tradition, written as a student in Leipzig, were published during his lifetime.

Many of Fleming's amatory poems relate to the sisters Elsabe and Anna Niehus, in Reval; others describe the art of kissing or the beauty of the female body, topics that established his reputation as a German-language Petrarchist. His reflective, spiritual poetry owed much to Lipsius's *De Constantia libri duo* (Two Books on Constancy, 1584), a transconfessional Christian primer that established Neo-Stoicism as the intellectual tool for coping with war and other crises in the first half of the seventeenth century:[126]

> LAß dich nur nichts nicht tauren
> mit trauren /
> Sey stille /
> Wie Gott es fügt /
> So sey vergnügt /
> mein Wille.

[Let yourself regret nothing with sorrows. Be still, as God insists. Be thus cheerful, my will.]

This simple ode contemplates the necessity of yielding to the divine plan, a sentiment also expressed by the song "In allen meinen Thaten laß ich den

Höchsten rahten" (In All My Deeds I Allow the Lord to Advise Me), which has been included in many Protestant hymnals. Fleming's self-referential sonnets reiterate his stoicism: the famous "An sich" (To Himself) begins with the memorable statement "Sey dennoch unverzagt" (Yet do not be afraid). The contradictory adverb "dennoch," which lacks an explicit antecedent, implies that the world is a wretched place — an idea apparently in need of no explanation.[127] But the epigrammatic closing lines express stoic confidence in the power of self-mastery:

> Wer sein selbst Meister ist / und sich beherrschen kan /
> dem ist die weite Welt und alles unterthan. (576)
>
> [Who's master of himself and rules his own desire
> Has subject unto him the mighty globe entire.][128]

Yet, the pseudorhyme of the last two lines alludes to an underlying dissonance, or asymmetry, of the usual baroque antithesis.[129] The same metaphysical unease also forms a subtext to his own "Grabschrifft" (Epicedium), written a few days before his death, in which he confidently states his immortal accomplishments as a poet, even as he submits to the divine order.

Andreas Gryphius. Andreas Gryphius is the most renowned, and representative, German poet of the seventeenth century.[130] He was the first to adopt fully the Opitzian reform program, which he applied to a far-reaching cultural vision; in his work, German poetry became emancipated from the Neo-Latin paradigm.[131] Gryphius engaged little in formal experimentation but excelled through mastery of established forms and rhetorical devices. Most of his poems focus on serious religious and philosophical themes, though he also authored a few light-hearted poems and many satirical epigrams. Love and nature have little place in his *oeuvre*. Gryphius organized his poetry for publication under three generic categories: sonnets, odes (mainly strophic songs, but also poems with irregular stanza patterns), and epigrams. Some books of poems appeared independently; others were incorporated in work editions, such as collections of plays. In 1698, his son Christian Gryphius edited the collection *Andreae Gryphii um ein merckliches vermehrte Teutsche Gedichte* (The Significantly Augmented Poems by Andreas Gryphius), which includes many occasional poems as well as seventy-one previously unpublished sonnets.[132]

Two philological problems are involved in the interpretation of Gryphius's poetry. First, many poems, particularly his sonnets, are part of cycles,[133] which forces us to read them in a specific context. Second, most exist in two or more versions, and often, in the later ones, the contexts have been changed (updated, altered in placement) and the texts stylistically and rhetorically improved.[134]

Gryphius's reputation as a poet rests primarily on his sonnets. His first youthful cycle, the Lissa sonnets of 1637, already show him as a master of the most complex poetic form of his time. The cycle is composed following numerological patterns — Gryphius did not replicate them in later editions. Traditionally, much of his poetry has been seen under the topoi of *vanitas mundi* (vanity of the world) and *memento mori* (remembrance of one's own mortality), occasionally counteracted by the topos of *carpe diem*.[135] The topos of life's vanity occurs, for instance, in his sonnet "Menschliches Elende" (Human Misery, 1637):[136]

> Was nach vns kompt / wird auch der Todt ins Grab hinzihn /
> So werden wir verjagt gleich wie ein Rauch von Winden.

> [What comes after us death also will pull into the grave. Thus we are chased away as smoke by the winds.]

Subsequent versions have modified endings, however, such as the final edition of 1663:

> Was nach vns kommen wird / wird vns ins grab nach zihn.
> Was sag ich? wir vergehn wie Rauch von starcken winden. (1,35)

> [What will come after us will follow us into the grave. What say I? We disappear like smoke among strong winds.]

Both versions use the alexandrine, the most common verse in his sonnets. The first redisposes the caesura in line 13 from its typical location after the third foot to after the second, while line 14 attains closure in a simile. Later versions change both lines: line 13 now has a regular caesura, contrasting and joining both halves by anadiplosis, the repetition of the word "wird"; line 14 achieves a pointed ending by setting it up with a rhetorical question in three syllables (beginning with a stress, which turns it into a trochee), thus shifting the caesura and making the closing statement more emphatic.

The centerpiece of the Lissa sonnets is "VANITAS, VANITATUM, ET OMNIA VANITAS" (Vanity of Vanities, and All Is Vanity), with the motto "Es ist alles gantz eytel" (Everything is completely vain; 1,7), based on Eccl. 1:2. This sonnet (no. 6) is the only one whose title is all in capital letters; it has thirty letters by analogy to the thirty sonnets of the collection, not counting the "Beschlus Sonnet" (Final Sonnet). The number six, the satanic number according to Revelation 13:18, is repeated three times and is the key to the structure of the collection.[137] By contrast, each word in the title of the collection — *ANDREAE GRYPHII Sonnete* — has seven letters and three syllables (both comprising divine numbers), adding to ten, the number of divine law; the numeric value of the entire title adds to thirty, the number of sonnets. This numerical strategy reinforces the central idea of salvation, which elevates the theme of *vanitas* beyond the general grievance of earthly transitoriness and the stoic response of resignation.[138] Gryphius has given the poem an eternal, even apocalyptic dimension,[139] culminating in the final line: "Noch wil / was ewig ist / kein einig Mensch betrachten!" (What is eternal, not a single human yet wants to consider; 1,8).

The sonnet "Die Hölle" (Hell, 1643) has a similar message, generated by the asyndeton (omission of linking conjunction) in the first quatrain (1,91):

Ach! vnd weh!
MOrd! Zetter! Jammer! Angst! Creutz! Marter! Würme! Plagen.
Pech! Folter! Hencker! Flamm! stanck! Geister! kälte! Zagen!
Ach vergeh!

[Alas! and Misery! Murder! Outcry! Lament! Fear! Cross! Torment!
Worms! Pains. Tar! Torture! Henchman! Flame! Stench! Spirits! Cold!
Hesitation! Alas, pass away!]

By beginning lines 2 and 3 with monosyllabic words, Gryphius creates the illusion of a more dramatic trochaic verse. The catalogue of images — a familiar technique of the early modern categorization of knowledge — conjures a horrific vision of hell.[140] Gryphius uses four different meters and verse forms here: alexandrine in the middle verses of the quatrains, cretic (foot or verse form with long-short-long syllable sequence) in the embracing verses of the quatrains, dactylic verse with eight feet in the first two verses of the tercets, and *vers commun* in the final verses of the tercets. The virtuosity of metric variety represents the chaos of hell, and the violent deformation of the sonnet form embodies its savagery.[141] The last line brings closure in a pointed formulation, true to generic norms: "O Mensch! Verdirb / vmb hier nicht zuverderben" (O Man! Perish, in order not to perish here; 1,91). Again, the eschatological message is central, conveyed by paronomasia (word play): physical suffering and death are prerequisites for securing eternal life.

"Threnen des Vatterlandes / Anno 1636" (Tears of the Fatherland, Anno, 1636), first published as "Trawrklage des verwüsteten Deutschlandes" (Lamentation on Devastated Germany) in 1637, is one of the most memorable and often quoted of Gryphius's war poems (1,48):

WIr sindt doch nunmehr gantz / ja mehr den gantz verheret!
　　Der frechen völcker schaar / die rasende posaun
　　Das vom blutt fette schwerdt / die donnernde Carthaun
Hatt aller schweis / vnd fleis / vnd vorrath auff gezehret.
Die türme stehn in glutt / die Kirch ist umgekehret.
　　Das Rahthaus ligt im graus / die starcken sind zerhawn.
　　Die Jungfern sind geschändt / vnd wo wir hin nur schawn
Ist fewer / pest / vnd todt der hertz vndt geist durchfehret.
　　Hier durch die schantz vnd Stadt / rint alzeit frisches blutt.
　　Dreymall sindt schon sechs jahr als vnser ströme flutt
Von Leichen fast verstopfft / sich langsam fortgedrungen.
　　Doch schweig ich noch von dem was ärger als der todt.
　　Was grimmer den die pest / vndt glutt vndt hungers noth
Daß auch der Selen schatz / so vielen abgezwungen.

[Entire, more than entire have we been devastated!
　　The maddened clarion, the bold invaders' horde,
　　The mortar thunder-voiced, the blood-anointed sword
Have all men's sweat and work and store annihilated.

The towers stand in flames, the church is violated,
  The strong are massacred, a ruin our council board,
  Our maidens raped, and where my eyes have scarce explored
Fire, pestilence, and death my heart have dominated.
  Here through the moat and town runs always new-let blood,
  And for three-times-six years our very rivers' flood
With corpses choked has pressed ahead in tedious measure;
  I shall not speak of that which is still worse than death,
  And crueler than the plague and torch and hunger's breath:
From many has been forced even the spirit's treasure.][142]

This poem follows the French sonnet form and the new metrics as prescribed by Opitz, including the alexandrine. Gryphius was well versed in humanist rhetoric, as the extensive use of topoi reveals. "Threnen" do not signify subjectivity or personal emotions; rather, the term is a metapoetic signal attributing the text to the generic tradition of lament.[143]

The first quatrain describes the acts of war in graphic detail. The second bemoans the breakdown of civic order and its impact on the civilian population: the city hall and the church, representing the two central institutions, which project social stability and spiritual safeguard, have been destroyed, and the subsequent loss of order leads to rape, illness, and death. The human path to salvation is marked by suffering in analogy to Christ's suffering.[144] This is not a strictly "realistic" poem, however, but a surrealistic vision of a material war world, to which is added an apocalyptic dimension, signaled by the occurrence of the satanic number — "three-times-six years" —[145] and concluding in eternal damnation marked by the pointed ending. The prophecy of the four last things — death, final judgment, hell, and joy of the elect — is an important motif in Gryphius's poetry.[146]

Among his other cycles, the *Son- undt Feyrtags Sonnete* (Sonnets for Sundays and Holidays, 1639) have a special place, as they are based on biblical pericopes.[147] They consist of two complete cycles organized according to the liturgical calendar. The sixty-five sonnets on Sundays and thirty-five sonnets on ecclesiastical feast days are rooted in Protestant devotional literature.[148] Gryphius's three books of odes, published in 1643, 1650, and 1657, contain twelve odes each: twenty strophic songs and sixteen Pindaric odes with uneven stanzas. They treat mostly biblical themes and were influenced by the Latin odes of the Jesuit Jacob Balde (1604–68). His cycle of odes *Thränen über das Leiden Jesu Christi* (Tears on the Suffering of Jesus Christ, 1652), which became the fourth book of odes in the 1657 edition, contains nineteen poems describing the suffering of Christ between the Last Supper and his death, and ending with his burial.

The final edition of his German epigrams, *Deutsche Epigrammata* (1663), includes three books with 100 epigrams each. The first book is dedicated to moral and devotional issues and often adduces biblical themes. The second book contains didactic, gnomic, contemplative, and elegiac epigrams. Fellow human beings, dead or alive, are targeted in the third book in both serious and jocular epigrams. "Grabschrift Laelii, welcher sich selbst erschossen" (Epitaph of Laelius, Who Shot Himself, 1663) is a fictitious epitaph, playfully alluding to the tomb inscriptions that stood at the beginning of the genre in Greek antiquity. It merges epitaph and riddle traditions to make light of a serious moral issue:[149]

> Hir ligt in einer Grufft / der Kläger / der beklagte /
> Der Recht sprach / der gezeugt / und der die Zeugen fragte /
> Und der das Recht außführt / und der so must erbleichen:
> Du zehlest siben zwar und findst nur eine Leichen. (2,214)

> [Here lies in one grave the plaintiff, the accused, the one who judged, who witnessed, and who queried witnesses, and who enforced the law, and who thus had to fade. You count seven, yet find only one corpse.]

His best-known epigram is "Uber Nicolai Copernici Bild" (On the Image of Nicolaus Copernicus) in its redaction of 1663. Its first version (1643) memorialized the centennial of the death of Copernicus (1473–1543) as well as of the publication of his renowned *De revolutionibus orbium coelestium libri VI* (On the Revolutions of Heavenly Spheres). Publication of the epigram may also have been motivated by the death of Galileo Galilei (1564–1642) the year before.[150] This epigram expresses praise in the device of a written portrait in the classical literary tradition of *laudatio*. Copernicus is likened to Hermes Trismegistus,[151] whose wisdom was rooted in sensual perception and empirical observation, rather than rational thinking. Copernicus was a hero of his time for having decided the struggle between the *antiqui* and the *moderni* by disproving the misconceptions of the ancients.[152] The earth's orbit has become his chariot, which will disseminate his fame in cosmic time. Copernicus thus displaces Phoebus, implying that the authority of modern natural philosophy has displaced that of classical mythology. Yet, the immobility of the sun — God's sun — implies that the centrality of the sun is not an astronomical but a theological issue. This releases Copernicus from the church's allegation of human *curiositas*, the inquisitiveness of the searching mind. The implication is that the scientific enterprise is in fact governed by divine providence.[153]

Innovators

Philipp von Zesen, like his teacher August Buchner, promoted the use of dactylic and anapestic verse and used them frequently in his own poetry, which became increasingly devotional as he grew older. He was both admired and reviled by contemporaries for his uncompromising efforts to reform German spelling and to cleanse the German language of foreign words.[154] Common German words like *Anschrift* (address) or *Augenblick* (moment) are his creations, but so are many rejected neologisms like *Gesichtserker* (facial bay) for "nose" or *Jungfenzwinger* (virgin kennel) for "nunnery." His experimentation with adventurous etymologies, exuberant word plays and sound effects (interior rhyme, alliteration, assonance), and correspondences between sounds and meanings were motivated by his search for the original Adamic language (*lingua adamica*).[155] The poet's explicit task, he explains in *Rosen-mánd* (Rose-Moon, 1651), his major theoretical work, is to free the Adamic language, the link to divine natural language in scripture, from obscurity. Poetry seeks to reclaim this natural language as a means of accessing nature as a source of divine revelation.[156]

The first stanza from Zesen's "Freudenlied" (Song of Joy), written in 1668 for a foundation festival of the Deutschgesinnete Genossenschaft and published in *Dichterisches Rosen- und Liljen-thal* (Poetic Valley of Roses and Lilies, 1670), illustrates some of his innovations:

> HAllet / ihr felder /
> erschallet / ihr wälder:
> singet / ihr sähler / ihr tähler erklingt:
> spielet ihr flüsse /
> durch töhnende güsse:
> springet ihr änger: ihr Sänger erschwingt
> lungen und zungen; seid heute bemüht /
> heute zu singen / zu bringen ein lied.
> Dichtet / ihr Dichter ein Meiengedicht /
> grüsset dis liebliche fröliche licht. (2,103)

[Sound, you fields; reverberate, you forests; sing, you fellows, you valleys, resound; be playful, you rivers, through resounding gushes; spring, you meadows; you singers, sway lungs and tongues. Endeavor today to sing today, to offer a song. Compose, you poets, a May poem. Greet this lovely, cheerful light.]

The dactylic verse and the uneven length of the lines give this poem a more direct, spoken quality, and transcend the realm of Opitzian poetics. Nature becomes anthropomorphic — it is asked to act autonomously, independently of artifice. Onomatopoeia reinforces this sense of immediacy of the language. Zesen became an important precursor and ally of the Nuremberg poets,[157] in particular, and he helped prepare the later mannerist style of Hofmannswaldau and others. The writers of the Nuremberg circle shared Zesen's joy of experimentation with sounds, rhyme, alliteration and assonance, and dactylic and anapestic verse. Like Zesen, Harsdörffer saw the German language as a system of signs in which the form of the word corresponded to its meaning. Given its presumed closeness to the Adamic origin, the German language was thought to have maintained its ability to express the secrets of nature. This enabled poets to generate meaning through numerological speculation, playful games with letters, sounds and words, onomatopoeia, and metaphors.[158]

Harsdörffer's crowning achievement in this regard was his "Fünffacher Denckring der teutschen Sprache" (Fivefold Ring for Thinking in the German Language). The fivefold ring exemplifies an adaptation of cabbalist thought deriving from the Spanish theologian Ramón Lull (ca. 1232–1315) and promulgated in the seventeenth century by the Jesuit Athanasius Kircher (1602–80). It became an indispensable tool for the poet to find rhymes and entire words suitable for poetry: the poet could discover word combinations by turning the five concentric discs and observing the indicator fixed in the center by a staple. The first (and smallest) disc lists forty-eight prefixes, the fifth twenty-four suffixes. The three middle discs form combinations of all possible monosyllabic German *Stammwörter* (root words), based on Schottelius's theory; they contain sixty initial letters or consonant clusters, twelve stem vowels or diphthongs, and 120 consonants or consonant clusters. The ring captured the entire German language in its simplicity and variety and reflected the language's capacity to represent nature in its entirety.

Harsdörffer displayed his aesthetically sensitized, if rather formulaic literary language in his pastoral writings. In the *Pegnesisches Schäfergedicht* (Shepherd Poem of the Pegnitz, 1644), a prose eclogue by Harsdörffer and the Buchner student Johann Klaj, two shepherds, Strefon (the society name for Harsdörffer) and Klajus, wander through a pastoral grove that resembles the surroundings of Nuremberg and engage in a singing contest on love, marriage, and fertility:[159]

> Sie sollen und wollen der Liebe geniessen /
> Das lange das bange Verlangen versussen.
> Eh kömmet der Meyen /
> Die Erden zu neuen /
> Eh gläntzet der Lentzen /
> Jn unseren Grentzen /
> Die Felder zu weyhen /
> Sie werden so ringen /
> Daß jederman höret die Wiegen besingen.

[They ought to and want to savor love, to sweeten the long and uneasy longing. Before May comes to renew the earth, before spring is glistening in our lands to bless the fields, they will toil such that everyone hears the celebration in song of the cradles.]

Prominent stylistic features, prototypical for the Nuremberg poetic style, are the extensive use of dactylic verse, the imitation of the sounds of nature through onomatopoeia, the heavily metaphoric language, and mannerist tendencies.

Mystical poetry was perhaps the most aesthetically innovative German poetry of the seventeenth century (it will be discussed in a separate section below). Speaking of innovators at this point, however, we must mention the unusually playful and metaphorical language of Catharina Regina von Greiffenberg, as well as the speculative, cabbalistic approach to literary language of Daniel Czepko and Johannes Scheffler and the exuberant verbal artistry of Quirinus Kuhlmann, all of whom will be discussed later in this chapter.

The Gallant Ideal: From Mannerist to Classicist Style

Two important shifts in poetic production took place in the second half of the seventeenth century. First, although the Opitzian reform continued to be held in high esteem, it affected practice less and less as the century progressed. Innovators — especially Harsdörffer and Zesen — became the new models, and influences from Spain and Italy are apparent. Second, we find increasingly diverse themes, poetic styles, and literary movements; in literary history these developments are often labeled as formalism, mannerism, Marinism, concettism, Second Silesian School, gallant poetry, French classicism, or early Enlightenment.

Literary styles came under the influence of the French system of behavioral norms: how one dressed, moved, talked, and comported oneself in good company. *Galante conduite*, or gallant conduct,[160] had a courtly origin but became increasingly obligatory for the urban middle classes as well. The adoration of women expressed itself, of course, in love poetry, typically in the Petrarchist vein. The signs of gallant behavior were prudence, skillful use of language, political acumen, and proper manners. Knowledge was no longer bookish or pedantic, but now worldly, witty, playful, tactful, and always suited to the situation.[161] The gallant ideal was essentially political in that it devised self-interested tactics, whether in the private or public realm, and required specific skills — cultural knowledge, appropriate conduct, and strategies for pursuing personal objectives.[162]

Most gallant poems were published either as occasional poems or as parts of anthologies; curiously, their publication peaked in the early eighteenth century, at a time when this poetry was in decline. Independent, single-author editions of gallant poetry were uncommon. The most significant anthology was Benjamin Neukirch's (1665–1729) *Herrn von Hofmannswaldau und andrer Deutschen auserlesener und bißher ungedruckter Gedichte* (Selected and Hitherto Unpublished Poems by Mister von Hofmannswaldau and Other Germans, 7 vols., 1695–1727). Only the first two volumes were edited by Neukirch; the remaining five were edited by Erdmann Uhse (1677–1730), Christian Hölmann (1677–1744), and others.[163] The gallant, mannerist poems by Hofmannswaldau and his followers assume a prominent place in the two Neukirch volumes. Subsequent volumes, however, show a tendency toward a more modest style influenced by French writers, especially Nicolas Boileau-Despréaux (1636–1711).[164]

As any writing was commonly seen as a public — that is, a political and gallant — act, an extraordinary preoccupation with style characterizes the seventeenth century. This promoted a particular style, beginning in the 1640s with writers like Harsdörffer and Klaj, which is commonly referred to as mannerist and which remained dominant until about 1700. Exuberant at best, it could become excessive; some modern scholars described it as pretentious, pompous, or bombastic. Toward the end of the century an increasing number of poets and critics called for a more restrained style for the sake of clearer communication.

Baroque mannerist style had two basic manifestations: the formal-artistic and the material.[165] The formal-artistic, or *concetto* style, pioneered by the Nuremberg writers and refined by Hofmannswaldau, derived from Romance literature, especially Giambattista Marino (1569–1625). Its main characteristics were flowery imagery, hyperbole, onomatopoeia, refined rhyme, varied metrics, and a particularly rich use of figures and tropes. In Germany it is especially associated with the Silesian writers of the second half of the seventeenth century. Ornate formulation tended to take precedence over subject matter, and the Opitzian balance of *res* and *verba* (things and words) was often ignored: clever, witty formulation became an end in itself; the boundaries between words and their meanings were blurred as poetic artistry became part of the message of the text.[166] Mannerist style could also reflect the *acutezza* and *argutezza* ideals of Emanuele Tesauro (1592–1675), Matteo Pellegrini (1595–1652), and Baltasar Gracián (1601–58), which emphasized ambiguity, pointedness, playful use of words and sounds, ironic affectation, and coquetry.

Hofmannswaldau was the originator of gallant poetry in Germany and its most significant representative. His work combines mannerist features and rational, but ironic, intellectualism. He is notable for working with an exceptional variety of stanza forms, for the musicality of his tone and meter, his mastery of the sonnet form and alexandrine verse, and the suppleness of his language.[167] A virtuosic handler of metaphors, he was careful, however, to apply them in moderation.[168] His lone edition of poems, *Deutsche Vbersetzungen vnd Getichte* (German Translations and Poems, 1679), which appeared posthumously, was actually an omnibus edition containing several discrete collections.[169] These include the early *Poetische Grab-Schrifften* (Poetic Funerary Writings), written in 1643; the *Heldenbriefe* (Heroic Letters), presumably completed in 1663; and the late, rather philosophical *Vermischte Gedichte* (Mixed Poems). He wrote many of his poems as early as the 1640s and circulated them among his colleagues in manuscript form. Hofmannswaldau, who was a patrician, apparently had no interest in achieving fame through poetry, unlike most writers of his time. It is also likely he feared that his more licentious poems — his "Lust-Getichte" (pleasure poems) — would provoke moral outrage. Hofmannswaldau's reputation as a great poet was ensured, however, by Neukirch's two volumes (1695 and 1697), which contained mainly work by Hofmannswaldau, including many of the poems he himself had not been prepared to publish.

Hofmannswaldau's *Heldenbriefe*, modeled on Ovid's *Heroides*, introduced a special form of epistolary writing into German literature. They consist of fourteen pairs of verse epistles between amorous noble couples from German history. Each epistle consists of 100 alexandrines with alternating rhyme.[170] They are replete with love imagery, simultaneously provocative and analytical, that stimulates the reader to reflect on the ironies of love and power, even as the rhetorical grandeur inspired by the lovers' suffering creates empathy for their vulnerable humanity.[171] Hofmannswaldau states in his introduction that love play should not be rejected on moral grounds, because erotic love is rooted in natural and divine law.

His later, more philosophical poems avoid the grim moral-religious pessimism of many of his peers. The first stanza of "Gedancken bey Antretung des funffzigsten Jahres" (Thoughts upon Entering the Fiftieth Year), while reflective about the natural loss of life's vitality, does so with cool detachment:[172]

> MEin Auge hat den alten Glantz verlohren /
> Ich bin nicht mehr / was ich vor diesem war /
> Es klinget mir fast stündlich in den Ohren:

Vergiß der Welt / und denck auf deine Baar /
Und ich empfinde nun aus meines Lebens Jahren /
Das funffzig schwächer sind als fünff und zwantzig waren.

[My eye has lost its old luster. I am not what I was before. It rings in my ears almost hourly: forget the world and think of your coffin. And I now sense from the years of my life that fifty are weaker than were twenty-five.]

The poem closes without indulging in *vanitas* topoi, instead praising God as the giver of life and sponsor of the eternal soul, which will endure once the body has been peeled away. This dichotomous worldview is illustrated in the paired poems "Die Wollust" (Lust) and "Die Tugend" (Virtue), which assume opposing viewpoints but are structurally interwoven and ultimately reconcilable through devices of antithesis and chiasm. In "Die Wollust," Epicurus is the teacher and interpreter of "Witz" (wit) and "Weltgeschmack" (universal taste). To reject him is to be an "Unmensch" (brute) and a "Scheusaal dieser Welt" (monster of this world). Erotic desire and the nude female body are gifts of nature and thus part of divine creation.[173] In "Die Tugend," on the other hand, Epicurus administers "Drachenmilch" (dragon's milk) as medicine and "gelbes Schlangengift" (yellow snake's poison) as sustenance. In the end, however, the two poems are compatible: the laws of virtue are restrictive, even tyrannical, but not without value; faith and earthly fulfillment are equally valid pursuits.

Some of Hofmannswaldau's poetic heirs, however, in their quest for rich rhetorical figures and clever word plays, far exceeded the bounds of rhetorical *aptum* (appropriateness) in producing grotesque images and outlandish formulations. For instance, in Heinrich Mühlpfort's (1639–81) "Sechstinne: Wettstreit der haare / augen / wangen/ lippen / halß und brüste" (Sestina: Competition of the Hair, Eyes, Cheeks, Lips, Neck, and Breasts), female breasts are personified as "DIß schwesterliche paar / das voll von flammen hencket / Von aussen vieler hertz mit liebes-öle träncket / Inwendig aber feur als wie ein Aetna schencket" (this sisterly pair that hangs full of flames, outwardly feeds the hearts of many with love's oil but internally dispenses fire like Aetna). The physical attributes of the parts — in their mannerist exaggeration — matter more than the beauty of the woman herself.

After the formal-artistic manifestation of baroque mannerism, the second operated predominantly in the material realm and elevated poetry to the grand style (*stilus grande*). Based on the polymathic ideal, which valued encyclopedic knowledge, this style reveled in the accumulation of obscure metaphors, exotic vocabulary, strained syntax, figures of repetition and contrast, and allusions to mythology, history, natural history, geography, and emblematics. This forced hyperbole owed to Kircher's metaphor machine designed in 1624: a rotating drum, hidden in a cabinet, projected images onto a mirror so that the viewer could see himself as random objects, thus demonstrating the connectedness and comparability of all material things.

The main representative of this form of mannerism was Daniel Casper von Lohenstein, one of the most eminent polymaths in Germany; his contemporaries compared him to a walking library and his works to a cabinet of curiosities. His erudition shaped an extremely ornate style, and he adorned learned and complex contents with a wealth of dazzling metaphors that mostly lacked the fine irony of those of Hofmannswaldau. His writings are full of allusions to mythology, history, natural history, geography, and emblems. Because his polyhistoric, hyperbolic style required texts of a comparable scale, Lohenstein cultivated the larger forms of novels and plays and a correspondingly intense rhetorical and philosophical discourse unsuited to the necessary subtlety of poetic expression.[174] His only collection of poems, *Blumen* (Flowers, 1680), was published as part of a larger work edition. Its three parts consist mainly of epithalamia (wedding poems), epicedia, and religious verse.

"Venus," Lohenstein's most important poem, appeared posthumously in 1695 in the first volume of Neukirch's anthology. It is an encomium to Venus in 1,888 alexandrines and follows the classical generic norms.[175] Lohenstein displays his erudition here by making some 230 different mythological references, mentioning several of them repeatedly. It opens with a dramatic show of erotic love with spring's fertile awakening:

> Izt liebt die gantze welt! des Titans glut wird mächtig
> Die erde zu vermähln / der himmel machet trächtig
> Mit regen ihren schooß / das blumen-gelbe jahr
> Beschwängert ihren bauch / der blumen sommer-haar
> Bekleidet allbereits die unbelaubten wipffel. (vv. 1–5)

[Now the whole world is in love. The Titan's fire rises in power to marry earth. The heavens infuse her womb with rain. The flower-yellow year impregnates her belly. Everywhere the flowers' summer hair clothes the leafless treetops.]

The beauty of Venus's nude body surpasses anything seen before: "Du machtest milch und schnee mit deinem halse grau/ Der marmolstein ward schwarz/ das helfenbein ward rauh" (You turned milk and snow grey with your neck, the marble stone turned black, the ivory became coarse; vv. 175–76). While milk, snow, white marble, and ivory were common metaphors to describe the ideal female complexion at the time, here Venus becomes the unmatched norm of beauty, the crowning metaphor that favors her mythological sensual power of love over cosmological, Neo-Platonic Eros. The poetic celebration of love in the highly metaphoric mannerist style appears as a secular ceremonial cult.[176]

Learned references, which would have been transparent only to readers trained in classical literature, are conspicuous throughout the poem. In one section, Lohenstein enhances an already elaborate geographic description with recondite allusions to mythology and an abundance of metaphors. A few examples may illustrate: Flora, the goddess of spring, is here also the bride of Zephyr and thus also the west wind; Calpe, an obscure name for Gibraltar, considered one of the pillars of Hercules, demarcates the western edge of the Mediterranean and thus of the ancient known world; Amphitrite and Doris are sea nymphs and stand metonymically for the ocean; Cypris is a poetic name for

Aphrodite (Greek for Venus), which indicates her provenance in the eastern Mediterranean; "Hundsstern" (Dog Star) presumably is a reference to Sirius, the brightest star in the sky and part of the constellation of *canis maior*, which rises with the sun during the hottest part of the year.

This level of erudition in poetry, although generally considered within the bounds of rhetorical norms, not only appealed to readers seeking encyclopedic knowledge but also had the social effect of setting apart the learned elite. On a purely intellectual level, however, Lohenstein was attempting to harmonize erotic love with reason, as expressed in his devotion to the tools of classical rhetoric. Finally, one may view his language use as part of a larger cultural argument — one that Leibniz especially will champion — that Germans are capable of witty and learned poetry and possess the requisite *bel esprit.*

The mannerist style and, to some extent, the gallant ideal were increasingly challenged in the years immediately before 1700. Informed by early Enlightenment ideas, theoreticians and poets began to demand more clarity in poetic expression; the demand led to a gradual transition to a leaner classicist style. Under the rubric of *iudicium* (good judgment), Christian Weise (1642–1708) criticized the mannerist style for failing to achieve the political objectives (noted above) of gallant communication and for using rhetorical tools injudiciously and thus obscuring the intended message. Instead, he favored a natural and clear language in the middle style. According to his guiding principle, the prose construction rule formulated in his *Curiöse Gedancken Von Deutschen Versen* (Curious Thoughts on German Verses, 1692), poetic constructions unsuited to prose should likewise be rejected in verse.[177] This principle was observed in the poetry of the prolific Johann Christian Günther (1695–1723), which was indebted to the gallant as well as traditional poetological discourses and humanist ideals. However, the intensity of Günther's language, the expression of personal emotions, and the cultivation of an individual voice identify him as a poet of the early Enlightenment.

This controversy motivated a range of new poetic styles around 1700 as literary production shifted from Silesia to the early enlightened cities, such as Hamburg and Leipzig, and the Saxon and Prussian courts. The new poetry arose as the century's defining crises (war, hunger, Turkish threat, plague) began to fade and optimism was inspired by revolutions in science (Kepler, Galileo, Newton) and secular philosophy (Decartes, Bacon, Leibniz). Influenced by French classicism, particularly by *L'art poétique* (1674) by Boileau-Despréaux, the new stylistic ideals were clarity and naturalness. Every gesture was to be informed by wit — and thus satire and the epigram returned to literary fashion. The *Scherzgedichte* (Jocular Poems, 1652) of Johann Lauremberg (1590–1658) went through numerous printings in the late seventeenth and early eighteenth century.[178] The French-inspired *Satirische Gedichte* (Satirical Poems, 1664) by Joachim Rachel (1618–69), known as the "deutscher Juvenal" (German Juvenal), also enjoyed widespread popularity.

The first poet to make the transition from the *concetto* to the natural-rational style was Friedrich Rudolf Ludwig von Canitz (1654–99), a diplomat by profession and the most important classicist poet in early modern Germany.

Canitz's poems were not published until after his death, in the collection *Neben-Stunden unterschiedener Gedichte* (Various Poems for Leisure Time, 1700). They gained popularity because of his witty and intelligent satires in the style of Boileau and continued to be published and read throughout the eighteenth century.[179] The baroque antithesis of earthly existence and eternal life is no longer in evidence in Canitz, who revealed the distinction between the appearance and the essence of things with candid language.[180] This is demonstrated in his eighth satire, "Der Hof" (The Court), in which the palace, the locus of princely power, is inhabited by the enchantress Circe, who turns it into a madhouse. Courtly life is a carnival where virtue is mocked and vice wears the mask of virtue:

> Denn schmeicheln heißt man hier: sich nach der Zeit beqvemen:
> Verleumden: ohnvermerckt den Gifft der Schlangen nehmen;
>   Den Hochmuth: Freund und Feind frey unter Augen gehn;
>   Den Geitz: mit Wolbedacht auf seine Wirthschafft sehn;
>   Die Pracht: den Purpur nicht mit Niedrigkeit beflecken;
>   Die Falschheit: mit Verstand des andern Sinn entdecken;
>   Den Soff: ein fremdes Hertz erforschen in dem Wein;
>   Die Unzucht: recht galant beym Frauenzimmer seyn. (294)

> [For to flatter here is called: to go with the flow: to slander: to take the poison of snakes unnoticed. Pride: to walk in plain view to friend and enemy. Avarice: to look after one's own finances with vigor. Splendor: not to soil purple with lowliness. Falsehood: to astutely discover the other's intentions. Drunkenness: to examine another's heart in wine. Indecency: to be gallant with women.]

While Logau and others had satirized the excesses of courtly life and the misguided courtier, Canitz's focus is the corrupt and immoral institution itself. However, in a clear departure from the baroque viewpoint, he does not see the world as a whole as being upside down, only the courts.

The general revival in satirical writing around 1700 found expression in the epigrams of the Swiss Johannes Grob (1643–97) and of Christian Wernicke, a particularly sharp critic of the overladen mannerist style.[181] In his poem "Auff Artemons Deutsche Gedichte" (On Artemon's German Poems), Wernicke scorns flaccid metaphors and mocks onomatopoeia as a tired gimmick:[182]

> Artemon hat gelernt an mehr als einem Ort
> Ein unverständlich Nichts durch auffgeblasne Wort'
> In wollgezehlte Reim' ohn' allen Zwang zu bringen;
>   In jedem Abschnitt hört man klingen,
> Schnee, Marmor, Alabast, Musck, Bisem und Zibeht,
> Samm't, Purpur, Seid' und Gold, Stern, Sonn' und Morgenröht'.
> Die sich im Unverstand verschantzen,
> Und in geschlossner Reihe tantzen:
> Zwar les' ich selten sie von Anfang biss ans End',

Doch klopf' ich lachend in die Händ',
Und denck' es sind nicht schlechte Sachen
Aus Schell'n ein Glockenspiel zu machen. (3,7)

[Artemon learned in more than one place to transform, through inflated
words, an incomprehensible nothing into well-measured rhymes without
restraints. In each section, one hears resounding snow, marble, alabaster,
musk ox, muskrat and civet, velvet, purple, silk and gold, stars, sun, and
morning glow. They hide behind incomprehensibility and dance in tight
circles. Of course, I rarely read them from beginning to end, yet I clap
my hands laughing and think that it is not a bad thing to make from bells
a glockenspiel.]

Wernicke reconfirmed the traditional rhetorical rules of *aptum* and *iudicium*
to restore the classical balance between *res* and *verba*. In an epigram called
"Lange Reden" (Long Speeches), he pokes fun at those who violate decorum:

Ein Redner ward gerühmt, der von geringen Sachen
Könt' eine lange Red' in schönen Worten machen;
Agesilaus sprach: Der Schuster wird verlacht,
Der, wenn die Füsse klein, doch grosse Schuhe macht. (10,21)

[An orator was praised if he could make a long speech in beautiful words
out of simple matters. Agesilaus spoke: A shoemaker is ridiculed when he
makes large shoes for small feet.]

Wernicke's critique of mannerist style amounted to more than merely an aesthetic difference. His rationally pragmatic worldview — a product of advances
in scientific thought[183] — fundamentally challenged the excesses of traditional
systems of knowledge represented by mannerist style, especially the material
character of Lohenstein's erudition.

Liturgical and Devotional Song

Seventeenth-century religious poetry of all confessions sought to deepen religious
experience rather than to engage in confessional polemics, which had driven
much religious poetry of the previous century.[184] Sixteenth-century precursors
included Martin Moller (1547–1606), Johann Arndt (1555–1621), Philipp
Nicolai (1556–1608), and Johann Matthäus Meyfart (1590–1642). As religious
poetry in the new century tended away from what had become a rigid Lutheran
orthodoxy and toward personal expressions of piety, its distinction from secular
poetry became less pronounced. Although few writers now specialized in religious poetry — defined primarily as liturgical or devotional — its volume rose.
Genre boundaries were quite fluid, as the poetry of Gryphius demonstrates, and
many poets published devotional and secular poetry side by side.

Liturgical song — including devotional poetry, which often was put to
liturgical use — is distinct from other religious or spiritual poetry: it functioned exclusively in an institutional setting, never merely for private devotion
or general Christian conduct.[185] Lutheran liturgical song, practiced by most of

the important Lutheran pastors, was the only form of poetry to evolve seamlessly out of a sixteenth-century poetic tradition, whether spiritual or secular.[186] Composed almost exclusively in the new standardized German language, it generally obeyed Opitzian norms, particularly alternating meter, and, unlike other poetic genres, did not engage in further formal experimentation. In its natural connection to the oral tradition of the sixteenth century, this genre constituted by far the largest group of poetry, which doubtless owed in part to the continuing condition of illiteracy in Germany.

The dissemination of hymns belonged increasingly to the domain of printed hymnals, however, such as the *Geistreiches Gesangbuch* (Spiritual Hymnal, 1704–11) of Anastasius Freylinghausen (1670–1739) or the Catholic collection, *Catholische Sonn- vnd Feyertägliche Evangelia* (Catholic Sunday and Holiday Evangels, 1653), of Johann Philipp von Schönborn (1605–73), the archbishop and elector of Mainz. Still, hymnals were not yet in general liturgical use, as congregations (still predominantly illiterate) sang few established hymns by heart. Rather, they served mainly a devotional function in the home; indeed, most religious songs were written for personal edification rather than for liturgical use, though many were eventually canonized as church hymns. This is particularly true for songs related to early pietist reforms; the gradual evolution of these songs from domestic to liturgical use further blurred the line between liturgical and devotional poetry.[187]

As the century progressed, hymn collections by single — and now usually named — authors began to appear. A substantial subset of the genre includes eloquent hymns by Weckherlin, Opitz, Gryphius, and Greiffenberg, not intended for liturgical use at all, but composed according to formal Opitzian poetic rules.[188] Johannes Heermann (1585–1647) was the first hymnist to write in accordance with the rules of the Opitzian reforms. His *Devota Musica Cordis, Haus- vnd Hertz-Musica* (Devout Music of the Heart: House and Heart Music, 1630) contains songs intended for private rather than public worship.[189] Heermann was also a pioneer of the *Erbauungslied* (edifying hymn), which could be read strictly as a lyric. His song "O Gott, du frommer Gott" (Oh God, You Righteous God, 1644) introduced the alexandrine to the church hymn,[190] and he experimented with dactylic verse. Martin Rinckart (1586–1649) is remembered today as the author of the chorale "Nun danket alle Gott" (Now Thank We All Our God, 1636). Many of Greiffenberg's later devotional poems belong to the type built around biblical pericopes, as does Logau's cycle of epigrams on the Sundays and feast days (1,9,1–69).

Paul Gerhardt (1607–76), the most significant hymnist since Luther, continued the tradition of devotional and edifying song started by Heermann. Even though only 134 of his hymns are extant, he remains an integral part of Lutheran church song. Many of his songs first appeared in Johannes Crüger's (1598–1662) *Praxis Pietatis Melica/ das ist Ubung der Gottseligkeit* (Practiced Lyrical Piety, that is Practice of Salvation in God, 1647), which was republished in many editions and became the first anthology of sacred songs in modern German. His main work was called *Geistliche Andachten* (Spiritual Devotions, 1667), a collection of 120 songs with musical settings mostly by Johann Georg

Eberling (1637–76). The book was conceived as a devotional book for the private, domestic articulation of piety, not as a hymnal for community performance. His songs were introduced into the Lutheran liturgy only in the eighteenth century. One of Gerhardt's most beloved songs is "An das Angesicht des HErrn JEsu" (To the Countenance of the Lord Jesus, ca. 1655), modeled on the thirteenth-century Latin hymn "Salve caput cruentatum." Its opening verse is typical of Gerhardt in how it combines simplicity of language with effective imagery and rhetorical figures (anaphora, repetition, expansion) to express trust in divine salvation, even in the gloomy hours of Christ's suffering:[191]

> O Haupt vol Blut und Wunden /
> Vol Schmertz und voller Hohn!
> O Haupt zum Spott gebunden
> Mit einer Dornen Krohn!
> O Haupt! sonst schön geziehret
> Mit höchster Ehr und Ziehr /
> Itzt aber höchst schimpfiret /
> Gegrüsset seyst du mir.

[O head covered with blood and wounds, full of pain and full of scorn! O head bound in derision with a crown of thorns! O head, previously beautifully adorned with highest honor and decor — but now utterly humiliated. I greet you.]

Two other writers of devotional songs deserve mention together with Gerhardt. Johann Rist, pastor in Wedel near Hamburg, published several collections of devotional songs with musical accompaniment.[192] The title of one of them, *Frommer und Gottseliger Christen alltägliche Haußmusik* (Everyday House Music for Pious and Devout Christians, 1654), suggests that the songs (with musical settings by various Hamburg composers) were meant for use in the home. Christian Knorr von Rosenroth (1636–89) was a scholar of hermetic, cabbalistic, Hebrew, and alchemical studies at the Sulzbach court northeast of Nuremberg, noted for its promotion of Jewish studies and religious tolerance. Knorr himself remained a steadfast Lutheran, as is evident in his collection of devotional and edifying songs, *Neuer Helicon mit seinen Neun Musen* (New Helicon with Its Nine Muses, 1684). It contains seventy devotional songs with melodies by anonymous composers, as well as a number of other poems. His famous "Morgen-Andacht" (Morning Devotion) is reminiscent of Gerhardt:[193]

> Morgen-Glantz der Ewigkeit
> Licht vom unerschöpften Lichte
> Schick uns diese Morgen-Zeit
> Deine Strahlen zu Gesichte:
> Und vertreib durch deine Macht
> unsre Nacht.

[Morning glow of eternity, light from unexhausted light, send us at this morning time your rays of light to see. And dispel with your might our night.]

The morning light — divine light — displaces the dark night — spiritual darkness. The last two lines of each stanza reflect on the presence of the divine light. Knorr's proclivity for nature mysticism made him a favorite of the Pietists.

Because the Catholic Church did not allow communal singing during Mass, the hymn was not of central importance in Catholicism. New songs were written mostly for nonliturgical religious purposes, such as procession, pilgrimage, vesper, and catechesis, and were disseminated by religious orders; likewise, fewer Catholic devotional songs were composed. Most important Catholic authors of songs were clerics active in southern Germany, notably Johann Khuen (or Kuen, 1606–75), Albert Graf Curtz (1600–1671), Jacob Balde (1604–68), Prokop von Templin (1608–80), and Laurentius von Schnüffis (1633–1702). The songs of Johannes Scheffler, collected in *Heilige Seelen-Lust Oder Geistliche Hirten-Lieder* (Holy Joy of the Soul, Or Spiritual Pastorals, 1657), were also received enthusiastically by Protestants well into the eighteenth century, despite his conversion to Catholicism in 1653. Friedrich Spee von Langenfeld (1591–1635) elevated Catholic devotional song aesthetically in his *Trvtz-Nachtigall* (Defiant Nightingale, completed 1634, published 1649). Many of Spee's songs appeared in both Catholic and Protestant hymnals.[194]

Calvinists limited congregational singing to the Psalter and generally excluded use of the organ from the Reformed service until the eighteenth century; in certain iconoclastic communities, church organs were destroyed. The Reformed movement thus did not contribute to the evolution of the hymn in the seventeenth century, but it helped promote the new nonconfessional genre of psalm song. The most successful and popular psalm translation was the 1573 version of the *Geneva Psalter* by Lobwasser.[195] Weckherlin borrowed the Lobwasser model for his *Gaistliche Gedichte* (Spiritual Poems, 1648); Opitz published his own version, *Die Psalmen Davids Nach den Frantzösischen Weisen gesetzt* (The Psalms of David, Set to French Airs, 1637). Neither translation, however, matched the popular appeal of the Lobwasser *Psalter*.[196]

Lutheran worship increasingly included the cantata after 1660 to provide a musical and poetic setting for the sermon. The early form, sometimes referred to as solo cantata, consisted of poems performed in the form of an aria, interrupted by ritornellos.[197] Its simple strophic form made it suitable for domestic use as well. The origins of the genre have been traced back both to earlier Italian forms, which were secular in character, and to chorale-based works by Michael Praetorius (1571–1621), Johann Hermann Schein, and Samuel Scheidt (1587–1654).[198] One of the most important centers for its early cultivation was the court at Weissenfels (Saxony), where Johann Philipp Krieger (1649–1725) was *Kapellmeister*. In the early eighteenth century a more complex form began to evolve that included narrative recitatives and da capo arias.[199] Major practitioners and innovators were Erdmann Neumeister (1671–1756), Georg Philipp Telemann (1681–1767), and, especially, Johann Sebastian Bach (1685–1750).

A related musical genre, the oratorio, also has its roots in the seventeenth century. The oratorio is cast with various performance roles, but the story, which is usually biblical, is told rather than acted out. The Lutheran *historia*, a musical setting of a scriptural story, was an early antecedent, though its function was strictly liturgical. One of the most successful compositions was the *Historia der frölichen und siegreichen Aufferstehung unsers einigen Erlösers und Seligmachers Jesu Christi* (Story of the Blessed and Victorious Resurrection of Our Only Redeemer and Savior Jesus Christ, 1623) by Heinrich Schütz (1585–1672). The genre was also known under the terms *actus oratorius* and *actus musicus*. The practice was to draw narrative and dialogue passages from a biblical story and to interpolate nonbiblical material, whether in chorale stanzas, freely composed poetry, or prose. Another form of oratorio was the passion, which reached its ultimate expression in the Leipzig compositions of Bach, most notably in his *Matthäus-Passion* of 1727 (revised 1736).[200] The first work to be explicitly designated an oratorio was *Der blutige und sterbende Jesus* (Bleeding and Dying Jesus, 1704) by Christian Friedrich Hunold (Menantes, 1681–1721). It was set to music by Reinhard Keiser (1674–1739), and when it was performed in Hamburg in the following year it was roundly criticized by the city fathers and the clergy as excessively theatrical and because it omitted the Evangelist's narrative.[201] The Nuremberg poet Johann Klaj invented and experimented with a type of declamatory oratorio (*Redeoratorium*). Several included musical settings by Sigmund Theophil Staden (1607–55). Klaj recited his first declamatory oratorio, *Aufferstehung Jesu Christi* (Resurrection of Jesus Christ), in a Nuremberg auditorium on Easter Sunday 1644.[202]

Mystical and Early Pietist Poetry

Baroque mysticism produced some of the most original and innovative poetry of the time, but it was not universally endorsed by theologians. Many mystics with a Lutheran background avoided institutional affiliation in their attempt to transcend sectarian issues and were consequently subjected to orthodox attacks and pressures, even censorship, whereas what few Catholic mystics there were tended to observe traditional doctrine. The Jesuit Johann Spee was the outstanding Catholic mystic.[203] He took as his inspiration the great German and Spanish mystics, such as Meister Eckhart and Ignatius of Loyola. Although he accepted most poetic reforms of the Protestant Opitz, Spee nevertheless aspired to create a specifically Catholic poetic discourse. His language is metaphorically complex, blending agonizing, Petrarchist love for Jesus, pastoral elements from Theocritus and Vergil, motifs from the tradition of the *laudes*,[204] and erotic imagery from the Song of Songs.[205] He often unites secular and spiritual imagery in contrafacta, as in "Hirtengesang, vber das Creutz, vnd Aufferstehung Christi" (Eclogue on the Cross and the Resurrection of Christ).[206] The antitheses of microcosm and macrocosm and of temporal and eternal life are central to his worldview.[207] His "bridal mysticism" integrates the sacred and the erotic into a union made possible by *Jesusminne* (love for Jesus).

Spee's most significant collection, *Trvtz-Nachtigall*, comprises fifty-two poems based on the *Spiritual Exercises* (1548) of Ignatius, the founder of the Society of Jesus. It contains songs of praise (*laudes*) for Christ and God's creation, from macrocosm to microcosm; lamentations for his suffering; and songs that offer penance. Finally, the love for Jesus, the good shepherd, is allegorized, in fifteen eclogues, as bucolic love. While this nature imagery may allegorize the yearnings of the soul for Jesus, it falls short of being able to express the glory of transcendent God.[208] The speaker as bride (*sponsa*) yearns for Christ, the groom (*sponsus*). In the third poem, "Anders Liebgesang der gespons JESV" (Another Love Song of the Spouse of Jesus), he describes the radiant flame of love:[209]

> Das Flämmlein das ich meine,
> Jst JESV süsser Nam:
> Es zehret Marck, vnd Beine,
> Frist ein gar wundersam.
> O süssigkeit in schmertzen!
> O schmertz in süssigkeit!
> Ach bleibe noch im hertzen,
> Noch bleib in Ewigkeit.

[The little flame that I have in mind is Jesus' sweet name. It devours marrow and bone, eats away wondrously. O sweetness in pain! O pain in sweetness! Alas, remain in my heart, remain throughout eternity.]

The love for Jesus remains bittersweet, for the desired union is unattainable.

Early modern mysticism in the Lutheran tradition was inspired by Neo-Platonism, which had entered Christian thought in Renaissance Florence. One of its seminal texts was the *Corpus hermeticum*, published in 1463 by Marsilio Ficino (1433–99) in a Latin translation; it was thought to have predated even the writings of Moses and was therefore held in great reverence.[210] Neo-Platonic natural philosophy helped to reveal the hidden forces behind nature and contributed to the rise of the disciplines of magic, alchemy, and astrology,[211] as described in *De occulta philosophia* (1533; written 1510) by Heinrich Cornelius Agrippa von Nettesheim (1486–1535) and in various writings of Theophrastus Philippus Bombastus von Hohenheim, known as Paracelsus (1493–1541). In one of his epigrams, Scheffler draws the analogy between the three Paracelsian primordial substances (*tria prima*) — fire (sulphur), salt, and mercury — which correlate to the Holy Trinity:[212]

> Die Dreyeinigkeit in der Natur.
> Daß GOtt Dreyeinig ist / zeigt dir ein jedes Kraut /
> Da Schwefel / Saltz / Mercur / in einem wird geschaut. (1,257)

["The Trinity in Nature." That God is Trinitarian every herb will show you, because sulphur, salt, and mercury are seen as one.]

Alchemy was rarely considered an actual science but rather an allegory of the transmutation of metals into pure matter, such as gold or the Philosopher's

Stone. Thus, in its search to transcend materiality and temporality, alchemy became symbolic of the transformation of the sinner and the purification of the soul. Alchemical language served as a source of imagery for the literary expression of spiritual and mystical beliefs.[213]

Protestant baroque mysticism focused on individual rather than collective experience. It was not practiced institutionally — in monasteries or church congregations — but rather in private circles.[214] The mystical experience was thought to occur in three stages: purification and cleansing (*via purgativa*), illumination (*via illuminativa*), and mystical union with the numinous (*via unitiva*). Important sixteenth-century precursors of mystical thought were the spiritualists Kaspar von Schwenckfeld (1489–1561), Valentin Weigel (1533–88), and the Paracelsian physician and theologian Johann Arndt. The Schwenckfeld biographer and educator Daniel Sudermann wrote more than 2,000 songs; in the 1620s, during the Thirty Years' War, he championed an eclectic approach to reaching peace, laying stress on the common basis of Christian faith.[215] Johann Valentin Andreae (1586–1654), a Lutheran theologian, promoted a general reform of Christian practice in his Rosicrucian writings; his prose parable *Chymische Hochzeit* (Chemical Wedding, 1616) lays out the path for the purification of the soul and ultimate mystical union. The theosophical and pansophical writings of Jacob Böhme (1575–1624), a cobbler in Görlitz (Silesia), exerted profound influence on an entire century of mystical thought, even though most of his writings circulated only in manuscript form, due to the opposition of Lutheran orthodoxy.[216]

The Böhme biographer Abraham von Franckenberg (1593–1652) was the leader of an important group of mystical poets in Silesia. Theodor von Tschesch (1595–1649), Czepko, and Scheffler were its most prominent members. Czepko's main work, the *Sexcenta Monodisticha Sapientum* (Six Hundred Single Couplets of Wise Men), written between 1640 and 1647 and circulated in manuscript form — it was suppressed in Breslau and not published until 1930 — was inspired by Tschesch's *Vitae cum Christo* (1644), a collection of 1,200 mystical Latin epigrams. Czepko's volume consists of six books, each containing an introductory sonnet and 100 couplets in alexandrines. The titles of the six sonnets refer to the six stages of illumination (after the six days of the creation) laid out in the thirteenth-century speculative theologian Bonaventure's *Itinerarium mentis in Deum* (Journey of the Mind into God). Czepko's collection ends before a seventh volume, since on the seventh day of creation God rested: the ecstatic union with God can occur only in silence and cannot be expressed with words.[217] The inherent paradox in mystical expression becomes evident here: its attempt to say with words what is ultimately inexpressible. Mystical poetry did not merely describe but created the mystical experience in language. The German baroque epigram is an ideal vehicle for this kind of expression, lending itself structurally (via pointed, brief, bipartite alexandrines) to antithetical or paradoxical statements, which are commonly conveyed through chiasm, paronomasia, or asyndeton, as in the following Czepko poem:[218]

Gott: Mensch:

und

Mensch: Gott

Mensch kleide dich in Gott: Gott wil sich in dich kleiden,
So wird dich nichts von IHM, auch IHN von dir nichts
   scheiden. (2,67)

["God — Man, and Man — God." Man, cloak yourself in God: God
wants to cloak himself in you. Thus, nothing will separate you from HIM,
and nothing HIM from you.]

In his long introductory poem, Czepko mentions the two books in which
divine will reveals itself: the Bible and the book of nature:

Gut: der Weißheit in der Natur nachschlagen:
Besser: Seeligkeit in der Schrifft erfragen:
An dem besten: Natur und Schrifft vergleichen,
Als der göttlichen Wahrheit feste Zeichen.

[Good: to look up wisdom in nature. Better: to query bliss in scripture.
Best: to compare nature and scripture as the sure signs of divine wisdom.]

This pantheistic view of the divine is central to Czepko's mystical poetry. The
soul does not seek the divine; rather the divine enters the soul, which is eager
to generate self-knowledge. This spiritual, divinely inspired subject is
autonomous, and the human, called "ICH" (I), thus a God-like creative being:

ICH.

I. Gott. C. Christus. H. Das ist der Heilge Geist:
Mensch, wann du sprichest: ICH: schau, wo es dich hin weist. (6,95)

["ICH." I. God. C. Christ. H. That is the Holy Ghost. Human, when
you say: I: look where it points you.]

Czepko suggests here that God, Christ, and the Holy Ghost reside in the individual's soul, because the letters of the word "ich" represent the persons of the
Trinity. The linguistic link, though speculative, serves as ontological proof.
The Neo-Platonic, cabbalistic, and hermetic traditions understood language as
a motivated system of signs: sounds and their graphic representations were
inherently bound to realities, just as God had empowered Adam to name
things according to their created properties.[219] The word had creative power,
as affirmed at the beginning of the Gospel of John; and human language,
which derived from the divine language, mirrored divine power and dignity.
Mystics therefore sought to understand and even recreate the Adamic language by focusing on etymologies, word roots, speculations, or onomatopoeia.
For Böhme and his followers, words engendered spiritual contemplation.[220]

Johannes Scheffler befriended Franckenberg in 1649 on his return to Silesia
after his studies abroad. In 1653, he converted to Catholicism and adopted the
name Angelus Silesius (Silesian Angel); in 1661, he was ordained as a priest.
Confessional issues thus were central in his writings. His *Cherubinischer*

Wandersmann (Cherubinic Wanderer, 1675), a collection of 1,666 epigrams (mostly couplets) and ten sonnets (at the beginning of the sixth book), was influenced by Böhme and Czepko. It was actually a republication of his earlier *Geistreiche Sinn- und Schlußreime* (Ingenious Epigrams and Apophthegms, 1657), expanded with a polemical sixth book that gives expression to the views assumed following his conversion. The wanderer's goal is that his soul be united with the pure divine essence; he will arrive at the desired state of eternal stillness only by overcoming his physical needs and human will. The cherubinic (angelic) path leads to mystical insight by intellectual means expressed through antithesis and paradox, as illustrated by the epigram "GOtt ist nicht tugendhafft" (God is not Virtuous):

> GOtt ist nicht tugendhafft: Auß ihm kombt tugend her /
> Wie auß der Sonn die Strahln / und Wasser auß dem Meer. (5,50)

[God is not virtuous. Virtue emanates from him, as out of the sun the rays, and the water out of the ocean.]

The ostensibly heretical statement "God is not virtuous" shocks until one recalls that, since God is the very essence of virtue, the word cannot be attributed to him. The implied syllogism in the double analogy from the natural world (sun and water) helps to resolve the paradox. Becoming one with God is possible only by abandoning one's self:

> Wenn man Vergöttet ist.
> Mensch / wann dich weder Lieb berührt / noch Leid verletzt /
> So bistu recht in GOtt / und GOtt in dich versetzt. (1,293)

["When One is Imbued by God." Human, if neither love moves you nor sorrow injures you, then you are properly transported into God, and God into you.]

The chiasm in the final line implies that the divine seeks the individual soul as much as the individual seeks God. Scheffler is the master of epigrammatic form and its economical demands on language; he brings the aesthetic norm of *argutia* into the service of the mystical experience of God.[221]

In the same year, Scheffler published another significant collection of mystical poetry: *Heilige Seelen-Lust Oder Geistliche Hirten-Lieder* (Holy Desire of the Soul, or Spiritual Pastoral Songs), a collection of 205 songs. Here, the path to the mystical experience may be called seraphic-affective, unlike the cherubinic-intellectual of the *Cherubinischer Wandersmann*. The poems are permeated by the imaginative sensuality of bridal imagery and the sufferings of Christ. As Scheffler avows in the *Cherubinischer Wandersmann*, however, both methods constitute a single path:

> Des GOttverliebten Wunsch.
> Drey wünsch' ich mir zu seyn: erleucht wie *Cherubim* /
> Geruhig wie ein Thron / entbrandt wie *Seraphim*. (3,165)

["Wish of the One in Love with God." Three things I wish to be: enlightened like cherubim, still like a throne, burning like seraphim.]

Catharina Regina von Greiffenberg was the most significant German woman poet of the seventeenth century and a major mystical poet.[222] Her largest work, comprising three books of twelve meditations each on the life, suffering, and death of Jesus, is *Andächtige Betrachtungen* (Devout Contemplations, 1672, 1678, 1693).[223] The text is mostly in prose, but numerous poems are interspersed. Greiffenberg's thought is anchored in Lutheran doctrine, but with motifs that oscillate between stoic *constantia* and mystical sensuousness.[224] Her collection *Geistliche Sonnette / Lieder und Gedichte* (Spiritual Sonnets, Songs, and Poems, 1662) contains 250 sonnets and 150 songs, nonstrophic poems, and epigrams. The first two quatrains of the sonnet "GOttlobende Frülings-Lust" (God-praising Spring Desire) demonstrate Greiffenberg's preference for euphoric imagery built on lively metaphorical and analogical constructions:[225]

> JAuchzet / Bäume / Vögel singet! danzet / Blumen / Felder lacht!
> springt / ihr Brünnlein! Bächlein rauscht! spielet ihr gelinden Winde!
> walle / Lust-bewegtes Träid! süsse Flüsse fliest geschwinde!
> opffert Lob-Geruch dem Schöpffer / der euch frisch und neu gemacht!
>   jedes Blühlein sey ein Schale / drauff Lob-Opffer ihm gebracht /
> jedes Gräslein eine Seul / da sein Namens-Ehr man finde.
> an die neu-belaubten Aestlein / GOttes Gnaden-Ruhm man binde!
> daß / so weit sein Güt sich strecket / werd' auch seiner Ehr gedacht.

> [Rejoice, trees! Birds, sing! Dance, flowers; fields, laugh! Leap, you fountains! Brooks, rush! Play, you mellow winds! Weave, lust-filled grain field! Sweet rivers, flow swiftly! Sacrifice praise-scents to the creator who made you fresh and new! Each blossom, be a bowl in which praise-sacrifices are brought to him; each blade of grass be a pillar, where one finds his name's honor. To the newly leaf-covered branches may one tie God's grace-fame! so that as far as his domain stretches his honor will be remembered.]

The verbal playfulness and onomatopoeia, along with the lively trochees, are typical of the Nuremberg manner and convey a sense of the fresh vitality of God's creation. However, the second quatrain has a decidedly pantheistic feel: the divine spirit permeates all of creation. Together with Spee and Scheffler, Greiffenberg thus stands at the beginning of pantheist nature poetry in Germany.[226]

The poetry of Quirinus Kuhlmann is peculiar because of its blend of religious ecstasy and excessive formalism. His linguistic eruptions arose from a combination of cabbalist and alchemist conceptions of language he had encountered in the writings of Athanasius Kircher and the thirteenth-century philosopher Ramón Lull. His early collection of sonnets, however, *Himmlische Libes-küsse* (Heavenly Love Kisses, 1671), was influenced by Harsdörffer, another student of combinatory technique (*ars combinatoria*). The first and last two lines from the sonnet "Der Wechsel Menschlicher Sachen" (The Change of Human Affairs) may serve as an example:[227]

Auf Nacht / Dunst / Schlacht / Frost / Wind / See / Hitz /
   Süd / Ost / West / Nord / Sonn Feur und Plagen/
Folgt Tag / Glantz / Blutt / Schnee / Still / Land / Blitz /
   Wärmd / Hitz / Luft / Kält / Licht / Brand und Noth:
[…]
Alles wechselt; alles libet; alles scheinet was zu hassen:
Wer nur disem nach wird-dencken / muß di Menschen
   Weißheit fassen.

[After night, haze, battle, frost, wind, ocean, heat, south, east, west,
north, sun, fire, and torment follow day, shine, blood, snow, calm, land,
lightning, warmth, heat, air, cold, light, fire, and woe. (. . .) All is changing; all is loving; everything seems to hate something: whoever contemplates this will grasp human wisdom.]

The message of life's transitoriness is reminiscent of the stoic poetry of
Gryphius. Kuhlmann, however, both here and in the collection's title, also
invokes a pantheistic concept of love that is both religiously and erotically
charged.[228] The sonnet shows formal innovation: verses with eight iambic feet,
with a closing couplet in trochees. Rather than following traditional German
usage of the Petrarchan structure (two quartets plus two tercets), Kuhlmann
opts (as did Shakespeare) for three quartets and a couplet. Except for the couplet, the entire sonnet is asyndetic, and each two lines form a pair, the images
of which contrast directly as an illustration of the changing nature of things
human.

    Kuhlmann encountered the writings of Böhme in 1673 in a way that
altered his life and work. He became convinced that Böhme's theory of the
interrelatedness of word sounds and their phonetic and graphic representations
was accurate. With messianic fervor, he began to speculate on the creator-like
powers contained in his own name. He proposes in his main work, the
Kühlpsalter (Kuhlmann's Book of Psalms, 1677–86), a chiliastic, visionary collection, to establish a "Kühlmonarchie" (or "Monarchia Jesuelitica"). With
himself at its head, as Jesuel (Son of God's Son) or "Kühlmonarch," he will
vanquish the antichrist and usher in the millennium, which will be a time of
"Erquickung" (revitalization) or "Kühlung" (cooling). In its earliest conception, the *Kühlpsalter* was to comprise ten books with 150 songs, by analogy to
the 150 biblical psalms. One hundred and fifteen of the songs, having together
more than 20,000 verses in innovative stanza form, were published between
1684 and 1668 in Amsterdam, a haven for religious dissidents.[229] Each song
and each subheading has a prose prologue with an autobiographical note,
which in turn is interpreted prophetically according to scriptural parallels and
personal speculations, producing a kind of autohagiography.[230] Since
Kuhlmann imagines that his language derives from divinity, he spares no effort
to discover appropriately expressive rhetorical devices: unusual metaphors,
asyndeton, anaphora, polyptoton (repetition of a word in its various possible
forms), among many others. His expressive reach for verbal-natural unity leads
to composing the final twenty-two songs without rhyme.[231]

He began to turn his speculations into reality by undertaking a fanatical mission of conversion of the Turks (undertaking a journey to Constantinople in 1678), Jews (suddenly abandoning his plan in 1681 to travel to Jerusalem), and Russians, leading him ultimately to Moscow, where he was burned at the stake as a conspirator and heretic in 1689. In "Jerusalemitische Geistreise" (Journey to Jerusalem in the Spirit), the struggle against the antichrist and for the "Kühlreich" takes the form of a prayerful journal: "Mein Vater, höhr! Ich schrei im Jesusnahm! / Di Kühlzeit kommt, um di mein Jesus kam" (My father, hear! I cry out in Jesus' name! The Kuhl time will come, for which my Jesus came; vv. 12477–78).

There is a political and social dimension to Kuhlmann's uncompromising call for reform, or revolt, at the end of the last extant *Kühlpsalm*, no. 117. Here he calls the seventy peoples, or tribes, who originated at Babel to overthrow their rulers and join the Jesus monarchy under his command.

> Fresst, Sibtzig Völker, fresst nun eure Könige!
> Gott gibt euch alle mir zum Jesu Kühlmannsthume!
> Ost, West, Nord, Sud ist mein zwölfeines Reich!
> Auf, Kaiser, Könige! Gebt her Kron, hutt und
>   Zepter! (vv. 20015–18)

> [Devour, you seventy peoples, now devour your kings! God gives you all to me for my Jesus Kuhlmanndom! East, west, north, south is my twelve-in-one empire! Onward, emperors, kings! Surrender crown, hat, and scepter.]

Furthermore, he bids the rulers of his time — calling them by the universal name of "Brüder" (brothers) — to ensure peace, unity, and an end to confessional strife: "Hasst euren unterscheid! Seid Brüder allesamt, Von einem Stamm erzeugt, von einem Christ erlöst!" (Hate your difference! Be brothers altogether, conceived from one tribe, redeemed by one Christ; vv. 16636–37). These demands echo those of the humanists and will become part of the Enlightenment program.[232]

The subjectivity of the seventeenth-century mystical poets seems to have anticipated the expression of personal experience in the poetry of the Age of Goethe, with Pietist poetry serving as an essential link.[233] The most important movement of Protestant religious renewal since the Reformation,[234] Pietism, a strong cultural force in Germany from about 1690 to 1750, shared with mysticism a focus on individual piety, personal religious experience, and opposition to institutional orthodoxy. However, in its quest to complete the spiritual ideals of the Reformation, Pietism also sought to overcome confessional divides, at least between Lutheranism and Calvinism, and to develop new forms of communal life that valued strict ethical norms and self-control.[235] Pietism shared the early Enlightenment's quest for blissful physical life, self-actualization, and self-sanctification; this was possible only by defying church authorities.[236] The work that best expressed the aspirations of German Pietism was *Pia desideria: oder Hertzliches Verlangen / Nach Gottgefälliger Besserung der wahren Evangelischen Kirchen* (Pia Desideria: or, Heartfelt Desire for a God-Pleasing Reform of the True Evangelical Church, 1675) by Jacob Spener (1635–1705). Spener hoped to find a spiritual path to ending confessional discord and to effect a turn from a Christianity of theology to one made vital through an active, faith-driven community of believers.[237]

While Pietist poetry continued in the mystical tradition of learned religious poetry, it also retained connections to the tradition of Lutheran devotional and liturgical song, which enhanced its emotional, even charismatic expression of faith and thereby promoted community building and the regeneration of society. Church hymns again, as they had for Luther, served as a vehicle for the communication and propagation of a religious reform movement. Pietist hymns, however, were sung not only in church but in secular institutions as well. August Hermann Francke (1663–1727), the founder of the *Franckesche Stiftungen* — a variety of educational and social institutions in Halle — institutionalized singing hours for his pupils at the orphanage by 1703.[238]

The two most important collections of early Pietist hymns were compiled by Freylinghausen and continued to be influential throughout the eighteenth century. The enlarged edition (1705) of the *Geist-reiches Gesang-Buch* (Spiritual Hymnal, 1704) contained 758 songs and 174 printed melodies; the sequel, *Neues Geist-reiches Gesang-Buch* (New Spiritual Hymnal, 1714), included 815 songs and 158 melodies. Heinrich Georg Neuss (1654–1716) and Johann Porst (1668–1728) compiled additional song collections during the period of early Pietism. Christian Friedrich Richter (1676–1711) contributed twenty-four songs to Freylinghausen's hymnals, both of which are still in use in Lutheran worship. Other significant authors of early Pietist songs were Joachim Neander (1650–80), Johann Kaspar Schade (1666–98), Johann Heinrich Schröder (1666–99), and Johann Burchard Freystein (1671–1718). Emilia Juliane von Schwarzburg-Rudolstadt (1637–1706) was one of several women who authored Pietist hymns. Among the most important later Pietist poets were Gerhard Teersteegen (1697–1769) and Nikolaus Ludwig von Zinzendorf (1700–1760).

Perhaps the most significant poet of early Pietism was Gottfried Arnold (1666–1714); he also authored important theoretical writings. Arnold published most of his poetry before 1701, during his radically anti-institutional period.[239] For Arnold, individual experience is decisive for a relationship with God, and he accordingly rejects the verbal re-creation of the *unio mystica*. Personal insight often stands in analogy with inspiration by nature, as in "Spatziergang mit JEsu" (Leisurely Walk with Jesus) from his first collection, *Göttliche Liebes-Funken* (Divine Love Sparks, 1698), which contains 169 poems and songs:[240]

> Es ist ja wahr / im Feld siehts lieblich aus /
> Wo alles sich mit Blumen kan bezieren:
> Ich aber geh auch hier in meinem Hauß
> In aller Still mit meinem Lamm spatzieren.
> Da scheint die Sonn / da singt die Nachtigal /

> Da grünts und blühts / da rauschen frische Quellen.
> Ich seh da nichts als Jesum überall /
> Sein Engel-Chor erfüllet alle Stellen.
> Er ist die Sonn / die Liebe / der Gesang /
> Dabey die Hoffnung grünt / und reine Wasser springen.
> Ist das nicht gnung bey meinem schönen Gang?
> Er soll mich ja zum Paradiese bringen.

[It is true; the meadow looks lovely, where everything can be adorned by flowers: I, however, go for a walk here in my house as well, in all silence, with my lamb. There the sun is shining, there the nightingale is singing, there it is greening and blossoming, there fresh springs rush. I see nothing but Jesus everywhere, his angelic choir filling all places. He is the sun, love, song, while hope is greening and pure waters springing. Is this not enough on my beautiful walk? Indeed, it should take me to paradise.]

The divine spirit permeates not just nature but the subject's personal space as well. Nature imagery addresses the affects and helps communicate the blissful feeling created by the divine presence, yet it is not an essential conduit. Arnold's language is less rhetoricized than that of mystical literature, and he makes less overt use of poetic devices. While the *vers commun* of this poem allows for antithetical treatment of the topic, it is lighter than Scheffler's alexandrines. Arnold expresses personal experience and individualized piety; but as he remained committed to humanist ideals of erudition, the imagery of his poetry is conventional. Many of his poems allude to bridal mysticism or are allegories based on the Song of Songs. In others, alchemical images of rebirth and transformation serve as allegories for the experience of the subject in search of the numinous.[241]

Conclusion

The tradition of learned poetry in the vernacular has distinct beginnings early in the seventeenth century, but it has no equally distinct ending. Rather, learned poetry gradually evolves into poetic forms of the Enlightenment. The time around 1700 is as much a period of continuity as it is a period of discontinuity. Many poetic traditions that we associate with the first half of the eighteenth century have their roots in the seventeenth: the gallant movement; the radical religious renewal of mysticism and pietism leading to personalized forms of religious expression, the first stirrings of an individualized *Empfindsamkeit* (sensibility), rational social critique, and not least a shared literary language. The lasting contributions of the seventeenth century, particularly of its second half, are the growing complexity of the literary landscape; the emerging pluralism of ideas, styles, genres, and modes of expression; and the increasing diversity of voices in poetry.

Notes

[1] Hans-Georg Kemper, *Epochen- und Gattungsprobleme*, vol. 1 of *Deutsche Lyrik der frühen Neuzeit* (Tübingen: Niemeyer, 1987), 11.

[2] For a discussion of early modern German poetics see the chapter by Joachim Knape in this volume. Also Peter Hess, "Dichtkunst," in *Historisches Wörterbuch der Rhetorik*, ed. Gerd Ueding (Tübingen: Niemeyer, 1994), 2:643–68.

[3] Ulrich Müller, "Sangverslyrik," in *Spätmittelalter, Reformation, Humanismus*, vol. 2 of *Deutsche Literatur: Eine Sozialgeschichte*, ed. Ingrid Bennewitz and Ulrich Müller (Reinbek: Rowohlt, 1991), 46–69, here 46; Dieter Burdorf, *Einführung in die Gedichtanalyse*, 2nd ed. (Stuttgart: Metzler, 1997), 3.

[4] Goethe mentions this in his *Noten und Abhandlungen zum West-östlichen Divan* (1819), here cited in Burdorf, *Einführung in die Gedichtanalyse*, 4.

[5] Michael Feldt, *Lyrik als Erlebnislyrik: Zur Geschichte eines Literatur- und Mentalitätsypus zwischen 1600 und 1900* (Heidelberg: Winter, 1990), 11.

[6] Emil Staiger, *Grundbegriffe der Poetik* (Zürich: Artemis, 1946), 13–44.

[7] Kemper, *Epochen- und Gattungsprobleme*, x.

[8] On the transition from the Middle Ages to the early modern see the chapter by Graeme Dunphy in this volume.

[9] Wilhelm Kühlmann, "Neo-Latin Literature in Early Modern Germany."

[10] See the detailed study by Rolf Wilhelm Brednich, *Die Liedpublizistik im Flugblatt des 15. bis 17. Jahrhunderts*, 2 vols. (Baden-Baden: Koerner, 1974–75).

[11] Thomas Cramer, *Geschichte der deutschen Literatur im späten Mittelalter* (Munich: DTV, 1990), 324.

[12] Burghart Wachinger, "Liebeslieder vom späten 12. bis zum frühen 16. Jahrhundert," in *Mittelalter und frühe Neuzeit: Übergänge, Umbrüche und Neuansätze*, ed. Walter Haug (Tübingen: Niemeyer, 1999), 1–29; for a contrasting view see Manfred Kern, "Hybride Texte — Wilde Theorie? Perspektiven und Grenzen einer Texttheorie zur spätmittelalterlichen Liebeslyrik," in *Deutsche Liebeslyrik im 15. und 16. Jahrhundert*, ed. Gert Hübner (Amsterdam: Rodopi, 2005), 11–45, here 16.

[13] Gert Hübner, "Die Rhetorik der Liebesklage im 15. Jahrhundert: Überlegungen zu Liebeskonzeption und poetischer Technik im 'mittleren System,'" in Hübner, ed., *Deutsche Liebeslyrik*, 83–117, here 87.

[14] Helmut Tervooren, *Sangspruchdichtung*, 2nd ed. (Stuttgart: Metzler, 2001), 127–30.

[15] Horst Brunner, *Die alten Meister: Studien zur Überlieferung und Rezeption der mittelhochdeutschen Sangspruchdichter im Spätmittelalter und in der frühen Neuzeit* (Munich: Beck, 1975), 1–12.

[16] Cramer, *Geschichte der deutschen Literatur*, 330.

[17] Eva Klesatschke, "Meistersang," in Bennewitz and Müller, eds., *Spätmittelalter, Reformation, Humanismus*, 70–80, here 70.

[18] Max Wehrli, *Vom frühen Mittelalter bis zum Ende des 16. Jahrhunderts*, vol. 1 of *Geschichte der deutschen Literatur von den Anfängen bis zur Gegenwart* (Stuttgart: Reclam, 1980), 730.

[19] In *Deutsche Literatur des 16. Jahrhunderts*, ed. Adalbert Elschenbroich (Munich: Hanser, 1981), 1:321–22.

[20] Barbara Könneker, *Hans Sachs* (Stuttgart: Metzler, 1971), 11–12.

[21] Robert W. Scribner, *For the Sake of Simple Folk: Popular Propaganda for the German Reformation*, 2nd ed. (Oxford: Clarendon, 1994), 59.

[22] Kemper, *Epochen- und Gattungsprobleme*, 4.

[23] For drinking songs see Norbert Haas, *Trinklieder des deutschen Spätmittelalters* (Göppingen: Kümmerle, 1991).

[24] Rebecca Wagner Oettinger, *Music as Propaganda in the German Reformation* (Aldershot, UK: Ashgate, 2001), 19–20; also Peter Burke, *Popular Culture in Early Modern Europe*, rev. ed. (Aldershot, UK: Ashgate, 1996), 24–27.

[25] On song books see Albrecht Classen, *Deutsche Liederbücher des 15. und 16. Jahrhunderts* (Münster: Waxmann, 2001).

[26] Cramer, *Geschichte der deutschen Literatur*, 313; extensive list of collections, 313–18; also Hans Rupprich, *Das Zeitalter der Reformation*, vol. 4/2 of *Geschichte der deutschen Literatur von den Anfängen bis zur Gegenwart* (Munich: Beck, 1973), 241–45.

[27] Oettinger, *Music as Propaganda*, 32.

[28] On this and other issues of Reformation (and early modern) music see the chapter by Steven Saunders in this volume.

[29] Klaus Düwel, ed., *Gedichte 1500–1600: Nach den Erstdrucken und Handschriften in zeitlicher Folge* (Munich: DTV, 1978), 149.

[30] Herbert Walz, *Deutsche Literatur der Reformationszeit: Eine Einführung* (Darmstadt: Wissenschaftliche Buchgesellschaft, 1988), 30–31.

[31] Communal song belongs under the heading of popular song, discussed above, since it cannot be separated from other forms of secular song.

[32] See, for example, Artur Göser, *Kirche und Lied: Der Hymnus "Veni redemptor gentium" bei Müntzer und Luther: eine ideologiekritische Studie* (Würzburg: Königshausen & Neumann, 1995).

[33] For instance the Marian sequence "Verbum bonum et suave," published ca. 1496 as a broadside entitled "Der Sequentz Verbum bonum getütscht durch Sebastianum Brant." Oettinger, *Music as Propaganda*, 90–92.

[34] Christopher Boyd Brown, *Singing the Gospel: Lutheran Hymns and the Success of the Reformation* (Cambridge: Harvard UP, 2005), 169. See also the comprehensive volume by Friedrich Blume et al., *Protestant Church Music: A History*, trans. F. Ellsworth Peterson (New York: Norton, 1974). For language and style of hymns see Waldtraut Ingeborg Sauer-Geppert, *Sprache und Frömmigkeit im deutschen Kirchenlied: Vorüberlegungen zu einer Darstellung seiner Geschichte* (Kassel: Stauda, 1984).

[35] Gerhard Hahn, *Evangelium als literarische Anweisung: Zu Luthers Stellung in der Geschichte des deutschen kirchlichen Liedes* (Munich: Artemis, 1981).

[36] In Elschenbroich, *Deutsche Literatur*, 1:20.

[37] For an introduction to Lutheran hymns and hymnals see Brown, *Singing the Gospel*, 1–25. On hymnals see Albrecht Classen, "The German Kirchengesangbuch: A Literary Phenomenon of the Sixteenth Century," *Daphnis* 30 (2001): 665–89.

[38] Mary Jane Haemig, "Elisabeth Cruciger (1500?–1535): The Case of the Disappearing Hymn Writer," *Sixteenth Century Journal* 32 (2001): 21–44.

[39] Walter Blankenburg, "The Music of the Bohemian Brethren," in Blume, *Protestant Church Music*, 591–607.

[40] Rupprich, *Das Zeitalter der Reformation*, 257–58.

[41] Rolf Wilhelm Brednich, "Hutterische Liedtraditionen des 17. Jahrhunderts," in *Literatur und Volk im 17. Jahrhundert: Probleme populärer Kultur in Deutschland*, ed. Wolfgang Brückner et al. (Wiesbaden: Harrassowitz, 1985), 2:589–600.

[42] Helmut K. Krausse, "Religiöse Lyrik," in *Zwischen Gegenreformation und Frühaufklärung: Späthumanismus, Barock 1572–1740*, vol. 3 of *Deutsche Literatur: Eine Sozialgeschichte*, ed. Harald Steinhagen (Reinbek: Rowohlt, 1985), 418–29, here 419.

[43] Walter Blankenburg, "Church Music in Reformed Europe," in Blume, *Protestant Church Music*, 507–90, here 517; Jan R. Luth, "Aulcuns pseaulmes et cantiques mys en chant: A Strasburg, 1539," in *Der Genfer Psalter und seine Rezeption in Deutschland, der Schweiz und den Niederlanden: 16.-18. Jahrhundert*, ed. Eckhard Grunewald et al. (Tübingen: Niemeyer, 2004), 9–19.

[44] Ralf Georg Czapla, "Transformationen des Psalters im Spannungsfeld von gemeinschaftlicher Adhortation und individueller Meditation: Paul Schedes Psalmen Davids und Psalmi aliquot," in Grunewald et al., eds., *Der Genfer Psalter*, 195–215.

[45] Lars Kessner, "Ambrosius Lobwasser: Humanist, Dichter, Lutheraner," in Grunewald et al., eds., *Der Genfer Psalter*, 217–28.

[46] Karina Kellermann, *Abschied vom 'historischen Volkslied': Studien zu Funktion, Ästhetik und Publizität der Gattung historisch-politische Ereignisdichung* (Tübingen: Niemeyer, 2000), 5.

[47] Cramer, *Geschichte der deutschen Literatur*, 318 and 327.

[48] Kellermann, *Abschied vom 'historischen Volkslied*,' 6.

[49] On rhymed speeches see Cramer, *Geschichte der deutschen Literatur*, with respect to this paragraph, esp. 101 and 321.

[50] The Latin genre is treated in this volume by Wilhelm Kühlmann in his chapter on Neo-Latin literature.

[51] In Elschenbroich, *Deutsche Literatur*, 1:334.

[52] Wilhelm Kühlmann, "Das Zeitalter des Humanismus und der Reformation," in *Geschichte der deutschen Lyrik vom Mittelalter bis zur Gegenwart*, ed. Walter Hinderer, 2nd ed. (Würzburg: Königshausen & Neumann, 2001), 49–73, here 56.

[53] Anthony J. Harper, *German Secular Song-Books of the Mid-Seventeenth Century: An Examination of the Texts in Collections of Songs Published in the German-Language Area between 1624 and 1660* (Aldershot, UK: Ashgate, 2003), 3–9.

[54] Eckhard Bernstein, "Humanistische Standeskultur," in *Hansers Sozialgeschichte der deutschen Literatur*, vol. 1, *Die Literatur im Übergang vom Mittelalter zur Neuzeit*, ed. Werner Röcke and Marina Münkler (Munich: Hanser, 2004), 97–129, here 97–102.

[55] Eckart Schäfer, "Conrad Celtis' Ode an Apoll: Ein Manifest neulateinischen Dichtens in Deutschland," in *Gedichte und Interpretationen*, vol. 1, *Renaissance und Barock*, ed. Volker Meid (Stuttgart: Reclam, 1982), 83–93.

[56] On the early modern German emblem see the chapter by Peter M. Daly in this volume.

[57] Wulf Segebrecht, *Das Gelegenheitsgedicht: Ein Beitrag zur Geschichte und Poetik der deutschen Lyrik* (Stuttgart: Metzler, 1977); Hans-Henrik Krummacher, "Das barocke

Epicedium: Rhetorische Tradition und deutsche Gelegenheitsdichtung im 17. Jahrhundert," *Jahrbuch der deutschen Schiller-Gesellschaft* 18 (1974): 89–147; Ruth Ledermann-Weibel, *Zürcher Hochzeitsgedichte im 17. Jahrhundert: Untersuchungen zur barocken Gelegenheitsdichtung* (Zürich: Artemis, 1984); Klaus Garber, *Göttin Gelegenheit: Das Personalschrifttums-Projekt der Forschungsstelle 'Literatur der Frühen Neuzeit' der Universität Osnabrück* (Osnabrück: Universitätsverlag Rasch, 2000), 13–15; Rudolf Drux, "Casualpoesie," in Steinhagen, ed., *Zwischen Gegenreformation und Frühaufklärung*, 408–17, here 408.

[58] Friedrich von Logau, *Deutscher Sinn-Getichte Drey Tausend* (1654; repr., Hildesheim: Olms, 1972), 3:176 (3,10,18). In epigram 3,8,59 he calls his poems "Nacht=Gedancken." See also Andreas Palme, *'Bücher haben auch ihr Glücke': die Sinngedichte Friedrich von Logaus und ihre Rezeptionsgeschichte* (Erlangen: Palm & Enke, 1998), 36–46.

[59] The formulation in Horace's poetics (v. 333) is "aut prodesse volunt aut delectare poetae."

[60] A cabbalistic method of interpretation "by interchanging words whose letters have the same numerical value when added" (OED).

[61] Umberto Eco, *The Search for the Perfect Language* (Oxford: Blackwell, 1995), 25–33; Veronika Marschall, *Das Chronogramm: Eine Studie zu Formen und Funktionen einer literarischen Kunstform: Dargestellt am Beispiel von Gelegenheitsgedichten des 16. bis 18. Jahrhunderts* (Frankfurt am Main: Lang, 1997), 178–232.

[62] Peter Hess, " 'Nachäffin der Natur' oder 'aller Völker Sprachen'? Zur Rolle visueller Bildlichkeit in Poetik und Rhetorik der Barockzeit," in *Künste und Natur in Diskursen der Frühen Neuzeit*, ed. Hartmut Laufhütte (Wiesbaden: Harrassowitz, 2000), 1047–62.

[63] Even Herder a century later called the seventeenth century emblematic: *Sämmtliche Werke*, ed. Bernhard Suphan (Berlin: Weidmann, 1887), 16:230.

[64] Peter Hess, " 'Ein lusthauß der Nimfen und Feldtgötter': Zur Rolle der Topik in der Erzählprosa des 16. und 17. Jahrhunderts," *Daphnis* 19 (1990): 25–40.

[65] Ferdinand van Ingen, "Zum Selbstverständnis des Dichters im 17. und frühen 18. Jahrhundert," in *Literary Culture in the Holy Roman Empire, 1555–1720*, ed. James A. Parente Jr. et al. (Chapel Hill: U of North Carolina P, 1991), 206–24; Barton W. Browning, "Poets Addressing Themselves: An Authorial Posture in Seventeenth-Century German Poetry," in Parente Jr. et al., eds., *Literary Culture*, 225–35. On poetic self-representation see Urs Herzog, *Deutsche Barocklyrik: Eine Einführung* (Munich: Beck, 1979), 89–148.

[66] Michael Schilling, "Höfische Lyrik," in *Hansers Sozialgeschichte der deutschen Literatur*, vol. 2, *Die Literatur des 17. Jahrhunderts*, ed. Albert Meier (Munich: Hanser, 1999), 316–32.

[67] Hans-Georg Kemper, "Von der Reformation bis zum Sturm und Drang," in Franz-Josef Holznagel et al., *Geschichte der deutschen Lyrik* (Stuttgart: Reclam, 2004), 95–260, here 143.

[68] Works written in German in the sixteenth century were mainly "populist." Peter Skrine, "The German-Speaking Countries," in *The Cambridge History of Literary Criticism*, vol. 3, *The Renaissance*, ed. Glyn P. Norton (Cambridge: Cambridge UP, 1999), 591–99, here 593.

[69] Ulrich Gäbler, *Huldrych Zwingli* (Munich: Beck, 1983), 48.

[70] Both *vers commun* and alexandrine are iambic verses, the former with five feet and a caesura after the second stressed syllable, the latter with six feet and a caesura after the third stressed syllable.

[71] Düwel, ed., *Gedichte*; on the Gessner poem, 172–73; on the following poem by Froe, 217.

[72] Volker Meid, *Barocklyrik* (Stuttgart: Metzler, 1986), 20.

[73] Düwel, ed., *Gedichte*, 174. This poem is a good example of an extreme confessional polemic of the early to mid-sixteenth century. Here, the Catholic Church is associated with chaos and godlessness.

[74] Düwel, ed., *Gedichte*, 222; Achim Aurnhammer, "Johann Fischarts Spottsonette," *Simpliciana* 22 (2000): 145–65, here 155.

[75] Gerald Gillespie, *German Baroque Poetry* (New York: Twayne, 1971), 26–33.

[76] On German Petrarchist poetry see the chapter by Gerhart Hoffmeister in this volume.

[77] Volker Meid, "Lyrik," in Steinhagen, ed., *Zwischen Gegenreformation und Frühaufklärung*, 367–84, here 367. For a systematic discussion of baroque song see Werner Braun, *Thöne und Melodeyen, Arien und Canzonetten: Zur Musik des deutschen Barockliedes* (Tübingen: Niemeyer, 2004).

[78] James A. Parente Jr., "German-speaking Centres and Institutions," in Norton, ed., *The Cambridge History of Literary Criticism*, 3:364–70, here 366.

[79] Kemper, "Von der Reformation," 152.

[80] Gillespie, *German Baroque Poetry*, 33; Eberhard Czucka, "Poetologische Metaphern und poetischer Diskurs: Zu Theobald Höcks 'Von Art der Deutschen Poeterey' (1601)," *Neophilologus* 71 (1987): 1–23.

[81] Christian Wagenknecht, *Weckherlin und Opitz: Zur Metrik der deutschen Renaissancepoesie* (Munich: Beck, 1971).

[82] On the relationship between Opitz and Zincgref see the chapter by Theodor Verweyen in this volume.

[83] Klaus Garber, "Martin Opitz," in *Deutsche Dichter des 17. Jahrhunderts: Ihr Leben und Werk*, ed. Harald Steinhagen and Benno von Wiese (Berlin: Schmidt, 1984), 116–84, here 165.

[84] Karl Otto Conrady, *Lateinische Dichtungstradition und deutsche Lyrik des 17. Jahrhunderts* (Bonn: Bouvier, 1962), 195–221.

[85] Paul Derks, "Deutsche Barocklyrik als Renaissancelyrik," in Steinhagen, ed., *Zwischen Gegenreformation und Frühaufklärung*, 385–93, here 387.

[86] Volker Meid, "Das 17. Jahrhundert," in *Geschichte der deutschen Lyrik vom Mittelalter bis zur Gegenwart*, ed. Walter Hinderer, 2nd ed. (Würzburg: Königshausen & Neumann, 2001), 74–138, here 79–80.

[87] Gunter E. Grimm, *Letternkultur: Wissenschaftskritik und antigelehrtes Dichten in Deutschland von der Renaissance bis zum Sturm und Drang* (Tübingen: Niemeyer, 1998), 247.

[88] Gary C. Thomas, "Musical Rhetoric and Politics in the Early German Lied," in *Music and German Literature: Their Relationship since the Middle Ages*, ed. James M. McGlathery (Columbia, SC: Camden House, 1992), 65–78, here 65.

[89] Martin Opitz, *Gesammelte Werke*, ed. George Schulz-Behrend (Stuttgart: Hiersemann, 1978), 2/2:392.

[90] Dirk Niefanger, *Barock* (Stuttgart: Metzler, 2000), 92.

[91] Roland Greene, "The Lyric," in Norton, ed., *The Cambridge History of Literary Criticism*, 216–28, here 217.

[92] Stefan Trappen, "Dialektischer und klassischer Gattungsbegriff bei Opitz: Ein übersehener Zusammenhang zwischen Aristoteles, Scaliger und der deutschen Barockpoetik," in *Martin Opitz (1597–1639): Nachahmungspoetik und Lebenswelt*, ed. Thomas Borgstedt and Walter Schmitz (Tübingen: Niemeyer, 2002), 88–98, here 96.

[93] Andreas Solbach, "Rhetorik des Trostes: Opitz' 'Trostgedichte in Widerwertigkeit deß Krieges' (1621/33)," in Borgstedt and Schmitz, eds., *Martin Opitz*, 222–35, here 224.

[94] Anna Carrdus, *Classical Rhetoric and the German Poet 1620 to the Present: A Study of Opitz, Bürger and Eichendorff* (Oxford: European Humanities Research Centre, 1996), 21.

[95] Martin Opitz, *Geistliche Poemata 1638*, ed. Erich Trunz (Tübingen: Niemeyer, 1966), 337.

[96] Klaus Garber, *Martin Opitz — 'Der Vater der deutschen Dichtung': Eine kritische Studie zur Wissenschaftsgeschichte der Germanistik* (Stuttgart: Metzler, 1976).

[97] Eberhard Mannack, "Opitz und seine kritischen Vertreter," in Borgstedt and Schmitz, eds., *Martin Opitz*, 272–79; Blake Lee Spahr, "Love and the Butcher's Son: Or, Martin Opitz and His Critics," *Daphnis* 24 (1995): 603–21.

[98] Justus Georg Schottelius, *Ausführliche Arbeit Von der Teutschen HaubtSprache*, ed. Wolfgang Hecht (Tübingen: Niemeyer, 1967). The discussion of Schottelius is based on vol. 2, pp. 868–997.

[99] Peter Hess, *Epigramm* (Stuttgart: Metzler, 1989), 4–8.

[100] Jutta Weisz, *Das Epigramm in der deutschen Literatur des 17. Jahrhunderts* (Stuttgart: Metzler, 1979), 23.

[101] Krystyna Wierzbicka, "Das geistliche Epigramm im Barock," in *Wege der Lyrik in die Moderne*, ed. Gunter Martens (Würzburg: Königshausen & Neumann, 2003), 23–30.

[102] Wilfried Barner, *Barockrhetorik: Untersuchung zu ihren geschichtlichen Grundlagen* (Tübingen: Niemeyer, 1970), 356–57.

[103] Logau, *Sinn-Getichte*, 2:65 (2,3,59).

[104] Gunter E. Grimm, *Literatur und Gelehrtentum in Deutschland: Untersuchungen zum Wandel ihres Verhältnisses vom Humanismus bis zur Frühaufklärung* (Tübingen: Niemeyer, 1983), 248–49; Hess, *Epigramm*, 43–44.

[105] Harper, *German Secular Song-Books*, 3; for Dach and Albert, 71–111; Brehme, Finckelthaus, and Greflinger, 111–222; Rist, 225–34; Zesen, 249–65; Schirmer, 169–90; Stieler, 303–16.

[106] Judith Aikin, "Caspar Stieler," in *Dictionary of Literary Biography*, vol. 164, *German Baroque Writers, 1580–1660*, ed. James Hardin (Detroit: Gale, 1996), 330–38, here 337.

[107] Harper, *German Secular Song-Books*, 5–6; Harper, *The Song-Books of Gottfried Finckelthaus* (Glasgow: Scottish Papers in Germanic Studies, 1988).

[108] Dorothea Glodny-Wiercinski, introduction to *Von den Madrigalen*, by Kaspar Ziegler (Frankfurt am Main: Athenäum, 1971), 10.

[109] János Riesz, *Die Sestine: Ihre Stellung in der literarischen Kritik und ihre Geschichte als lyrisches Genus* (Munich: Fink, 1971), 165–76.

[110] Greene, "The Lyric," 222: "The early modern sonnet becomes the semi-official vehicle of contemporaneous lyric."

[111] Flora Kimmich, "Sonnets Before Opitz: The Evolution of a Form," *German Quarterly* 49 (1976): 456–71.

[112] Hans-Jürgen Schlütter, *Sonett* (Stuttgart: Metzler, 1979), 79.

[113] So called because the collection was published in the Polish city of Leszno (Lissa), located between Poznań (Posen) and Wrocław (Breslau).

[114] For early modern courtly literature see the chapter by Helen Watanabe-O'Kelly in this volume.

[115] David G. Halsted, *Poetry and Politics in the Silesian Baroque: Neo-Stoicism in the Work of Christophorus Colerus and His Circle* (Wiesbaden: Harrassowitz, 1996).

[116] Jane O. Newman, *Pastoral Conventions: Poetry, Language, and Thought in Seventeenth-Century Nuremberg* (Baltimore: Johns Hopkins UP, 1990), 132–33.

[117] Willard James Wietfeldt, *The Emblem Literature of Johann Michael Dilherr (1604–1669): An Important Preacher, Educator and Poet in Nürnberg* (Nuremberg: Korn und Berg, 1975), 43–57.

[118] Helen Watanabe-O'Kelly, *Court Culture in Dresden from Renaissance to Baroque* (Houndmills, Basingstoke: Palgrave, 2002).

[119] Meid, *Barocklyrik*, 85–87.

[120] Albrecht Schöne, *Kürbishütte und Königsberg: Modellversuch einer sozialgeschichtlichen Entzifferung poetischer Texte: Am Beispiel Simon Dach* (Munich: Beck, 1982). The pumpkin, which quickly flourished but also quickly decayed, became a fitting symbol. For this see George C. Schoolfield, "Simon Dach," in Hardin, ed., *German Baroque Writers, 1580–1660*, 88–106, here 94–95.

[121] Barbara Sturzenegger, *Kürbishütte und Caspische See: Simon Dach und Paul Fleming: Topoi der Freundschaft im 17. Jahrhundert* (Bern: Lang, 1996).

[122] Eberhard Mannack, "Barock-Dichter in Danzig," in *Wahrheit und Wort*, ed. Gabriela Scherer and Beatrice Wehrli (Bern: Lang; 1996), 291–305.

[123] Elio Brancaforte, *Visions of Persia: Mapping the Travels of Adam Olearius* (Cambridge: Harvard UP, 2003), 1–21.

[124] Gillespie, *German Baroque Poetry*, 8, states that Fleming "could write with equal ease lilting Cavalier and student songs, Petrarchistic broodings, meditative sonnets, and dynamic epistles on his adventures."

[125] Jörg-Ulrich Fechner, "Paul Fleming," in Steinhagen and Wiese, eds., *Deutsche Dichter des 17. Jahrhunderts*, 365–84, here 376.

[126] Paul Fleming, *Teütsche Poemata* (1646; repr., Hildesheim: Olms, 1969), 576.

[127] Konstanze Fliedl, "Das Gedicht an sich: Paul Flemings Trostsonett," *MLN* 117 (2002): 634–49, here 641.

[128] Translation by George C. Schoolfield, *The German Lyric of the Baroque in English Translation* (Chapel Hill: U of North Carolina P, 1961), 103.

[129] Fliedl, "Das Gedicht an sich," 645–46.

[130] Robert M. Browning, *German Baroque Poetry 1618–1723* (University Park: Pennsylvania State UP, 1971), 89.

[131] Conrady, *Lateinische Dichtungstradition*, 222–24; on Gryphius's cultural vision see Kemper, "Von der Reformation," 161.

[132] Eberhard Mannack, *Andreas Gryphius*, 2nd ed. (Stuttgart: Metzler, 1986), 45.

[133] Robert M. Browning, "Towards a Determination of the Cyclic Structure of the Secular Sonnets of A. Gryphius," *Daphnis* 14 (1985): 303–24.

[134] Nicola Kaminski, *Andreas Gryphius* (Stuttgart: Reclam, 1998), 53–54.

[135] Ferdinand van Ingen, *Vanitas und Memento Mori in der deutschen Barocklyrik* (Groningen: Wolters, 1966); Wolfram Mauser, *Dichtung, Religion und Gesellschaft im 17. Jahrhundert: Die 'Sonnete' des Andreas Gryphius* (Munich: Fink, 1976).

[136] Andreas Gryphius, *Gesamtausgabe der deutschsprachigen Werke*, ed. Marian Szyrocki (Tübingen: Niemeyer, 1963), 1:9. All further Gryphius poems are taken from this edition.

[137] Marian Szyrocki, *Der junge Gryphius* (Berlin: Rütten & Loening, 1959), 88–89; see Szyrocki further on Gryphius's numerology, 84.

[138] Blake Lee Spahr, *Andreas Gryphius: A Modern Perspective* (Columbia, SC: Camden House, 1993), 28.

[139] Kaminski, *Andreas Gryphius*, 61.

[140] Peter Hess, "Zum Toposbegriff in der Barockzeit," *Rhetorik: Ein internationales Jahrbuch* 10 (1991): 71–88, here 78–81.

[141] Moritz Bassler, "Zur Sprache der Gewalt in der Lyrik des deutschen Barock," in *Ein Schauplatz herber Angst: Wahrnehmung und Darstellung von Gewalt im 17. Jahrhundert*, ed. Markus Meumann and Dirk Niefanger (Göttingen: Wallstein, 1997), 125–44, here 131.

[142] Translation by Schoolfield, *The German Lyric*, 146–47.

[143] Theodor Verweyen, " 'Thränen des Vaterlandes / Anno 1636' von Andreas Gryphius — Rhetorische Grundlagen, poetische Strukturen, Literarizität," in *Traditionen der Lyrik*, ed. Wolfgang Düsing et al. (Tübingen: Niemeyer, 1997), 31–45, here 35–39 and 40–41.

[144] Peter Nusser, *Deutsche Literatur von 1500 bis 1800: Lebensformen, Wertvorstellungen und literarische Entwicklungen* (Stuttgart: Kröner, 2002), 203.

[145] Kaminski, *Andreas Gryphius*, 62–63.

[146] Gunter Ott, *Die 'Vier letzten Dinge' in der Lyrik des Andreas Gryphius: Untersuchungen zur Todesauffassung des Dichters und zur Tradition des eschatologischen Zyklus* (Frankfurt am Main: Lang, 1985).

[147] Pericopes are lessons, based on specific sections of the Bible, which are written out in their liturgical order for each Sunday and feast day in the church calendar.

[148] Renate Gerling, *Schriftwort und lyrisches Wort: Die Umsetzung biblischer Texte in der Lyrik des 17. Jahrhunderts* (Meisenheim am Glan: Hain, 1969), 53.

[149] Hess, *Epigramm*, 71–72.

[150] Wilhelm Kühlmann, "Neuzeitliche Wissenschaft in der Lyrik des 17. Jahrhunderts: Die Kopernikus-Gedichte des Andreas Gryphius und Caspar Barlaeus im Argumentationszusammenhang des frühbarocken Modernismus," *Jahrbuch der Deutschen Schillergesellschaft* 23 (1979): 124–53, here 124.

[151] Counted among the Egyptian gods, Hermes Trismegistus ("the thrice-great"; Latin: Mercurius ter Maximus) is considered the originator of hermeticism.

[152] Jörg Jochen Berns, "Naturwissenschaft und Literatur im Barock unter besonderer Berücksichtigung der Sulzbacher Kulturregion zwischen Amberg, Sulzbach und Nürnberg," *Morgen-Glantz* 5 (1995): 129–73, here 143.

[153] Bruno Rieder, *Contemplatio coeli stellati: Sternenhimmelbetrachtung in der geistlichen Lyrik des 17. Jahrhunderts* (Bern: Lang, 1991), 18–19.

[154] On the evolution of German in the early modern period see the chapter by Renate Born in this volume. Further, Ferdinand van Ingen, "Philipp von Zesen," in Steinhagen and Wiese, eds., *Deutsche Dichter des 17. Jahrhunderts*, 497–516, here 498–99.

[155] Renate Weber, "Die Lautanalogie in den Liedern Philipp von Zesens," in *Philipp von Zesen 1619–1669: Beiträge zu seinem Leben und Werk*, ed. Ferdinand van Ingen (Wiesbaden: Steiner, 1972), 156–81.

[156] *Sämtliche Werke*, ed. Ferdinand van Ingen (Berlin: de Gruyter, 1974), 11:111. Further references to Zesen's works are taken from this edition.

[157] Josef Keller, *Die Lyrik Philipp von Zesens: Praxis und Theorie* (Bern: Lang, 1983), 160–63.

[158] Peter Hess, "Georg Philipp Harsdörffer," in Hardin, ed., *German Baroque Writers, 1580–1660*, 145–60, here 152.

[159] Georg Philipp Harsdörffer and Johann Klaj, *Pegnesisches Schäfergedicht* (1644), ed. Klaus Garber (repr., Tübingen: Niemeyer, 1966), 38.

[160] Peter Hess, "Galante Rhetorik," in *Historisches Wörterbuch der Rhetorik*, ed. Gerd Ueding (Tübingen: Niemeyer, 1996), 3:507–23; Dirk Niefanger, "Galanterie: Grundzüge eines ästhetischen Kozepts um 1700," in *Künste und Natur in Diskursen der Frühen Neuzeit*, ed. Hartmut Laufhütte (Wiesbaden: Harrassowitz, 2000), 1:459–72.

[161] Horst Albert Glaser, "Galante Poesie," in Steinhagen, ed., *Zwischen Gegenreformation und Frühaufklärung*, 394–407, here 394.

[162] Hess, "Galante Rhetorik," 511.

[163] Franz Heiduk, *Die Dichter der galanten Lyrik: Studien zur Neukirchschen Sammlung* (Bern: Francke, 1971), 15–22.

[164] Gillespie, *German Baroque Poetry*, 178, says that later volumes fluctuate between "bombastic," "gallant," and "enlightened" style. The Neukirch anthology, available in a reprint edition, has largely framed the scholarly debate on the poetry of the latter part of the century and contributed to the assessment of the late century as a cohesive period in spite of significant differences in style and content. Neukirch, Johann von Besser (1654–1729), and Otto Christoph Eltester (1666–1738) started out writing mannerist poetry but evolved in the direction of classicist writing. Other gallant poets who practiced forms of mannerist style at least in some of their poetry include Assmann von Abschatz, August Adolph von Haugwitz (1647–1706), Christian Gryphius, Johann Christoph Männling (1658–1723), Neumeister, Gottfried Stolle (Leander, 1673–1744), Johann Burchard Mencke (Philander von der Linde, 1674–1732), Hölmann, Gottlieb Siegmund Corvinus (Amaranthes, 1677–1746), and Hunold.

[165] Grimm, *Letternkultur*, 247.

[166] Rüdiger Zymner, "Zwischen 'Witz' und 'Lieblichkeit': Manierismus im Barock," *LiLi: Zeitschrift für Literaturwissenschaft und Linguistik* 25:98 (1995): 52–79, here 56.

[167] Gillespie, *German Baroque Poetry*, 156.

[168] Veronique Helmridge-Marsillian, "The Philosophical Implications of Hofmannswaldau's 'Albanie,'" *Daphnis* 19 (1990): 687–714, here 689: He "was raising German poetry to its apogee of ornamental euphony and eurhythmic grandeur."

[169] Lothar Noack, *Christian Hoffmann von Hofmannswaldau (1617–1679): Leben und Werk* (Tübingen: Niemeyer, 1999), 452–72.

[170] Erwin Rotermund, *Affekt und Artistik: Studien zur Leidenschaftsdarstellung und zum Argumentationsverfahren bei Hofmann von Hofmannswaldau* (Munich: Fink, 1972), 36.

[171] Michael M. Metzger, "Christian Hoffmann von Hofmannswaldau," in Hardin, ed., *German Baroque Writers, 1580–1660*, 194–202, here 199.

[172] *Gedichte*, ed. Manfred Windfuhr (Stuttgart: Reclam, 1969), 132.

[173] Anselm Schubert, "Auf der Suche nach der menschlichen Natur: Zur erotischen Lyrik Hofmannswaldaus," *Daphnis* 25 (1996): 423–65, here 436–37.

[174] Barton W. Browning, "Daniel Casper von Lohenstein," in *Dictionary of Literary Biography*, vol. 168, *German Baroque Writers, 1661–1730*, ed. James Hardin (Detroit: Gale, 1996), 266–80, here 276: "His grandiloquent, rhetorically, and philosophically intense style often seems too powerful for the genre. There is little place in his verse for subtle or intimate tones."

[175] Charlotte Lang Brancaforte, *Lohensteins Preisgedicht 'Venus': Kritischer Text und Untersuchung* (Munich: Fink, 1974), 75–78.

[176] Kemper, "Von der Reformation," 177.

[177] Weise first formulated this idea in *Der Grünen Jugend Nothwendige Gedancken* (1675), in *Sämtliche Werke*, ed. John D. Lindberg (Berlin: de Gruyter, 1978), 21:306–7.

[178] Winfried Freund, *Die deutsche Verssatire im Zeitalter des Barock* (Düsseldorf: Bertelsmann, 1972), 38.

[179] Documented in the appendix "Zeugnisse zur Wirkungeschichte der Gedichte von Canitz," in *Gedichte*, ed. Jürgen Stenzel (Tübingen: Niemeyer, 1982), 535–62.

[180] Freund, *Die deutsche Verssatire*, 121.

[181] In a multipage footnote to the epigram "Auf die Schlesische Poeten" (Regarding the Silesian Poets), he offers a comprehensive critique of Hofmannswaldau's style.

[182] Christian Wernicke, *Epigramme*, ed. Rudolf Pechel (Berlin: Mayer & Müller, 1909), 215–16.

[183] Grimm, *Literatur und Gelehrtentum*, 532–33.

[184] Irmgard Scheitler, "Geistliche Lyrik," in Meier, ed., *Die Literatur des 17. Jahrhunderts*, 347–76, here 347.

[185] Hans-Georg Kemper, "Das lutherische Kirchenlied in der Krisen-Zeit des frühen 17. Jahrhunderts," in *Das protestantische Kirchenlied im 16. und 17. Jahrhundert: Text-, musik- und theologiegeschichtliche Probleme*, ed. Alfred Dürr and Walther Killy (Wiesbaden: Harrassowitz, 1986), 87–108, here 87–88.

[186] Kemper, *Epochen- und Gattungsprobleme*, 44.

[187] Scheitler, "Geistliche Lyrik," 351, 352, and 355. On their canonization as hymns see Kemper, "Das lutherische Kirchenlied," 89.

[188] Hans-Henrik Krummacher, "Überlegungen zur literarischen Eigenart und Bedeutung der protestantischen Erbauungsliteratur im frühen 17. Jahrhunderts," *Acta Litteraria Academiae Scientiarum Hungaricae* 26, nos. 1–2 (1984): 145–62, here 147.

[189] Carl-Alfred Zell, *Untersuchungen zum Problem der geistlichen Barocklyrik mit besonderer Berücksichtigung der Dichtung Johann Heermanns (1585–1647)* (Heidelberg: Winter, 1971), 155–71.

[190] Helmut K. Krausse, "Religiöse Lyrik," in Steinhagen, ed., *Zwischen Gegenreformation und Frühaufklärung*, 418–29, here 420.

[191] Volker Meid and Ulrich Maché, eds., *Gedichte des Barock* (Stuttgart: Reclam, 1980), 168–71.

[192] Irmgard Scheitler, *Das geistliche Lied im deutschen Barock* (Berlin: Duncker & Humblot, 1982), 230–71.

[193] Commonly translated as "Dayspring of Eternity." Renate Fischetti, ed., *Die deutsche Literatur: Ein Abriß in Text und Darstellung*, vol. 4, *Barock* (Stuttgart: Reclam, 1975), 124.

[194] Bernhard Schneider, "Die Wirkungsgeschichte der Lieder Friedrich Spees in katholischen Gesangsbüchern vom Barock bis zur Gegenwart," in *Friedrich Spee zum 400. Geburtstag*, ed. Gunther Franz (Paderborn: Bonifatius, 1995), 265–348; Gunter Franz, "Spee-Lieder in evangelischen Gesangbüchern," in ibid., 349–76.

[195] Irmgard Scheitler, "Der Genfer Psalter im protestantischen Deutschland des 17. und 18. Jahrhunderts," in Grunewald et al., eds., *Der Genfer Psalter*, 263–81.

[196] Jörg-Ulrich Fechner, "Martin Opitz und der Genfer Psalter," in Grunewald et al., eds., *Der Genfer Psalter*, 295–315.

[197] A *ritornello* is a refrain-like group of two, sometimes three, lines at the end of a stanza.

[198] Friedhelm Krummacher, "The German Cantata to 1800," in *The New Grove Dictionary of Music and Musicians*, ed. Stanley Sadie, 2nd ed. (New York: Grove, 2001), 5:21–32.

[199] An A-B-A form in which the direction "da capo" occurs at the end of the B-section, so that the singer returns to and repeats the A-section.

[200] Howard E. Smither, "Oratorio (Protestant Germany: Baroque)," in Sadie, ed., *The New Grove Dictionary*, 18:512–15.

[201] Scheitler, "Geistliche Lyrik," 369, and Smither, "Oratorio," 514b. In 1712 Barthold Heinrich Brockes based a new passion oratorio on the same text, and it was also set to music by Keiser.

[202] Max Reinhart, "Johann Klaj," in Hardin, ed., *German Baroque Writers, 1580–1660*, 195–205, here 198.

[203] Hans-Georg Pott, "Friedrich Spee und die Mystik," in *Friedrich Spee (1591–1635)*, ed. Theo G. M. van Oorschot and Martin Gerlach (Bielefeld: Aisthesis, 1993), 30–50.

[204] The *laudes*, or *laudes divinae*, are a form of morning prayer; more generally also prayers of acclamation praising God, Jesus Christ, the Holy Spirit, Mary, angels, and saints.

[205] Spee alludes to this interplay of spiritual and worldly motifs in the subtitle of the collection: *Geistliches poëtisch Lvst-Waeldlein* (Spiritual Poetic Forest of Desire). See Manfred Windfuhr, " 'Coincidenta oppositorum': Die barocke Grundspannung profan/geistlich in Spees Werken," in Oorschot and Gerlach, eds., *Friedrich Spee*, 67–92.

[206] Hans-Georg Kemper, *Barock-Mystik*, vol. 3 of *Deutsche Lyrik der frühen Neuzeit* (Tübingen: Niemeyer, 1988), 166–70.

[207] Andrea Rösler, *Vom Gotteslob zum Gottesdank: Bedeutungswandel in der Lyrik von Friedrich Spee zu Josef von Eichendorff und Annette von Droste-Hülshoff* (Paderborn: Schöningh, 1997), 39. Rösler refers to Spee's "antithetisches Lebensgefühl" (antithetical outlook on life).

[208] On nature imagery see G. Richard Dimler, *Friedrich Spee's Trutznachtigall* (Bern: Lang, 1973).

[209] Friedrich von Spee, *Trutz-Nachtigall*, vol. 1 of *Sämtliche Schriften*, ed. Theo G. M. van Oorschot (Bern: Francke, 1985), 22.

[210] A related intellectual tradition, cabbala, was promoted among German humanists by the Hebraicist Johannes Reuchlin (1455–1522).

[211] Rieder, *Contemplatio coeli stellati*, 1–41.

[212] Johannes Scheffler, *Cherubinischer Wandersmann: Kritische Ausgabe*, ed. Louise Gnädinger (Stuttgart: Reclam, 1984), 64.

[213] Fred Ehrman, "Alchemical Images of Rebirth in Pietist Hymns: Overcoming the Duality of Heaven and Earth," *Colloquia Germanica* 28 (1995): 219–43, here 220.

[214] Bernard Gorceix, "Mystische Literatur," in Steinhagen, ed., *Zwischen Gegenreformation und Frühaufklärung*, 206–18, here 208–9.

[215] Kemper, *Barock-Mystik*, 63–70, and Kemper, "Von der Reformation," 127–28.

[216] A comprehensive edition of Böhme's works was not published until 1682, in Amsterdam. A few of his works were published before that, either in Amsterdam or in English translation in London.

[217] Annemarie Meier, *Daniel Czepko als geistlicher Dichter* (Bonn: Bouvier, 1975), 98.

[218] Daniel Czepko, *Sämtliche Werke*, ed. Hans-Gert Roloff and Marian Szyrocki (Berlin: de Gruyter, 1989), 1/2:581.

[219] Gen. 2:19–23. Steffen Martus, "Sprachtheorien," in Meier, ed., *Die Literatur des 17. Jahrhunderts*, 140–55.

[220] Steven A. Konopacki, *The Descent into Words: Jakob Böhme's Transcendental Linguistics* (Ann Arbor: Karoma, 1979), 71.

[221] Wilfried Barner, "Vergnügen, Erkenntnis, Kritik: Zum Epigramm und seiner Tradition in der Neuzeit," *Gymnasium* 92 (1985): 350–71, here 364.

[222] See the chapter on German women poets by Anna Carrdus in this volume.

[223] It is now regarded as her most important work. Lynne Tatlock, "Catharina Regina von Greiffenberg (1633–1694)," in *Deutsche Frauen der frühen Neuzeit: Dichterinnen, Malerinnen, Mäzeninnen*, ed. Kerstin Merkel and Heide Wunder (Darmstadt: Primus, 2000), 93–106, here 104.

[224] Burkhard Dohm, *Poetische Alchimie: Öffnung zur Sinnlichkeit in der Hohelied- und Bibeldichtung von der protestantischen Barockmystik bis zum Pietismus* (Tübingen: Niemeyer, 2000), 19–129.

[225] *Sämtliche Werke*, ed. Martin Bircher and Friedhelm Kemp (Milwood, NY: Kraus Reprint, 1983), 1:225.

[226] Rieder, *Contemplatio coeli stellati*, 175–237.

[227] In Meid and Maché, *Gedichte des Barock*, 268–69.

[228] Sabine Kyora, "Erotischer Genuß, religiöses Ergriffensein: Körperinszenierungen in barocker Lyrik," *Euphorion* 97 (2003): 405–17, here 414.

[229] Johann Nikolaus Schneider, "Kuhlmanns Kalkül: Kompositionsprinzipien, sprachtheoretischer Standort und Sprechpraxis in Quirinus Kuhlmanns Kühlpsalter," *Daphnis* 27 (1998): 93–140, here 96–101. On the structure of the Kühlpsalter see

Gerhart Hoffmeister, "Quirinus Kuhlmann," in Hardin, ed., *German Baroque Writers, 1661–1730*, 230–38, here 236.

[230] Schneider, "Kuhlmanns Kalkül," 97.

[231] Kuhlmann also started work on follow-up projects. In the last two years of his life he published a number of texts under the rubric of *Kühl-Jubel* (Kuhl Jubilations), and in 1687 he worked out a plan for his *Kühlapokalypse* (Kuhl Apocalypse), which was meant to surpass the *Kühlpsalter*.

[232] Kemper, "Von der Reformation," 143.

[233] Steffen Arndal, "Mystik und Dichtung bei Gottfried Arnold," *Gottfried Arnold (1666–1714): Mit einer Bibliographie der Arnold-Literatur ab 1714*, ed. Dietrich Blaufuss and Friedrich Niewöhner (Wiesbaden: Harrassowitz, 1995), 5–19, here 5.

[234] Johannes Wallmann, *Philipp Jakob Spener und die Anfänge des Pietismus*, 2nd ed. (Tübingen: Mohr, 1986), vii. Important precursors of Pietism were William Perkins (1558–1602) in England and Johann Arndt (1555–1621) in Germany, particularly his *Vier Bücher vom wahren Christentum* (Four Books of True Christianity, 1605–10), which was republished by Pietists several times.

[235] Johannes Wallmann, *Der Pietismus* (Göttingen: Vandenhoeck & Ruprecht, 1990), 7.

[236] Hans-Georg Kemper, *Aufklärung und Pietismus*, vol. 5/1 of *Deutsche Lyrik der frühen Neuzeit* (Tübingen: Niemeyer, 1991), 42.

[237] Panajotis Kondylis, *Die Aufklärung im Rahmen des neuzeitlichen Rationalismus* (Munich: DTV, 1986), 563.

[238] He did so perhaps as early as 1698, when the *Stiftungen* were founded. Friedrich de Boor, "Von den privaten 'Singestunden' im Glauchaer Pfarrhaus (1698) zu den öffentlichen 'Ermahnungs=Stunden' im Waisenhaus (1703)," in *Pietismus und Liedkultur*, ed. Wolfgang Miersemann and Gudrun Busch (Tübingen: Niemeyer, 2002), 1–46, here 18–26.

[239] Dohm, *Poetische Alchimie*, 193.

[240] Erich Seeberg, ed., *Gottfried Arnold: Auswahl* (Munich: Langen, Müller, 1934), 269.

[241] Ehrman, "Alchemical Images," 225–27, and Dohm, *Poetische Alchimie*, 215–50.

Early Modern German Narrative Prose

Andreas Solbach

U NTIL THE 1960S RELATIVELY LITTLE WORK had been devoted to the study
of German prose written before the eighteenth century, with the exception of *Simplicissimus Teutsch* (1669), the picaresque novel by Hans Jakob
Christoffel von Grimmelshausen, which will be discussed below. The prevailing opinion was that the *Agathon* (1766) of Christoph Martin Wieland
(1733–1813) was the first German novel of aesthetic quality deserving the
attribute of originality and worthy of broad attention. However, with the
advent of the sociohistorical school of research, which was driven in part by an
inquiry into the origins of modernity,[1] researchers began to show interest in
earlier contexts and mentalities previously ignored. Since the 1970s a surge of
critical text editions, reprints, series, and monographs have introduced many
important writers from the fifteenth, sixteenth, and seventeenth centuries:[2]
Elisabeth von Nassau-Saarbrücken, Hermann Bote von Braunschweig, Jörg
Wickram, Johann Michael Moscherosch, Christian Weise, Duke Anton Ulrich,
Johann Riemer, and Johann Beer, to name only a few.

A German literary prose began to emerge in the late Middle Ages.[3]
Whether anecdotes, short tales, or novelistic forms, late medieval prose narratives bore witness to the continued vitality of German vernacular traditions
into the early modern period. The literary impulses coming from Renaissance
Italy, transmitted almost exclusively in Latin, also had an impact on German
prose narrative.[4] With the spread of mechanical printing throughout Europe
in the second half of the fifteenth century, however, things changed dramatically, if slowly over a considerable period of time. Not only form and content,
including new textual and intertextual combinations, but the modes of production and dissemination experienced profound transformation. Together,
they demonstrate that the early modern intertextual relationships comprised a
Europe-wide web of regional and national literatures.

The slow pace with which this profound transformation took place makes
it difficult to determine a precise *terminus a quo* for the emergence of early
modern German prose. Some scholars take the anonymously authored
Volksbuch (folkbook or chapbook) *Fortunatus* (1509) as the authentic starting
point; others, Wickram's novels from the 1550s. Yet, there are other early
modern prose works as well, some of them considerably older, that could serve
equally well as points of origin: for example, the mid-fifteenth-century writings
of Eleonore von Österreich and Elisabeth von Nassau-Saarbrücken, or the so-
called *Prosaauflösungen* (prose translations) of Middle High German verse

epics, such as the Arthurian folkbook *Wigalois* (1210/20) of Wirnt von Gravenberg, the *Heldengeschichte* (heroic tale) *Wilhelm von Österreich* (1314, prose 1481) of Johann von Würzburg, or the courtly epic *Tristrant und Isalde* (ca. 1170, prose 1484) of Eilhart von Oberg.[5] Older scholarship generally disparaged these texts as trivializations of "genuine" epics, as examples of *gesunkenes Kulturgut* (sunken literary taste),[6] and ordered them according to crude linguistic lines of transmission — French, Latin, or German. Of these, the Latin prose translations were most numerous, though the French tradition was particularly fruitful for scholarship; prose versions of German verse epics were thought to have been of little consequence.[7]

Fifteenth-Century Prose Narration

With the singular exception of the prose version of *Lancelot* of the thirteenth century, the appearance of epic narrative in prose was a phenomenon of the late fourteenth century. With the advent of mechanical print, which contributed to the practice of silent, individualized reading, appreciation for oral epic verse decreased rapidly. But because the prose of Countess Elisabeth von Nassau-Saarbrücken (1393–1456) predates the printing revolution and because scholars previously assumed that prose was the characteristic form of expression for the rising bourgeoisie, one wondered why a noble ruler should employ a decidedly bourgeois literary form.[8] Some scholars believe that Elisabeth embraced the new literary form of expression in order to convey to her peers — and specifically to her son, Johann III — that the rise of a potent urban bourgeoisie made it historically necessary to shift from a confrontational (top-down) to a cooperative (horizontal) type of politics based on a shared form of communication. In her four prose translations (*Herpin, Loher und Maller, Sibille,* and *Hug Schapler*), all probably undertaken before 1437, Elisabeth forces her courtly protagonists to reap the consequences of failing to control their passions, particularly their sexual intemperance and physical violence. Only Hug Schapler overcomes his affective instincts and is rewarded accordingly. Because he extracts himself from dangerous situations, provides unflinching support for the rightful queen, and adapts to the new mores of the court, Hug wins the hand of the princess and the throne.

However, the purpose of *Hug Schapler* was not only to illustrate that brute force must be complemented by the finesse of modern politics; the internal issue of family character and status is also at stake. Hug is the grandson of a butcher, and although his father counts among the nobility, he himself must yet overcome the lingering stigma of his deeper pedigree. These sensational parts of the story in particular, including the hero's erotic adventures, clearly must have captured the attention of the readers of the first printed editions.[9] Although Elisabeth's social message is timely, the composition itself is by no means original but indebted to French sources; her adaptation can unfold only within the framework of the received plot. Nor was her choice of prose unprecedented, for the earlier French translators had already used the vernacular.[10]

Elisabeth's private intentions, therefore, cannot fully account for the meaning of the text and its prose form. Ultimately, one must ponder to what extent the several translations affected the meaning of the original texts.[11]

It is obvious that the prose adaptations both shortened and clarified the text. Descriptive passages and redundant material were often pruned in order to shape the text to the needs and habits of the growing audience of silent readers. For instance, plots were made linear and ambiguities were dissolved.[12] As a result of the gradual reduction in prose of rhetorical ornamentation and stylistic brilliance of the original verse epics, the plot-bearing elements themselves achieved sharper profile, and straight narrative telling became more important than eloquence (*elocutio*). *Telling* (indirect speech) effected a general reduction in *showing* (direct speech); dialogue, in other words, gave the narrator a more "neutral" or "objective" voice. The brilliance of style in the original epics faded in the sobering light of moral-political didacticism. By reducing the subjective features of the verse source, the prose texts achieved greater homogeneity and historical veracity. These changes are present in different degrees from text to text. In sum, the strategies aimed to provide easier access to the text and to make reading in solitude an enjoyable pastime.

Thüring von Ringoltingen's (ca. 1415–83) prose narration *Melusine* (1456, printed 1474) was the most successful prose narrative of the time: sixteen manuscripts, more than ten incunabula, and sixteen editions in the sixteenth century alone testify to its having attracted a large audience.[13] The original source of the story was the verse epic *Mellusine* (ca. 1401–5; only one manuscript survives) by a man known as Couldrette, a French cleric, about whom little is known. Thüring's narrative employs the same method of antirhetorical abbreviation and clarification found in other prose translations. As Hans-Gert Roloff has shown, most early modern prose texts exhibit a characteristic montage technique: prefabricated story elements assembled in linear fashion.[14] In the case of *Melusine*, which has at least three such story elements, the last provides the explanation for the first. The story features a beautiful and mysterious creature (Melusine's origins are uncertain; her mother may have been a water sprite) and a supernatural pact that promises earthly riches and success; it also involves sensational elements of fratricide, infanticide, and dreadful loss (the result of uncontrolled passion), not to mention monstrous entities and ubiquitous battle scenes — all of that in a text that is easy reading for an afternoon. Research first focused on its genealogical implications, which seemed to be transparent to modern structuralist methodology. That the noble lineage of a historical family should include spirits was extraordinary if not unprecedented in literature. Interpretations that focus on the spectacular content usually make much of the narrative's montage technique; others argue that the "de-demonizing" of Melusine was meant to comprise the story's primary focus, and interpret the heroine as belonging to the group of fallen angels that act as God's adversaries.[15] However, Melusine is depicted as a sincere Christian believer, meaning that Thüring includes the realm of spirits among the positive religious experiences. The main import of the story therefore lies elsewhere. Our first clue is the narrative structure itself. When Reymund first meets Melusine he is in distress, having accidentally killed his benefactor, his uncle, the count of Poitiers. Melusine offers to bless him with her love and a prosperous family, but under the condition that he marry her and never inquire how she spends her Saturdays. Reymund is skeptical, but having convinced himself that the pact does not violate his Christian faith, he agrees. Everything begins to happen as Melusine has promised. However, Reymund's brother provokes his suspicions of Melusine, and he spies on her in violation of his pact. He discovers not that she is involved in some illicit activity, but that she is a spirit, half woman, half fish. The pact broken, Reymund fears he may lose everything and sends his brother away in anger. A catastrophe ensues involving Reymund's two sons: Goffroy, angered by the decision of his brother Freymund to take monastic vows, and suspecting the monks' complicity, burns down the monastery, killing not only the monks but his brother as well. Reymund thereupon publicly denounces Melusine. Immediately, the curse takes effect. Reymund realizes that his betrayal means losing both Melusine and his fortune.

One may wonder why Melusine ever established the taboo, since the story offers no hint that she could not have tolerated Reymund's knowledge of her secret. Apart from simply not wanting it to become common knowledge (social shame), there is a potent hidden motive, explained by Goffroy only in the last part of the story. He has found out that Melusine is one of three daughters of Helwas, the king of Albanie, and Persina, who forbade her husband to see her in childbed. Helwas violated this condition and consequently lost his wife and daughters. When they came of age at fifteen, Persina revealed their father's betrayal. In anger, Melusine had him imprisoned in a mountain, and for this misdeed Persina placed a curse on all three daughters. This curse included a taboo. Thus, the taboo around Melusine is the result of the violation of a previous taboo and her subsequent emotional overreaction toward the violator.[16]

Taboos were always a vital part of the sociocultural structure of societies. In *Melusine* the structure of the taboo undergoes a modern shift: the taboo of vision turns into a taboo of doubt. "Thou shalt not see" becomes "Thou shalt not doubt." Doubt, or skepticism, the most prominent intellectual feature of modern thought, arises out of early modern political and rhetorical theories of *dissimulatio* (deception). The art of deceiving becomes the primary cultural technique of acquiring and maintaining power; it results in doubt and the loss of sincerity. In this story it proceeds in three stages. Reymund is at first beset by anxiety over being suspected of the premeditative murder of his benefactor: "so mag ich auss argwon nimmer kommen" (I may never again appear without suspicion); later, he cannot overcome his own suspicion of Melusine; and finally, Goffroy is suspicious of his brother's decision to become a monk. In each instance, doubt causes affective misbehavior that wrecks the good fortune of the protagonists. The anthropological structure of taboo now serves as the basis for the solution to the intellectual dilemma: refuse to doubt. The story of Melusine is convincing precisely because it uses this structure to solve the most important problem in modern thought, the taboo on doubt.

The other especially important early modern prose narrative was *Fortunatus*.[17] Its theme, which originated in the late medieval quests for adventure, shares the concern of *Melusine* with the relationship between wisdom and wealth. The titular hero is given the choice between several kinds of good fortune, and chooses wealth over wisdom. Fortunatus possesses the bag of fortune, which guarantees boundless wealth, and steals the wishing hat, which enables him to wish himself to any place on earth; he also marries, but above his station. His children are equally irresponsible in dealing with the goods they inherit. Andolosia, a victim of his passions, only narrowly escapes multiple catastrophes, and in the end his arrogance provokes an envious nobleman to murder him. His brother Ampedo, while more rational, is ineffectual and less interesting as a moral and literary character. Ultimately, it is Andolosia who exemplifies the message of the story: that wisdom should be chosen over riches; wealth, after all, will naturally flow from wisdom:

> BEy diser hystoria ist tzu vermercken / hette der jung Fortunatus im walde betrachtlichen Weißhait / für den seckel der reichtumb / von der junckfrawen des gelücks erwölt unnd begert / sy wâre ym auch mit hauffen gegeben worden / den selben schatz ym nyemandt hett mügen enpfieren.[. . .] Dem nach ain ygklicher dem solliche wal gegeben wurde / bedencke sich nit lang / volge der vernunfft und nit seinem frechen torechten gemût / und erkyeß Weißhait für reichtumb. (194–95)

> [As this story shows, had young Fortunatus asked the maiden of fortune in the forest for wisdom instead of the wish bag, he would have received riches in abundance that nobody could have taken from him. Thus, anybody faced with such a decision should not ponder long but follow his reason, not his impetuous and foolish mind, and choose wisdom over wealth.]

This prose novel offers much more than conventional moralizing, to be sure. Its plot is carried forward by a series of popular travel stories and in the process dispenses a great deal of information about exotic lands and travel routes.[18] *Fortunatus* remained popular well into the eighteenth century.

An implicit distinction between origin and claim affects the plot of *Fortunatus* throughout. Although the second part of the novel, the story of Ampedo and Andolosia, at first appears to be an inorganic supplement following the death of the titular hero, it is in fact of seminal importance. For one thing, the claims of a *nouveau riche* bourgeoisie are denounced here in religious terms; more importantly, however, it is only in this second part, which deals with the second link of the generational chain, that the ultimate consequences of Fortunatus's faulty judgment are revealed. His original failing lay in his fatal choice of wealth over wisdom. Even if Fortunatus had sensibly handled the magical objects placed at his disposal by fate, the self-invited calamity must inevitably be visited on his children. In the end, Andolosia somewhat redeems the family name by winning back the treasure and doing the good deed of facilitating a royal marriage — hence the final epithet applied to the sinner Andolosia: he is "pious Andolosia."

What connects this novel with *Melusine* is not simply the presence of magical elements, but magical behavior. In *Fortunatus* this behavior is associated with the ostensibly magical power of money in early capitalism, a power itself associated with the wondrous ability to change locations quickly (thus the deeper significance of the travel episodes). In the sixteenth century, people and information began to move with unheard-of speed — some even called it devilish! This rapidly expanding world called forth religious and moral strictures, and the author of *Fortunatus* appeals to these authorities to help rein in the bewildering and seductive powers of this new age. On the other hand, many contemporary readers, while acknowledging the moral dangers, yielded with pleasure to a story that combined the allure of modern worldly possibilities with the tradition of farce.

Sixteenth-Century Prose Narration

Four indigenous prose traditions developed over the course of the fifteenth and sixteenth centuries: farce, prose satire, the prose novel, and the novels of Jörg Wickram. The subject matter of these literary traditions was concentrated around love, history, and society; the topics of society and love were usually treated within the framework of satire and oriented rhetorically around an instructional postulate (*docere*). The sixteenth century was especially receptive to farce, both in its late medieval German form, the *Schwank*, and in its Neo-Latin lines of transmission (*facetiae*).[19] This humorous form of narrative offered a lively repertoire of stock figures, including the cuckolded husband, the lusty vicar, the shrew, the simpleton farmer, and the miser. Its popularity remained high throughout the early modern period, and a generic category of "lower literature" of the farcical type arose in the seventeenth century, when farcical elements formed a montage of episodes in the picaresque novel. The Romance novella, which evolved more or less simultaneously in Europe as a longer form of prose narrative, was largely rejected by German writers in favor of episodic and other smaller forms typical of farce.

The most effective use of episodic *Schwank* is exemplified in the Low German prose novel *Till Eulenspiegel* (1510 or 1511), presumably written by Hermann Bote von Braunschweig (ca. 1460–ca. 1520).[20] Bote collected regional tales about the legendary Till Eulenspiegel and worked them into one of the most significant prose narratives in early modern Germany. Eulenspiegel's pranks typically spring from a literal interpretation of figurative language or statements and commonly result in social mayhem. In the "47. Histori" (47th Story), which takes place in a brewery, he is ordered to boil hops ("Hopffen") for the beer. The brewer's dog is named "Hopff," so Eulenspiegel throws him into the vat. He is astonished that he does not receive praise for his action!

Ulenspiegel sagt: Ja, Her, Ihr haben mich das so geheissen. Ist es nit ein grose Plag, ich thun alles, was man mich heisset, noch kann nienen Danck verdienen. (139)

[Eulenspiegel says: But Master, you told me to do so. Isn't it a great pity: I do everything as told but never receive any thanks.]

Eulenspiegel's pranks both satirize his witless audience and illuminate their intellectual and moral shortcomings. Eulenspiegel — the name means Owl Glass — holds up a mirror to his audience: they must recognize fools not only in the duped victims of his pranks but in themselves. In the "14. Histori" he summons the townspeople to the marketplace to witness that he can fly. His purpose is to ridicule their gullibility, since they should know that humans cannot fly. Nevertheless, here and in his other stories, many of which are heavily scatological, Bote always aims for his readers to enjoy them as entertainment. His didactic thrust reckons with the persuasive power of the damage Eulenspiegel causes, which throws a sharp light on the problems: the stories are inscribed in memory as painful corporeal events. This strategy corresponds to the dominant contemporary pedagogical theory of corporal punishment for errors committed. As a measure administered through the medium of the text, however, its effect remained limited.

In the early prose works of the sixteenth century, a pattern of double, or complementary, reading thus developed: by placing religious and moral aims within a humorous narrative, even heavily didactic texts could be absorbed with pleasure (rhetorical *delectare*). The phenomena of gaps and incongruities that complementary reading sought to bridge stimulated imagination in German writers of prose narrative for the next hundred years. The seventeenth-century novelists Grimmelshausen, Christian Weise (1642–1708), and Johann Beer (1655–1700) continued to work out the implications of this narrative theory. Perhaps for this reason it has been the popular sixteenth-century texts (as well as the novels they inspired in the seventeenth century), not the aesthetically elaborate, presumably more ambitious prose narrations of the later seventeenth and eighteenth centuries (most notably the novels of state, also known as courtly-historical novels), that have enjoyed the most enduring reception down to the present day. Besides *Till Eulenspiegel*, two of the most successful of these sixteenth-century prose narratives were the *Lalebuch* of 1597 and the anonymously authored *Historia von D. Johann Fausten* of 1587, the most famous chapbook of the century.

The farcical themes emanating from the Alsatian small-town community of the Laleburghers continued this tradition of popular texts that generated near mythic power. While their influence on later writers extended beyond the sixteenth century in only a few cases, they exerted lasting influence on the practice of satire. The *Lalebuch* actually achieved its greatest popularity in the slightly altered version of 1598, in which Laleburg and its citizens were renamed *Schilda* and *Schildbürger*. The Schildburghers, or Laleburghers, are the embodiment of harmless stupidity, as symbolized, for example, in their doorless and windowless city hall (constructed, moreover, in triangular shape).

To bring light into their government building they attempt to catch the daylight in sacks; when this fails they remove the roof, though this creates certain problems when it rains. Thus it goes in Schilda. However, the major interest of this folkbook derives less from its entertaining stories — the same can be found in many contemporary collections of short prose — than from the elaborate frame within which the history of the Schildburghers is told. Once upon a time they had been renowned for their wisdom and were in demand as advisers for regional courts and towns. But because the men had to be absent from home much of the time, domestic duties were left in the hands of the women, and as a result the economy deteriorated and the men had to be called home. To prevent this from recurring, the Schildburghers adopted the mask of foolishness; in time, however, they turned into real fools. Such humor made for delightful reading, of course, though what the text actually intended remains unclear, since the message seems to run against the interests of the small community and the state as well. As a work of artistic complexity, however, the *Lalebuch* has been equated with Erasmus's great satire *Praise of Folly* (1511).[21]

In the *Historia von D. Johann Fausten* too,[22] a powerfully didactic work, complementary reading is the basic narrative principle. Faust's damnation and descent into hell allow no doubt as to the sinfulness of his life and deeds. His boundless curiosity leads him into the clutches of the devil, through whose magic he gains access to knowledge and experiences beyond what is humanly permissible. Complementarily, however, the literary Faust functions in the tradition of the adventurous world traveler, whose life and death encompass, in graphic extreme, both fantastic promise and hellish damnation. It is this fascinating tension between the temptations of knowledge and the threat of hell that made this folkbook into a myth-creating exemplar.

The first of the story's three parts explains how Faust conjures up Mephistopheles, one of the underlings in the kingdom of hell; Faust himself is at first of only secondary interest to the more colorful Mephistopheles. The narration then proceeds as a kind of biography. One of its most sensational elements is the precise formulation of the pact with the devil, which provides information about what hell is really like. A strategic problem for the author is to find a way to grant Faust's wish to learn about eternal truths without allowing this learning to conflict with biblical teaching. This is further complicated by the condition that the pact holds only as long as the devil can continue to offer Faust new knowledge. Three narrative strategies are invented to solve this dilemma: Faust's initial interest in the kingdom of hell; the devil's frequent prevarications; and the use of marginalia for commentary. It becomes apparent that the knowledge provided the hero is fundamentally flawed, since it is both patently false and rhetorically manipulated: Faust falls victim to the rhetorical conventions of oratory — yet another illustration of the antagonism between being and appearance. This is borne out by the insubstantiality of the fulfillment of Faust's wishes. The devil in fact has no generative power. Whatever he procures for Faust is either material, and stolen, or it is a figment of fantasy (the women Faust conquers are only guises of the devil himself). Faust learns little of importance that he did not previously know.

The second part of the folkbook presents Faust as astrologer and petty magician who astonishes his audience with cheap tricks. The third part depicts his repentance and downfall after the twenty-four-year pact has expired. A philological problem arising from Luther's translation of Gen. 4:13 lies behind Faust's predicament: "KAin aber sprach zu dem HERRN / Meine Sünde ist grösser / denn das sie mir vergeben werden müge" (But Cain said to the Lord, My sin is greater than can be forgiven me). This rendering implies that Cain's sin of fratricide is too heavy to be forgiven, thus implying the limitations of God's power and grace, whereas the pre-Lutheran interpretation had been simply that Cain could not bear God's punishment. As in *Melusine*, the issue of doubt is central. If Faust can overcome his skepticism, redemption may yet be possible; but he doubts God's grace and thus manifests the ultimate hubris. It is therefore not surprising that the realm of the devil is associated with rhetorical and artistic devices, including fantasy, illusion, and make-believe. Artist and devil are alike in their ability to persuade and manipulate. Given the entertaining mood of the story only straight commentary can drive home the moral:

> Also endet sich die gantze warhafftige Historia vnd Zåuberey Doctor Fausti / darauß jeder Christ zu lernen / sonderlich aber die eines hoffertigen / stoltzen / fürwitzigen vnd trotzigen Sinnes vnnd Kopffs sind / GOtt zu förchten / Zauberey / Beschwerung vnnd andere Teuffelswercks zu fliehen / so Gott ernstlich verbotten hat / vnd den Teuffel nit zu Gast zu laden / noch jm raum zu geben / wie Faustus gethan hat. (123)

> [Thus ends the complete and truthful history and magic of Dr. Faustus, from which each Christian, particularly those who have an unruly, proud, curious, and spiteful mind, may learn to fear God and flee from sorcery, conjuring, and other works of the devil, which God sternly forbids, and not to invite the devil or cede him room as did Faustus.]

During the seventeenth century the Faust topic occupied only a minor place in literature, simply because the problem of doubt it embodied had become ubiquitous in the new scientific age. In the eighteenth century, in works by Lessing and Goethe, the figure of Faust achieved truly mythical dimensions.[23]

Jörg Wickram

Unlike *Faust*, the novels of sixteenth-century Germany's outstanding moralist writer, Jörg Wickram (ca. 1505–61), despite their wide popularity during his lifetime, were quickly forgotten. Later attempts by the Romantics to resurrect interest in Wickram were unsuccessful, and the merits of these works were not appreciated until the methodological reform of the 1960s mentioned at the beginning of this chapter.[24] Wickram was not a *poeta doctus* (learned poet) but an educated craftsman who wrote within the medieval traditions of *Meistergesang* and *Schwank*. In *Ritter Galmy uss Schottland* (Knight Galmy from Scotland, 1539) he created an exceptionally popular novel from the motif of the late medieval knight. In this novel, as well as in the later *Gabriotto und Reinhart* (1551) and *Der Goldtfaden* (The Golden Thread, 1557),[25] Wickram addresses two themes: love that transcends the bounds of class, and the possibility of social ennoblement.[26] An ethos of behavior arises here that is grounded in chaste love and loyalty, the proper aims of and correct path to nobility. This idea of virtuous behavior sometimes makes use of the amorous topos, with its chivalric conventions, as a metaphor for the propagation of bourgeois notions of moral reform. *Der jungen Knaben Spiegel* (Mirror for the Young Man, 1554) and *Von guten und bösen Nachbarn* (Good and Bad Neighbors, 1556), while eschewing love as the central theme, likewise seek such reform. Virtuous behavior becomes a class-transcendent moral and social principle: improper behavior threatens the aristocrat's privilege and wealth, while good and just behavior give the commoner a strategy for prosperity, security, and even social mobility.

The love story in *Galmy* and *Gabriotto und Reinhart* transcends social station. In *Galmy*, Wickram's first novel, the success of this love stands out against received tradition, represented by Enea Silvio Piccolomini's (1405–64) novella *Eurialus und Lucretia* (1444), in which social aspirations failed. Galmy's chaste love for the duchess of Britania corresponds to the medieval ideal of courtly *minne* and, as a test of both his and her honor, is the prerequisite — along with the necessity of keeping their love secret — for the relationship's happy outcome. Although no one can find fault with their relationship, the lovers themselves can hardly expect understanding, and certainly not from the duke. To avoid attracting suspicion, Galmy leaves the court of the duke, who himself shortly thereafter sets off on a pilgrimage. In their absence the marshal tries to seduce the duchess, is rejected, and finds his retribution in accusing her of a relationship with a young man who works in the kitchen. The accuser is later defeated by Galmy in a judicial battle, the duchess regains her honor, the duke dies, and Galmy is able to marry the duchess once he has identified himself as her champion. While chastity and deceitful rationality contribute to this success, only the fortuitous death of the duke makes their marital happiness possible. Chance, indeed, is the all-important factor.

Twelve years passed before Wickram returned to the amorous novel. As in the case of *Galmy*, in which the hero has an adviser and friend in the person of Friedrich (a nonparticipant in the amorous plot), the new novel also features a pair of friends. Gabriotto and Reinhart fall in love, respectively, with the sister of the queen of England and her mistress. This time it is clear from the beginning that the way to happiness will not be eased by the fortuitous death of a ruler. In *Galmy* the *bona fortuna* is predicated on the rationality and virtuousness of the protagonists. The *mala fortuna* of the two pairs of lovers in *Gabriotto und Reinhart* (in explicit comparison with Tristan and Isolde, Euryalus and Lucretia, Pyramus and Thisbe, or Guiscardo and Sigismunda), results from concealed irrational forces within the protagonists themselves. Having dared to marry above their station and fallen victim to their passions and absolutist attitudes, they provoke the king's disfavor and must die. A fatal connection exists between absolute love and death. Only a *Liebestod* can be the commensurate outcome for absolute love. The death of the lovers ultimately owes to the temptation to exceed all boundaries for the sake of an apotheosis in the realm of art. *Galmy* is superior to *Gabriotto und Reinhart* inasmuch as the improbability of love's success may be ascribed to chance; in *Gabriotto und Reinhart* its failure is all too predictable.

Social mobility, while still exceptional in Germany in the mid-sixteenth century, constitutes the central action in *Der Goldtfaden*, the third of Wickram's novels, and his most humorous. Here he has managed to free himself from conventional postulates of virtue and the binary pattern of reward and punishment. One of the most complex and artistic prose texts of the early modern period, this novel was also later esteemed by the Romantics for its poetic quality, especially as expressed in the symbolic value of the golden thread, and for its integration of traditional images. Its love story is indeed exceptionally poetic for the sixteenth century. *Goldtfaden* continues the theme of virtuous love rewarded that had been established in *Galmy* and in *Gabriotto und Reinhart*, but it surpasses them in offering the possibility of a genuinely transcendental love that overcomes social barriers without having to rely on mere chance.

Goldtfaden tells the story of Lewfrid, son of a poor shepherd couple, who marries the countess Angliana and becomes an exemplary prince. Prior to his birth his mother had encountered a tame lion, called Lotzmann, whose calm manner of protection was heralded as miraculous, "so dann zuovor von niemans vormals erhoert was" (to a degree never before heard of by anyone).[27] This unprecedented event is an essential component of the novella genre, as Goethe later observed,[28] and no other Wickram novel reflects as many traits of the Renaissance novella as *Goldtfaden*. (Wickram in fact employs three unprecedented events here: the encounter with the peaceful lion, the appearance of the golden thread, and the marriage of a shepherd's son to a princess.) The lion, as friend, alter ego, and protector (at one point he helps Lewfrid escape an assassination attempt), represents the symbolic center of Lewfrid's world. The shepherd's son is adopted by a wealthy merchant, but he must interrupt his education and flee to the court of a count in order to escape undeserved punishment. Thus, Lewfrid's initial, unmotivated advantage is cancelled. His wondrous birth is now visible only by a lion's-claw birthmark on the left side of his chest; otherwise, he appears to be nothing more than kitchen help. A fight between the boys of his school and the noble boys of another, who hurl disdainful remarks at Lewfrid and his peers, occasions his flight. Lewfrid wins this symbolic battle but in the process discovers a traitor within his school's ranks and has him severely punished. On the one hand, this punishment manifests Lewfrid's sense of justice and his inherently noble pride; on the other hand, it reveals his ruthlessness, and he himself must therefore be subjected to corporal punishment. Among soldiers in early modern Europe, corporeal punishment represented loss of honor, and because Lewfrid unconsciously sees himself as an aristocratic knight, he is compelled to flee his punishment.

At the court Lewfrid's beautiful singing voice and noble bearing signify his exceptional character. Appointed chamberlain to the count's daughter Angliana, he falls in love with her. In this case too, the hero's love is unconditional, though it does not dissolve, as in *Gabriotto und Reinhart*, into mythical pathos. Lewfrid does not aspire to outdo Tristan's love in a grand *Liebestod*. His love manifests itself rather in the symbol of the golden thread. Essentially worthless, this sparkly bagatelle from a *wirckrammen* (hand-loom, a pun on *Wickram*) serves Angliana as a New Year's gag gift, namely, to provoke Lewfrid to compose another love song (the previous New Year's she had not offered her love, and he had made that fact the theme of a moving song). Angliana is thus playing a terrible game with him in order to determine whether he is suffering over her but also to insinuate herself into his poetic work. Lewfrid accepts the golden thread with delight, ignoring its mischief; he makes an incision over his heart and closes the thread inside the wound. The song thus inspired is therefore not a lament but a validation of his love. When at last Angliana inquires into the whereabouts of the golden thread, he opens the wound, now healed, before her eyes and presents her with the intact thread. The impact of this gesture on her is profound:

> Deß kond sich die junckfraw nit genuog verwunderen, und aber wundert sie sich noch vil mehr an dem jüngling, der sich jetzund zweymal mit scharpffem messer an seinem leib verseert hatt. Von der stund an ward Angliana gar hart mit dem pfeil der liebe Cupidinis verwundet.[29]

> [The young lady could not cease to be amazed at this, and yet her wonder was greater still for the young man who had wounded his body twice with a sharp knife. From that moment on, Angliana was sorely wounded by Cupid's arrow of love.]

While the astonishment over the peaceful lion relates to a fairy-tale motif, Angliana's wonder in this instance may be explained by what classical novella theory calls the concrete object, or *Dingsymbol*. Fairy-tale motif and concrete object alike relate to what is unprecedented, though this does not imply that it is unrealistic, at least from the early modern perspective. Accordingly, mutual love remains not only a more abstract, if passionate, aspiration, but is implicit in a symbolic act of self-denial: its purity and strength are not simply asserted but actually concretized in the symbol and validated in the heart's blood. What is new in this is the lover's poetic action, which stands as a virtue equal to the knightly virtues that he demonstrates only later; it is similar to the anagrammatical play on *Wickram* and *wirckrammen*, which places the author and the threads of his narration in a symbolic relationship. The author holds the narrative threads together as a texture, or text.

Predictably, the further course of the action is dedicated to removing the impediments to marriage, including the count's objections. Unlike *Gabriotto und Reinhart*, the count's opposition does not lead to the death of the lovers. Their fortitude, flexibility, and, especially, Lewfrid's wondrous distinction, activate the decisive and unprecedented miracle: the count quits his opposition and agrees to the marriage. Whereas in *Galmy* only chance can make a positive outcome possible, and whereas in *Gabriotto und Reinhart* necessity leads to catastrophe, in *Goldtfaden* it is the veritable fairy-tale wonder — the unprecedented moment of the novella — that motivates the happy turn.

With the works of Wickram, German literature at last achieved the artistic quality and scope necessary to generate an indigenous development. Following his death a literary hiatus formed that lasted until the reforms of Martin Opitz (1597–1639) in the 1620s. Only one significant novel appeared during this time. *Affentheurlich naupengeheurliche Geschichtklitterung* (Adventuresome Narrative Scribbling, 1582; this canonical version represents a revision of the 1575 original) by Johann Fischart (1546/47–1590/91) was an adaptation, doubled in length through amplification of existing and added material, of François Rabelais's *Gargantua et Pantagruel* (1532–52). It is a work of stunning stylistic and thematic originality that defies ordering into any established genre. Given its many outrageous obscenities, it may be categorized as a lower novel. Although it is now acknowledged as a literary-historical monument, at the time the *Geschichtklitterung* had practically no effect on the larger world of German narrative writing.

European Genre Conventions and the German Tradition: Transitions and Translations

Wickram's novels had little impact on subsequent German novelists. This tepid reception, attributable in part to his early death, represents a serious gap in the history of German literature. As we have seen, *Goldtfaden* suggests what quality of writing Wickram was capable of, and one can only speculate on how the early modern German novel might have developed had he lived to write others. By the time of his death he was moving away from farce and satire and toward the Romance novel. The evolution of the Romance novel itself, however, was cut short after midcentury and its place filled by the translations of *Amadis*, a Spanish-Portuguese serialized novel — the earliest printing was a version by Garci Rodríguez de Montalvo, *Amadis de Gaulla*, in Zaragoza in 1508 — full of tales of knight-errantry. Originally intended for aristocratic readers, the provocative *Amadis* — its erotic details included descriptions of pre- and extramarital sex — split reception into two camps. Moral critics claimed that its sensational elements exemplified the dangers inherent in the novel *qua* genre, undermining Christian values and promoting lasciviousness; its defenders praised its vigorous style and the unfailing *courtoisie* of its hero. By late century, *Amadis* had come to represent the standard for the modern European novel. Its phenomenal popularity created a hunger for sequels: the French version extended to a dozen volumes, the German to twenty-four.[30] The Frankfurt publisher Sigmund Feyerabend's 1587 *Amadis* edition, called *Buch der Liebe* (Book of Love, 13 vols.)[31] is an anthology of "modern" romances of the sixteenth century from various foreign sources but treated as purely German texts: *Melusine, Ritter Pontus, Herpin, Magelone,* and *Kaiser Octavianus,* among others. Johann Fischart translated the sixth volume of Feyerabend's edition as early as 1572.[32] These texts remind us that German literature of the sixteenth century was richly nourished by French sources and styles.

Aside from the folkbooks *Faust* and *Lalebuch* and the farce book *Hans Clawerts Werckliche Historien* (Hans Clawert's True Stories, 1587) by Bartholomäus Krüger (ca. 1540–97), most German prose narratives published before 1630 were translations. This reception of foreign models had the effect of retarding the growth of an indigenous German love novel until the mid-seventeenth century, when the *Adriatische Rosemund* (The Adriadic Rosemund, 1645) of Philipp von Zesen (1619–89) appeared.[33] This delay no doubt explains the urgency felt by the new generation of writers in the early seventeenth century to catch up. "Close the gap, cross the border!" could have been their motto.[34] That task of bringing German literature up to international standards could be accomplished only after an authoritative poetics for German writing had been established with Opitz's *Buch von der Deutschen Poeterey* (Book of German Poetics, 1624) and after the German language itself had become a supple enough instrument to compete with other European literary languages. These questions are dealt with in greater detail elsewhere in this volume.[35]

By the time the German literary reform began,[36] the novel was already considerably advanced elsewhere in Europe. On the one hand, the suddenness of the appearance of fully formed European novels in Germany abetted Opitz's ambitious goal of catching up with European developments within a single generation. On the other, it extracted a heavy cultural price, since the uncoupling from the sixteenth-century tradition of German prose narration and the substitution of international models and genre conventions retarded its independent national development. The translations by Opitz, Harsdörffer, Zesen, Hans Ludwig von Kuffstein (1582–1656), Johann Wilhelm Freiherr von Stubenberg (1619–88), and others contributed to the importation and practice of certain prose forms that the literary reformation had claimed to wish to reject. Nevertheless, German authors built on this ready-made foreign foundation, which had the advantage of allowing them to concentrate efforts on writing native adaptations. The history of German prose narration in the seventeenth century is thus essentially one of inventing uniquely indigenous combinations, or hybrids, from borrowed forms. Viewed negatively, this mutation represents an unrealistic striving to attain to the European ideal; viewed positively — as recent scholarship has done — it manifests the subversive, creative power of previously marginalized German genre traditions.[37]

Older scholarship organized seventeenth-century German narrative prose according to genre, a conception that rested primarily on non-German traditions and focused on the interplay of literary raw materials and the genres to which they could be fitted. Accordingly, the novel of low culture was said to deal mainly with comical plots and actions of the lower classes (peasants, laborers, artisans), often with satirical intentions. The novel of high culture, by contrast, presented serious scenarios from the lives of noble and other elevated personages. Finally, the pastoral or bucolic novel, which treats mainly aristocratic protagonists in rustic disguise, was identified as cultivating a middling form and style. However, in practice no consistent division was observed between higher (courtly-historical), lower (satirical, political, picaresque), and pastoral novels; nor did the complex structures of intertextual forms fit neatly into the predisposed genre triad.[38] Opitz's translation (1626) of John Barclay's Latin *Argenis* (1621), together with the anonymous translation in 1629 of Sidney's *Arcadia* (1590), provided a basis for the later courtly novels in German, though none of these adhered to strict genre prescriptions.

In Germany, the liveliest interest was shown in the pastoral novel, with its love stories, its setting in a rustic idyll, and its noble protagonists costumed as shepherds conversant in the topics of love and happiness.[39] Pastoral literature is somewhat exceptional among the narrative forms, in that it is not bound to a specific genre (one speaks more often of a pastoral *mode*) but is situationally adapted: in a beautiful, idyllic landscape, peaceable, unencumbered shepherds converse about the proper conduct of life and about true love. The ideal of a golden age serves only as a historically distant reference point for the standard of a well-lived life. Nicolas de Montreux's *Les Bergerie de Juliette* was translated into German in 1615,[40] Jorge de Montemayor's *Diana* in 1619,[41] Honoré d'Urfé's *L'Astrée* between 1619 and 1635,[42] Diego de Pedro's *Cárcel de Amor* in 1624,[43] and Philip Sidney's *Arcadia* in 1629.[44] A critical mass of foreign models for pastoral literature was reached by 1630, after which original works in German began to appear with regularity. These included Martin Opitz's *Schäfferey von der Nimfen Hercinie* (Pastoral of the Nymph Hercinie, 1630), Georg Christoph von Gregersdorf's (d. after 1664) *Jüngst-erbaute Schäfferey* (New Pastoral, 1632) and *Winter-Tags Schäfferey* (Pastoral of a Winter's Day, 1636),[45] Georg Neumark's (1621–81) *Filamonin* (1640), August Augspurger's (fl. 1642–44) *Arnalte und Lucenda* (1642), and the anonymous *Verwüstete und verödete Schäferey* (Barren and Deserted Pastoral, 1642). In the 1640s, the pastoral underwent significant developments under the influence of the French courtly-historical novel and because of experimentation by a new generation of gifted German poets, especially in Nuremberg.

The German traditional pastoral literature manifests a proclivity for learned, often panegyrical, discourse. The tone was set by Opitz's *Hercinie*, the prototype of the so-called *Prosaekloge* (prose eclogue).[46] In *Hercinie* the narrating poet wanders in shepherd's costume through the Silesian *Riesengebirge* (the Bohemian Krkonose, or Giant Mountains, between the Elbe and Oder). Along the way he meets three other shepherds, identifiable as Opitz's real-life friends August Buchner, Wilhelm Nüssler, and Balthasar Venator. The four converse in learned fashion about love, reason, and travel. At last they come upon the local nymph Hercinie, who leads them through a subterranean network of grottos as she discourses on the merits of the House of Schaffgotsch. The work is, in fact, dedicated to Hans Ulrich von Schaffgotsch, Opitz's patron at the time. At the work's literal center, a panegyric on the Schaffgotsch family marshals elements from the medieval tradition of the mirror of princes (*Fürstenspiegel*). After Hercinie disappears, and before they are frightened away by the appearance of a witch, the friends engage in a discussion about spirits and death. Their walk ends at last at the Schaffgotsch medicinal springs, which they praise with another round of observations in prose and verse.

Opitz's immediate structural model was Jacopo Sannazaro's *Arcadia* (1504), a work that alternates prose narrative and verse inlays, though *Hercinie* can trace an ancestry of erudition in rustic garb all the way back to Vergil's *Eclogues* and Theocritus's *Idylls*. Many imitations of and developments on *Hercinie* followed over the next several decades, beginning with Buchner's *Orpheus und Euridice* (1638). The most active center for production of pastoral after Opitz was Nuremberg, however, around the brilliant experimentalists Georg Philipp Harsdörffer (1607–58), Johann Hellwig (1609–74), Johann Klaj (1616–56), and Sigmund von Birken (1626–81). The *Pegnesisches Schäfergedicht* (Pegnitz Pastoral, 1644) of Harsdörffer and Klaj was composed as the founding work of the *Pegnesischer Blumenorden*, one of the century's leading language and literary societies. It inspired two sequels of lasting quality within the order itself: *Fortsetzung der Pegnitz-Schäferey* (Continuation of the Pegnitz Pastoral, 1645) by Birken and *Die Nymphe Noris* (The Nymph Noris, 1650) by Hellwig.[47] With the Nuremberg poets, the traditional pleasant ambience of prose eclogue often masks a serious, even critical, purpose.[48] Precisely because the action of prose eclogue occurs in a fictive *locus* remote from reality, in a kind of counter-world, it lends itself to reflection on the real sociopolitical world. The practice in Germany of the pastoral novel as a critical-reflective genre was intense in the seventeenth century.[49]

After Opitz's *Hercinie* a large number of bucolic prose works arose in the European pastoral tradition of "individual pastorals" — so named because of their mainly private intentions, by contrast with the broader worldly interests of the European pastoral novel; some individual works were written simply to practice or illustrate a single aspect of the pastoral mode (the rhetorical expression of its panegyrical component, for instance). Sidney's *The Lady of May*, written about 1578 as an entertainment for Queen Elizabeth, is a classic example from the European tradition of individual pastoral.[50] German individual pastorals are usually set in the sphere of the petty rural aristocracy (*Landadel*), are conceived as moral cautionary tales, and avoid engaging larger questions of history and politics. They may deviate widely from, because they are unconcerned with, conventional pastoral narrative structures. Their reception was accordingly limited mainly to readers who knew or enjoyed trying to identify the actual people behind the literary masks. Very few pastorals of this type are of literary quality; their interest lies rather more in their value as social documents.[51]

The Novel of State

By the mid-seventeenth century a new literary trend toward courtly themes and ambience was developing. Zesen's *Adriatische Rosemund* (1645),[52] a work of deep psychological penetration, employs pastoral settings together with elegant courtly conceits in the tradition of *L'Astrée* (1607–23) of Honoré d'Urfé.

Written the year after Zesen translated Vital d'Audiguier's *Les Amours de Lysander et Caliste* and Madeleine de Scudéry's (1607–1701) *Ibrahim Bassa*, it may be seen as a transitional novel of a hybrid type.[53] While Zesen was following the general practice of imitating European models, this novel is not based on any specific source; moreover, his models enabled him to escape the genre's conventional limitations, given that they themselves defied European conventions. But what was good for the French was not necessarily good for the Germans, as Zesen realized. He therefore combines various historical, social, and aesthetic tendencies — confessional conflict, which had been shaping the wider culture for some time; bucolic setting, a newly popular trend; and aristocratic elements — to form a type of novel with uniquely German features. Zesen's goal was to integrate the autobiographical, symbolic, learned, and idealized aspects — thus, the hybrid form. In this, he seems to have taken up the trends and challenges of the novels of the sixteenth century. As a translator also, Zesen regarded the European examples of this genre as common property, available to an informed readership, a circumstance that relieved him of any obligation to try to develop an original novel. *Adriatische Rosemund* thus became the most important model, one based on montage technique, for the new German novel.[54]

In its extraordinary openness to these tendencies, the text represents a kind of mosaic of intentionalities. These are concretized as narrative particles (*Erzählpartikel*). We see this technique at work, for example, in the description of the city of Venice, which is essentially an imbedded story that serves Zesen's wish to reflect on the character of the German nation. The action of the novel is quite sparse and is to a great extent given only second hand through the inlaid, or particle, stories. The plot tells an unfortunate love story: In Amsterdam the honorable young Silesian Markhold falls in love with Rosemund, the daughter of the Venetian aristocrat Sünnebald. Their love is complicated, however, by confessional differences: he is Protestant, she is Catholic. Markhold journeys to Paris, and the correspondence that ensues reveals the depths of their feelings and the ups and downs of their relationship. In spite of his promise to marry her, Markhold does not actually think of himself as her suitor, and Rosemund, beginning to question the sincerity of his love, withdraws to an idyllic locale. Markhold succeeds in allaying her jealousy and doubt, but Rosemund's father continues to withhold his blessing, thus keeping the future of the lovers in doubt. A number of narrative particles are inserted now that constitute the bulk of the remaining plot of the novel. Rosemund's attempts to resolve the confessional conflict fail, and at last she resigns herself to the realization that their love can never be consumated:

> was ich begähre, das hab' ich; was ich wündsche, das säh' ich fohr meinen augen: aber dehr einige schaz, dehr mihr so manche trähnen und so manchen kummer veruhrsachchet, dehn kan ich nicht erlangen, wi sehr ich mich auch dahrüm bemühe. Ich darf nuhn nicht mehr hoffen, daß sich mein verhängnüs ändern wärde: es ist aus; aus ist es, und ich wärde das ände bald sähen. (226)

[All that I should desire, I have; all I should wish for, I see before my very eyes. But that one treasure, which causes me so many tears and so much grief, that one I cannot obtain, no matter how much I strive for it. I can no longer hope that my fate will change: it is over, over, and I shall soon see how it ends.]

Very little theory preceded the actual writing of novels in the seventeenth century. That Opitz did not deal explicitly with the novel in his *Buch von der Deutschen Poeterey* was no oversight; it owed, despite its vigorous practice outside of Germany, to the lack of any sense of the novel as genre. The introduction to Scudéry's *Ibrahim Bassa* of 1641 constituted the dominant theoretical statement on the courtly novel in Europe until the *Traité de l'origine des romans* (1670, German translation 1682) by the Jesuit scholar Pierre Daniel Huët (1630–1721). Scudéry's introduction deals especially with the questions of probability, narrative structure of *in medias res*, organic connection of plots and subplots, time (action occurring within a single year), variety of characters, and embedding of cultural content. Scudéry derived these elements predominantly from the Greek romance *Aithiopika* (3rd c. A.D.) of Heliodorus, and they subsequently became normative for the modern novel of state. For Scudéry, the novel of state should both instruct and entertain;[55] in short, it should provide a kind of manual for good living.

The second important theoretical document on the German novel was Sigmund von Birken's preface (1669) to Duke Anton Ulrich's *Aramena* (discussed below). Birken differentiates three kinds of historical writing: traditional historiography, a metered combination of history and fiction, and the prose novel. Some novels are conceived as *Geschichtgedichte* (representations of historical events), which combine history and fiction; others as *Gedichtgeschichten* (fictional histories), in which the author has license to speak of true and moral things from behind the mask of contrived characters and situations. Although most novels of state rest on a historical base, the genre itself was constantly challenged as to its utility and morality. Birken's response to this question is standard: in the end the novel must lead to virtue, greater knowledge of God (*Gotteserkenntnis*), and noble speech and manners. On formal issues Birken is largely silent, recommending only "die Mänge und Mängung der Geschichten" (a multiplicity of stories and their interweaving).

The actual corpus of German novels of state was extremely small, but several rose to the European standard of quality.[56] Most follow the Heliodoran model, in which noble lovers are separated by fate and eventually reunited.[57] This narrative kernel of lover-pairs may be multiplied many times, all of whom are somehow connected with each other. Political interests, wars, machinations, intrigues, and personal passions draw the massive personnel into a chaotic whirlpool until virtue is at last rewarded, vice punished, and order restored.

The first of the major German novels of state is *Herkules und Valiska* (1659) by Andreas Heinrich Buchholtz (1607–71).[58] Herkules, son of the German king Henrich, and his friend Ladisla, son of the king of Bohemia, set out from Rome for the Holy Land, where Herkules is to be baptized. On their way they free two noble virgins from abductors; one of the virgins, Sophia, daughter of the Roman governor of Padua, becomes the wife of Ladisla. Herkules meets Ladisla's sister, Valiska; soon thereafter, however, Valiska, traveling in male disguise under the name Herkuliskus, is abducted and taken to the Parthian king Artabanus. When they reach the Holy Land, Herkules is baptized by the bishop of Jerusalem. Meanwhile, Valiska is brought before the Medean king Mazens, who is impressed by the chivalric abilities of the "young man"; Artabanus is similarly infatuated and wishes to include "him" among his eunuchs. Soon Valiska's real gender is discovered and Artabanus woos her. Valiska secures a moratorium of one year, and Herkules succeeds in freeing her before the time is up. Then he, Ladisla, and Fabius join German, Roman, and Bohemian troops in an uprising of mostly Persian vassals against Artabanus. They return via Jerusalem, where most of the party convert to Christianity before proceeding to Italy; they are accompanied by Arbianus, the son of Mazens, who has been smitten by the portrait of Klara, sister of Herkules. The Roman emperor declares Herkules and Ladisla his equals, and together with the newly arrived Siegward, son of the Swedish king, and Herkules' brother Baldrich, they all travel to Prague for Ladisla's coronation, his father having died in the meantime. In Prague they learn that the rebel Frisians under the leadership of Krito and his son Gotschalk, both of whom desire Klara, have abducted her. Herkules and his friends defeat and kill Krito and Gotschalk, and Baldrich becomes the king of Frisia. Meanwhile, they have to discipline their own troops, who are dissatisfied with the new Christian belief of their leaders, eventually pacifying them with a guarantee of religious freedom. Upon their return to Prague, however, Herkules and Ladisla must battle the Pannonian king Mnata as well as the prince Dropion, who secretly plans to overthrow the king. Herkules and Ladisla are captured but later freed by their ally, Prince Olaf, along with Valiska and Prince Markomir, whose unsuccesful wooing of Valiska rendered him mad until her sincere friendship cured him. Mnata is defeated and then befriended by Herkules and Ladisla; the treacherous Dropion is executed; and Ladisla's and Valiska's father, the Bohemian king Notesterich, believed dead, suddenly reappears. His former abductor, the infidel vassal Prinisla, is executed, and order is restored.

The derivative nature of this novel is striking. Composed in the 1640s, *Herkules und Valiska* belonged to the first wave of the German reception of foreign, mainly French, novels. Most of Buchholtz's characters are drawn from the traditions of *Amadis* and the subsequent French courtly-historical novel. As a Protestant clergyman, Buchholtz's primary intention was by no means to imitate the famous (Catholic) love novel, but rather to adapt the tradition into a political work of Christian edification. Scudéry's theory provided his theoretical basis. Buchholtz sought to create a kind of program for illuminating the presence of divine truth.[59] His patriotic themes, furthermore, reflect his conviction that the German novel of state had to find its own legitimacy as a historical novel, or *Zeitroman*. To be sure, some of his political views, expressed here in the form of the antiquated world of chivalry, were long obsolete.[60]

A more current and formally more sophisticated approach to the novel of state characterizes the work of Anton Ulrich of Braunschweig-Wolfenbüttel (1633–1714).[61] His two epic novels, *Die durchleuchtige Syrerin Aramena* (The Noble Syrian Woman Aramena, 5 parts, 1669–73), and *Römische Octavia* (The Roman Octavia, 1677–79, 1703–4, 1712–14), stand unapologetically in the French tradition. Together with his sister Sibylla Ursula (1629–1714), Anton Ulrich translated Gautier de Costes de La Calprenède's's austere moral romances *Cassandre* (10 vols., 1642–45) and *Cléopâtre* (12 vols., 1646–58) and carried on a correspondence with Mlle. de Scudéry.

Aramena adopts the Heliodoran scheme. Over the course of some 3,200 pages, the princely author first complicates and then untangles — with the assistance of divine providence — a complex web involving thirty-four protagonists (seventeen pairs of lovers).[62] The time of the novel is the second millenium B.C. Beginning in Europe and ranging across Palestine and beyond, it explores the fate of Marsius and his sister Hercinde, children of the king of the Celts and the Germans. The children follow their father as he goes to war against the tyrant Belochus, ruler of Assyria and usurper of Syria. After many battles, intrigues, disguises, and misunderstandings, the main protagonists at last find happy marriages that help to restore order and promote a stable religious life. Notwithstanding this familiar pattern, *Aramena* represents a unique German version of the European novel of state. Anton Ulrich concentrates on historical, religious, and teleological aspects far more than did his French precursors. He also radicalizes the principle of *Fortuna* as an autonomous power, whose negative capability, realized in a senselessness bordering on evil, threatens to destroy not only the mundane but the divine order as well. An unprecedented philosophical seriousness thus arises from what seemed to begin as just another intellectually spirited but predictable game. Ultimately, providential salvation triumphs; meanwhile, however, the danger of the fall from grace is philosophically intensified and deepened so that the process becomes singularly affecting. By enlivening this radical pattern with a plot that makes the German empire the direct descendent of the nation of Israel, with full sovereignty and autonomy, Anton Ulrich implies that the Germans are a chosen people. His interest is not so much in portraying charismatic leaders and savior figures, but rather to show the German nobility as an independent and indeed theologically privileged class, even above their European counterparts. While this is not the central idea in the novel, it does throws light on the broader ideological context: the dignity and historical destiny of the Germans is manifested out of the radical antitheses of good and evil.[63]

Römische Octavia,[64] which remained unfinished after some thirty-five years and more than 6,000 printed pages in six parts, turned away from the bewildering and often bizarre Oriental-Germanic interfusion to engage the rising enlightened ideology of *Humanität*.[65] The action takes place in Rome during the late empire period between Nero and Vespasian and sets Christian and pagan ethics in striking contrast. Although intrigue, ruthless ambition, and treachery characterize the political world of the pagan court, Octavia (who had

been engaged to Nero as a child), becomes a Christian and exhibits the opposite behavior: friendship, charity, and selflessness. Falsely accused by her enemies and threatened with death, her faith only grows stronger in adversity. She
embodies Christian conscience wed to political prudence and represents for
Anton Ulrich the correct ethos of the new order called for by the modern
enlightened state.[66]

The novel *Arminius*[67] by Daniel Casper von Lohenstein (1689/90), one
of the century's great polymaths, entertains a similar hope for Germany by
invoking once again the spirit of the great tribal leader praised by the Roman
historian Tacitus for his military genius in overcoming Rome's forces under the
general Varus. The loss of three entire legions under Publius Quinctilius Varus
in the Battle of Teutoburg Forest was one of the greatest military disasters in
Roman history. In September of the year 9 A.D. Varus marched into the forests
of northern Germany and into a trap set by Hermann the Cherusker (also
known in literature as Arminius). The battle became a rout. As a result, the
Roman Empire never again attempted to annex the land east of the Rhine
frontier. The novel clearly has a hidden agenda: it paints a utopian vision of
Germany as a unified nation able to stand up to the hegemonism of Louis XIV.
After the description of the battle the various leaders, both German and foreign, narrate their personal and national histories. Lohenstein generally shapes
these narratives as prefigurations of modern historical events. An account of
Arminius's marriage to Thusnelda concludes the first part of the novel. The
second part tells of the discord that arises around Arminius's brother Flavius,
who falls in love with Erato, who is betrothed to Zeno, who is pursued in turn
by Flavius's sister Ismene. After Erato's abduction Flavius joins the German
prince Adgandester, who was expelled from Arminius's court for fomenting
intrigue, and both side with the Romans in a new invasion of Germany;
Thusnelda is abducted during these actions. Eventually, Flavius suffers remorse
for his actions and helps Thusnelda escape fom Rome. In the end it is revealed
that Erato and Zeno are siblings and thus free to marry Flavius and Ismene.
Arminius resigns as king of the Cheruskers and becomes king of the Chatten
after their former ruler, Marbod, has been dethroned; Flavius succeeds
Arminius as king of the Cheruskers.

Formally, *Arminius* follows the Heliodoran pattern only minimally, and
that only in part one, after which it switches to chronological narration.[68] This
turn implies an increased alertness to historical-philosophical implications of
narrative in Lohenstein. *Fortuna* is also transformed from a force of blind luck
to one of doom, further influencing the structural change in the direction of
universal history, which has no predictable ending. Lohenstein goes beyond
Anton Ulrich's program of national legitimization by integrating and elevating
the history of the Germans into the context of world history. *Arminius* is a
roman à clef, in part, in which some of its characters are identifiable with certain historical personalities. The central figure of identification is Leopold I.
But from a literary standpoint, more important than the unmasking of the
many veiled characters is the immense range of discourse and the rhetorical
sophistication, often mixed with stunningly erotic imagery, which comes from

Lohenstein's vast erudition. He begins his description of the Thracian princess Ada as follows:

> An statt des Zeither aus gedörtem und im Flüß-Wasser lange abgewasch-enem Baum-Mooße oder aus gefeiltem Helffenbeine gebrauchten Haar-Staubes / stäubete die Fürstin Ada ihr nach dem Beyspiele der Persischen Könige mit Narden-Wasser und Myrrhen-Oele angefeuchtetes / wie auch nach Phrygischer Art mit heissen Eisen gekräuseltes Haar mit gemahlenem Golde ein.[. . .] Ihre Brüste trug sie alleseit gantz bloß / und ihre Unter-Röcke waren von so dünnem seidenen Flore: daß sie mit diesem mehr gewebten Winde als Kleide weniger / als eine Ehbrecherin ihrem Buhlen im Bette verdeckte.[69]

> [Instead of making use of the older fashion of moss thinned and distilled with running water or hair powder from crushed ivory, Princess Ada treated her hair, in the manner of Persian kings, with spikenard water and oil of myrrh, and, in the Phyrgian style, she curled with a hot iron crushed gold into her hair. She wore her breasts completely bare, and her under-garments were of such fine floral silk that it — more like a subtle breeze than clothing — covered her less than an adulteress clothes herself in bed for her paramour.]

Putting this erudition on such conspicuous display doubtless meant to reflect the powerful role — heretofore concealed — of the Germans in world history. Lohenstein self-consciously assumes the role as historical mediator of German destiny. The formal genre traditions became for him an abstract structure to be filled with the themes of the new national traditions. His singular achievement, however, had no influence on the subsequent aesthetic development of the German novel.[70]

Heinrich Anshelm von Ziegler und Kliphausen's (1663–96) *Die Asiatische Banise* (1689)[71] was the most popular of the German courtly-historical novels. Ziegler's immediate model was a work by the Spanish emblematist Diego Saavedra Fajardo (1584–1648); but he also undertook his own investigation of historical sources pertaining to the action of the story (the text is based on actual events that took place in the Asian kingdom of Siam in the late sixteenth century). Ziegler simplifies the weighty cast of characters found in most other German novels of state, concentrating instead on flashbacks on a single main character. Like Lohenstein, he also turns to chronological narration in the second half of the novel. The introductory scene in which Balacin of Ava laments his sorry fate and curses his tyrannical opponent, the cruel king Chaumigrem of Siam, became paradigmatic in literary history for courtly-historical exposition. Older scholarship assumed that Ziegler had modeled his novel on Lohenstein, but recent research has shown that, while Lohensteinian stylistic and formal influences are present (for example, in the chronological narration), he diverges in significant ways. As in the familiar Heliodoran scheme, Ziegler aims at a happy ending with multiple marriages following the usual machinations. The story involves extreme levels of violence, though the scenes of mass slaughter are made less horrible by a quasi-picaresque servant figure, Scandor.

The affectionate descriptions of the lovers Balacin and Banise also help to elevate the story. Significantly, the Buchholtzian-Ulrichian ideology of the transhistorical legitimization of German destiny has no place in this novel.

The Picaresque Novel

We have seen that the history of the novel of state in Germany did not constitute a unified genre tradition but essentially only a small corpus of special cases, as it were. Much the same could be said of the picaresque novel, certain important differences notwithstanding.[72] For one thing, the picaresque novel did not count among the established genres; second, it lacked a genre tradition comparable to that of the novel of state; third, it was primarily Spain, not France, that provided the exemplary texts; and fourth, the German picaresque novel superimposed even more indigenous forms and content on the intentions of the original foreign texts than did the German novels of state.

Scholarship usually distinguishes two types of picaresque novel. The older type presents a young and naïve protagonist, usually orphaned, who gains knowledge of the world and its various classes of people as he — always a male except in the case of Grimmelshausen's renowned female picara, Courasche — moves through life, horizontally through the land, vertically through society. Through repeated confrontation with extreme hardship the picaro develops a worldly-wise strategy of deceit (*dissimulatio*) that helps him survive and eventually secure for himself a position in society. Because the picaro's existence depends on the ability to adapt to the world's deceitfulness and falsity, his eternal soul is constantly at risk. Although he may commit grievous sins, he ordinarily does so only out of the necessity for survival, or to escape danger; moreover, his questionable behavior serves the reader's wish for justice and is often uproariously funny to read. As it was in sixteenth-century prose fiction, the technique of complementary reading is fundamental to the picaresque novel.

The second, newer, type of picaresque novel is based on the truncated 1573 version of *Lazarillo de Tormes* (1553) — a racy colloquial work of obscure authorship in autobiographical style[73] — the so-called *Lazarillo castigado* (Lazarillo chastened), in which the radically critical tone and themes of the original, under the conviction of religious certainty, are modified and softened. This "chastened" version, translated into German in 1617, three years after the translation of the unexpurgated work, accepts the groundwork of the earlier type but has the hero undergo a religious conversion and repudiate his former sinful life. This changes the tone and message of the picaresque worldview, for its religious instruction is far less heavy-handed.

The seminal line of influence for the German picaresque novel came from the medieval tradition of moral satire, however. In this tradition, condemnation of exemplary sins frame the sinner as fool in a religiously determined dichotomy between good and evil. Sebastian Brant's *Narrenschiff* (1494) was the most powerful model for this European form of narration based on the topos of the fool. This so-called fool's literature was used to brilliant advantage especially by Counter-Reformation authors from the Franciscan Thomas Murner (1475–1537) to the Munich chancery officer Ägidius Albertinus (ca. 1560–1620). Although an anonymous German translation in 1614 of *Lazarillo de Tormes* sparked initial interest in the Spanish picaresque novel in Germany, it was Albertinus who definitively established the picaresque novel in Germany with his didactic translation of Mateo Alemán's *Guzmán de Alfarache* (1599–1604) as *Der Landstörtzer* (The Vagrant; sometimes translated as The Runagate): *Gusman von Alfarache oder Picaro genannt* (1615), in which he turns the conversion of the first-person narrator into an example of Christian decisionism. Albertinus concentrates on the picaro's stations of sin, contrition, penitence, and change in lifestyle, while essentially ignoring potential psychological motivations. Alemán's *Guzmán de Alfarache* can be read as a conversion story; however, the story's pessimistic undercurrent is unmistakable and throws into doubt the first-person narrator's religious self-critique.

The translations by Niclaus Ulenhart (about whose life nothing is known) of Cervantes's 1613 novella *Rinconete y Cortadillo* (German 1617) as well as López de Úbeda's 1605 *Pícara Justina* (German 1620–27) belong to the first generation of German reception of the picaresque novel. The influence of these works helped to inspire the vivid use of local color in Grimmelshausen's (second-generational) writings; it helped to promote, for example, his realistic manner of speech and treatment of gender. The first original German work in the picaresque tradition did not appear until 1640, with Johann Michael Moscherosch's (1601–69)[74] *Gesichte Philanders von Sittewalt* (Visions of Philander of Sittewalt). The first part, consisting of seven dream visions, was freely adapted from Francisco de Quevedo's *Los Sueños* (written 1606–22, published 1627), but the second part was wholly original with Moscherosch. Moscherosch does not tell the life's story of a picaro but rather relates the narrator's dream visions, thereby adapting the moral satire of the sixteenth century to the seventeenth-century literature of visions. Similarly to the novel of state, Moscherosch's picaresque novel displays patriotic tendencies. His purpose, however, is not the historical legitimization of the Germans (as in Buchholtz and Anton Ulrich), but a reassertion of the ancient Germanic virtues of integrity and honesty. In contrast to the allegedly brilliant but treacherous superficiality of the French national character, Moscherosch celebrates the quintessential Germanic virtue of *Aufrichtigkeit* (honesty, sincerity):

> Dann einmahl last sich alte Teutsche Redlichkeit vnd Auffrichtigkeit nicht bergen noch vertuschen. Ein mahl weiß man das diese Gramanzische Sucht den Teütschen nicht angebohren.[. . .] Einmahl erfahret man das solche Hertzen vntüchtig sind / vnd in der Heücheley also erweichet / daß sie zu waß dapffers schwerlich mehr mögen angezogen werden.[75]

> [For one thing, the ancient German honesty and sincerity can be neither hidden nor dissimulated. For another, everyone knows that this [French] habit of grimacing and gesticulating does not come naturally to the Germans. And for another, we have learned that such hearts are untrustworthy,

that they grow soft with hypocrisy, and that they can therefore hardly be trained to behave courageously.]

Moscherosch dispenses with the distinction between a narrating and an experiencing first-person by replacing the commentary with an experiencing protagonist whom he accordingly calls Expertus Robertus (Experienced Robert). The value of this novel lies less in its depiction of the picaresque life as in its clear-eyed look at social values and their moral consequences, as discerned and expressed by the visionary hero.

Hans Jakob Christoffel von Grimmelshausen (1621 or 1622–76)[76] is the best known prose author of the early modern period. His picaresque novel *Der abentheuerliche Simplicissimus Teutsch* (The Adventurous Simpleton, German), which appeared in 1668, is considered a work of world literature and is still read with great pleasure by many, either in the original or in translation. It is the central work, in five books, of a ten-book corpus of so-called Simplician novels (thus, the "Simplician Cycle"). In 1669 the sequel (book six) appeared, called *Continuatio des abentheuerlichen Simplicissimi,* and it in turn was followed in 1670 by *Trutz-Simplex: oder Ausführliche und wunderseltzame Lebensbeschreibung Der Ertzbetrügerin und Landstörzerin Courasche* (Anti-Simplex: Or Exhaustive and Curious Life-Description of the Arch-Deceiver and Vagrant Courage). In that same year *Der Seltzame Springinsfeld* (Strange Springinsfeld) was published, and in 1672–73 the two volumes of *Wunderbarliches Vogelnest* (The Miraculous Birds Nest).[77] Grimmelshausen's works are sometimes said to exemplify a uniquely German type of literature. This category is distinguished, first of all, by the presence of patriotic themes. We have seen this in the genre of the novel of state, in both its German and its foreign versions; but the German reception of picaresque novels exhibits a still greater insistence on the *partiality* for German forms and themes. This helps to explain why the European picaresque novel had its most enthusiastic and profound reception in seventeenth-century Germany.

Grimmelshausen was much affected by Albertinus's *Landstörzer,* which combines Albertinus's translation of the first part of Alemán's novel with his translation of a portion of a sequel to it (1602) by a certain Juan Martí; Albertinus himself independently contributed the second part, writing in the militant spirit of the Counter-Reformation. A third part (1626), masquerading as a translation from the Spanish by one Martin Frewdenhold, transformed the original story into a travelogue. The combined first two parts may be considered the founding document of the German picaresque tradition. Both *Simplicissimus* and *Guzmán* are stories of conversion, but they are also much more. While both authors pursue moral and religious aims, their plots move as a succession of crises that show the hero in conflict with a hypocritical world. Grimmelshausen follows the genre rule of first-person narration, which establishes a distance between the older, morally reformed Christian narrator and his younger, rambunctiously sinning self.

Simplicius (simpleton), known at first only as "Bub" (boy), grows up in poverty among peasants during the Thirty Years' War. So profound is his naiveté that he takes literally — much as Eulenspiegel did, to hilarious effect — his (supposed) father's fanciful description of the farm as a royal estate:

Mein Knan [. . .] hatte einen eignen Palast, so wohl als ein anderer, ja so artlich, dergleichen ein jeder König mit eigenen Händen zu bauen nicht vermag, sondern solches in Ewigkeit wohl unterwegen lassen wird; er war mit Leimen gemalet und anstatt des unfruchtbaren Schiefers, kalten Blei und roten Kupfers mit Stroh bedeckt, darauf das edel Getreid wächst [. . .]. Wo ist ein Monarch, der ihm dergleich nachtut? Seine Zimmer, Säl und Gemächer hatte er inwendig vom Rauch ganz erschwarzen lassen, nur darum, dieweil dies die beständigste Farb von der Welt ist und dergleichen Gemäld bis zu siner Perfektion mehr Zeit brauchet, als ein künstlicher Maler zu seinen trefflichsten Kunststücken erfordert.[78]

[My dad owned a palace as good as the next man's. It was so attractive that not one single king could have built one like it with his own two hands; he would rather have put off the construction for all eternity. It was well chinked with adobe, and instead of being covered with barren slate, cold lead, or red copper, it was thatched with straw, on which grows noble grain. Where is the monarch to imitate that? Where is the sovereign wanting to do likewise? The rooms, halls, and chambers had been tinted black by smoke — only because black is the most durable color in the world, and paintings in that color need more time to acquire perfection than even the most skillful painters give their best work.]

His "education" is similarly imaginary, which gives him the greatest pride: "Ja ich war so perfekt und vollkommen in der Unwissenheit, daß mir unmüglich war zu wissen, daß ich so gar nichts wußte" (I was so perfect and excellent in ignorance that I could not possibly have known that I knew nothing at all; I, 1). When soldiers ransack the farm he flees into the woods, where he spends his preadolescent years with a hermit who acquaints him with Christian teachings. This hermit, a Scottish nobleman, serves as Simplicius's spiritual father; later it will be revealed that he is in fact the hero's real father. When the hermit dies, Simplicius must leave his secluded life and enter the real world outside. There he is made to play the fool to various officers of the Protestant and Catholic armies. Simplicius keeps his wits, however, survives, and finally, with the help of his true friend "Hertzbruder" (Heart-brother), achieves a measure of success. After they become separated, Simplicius, as "The Huntsman of Soest," becomes a notorious thief, a role that leads him to Paris, Russia, and Asia. Along the way he is occasionally reminded of his true parents. He eventually adopts the life of a hermit and pilgrim and in the course of his wanderings is abducted, taken to Egypt, freed, and finally stranded on an island. When he is discovered and given the chance to leave the island he refuses. Instead, he entrusts the captain of the rescue ship with his autobiography — the very book the reader is holding in his hands. His final statement sounds a call for renunciation of the sinful world:

O Welt! du unreine Welt, derhalben beschwöre ich dich, ich bitte dich, ich ersuche dich, ich ermahne und protestiere wider dich, du wollest kein

Teil mehr an mir haben; und hingegen begehre ich auch nicht mehr in dich zu hoffen, dann du weißt, daß ich mir hab fürgenommen, nämlich dieses: Posui finem curis, spes et fortuna valete. (V, 24)

[O World, you unclean world! For these reasons I pray, I beg, I ask, I admonish you, and I protest against you. May you have no part of me any more. I, for my part, do not desire to place any hope in you, for you know I have determined to put an end to care. Hope and fortune, farewell!]

Grimmelshausen is not advocating the idea of ascetic renunciation, however, but of an ongoing confrontation with human frailties and delusions. More profoundly than any other novel of the early modern period, *Simplicissimus* penetrates into the realm of the inevitability of earthly failure. Self-awareness — the classical imperative of *nosce te ipsum* — is temporary and imperfect and requires constant reflection. Hermetic withdrawal is not a viable solution. For the practical-minded Grimmelshausen, who was himself a family man, innkeeper, and mayor in Renchen, people must live out their Christian lives in a social environment built around moral reflection and compassion. The continuing popularity of this novel is proof enough that modern readers are still able to draw useful secular lessons from its religiously coded messages. The same may be said of the remainder of the Simplician cycle only to a limited degree.

The novel *Trutz-Simplex*, commonly known as *Courasche* after its heroine, is a special case. It too is set during the Thirty Years' War and is told from the end-of-life perspective of the heroine, Libuschka from Bohemia. The story of this picara begins with her having disguised herself as a boy for safety's sake as well as for greater mobility in the world; her secret is found out, however, and soon thereafter she loses her virginity. It is from this event that she receives her nickname, Courasche (courage), ironically, meant to imply that she has boldly given up her virginity voluntarily. In truth, she is as much opportunist as victim. She possesses an avid appetite for material gain, and through a succession of conquests and failures in battle zones together with a series of marriages and betrayals, she gains notoriety and wealth. Eventually, she loses everything. Courasche conforms to the Lazarillo type of picaresque hero, but ultimately surpasses it in two ways: she refuses to repent, mocking all attempts at her religious conversion; and she seeks to avenge herself on Simplicissimus, who has insulted her in his "autobiography" by seducing and denigrating her (*Simplicissimus*, book 5, chapter 6). Despite many reversals of fortune, Courasche remains confident. Over the course of events, indeed, she is transformed into a quasi-mythical gypsy queen. In the newer scholarship the trend has been away from moralistic criticism in favor of a more nuanced view. For example, some argue that her spite ("Trutz") is psychologically understandable in light of the indignities she suffered, especially at the hands of Simplicissimus, and that it sheds historical light on contemporary realities. While her conduct may remain abhorrent, this deeper understanding humanizes her and makes her a recognizably modern figure.

The cycle's last two books, comprising the *Wunderliches Vogelnest*, do not maintain the level of narrative complexity of the earlier books but rely on a series of moral examples. The novel that immediately precedes them, however, *Der Seltzame Springinsfeld*, does offer something new: in the end, it is left ambiguous whether Springinsfeld really undergoes a conversion. Both Springinsfeld and Courasche are complex and memorable characters — Luther might have called them "pious sinners" — and represent the modern possibility of a failure of religious confidence, possibly even unbelief, in response to new historical and social developments.[79] This radical proposition may be seen as a corollary to the powerful and chaotic Fortuna of Anton Ulrich's *Aramena*.

Grimmelshausen's successors demonstrated little interest in conforming to the classical genre model of the picaresque novel. Johann Beer (1655–1700) is the most notable among them. His style is so idiosyncratic, indeed, that it would be misleading to say that he belongs to the Grimmelshausen school of picaresque writing. He has no real predecessor.[80] Born into a poor Austrian peasant family, Beer was an innately talented and energetic figure. His musical talents got him a stipend at a Gymnasium in Nuremberg where he spent many a night — based on autobiographical statements found in his novels — spinning fantastic tales for his fellow students. He went on to university for a short time but obtained a steady position as a musician at the new court in Weissenfels and rose to the rank of *Kapellmeister*. There he composed a body of music that is still occasionally performed. In the meantime, he wrote a number of novels that were published anonymously and undoubtedly motivated by the need for additional income. It was only with the brilliant scholarly detective work of Richard Alewyn in 1932–33 that Beer's identity as the author of the picaresque novels came to light. For unknown reasons Beer dropped his novel writing abruptly in the 1680s and turned to more serious musical satire. He was unique among German baroque authors in that he maintained a detailed diary; it was found after his death in 1700, and later published in an incomplete edition. In its last pages he relates the incident that would lead to his death several days later: an accidental shot fired by an officer at a shooting contest.

Beer's first works reference the formulas of the European courtly novel, but they subvert and parody them. His first novels, *Ritter Hopffen-Sack* (Knight Hop-Sack, 1677), *Prinz Adimantus* (1678), *Ritter Spiridon* (Knight Spiridon, 1679), and *Artlicher Pokazi* (The Courteous Pokazi, 1679), display a sovereign disregard for causality, taking their willful pleasure in narration for its own sake instead. *Simplicianischer Welt-Kucker* (The Simplician World-Observer, 1677–79) is considerably longer and more ambitious in scope and purpose and represents a development in Beer's narrative craft. It introduces a number of motifs and themes that are typical of his mature work: the unforgettable seduction scenes, the rich descriptions of musician figures, and the theme of the rise to nobility of a character who reveals previously hidden aristocratic qualities. *Corylo* (1679–80) and *Jucundus Jucundissimus* (1680), both of which revel in fancy and avoid clearly delineated plots, are brilliant examples of Beer's style of narrative free play, abounding in delightful particulars. Alewyn speaks of its "Fülle an Gegenständlichkeit" (fullness of detail and local color) and offers an example from *Jucundus Jucundissimus* (abbreviated here; Alewyn's own summary is given in brackets in the German quotation):[81]

Eines Abends als ich nächst an der Mühle gesessen / und daselbsten meine Gänse gehütet / damit sie mir nicht in das Wasser / und also unter die Räder geriethen / ritte eine Frau den hohen Berg (den Tschaukner) herunter. [Sie arbeitet sich mühsam über die Felsen und durch die hoch aufgeschossenen Tannenzweige hinunter. Sie bleibt stehen, sieht sich um, ruft zweimal, aber bei dem Geklapper der Mühle kann J. nichts verstehen. Das Dorf ist so "leutselig" (menschenleer), daß man tagsüber kaum mehr als drei Menschen auf der Straße sehen kann; daher muß sie lange rufen und wird doch von niemandem gehört als von Jucundissimus, der sich nicht getraut, seine Gänse allein zu lassen. Er macht daher seine Mutter aufmerksam, die gerade "auf dem Gang" die Wäsche von der Stange nimmt. Sie hat nämlich gewaschen, weil am nächsten Tag Feiertag ist, an dem gewöhnlich in der Dorfkirche eine Predigt gehalten wurde, und die Kinder zum Kirchgang weiße Hemden tragen sollen.]

[One evening as I was sitting by the mill and tending my geese, so that they did not wander into the water and get under the water-wheel, a lady came riding down the high mountain (the Tschaukner). She works her way with difficulty over the rocks and down through the tall-grown branches of the pines. She stops, looks around, calls out twice, but Jucundissimus cannot understand her over the rattling of the mill. The village is so "people-poor" that one can see hardly more than three on the street over the length of a whole day. She therefore has to call a long time and nobody hears her except Jucundissimus, but he is afraid to leave his geese alone. So he tells his mother, who just now is "on the way" to take the wash down from the pole. She has been washing because the next day is a holiday on which a sermon is always held in the village church and the children will need to wear white shirts to the processional.]

Beer also delights in practical jokes by his youthful heroes — a kind of aesthetic infantilism that sometimes prompts him to abandon the plot design in the middle of things. Such radical or iconoclastic satirizing tends to destabilize the narrative and cause plots to spiral into absurdity. Some of his writings gather a kind of zealous force that can border on misanthropy. At his best, as in the short work *Der Berühmte Narrenspital* (The Famous Hostel of Fools, 1681), he controls the grotesque and makes it exceptionally effective, like no other narrative style before Goethe. *Narrenspital*, which is full of ribald and scatological humor, presents lazy Lorentz, whose main pleasures in life consist in back-scratching, wind-letting, and storytelling. He rejects all religious beliefs and restrictions on his life. In the end, the young narrator who works as a servant to Lorentz becomes so fearful for his immortal soul if he stays with Lorentz that he takes leave of his post.

Beer's double novel of 1682–83, *Teutsche Winternächte* (German Winter Nights)[82] and *Kurtzweilige Sommer-Täge* (Summer Tales),[83] transports elements of the courtly novel into the milieu of the petty nobility and adds features of the picaresque. The plot concerns the narrator-hero Zendorio, who is in love with the noblewoman Caspia, though he considers himself to be a social outcast. After a number of misunderstandings, Zendorio and his noble friends learn that he was actually born into a noble family. This revelation motivates a series of marriage stories, and these in turn constitute the frames for further imbedded stories. At the end of the first volume the feasting comes to a close when a befriended hermit persuades everybody to retire from secular life. The second part concerns the further lives of the protagonists after their attempts to live as hermits have failed. The structure of the novel is dominated by a great number of loosely connected life stories held in a certain focus by the biography of the narrator. Eventually, after many mistakes and much suffering, the protagonists retire to their castles or to a hermitage and lead quiet and solitary lives. Beer's quasi-picaresque worldview threatens to transgress the expectations of the standard picaresque novel, however, in that its subject is the landed lower aristocracy of his Upper Austrian homeland. The numerous biographies of aristocratic, but also bourgeois and artistic, personalities make entertaining reading and integrate well into what becomes a polyphonic structure. As amusing as we may find Beer's stories now, however, they did not appeal to a broad audience in his time.

One of Beer's few kindred successors, as it were, was Christian Reuter (1665–after 1712), a contemporary of the great English satirist Jonathan Swift.[84] Reuter seems to have been familiar with the novels later attributed to Beer. His comedic novel *Schelmuffsky* (1696)[85] — the name combines the ideas of the picaro (*Schelm*) and the fool — is a grand story of lies and fantasy that so disturbed church authorities that it was placed on the papal index of banned books. Schelmuffsky is the inept son of a wealthy innkeeper. His doting mother finances his Grand Tour, traditionally the capstone experience for young men who had completed their formal education. Schelmuffsky's "travels" take him only a few miles from home, however, and are dulled by excesses of tobacco and brandy. Returning home penniless, he regales everybody with tall tales of fantastic journeys around the world. At the end of chapter 1 he boasts: "Was ich nun in der Fremde zu Wasser und Lande überall gesehen, gehöret, erfahren und ausgestanden, das wird in folgenden Capiteln mit höchster Verwunderung zu vernehmen seyn" (Whatever I saw, heard, experienced, and survived abroad, on water and on land, all of that you will be amazed to learn over the following chapters). Reuter actually set out to write an invective against his unpleasant landlady in Leipzig, one Rosina Müller, but the narrative — which is based on the topos of the artist versus an unartistic, or ignorant, antagonist[86] — developed into a complex work of irony with universal implications.

In the works of Beer we can still see the genuine, if insatiable, longing of the citizen and the artist for social recognition and ennoblement, even if it is perhaps no longer attainable through virtuous acts but only through a wish-fulfilling hidden genealogy. By contrast, Reuter's Bakhtinian liar-hero completely discredits this fantasy through his grotesque inversion of the material world.[87] Reuter's purpose in borrowing the narrative traditions of the sixteenth century was to subvert the canonical genre forms of the seventeenth to reveal their ineffectiveness. But just as the earlier seventeenth-century reform movement had ignored the narrative traditions of the sixteenth century, the eighteenth century similarly excluded those of the seventeenth century from its own canon. It remained for the Romantics of the nineteenth century to begin to rediscover the qualities of the sixteenth-century narrative tradition and its great seventeenth-century successors.

The Political Novel

Beer was also the author of several political novels including *Der Politische Feuermäuer-Kehrer* (The Political Chimney-Sweep, 1682) und *Der Politische Bratenwender* (The Political Turnspit, 1682). However, the political novel is most closely associated with the narrative work of Christian Weise; indeed, he is considered its progenitor through the following three titles: *Die drey ärgsten Ertz-Narren in der gantzen Welt* (The Three Worst Arch-Fools in the Whole World, 1672), *Die drey klügsten Leute in der gantzen Welt* (The Three Cleverest People in the Whole World, 1675), and *Der Politische Näscher* (The Political Nibbler, 1678). The political novel flourished (if only for a short time) owing mainly to the success of Weise's books, including a kind of genre poetics that he wrote called *Kurtzer Bericht vom Politischen Näscher, wie nehmlich dergleichen Bücher sollen gelesen, und vor andern aus gewissen Kunst-Regeln nachgemacht werden* (Brief Commentary on the *Political Nibbler*: Namely, how these kinds of books should be read and according to what aesthetic principles they should be constructed, 1680). For Weise, "politisch" implies the use of actions and behaviors whose ends justify their means, which may often enough be morally questionable, such as deception, intrigue, or treachery, or even downright illicit. If, however, such behaviors are only temporary and result in some ultimately intended good, they are justifiable.

The political novel was directed at the bourgeoisie and at the officialdom in the service of princely nobility, whereas the mirror of princes targeted the rulers themselves; its purpose was to demonstrate how to live simultaneously both virtuously and pragmatically in the real world. *Die drey ärgsten Ertz-Narren* presents models, as it were, of foolish behaviors that readers should take care not to emulate. It concludes with a definition of the greatest of fools: "Nemlich derselbe / der umb zeitliches Kothes willen den Himmel verschertzt. Nechst diesem / der umb lüderlicher Ursachen willen entweder die Gesundheit und das Leben / oder Ehre und guten Nahmen in Gefahr setzet"[88] (Namely, the person who, for the mere sake of a shabby earthly dwelling, gives up hope of heaven. Or the person who, for any foolish reason, risks health and life or honor and a good name). By the same token, *Die drey klügsten Leute* presents an ideal of political prudence, though this pragmatism ultimately fails to be convincing: among all of the presumptively clever people, who in fact turn out to be simply fools in disguise, only one proves worthy of imitation as a model of genuinely prudent conduct. The idyll *Coridonus und Tityras* offers a lovely contrast to the real world, but its utopian vision is hardly a workable alternative for the political novel. Political prudence consists essentially in making choices between what is good and what is bad, such that the prudent ruler or official can avoid danger on the one hand and can on the other "seinen Nutzen in allen Stücken befördern" (take advantage of every opportunity; 291). The plots of these novels are filled with instances of deceitfulness in which evil actually lurks behind what ostensibly is good. Thus, the world becomes a stage for fools, on which the individual actor must come to understand the roles and costumed disguises if he is eventually going to be able to protect the society that he will serve. Besides the contemplation of death and the salvation of one's own soul, the most important element of this political ethos is the exercise of reason. That is, the political novel is concerned not only with justifying deceit as useful — as in "frommer Betrug," a good deception — but actually employing it as a method by which readers learn the proper practice of a *politica christiana*, or Christian politics. The narrative scheme is thus similar in all political novels: a group of young persons set out on a journey in search of, say, the three cleverest or the three most foolish examples they can find and describe. A number of times Weise provides accounts of situations that exemplify these sorts of misbehavior in a kind of journey review. No general political theory is yielded from this bundle of examples, however, which makes it necessary for the author to interpolate longer nonfictional commentaries in order to achieve the desired point of it all. This has a negative effect on the quality of the narrative *qua* novel.

The most important successor to Weise was Johann Riemer (1648–1714), whose three political novels sustained the tradition: *Der Politische Maul-Affe* (The Political Gaping Fool, 1679) imitates Weise's scheme of the journey review; accordingly, the "gaping fools" here are those "welche am Verstande schwach / und der Einbildung nach die klügsten seyn wolten. Und darinnen eben bestünde die gröste Narrheit der Welt"[89] (who have little power of discernment but who imagine themselves to be the most clever. And precisely in this consists the greatest foolishness in the world). A number of imitations in the manner of Weise follow, most of them published anonymously: *Der Politische Grillenfänger* (The Political Melancholic, 1682), *Der Politische Leyermann* (The Political Organgrinder, 1683), *Der lustige Politische Guckguck* (The Cheerful Political Cuckoo, 1684), *Die drey Lasterhafftigsten Leute der Welt* (The Three Most Depraved People in the World, 1685), *Der Politische Freyersmann* (The Political Suitor, 1686), and *Das Politische Kleppel-Mädgen* (The Political Hammer-Girl, 1688), to name only a few.

A special subset of the political novel addresses a particular profession, usually with some satirical or polemical purpose, though not necessarily harshly intended; it often consists of a series of related works by a single author. Johann Christoph Ettner's (1654–1724) six-volume *Des getreuen Eckharts Medicinischer Maul-Affe* (Loyal Eckhart's Medical Gaping Fool, 1694–1715), modeled in part on Riemer's *Politischer Maul-Affe*, is one example.[90] While the usual types of charlatans receive their due ridicule, the heart of the series actually concerns a friendship between friends whose loyalty to each other is expressed in sentimental, often very touching, conversations over the course of an educational journey through Bohemia and Austria. The various stations along the way, where they encounter certain medical quacks and other risible imposters, offer ample opportunity for satire.

Most important to this subgenre of the political novel, however, are the works by the Dresden *Kapellmeister* Wolfgang Caspar Printz (1641–1717)[91] and Johann Kuhnau (1660–1722).[92] In his three musician novels, *Musicus Vexatus* (1690), *Musicus Magnanimus* (1691), and *Musicus Curiosus* (1691), Printz describes the interconnected lives of three musicians who must overcome social rejection. Through clever political actions they finally achieve their goal of having their craft recognized as an honorable profession. Printz tends to follow the narrative scheme of the picaresque novel as practiced by Grimmelshausen. In his first novel, *Güldner Hund* (The Golden Hound, 1675), a Bohemian knight is turned into a dog in imitation of a legend from Apuleius.

Kuhnau's first novels, *Der Schmid seines eignen Unglückes* (The Maker of His Own Misfortune, 1695) and *Des klugen und thörichten Gebrauchs der Fünf Sinnen* (On the Clever and Foolish Use of the Five Senses, 1698), follow the traditional episodic scheme of the journey. In his strikingly realistic and historically informative *Musicalischer Quacksalber* (1700),[93] however, one of the most humorous works of German baroque fiction, he introduces a negative hero of the gaping-fool type, a musical quack, by the name of Caraffa. Caraffa, a German, fancies himself an Italian since, as he believes, only an Italian is capable of achieving renown in the world of music in Germany. His devotion to Italian opera is ridiculously overblown and provides scenes of especially effective comedy. Remarkably, most of his naive countrymen swallow his conceits, and he, unlike his counterparts in Weise and Riemer, is rewarded with social success. Kuhnau was by far the most renowned and successful of contemporary writers and musicians; his successor in Leipzig as cantor at the St. Thomas Church was none other than Johann Sebastian Bach.

Translated by Michael Swisher and Max Reinhart

Notes

[1] The question of the search in the 1960s for the origins of modernity is taken up in this volume by Klaus Garber.

[2] On early modern text editions see the chapter by Hans-Gert Roloff in this volume.

[3] Almost all literary histories of the late middle ages include the literature of the fifteenth and sixteenth centuries, for example, Thomas Cramer, *Geschichte der deutschen Literatur im späten Mittelalter* (Munich: dtv, 1990), and *Von der Handschrift zum Buchdruck: Spätmittelalter, Reformation, Humanismus 1320–1572*, ed. Ingrid Bennewitz and Ulrich Müller, vol. 2 of *Deutsche Literatur: Eine Sozialgeschichte* (Reinbek: Rowohlt 1991). On this transition see the chapter by Graeme Dunphy in this volume.

[4] Some scholars argue that the impact was greater than I judge it to have been. For example, see Rüdiger Schnell, "Prosaauflösung und Geschichtsschreibung im deutschen Spätmittelalter: Zum Entstehen des frühneuhochdeutschen Prosaromans," in *Literatur und Laienbildung im Spätmittelalter und in der Reformationszeit*, ed. Ludger Grenzmann and Karl Stackmann (Stuttgart: Metzler, 1984), 214–48.

[5] Alois Brandstetter, *Prosaauflösung: Studien zur Rezeption der höfischen Epik im frühneuhochdeutschen Prosaroman* (Frankfurt am Main: Athenäum, 1971). See also Hans-Joachim Koppitz, "Zur Überlieferung der Drucke des Prosaromans *Wilhelm von Österreich*," *Gutenberg Jahrbuch* 38 (1963): 53–59; Veronika Straub, *Entstehung und Entwicklung des deutschen frühneuhochdeutschen Prosaromans: Studien zur Prosaauflösung* Wilhelm von Österreich (Amsterdam: Rodopi, 1974); Hartmut Beckers, "Zur handschriftlichen Überlieferung des *Wilhelm von Österreich* Johanns von Würzburg," Sonderheft, *Zeitschrift für deutsche Philologie* 93 (1974): 156–85; Bernward Plate, "Gottfried-Rezeption im Prosa-Eilhart?" *Euphorion* 71 (1977): 250–68; Plate, "Verstehensprinzipien im Prosa-Tristrant von 1484," *Literatur — Publikum — historischer Kontext*, ed. Gert Kaiser (Frankfurt am Main: Lang, 1977), 79–89; Carola Voelkel, *Der Erzähler im spätmittelalterlichen Roman* (Frankfurt am Main: Lang, 1978); and Xenja von Ertzdorff, *Romane und Novellen des 15. und 16. Jahrhunderts in Deutschland* (Darmstadt: Wissenschaftliche Buchgesellschaft, 1989).

[6] Helmut Melzer, *Trivialisierungstendenzen im Volksbuch: Ein Vergleich der Volksbücher* Tristrant und Isalde, Wigoleis *und* Wilhelm von Österreich *mit den mittelhochdeutschen Epen* (Hildesheim: Olms, 1972).

[7] Barbara Weinmayer, *Studien zur Gebrauchssituation früher deutscher Druckprosa: Literarische Öffentlichkeit in Vorreden zu Augsburger Frühdrucken* (Munich: Artemis, 1982).

[8] Bernhard Burchert, *Die Anfänge des Prosaromans in Deutschland: Die Prosaerzählungen Elisabeths von Nassau-Saarbrücken* (Frankfurt am Main: Lang, 1987).

[9] The first edition was published by Conrat Heyndörffer, who was subsidized by Elisabeth's son Johann III.

[10] Prose translations of verse epics were fairly common in France and elsewhere in Europe. Elisabeth's opting for prose followed the fashion of the day.

[11] Aside from Burchert, Brandsteller, Straub, and Melzer, this problem has been treated by Jan-Dirk Müller, "Held und Gemeinschaftserfahrung: Aspekte der Gattungstransformation im frühen deutschen Prosaroman am Beispiel des *Hug Schapler*," *Daphnis* 9 (1980): 393–426; Müller, "Gattungstransformation und Anfänge des literarischen Marktes: Versuch einer Theorie des frühen deutschen Prosaromans," in *Textsorten und literarische Gattung*, ed. Vorstand der Vereinigung der deutschen Hochschulgermanisten (Berlin: Schmidt, 1983), 432–49; Hans-Gert Roloff, "Anfänge des deutschen Prosaromans," in *Handbuch des deutschen Romans*, ed. Helmut Koopmann (Düsseldorf: Bagel, 1983), 54–79.

[12] Weinmayer, *Studien*; Jan-Dirk Müller, " 'Ich Vngenant und die leit': Literarische Kommunikation zwischen mündlicher Verständigung und anonymer Öffentlichkeit in Frühdrucken," in *Der Ursprung von Literatur: Medien, Rollen, Kommunikationssituationen zwischen 1450 und 1650*, ed. Gisela Smoltker-Koerdt, Peter M. Spangenberg, and Dagmar Tillmann-Bartylla (Munich: Fink, 1988), 149–74.

[13] Edition: Thüring von Ringoltingen, *Melusine*, ed. Hans-Gert Roloff (Stuttgart: Reclam, 1991). Studies: Hans Gert Roloff, *Stilstudien zur Prosa des 15. Jahrhunderts: Die Melusine des Thüring von Ringoltingen* (Cologne: Böhlau, 1970); Xenja von Ertzdorff, "Die Fee als Ahnfrau: Zur *Melusine* des Thüring von Ringoltingen," in *Festschrift für Hans Eggers zum 65. Geburtstag*, ed. Herbert Backes (Tübingen: Niemeyer, 1972), 428–57; Jan-Dirk Müller, "Melusine in Bern: Zum Problem der 'Verbürgerlichung' höfischer Epik im 15. Jahrhundert," in *Beiträge zur älteren deutschen Literaturgeschichte 1: Literatur, Publikum, Historischer Kontext*, ed. Joachim

Bumke (Bern: Lang, 1977), 29–77; Kurt Ruh, *Die "Melusine" des Thüring von Ringoltingen* (Munich: Bayerische Akademie der Wissenschaften, 1985).

[14] Roloff, *Stilstudien.*

[15] Ruh, *Die "Melusine."*

[16] Childbed taboos belong to common taboos observed by anthropologists, and they can be regarded as a standard example of the meaning of taboo. The Melusine episode is not a perfect mirror image of the Persina episode, of course, since the violator of the taboo is not punished. Affective misbehavior occurs at various points, two of which are particularly important: Goffroy's ill-tempered assault on the monks, and Reymund's spying on and later denunciation of Melusine.

[17] *Fortunatus: Studienausgabe nach der Editio Princeps von 1509,* ed. Hans-Gert Roloff (Stuttgart: Reclam, 1981). Roloff cites the entire older literature. See also Hannes Kästner, *Fortunatus — Peregrinator mundi: Welterfahrung und Selbsterkenntnis im ersten deutschen Prosaroman der Neuzeit* (Freiburg: Rombach, 1990). Kästner thinks the author may have been the Nuremberg Franciscan Stephan Fridolin.

[18] See in this volume the chapter on travel literature by Wolfgang Neuber.

[19] Further on *facetiae,* see in this volume the chapter on Neo-Latin literature by Wilhelm Kühlmann.

[20] *Ein kurtzweilig Lesen von Dil Ulenspiegel,* ed. Wolfgang Lindow (Stuttgart: Reclam, 1978).

[21] On Erasmus's *Laus Stultitiae* see the chapter on early modern education by Wilhelm Kühlmann in this volume.

[22] *Historia von D. Johann Fausten,* ed. Stephan Füssel and Hans Joachim Kreutzer (Stuttgart: Reclam, 1988). The editors cite a complete list of the secondary literature. For a discussion of this novel seee the chapter by Gerhild Scholz Williams in this volume.

[23] Goethe's *Faust* will be known to most readers. The mention of Lessing refers to the so-called *Faust-Fragment* in his seventeenth *Literaturbrief* of 1759, which represents an important model in the development of Goethe's conception of the character of Faust.

[24] See Georg Wickram, *Sämtliche Werke,* 9 vols., ed. Hans-Gert Roloff (Berlin: de Gruyter, 1967–93). Important studies from this initial period of research included G. J. Martin-ten Wolthuis, "Der *Goldtfaden* des Jörg Wickram von Colmar," *Zeitschrift für deutsche Philologie* 87 (1968): 46–85, and Reinhold Jacobi, *Jörg Wickrams Romane: Interpretation unter besonderer Berücksichtigung der zeitgenössischen Erzählprosa* (Ph.D. diss., University of Bonn, 1970). The early study by Clemens Lugowski, *Die Form der Individualität im Roman* (Berlin: Junker & Dünnhaupt, 1932), remains indispensable.

[25] Translated by Pierre Kaufke as *The Golden Thread: An Agreeable & Entertaining Tale of Lionel, Son of a Poor Shepherd [. . .]* (Gainesville: UP of Florida, 1991).

[26] On love in Wickram as well as in the entire early modern period see in this volume the chapter by Gerhart Hoffmeister.

[27] Wickram, *Werke,* 5:2.

[28] In a conversation with Eckermann of 29 January 1827: "denn was ist eine Novelle anders als eine sich ereignete unerhörte Begebenheit. Dies ist der eigentliche Begriff, und so Vieles, was in Deutschland unter dem Titel Novelle geht, ist gar keine Novelle, sondern bloß Erzählung oder was Sie sonst wollen."

[29] *Werke* 5:34.

[30] See Volker Meid, *Der deutsche Barockroman* (Stuttgart: Metzler, 1974), 11–12. Volumes 1–21 of the German version were translations of the French *Amadis*. Volumes 22–24 seem to have been the source for later French versions.

[31] Feyerabend was also the publisher of Wickram's *Goldtfaden* in 1557.

[32] *Das sechste Buch, der Historien vom Amadis auß Franckreich, auch seinen Nachkommen und Söhnen: Gantz nützlich von guten Lehren und lieplich von Geschichten zulesen. Auss frantzösischer Sprach newlich in Teutsche durch J. F. G. M. gebracht.*

[33] This novel will be discussed below. The argument that German-language narrative prose of the seventeenth century had no generally recognized national tradition to which it could appeal is partially accurate, though it does not adequately account for genre tradition or, more specifically, the traditions of theme and form. See Dirk Niefanger, *Barock* (Stuttgart: Metzler, 2000), 176–77; also Meid, *Barockroman*, 9.

[34] The allusion here is to Leslie Fiedler's slogans from his *Cross the Border — Close the Gap* (New York: Stein and Day, 1972): "cross the gap," that is, between high and low culture, and "cross the border" between canonical and popular literature.

[35] See in particular the chapters by Renate Born, Wilhelm Kühlmann ("Education"), Joachim Knape, and Theodor Verweyen in this volume.

[36] For discussions of the literary reform see in this volume especially the chapters by Kühlmann ("Education") and Knape.

[37] There was also another reason for the special path taken by the German novel: neither Wickram nor Grimmelshausen, the greatest novelist of the seventeenth century in Germany, belonged to the academically educated bourgeoisie. Both achieved significant learning, but it was probably their distance from the European humanistic tradition that most ensured their distinctive contribution to the history of German literature. Nowhere in Europe was the tension between scholarly and nonacademic literature so pronounced as in Germany. Even after the triumphant success of the *poeta doctus* this tension remained in place. The longing for things folksy, original, and natural helped authors such as Christian Fürchtegott Gellert (1715–69), who was himself a professor, and Heinrich Jung-Stilling (1740–1817) gain fame and recognition. One could even claim that large parts of the history of literature of the eighteenth century were inspired by the attempt to bridge this gap, often reflected as a duality between the naïve and the sentimental. On seventeenth-century theories of the novel see Wilhelm Voßkamp, *Romantheorie in Deutschland: Von Martin Opitz bis Friedrich von Blanckenburg* (Stuttgart: Metzler, 1973). Further: Hans Gerd Rötzer, *Der Roman des Barock 1600–1700: Kommentar zu einer Epoche* (Munich: Winkler, 1972), and Meid, *Barockroman*.

[38] This applied equally to the new "bourgeois" novel toward the end of the century. "Mixed forms" and the "political" novel were recognized as exceptions to the classical triadic typology. The question of triadic genre is often discussed as part of inquiries into the origins of the German baroque novel.

[39] Because the pastoral novel, including the prose eclogue, occupied a position outside of the prose narrative tradition, however, its influence did not extend much beyond the seventeenth century. Indeed, there are both historical and systematic reasons to doubt that the pastoral novel contributed directly to the establishment of the modern novel as a genre. Pastoral texts cannot be viewed as novels *sui generis*; nor is it possible to reconstruct a historical or causal connection between pastoral antecedents and the modern novel. The novel entered Germany strictly through translations and was not guided by genre conventions but by subject matter.

[40] As *Die Schäffereyn Von der schönen Juliana*; the evidence of the initials "J. B. B. B." given in the later volumes suggests J. B. B. von Borstel as the translator.

[41] As *Erster unnd anderer Theil Der newen verteutschten Schäfferey, von der schönen verliebten Diana, und dem vergessenen Syreno*; translated by Hans Ludwig von Kuffstein.

[42] As *Von der Lieb. Astreae und Celadonis Einer Schäfferin und Schäffers*; probably translated by J. B. B. von Borstel.

[43] As *Gefängnüss der Lieb* (Prison of Love); translated by Hans Ludwig von Kuffstein.

[44] As *Arcadia der Gräffin von Pembrock*; translation formerly sometimes attributed to Martin Opitz though now considered anonymous.

[45] See Ulrich Seelbach, "Logun, Gruttschreiber, Gregersdorf: Zum Verfasser der *Jüngsterbauten Schäfferey*," *Daphnis* 18, no. 1 (1989): 113–24.

[46] *Hercinie* and the subsequent works in the tradition of the prose eclogue, however, do not fit well into the category of the novel, precisely because prose eclogue mixes prose and verse freely. More on this mixed genre in the introduction to the present volume.

[47] For a close analysis see Klaus Garber, "Nuremberg, Arcadia on the Pegnitz: The Self-Stylization of an Urban Sodality," trans. Karl F. Otto Jr., Michael Swisher, and Max Reinhart, in *Imperiled Heritage: Tradition, History, and Utopia in Early Modern German Literature*, ed. Max Reinhart (Aldershot: Ashgate, 2000), 117–208.

[48] See Garber, "Utopia and the Green World: Critique and Anticipation in Pastoral Poetry," in *Imperiled Heritage*, 73–116; also Max Reinhart, "Poets and Politics: The Transgressive Turn of History in Seventeenth-Century Nürnberg," *Daphnis* 19, no. 1 (1990): 41–66, and "Welt und Gegenwelt im Nürnberg des 17. Jahrhunderts: Ein einleitendes Wort zur sozialkritischen Funktion der Prosaekloge im Pegnesischen Blumenorden," in *Pegnesischer Blumenorden in Nürnberg: Festschrift zum 350jährigen Jubiläum*, ed. Werner Kügel (Nuremberg: Tümmel, 1994), 1–6.

[49] Gerhard Spellerberg, in *Damon und Lisille*: Eheroman und Vorläufer des bürgerlichen Privatromans des 18. Jahrhunderts?," *Chloe* 7 (Amsterdam: Rodopi, 1988), 703–31, rejects the genre name of "pastoral novel" in favor of the prose eclogue. Spellerberg there discusses all the relevant secondary literature. Regarding Opitz's *Hercinie* as origin of prose eclogue see Klaus Garber, *Der locus amoenus und der locus terribilis: Bild und Funktion der Natur in der deutschen Schäfer- und Landlebendichtung des 17. Jahrhunderts* (Cologne: Böhlau, 1974); also Anke-Marie Lohmeier, *Beatus ille: Studien zum* Lob des Landlebens *in der Literatur des absolutistischen Zeitalters* (Tübingen: Niemeyer, 1981); Garber, "Formen pastoralen Erzählens im frühneuzeitlichen Europa," *Internationales Archiv für Sozialgeschichte der deutschen Literatur* 10 (1985): 1–22. *Hercinie* is not even mentioned in the most recent representative literary history of the seventeenth century: in fact, *Die Literatur des 17. Jahrhunderts*, ed. Albert Meier (Munich: Hanser, 1999), lacks a chapter on pastoral prose. For more on Opitz's *Hercinie* see Garber, "Martin Opitz' *Schäferei von der Nymphe Hercinie*: Ursprung der Prosaekloge und des Schäferromans in Deutschland," *Daphnis* 11 (1982): 547–603; Peter Rusterholz, "Der "Schatten der Wahrheit' der deutschen Schäferdichtung," *Compar(a)ison* 2 (1993): 239–59; and Silvia Serena Tschopp, "Die Grotte in Martin Opitz' *Schäfferey von der Nimfen Hercinie* als Kreuzungspunkt katholischer Diskurse," in *Martin Opitz (1597–1639): Nachahmungspoetik und Lebenswelt*, ed. Thomas Borgstedt and Walter Schütz (Tübingen: Niemeyer, 2002), 236–49. Garber correctly points out that a courtly pastoral novel never came to fruition in Germany. For analyses of the few so-called individual or private pastoral novels see Arnold Hirsch, *Bürgertum und Barock im deutschen Roman: Ein Beitrag zur Entstehungsgeschichte des bürgerlichen*

Weltbildes (Cologne: Böhlau, 1957), and Wilhelm Voßkamp, "Der deutsche Schäferroman des 17. Jahrhunderts," in *Handbuch des Romans*, ed. Helmut Koopmann (Düsseldorf: Bagel, 1983), 105–16, 604–6.

[50] See S. K. Orgel, "Sidney's Experiment in Pastoral: *The Lady of May*," *Journal of the Warburg and Courtauld Institutes* 26, nos. 1–2 (1963): 198–203.

[51] See especially Klaus Garber, "Forschungen zur deutschen Schäfer- und Landlebendichtung des 17. und 18. Jahrhunderts," *Jahrbuch für Internationale Germanistik* 3 (1971): 226–42; *Der locus amoenus und der locus terribilis*; and "Vorwort," *Europäische Bukolik und Georgik*, ed. Garber (Darmstadt: Wissenschaftliche Buchgesellschaft, 1976), vii–xxii.

[52] Edition: *Adriatische Rosemund*, in *Sämtliche Werke* 4/II, ed. Volker Meid (Berlin: de Gruyter, 1993). Studies: Paul Baumgartner, *Die Gestaltung des Seelischen in Zesens Romanen* (Frauenfeld: Huber, 1942); Klaus Kaczerowsky, *Bürgerliche Romankunst im Zeitalter des Barock: Philipp von Zesens* Adriatische Rosemund (Munich: Fink, 1969); Ferdinand van Ingen, *Philipp von Zesen* (Stuttgart: Metzler, 1970); *Philipp von Zesen 1619–1969: Beiträge zu seinem Leben und Werk*, ed. Ferdinand van Ingen (Wiesbaden: Steiner, 1972); Jean Daniel Krebs, "Manieren und Liebe: Zur Dialektik von Affekt und Höflichkeit in Philipp von Zesens 'Adriatische Rosemund,'" in *Geselligkeit und Gesellschaft im Barockzeitalter*, ed. Knut Kiesant et al. (Wiesbaden: Harrassowitz, 1997), 1:401–10; and Sandra Krump, "Zesens 'Adriatische Rosemund': Gesellschaftskritik und Poetik," *Euphorion* 94, no. 4 (2000): 359–402.

[53] Zesen omitted from his translation of Scudéry's novel the important introduction, which presents nothing less than a poetological program of the courtly novel. Von Ingen, *Zesen*, 45, states that "*Adriatische Rosemund* cannot be classified as one of the current novel types.[. . .] It remains above all an exception to the rule."

[54] This held true in a limited fashion for the novels written a generation later: *Assenat* (1670) and *Simson* (1679). *Assenat* clearly follows the pattern of the political novel and attempts to borrow authenticity from the historicity of its biblical source, while *Simson* shows no structural unity. *Assenat* modifies the classical technique of *in medias res* and creates two parallel plots while significantly reducing the number of protagonists. *Simson* does something similar but is unable to integrate the main and subplots, thereby yielding an episodic sequence, which van Ingen, *Zesen*, 41, nonetheless calls a "remarkable experiment."

[55] The focal point of the epos, by contrast, is war.

[56] One cannot speak of popularity in its literal sense, for these texts were aimed at a public of rank and education, which was to prepare the way for a broad reception. The novel of state was written by and for the nobility, and the educated higher bourgeoisie could not afford to buy these texts.

[57] For more on the Heliodoran model and tradition see James J. Lynch, "Romance Conventions in Voltaire's *Candide*," *South Atlantic Review* 50, no. 1 (1985): 35–46.

[58] Andreas Heinrich Buchholtz, *Des Christlichen Teutschen Großfürsten HERKULES Und Der Böhmischen Königlichen Fräulein VALISKA Wunder-Geschichte* (1659). Niefanger, *Barock*, 187 is among the literary historians who take Buchholtz's *Hercules* novel of 1659 as the starting point. However, Zesen's *Rosemund* appeared in 1645, some fifteen years earlier, and Gregersdorf's *Jüngst-erbaute Schäfferey* was written still earlier, in 1632. While bucolic narrations may not generally be considered actual novels, Zesen's *Rosemund*, undertaken in the context of his translation work, offers strong contradictory evidence.

⁵⁹ For more on Buchholtz see Ingeborg Springer-Strand, *Barockroman und Erbauungsliteratur: Studien zum Herkulesroman von Andreas Heinrich Buchholtz* (Bern: Lang, 1975); also Ulrich Maché, "Die Überwindung des Amadisromans durch Andreas Heinrich Buchholtz," *Zeitschrift für deutsche Philologie* 85 (1966): 542–59.

⁶⁰ Gerhard Spellerberg, "Höfischer Roman," in *Zwischen Gegenreformation und Frühaufklärung: Späthumanismus, Barock 1572–1740*, ed. Harald Steinhagen, vol. 3 of *Deutsche Literatur: Eine Sozialgeschichte* (Reinbek: Rowohlt, 1985), 320.

⁶¹ On Anton Ulrich see especially Blake Lee Spahr, "Herzog Anton Ulrich von Braunschweig-Lüneburg," in *Deutsche Dichter des 17. Jahrhunderts: Ihr Leben und Werk*, ed. Harald Steinhagen and Benno von Wiese (Berlin: Schmidt, 1984), 597–614.

⁶² On Anton Ulrich's novels see Harry Gerald Haile, "Octavia, Römische Geschichte: Anton Ulrich's use of the episode," *Journal of English and German Philology* 57 (1957): 611–32; Wolfgang Bender, "Verwirrung und Entwirrung in der *Octavia / Römische Geschichte* Herzog Anton Ulrichs von Braunschweig-Wolfenbüttel" (Ph. D. diss., University of Cologne, 1964); Blake Lee Spahr, *Anton Ulrich and Aramena: The Genesis and Development of a Baroque Novel* (Berkeley: U of California P, 1966); Adolf Haslinger, *Epische Formen im höfischen Barockroman: Anton Ulrichs Romane als Modell* (Munich: Fink, 1970); Fritz Martini, *Der Tod Neros: Suetonius, Anton Ulrich von Braunschweig-Wolfenbüttel, Sigmund von Birken oder: Historischer Bericht, erzählerische Fiktion und Stil der frühen Aufklärung* (Stuttgart: Metzler, 1974); Giles Reid Hoyt, *The Development of Anton Ulrich's Narrative Prose on the Basis of Surviving "Octavia" Manuscripts and Prints* (Bonn: Bouvier, 1977); *Monarchus Poeta: Studien zum Leben und Werk Anton Ulrichs von Braunschweig-Lüneburg*, ed. Jean-Marie Valentin (Amsterdam: Rodopi, 1985); and Stephan Kraft, *Geschlossenheit und Offenheit der Römischen Octavia von Herzog Anton Ulrich: "der roman macht ahn die ewigkeit gedencken, den er nimbt kein endt"* (Würzburg: Königshausen, 2004).

⁶³ This is clearly underscored by Anton Ulrich's extraordinarily successful politics of marriage.

⁶⁴ A summary of the immense complexity of this work (author, history of publication — including possible collaborations — structure, reception, and bibliography) is provided by Stephan Kraft in the web-based *Marteau Encyclopedia of the Early Modern Period* at http://www.pierre-marteau.com/library/g-1677–0001.html.

⁶⁵ Thomas Saine, "J. G. Herder: The Weimar Classic Back of the (City) Church," in *The Literature of Weimar Classicism*, ed. Simon Richter, Camden House History of German Literature, vol. 7 (Rochester, NY: Camden House, 2004), 113–31, here 126, remarks that *Humanität* may be best described as "the true nature of humanity and the human race."

⁶⁶ This ideal springs the bounds of the baroque worldview. Insofar as Anton Ulrich has been taken as a baroque author, some scholars, such as Martini in *Der Tod Neros* and Kraft in *Geschlossenheit und Offenheit*, have considered him to be an "anomaly" and see him more as an example of early bourgeois literature.

⁶⁷ *Großmüthiger Feldherr Arminius oder Hermann Als ein tapfferer Beschirmer der deutschen Freyheit / Nebst seiner Durchlauchtigen Thusnelda In einer sinnreichen Staats-Liebes-und Helden-Geschichte Dem Vaterlande zu Liebe Dem deutschen Adel aber zu Ehren und rühmlichen Nachfolge [. . .].*

⁶⁸ For more on Lohenstein see in this volume the section "The Gallant Ideal: From Mannerist to Classicist Style" in the chapter by Peter Hess. Further: Dieter Kafitz, *Lohensteins Arminius: Disputatorisches Verfahren und Lehrgehalt in einem Roman*

zwischen Barock und Aufklärung (Stuttgart: Metzler, 1970); Gerhard Spellerberg, *Verhängnis und Geschichte: Untersuchungen zu den Trauerspielen und dem* Arminius-*Romans Daniel Caspers von Lohenstein* (Bad Homburg: Gehlen, 1970); Elida Maria Szarota, *Lohensteins* Arminius *als Zeitroman: Sichtweisen des Spätbarock* (Bern: Francke, 1970); Bernhard Asmuth, *Daniel Casper von Lohenstein* (Stuttgart: Metzler, 1971); Wolfgang Bender, "Lohensteins *Arminius*: Bemerkungen zum 'Höfisch-Historischen' Roman," in *Rezeption und Produktion zwischen 1570 und 1730: Festschrift für Günther Weydt*, ed. Wolfdietrich Rasch et al. (Bern: Francke, 1972), 381–410; Wolf Wucherpfennig, *Klugheit und Weltordnung: Das Problem politischen Handelns in Lohensteins* Arminius (Freiburg: Becksmann, 1973); Spellerberg, "Daniel Casper von Lohenstein," in Steinhagen and von Wiese, eds., *Deutsche Dichter des 17. Jahrhunderts*, 640–89; Adalbert Wichert, *Literatur, Rhetorik und Jurisprudenz im 17. Jahrhundert: Daniel Casper von Lohenstein und sein Werk: Eine exemplarische Studie* (Tübingen: Niemeyer, 1991); Thomas Borgstedt, *Reichsidee und Liebesethik: Eine Rekonstruktion des Lohensteinschen Arminiusromans* (Tübingen: Niemeyer, 1992); Cornelia Plume, *Heroinen der Geschlechterordnung: Weiblichkeitsprojektionen im epischen und dramatischen Werk Daniel Caspers von Lohenstein und die Querelle des femmes* (Stuttgart: Metzler, 1996).

[69] Quoted from *Barock*, vol. 3 of *Die deutsche Literatur: Texte und Zeugnisse*, comp. Albrecht Schöne (Munich: Beck, 1963), 409.

[70] This was also the case for the relatively vital form of the "chivalric novel," whose best known representatives were August Bohse (1661–1742), pseudonym Talander, and Christian Friedrich Hunold (1681–1721), pseudonym Menantes. They continued the courtly-historical novel as a pure love story, which often appeared as a *roman à clef*, and thereby connected more directly with the French tradition; *fortuna* and *providentia* were transformed back into stories of intrigue as the plots became generally individualized and lost universal significance. See Herbert Singer, *Der deutsche Roman zwischen Barock und Rokoko* (Cologne: Böhlau, 1963); Singer, *Der galante Roman*, 2nd ed. (Stuttgart: Metzler, 1966); and Wilhelm Voßkamp, "Christian Friedrich Hunold (Menantes)," in Steinhagen and von Wiese, eds., *Deutsche Dichter des 17. Jahrhunderts*, 852–70.

[71] Of the little scholarly work done in this area see Wolfgang Pfeiffer-Belli, *Die Asiatische Banise: Studien zur Geschichte des höfisch-historischen Romans in Deutschland* (Berlin: Ebering, 1940); Gerhart Hoffmeister, "Transformationen von Zieglers *Asiatischer Banise*: Zur Trivialisierung des höfisch-historischen Romans," *German Quarterly* 49 (1976): 181–90; Hans-Gert Roloff, "Heinrich Anselm von Ziegler und Kliphausen," in Steinhagen and von Wiese, eds., *Deutsche Dichter des 17. Jahrhunderts*, 798–818; Irmgard Wirtz, "Galante Affektinszenierung im spätbarocken Roman: Heinrich Anselm von Ziegler und Kliphausens *Asiatische Banise*," in *Der galante Diskurs:Kommunikationsideal und Epochenschwelle*, ed. Thomas Borgstedt and Andreas Solbach (Dresden: Thelem bei w.e.b., 2001), 331–45.

[72] On the picaresque novel see especially Matthias Bauer, *Der Schelmenroman* (Stuttgart: Metzler, 1994).

[73] *Leben und Wandel Lazaril von Tormes: Und beschreibung, Wasz derselbe fur unglück und widerwertigkeit auszgestanden hat*. The translator seems to have been a native of Silesia and based his translation on the Antwerp edition of the original.

[74] Walter E. Schäfer, *Johann Michael Moscherosch: Staatsmann, Satiriker und Pädagoge im Barockzeitalter* (Munich: Beck, 1982), and Claudie Bubenik, "*Ich bin, was man

will": Werte und Normen in Johann Michael Moscheroschs Gesichten Philanders von Sittenwald (Frankfurt am Main: Lang, 2001).

[75] Edition: *Wunderliche und Wahrhafftige Gesichte Philanders von Sittewalt,* ed. Wolfgang Harms (Stuttgart: Reclam, 1986), 129–30.

[76] On Grimmelshausen see Volker Meid, *Grimmelshausen: Epoche — Werk — Wirkung* (Munich: Beck, 1984), Dieter Breuer, *Grimmelshausen-Handbuch* (Munich: Fink, 1999), and *A Companion to the Works of Grimmelshausen,* ed. Karl F. Otto Jr. (Rochester, NY: Camden House, 2003).

[77] Grimmelshausen's devotional novels *Histori vom Keuschen Joseph* (1666), *Dietwald und Amelinde* (1670), und *Proximus und Lympida* (1672) can be ignored here.

[78] Book 1, chap. 1. The translations that follow are by George Schultz-Behrend, *The Adventures of Simplicius Simplicissimus,* 2nd rev. ed. (Columbia, SC: Camden House, 1993).

[79] See Lucien Febvre, *The Problem of Unbelief in the Sixteenth Century: The Religion of Rabelais,* trans. Beatrice Gottlieb (Cambridge: Harvard UP, 1982).

[80] Modern research on Beer goes back to the 1960s with the editions by Richard Alewyn. For a first summary of research and new beginnings see James Hardin, *Johann Beer* (Boston: Twayne, 1983). See also Hardin's *Johann Beer: Eine beschreibende Bibliographie* (Bern: Francke, 1983), which lists all known copies of works by Beer and those attributed to him. More recently see Andreas Solbach, *Johann Beer: Rhetorisches Erzählen zwischen Satire und Utopie* (Tübingen: Niemeyer, 2003), and *Johann Beer: Schriftsteller, Komponist und Hofbeamter, 1655–1700* (Frankfurt am Main: Lang, 2003), which also provides secondary literature.

[81] In "Realismus und Naturalismus" (1932), in *Deutsche Barockforschung,* 2nd ed., ed. Alewyn (Cologne: Kiepenheuer & Witsch, 1966), 358–71, here 364–65.

[82] Translated by John Russell (Columbia, SC: Camden House, 1999).

[83] Translated by James Hardin and Gerda Jordan (New York: Lang, 1984).

[84] Another was Johann Kuhnau, a writer of great wit and a musician (he will be discussed below).

[85] *Schelmuffskys wahrhafftige curiöse und sehr gefährliche Reisebeschreibung zu Wasser und Lande,* ed. Ilse-Marie Barth (Stuttgart: Reclam, 1992). See Eckart Oehlenschläger, "Christian Reuter," in Steinhagen and von Wiese, eds., *Deutsche Dichter des 17. Jahrhunderts,* 819–38. English translation: *Schelmuffsky,* trans. Wayne Wonderley (Chapel Hill: U of North Carolina P, 1962).

[86] On Reuter's exploitation of this topos in *Schelmuffsky* and the related drama *Die ehrliche Frau zu Plissine* see the older but still useful study by Helen Walden, "Christian Reuter: Is He a Baroque Poet, or Not?" *German Quarterly* 9, no. 2 (1936): 71–77.

[87] The allusion here is to Mikhail Bakhtin's theories of laughter and the grotesque in *Rabelais and His World* (written during the Second World War but not published until 1965).

[88] *Sämtliche Werke,* vol. 17, *Romane I,* ed. Hans-Gert Roloff and G.-H. Susen (Berlin: de Gruyter, 2006), 294.

[89] Johannes Riemer: *Werke,* vol. 1, *Romane,* ed. Helmut Krause (Berlin: de Gruyter, 1979), 45.

[90] On Ettner see *Johann Christoph Ettner: Eine beschreibende Bibliographie,* ed. James Hardin (Bern: Francke, 1988).

[91] See Susanne Stöpfgeshoff, *Die Musikerromane von Wolfgang Caspar Printz und Johann Kuhnau* (Ph.D. diss., University of Freiburg im Br., 1960), and Helmut K. Krausse, ed., Wolfgang Caspar Printz, *Ausgewählte Werke* (Berlin: de Gruyter, 1974–93).

[92] See James Hardin, ed., *Johann Kuhnau: Ausgewählte Werke*, 3 vols. (Bern: Lang, 1992).

[93] *The Musical Charlatan [Der musikalische Quacksalber]*, trans. John R. Russell, ed. James Hardin (Columbia, SC: Camden House, 1997). Romain Rolland called this novel one of the most interesting and amusing of the Baroque.

The Emblem and Emblematic Forms in Early Modern Germany

Peter M. Daly

Genre, Sources, and Functions

THE EMBLEM IS NO LONGER REGARDED as a no man's land between literature and the graphic arts. Scholars in different disciplines now recognize the emblem as an important expression of the cultural life of the Renaissance and the Baroque, reflecting a panoply of interests, ranging from war to love, from religion to philosophy and politics, from the sciences and natural history to the occult, from social mores to encyclopedic knowledge, and from serious speculation to entertainment. Poets and preachers, writers and dramatists frequently employed emblems and emblem-like structures in speeches, sermons, and conversations as well as in written texts. Emblems and imprese[1] were also used in the significant decoration of buildings and household wares; they helped to shape virtually every form of verbal and visual communication during the early modern period.

A typical emblem consists of a motto, a symbolic picture, and two or more brief texts. Their Latin terms are, respectively, *inscriptio, pictura,* and *subscriptio,* neutral labels that do not specify a particular form or function for the part so named. "Emblem" can be regarded as a mode of thought that combines picture and word into a meaning, or an art form that joins visual image and text. Attempts to define the genre of illustrated books, called "emblem books," have been less than successful. If definitions are too narrow they exclude too much; if they are too wide they embrace too much. There is also the problem of normative definitions that may exclude works considered emblematic by their creators. The term itself and its various synonyms have undergone mutations of meaning and use, often differing from country to country or language to language. For some people the word *emblem* calls to mind the badges of schools, universities, armed services, coats of arms, and national symbols, which consist of a motto and a symbolic picture. Badges are often descendants of the emblem, survivors of a tradition of verbal and visual symbolism that was all-pervasive during the sixteenth and seventeenth centuries in Europe.

As a miniature form of allegory the emblem communicates through words and pictures simultaneously.[2] These two symbol systems collaborate in the production of emblematic meaning. The reciprocal cross-referencing of text and image in the act of reading suggests that the *pictura* is more than a mere illustration of the text. The sketchy nature of some *picturae* can have the effect of engaging the reader to piece out the full import. The texts do not always repeat or develop the visual codes, which depend for their effect on the ability of the reader/viewer to identify picture content and recognize its inherent or assumed meaning. Only a slight extension of the concept of intertextuality is required to account for some of the semantic activity in emblem *picturae;* for the emblem, though illustrated, is essentially a literary genre, and sixteenth-century readers approached illustrations with much the same verbal-symbolic suppositions as they did painting.[3]

Every emblem is a mixed-media communication, and emblem images often bear meanings not expressly stated in the words of the *inscriptio* or *subscriptio*. Such visual meaning may enrich, complicate, or even undercut textual communication. Indeed, the very notion of emblematic "meaning" can be problematic. Equating an emblem with a single meaning is the chief error in Henkel and Schöne's otherwise invaluable handbook, *Emblemata,* analyzing emblems in the sixteenth and seventeenth centuries.[4] Their "Bedeutungsregister" (Index of Meanings) presents one meaning or subject for each emblem, which tends to oversimplify or flatten multivalence.[5] While reducing emblems to meaning or signification is almost unavoidable, concepts are rarely identical with words in an emblem, and they are virtually never identical with visual motifs. We may say that the Brutus who falls on his sword in an emblem "means" suicide, or fickle fortune, or something else, depending on the *scriptura* (textual parts) of the emblem. But what is pictured is Brutus, not a concept. Listing emblems by their meanings is a kind of shorthand, but an approach that cannot be justified.

The first emblem book, entitled appropriately *Emblematum liber* and containing Latin texts, was published in 1531 in Augsburg, Germany for the noted Italian lawyer Andrea Alciato, who is rightfully known as *pater et princeps* (father and prince) of the emblem. At least 6,400 books of or about emblems and imprese, starting with Alciato, have been published, both in Neo-Latin and in many vernacular languages.[6] Alciato's emblems provide evidence of ethical, social, political, and religious principles, and occasionally of economic concerns.[7] In general, however, emblems and imprese tend to reflect dominant cultures, whether political or religious, rather than advocate for change. From the beginning, emblems were printed in books containing scores, even hundreds, of discrete and usually unrelated statements. Only from the end of the sixteenth century did specialized emblem books on love, religion, Stoicism, political statecraft, and princely power and achievements begin to appear.

The emblem combines symbolic graphics and texts in a special way (fig. 1). The *pictura* is usually framed between *inscriptio* and *subscriptio*. Typically, the emblem begins with an abstract statement of theme in the *inscriptio*. Alciato's Prometheus emblem, which draws its symbol from Greek and Roman tradition, bears the *inscriptio* "Quae supra nos, nihil ad nos" (What is above us is no concern to us). The *pictura* embodies this abstract notion symbolically in a male figure attacked by an eagle. The knowing reader will recognize the figure as Prometheus even before reading the text, which relates briefly the situation:

Quos tibi donamus fluuiatiles accipe cancros,
Munera conueniunt moribus ista tuis.
His oculi uigiles, & forfice plurimus ordo
Chelarum armatus, maximáq; aluus adest.
Sic tibi propensus stat pingui ab domino uenter,
Pernicesq; pedes, spiculáq; apta pedi.
Cum uagus in triuijs, mensǽq; sedilibus erras,
Inq; alios mordax scommata salsa iacis.

CONCORDIA

In bellum ciuile duces cum Roma pararet,
Viribus & caderet Martia terra suis.
Mos fuit in partes turmis coëuntibus hasdem,
Coniunctas dextras mutua dona dare,
Foederis hæc species, id habet concordia signum,
Vt quos iungit amor iungat & ipsa manus.

QVAE SVPRA NOS NI-
bil ad nos.

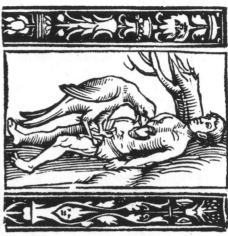

Caucasia æternū pendens in rupe Promethæus
Dirripitur sacri præpetis ungue iecus
Et nollet fecisse hominem, figulosq; posus
Accensa rapto damnat ab igne facem
Roduntur uarijs prudentum pectora curis
Qui cœli affectant scire deumq; uices

IN AMATORES MERE-
tricum.

Figure 1. *Alciato*, Emblematum liber *(Augsburg, 1531), fols. B4r and B4v.*

Caucasia aeternum pendens in rupe Prometheus
   Diripitur sacri praepetis ungue iecur.
Et nollet seasse hominem, sigulosque perosus
   Accensam rapto damnat ab igne facem.

[Prometheus hangs eternally on the Caucasian rock; his liver is being shredded by the talon of the sacred bird. And he would wish not to have created man; despising potters, he renounces the spark enkindled from the stolen fire.]

That in all brevity explains why Prometheus suffered the eternal punishment of having his liver torn out daily by Zeus's eagle: he had aspired too high; he had vied with the gods in creating man and stealing divine fire for mortals. The concluding lines apply the meaning of the symbol in the human sphere, but not as a simple prohibition:

Roduntur uarijs prudentum pectora curis,
Qui coeli affectant scire deumque uices.

[The hearts of wise men, who aspire to know the changes of heaven and the gods, are gnawed by various cares.]

The message of this humanist emblem is addressed to "prudentes" (wise men), who aspire to know things supernatural and divine, though their quest is fraught with cares. When we combine this final sentence with the statement in the *inscriptio,* recalling that Prometheus had been punished for betraying the secrets of the gods, we are likely to draw the conclusion from the emblem as a whole that, even for wise men, divine mysteries should remain mysteries and that there are some things humankind should not know or do. This emblem is typical insofar as a general moral is enunciated in the *inscriptio,* embodied in the *pictura* through the fate of Prometheus, and elucidated in the *subscriptio.* It is also characteristic of the emblem at its best that the three parts cooperate in communicating a complex notion not fully contained in any one of the parts.

Another major source of emblem motifs is nature, or natural history, as understood in the medieval Christian tradition. Animals, plants, and stones, in fact all things, belong to a *mundus symbolicus,* a symbolic world. Everything bears a significance implanted by God at creation. Thus, the chameleon can signify flattery, for it feeds on thin air and changes its color according to its environment, taking on every hue except red and white, the latter being the color of virtue and honesty. In Alciato's chameleon emblem (fig. 2) he is not inventing an equation between the chameleon and the concept of flattery but applying accepted inherent qualities of the creature to moral concepts. This is an exercise, not of private symbolism, but rather of public allegory.

The Bible and Christian tradition also supplied motifs, as did literary topoi and proverbs. Although writers were slow to press the emblem into the service of religion — forty years would elapse before the French noblewoman Georgette de Montenay (ca. 1540–1607) published *Emblemes, ou deuises chrestiennes* (1571), the first wholly Christian emblem book — the Society of Jesus eventually used the new form in hundreds of books and pamphlets, published in Latin and all vernacular languages of Europe. Jesuits produced over 1,500 editions of emblem books, most illustrated, but some not.[8] That figure represents about a quarter of all known books of imprese and emblems.

The emblem did not spring into existence from nowhere. There were many important forerunners and other forms that, like tributaries, fed the mainstream of emblem literature.[9] Emblems incorporated ideas and materials from the Greek epigram, classical mythology and history, Renaissance collections of *loci communes* (commonplaces), the *Tabula Cebetis* (The Tablet of Cebes, an allegorical work by the Theban philosopher Cebes, a pupil of Socrates), Egyptian and Renaissance hieroglyphics,[10] imprese, commemorative medals, heraldry, medieval nature symbolism, and Bible exegesis. The emblematists of the sixteenth and seventeenth centuries drew upon these materials in different degrees, and their prefaces do not always adequately account for their actual practices.

196 AND. ALC. EMBLEM. LIB.

In adulatores. LXXXVIII.

Semper hiat,semper tenuem quae uesatur auram,
 Reciproc*at* chamaeleon,
Et mutat fidem,uarios sumitꝗ; colores,
 Praeter rubrum uel candidum:
Sic & adulator populari uescitur aura,
 Hiansꝗ; aucta deuorat,
Et solium mores imitatur principis atros,
 Albi & pudica nescius.

*Das buechle derverschroten werck.*197

Der Furſten heuchler. LXXXVIII.

Chameleon von lufft ſich nert,
Den er ſtet vacht in offnen ſchlund,
Auch on rot vnd weyſs er ſich kert
In alle farb in ainer ſtund:
Alſo hat allzeyt offnen mund
Ein ſchmaychler, friſt die arm gemain,
Vnd lobt dem Furſten all ſein fund
On frumbkeyt, vnd die warheyt rain.
 N iij

Figure 2. *Alciato*, Emblemata *(Paris, 1542), no. 88.*

The function of the emblem is didactic in the broadest sense: it is intended to convey knowledge and truth in a brief and compelling form that will persuade the reader and imprint itself on the memory. In this process the choice of picture symbol is essential, since it embodies the meaning of the emblem. The term *emblem* originally meant mosaic, insert, or inlay, and it is no coincidence that individual emblems make miniature statements that are complete in themselves. Emblems are closely related to popular collections (German: *Florilegien*) of sayings, epigrams, and commonplaces; indeed they often derive from such collections, only later to be plundered for commonplace books and used in various ways in schools. There are, of course, many different manifestations of the emblem. Most emblem and impresa literature of early modern Europe can be divided into five main groupings:

1. illustrated emblem books in the strict sense, that is, the tight three-part form associated with Alciato;
2. unillustrated collections of emblems or imprese, where the graphic element is replaced with a verbal description, for example, with Andrew Willet (1562–1621, prebendary of Ely and controversialist);
3. expanded forms, in the case, for example, of the Flemish poet Jan Van der Noot (1540–95), who adds a book-length prose commentary; or the Nuremberg poet Georg Philipp Harsdörffer (1607–58), who often works with multiple emblems, as we shall see below;

4. emblematically illustrated works such as meditations, where the plate becomes an integral if minor part, as seen in works of the Jesuit court preacher Jeremias Drexel (1581–1638) and the baroque poetess Catharina Regina von Greiffenberg (1633–94);
5. theoretical discussions of emblem and impresa — these may also be contained in poetological works — which provide many examples, as in the works by the Italian historian Paolo Giovio (1483–1552) or the French grammarian Dominique Bouhours (1628–1702).

Sixteenth-century treatises reveal a confusing use of terms, but the more personalized function of the two-part impresa clearly distinguishes it from the standard three-part emblem. The impresa, which comprises an image and a motto, is the personal badge of an aristocratic or powerful bourgeois personage. It makes a personal statement and is an aspect of self-fashioning or self-representation. Initially, imprese were symbolic statements inscribed on objects, which is to say, they belonged to material culture rather than print culture.[11] They were nonetheless intended to be "read." The picture motif carried symbolic, that is, verbal significance related to the bearer; hence the occasional relation to heraldry. Some imprese, such as the tournament imprese at the Accession Day Tilts in Elizabethan London,[12] were unique to the event; they can be interpreted only when we know exactly who used the impresa on which occasion and under what circumstances. Other imprese became permanent badges of the person, and the special meanings of the motif were thus appropriated by the wearer. Often worn by aristocrats on their clothing, as in the *Portrait of a Courtier* by Bartolomeo Veneto,[13] imprese could take a variety of forms, of which jewelry and brooches are the most obvious. Imprese also often adorned weapons and armor worn by man and horse, playing a symbolic role in jousts and tournaments. Many products of material culture, including armor, garments and jewelry, embroidery and tapestry, carvings in stone and wood, stained glass, paintings and portraits, wall and ceiling decorations, even tombstones, were often embellished with decorations deriving from the emblem tradition.

The German Translations

The bibliographical procedures for determining "German" emblems have not been normalized. Different bibliographers take different tacks. For John Landwehr, who has produced the only printed bibliography of German emblems,[14] "German" applies to emblem books in any language produced in German-speaking countries as well as emblem books with German texts printed anywhere. His bibliography contains 661 items, many of them with Latin texts. For other bibliographers "German" applies only to German-language texts printed anywhere. The Union Catalogue of Emblem Books database presently contains more than 1,000 records of works with German texts, of which nearly 600 were published in the early modern period; those books include bilingual editions and polyglot collections. The publication statistics strongly suggest that there was a vigorous market for emblem books with German texts. As we shall see, Wolfgang Hunger and Jeremias Held provided German versions of Alciato's emblems in the sixteenth century.

The German translations of Alciato's emblems, whether printed in Paris or Frankfurt am Main, were bilingual.[15] They may be organized under thematic headings (classical, political, religious) and examples may be selected to show how word-image relationships change in the process. By "classical" is meant the mythology, literature, and history of ancient Greece and Rome, which plays a central role in Alciato's *subscriptiones*. The *Greek Anthology,* which Alciato was translating into Latin in the 1520s, is the most important but not the only source.[16] It is possible to identify the intended reader by investigating the educational and cultural information conveyed by the emblems. Classical allusions presuppose a reader who has enjoyed a humanistic education.

Wolfgang Hunger was, like Alciato, a teacher and lawyer. Born in 1511, he studied at Freiburg, spent the years 1535 to 1537 in France as tutor to Balthasar and Werner von Seibolsdorf, to whom the Wechel bilingual edition (Latin and German; Paris, 1534) of his *Emblematum libellus* (Little Book of Emblems) is dedicated.[17] He began his translation, the first in German, after returning to Germany in 1537.[18] In 1539 he was at Bourges completing his law degree under Alciato,[19] and here he finished the translation for the well-known Wechel printing house in 1542. One wonders whether he ever discussed the project with Alciato. In 1540 Hunger was appointed to the University of Ingolstadt and served as rector there from 1541 to 1549. He then became an assessor for the imperial tribunal of Speyer, and from 1552 until his death in 1555 he was chancellor to the bishop of Freising. His translation of Alciato's emblems was the only work he published during his lifetime.

Little is known about Jeremias Held; even his dates are not certain. The assumption that he was a doctor of medicine or an apothecary derives solely from a book he wrote on herbs, printed by the renowned Frankfurt am Main publisher Sigmund Feyerabend in 1566. Presumably, Held was born in Nördlingen, an imperial free city, a center of wool production with an important trade fair, at the beginning of the sixteenth century, where he probably attended the local Gymnasium. The literature dealing with Nördlingen, however, provides no information on Jeremias Held or his family.[20] If he studied at a German university, then probably at Altdorf, though this cannot be established because no matriculation records are available for the period in question. He published his translation, *Liber Emblematum [. . .] Kunstbuch* (Book of Emblems: Book of Art) in 1566.[21]

Should the two German versions of Alciato be regarded as actual translations? We have to be on guard against modern assumptions concerning the nature, process, and purpose of translation. We know little, if anything, about the actual process of translation that produced these new vernacular texts.[22] Even when translators explain their intentions in prefaces or introductions, these are usually so brief or general as to afford little insight. In any case, authorial statement must be compared closely with actual practice. Alciato wrote in Neo-Latin for a humanistically schooled elite who read Latin and Greek and thus knew well the literature and mythology of the Greeks and Romans. His translators, whether writing in French, German, Italian, or Spanish,[23] used an early modern vernacular and evidently did not expect their readers to catch all of Alciato's learned allusions.

Another question: what happens to the intertextuality of word and image in the emblem when a learned Neo-Latin emblem book is translated into German and enters a more popular culture? In presenting these often allusive emblems to a German audience these books had to be adapted to the level of knowledge and the concerns of the new readership: the German mercantile and professional middle class with little understanding of Latin. The *picturae* of course remained unchanged; only the German texts were new. Translation involved adaptation in two ways: the Latin text was rendered into German for a German readership; and this process was often complicated by virtue of having both the Latin and a French text at hand, so that, in effect, the translator actually conceived of the new edition as trilingual.[24]

Hunger was the first to recognize the pedagogical and linguistic potential of the emblem. According to his preface, the translation was prompted by his reading of the French edition of Alciato's emblems.[25] He initially seems to have considered producing a trilingual edition in the expectation that this would demonstrate the qualities of the two vernacular languages when compared with Latin. In general, Hunger downplays the classical content for his German readership by simplifying, explaining, or omitting some of the allusions, which in fact often embody the meaning of the whole Latin emblem. Except in the rare instances where the name of the figure is printed in the *pictura*, his German reader probably could not identify the figure from the *pictura* alone unless that figure is engaged in an action uniquely associated with his name: a Roman soldier falling on his sword (Brutus); a male figure carrying a club and wearing a lion's skin and beset by pigmies (Hercules). Brutus emblems provide telling examples, even as early as the first Alciato edition, where the printer Steyner had a crude woodcut made that shows a soldier plunging a knife into his chest. Above the figure appears the abbreviation "M. BR." (Marcus Brutus). Presumably, the figure was deemed not to be self-explanatory. By contrast, the woodcut devised for Hunger's edition depicts an unnamed soldier (but recognizable as Brutus) falling on his sword.[26] Often, however, the *pictura* only provides the viewer with a generalized figure, and the Latin text only supplies an allusive name, such as Dione (mother of Aphrodite), thus engaging the reader in an intellectual exercise.

Hunger also changes the intertextual relation of picture and text by providing more commonly known names and additional information. Alciato names the figure in emblem 20 wearing an animal skin Alcides, whereas Hunger calls him by the name familiar to the German reader, Hercules. Hunger refers to the goddess of love in emblem 95 directly as Venus rather than, say, "Daughter of Dione," and he calls the poet in emblem 4 Homer rather than Maeonius. He may also provide new identifications where Alciato

38 AND. ALC. EMBLEM. LIB.

38 AND. ALC. EMBLEM. LIB.

In auaros,uel quibus melior condi-
tio ab extraneis offertur. XI.

Delphini infidens uada cœrula fulcat Arion,
  Hocq; aures mulcet,frœnat & ora fono.
Quàm fit auari hominis,nõ tã mens dira ferarũ eſt,
  Quiq; uiris rapimur,pifcibus eripimur.

Das buechle der verfchroten werck. 39

Wider die geytzigen,oder von den,
welchen beſſer ſtand von frembden angeboten. XI.

Ee dann Arion in das meer
Von den fchiffleuten gſtoſſen ward,
Bat er,das im vergunnet wer,
Sein harpffen zſchlagen noch ein fart:
Nach feinnem gfang er nit verhart,
Springt in das meer,kumbt ein Delphin,
Fuert in zu land freundlicher art:
Hye fich deſß geytz greulichen fin.
  C iiij

Figure 3. Alciato, Emblemata *(Paris, 1542), no. 11.*

had resorted to indirection, circumlocution, or allusion. In the Latin *subscrip-tio* of emblem 32 Alciato paraphrases his subject as the "Trojan boy [. . .] borne aloft by the bird of Jove"; Hunger identifies him directly as Ganymede. Ithacus becomes Ulysses in emblem 37, which focuses on the blinding of the Cyclops, also renamed and described as "Polyphem der einaugig ryß" (Polyphemus, the one-eyed giant). Similarly, Hunger often assists his less-educated reader by explaining the mythological figure or story that embodies the meaning of the emblem. This can be as simple as adding a word or two to reveal the identity of the figure. Who was Lais? Alciato does not need to tell his sophisticated reader, but Hunger informs his reader, in emblem 25, that Lais was "die schoen huer von Corinth" (the beautiful whore of Corinth). In emblem 11 (fig. 3) Alciato mentions Arion sitting on the dolphin, which suffices to remind the humanistically schooled reader of the situation. Hunger, however, recollects the story in the first seven lines of his *subscriptio:*

> Ee dann Arion in das meer
> Von den schiffleuten gestossen ward,
> Bat er, das im vergunnet wer,
> Sein harpffen zschlagen noch ein fart:
> Nach seinem gsang er nit verhart,
> Springt in das meer, kumbt ein Delphin,
> Fuehrt in zu land freundlicher art.

62   AND. ALC. EMBLEM. LIB.

Ex arduis perpetuum nomen.   XXIII.

Crediderat platani ramis sua pignora passer,
  Et bene,ni seuo uisa dracone forent.
Glutijt hic pullos omnes,miseramq; parentem
  Saxeus,er tali dignus obire neæ.
Hæc,nisi mentitur Calchas,monumenta laboris
  Sunt longi,auius fama perennis eat.

Das buechle der verschroten werck. 63

Ewig ehr,auß schwaren thaten.
                        XXIII.
Ein werck das sol vil iar bestan
In lob vnd ehr vor aller welt,
Das wil vil zeyt vnd arbeyt han,
Wie Calchas seinen Griechen meldt,
Sy muesten zehen iar zu veld
Vor Troia ligenn,eé es in gluckt:
Dem zu prob er ein Drachen stelt,
Der einn spatz vnd neun iunge schluckt.

Figure 4. Alciato, Emblemata *(Paris, 1542), no. 23.*

[Before Arion was pushed into the sea by the sailors, he asked that he be allowed to play his harp again. After his song, he did not delay, but jumped into the sea; a dolphin comes, takes him to land in a friendly manner.]

Alciato's emblem 23 (fig. 4) on the subject of fame through deed and effort has as its *inscriptio* "Ex arduis perpetuum nomen" (Eternal fame through difficult deeds). The emblem pictures a large snake, called in the *subscriptio* Draco, which devours a sparrow, while in the nest above, young birds flutter nervously. No doubt the sixteenth-century German reader would be puzzled as to the relationship here of motto to *pictura*. How does this *pictura* of a serpent devouring a sparrow and its young signify eternal fame through difficult deeds? Alciato's Latin *subscriptio* supplies only one hint: it was Calchas, the diviner who accompanied the Greeks to Troy, who "gave this sign of long labor." The learned reader could combine this single reference with the pictorial motif and thus recognize the symbolic reference to the Trojan War — alluded to in the *subscriptio* but not depicted in the *pictura* — and understand its meaning. For his part Hunger explicitly names the Greeks, Troy, and the war. Indeed, he recounts the story for his German readers (no. 23):

Wie Calchas seinen Griechen meldt,
Sy muesten zehen iar zu veld

> Vor Troia ligenn ee es in gluckt:
> Dem zu prob er ein Drachen stelt
> Der einn spatz vnd neun iunge schluckt.

[As Calchas told his Greeks, they would have to spend ten years in front
of Troy before they succeeded; as a demonstration, he placed a dragon
that devoured a sparrow and nine young.]

Hunger thus creates a completely new text, in which he resolves the enigmatic
combination of text and picture by telling the story that Alciato left untold.

Jeremias Held rendered Alciato's Latin emblems into German some years
later, published in a 1566–67 and a 1580 edition. It too is bilingual and contains two prefaces in German; the Latin emblem texts are followed by Held's
German version. The first preface, dated 9 September 1566 and dedicated to
the lawyer Dr. Raymund Graff, opens with a long discussion of gratitude and
ingratitude, citing instances from classical history and mythology as well as
from nature. In his continuing statements on gratitude, Held returns to
Alciato, noting that Alciato's original dedication was to the well-known jurist
Conrad Peutinger of Augsburg.

The second preface addresses the reader and the question of what was
expected of emblems in Germany in the 1560s. Held says he knows that his
translation of Alciato will provoke envious critics,[27] who will consider his work
only suitable for "Handwercker" (artisans), such as painters and goldsmiths.
His explanation of the values of the book comprises thirteen numbered points
and a longer final discussion. He begins by appealing to the ancient provenance of emblems among the Egyptians, who possessed not only a common
vernacular language but also a sacred language reserved to the priests, which
used only images "von den Thieren vnd gewechsen / etc vnd deren Gliedern
vnd theilen" (of creatures and plants etc., and their limbs and parts). In the
pages of these emblems "das stummend redt" (that which is silent speaks), and
"das on vernunfft / gibt eine grosse vernunfft von sich" (that which is without reason gives expression to great reason). Emblems contain "grosser ver-
standt vnd geheimnuß" (great understanding and mystery); the book contains
the very "geheimnuß der Natur" (secret of nature). The theologian, the
lawyer, the medical doctor, physicist, mathematician, astronomer, and
astrologer all require knowledge of the secrets of nature that emblems can
impart. As to the importance of this modern translation Held stresses the novelty of the book. Although its content is of ancient origin, his translation will
present that which is new and "vor bey uns Teutschen nit viel gesehen" (previously not seen much by us Germans). The beautiful illustrations will be
"offter besehen vnd der gedechtnuß fleissiger befohlen werden" (frequently
looked at and recommended to memory). He thus makes a claim for the value
of pictures, which many twenty-first-century readers, bombarded by illustrations from magazines, billboards, and television, will find difficult to appreciate. The verses also serve the memorial function of the emblem. The book,
moreover, has an ethical purpose, namely, to promote "gutte sitten" (good
customs). Held expands on this notion by insisting that readers will learn here

various "Lehr / Vermahnung / Zucht / Tugend / gute Sitten vnd alle Bürgerliche ehrlichkeit" (teachings, warnings, breeding, virtue, good customs, and all civic [i.e., middle-class] honorableness). Finally, as Alciato himself did in his poem to Peutinger, Held emphasizes the practical application of emblems in material culture, recommending their use on "Haußrath / Gewand / Teppich / Schild / Wappen / Helm / Bitschier / Wend / Pfosten / Küssin vnd ander ding mehr" (household goods, clothing, wall hangings, shields, helmets, walls, posts, cushions, and other things).

Finally, Held explains that he has undertaken this work because noble and honorable people who did not know Latin had seen Alciato's emblems and asked him for the meaning of the illustrations and for a German version in rhyme. He acknowledges that the material is difficult, "darinnen vil verborgner alter Historien / Geschicht / Fabeln vnd Gedicht [. . .] die uns Teutschen unbekannt" (with many hidden old stories, histories, fables, and poems unknown to us Germans). Thus, although the intended readership includes "den gemeinen Mann" (the common man), the material is not "Kindisch" (childish) and may not be entrusted to "leichtfertige Personen" (frivolous persons). After all, not only Alciato, but also Erasmus and Melanchthon had drawn on the *Greek Anthology,* and Luther had translated Aesop's fables. These names may be considered authorities for Held and his readers.

Held offers his German version as a "Kunstbuch" (art book) for all amateurs of the fine arts. Just how seriously he may have been referring to the extraliterary use of emblems in material culture, or to what extent it may have been rather an advertising ploy, is difficult to know. The Latin text on Held's title page makes no reference to the use of emblems in material culture, even though Alciato's original poem of dedication to Peutinger had mentioned "badges" attached to "hats." Nonetheless, Held's title page, with its specific mention of artists, goldsmiths, silk-embroiderers, and sculptors, suggests his intended readership: mainly artisans and craftsmen, not in the first place learned individuals with knowledge of Latin and Greek. Held's German is simple and colloquial; in fact it is careless in both orthography and rhyme. Some literary evaluations of Held's language have criticized its crude or arbitrary rhyming and even accused it — by contrast with Hunger's more elegant version — of barbaric linguistic violations. But Max Rubensohn, who is otherwise also critical of Held's infelicities, does allow that the very absence of artistry gives the work a certain folksy sincerity.[28]

Similarly, Held's *inscriptiones* seem to have been written with an audience of German craftsmen in mind. He omits certain classical figures and references that his readership would be unlikely to know. Greek Anteros becomes "Wider Lieb" (Against Love); Invidia is no longer the classical personification but the abstract German noun "Verbunst" (envy). There is a homely, often proverbial quality about many of Held's German *inscriptiones;* indeed he sometimes uses actual proverbs to render Alciato's Latin *inscriptiones.* For "Maturandum" (One must ripen/mature), Held, like Hunger before him, uses the proverb "Eil mit weil" (Hurry with tarrying), still current today as "Eile mit Weile"; "Qui alta contemplatur cadere" (Those who contemplate things on high, fall) becomes the homely "Wer zu hoch steigt der felt" (He who climbs too high, falls); "ganeo" (gluttons) becomes "Tellerlecker" (plate lickers). Literary German of the sixteenth and seventeenth centuries exhibits a tendency toward double expressions. Thus in Held's emblems "incolumitatem" (safety) becomes "nutz vnd heil" (usefulness and well-being); "fortitudine" (courage) becomes "künheit vnd sterk" (bravery and strength).

It is among the 217 *subscriptiones* that one finds most evidence of Held's purposes and procedures. His *subscriptiones* are, with few exceptions, twice the length of the original Latin ones. The brevity of the Latin reflected the taste associated with courts and those who served them; the German reflects the verbosity associated with the middle class. Like Hunger, Held was committed to rhyme, which imposes particular difficulties that lead almost always to verbal padding. Also like Hunger, Held does not expect the sixteenth-century German reader to be able to recognize all of Alciato's references to historical or mythological figures, and devises various solutions:

1. An identifying word. In emblem 12 Thetis has the added epithet "sein [sic] Mutter" (his mother), and Achilles that of "Held" (hero); whereas Alciato calls Chiron by name (114), Held explains that he is "Der Centaur Chiron" (Chiron, the centaur); Held adds the word "Vogel" (bird) to the Ibis, and he identifies Faunus as "der WaldGott" (the god of the forest, 176).
2. Avoidance of classical names. Alciato's "garland of Pallas" becomes a "Kranz auß ölzweig" (garland of olive branches, 14); Nemesis is paraphrased as the "Göttin der Rach" (goddess of vengeance, 70, 71, 103).
3. Addition of the implied noun or name by circumlocution. The "king of Pella" becomes "der groß Alexander" (the great Alexander, 1); the "old man of Ascra" as the readily recognizable "Hesiod" (69).
4. Preference for the more common name over Alciato's use of the patronymic: "son of Aeacides" becomes "Achilles" (66); "son of Telamon" is rendered as "Ajax ein Son Thelamonis (Ajax, a son of Telamon, 66).
5. Addition of middle-class allusions to replace classical and mythological references. Some have political or economic overtones. Held augments "toga" into "Dem Burgerlichen Rock vnd Kleid" (the citizen's dress and clothing, 18); replaces "populus" with "Vnderthon" (subjects, 28); Alciato's Fortuna presides over chance events, Held's presides over "Gut" (property, or goods, 58). Held avoids references to kings and princes, changing "rex" to "Oberkeit" (superiors, 153) and "princeps" to "Herrn" (lords, 164).

The Emblem Book in German[29]

The first emblem book with German texts after the German translations by Hunger and Held was published in 1581 in Strasbourg under the name of

Figure 5. Title page to Holtzwart's Emblematum
Tyrocinia [. . .] Gemälpoesy *(Strasburg, 1581).*

Mathias Holtzwart (ca. 1540–ca. 1590/94). *Emblematum Tyrocinia* [. . .]
Gemälpoesy (Emblematic Trials: Pictured Poetry; fig. 5) is a bilingual edition
with Latin and German texts of the seventy-one emblems.[30] The German texts
are invariably longer than the Latin texts and probably not Holtzwart's own
translations. Holtzwart is concerned in the first place with moralizing and
middle-class values.

Emblems 2 through 11 deal with childhood, education, and learning. Many others treat common aspects of human life and reinforce folk wisdom: people are born in tears and depart in tears (22); beauty can bring destructive results (25); the three Fates are blind, deaf, and dumb (29); envy, anger, greed, and adultery can destroy a man (31); the four passions (Stoicism's *quatuor affectus*) beset mankind (66); good fortune quickly turns to misfortune (49); there is no joy without suffering (60); life is more gall than honey (32); truth resides in wine (16), and so forth. The message of emblem 12 is that governance should be accompanied by mercy and generosity. Holtzwart also treats various virtues and vices. The virtues include praiseworthy behavior (13); eloquence (14); virtue itself (15, 39, 40); friendship (20); honorable love (23); freedom (29); piousness (44, 50); and wisdom (56). As for the vices, they include false friendship (21); whoredom (26, 31); anger, envy, greed, adultery (31); voluptuous women (5); prodigality (54); ambition leading to a fall (37); ingratitude (42); flattery (64); deceptive good works (51); and evil in all forms, which will always be punished (36).

The few religious themes occur mainly toward the end of the collection. The priesthood is celebrated in emblem 62; the three ages of the world in 69; resurrection in 70; eternal life in the last emblem, 71. The criticism of court (30) is conventional. There are also economic concerns that surface, somewhat unexpectedly: the phrase "Reich und Arm" (rich and poor) occurs repeatedly; one of the justifications of marriage is economic (24); home ownership is the subject in 27, and the emblems on misers (53) and prodigality (54) both have economic ramifications.

It is perhaps understandable that the majority of emblematic books printed in the German lands at the beginning of the early modern period were bilingual editions or translations of emblem books that had been successful elsewhere. Some editions contain texts in three or even four languages. The *Pia desideria* (Blessed Desire) of the Flemish Jesuit Herman Hugo (1588–1629), written in Latin and published in Antwerp in 1624, became probably the most popular and most influential of all religious emblem books, among Catholics and non-Catholics alike. It was first translated into German and French in 1627; at least thirty-seven printings of German translations alone are verifiable.[31] These translations helped to fuel the rise in popularity in the seventeenth century of religious emblem books.

Increasingly, collections of meditations were enhanced with emblematic plates. Many of the widely read and translated books of the converted Jesuit Jeremias Drexel,[32] a preacher at the court of Maximilian of Bavaria, contain emblematic plates in abundance. Drexel's works, including their German translations, are recorded in the illustrated bibliography of Jesuit emblematic books.[33]

Daniel Cramer (1586–1637), a Protestant theologian and Rosicrucian, published in 1617 a bilingual edition of forty religious emblems with the title *Iesv et Roseæ Crucis Vera: Hoc est Decades Quatuor Emblematum Sacrorum.* [. . .] *Wahrhaffte Bruderschafft Jesu vnd deß Rosen Creutzes* (Jesus and the True Cross of the Rose: That is, Forty Sacred Emblems. The True Brotherhood of Jesus

VELLE, AT NON POSSE, DO-
LENDUM EST.

Velle, & poſſe, mihi non lance appenditur aquâ:
Vt ſi proficiam, plus ego deficiam.

  𝕿   𝖉𝖎𝖙   )𝖚

Figure 6. Cramer, Octoginta Emblemata Moralia Nova
(Frankfurt am Main, 1630), no. 73.

and the Rosy Cross).[34] As the bilingual title suggests, the emblems' texts are in both Latin and German. Each engraved emblem has an engraved Latin *inscriptio,* above which is printed in both languages a biblical text with reference; below the *pictura* a couplet *subscriptio* stands in Latin. The same publisher, Lucas Jennis, also published in 1617 Andreas Friedrich's (ca. 1560–ca. 1617) *Emblemata nova; Das ist / New Bilderbuch* (New Emblems; That is, New Picture Book), a collection of eighty-seven emblems, all in German. In Cramer's *Octoginta emblemata moralia Nova* (Eighty New Moral Emblems, 1630) the *picturae* are printed on rectos with Latin *inscriptiones* and captions above and a brief Latin text beneath. On the facing versos are quatrains in German, French, and Italian, introduced by a biblical quotation with its reference. Cramer's emblems are religious or moral; thus Alciato's motif of the man with winged hand flying upwards while the other hand is weighed down by a stone finds a moral application here (fig. 6).

Nuremberg: New Center of Emblem Theory

The importance of early modern Nuremberg as a free imperial city can hardly be overestimated. The Kaiser may have been elected in Frankfurt and crowned in Aachen, but the insignias of the empire were preserved in Nuremberg, which was regularly the seat of the imperial diets. Charles IV visited the town some fifty times; the peace negotiations that ended the Thirty Years' War were held here; the first festive banquet to celebrate the new peace was hosted by the Swedish delegation in the Great Hall of the *Rathaus;* not to be outdone, the imperial party held a similarly splendid banquet in the castle above the town.

Nuremberg was particularly renowned as a center for the emblematic embellishment of material culture. The Heilig Geist Spital (Hospital of the Holy Spirit) was decorated with emblematic paintings, and these were published in book form in 1626 in Johann Pfann's *Biblische Emblemata und Figuren.* Perhaps the most famous example is the town hall, the council room of which was decorated with a series of emblematic paintings; these were recorded in a book entitled *Emblematica politica,* printed in Nuremberg in 1617 and again in 1640.[35] Whereas the book was probably issued in only 200 or 300 copies, thousands of persons actually visited the town hall where, waiting for appointments with officials and judges, they doubtless pondered the emblematic decorations, which represent the social and political program of the governing oligarchy, as well as the virtues expected of rulers.

Many writers, artists, and publishers of emblems and emblem books were active in Nuremberg by the turn of the seventeenth century.[36] As early as 1590 the humanist physician and botanist Joachim Camerarius the Younger (1534–99) began publishing his *Symbole et Emblemata* (Symbols and Emblems, 1590, 1595, 1596) in Nuremberg. Johann Mannich (fl. 1624), deacon of the Heilig Geist (Catholic) Church and preacher at St. Walburg's (Catholic) Church in Nuremberg, published his *Sacra emblemata* (Sacred Emblems) there in 1624, and Johann Saubert, senior pastor at St. Sebald's Church, his own *Emblematum sacrorum* between 1625 and 1630. In 1647 Hieronymus Ammon (b. 1591) published his *Imitatio Crameriana,* imitations of the emblems of Daniel Cramer.[37] The religious poet Johann Vogel (1589–1663) dedicated his celebration of peace after the Thirty Years' War, *Meditationes emblematicae* (1648), to the senate of Nuremberg.[38] The Pegnesischer Blumenorden (Flower Order on the Pegnitz), founded by Harsdörffer in 1644, became one of Germany's most important *Sprachgesellschaften* (language and literature societies); it is still in existence today in Nuremberg. The multiple form known as *mehrständige* (multiple) emblems was primarily Harsdörffer's invention.[39]

Emblematic practice takes many forms. Nuremberg produced not only emblem books proper but also emblematically devised frontispieces and other emblematically illustrated works. These included the poetic meditations of the Austrian Protestant exile Catharina Regina von Greiffenberg, mentioned above,[40] and the sermons of Johann Michael Dilherr (1604–69), the brilliant new pastor, as of 1646, of St. Sebald's Church and director of the Egidien School.[41]

No discussion of emblematic Nuremberg is complete without taking into account the renowned Altdorf Academy, which was attended by many sons of Nuremberg's patrician and middle class.[42] No fewer than sixteen of the thirty-two emblems that adorned the Nuremberg town hall may be traced to Altdorf medals. The brother of the emblem writer Camerarius was pro-chancellor at Altdorf, and the emblem writer Nicolaus Taurellus (1547–1606) was a professor there.

Nuremberg was likewise — and this is perhaps even more significant for the history of early modern German literature — a center for theoretical discourse. Harsdörffer combined theory, drawn from his extraordinarily wide reading, especially of the Italians and Jesuits, with practice, and was perhaps the most important mediator to German baroque culture of emblematic theory.[43] His reflections on emblems are scattered throughout the eight volumes of his *Frauenzimmer Gesprächspiele* (Playful Colloquies for the Ladies, 1641–49)[44] and in his *Bericht von den Sinnbildern* (Report on Emblems), published as an appendix to *Der Große SchauPlatz jämmerlicher Mordgeschichte* (Grand Theater of Lamentable Murders, 1650); many of his other writings as well include emblematic frontispieces, individual emblems, and small collections of emblems.

The *Frauenzimmer Gesprächspiele* is not a philosophical work with precise definitions but a social discourse in the form of conversations among a group of six individuals, three men and three women, who meet at an idyllic country estate. Their host is Vespasian, an older courtier. Together they discuss all manner of subjects of interest to socially and culturally engaged Germans, ranging from history to books to society to the natural world. The manner of their discussions is informal, even playful, but always educational.

Emblematics is one such topic of special interest, and it arises with regularity throughout all but one of the eight volumes. Some of the "rules" or "laws" of the emblem described there derive specifically from Italian impresa theory and do not conform to the more conventional views of the emblem; they are also at times somewhat at odds with the practice of Alciato. Although Harsdörffer's discussions, conversations, and commentaries on emblems in the *Frauenzimmer Gesprächspiele* are the most thorough in German literature of the seventeenth century, scholarship has never adequately dealt with them in terms of a unified theory. They deserve, therefore, to be presented here at length.

In part 1 of the *Frauenzimmer Gesprächspiele* Vespasian suggests six different ways of organizing a conversation game of emblems. In effect, they comprise the various ways of inventing emblems, but they are converted here into a social and educational game:

1. naming a thing as the basis of an emblem;
2. choosing a *pictura* and inventing an *inscriptio;*
3. choosing an *inscriptio* and inventing a *pictura;*
4. illustrating chapters of the Bible;
5. going through nature and making emblems as Camerarius and Aldrovandus did;[45]
6. choosing suitable sayings from the poets as *inscriptiones.*

Harsdörffer (through Vespasian) comments that emblems are so named, "weil selbe von Bildern / vnd wenig Worten / darinn der Sinn / Meinung und Verstand deß Erfinders begriffen / zusammengesetzet: welche dann mehr weisen / als gemahlet oder geschrieben ist / in demselbe zu ferneren Nachdencken fügliche Anlaß geben" (because they are composed of pictures and a few words, which contain the sense, opinion, and understanding of the inventor; they point to more than is depicted or written and give occasion to further contemplation). This is an unusually inclusive description. Because emblems have greater significance than is expressly stated in the texts or depicted in the emblem *pictura*, Harsdörffer expects his readers to apply all necessary intellectual energy to understand their full meanings.[46]

In this conversation on *Sinnbildkunst* (the art of the emblem) eight theoretical points are made, quite eclectically. Certain of them derive from Italian impresa theory:

1. Jedes Sinnbild sol bestehen in Figuren und etlichen beygeschriebenen Worten (Each emblem should consist of figures and a few words).
2. Der Figuren sollen auf das meiste drei seyn / auf das wenigste eine (The figures should be at most three, and at least one).
3. Die Figuren sollen in ihrer deutenden Gestalt scheinlich und sichtig ausgemahlet werden (In their pointing form the figures should be depicted clearly and visibly).
4. Die Figuren sollen nicht gantz unbekant seyn / und keine Gestalt von einem Menschen haben (The figures should not be completely unknown, and they should not have the form of a human being).
5. Die Schrift sol in wenig Worten bestehen / und aus bekanten Scribenten entnommen / oder im Nohtfall von dem Erfinder des Sinnbilds verständig ersonnen seyn: doch dergestalt / daß es über einen halben Vers nicht belauffe / zum wenigsten aber zwei / selten ein einiges Wort begreiffe (The writing should consist of a few words, taken from well-known authors, or if necessary, conceived by the inventor of the emblem, but not exceeding half a verse, containing at least two and seldom only a single word).
6. Die Schrift sol niemals in der andern Person / sondern allzeit in der ersten oder dritten reden. [. . .] Diese Gleichniß ist die Seele des Sinnbildes / dessen Dolmetscher die Obschrift / und der Leib ist das Bild oder die Figur an sich selbsten (The writing should never speak in the second person but always in the first or third person. This comparison is the soul of the emblem, whose translator is the *inscriptio*, and the body is the *pictura* or the figure itself).
7. Die anmutigsten Vberschriften sind diese / welche von den Poeten entnommen / in Betrachtung / zwischen der Mahlerey / und der Poeten Dichtkunst eine genaue und Lustreitzende Vereinigung ist (The most charming *inscriptiones* are those taken from poets, in consideration that between painting and the art of poetry there is an exact and pleasure-provoking unity).

8. Diese Figuren und Schrift sollen also miteinander verbunden seyn / daß keines ohne das ander könne verstanden werden (These figures und text should also be so conjoined that neither can be understood without the other).[47]

Although these rules together constitute the "perfect emblem," Harsdörffer sometimes ignores them in his own creations. In "Der Waffen Elend / frölich End" (A Happy End to the Misery of Weapons), for example, the *picturae* suggested to embody this motto include a dove with an olive branch over a calm sea; a garden in which the "Eisenkraut" (iron plant) has withered and been replaced with a "Friedelar" (*Friede* "peace"); the temple of peace at Rome; and a crown surmounting a flourishing olive tree, at the base of which lie broken weapons of war.

Conversations devoted to other subjects may also contain references to emblems. The discussion of tournaments includes mention of the dog as emblem of loyalty, and this leads to the important remark: "So kan man bey fast allen Sinnbildern unterschiedliche Deutungen suchen" (Thus one can discover different interpretations in almost all emblems). Harsdörffer will elaborate on this point in part 4 in observing that the recognition of meaning in an emblem depends on an understanding of the thing portrayed and its qualities. Harsdörffer comments, "daß von keinem Sinnbilde kan geurtheilt werden / man habe dann der Figuren Eigenschaften alle und jede erlernet / und betrachtet (that one cannot judge an emblem unless one has first learned and considered each and every quality of the figure). But Harsdörffer insists on the reader's ability to identify the figures in order to guarantee understanding: "man [kan] von keinem Sinnbilde urtheilen [. . .] / man habe dann zuvor der Figuren Natur und Eigenschaften gründlich erlernet / welche vielmals verborgen ist / und nicht ausgemahlet werden kan / daher dann des Sinnbildes Verstand schwer und tunkel wird" (one cannot judge an emblem unless one has previously learned thoroughly the nature and qualities of the figures, which is often hidden and cannot be depicted, from whence the meaning of the emblem becomes difficult and dark). Harsdörffer's reader is thus knowledgeable and an active participant in the production of emblematic meaning.

In part 2 the conversation "Von Fremden Sinnbildern" (On Foreign Emblems) focuses on the imprese of Italian academies. The Intronati Academy of Sienna, for instance, chose as its impresa the dried pumpkin used by peasants to hold salt. Its motto, "Meliora latente" (The Best is Hidden Within), refers to the hidden "Saltz der Weißheit / Verstand und Wissenschaft" (Salt of Wisdom, Understanding, and Knowledge). In another conversation, on "Der Sinnbilder Figur und Obschrifft" (Figure and *Inscriptiones* of Emblems), Vespasian observes that the sun can be used for different themes.

Part 3 is concerned with related problems. With respect to the topic "Von der Welt Eitelkeit" (On the Vanity of the World) the anchor is an emblem of hope, and the white swan with its black flesh an image of the deceptive world. In clarification of the generally held opinion that human limbs should have no place in emblems, Harsdörffer explains that individual limbs are "ownerless," by which he means that in emblems it is unnatural and therefore wrong to depict only individual parts, rather than the whole body.

Part 4 is particularly rich in emblematic theory and practice. It opens with an emblematic frontispiece and a dedicatory emblem to August the Younger, duke of Braunschweig, known in the Fruchtbringende Gesellschaft as "der Befreiende" (the Liberator); hence the *inscriptio* "Mit Freuden Befreyet" (Freed with Joys). The engraving is framed by twelve heraldic shields surrounding a centered motif cluster comprising a staff supporting a flourishing bean plant surmounted by a winged hat; at the base of the staff two snakes hiss at the plant; in the background may be seen a walled city with a castle on a hill. The *subscriptio* takes the form of a sonnet and explains the image. The topic "Die Erfindung der Sinnbildkunst" (The Invention of the Art of Emblems) raises the question of whether anything and everything can be used in emblems. Vespasian replies positively: "Alles / was sichtbarlich ist / unterfangt die Mahlerey vorzustellen; was aber unsichtbarlich ist / kan mit der Sinnbildkunst / vermittelst der Umschrift / verstanden werden" (Painting undertakes to represent everything that is visible; but that which is invisible can be understood by means of the art of the emblem through the *inscriptio*). Still, questions of obscurity, enigma, and obviousness remain. "Es ist nicht zu laugnen daß ein Sinnbild leicht / das ander schwer; eines gut und eingrifflich das ander schlecht und einfältig; eines auf eine gewiese Sache / das ander auf viel unterschiedliche Händle zu deuten" (It may not be denied that one emblem is easy, another difficult; one is good and penetrating, another poor and simple; one indicates a specific thing, another many different matters). Arguing for a middle way Vespasian says: "Die besten aber sind meines Bedunkens / welche in dem Mittelstande nicht allzuhoch / nicht allzunieder kommen; die wohl verstanden werden können / aber nicht gleich einem jeden eröffnet darliegen" (In my opinion the best are those which in the middle way are neither too high nor too low, which can certainly be understood, but which do not lie open for everyone). Harsdörffer is careful not to insult readers by calling them "plebeians" as Paulo Giovio did when formulating the level of difficulty in an impresa.

Of other emblematic themes addressed in part 4 the following are among the most significant for the interpretation of the emblem: the *inscriptio* as the *Seele* (soul) of the emblem;[48] certain material culture uses of the emblem in processions, tournaments, and coins; objects of print culture, including *alba amicorum* (albums of friends), which often took the form of emblem books printed with interleafed blank pages; the number of figures, or motifs, that may be allowed: "Es sollen nicht mehr als drey bedeutende Figuren / unterschiedliches Geschlechtes in einem wolgestalten Sinnbild seyn" (There should be no more than three meaningful figures of different species in a well constructed emblem).[49] And finally, Harsdörffer stresses, in what has become a canonical statement, the great variety that is possible in emblematic art: "Die Sinnbildkunst ist eine nachdenkliche Ausdruckung sonderlicher Gedanken / vermittelst einer schicklichen Gleichniß / welche von natürlichen oder künstlichen Dingen an- und mit wenig nachsinnlichen Worten ausgeführt ist" (The art of the emblem is the considered expression of unusual thoughts by means of an appropriate comparison, which is introduced by natural or artificial things and elucidated in a few thoughtful words).

Vespasian repeats his rule number 3 from part 1 about the clear depiction of figures, then rule number 4 regarding necessary minimal familiarity with (nonhuman) figures. The term "ungestaltet" (ill-formed) is applied to "Mißgeburten" (freaks) in general and half-eagles in particular; anything unknown in nature, including winged snails and winged tortoises, is subsumed under this term. Various reasons are given for excluding the human figure. One speaker argues, however, that the human figure should be admissible since man is the noblest of all creatures,[50] and it is concluded that the human figure, including body parts, be accepted as appropriate to emblem-like "Geistliche Gemählden" (also: "Andachts-Gemählen," spiritual pictures). A multiple emblem is shown with *inscriptiones* that derive from the Bible and *picturae* that come from a German version of Hugo's *Pia desideria*. Conversation turns to a series of biblical sayings that are then illustrated by various pictorial motifs; these motifs are featured graphically in the illustrated initials that start each text.

As to the topic of "der Sinnbilder Obschrift" (the *inscriptio* of emblems), Vespasian repeats his rule number 5 about the recommended brevity of emblematic texts. One speaker rejects the idea that the number of words may be prescribed. Giovio is quoted as preferring a foreign language for *inscriptiones*, a notion that is defeated in favor of writing in one's mother tongue; we recall that the cultivation of German was a major concern of the *Sprachgesellschaften*. The use of puns, anagrams, and wordplay is encouraged in the ensuing discussion with the pictorial motifs again reproduced in the illustrated initials. A triple emblem (fig. 7) is reproduced and discussed. Vespasian concludes the conversation with a repetition of his rules 6–8 with occasional additions.

Part 4 concludes with a collection of thirteen numbered unillustrated Latin emblems, printed as an unpaginated appendix following the list of writers and theorists — it reads like a who's who of writers of emblems and imprese. The Latin emblems have illustrated initials that bear the central pictorial motif of the unillustrated emblems. Anagrams on the names of the person celebrated provide captions or *inscriptiones*. Several Nuremberg writers of emblems are celebrated, including Johann Michael Dilherr, Johann Rist, Johann Saubert, and Johann Vogel.

Part 6 (part 5 has no conversations relative to the emblem) includes a revealing conversation that begins with the question, whether there is anything new under the sun and then promptly turns to multiple emblems. Four-, five-, or six-fold emblems may be devised to decorate a clock, candleholder, box, glasses, even tapestries — in other words, on products from material culture. In the example of a four-fold emblem, the four seasons are carved into a drinking glass. The suggestion that even an eight-fold emblem would be possible is too much for Vespasian. At some point, he insists, this terminological inexactitude threatens the very definition of the emblem, putting it in danger of breaking down into meaninglessness: "Ob sich gleich viel finden / welche von

Figure 7. Harsdörffer, Frauenzimmer Gesprächspiele *4, 222.*

den Sinnbildern wenig halten / so können sie doch meines Erachtens / niemand mißfallen / als dem / der keinen Verstand darvon hat / und ein jedes Gemähl ein Emblema nennet" (Although there are many who do not hold emblems in high regard, in my view they can displease no one except him who has no understanding of them, and who calls every picture an emblem).

The ensuing discussion deals with the value of the accompanying poetic *subscriptio* or epigram. The examples, all of which come from material culture, give prominence to the question of the objective space for interpretation. "Ist es ein Glas / Kandel / oder dergleichen / so muß die Erfindung also beschaffen seyn / daß es keiner fernern Auslegung von nöhten hat" (If it is a glass, candle or something like that, the invention must be so constructed that no further interpretation is necessary). An emblem on a material object is likely to have space only for a *pictura* and *inscriptio,* and this must suffice to present a clear meaning. By contrast, a book emblem allows for the addition of poems.

Part 6 concludes with an appendix of Harsdörffer's "spiritual pictures," twelve in number. Each has an *inscriptio* comprising a saying from the Bible (with a marginal reference to the source), a *pictura* with two, sometimes three motifs, and an explanatory poem.

The discussion of emblems in Part 7 begins with reflections on the ideogram and Chinese languages before turning to matters of interpretation and meaning. The often-heard modern criticism that emblematic images are contrived or arbitrary may result from the confusion that arises when one is confronted with an image carrying different, at times contradictory, meanings. Harsdörffer sometimes speaks about such contradictions in terms of good or evil qualities. Of the snake he observes: "Die Deutung ist auch mehrmals als zweiffelhafftig / und kan / wie vor von den Löwen gesagt worden / gut und böß seyn. Die Schlange ist ein Bild der Klugheit / der gifftigen Verleumdung / und wann sie den Schwantz in dem Mund hat / eine Abbildung der Ewigkeit" (The interpretation is also sometimes doubtful, and as was said earlier of the lion it can be good or evil. The snake is an image of cleverness, of poisonous slander, and when it has its tail in its mouth, an illustration of eternity). With respect to the eagle Harsdörffer insists that "Gutes und Böses" (good and evil) can be created in accordance with what naturalists have written of the bird. The various birds, fish, and trees in emblems have similar "meanings."

A conversation devoted to "Die Bildkunst" (The Art of Images) is not directly concerned with the emblem, but each of the fourteen full-page engravings features three personifications whose attributes are often found in emblems, and these are identified and explained in the text. In discussing one of these plates Harsdörffer remarks, in keeping with received opinion, that "diese Gleichniß [. . .] muß nicht von zufälligen / sondern wesentlichen Eigenschaften eines Dings hergenommen seyn" (this comparison must not be drawn from accidental, but rather from essential qualities of the thing). Harsdörffer frequently uses the term *Gleichniß* (comparison, or analogy; not simile) to name the basis of an emblem. To the objection that such comparisons are difficult to understand without a text, far from denying it, Harsdörffer welcomes it as a fruitful stimulus to imagination and thought: "Man kann durch eine Obschrift [. . .] die Deutung ausfündig machen; doch ist mehrmals das verborgene angenehmer / und verursachet mehr Nachfrage / als das was gleich in dem ersten Anblikk erkennet wird" (One can make the meaning accessible through the *inscriptio*; but frequently the concealed is pleasanter and causes more questioning than that which is recognized at first glance). Again the application of such images is recommended for material culture, such as triumphal arches; products of print culture, such as poems, emblems, and book titles, are also included.

In the eighth and final part of the *Frauenzimmer Gesprächspiele* Harsdörffer places emblems — a wall clock and a sundial — at its beginning and conclusion. A discussion arises concerning "Kriegsgemähl" (images of war), here in the form of triple emblems etched on six drinking glasses. Each circular *pictura* has its own *inscriptio* and a couplet *subscriptio*. The conversation moves on to how *inscriptiones* may be added to *picturae* to make a certain kind of emblem, in this case, one from material culture: "so kan man auch in Fürstlichen Zimmern über allerhand Saidenspiele / Bilder und Geretschaften schikkliche Vberschriften machen" (thus also in princely rooms one can set appropriate *inscriptiones* above all kinds of stringed instruments, pictures, and objects). The four lyres, or violins, represent different stages in the development of a male. Each instrument bears a short *inscriptio* that depicts, in its illustrated initial letter, the motif. Triple emblems on the subject of each of the twelve months are presented, each circular *pictura* provided with a Latin *inscriptio*, the motifs and *inscriptiones* stated in German (fig. 8).

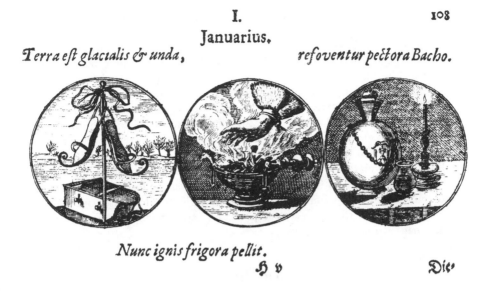

Figure 8. Harsdörffer, Frauenzimmer Gesprächspiele *8, 108.*

Harsdörffer published both religious and secular emblem books. *Hertzbewegliche Sonntagsandachten: das ist, Bild- Lieder- und Bet-Büchlein, aus den Sprüchen der H. Schrift* (Heart-moving Sunday Sermons: That is, A Little Book of Images, Songs, and Prayers from the Sayings of the Holy Scriptures, 1649) contains seventy-six woodcut emblems. Under the pseudonym Fabianus Athyrus he published several books of heart emblems after the mid 1640s. *Stechbüchlein: Das ist Hertzenscherze, in welchen der Tugenden und Untugenden Abbildungen zu wahrer selbst Erkantnis, mit erfreulichem Nutzen auszuwehlen* (Little Book for Stabbing: That is, Jests of the Heart in which may be Selected with Pleasurable Usefulness the Representations of Virtues and Vices for True Self-Knowledge,[51] 1645) contains fifty heart-shaped emblems. *Das erneuerte Stamm- und Stechbüchlein: Hundert Geistliche Hertzens Spiegel Weltliche Hertzens Spiegel Zu eigentlicher Abbildung der Tugenden und Laster vorgestellet* (The Renewed Little Album and Book for Stabbing: One Hundred Spiritual Mirrors of the Heart/Secular Mirrors of the Heart Representing the True Image of the Virtues and Vices, 1654) is a collection of 100 emblems. These were reprinted as *Lehr- und Sinnreicher Herztens-Spiegel in Hundert Geist und Weltlichen Hertzens Bewegungen Zu eigentlicher Abbildung der Tugenden und Laster vorgestellet* (Instructive and Perspicacious Mirrors of the Heart in One Hundred Spiritual and Secular Motions of the Heart Representing the True Image of the Virtues and Vices; no date). The emblems here serve as a kind of educational social game, reminiscent of those in the

Frauenzimmer Gesprächspiele: the rule is that each participant "muß [. . .] in dem ersten Theil / wann es eine Weibs-Person / und in dem andern / wann es eine Manns-Person / mit einem Stefft / Messer oder Steck-Nadel einstechen / seine Hertzens-Spiegel-Bild auswehlen / ablesen und bemercken" (must stick in a knife or needle — a female in the first part, a male in the second part — choosing, reading, and noting the image of his or her heart's mirror). Hence the word "Stechbüchlein" in the titles of these works. Harsdörffer also contributed the eighty-one exceptionally complex triple emblems in *Dreiständige Sonn- und Festtag-Emblemata, oder Sinne-bilder* (Triple Emblems for Sundays and Feast Days), which first appeared, two years after his death, in Dilherr's voluminous *Heilige Sonn- und Festtags-Arbeit* (Holy Work for Sundays and Feast Days, 1660).[52] If Harsdörffer was the leading light among Nuremberg's men of letters, Dilherr was certainly, besides being one of the city's most productive writers and preachers, an indefatigable producer of emblematic works.[53]

Conclusion

Formerly an unclaimed territory straddling literature and the visual arts — the nineteenth century paid it virtually no critical attention, thus its important role in earlier cultures was largely ignored — the emblem is currently being rediscovered and remapped.[54] Modern perspectives from semiotics, the sociology of production and reception, and communications theory are being applied to the emblem in an attempt to arrive at a better understanding of its role in society and of the interaction between emblems proper and other cultural forms.

With respect to how the emblematic mode helped shape the print and material cultures of Europe of the sixteenth to eighteenth centuries, one line of scholarship is focusing on the discovery of emblematic modes in title pages and frontispieces, but also in printers' and publishers' devices.[55] To literary historians emblem books are the most widely known manifestation of this allegorical mode, but for historians of art and architecture the use of emblems and imprese in material culture is even more important. With regard to the reception of images and their meanings, buildings — especially ecclesiastical buildings, because they were open to all — may have been even more influential than books. Veritable emblem programs adorn the walls and ceilings of many buildings in the German-speaking lands from the sixteenth to the nineteenth centuries.[56] South Germany, Austria, and Switzerland have churches and chapels that contain important emblematic programs.[57] Many of the inscriptions are in Latin, but not all.

A small Catholic baroque church, a pilgrimage church, called Maria Brünnlein Zum Trost (Mary, the Little Fountain of Consolation), stands near Eichstätt in Bavaria. The emblematic images there were once recognized as public symbols. Each *pictura* is accompanied by a brief Latin *inscriptio* naming the image and identifying a biblical source as well as a longer German explanation. The combination of symbolic picture and text was evidently

*Figure 9. Mary as fountain, Bavarian pilgrimage church Maria Brünnlein
Zum Trost.*

intended to be received and understood by not only the learned but also the
less learned who could read German. It is perhaps noteworthy that many of the
biblical sayings, earlier applied to Christ, are applied here to Mary, the "little
fountain" (fig. 9). Some foreign observers may be startled at the sight of a
demure, blond-haired Mary out of whose covered breasts two streams issue
over her traditional blue garment. She is, in fact, a garden fountain figure, representing visually the abstract theological notion "In me gratia omnis" (In me
is all grace).[58] The German is simpler if longer: "Niemand ist, der Hilff
begehrt, den Maria nit erhört" (There is no one who desires help, whom Mary
does not hear). A fresco emblem depicts a pink rose with the title "Rosa mystica" (The Mystical Rose), as described in the apocryphal book of Sirach, chapter 24. For the less educated in the congregation an instruction is provided in
German: "Ein Gehaimnus der natur die Edle Rosen ist, das Geheimnus aller
gnad du, o Maria bist" (The noble rose is a mystery of nature; you, O Mary,
are the mystery of all mercy; fig. 10).

But not only architecture, also more humble objects in everyday use, such
as cabinets and cupboards, drinking glasses and trenchers, and other household wares, could be enhanced with emblems.[59] The Benedictine monastery
named Kloster Lüne outside of Lüneburg preserves a set of narrow woven

Figure 10. Mary as rose, Bavarian pilgrimage church
Maria Brünnlein Zum Trost.

panels, sewn together and used as a bench edging. Dating from around 1500 it includes the Pelican-in-her-Piety.[60] The Nuremberg Nationalmuseum possesses a number of glass drinking goblets decorated with emblems. In their pioneering essay of 1959 on emblems and emblem books Heckscher and Wirth reproduced a glass goblet made for the golden wedding anniversary of the patrician Kress couple around 1635.[61] Most artifacts with such emblematic decorations are now lost.[62] The book is the primary medium through which the emblematic combination of text and picture was disseminated.

A mode of symbolic communication, the emblem is today a subject of interdisciplinary study embracing the Neo-Latin and vernacular literatures, the visual arts and material culture. The books have become rare, scattered throughout the world's libraries, and this has hampered research. Digitization is the latest technology that can render emblematic books more accessible.[63]

Not long ago microforms were being used for a similar purpose.[64] Perhaps the most important difference between print or microform editions and online or CD-ROM editions lies in the simple fact that editions in print and microform are static and fixed whereas online and CD-ROM versions can readily be brought up to date.

Opinions are likely to continue to differ on what constitutes an emblem, and this will have an influence on bibliography. Mario Praz, in his *Studies in Seventeenth-Century Imagery*, has a broad understanding of the emblem, and his is still the most valuable and informative general bibliography. Opinions will also doubtless be divided on which verbal constructions can usefully be called emblematic. Some verbal images in poetry can be labeled emblematic as can certain episodes in prose fiction, and even effects on stage.[65] Naturally, the purely verbal or literary effect lacks the visual component of the emblem and must either assume it or replace it with a verbal description. Albrecht Schöne's *Emblematik und Drama* is dedicated to the emblem and emblematic constructions in German drama of the early modern period. The poetry of most German baroque poets reveals similar structures.[66]

The seventeenth century was the heyday of the emblem in Europe. But bibliographical evidence demonstrates that religious emblem books, especially, were published continuously during the eighteenth and nineteenth centuries. In the twentieth century some poets created montages of images and texts that harkened back to emblematic practice. Berthold Brecht constructed a *Kriegsfibel* (A Primer of War) out of war photographs and his own new texts, using a procedure that may be called emblematic.[67] Emblems and imprese will also be discovered, or perhaps one should say rediscovered, on the flags and seals of counties, provinces and states, schools and universities, not to speak of nation states. And modern advertising can at times create effects reminiscent of the emblem.[68]

Notes

[1] The impresa (pl.: imprese) is an emblematic device that comprises an image and a motto; it typically lacks the third feature of the emblem: the *subscriptio,* the explanatory verse (or narrative) below and is thus often considered an ephemeral art form.

[2] Some of these reflections derive from Peter M. Daly, "The Intertextuality of Word and Image in Wolfgang Hunger's German Translation of Alciato's *Emblematum liber,*" in *Intertextuality: German Literature and the Visual Arts,* ed. Ingeborg Hoesterey and Ulrich Weisstein (Columbia, SC: Camden House, 1993), 30–46.

[3] Charles Moseley, *A Century of Emblems: An Introductory Anthology* (Aldershot: Scolar Press, 1989), 9. See also elsewhere in the present volume the chapter by Jeffrey Chipps Smith.

[4] *Emblemata: Handbuch zur Sinnbildkunst des XVI. und XVII. Jahrhunderts,* 2nd ed. (Stuttgart: Metzler, 1976), contains fifteen books with German texts — usually translations of the emblems originally in another language — among the total of forty-six books indexed and reproduced.

[5] "Bedeutung" is the only subjective category in the Henkel/Schöne *Handbuch*. However, I have found it difficult to reduce a whole emblem to a single statement of "meaning," which is typically either redundant or subjective.

[6] The statistic derives from the bibliographic database known as The Union Catalogue of Emblem Books. An early account of that database project is found in Peter M. Daly, "The Union Catalogue of Emblem Books and the *Corpus Librorum Emblematum*," *Emblematica* 3 (1988): 121–33. This number includes the various printings and translations of a single work, and books that were reissued under a single and different cover title are listed as many times as they were printed.

[7] Peter M. Daly, *Andrea Alciato in England: Aspects of the Reception of Alciato's Emblems in England* (New York: AMS Press, forthcoming).

[8] In unillustrated emblem books verbal description replaces the visual element. An illustrated bibliography of Jesuit emblem books is appearing under the title *The Jesuit Series*, edited by Peter M. Daly and G. Richard Dimler, S.J. The series is part of the *Corpus Librorum Emblematum* and is now being published by the University of Toronto Press.

[9] Peter M. Daly, *Literature in the Light of the Emblem: Structural Parallels between the Emblem and Literature in the Sixteenth and Seventeenth Centuries*, 2nd rev. ed. (Toronto: U of Toronto P, 1998).

[10] The term here, "renaissance hieroglyphics," refers to the creation of new hieroglyphs during the Renaissance — not to the discussion of ancient Egyptian hieroglyphics.

[11] Material culture is comprised of human artifacts, including commodities — furniture, goods for consumption, and the like — as opposed to objects intending symbolic value (literary texts, *objets d'art*), though the line between them is by no means absolute.

[12] Alan R. Young, *The English Tournament Imprese* (New York: AMS Press, 1988), and "The English Tournament Imprese," in *The English Emblem and the Continental Tradition*, ed. Peter M. Daly (New York: AMS Press, 1988), 61–81. Also by Young, *Tudor and Jacobean Tournaments* (London: George Philip, 1987).

[13] The painting is reproduced in Mario Praz, *Studies in Seventeenth-Century Imagery*, 2nd ed. (St. Clair Shores, MI: Scholarly Press, 1979), facing p. 8.

[14] Landwehr, *German Emblem Books 1531–1888: A Bibliography* (Utrecht: Haentjens Dekker & Gumbert, 1972). Some seventy German titles in Praz, *Studies*, are not to be found in Landwehr, which means that one must consult both bibliographies.

[15] In quick succession, the Paris publisher Chrestien Wechel also produced a bilingual French-Latin edition, then in 1542 Hunger's German-Latin edition utilizing the same illustrations.

[16] The *Greek Anthology* was comprised of cycles of Greek epigrammatic and other poetry from antiquity through the Middle Ages. Alciato seems to have made use of the so-called Planudean version, which had been discovered in the fifteenth century and published by the Hellenist Janus Lascaris in Florence in 1494.

[17] Hunger's German version was reprinted in facsimile in 1967 and 1980 by the Wissenschaftliche Buchgesellschaft in Darmstadt.

[18] See Denis L. Dysdall, "Defence and Illustration of the German Language: Wolfgang Hunger's Preface to Alciati's Emblems (text and translation)," *Emblematica* 3 (1988): 137–60, and Peter M. Daly, "The Intertextuality of Word and Image in Wolfgang Hunger's German Translation of Alciato's *Emblematum liber*," in Hoesterey and Weisstein, eds., *Intertextuality*, 30–46.

[19] Steven Rowan observes: "Wolfgang Hunger studied under Zazius for a while after 1533, but he left for Bourges to finish his degree under Andrea Alciato." *Ulrich Zazius: A Jurist in the German Renaissance 1461–1535* (Frankfurt am Main: Klostermann, 1987), 84.

[20] Heinz Berger, "Die Entwicklung einer Stadt von den Anfängen bis zum Beginn der sechziger Jahre des 20. Jahrhunderts" (Ph.D. diss., Erlangen, 1969); Dieter Kudorfer, *Nördlingen: Historischer Atlas von Bayern: Schwaben* (Munich: Kommission für Landesgeschichte, 1974); Hans-Christoph Rublack, *Eine bürgerliche Reformation: Nördlingen* (Gütersloh: Gerd Mohn, 1982); Dietmar Vosges, *Die Reichsstadt Nördlingen: 12 Kapitel aus ihrer Geschichte* (Munich: Beck, 1988).

[21] The colophon is dated 1567. A facsimile edition, accompanied by an introduction and indexes, is forthcoming in the series Imago Figurata with Turnhout Press in Brepols.

[22] As John Manning has observed in his discussion of Thomas Palmer's manuscript collection of emblems, "we do not know to what extent the original was regarded as authoritative, or merely as a stimulus to fresh composition." *The Emblems of Thomas Palmer: Two hundred poosees: Sloane MS 3794* (New York: AMS Press, 1988), xiii.

[23] Oddly enough there were no vernacular translations into early modern Dutch or English.

[24] Additionally the translation frequently fulfilled the new function of making the semiotics of the *picturae* accessible to a different audience.

[25] As Drysall, "Defence and Illustration," 138, puts it, it was precisely "at a moment when Hunger was looking for a means to refresh his own German, to maintain his French, and to satisfy his interest in poetry."

[26] Useful though this example is for my immediate purpose it does not represent a pattern, as the Ganymede emblem testifies. In Steyner's *pictura* (B6ʳ) an unnamed figure is seated on the back of an eagle in flight, whereas in Wechel's cut (XXXII) the name is printed in Latin above the figure and in Greek below. And the *pictura* was designed to accompany the Latin texts, not the vernacular translations.

[27] The German diatribe reads: "verbunstige Mißgünner / lose Tadler / Meister klügel / neidische / höhnische Spötter vnd Gaufferer" (A7r).

[28] Max Rubensohn devotes most of his discussion of Held to a criticism of his poor rhymes and imperfect language. He offers many examples, often contrasted with Hunger's version, listing the primary failures as "Roheit der Reimbildung" (clxxi), "willkürliche Reime" (clxxiv), "barbarische Gleichgiltigkeit gegen die einfachsten Regeln der Rhythmik" (clxxi), and "Vergewaltigung der Sprache" (clxxi).

[29] Another view of German emblems with a different accentuation will be found in Dietman Peil, "The Emblem in Germany and the German-speaking Countries," in *The Companion to Emblem Studies,* ed. Peter M. Daly (New York: AMS Press, forthcoming).

[30] Other than the excellent edition produced by Peter von Düffel and Klaus Schmidt (Stuttgart: Reclam, 1968) there are relatively few studies of Holtzwart's emblems. See especially Holger Homann, *Studien zur Emblematik des 16. Jahrhunderts* (Utrecht: Haentjens Dekker and Gumbert, 1971), with essays on Brant, Alciato, the Hungarian humanist Joannes Sambucus (Zsámboky, 1531–84), Holtzwart, and Taurellus; also Ken Fowler, "Social Content in Mathias Holtzwart's *Emblematum Tyrocinia*," *Emblematica* 4 (1989): 15–38; and Elisabeth Klecker and Sonja Schreiner, "How to Gild Emblems: From Mathias Holtzwart's *Emblematum Tyrocinia* to Nicolaus Reusner's *Aureola Emblemata*," in *Mundus Emblematicus,* ed. Karl A. E. Enenkel and Arnoud S. Q. Visser (Turnhout: Brepols, 2003).

[31] Daly and Dimler, eds., *The Jesuit Series,* Part 3 (F-L, 2002), nos J. 712 to J. 749. A selection of Hugo's *Pia desideria* is available in English in a paperback edition: *A Selection of Emblems: From Herman Hugo, Pia Desideria; Francis Quarles, Emblemes* (Brooklyn, NY: AMS Press, 1992).

[32] To take but one example: Drexel's *Zodiacus, das ist Christlicher Himmelcirckel* (Munich, 1619), has an engraved title page and fourteen engravings. Subsequent editions: 1622, 1624, 1627, 1630.

[33] Daly and Dimler, eds., *The Jesuit Series,* Part 1 (A-D) (Montreal: McGill-Queen's UP, 1997), nos J. 164 to J. 238; and *The Jesuit Series,* Part 2 (D-E) (Toronto: U of Toronto P, 2000), nos J. 239 to J. 500.

[34] There is a recent translation by Fiona Tait of Cramer's Rosicrucian emblems: *The Rosicrucian Emblems of Daniel Cramer: The True Society of Jesus and the Rosy Cross,* Magnum Opus Hermetic Sourceworks 4 (Grand Rapids: Phanes, 1991).

[35] See the facsimile edition by Wolfgang Harms of *Emblemata politica,* Nachdrucke deutscher Literatur des 17. Jahrhunderts 35 (Bern: Lang, 1982).

[36] Although today emblematics have experienced a renaissance of interest, no studies have yet focused on larger issues; none for instance on a given publisher or center of production, such as Antwerp, Lyons, Paris, Munich, or Nuremberg.

[37] Reprint edition by Sabine Mödersheim (Turnhout: Brepols, 1999).

[38] Full title, *Meditationes emblematicae de restaurata pace Germaniae cum breve explicatione: Sinnbilder von den widergebrachten Teutschen Frieden* (Frankfurt am Main: Johann David Zunner, 1648).

[39] Ingrid Höpel, "Harsdörffers Theorie und Praxis des dreiständigen Emblems," in *Georg Phillip Harsdörffer: Ein deutscher Dichter und europäischer Gelehrter,* ed. Italo Michele Battafarano (Bern: Lang, 1991), 221–23. The multiple emblem will be further discussed below.

[40] The emblematic frontispieces and illustrations, accompanied by textual explanations, to Greiffenberg's meditations are printed in Peter M. Daly, *Dichtung und Emblematik bei Catharina Regina von Greiffenberg* (Bonn: Bouvier, 1976), 166–249. See also Hartmut Laufhütte, "Geistlich-literarische Zusammenarbeit im Dienste der 'Deoglori': Sigmund von Birkens Emblem-Erfindungen für die Andachtswerke der Catharina Regina von Greiffenberg," in *Polyvalenz und Multifunktionalität der Emblematik: Multivalence and Multi-functionality of the Emblem,* 2 vols., ed. Wolfgang Harms and Dietmar Peil, Mikrokosmos 35 (Frankfurt am Main: Lang, 2002), 581–96.

[41] For the only book-length study of Dilherr in English see Willard James Wietfeldt, *The Emblem Literature of Johann Michael Dilherr (1604–1669)* (Nuremberg: Schriftenreihe des Stadtarchivs Nürnberg, 1955); additionally see Silke Falkner, "Hens and Snails: Emblematic Representations of Women in Johann Michael Dilherr's Sermons on Matrimony," *Emblematica* 12 (2002): 185–221.

[42] Its emblematic medals and orations have been studied by Frederick John Stopp, *The Emblems of the Altdorf Academy: Medals and Medal Orations 1577–1626,* Publications of the Modern Humanities Research Association 6 (London: Modern Humanities Research Assoc., 1974).

[43] Although Harsdörffer's mediational theorizing in German is extremely important, after the now dated study by Erich Kühne, "Emblematik und Allegorie in Georg Philipp Harsdörffers Gesprächspielen" (Ph.D. diss., Vienna, 1932), little attention was paid to his emblem theory until recently. The observations of Jean-Daniel Krebs in *Georg*

Philipp Harsdörffer (1607–1658): Poétique et Poésie (Bern: Lang, 1983), 260–323, add little to our understanding. More important: Albrecht Schöne, *Emblematik und Drama im Zeitalter des Barock,* 3rd ed. (Munich: Beck, 1993); Dietrich Walter Jöns, *Das "Sinnen-Bild": Studien zur allegorischen Bildlichkeit bei Andreas Gryphius* (Stuttgart: Metzler, 1966); Dieter Sulzer, *Traktate zur Emblematik: Studien zu einer Geschichte der Emblemtheorien,* ed. Gerhard Sauder (St. Ingbert: Röhrig, 1992); Ingrid Höpel, *Emblem und Sinnbild: Vom Kunstbuch zum Erbauungsbuch* (Frankfurt am Main: Athenäum, 1987); Max Reinhart, "Battle of the Tapestries: A War-Time Debate in Anhalt-Köthen (Georg Philipp Harsdörffer's *Peristromata Turcica* and *Aulaea Romana,* 1641–1642)," *Daphnis* 27, nos. 2–3 (1998): 291–333; and most recently, Sabine Mödersheim, *Dekor und Decorum: Zur Analogie von Architektur und Rhetorik in Rathausdekorationen der Frühen Neuzeit* (Turnhout: Brepols, forthcoming).

[44] Harsdörffer, *Frauenzimmer Gesprechspiele,* 8 vols., ed. Irmgard Böttcher (Tübingen: Niemeyer, 1968–69). The title pages of the first six volumes have in capital letters *GESPRECHSPIELE,* whereas the title pages of the last two volumes are written *Gesprächspiele,* set in lower case and with "ä."

[45] Camerarius (discussed above) created the first scientifically ordered botanical garden in Germany (in Nuremberg) and wrote *Hortus medicus et philosophicus* (Medical and Philosophical Garden). Ulissa Aldrovandus (1522–1605), Italian naturalist, wrote *De animalibus et insectis libri septem, cum singulorum iconibus ad vivum expressis* (Seven Books of Animals and Insects, 1602).

[46] Vespasian asserts in passing that the distinction between *emblem* and *symbolis heroicis,* which he renders as "Fahnen-Bilder" (flag-pictures), is not important and not much observed.

[47] The following commentaries pertain to points 2 through 8: 2: This provokes a discussion of emblems or imprese with no figures, such as the black shield with no motif and accompanied only by the phrase "Par nulla figura dolori." 3: This may appear obvious, but "deutend Gestalt" suggests that the motif depicted in the picture "points" to a meaning that may not be immediately observable. 4: The quarrel over the exclusion of the human form from such images was an issue in impresa theory: for Harsdörffer a human figure is at best an "Exempel" but not a "Sinnbild" (emblem). 5: The number of words permitted had been a sore point among theorists of the impresa; some of Alciato's one-word *inscriptiones* would fail to meet this standard, especially where they name the personification shown in the *pictura.* 6: It was in fact usual for *inscriptiones* to be in the first or third person. 7: This is the old commonplace that virtually equates poetry with visual art. 8: This certainly describes the emblem at its best, although it will not always account for the actual practice of Alciato.

[48] Various Italian theorists of the impresa are cited, including the Venetian cartographer Girolamo Ruscelli (ca. 1504–66), author of *Le imprese illustri;* Scipione Bargagli (1537–86), of *Dell'impresse;* Stefano Guazzo (1530–93), of *De conversatione civili;* and Giulio Caesare Capaccio (fl. 1592), of *Delle imprese trattato.*

[49] To illustrate his meaning he refers to the engraved frontispiece emblem of the sundial and flowers with the motto: "Es nutzet und behagt" (It is useful and pleasing).

[50] This topic comes up again in Part 7. The speaker here, as before, argues that "der Mensch / als das Meisterstükk unter aller Geschöpfen / kan von dieser Kunst nicht wol ausgeschlossen" (the human being as the masterpiece among all creatures cannot be excluded from this art).

[51] As often in Harsdörffer the title plays with double-entendre. The word *Stech* (literally "stitch") in *Stechbüchlein* is ambivalent, for this is not a stitching manual; as for *stechen*, Harsdörffer uses it in the following quotation, clearly referring to the sticking of a pin or knife or needle into the book.

[52] This work, evidently a joint production of Dilherr and Harsdörffer, was probably printed in Nuremberg around 1660. For an excellent discussion see the facsimile edition by Dietmar Peil of the *Drei-ständige Sonn- und Festtag-Emblemata, oder Sinnebilder* (Hildesheim: Olms, 1994). Peil discusses the complex nature of these emblems and the broad spectrum of uses to which emblems were assigned in his "Nachwort" to the facsimile edition.

[53] In his *Personalbibliographien zu den Drucken des Barock*, 2nd ed. (Stuttgart: Hiersemann, 1990), Gerhart Dünnhaupt lists 467 titles for Dilherr, considerably more than in Wietfeldt's monograph (pp. 292–328), which lists seventy-two German and eighteen Latin titles. Among his emblematically illustrated works, all printed in Nuremberg, are the following: *Weg der Seligkeit* (1624); *Christliche Feld- und Gartenbetrachtung* (1647); *Göttliche Liebesflamme* (1651); *Frommer Christen Täglicher Geleitsmann* (1653); *Heilige Sonn- und Festtags-Arbeit* (1660); *Hertz- und Seelen-speise* (1661); *Augen- und Hertzens-Lust* (1661); *Heilig-Epistolischer Bericht* (1663); and *Himmel und Erden* (1667).

[54] It is only within the last forty years, with the advent of interdisciplinary approaches, that this bimedial form has been accorded its due of attention.

[55] Title pages: see Alfred Forbes Johnson, *A Catalogue of Engraved and Etched English Title Pages down to the Death of William Faithorne, 1691* (Oxford: Oxford UP, 1934). Frontispieces: Margery Corbett and R. W. Lightbown, *The Comely Frontispiece: The Emblematic Title Page in England 1550–1650* (London: Routledge & Kegan Paul, 1979); Karl Josef Höltgen, "Emblematic Title Pages and Brasses," in *Aspects of the Emblem: Studies in the English Emblem Tradition and the European Context* (Kassel: Edition Reichenberger, 1986), 91–140; Dietmar Peil, "Architectural Motifs as Significant or Decorative Elements in Emblems and Frontispieces," in *The Emblem and Architecture: Studies in Applied Emblematics from the Sixteenth to Eighteenth Centuries*, ed. Peter M. Daly with Hans J. Böker, Imago Figurata Studies 2 (Turnhout: Brepols, 1999), 209–29. Publishers' devices: Ronald B. McKerrow, *Printers' and Publishers' Devices in England and Scotland, 1485–1640* (London: The Bibliographic Society, 1949); P. van Huisstede and J. P. J. Brandhorst, *Dutch Printers' Devices: 15th–17th Century: A Catalogue* (Nieuwkoop: De Graaf Publishers, 1999), accompanied by a CD-ROM; Anja Wolkenauer, *"Zu schwer für Apoll": Die Antike in humanistischen Druckerzeichen des 16. Jahrhunderts*, Wolfenbütteler Schriften zur Geschichte des Buchwesens 35 (Wiesbaden: Harrassowitz, 2002). *The Library Quarterly* has also published a series of short essays devoted to the individual devices of many English and continental printers. From 1931 to 1975 the journal published 176 printers' marks, and John L. Sharpe III produced an alphabetical index to them in *Library Quarterly* 48 (1978): 40–59. The index concludes with a useful list of studies of European printers' devices.

[56] There has been considerable interest shown in the emblematic decoration of secular buildings in the German-speaking lands. See Hartmut Freytag, Wolfgang Harms, and Michael Schilling, with Wolfgang Carl and Deert Lafrenz, *Gesprächskultur des Barock: Die Embleme der bunten Kammer im Herrenhaus Ludwigsburg bei Eckernförde* (Kiel: Ludwig, 2001); Hartmut Freytag and Dietmar Peil, eds., *Das Kügelgenhaus in Dresden und seine emblematische Deckendekoration* (Neustadt a.d.A.: Schmidt, 2001); Wolfgang Harms, introduction to the 1640 facsimile edition of *Emblemata politica* (Bern: Lang, 1982);

Wolfgang Harms and Harmut Freytag, eds., *Außerliterarische Wirkungen barocker Emblembücher: Emblematik in Ludwigsburg, Gaarz und Pommersfelden* (Munich: Fink, 1975); Matthias Mende, *Das alte Nürnberger Rathaus: Baugeschichte und Ausstattung des großen Saales und der Ratsstube,* Ausstellungskataloge der Stadtgeschichtlichen Museen Nürnberg, vol. 15 (Nuremberg: Stadtgeschichtliche Museen Nürnberg, 1979), 383ff.; Werner Meyer, "Studien zur emblematischen Deckenmalerei an Beispielen aus dem Landkreis Dillingen an der Donau," *Bericht des Bayerischen Landesamtes für Denkmalpflege* 26 (1967): 133–69; Sabine Mödersheim, "Duke Ferdinand Albrecht's Self-Portrayal in the Emblematic Programme of Castle Bevern," in Daly and Böker, eds., *Emblem and Architecture,* 125–47; Eric Garberson, "The Relation between Decoration and Books in Early Modern Libraries: Three Examples from Germany and Austria," in Daly and Böker, eds., *Emblem and Architecture,* 107–22; Sabine Mödersheim, "Matthäus Rader und das allegorische Programm im Augsburger Rathaussaal," in *Emblematik und Kunst der Jesuiten in Bayern: Einfluß und Wirkung,* ed. Peter M. Daly, G. Richard Dimler S.J., and Rita Haub, Imago Figurata Studies 3 (Turnhout: Brepols, 2000), 227–47; Johannes Köhler, *Angewandte Emblematik im Fliesensaal von Wrisbergholzen bei Hildesheim,* Beiträge zur Historischen Bildungsforschung 7 (Hildesheim: August Lax, 1988); Fritz Graf, "Emblemata Helvetica: Zu einer Sammlung angewandter Embleme der deutschsprachigen Schweizer Kantone," *Zeitschrift für Schweizerische Archäologie und Kunstgeschichte* 31 (1974): 145–79; and Reinhard Frauenfelder, "Vorlagen für die emblematischen Bilder am Hause zum Großen Käfig in Schaffhausen," *Zeitschrift für schweizerische Archäologie und Kunstgeschichte* 14 (1953): 103–6.

The theoretical issues have also been discussed by Wolfgang Harms, "The Investigation of Emblem Programmes in Buildings: Assumptions and Tasks," in Daly and Böker, eds., *Emblem and Architecture,* 3–16, and by Judi Loach, "Architecture and Emblematics: Issues in Interpretation," in *Emblems and Art History,* ed. Alison Adams (Glasgow: Glasgow Emblem Studies, 1996), 1:1–21.

[57] Ecclesiastical buildings have also attracted the attention of emblem scholars. See Dieter Bitterli, "Barockemblematik, *Memento mori,* und Totentanz: Die Embleme in der Beinhauskapelle von Ettiswil (LU)," *Zeitschrift für Schweizerische Archäologie und Kunstgeschichte* 58 (2001): 143–58; Joseph Imorde, "Gebaute Emblematik: Die Jesuitenkirche Franz Xaver in Luzern," in Daly, Dimler, and Haub, eds., *Emblematik und Kunst,* 209–25; Bitterli, *Der Bilderhimmel von Hergiswald* (Basel: Wiese, 1997); Cornelia Kemp, *Angewandte Emblematik in Bildprogrammen süddeutscher Barockkirchen,* Kunstwissenschaftliche Studien 53 (Munich: Deutscher Kunstverlag, 1981); Kemp, "Die Embleme des Klosters Wessobrunn und ihre Vorlage: Ein Beitrag zur Marienverehrung des 18. Jahrhunderts in Süddeutschland," *Das Münster* 28 (1975): 309–19; Kemp, "Cycles d'emblèmes dans les églises de l'Allemagne du Sud au dix huitième siècle," in *Figures du Baroque,* ed. Jean-Marie Benoist (Paris: Presse universitaire de France, 1983), 57–72; Ulrike Köcke, "Protestantische Barockemblematik am Lettner der Buttforder Kirche," *Niederdeutsche Beiträge zur Kunstgeschichte* 14 (1975): 205–16; Grete Lesky, *Barocke Embleme in Vorau und anderen Stiften Österreichs: Ein Vademecum für den Kunstwanderer* (Graz: Chorherrenschaft Vorau, 1963); Lesky, "Barocke Embleme der Chorherrenkirche in Ranshofen," in *Jahrbuch des Stiftes Klosterneuburg* N.F 6 (1966): 179–219; Lesky, *Die Bibliotheksembleme der Benediktinerabtei St. Lambrecht in Steiermark* (Graz: Imago, 1970); Lesky, *Die Marienembleme der Prunkstiege im Grazer Priesterhaus* (Graz: Moser in Komm., 1970); Hermann Oertel, "Die emblematische Bildausstattung der Kirche des Deutschen Ritterordens zu Lucklum," *Niederdeutsche Beiträge zur Kunstgeschichte* 14 (1975): 175–204; Oertel, "Die protestantischen Bilderzyklen im niedersächsischen Raum und

ihre Vorbilder," *Niederdeutsche Beiträge zur Kunstgeschichte* 17 (1978): 102–32; Oertel, "Die emblematische Bilderpredigt in der Ordenskirche zu Lucklum am Elm," *Niederdeutsche Beiträge zur Kunstgeschichte* 20 (1981): 101–26.

[58] Sirach (Ecclesiasticus) 24:25: "in me gratia omnis vitae et veritatis in me omnis spes vitae et virtutis."

[59] See Ingrid Höpel, "Emblemprogramme auf nordfriesischen Bauernschränken des 18. Jahrhunderts," in *The Emblem Tradition and the Low Countries,* ed. John Manning, Karel Porteman, and Marc van Vaeck, Imago Figurata Studies 1B (Turnhout: Brepols, 1999), 389–421.

[60] Representation of a pelican in the act of wounding her breast in order to sprinkle her young with her blood. It is reproduced in the catalogue of the Landesausstellung Niedersachsen 1985 by Marianne Zehnpfennig, *Stadt im Wandel: Kunst und Kultur des Bürgertums in Norddeutschland 1150–1650* (Braunschweig: Braunschweigisches Landesmuseum, 1985), 72. See also Peter M. Daly, "The Pelican-in-her-Piety," in *Emblem Scholarship: Directions and Developments: A Tribute to Gabriel Hornstein,* ed. Daly (Turnhout: Brepols, 2005), 83–108.

[61] Illustration 42 in William S. Heckscher and Karl-August Wirth, "Emblem, Emblembuch," in *Reallexikon zur Deutschen Kunstgeschichte* (Stuttgart: Metzler, 1959), 5: col. 196. The goblet is in the collection of the Germanisches Nationalmuseum in Nuremberg.

[62] One of the few discussions of such emblematically embellished works of glass is the essay by Carsten-Peter Warncke, "Erörtende Embleme auf dem Satz Nürnberger Silberbecher aus dem Jahr 1621," *Anzeiger des Germanischen Nationalmuseums* (1982): 43–62.

[63] There are now many web sites with emblems, and at the end of 2004 Google announced an ambitious plan to scan millions of pages of books at the university libraries of Stanford, Michigan, Harvard, Oxford, and the New York Public Library. On the subject of emblem digitization see Peter M. Daly, *Digitizing the European Emblem* (New York: AMS Press, 2002).

[64] One of the greatest differences between the two forms of technology lies in the initiative behind the enterprises and, in a sense, in the ownership of the results. Whereas publishing firms such as IDC took the initiative to make microfiches of many emblem books and sold the resulting products, it seems to have been individual scholars or small teams of scholars rather than companies who have taken the lead in digitizing emblems, especially when they take the form of online editions. This is likely to change again as publishing companies recognize the commercial value of digital versions; CD-ROM rather than Internet versions are more likely to interest firms driven by economic considerations. But some scholars also find CD-ROM distribution a valuable alternative. It costs too much to reprint the small-run emblem edition when improvements could subsequently be made. On the other hand, online or CD-ROM editions can be updated at no or little cost to the user.

[65] Daly, *Literature in Light of the Emblem.*

[66] On Catharina Regina von Greiffenberg see Daly, *Dichtung und Emblematik;* Laufhütte, "Geistlich-literarische Zusammenarbeit." On Gryphius see Dietrich Walter Jöns, *Das "Sinnen-Bild": Studien zur allegorischen Bildlichkeit bei Andreas Gryphius* (Stuttgart: Metzler, 1966), and Friedrich-Wilhelm Wentzlaff-Eggebert, "Die Bedeutung der Emblematik für das Verständnis von Barock-Texten: Mit Beispielen aus der Jugenddichtung des Andreas Gryphius," *Argenis* 2 (1978): 263–307.

[67] Reinhold Grimm, "Marxistische Emblematik: Zu Bertolt Brechts 'Kriegsfibel,'" in *Wissenschaft als Dialog: Studien zur Literatur und Kunst seit der Jahrhundertwende,* ed. R. von Heydebrand and K. G. Just (Stuttgart: Metzler, 1969), 351–79, 518–24, reprinted in *Emblem und Emblematikrezeption,* ed. Sibylle Penkert (Darmstadt: Wissenschaftliche Buchgesellschaft, 1978), 502–42.

[68] Peter M. Daly, "Modern Illustrated Advertising and the Renaissance Emblem," in *Word and Visual Imagination: Studies in the Interaction of English Literature and the Visual Arts,* ed. Karl Josef Höltgen, Peter M. Daly, and Wolfgang Lottes, Erlanger Forschungen, Reihe A, Geisteswissenschaften 43 (Erlangen: Universitätsbund Erlangen-Nürnberg, 1988), 349–71. Also Daly, "Telling Images in Emblems, Advertisements and Logos," in *Telling Images: The Ages of Life and Learning,* ed. Ayers Bagley and Alison M. Saunders (Minneapolis: U of Minnesota P, 1996), 109–20, 151–55; Daly, "The *Nachleben* of the Emblem: Emblematic Structures in Modern Advertising and Propaganda," in Harms and Peil, eds., *Polyvalenz und Multifunktionalität,* 47–69; and Daly, "The European Impresa: from Fifteenth-Century Aristocratic Device to Twenty-First-Century Logo," *Emblematica* 13 (2003): 303–32.

Part IV:

Representations

Figure 1. Anonymous South German (Swabian?) Artist,
Buxheim St. Christopher, *1423, colored woodcut. 29.3 3 20.5cm.*
Manchester, John Rylands Library of the University of Manchester.

The Pictorial Language of German Art, 1400–1650

Jeffrey Chipps Smith

THE *BUXHEIM ST. CHRISTOPHER* (1423, fig. 1) is a simple yet elegant print.[1] When conceiving this image the south German (Swabian?) artist had to consider the choice of medium (a woodcut), of subject (St. Christopher carrying the Christ Child across a river), of mood (the surprised expression of St. Christopher contrasted with the calmness of the Christ Child), of composition (where to place the figures, the river, and other secondary features), and of aesthetics (a qualitative and economic-based decision to add delicate color washes to supplement the black ink on white paper). Each determination affected the potential audience for and functions of the print.

These decisions are integral features of a pictorial language that is unique to every work of art and its maker. Much like a writer choosing a genre of literature and a distinctive way of phrasing words, the artist, whether alone or in collaboration with other masters, devises a visual text. The following essay does not pretend to be a balanced survey of German art of the early modern period, which would be impossible to do in a single essay. Instead, I wish to use both familiar and unfamiliar images to consider the creative means by which artists and audiences communicated. The style of an object was individual to a particular master yet part of the broader visual language of the period. One must learn how to read such images. The nuances of form and the expectations of the reader/viewer can be just as varied as a poem is to an epic text. Frequently, as in the St. Christopher woodcut, image and text are combined to enhance the possible dialogue between audience and object. The occasional duet between visual and verbal languages will be a subtheme of our discussion.

The *Buxheim St. Christopher*, dated to 1423, is one of the oldest extant woodcuts made in the German-speaking lands. During the late fourteenth century, blocks of wood were cut to make designs that could be stamped onto textiles. As paper gradually became more available following the establishment of the first documented paper mill in Nuremberg in 1390, the artistic and commercial possibilities of printmaking soon became evident. An image like St. Christopher could be produced inexpensively in large quantities. Often several hundred copies could be pulled before the woodblock physically wore down. For the first time, a work of art was widely reproducible. Unlike a painting or sculpture, a print was affordable to a much broader segment of the population. Since an artist's investment in materials was small, he generally made woodcuts for the open market rather than on commission. This resulted in the creation of 10,000 or more different prints during the fifteenth century. Although the majority depicted religious subjects, new themes and uses for prints were continually being found.

Johann Geiler von Kaisersberg (1445–1510), Strasbourg's cathedral preacher, urged his audience,

> [N]imm ein Bild von Papier, darauf Maria und Elisabeth gemalt stehen, wie sie zusammenkommen, du kaufft eines um einen Pfennig. Siehe es an und gedenke daran, wie sie fröhlich gewesen sind und guter Dinge, und erkenne das im Glauben! Danach erzeige dich gegen sie in äusserer Ehrerbietung, küsse das Bild auf dem Papier, neige dich vor dem Bilde, knie davor nieder! Rufe Maria an, gib einem armen Menschen ein Almosen um ihretwillen! Das heisst Maria ehren und ihre Muhme Elisabeth.[2]

> [Take a picture on paper where Mary and Elizabeth are depicted as they meet each other — you buy it for a penny. Look at it and think how happy they were and of good spirits, and believe that. Thereafter show yourself to them in great reverence, kiss the image on the paper, bow in front of the image, kneel before it. Call upon Mary, give alms to some poor fellow human being in her name. That is to honor Mary and her relative Elizabeth.]

A woodcut like the St. Christopher was a devotional aid. The artist and Geiler von Kaisersberg both recognized the inherent power of visual images to stimulate memory and prayer. For most individuals the eye is the strongest of the senses. With his vivid composition and subtle hand coloring our artist has made this St. Christopher appealingly memorable. One can almost hear the dialogue between the giant and the Christ Child. In turn, the viewer is exhorted by the accompanying written text:

> Christofori faciem die quacumq[ue] tueris
> Illa nempe die morte mala non morieris.

> [If you look upon the face of Christopher any day, On that day you will surely not die an unlucky death.]

A short prayer asking for protection by Christopher, the patron saint of travelers, would surely follow. Monumental paintings of St. Christopher adorned church or public walls in most towns. A contemporary viewer literally interacted with the print by holding or kissing it. This practice helps to explain why so many early woodcuts exist in just one or two copies. This unique impression, preserved at the University of Manchester, survived because it had been placed into a book. Most woodcuts were simply discarded when worn out and replaced. The valuing of some prints as collectible objects, whether for practical or aesthetic reasons, occurred only later in the century.

Art as a direct mediator between the individual and the divine is illustrated in an anonymous contemporary painting, *Christ Carrying the Cross* (ca. 1420, fig. 2) made for a nun, perhaps a member of the Franciscan convent of Kamp, near Boppard.[3] This panel was the exterior of either a small devotional diptych

Figure 2. Anonymous Middle Rhine Artist, Christ Carrying the Cross,
ca. 1420, oil on pine panel. 62 × 30 cm. Madrid, Museo Thyssen-Bornemisza.

or triptych. Its obverse shows an emotional Descent from the Cross. Like the master of the *Buxheim St. Christopher*, this unknown artist, perhaps active in or near Mainz, presents a simple composition with strong contour lines and clear, if subdued, colors. Christ, clad in a green robe tied with a rope, bears the cross. Thick drops of blood cover his head, hands, and feet as tangible records of his scourging while in prison. Blood stains even the grass beneath his feet. This is the beaten, human form of Christ. His divinity is not immediately obvious. Upon closer scrutiny the viewer discovers that the artist has painted three wood knots on the arms of the cross and lightly incised the surface of the painting with the tripartite rays of light about his head. Christ glances toward the nun, dressed in a black habit, who follows carrying her own cross. She is slightly smaller than Christ. Her expression is one of both sadness and humility.

Mystic literature of the fourteenth and fifteenth centuries often stressed the individual Christian's need to pick up the cross and follow Christ. This was a means for stimulating one's empathetic engagement with Christ's suffering. Beneath the picture are two columns of texts constructed as a dialogue between Christ and the nun. The sequence of the words is marked by connecting red lines. Christ strictly guides her spiritual formation. The text begins:

> (Christ:) Hebe uff din crutze und gange nach mir
> Odder gange vor. ich volge dir
> Ich muß dich czwingen und lemen
> Du bist wilde ich muß dich zemen
>
> (Nun:) Ich bin noch jung zart und krang
> Wie mocht ich gelyden den betzwang
> En schwere burden kann ich nit gedragen
> Schone min here in mynen jungen dagen
>
> (Christ:) Ich muß nidder biegen dinen hohen mut und lypp
> Sol vst guts oder heils an dir becliben
> Du wurdest anders gar zu geyle
> Dede ich des nit du wurdest myme fiende zu deyle
>
> (Nun:) O here wie bistu mir also recht hart
> Ich wont du werest myneclich und zart
> Zu mal schwere und hart ist mir die fart
> Wan noch zumals. e bin ich uff mich gekart.

> . . . .

And it concludes:

> (Christ:) Liebes kint din hertze gib mir
> Wis sicher daz ich numer gelaßen dir.
> Und solt ich darumb zu dem andern male sterben
> In dynen sunden laß ich dich nit verderben
>
> (Nun:) Ach here myn notdurfftigkeit laß dich erbarmen
> Versmehe nit mich elende und armen.

Dynen liebsten willen volbringe an mir
Mich glustet wol zu gefallen dir. Amen

[(Christ:) Lift up your cross and walk after me
Or go before; I shall follow you.
I must force and break you;
You are wild, I must tame you.

(Nun:) I am still young, tender, and weak;
How can I bear this burdening?
I cannot carry a heavy load;
Spare me, Lord, in my days of youth!

(Christ:) I must bend down your pride and body
If anything good or saving is to cling to you.
You would otherwise be far too shameless;
If I did not do this, you would fall as property to my enemy.

(Nun:) O, Lord, how very hard you are to me!
I thought you were loving and gentle;
The journey is too difficult and hard for me,
And all at once, I am on my own!

(Christ:) Beloved child, give me your heart;
Know for certain that I will never leave you,
And should I for this cause die again,
I will never let you see corruption in your sins.

(Nun:) Ah, Lord, let my need make you have mercy;
Do not despise me, the lost and poor.
Let your sweetest will be perfected in me;
I well desire to please you. Amen.]

Text and image present the necessary path, however rough, that the nun must follow to achieve salvation and union with Christ. Intended for private meditation by an individual or by a limited group of nuns, the panel offered a daily reminder of the hardships but also the rewards of following Christ. In this instance, the gold background, a stylized feature in contemporary German painting, implied a hope of heavenly reward.

Martin Schongauer (ca. 1435/50–1491) of Colmar, Germany's foremost printmaker before Albrecht Dürer, imagined *Christ Carrying the Cross* (ca. 1480–85, fig. 3) quite differently.[4] Instead of an iconic and intimate presentation, as in the panel, he wove an epic account. Schongauer employed a technique known as simultaneous narrative in which he represented an instant frozen in time. This permits the viewer leisurely to observe the many different actions occurring at that single moment. Schongauer mixed the gospel accounts of this event with his own vivid invention. Certainly the artist was responding to writers, such as Thomas à Kempis (ca. 1379–1471), who admonished Christians to imitate Christ by using their own imaginations to place

Figure 3. Martin Schongauer, Christ Carrying the Cross, ca. 1480–85, engraving. 28.6 × 43 cm. Berlin, Kupferstichkabinett.

themselves with their savior.[5] What would the viewers see, hear, and even smell if they had been on the route to Golgotha as Christ passed by? Dozens of people, horses, and dogs make their way from Jerusalem, seen at the upper right, to Calvary, which still is out of sight. Christ stumbles beneath the weight of the cross. As he calmly, if sadly, stares directly at the viewer, he is subjected to the curses and beatings of his guards. Amid the immediate throng, Simon of Cyrene is scarcely noticed quietly carrying the foot of the cross. Schongauer gives even more prominence to the horse walking by Simon's side. The artist fills his composition with a myriad of details, some moving and some mundane yet each potentially fascinating to the observer. He presents exotic costumes, complex and almost endlessly varied poses, and a wide range of human emotions. Many of the participants are bored or angry or simply curious. Some talk with each other, oblivious to the importance of this religious episode. As the path begins to dip, St. Veronica waits patiently for Christ to pass. Meanwhile in the clearing beyond her the Virgin Mary, John the Evangelist, and the Holy Women sob helplessly. Farther on in the procession the two thieves ride on horses. Seemingly overlooked by all except the viewer the sky begins to darken. The clouds gather over Golgotha and move toward Jerusalem.

Schongauer's engraving is exceptionally ambitious. The print is unusually large and complex. It intentionally rivals small paintings or sculptures, but at a fraction of the cost. Trained as both a goldsmith and a painter — as were most early engravers — Schongauer sought to make this print pictorially expressive. Using just black ink on white paper, rather than colors, he adroitly varies the character of his lines and his shading. In the *Buxheim St. Christopher* thick lines merely described contours and some shadows. Schongauer's lines range from the lightest traces that suggest the distant hills beyond the city to densely hatched and crosshatched passages describing the lighting effects around Christ. Consider the tormenter about to whip Christ with a rope. His left leg is clearly if subtly outlined. Small stipples imply the different calf and thigh muscles. At the same time Schongauer contrasts the highlights, created using just the white paper, with gradated shadows. The billowing drapery accents the man's agitated movement toward Christ. The sheer diversity of figures, complex poses, and emotional contrasts exhibited here had never before been attempted to this degree in a print.

With this and other pictorially sophisticated engravings Schongauer and some of his talented contemporaries altered the period's attitudes toward prints. High quality engravings were avidly collected. Most of Schongauer's prints exist in numerous impressions. Frequently other artists borrowed both whole compositions and individual details. Schongauer's designs can be found copied on everything from wooden furniture and ceramic wares to large-scale sculpted altarpieces and intricate goldsmith pieces. Schongauer was among the first German artists to enjoy an international reputation, a fact not lost on the young Albrecht Dürer, as we shall see.

Although most prints depicted religious subjects, there developed a rapidly growing market for playing cards and images of all sorts of secular themes. Master E. S., active along the Upper Rhine and in Switzerland

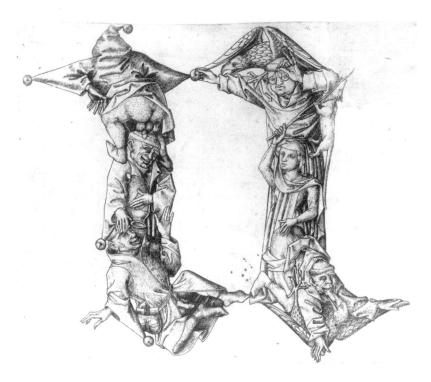

Figure 4. Master E. S., Letter N *from the* Figure Alphabet, *ca. 1465–66, engraving. 13.8 × 17.5 cm. Berlin, Kupferstichkabinett.*

between about 1450 and 1467, fashioned a whimsical figured alphabet of twenty-three letters.[6] This tradition may be found in late medieval manuscripts, including the late-fourteenth-century *Sketchbook of Giovannino de Grassi*, which Master E. S. knew either directly or through an intermediary source. Master E. S.'s letters, formed from twisted human and animal forms, range from saints to jousting knights. *Letter N* (ca. 1465–66, fig. 4) is distinctly ribald in poking fun at the sins of the clergy. Several of the tonsured friars sport fool's bells as they engage in acts of gluttony and lechery. Another with a full purse has apparently forgotten his vow of poverty. One monk adjusts his glasses yet cannot see his company's moral failings. At right, a nun or a concubine prepares to beat another friar's bare buttocks. Accusations of clerical sexual misconduct were voiced frequently before the Reformation. Master E. S.'s alphabet, while good-natured, anticipates the polemical role that prints will play in the next century. His technical and pictorial skills, notably the cruder handling of lines, were not as developed as Schongauer's but were ideal for his expressive compositions.

The *Hausbuchmeister* (Housebook Master, also known as the Master of the Amsterdam Cabinet; active ca. 1470–1500), another of Schongauer's contemporaries, worked in a courtly rather than burgher environment, perhaps in Heidelberg or Mainz. Many of his drawings and drypoint prints depict banquets, jousts, and, of course, lovers. He painted the *Gothaer Liebespaar* (Gotha Pair of Lovers; ca. 1480–85, fig. 5), an attractive couple about whom there has been considerable speculation concerning their identification and the painting's intent.[7] Drawing upon the tradition of *Minne*, or courtly love, the pair, both rendered life-size, express their mutual affection. The young man stares intently at the woman while gently embracing her. Demurely, she looks down at the wild rose in her hand. The flower, associated with Venus, symbolizes their bond. The young man sports a wreath of matching roses on his head. She also grasps a gold band, known as a *Schnürlein*, with which she binds the tassel of the man's brown cap resting on his left shoulder. This signified his willing fidelity as acknowledged too by his raised right hand. These meaningful gestures conform to popular conventions often observed in betrothal or marriage portraits. Both are fashionably dressed. The golden suns woven into her *Haube*, or kerchief, are painstakingly handled.

Two banderoles flutter wildly above their heads. Their agitation hints at the couple's passion so carefully constrained in the demure portrait. The inscribed texts offer a dialogue. He says, "Vn byllich het Sye esz gedan, wann jch han esz sye genissen lan" (Wrongfully has she done it / equally well have I worried for her welfare). She replies, "Sye hat uch nyt gantz veracht, Dÿe uch dasz schnurlin hat gemacht" (You have your own love / Who has made this gold band).[8] The coat of arms at the top of the painting has been identified as that of Philip the Younger, count of Hanau-Münzenberg, who lived from 1449 to 1500. Following the early death of his wife Adriana von Nassau in 1477, Philip took Margarethe Weiskircher, a commoner, as his mistress. The couple had three children to augment the six that Philip sired in his marriage. The painting is undated. It has been suggested that Philip commissioned the picture prior to his departure in 1484 for the dangerous pilgrimage to Jerusalem. If so, the painting may document their relationship, though the man looks much younger than the thirty-five-year-old prince.

Independent portraits, those that were made separate from an altarpiece or a funerary monument, appeared slowly during the last third of the fifteenth century in Germany. With few exceptions German artists and their patrons lagged well behind their Italian and Netherlandic counterparts. Although some pictures were inscribed as being a true *contrafett* (counterfeit), the contemporary term for a life-like image, most were rather stylized.[9] This makes Albrecht Dürer's *Self-Portrait* of 1500 (fig. 6) all the more remarkable.[10] The young Nuremberg master (1471–1528), trained as a goldsmith by his father, Albrecht the Elder, and as a painter-printmaker by Michael Wolgemut (1434–1519), had already executed several notable drawn or painted self-likenesses. Not content with the standard poses, Dürer here presented himself frontally. His models were images of Christ as the Savior of the World (*Salvator Mundi*). In one sense, he and the cross-carrying nun discussed earlier are both quite consciously emulating Christ for pious reasons.[11]

Figure 5. Housebook Master, Gotha Pair of Lovers, *ca. 1480–85, oil and tempera painting on panel. 118 × 82.5 cm. Gotha, Schlossmuseum.*

Figure 6. Albrecht Dürer, Self Portrait, *1500, oil on panel. 67 × 49 cm.*
Munich, Alte Pinakothek.

Dürer's pictorial language is strikingly naturalistic. He faithfully mimics the fur and fabric of his cloak. Each hair of the trim looks individually delineated. These textures are juxtaposed with those of his own hair, beard, and veined hand. Light draws the viewer to Dürer's face, with its subtle shading and three-dimensional structures, and reflects off his moist eyes. A few dabs of white paint suffice to indicate the presence of a fictive window, the source of the picture's light, to the upper left on the viewer's side of the picture plane. Dürer focuses too on his broad forehead and right hand, both located on the central vertical axis. A few years later in his theoretical writings Dürer will make a distinction between a true artist and a craftsman. The latter has skill but the former has both skill and knowledge. He supposedly coined the modern German word for art — *Kunst*, which derives from *können* (to know or to understand).[12] The painting conveys his mind, the seat of his creativity, and his right hand, the skilled tool that transforms ideas into works of art. The artist's frontal pose is carefully based on mathematical ratios and strict symmetry, lessons that he learned while in Italy in 1494–95, as he intentionally offers here a studied example of this knowledge.

Like several of the works discussed so far this one is inscribed. The intent of his words is, however, much different. To the left he writes the composition date "1500" and his monogram "AD." Both Schongauer and Master E. S. had earlier placed monograms on most of their works as a means of clearly establishing authorship. Writing in Latin, the international language of scholars, rather than in German, he identifies himself as the sitter and gives his age: "Albertus Durerus Noricus ipsum me proprijs sic effingebam coloribus aetatis anno xxviii." (I, Albrecht Dürer of Nuremberg painted myself thus, in undying colors, at the age of twenty-eight years.) Interestingly, he alludes to the picture's role as a record of his likeness, which would survive much longer than his mortal body. It was akin to a writer's conceit that one's words, and hence one's fame, endure long after one's death. This remarkable painting hung in the artist's house until at some point it was presented to the Nuremberg city council and displayed in the *Rathaus* (city hall); it was sold in 1805.

Dürer's preoccupation with both the technical and the theoretical aspects of art is beautifully evident in *Adam and Eve* (1504, fig. 7), his most famous print.[13] The pair stands before the tree of knowledge at the edge of a dense forest. Light dances across their bodies. Although Dürer was influenced generally by Schongauer's style, his ability to define forms through almost infinitely varied lines and sophisticated chiaroscuro was without precedent. Notice the detailed structure of Adam's legs in which the individual muscles are carefully articulated. Adam's right leg casts a shadow on the left one, a feature that Dürer exploited to stress the three-dimensionality of both limbs. The brilliant tonalities of Adam and Eve's bodies stand in luminous contrast with the velvety gloom of the forest behind. Surviving trial proofs, or test impressions pulled during intermediate stages of production, reveal that the artist completed all of the background before working on Adam and then Eve.

As God's creations, Adam and Eve were physically perfect in Dürer's eyes. For that reason he sought famous classical models, which he knew mainly

Figure 7. Albrecht Dürer, Adam and Eve, *1504, engraving. 24.9 × 19 cm. Albertina, Vienna.*

through the prints and drawings of Italian artists. Adam derives from the *Apollo Belvedere* (Vatican Collection), and Eve is a variation akin to the *Medici Venus* (Uffizi in Florence). These embodied ideal beauty and the Vitruvian canon of proportions. Vitruvius, an ancient Roman architect who was active in the later first century B.C., was best known in the Renaissance as the author of *De architectura*, commonly called the *Ten Books on Architecture*.[14] This theoretical treatise also contains a discussion about the proper ratio of the parts of the body to the whole. Ideally, the head is one-eighth the length of the body, the face is one-tenth, and the foot is one-seventh. Dürer was the first German master to be intensely interested in contemporary Italian artistic theory, which he sought to apply to his own art. His engraving also references Galenic medicine, which was based on the balancing of the four bodily humors.[15] This served as the foundation of medicine from the second to the sixteenth century. Before biting into the fruit Adam and Eve were immortal; however, with knowledge came mortality. It was presumed that while in a state of grace Adam and Eve possessed perfect humoral equipoise. Only when they were expelled from paradise did one humor or temperament predominate. In the print, the cat (choler or yellow bile), rabbit (sanguine or blood), elk (melancholy or black bile), and ox (phlegm) symbolize the humors, whose imbalance resulted in illness. So as conceived by the Nuremberg master, Adam's and Eve's physical perfection, albeit briefly, was external and internal.

Dürer used this engraving to demonstrate his creativity and his talents as a printmaker. Skill and knowledge are beautifully combined. The *Adam and Eve* engraving was avidly collected and widely emulated on both sides of the Alps. This print, following fairly soon after his expressive *Apocalypse* woodcuts of 1498, made Dürer famous across all of Europe. He was hardly shy about his accomplishments. Adam and Eve are not alone in his Eden. The cartellino, or small sign, beside Adam reads "Albertus Durer Noricus Faciebat AD 1504" (Albrecht Dürer of Nuremberg made this. AD 1504). It signals his presence in paradise and, not without a bit of humor, the God-like perfection of his art. Some humanists, such as Willibald Pirckheimer (1470–1530), his closest friend, must have enjoyed discussing the possible meanings of this sign. God created the first couple but Dürer depicted their perfection before the Fall. Perhaps too Dürer alluded to melancholy, the artist's curse from which he occasionally suffered, which came with his own quest for knowledge.

The Nuremberg master was the most dominant artist of the Renaissance in Germany. Yet his was hardly the only voice. Several of his contemporaries had different intentions and different pictorial languages. Gothart Nithard, or Neithart (ca. 1480–1528), better known from later biographers as Mathias Grünewald (also: Mathis von Aschaffenburg), had a far more immediate, more emotional style than Dürer. His *Crying Head* (1520, fig. 8), probably that of an angel sobbing over Christ's death, was likely a study for an altarpiece in Mainz Cathedral; it was stolen between 1631 and 1632 by Swedish troops and subsequently lost.[16] The head has a raw, primal quality; the entire body, seen and implied, seems to participate in the agony. Its sobs pierce the very silence of the viewer's imagination and elicit an empathetic response. The clarity and

Figure 8. Mathias Grünewald (Mathias Gothart Neithart), Crying Head, *ca. 1520, black chalk drawing with gray wash and white highlights. 24.4 × 20 cm. Berlin, Kupferstichkabinett.*

absolute control of Dürer's lines are absent here. Grünewald preferred to use bold, expressive wavy outlines that often fail to contain the adjoining shading strokes. This fluidity animates the features, especially since the artist reworked many passages. The same style, though augmented by intense colors, may be observed in his paintings, such as the famous *Isenheim Altarpiece* (completed 1515), now in Colmar (Unterlinden Museum).[17] Grünewald's uninhibited and extremely human emotionalism is the essence of his appeal.

Albrecht Altdorfer (ca. 1480–1538) found his spiritual inspiration in the Danube valley landscape around his native Regensburg. He reveled in the verdant abundance of nature. *Landscape with Castle* (ca. 1522–25; fig. 9) is framed by two tall trees.[18] This implicates the viewer by suggesting that he or she is just emerging from the forest. The scene suddenly opens up to reveal a compelling vista with a nearby castle (Schloss Wörth?). Other than the castle and the winding road there are no signs of human presence. Rather it is the dense forest with its pendulous fir trees that captured Altdorfer's attention. He patiently described the shapes of the leaves and branches. Their irregular quality coupled with the highlights animate the trees. Altdorfer employed an effective if not always realistic color scheme with browns dominating the foreground, greens the middle tier, and blues the background. He was the first of the so-called Danube school of artists, who specialized in landscapes.

For Altdorfer the forests may have had a nationalistic quality as well. Conrad Celtis (1459–1508) and other German humanists around 1500 were angered by the dismissive comments about their culture voiced by their Italian counterparts. In his *Germania*, Tacitus, the classical Roman historian, described the ancient Hercynian forests that once covered the German lands. Celtis, who published this text in Vienna in 1500, celebrated the Germanness of the tree-covered landscape.[19] This debate may have inspired some of Altdorfer's landscapes populated with satyrs, wild men, and virtuous saints.

Hans Baldung Grien (1484/85–1545) of Strasbourg, once a pupil of Dürer's, found a very different use for the forest. It served as the setting for wild animals, for death, and for witches. Where Dürer typically celebrated the rational accomplishments of the mind, Baldung explored the darker sides of human nature. In his *Witches' Sabbath* (1510, fig. 10), a group of naked women gather in a forest clearing.[20] The blasted, moss-covered tree — Baldung's own cartellino in homage to Dürer hangs here — sets the malevolent tone. Prior to the publication in Strasbourg of Heinrich Kramer's *Malleus maleficarum* (The Witches' Hammer, 1487),[21] there was no real tradition of showing witches. More than those of any other artist, Baldung's many images shaped posterity's vision of the witches' secret nocturnal gatherings. He also capitalized upon the titillating quality of nude females doing unthinkable things.

In the foreground three women gather around a ceramic pot adorned with pseudo-Hebraic letters. From this witches' brew spews a dense vapor containing toads, vermin, and other noxious ingredients. It forms a cloud that fills half of the composition. The left-hand witch raises her cup as she prepares to drink from this diabolic draught. Appropriately, Baldung's dark woodcut yields its details only slowly, much like one's optical experience upon entering a dim place. The central crone holds a platter filled with unpalatable meats. She appears to be shouting a spell. Obscured behind her are another witch and a goat. Yet another younger witch flies through the air on the back of a goat, a symbol of the devil. In her staff she holds another pot. From these concoctions the witches draw their powers to affect the weather, to cause infertility, and to inflict other damages upon the world. Baldung includes several limp sausages roasting over the fire at the far left, a reference to male impotency.

Figure 9. Albrecht Altdorfer, Landscape with Castle, *ca. 1522–25, oil on parchment attached to panel. 30.5 × 22.2 cm. Munich, Alte Pinakothek.*

Figure 10. Hans Baldung Grien, Witches' Sabbath, *1510, chiaroscuro woodcut with gray tone block. 37.9 × 26 cm. Boston, Museum of Fine Arts.*

The artist has devised a nightmare, yet one at which the viewer eagerly stares. Baldung introduced printed, not hand-applied, color into his woodcut. The chiaroscuro woodcut, experimented with a few years earlier by Hans Burgkmair (1473–1531) and Lucas Cranach the Elder (1472–1553), involves a line or key block and a tone block. The line block supplies the essential black lines, much as in the *Buxheim St. Christopher*. The tone block, which involves carefully reprinting each sheet of paper, adds color accents, whether for shading or highlighting. This impression of the *Witches' Sabbath* employs gray ink, which affects both the overall mood of the composition and the modulations of light, as nicely observed in the two foreground witches and in the tree. Another impression in the British Museum in London was made with an orange tone block. It possesses a different, indeed quite eerie character.

While Baldung's nocturnal scene was wholly imaginary, Dürer experienced a vivid nightmare so disturbing to him that he prepared a watercolor drawing of it, called *Dream Vision* (1525, fig. 11), the following morning.[22] Here image and text are equally necessary for conveying the horror of the vision. Beneath the drawing he writes:

Im 1525 Jor nach dem pfinxstag zwischen dem Mitwoch und pfintzdag in der nacht im schlaff hab ich / dis gesicht geschen wy fill großer wassern vom himell fillen Und das erst traff das erthrich ungefer 4 meill fan / mir mit einer solchen grausamkeitt mit einem ubergroßem raüschn und zersprützn und ertrenckett / das gantz lant In solchem erschrack ich so gar schwerlich das ich doran erwachett e dan dy andern wasser filn / Und dy wasser dy do filn dy warn fast gros und der fill ettliche weit etliche neher und sy kamen so hoch herab das sy / im geduncken gleich langsam filn. aber do das erst wasser das das ertrich traff schir herbey kam do fill es mit einer / solchen geschwindikeit wy(n)t und braüsen das ich also erschrack do ich erwacht das mir all mein leichnam / zitrett und lang nit recht zu mir selbs kam Aber do ich am morgen auff stund molet ich hy oben wy ichs / gesehen hett. Got wende alle ding zu(m) besten. Albrecht dürer[23]

[In 1525 in the night between Wednesday and Thursday, after Whitsunday,[24] I saw this vision in my sleep — how many great waters fell from heaven. The first struck the earth about four miles away from me with terrific force and tremendous noise, and it broke up and drowned the whole land. I was so sore afraid that I awoke from it. Then the other waters fell, and as they fell they were very powerful and there were many of them, some further away, some nearer. And they came down from so great a height that they all seemed to fall with an equal slowness. But when the water that touched the earth had very nearly reached it, it fell with such swiftness, with wind and roaring, and I was so sore afraid that when I awoke my whole body trembled and for a long while I could not recover myself. But when I arose in the morning I painted it above here as I saw it. God turn all things to the best. Albrecht Dürer]

Dürer's watercolor, recorded before the clarity of his memory faded, shows a panoramic landscape dotted with a few trees and a distant skyline of a city, not

Figure 11. Albrecht Dürer, Dream Vision, 1525, watercolor: 30.5 × 42.5 cm. Vienna, Kunsthistorisches Museum.

unlike his native Nuremberg. At the horizon a great blue wall of water explodes on impact with the ground. The flood envelops everything and everyone beneath it. Further aqueous projectiles fall. Some are scarcely brushed on, suggesting their great distances; others are closer. The devastation will be immense. One can easily imagine the roaring noise. Indeed, for a modern viewer this vision is frighteningly reminiscent of recordings of an atomic explosion.

Unlike a print, this was a private document. Dürer likely shared it with his wife, Agnes Frey, and with his closest friends, notably Willibald Pirckheimer. Dreams, much like such irregular natural occurrences as comets or monstrous births, were viewed as portents of potentially horrific events. In 1525 Germany was in the midst of great upheavals. Peasants demanding more rights and opportunities had revolted across southern and central Germany. Their rebellion, begun a year earlier, was being brutally suppressed, especially in the nearby territories of the prince-bishop of Würzburg. Dürer designed at least one biting critique of the peasants in the form of a mock memorial, so it was unlikely that he was sympathetic to the peasants' challenge to the social order. Although it is impossible to know what event triggered Dürer's nightmare, the more plausible impetus was the Protestant Reformation, which shook the foundation of Dürer's world. On 17 March 1525, after listening to twelve days of debate between Protestant and Catholic preachers, the council of Nuremberg officially declared the city to be Lutheran.[25] As one of the largest and most powerful cities in the Holy Roman Empire, Nuremberg's decision had immediate repercussions for the future courses of both the city and the spread of the Reformation. Dürer and Pirckheimer, as individuals and as members of the Sodalitas Staupitziana (Staupitz Society) in 1516–17, were both deeply engaged in the local religious debate.[26]

The Reformation's impact on art and artists was immediate.[27] Martin Luther, Andreas Karlstadt (Bodenstein, ca. 1477–1541), Huldrych Zwingli (1484–1531), and, later, Jean Calvin (1509–64) all questioned the legitimacy of religious art. Many radical Protestant preachers viewed the art adorning churches as idolatrous, a sin against God's commandment to have no graven images. The fine line between using an image to aid in one's devotions and the misplaced belief that the individual painting or statue had its own intrinsic power to help or to harm, through the giving or the withholding of its assistance, was often blurred. Most communities had an image known for its miraculous efficacy. Stories of statues or pictures that briefly had "come alive" to help the worshiper were legion. Others complained about the expense of art. Even after a painted or carved altarpiece was placed in a church, its "appetite" continued forever. That is, an endowment had to accompany every altar to pay for the officiating priest(s), the cost of wax for candles and other liturgical expenses, and the maintenance of the accompanying work of art. Such funds, reformers held, would be better spent aiding the community's needy. The cure, many felt, was the abolition of most religious art. Incidents of *Bildstürmerei* (iconoclasm) swept across the German-speaking lands from 1522. Some were spontaneous while others were sanctioned by civic officials. Zwingli boasted of the pure whitewashed interior of the cathedral in Zurich. The Münster in Ulm had fifty-one of its fifty-two altars stripped of their art on 19 June 1531; only one family successfully retrieved the altar that it had given to the church. The artistic patrimonies of many cities and entire regions were irreparably damaged.

The Reformation challenged artists' very livelihood. Upward of 90% of many artists' commissions had been for religious objects. In Protestant controlled areas demand for new religious images virtually ceased. Even in Catholic towns, especially from 1525 onward, orders for religious art were scarce. Artists had either to adapt to the new realities or seek other employment. Both scenarios occurred. Writing in 1526 from Basel, Erasmus asked his friend Sir Thomas More in London to assist the talented young artist Hans Holbein the Younger (1497/98–1543). He remarked in a related latter to Antwerp humanist Pieter Gillis that "the arts are freezing in this part of the world."[28] Holbein traveled twice to England in pursuit of a better working environment. The majority of his pre-English works were religious; in England, however, he specialized in portraiture.

In 1532, shortly after arriving in London a second time, Holbein painted Georg Gisze of Danzig (fig. 12).[29] Seated at his worktable the German merchant is surrounded by ledgers, letters, and other accoutrements of his business. Holbein's painstaking attention to each object, notably to the textures and colors of each, served several purposes. First, it established his absolute skill at faithfully replicating material items. Indeed, he was showing off; the glass flower vase, for example, is both translucent and reflective. Second, he used these props to position Gisze in a believable space, one illuminated with light from the upper right. Third, the inscriptions on the papers cleverly identify the sitter. The letter in his hand is from his brother Thadman, who was then the bishop of Danzig. Scrawled on the wall at left is Gisze's motto "Nulla sine merore voluptas" (No pleasure without regret). The sheet affixed with red wax to the back wall reads, "The picture that you see here records the features of Georg, such are his lively eyes, such is his face." This documents both the veracity of Holbein's portrait and, of course, the painter's artistic talents. The success of this picture was immediate, as it led to other commissions; it was also enduring, as it led soon to his appointment as the painter of King Henry VIII. The life-like character of his portraits with their stress on decorative attire revolutionized contemporary English painting. Not until Anthony van Dyck's arrival a century later would England have another portraitist of comparable international stature. Yet Holbein's career is a fascinating case study of how the artist adapted his pictorial language, which once delighted in elaborate perspectival caprices and moving images of Christ, to fit the new cultural realities.

Although Lucas Cranach the Elder grew quite rich in Wittenberg from making portraits of Saxon nobles and burghers as well as innumerable female nudes, typically under the guise of Venus, he is best known as the painter of the Lutheran Reformation. He anonymously illustrated many of Martin Luther's or Philipp Melanchthon's polemical treatises and anti-Catholic broadsheets. In works such as the *Passional Christi und Antichristi* (Wittenberg 1521), he excelled at distinguishing in clear, immediate compositions what he considered

Figure 12. Hans Holbein the Younger, Portrait of Georg Gisze, *1532, oil painting on oak panel. 96.3 × 85.7 cm. Berlin, Gemäldegalerie.*

to be the papal perversion of the Christian Church. In one pair of scenes Christ humbly washes the feet of his disciples while, on the facing page, the pompous pope seated on his throne receives the homage of princes and prelates alike.

Due doubtless to Cranach's influence, Luther was one of the few Protestant leaders who recognized the pedagogical benefits of permitting at least some religious art. Cranach gradually developed new themes that emphasized Luther's ideas on baptism, communion, and the Word of God. In 1529 he painted *The Law and the Gospel* (fig. 13), which illustrates one of Luther's critical tenets about human salvation through Christ.[30] Here as in his satirical works Cranach employed visual antithesis to contrast the teaching of the Old and New Testaments. A tree divides the composition. The left-hand branches

Figure 13. Lucas Cranach the Elder, The Law and the Gospel,

1529, oil painting on linden wood panel. 82.2 × 118 cm. Gotha, Schlossmuseum.

are dead, signifying the passing of the Old Law. At the lower right of this side Moses holds the tablets of the Ten Commandments. Because of the original sin of Adam and Eve, mankind is unable to keep God's laws. Death and Devil push Everyman toward the pit of hell and eternal damnation. Under the old, pre-Christian dispensation, salvation, as represented in the sky above, was impossible for the fallen individual. On the right side, with its flourishing tree, John the Baptist directs Everyman's attention to the crucified Christ. In the guise of the Lamb of God the sacrificial Christ tramples on Death and Devil. Lutheran art, starting with early works such as this, includes scriptural citations. Six panels beneath the scene supply the dialogue for each of the protagonists. These explain that under the old dispensation salvation was unachievable, but now, by the grace of God through Christ, forgiveness and redemption are available. In the background the Hebrew encampment with the brazen serpent is contrasted with a Christian city with its church towers.

Cranach also made a woodcut of this composition since he knew that it would reach a far broader audience. Unlike Dürer's woodcuts and engravings, the aesthetic level of such popular prints was considerably less refined. Rather, clarity and, when possible, visual novelty were important. Consider *Rabbits Catching the Hunters* (ca. 1534–35; text 1550, fig. 14), a sizeable broadsheet with a lengthy text by Hans Sachs and an eye-catching woodcut likely by Georg Pencz (ca. 1500–1550), both of Nuremberg.[31] Pencz was a highly refined painter of portraits and mythological pictures, yet his woodcuts employed a much simpler style with only a modicum of detail or shading. He focuses on the action as hares get revenge against their normal adversary, the hunter. The hare at the table signs the old hunter's death warrant. Meanwhile, another hunter is being roasted and the dogs are trussed, butchered, smoked, and stewed. The exquisitely colored woodcut illustrates the world upside down, an episode, or topos, when the normal order of life is reversed.

Sachs's accompanying text is titled simply *Ein yeder trag sein Joch dise Zeit/ Und uberwinde sein ubel mit gedult* (Let Everyone Bear His Yoke at This Time and Overcome His Misfortune with Patience), which initially seems at odds with the image. It opens with a narrative explaining the scene:

> Eins morgens gieng ich durch einn Wald /
> Es het geschneit vnd war grimm Kalt /
> Neben der strassen hort ich wispern
> Etwas hind' einem gestreuß laut zispern /
> Ich gugt hin durch / sah das da sassen
> Etwas in die zwey hundert Hasen /
> Hetten sam da fren Reichstag /
>
> Ein alter Haß erzelt die clag
> Uber einn gar vralten Jeger /
> Der sie teglich in jrem Leger
> Uberfiel mit lauschen vnd hetzen /
> Mit geschoß / Falcken / Hunden vnd Netzen /

Figure 14. Georg Pencz (attributed), Rabbits Catching the Hunters, ca. 1534–35 (text 1550), hand-colored woodcut. 25.4 × 39.3 cm. (woodcut). 52.3 × 39.5 cm. (sheet). Boston, Museum of Fine Arts.

Da mit sie vilfeltig verstricket /
Und sie on all erbarmung knicket /

. . . .

War ist es / wie Seneca spricht /
Welcher Man treibt groß Tyranney /
Macht vil auffsetz vnd schinderey /
Maint zu drucken sein vnderthann
Auff das sie förchten sein person /
Der selb můs jr auch förchten vil /
Und wenn ers gar vbermachen wil /
Wirts etwan mit vngstům gerochen /
Und hart gespannterbogen brochen.

[One morning I went through a wood;
It had snowed and was horribly cold.
Next to the road I heard a whispering,
Something behind a bush talking loudly.
I looked through, saw that sitting there
Were something like two hundred hares.
They'd assembled their imperial diet there.

An old hare was reading the charge
Against a very old hunter,
Who every day in their encampment
Attacked them with ambush and chase,
With shooting, falcons, hounds and nets,
So that they were caught in myriad ways
And without any mercy killed.

It is true, as Seneca says,
Any man who practices great tyranny,
Levies high taxes, and exploits his people,
Thinking to oppress his subjects
So that they fear his person,
Must himself fear them greatly.
And if he should overdo it,
He will eventually be rewarded with violence
And, as a hard-drawn bow, be broken.]

The print now assumes a political meaning with the hare signifying the burghers and peasants while the hunters stand for tyrannical rulers. If oppressed too much, even the worm will turn, the mild citizenry will rise up against its leaders. The Peasant Revolt of 1524–25, with its suppression of traditional rights, was at this moment still a recent event. Pencz himself had been expelled from Nuremberg on 12 January 1525 for denying Christ. The "godless" artist was permitted to return only later in the year.

German noble patronage, although already significant in the 1400s and early 1500s, became more active in the mid-sixteenth century as several notable palaces were erected or expanded. Unlike France or England no single court dominated artistic tastes. In 1536 Ludwig X, duke of Bavaria-Landshut and Straubing (r. 1516–45), started the construction of a new palace in the heart of Landshut.[32] This was to be an alternative to his heavily fortified Burg Traunsnitz, which overlooks the town. During the initial building phase the duke visited the Palazzo del Te, Federigo II Gonzaga's new pleasure palace (1525–35) in Mantua. Excitedly he wrote to his brother, "The like, I believe, has never been seen."[33] Giulio Romano's architecture and decoration embodied the latest *Welsch*, or Italian, Renaissance style.[34] As a result of this visit the entire character of the Landshut palace changed. New plans and masons were imported from Mantua. The courtyard has an elegant Doric loggia that was unprecedented in Germany.

The rooms and their decorations were dedicated to various classical deities. The duke's bedroom honored Venus. The *Italian Hall*, or *Banqueting Hall* (ca. 1540–43, fig. 15) exhibits a great coffered barrel vault and marble-sheathed walls. The latter were slightly altered in the eighteenth century. The form of the ceiling and the running frieze below also were inspired by rooms in the Palazzo del Te. The hall's paintings, by Hans Bocksberger the Elder (ca. 1510–before 1569), present a mirror of proper princely conduct. It celebrates the benefits of Concord and human achievements. Sixty imaginary portraits of great classical rulers and intellectuals accompany the central figure of Fama. The north lunette shows Apelles, Zeuxis, Archimedes, Vitruvius, Praxiteles, and Phidias, who represent the arts of painting, architecture, and sculpture. Many of Bocksberger's figures are skillfully foreshortened so they will appear in correct perspective when seen from below. The south lunette presents Minerva with Clio, the Muses of History and Philosophy. Thomas (Doman) Hering (ca. 1510–49) carved the chimney reliefs depicting the gifts that the classical gods bestowed on humanity. Saturn presented agriculture while Mercury gave eloquence to aid the merchant. His twelve solnhofen (very fine-grain limestone) roundels depicting the feats of Hercules, another princely model, line the walls. In this instance the choice of erudite subject matter as well as the latest pictorial and architectural styles marked Ludwig as a sophisticated and modern prince. Alas, he died without direct heir two years later, and the immediate impact of the Landshut palace was far more limited than might be expected. It did signal the growing mix of artistic styles available in Renaissance Germany.

Gardens became a requisite feature of German palaces. Again, the initial inspiration came from Italy where, for instance, lavish gardens were created to accompany new city palaces, such as the Pitti in Florence, and country residences. Salomon de Caus's design for Heidelberg (before 1620, fig. 16) brilliantly fits the castle's unique setting.[35] De Caus (1576–1628), from a French Huguenot family, grew up in England and studied in Italy. Through his work for the English royal family he was selected by Friedrich V, elector of the Palatinate, and his wife Elisabeth Stuart, to build a garden at their new

Figure 15. Hans Bocksberger the Elder, Thomas Hering, and assistants, Italian Hall, *ca. 1540–43. Landshut, Stadtresidenz.*

Figure 16. Jacques Fouquier, Heidelberg Castle and Gardens, *1620, painting. Heidelberg, Kurpfälzisches Museum der Stadt Heidelberg.*

residence in Heidelberg. Between 1614 and autumn 1619, when Friedrich was elected king of Bohemia and the couple moved to Prague,[36] de Caus devised different terraces, each yielding new visual experiences. Perched against and contrasted with the rugged, forested hillside, de Caus's nature is tamed. Beyond the individual plantings and the changeable character that these provided during the course of the year, his gardens exhibit a mathematical regularity; hedges and flowerbeds are formed to make intricate geometric patterns. The visitor experienced open vistas across the terraces, private trellised spaces and arbors, a maze, and — not visible at the extreme lower left of Jacques Fouquier's painting — a great grotto constructed partially in the hillside. Animating the entire garden were fountains and diverse statuettes. De Caus used nature rather than pigments to paint this natural canvas. As a landscape architect he developed a distinctive personal style, one that he disseminated through his publications, such as the *Hortvs Palatinvs* (Palatine Garden, Frankfurt 1620) on the Heidelberg garden.

Christoph Jamnitzer (1563–1618) of Nuremberg supplied lavish goldsmith pieces for nobles and wealthy patricians. His challenge was to delight his patrons through exquisite craftsmanship, expensive materials, and novel compositions. Consider Jamnitzer's *Moor's Head Drinking Cup* (ca. 1595–1600, fig. 17), which may have been created as a wedding present for members of the Strozzi and Pucci families in Florence.[37] The Pucci's coat of arms included the bust of a Moor sporting a fillet on its head. Jamnitzer's figure functions as a drinking vessel. The top of the head may be removed to reveal a cup for wine.

Figure 17. Christoph Jamnitzer, Moor's Head Drinking Cup, *ca. 1595–1600, gilt silver, partially painted, gold, rock crystal, enamel or glass, and shell. 51.9 cm. tall. Munich, Bayerisches Nationalmuseum.*

There is an intentional verbal play operating here since *Kopf* (head) was also employed occasionally to mean a drinking cup. A *Doppelkopf* was a vessel that could be separated to make two identical or similar cups for use by a host and a guest. The *Moor's Head* is also a conversation piece intended to be admired on a table or cupboard. Jamnitzer's vivid portrayal suggests that he used a

Figure 18. Georg Flegel, Still Life with Cherries, *1635, oil on panel. 18.3 × 24.8 cm. Stuttgart, Staatsgalerie.*

model. Indeed, it is one of the most dignified depictions of a black man during this period. Unlike a painted portrait by Dürer or Holbein this life-size representation transcends the inherent limits of two-dimensional media, since it exists in real space. Its tactility encourages the viewer to hold and slowly turn the cup in order to study the Moor's features. Yet as much as one might admire the stunningly crafted head, its mounting on the intricately worked silver base reveals its artifice. The true subject here is Jamnitzer's *inventio*, his inventiveness.

This interplay between reality and artifice is evident too in the pictorial language of the still-life paintings of Georg Flegel (1566–1638), who was active in Frankfurt.[38] Small pictures such as this, referred to as cabinet pieces, were intended for intimate scrutiny by the fortunate viewer. Flegel's works were admired for their mimicry of nature. In *Still Life with Cherries* (1635, fig. 18) he created an intimate mood through the composition's tight framing and lighting effects. The wine, nuts, cherries, cheese, and bread are set out for the viewer's optical and, perhaps, gustatory delectation. Is this food for us or for another diner who is temporarily absent? Unlike Jamnitzer's Moor, Flegel's subject seems so ordinary. It is easy to forget that you are looking at a picture rather than at the actual objects. Holbein's *Georg Gisze* (fig. 12) is replete with marvelous still-life details; however, these are subordinate to the portrait. Still life as an independent genre of painting evolved gradually during the later sixteenth and early seventeenth centuries, especially in the Low Countries. Flegel was Germany's foremost practitioner.

A composition, as here, that seems accidental is in reality a carefully choreographed balancing of different elements. The table establishes the scene's immediacy. Flush with the bottom of the picture the table abuts the viewer's space and seems to extend to the left and right. The wood grain and knots, painstakingly rendered, stimulate the viewer's memory of having seen similar tables. The Venetian wine glass provides the dominant vertical element. It is perfectly divided into two halves as the busy, intertwined stem yields to the clean lines of the simple yet attractive bowl. Glass and wine alike reflect the light and reveal its source as an unseen window behind the viewer's left side. The pewter plate, the knife, the cherries, and even the creamy soft cheese are enlivened by the light as well. Flegel accented the different textures and colors of his foods.

Six centuries earlier Pliny the Elder had told of a famous rivalry between Zeuxis and Parrhasios.[39] Zeuxis painted fruit so carefully that birds tried to pluck the fictive cherries, yet Parrhasios won this game of mimesis by crafting a picture whose painted curtain fooled even Zeuxis, who sought to push it aside. This classical pictorial topos proved popular in the Renaissance and Baroque periods. The painter's powers of observation and his skill in artfully reproducing nature stand at the core of his *Kunst*, to borrow Dürer's term. Flegel added a dragonfly that has landed on the bread, behind. Whether fictive or real, the viewer is tempted to shoo it away. Insects often were inserted as reminders of the transience of the material world, though Flegel here does not overly emphasize the *vanitas* character or overt moralization implicit in many still-life pictures. Unlike Dürer's *Self-Portrait* (fig. 6), where the artist calls attention to himself in both the subject and its execution, Flegel did not want his hand to be evident. By disappearing, so to speak, his artifice and his intention are masterfully realized. Unobtrusively, Flegel monogrammed and dated his picture at the lower right.

During the final decades of the sixteenth century, German Catholics started building new churches and redecorating older ones. In 1563 the Council of Trent issued an edict reaffirming art's historic role within the church while also empowering bishops to curb any abuses. The Society of Jesus, aided by powerful princely patrons, took the lead in creating stunning new churches, such as St. Michael's in Munich (1583–97), which asserted Catholicism's active, indeed often militant, presence in many communities.[40] Many of the monastic orders that had been repeatedly decimated by the loss of personnel and property during the Reformation rebounded as well, if slowly. The Benedictine monastery of Sts. Ulrich and Afra in Augsburg (fig. 19), founded in the eleventh century, began construction of a new building in 1500. Because of Augsburg's confessional upheavals as it moved between Catholic and Protestant affiliations and finally to an acceptance of both, the structure remained incomplete for almost a century. It was finished in a late-Gothic style.

Figure 19. Hans Degler, Adoration of the Magi *(high altar), completed 1604,* Pentecost *(St. Afra Altar), and* Resurrection *(St. Ulrich Altar), both finished in 1607, polychromed wooden sculpture.* Hans Reichle, Crucifixion *(Cross Altar), completed in 1605, bronze. Augsburg, Sts. Ulrich and Afra.*

The decoration of the choir and crossing (the intersection of the nave and transept) of this church, more than its architecture, expresses the Catholic Church's new resolve. Abbot Johann Merk (r. 1600–1632) commissioned Hans Degler (1564–ca. 1635), a sculptor from nearby Weilheim, to make three great altarpieces, each measuring about twenty-two meters high, for these spaces. Individually and collectively Degler's altarpieces (1604–7; also fig. 19) display biblical narratives as grand sacred theater (*theatrum sacrum*). In the corpus, or central parts of each, life-size wooden statues, vividly polychromed by Elias Greither I (1565/70–1646) also of Weilheim, dramatically reenact the Adoration of the Magi (high altar), Resurrection (St. Ulrich Altar to the right, or south side), and Pentecost (St. Afra Altar to the left, or north side). As the three kings venerate the Christ Child the heavens seem to explode with a host of joyous angels. The gestures are exaggerated for dramatic effect and also to ensure the sculptures' visibility throughout the church. Likewise, as Christ rises triumphantly from his tomb in the Resurrection the guards can only look on helplessly. Each of the three altars has a clear architectural frame that recalls a triumphal arch. Innumerable saints and angels, like noisy witnesses, fill the margins of each retable. Degler adroitly used the daily movement of light within the church to animate his figures, which he set within a mix of open and closed spaces.

Degler's altars also frame the bronze *Crucifixion* group that Hans Reichle (ca. 1565/70–1642), originally from Schongau, created for the Cross Altar in 1605 (also fig. 19). The elevated figure of Christ is silhouetted against the backdrop of the high altar. As the Virgin Mary and John the Evangelist grieve, Mary Magdalene, seen initially only from the back by viewers in the nave, desperately embraces the cross. Sinner and penitent, she becomes the emotional and spiritual Everyman for the worshiper.

Degler and Reichle employed highly theatrical forms to attract and sustain the viewer's attention. The biblical stories are brought alive with a new poignancy. Both masters exploited art's inherent ability to form memorable images capable of moving the viewer. Through works such as these the Catholic Church energetically reasserted its spiritual authority in Augsburg, a dual-confessional city.

While most Protestant communities simply reused former Catholic churches for their worship, around 1600 a few new edifices arose in direct response to new Catholic architecture. The Hauptkirche Beate Mariae Virginis (Central Church of the Blessed Virgin Mary) in Wolfenbüttel, begun in 1608, and the Stadtkirche in Bückeburg (1609–15, fig. 20) are the outstanding early examples. The Stadtkirche was erected soon after Count Ernst of Schaumburg-Lippe (r. 1601–22) moved his residence to Bückeburg from Stadthagen in 1608.[41] The edifice is a fascinating mélange of Gothic, Renaissance, and early baroque architectural forms, as evident from the showy façade. The scroll work, masks, obelisks, and other decorative motifs derive loosely from Wendel Dietterlin's (1550/51–99) *Architectura* of 1598, an engraved architectural manual that inspired artists working in various media.[42] This overloading of ornamental forms, probably done under the direction of sculptor Hans Wulff

Figure 20. Bückeburg, Façade of the Stadtkirche, 1609–15.

the Elder (fl. 1612–22), was considered the height of modernity, especially in northern Germany where it most often appeared. It is a self-conscious blending of different architectural traditions. The busyness of its ornamentation almost obscures the church's attractive tripartite division. The explicit ostentation extends to the main portal, where two carved reclining angels hold Ernst's coat of arms. The patron's name, in underlined golden letters, is inscribed prominently across the façade: EXEMPLUM RELIGIONIS NON STRUCTURAE (Example of Religion not Architecture). Ernst and his artists selected a pictorial idiom that draws attention to the new Lutheran church and to its benefactor.

The churches in Bückeburg and Augsburg were completed shortly before the start of the Thirty Years' War (1618–48), one of the darkest chapters in German history. Catholic victories in the 1620s were followed in the early 1630s by the invasion of central and southern Germany by Protestant armies under the direction of Gustavus Adolphus, king of Sweden (r. 1611–32). Hans Degler was just one of many artists whose livelihoods were destroyed by the war. Georg Petel (ca. 1601/2–ca. 1634), Germany's finest sculptor of his time, died in the famine and plague of the early 1630s.

One of the period's most successful artists was Leonhard Kern (1588–1662) of Schwäbisch Hall. He began as a sculptor of monumental figures, such as the allegorical stone statues over the three portals of the Nuremberg *Rathaus* in 1616–17 that follow designs by Christoph Jamnitzer. Yet with the outbreak of hostilities he soon adapted his art to the political realities in which he lived. Kern switched to making small-scale collectible sculptures. These were portable and made of materials such as ivory, alabaster, boxwood, or fine-grained limestone. Their refinement made Kern rich, and in 1648 he was appointed court sculptor to Friedrich Wilhelm von Hohenzollern, elector of Brandenburg.

Kern's *Officer and Naked Woman* (1656–59, fig. 21) seemingly recounts one of the horrific incidents of the recent war.[43] The soldier forces the unwilling woman forward. He has her arms pinned behind her back. The point of his dagger touches her flesh as well. While she looks upward in resignation, the officer, mouth open, speaks to someone. Presumably, her clothes are heaped on the ground between them. Removed from any specific narrative, the ensemble reflects the physical assaults, especially against women, endemic to war.[44] The immediacy of their contact renders any possible allegorical reading, such as the woman representing Germania ravaged by War, as wholly secondary.

This statuette was documented in the 1659 inventory of Archduke Leopold Wilhelm of Austria in Vienna. Subject aside, it is an exquisite work of art. As one turns it each side reveals something new. A straight frontal view shows off the woman's body but obscures the soldier's knife and the real threat of her death. As illustrated here the officer's expression is clearer than hers. Kern plays with the rhythms of his figures. The officer's assured step forward is contrasted with her small, hesitating movements. His boot with its spur is set beside her vulnerable bare foot. The soft curving lines of her body are juxtaposed against the stiffness of his leather boots, pants, and jacket. The line

Figure 21. Leonhard Kern, Officer and Naked Woman, *between 1656 and 1659, alabaster sculpture. 34.3 cm. high; plinthe ca. 21.5 × 12 cm. Vienna, Kunsthistorisches Museum.*

of her hair plays off the soldier's elaborate curls, which are further accented by the ostrich feather in his cap and the cape that trails over his shoulder. Kern used the open passages between the figures and between their respective limbs to create a convincing sense of motion through space.

Art and literature have always been closely intertwined. Both are expressions of individuals grappling to articulate the expectations and aspirations of their age. Artists and writers alike must choose the appropriate pictorial media or verbal genre to work in. Finally, period style and personal formal particularities have their impact on the finished work of art. In this brief essay I have attempted to explain some of the technical, conceptual, and intellectual considerations that shaped German art from the late Gothic to Baroque periods or, roughly, from about 1400 to 1650. I have avoided making sweeping or blanket comments about the evolution of art, since such truisms are rarely true — at best, such comments would minimize the creative diversity operating at any particular moment in time. The sophistication of Holbein's *Georg Gisze* (fig. 12) and Christoph Jamnitzer's *Moor's Head Drinking Cup* (fig. 17) comfortably coexisted respectively with the emotional expressiveness of Grünewald's *Crying Head* (fig. 8) or Hans Degler's three altars in Augsburg. Commonalities of pictorial languages are often more helpful than strict chronological progressions for understanding artistic intent and audience reception. Taken collectively, these German-speaking artists forged a varied and rich artistic heritage, one that continues to resonate across time and to engage new audiences.

Notes

[1] Wilhelm Ludwig Schreiber, *Handbuch der Holz- und Metallschnitte des XV. Jahrhunderts* (1927; Stuttgart: Hiersemann, 1969), 3: no. 1349; Peter Parshall and Rainer Schoch, eds., *Origins of European Printmaking: Fifteenth-Century Woodcuts and Their Public*, exhibition catalogue, National Gallery of Art, Washington, DC (New Haven: Yale UP, 2005), 153–56 (with a possible later dating of ca. 1450). The literature on most of the works discussed in this essay is extensive. I have listed only the most relevant or the most recent sources. These in turn will contain additional bibliographic references. Unless indicated otherwise the respective photograph was supplied by the museum or library listed in the captions. I wish to thank the many individuals who assisted me in gathering these images. Funding for the photographs was supplied by the University of Texas at Austin and by the Kay Fortson Chair in European Art.

[2] Quoted in Otto Clemen, *Die Volksfrömmigkeit des ausgehenden Mittelalters* (Dresden: Ungelenk, 1937), 14; quoted in English by Sixten Ringbom, *From Icon to Narrative*, rev. ed. (Doornspijk: Davaco, 1984), 29, note 40.

[3] Isolde Lübbeke, *The Thyssen-Bornemisza Collection: Early German Painting 1350–1550*, trans. Margaret Thomas Will (London: Sotheby's Publications, 1991), no. 12. I wish to thank Lisa Kirch for the translation. Because formal titles were not typically given to early works of art, standard English-language titles, derived from the subject matter, are provided.

[4] Pantxika Béguerie, ed., *Der hübsche Martin: Kupferstiche und Zeichnungen von Martin Schongauer (ca. 1450–1491)*, exhibition catalogue, Unterlinden Museum, Colmar (1991), no. K. 83. For a superb introduction to German prints see David Landau and Peter Parshall, *The Renaissance Print, 1470–1550* (New Haven: Yale UP, 1994).

[5] Thomas à Kempis, *The Imitation of Christ*, trans. Leo Sherley-Price (Harmondsworth: Penguin, 1952).

[6] Holm Bevers, *Meister E. S.: Ein oberrheinischer Kupferstecher der Spätgotik*, exhibition catalogue, Staatliche Graphische Sammlung, Munich (1986), nos. 110–32; Jürgen Alexander Wurst, *Das Figurenalphabet des Meisters E. S.* (Munich: Tuduv, 1999). The *Sketchbook of Giovannino de Grassi* is in the Bibliotheca Civica in Bergamo.

[7] J. P. Filedt Kok, ed., *Livelier than Life: The Master of the Amsterdam Cabinet or the Housebook Master ca. 1470–1500*, exhibition catalogue, Rijksprentenkabinet, Amsterdam (Maarssen: Schwartz, 1985), no. 133; Daniel Hess, "Das Gothaer Liebespaar oder die gesellschaftliche Absicherung einer gräflichen Konkubine," in *Jahreszeiten der Gefühle: Das Gothaer Liebespaar und die Minne im Spätmittelalter*, ed. Allmuth Schuttwolf (Ostfildern-Ruit: Hatje, 1998), 14–20, and no. 8; and Michael Camille, *The Medieval Art of Love* (New York: Harry Abrams, 1998), 156–58.

[8] Hess, "Das Gothaer Liebespaar," 15, offers this paraphrase: "die Frau unrechtmässig mit Philipp zusammengelebt habe, weil dieser es so gewollt habe und um ihr Wohl besorgt gewesen sei. Sie habe ihn sehr geliebt und habe ihm deshalb das Schnürlein geschenkt."

[9] Peter Parshall, "*Imago Contrafacta*: Images and Facts in the Northern Renaissance," *Art History* 16 (1993): 554–79. See also Jeffrey Chipps Smith, *The Northern Renaissance* (London: Phaidon, 2004), passim.

[10] Joseph Koerner, *The Moment of Self-Portraiture* (Chicago: U of Chicago P, 1993); Gisela Goldberg, Bruno Heimberg, and Martin Schawe, *Albrecht Dürer: Die Gemälde der Alten Pinakothek* (Munich: Edition Braus, 1998), 314–53.

[11] In fact Dürer's portrait served as the literal model for Christ's own likenesses occasionally from the seventeenth to the twentieth centuries. See Jan Bialostocki, *Dürer and His Critics, 1500–1971* (Baden-Baden: Koerner, 1971), fig. 35.

[12] Peter Strieder, " 'Schri. kunst. Schri. vnd klag. dich. ser': Kunst und Künstler an der Wende vom Mittelalter zur Renaissance," *Anzeiger des Germanischen Nationalmuseums* (1983): 19–26, esp. 19.

[13] Charles Talbot, ed., *Dürer in America*, exhibition catalogue, National Gallery of Art, Washington, DC (1971), no. 30.

[14] Erwin Panofsky (with a new introduction by Jeffrey Chipps Smith), *The Life and Art of Albrecht Dürer* (1943; Princeton: Princeton UP, 2005), 261–64; Thomas Noble Howe, Ingrid D. Rowland, and Michael J. Dewar, *Vitruvius Pollio: De architectura English* (New York: Cambridge UP, 1999).

[15] Blood was associated with the sanguine personality; phlegm with the sluggish; yellow bile with the choleric; and black bile with the melancholic.

[16] Öffentliche Kunstsammlung Basel and Staatliche Museen zu Berlin — Preussischer Kulturbesitz, *From Schongauer to Holbein: Master Drawings from Basel and Berlin*, exhibition catalogue, National Gallery of Art, Washington, DC (Ostfildern-Ruit: Hatje Cantz Publishers, 1999), no. 97.

[17] Horst Ziermann, *Matthias Grünewald*, trans. Joan Clough-Laub (Munich: Prestel, 2001), 74–152.

[18] Erich Steingräber, introduction to *Bayerische Staatsgemäldesammlungen — Alte Pinakothek München* (Munich: Lipp, 1983), 38, inventory no. WAF 30; Christopher S. Wood, *Albrecht Altdorfer and the Origins of Landscape* (Chicago: U of Chicago P, 1993), 138, fig. 100.

[19] Larry Silver, "Forest Primeval: Albrecht Altdorfer and the German Wilderness Landscape," *Simiolus* 13 (1983): 4–43.

[20] James H. Marrow and Alan Shestack, eds., *Hans Baldung Grien — Prints & Drawings*, exhibition catalogue, National Gallery of Art, Washington, DC (New Haven: Yale University Art Gallery, 1981), no. 18; and Saskia Durian-Ress, ed., *Hans Baldung Grien in Freiburg*, exhibition catalogue, Augustinermuseum Freiburg i.B. (2001), no. 34.

[21] *Malleus maleficarum* is sometimes attributed, wrongly, to both Heinrich Kramer and Jakob Sprenger. Kramer was the sole author. Sprenger collaborated with Kramer, having been charged to do so by Pope Innocent VIII, in identifying and prosecuting witches in southwestern Germany and certain parts of Austria. See in this volume the chapter by Gerhild Scholz Williams.

[22] Fedja Anzewelsky, *Dürer: His Art and Life*, trans. Heide Grieve (New York: Alpine Fine Arts Collection, 1980), fig. 239; Karl Schütz, *Albrecht Dürer im Kunsthistorischen Museum* (Vienna: Kunsthistorisches Museum Wien, 1994), 99–101.

[23] Transcription from *Albrecht Dürer Kunsthistorisches Museum*, 99–100: catalogue no. 9F.

[24] Whitsunday is Pentecost, seventh Sunday after Easter; in 1525, the first week of June.

[25] *Reformation in Nürnberg: Umbruch und Bewahrung*, exhibition catalogue, Germanisches Nationalmuseum, Nuremberg (1979); Jeffrey Chipps Smith, *Nuremberg, A Renaissance City, 1500–1618*, exhibition catalogue, Huntington Art Gallery, University of Texas (Austin: U of Texas P, 1983), 30–36.

[26] Staupitz presented Advent sermons in Nuremberg in the winter of 1516 and more sermons during Lent 1517. The group around Pirckheimer referred to itself as the Sodalitas Staupitziana in 1516–17 and from 1519 on as the Sodalitas Martiniana. See Jane Campbell Hutchison, *Albrecht Dürer: A Biography* (Princeton: Princeton UP, 1990), 123–24.

[27] This is a rich and complicated topic. See Sergiusz Michalski, *The Reformation and the Visual Arts* (London: Routledge, 1993); Jeffrey Chipps Smith, *German Sculpture of the Later Renaissance, c. 1520–1584: Art in an Age of Uncertainty* (Princeton: Princeton UP, 1994), chapters 1–4 with additional literature; and C. Scott Dixon's essay in the present volume.

[28] Derek Wilson, *Hans Holbein: Portrait of an Unknown Man* (London: Weidenfeld & Nicolson, 1996), 126.

[29] Paul Ganz, *The Paintings of Hans Holbein* (London: Phaidon, 1950), 238, no. 61; John Rowlands, *Holbein: The Paintings of Hans Holbein the Younger — Complete Edition* (London: Phaidon, 1985), 82–83 and 137, no. 38.

[30] Carl C. Christensen, *Art and the Reformation in Germany* (Athens: Ohio UP, 1979), esp. 124–27. For a good discussion of the role of prints, including a woodcut after Cranach's composition, see Robert W. Scribner, *For the Sake of Simple Folk: Popular*

Propaganda for the German Reformation (Cambridge: Cambridge UP, 1981), 216–18, fig. 171 and passim.

[31] Smith, *Nuremberg*, no. 106; Susan Dackerman, ed., *Painted Prints: The Revolution of Color in Northern Renaissance & Baroque Engravings, Etchings, & Woodcuts*, exhibition catalogue, Baltimore Museum of Art (University Park: Penn State UP, 2002), no. 21. Sachs's text was added to the print only in 1550. I wish to thank Lisa Kirch and Hubert Heinen for the translations.

[32] Smith, *German Sculpture of the Later Renaissance*, 247–51; Gerhard Hojer, ed., *Der Italienische Bau: Materialien und Untersuchungen zur Stadtresidenz Landshut*, exhibition catalogue (Landshut: Bayerische Verwaltung der Staatlichen Schlösser, Gärten und Seen, 1994); and Iris Lauterbach, Klaus Endemann, and Christoph Luitpold Frommel, eds., *Die Landshuter Stadtresidenz: Architektur und Ausstattung* (Munich: Zentralinstitut für Kunstgeschichte, 1998).

[33] "Der gleichen glaube ich dass kain sollicher gesehen worden," in *Stadtresidenz Landshut: Amtlicher Führer*, ed. Hans Thoma, Herbert Brunner, and Theo Herzog (Munich: Bayerische Verwaltung der Staatlichen Schlösser, Gärten und Seen, 1980), 6.

[34] For a good discussion of the term *Welsch*, see Michael Baxandall, *The Limewood Sculptors of Renaissance Germany* (New Haven: Yale UP, 1980), 135–42.

[35] Gerhard Wather, *Der Heidelberger Schlossgarten* (Heidelberg: Heidelberger Verlagsanstalt, 1990).

[36] The move lasted hardly a year, when Friedrich's army was destroyed by imperial forces at Weissenberg and he fled back to Germany.

[37] Renate Eikelmann, ed., *Der Mohrenkopfpokal von Christoph Jamnitzer*, exhibition catalogue, Bayerisches Nationalmuseum, Munich (2000); in that volume, see esp. Lorenz Seelig, " 'Ein Willkomme in der Form eines Mohrenkopfs von Silber getriebener Arbeit': Der wiederentdeckte Mohrenkopfpokal Christoph Jamnitzers aus dem späten 16. Jahrhundert," 19–123.

[38] Kurt Wettengl, ed., *Georg Flegel, 1566–1638: Stilleben*, exhibition catalogue, Historisches Museum, Frankfurt am Main (Stuttgart: Hatje, 1993), no. 52.

[39] Olaf Koester, ed., *Illusions: Gijsbrechts — Royal Master of Deception*, exhibition catalogue, Statens Museum for Kunst, Copenhagen (1999), 14.

[40] Jeffrey Chipps Smith, *Sensuous Worship: Jesuits and the Art of the Early Catholic Reformation in Germany* (Princeton: Princeton UP, 2002), 57–101 (for St. Michael's in Munich) and passim.

[41] Thorsten Albrecht, *Die Bückeburger Stadtkirche* (Petersberg: Imhoff, 1999), esp. 14–23 and 34–38.

[42] Christoph Jamnitzer's *Moor's Head* (fig. 17) shares some of the same decorative vocabulary. Adolf K. Placzek, introduction to *The Fantastic Engravings of Wendel Dieterlin: The 203 Plates and Text of His Architectura* (New York: Dover, 1968).

[43] Harald Siebenmorgen, ed., *Leonhard Kern (1588–1662)*, exhibition catalogue, Hällisch-Fränkisches Museum, Schwäbisch Hall (Sigmaringen: Thorbecke, 1988); and 1648 catalogue, no. 441.

[44] On 6 February 1634, Protestant and Swedish troops under the direction of the count of Hessen-Darmstadt entered the episcopal city of Eichstätt. Clara Staiger, the prioress

of Mariastein, an Augustinian convent, kept a diary in which she described the occupation. Although she and her fellow nuns were not subjected to the indignities of the woman portrayed by Kern, her account of the fears and uncertainties that all experienced, especially in the first month, is quite gripping. See Joseph Schlect, ed., *Eichstätt im Schweden Kriege: Tagebuch der Augustinernonne Clara Staiger, Priorin des Klosters Mariastein, über die Kriegsjahre 1631 bis 1650* (Eichstätt: Verlag der Ph. Brönner'schen Buchhandlung, 1889), esp. 90–97.

Eros in Early Modern German Literature

Gerhart Hoffmeister

U NTIL FRENCH BEGAN TO DISPLACE NEO-LATIN as the chief instrument of literary culture around the middle of the seventeenth century, the use of Latin in early modern Europe ensured both the continuity of ancient intellectual traditions as well as the coherence of humanistic endeavors within the republic of letters, or *respublica litteraria*. This international use of a common language served to challenge Italy's cultural claim to primacy in the renewal of language and literature on modern soil. On the other hand, it also meant that scholars and poets outside Italy had to cope with multiple traditions — classical, Italian, and contemporary foreign practices — in striving to understand, translate, or rework their sources, a reality that delayed the arrival in northern Europe of aesthetic equality with Italian humanism. Once that had happened, however, the works of the modern erudite poets — *poetae docti et eruditi* — whether written in Neo-Latin or in the vernacular, were produced within a unified literary world. Not surprisingly, the modern reader faces complicated lines of transmission. Early modern love poetry, which Hans-Gert Roloff has recognized to be the essential domain of Neo-Latin poetry,[1] is a case in point. Johannes Secundus's formulation, "Mollia Romulidum uerba loquetur Amor" (Love speaks the gentle words of the Romans),[2] despite its elegance, is misleading; for Renaissance love, eros, was multifaceted, both in theory and in practice. This is true not only with respect to the origins, reception, and adaptation of the Renaissance concept of love but to the erotic *raison d'être* in the lives of many early modern poets as well, in Germany as elsewhere.

The Italian Revival of Ancient Eroticism

Fourteenth-century Italian scholars rediscovered in pre-Christian Greece and Rome a model for leading life in keeping with natural reason. With this classical ideal before them they gradually liberated themselves from the hold of religious doctrine and worked out an aesthetic approach to the arts that accounted for the presence of divine forces in both nature and man. In doing so they revived the entire spectrum of ancient love literature from Sappho and Plato to the Roman poets Catullus, Tibullus, Propertius, and Ovid; while these various traditions were understood as a distinct heritage, in the course of adaptation they often were integrated with specific Renaissance varieties. Three of the most vigorous erotic strains received or inaugurated in Italy and further developed in transalpine countries until 1700 were the Catullan Renaissance, Neo-Platonism, and Petrarchism.

The Catullan Renaissance

Catullus exerted a profound influence on Renaissance and baroque poetry in all European languages. This is especially true of the love lyrics in the first section of his *Carmina*, such as the celebrated poems "Vivamus, mea Lesbia, atque amemus" (Let us live, my Lesbia, and love),[3] "Passer, deliciae meae puellae" (Sparrow, delight of my girl), and "Ille mi par esse deo videtur" (Like a god he seems to appear to me; based on Sappho). The varieties of love presented in this anthology — it consists of three sections: songs, elegies and epithalamia, and epigrams — prefigure all subsequent kinds of love, from the outright sexual (c. 32, 94), to the experience of profound suffering and loss of self (c. 51), to the mythological extolling of one's beloved (c. 7). If his desire for "mille basia" (a thousand kisses, c. 8) is not met, the poet may revoke his love (c. 76) or denigrate his lover (c. 41), sometimes seriously, other times playfully (c. 2, 67). Catullus revived Sappho's bittersweet love, compressed in the famous "Odi et amo" (I hate and love, c. 85), and was responsible for a strongly sensual type of fulfilled love. He also brought many Greek rhythms and lyric meters into Latin literature; it is therefore not surprising to see Cristoforo Landino, in the *Xandra* elegies (1443–44) addressed to his beloved, deliberately attempting, for the first time in the Renaissance, to imitate Catullus's style and meter. Giovanni Pontano's *De amore coniugali* (On Married Love, before 1503), Marc Antonio Flaminio's *Carmina* (before 1500), and Michelle Marullo's *Epigrammata* (1497) followed Landino's practice and established a Catullan manner of writing Neo-Latin erotic poetry that vied with the earlier idealistic-courtly vernacular form of the troubadours and, later, Petrarch. This functional differentiation[4] of preferred topics according to the choice of language and the education of the intended audience is discernible throughout most of the sixteenth century and remains visible until various "schools of love" merge in the Age of the Baroque.

No direct link has been established between Catullus and Boccaccio, Petrarch's cofounder of Italian Renaissance Humanism, who had studied Roman antiquity as well as Homer by the time he embarked on his collection of novellas known as *Il Decamerone* (1353). He does share with Catullus, however, the distinction of being placed on the Index of Books prohibited for school use, given the offensive eroticism of so many of his stories (especially those of the third and fourth days). Both poets recognize love as a force of nature that requires rational and ingenious management if it is to survive social pressures until its fulfillment. Boccaccio does not limit the adventurous nature of amorous desire to men; women too, who must use their wits to obtain their desires, are included. This shared attitude among the sexes appears to reflect the pragmatism of the rising merchant class in Florence, represented by Boccaccio as being superior to the clergy and nobility in the game of love making.[5]

The Boccaccian novella, with its imitation in Italian of rhetorical Latin prose and its erotic content, served as a model for many Neo-Latin authors, such as Enea Silvio Piccolomini (1405–64), the future Pope Pius II, who wrote his *De duobus amantibus historia Eurialo et Lucretia* (On the History of Two Lovers, Eurialus and Lucretia) in Vienna in 1444. The plot describes a passionate love story between a Franconian nobleman and a Siennese married woman. Though hesitant at first, Lucretia arranges several Boccaccesque rendezvous and is prepared to sacrifice everything for his love; Eurialus must return to the north, however, and Lucretia dies of a broken heart. What turned this tale into a European bestseller was its presentation of love as an overpowering force, reminiscent of Ovid's avowal that "Amor vincit omnia" (Love conquers all). The sentimental and amorous correspondence between Eurialus and Lucretia casts a revealing light upon the psychological motivation of the lovers.[6]

Neo-Platonism

On the threshold of the early modern period Francesco Petrarch (1304–74) asked the key question for his and subsequent generations of scholars: Who was the greater genius, Plato or Aristotle? His answer: "A maioribus Plato, Aristotiles laudatur a pluribus" (Plato is praised by more distinguished men, Aristotle by the crowd).[7] He considered Plato divine because closer to Christian truth — and this was the decisive attitude behind the revival, beginning in 1459, of Plato's philosophy at the Platonic Academy in Florence. Plato had been transmitted to Petrarch's time by way of Cicero and St. Augustine (Petrarch himself owned copies of Greek and Latin manuscripts of Plato). The systematic translation of the philosopher's *oeuvre* into Latin, however, had to wait until the complete manuscript arrived in Venice from Constantinople in 1428. Greek orthodox participants in the Church Council in Florence in 1438–39 added to this manuscript transmission. It was at this point that Cosimo de Medici, ruler of the Florentine Republic between 1434 and 1464, decided to employ the Greek scholar Marsilio Ficino (1433–99) as interpreter and translator of Plato as well as director of the Medici academy. Ficino published *De amore*, his commentary on Plato's *Symposium*, in 1469 and his *Theologia Platonica* in 1482. As the title of the later work suggests, Ficino understood this synthesis of Platonic and Christian spiritualism as a *philosophia pia*, whereby eros and grace possess equal status. Ultimately, therefore, Ficino's philosophy must be called Neo-Platonism, since it adapted and modified seminal Platonic ideas to his modern worldview. The idea of the unity of the cosmos, for example, imagines a hierarchy of beings with God and angels above nature, the corporeal world of animals and inanimate matter below, and the human soul in the center, free to move up or down but ideally ascending to God. According to Ficino's *De amore*, eros is the divine ray of love that pervades and connects the cosmos; it emanates from God, becomes matter, and returns at last, with the help of the soul, to God. What drives the purification of the soul and the world it inhabits is love, which may be defined as the desire for the beauty of the universe and of God, as manifest in beautiful persons, who are the mirrors of divine splendor. This is not sensual love in the Catullan tradition but intellectual love, the ultimate goal of which is the mystical union of the soul and God. Love raises man to God. Thus Ficino's *amore Platonico* keeps its original meaning of pure spirituality, although his language of love merges with that of the troubadours and Petrarch in describing love's progress from the heart through the eyes and back to the heart.[8] This philosophy in fact recognizes multiple types of love: cosmic eros that links the heavens and the material world through a process of emanation and return; extreme sensual earthly love or, at the extremes, the love of brutes; and human love that constantly purifies itself on the way to God.[9]

Ficino's disciple, Pico della Mirandola (1463–94), confirmed and strengthened Ficino's worldview by emphasizing in his *Oratio de hominis dignitate* (*Oration on the Dignity of Man*, 1486) its religious connotations while simultaneously promoting the dignity of man. Both men played key roles in the dissemination of Neo-Platonism as a cosmological theory as well as a theory of love. Their influence on essayists such as Cardinal Pietro Bembo (1470–1547) and Count Baldassare Castiglione (1478–1529) was powerful and extended to Neo-Latin and vernacular poets in most European literatures down to the eighteenth century. Not the least of these were the Cambridge Platonists, as well as representatives of the so-called New Humanism in the Age of Goethe, such as Johann J. Winckelmann and Friedrich Schiller.[10]

Castiglione, renowned for his *Il libro del Cortegiano* (The Book of the Courtier, 1528), was a crucial figure in the transmission of Neo-Platonism to transalpine countries. The fourth section of these dialogues is devoted to Platonic love at an imaginary courtly gathering at Urbino, the most chivalrous and splendid court of the Italian Renaissance; the main speaker is Bembo, who had in fact once lived at Urbino and was the writer of an earlier Platonic dialogue on love, *Gli Asolani* (1505). Although the integrated group of courtly men and women in his *Cortegiano* harkens back to Boccaccio, Castiglione's purpose is rather to confirm, strengthen, and alter Platonic precepts. Bembo explains eros as divine energy that binds the "chain of beings" together to form a harmoniously ordered cosmos; everything emanates from God and, desirous of beauty, longs for God, creating thereby a circle of love. From his central position in the cosmic chain, man must exert free will in order to ascend the ladder of love from the bottom (sensual love), to the middle via reason (rational love), and at last to the heights of the intellectual contemplation of divine beauty.[11] Thus the tripartite division of the soul's faculties corresponds to three types of love and beauty: body, mind, and God. Unlike Plato, and differently from Ficino's intellectual concept of friendship, Castiglione gives significant value to heterosexual courtly love in which love longs for beauty; guided by reason, partners are led into the realm of perfection.

Petrarchism

Petrarch synthesized the dominant erotic traditions and transferred Roman and Greek motifs to his mother tongue. One line of tradition extended from antiquity (Sappho, Plato, Catullus, Ovid), with Plato transmitted by Cicero and Augustine; the other from the Middle Ages (the troubadours, the Sicilian school), the key locations being trecento Palermo (Emperor Friedrich's court) and quatrocento Florence (the Tuscan *dolce stil nuovo* of Dante and Guido Cavalcanti). Disciples by the hundreds across Europe, whether writing in Neo-Latin or the respective vernacular, emulated this "master of love" until well into the eighteenth century.[12] Petrarch's *Canzoniere* (concluded shortly before his death), composed at the threshold of the early modern period, provides more than a lyrical summation of the poetry of his predecessors. It is an unprecedented analysis of the divided self. His ambivalence toward the beloved Laura — are these the feelings of sensual temptation or divine virtue? — allows a struggle to erupt between conflicting loyalties: of love and reason, desire and salvation, Laura and St. Mary, heaven and earth, which mirror both the human condition of his time and his own growth as a poet. From the early individual sonnets after 1327, when he encountered Laura (especially "Era il giorno" and "Benedetto sia 'l giorno"), through their final assignment within an anthology of 366 poems, a "love novel in sonnets" emerges,[13] having dimensions sufficient to tell a tale of inner development from unhappy love, to death of the beautiful beloved, to repentance, to the final union of Laura and Mary in a grand vision of divine beauty (c. 362, 366). In the end a great integration has occurred — on the Platonic model in Petrarch's venerated master Augustine — of the erotic and the psychological "novels" together with the religious narrative of salvation. Not the life story itself is important, but the fiction of a love story for the sake of a work of art.[14] The essential features of this love are traditional (revival of the *dulce malum* of Sappho and the Roman erotic poets, troubadour worship of the lady, divine love and beauty as the ultimate Platonic goal), but they are adapted to a distinctive elegiac mood of narcissistic remembrance, which unfolds in a continuous dialogue of the soul with itself.

The irony in this reception was that Petrarch, the synthesizer and innovator, achieved greater fame as a love poet than did his renowned predecessors; indeed he eventually replaced them as the chief authority, especially in vernacular poetry, and kept his followers in thrall for centuries to come. Urged on by laudatory commentaries on the *Canzoniere*, especially Bembo's *Le Prose della volgar lingua* (On Writing in the Vernacular, 1525), and even dictionaries, such as the *Epiteti del Petrarca* (1560) of Lodovico Beccadelli, poets, painters, and composers of art songs all imitated Petrarch.[15] Poets in particular, ambitious to acquire expertise in poetic diction and to vie with past and contemporary rivals for poetic laurels,[16] sought to reproduce his melancholy tone and borrowed heavily from the Petrarchist[17] repertoire of love motifs, employing them not only in the standard poetic forms (sonnet, madrigal, epigram, canzone) but in other genres as well (drama, epic, novel). The classic Petrarchist poem is a love sonnet that praises an angelic but cruel lady, whose suitor, rejected, suffers desperately, even while taking narcissistic pleasure in his predicament.

Of course, the imitation of Petrarch was not the only erotic current flourishing around 1500. Bembo, for instance, dedicates one chapter of *Gli Asolani* to the Petrarchist lament of unhappy love, one to Catullan hedonism, and one to Neo-Platonic love. Yet, by 1600, versions of Petrarchism dominated love poetry; in fact so pervasively that it absorbed most other traditions — Ovidian, pastoral, emblematic, political, and Anacreontic — into new erotic blends. This breadth of imitation and emulation precludes any attempt at a normative definition of Petrarchism, for its features were nothing if not changeable and could be readily discarded upon the invention of some new and ingenious combination of motifs from the *Canzoniere* or its imitators. Individual success, measured by the degree to which a poet could entertaining or otherwise impress his audience, hinged on his ability to achieve maximum cleverness through striking antitheses, metaphors, epigrammatic punch lines, and the like. Indeed, love poetry was the perfect vehicle for entertaining the leisure class,[18] first at the Italian courts and thereafter in the courts and cities of Europe, where the madrigal and other kinds of art song were cultivated, inspired by the *musa iocosa*, the playful, witty muse.[19] Petrarchism soon provoked its opposite, its inversion, or contrafacture. This "anti-Petrarchism" could take various forms: rejection by one's mistress, usually accompanied by burlesque mockery, as in Francesco Berni's "Sonetto contro la moglie" (Sonnet Against a Wife, before 1535);[20] the objectification of the mistress for carnal lust, as in Giambattista Marino's *Rime* (1602); or the transformation of eroticism into either a Christian mysticism of the kind found in *Jesusminne* (Jesus love poetry) or spiritual *Hirtendichtung* (pastoral poetry).

Petrarchism not only transmitted Petrarch's adaptations of ancient eroticism, mythology, and metric forms, it also provided training in the fully developed Neo-Latin poetic diction, which in turn served as a model for the vernacular poetry that had replaced Neo-Latin in all of Europe by the end of the seventeenth century. Moreover, the rise of Petrarchism as the dominant love conception furthered the acceptance of lyrical poetry as an independent genre. Because the topic of love was central to the self-understanding of the learned upper class, Petrarchism, it may be said, contributed to the sophistication of social manners, language, and taste.[21]

Reception and Adaptation in German Literature: Neo-Latin Mediators

After the decline of the High Middle Ages the re-creation of a viable literature in the German language depended in significant part on how Renaissance ideas and practices, both in Latin and Italian, were transferred to Neo-Latin scholar-poets north of the Alps. These academically trained authors constituted a thin but all-important layer of elite culture above the popular base of German-language writers. Most early German humanists went to study at Padua, Pavia, or Bologna, and returned with a deep admiration for the revival of antiquity that had been promoted by Petrarch. Of equal importance were the Italian humanists who traveled north in search of manuscripts and who frequently stayed on to fill administrative positions at German courts, universities, or cities. Petrarch's Latin works on ethics, philosophy, and humanist education, first appreciated and cultivated north of the Alps at the court of Emperor Charles IV (r. 1355–78) in Prague, became the primary models for the renewal of transalpine letters for the following century and a half. Initially received only warily by Charles, Petrarch eventually developed a friendship with the emperor that would endure for more than twenty years; his correspondence with the imperial chancellor, Johann von Neumarkt (ca. 1310–80), remained intense and productive.[22]

Two German texts in particular represent the brief flourishing of Prague humanism under the influence of Petrarch and later Italian visitors. The first, Neumarkt's translation — influenced by Petrarch's style even before his first visit to the court in 1356 — of the pseudo-Augustinian *Buch der Liebkosung* (Book of Adoration, 1355), takes the form of a mystical monologue on the union between the soul and God.[23] The second, Johann von Tepl's *Der Ackermann aus Böhmen* (The Plowman from Bohemia), composed about 1400, is a work of great rhetorical skill in the chancery style of Neumarkt. Tepl (ca. 1350–1414) elegantly portrays the dignity of man in the person of the grieving plowman who has lost his wife to Death, with whom he exchanges arguments throughout the book. In chapters 27 and 29 the Plowman offers a powerful defense of women and their ennobling role in marriage:

> So manlichen man gesach ich nie, der rechte mutig wurde, er wurde dann mit frawen troste gesteuret. Wo der guten samenung ist, da sihet man es alle tage: auf allen planen, auf allen hofen, in allen turnieren, in allen her-farten tun die frawen ie das beste. Wer in frawen dienste ist, der muss sich aller missetat anen. Rechte zucht vnd ere lernen die werden frawen in irer schule. Irdischer freuden sint gewaltig die frawen.[24]

> [I never saw any man, however valiant, come to achievement except with a woman's help and guidance. One sees it every day, wherever there is good company, in all places, at all courts, at all tourneys, on all campaigns, it is the women who do the greatest things. He who is in the service of women must shun any evil deed. Noble women teach dignity and honor in their school. Women command earthly joys.]

Among the most influential mediators between the south and the north were poets and scholars who studied in Italy and upon their return published their writings in Neo-Latin, which were immediately disseminated to all of their colleagues across the European republic of letters. In the late fifteenth century this group included Conrad Celtis, Johannes Secundus, and Petrus Lotichius. During his decade of itinerancy, Celtis (1459–1508), "the German arch-humanist,"[25] lived for two years in Italy (1487–89), where he frequented Ficino's Accademica Platonica, a group of scholars who gathered in Florence, and subsequently studied Latin, Greek, and Hebrew in Florence, Ferrara, and

Rome. In 1495 Celtis was instrumental in founding his own Platonic academy in Heidelberg.[26]

In 1502 he published his masterpiece, *Quattuor libri amorum* (Four Books of Amores), based on his years of wandering. Constructed according to Pythagorean numerical symbolism, the *Amores* are divided into four cycles, each having its own female lover (Hasilina, Elsula, Ursula, and Barbara) of different temperament and age who lives in a different city on a major river. Given Celtis's exposure to Neo-Platonism one might expect that he would integrate this philosophy into his love stories; most of his subject matter, however, appears to have been inspired by ancient erotic poets, most notably Ovid and Catullus. His writing has the force of personal experience, though this impression can be extremely misleading. A good example is the famous Hasilina poem "De nocte et osculo Hasilinae, erotice" (Of the Night and Hasilina's Kiss, in an erotic manner).[27] On the evidence of a Czech letter from a woman named Hasilina, who complains in embarrassment about a reading of the poem at a Kraków inn, scholars long accepted the biographical interpretation that the letter reflected real experience. Alas, it was a hoax, perpetrated by none other than Celtis himself![28] The poem in fact exemplifies the transfer of ancient eroticism in the manner of mythological embellishment of the beloved as seen in Catullus's *Carmina* (e.g., "Quaeris, quot mihi basiationes"). For literary history the Hasilina poem represents a high-water mark of aesthetic accomplishment: the moment at which German Neo-Latin poets drew even with their Italian counterparts.

Scholarship is also divided over the quality of Celtis's Neo-Platonism. Some scholars speak of Celtis as an important mediator, others claim that his Platonic ideas are nebulous and poorly presented. The clearest answer to this question comes from Celtis himself in his dedication to the *Amores*, in which he says that cosmic eros pervades the entire chain of beings.[29] Elsewhere Celtis refers repeatedly to the divine order of the cosmos and the ascent of the soul to heaven, though he does not elaborate the details.[30]

Johannes Secundus (1511–36) is often missing from histories of Neo-Latin German humanists owing to the circumstance of having been born in the Netherlands rather than Germany proper. Goethe had the highest regard for Secundus, holding him for a poet of European stature who drank deeply at the fountain of life and love. In his Storm and Stress period the young Goethe wrote a poem "An den Geist des Johannes Secundus" (To the Spirit of Johannes Secundus), in which he invoked the Neo-Latinist as "Lieber, heiliger, grosser Küsser" (Beloved, holy, great kisser), in honor of his *Basia*, a cycle of nineteen kiss poems that had achieved instant notoriety upon its publication in 1539. In *Basium* 16, Secundus demands, significantly, as many kisses from his mistress Neaera as Lesbia had once given to Catullus: "Da tot basia, quot dedit / Vati multiolo Lesbis."[31] The genius, and the true originality, of this young poet — he died at only twenty-four years of age — lay less in his superb imitation of Roman erotic poetry than in his witty allusions to the ancient models, which so heightened the erudite reader's enjoyment.[32]

According to Martin Opitz (1597–1639), the *Elegiarum liber, eiusdem carminum libellus* (Book of Elegies, and His Short Book of Poems, 1551) of

Petrus Lotichius Secundus (1528–60; generally known as Lotichius) made him the equal of Celtis and Johannes Secundus.[33] These ten *carmina*, or love songs, to Claudia are clearly modeled on the Lesbia poems of Catullus, both in their intensity and in the ultimate failure — despite the greater decency observed by Lotichius — of the love relationship. In his subsequent *Elegiae* as well (1553), which take him from Germany (no. 1) to France (no. 2) and finally to Italy (no. 3),[34] Lotichius continues to cope with his devastating relationship with Claudia. Like Celtis, Lotichius appears always to have been on the move; one finds in his poetry greater topical diversity, however, and less reliance than in Celtis on fiction.

With respect to the subsequent development of German literature, two important observations are in order at this point: First, as later poets returned to Roman — and Neo-Latin — models for inspiration they exploited favorite images, metaphors, and motifs that were also commonplace in the parallel vernacular Petrarchist tradition. The question arises, however, as to whether the Germans were using the Roman erotic repertoire exclusively or rather blending it with the Petrarchan strain. If the latter, then how may we distinguish between Catullan and Petrarchan influences? One answer would be that the Roman and Neo-Latin kiss poems belong to one tradition, while the frame of memory and dream are unique to Petrarchism. But there are too many exceptions, such as Celtis's Hasilina, who captures her lover's heart with her eyes or, in her feminine cruelty ("femina cruda"), dissolves his bones and roasts his tender heart upon a pitiless flame ("Igneque non facili mollia corda coquis").[35] The *Basia* poems of Johannes Secundus provide an even more striking example. Here the "dura puella," the cruel girl, with her rosy cheeks, red lips, and milky breasts — Venus herself must stand by in envy! — pierces her lover with arrows and inflames him until he loses his senses and dies in her kisses. Icy fire grips him, but he recovers in her sexual embrace. There is little doubt here that Secundus is exploiting both traditions.[36]

The second observation with respect to the subsequent development of German literature is that, given their creative adaptation of the ancients' *voluptas mundi* (worldly pleasure),[37] all three of these outstanding Neo-Latin German poets must be viewed as early precursors of Goethe's erotic poetry. His *Römische Elegien* (Roman Elegies), published in 1795, were inspired by personal experiences in Italy.

German Translators of Renaissance Eroticism

Early German humanists translated the Latin and Italian works of Petrarch, Boccaccio, and Enea Silvio Piccolomini to the near exclusion of ancient Roman literature. The most accomplished of these, Niklas von Wyle, Albrecht von Eyb, Heinrich Steinhöwel, and Heinrich Schlüsselfelder, are known as the "Italianized Germans."[38] Wyle (ca. 1415–79) was among the first to transfer significant material from Italian Neo-Latin literature to Germany. In his civic role as municipal secretary Wyle corresponded with and made the acquaintance of Enea Silvio, who was at that time imperial secretary in Vienna. As Petrarch had inspired Johann von Neumarkt, so was Wyle challenged by Enea Silvio — the apostle of humanism to Germany, as he is traditionally known — to reintroduce to Germany the forgotten art of eloquence.[39] Enea Silvio's novella of illicit love, *Eurialus et Lucretia*, opens Wyle's *Translationen* (1478), a collection of eighteen translations. Both Enea Silvio and Wyle agreed that the love was adulterous and, while taking obvious pleasure in the narration, sought to provide a moral framework for it.[40] Once he became pope, as Pius II (r. 1458–64), Enea Silvio renounced the tale as a sin of his youth; Wyle, for his part, used the fact that a future pope had written it to buttress his own apology.[41] Two things helped to turn this unhappy love story into a European bestseller — in Neo-Latin as well as all major vernaculars — until well into the sixteenth century: the historical claim of author and translator that the story had actually taken place during a visit by Emperor Sigismund to Siena,[42] and the soul-revealing letters of the suffering lovers. These remarkable letters employ a blend of troubadour, Petrarchist, and classical motifs, with eros presented as an overwhelming force that endangers social conventions and, in the end, almost destroys the protagonists. However, it is the adulterous Lucretia — a modern Helen — who has to pay the price for her lover's infidelity, since Eurialus rejects her in favor of career, fame, and marriage of convenience at the imperial court.

As the first translator of Italian Renaissance literature Wyle influenced its reception down through the Baroque. He had great influence on chancery style. His German descriptions of voluptuous love, moreover, were taken up in the 1537 German edition of the popular *Hug Schapler* chapbook (a French folk epic), and as late as 1645 in *Die Adriatische Rosemund* (The Adriatic Rosemund) of Philipp von Zesen (1619–89), a sentimental novel about two unhappy lovers that shows remarkable affinities with *Eurialus et Lucretia*.[43]

Like Wyle, the German translators of the *Decamerone* encouraged their readers to avoid weighty moral judgments. Over the course of the Reformation century that followed, however, a general increase in moral fundamentalism severely affected procedures of translation and adaptation; the subjective amorality of the free Renaissance artist, as exhibited in Boccaccio, was no longer tolerated in the Reformation. The most popular novellas from the *Decamerone* in German translation were *Guiscardo e Sigismunda* and *Griselda*. *Guiscardo e Sigismunda* relates the story of an outraged father who kills his widowed daughter's lover of inferior social rank and presents her with his heart, whereupon she poisons herself. *Griselda* is the story of a patient wife who is subjected to excessively harsh tests of loyalty by a patriarchal husband. Boccaccio's intention had been to criticize male chauvinism; Petrarch turned his Latin version, *De obedientia ac fide uxoria mythologia* (Fable on Obedience and Marital Fidelity, 1373), into an allegory of Christian obedience to God. In the German translations of the Reformation the stories were adapted as cautionary tales against moral license.

Andreas Capellanus's *Liber de arte honeste amandi* (Book on the Art of Courtly Love, ca. 1300) had long provoked discussion on the basic conflict between love and marriage in real life. In Germany attention focused more on Boccaccio, especially in adaptations of the Latin translations by Petrarch and Leonardo Bruni. Wyle's rendering of *Decamerone* 4.1 (as *Translatze* 2) shifts the emphasis from love as elemental force to love as personal weakness, as exemplified by Sigismunda, who yields before marriage to sexual desire.[44] Albrecht von Eyb (1420–75), educated in Italy, offers a practical solution to this temptation in his *Ehebüchlein* (Little Book on Marriage, 1472). In the exemplary tale *Guiscardus und Sigismunda* he advises, "das man frawen und iunckfrawen zu rechter zeit menner geben soll" (that husbands be provided to women and virgins at a reasonable time). It is interesting to compare two fifteenth-century German adaptations of Petrarch's *Griseldis* of 1373. Heinrich Steinhöwel of Ulm (1411/12–1479) admonishes women to learn patience, a principle that ensured the popularity of his novella of the same title (1471) for several generations to come. By contrast, in an earlier adaptation called *Grisardis* (1432), the Nuremberg Carthusian Erhart Gross (died 1450) had strengthened the religious content beyond Petrarch's allegory by changing the noble husband into a saintly figure and Grisardis into a hagiographic martyr.[45] None of the other four *Griseldis* translations matched this drastic change,[46] yet all contributed significantly to the view of the period that women's inconstancy needed to be kept under constant surveillance.

The Nuremberg patrician Heinrich Schlüsselfelder (fl. 1442–72), under the pseudonym Arigo, published a translation of the entire *Decamerone* in Ulm in 1473. Here the playful, ironic, amoral character of the original has been over-written in a moral tone that emphasizes utility, decency, and honesty for the sake of upholding social convention.[47] This rendition became one of the most widely read and reprinted books of the sixteenth century — next to Luther's Bible and the Alsatian monk Johannes Pauli's (ca. 1455–after 1530) collection of anecdotes *Schimpf und Ernst* (Mischief and Morality, 1522) — though not until after the Reformation, when a revised and updated version appeared.

For sheer readerly entertainment the popular *Schwankbücher*, or books of farces, such as *Schimpf und Ernst* or the *Rollwagenbüchlein* (Carriage Booklet, 1555) of the early novelist Jörg Wickram (ca. 1505–61), exploited the new Italian subject matter, reducing it to anecdotal form and adding moral caveats. Hans Sachs (1494–1576) adapted more than sixty of Boccaccio's novellas into a variety of genres, including tragedy, as in *Tragedi dess Fürsten Concreti und Gismunda* (Tragedy of Prince Concreti and Gismunda, 1545), and comedy, as in *Comedi Griselda* (1546). The reductive operation is typified by Pauli's number 228, which trims Boccaccio's tale about *Nastagio degli Onesti* to an eighth of its original length even as it reorients the plot from unrequited love and revenge to adultery.[48]

From these adaptations two points can be deduced for the development of German literary history. First, using Italian Renaissance masters as their models, German translators attempted to streamline the emerging German *Kunstprosa*, or literary prose, by adhering to the style of the mostly Latin sources, thereby elevating their vernacular to a literary language. Second, the reinforcement of strict ethical norms in the more conservative patriarchal society of sixteenth-century Germany had a sobering effect on Renaissance *joie de vivre.*

While the flood of translations and adaptations from foreign literatures continued at least until the *Sturm und Drang* of the 1770s, the narration of love stories began to demonstrate decidedly greater creativity around the middle of the sixteenth century in the work of Jörg Wickram, who is credited with publishing the first original novels in German literature.[49] *Ritter Galmy uss Schottland* (1539) and *Gabriotto und Reinhart* (1551) were republished in Sigmund Feyerabend's collection of the most popular romances of the sixteenth century: *Buch der Liebe* (Book of Love, 1587); *Der Goldtfaden* (The Golden Thread) appeared in 1557.[50] Wickram often makes use of love relations as a means of commenting on the social class system and its detrimental effect on individual lives. In *Ritter Galmy* a triangular relationship is guided by decency and reason to a happy end. Although he uses narrative techniques, such as letters and dialogues, similar to those employed by Boccaccio and Enea Silvio, Wickram turns the stories of *Eurialus et Lucretia* and *Guiscardo et Sigismunda* into warnings to Galmy and his virtuous duchess. In *Der Goldtfaden* the count is reminded by way of the novella *Guiscardo et Sigismunda* that disaster may befall his family if he should have his prospective son-in-law Lewfrid, an upstart shepherd's son, murdered; consequently, he offers Lewfrid the chance to prove his virtues as a prince and husband. By contrast, Gabriotto and Reinhart, both men of the middle class, overreach their social boundaries by falling in love with noble women. Both couples fall victim to their passions, violate societal mores, and will their own deaths in a manner reminiscent of Tristan and Isolde or Guiscardo and Sigismunda.[51]

Petrarchist Love Literature: Imitation, Emulation, Synthesis

After 150 years of Petrarch's rule as the master of Latin works, his Italian poetry, especially the *Canzoniere*, became the model — codified by Bembo in *Le Prose della volgar lingua* (1525) — for poetic diction in the so-called vulgar languages as well. Composers from the Netherlands, such as Philipp de Monte, Orlando de Lassus, and Adrian Willaert, as well as from Germany, such as Hans Leo Hassler (1564–1612) and Heinrich Schütz (1585–1672), having studied and traveled in Italy, brought to the northern courts a madrigal form based on the Petrarchan sonnet.[52] The Reformation and Counter-Reformation, however, introduced significant changes in the intellectual climate. Whereas erotic motifs in painting and in music enjoyed ready acceptance at the courts and within the Neo-Latin *respublica litteraria*, love poetry in the mother tongue was less warmly received. Two German humanists in particular contributed to the spread of amorous lyrics in the vernacular by integrating Petrarchist motifs into existing literary strains. In the 1580s Paul Schede-Melissus (1539–1602), upon his return from Italy and the Netherlands, mixed

Neo-Platonic and Petrarchist motifs into German song, as in "Rot Röslein."[53] Schede goes beyond the conventional Petrarchist features, addressing his beloved as a beautiful and virtuous, yet thorny, rose. He invokes her as "liebster Schatz" (most beloved treasure) and promises to remain faithful after their wedding, thus transforming Petrarchist convention into the more traditional German *Treue-Thematik* (theme of faithfulness) prevalent in art and folksong. In the 1620s the philologist Kaspar von Barth (1587–1658) combined elements of Petrarchist lady worship and the Roman *carpe diem* topos, translating the inlaid Spanish poems of Gaspar Gil Polo's *Diana enamorada* into Latin, with an emphasis on eroticism.[54]

The first Petrarchist poems in German began to appear as early as the 1570s — the earliest a sonnet by one Balthasar Froe in 1573 — and continued to increase in number into the early seventeenth century. Notable examples are the *Schönes Blumenfeldt* (Beautiful Field of Flowers, 1601) collection of Theobald Hock (1573–ca. 1624) and poems by Georg Rudolf Weckherlin (1584–1653) and Schwabe von der Heyde in the years 1616 and 1617, respectively. Germany continued to lag behind its Romance neighbors by two generations, however, until Opitz, finding himself amid multiple erotic traditions in various states of integration or contradiction, officially inaugurated the practice of *Petrarquiser*. Defined by Opitz as "wie Petrarcha buhlerische reden brauchen" (to use erotic language like Petrarch),[55] *Petrarquiser* opened the floodgates of imitation in Germany and earned for him the label of the "German Petrarch." Thus, it was at this very belated moment that German love poetry could at last claim equality with that of the other European literatures.

To provide paradigms for German imitation Opitz continued to translate poetry from Italian (Veronica Gambara), French (Pierre de Ronsard), and Dutch, especially the strict Petrarchist alexandrines of the *Nederduytsche Poemata* (1616) of Daniel Heinsius (1580–1655). Opitz himself composed only two Petrarchist sonnets in German. Paul Fleming (1609–40), in full command of the Catullan — "Wie Er wolle geküsset seyn" (How He Wished to Be Kissed) — and Petrarchist — "An Dulkamaren"(To Dulkmara) — traditions, and an able emulator of Johannes Secundus, was more prolific than Opitz and wrote love lyrics in both Latin and German. One hears an echo of the self-assured Celtis in Fleming's self-penned "Grabschrifft" (Epitaph): "Kein Landsmann sang mir gleich" (No countryman ever sang like me), he declares. Other poets offered equally striking examples of this fusion. Zesen and Georg Philipp Harsdörffer (1607–58) deemphasized Petrarchist antitheses and oxymora in favor of *Klangmalerei* (sound painting), a unique kind of onomatopoeia, in order both to demonstrate their preference for constant and reciprocal love as well as to show the rich expressivity of the German language. It is difficult to decide whether Harsdörffer was motivated to write anti-Petrarchist poems more because of this deeply ingrained German ethical tradition or because of the *musa iocosa*, the playful art practiced by Nuremberg pastoral poets.[56] For some poets earthly beauty inspired pessimism. Andreas Gryphius (1616–64), for example, creates hellish distortions of Petrarchist praise, as in "Uber die Gebaine der aussgegrabenen Philosetten" (On the Remains of Exhumed Philosette):[57]

> O Hässlich' Anblick! ach! wo sind die güldnen Haar!
> Wo ist der Stirnen Schnee? wo ist der Glantz der Wangen?
> Der Wangen / die mit Blut und Lilien umbfangen?
> Der Rosen rote Mund! wo ist der Zähne Schaar?

[Oh, ugly sight! oh! Where is the golden hair? Where is the forehead's snow? where the shining cheeks? The cheeks now surrounded by blood and lilies? The rosy red mouth! where is the array of teeth?]

Christian Hofmann von Hofmannswaldau (1616–79), as Giambattista Marino before him, at times inverts erotic Petrarchist topoi for the sake of a witty and sensual point, as in his poem "An Lauretten" (To Little Laura). Here he admonishes the angelic but cruel lady to yield to his desire, even though to obey the *carpe diem* principle may lead to the loss, and even "death," of his self:

> [Wer] hören wird / wie ich gestorben /
> Wird sagen: Wer also verdirbt /
> Und in dem zarten schoosse stirbt /
> Hat einen sanfften tod erworben.[58]

[Whoever will learn how I died will say: Who perishes thus dying in a tender lap has earned a gentle death.]

The idealized beauty of the beloved mistress, her face bathed in sunlight, her voice that of an angel, provided frequent occasion for reflections on eternal beauty — a Neo-Platonic legacy audible in love poetry since Petrarch, introduced to Germany by Celtis. Until Bembo's exposition, in book 4 of Castiglione's *Il Cortegiano*, was translated into German (1565) and Latin (1569),[59] this Neo-Platonic-Petrarchist symbiosis had been known in Germany through Italian poetry, such as that of Giovanni Battista Guarini, and in French, such as that of Joachim Du Bellay (*Olive*, 1550). Among the German poets following their lead were Weckherlin and Fleming. Both eventually left the Petrarchist "code" behind, perhaps as a result of their distant travels: Weckherlin to London, Fleming to Persia. In the country where they had once perfected them, however, the conventions remained strong.

The Petrarchist repertoire also lent itself to mystical poetry. Baroque mystics, such as Friedrich von Spee (1591–1635) — in his *Trutznachtigall* (Defiant Nightingale, 1649) — Daniel Czepko (1605–60), Johann Scheffler (also called Angelus Silesius, 1624–77), and Quirinus Kuhlmann (1651–89), fused the traditions of *Jesusminne*, the *Song of Songs*, and Petrarchism in such a way that Jesus could assume the role of the beloved mistress and shoot his own arrows, Cupid-like, at the stony-hearted soul.[60] At the end of the seventeenth century, Johann Christian Günther (1695–1723) inverted the convention by declaring the passionate lover a failure in comparison with the faithful beloved, a transformation that reflected his personal experience and severed all ties to the previous erotic tradition. Günther's "An Leonoren" (To Leonore;

one of the late versions of his many poems with this title) culminates in the lines:

> Vergiss mich stets und schlag mein Bild
> Von nun an aus dem Sinne,
> Mein letztes Wünschen ist erfüllt,
> Wofern ich diß gewinne,
> Das mit der Zeit noch jemand spricht:
> Wenn Philimen die Ketten bricht,
> So sinds nicht Falschheits-Triebe,
> Er haßt sie nur aus Liebe.[61]

[Forget me and dismiss my image from your mind from now on. My last wish is granted if I should gain one thing: That someone will say this afterwards: When Philimen breaks his chains, it is not out of deceitfulness; he hates her out of love.]

Dissemination of Petrarchism: Frontiers and Genres

Typically, Petrarchism is thought of as a codified system of love that dominated erotic sonnet composition in the early modern period. However, the textual evidence presented here suggests rather that it is best viewed as a repertoire of motifs that could be infinitely varied and combined. At its center, as Opitz observed in the third chapter of the *Buch von der Deutschen Poeterey* (Book of German Poetics, 1624), resides "Liebe als Wetzstein des Verstandes" (Love as the whetstone of the mind). The burlesque form of anti-Petrarchism must not be overlooked; nor can Petrarchist manifestations be restricted to the sonnet. The essence of Petrarchism was always its mutability, its fusion with other conceptions of love, a quality that manifested itself in a rich exchangeability of generic forms. Its coexistence, on the one hand, and merger, on the other, with various currents in German literature owed much to the fact of its belated reception and simultaneous expansion in the poetry of Marino, acknowledged since his *Rime* (1602) and *Adone* (1623) as the king of the witty baroque metaphor.[62]

Although Renaissance eroticism came to Germany first and most directly from Italy, other advanced cultures, particularly French, Spanish, and Dutch, also influenced its dissemination. Its impact is especially visible in the German sonnet, yet it is by no means lacking in most other lyrical forms, including the madrigal, epigram, and canzonetta; that is to say nothing of how it affected the fashion of *Petrarquiser* in plays and novels. To take only the example of the Silesian Hans Assmann von Abschatz (1646–99): Abschatz emulated Italian, French, English, and Roman erotic poets, though Marino and Guarini stand out in his work as models. Abschatz makes particularly effective use of the technique of raising questions repeatedly, as if conversing with his lyrical protagonists, as a means of intensifying the expressivity of his great predecessors. His translation of Guarini's tragicomedy *Il pastor fido* (1596) as *Der getreue Schäfer*

(The Faithful Shepherd, 1678), a pastoral play that tells the story of the mythological shepherd Mirtillo and his beloved Amarilli, mixes masquerade, sensuality, fidelity, and Petrarchist motifs in the baroque manner.[63]

The German Reception of
Spanish Golden Age Eroticism

The dynastic connection between the Habsburg courts in Madrid and Vienna positioned Germany to become an early recipient of Spanish Golden Age culture and literature. Foremost among the Spanish genres by which Petrarchism was transmitted to Germany were the pastoral and sentimental novels. The steady rise of courtly culture demanded a greater variety of reading materials suitable to the evolving literary taste and the more sophisticated lifestyle. Whoever did not know the art of love had no place in high society; whoever could not withstand the vicissitudes of fortune lacked nobility of soul. The age in which the short pastoral novel thrived enjoyed a peculiar morbidity of emotion to a degree that later times have found pathological. Certain recurrent features are characteristic of this subgenre: love as a cosmic force threatens a fatal outcome inasmuch as it releases its followers from the conventional ties of rank and moral code; the unhappy ending, adumbrated in the repeated forebodings of separation, concludes with a final farewell and death. "Wer nicht weinen kann, der kann auch nicht lieben" (Those who cannot weep cannot love) could serve as the motto of this genre,[64] since it reveals a shift away from an external plot to an internal world of emotions, expressed in fervent letters that momentarily cheer the soul but help to destroy it in the end. These novels adopt from the Neo-Platonic-Petrarchist symbiosis the notion of a cosmic eros that imprisons lovers and strips them, through anguish, of their very selves. Reminiscent of the strict Petrarchism of Bembo, the protagonists never reach love's fulfillment, either because the lady refuses to yield to her suitor, in effect sentencing him to die of grief, or because he deserts her for the sake of honor, leaving her victim to the mores of society as represented by her parents or her lover. Sometimes lovers elect for self-sacrifice. In contrast to the idealized courtly novel, these short unhappy novels end as anti-fairy tales.

Jorge de Montemayor's *La Diana enamorada* (1559) — the only pastoral novel not thrown into the fire in *Don Quixote*! — was translated into German in 1619 by Hans Ludwig von Kuffstein (1582–1656), an important intermediary in the German reception of Renaissance eroticism. Kuffstein's translation seems to have been a major vehicle for introducing the Neo-Platonic-Petrarchist concept of love to Germany, that is, even before Opitz brought it to general attention. The *Diana* also appeared six years later in a curious Latin translation called *Erotodidascalus* (Teacher of Love) by the eccentric Kaspar von Barth, and then in 1646 in Harsdörffer's continuation of the Kuffstein translation. A comparison of the various texts with inlaid poems reveals two tendencies unique to Kuffstein: the reduction of Petrarchist topoi in favor of mutual love, with marriage the reward for loyal courting; and the elaboration on Spanish courtly customs, adding decorum to the innocent pastoral companionship, probably as a means of encouraging the gentry to keep coarse behavior out of noble parlors.[65]

Kuffstein also translated Diego de San Pedro's *Cárcel de amor* (1492) as *Gefängnüss der Lieb* (Prison of Love, 1624), a sentimental love novel with an unhappy ending. As the title implies, the lovers are enslaved to a cosmic force that sometimes causes bliss, sometimes ruin, as their passion collides with social convention. Kuffstein's modest sense of proportion prompted him to lower the status of the lady from her elevated Neo-Platonic position as mystical and divine; nevertheless, he maintains the traditional excessive laments of Petrarchist lovers. For Kuffstein, fulfilled love is the remedy for melancholy. Interestingly, in 1678 a troupe of itinerant actors created a stage version, entitled *Liebs-Gefängnüs Traur-Freuden-Spiel* (Love's Prison: A Tragicomedy, 1678), of Kuffstein's popular novel, albeit with the substitution of a happy ending.[66]

Kuffstein's *Gefängnüss der Lieb* constitutes a significant link in the chain of short sentimental love novels. This development had begun with Boccaccio's novellas and Enea Silvio's *Eurialus et Lucretia*, flourished in Spain with Juan de Flores and Diego de San Pedro[67] and in sixteenth-century France in the *tragiques amours*, before at last establishing a subgenre within the baroque novel in Germany. Inspired by these foreign models, the first original German novels after Wickram's *Gabriotto und Reinhart* appeared during the Thirty Years' War; the direct influence of Enea Silvio is obvious in the anonymous pastoral *Amoena und Amandus* (1632) and in Zesen's *Adriatische Rosemund*. Another typical tale in this genre was the *Unglückselige Liebes-und Lebens-Geschichte des Don Francesco und Angelica* (The Unhappy Story of the Love and Life of Don Francesco and Angelica, 1667) by Fortunatus.[68] A century later Goethe's *Die Leiden des jungen Werthers* (The Sorrows of Young Werther, 1774) will become simultaneously the crowning achievement and nemesis of this sentimental vogue in German literature.

Generic crossovers from the ideal Petrarchist sonnet to other literary forms can be traced beyond the novel to include epic poems and plays. For instance, Petrarchist love language pervades the crude adaptations of Shakespeare by the so-called English Comedians[69] as well as the high baroque dramas of Gryphius and his Silesian compatriot Daniel Casper von Lohenstein (1635–83). But Petrarchism was not limited to the realm of literature or to the purpose of reviving ancient erotic and mythological formulas as a new instrument of introspection and self-analysis; its influence extended to real life as well by contributing to the refinement of language, taste, and courting customs. Courtly etiquette required ladies and gentlemen not only to be up to date in their behavior but capable also of turning out poems and letters to their lovers in suitably fashionable language and style. Elizabeth I received laudatory sonnets from Walter Raleigh and George Puttenham and used her position, as Laura incarnate, to political advantage. The love correspondence between Count Königsmarck of Sweden and Princess Sophie Dorothee of Hanover in the late years of the seventeenth century — conducted in French, of course, since German still lacked the prestige of elegance — offers an example of "real-life Petrarchism."[70] By 1700, literary tradition in which convention had become life, and life literature, was nearly three centuries old.

Counterthrusts to Petrarchism

Petrarchism was by no means the only erotic literary tradition available in the early modern period; nor did it enjoy universal favor. Anti-Petrarchist practice took various forms, including a distinctive use of language derived from Petrarch himself, thereby undermining Petrarchism from within, as it were. Such a goal had been the purpose of Marino's *Rime*, an anthology of poems that supplanted Neo-Platonic and Ciceronian versions of Petrarchism by the end of the seventeenth century. This was true even in Germany in the high baroque school of Silesian hyperbolism, which included Lohenstein, Angelus Silesius, and Hofmannswaldau, among others.

An equally subversive foreign incursion into Germany came in the form of the picaresque novel in the early 1600s. *La novela picaresca* arose in Spanish literature as a response to the observation of the misery and exploitation of people on the periphery of society. Consciously rejecting all idealization, this new subgenre parodied courtly and hagiographic literature by portraying society and the world from the point of view of the lowly stations of life. These new protagonists observe the hypocrisies of the upper classes and must use their wits to survive hunger, cold, and lack of love on their journey through life. Love is not spiritualized here; but the picaresque novel does take a non-moralizing approach to love as sex and to life as grounded in hard reality, whereby the hero — or rather, anti-hero — often has no recourse but to resort even to criminal means for survival. Knavish behavior toward women thus became the rule in the genre and spread from the first adaptations — the anonymous *Lazarillo de Tormes* (1554) and the *Rinconete y Cortadillo* (1613) of Cervantes, both translated in 1617 into German[71] — to the novels *Der Abentheurliche Simplicissimus Teutsch* (The Adventurous German Simpleton, 1669) and *Landstörtzerin Courasche* (The Runagate Courage, 1669) of Hans Jakob Christoffel Grimmelshausen (1621/22–76). In *Simplicissimus* an unknown mistress pays Beau Alman for his services and turns him into a male prostitute. In *Courasche* the anti-heroine thrashes her husband and renounces the institution of marriage; then, having prostituted herself in order to escape sexual exploitation during the war, she descends to the counterculture of the Gypsies. The book culminates in a view of society that is the very opposite of patriarchal order. Grimmelshausen emphasizes the co-responsibility of men in love relationships and the equality of women. It must be noted, however, that in the end he warns his readers not to succumb to the snares of his book, which is an allegory of the inconstancy of the world (Courasche is a version of the illusory, seductive *Frau Welt*).

The late-century court musician and novelist Johann Beer (1655–1700), unlike Grimmelshausen before him, had little interest in questions of salvation or metaphysics. He wished rather to describe life as it is, with a satirical eye to the foibles of real men and women. With Beer, the moral tone often gives way quickly to sheer amusement: "Ich schreibe hier sehr lose Stück, nicht wie es die Welt machen soll, sondern wie sie es gemacht hat. Lerne also keinen folgen" (I am writing here quite ribald tales, not about how the world should behave, but how things are in reality. Therefore, learn not to follow any of them).[72] His Corylo stumbles into a whore's nest managed by a lascivious lady of the gentry, and the story serves to unmask the hypocrisy common to both bourgeois and courtly marriage. While taking lively enjoyment in spinning his narratives, Beer sought to dispel the illusion of respectability and the treacherous glamour of love. In this sense he shared the anti-Petrarchist bias of Grimmelshausen in *Simplicissimus*, with its "überzwerches Lob einer schönen Damen" (inverted praise of a beautiful lady).

In the fairy-tale realm of the courtly novel between *Hercules und Valiska* (1659) of Heinrich Bucholtz (1607–71) and *Die Asiatische Banise* (The Asiatic Princess Banise, 1689) of Anselm von Ziegler (1663–96), the superhuman virtue of angelic ladies is tested repeatedly. Controlled by reason, passion cannot upset courtly decorum. Accordingly, the theme of these novels is not love but constancy in the face of all odds. Picaresque novels and their satirical offshoots, often written in times of war or its aftermath, were the perfect media for presenting a world out of joint; Platonic beauty and virtue are betrayed as fraudulent. The dichotomous views of the courtly and picaresque novel types further reflect the dualistic attitude toward women and love that prevailed between the Middle Ages and the Thirty Years' War: idealization and denigration, virtue and lust. Strict conventions of genre and class — the angelic lady dominates the courtly world, the evil temptress the picaresque — reinforce the traditional dichotomy. By the second half of the seventeenth century, however, startling phenomena, such as the appearance of prostitutes of noble rank, occur with some regularity; class differences are blurred; the moorings of poetic and moral conventions have been deeply disturbed.[73]

Unmasking the lofty language and stilted behavior of courtly lovers had long been a target of caricature, particularly in lyric poetry but also in drama. In sonnet 130, "My mistress' eyes are nothing like the sun," Shakespeare debunks the conventions of outward beauty; in *Twelfth Night* he deflates the Italianate lover Malvolio, who is full of Petrarchist conceits and foolish pomposity. In *Love's Labour's Lost*, Lord Berowne, a sensualist and realist, makes fun of Petrarchist conceits. Don Adriano de Armando, a "fantastical Spaniard" and master of extravagant language, is an early parody on the Don Quixote character.[74] Around 1613 this kind of figure began to appear as satire in German broadsheets, plays, and novels. The comic dramas *Absurda Comica oder Herr Peter Squentz* (1657–58) and *Horribilicribrifax* (1663) of Gryphius provide good examples of the parodistic deflation of courtly lovers. The shepherd Don Hylas, a mostly French-inspired caricature, is well known from Honoré d'Urfé's sentimental pastoral *L'Astrée* (1607–27).[75] The Nuremberg Pegnitz Shepherds, as they were called, Harsdörffer and Sigmund von Birken (1626–81), introduced Don Hylas in their prosimetric (prose-and-verse) pastorals — known as prose eclogues — as a Don Quixote-like figure, full of fustian praise for his beloved. Goethe tried to distance himself from pathological Petrarchist lovers, including his own Werther,[76] by adding a cautionary motto poem to book 2 of his sensational Storm and Stress novel:

> Sieh, dir winkt sein Geist aus seiner Höhle:
> *Sei ein Mann, und folge mir nicht nach.*[77]

[See, his ghost is waving to you from his cave: Be a man and do not follow me.]

Nevertheless — as manifested in Goethe's subsequent attack on sentimental fools in *Der Triumph der Empfindsamkeit* (The Triumph of Sentimentality, 1787) — the demise of the Petrarchist manner was a slow one indeed. In this short work Prince Oronaro, the key figure, invents an artificial cosmos in his room that enables him to worship the moon along with the doll-like image of his mistress; the books that mislead him end up in the fireplace in a scene that signals the decline of cosmic eros. Heinrich Heine (1797–1856) was not only the last romantic, but also the last Petrarchist, for he experienced the same dualistic forces of love — the cruel mistress, the lover's torment — that had been the fate of so many lovers since Petrarch. Heine's greatness as a poet lay in his ability to rise above his dismal situation by wielding a devastating wit that demolished the entire school of Petrarchism.

New-Platonism distinguished between brutish love and heavenly love, and a trend developed in the sixteenth and seventeenth centuries in Germany to separate chaste and sinful love according to social class and literary genre. As a consequence, the image of woman remained divided between Eve and Mary, with the former representing the lower social strata, the latter courtly society. This dualistic vision manifested itself in strong misogynistic impulses and in the worship of the ideal lady at the expense of appreciating the real life of married women. Until the artificial barriers of gender, class, and genre began to erode, fairy tale and satire stood at opposite ends of the spectrum, with satire providing a counterthrust to the idealization of love and women. Religion and misogyny also often combined into a formidable mix that bedeviled women until the eighteenth-century Enlightenment. This revealed a portion of the dark and dangerous underside of the Renaissance in contrast to its more often proclaimed *joie de vivre*, the discovery of the individual, and the adoration of women. Neither the extravagant worship of women in upper class and courtly circles nor their vilification in the lower strata of society accurately illuminated the reality of women's' general subservience in early modern Europe.

One thing is certain, moreover: the witch craze that swept early modern Europe provided a terrible counterpoint to courtly love and its successor philosophy, Petrarchism. The Dominican Order created the image of evil witches in pact with the devil. In his *Malleus maleficarum*, or *Hexenhammer* (Witches' Hammer, 1487), the Dominican Heinrich Kramer (Institoris, 1430–1505) describes in much fanciful detail the malignant nature of witchcraft and trial proceedings.[78] Eve, he claims, has continued to tempt God-loving men ever since the Garden of Eden. Women are the weaker sex, easily corrupted, tempted, and seduced because of their lack of faith, their carnal desires, their talkativeness, and their fragility. Only much later in history did the irony of this assessment become evident, namely, that the women taken for witches typically did not conform to the established norms. Many were poor single women, ostracized by village society; others were harassed because they exuded so much self-confidence, courage, and strength that they were regarded as a menace to authority. The world depicted in the witch literature is divided into kingdoms of good and evil, angelic ladies and devilish women. And wherever the gods, among them cosmic eros, have fled back to Olympus, ghosts terrify superstitious people at all levels of society.

During the period of the Counter-Reformation in Germany this anti-feminist trend found a champion in the Jesuit-educated Ägidius Albertinus (ca. 1560–1620), who is more commonly known for having introduced the picaresque novel to Germany from Spain (*Gusman von Alfarache oder Picaro*, 1615; based on Mateo Alemán). Albertinus was also the author of moralizing writings, such as *Lucifers Königreich und Seelengejaidt* (Lucifer's Kingdom and Hunt for Souls, 1616),[79] whose misogynistic diatribes subvert the positive courtly admiration of women. According to Albertinus, women are the devil's tools: their beauty is a cosmetic for the seven deadly sins, and their angelic faces disguise their true identity as the devil's concubines.

But such voices did not go unchallenged in seventeenth-century Germany. Friedrich von Spee, a Jesuit poet and philosopher, attacked the judicial procedures of church and state against witches in his anonymously published *Cautio criminalis* (Precautions in Criminal Matters, 1631), though without immediate success.[80] It was left to Christian Thomasius (1655–1728) of the University of Halle at the turn of the eighteenth century to undermine definitively the construct of witchcraft with his *Theses de crimine magiae* (Theses on Witchcraft, 1701).[81] An enemy to all prejudice and superstition, Thomasius regularly questioned authority from a position of common sense, powerfully objecting to any collusion of government, church, and university. His personal involvement with a witch trial set him upon a relentless investigation of the history and fictions of witchcraft and brought him at last to the conclusion that, if the cornerstone doctrine of the devil incarnate were removed, the conceptual edifice of witchcraft would crumble. Inspired by his stand, Prussia discontinued the trials of witches after 1714.[82]

By the end of the seventeenth century, Renaissance eroticism had branched into multiple poetic currents, sometimes merging, sometimes canceling each other out. A more realistic approach to love poetry arose simultaneously with the waning of the witch craze. In fact, this new realism of love had been gathering strength since the Reformation. The young Luther shared the Renaissance belief in an all-powerful, all-consuming love that burns like fire and demands everything or nothing. Instead of sublimating it, however, that is, instead of advocating chastity and the worship of one's lady, whether in real life or in fiction, Luther came to advocate marriage as the greatest love on earth. Husband and wife are to enjoy equality in sexual matters, though the wife should remain obedient to her husband-master in all other matters, be they legal, financial, or educational.[83]

Didactic marriage tracts, known as *Ehezuchtbücher*, enjoyed great popularity in the sixteenth century, though apart from Hans Sachs's domestic plays marriage was rarely made the subject of serious fiction, for it simply did not hold general interest. In the seventeenth century, however, one great exception, the novel *Damon und Lisille* (1663) by Johann Thomas (1624–80) avoided the multiple voices of Renaissance eroticism, courtly extravagance, picaresque carnality, and sentimental foolishness. A post-wedding-day narrative of everyday life, written in simple, lyrical German, *Damon und Lisille* is the very antithesis of the lofty courtly novel of the *Amadis* type or *Die Asiatische Banise*, the plots of which invariably resolved in an ostentatious wedding celebration. This redirection toward real domestic love defines a major change in German literary history, for it crowned all previous efforts to mold German into a confident literary language able to stand shoulder to shoulder with its European counterparts. The language, topics, and forms of eros proved to be one of the chief means to this end. Thomas admonishes his readers to imagine the arrival of a new age in terms of simple honesty and liberality:

> Denkt, die Liebe der Lisillen,
> Und dann die Poeterey,
> Seyn von allen Regeln Frey.[84]

[Remember, Lisille's love, like that of poetry, is free of every rule.]

Notes

[1] Hans-Gert Roloff, "Neulateinische Literatur," in *Propyläen-Geschichte der Literatur: Renaissance und Barock, 1400–1700*, ed. Erika Wischer (Berlin: Propyläen, 1984), 3:216.

[2] Fred J. Nichols, comp., *An Anthology of Neo-Latin Poetry* (New Haven: Yale UP, 1979), 486–87.

[3] I am using *Catull: Liebesgedichte Lateinisch Deutsch*, ed. Otto Weinreich, Rowohlts Klassiker der Literatur und Wissenschaft (Reinbek: Rowohlt, 1960); "c." = *carmen* (poem) or *carmina* (poems).

[4] The term "funktionale Differenzierung" comes from Alfred Noe, *Der Einfluss des italienischen Humanismus auf die deutsche Literatur vor 1600*, Internationales Archiv für Sozialgeschichte der deutschen Literatur 5. Sonderheft (Tübingen: Niemeyer, 1993), 280.

[5] See in particular Novella 5.10, "Pietro di Vinciolo."

[6] Eckhard Bernstein, *Die Literatur des deutschen Frühhumanismus*, Sammlung Metzler 168 (Stuttgart: Metzler, 1978), 47–48.

[7] Petrarca, *Opere latine*, ed. Antonietta Bufano (Turin: Unione tipografico, 1975), 2:1118.

[8] For a complete assessment of Ficino see Paul Oskar Kristeller, *The Philosophy of Marsilio Ficino* (Gloucester, MA: Peter Smith, 1964). Kristeller quotes *Platonic Love* at 285–86.

[9] Ficino, "How the soul is raised from the beauty of the body to the beauty of God," in *Commentary on Plato's Symposium*, trans. Sears Jayne (Dallas: Spring Publications, 1985), 141.

[10] David Pugh, *Dialectic of Love: Platonism in Schiller's Aesthetics* (Montreal: McGill-Queen's UP), 1997.

[11] Baldassare Castiglione, *Il Cortegiano* (Novara: Il Club del Libro, 1968), chap. 68, 576; *The Book of the Courtier*, trans. Charles S. Singleton, Anchor Books 186 (Garden City, NY: Doubleday, 1959), 354.

[12] Friedrich Schlegel, in his *Literary Notebooks, 1797–1801*, ed. Hans Eichner (Toronto: U of Toronto P, 1957), no. 1553, called Petrarch "der Erfinder (Meister) der Liebe, nämlich er hat ihr die Form gegeben, die noch besteht."

[13] The characterizing phrase comes from August Wilhelm Schlegel, in his *Kritische Schriften und Briefe*, ed. Edgar Lohner (Stuttgart: Kohlhammer, 1962), 4:204, who speaks of a "Liebesroman in Sonetten."

[14] Hugo Friedrich, *Epochen der italienischen Lyrik* (Frankfurt am Main: Klostermann, 1964), 164.

[15] See "das Kunstlied" in Gerhart Hoffmeister, *Petrarca*, Sammlung Metzler 301 (Stuttgart: Metzler, 1997), 116–18.

[16] Leonard W. Forster, *The Icy Fire: Five Essays in European Petrarchism* (London: Cambridge UP, 1969), 61.

[17] *Petrarchist* is used here in the sense of deriving from the imitative tradition after Petrarch; later in this chapter the term *Petrarchan* will be used to refer to whatever flows primarily from Petrarch himself and his poetry.

[18] Friedrich, *Epochen der italienischen Lyrik*, 670, uses the Latin phrase "lusi per otium."

[19] See Heinz Schlaffer, *Musa iocosa: Gattungspoetik und Gattungsgeschichte der erotischen Dichtung in Deutschland*, Germanistische Abhandlungen 37 (Stuttgart: Metzler, 1971).

[20] Text in Johannes Hösle, ed., *Texte zum Antipetrarkismus* (Tubingen: Niemeyer, 1970).

[21] Hoffmeister, *Petrarca*, 125.

[22] Agostino Sottili sketches this fascinating history in his study "Wege des Humanismus: Lateinischer Petrarkismus und deutsche Studentenschaften italienischer Renaissance-Universitäten," in *From Wolfram and Petrarch to Goethe and Grass: In Honor of L. Forster*, ed. D. H. Green et al. (Baden-Baden: Koerner, 1982), 125–50. See also Hoffmeister, "Der lateinische Petrarca in Deutschland," in *Petrarca*, 106–12.

[23] Excerpts in Hans Rupprich, ed., *Die Frühzeit des Humanismus und der Renaissance in Deutschland* (1938; repr., Darmstadt: Wissenschaftliche Buchgesellschaft, 1964), 93–104.

[24] Johannes von Tepl, *The Plowman from Bohemia*, trans. Alexander and Elizabeth Henderson (New York: Ungar, 1966), chap. 29.

[25] So called by Lewis W. Spitz, *Conrad Celtis: The German Arch-Humanist* (Cambridge: Harvard UP, 1957). As evidence see the excerpts (with German translation) in *Spätmittelalter Humanismus Reformation: Texte und Zeugnisse*, ed. Hedwig Heger (Munich: Beck, 1978), 2:31–33.

[26] On early modern literary soceities see the introduction to this volume by Max Reinhart.

[27] "Amorum 1," in Nichols, ed., *Anthology of Neo-Latin Poetry*, 440–41.

[28] Ursula Hess, "Erfundene Wahrheit: Autobiographie und literarische Rolle bei Conrad Celtis," in *Bildungsexklusivität und volkssprachliche Literatur: Literatur vor Lessing — nur für Experten?*, ed. Klaus Grubmüller and Günter Hess (Tubingen: Niemeyer, 1986),

136–47; the partial German translation of this bogus letter is in Heinz Otto Burger, *Renaissance Humanismus Reformation* (Bad Homburg: Gehlen, 1969), 236.

[29] Spitz, *Conrad Celtis*, 106–8; dedication quoted 114.

[30] For proof see Celtis's poem "Ad se ipsum" in Heger, ed., *Spätmittelalter Humanismus Reformation*, 2:23–24.

[31] In Nichols, ed., *Anthology of Neo-Latin Poetry*, 508.

[32] Clifford Endres, *Joannes Secundus: The Latin Love Elegy in the Renaissance* (Hamden, CT: Archon Books, 1981), 58, calls it essentially "a poetry of quotation and allusion."

[33] Some of the songs and elegies are reproduced and translated in Nichols, ed., *Anthology of Neo-Latin Poetry*, 546–67.

[34] Eckart Schäfer, "Lotichius' Liebesdichtung — ein Experiment mit dem Leben," in *Lotichius und die römische Elegie*, ed. Ulrike Auhagen and Eckhart Schäfer (Tubingen: Narr, 2001), 241–300; see also *Des Petrus Lotichius Secundus Elegien*, trans. Ernst G. Köstlin (1826; repr., New York: Royal Press, 1968).

[35] Eventually he may die of the disease of lovesickness! "Ad Hasilinam de Aborta Tempestate," in Nichols, ed., *Anthology of Neo-Latin Poetry*, 440–41.

[36] See Endres, Johannes Secundus, 71 and 92, with reference to Elegy 1.3: "We may consider this kind of delight in opposites as one result of the Petrarchan influence." Of the nineteen *Basia*, see especially nos. 10 and 14. In Lotichius's elegies there is less of a Petrarchist incursion, except perhaps in his elegy "De puella formosissima." See Adalbert Elschenbroich, ed., *Deutsche Literatur des 16. Jahrhunderts* (Munich: Hanser, 1981), 1:274–79, a bilingual edition in two volumes.

[37] Interestingly, Max Baeumer (following Burger, *Renaissance*, 34) affirms *voluptas* as a key principle, in "'Voluptas' und frühbürgerliche Revolution: Neue Sichtweisen der Literatur des 15. und 16. Jahrhunderts," *Monatshefte* 65 (1973): 393–415.

[38] For a fuller discussion of this topic see elsewhere in this volume the chapter by John Flood.

[39] Silvio is called "the apostle of humanism to Germany" by Georg Voigt in his *Enea Silvio de' Piccolomini als Papst Pius der Zweite und sein Zeitalter* (1856–63; repr., Berlin: de Gruyter, 1967). Cf. Bernstein, *Frühhumanismus*, 9. Wyle's method of translation keeps closely to Latin syntactical patterns with the intention of disciplining German into a concise and elegant chancery language, much as Chancellor Neumarkt had sought to do a century earlier. His efforts culminated in a literary prose, or *Kunstprosa*, best described as a Latinized German.

[40] In his dedication Wyle admonishes the reader that "bulsch[e] liebe . . . billig sin zefliehen" (lascivious love is to be avoided) and advises to use the discrimination of a bee in dealing with the text. In *Translationen*, ed. A. von Keller (1861; repr., Hildesheim: Olms, 1967), 14; more recently see Eric J. Morrall, ed., *Aeneas Silvius Piccolomini (Pius II) and Niklas von Wyle: The Tale of Two Lovers, Eurialus and Lucretia* (Amsterdam: Rodopi, 1988), a bilingual edition.

[41] At about this same time the archduchess Mechthild of Rottenburg, a patroness of humanism, also asked Wyle to translate several contemporary Latin works into German.

[42] See Silvio's "Dedication to Schlick" in Morrall, ed., *Aeneas Silvius*, 72. Walter Pabst rightfully claims, however, in *Novellentheorie und Novellendichtung*, 2nd ed. (Heidelberg: Winter, 1967), 51, that this is nothing but the application of the medieval topos of attestation.

[43] Volker Meid, "Zesens Romankunst" (Ph.D. diss., Frankfurt am Main, 1966), 19–21. On *Hug Schapler*, see Burger, *Renaissance*, 108–9.

[44] "Die traditionelle Psychologie der Frau als triebhaftes Wesen hat die Geschichte des Boccaccio in dieser Übersetzung wieder eingeholt." Xenja von Ertzdorff, *Romane und Novellen des 15. und. 16. Jahrhunderts in Deutschland* (Darmstadt: Wissenschaftliche Buchgesellschaft, 1989), 24.

[45] Bernstein, *Frühhumanismus*, 80.

[46] Ursula Hess, *Heinrich Steinhöwels "Griseldis": Studien zur Text- und Überlieferungsgeschichte einer frühhumanistischen Prosanovelle* (Munich: Beck, 1975); also Käte Laserstein, *Der Griseldis-Stoff in der Weltliteratur* (1926; repr., Hildesheim: Gerstenberg, 1978).

[47] See Jan-Dirk Müller, "Boccaccios und Arigos 'schöne Gesellschaft': Italienische Renaissanceliteratur im spätmittelalterlichen Deutschland," *Fifteenth-Century Studies* 7 (1982): 281–97.

[48] "Instead of an amoral novella reproving cruel women, we end up with a moral example in the strictest sense of the church dogma." Gerhart Hoffmeister, "The Pagan Influence of the Italian Renaissance on German Life and Letters, 1450–1520," in *The Renaissance and Reformation in Germany*, ed. Hoffmeister (New York: Ungar, 1977), 63; see Ertzdorff, *Romane und Novellen*, 95–98, about the romance *Florio und Biancefora* (1499) modelled on Boccaccio's *Il Filocolo*.

[49] For prose narrative of the early modern period in Germany see the chapter by Andreas Solbach in this volume.

[50] *Sämtliche Werke*, ed. Hans-Gert Roloff (New York: de Gruyter, 1967–73).

[51] Ertzdorff, *Romane und Novellen*, 107–24.

[52] Hasler resided in Venice in 1584–85; Schütz later resided there between 1609 and 1612. See poems by Hasler and Johann-Hermann Schein in *Die deutsche Literatur, Texte und Zeugnisse: Das Zeitalter des Barock*, ed. Albrecht Schöne (Munich: Beck, 1968), 697–98.

[53] Text in *Epochen der deutschen Lyrik 1600–1700*, ed. Christian Wagenknecht, dtv 4018 (Munich: Deutscher Taschenbuch Verlag, 1969), 57–58.

[54] Gerhart Hoffmeister, *Die spanische Diana in Deutschland*, Philologische Quellen und Studien 68 (Berlin: Schmidt, 1972), 118–19; see also Barth's poem "Ad Neaeram" in *Lateinische Gedichte deutscher Humanisten*, ed. Harry Schnur (Stuttgart: Reclam, 1966), 8–9.

[55] In chapter 6, which deals with verbal ornamentation, of his *Buch von der Deutschen Poeterey*, ed. Cornelius Sommer, UB 8397 (Stuttgart: Reclam, 1980), 36. On love as virtue see Georg Philipp Harsdörffer, "Ein Christlicher Poet handelt von der Liebe / als von einer Tugend," in Schöne, ed., *Die deutsche Literatur*, 30.

[56] See Harsdörffer's "Reim-dich-Bundschuh" poems (e.g., "Schöne, wie des Ofens Grund euer Mund"), in *Poetischer Trichter* (1650; repr., Darmstadt: Wissenschaftliche Buchgesellschaft, 1969), Part 2, 10th Stunde (Hour), 61; also his letter "An eine sehr hässliche Jungfrau," in *Die Pegnitz-Schäfer*, ed. Eberhard Mannack, UB 8545 (Stuttgart: Reclam, 1968), 222.

[57] Sonette 1.33 in *Andreas Gryphius: Dichtungen: Texte deutscher Literatur, 1500–1800*, ed. Karl Otto Conrady, Rowohlts Klassiker 500–501 (Reinbek: Rowohlt, 1968), 26.

[58] Stanza 5; for the entire text see Wagenknecht, ed., *Epochen*, 332.

[59] Klaus Ley, "Castiglione und die Höflichkeit: Zur Rezeption des Cortegiano im deutschen Sprachraum vom 16. bis zum 18. Jahrhundert," in *Beiträge zur Aufnahme der italienischen und spanischen Literatur in Deutschland im 16. und 17. Jahrhundert*, ed. Alberto Martino (Amsterdam: Rodopi, 1990), 3–108.

[60] Gerhart Hoffmeister, "Barocker Petrarkismus: Wandlungen und Möglichkeiten der Liebessprache in der Lyrik des 17. Jahrhunderts," in *Europäische Tradition und deutscher Literaturbarock*, ed. Hoffmeister (Bern: Francke, 1973), 44–48; on Kuhlmann see the entry by Gerhart Hoffmeister in *German Baroque Writers, 1661–1730*, ed. James Hardin, vol. 168 of *Dictionary of Literary Biography* (Detroit: Gale, 1996), 230–38.

[61] *Johann Christian Günther: Gedichte*, ed. Manfred Windfuhr (Stuttgart: Reclam, 1967), 30–31.

[62] Gerhart Hoffmeister, "Marinismus," in *Deutsche und europäische Barockliteratur*, Sammlung Metzler 234 (Stuttgart: Metzler, 1987), 147–55.

[63] Not surprisingly, Hans Abschatz was only one of many verse- and prose-translators of *Il pastor fido*, among them Hofmannswaldau (also in 1678). On Abschatz's Guarini-renditions see Gerhart Hoffmeister, "Italienische Vorlagen und petrarkistische Topoi," in *Studia neophilologica* 42 (1970): 435–50; on Guarini's play see Elida Maria Szarota, "Deutsche Pastor Fido-Übersetzungen und europäische Tradition," in Hoffmeister, ed., *Europäische Tradition*, 305–27.

[64] Quoted from *Don Francesco und Angelica*, ed. Gerhart Hoffmeister (Tubingen: Niemeyer, 1985), 377.

[65] Hoffmeister, *Die spanische Diana*, 96–108; also the following by Hoffmeister: "Courtly Decorum: Kuffstein and the Spanish Diana," *Comparative Literature Studies* 8 (1971): 214–23, and "Hans Ludwig von Kuffstein," in *German Baroque Writers, 1580–1660*, ed. James Hardin, vol. 164 of *Dictionary of Literary Biography* (Detroit: Gale, 1996), 206–9.

[66] Hans Ludwig von Kuffstein, *Gefängnüß der Lieb*, ed. Gerhart Hoffmeister, Nachdrucke deutscher Literatur des 17. Jahrhunderts 7 (Bern: Lang, 1976), and Hoffmeister, "Kuffstein und die Komödianten," *Daphnis* 13 (1984): 217–28.

[67] Gerhart Hoffmeister, "Juan de Flores' Grisel y Mirabella und Christian Pharemunds Aurelio und Isabella: Zur Rezeption der 'novela sentimental' in Deutschland (1492; 1630)," in Martino, ed., *Aufnahme der italienischen und spanischen Literatur*, 235–56; see also Hoffmeister's edition, based on Diego de San Pedro's novel of 1492, of August Augspurger, *Arnalte und Lucenda* (Bern: Lang, 1988).

[68] Fortunatus is the name given to this anonymous author by a Hamburg literary circle; his real name appears only in abbreviation as J.F.R.V.E.

[69] Gerhart Hoffmeister, "The English Comedians in Germany," in *German Baroque Literature*, ed. Hoffmeister (New York: Ungar, 1983), 142–58. The English Comedians are also known in literary historiography as the "English Players" as well as the "English strolling players."

[70] The term "gelebter Petrarkismus" comes from two sources by Leonard Forster: *The Icy Fire*, 122, and "Gelebter Petrarkismus," *Daphnis* 9 (1980): 517–56.

[71] Gerhart Hoffmeister, ed., *Niclas Ulenhart: Historia von Isaac Winckelfelder vnd Jobst von der Schneid* (Munich: Fink, 1983); also the following by Hoffmeister: "Grimmelshausens Simplicissimus und der spanisch-deutsche Schelmenroman,"

Daphnis 5 (1976): 275–94; "Adaptation as Acculturation: The Picaro's Rebirth as Schelm in German Literature," *Prism(s)* 7 (1999): 105–16; and "Schelmenroman," in *Enzyklopädie des Märchens*, ed. Ulrich Marzolph (Göttingen: de Gruyter, in press).

[72] Johann Beer, *Beschreibung eines Ertz-Landstreichers Coryli*, ed. Ferdinand van Ingen and Hans-Gert Roloff (Bern: Lang, 1981), 13.

[73] For more details see Gerhart Hoffmeister, "Dirnen-Barock: On Misogyny in 17th-Century German Prose and its Roots in Reality," in *Studies in German and Scandinavian Literature after 1500: Festschrift for George Schoolfield*, ed. James A. Parente and Richard E. Schade (Columbia, SC: Camden House, 1993), 67–80.

[74] See Hoffmeister's "Profiles of Pastoral Protagonists, 1504–1754: Derivations and Social Implications," in *From the Greeks to the Greens: Images of the Simple Life*, ed. Reinhold Grimm and Jost Hermand (Madison: Wisconsin UP, 1989), 18–33.

[75] Gerhart Hoffmeister, "Versuch einer Typologie des 'spanischen Narren' zwischen 1613 und 1787," in *Literary Culture in the Holy Roman Empire, 1555–1720*, ed. James Parente, Richard Schade, and George Schoolfield (Chapel Hill: North Carolina UP, 1991), 89–106.

[76] Jorg-Ulrich Fechner, "Die alten Leiden des jungen Werthers: Goethes Roman aus petrarkistischer Sicht," *Arcadia* 17 (1982): 1–15.

[77] These lines open book 2 of the "zweyte ächte Auflage" (second authorized edition) of 1775, printed by Weygand in Leipzig.

[78] *Malleus maleficarum* is sometimes attributed, wrongly, to both Heinrich Kramer and Jakob Sprenger.

[79] Rochus Freiherr von Liliencron, ed., *Deutsche National-Litteratur 26* (Berlin: Spemann, 1884).

[80] For a fuller discussion of the literature surrounding magic and witchcraft see the chapter by Gerhild Scholz Williams in this volume.

[81] *Über die Hexenprozesse: "De crimine magiae,"* ed. Rolf Lieberwirth (Weimar: Böhlau, 1967).

[82] Robert Spaethling, "Christian Thomasius," in Hardin, ed., *German Baroque Writers, 1661–1730*, 380–90.

[83] Eberhard Berent, *Die Auffassung der Liebe bei Opitz und Weckherlin und ihre geschichtlichen Vorstufen* (The Hague: Mouton, 1970), 29–33.

[84] *Johann Thomas: Damon und Lisille*, ed. Herbert Singer and Horst Gronemeyer (Hamburg: Maximilian Gesellschaft, 1966), 146.

Literature and the Court, 1450–1720

Helen Watanabe-O'Kelly

The Court as Institution

Definition and Development

DISCUSSION OF THE EARLY MODERN COURT in the Holy Roman Empire is complicated by the sheer number of courts and their political and cultural diversity. At a conservative estimate there were 100 courts in the empire during our period, of which the most important was the imperial court, followed by the courts of the secular electors (Saxony, Brandenburg, the Palatinate, Bohemia, later Bavaria, and later still Hanover); of great lords such as the dukes of Württemberg or the landgraves of Hesse-Kassel and Hesse-Darmstadt; and of the three ecclesiastical electors, Trier, Cologne, and Mainz. Since primogeniture was not the rule, territories were constantly being subdivided, and these smaller territories had their own courts. A particular court could have a cultural importance out of all proportion to its size. Rottenburg on the Neckar under Mechthild of the Palatinate (1418–82, r. in Rottenburg 1452–82), Wolfenbüttel during the reign of August of Braunschweig-Lüneburg (1579–1666, r. 1635–66), Gottorf in Schleswig-Holstein under Friedrich III of Schleswig-Holstein-Gottorf (1597–1659, r. 1616–59), or Weissenfels under August of Saxony-Weissenfels (1614–80, r. 1656–80) are cases in point.

Another complicating factor is that the court as an institution underwent a remarkable transformation from the fifteenth to the early eighteenth century.[1] At the beginning of the fifteenth century the term *court* denoted the ruler's household, that is, his family and personal servants augmented by those nobles who had access to him. The court meant therefore the group of people that moved around from place to place with the ruler. As the early modern territorial state developed and the prince set about consolidating his power, a centralized governmental apparatus became necessary, consisting of increasing numbers of officials appointed for their specialized knowledge in such subjects as law, fortification techniques, or mining. The court thus gradually came to mean the government of a particular territory with its attendant civil service; often too it was the seat of justice and social control, a function still apparent in the phrase "a court of law."

As time went on, princes fixed on a particular city as their capital, or *Residenz*, and the court took up permanent residence there. "Going to court" thus meant visiting the ruler in one particular city rather than waiting upon him wherever he happened to be "holding court." The imperial court, for instance, became fixed in Vienna at the beginning of the seventeenth century. Before then it had moved around with the emperor to those cities such as Augsburg, Nuremberg, Regensburg, Aachen, and Frankfurt am Main that had an official function in imperial ceremonial, while the principal seat of Maximilian I (1459–1519, r. 1508–19) was Innsbruck and that of Rudolf II (1552–1612, r. 1576–1612) Prague.

During the course of the sixteenth century the expansion of centralized government and administration meant that court personnel grew ever more numerous. In 1554 under Charles V (1500–1558, r. 1519–56) the imperial court consisted of 451 people. By the reign of Charles VI (1685–1740, r. 1711–40) it had grown to 2,175. Volker Bauer points out that this figure would be as great as 25,000 if the retinues of the empress, the dowager empresses, and the princes and princesses were included.[2] Other courts expanded at a similar rate. This expansion was accompanied architecturally by the addition of palaces and other edifices connected to the court, so that gradually the court dominated the capital city. This development was not continuous, however, for the Thirty Years' War generally led to a hiatus, with building and expansion only beginning again after 1660.

Which dynasties and courts were important at any one time was also subject to fluctuation. The Habsburgs, for instance, only began their dominance on the imperial throne with the short reign of Albrecht II (r. 1438–39) and only really established themselves during the fifty-three-year reign of his successor Friedrich III (r. 1440–93). During this reign there were several serious political crises, the first in 1470 and another toward the end of the reign, leading in 1495 to the so-called *Reichsreform* (Imperial Reform), in which the *Reichstag* (Imperial Diet) and the *Reichskammergericht* (Imperial Cameral Court) were created, thus depriving the emperor of several important powers.

The Hohenzollerns, so firmly associated today with Brandenburg, came to that territory for the first time only in 1417 when Burgrave Friedrich of Nuremberg (1371–1440, r. 1417–40) succeeded as margrave and elector of Brandenburg. It was his successor, Friedrich II (1413–71, r. 1440–71), who established the twin town of Berlin-Cölln as his capital. The seventeenth century saw the constant rise of this dynasty and the expansion of its power and territory until Friedrich I had himself crowned king of Prussia in Königsberg in 1701.

The Albertine branch of the Wettin dynasty came to prominence only when Duke Moritz (1521–53) wrested the title of elector of Saxony from the Ernestine branch of the family in 1547 at the Battle of Mühlberg, whereupon Dresden became the capital city of Electoral Saxony. The Wettins saw the culmination of their rise to power in 1697 in the election and coronation of Friedrich August I, elector of Saxony ("August the Strong," 1670–1733, r. 1694–1733) as August II, king of Poland. On his death in 1733 his son Friedrich August II (1696–1763, r. 1733–63) was elected as his successor in

Poland and reigned as August III. Another court that rose to prominence toward the end of our period was Hanover, whose dukes were created electors in 1692 and who, in 1714, became kings of Great Britain and Ireland.

Another important agent for change from the beginning of the sixteenth century was the Reformation. The fortunes of a court were thereafter determined by which of the three confessional groupings it belonged to — Catholic, Lutheran, or Calvinist. The principle had been established at the Peace of Augsburg in 1555 that the prince should determine the religion of his people and that Lutheranism should be accorded the status of a recognized religion. A court thus belonged to a particular power bloc by virtue of the confessional allegiance of the prince. This in turn influenced the cultural network to which a given court belonged and the dynastic marriages its rulers made. Catholic dynasties such as the Habsburgs and the Bavarian Wittelsbachs intermarried with each other and with Italy, Spain, Poland, or Savoy, to whom they looked for political support and cultural impulses. The Protestant courts such as Brandenburg, Saxony, or Württemberg intermarried with each other and with Denmark, the Protestant Netherlands, or England.

The difference that confessional allegiance could make to the fortunes of a court can be seen by looking at the two most important Wittelsbach courts, the Bavarian court in Munich and the Palatine court in Heidelberg. Each had a charismatic and strong-minded ruler in the fifteenth century, Friedrich the Victorious of the Palatinate (r. 1449–76) and Albrecht IV of Bavaria (r. 1467–1508). The court of Heidelberg (the capital of the Palatinate or *Pfalz*, ruled over by the Electors Palatine) went over to Lutheranism under Friedrich II (1482–1556, r. 1544–56) and then to Calvinism under Friedrich III (r. 1559–76). Friedrich V (r. 1610–32) became the leader of the Protestant Union, the power bloc of Protestant princes who opposed the emperor, and had himself crowned king of Bohemia in Prague in 1619. He was routed at the Battle of the White Mountain near Prague in 1620, Heidelberg was overrun by imperial forces under Tilly in 1622, and Friedrich's electoral title and his territory were given to the Bavarian branch, which had remained Catholic, in 1623. Maximilian I, duke of Bavaria (r. 1597–1651), thus became the first elector of Bavaria, and Munich flourished as a court city. Though Karl Ludwig (1617–80, r. 1649–80), Friedrich V's son, tried to rebuild Heidelberg after the Thirty Years' War and restore court culture, it was again devastated by the French at the end of the seventeenth century.

The fortunes of Stuttgart, the capital of Württemberg, were similarly affected. The Reformation was introduced by Duke Ulrich (r. 1498–1520 and r. 1534–50) in 1534. Stuttgart was the site of a culturally important court throughout the second half of the sixteenth century and up to the Thirty Years' War, but as a center of Protestant dissent it too was overrun by the imperial troops in 1634 and did not begin to recover until the 1670s. It was not until the mid-eighteenth century under Duke Karl Eugen (1728–93, r. 1737–93) that Stuttgart again experienced a period of great cultural and architectural development, achieved not without internal political conflict.

The Emergence of the Courtier

The nature of court society also changed during our period, because German-speaking courts, whether Protestant or Catholic, took the northern Italian courts as their models throughout the fifteenth, sixteenth, and the first half of the seventeenth centuries; the French court became a dominant influence only toward the end of the seventeenth century. The enthusiasm with which leading courts adopted humanism is the first and most obvious manifestation of this Italian influence.[3] They frequently employed Italian scholars or else Germans who had studied in Italy. Examples of the former are Enea Silvio Piccolomini (1405–64), brought to Vienna in 1443, and Petrus Antonius Finariensis (Antonio de Clapis, ca. 1440–1512), employed in Heidelberg from 1465. An example of the latter is Peter Luder (ca. 1415–72), brought to Heidelberg in 1456; the team of scholars and artists that Emperor Maximilian I brought together in Vienna around 1500 is another example.

But it was not only a learned Latin culture that the German-speaking courts borrowed from Italy.[4] They also adopted the social norms and conventions of the northern Italian courts, collected Italian art, listened to Italian music, imitated Italian architecture, and imported Italian painters and sculptors. The scientific advances of the Renaissance were just as enthusiastically received, not least because German princes had a practical need of them: the new understanding of perspective and the development of the science of optics, for instance, were fundamental to the development of ballistics and fortification techniques, of architecture, cartography, and mining. Florence, Ferrara, Mantua, and Vicenza were the sources of innovation for courts in the empire. Because of their geographical position, these new impulses reached Innsbruck, Munich, and Vienna first, Dresden, Berlin, and Rostock later; but by the end of the sixteenth century it is safe to say that any court with cultural ambitions had its Italian *Kapellmeister* (director of music), its Italian painter or sculptor, its Italian architect and fortifications engineer.

A new social ideal was also imported from Italy, according to which the medieval knight was transformed into the modern courtier. At the Diet of Worms in 1495 the knights lost their *Fehderecht*, that is, the right to take up arms in pursuit of their own aims and in self-defense. This right had hitherto been a defining characteristic of the knightly estate. At the same time, military force was becoming ever more concentrated in the hands of the princes and increasingly professionalized. Technical developments in warfare, such as the success of pikemen and crossbowmen on the battlefield, the development not only of cannon but, during the sixteenth century, of viable handguns, and the introduction of new fortification techniques such as the bastion, were also changing the role and self-understanding of the knight.[5] A knight could now either take up service as a professional soldier in the army of a prince or he could become a civil servant and courtier.

It was Baldassare Castiglione (1478–1529) who most famously set down the ideal of the courtier in his *Libro del Cortegiano* (1528).[6] Each of the four sections describes an evening gathering at the court of Urbino in the year 1507, at which a group of aristocrats and intellectuals, under the direction of the duchess Elisabetta Gonzaga (1471–1526) and her niece Emilia Pia (died 1528), describes and defines the courtier. He must be of noble birth, a capable soldier and horseman, adept at literature, music, drawing, and the arts, and must know Latin and Greek. He must always aim to please his prince, though he must hide the effort this costs him. This appearance of ease Castiglione termed *sprezzatura*. The successful courtier must be able to dissimulate, to control his passions, and to be prudent in his actions.[7] He should not be an amoral opportunist as advocated by Machiavelli in his *Il Principe* (The Prince, 1513), however. Virtue and nobility of mind are important characteristics. *Il Cortegiano* was first translated into German by Laurentz Kratzer in 1565 and dedicated to Albrecht V of Bavaria.[8] A Latin translation by Hieronymus Turler appeared four years later in Wittenberg, dedicated to August, elector of Saxony.[9] A second Latin translation by Johannes Richius (Reiche) appeared in two versions, in 1577 and 1584 respectively, dedicated to Emperor Rudolf II.[10]

Another influential work was Giovanni della Casa's courtesy book or treatise *Galateo* (1559).[11] The German humanist Nathan Chytraeus (1543–98) translated it into Latin in Rostock in 1578, a translation that ran into several editions;[12] in 1597 he published a revised edition, which he himself translated into German.[13] Two years before this so-called first German edition, the Helmstedt scholar Friedrich von Gelhorn translated *Galateo* from Italian into German for the three young sons of the deceased elector Christian I of Saxony (1560–91, r. 1586–91).[14] *Galateo* is concerned not with morals but with manners, with what it calls *civil conversazione*. It promulgates a vision of a civilized society from which vulgarity and pomposity are equally banned and in which the man of manners distinguishes himself by concern for others, by avoiding embarrassing and hurtful situations, by self-control and eloquent speech. He lives in harmony with himself and can thereby better influence others. Where Castiglione deals with the inner man, della Casa concentrates on the outer, but both are necessary to produce the man (or woman) who can successfully perform what Castiglione calls *cortegiania*, service at court. To be a courtier is now a profession in itself.

Women also became an important cultural force at court during the Renaissance. Throughout our period, princesses and great ladies collected books, acted as patrons, and wrote themselves, being particularly active in the fields of devotional literature, novels, and court entertainments.

Books and Learning at Court

In the Middle Ages courts were among the few places where people had access to the written word, but it was not until the early modern period that the ability to read and write German, as well as at least a basic knowledge of Latin, first became essential skills for a nobleman. Learning had been the preserve of the clergy in the Middle Ages and therefore incompatible with the knightly estate, but now a prince needed learning to enable him to rule well and with political acumen. He also needed courtiers and officials with an academic training that would equip them to perform the administrative tasks of the early modern state. All the universities founded between 1450 and 1510, apart from Basel, were princely foundations. Among them are Freiburg in Breisgau, Tübingen, Ingolstadt, Rostock, Greifswald, Wittenberg, and Frankfurt on the Oder.

Princely and noble education constantly improved throughout the period. Noblemen went to university in ever greater numbers during the sixteenth century, though if they were Catholic they were often sent instead to the Jesuit colleges that began to be founded in the empire after 1550. In addition, a new type of educational institution was created at the end of the sixteenth century, the *Ritterakademie*, or noblemen's academy. The earliest of these, the Collegium Illustre, founded in Tübingen in 1589, and the Collegium Mauritianum, founded in Kassel in 1599, had to close because of the Thirty Years' War. A whole series of such academies was founded after the war, among which were Lüneburg in 1655, Halle in 1680, Wolfenbüttel in 1687, Erlangen in 1699, Brandenburg in 1704, Berlin in 1705, and Kassel in 1709. Academies for noblemen continued to be created throughout the first half of the eighteenth century, for instance in Dresden in 1725, in Braunschweig in 1745, and in Vienna in 1746. Subjects studied included law, history, geography, mathematics, Italian, French, fortification techniques, heraldry, and genealogy; great stress was also placed on dancing, fencing, riding, the art of conversation, and the social graces. Some of these academies, such as Halle and Erlangen, were later transformed into universities; others, such as Dresden, became cadet schools for the training of young officers. Training at such an academy was rounded out by the Grand Tour, a journey to foreign courts and centers of learning and culture. All these educational opportunities were reserved for men. Noble ladies were taught by governesses and private tutors, and their education was principally designed to make them devout and decorative, and thus suitable future consorts and mothers.

The court was also a place where new branches of knowledge were actively promoted. Some were of practical importance, but knowledge also formed an important part of the panoply of a prince's power. Just as he had to have certain cultural functionaries (a *Kapellmeister*, a court poet, a court painter), so too a prince needed to show that he was at the forefront of modern knowledge. Princes therefore gathered round them scholars and specialists of all kinds — physicians, mathematicians, cartographers, fortification engineers. They built up libraries and scientific collections, and they engaged actively in the study and practice of such important branches of knowledge as alchemy and astronomy.[15] The interests of the prince, as well as the various functions that the court had to fulfill as seat of government, as military center, and as entrepreneur, demanded a wide range of factual and technical books. Many important treatises on law and political philosophy, medicine and farriery, cartography, surveying, mathematics and astronomy, metallurgy and mining, agriculture, horticulture and animal husbandry, military matters and fortification, artillery and fireworks were commissioned by or written at early modern courts.

The Court Poet

It would be more correct to refer to the court poet as the court intellectual, for his services covered a far wider range than is implied by the term *poet*. His official function was often something different.[16] He might be the chaplain, like Matthias von Kemnat (ca. 1430–76) at Heidelberg; the tutor, like Sigmund von Birken (1626–81) at Wolfenbüttel; the librarian, like David Schirmer (1623–86) at Dresden; or the court scientist, like Adam Olearius (1599–1671) at Gottorf. Olearius's official title was actually *Hofmathematicus* (court mathematician), and he was in charge of the scientific collection or *Kuriositätenkabinett*. The court poet could be the ducal secretary, like Kaspar Stieler (1632–1707) at Rudolstadt or Christian Weise (1642–1708) at Leiningen, later Weissenfels; or the court historiographer, like Jacob Balde (1604–68) at Munich. Georg Rudolf Weckherlin (1584–1653), after working as a court poet in Stuttgart before the Thirty Years' War, went to England, where he was employed for twenty-eight years as the "Secretary for Foreign Tongues," a kind of secret service chief, collecting material from his agents in the field. Some court poets worked for most of their professional lives at one court, others were freelance experts who hired themselves out to whichever court needed them.

An example of the former is David Schirmer. He arrived in Dresden in 1650 to take up the post of librarian, which he held until 1682, but he functioned as a court poet at least up to 1663, writing occasional verse in honor of members of the electoral family as well as libretti for a considerable number of dramatic works: ballets, musical entertainments, operas, and firework dramas. It is likely that some of the ballets performed in Dresden after 1663 are also by him, so that his career as a court poet lasted almost twenty years. He was also writing considerable quantities of accomplished poetry, which he published in two collections, the most famous of which is the *Poetische Rosen-Gepüsche* (Poetic Rose Bushes) of 1657.[17] In 1663 Schirmer brought out a collection of his occasional poetry and dramatic works for the court under the title *Poetische Rauten-Gepüsche* (Poetic Rue Bushes), the rue being the emblem of the Albertines.[18] It is dedicated to the elector and his family and presents the texts in chronological order, so that we see a busy court poet at work, writing libretti for firework dramas, ballets, and operas, as well as a stream of occasional verse, and doing it all with great technical proficiency and inventiveness.

Sigmund von Birken is an example of the international freelance literary consultant.[19] He came to the court of Wolfenbüttel as a twenty-year-old to tutor the young Dukes Anton Ulrich and Ferdinand Albrecht. Though he did not spend long in Wolfenbüttel, he remained in touch with the court for the rest of his life. He moved back to the free city of Nuremberg in 1648, where he lived until his death. From here he acted as historiographer, genealogist, court poet, and consultant to the courts of Vienna, Wolfenbüttel, Brandenburg-Bayreuth, and Dresden; he composed genealogies for the Habsburgs (1656), for the dukes of Braunschweig and Lüneburg (1669), and for the electors of Saxony in 1677. He wrote plays such as *Androfilo* (1656), ballets such as *Ballet der Natur* (1662), and opera libretti such as *Sophia* (1662), the two last-named for the wedding of Christian Ernst of Brandenburg-Bayreuth and Erdmuthe Sophie, duchess of Saxony. In 1664 he wrote an illustrated geographical work about the Danube and the cities along it entitled *Der Donau-Strand* (The Banks of the Danube) and in 1668 published a compilation of the travel journals of Christian Ernst under the title *Hoch Fürstlicher Brandenburgischer Ulysses* (The Prince of Brandenburg as Ulysses). In the same year he wrote *Spiegel der Ehren des Höchstlöblichsten Kayser- und Königlichen Erzhauses Oesterreich* (Mirror of Honors of the Most Praiseworthy Royal and Imperial House of Austria), a history of the House of Habsburg up to 1519, which he says is a greatly augmented version of a work by Johann Jacob Fugger. It combines some of the features of genealogy and heraldry and is dedicated to Emperor Leopold I and his bride, the Spanish Infanta Margarita Teresa, on the occasion of their marriage in 1667. Birken also acted as ghost writer to Count Gottlieb von Windischgrätz (1630–95), an influential figure at the Viennese court. We also find him writing occasional verse of all kinds, including epicedia for deceased nobles, all this in addition to festive pieces in celebration of the Peace of Westphalia and a number of pastoral works.

The *oeuvre* of Schirmer and that of Birken can only be properly understood within the context of how literature was used at court. It is equally important, however, to recognize that most early modern writers, including Weckherlin, Martin Opitz, Andreas Gryphius, Paul Fleming, and Casper von Lohenstein, wrote at least some of their works for a court or at some stage in their lives enjoyed court patronage.

Literature as Dynastic Tool

The inherently unstable grip on power of dynasties, courts, and individual rulers explains the existence of a number of genres concerned with defining the nature of the court and giving legitimacy to individual rulers and dynasties. Works of genealogy and heraldry, chronicles, and histories justify the claims of a particular dynasty, ruler, or noble to power and superior standing, while *Fürstenspiegel* (mirrors for princes) define the prince's role and regulate his behavior. This type of writing, in contrast to the genres discussed below (in the section "Literature and Power"), purports to be factual. Indeed, that is its point.

Genealogy and Heraldry

A work of genealogy marks a particular family or dynasty off from all others by tracing the descent of the whole group from one original ancestor, who is the absolute beginning of the dynasty and the link between all its members down the centuries.[20] Works of genealogy constantly refer to him, so that the distant past is still alive in the present. Descent is an unbeatable criterion of class distinction, for those who do not have it can never acquire it, no matter how wealthy or successful they become. Descent was used to differentiate between those members of the nobility who were allowed to take part in tournaments, as well as to create degrees of precedence between different families and different branches of the same family. Descent determined who could rule and who could not and who was fit to marry whom. The coat of arms embodies these distinctions, just as it also presents in visual form the connections between dynasties.

Many noble families commissioned genealogical works. Ernst Brotuff's (1497–1565) genealogy of the princes of Anhalt, published in 1556, is one example.[21] It intersperses short chronicle-like passages with family trees and with many illustrations of coats of arms. Comparable works are Wolffgang Jobst's (1521–75) *Genealogia oder Geburtlinien und Ankunfft des löblichen Chur und fürstlichen Haus zu Brandenburgk* (The Genealogy or Family Tree and Origin of the Praiseworthy Electoral and Princely House of Brandenburg, 1562) and his *Genealogia, oder Stam vnd Geburtlinia, der [. . .] Fürsten und Hertzogen in Pommern / Stettin / der Cassuben und Wenden* (Genealogy or Family Tree of the Princes and Dukes of Pomerania, Stettin, the Kashubians, and Wends, 1573), and the many works written by Cyriacus Spangenberg (1528–1604), such as *Die Manßfeldische Chronica* (The Mansfeld Chronicle, 1572, republished unchanged in 1583 as the *Sächssische Chronica*, or Saxon Chronicle), *Die Hennebergische Chronica* (The Henneberg Chronicle, 1599), and the posthumously published *Chronicon [. . .] der Hochgebornen Uhralten Graffen Zu Holstein Schaumburgk* (Chronicle of the Noble and Ancient Counts of Holstein and Schaumburg, 1614).[22]

In some cases these genealogies had a precise political aim. The Ernestine branch of the Wettin dynasty, which had lost the electorship of Saxony to the Albertine branch in 1547, tried to reestablish its claim in a series of genealogical works commissioned from Balthasar Mentz (1537–1617).[23] Mentz's *Genealogia und Geburts Linia* (Genealogy and Family Tree, 1594) consists of woodcut portraits of the electors going back to the Germanic hero Wittekind; a first-person verse monologue in nine couplets of rhyming doggerel stands under each portrait. His *Stambuch* (Genealogy) of 1597 presents coats of arms as well as portraits, thus combining heraldry and genealogy, while his *Stambuch und Kurtze Erzehlung* (Genealogy and Short Account) of 1598 is actually a work of history, though with some of the same genealogical and heraldic material. Such works naturally demonstrated that the Albertine branch of the family had only had the electorship for a mere forty years at this point.

Genealogy continued to expand during the seventeenth century and well into the eighteenth, with noble houses of all ranks bringing their family tree up to date every so many decades in works that chronicled the succession and displayed the marriage alliances made by the family in question. In the seventeenth century too, certain writers worked as genealogical experts, composing genealogies for several very different dynasties. Johann Ulrich Pregitzer (1647–1708), for instance, is the author both of *Teutscher Regierung- und Ehren-Spiegel* (German Mirror of Governance and Honor, 1703) for the house of Hohenzollern and of *Wirttembergischer Cedern-Baum* (The Württemberg Cedar Tree, 1703) for the dukes of Württemberg.[24] Birken composed *Ostländischer Lorbeerhäyn von dem Höchstlöblichen Erzhaus Österreich* (Eastern Laurel Grove of the Most Praiseworthy House of Austria) for the Habsburgs in 1656, *Guelfis oder NiderSächsischer Lorbeerhayn* (Guelfis; or, Lower Saxon

Laurel Grove) for the Guelf dynasty in Braunschweig and Lüneburg in 1669, and *Chur- und Fürstlicher Sächsischer Helden-Saal* (Gallery of Saxon Electoral and Princely Heroes) for the Wettin dukes of Saxony in 1677.

Works of heraldry form another characteristic early modern genre closely related to genealogy. In the fifteenth century, coats of arms are depicted in the Ingeram Codex (now in the Kunsthistorisches Museum in Vienna), which was composed for the wedding of Mechthild of the Palatinate and Albrecht of Austria in 1452, and in Jakob Püterich von Reichertshausen's (1400–1469) *Ehrenbrief* (Letter of Honor, 1462), whose middle part consists of the coats of arms of the noble Bavarian families. The invention of printing made it possible to publish ambitious large-scale compendia, such as the *Wappenbuch des Heiligen römischen Reichs, und allgemainer Christenheit in Europa* (The Coats of Arms of the Holy Roman Empire and All of Christendom) by Martin Schrot (d. 1581) in 1580. Such compendia continued to be produced at regular intervals throughout the next century and a half, often massive folio volumes running to close on seven hundred pages, such as the *Einleitung zur Wapen-Kunst* (Introduction to Heraldry, 1714) of Johann Wolfgang Trier (1686–ca. 1750).[25]

Heraldry is often mixed in with other genres. The so-called *ThurnierBuch* by the herald Georg Rüxner (Rixner), a compendium of descriptions of thirty-six tournaments held between 938 and 1487, purports also to be a work of genealogy and of heraldry; each begins with the depiction of a coat of arms and a list of the participants.[26] Mentz's *Stambuch und Kurtze Erzehlung* and Birken's *Chur- und Fürstlicher Sächsischer Helden-Saal* also demonstrate how difficult it is to separate genealogy from history.

Historiography

While genealogy focuses on birth, a passive criterion, historical works are concerned with the deeds, the *res gestae*, of a particular ruler and with the political circumstances of his reign. The emergence of territorial states favored the development of regional history rather than of world history, and of a regional history that was presented as identical with the history of the ruling house.[27] In contrast to modern historiography, early modern historians had no intention of reporting objectively or weighing events up in a spirit of neutral inquiry. Rather, they aimed to justify and provide evidence for the claims to hegemony of the ruler who was their patron by showing him to be the culmination of a long tradition. In the fifteenth century, chronicles of individual territories still often began with the creation of the world, with Noah's ark, or with the founding of Rome, before they proceeded to the deeds of a particular prince. Histories had the function of providing members of a court with a common past. Again, in contrast to modern historiography it was the typical features that were emphasized. The behavior and deeds of a particular prince were praised not for their specificity but because they corresponded to a preexisting ideal. The prince could then function as a model for his descendants, and the history could take on some of the characteristics of a mirror for princes.

Historiography in Heidelberg in the fifteenth century took the outstanding personality of Friedrich the Victorious as its starting point.[28] Matthias von

Kemnat, from about 1460 court chaplain, initiated the tradition, dedicating the last years of his life to his principal work, the *Chronik Friedrichs I. des Siegreichen* (The Chronicle of Friedrich I the Victorious). The first part, completed in 1475, narrates the history of the popes and the emperors from the birth of Christ to the death of Ludwig IV (r. 1435–59), Friedrich's brother and predecessor, and contains passages on the duchy of Bavaria and on the Wittelsbachs, based on Andreas of Regensburg's (1380–1438) *Chronik von den Fürsten zu Bayern* (Chronicle of the Dukes of Bavaria, 1428). The second part consists of the actual chronicle of Friedrich's life and deeds, covering a much shorter period of about twenty-five years, beginning with a translation of a notable panegyric to Friedrich by Peter Luder.[29] Both Luder and Matthias present the elector as a successful warrior comparable to Alexander the Great, but both feel themselves obliged to justify and excuse the maneuver (the so-called "arrogation") by means of which Friedrich came to power as the regent for his underage nephew. Matthias lent his source materials to the *Meistersinger* Michel Beheim (1416–ca. 1474), who came to Heidelberg in 1467 and wrote a rhymed chronicle between 1469 and 1471, the *Pfälzische Reimchronik* (Palatine Verse Chronicle), another work concentrating on the deeds of Friedrich.

Another example of historiography that is similarly focused on one man also comes from the Palatinate. Hubertus Thomas (ca. 1495–1555) was court historiographer to Friedrich II and wrote a history of his reign in fourteen books, the *Annales de vita et rebus gestis illustrissimi principis Friderici II.* (The Annals of the Life and Deeds of the Most Noble Prince Friedrich II).

In Bavaria, historiography focused on the dynasty. It began with Andreas of Regensburg's aforementioned chronicle. In 1478, almost simultaneously with the works of Matthias and Beheim, the painter and poet Ulrich Fuetrer (ca. 1430–96) began his *Bayerische Chronik* (Bavarian Chronicle) at the instigation of Albrecht IV of Bavaria-Munich. His chronicle covers the period from 60 B.C. to 1481. One of his aims is to justify the hegemony of the Bavarian Wittelsbachs by means of his account of the origins of the territory and of the dynasty. Two further installments after his death take the history up to 1502 and 1511 respectively.

This Bavarian tradition was continued in *De bello palatino-boico libri tres* (The Palatine-Bavarian War in Three Books) by August Kölner, private secretary to Albrecht IV, in the *Chronicon Bavarorum* (Bavarian Chronicle) composed in 1505/6 by Veit von Ebersberg, and above all in the historical writings of Johannes Turmair (known as Aventinus, 1477–1534).[30] Aventinus was a pupil of famed humanist Conrad Celtis (1459–1508), spent the years 1497–1502 in Vienna (the first three at the university), and later studied in Paris with the historian Beatus Rhenanus (1485–1547). In 1517 he was appointed court historiographer to the duke of Bavaria. His *Annalium Boiorum libri septem* (Annals of Bavaria in Seven Books), completed in 1524, as well as his *Bayerische Chronik* (Bavarian Chronicle), written in German and completed in 1533, were not printed until 1554 and 1566 respectively, long after his death.[31] Aventinus, in contrast to most other historians of the age, wanted to present historical truth, and he derided Fuetrer's chronicle as pure invention. He claims to have carried out real historical research, looking at all possible manuscripts, printed, official, ecclesiastical, native and foreign documents and chronicles. Aventinus also wanted to interpret events, not just catalogue them, and he makes his own opinions clear on every page. But this did not suit his patrons and, together with his tolerance toward the Reformation, prevented the *Bayerische Chronik* from being printed during his lifetime.

One ruler above all others involved himself personally in creating an image for posterity of himself and his court, namely, Emperor Maximilian I. He called this public relations program *Gedechtnus* (commemoration), and historiography played a central part in it.[32] He employed a whole team of scholars both to research and to write history. Among them were Johannes Stabius (died 1522), his adviser and historian from 1503 and the composer of the verses on Albrecht Dürer's (1471–1528) *Triumphal Arch*; Johannes Trithemius (1462–1516), abbot of Sponheim, who undertook genealogical research and who, when he could not find suitable sources, invented them; Josef Grünpeck (1473–1540), Maximilian's secretary from 1497 to 1501, who wrote the *Historia Friderici III. et Maximiliani* (History of Friedrich III and Maximilian); Conrad Celtis, who also worked as a genealogist for the emperor; Jakob Mennel (1450–1525), who attempted a *Chronik des Hauses Österreich und der Grafen Habsburg* (Chronicle of the House of Austria and of the Habsburg Counts, 1507) and wrote a *Habsburgische Reimchronik* (Verse Chronicle of the Habsburgs) as well as a five-volume *Fürstliche Chronik* (Princely Chronicle); and Johannes Cuspinian (1473–1529), who also worked for Maximilian as a historian and published *Austria [. . .] cum omnibus eiusdem marchionibus, ducibus, archiducibus* (Austria, with All Its Counts, Dukes, Archdukes) at Frankfurt in 1601. The Augsburg humanist Conrad Peutinger (1465–1547) wrote an unfinished *Vitae imperatorum* (Lives of the Emperors, 1510). In addition to all this, Maximilian turned his own life into history in a series of works in which he appears as a knight: the richly illustrated *Theuerdanck* (printed in 1517), the courtly verse epic *Freydal* (begun in 1502 and for which 255 drawings survive), and the prose romance *Weißkunig*, which tells the story of his courtship illustrated with 236 woodcuts. In all of these works Maximilian appears as the ideal prince, a great general, successful warrior and jouster, and loving father to his people. At the same time, he embodies the ideal of the *rex litteratus*, the learned and cultivated king. Here historiography takes on the character of a mirror for princes.

Dynastic history and chronicle writing among noble families[33] continued to be important as a propaganda tool during the seventeenth century but was greatly affected by the Thirty Years' War, which meant that there was a hiatus roughly from 1620 to 1680. The decades from the end of the sixteenth century to the beginning of the war were characterized by such works as Reinerus Reinbek's sixty-page summary, *Chronica Des Chur und Fürstlichen Hauses zu Brandenburg* (Chronicle of the Electoral and Princely House of Brandenburg, 1580), or Mathaeus Dresser's (1536–1607) *Sächsisch Chronicon* (Saxon Chronicle), a history of Saxony that begins with the creation of the world and takes the reader up to 1596, the year in which it appeared,[34] or Johann Carl

Unckel's (active as a publisher 1615–34) history of the Palatinate, Saxony, and Brandenburg, published a year after the war began.[35] The years around 1700, however, saw the appearance of large and ambitious historical overviews, often covering the history of more than one dynasty or at least of all the branches of a dynasty. This is the period when Saxony, Brandenburg, and Hanover were jockeying for position in the empire and in Europe. Characteristic examples are the two enormous folio histories: Johann Sebastian Müller's (1634–1708) *Des Chur- und Fürstlichen Hauses Sachsen/ Ernestin- und Albertinischer Linien/ Annales von Anno 1400. bis 1700* (The Annals of the Ernestine and Albertine Branches of the Electoral and Princely House of Saxony, 1700) and Jacob Paul Gundling's *Leben und Thaten Des Durchlauchtigsten Markgrafens Zu Brandenburg Friderichs des Ersten* (Life and Deeds of Friedrich I, the Most Noble Margrave of Brandenburg, 1715). Müller's work, a mixture of genealogy and chronicle, covers the two main branches of the Wettin dynasty as well as the fourteen other branches into which they had split. Gundling's account purports to be a history of the first Hohenzollern margrave to come to Brandenburg in 1415 but in fact covers the history of Brandenburg, Saxony, Bavaria, Braunschweig-Lüneburg, Pomerania, Franconia, and other territories in 500 folio pages.

Mirrors for Princes and Political Treatises

Fürstenspiegel (mirrors for princes) were didactic works whose aim was to teach the ruler virtue and to define his duties.[36] It was a genre with a tradition going back to antiquity, for learned counselors had always tried to influence their rulers. Humanism and the Reformation, the advent of printing, the development of a written culture at court, and the emergence of the territorial state and of the court as an institution led to a huge expansion in the genre throughout the period discussed here.

Humanist works of instruction for the prince, generally written in Latin, took the educability of the individual as their basic premise. Their aim was to turn him into a truly virtuous man by means of the study of ancient literature, for a virtuous ruler was necessary for a well-governed polity. Enea Silvio Piccolomini's didactic letter to Duke Sigmund of Tyrol and his *Tractatus de liberorum educatione* (Treatise on the Education of Free Men, 1450) addressed to the future king of Bohemia and Hungary, Ladislaus Postumus, laid down the central tenets of a humanist education for the good ruler: a thorough grounding in morals and religious precepts, and acquaintance with the classical authors as the source of virtue and moderate behavior. Petrus Antonius Finariensis propounds the same ideal in his dialogue on princely governance, *De dignitate principium* (The Dignity of Princes, 1464), which he sent to Friedrich the Victorious from Basel. A year later at Friedrich's instigation Finariensis wrote a treatise for Charles the Daring of Burgundy called *De principatus conservacione* (On the Preservation of Government, published 1466), which puts forward the ideal of the Christian prince. His *De virtutum civitate* (On the Virtues of the State, 1466), directed at Johann of Cleves, a military ally of Friedrich's, advocates another central humanist idea, that of peace.

The works of Jakob Wimpfeling (1450–1526) were also written in the context of the Heidelberg court. Friedrich the Victorious brought Wimpfeling to Heidelberg for the first time in 1469. In 1483 he went to Speyer Cathedral as a preacher, where he served until Elector Philipp (1448–1508, r. 1476–1508) brought him back to Heidelberg in 1498. In Speyer Wimpfeling wrote two treatises for princes and a pedagogical work for his patrons in Heidelberg. They were *Philippica* (1498), *Agatharchia* (1498), and *Adolescentia* (Youth, 1500). The six dialogues of the *Philippica*[37] are dedicated to Philipp, the second-eldest son of Elector Philipp, and emphasize the significance of a humanist education for the good ruler, while *Agatharchia*,[38] dedicated to Ludwig, the eldest son of the elector, concentrates rather on the duties of the ruler. *Adolescentia* is a lengthy treatise on the education of young noblemen, a compendium of ideas from classical, medieval, and humanist works.

One of the best known mirrors for princes is Erasmus's *Institutio principis Christiani* (The Institution of the Christian Prince, 1516), written for the future emperor, Charles V, then aged sixteen. After a lengthy first part dealing with the education of a ruler, Erasmus calls for peace. The chief task of the ruler should consist not in going to war, he says, but in conducting his political affairs with so much skill and virtue that peace and harmony are the result.

Because the humanists had such high expectations of the ruler and his court, their criticisms were correspondingly sharp. Enea Silvio Piccolomini's *De miseriis curialium* (On the Miseries of Courtiers, 1458), translated into German by Wilhelm von Hirnkofen in 1478, mocks the ambition, greed, and lust for power of the courtier, as well as the dissimulation and flattery necessary to make a successful career at court. Ulrich von Hutten's (1488–1523) critical dialogue *Aula* (The Court, 1518) tries to steer a middle course.[39] The well-known vices of the court are depicted, but he claims that there are wise rulers and thoughtful courtiers. In this dialogue and in his letter about court life to Willibald Pirckheimer of 25 October 1518, Hutten is clearly having some difficulty reconciling courtly values with his own idea of virtue. The sharpest critique of the court comes from Cornelius Agrippa of Nettesheim (1486–1535). Chapter 68 of his *De incertitudine & uanitate scientiarum declamatio inuective* (Diatribe on the Uncertainty and Vanity of Learning), written in 1526 and published in 1530, portrays the court as the quintessence of vice.

Mirrors for princes after the Reformation still contained humanist ideas but orientated themselves principally according to Luther's teaching on *Obrigkeit*, or secular authority. These works were more likely to be written in German. One of the earliest was the theologian Urban Rhegius's (Rieger, 1489–1541) *Enchiridion odder handtbüchlin eines Christlichen Fürstens, darinnen leer und trost aller Oberkeit [. . .] zusamen gezogen* (Manual or Little Handbook of a Christian Prince, which contains teaching and comfort for all those in government, 1535), translated into Latin three years later by the court preacher and friend of Luther, Georg Spalatin (1484–1545). Leonhardt Werner's *Fürstlicher Trostspiegel* (Mirror of Comfort for Princes), published in 1562, exemplifies the different purpose of a Protestant mirror for princes. It aims to warn the prince of sin, to arm him against the temptations of the devil, and to comfort him in the difficulties of his office. The stoic calm of a Renaissance prince is no longer the right stance to take when the devil stalks the earth, and the prince must defend the new Protestant religion against its enemies.

Many mirrors for princes contained discussions of the legal foundation of political power and so began to take on the character of works of political theory. Examples include Reinhard Lorich's (1500–1564) *Loci communes de institutione Principum* (Commonplaces Relating to Princely Government, 1538), Jakob Omphalius's (1500–1567) *De Officio et potestate Principis in Republica bene [. . .] gerenda libri duo* (Two Books on the Office and Power of the Prince in a Well-Run Polity, 1550), Melchior von Osse's (1506–57) so-called *Politisches Testament* (Political Testament, written in 1555 but not published until 1607), Georg Lauterbeck's (ca. 1505–70) *Regentenbuch* (Book of Governance, 1556), and Konrad Heresbach's (1496–1576) *De educandis erudiendisque Principum liberis* (Of the Education and Learning of Free Princes, 1570). As time went on, the focus on the conduct of the prince, so characteristic of the mirror for princes, gave way more and more to a general discussion of the conduct and organization of the state and of the good management of the court. The mirror for princes became rather a political treatise and a handbook of government, a development that coincided with the consolidation of the territorial state and with the expansion of the court as an institution.

Two seventeenth-century works of very different character that illustrate this point are Georg Engelhard von Löhneyss's (1552–1622) *Aulico Politica* (Courtly Polity, 1622) and Veit Ludwig von Seckendorff's (1626–92) *Teutscher Fürsten-Stat* (The German Princedom, 1656). Löhneyss begins in the classic manner of the mirror for princes by enumerating sixty-eight separate things a young prince needs in order to be able to govern well. These range from virtues through branches of knowledge to practical skills. Löhneyss then sets out how the prince should behave and how he should rule in practice, laying particular emphasis on the choice of counselors and officials, to which he devotes nearly 600 of his 777 folio pages. His description of the various offices and tasks implies, of course, a particular view of how government is to be organized. Seckendorff's work is a combination of a practical manual for the German princedoms and duchies, and a mirror for princes.

By the early eighteenth century the organization of the court had become so complicated and its ritual so elaborate that the science of *Zeremoniellwissenschaft*, the theory and practice of court ritual and etiquette, had come into being. Elaborate ceremonial implied an underlying set of constitutional and legal principles, for its purpose was to surround the prince with an aura of majesty.[40] For ceremonial to be deployed effectively, officials, diplomats, and courtiers needed a small reference library of manuals at their elbow. Gottfried Stieve's *Europäisches Hoff-Ceremoniell* (European Court Ceremonial, 1715), Johann Christian Lünig's (1662–1740) two huge folio volumes — containing together some 3,500 pages — *Theatrum Ceremoniale Politicum* (Theater of Political Ceremonial, 1719–20), and Julius Bernhard von Rohr's (1688–1742) *Einleitung zur Ceremonialwissenschaft der grossen Herren* (Introduction to the Theory of the Ceremonial of Great Lords, 1729) are the classic works to which they turned. Lünig provides the largest possible treasury of examples from as many different European courts as possible and embracing every kind of social gathering in which a nobleman or prince could be involved. Rohr, on the other hand, elucidates general principles.

Literature and Power

Court Theater and Spectacle

Spectacle is a central element of court culture. It embraces older forms such as the tournament and the drama and new ones such as the opera, the firework drama, and the *ballet de cour*. All of these were often presented in succession over a period of days or weeks as part of one great festival, sometimes with an overarching theme. The pronounced development of spectacle at German-speaking courts from the middle of the sixteenth century on was due in large part to the influence of the Italian courts. This growth continued throughout the next two centuries.

It is important to distinguish between ceremonies and spectacle. Ceremonies are ritual acts that bring power into being. The king actually becomes a king by means of the coronation ritual, a feudal contract between prince and people is sealed in the ceremonial of the royal entry, and dynastic alliances are created in the marriage ceremony. Ceremonies may be accompanied by theatrical presentations, may even embody some of the elements of theater such as costumes and set speeches, but they are different in essence and are not what is meant by spectacle here.

Spectacle fulfilled a variety of functions, usually more than one at a time. It entertained the courtiers and the princely family, who both watched and took part in it. They were the only social group in the early modern period with conspicuous and guaranteed leisure time and, then as now, leisure brought into being a series of mechanisms to fill it. Spectacle was also an important medium of social discipline and control, in which the prince could present precepts he wished to put across to his people or to his court or in which he could have his courtiers act out their subordinate relationship to him. Theatrical displays at court often presented the relationship between ruler and people in a state of disorder, thereby to demonstrate how this malfunction might be addressed and order restored. Another important function of spectacle was panegyric, presenting the majesty of the prince in symbolic form.

Spoken Drama

Religious drama was one of the standard elements of court spectacle, a fact that should not surprise us when we remember that the public display of piety was one of the primary duties of the prince.[41] In the case of a Protestant court this meant Lutheran biblical drama, presenting Old Testament stories and New Testament parables. At Kassel there are records of biblical plays being performed for at least fifty years beginning in 1570, and we know that the young landgrave Moritz of Hesse-Kassel (1572–1632, r. 1592–1627) dramatized at least four Old Testament stories himself. In Dresden, biblical plays were performed continuously up to at least 1680 as part of every major celebration at court.[42] The greatest original contribution was made in Dresden by Constantin Christian Dedekind (1628–1715), composer, writer, bass, violinist, and director of the court orchestra from 1666 to 1675. Dedekind published his first collection of biblical plays, *Neue geistliche Schau-Spiele, bekwehmet zur Music* (New Religious Plays Set to Music), in 1670 and dedicated them to Elector Johann Georg II (1613–80, r. 1656–80). As far as we know, these works, which lie somewhere between plays and operas and dramatize the Passion, Resurrection, and Nativity, were never performed. Dedekind brought out a second collection in 1676, *Heilige Arbeit über Freud und Leid der alten und neuen Zeit / in Music-bekwehmen Schau-Spielen ahngewendet* (Sacred Reworking of Joyful and Sorrowful Events in Ancient and Modern Times, in plays suitable for music), dedicated this time to Johann Georg's younger brother August of Saxony-Weissenfels, and concentrating on themes from the Old Testament.

Johann Georg II also used biblical drama as a tool of social control within his own family. He felt threatened by his three younger brothers, to whom his father had given territories in the west of Saxony that would otherwise have belonged to his patrimony, and his rivalry with his brother, August, was particularly intense. Johann Georg II made his brothers and their families sit through plays on the topic of Joseph and his brothers in 1665, 1669, 1671, 1672, and 1678. Each time the plays got longer and more vehement, taking up three evenings by the end, and each time they stressed the hatred of the envious brothers for the virtuous Joseph, their father's favorite son, and rejoiced in Joseph's ultimate triumph over their wicked wiles.

Jesuit drama played a correspondingly central role at Catholic courts and, at the two most important Catholic courts of Munich and Vienna, formed part of the celebrations on all important dynastic occasions. Andreas Brunner's (1589–1650) *Nabuchodonosor* (Nebuchadnezzar, 1635) for the Munich court illustrates how this worked in practice. It celebrates the wedding of Maximilian, elector of Bavaria (1573–1651), and Maria Anna (1610–65), the daughter of Emperor Ferdinand II, in a work that Ruprecht Wimmer has called a mixture of biblical tragedy, encomiastic drama, and mirror for princes.[43] The Jesuit dramatist Nicolaus Avancini (1611–86) created a kind of panegyric drama, the *ludus caesareus* (imperial play), for the Viennese court, in which figures from antiquity or the Bible are presented as prefigurations of Habsburg emperors, who appear as the Catholic saviors of Europe. *Curae Caesarum* (The Cares of the Emperors, 1644) does this with Theodosius; *Imperii Pax* (The Peace of the Empire, 1650) with Joseph, the mediator between Canaan and Egypt, who prefigures Ferdinand III's efforts to bring about the Peace of Westphalia; and *Pietas victrix* (Piety Victorious, 1659), which celebrates the election and coronation of Leopold I, with Emperor Constantine.

A very different kind of spoken drama was the professional theater of the Italian *commedia dell'arte* troupes and of the English strolling players (sometimes called the English Players). The first record of a *commedia dell'arte* performance in the empire is at the Munich court in 1568 for the wedding of Wilhelm, duke of Bavaria (1548–1626, r. 1579–97), and Renée, princess of Lorraine (1544–1602), and the English strolling players (*Englische Komödianten*) made some of their first appearances in the empire at the Dresden court in 1586.[44] These English players were often highly proficient professional actors and musicians who had already made a name for themselves on the London stage. They toured the important fairs from the Netherlands to the Baltic, but they usually spent the winters, when the roads were impassable, at court. Thomas Sackville and John Bradstreet from Robert Browne's troupe came to Wolfenbüttel to the court of Heinrich Julius, duke of Braunschweig (1564–1613) in 1592 and seem to have returned repeatedly over the next ten years. Heinrich Julius's own eleven dramas, in which he put across ideas that he was simultaneously enshrining in law, were greatly influenced by these actors. *Von Vincentio Ladislao* (Vicentius Ladislaus, 1594) presents a boastful humbug at court and is related to the Duke's Court Ordinance, the *Hofordnung* of 1589. His four plays about marriage (e.g., *Von einem Weibe* [A Wife, 1593]) relate to his laws against adultery of the same year, called the *Constitutio der Hurerey vnd Ehebruchs halber* (Regulations on Whoring and Adultery); his plays about a butcher (*Von einem Fleischhawer*) and an innkeeper (*Von einem Wirthe*), both from 1593–94, are related to other legislation he was promulgating. Moritz of Hesse-Kassel had English players in his service from 1594 to 1613, among whom in the early years was the composer John Dowland. Moritz erected a permanent theater, the Ottoneum, for the strolling players between 1604 and 1606. The text over the entrance stressed that the plays performed there would function as instruments of social control.

Strolling players were frequent visitors to Dresden, performing at court there in 1600, 1601, 1605, 1609, 1610, 1617, 1626–27, and 1630–32. John Spencer's company, which came to Dresden in 1609, may have stayed there for almost two years, and returned to perform for the visit of Emperor Matthias and his family in 1617. John Green's troupe, which spent the season of 1626–27 at Dresden, was brought to Torgau to perform at the wedding in 1627 of Sophie Eleonore of Saxony (1609–71), and Georg, landgrave of Hesse-Darmstadt (1605–61).

If these players made a wide range of Elizabethan and Jacobean plays known in German prose versions, it was Johannes Velten's (1640–92) troupe that introduced Molière to the German-speaking world, via the Dresden court, in the 1670s and 1680s. He was a much more highly educated kind of actor-manager, and from 1678 on his troupe was allowed to call itself the *Chursächsische Comödien-Bande* (Elector of Saxony's Players). In his repertoire were no fewer than ten Molière comedies, of which he presented eight for the first time in German translation.

Dramatists known chiefly today for their school dramas also wrote for a court audience. Andreas Gryphius (1616–64) is one such figure. His dramatic works for the Piast dynasty in Silesia show a skillful combination of translations from the French with original German material. His *Verlibtes Gespenste* (Ghost in Love) and *Die gelibte Dornrose* (The Beloved Briar Rose, 1660), a delightful double comedy, was composed for the wedding of Countess Palatine Elisabeth Maria Charlotte (1638–64) and Duke Georg III of Liegnitz and Brieg (1611–64, r. 1639–64) and was performed in Glogau on 10 October 1660. *Verlibtes Gespenste* is an elevated operatic work, or *Singspiel*,[45] based on Philippe Quinault's *Fantôme amoureux* (1658), while *Die gelibte Dornrose* is a dialect comedy. The message of the play is that the god of love rules the whole social pyramid, and this is underlined by the presence of the aristocratic bride and bridegroom as spectators of honor, watching the love intrigues of their inferiors on stage.

Much court spectacle had as its central function the glorification of the prince and the symbolic representation of his power. This is the point of Gryphius's festive tribute, *Majuma*, which he wrote for the coronation of Ferdinand IV as Roman king in June 1653 in Regensburg, Ferdinand having been elected in May 1653 in Augsburg. This short work, which was at least partly sung, rejoices that the Thirty Years' War is over and that love and nature can return to normal under Ferdinand's rule. *Piastus* was written in 1660 for Christian von Wohlau (1618–72) and his wife Luise von Anhalt-Dessau (1631–80) during the latter's pregnancy.[46] When the pregnancy had a happy outcome and an heir was born, Gryphius wrote *Der schwermende Schäfer* (The Raving Shepherd), a translation of Thomas Corneille's *Le Berger extravagant* (1653), for the first birthday of little Georg Wilhelm, duke of Liegnitz and Brieg (1660–75), in September 1661.

Daniel Casper von Lohenstein (1635–83), who represented the Silesian town of Breslau (Wrocław) at the Viennese court in 1675 and was ennobled by the Habsburgs, included tributes to the dynasty in his long, learned plays *Sophonisbe* (1669) and *Cleopatra* (1661; second version 1680) and wrote *Ibrahim Sultan* for the wedding of Emperor Leopold to his second wife Claudia Felicitas, archduchess of Austria, in 1673. It is instructive to see Lohenstein's works, whose central theme is so often the nature of governance and the importance of *prudentia* and reason for the good ruler, against the background of the political literature of his day. That he himself was *au fait* with the current debate can be seen in his translation in 1672 of Baltasar Gracián's *El Político D. Fernando el Católico* (1640) as *Staats-Kluger Catholischer Ferdinand* (The Clever Statesman, the Catholic Ferdinand, 1672), which he dedicated to the young Piast duke of Liegnitz and Brieg, Georg Wilhelm.

Opera

Opera is the quintessential court spectacle, for it demands vast resources in terms of staging and musical competence, thus bearing witness to the splendor of the court concerned.[47] Its artificiality fits well with the consciously regulated nature of all social interaction at court, while its mythological and pastoral plots provide a safe way to test and resolve politically and socially threatening situations.[48]

Italian opera in the shape of Monteverdi's *Orfeo* (1607) was first performed in the empire at the court of Prince Archbishop Marx Sittich von Hohenems in Salzburg in 1618 and again in Vienna in 1619 at the imperial court. In 1627 the first opera in German, Martin Opitz's (1597–1639) translation of the libretto of Rinuccini's *Dafne* with music (now lost) by Heinrich Schütz (1585–1672), was performed in 1627 at Torgau for the wedding of Sophie Eleonore of Saxony and Georg, landgrave of Hesse-Darmstadt, mentioned above. These were small beginnings, for Opitz and Schütz's *Dafne* is a small-scale pastoral entertainment. It was not until after the hiatus caused by the Thirty Years' War that opera meant grand Italian opera. The prominence of musical entertainments in general was given added impetus by the fact that the ruling princes in Vienna (Emperor Leopold I, r. 1658–1705), in Munich (Ferdinand Maria, elector of Bavaria (r. 1651–79), and in Dresden (Johann Georg II, elector of Saxony) were all proficient musicians themselves. Seventy-five operas were staged in Vienna between 1656 and 1700 and about fifty in Munich in the same period. The great courts hired not only Italian singers, instrumentalists, and set designers, but also *Kapellmeister*: Ercole Bernabei (1622–87) in Munich from 1674 to 1684, Antonio Draghi (1635–1700) in Vienna, and Giovanni Angelini Bontempi (ca. 1624–1705) in Dresden. The themes of the Italian operas they composed were in general taken from either mythology, ancient history, or the pastoral tradition. They usually illustrate the disorder wrought by the passions, which have to be controlled before the prince can govern well, and then glorify him as a latter-day Paris, Apollo, or Theseus. But these great courts were only the tip of the iceberg: Renate Brockpähler lists no fewer than fifty-one separate courts at which opera was performed during the seventeenth and early eighteenth centuries.[49]

Ballet de cour

This genre, invented at the French court in 1581, recreated the dance of antiquity and was intended to represent "cosmic harmony."[50] It combined music, dance, and text and could be performed in the theater, either on its own or as part of an opera or play, or in the Great Hall of a palace. It frequently presented plots that illustrated the theme of order and disorder in the state. The first ballet known to have been performed at a German court, *Die Befreiung des Friedens* (The Liberation of Peace), staged in 1600 in Darmstadt at the court of the landgrave of Hesse-Darmstadt, exemplifies this. It is clearly indebted to the *Balet comique de la royne* (The Queen's Comic Ballet), the first *ballet de cour* danced in Paris in 1581. Another court at which ballet flourished before the Thirty Years' War was Stuttgart. Ballets were staged there in 1609, 1616, 1617, and 1618. The last three of these were composed by Georg Rudolf Weckherlin, mentioned above, and he is thought to have had a hand in the first. Weckherlin had traveled in France and England, and his knowledge of the English masque and of the French ballet influenced the Stuttgart ballets. All these early ballets were danced by men.

From the 1620s, however, ballet became the form that court ladies — who frequently both danced in and arranged ballets — could call their own.

Eleonora Gonzaga (1598–1655), consort of Emperor Ferdinand II, brought ballet to Vienna in 1622, and the first performances of ballet in Dresden at around the same time are associated with Magdalena Sibylle of Brandenburg (1587–1659), the wife of Johann Georg I (1585–1656); from the 1650s on, Henriette Adelaide of Savoy (1636–76) and Elisabeth Dorothea of Saxony-Gotha (1640–76) played a central role in the development of ballet in Munich and in Darmstadt respectively. At Dresden too, the Saxon princesses participated actively. In 1655, for instance, the *Ballet der Glückseligkeit* (Ballet of Happiness) in honor of Johann Georg I was danced by Johann Georg II's wife — another Magdalena Sibylle, margravine of Brandenburg-Bayreuth (1612–87) — her sister-in-law Sophie Eleonore of Saxony, and five of the latter's seven daughters.

Professional dancing masters had always danced the more complicated steps, and ballet on stage tended to be more professional than ballet in the Great Hall. By the end of the century the move toward professionalization had developed further, as evidenced by August the Strong's engagement of a troupe of professional French dancers to perform for festivities in Dresden in 1699 and 1709.

Tournaments

Medieval tournament forms such as jousts (one-to-one combat on horseback with the lance) and tilts (jousting over a solid wooden barrier) were still practiced at the beginning of the seventeenth century but by about 1570 were being superseded by combats against inanimate objects.[51] These consisted of such exercises as the running at the ring and at the quintain, in which lances were used, and at the head, in which lances, swords, javelins, and even pistols were employed. In the foot tournament, groups of combatants did battle with pikes over a low barrier. These forms of contest trained and tested skills that were now needed on the battlefield as a consequence of new weaponry, new types of riding, and different breeds of horse.

Over time these tournaments or equestrian festivities began to acquire a theatrical framework. The participants wore elaborate costumes and, in the initial parade into the lists, which could take several days, each group was accompanied by a float representing a mythological or allegorical theme. This theatrical element was often used to promulgate a set of political ideas. Examples would include the tournaments of the Protestant Union, held at the courts of Stuttgart in 1609, 1616, 1617, and 1618; Jägerndorf in 1610; Heidelberg in 1613; Dessau in 1613 and 1615; and Halle in 1616.[52] Here members of the Union presented a specifically German and Protestant political iconography.

The ultimate in theatrical tournaments was the tournament opera, which came to Munich in 1654 from Italy. Here arias moved the action forward, which in turn motivated the tournament contests. Tournament opera was performed in Munich in 1658 and 1662, in Vienna in 1667, and in Dresden in 1719.

Courtly panegyric also formed an important part of equestrian festivals. In the equestrian ballet held in Vienna in 1667 for the wedding of Emperor

Leopold I and the Spanish infanta Margarita Teresa, for instance, the emperor rode at the center of a formation in which his courtiers radiated out from him like rays. In Munich in 1658 Ferdinand Maria of Bavaria and his brother appeared as the Sun and Moon respectively in the tournament opera known as *Applausi festivi* (Festive Acclamations), and in Dresden in 1678 Electoral Prince Johann Georg III (1647–91, r. 1680–91) was costumed as Sol and his uncle Moritz of Sachsen-Zeitz (1619–81) as Luna in one of the tournaments that formed part of the *Durchlauchtigste Zusammenkunft* (Most Noble Gathering).

Tournament Books and Festival Books

An extremely widespread and numerous textual genre that arises out of court spectacle was the festival book. It has its origins in the illuminated manuscript tournament books of the Middle Ages. Such works usually depict a series of encounters between two mounted and armored knights jousting or tilting, showing the combatants at the very moment when one unhorsed the other, and they continued to be produced long after the advent of printing. Emperor Maximilian I commissioned such a work from Hans Burgkmair the Elder (1453–1530), as did Johann the Constant of Saxony (1468–1533, r. 1525–33), whose book depicts tournaments in which he participated between 1487 and 1527.[53] The tournament book of his son, Johann Friedrich the Magnanimous (1503–54, r. 1532–47), dates to 1543 and depicts him in 146 jousts and tilts, while that of Wilhelm IV of Bavaria (1493–1550, r. 1508–50), dating to 1541, shows him in thirty-one tournaments.[54] In 1584 Elector August of Saxony (1526–86) commissioned a tournament book from his court painter Heinrich Göding, depicting him in fifty-five tournaments in which he took part between 1543 and 1566.[55] Karl Albrecht, elector of Bavaria (1697–1745, r. 1726–45, emperor from 1742), staged thirty tournaments and equestrian festivities at the Munich court between 1717 and 1734 and had them set down for posterity in 1734 in an illuminated vellum codex.[56]

Printed tournament books were in existence long before this. The *ThurnierBuch* (Tournament Book, 1530) by the herald Georg Rüxner, mentioned above under "Genealogy and Heraldry," is a compendium of thirty-six tournaments held in the empire between 938 and 1487. It was reprinted in 1532, 1566, 1570, 1578–79, and 1586, and an extract from it was inserted by Bartholomäus Clamorinus into his *Thurnirbüchlein* (Little Tournament Book, Dresden 1590). It presents the tournament as the defining activity of the knightly class, whose members are entitled to take part in tournaments because of their aristocratic blood. Hans Francolin's *Turnier Buech* (Tournament Book),[57] on the other hand, embellished with fourteen large woodcuts, describes the great tournament put on by Ferdinand I in 1560 in Vienna in honor of his son-in-law Albrecht V of Bavaria, and belongs to the genre of the printed festival book.

This new genre had its origins in the last decades of the fifteenth century but really only became established across Europe between 1510 and 1520,[58] principally thanks to Emperor Charles V. His entry into Bruges in 1515 as a young prince was recorded in Dutch in a printed account. His entry into

Aachen for his coronation as Roman king in 1519; into various Spanish cities in 1526; into Bologna and his double coronation there in 1530; after his coronation into Innsbruck, Munich, Augsburg, and Nuremberg; into Messina and Naples in 1535; into Rome, Florence, and Siena in 1536; into Nice in 1538; into Utrecht in 1540; and his progress through France in 1539 were all recorded in short, simple, printed chronicle-like accounts and widely disseminated. Usually the vernacular of the country in question was used, sometimes Latin, but often German.

Manuscript accounts of festivals continued to be produced, whether because they were more exclusive or because of local tradition. Right up to the eighteenth century the Dresden court recorded its festivals in large gouache paintings on sheets of paper, which were then bound together to form codices. At other courts, entries, tournament processions, and funeral cortèges were depicted on illuminated scrolls. In general, culturally ambitious courts realized that if their festivals were to become known outside their own territories, they would have to print accounts of them. The excellence of German woodcut artists and copper engravers meant that these accounts were sometimes much more lavishly illustrated than was common in other countries.

The wedding of Wilhelm V of Bavaria to Renée of Lorraine in 1568, for instance, was recorded in three separate printed festival books: Heinrich Wirre's *Ordenliche Beschreibung* (Careful Description)[59] containing forty-four woodcuts, Hans Wagner's *Kurtze doch gegründte beschreibung* (Short but Authentic Description)[60] with fourteen woodcuts, and the singer Massimo Troiano's dialogue *Discorsi delli trionfi, giostre, apparati* (Account of the Triumphs, Jousts, and Spectacles).[61] Wirre is still writing in the older tradition of what was called *Pritschmeisterdichtung*, a *Pritschmeister* being a kind of master of ceremonies whose name derived from his wooden clappers, or *Pritsche*, and who afterwards composed an account of the festival in rhyming doggerel. Such accounts were still being printed up to the early years of the seventeenth century.[62] Wenzel Sponrib's description of the entry of Archduke Karl and his bride Maria of Bavaria into Graz in 1571 was embellished with thirty-six woodcuts,[63] and Diederich Graminäus's account of the wedding of Wilhelm of Jülich, Cleve, and Berg to Jacobe of Baden in 1585 with thirty-seven.[64] In 1596 and 1600 Moritz the Learned, margrave of Hesse-Kassel, held two christening celebrations in Kassel and marked them with large-scale tournaments. They are recorded by Wilhelm Dilich (1571–1650) in accounts so lavishly illustrated that, as we turn the pages, we get the impression that we are seeing the festivity taking place before our eyes. As well as depictions of floats or particular scenes there is plate after plate representing each identical group of pages, grooms, or musicians, no matter how many times such a group has already appeared.

This then became the norm for the great series of Stuttgart festival books, which began in 1609 with the account of the wedding of Johann Friedrich, duke of Württemberg, and Barbara Sophia, margravine of Brandenburg. As discussed above, these festivals articulated the iconography of the Protestant Union in the tense decade before the Thirty Years' War. It was therefore essential that it be disseminated via the printed page. The main visual record came in a separate book of 214 plates by Balthasar Küchler (1571–1641).[65] In 1616 and 1617 two other similar volumes in the same format — oblong folio — were produced for other festivals in Stuttgart. The 1616 volume has seventy-seven plates, mostly by Matthäus Merian the Elder (1593–1650),[66] while the 1617 volume contains ninety-two plates.[67] These works were far in advance of those produced at any other contemporary European court in the lavishness and technical excellence of their illustrations.

Most festivals were recorded in simple, purportedly factual accounts without illustrations; occasionally German festival books used the actual description of the festival as a launching pad for a series of philosophical or moral reflections. Examples of this purely German phenomenon are Johann Oettinger's (1577–1633) account of the Stuttgart festival of 1609[68] and Gabriel Tzschimmer's (1629–94) account of the gathering of Johann Georg II of Saxony and his three younger brothers and their families in Dresden in 1678.[69] The actual account consists of 316 folio pages with thirty huge foldout plates depicting tournaments, hunts, processions, ballets, and theatrical scenes; the discursive second part consists of 562 pages in much smaller print.

Festival books purport to be a form of historiography, claiming in their very titles to be true and unadorned accounts.[70] But the chronicle-like quality of many of them should not lead us to treat them as reliable factual accounts. Their aim is to present the prince or the court that commissioned them in the most favorable light possible, and distortions of fact are therefore perfectly permissible; to explicate the political program of the festival and so provide the reader with a ready-made interpretation; and to constitute a monument to the festival that would mitigate its transience by recording it for posterity.

Panegyric Poetry

Modern readers are often baffled by panegyric, dismissing it as insincere flattery or empty phrase making. But the praise of the prince was a central branch of early modern (as of classical) rhetoric and presented the artist with one of his most important tasks. Since the prince was not regarded as an individual human being but as a representative figure, playing a vital role on earth within the divinely ordained system of the universe, praise of him was only one step below praise of God and just as much of a duty. Every conceivable event at court or in the lives of the princely family — births and christenings, engagements and marriages, convalescences and deaths, progresses and entries, coronations and acclamations, name days and birthdays, victories and state visits — was marked by a number, sometimes a very large number, of panegyric poems. These were an indispensable accompaniment to the event. This does not necessarily mean that the prince or his family read them. It was more likely that, after their formal presentation, they were placed in the court archive for posterity.[71] Their point was that they existed. It is no exaggeration to say that all early modern poets at some stage wrote panegyric verse, whether in praise of their own overlord, of a ruler they were hoping would be their patron, or to honor a visiting dignitary. So universal is this activity that it is pointless to single out any one poet. Panegyric verse grew in intensity and in quantity throughout the seventeenth and into the eighteenth century and could be written in the vernacular or in Latin.[72]

In the same way that there is a world of difference between the courtly portraiture of a Titian and that of a second-rate master, such verse can vary greatly in quality. The best examples are characterized by learning, graceful allusion to the event or person being celebrated, wit and inventiveness in the use of metaphors and conceits, and technical competence. Simon Dach's (1605–59) poems on the entry of Friedrich Wilhelm, elector of Brandenburg, into Königsberg in 1641, Gryphius's sonnet on the entry of Maria Henrietta, deposed queen of England, into Antwerp in 1644, or Johann Christian Günther's poem of fifty ten-line stanzas on the peace made in 1718 between the emperor and the Turks are some worthy examples.

Conclusion

The wide and ever-expanding range of activities and functions encompassed by the early modern court was reflected in and supported by the varied literary forms the court produces. Works of instruction for the prince, his ministers, courtiers, and servants were designed to develop the court as an institution and enable it to function better. Works of genealogy, heraldry, and historiography aimed to legitimate the prince's power, which was the *raison d'être* of the court in the first place. Theater and spectacle in their many forms as well as panegryric poetry displayed that power using rhetorical and artistic means.

Notes

[1] Ronald G. Asch and Adolf M Birke, eds., *Princes, Patronage and the Nobility: The Court at the Beginning of the Modern Age c. 1450–1650* (Oxford: Oxford UP, 1991); Volker Bauer, *Die höfische Gesellschaft in Deutschland von der Mitte des 17. bis zum Ausgang des 18. Jahrhunderts* (Tübingen: Niemeyer, 1993); Rainer A Müller, *Der Fürstenhof in der Frühen Neuzeit* (Munich: Oldenbourg, 1995); and John Adamson, ed., *The Princely Courts of Europe: Ritual, Politics and Culture Under the Ancien Régime 1500–1750* (London: Weidenfeld & Nicholson, 1999).

[2] Bauer, *Die höfische Gesellschaft*, 65. Figures for other courts are given by Müller, *Der Fürstenhof*, 30–31.

[3] Jan-Dirk Müller, "Der siegreiche Fürst im Entwurf der Gelehrten: Zu den Anfängen eines höfischen Humanismus in Heidelberg," in *Höfischer Humanismus*, ed. August Buck (Weinheim: VCH, 1989), 20 and 47.

[4] Alfred Noe, *Der Einfluß des italienischen Humanismus auf die deutsche Literatur vor 1600*, Sonderheft, Internationales Archiv für Sozialgeschichte der deutschen Literatur 5. (Tübingen: Niemeyer 1993).

[5] Roger Sablonier, "Rittertum, Adel und Kriegswesen im Spätmittelalter," in *Das ritterliche Turnier im Mittelalter: Beiträge zu einer vergleichenden Formen- und*

Verhaltensgeschichte des Rittertums, ed. Josef Fleckenstein (Göttingen: Vandenhoeck & Ruprecht, 1985), 542.

[6] Klaus Ley, "Castiglione und die Höflichkeit: Zur Rezeption des *Cortegiano* im deutschen Sprachraum vom 16. bis zum 18 Jahrhundert," in *Beiträge zur Aufnahme der italienischen und spanischen Literatur in Deutschland im 16. und 17. Jahrhundert*, ed. Alberto Martino, Chloe 9 (Amsterdam: Rodopi, 1990), 3–108.

[7] August Buck, "Baldassare Castigliones 'Libro del Cortegiano,'" in Buck, ed., *Höfischer Humanismus*, 5–16.

[8] *Hofman / Ein schon holdseldig Buch / in Welscher sprach der Cortegiano / oder zu Teutsch der Hofman genannt / Welches seinen ursprung und anfang / an dem Fürstlichen Hof zu Urbino empfangen / lustig zulesen / Etwa in Italiänischer Sprach durch Graf Balthasern Castiglion beschriben worden.* Nunmals in schlecht Teutsch / durch Laurentzen Kratzer Mautzaler zu Bruckhausen transferiert. Anno 65. Mit Rö. Kay. May. Freiheit nicht nach zetrucken (Munich, 1565).

[9] *Aulicus Balthasaris Castilionii; factus ex Italico sermone latinus.* Autore Hieronymo Turlero. Cum gratia & privilegio Caesareae Majestatis ad annos X. (Wittenberg, 1569).

[10] *Baldessaris Castilionii comitis ad Alphonsum Ariostum de Aulico libri IIII. Ioanne Riio Annoberense interprete* (Frankfurt, 1584).

[11] *Galateo* appeared first in *Rime e prose di Monsignor Giovanni Della Casa* (Venice, 1558). The first full edition appeared in Milan in 1559.

[12] *Io. Casæ V. Cl. Galateus. Seu de morum honestate & elegantia, liber ex Italico Latinus*, Interprete Nathane Chytræo (Rostock, 1578).

[13] *Ioannis Casae Galateus seu de morum honestate, et elegantia, liber ex italico latinus, interprete Nathane Chytraeo, cum eiusdem notis, nuper additis* (Frankfurt, 1597).

[14] *Galatheus oder von Erbarkeit, vndt Höfflikeit der Sitten. Erstlichen in Welscher sprach geschrieben vndt itzundt erst, mit sonderem fleis aus dem Welschen in unsere hochdeutsche sprach vertiret vndt gebracht.* Shelf number: SLUB Mscr.Dresd.M 222.

[15] See the discussion of princely alchemists in chapter IV of Helen Watanabe-O'Kelly, *Court Culture in Early Modern Dresden from Renaissance to Baroque* (Basingstoke: Palgrave Macmillan, 2002).

[16] Sara Smart, "On the diverse duties of the servants of princes: Lorenz Beger (1653–1705), librarian, antiquarian, and court poet in Heidelberg," *The Modern Language Review* 94 (1999): 1025–40.

[17] *David Schirmers Churfürstlichen Sächsischen Bibliothecarii Poetische Rosen-Gepüsche. Von Ihm selbsten aufs fleißigste übersehen / mit einem gantz neuen Buche vermehret und in allem verbesserten heraus gegeben* (Dresden, 1657). The subsequent volume's title reads: *David Schirmers Poetischer Rosen-Gepüsche Neues oder Ander Buch / Von Ihm selbsten herauß gegeben* (Dresden, 1657). A modern edition of this work is by Anthony J. Harper, ed., *Singende Rosen, oder, Liebes- und Tugend-Lieder 1654; Poetische Rose-Gepüsche 1657* (Tübingen: Niemeyer, 2003).

[18] *David Schirmers Churfürstlichen Sächsischen Bibliothecarii Poetische Rauten-Gepüsche in Sieben Büchern* (Dresden, 1663).

[19] Klaus Garber, "Sigmund von Birken," in *Literaturlexikon: Autoren und Werke deutscher Sprache*, ed. Walther Killy (Munich: Bertelsmann, 1998), 1:517.

[20] Kilian Heck and Bernhard Jahn, eds., *Genealogie als Denkform in Mittelalter und Früher Neuzeit* (Tübingen: Niemeyer, 2000).

[21] Ernst Brotuff, *Genealogia Und Chronica / des Durchlauchten Hochgebornen / Königlichen und Fürstlichen Hauses / der Fürsten zu Anhalt / Graffen zu Ballenstedt und Ascanie / Herrn zu Bernburgk und Zerbst / auff 1055. Jar. in sechs Büchern / mit viel schönen alten Historien / Geschichten / Königlichen und Fürstlichen Wopen* [sic!] *gezieret / und beschrieben*. Mit einer Vorrede Herrn Philippi Melanthon (Leipzig, 1556).

[22] Bernhard Jahn, "Genealogie und Kritik: Theologie und Philologie als Korrektive genealogischen Denkens in Cyriacus Spangenbergs historiographischen Werken," in Heck and Jahn, eds., *Genealogie als Denkform*, 69–85.

[23] Balthasar Mentz, *Genealogia und Geburts Linia / der Durchlauchtigsten Hochgebornen und in aller Welt berhümbten Hertzogen und Churfürsten zu Sachsen* (Wittenberg, 1594); *Stambuch und Kurtze Erzehlung Vom Ursprung und Hehrkommen der Chur unnd Fürstlichen Stämmen / Sachsen / Brandenburg / Anhalt und Lauenburg sampt etlichen derselben Bildnussen / wie sie im Schloß zu Wittenberg zu finden* (Wittenberg, 1597); and *Stambuch Dorinnen der Chur unnd Fürsten zu Sachsen Hochlöbliche / Ritterliche Thaten / Bildnüsse und Wapen [. . .] Und das der Keyser Thurnier und Cammergerichts zu Speyr / neben der Churfürsten zu Sachsen Hoffgerichts zu Wittenberg / wolbestalte ordnung / kurtz zusamen / unnd in druck gebracht* (Wittenberg, 1598).

[24] Johann Ulrich Pregitzer, *Teutscher Regierung- und Ehren-Spiegel vorbildend d. Teutschen Reichs, und desselben Staende, ersten Anfang, Fortleitung Hoheit, Macht, Recht, undFreyheit; [. . .] besonders des Hauses Hohenzollern, Ursprung, Wuerde, und Herrlichkeiten* (Berlin, 1703); and *Wirttembergisher Cedern-Baum Oder Vollständige Genealogie Des Hoch-Fürstlichen Hauses Wirttemberg In sechs Theilen, Aus denen besten und bewährtesten Authoribus und Genealogisten, documentis publicis [. . .]*, 2nd ed. (Stuttgart, 1734). This edition, begun by his father, Johann Ulrich Pregitzer the Elder, was augmented by Johann Ulrich the Younger and continued by his brother Johann Eberhard.

[25] Johann Wolfgang Trier, *Einleitung zur Wapen-Kunst, darinnen diese Wissenschaft durch deutliche Regeln und Exempel vorgetragen und die Wapen der gekrönten Häupter in Europa [. . .] erläutert werden [. . .]* (Leipzig, 1714).

[26] Georg Ruexner, *ThurnierBuch. Von Anfang, Ursachen, ursprung, und herkommen / Der Thurnier im heyligen Römischen Reich Teutscher Nation [. . .] Mit schönen neuwen Figuren / sonderlich auch der Adelichen Wappen / auffs schönest zugericht / und allen Adels-Personen der hochberühmtesten Teutscher nation / hohes und nidern Stands / zu ehren [. . .]*, 5th ed. (Frankfurt am Main, 1566). The first edition appeared in 1530 in Simmern, published by Johann II., Count Palatine of Pfalz-Simmern.

[27] Horst Wenzel, "Alls in ain summ zu pringen: Füetrers 'Bayerische Chronik' und sein 'Buch der Abenteuer' am Hof Albrechts IV.," in *Mittelalter-Rezeption: Ein Symposion*, ed. Peter Wapnewski (Stuttgart: Metzler, 1986), 10–31; Horst Wenzel, *Höfische Geschichte: Literarische Tradition und Gegenwartsdeutung in den volkssprachigen Chroniken des hohen und späten Mittelalters* (Bern: Lang, 1980).

[28] Maren Gottschalk, *Geschichtsschreibung im Umkreis Friedrichs I. des Siegreichen von der Pfalz und Albrechts IV. des Weisen von Bayern-München* (Munich: Fink, 1989), and Birgit Studt, *Fürstenhof und Geschichte: Legitimation durch Überlieferung* (Cologne: Böhlau, 1992).

[29] Jan-Dirk Müller, "Sprecher-Ich und Schreiber-Ich: Zu Peter Luders Panegyricus auf Friedrich d. S., der Chronik des Mathias von Kemnat und der Pfälzer Reimchronik des Michel Beheim," in *Wissen für den Hof: Der spätmittelalterliche Verschriftungsprozeß am*

Beispiel Heidelberg im 15. Jahrhundert, ed. Jan-Dirk Müller (Munich: Fink, 1994), 289–321.

[30] Gerald Strauss, *Historian of an Age of Crisis: The Life and Work of Johannes Aventinus 1477–1534* (Cambridge, MA: Harvard UP, 1963); Friedrich Merzbacher, "Aventin und das Recht," *Zeitschrift für bayerische Landesgeschichte* 40, Heft 2/3 (1977): 373–90.

[31] *Annales Boiorum / Joanne Aventino auctore. Acc. Rerum & verborum memorabilium index copiosus* (Ingolstadt, 1554); Johannes Aventini [. . .] *Chronica / Darinn nit allein deß gar alten Hauß Beyern / Keiser / Könige / Hertzogen / Fürsten / Graffen / Freyherrn Geschlechte / Herkommen / Stamm und Geschichte / sondern auch der vralten Teutschen Ursprung / herkommen / Sitten / Gebreuch / Religion / mannliche und trefliche Thaten / [. . .] zusammen getragen und in acht Bücher getheilt [. . .].* (Frankfurt am Main, 1566).

[32] Jan-Dirk Müller, *Gedechtnus: Literatur und Hofgesellschaft um Maximilian I.*, Forschungen zur Geschichte der älteren deutschen Literatur 2 (Munich: Fink, 1982).

[33] The famous chronicle of the noble family of Zimmern from Swabia, written probably by various family members in the sixteenth century, is the best-known example of this genre.

[34] Mathaeus Dresser, *Sächsisch Chronicon. Darinnen ordentlich begriffen die fürnembsten und denckwirdigsten Sachen, so von Anbeginn der Welt sich begeben, allermeist aber die in dem Römischen Reiche und Sachsen bis uff den Monat Majum 1596* (Wittenberg, 1596).

[35] Johann Carl Unckel, *Pfaltz / Sachsen / Brandenburg. Historische Beschreybung / dero dreyen Hochlöblichen / Weltlichen Churfürstlichen / Pfaltz / Sachsen / Brandenburg / Ankunfft / Geschlechten / Succession, Gemahlin / Kindern / Geschichten / Thaten / Leben / und endtlichen Absterben [. . .]* (Frankfurt, 1619).

[36] Bruno Singer, *Die Fürstenspiegel in Deutschland im Zeitalter des Humanismus und der Reformation* (Munich: Fink, 1980); Bruno Singer, "Fürstenspiegel," in *Theologische Realenzyklopädie*, ed. Gerhard Krause and Gerhard Müller (Berlin: de Gruyter, 1982), 11:707–11; Michael Philipp, "Regierungskunst im Zeitalter der konfessionellen Spaltung: Politische Lehren des mansfeldischen Kanzlers Georg Lauterbeck," in *Politische Tugendlehre und Regierungskunst: Studien zum Fürstenspiegel der Frühen Neuzeit*, ed. Hans-Otto Mühleisen and Theo Stammen (Tübingen: Niemeyer, 1990), 71–115.

[37] *Philippica in laudem et defensionem philippi comitis Rheni Palatini, Bavarie ducis* (Strasbourg, 1498).

[38] *Agatharchia. Id est bonus Principatus: vel Epithoma condicionum boni Principis* (Strasbourg, 1498).

[39] Wilhelm Kühlmann, "Edelmann — Höfling — Humanist: Zur Behandlung epochaler Rollenprobleme in Ulrich von Huttens Dialog 'Aula' und in seinem Brief an Willibald Pirckheimer," in August Buck, ed., *Höfischer Humanismus*, 161–82.

[40] Miloš Vec, *Zeremoniellwissenschaft im Fürstenstaat: Studien zur juristischen und politischen Theorie absolutistischer Herrschaftsrepräsentation* (Frankfurt am Main: Klostermann, 1998).

[41] For a general review of early modern German drama see in this volume the chapter by John Alexander.

[42] Watanabe-O'Kelly, *Court Culture in Dresden*, 26–34.

[43] Ruprecht Wimmer, "Le théâtre néo-latin en Europe," in *Spectaculum Europaeum: Theater and Spectacle in Europe (1580–1750): Histoire du Spectacle en Europe*

(1580–1750), ed. Pierre Béhar and Helen Watanabe-O'Kelly (Wiesbaden: Harrassowitz, 1999), 41.

44 Jerzy Limon, *Gentlemen of a Company: English Players in Central and Eastern Europe, 1590–1660* (Cambridge: Cambridge UP, 1985).

45 *Singspiel*: "A musico-dramatic work with a German text [. . .] in which spoken dialogue alternates with songs and sometimes with ensembles, choruses, or more extended musical pieces." Charlotte Greenspan, "Singspiel," in *The New Harvard Dictionary of Music*, ed. Don Michael Randel (Cambridge: Belknap Press of Harvard UP, 1986), 750.

46 It is not clear if it was ever performed, and Gryphius did not include it in the collected edition of his works published in 1663.

47 For a general overview of music in this period, including opera, see in this volume the chapter by Steven Saunders.

48 For a full discussion of opera as a genre see Werner Braun's article "Opera in the Empire" in Béhar and Watanabe-O'Kelly, eds., *Spectaculum Europaeum*, 437–70; also Manfred Brauneck, *Die Welt als Bühne* (Metzler: Stuttgart, 1996), 2:442–59.

49 Renate Brockpähler, *Handbuch zur Geschichte der Barockoper in Deutschland* (Emsdetten: Lechte, 1964). Though superseded in many details, this work is still a useful starting point.

50 For a detailed history of ballet at German-speaking courts see Sara Smart, "Ballet in the Empire," in Béhar and Watanabe-O'Kelly, eds., *Spectaculum Europaeum*, 547–70.

51 Helen Watanabe-O'Kelly, *Triumphall Shews: Tournaments at German-speaking Courts in their European Context 1580–1750* (Berlin: Gebr. Mann, 1992), and "Tournaments in the Empire," in Béhar and Watanabe-O'Kelly, eds., *Spectaculum Europaeum*, 598–603.

52 See the section "The Protestant Union" in *Europa Triumphans: Court and Civic Festivals in Early Modern Europe*, ed. J. R. Mulryne, Helen Watanabe-O'Kelly, and Margaret Shewring (London: Ashgate, 2004), 2:15–113, which contains extracts from these works with English translations.

53 The tournament book of Johann the Constant (Mscr. Dresd. J16) still exists though badly damaged in the Sächsische Landesbibliothek — Staats- und Universitätsbibliothek (hereafter: SLUB) in Dresden. Some of the illustrations are reprinted in Erich Haenel, *Der sächsischen Kurfürsten Turnierbücher* (Frankfurt am Main: Keller, 1910).

54 Hans Schenckh, *Das Turnierbuch Wilhelms IV. Von Bayern.* (Illustriert von Hans Ostendorfer). 1541 (cgm 2800 Bayerische Staatsbibliothek, Munich).

55 Heinrich Göding, *Vorzeichnus vnd warhafftige eigentliche Contrafacturen aller Scharff rennen vnd Treffen, so der Durchlauchtigste hochgeborne Fürst vnd Herr Herr Augustus Hertzog zu Sachßen etc. vor vnnd inn S. Churf. G. Churfürstlichen Regierung mitt sonderlicher geschicklichkeit auch großer Lust vnnd verwunderung aller Zuseher gantz Ritterlich vnd rühmlich gethan vnd verbracht hat [. . .].* In the SLUB Dresden: Mscr.Dresd. J 44.

56 Das Turnierbuch Karl Albrechts von Württenberg, Bayr. Staatsbibliothek, cgm 8009a.

57 Hans von Francolin, *Thurnier Buech Warhafftiger Ritterlicher Thaten / so in dem Monat Junij des vergangnen LX. Jars in vnd ausserhalb der Statt Wienn zu Roß vnd zu Fueß / auff Wasser vnd Lannd gehalten worden / mit schönen figuren contrafeit / vnd [. . .] durch Hannsen von Francolin Burgunder / Hochstgedachter Rö: Kay:Mayt: &c. Ernholden &c. zu Ehren beschriben* (Vienna, 1561).

[58] Helen Watanabe-O'Kelly and Anne Simon, *Festivals and Ceremonies: A Bibliography of Printed Works relating to Court, Civic and Religious Festivals in Europe 1500–1800* (London: Mansell, 2000).

[59] Heinrich Wirre, *Ordenliche Beschreybung der Fürstlichen Hochzeyt / die da gehalten ist worden / durch den Durchleüchtigen Hochgebornen Fürsten und Herrn / Herrn Wilehlm Pfalzgraf beim Reyn [. . .] Mit dem Hochgebornen Fräwlin Renata / geborne Hertzogin auß Luttringen / den 21. Tag Februarij / des 1568. Jars / in der Fürstlichen Statt München [. . .]* (Augsburg, 1568).

[60] Hans Wagner, *Kurtze doch gegründte beschreibung des Durchleuchtigen Hochgebornnen Fürsten vnnd Herren / Herren Wilhalmen / Pfaltzgrauen bey Rhein [. . .] Und derselben geliebsten Gemahel / der Durchleuchtigisten Hochgebornnen Fürstin / Frewlein Renata gebornne Hertzogin zu Lottringen vnd Pari / &c. gehalten Hochzeitlichen Ehren Fests [. . .] Und dann was für Herrliche Ritterspil / zu Roß vnd Fueß / mit Thurnieren / Rennen vnd Stechen [. . .] in der Fürstlichen Haubtstat München gehalten worden sein / den zwenvndzwaintzigisten vnd nachuolgende tag Februarij. / Im 1568. Jar* (Munich, 1568).

[61] Massimo Troiano, *Discorsi delli trionfi, giostre, apparati, é delle cose piu notabile fatte nelle sontuose Nozze, dell'Illustrißimo & Eccellentißimo Signor Duca Guglielmo. Primo genito del generossissimo Alberto Quinto, Conte Palatino Del Reno, e Duca della Bauiera alta e Baßa, nell' Anno 1568, à 22. Di Febraro* (Munich, 1568).

[62] For instance, Jakob Frischlin, *Drey schöne vnd lustige Bücher / von der Hohen Zollerischen Hochzeyt / welcher gestalt: Der Hoch vnd- Wolgeborne Herr / Herr Eytel Friderich / Graffe zu Hohen Zollern [. . .] Gnaden geliebten Son / Herrn Johann Georgen Graffen zu Zollern / etc. Hochzeyt gehalten hab / mit dem Hoch vnd Wolgebornen Fräwlin / Fräwlin Francisca. Des [. . .] Herrn Friderichs Wild Graffens zu Dhaum vnd kürburg [. . .] geliebten Tochtern: Wie die gantze hochzeyt zu Hechingen den 11. Octobris Anno 1598. gehalten worden* (Augsburg, 1599).

[63] Wenzel Sponrib, *Wahrhaffte Beschreibung / was vor der Fürstl: Durchleucht Ertzherzogen Carls zu Osterreich etc. Hochzeitlichen haimfuerung in der Hauptstadt Grätz in Steyer vom 17 August biß auff den 8 September / von Porten vnd andern Triumphirenden zierligkhaiten zuegerichtet* (Graz, 1572).

[64] Diederich Graminäus, *Fvrstliche Hochzeit So der Durchluchtig hochgeborner Furst vnd Herr, herr Wilhelm Hertzog zu Gulich Cleue vnd Berg [. . .] dem Durchleuchtig hochgebornen Fursten vnd hern, hern Johann Wilhelm Hertzogn zu Gulich etc hochermelten Ihrer F. G. geliebten Sohn Vnd der Durchleuchtigen Furstinen Frewlin Jacobae gebornen Marggraffinen zu Baden etc. In Ihrer F. G. Statt Dußeldorff gehalttenn* (Cologne, 1587).

[65] Balthasar Küchler, *Repraesentatio der fürstlichen Auffzug und Ritterspil. So bei des Durchleuchtigen Hochgebornen Fürsten und Herren Herrn Johann Friderichen Hertzogen zu Württemberg und Techk [. . .] Und der Durchleuchtigen Hochgebornen Fürstin und Freülin Frewlin Barbara Sophien geborne Marggravin zu Brandenburgi Hochzeitlich. Ehrenfest den 6. Nouemb. A° 1609. In der Fürstl. Hauptstat Stutgarten mit grosser Solennitet gehalten worden* (Schwäbisch-Gmund, 1611).

[66] Georg Rudolf Weckherlin, *Triumf Newlich bey der F. Kindtauf zu Stutgart gehalten* and *Triumphall Shews set forth lately at Stutgart* (Stuttgart, 1616); Esias von Hulsen and Matthaeus Merian, *Repraesentatio der Furstlichen Aufzug und Ritterspil, So [. . .] Herr Johan Friderich Hertzog zu Württemberg und Teckh [. . .] bey Ihr. F. G. neüwgebornen Sohn, Friderich Hertzog zu Württemberg, etc. fürstlicher Kindtauffen, denn 10. Biss auff den 17. Martij, Anno 1616. Inn Stuetgarten, mit grosser solennitet gehalten.*

⁶⁷ Esaias von Hulsen, *Aigentliche Wahrhaffte Delineatio unnd Abbildung aller Fürstlichen Auffzüg und Rütterspilen. Beÿ Deß Durchleüchtigen Hochgebornen Fürsten unnd Herren, Herren Johann Friderichen Hertzogen zu Württemberg unnd Teck [. . .] Jungen Printzen und Sohns Hertzog Ulrichen wohlangestellter Fürstlichen Kindtauff: und dann beÿ Hochermelt [. . .] Bruoders [. . .] Herrn Ludwigen Friderichen Hertzogen zu Württemberg etc. mit [. . .] Fraw Magdalena Elisabeth Landtgräffin auss Hessen etc. [. . .] Fürstlichem Beylager und Hochzeÿtlichem Frewdenfest Celebrirt und gehalten, In der Fürstlichen Hauptstatt Stuetgartt Den 13.14.15.16. unnd 17. Julÿ Anno 1617* (Stuttgart, 1617), and the account is by Weckherlin again, entitled *Kurtze Beschreibung / Dess zu Stutgarten / bey den Fürstlichen Kindtauf und Hochzeit / Jüngst / gehaltenen Frewden-Fests* (Tübingen, 1618).

⁶⁸ Johann Oettinger, *Warhaffte Historische Beschreibung Der Fürstlichen Hochzeit / und deß Hochansehnlichen Beylagers So Der Durchleuchtig Hochgeborn Fürst vnnd Herr / Herr Johann Friderich Hertzog zu Würtemberg vnd Teck [. . .] mit Der auch Durchleuchtigen Hochgebornen Fürstin vnnd Frewlin / Frewlin Barbara Sophia Marggrävin zu Brandenburg [. . .] In der Fürstlichen Haubtstatt Stuttgardten Anno 1609. den 6. Novembris vnd etliche hernach volgende Tag Celebriert vnd gehalten hat* (Stuttgart, 1610).

⁶⁹ Gabriel Tzschimmer, *Die Durchlauchtigste Zusammenkunft / Oder: Historische Erzehlung / was der Durchlauchtigste Fürst und Herr / Herr Johann George der Ander [. . .] Bey Anwesenheit Seiner [. . .] Herren Gebrüdere / dero Gemahlinnen / Prinzen / und Princessinnen / zu sonderbahren Ehren / und Belustigung / in Dero Residenz und Haubt-Vestung Dresden im Monat Februario, des M.DC.LXXVIIIsten Jahres An allerhand Aufzügen / Ritterlichen Exercitien, Schau-Spielen / Schiessen / Jagten / Operen, Comoedien, Balleten, Masqueraden, Königreiche / Feuerwercke / und andern / Denkwürdiges aufführen und vorstellen lassen* (Nuremberg, 1680).

⁷⁰ For a more detailed discussion of the genre of the festival book see Helen Watanabe-O'Kelly, "Early Modern European Festivals — Politics and Performance, Event and Record," in *Court Festivals of the European Renaissance: Art, Politics and Performance*, ed. J. R. Mulryne and Elizabeth Goldring (Aldershot: Ashgate, 2002), 15–25, and "The Early Modern Festival Book — Function and Form," in Mulryne, Watanabe-O'Kelly, and Shewring, eds., *Europa Triumphans*, 1: 3–17.

⁷¹ Kestin Heldt, *Der vollkommene Regent: Studies zur panegyrischen Casuallyrik am Beispiel des Dresdner Hofes Augusts des Starken* (Tübingen: Niemeyer, 1997), 14.

⁷² Wilhelm Kühlmann treats panegyric poetry in its Neo-Latin tradition in this volume in "Neo-Latin Literature in Early Modern Germany."

Discant (soprano) part of the funeral composition,
"O Gott, du liebster Vatter mein" (1620) by Andreas Rauch.

Music in Early Modern Germany

Steven Saunders

M USIC IN EARLY MODERN GERMANY RESOUNDED from courtyards, city walls, and village squares and was heard in church, chapel, chamber, and theater. It accompanied activities as diverse as coronations, banquets, weddings, funerals, tournaments, military campaigns, theatrical productions, hunting expeditions, school instruction, dancing, social singing, and public and private religious observances. Music served as entertainment, liturgical and devotional aid, educational tool, and instrument of political representation, and its sonic patterns conveyed messages concerning social standing, confessional creed, and political allegiance. Music and the literary texts that it made audible formed more than a sonic backdrop to daily activity; they gave voice to — indeed shaped — many of the ideals and aspirations of early modern life.

Defining Early Modern Germany Musically

The autonomy that characterized territories within the Holy Roman Empire contributed to an oft-remarked cultural fragmentation that has militated against viewing early modern German music as a whole. The social and institutional bases for music and music making at the secular courts, with their need for grandeur and public representation, were quite different from those in the *Reichsstädte* (imperial cities), for example, and these, in turn, diverged from the requirements at centers ruled by ecclesiastics. Moreover, the Reformation led to two distinct, if often overlapping, traditions of sacred composition. Such diversity created musical genres that were less quintessentially German than courtly (Italian opera, madrigal, chamber duet), civic (*Meistergesang,* continuo lied), or Protestant (chorale-based composition).

 Dynastic intermarriage, the itinerant character of secular courts, and shifting political allegiances likewise ensured that composers, performers, and music from France, Flanders, Italy, England, and Central Europe were dispersed throughout Germany. Art music in early modern Germany was often in a language other than German and frequently composed or performed by imported musicians. Thus Orlando de Lassus (1532–94), the Dutch *Kapellmeister*, or chapel master, at the Bavarian court, arguably the most influential "German" composer of the sixteenth-century, published works with texts in French, Italian, and Latin, turning to German compositions only late in his career.

During the fifteenth and sixteenth centuries, in fact, the most highly sought musicians at German courts came from northern France and the Low Countries. This predilection for Netherlandic composers is seen most strikingly at the courts of the Habsburg emperors, whose chapels provided a model for other German rulers throughout much of the era: prominent Habsburg musicians of the early modern era included Heinrich Isaac, Arnold von Bruck, Pieter Maessens, Jean Guyot, Jacobus Vaet, Philippe de Monte, Carl Luython, Jacobus de Kerle, and Lambert de Sayve. The pattern was followed belatedly elsewhere, for example at the courts at Graz (Johannes de Cleve), Munich (Lassus), and Dresden (Matthaeus Le Maistre and Rogier Michael). By the seventeenth century, tastes had shifted, but the predilection for imported music remained strong; much German music after 1650 was based on styles or genres whose musical and linguistic roots were Italian.

Traditional disciplinary fault lines within musicology — sacred/secular, vocal/instrumental, Catholic/Protestant, courtly/civic — have further conspired to discourage a unified view of German music of the early modern period. German music historiography, moreover, has a strong tradition of favoring local and regional histories over national ones. Revealingly, the bibliography under "Art music" for Germany in the standard English-language reference work in music history, *The New Grove Dictionary of Music and Musicians*, lists only three works under the heading "Germany — General": two books devoted exclusively to the nineteenth century, and a third on the eighteenth.[1]

Early modern Germany's cultural diversity and its reliance on imported musical models have spawned two related tropes. Germany is characterized as participating, albeit belatedly, in a European mainstream whose artistic roots lay elsewhere, and also conversely as harboring a handful of unique but implicitly peripheral musical traditions.[2] The major figures of sixteenth-century music in Germany — Heinrich Isaac (ca. 1450–1517), Ludwig Senfl (ca. 1486–1542/43), and Orlando de Lassus — were not German-born, and the native composers who dominate the historiography of German music in the seventeenth and eighteenth centuries — Heinrich Schütz (1585–1672), Dieterich Buxtehude (1637–1707), and even Johann Sebastian Bach (1685–1750) — are typically seen as forging a distinctly German art through the synthesis of indigenous and foreign elements. Even in the eighteenth century the composer and theorist Johann Joachim Quantz (1697–1773) claimed that Germans had not developed a true national style but rather, "wissen sich das Gute von allen Arten der ausländischen Musik zu Nutzen zu machen" (know how to make use of the good things in all types of foreign music).[3]

If the concept of a unified Germany remains problematic musically, so too is the notion of an early modern period for music. Music historians, particularly those working on German music, have been slow to embrace the idea of an early modern era, adhering instead to a historiographic tradition, derived from August Wilhelm Ambros's influential *Geschichte der Musik* (History of Music, 1862–82), that sees pronounced cultural and stylistic divides between medieval, Renaissance, and Baroque.[4] The traditional boundaries have been challenged recently by a number of scholars, notably Reinhard Strohm in his magisterial *Rise of European Music, 1380–1500*, which views the fifteenth century as an independent period, whose links to the late Middle Ages are as strong as those to later epochs.[5] Nonetheless, the time-honored divisions between stylistic periods have proven remarkably durable, particularly because music's supposed autonomy and lack of obvious signification was, until recently, taken for granted; under such a view, music history tended to chronicle changes in compositional practice rather than engage broader issues of cultural or intellectual history.

The following survey begins with a view of the institutional and social contexts for music, and continues with overviews of the major genres of German-texted music both secular and sacred. Chronological coverage reaches from the establishment of polyphonic composition in Germany in the late fifteenth century to the full adoption of Italian seventeenth-century vocal idioms in the last years of the century, a development that even contemporary writers noted;[6] Quantz, for example, did not hesitate to assign a precise year, 1693, to this change.[7]

Institutional and Social Contexts

The earliest manuscripts containing German polyphony evince features that would characterize most repertoires throughout the early modern period: the music was international, much of it originating outside Germany from a variety of institutional contexts, including court, monastery, university, and cathedral. The so-called St. Emmeram Codex, for example,[8] preserves works by English and continental composers of the early fifteenth century, alongside a few works of German and Bohemian origin.[9] The codex not only contains compositions from academic circles at the University of Vienna, where its owner, Hermann Pötzinger, was active, but also transmits music from the chapels of rulers who attended the Council of Basel (1431–49).

Such diversity mirrored the varied needs of the institutions for which music was created. We are least well informed about music in the universities. Instruction naturally stressed music's traditional role as a speculative discipline within the *quadrivium,* yet teachers at many German universities were also composers or choirmasters with firsthand knowledge of *musica practica.* At Cologne, for example, there was required study of "music in two parts" as early as 1398;[10] and many universities were linked administratively to a cathedral choir school, or *Kantorei.* Increasingly after the middle of the sixteenth century, the study of mathematically based *musica speculativa* was supplanted by the study of music as a liberal art, including instruction in notation, the modes, and the rudiments of composition. There was thus an early German theoretical tradition that combined the study of practical music making, particularly polyphonic composition, with the mathematical and cosmological view of music. The tendency among German musicians to retain the quadrivial conception of music, however, was remarkably strong. Even in the mid-seventeenth century, when music treatises typically contained practical advice on notation and performance (and when very few major musical figures held a university degree), Athanasius Kircher's (1602–80) monumental *Musurgia universalis* (1650) remained steeped in the medieval notion of music as a manifestation of God's order expressed through number.[11]

In stark contrast to other parts of Europe, Germany's cathedrals played a relatively modest role in musical life after the late Middle Ages. Following the Reformation many cathedrals in Protestant centers became civic institutions under the administrative control of the cities, and these often had impressive musical establishments. In Catholic areas, however, a nearby court often usurped the cathedral's role of principal artistic patron, while in some cities the cathedral's centrality was reduced because its bishop spent relatively little time in residence. Moreover, clerics who provided music, usually plainchant (the monophonic, unison chant of liturgies), in the cathedrals enjoyed relatively low status. All these factors conspired to reduce the role of the cathedrals, so that there was virtually no development of liturgical polyphony, even on major feast days, in most cathedral churches.[12]

In general the secular courts maintained the largest, most cosmopolitan musical establishments and cultivated the most adventurous musical styles. As the sixteenth century progressed, *Hofmusik-Kapellen* (court music chapels) gradually shed their traditional character as "chapels," whose principal duty was to provide music for the liturgy. Administration of the chapels passed from clerics to *Hofkapellmeister* (court chapel masters), whose qualifications were principally musical. By the seventeenth century a music chapel might include chamber musicians who had little role in sacred music making, as well as Italian *virtuosi*, including women singers, whose primary role was to perform at court festivities such as tournaments, ballets, and operas. Indeed, court music making became increasingly public over the course of the early modern period, centering less on the chapel interior and more on princely chambers, banquet halls, and even outdoor stages, eventually providing a kind of *klingende Architektur* (sounding architecture) of the monarchy.[13] The increasing secularization of courtly chapels can also be read in the higher incidence of musically competent rulers; the Habsburg emperors Ferdinand III and Leopold I and Landgraf Moritz der Gelehrte (the Learned) of Hesse-Kassel, for example, were all composers of some accomplishment.

In contrast to the court's centralized model, the musical topography at urban centers was more complex; nevertheless, the tendency toward specialization and professionalization mirrored trends at court. In many towns the responsibility for preparing sacred music passed from the local *Schulmeister* (schoolmaster) or rector to a trained *Kantor*, or *regens chori* (choir director) — a shift that mirrored the growing importance of complex figural music. The duties of the Kantor, however, still included training boy singers and usually teaching music (and often other subjects) in the local schools. Later, particularly in larger cities, a slightly different model evolved, that of the more autonomous civic Kapellmeister, or *director musices*, whose role in academic instruction was secondary to his duties as the chief civic musician. Vestiges of the older system survived, however; J. S. Bach and Georg Philipp Telemann (1681–1767) were both nominally in charge of Latin instruction in Leipzig, though they were allowed to hire a stand-in for these duties. Many of Bach's disputes with his employers were provoked, in fact, by tensions between these two models; factions on the Leipzig town council that preferred a virtuoso or composer along the lines of a typical *director musices* often squared off against civic-oriented councilors who preferred a more traditional Kantor.[14]

A typical *director musices* provided music for both religious and civic functions, often engaging smaller ensembles of professional players drawn from the ranks of the *Stadtmusiker* (town musicians) or *Ratmusiker* (council musicians). These civic musicians were the latter-day successors to the *Türmer* (tower watchmen), who typically marked the hours with fanfares, popular tunes, and eventually with more complex compositions. The town musicians were usually organized as trade guilds and participated in civic celebrations such as processions and entries into the town, often augmenting their income by playing at private entertainments or in the churches. Particularly in the seventeenth century the organists at important churches became figures of some consequence, often contributing to the burgeoning repertoire of solo music for the instrument and serving as mediators between civic and church authorities. Buxtehude in Lübeck, Matthias Weckmann (ca. 1616–74) in Hamburg, and Johann Pachelbel (1653–1706) in Erfurt and Nuremberg provide examples of such influential composer-organists.

Many towns also had ensembles made up of students, amateurs, and in some cases professionals, who met to perform vocal, chamber, and instrumental music. Nuremberg's fabled *Meistersinger*, for example, were closely tied to the trade guilds and specialized in improvised monophonic song of sacred or moral character; the patrician Kränzleingesellschaft (Society of the Garland) of the same city, in contrast, resembled an artistic academy, even commissioning musical works on occasion.[15] Still more professional were the *collegia musica*, groups of university students, professional musicians, and talented amateurs who often performed under the leadership of a town's most prominent composer. The seventeenth-century Hamburg collegium, for example, founded by Weckmann, had fifty members and became renowned for performances at leading musical centers of Europe, including Venice, Rome, and Vienna. The composer-critic Johann Mattheson (1681–1764) claimed that famous composers actively sought to have their works associated with the Hamburg collegium. Leipzig, too, had a number of such collegia, and its leaders read like an honor roll of seventeenth- and eighteenth-century German musicians: Adam Krieger (1634–66), Johann Rosenmüller (1619–84), Sebastian Knüpfer (1633–76), Johann Kuhnau (1660–1722), Telemann, and Bach.

In addition to such institutions, early modern German cities supported lively cultures of popular music. Dance music and popular song have received scant attention from musicologists, since much of the transmission was oral and most of the music was written for a single line and was thus structurally unpretentious. Yet popular song was an important constituent of the early modern mass media, transmitting news, spiritual edification, moral instruction, political propaganda, and popular entertainment.[16] Moreover, boundaries between high and low culture were quite permeable. Court composers such as Isaac and Senfl prepared refined polyphonic settings of folk songs, while conversely, songs from the oral tradition passed into the chorale repertoire of the early Lutheran church.

The institution of music printing also had profound effects on the preservation and transmission of music, producing effects analogous to those for the printed book. Prints of polyphonic compositions ensured that works were circulated more widely, rapidly, and economically than before, gave composers at least a modicum of control over the form in which their works circulated, and allowed musical styles to spread more rapidly. Yet music's print culture was in other respects quite different from the culture of the printed word, owing to the technical demands of music typography, the divergent requirements of various repertories and institutions, the extent of musical literacy, and economic factors.

Although music printing from woodcuts began in Germany as early as the 1470s, it was not until the first two decades of the sixteenth century — when Erhard Oeglin (d. 1520) and Peter Schöffer the Younger (1475/80–1547) pioneered multiple-impression typography (one impression for the staff lines, additional impressions for notes and text) — that the publication of polyphony became economically viable. Music printing was widespread: over a thousand music printers from over 200 German cities issued music prints during the sixteenth and seventeenth centuries.[17] Nuremberg established itself as the center for music publishing in the sixteenth century and became home to prominent music printers such as Hieronymus Formschneider (d. 1556), Johann Petreius (1497–1550), Johann Berg (ca. 1500–1563), and Ulrich Neuber (d. 1571).

Nevertheless, much of the publishing activity in German focused on hymnals and other liturgical collections destined for local markets.[18] In fact, the output of the major German publishers represented only a small fraction of the music that circulated in Germany. Manuscripts remained the fundamental source of transmission for many types of music, including large-scale works, most instrumental music, and, in the seventeenth century, dramatic genres such as cantata, opera, and oratorio. Music printing reached its peak before the turn of the seventeenth century and declined significantly in the wake of the Thirty Years' War (1618–48). Manuscript transmission, on the other hand, retained an important place in musical commerce into the early nineteenth century.

Another constraint on the impact of Germany's music printers was foreign competition. Latin church music and Italian secular song were widely available in economical editions from Venice and Antwerp, cities whose output of music dwarfed that of the German centers. Surviving inventories from the late sixteenth and seventeenth centuries suggest that imported music prints far out-numbered indigenous ones at many centers, particularly in southern Germany. Even collections printed in Germany often contained a high percentage of works that had first been published elsewhere.

The repertories that predominated in Germany's music print culture were distinctly limited, favoring genres that lent themselves to publication in the economical partbook format, in which the parts for each individual voice or instrument were written out, usually by hand, but also sometimes published together in separate octavo-size volumes.[19] Small-scale vocal music was the most common type of music transmitted in print; collections of psalms and motets and, in the secular realm, the polyphonic *lied* (song), were particularly favored. The predominance of partbook printing created another signal differ-ence between the transmission of music and the transmission of the printed word. Most published genres (with the exception of the occasional lute or key-board intabulation[20]) were of little use to a single "reader"; polyphonic music, by its nature, required realization by a group in performance. Thus the market for music prints was, in the broadest sense, institutional and not directed toward a public consisting of individual readers.

Secular Song I: Tenor Lied

German lyric verse and monophonic song in the later Middle Ages were inter-twined, for poetic recitation implied singing. Some of the earliest polyphonic settings of German texts are linked to prominent literary figures, notably the Monk of Salzburg (ca. 1350–75) and Oswald von Wolkenstein (1376–1445). Attributions of music to significant authors, however, are the exception rather than the rule; most polyphonic pieces in German from the later Middle Ages were anonymous, and attributions, when they appear, can be misleading. Many German-texted works attributed to Oswald, for example, were mere rework-ings of French chansons or Italian *ballatas*.[21]

Only in the second half of the fifteenth century did German lyric verse begin to be set polyphonically with some frequency; yet German sources were still dominated by Latin sacred music and French song. Even within the German-speaking regions of the empire German-texted music constituted a distinctly secondary repertoire — manuscript "filler" as one scholar has described it.[22] Nonetheless, by the second half of the fifteenth century the practice of setting German poetry to music for more than one voice had coalesced into a distinct tradition. This genre, the so-called tenor lied, would eventually com-prise some 1,300 compositions, many of them elaborations of a core repertoire of well-known melodies, making it the prototypical song type in Germany between 1450 and 1550. The sources for the tenor lied are fascinating both on musical grounds and as documents of social and intellectual history, for they illuminate the conditions surrounding the creation, transmission, and consumption of music in Germany.

The tenor lied — the term is of modern coinage, as most contemporary sources used designations such as *teutsches Lied* or *Liedlein* (German song) — seems at first glance to have emerged fully formed in a series of seminal anthologies from the early years of German music printing; yet earlier manuscript sources, including the Lochamer and Schedel songbooks, provide tantalizing if fragmentary evidence about the emergence of this song type.[23] Most of the two- and three-voice German songs from the Lochamer songbook, copied at Nuremberg between 1452 and 1460, are musically unassuming; their frequent inclusion of a voice that mirrors the melody in parallel motion (a feature that persists in later examples of the tenor lied) suggests written-out versions of an improvised practice, or *Übersingen*, a practice in which performers added a line in parallel motion to an existing tune.[24] Nonetheless, the three-voice pieces anticipated the typical disposition of parts found in the later four-voice tenor lied: a principal melody in a middle voice framed by more florid outer parts.

The Schedel songbook, assembled mainly in the 1460s, shows the mixture of Latin sacred works along with French and Italian song common to German manuscripts of the fifteenth century. Some German songs with the melody in the top voice (a typical arrangement in the chanson) are musically nearly indistinguishable from the chansons in the collection; yet other settings exhibit features that came to identify the mature tenor lied, including a melody in a middle voice surrounded by somewhat more elaborate lines, and texts cast in bar forms (AAB) that hark back to the courtly tradition of *Minnesang* (literally "love song," courtly song of the twelfth to fourteenth centuries). Although most pieces in the Schedel songbook are musically unpretentious, the handling of the vocal writing is generally polished, without the coarse voice leading found at times in the Lochamer songbook.[25] The early sources for German polyphonic song, then, suggest that early polyphonic lieder drew on numerous traditions, including courtly monophonic song of the later Middle Ages and its poetic traditions, French chanson, and indigenous traditions of vocal improvisation.

The form of the tenor lied in the early sixteenth century was captured, indeed crystallized, in a trio of printed collections from the second decade: the anthologies of Oeglin (Augsburg, 1512), Schöffer the Younger (Mainz, 1513), and Arnt von Aich (Cologne, 1519). Each print transmits works from a different circle: Oeglin's from the imperial *Hofkapelle* of Maximilian I, Schöffer's from the music chapel of Duke Ulrich of Württemberg, and that of von Aich (d. ca. 1528) from the chapel of the Augsburg bishop Friedrich II of Zollern.[26] Many of the works are by minor figures, but two of the major composers of this generation, Heinrich Isaac and Paul Hofhaimer (1459–1537), are represented in volumes of all three publishers.

The essential features of the genre are encapsulated neatly in a short setting by Hofhaimer of "Mein's trawrens ist," first published by Schöffer, and frequently reprinted.[27] Texts typically contain three or more verses set strophically (having the same music for each verse of text). Individual verses are cast in the tripartite form that had characterized much German poetry since the

Middle Ages: two paired *Stollen* (combining to form the *Aufgesang*) with similar scansion and rhyme scheme are followed by a concluding *Abgesang* with different rhyme scheme and often a different poetic meter, as in the first strophe of "Mein's trawrens ist":

> Mein's trawrens ist Vrsach mir g'brist
> das ich niemandts darff klagen,
> dann dir alleyn, mein clarer schein,
> pein muß ich deinthalb tragen.
> Ich wolt glaub mir, schir ee den tod erkiesen,
> dann dich also verliesen.

[My misery is the cause of my infirmity that I must not complain to any one but to you alone, my shining light. On your behalf I must bear this pain. I should, believe me, prefer to choose death, than thus to lose you.]

Such texts translated naturally into a musical setting in bar form, with the same music used for both *Stollen* and contrasting music for the *Abgesang*.

Four-voice settings with melody in the tenor voice became standard by the sixteenth century. Many settings drew on a common stock of frequently set tunes, though others were based on new melodies cut from the same rough-hewn cloth: short, rhythmically foursquare in duple meter, and predominantly syllabic, except perhaps for a short melisma (vocal roulade, or run, on a single syllable) before cadences. With the main melody effectively buried in the tenor, the remaining voices are free to surround the tune with more disjunct and animated contrapuntal lines. Often these outer voices, particularly the upper pair, continue their activity across the cadences that mark the ends of poetic lines in the main melody, lending settings a seamless quality articulated by clear cadences only at the ends of the two *Stollen*. The tenor melody might enter with the other voices at the beginning of the piece, particularly in simpler homorhythmic settings or, as in "Mein's trawrens ist," might be introduced by pre-imitation, where other voices anticipate the main tenor melody in a series of staggered entries.

Between the seminal anthologies of the 1510s and the next significant tenor lied publications of the 1530s, there was a fifteen-year hiatus, due in part to the diversion of the resources of the music printing trade to the musical needs of the early Reformation. The first collection from this second generation was an anthology, *Hundert und ainundzweinzig newe Lieder* (One Hundred and Twenty-One New Songs, 1534), assembled by the Nuremberg publisher and bibliophile Hans Ott (d. 1546). Ott's collection was followed in short order by several others, notably those of Christian Egenolff (1502–55; Frankfurt am Main, 6 vols., ca. 1535) and Georg Forster (1510–68; Nuremberg, 5 vols. 1539–60). Pieces of considerable artistic merit by Isaac and Senfl rub shoulders in these collections with works written by composers from more modest urban backgrounds, and courtly lyrics praising constancy in matters of the heart appear alongside lieder with unabashedly vulgar lyrics.

Of the younger composers represented in the lieder prints of the 1530s the most prolific and engaging was the Swiss-born Ludwig Senfl, Isaac's colleague and eventual successor as principal composer in the imperial chapel of Emperor Maximilian I. Some of Senfl's compositions are similar to those of the previous generation. Others, however, show considerable sophistication and compositional craft, including the use of pervasive imitation (all voices presenting the same musical material successively at different times and/or pitch levels), canon (exact imitation), and other contrapuntal devices. Many of Senfl's lieder open with passages that would be equally at home in a sacred motet, with all the voices presenting the lied melody in imitation; some, such as "Was wird es doch des Wunders noch" (What Wonder yet) or "Gottes Gewalt, Kraft, und auch Macht"(God's Power, Strength, and Might) present the lied melody in strict canon in two voices preceded by looser pre-imitation in other voices; others, such as "Mit Lust tät ich ausreiten" (I Rode Out with Pleasure) feature textural contrasts between passages for two of three voices and more thickly scored passages where all of the voices are active; still others have a migrating *cantus firmus* (the melody around which a polyphonic musical work is constructed) where successive phrases of the tune are passed between voices, as in the popular "Das Gläut zu Speyer" (The Bells at Speyer). Here the migrating melody is surrounded by a playful halo of onomatopoeic lines (for example, "gluing, gang" or "murk, main"). Senfl's best works transfigure popular song into art.

Tenor lieder open a window onto several aspects of early modern German society. As we have seen, the early manuscript sources for the genre show that German polyphonic secular song was an amalgam of various traditions including French chanson, unwritten performance traditions, courtly poetry, and folk song. Although a significant portion of the early repertoire seems to have been created by composers associated with secular courts, the tenor lied's distribution via music printing allowed it to be consumed and, very quickly, imitated in ecclesiastical, urban, and university settings. Indeed, by midcentury the theorist Hermann Finck (1527–58) lamented that even incompetent composers were rushing their works into print in an attempt to garner recognition.[28] Renowned court composers infused the genre with features of music cultivated in courtly contexts, particularly the techniques of imitation found in sacred polyphony; yet conversely, musicians as capable as Isaac and Senfl penned more modest and even vulgar pieces that responded unapologetically to market forces.

The transmission and performance of tenor lieder also illuminate music's status in early modern culture. Important clues can be gleaned from the text-underlay in the sources. In the earliest manuscripts tenor lieder are often textless, bearing only a title or short incipit. Such pieces were conceived less as settings of a particular poetic text than as arrangements of an existing melody, suitable for performance in a variety of ways according to local needs: on instruments alone, in combinations of voices and instruments, or by voices singing a text other than the original. In the early printed sources, by contrast, the tenor's melody line generally received text for the first verse, though most often the remaining verses were printed separately below the music. The remaining vocal parts, however, usually remained textless; indeed, the verbal text often fit these lines far less comfortably than it did the tenor. The faster moving, sometimes athletic character of these parts suggests instrumental performance. By the 1530s the physical presentation of the music had changed again, increasingly providing text underlay for all the parts. The first volume of Forster's *Frische teutsche Liedlein* (New German Songs, 1539) provides text for all four voices, including full texting for the many retrospective pieces in the print. In fact, Forster improved the text underlay and composed his own texts for pieces whose texts were lacking or unsuitable in the earlier sources.

Such evidence has usually been read as an indication of musical performance practice.[29] Yet the physical presentation of the tenor lied suggests something more — that modern conceptions of music itself correspond imperfectly to early modern notions. The tenor lied fits poorly with our ideal of a musical "artwork" that manifests the unique creative vision of a single composer, who conceives particularized sonic ideas and gives them stable form via music notation. The tenor lied takes as its starting point not the invention of an individual, but a communal stock of familiar melodies. In fact, the presumption that a new musical work was in some measure based on a preexisting model undergirded most medieval music and survived in numerous forms in early modern genres (see "Church Music from Isaac to Lassus," below). This meant that the melodies of many tenor lieder would enjoy an afterlife, serving as the basis for instrumental arrangements and intabulations, *cantus firmus* Mass settings, and as chorale melodies.

The idea of music having a fixed or final form was also not current in the early modern world, as can be seen from the various reworkings of tenor lieder. Some versions of a single tune are similar enough to suggest common origin, yet it is often impossible to untangle the exact relationship between competing readings — or even to say when variants diverge enough to constitute a new musical work. The Oeglin print of 1512, for example, added a new vocal line to lieder that had previously circulated in three-voice versions, bringing them into line with the fashion for the fuller texture prevalent after the turn of the sixteenth century.[30]

Even the pitches themselves were not wholly fixed. Many accidentals (sharps or flats), particularly at cadences, were not notated but instead left to performers to realize according to their experience, judgment, and taste. While the addition of accidentals in many contexts was formulaic under the rules of so-called *musica ficta* (unwritten accidentals), divergent solutions were also possible. The early modern concept of a musical work, then, did not embrace a number of dimensions that we usually consider central, for example the association of music with a particular verbal text, a single composer, an instrumental or vocal color, or specific pitches. For all music's practical importance to German society there remained a flicker of life in the quadrivial ideal of music as sounding number — an abstract representation of pattern, distinct from any particular sounding realization.

Secular Song II: The Italianization of the Polyphonic Lied

The demise of the tenor lied, like its origin, was due in some measure to the assimilation of foreign influences. Beginning in the 1560s the tradition of setting German texts as tenor lieder was challenged by settings that mimicked the poetic forms and musical gestures of currently fashionable genres of Italian secular music, particularly *villanella* and *canzonetta*.[31] There were several aspects to this transformation: the enthusiastic reception of Italian vocal music, especially in courtly and aristocratic circles in southern Germany; the appearance of collections of Italian secular music printed in the empire; the publication of Italian pieces by German composers trained in Italy; arrangements and contrafacta[32] of Italian songs by Germans; and original compositions to German texts set in the style of the villanella, canzonetta, and later, madrigal.

Italian secular music was cultivated at a few centers in southern Germany during the period between 1540 and 1560, particularly at the Habsburg courts and at Augsburg, Regensburg, and Nuremberg. Raimund Fugger's music collection, for example, contained nearly seventy madrigal and villanella prints by 1566.[33] By the 1560s the Catholic courts at Munich, Graz, and Innsbruck began to recruit Italian musicians rather than northerners, and in the same decade, the first complete print devoted to Italian music appeared in Germany, *Il primo libro delle canzone napolitane* (The First Book of Neopolitan Songs, 1566) by the Dresden Kapellmeister Antonio Scandello (1517–80). German printers capitalized on the vogue for Italian music by reprinting many of the most successful Italian vocal collections. From the 1580s Orazio Vecchi's canzonettas, Giovanni Gastoldi's *balletti*, and Luca Marenzio's madrigals received enthusiastic receptions north of the Alps, and it became an important selling point for prints of secular music to tout works composed in the Italian manner.

German translations and contrafacta of fashionable Italian pieces also took hold; Vecchi's canzonettas were especially popular, providing the source for no fewer than 150 German contrafacta.[34] German translations and adaptations of Italian texts took a variety of forms. At one extreme were those like Hans Leo Hassler's (1564–1612) *Neüe teütsche Gesang* (New German Songs; Augsburg, 1596) and *Lustgarten neuer teutscher Gesäng* (Pleasure Garden of New German Songs; Nuremberg, 1601), which contain faithful, rhymed translations of poems by Giovanni Battista Guarini and Torquato Tasso. At the other end of the spectrum were free German reworkings of Italian poems, like those published by Valentin Haussmann (1560–ca. 1611/13) — adaptations that retained little more than the meter and scansion of the originals. Haussmann built a career around the creation of contrafacta of Italian compositions with collections such as *Ausszug auss Lucae Marentii* [. . .] *italianischen dreystimmigen Villanellen* [. . .] *mit teutschen Texten gezieret* (Selections from Luca Marenzio's Three-voice Italian Villanellas Adorned with German Texts; Nuremberg, 1606), and his numerous editions of Vecchi's canzonettas.[35] Haussmann's procedures can be deduced by examining the following stanzas from his contrafactum of Vecchi's "Cosa non vada più":[36]

Vecchi, "Cosa non vada più"	Haussmann, "Mein Hertz habt ihr"
Cosa non vada più come solea, Poi che quel nodo si possente et forte Rotto spezzato sento, Ond'hor vivo contento.	Mein hertz habt ihr mit Liebesflamm versehret, Welches mit angst und schmertz is gar umbgebn. Ihr thut es hart verwunden, Tag und nacht, so vil stunden.
Amor scalda Leon, Tigri, e serpenti, Ma come è spenta qualla ardente fiamma, Più non si sente mai Ne martello ne guai.	Dess hab ich über euch mich hart beschweret, Und euch umb linderung gebettn hienebn. Die kan ich nicht erlangen; Im schweiss last ihr mich hangen.
[Something is not going as it used to, for I feel that bond, strong and powerful, broken, so that I live contented.	[You have wounded my heart with love's flame; it is surrounded with fear and pain. You injure it gravely, day and night, for so many hours.
Love burns lions, tigers, and serpents, but when that ardent flame is burned out, one feels no more pains and torments.]	I have suffered much from you, and have begged you for mercy besides, but I cannot achieve it; you leave me hanging in sweat.]

Haussmann makes no attempt at literal translation; in fact, the original sense is inverted. Yet he retains the strophic form based on lines of seven and eleven syllables, the original rhyme scheme, and the characteristic feminine endings of the original. Equally telling, Haussmann's translations assimilate the mordant imagery of Marino and Guarini, adopting the images of inflamed hearts, piercing glances, and wounds of love that would permeate German poetry into the seventeenth century.[37]

Musicians in Germany freely adapted not only the texts but also the music of Italian compositions; the early *villanesche* of Lassus, for example, were arrangements of existing works.[38] In a slightly later phase, German composers published musical settings of Italian poetry as part of the journeyman phase of their training in Italy. As an outgrowth of his studies in Venice with the renowned organist at St. Mark's, Andrea Gabrieli, Hassler published a collection of Italian canzonettas (1590) and a group of *Neüe teütsche Gesang* (1596); the latter bears the predictable subtitle "nach Art der welschen Madrigalien und Canzonetten" (in the manner of the Italian madrigals and canzonettas). The northern pupils of Giovanni Gabrieli routinely produced Italian madrigals to mark the end of their studies; such musicians included Heinrich Schütz, who published his *Primo libro de madrigali* (First Book of Madrigals, 1611) during an early sojourn in Italy.[39]

The decisive stage in the reception of Italian secular music was the composition of original lieder in the style of popular Italian models. Lassus's first collection of lieder, the *Neue teütsche Liedlein* (New German Songs; Munich, 1567), published just a year after Scandello's seminal collection, receives pride of place in this development. Although the poetic texts of the Lassus collection are largely those of tenor lieder, his musical settings are anything but traditional. They use five voices instead of the customary four, and only one of the settings could be called a conventional tenor lied, with the tune treated as a *cantus firmus* in the tenor. Lassus rejects the traditional bar form and uses a lively style of declamation (with syllables mostly assigned to eighth notes) that recalls the canzonetta or madrigal rather than the more staid rhythmic pacing of the traditional tenor lied. Significantly, many of the most important lied composers of the last quarter of the sixteenth century were from Lassus's circle, including Johann Eccard of Königsberg (1553–1611), Anton Gosswin, probably of Liège (ca. 1546–97), Leonhard Lechner of the South Tirol (ca. 1553–1606), and the Munich court organist Ivo de Vento (ca. 1544–75).

The future mainstream of the polyphonic lied, however, was charted in a set of seemingly less pretentious prints, Jakob Regnart's (1540–99) *Kurtzweilige teutsche Lieder zu dreyen Stimmen, nach Art der Neapolitanen oder Welschen Villanellen* (Entertaining German Songs for Three Voices, in the Manner of the Neapolitan or Italian Villanellas), which appeared in three volumes (Nuremberg, 1574, 1577, 1579); a complete edition followed in 1583, with more than a dozen reprints until 1611. Regnart, a musician in the service of Emperor Rudolf II (r. 1576–1612), had previously published Italian canzonettas that were later reissued in German translation (Nuremberg, 1595) "ohn einige verenderung der composition" (with no compositional changes). His *Kurtzweilige teutsche Lieder*, however, linked the late-sixteenth-century lied inextricably with the villanella, a song type with roots in Neapolitan popular melody, its humble origins embedded in the etymology of the word *vile* (low, base, or vulgar). Regnart's verse preface is apologetic about this genre's lack of pretense:[40]

Lass dich darumb nit wenden ab,
Das ich hierinn nit brauchet hab
Vil Zierligkeit der Music.
Wiß, das es sich durchauß nit schick,
Mit Villanellen hoch zu prangen,
Und wöllen dardurch Preiß erlangen
Wirdt sein vergebens und umbsunst;
An andre ort gehört die Kunst.

[Do not be put off if here I have not employed many of music's graces. Know that it is not naturally befitting to make pretenses in villanellas, for whoever seeks glory there does so in vain and for naught; art belongs in other places.]

Regnart's compositions affect most features of the Italian villanella: strophic musical settings for three voices, usually cast in four verses in simple homophonic style (block chords without imitation). The top voice carries the melody, supported by the lower two voices in relatively high registers. Common forms include three-line stanzas of eleven syllables rhyming *aaa*, *aba*, or *abb*, or six-line stanzas with six- and seven-syllable lines that form paired couplets.[41] Although each line of the poem receives its own music, many of the musical phrases repeat. Voices sometimes proceed in parallel fifths (a practice banned in conventional counterpoint); the parallel motion was probably an outgrowth of performances accompanied by stringed instruments, where the movement of the hand in a fixed configuration along the fingerboard would have produced similar progressions.[42]

It was this type of modest setting, together with settings related to the canzonetta (usually set for four voices) and *balletto* that became the predominant lied type in Germany between 1575 and 1625. Germans tended to mix elements of the Italian forms freely, so that the distinctions between villanella, canzonetta, balletto, and even madrigal were less pronounced than in Italy. An early example of such hybrid forms are found in Lechner's reworking of Regnart's villanellas.[43] Lechner adds two new voices and smoothes over many of the unrefined voice leading quirks in Regnart's originals. He also introduces imitative entries, textural contrasts, and repetition of short text fragments, so that the result represents a mixture of villanella and madrigal.

The central tradition of setting German texts in the popular, homophonic style of the villanella and canzonetta continued in collections such as Hassler's *Lustgarten neuer teutscher Gesäng* and Johann Hermann Schein's *Musica boscareccia* (Music of the Forest; Leipzig, 3 vols., 1621–28), with its evocation of Marino's *rime boscherecce*. A text such as Schein's "O Scheiden, o bitter Scheiden" (below) from the *Musica boscareccia* shows how thoroughly Germany had absorbed the conceits of Italian pastoral, including the fawning diminutives, the antithesis between pain and pleasure, and the imagery focused on physical attributes of the beloved:

O Scheiden, o bitter Scheiden,
wie machst Du mir so grosses Leiden!
O schöne Augelein
ach soll eur Blickelein
ich den sie garfort meiden!
O süsser Mund, o süsser Mund
dein Lippen rund tun mir mein Herz
zerschneiden.

[O parting, O bitter parting,
you cause me such great pain!
O beautiful little eyes,
ah, should I henceforth avoid
the gaze of your little glance!
O sweet mouth, O sweet mouth,
your rounded lips tear my heart
asunder!]

Although the Italian madrigal was cultivated at Catholic courts of the South, it was far less influential than the lighter forms of villanella and canzonetta for settings of German texts. Its more complex musical style and poetic form (a single strophe without a fixed number of lines or set rhyme scheme; lines of seven and eleven syllables; relatively elevated poetry; five voices; freely changing textures) proved inimical to most German poetry. Ironically, when Kaspar Ziegler (1621–90), a professor of law in Wittenberg and composer of occasional music, began to advocate forms based on Italian madrigalian verse after the middle of the seventeenth century, the madrigal was moribund as a musical genre. By the time German poets and musicians adopted madrigalian verse, the conventions for setting German secular texts had undergone yet another metamorphosis — lied had become aria.

Secular Song III: From Lied to Aria

Connections between German poetry and song grew particularly intense after 1624 in the wake of Martin Opitz's (1597–1639) verse reforms, which in effect dictated that natural stress should obtain in a poetic text rather than artificial syllable stress.[44] Music often augmented the print media as a means of transmitting poetic texts, and frequently the dividing line between *lesen* (reading) and *singen* (singing) was nebulous or even nonexistent. Many baroque poems were conceived as singable lyrics and transformed only retrospectively into written lyrics. The first edition of Opitz's *Teutsche Poemata* (German Poems; Strasbourg, 1624), for example, contained indications of the tunes to which the poems were to be sung, though these rubrics were eliminated in later reprintings.[45] Similarly, the poems of the mystic Angelus Silesius (Johann Scheffler, 1624–77) in *Heiligen Seelen-Lust* (Holy Joy of the Soul, 1657) were originally intended for musical setting; only with the second edition of 1668 was a notice added to the title page: "allen denen die nicht singen können statt eines andaechtigen Gebets Buchs zu gebrauchen" (to be used instead as a devotional prayer book by all those who cannot sing).[46] Poets' use of familiar rhymes, metrical schemes, or alliteration enabled them to conjure up familiar melodies; anyone who knows the tune to "Jesu meine Freude" (Jesus, My Joy) will mentally supply the tune upon reading the lines:[47]

> Chloris / meine Sonne
> Meine Lust / und Wonne /
>   Ursprung meiner Pein /
> Meine Gunst dir bleibet
> Deine Tugend treibet /
>   Dass ich dein muß seyn

[Chloris, my sun, my desire, and bliss, source of my suffering, my affection remains with you, your virtue means that I must be yours.]

Poetry could even evoke music without alluding to a specific melody. The rhythmical, quasi-musical quality of many of Philipp von Zesen's (1619–89) poems is often noted,[48] and his poems were set by Hamburg composers including Weckmann and Johann Schop (ca. 1590–1667). The dactyls of Zesen's "Maienlied" (May Song), for instance, dictate their own musical rhythms, evoking an imaginary musical setting in the fast triple-meter aria style that became common in the mid-seventeenth century:

> Glímmĕrt ĭhr Stérnĕ,
> Schímmĕrt vŏn férnĕ,
> Blínkĕrt nĭcht trŭbĕ,
> Flínkĕrt zŭ Líebĕ
> Díesĕr ĕrfréulĭchĕn líeblĭchĕn Zéit.

[Glimmer, you stars, shimmer from afar, do not blink dully, flash with love for this joyful, lovely time.]

From the standpoint of composers, however, seventeenth-century reform poetry was a decidedly mixed blessing. The strophic texts nearly always called forth strophic musical settings, whose musical repetitions precluded close correspondence between musical gestures and textual meaning. Composers occasionally engaged in madrigalism or word-painting, for example by setting *hoch* (high) to a high note or using a melisma to portray a word like *fliehen* (flee), even though the device became superfluous or even incongruous for subsequent verses.[49] Heinrich Albert (1604–51) noted in the preface to his fifth book of *Arien* (Arias; Königsberg, 1642) that some of the texts really required different music for each strophe, but that he had only provided a single verse because of the prohibitive cost of printing such through-composed music.[50] In addition, the metrical regularity and regular rhyme schemes that seemed to elevate the newer poetry above the old *Knittelvers* (doggerel) — while ensuring lucid, symmetrical phrase structures — made it difficult to avoid musical settings that fell into repetitious patterns. Even settings by the gifted Albert often contain successive paired phrases that collapse into nearly identical rhythms. Finally, most German poetry lacked the pithy, epigrammatic focus on a single image or antithesis found in Italian madrigal verse, the madrigal's epigrammatic tendency toward (in Ziegler's formulation) "wenig Worte und weitläufftige Maynungen" (few words and many meanings).[51] Little wonder, then, that Schütz wrote to Ziegler — in the same year that the poet published *Von den Madrigalen, einer schönen und zur Musik bequemsten Art Vers* (On Madrigals, a Beautiful Verse Form Highly Suited to Music, 1653) — to lament the difficulties he had encountered in fitting the verse of Opitz and other reform poets into the forms of Italian music.[52]

In part because of such tensions and in part because of certain musical developments (to be discussed below), German poems of the seventeenth century were most often set as continuo lieder; that is, as songs for solo voice with basso continuo accompaniment, sometimes with one or two additional parts for treble instruments. Simplicity was the rule: most settings were strophic, and many were almost entirely syllabic. Schütz commented disparagingly, and with irony, that there was scarcely a musician incapable of writing a strophic song.[53] Poets typically recruited local musicians to provide music for their collections, so that even the most renowned poets often had their verses set by relatively minor musical figures. When more gifted composers selected the poetry for their collections the music was often more ornate, though the literary quality was usually more uneven. Collaborations between gifted poets and musicians, like that of Heinrich Albert and Simon Dach (1605–59) in Königsberg, were the exception rather than the rule.

In contrast to Italian monody, a fundamentally aristocratic genre, the continuo lied was cultivated relatively infrequently by composers working in court settings, where Italianate forms still held sway.[54] In fact, despite the literary pretentiousness of some of the poetry, the continuo lied was essentially a genre of *Gebrauchsmusik* (literally, music for use), written for the amusement of students and literati of the urban middle class, particularly at important trading centers such as Hamburg, Königsberg, Leipzig, and Nuremberg. Nonetheless, two of the earliest collections of continuo lieder were by court composers, Johann Nauwach's (1595–1630) *Teutsche Villanellen* (German Villanellas; Dresden, 1627) and Caspar Kittel's (1603–39) *Cantade und Arien* (Cantatas and Arias; Dresden, 1638). Although their songbooks include some settings of reform poems, including many by Opitz, the music forces the newer verse into the molds of Italian monody now over a quarter-century old. The collections include strophic variations (the bass line remains constant between strophes, while the vocal line is varied), pieces built on repeating ostinato basses, solo madrigals, and short strophic songs reminiscent of the arias of the Florentine Giulio Caccini's famous *Le nuove musiche* of 1601.

The German continuo lied anticipated by Nauwach and Kittel was firmly established in the eight books of *Arien* published by Albert between 1638 and 1650. His settings include a large number of settings of poems by Dach, along with songs based on the poetry of other Königsberg colleagues including Andreas Adersbach (1604–51), Robert Roberthin (1600–1648), and Christoph Kaldenbach (1613–98). Albert's *Arien* provide a virtual compendium of the song types that comprised seventeenth-century continuo lieder: songs set to simple dance tunes, short triple-meter arias, chorales, settings where the continuo imitates the voice, pieces reminiscent of the French *air de cour*, old-fashioned lieder in bar form, and even declamatory settings that hint at operatic recitative. Some of the *Arien* are set in polyphony for two to five voices, and some also have short instrumental interludes, called *symphonien*; but many are simple strophic songs of the type that became standard for the German continuo lied in its efflorescence between about 1640 and 1670.

In its typical incarnation a continuo lied sets its text syllabically, with few text repetitions, melismas, or madrigalisms. The music carefully mirrors the poetic scansion and is clearly indebted to French musical models, just as Opitz's reforms relied heavily on French poetry: unaccented syllables fall on weak beats or are set to short note values; the last accented syllable of a line tends to fall on a downbeat (with feminine line-endings therefore concluding on a weak beat). Line breaks (and caesuras in longer lines) are marked by a rest, long note, and/or cadence; rhymes are mirrored musically by similar melodic contours at the ends of the rhyming lines. This model was adopted, with few deviations, by other important composers of the continuo lied from the 1640s and 1650s, including the Zittau organist Andreas Hammerschmidt (1611/12–1675) and his friend Johann Rist (1607–67), one of the German Baroque's leading authorities on poetic norms.

With the more ornate settings of Adam Krieger (1634–66), perhaps the most talented composer of continuo lieder, the unpretentious genre began its metamorphosis into the aria, reestablishing the links with the Italian models that had largely been abandoned after the early collections of Nauwach and Kittel. Some of Krieger's compositions adhere to the older Albert-type lied, yet others show the influence of Italian opera aria; they have obbligato (indispensable accompanying) instrumental parts and often prolong or repeat terse motives or set off short sections of texts with rests. Melodic lines are carefully crafted, featuring sequences, short melismas, expressive leaps, and phrases that build to a clear climax on a high note.

By the 1670s two new musical stimuli transformed the continuo lied in ways that would eventually lead to its near disappearance. One was the renewed interest in modeling German poetry on Italian madrigal verse in the wake of Ziegler's *Von den Madrigalen*. Ziegler advocated short, nonstrophic poetry, without fixed rhyme schemes, and based on lines of seven and eleven syllables (optionally eight or twelve syllables in lines with feminine endings). The Leipzig cantor Sebastian Knüpfer, in his *Lustige Madrigalien und Canzonetten* (Leipzig, 1663) followed Ziegler's principles, but this tradition was less important for the madrigal itself than as the model for German recitative. The second stimulus was the increasingly important Italian cantata and opera. Under the influence of these dramatic genres, settings of German verse became more ornate, expressive, and complex, effectively leading to a new genre, the German baroque aria. The following table encapsulates two prototypes, which are best viewed as extremes on a musical continuum. Although composers continued to cultivate a wide variety of solo song types in the second half of the century, the trend toward aria-like settings was never reversed, and the lied was essentially absorbed by settings of various aria types.

Lied	Aria
strophic text	increasingly through-composed after midcentury
syllabic text-setting	florid, melismatic text-setting
short phrases	longer phrases repeat or develop melodic ideas
little text repetition	considerable text repetition
affectively neutral	music reflects *Affekt* of the text
written for private entertainment	written for public performance
linked to popular song, dance music	linked to Italian vocal music
poetic models French, Dutch	poetic models Italian
instrumental participation rare	instrumental participation common

By the end of the seventeenth century, norms that would obtain throughout the eighteenth century had been established. The dramatic genres based on aria, including opera, oratorio, and cantata — long cultivated in Catholic centers like Vienna, Munich, and Innsbruck — now held sway throughout Germany. Secular vocal music adopted one of two distinct vocal styles: recitative or aria. Recitative (narrative texts in madrigalian forms) was set to declamatory music for voice and continuo, and aria (two strophes, often based on shorter lines) was set in more melodious style and often in *da capo* (ABA) form. Even near the close of the early modern era Germany's receptiveness to foreign cultural models continued to shape, and even to define, the nation musically.

The Chorale and Music in the Early Reformation Church

Martin Luther's historical centrality in the realm of music rivals his significance as a major influence on the development of a standard German language, as masterful translator of the Bible, and as a mighty cultural and political force.[55] Luther's translations of the Old and New Testaments provided a rich fount of sacred texts for generations of German composers, and his redefining of the role of music within Christian liturgy had transforming effects on nearly every aspect of Protestant sacred music.[56] Moreover, the corpus of evangelical chorales, which Luther was instrumental both in commissioning and in writing, quickly assumed musical significance beyond mere congregational song. The chorale melodies became a musical canon that provided the foundation for elaborations in a variety of musical styles and genres throughout the early modern period and beyond.

Although Lutheranism defined itself primarily by its various doctrinal oppositions to Catholicism, it retained most of the outer forms of the Catholic rite, including numerous musical traditions. Moreover, although the congregational hymn or chorale tends to receive pride of place in discussions of Reformation music, the role of music in the early Lutheran liturgy was much broader, embracing traditional Catholic plainchant, new recitation formulas based on plainsong, an international, cross-denominational repertoire of Latin sacred polyphony, and diverse types of nonliturgical song. The publications of sacred music by the Wittenberg publisher Georg Rhau (1488–1548), whose press provided much of the music for the early Lutheran movement, attest eloquently to this diversity. His collections included music in simple and complex musical styles for a variety of liturgical contexts, settings of texts in both Latin and German, and works by both Protestant and Catholic composers.[57]

Luther's profound love of music is well documented; he was not only a competent singer, recorder player, and lutenist, but also had broad knowledge of the music of his era. He expressed particular admiration for the music of Josquin des Prez (ca. 1450/55–1521), the most prominent master of the Franco-Flemish polyphonic style in the years around 1500,[58] and he corresponded with Senfl, requesting, in one letter, that the composer arrange the antiphon "In pace in idipsum dormiam et requiescam" (I Will Lie Down and Sleep in Peace, Ps. 4:8) upon Luther's death.[59] Underlying his fondness for music was an ardent belief in music's efficacy as an instrument of education, spiritual edification, and faith.[60] Luther sketched his musical aesthetics most fully in the preface to Rhau's *Symphoniae iucundae* (Joyful Sinfonias, 1538), where he praised music as a gift of God that was capable both of moving the emotions and of transcending human eloquence.[61] Such convictions shaped Luther's ambitious program for music; seldom, in fact, had music been deployed more effectively as an agent of theological, educational, and social change.

Luther established a new role for music in public worship in the *Formula missae et communionis pro Ecclesia Wittembergensi* (Formula of the Mass and Communion for the Church in Wittenberg, 1523), which adapted the basic structure of the Catholic Mass to the new dogma in ways that were, in the words of Robin Leaver, "liturgically conservative but theologically radical."[62] The *Formula missae* retained not only the Latin language but also most of the structure and even individual texts of the Mass. Luther's fundamental textual changes involved portions of the Mass, particularly the Canon, that lacked strong traditions of musical elaboration.[63] The *Formula missae* also preserved the central distinction between Ordinary and Proper along with the structure of most individual items.[64] The practical result of retaining so many textual features of the Catholic Mass was that existing music conceived for use in Catholic worship, particularly settings of the Psalms and Mass Ordinary, remained equally at home within the new Protestant liturgies; indeed, Luther was explicit in his desire to use the best music, regardless of the composer's confession.[65]

The liturgical transformation of greatest musical consequence was the interpolation of chorales — an introduction that, at one stroke, elevated both congregational singing and the use of the vernacular. The *Formula missae* contains only general suggestions about the use of congregational songs, recommending that they be inserted after the Gradual, Sanctus, and Agnus Dei (*Luther's Works*, 53:36). The centrality of the chorale increased with the issuance of the *Deudsche Messe und Ordnung Gottesdiensts* (German Mass and

Order of Worship, 1526), which provided a service order entirely in German for use by smaller congregations. The *Deudsche Messe* eliminated some items from the Mass entirely; of greater significance, however, it included more spiritual songs in the vernacular than had the *Formula missae*.

Luther's provision of two models for public worship, together with his rejection of a centralized hierarchy, led to the proliferation of local traditions in both liturgy and music. Nearly every major city eventually had its own hymnal and *Kirchenordnung* (one of the evangelical church constitutions); yet everywhere the reformed liturgy demanded new types of music: new recitation tones (formulas used to chant prayers and biblical readings), new chorales for unison congregational singing, and more elaborate polyphonic versions of these chorales for churches with trained choirs.

Luther took pains in revising the traditional recitation tones published with the *Deudsche Messe*. Despite their musical simplicity — most of the reciting formulas are based on a single pitch, with more elaborate opening and closing flourishes serving as musical punctuation — he was deeply concerned that the recitation tones possess a sensitive union of text and music. The recollections of Johann Walter (1496–1570), Luther's friend and principal musical adviser, emphasized Luther's sensitivity to the affective character of the modes,[66] and Luther's own musings in *Wider die himmlischen Prophete* (Against the Heavenly Prophets, 1524) insist that, "es mus beyde text und notten, accent, weyse und geperde aus rechter mutter sprach und stymme komen, sonst ists alles eyn nachomen, wie die affen thun" (the text and notes, accent, melody, and manner of rendering ought to grow out of the true mother tongue and its inflection; otherwise all of it becomes an imitation as monkeys do).[67]

Luther's belief in the importance of congregational song reflected core convictions of the Reformation. Communal singing reinforced the concept of a priesthood of believers, allowing the congregation to assume a function previously reserved for choirs comprised of priests or lay clerics (*Luther's Works*, 53:36). Chorales also stressed the centrality of the Word, since most of Luther's chorales are metrical paraphrases of biblical passages. Additionally, congregational participation underscored the idea of the *Gottesdienst* (worship) as a gift of God to all of the faithful, rather than as a sacrifice by the priest acting as intermediary.

As early as the winter of 1523 Luther and his circle began to create songs for use in Wittenberg, assembling, adapting, and arranging textual and musical materials that were close at hand rather than forging an entirely new repertoire. The reformers translated Latin songs into German, provided vernacular tunes with sacred verses, and edited and improved other texts. Their musical approach was similarly eclectic: some melodies were taken over without change, existing texts were set to new tunes, while other melodies were rewritten to accommodate the inflections of new poetry.

Gregorian chant melodies provided one rich source for the chorales. The Gregorian hymns were especially important since their strophic forms, clear metrical patterns, and relatively tuneful melodies made them suitable for singing by musically untutored congregations. "Nun komm, der Heiden Heiland" (Come now, Savior of the Nations), for example, is Luther's reworking of the Latin hymn "Veni Redemptor gentium," and "Komm, Gott Schöpfer, heiliger Geist" (Come, God Creator, Holy Spirit), is based on "Veni creator Spiritus."

Latin *cantiones* — strophic spiritual songs used as accretions to the Mass or as private devotional songs — were also taken over enthusiastically by the early Lutheran church. Some of these Latin songs were already well known in German translation even before the Reformation, making them immediately useful. Particularly noteworthy examples of this category are the Christmas and Advent songs "Der Tag der ist so freudenreich" (The Day is so Joyful), "Ein Kind geborn zu Bethlehem" (A Child Born in Bethlehem), and "Joseph, lieber Joseph mein" (Joseph, My Dear Joseph). There was also a well-established tradition of sacred songs in German by the early sixteenth century, and many of these melodies, particularly the *Leisen,* seasonal songs performed as extra-liturgical additions to the Catholic Mass, were included in early Lutheran hymnals. The best known of these is the Easter melody "Christ ist erstanden" (Christ is Risen).[68] Even the tenor lied contributed to the early chorale repertoire. Isaac's "Innsbruck, ich muss dich lassen" (Innsbruck, I Must Leave You) appears in early Protestant hymnals with the text "O Welt, ich muss dich lassen" (O World, I Must Leave You).

Some early chorales had original text and music, yet even these were often free metrical paraphrases of biblical passages, especially the psalms, set to music that drew heavily on a stock of common melodic formulas. The text of Luther's best known original chorale, "Ein' feste Burg ist unser Gott" (A Mighty Fortress is Our God), for example, is based on Psalm 46, and its melody may derive many of its gestures from a song by the Meistersinger Hans Sachs (1494–1576), his "Salve, ich grus dich" (Hail, I Give You Greetings). Whatever the relationship between the two works, it is clear that even the original chorales drew on a store of well-worn melodic materials, even when they were not directly modeled on a particular song.[69]

Neither Luther's role in the creation of text and music for the earliest chorales nor his working relationship with Johann Walter have been entirely clarified. Recent scholarship, however, credits Luther himself with considerable activity both as poet and as composer, even if the final form of some melodies may have resulted from collaboration with Walter.[70] Among the works whose complete attribution to Luther seems secure are some fifteen chorales including "Aus tiefer Not schrei ich zu dir" (Out of Deep Despair I Cry Unto You), "Ein' feste Burg," and "Vom Himmel hoch da komm ich her" (From Heaven on High I Come).[71] Luther made his requirements and priorities for the texts of the new chorales clear in a letter to Georg Spalatin, whose help he sought to enlist in this program:

> Consilium est [. . .] psalmos vernaculos condere pro vulgo, id est spirituales cantilenas, quo verbum dei vel cantu inter populos maneat. Oro, vt nobiscum in hac re labores, & tentes aliquem psalmorum in cantilenam

transferre, sicut hic habes meum exemplum. Velim autem nouas & auli-
cas voculas omitti, quo pro captu vulgi quam simplicissima vulgatissi-
maque, tamen munda simul & apta verba canerentur, deinde sententia
perspicua & psalmis quam proxima redderetur. Libere itaque hic agen-
dum & accepto sensu, verbis relictis, per alia verba comoda vertendum.
Ego non habeo tantum gratie, vt tale quid possem, quale velleum.[72]

[Our plan is to compose psalms for the people in the vernacular, that is,
spiritual songs, so that the Word of God may be among the people also
in the form of music. I ask you to work with us on this project; try to
adapt any one of the psalms for use as a hymn, as you may see I have done
in this example. But I would like you to avoid any new words or the language used at court. In order to be understood by the people, only the
simplest and most common words should be used for singing; at the same
time, however, they should be pure and apt; and further, the sense should
be clear and as close as possible to the psalm. You need a free hand here:
maintain the sense, but don't cling to the words; rather translate them
with other appropriate words. I myself do not have so great a gift that I
can do what I would like to see done here.]

Luther's claim to "not have so great a gift" contains more than a touch of false
modesty, for his chorale texts are faithful to the demands outlined to Spalatin.
Luther's chorales set standards for the genre: several strophes of rhymed, metrical poetry, often in bar form. They show his expressed preference for simplicity and directness and are notable for their striking imagery, direct locutions,
and compact lines that use adjectives sparingly. Many are based on psalms, with
each strophe furnishing a free metrical translation of one or more psalm verses.

Musically, the early chorales evince a straightforward ruggedness consistent with the tone of the verbal texts. They set lyrics syllabically, eschewing
elaborate flourishes, and the melodies frequently have a jagged leap near the
beginning of the melody that lends the tune a characteristic shape. Moreover,
Luther's concern for matching the rhythmic structure of the music to the scansion of the poetry leads to frequent syncopations, since the note lengths,
chosen to reflect the stress of the poetry, sometimes conflict temporarily with the
musical meter. The rhythmically uniform versions of the chorales sung today
smooth over the asymmetrical, often swaggering rhythms of the originals.

Despite Luther's desire to encourage communal singing, the first published
monument of the Lutheran chorale literature was not a congregational hymnal
but rather a book of polyphonic chorale settings designed for accomplished
singers.[73] With Luther's sanction Walter compiled the *Geystliches gesangk
Buchleyn* (Small Book of Spiritual Songs, 1524), often known simply as the
Chorgesangbuch (Choir-Songbook).[74] Its thirty-eight chorale settings in three
to five voices (plus five Latin motets) were issued in separate partbooks and thus
designed for performance either by students learning to sing figural music or by
institutions with trained choirs capable of performing polyphony. The format
seems to have been part of a strategy of first providing music for students and
for the choir, who could subsequently teach the congregation the new chorales.

A congregational version of the *Chorgesangbuch*, with text and melodies only, appeared a year later, and its derivation from Walter's partbooks is immediately clear: its chorales appear in the same order as in the *Geystliches gesangk Buchleyn*, and the hymnal even reprints Luther's preface to the earlier publication.

The polyphonic settings of the *Chorgesangbuch*, with only two exceptions, have the chorale melody in the tenor voice; indeed, Walter's settings adopt one of two compositional approaches already well established in the tenor lied. The more modest type resembles the block homophonic settings of tenor lieder by Isaac or Finck described above. It is characterized by clear-cut phrase structures, with all voices moving in nearly identical rhythms, the occasional light ornamentation failing to conceal the underlying note-against-note conception. In Walter's more elaborate settings the tenor presents the chorale melody in long notes. The framing voices generally anticipate the entry of the tenor's entry chorale tune with imitative entries based loosely on the chorale, though there is little systematic imitation. Instead, the ornamenting voices surround the chorale with florid lines that generally have rhythmic values two to four times as fast as the measured unfolding of the tenor. Luther expressed his admiration for such settings, writing that when three, four, or five voices decorate a chorale, the effect is so wonderful that it creates "himlische Tantzreien" (divine roundelays) unlike anything else in the world (*Luther's Works*, 53:324). The musical choices that Luther encouraged for the first polyphonic settings of chorales are revealing. Many of the melodies, as we have seen, were already known to the congregation, helping to ensure a degree of familiarity and acceptance. Moreover, when these melodies were sung by the choir, sometimes alternating verse-by-verse with the congregation, the style often retained the basic musical gestures of the tenor lied that characterized convivial music making, thus reinforcing social bonds among the faithful.

The central corpus of early Lutheran chorales began to take shape in the Wittenberg congregational hymnals published by Joseph Klug, beginning with the *Geistliche Lieder* (Spiritual Songs, 1529), which organized the chorales into three groups: Luther's chorales, "Lieder der unsern" (chorales by Luther's associates), and chorales based on pre-Reformation German and Latin melodies. Hymnals proliferated rapidly; nearly one hundred appeared between 1524 and Luther's death in 1546, including a number of volumes prepared under Luther's supervision (*Luther's Works*, 53:194).

Another seminal collection of early chorale settings was Rhau's collection *Newe deudsche geistliche Gesenge für die gemeinen Schulen* (New German Spiritual Songs for the Common Schools, 1544), an anthology containing 123 compositions by an international roster of composers including Balthasar Resinarius, Arnold von Bruck, Ludwig Senfl, Benedictus Ducis, Sixt Dietrich, and Thomas Stoltzer. The settings adhere to the same two compositional types cultivated by Walter and are musically interesting mainly for their high quality.[75] As a social document, however, the collection confirms the spread of chorale-based composition beyond Lutheran circles; the three best-represented composers — Resinarius, Bruck, and Senfl — all had ties to the Habsburg courts.

The prototype for the modern Protestant hymnal did not appear until 1586, in Nuremberg, with the *Funffzig geistliche Lieder und Psalmen mit vier Stimmen auff contrapunctsweise* [. . .] *gesetzt* (Fifty Spiritual Songs and Psalms for Four Voices Set in Counterpoint) of Lucas Osiander (1534–1604), son of the well-known if controversial preacher Andreas Osiander. The signal change in this collection is that the chorale melodies appear consistently in the top voice rather than in the tenor. The settings are musically unassuming: the melody, with its original rhythms preserved, is harmonized in four parts, with simple chords set "auff contrapunctsweise" (in note-against-note fashion), and almost exclusively with root-position triads. This style of chorale setting, the so-called *Cantionalsatz* (cantional style: homophonic with melody in the top voice), became standard, displacing the increasingly archaic configuration having the tune in the tenor. It led eventually to musically more substantial settings in cantional style, such as the Berlin Kapellmeister Johann Eccard's *Geistliche Lieder auff den Choral* (Spiritual Songs on Chorale Tunes, 1597), Hassler's *Kirchengesänge, Psalmen und geistliche Lieder* [. . .] *simpliciter gesetzt* (Church Songs, Psalms, and Spiritual Songs Simply Set; Nuremberg, 1608), and settings in parts VI through VIII of Michael Praetorius's *Musae Sioniae* (Muses of Zion, 1609–10).

Although the corpus of Lutheran chorales continually changed through accretion and deletion, its liturgical, didactic, devotional, and social import was certain by the middle of the sixteenth century. Musicians' energies shifted from the creation of new chorales to fashioning polyphonic settings based on a canon of established chorale melodies. The history of the congregational chorale thus merges with the development of other genres, such as the chorale variation, chorale motet, and chorale concerto.

Church Music from Isaac to Lassus

Chorales and chorale-based compositions were Germany's most characteristic contribution to sacred music of the post-Reformation era, yet an international tradition of Latin liturgical music, particularly settings of texts useful in both Catholic and Lutheran liturgies, retained their preeminence long after Luther's reforms.[76] The compositional strategies used to set Latin liturgical texts became a musical *lingua franca*, adopted (and later adapted) in Germany not only for church music, but also for other genres.

Early sacred polyphony from the German-speaking lands reached its first maturity in the second half of the fifteenth century, just as a significant stylistic shift was taking place. Before turning to developments in German music, it will be useful to sketch these broad, international trends. Put baldly, a desire for music to mirror the structure and meaning of a verbal text superseded a more abstract compositional approach based on the idea of providing a musical setting — much like the setting of a precious gemstone — to a preexisting melody. Nevertheless, the idea of incorporating a borrowed model melody into a sacred work endured in various forms throughout the early modern period, although the nature and treatment of both the borrowed material and the newly composed parts were subject to nearly limitless displays of compositional ingenuity.

By the 1440s cyclic masses, settings of the Ordinary whose sections were unified by common musical material, were most often based upon a French chanson rather than a Gregorian chant, though the practice of using a chant *cantus firmus* remained tenacious in Germany. When the model tune for a mass was a secular song, the melody was typically placed in the tenor voice and purged of its secular lyrics, creating a so-called *cantus firmus* mass or tenor mass. The *cantus firmus* might be presented in a series of long, equal notes — an older procedure more typical of settings based on chant — or could be given a more flexible rhythmic shape. The borrowed tune could also be graced through the addition of ornamental notes (the paraphrase mass), or split among several voices rather than being assigned to a single part (the migrating *cantus firmus*). Moreover, the model melody could be manipulated through a variety of processes: it might be sung under different mensuration signs (the precursors of modern time signatures, which in the prevailing system of mensural notation also altered the rhythm); segmented and treated in augmentation, diminution, retrograde, inversion, or canon; or sung on different starting pitches. Reliance on borrowed material was hardly an exercise in shopworn scholasticism; *cantus firmus* procedure offered numerous appeals, containing a bow to the conventions of genre, setting abstract compositional challenges, evoking associations from a secular work in a sacred context,[77] and creating intertextuality with other works based on the same model.[78] Indeed, some melodies became, effectively, standards; the most widely borrowed melody was the French song "L'homme armé" (The Armed Man), which served as the basis for over forty masses from the fifteenth to seventeenth centuries, including a cycle by Senfl.

The later, more progressive stream in sixteenth-century Latin sacred composition gradually rejected the idea of works based on preexisting compositions. The ideal of composition on a *cantus firmus* gradually yielded to an approach, influenced by humanistic concerns, by which the syntax, accentuation, and meaning of the verbal text became the pivotal factors in shaping both small-scale musical gestures and larger forms. This style had already begun to appear by the last quarter of the fifteenth century in works by a handful of northern composers, most of whom had spent a portion of their careers in Italy, but was disseminated in Germany only somewhat later. For Germany, the *fons et origo* of such music was Josquin des Prez. Josquin's towering position in music historiography is indeed due in large measure to the reception of his music by humanists in southern Germany in the decades following his death.[79] Other composers who belonged to Josquin's generation and whose works appeared prominently in the motet anthologies of Berg and Neuber, Formschneider, Ott, and Petreius included Pierre de la Rue, Jean Mouton, Jacob Obrecht, and most crucial for German music, Heinrich Isaac.

The new techniques cultivated by these composers at first centered on the motet (settings of words other than the fixed texts of the Mass Ordinary, or the psalms, hymns, and canticles of the Offices). Similar traits soon appeared in masses and other sacred genres, however. In the archetypical motet texture, the voices present the same musical phrase — often a short, syllabic idea carefully crafted to fit the accentuation of the text — in staggered imitative entries, creating a short section or point of imitation. In addition to such pervasive imitation, the new language is characterized by clear-cut cadences and seamless overlapping phrases. Composers introduced variety by alternating such points of imitation with other textures, including duets, trios, and block homophony. This general approach, based on all parts sharing similar melodic material presented contrapuntally, continued to serve composers of sacred music for several hundred years, because of its essential simplicity and flexibility. A composer could set a text "left-to-right" — in much the same way as a reader would read it — dividing longer texts into short syntactical units, and then allowing the words to suggest a suitable melodic motive, contrapuntal technique, or musical texture for each section.

As this type of pervading imitation came to predominate, a new sort of ordinary setting developed. After about 1520, masses were typically based on all the voices in the polyphonic fabric of a model composition rather than on a single melodic line of a song or chant. In such parody or imitation masses, the borrowed material consisted not only of an isolated line but of a contrapuntal complex, a web of relationships between several voices. This technique was also applied to texts other than those of the Mass; Lassus, for example, composed forty imitation Magnificats.[80]

The reception of these trends took unique forms in Germany. German composers of the sixteenth century have sometimes been treated in three categories: an early group whose musical language was formed by the older Franco-Flemish style (Adam von Fulda, Paul Hofhaimer, and the early works of Heinrich Finck); a slightly later generation, born in the last two decades of the fifteenth century, whose creative lives straddled the stylistic divide (Stolzer, Resinarius, and Bruck); and a more forward-looking group, represented most characteristically by Senfl and his successors.[81] A comparison of three settings of a single text, the Christmas Responsory "Verbum caro factum est" (the Word was made flesh) illustrates such stages.

The earliest setting, a three-part piece by Fulda, is the most archaic, presenting the notes of the chant strictly, in long, equal notes in the tenor, while the surrounding voices present flowing, animated lines characterized by long melismas that can accommodate virtually any text.[82] This sort of layered texture, with the borrowed chant melody moving more slowly than the free, added voices, was widely used in the late fifteenth century, and was particularly associated with hymn settings.[83]

A setting by Stoltzer for five voices, in striking contrast, uses the chant melody twice: in long notes in the bass voice, as well as in lightly ornamented form in the middle voice. The remaining free voices even mimic the basic shape of the chant's opening gesture, though the imitation is not carried out strictly or systematically. This composition, however, preserves two distinct levels of rhythmic activity, with the chant-bearing voices moving more slowly than the free voices.

Senfl's six-voice setting of the text from the same responsory, beginning "in principio erat verbum" (in the beginning was the Word), immediately shows greater textural variety, beginning with a duet for the upper two voices that paraphrases the chant rather than presenting it with note-for-note faithfulness. When the lower voices enter, they present similar motives in quick imitation, all moving at the same speed. Although some entries begin with the chant in equal notes, such entries quickly break off as the chant-bearing voice joins the others in presenting faster moving lines. Other portions of Senfl's setting, for example the opening of the *secunda pars*, "Plenum gratiae et veritatis" (full of grace and truth), have even more systematic and strict imitation; indeed, the voices sing virtually identical melodies in a series of staggered entries.

The overall tendency in these three settings is remarkably clear: In the earliest, the chant is treated as an object of veneration — displayed openly and in pristine form, starkly contrasted from the two decorating voices, which diffidently accommodate themselves to its shape. In the later two works the original chant has been progressively transformed into raw melodic material that the composer molds and refigures, allowing it to permeate all parts of the musical fabric.

The German reception of the so-called Netherlands style, however, was neither as tidy nor as simple as these three examples suggest. The overall trend toward less reliance on chant melodies and greater equality of the vocal lines is clear; nonetheless, the older tenor mass and the music written in the style of Josquin's era continued to predominate in German prints designed for Protestant use long after it had become outmoded at the more progressive Catholic courts. Rhau's *Opus decem missarum* (Ten Masses; Wittenberg, 1541), for instance, concentrates on tenor masses rather than the more up-to-date imitation mass.[84] And his comprehensive series of anthologies of Latin church music, which assumed near canonical significance for Protestant Germany, contained many works that were old-fashioned by the time they were published.[85] It was characteristic of Germany that new approaches supplemented but never entirely supplanted established styles. German composers were generally slow to abandon the older layered, *cantus firmus* style, often incorporating elements of the new language rather than embracing it completely. Such tensions are evident in Senfl's reworking of Josquin's "Ave Maria [. . .] virgo serena" (Ave Maria, Virgin Serene). The piece begins almost identically with the celebrated motet except for shifts in register, yet the pervasive imitation of the opening turns out to be an extended introduction to a passage where the opening melody is presented as an old-fashioned long-note *cantus firmus* in the tenor.[86]

A number of other traits are often cited to characterize Renaissance sacred music in the German-speaking lands as conservative or out of touch with the latest developments, including the use of long-note *cantus firmus*, the introduction of a migrating *cantus firmus*, and the practice of employing more than one borrowed melody. Yet recent research has suggested that all of these features occurred within the broader Western tradition. Strohm argues that the use of monorhythmic *cantus firmi* (pieces with the Gregorian chant presented in long, equal notes), was less a specifically German trait than a general European solution to the problem of allowing trained and untrained choristers to perform together.[87] In fact, one can find similar parallels for nearly all of the other approaches that have been singled out as specifically Teutonic.

There is, however, an alternative to the traditional negative view of the reception of Latin church music in the empire. From this perspective, works that incorporate a chant or chorale melody are not manifestations of out-moded compositional practices but rather embellishments of a portion of the liturgy through music. Such compositions remained elaborations or intensifi-cations of a sanctioned liturgical melody, and as a result were bound to a par-ticular time and place through local variants in the melody. (In contrast, works lacking a *cantus firmus* altogether became more independent and universal, marking a major step toward the autonomy that we understand as part and parcel of the modern musical masterwork.)

The predilection for settings of revered melodies is likewise evident in two other traditions centered in Germany: proper cycles and *alternatim* masses. Settings of proper cycles were understandably rarer than settings of the Ordinary, since they were generally useful for only a single feast day. Yet they were in use in the Habsburg chapels as early as the 1430s, and the form was monumentalized in the three volumes of Isaac's *Choralis Constantinus* (1550–55), a collection that has justifiably been called a musical counterpart to the literary and iconographic monuments commissioned by Emperor Maximilian I: *Weisskunig* (White King, 1514), *Teuerdank* (literally, Loyal Thanks, 1505–12; published 1517), and *Triumphzug* (Triumphal Procession, 1516–18).[88] The collection contains nearly 100 settings of the main items from the Proper (usually the Introit, Alleluia or Tract, Sequence, and Communion) for Sundays and major feasts of the year.

Stylistically, Isaac's collection is a virtual compendium of procedures for creating works based on a chant *cantus firmus*. Most of the settings are in four voices, with the chant sometimes presented in long notes, at other times given a freer rhythm. In some settings the chant is worked out in two- or even three-part canonic imitation, a feat of considerable compositional virtuosity. Pervasive imitation is evident throughout, and even the so-called free voices often mimic the most characteristic gesture of the chant. The settings are also striking for their sensitivity to the structure and meaning of the verbal texts. Isaac's cycle was followed by settings of proper cycles by others, including Sixt Dietrich (ca. 1493–1548) and Adam Rener (ca. 1485–ca. 1520).[89]

During the second half of the sixteenth century, Catholic courts in south-ern Germany increasingly employed composers whose Latin church music took on a new expansiveness and expressiveness, most notably Lassus at the Bavarian court, and Philippe de Monte (1521–1603), Kapellmeister under Emperor Rudolf II. Lassus placed an indelible stamp on German music for the next several generations. Most of his mature works were written during his long service at the court of Duke Albrecht V (r. 1550–79), where he con-tributed to nearly every important genre of the period, including Mass, motet, Magnificat, chanson, madrigal, and lied.

Lassus's motets (his contribution to the German polyphonic lied was discussed above) assumed paradigmatic status for the later sixteenth and early seventeenth century. They are admired especially for their imaginative use of varied textures, the carefully crafted declamatory rhythms, a masterly handling of counterpoint, and, in some works, the judicious use of chromaticism[90] to underline deeply emotive texts. Above all, it was the rhetorical qualities of the music that influenced later composers — an ability already recognized in the *Musica poetica* (1606) of the influential theorist and poet laureate Joachim Burmeister (1564–1629).[91] Lassus was most influential both for his ability to reflect textual meaning via conventional word painting and also for that harder-to-define ability to project the underlying *Affekt* through mode, texture, melody, and rhythm. The authority of his music was increased with the posthumous publication of 516 motets as the *Magnum opus musicum* (1604). Two of the most influential Italian composers of the following generation, Andrea and Giovanni Gabrieli, worked at Munich during their formative years, and, as we shall see, it was the axis formed by Lassus and the Gabrielis that constituted a central strain of influence for German composers of the early seventeenth century.

Church Music in the Seventeenth Century

The vogue for Italian music that shaped German secular music in the late sixteenth century pervaded the music of the seventeenth. A music chapel staffed with Italian musicians became a near requirement for any ruler with serious artistic aspirations; by early in the century the courts at Graz, Innsbruck, Munich, Salzburg, and Vienna were dominated by Italians. Dresden, Hanover, and Kassel soon followed suit. Competition for Italian musicians could be intense, even dangerous; the Jesuit Priest Giacinto Cornacchioli reported to his patron, Habsburg Archduke Leopold Wilhelm, that his recruiting mission in Venice had become endangered when word circulated that his intention was to "plunder Saint Mark's of musicians."[92] German princes and civic patrons like the Fugger family routinely sent promising musicians to Italy for study, and Quantz claimed that the prejudice against German music, as *un gusto barbaro*, diminished only after numerous German composers had undertaken journeys to Italy.[93] Even composers who had never set foot in Italy were eager to advertise that their works were "auff italiänische *Invention* componirt."[94]

The influence of Italian music was most obvious in the Catholic South, but it eventually infiltrated other regions of Germany as well. By the 1670s Dresden's musical life was dominated by Italian music (lists of prints and manuscripts consist almost entirely of Italian titles), and nearly all of the major composers were Italians.[95] Music treatises showed this growing Italianization, devoting ever increasing space to the latest Italian singing styles and the art of improvising from a basso continuo rather than to theories of mode or rules of academic counterpoint. Performances of Italian opera had been staged at Salzburg, Prague, Vienna, and Innsbruck by the 1620s,[96] and the earliest attempt at German opera followed in 1627 with the performance of Opitz's translation and reworking of an Italian libretto, *Dafne*, set to music (now lost) by Schütz. By the end of the century Italian opera still dominated at the major cultural centers of Dresden, Hanover, Munich, and Vienna. German-language theatrical works, however, had been performed at courts throughout Germany, including Bayreuth, Breslau, Braunschweig-Wolfenbüttel, Lüneburg, Hamburg, Weissenfels, Rudolstadt, Gotha, Jena, Coburg, and Nuremberg.[97]

Among the most enduring Italian influences on German sacred music in the seventeenth century were the polychoral style and basso continuo accompaniment. The predilection for polychoral music was especially intense among German musicians with ties to Venice and to the circle of musicians around Andrea and Giovanni Gabrieli.[98] Such composers included Schütz, Hassler, and Gregor Aichinger (1564–1628). Gabrieli's works were widely transmitted in German manuscripts;[99] one of the most important printed sources for his music, the *Reliquiae sacrorum concentuum* (Collection of Sacred Concertos), was published by Georg Gruber (d. 1631) in Nuremberg in 1615. The Gabrielian polychoral motet, with large, colorful scorings that mix voices and instruments, antiphonal exchanges, flexible, declamatory rhythms, and sonorous *tutti* climaxes, all found echoes in German compositions.[100] By 1620 polychoral composition had become so widespread in sacred music that the terms *motet* and *double-choir* had become virtually synonymous in German anthologies.[101]

Part of the appeal of the polychoral style lay in the sonorous, contrasting colors of the divided choirs, or *cori spezzati*. Yet another of its attractions was its flexibility; a polychoral composition often amounted to an elaboration of the textures of the late-sixteenth-century motet, with its material distributed among multiple choirs that mixed instruments and voices. When these choirs performed simultaneously, one of them usually contained most of the essential melodic and harmonic material while the others functioned as doubling or reinforcement. Even one of the most imposing German incarnations of the polychoral style, Schütz's *Psalmen Davids* (Dresden, 1619), follows this model.

A characteristic German adaptation of the polychoral style was the addition of trumpets and drums. Michael Altenburg (1584–1640) published a motet with optional trumpets in his *Gaudium Christianum* (Christian Joy, 1617);[102] Michael Praetorius's motet "In dulci jubilo" from the *Polyhymnia caduceatrix* (Polyhymnia, the Herald, 1619) has a choir of trumpets; and Samuel Scheidt's (1587–1654) setting of the same text from 1620 includes two clarino parts.[103] Schütz conducted and probably composed similar works for the Dresden commemoration of the Reformation centennial in 1617.[104] Around the same time the imperial musician Giovanni Valentini (ca. 1582–1649) composed huge polychoral works with trumpets for court celebrations (collected in his *Messa, Magnificat et Iubilate Deo a sette chori concertati con le trombe*; Vienna, 1621). It is no coincidence that so many works with notated trumpet parts appeared in Germany precisely at the onset of the Thirty Years' War, at a time when confessional interests became so closely intertwined with political and military concerns. The trumpet's military connotations (trumpet corps were usually attached to the court stables rather than to the chapel), which proved so useful in Germany, led the procurators at St. Mark's in Venice to ban the instrument's use there in 1639 as being too "warlike [. . .] [and] more suitable for armies than for the house of God."[105]

Even more fundamental than the polychoral idiom to the musical transformation around the turn of the seventeenth century was the advent of basso continuo accompaniment and figured bass notation. Basso continuo, the practice of improvising full harmonies above a bass line on keyboard or plucked string instruments, and figured bass notation, the related practice of indicating harmonies via figures above each bass note, were at once symptoms and causes of a revolution in musical thinking. In the typical texture of sixteenth-century sacred music, a polyphonic web of equal parts created full harmonies through the interaction of individual melodic lines. In contrast, basso continuo accompaniment automatically provided full harmonies, which freed composers from the obligation to keep three or four voices "in play" in order to create full sonorities. This freedom enabled composers to emphasize one or two treble melodies supported by a harmonically conceived bass, leading to the development of monody (solo song) and recitative. The basso continuo also made possible various contrasts known collectively as concerting, or the *concertato* style. Such practices included the juxtaposition of instrumental and vocal forces; the contrasting of groups of various sizes within compositions scored for larger forces; the mixture of solo, duet, and *tutti* textures; and the use of concertists, singers who reinforced instrumental soloists' lines at various points.

The most influential source for the transmission of early continuo practice in Germany was Ludovico Viadana's (1560–1627) three-volume *Cento concerti ecclesiastici* (One Hundred Sacred Concerti; Venice, 1602), the first collection of sacred music to exploit the basso continuo. Four German editions of the *Concerti* appeared between 1609 and 1626, and the foreword to the collection became a touchstone for German theoretical writings on continuo practice. Basso continuo accompaniments to church music appeared in the German-speaking lands, beginning with Aichinger's *Cantiones ecclesiasticae* [. . .] *cum basso generali* (Sacred Concertos with Basso Continuo, 1607), and the practice rapidly became obligatory. A *bassus ad organum* part for Lassus's *Magnum opus musicum* appeared in 1625, for example, and Schütz, at the insistence of his publishers, included figured bass parts to his most conservative collections, *Cantiones sacrae* (Sacred Songs, 1625) and *Geistliche Chor-Music* (Spiritual Choir Music, 1648).

Seventeenth-century music with continuo accompaniment often consisted of series of phrases set off by contrasts in texture, performing forces, or harmony. Several types of writing became markers of the new continuo-derived style: "perforated" melodies, with short clauses separated by rests; motives declaimed syllabically in quick note values; repetitions or transpositions of short sections of text and the associated music; and written-out ornamentation derived from Italian solo song.

Such continuo-inspired music did not lead to the atrophy of the sixteenth-century polyphonic style in Germany, however. Sacred music in the *a cappella* style of Lassus's generation was regularly performed, emulated, and upheld as the pedagogical foundation for composers. Sixteenth-century music continued to be performed from retrospective collections, such as the first volume of

Erhard Bodenschatz's (1578–1636) *Florilegium portense* (Marvelous Harvest of Flowers, 1603), which includes motets by Lassus, Jacob Handl (1550–91), and other sixteenth-century composers. The *Florilegium* was used for generations at Bremen, Dresden, Grimma, Halle, Lüneburg, and Pirna, and still formed part of the repertory in Leipzig during J. S. Bach's tenure.[106] Even at more progressive Catholic centers such as Munich, Innsbruck, and Vienna, sacred works by Lassus and Palestrina remained in the repertoire until the eighteenth century.[107] Moreover, Latin and German motets heavily indebted to Lassus and to sixteenth-century Italian practice continued to be written throughout the century. As late as 1673 Johann Theile (1646–1724) published masses "sine basso continuo juxta veterum contrapuncti stylum" (without basso continuo and in the old style of counterpoint),[108] and Schütz asked Christoph Bernhard (1628–92) to write a funeral motet for him in the contrapuntal style of Palestrina.

Initially, the *stile antico* (old style) was considered one of several appropriate options for composing solemn church music. German composers of the early seventeenth century were expected to be musically bilingual — equally capable of writing works in the older and newer manners. By the second half of the century, however, the cultivation of the *stile antico* took on an air of self-conscious historicism, erudition, and even connoisseurship. This coexistence of old styles and multiple new compositional approaches led to a preoccupation with classifying and disputing the appropriateness of these practices. Theorists proposed classifications based on compositional distinctions between old style and new style (*stile moderno*); on national character (French, Italian, German, mixed); on location or function (church, chamber, theater); on genre (motet style, madrigal style); and, like literature, on the level of decorum (high, middle, low).

The idea of two practices — the first (*prima prattica*) based on the contrapuntal style of the sixteenth century, emphasizing imitative writing, lack of an obligatory continuo, rhythmic composure, and the careful treatment of dissonance; the other (*seconda prattica*) incorporating various innovations found in the word-based Italian vocal music of the late sixteenth and early seventeenth centuries — was adopted and modified by German theorists.[109] In the grave, contrapuntal style, dissonance was introduced and quitted discretely, while in the modern luxuriant style dissonances could be introduced with considerably more freedom.

In another fundamental distinction, articulated most fully and influentially by the Polish chapel master Marco Scacchi (ca. 1600–1662), a three-fold division obtained between the *stylus ecclesiasticus* (church style), *stylus cubicularis* (chamber style), and *stylus scenicus seu theatralis* (stage or theatrical style, embracing mainly recitative).[110] Scacchi's scheme became widely influential, in part because of its ability to encompass a variety of musical parameters, including function, compositional approach, and scoring. Athanasius Kircher's *Musurgia universalis* (1650) proposed a nine-fold scheme that was even more eclectic:[111]

1. *stylus ecclesiasticus*: for the church; full of majesty, solemn and grave
   a. *stylus ligatus* (with *cantus firmus* or chorale)
   b. *stylus solutus* (lacking a *cantus firmus*)

2. *stylus canonicus*: compositions in canon
3. *stylus moteticus*: more varied and florid version of the *stylus ecclesiasticus*
4. *stylus phantasticus*: improvisatory instrumental music
5. *stylus madrigalescus*: madrigal style; joyful, lively, used for portraying love, affection, and pain
6. *stylus melismaticus*: simple settings of strophic texts such as villanellas
7. *stylus choriacus et theatralis*: music for theater, and music for dance and ballet
8. *stylus symphoniacus*: instrumental ensemble music
9. *stylus dramaticus sive recitativus*: recitative style

Even schemes as wide-ranging as Kircher's, however, failed to embrace the diversity of actual compositional practice. In a polemical attack on Johann Mattheson's updated version of Scacchi's scheme, the Erfurt organist Johann Heinrich Buttstett (1666–1727) identified this inadequacy, trenchantly observing that distinctions between church, theater, and chamber music had vanished. "Es ist ja fast eine wie die andere. Bringet man doch jetzo nebst dem *Stylo recitativo Theatrali* fasst allen liederlichen Krahm in die Kirche / und je lustiger und tantzlicher es gehet / je besser gefallet es theils Personen" (One is pretty much the same as the other. Nearly every kind of songful stuff is presently brought into the church along with the *stylus recitativus theatralis*, and the more merrily and dancingly it goes, the better it pleases some people).[112] Buttstett's critique underscores the reason for German theorists' failure to produce a satisfactory classification scheme, namely the shifting relationship between style and genre. Musical genre distinctions suffered a fate similar to Opitz's literary genre distinctions: a loosening of bonds between specific types of texts and particular compositional styles. Religious texts were now set variously in the *stile antico*, in the polychoral style, and as modern *concertato* compositions for forces ranging from a single vocal soloist to large forces with obbligato instruments. Bernhard isolated this problem in discussing the pitfalls of classification schemes based on genres: "Sonsten aber könnte der Contrapunct mehr Divisiones leyden als in Motetten, Madrigalen, Canzonetten, Arien, Sonaten; etc. allein solches sind nicht sowohl Species des Contrapunctes als Themata der Componisten" (Counterpoint could otherwise admit even more divisions than into motets, madrigals, canzonettas, arias, sonatas, etc., yet such divisions are not so much types of contrapuntal composition as topics of the composers).[113] Schein's *Israelsbrünnlein* or *Fontana d'Israel* (Fountain of Israel, 1623) set Old Testament texts not in the time-honored style of the polyphonic motet, or even in the newer manner of the motet for solo voice and continuo, but rather for five voices "auf eine sonderbar Anmutige Italian Madrigalische Manier" (in a special, agreeable Italian madrigal manner). As we have seen, seventeenth-century lieder texts might be set in old or new styles, for solo voice, or even polyphonically. Even solo continuo lieder could draw on the melodic conceits of dance music, Italian monody, chorales, canzonettas, or even *stile antico* counterpoint.[114] This diversity, along with the tendency to mix compositional approaches within even a single work, proved to be the most characteristic trend in German music at the close of the early modern era.

Schütz's major published collections provide a concise overview of the range that characterized Protestant sacred music in the first half of the seventeenth century. His works included settings of German biblical texts as polychoral motets for as many as twenty voices (*Psalmen Davids*); Latin devotional literature in strict contrapuntal style (*Cantiones sacrae*); settings of Cornelius Becker's (1561–1604) rhymed Psalter in simple cantional style (*Becker Psalter*, 1628); Latin pieces for three to six voices and obbligato instruments heavily indebted to Italian music of the 1620s; smaller-scale German motets for a few voices and continuo; German compositions in *concertato* style for a variety of scorings; and a mixture of traditional and modern concertato motets for five to seven voices.

Seventeenth-century music based on traditional chorale tunes was equally varied. Cantional settings for congregational singing continued throughout the seventeenth century, and although many publications were simply reprintings of older settings, there were also distinguished new collections like Hassler's *Kirchengesänge*, Schein's widely used *Cantional oder Gesangbuch Augspurgischer Confession* (Songbook of the Augsburg Confession, 1627), and Schütz's *Becker Psalter*. Chorale melodies also began to be treated in unassuming settings for solo voice, often in "improved" versions where the metrical irregularities of the traditional tunes were replaced by regular metrical movement.[115] The most influential procedure, however, was pioneered by Schein in his *Opella nova I*, and even more systematically in the chorale concertos of Scheidt: each phrase of the chorale is heard in its original form in long, even notes only after being introduced by *Vorimitation* (fore-imitation), fugue-like imitation based on subjects derived by speeding up and ornamenting the chorale melody. Fore-imitation remained characteristic of chorale-based compositions throughout the Baroque.

In addition to a penchant for classifying musical styles, seventeenth-century musicians tried to justify their musical innovations by analogy to the tropes and figures of classical rhetoric.[116] Musical *inventio*, for example, was often identified with devising the appropriate musical motive, key, and rhythm; *dispositio* connoted the working-out and arrangement of these ideas within a composition. Similarly, the form of a musical work could be compared to the structure of an oration, as in Mattheson's comparison of the successive parts of a musical composition to the orational stages of *exordio, narratio, propositio, confirmatio, confutatio*, and *peroratio*.[117] The fundamental alliance between music and rhetoric, however, lay in their mutual use of *figura*. Seventeenth-century German theorists eagerly mapped architectonic devices onto the figures of classical rhetoric; for example, *anadiplosis* (repetition of the conclusion of one passage to begin the following one) was applied to the repetition of the cadential close of one phrase at the beginning of the next; *noema* (a phrase having greater meaning than its surface denotation) signified a passage in block homophonic chords within an otherwise imitative texture. The most prevalent figures represented local melodic ornaments, especially those that breached the rules of counterpoint for the sake of variety and grace: *superjectio* (exaggeration or overstatement) acquired the musical meaning of a dissonant ornamental note following a consonance; *abruptio* an unexpected break or rest. Such techniques for emphasizing or intensifying semantic features of a verbal text were repositioned by Mattheson and other writers in the early eighteenth century as resources for arousing human affections in both vocal and instrumental music. *Figurenlehre* (doctrine of figures), under the influence of a rising modern anthropology, was reinterpreted as *Affektenlehre* (doctrine of emotions) with the crucial result that music without words now assumed the power to mimic or represent ideas and emotional states, much like an oration.

A final development in seventeenth-century sacred music was the creation of dramatic genres, particularly cantata. For all their dazzling stylistic range, most works from the earlier half of the century were based on the common presupposition that the text should be of a single type: *Spruch* (biblical text), devotional prose, chorale, or strophic poetic text. Around midcentury, however, music both sacred and secular began to incorporate mixed, or prosimetric (combined prose and verse) texts, a practice reminiscent of the pastoral poetry of the Nuremberg *Pegnitz Schäfer* (Pegnitz Shepherds) that linked narrative with lyrical verses,[118] or of the lied texts incorporated into — to name but one work of many — the novel *Simplicissimus* (1669) by Hans Jacob Christoffel von Grimmelshausen (1621/22–1676). The mixed or multimovement cantata thus grew from two related tendencies: the uniting of different textual types within a single composition, and the sectionalizing of longer works. Intermediate stages in this process are audible around midcentury in sacred concertos having sections that are highly contrasted while retaining structural links to the surrounding material. Examples are Johann Rosenmüller's "Seine Jünger kamen des Nachts" (His Disciples Came by Night) and the works of Matthias Weckmann.[119]

Sacred cantatas (nondramatic religious works combining poetic and prose texts) assumed various shapes in the seventeenth century. Some juxtaposed a sacred concerto with a chorale setting (chorale cantata); others mixed concerto with aria (the concerto-aria cantata); still others combined chorale, concerto, and aria (the "older mixed cantata"). Only at the turn of the eighteenth century did German texts begin to be set in the manner of the Italian secular cantata, with recitative alternating with arias; the Weissenfels poet Erdmann Neumeister (1671–1756) experimented with a particularly complex mixture of recitative, aria, chorale, and concerto movements. Such designs would soon become standard in works by Bach, Händel, and Telemann.

Of these mixed types in the seventeenth century, the most commonly heard was the concerto-aria cantata, in which a strophic aria (setting a poetic text) was framed by outer movements of biblical prose set in the style of the traditional sacred concerto. The appeal of the concerto-aria cantata form lay not only in the neatly symmetrical arrangement of the movements but also in its juxtaposition of Bible verses with a poetic gloss, providing a musical commentary on the Word.[120] After 1670 the concerto-aria was cultivated by nearly all important Protestant composers; Buxtehude, for instance, wrote no fewer than twenty-one.[121] Although the form has long been considered a German invention, it may in fact have originated in the works of Italian composers at Dresden, particularly of Vincenzo Albrici (1631–96), who was writing concerto-aria cantatas as early as 1660.[122] It is fittingly emblematic that, at the close of the early modern era, Germany's most characteristic sacred music was an amalgam of traditional texts harking back to the time of Luther and operatic gestures that seemed to gaze enviously southward across the Alps.

Notes

[1] *The New Grove Dictionary of Music and Musicians*, 2nd ed. (London: Oxford UP, 2001), 709–34, here 709 and 733. Hereafter cited as NG2. The counterpart authority in German is *Musik in Geschichte und Gegenwart*, 17 vols., 2nd ed., ed. Friedrich Blume (Kassel: Bärenreiter und Metzler, 2005).

[2] An influential critique of this model of "diffusion" and of "center/periphery" is mounted in Reinhard Strohm, *The Rise of European Music, 1380–1500* (Cambridge: Cambridge UP, 1993), esp. 5–10; and in his "Centre and Periphery: Mainstream and Provincial Music," in *Companion to Medieval and Renaissance Music*, ed. Tess Knighton and David Fallows (New York: Schirmer Books, 1992), 55–59.

[3] Quantz, *Versuch einer Anweisung die Flöte traversiere zu spielen* (1789; repr., Kassel: Bärenreiter, 1953), 328; Quantz, *On Playing the Flute*, trans. and ed. Edward R. Reilly (New York: Schirmer Books, 1966), 338.

[4] Wilhelm Ambros, *Geschichte der Musik*, 5 vols., 3rd rev. ed. (Leipzig: Leuckart, 1887–1911).

[5] Strohm, *The Rise of European Music*, 1–11.

[6] The history of German opera, oratorio, and related genres is taken up by Sarah Colvin, "Musical Culture and Thought," in *German Literature of the Eighteenth Century: The Enlightenment and Sensibility*, ed. Barbara Becker-Cantarino, Camden House History of German Literature, vol. 5 (Rochester: Boydell & Brewer, 2005), 185–220.

[7] Quantz, *On Playing the Flute*, 340.

[8] Munich, Bayerische Staatsbibliothek, CLM 14274; (formerly Mus.ms.3232a).

[9] Tom R. Ward, "A Central European Repertory in Munich, Bayerische Staatsbibliothek, CLM 14274," in *Early Music History*, ed. Iain Fenlon (Cambridge: Cambridge UP, 1981), 1:325–44.

[10] NG2, "Universities I: Middle Ages and Renaissance," by Christopher Page.

[11] Athanasius Kircher, *Musurgia universalis*, ed. Ulf Scharlau (Hildesheim: Olms, 1970).

[12] Klaus Hortschansky, "Regionen und Zentren," in *Die Musik des 15. und 16. Jahrhunderts*, ed. Ludwig Finscher (Laaber: Laaber-Verlag, 1990), 2:45.

[13] Werner Braun, *Die Musik des 17. Jahrhunderts* (Wiesbaden: Akademische Verlagsgesellschaft, 1981), 46.

[14] Ulrich Siegele, "Bach and the Domestic Politics of Electoral Saxony," in *The Cambridge Companion to Bach*, ed. John Butt (Cambridge: Cambridge UP, 1977), 17–34.

[15] Susan Gattus, "16th-Century Nuremberg," in *The Renaissance: From the 1470s to the End of the 16th Century*, ed. Iain Fenlon (Englewood Cliffs, NJ: Prentice Hall, 1989), 288–93.

[16] Rebecca Wagner Ottinger, *Music as Propaganda in the German Reformation* (Aldershot: Ashgate, 2001).

[17] D. W. Krummel and Stanley Sadie, *The Norton/Grove Handbooks in Music: Music Printing and Publishing* (New York: Norton, 1990), 86.

[18] The scope of such publishing activity can be gauged from Konrad Ameln, Markus Jenny, and Walter Lipphardt, eds., *Das deutsche Kirchenlied: Verzeichnis der Drucke von den Anfängen bis 1800*, Répertoire international des sources musicales, B/VIII/1 (Kassel: Bärenreiter, 1975).

[19] Generally there were four partbooks, one for each of the parts: *cantus firmus, altus, tenor*, and *bassus*.

[20] Intabulation is the translation of vocal music into characteristic instrumental notation.

[21] NG2, "Wolkenstein, Oswald von," by Lorenz Welker.

[22] Martin Staehlin, "The German Tenor Lied: Drafting the History of a Genre," in *Music in the German Renaissance: Sources, Styles, and Contexts*, ed. John Kmetz (Cambridge: Cambridge UP, 1994), 176.

[23] The two manuscripts are, respectively: Berlin, Staatsbibliothek zu Berlin, Preussischer Kulturbesitz, Mus.40613; and Munich, Bayerische Staatsbibliothek, Cgm 810 (formerly Mus.ms.3232; Cim.351a).

[24] Staehlin, "The German Tenor Lied," 179–81.

[25] Ludwig Finscher and Silke Leopold, "Volkssprachige Gattungen und Instrumentalmusik," in Finscher, ed., *Die Musik des 15. und 16. Jahrhunderts*, 548; Strohm, *The Rise of European Music*, 496–99. "Voice leading" relates to how the various notes, or voices, of a chord progress linearly to the next according to stylistic rules of harmony.

[26] Finscher and Leopold, "Volkssprachige Gattungen und Instrumentalmusik," 552.

[27] The text follows Leopold Nowak, ed., *Das Deutsche Gesellschaftslied in Österreich von 1480–1550*, Denkmäler der Tonkunst in Österreich, XXVII/2, vol. 72 (Graz: Akademische Druck- und Verlagsanstalt, 1960), 41.

[28] Hermann Finck, *Practica musica* (Wittenberg, 1556); quoted in Jane A. Bernstein, "Financial Arrangements and the Role of Printer and Composer in Sixteenth-Century Italian Music Printing," *Acta musicologica* 63 (1991): 48.

[29] Stephen Keyl, "Tenorlied, Discantlied, Polyphonic Lied: Voices and Instruments in German Secular Polyphony of the Renaissance," *Early Music* 20 (1992): 434–45. Keyl questions the traditional assumption that the normative performance practice was to have a solo tenor voice accompanied by a group of instruments.

[30] Robert Eitner, ed., *Erhart Oeglin's Liederbuch* (1880; repr., New York: Broude Brothers, 1996), col. v.

[31] The *villanella* is a light rustic genre of secular vocal music; the *canzonetta* is related to the madrigal, but stylistically lighter.

[32] Contrafactum is usually a vocal composition whose text is changed or reworked to make it useful in a new context. The most common procedure is fitting a secular work with a sacred text, but retexting (but not "translating") in a different language is called the same thing.

[33] Ludwig Finscher, "Lied und Madrigal, 1580–1600," in Kmetz, ed., *Music in the German Renaissance*, 185.

[34] Orazio Vecchi, *The Four-Voice Canzonettas with original Texts and Contrafacta by Valentin Haussmann and Others*, ed. Ruth I. DeFord, Recent Researches in the Music of the Renaissance, vol. 92 (Madison: A-R Editions, 1993).

[35] For a list of Haussmann's publications see NG2, "Haussmann, Valentin," by Martin Ruhnke and Klaus-Peter Koch.

[36] Texts from Vecchi, *The Four-Voice Canzonettas*, 36 and 78.

[37] For this Petrarchist practice see in this volume the chapter by Gerhart Hoffmeister.

[38] Vecchi, *The Four-Voice Canzonettas*, 8.

[39] Denis Arnold, *Giovanni Gabrieli and the Music of the Venetian High Renaissance* (London: Oxford UP, 1979), 211–30; Konrad Küster, *Opus primum in Venedig: Traditionen des Vokalsatzes 1590–1650*, Freiburger Beiträge zur Musikwissenschaft, vol. 4 (Laaber: Laaber-Verlag, 1995).

[40] Jakob Regnart, *Deutsche dreistimmige Lieder nach Art der Neapolitanen nebst Leonhard Lechner's Fünfstimmiger Bearbeitung*, ed. Robert Eitner, Publikation aelterer praktischer und theoretischer Musikwerke, vol. 19 (1895; repr., New York: Broude Brothers, 1966), 7.

[41] R. Hinton Thomas, *Poetry and Song in the German Baroque: A Study of the Continuo Lied* (Oxford: Clarendon, 1963), 8.

[42] Nino Pirrotta, "Willaert and the Canzone Villanesca," in *Music and Culture in Italy from the Middle Ages to the Baroque, A Collection of Essays* (Cambridge: Harvard UP, 1984), 175–97; esp. 411, note 25.

[43] *Neue teutsche Lieder, erstlich durch [. . .] Jacob Regnart [. . .] componirt mit drey Stimmen nach Art der welschen Villanellen. Jetzund aber [. . .] mit fünf Stimmen gesetzt* (Nuremberg: Gerlach, 1579); modern edition in Regnart, *Deutsche dreistimmige Lieder*.

[44] Martin Opitz, *Buch von der Deutschen Poeterey* (1624), ed. Cornelius Sommer, UB 8397 (Stuttgart: Reclam, 1980).

[45] Ferdinand van Ingen, "Der Stand der Barocklied-Forschung in Deutschland," in *Weltliches und geistliches Lied des Barock: Studien zur Liedkultur in Deutschland und Scandinavien*, ed. Dieter Lohmeier (Amsterdam: Rodopi, 1979), 3–18. The first, so-called Strasbourg, edition of 1624 was published without Opitz's approval; he made improvements and republished the collection in Breslau as *Deutsche Poemata* so as to distinguish it from the first edition. On the controversy surrounding this situation see in this volume the chapter by Theodor Verweyen.

[46] van Ingen, "Der Stand der Barocklied-Forschung," 7.

[47] Quoted after van Ingen, "Der Stand der Barocklied-Forschung," 10.

[48] Thomas, *Poetry and Song*, 73–77.

[49] For examples, see John Herschel Baron, "Foreign Influences on the German Secular Solo Continuo Lied of the Mid-Seventeenth Century" (Ph.D. diss., Brandeis University, 1967), 100–104.

[50] Albert, *Arien II*, ed. Eduard Bernoulli, Denkmäler deutscher Tonkunst, ser. 1, vol. 13 (Wiesbaden: Breitkopf & Härtel, 1958).

[51] Quoted after Marian Szyrocki, *Die deutsche Literatur des Barock*, UB 9924 (Stuttgart: Reclam, 1979), 89.

[52] Hans Joachim Moser, *Heinrich Schütz: His Life and Work*, trans. Carl F. Pfatteicher (St. Louis: Concordia, 1959), 382.

53 Moser, *Heinrich Schütz*, 382.

54 But see Heinrich W. Schwab, "Zur Liedkunst Gabriel Voigtländers," in Lohmeier, ed., *Weltliches und geistliches Lied*, 185–88.

55 See in this volume the chapter by Renate Born on linguistic standardization.

56 The seminal work on music for the Lutheran Church is Friedrich Blume, et al., *Protestant Church Music: A History* (New York: Norton, 1974). This volume is an expanded translation of Blume's *Geschichte der evangelischen Kirchenmusik*, 2nd ed. (Kassel: Bärenreiter, 1965).

57 For a listing of Rhau's major collections and their contents see Blume, *Protestant Church Music*, 114–19; see also the works list in NG2, "Rhau, Georg," by Victor H. Mattfeld.

58 Jaroslav Pelikan and Helmut T. Lehmann, gen. eds., *Luther's Works* (Philadelphia: Fortress, 1967), 54:129–30. (Hereafter cited as *Luther's Works*.)

59 *Luther's Works*, 49:427. Translation according to the NIV.

60 On Luther's views of music see especially Walter E. Buszin, "Luther on Music," *Musical Quarterly* 32 (1946): 80–97; Carl Schalk, *Luther on Music: Paradigms of Praise* (St. Louis: Condordia, 1988); and Robin A. Leaver, "The Lutheran Reformation," in Fenlon, ed., *The Renaissance*, 263–85.

61 Full translations of Luther's preface are found in *Luther's Works*, 53:321–24.

62 Leaver, "The Lutheran Reformation," 267.

63 Leaver, "The Lutheran Reformation," 267, for example; and *Luther's Works*, 53:28.

64 On Luther's liturgical reforms see esp. Robin A. Leaver: "Theological Consistency, Liturgical Integrity, and Musical Hermeneutic in Luther's Liturgical Reforms," *Lutheran Quarterly* ix (1995): 117–38.

65 See, for example, Blume, *Protestant Church Music*, 13.

66 Michael Praetorius, *Syntagma musicum I* (Wolfenbüttel, 1615; facsimile reprint, Kassel: Bärenreiter, 1988), 451–53; translated in Piero Weiss and Richard Taruskin, eds., *Music in the Western World: A History in Documents* (New York: Schirmer Books, 1984), 104–5.

67 *D. Martin Luthers Werke: Kritische Gesamtausgabe* (Weimar: Böhlaus Nachfolger, 1908), 18:123; *Luther's Works*, 53:54.

68 The original melodies are transcribed in Johannes Riedel, ed., *Leise Settings of the Renaissance and Reformation*, Recent Researches in the Music of the Renaissance, vol. 35 (Madison: A-R Editions, 1980), vii.

69 NG2, "Chorale," by Robert L. Marshall and Robin A. Leaver.

70 NG2, "Luther, Martin," by Robin A. Leaver.

71 NG2, "Luther, Martin," by Leaver.

72 *Luther's Works*, 49:68–69; *D. Martin Luthers Werke, Briefwechsel*, 3:220.

73 Blume, *Protestant Church Music*, 46–47.

74 Otto Kade, ed., *Johann Walther (1496–1570): Wittembergisch geistlich Gesangbuch von 1524*, Publikation aelterer praktischer und theoretischer Musikwerke, vol. 7 (1878; repr., New York: Broude Brothers, 1966).

75 Blume, *Protestant Church Music*, 80–96.

76 Blume, *Protestant Church Music*, 113–21.

[77] See, for example, Flynn Warmington, "The Ceremony of the Armed Man: the Sword, the Altar, and the L'homme armé Mass," in Antoine Busnoys, *Method, Meaning, and Context in Late Medieval Music*, ed. Paula Higgins (Oxford: Clarendon, 1999), 89–130.

[78] Howard Mayer Brown, "Emulation, Competition, and Homage: Imitation and Theories of Imitation in the Renaissance," *Journal of the American Musicological Society* 35 (1982): 1–49.

[79] Jessie Anne Owens, "How Josquin became Josquin," in *Music in Renaissance Cities and Courts: Studies in Honor of Lewis Lockwood*, ed. Owens and Anthony M. Cummings (Warren, MI: Harmonie Park, 1997) 277–79; and Stephanie Schlagel, "Josquin des Prez and His Motets: A Case-Study in Sixteenth-Century Reception History" (Ph.D. diss., University of North Carolina at Chapel Hill, 1996).

[80] David Crook, *Orlando di Lasso's Imitation Magnificats for Counter-Reformation Munich* (Princeton: Princeton UP, 1994).

[81] Lothar Hoffmann-Erbrecht, "Stufen der Rezeption des niederländischen Stils in der deutschen Musik der Dürerzeit," in *Florilegium Musicologicum: Hellmut Federhofer zum 75. Geburtstag*, ed. Christoph-Hellmut Mahling (Tutzing: Schneider, 1988), 155–66.

[82] Modern edition in Martin Just, ed., *Der Kodex Berlin 40021, Erster Teil*, Das Erbe deutscher Musik, vol. 76 (Kassel: Bärenreiter, 1990), 137–38.

[83] Martin Just, "Polyphony based on Chant in a Late Fifteenth-Century German Manuscript," in Kmetz, ed., *Music in the German Renaissance*, 131.

[84] Blume, *Protestant Church Music*, 116–17.

[85] Blume, *Protestant Church Music*, 113–19.

[86] Modern edition in Gerstenberg, ed., *Ludwig Senfl*, 11:12–27.

[87] Strohm, "Heinrich Isaac und die Musik in Deutschland vor 1492," in *Heinrich Isaac und Paul Hofhaimer im Umfeld von Kaiser Maximilian I.*, ed. Walter Sallmen (Innsbruck: Edition Helbling, 1997), 24.

[88] NG2, "Isaac, Henricus," by Reinhard Strohm and Emma Kempson.

[89] Isaac also wrote *alternatim* masses, which, like the *Choralis Constantinus*, were based on chants for the Ordinary of the Mass rather than on secular tenors. However, in an *alternatim* mass the entire text of the Ordinary is not set to vocal polyphony; instead, short sections or versets are left to be sung in plainchant or replaced by short organ pieces. One source explicitly labeled such a setting "Missae ad Organum," a rubric that reflects the performance practice of the imperial chapel of Maximilian I. This practice of inserting organ versets seems to have been particularly important in the circles around Hofhaimer, a renowned organist who served Maximilian at several points during his career.

[90] From Greek *chromos* "color"; chromaticism makes use of tones that fall outside of the regular diatonic scale, thereby lending greater color or emotional expression.

[91] Joachim Burmeister, *Musical Poetics*, trans. Benito V. Rivera (New Haven: Yale UP, 1993), esp. 155–99.

[92] Vienna, Haus-, Hof- und Staatsarchiv, Habsburgisch-Lothringisches Familienarchiv, Familienkorrespondenz A, Karton 49, No. 78, fol. 8r.

[93] Quantz, *On Playing the Flute*, 341.

[94] From the title page of Johann Hermann Schein's *Opella nova I* (Dresden, 1618); facsimile in *Opella nova: Erster Teil Geistlicher Konzerten, 1618*, ed. Adam Adrio and Siegmund Helms (Kassel: Bärenreiter, 1973), viii.

[95] Gina Spagnoli, *Letters and Documents of Heinrich Schütz 1656–1672: An Annotated Translation* (Ann Arbor: UMI Research, 1990), 223–38. Compositions by Italian musicians, particularly small-scale Latin motets, were widely anthologized in German collections, for example in the printed collections assembled by Georg Victorinus (d. 1639), Johann Donfried (1589–1661), and Ambrosius Profe (1589–1661). See Jerome Roche, "Anthologies and the Dissemination of Early Baroque Italian Sacred Music," *Soundings* 4 (1974): 6–11.

[96] Herbert Seifert, "Frühes italienisches Musikdrama nördlich der Alpen: Salzburg, Prag, Wien, Regensburg, und Innsbruck," in *In Teutschland noch gantz ohnbekandt: Monteverdi-Rezeption und frühes Musiktheater im deutschsprachigen Raum*, ed. Markus Engelhardt (Frankfurt am Main: Lang, 1996), 29–44.

[97] Getraut Haberkamp, "Werke mit Musik für die deutschsprachige Bühne des 17. Jahrhunderts — der aktuelle Quellenstand," in Engelhardt, ed., *In Teutschland*, 1–28.

[98] For a list of the students and associates of Giovanni Gabrieli see Richard Charteris, *Giovanni Gabrieli (ca. 1555–1612): A Thematic Catalogue of His Music with a Guide to the Source Materials and Translations of His Vocal Texts*, Thematic Catalogues, no. 20, gen. ed. Barry S. Brook (Stuyvesant, NY: Pendragon, 1996), xi–xiii.

[99] Charteris, *Giovanni Gabrieli*, passim.

[100] The Graz court of Archduke Ferdinand (later Holy Roman Emperor Ferdinand II, r. 1619–37) was an important hub for the copying and transmission of large-scale polychoral works from Venice; other important centers included Augsburg (with works by Hassler, Aichinger, Christian Erbach, and Adam Gumpelzhaimer) and Hamburg (Hieronymus Praetorius and Heinrich Scheidemann).

[101] Braun, *Die Musik des 17. Jahrhunderts*, 186.

[102] Don L. Smithers, *The Music and History of the Baroque Trumpet before 1721*, 2nd ed. (Carbondale: Southern Illinois UP, 1988), 133–34.

[103] Modern editions in Wilibald Gurlitt, ed., *Gesamtausgabe der musikalischen Werke von Michael Praetorius*, vol. 17/2 (Wolfenbüttel: Kallmeyer, [1933]); and Gottlieb Harms and Christhard Mahrenholz, eds., *Samuel Scheidt: Werke*, vol. 4 (Leipzig: Deutscher Verlag für Musik, 1933).

[104] On the works performed at the Reformationsjubiläum see Christhard Mahrenholz, "Heinrich Schütz und das erste Reformationsjubiläum 1617," in *Musicologica et liturgica: Gesammelte Aufsätze von Christhard Mahrenholz*, ed. Karl Ferdinand Müller (Kassel: Bärenreiter, 1960), 198–204.

[105] Lorenzo Bianconi, *Music in the Seventeenth Century*, trans. David Bryant (Cambridge: Cambridge UP, 1987), 113.

[106] NG2, "Bodenschatz, Erhard," by Otto Riemer and Clytus Gottwald.

[107] Orlando di Lasso, *Das Hymnarium aus dem Jahre 1580/81*, ed. Marie Louise Göllner, Sämtliche Werke, new ser., vol. 18 (Kassel: Bärenreiter, 1980), vii.

[108] Kerala J. Snyder, *Dieterich Buxtehude: Organist in Lübeck* (New York: Schirmer Books, 1987), 223.

[109] Notable among them was Schütz's colleague Bernhard, who identified the hallmark distinction between *contrapunctus gravis*, or *stylus antiquus*, and *contrapunctus luxurians*, or *stylus modernus* as a matter of how dissonance was treated. Walter Hilse, "The Treatises of Christoph Bernhard," *The Music Forum* 3 (1973): 1–196.

[110] Claude V. Palisca, "Marco Scacchi's Defense of Modern Music (1649)," in *Words and Music: The Scholar's View*, ed. Laurence Berman (Cambridge: Harvard UP, 1972), 189–235.

[111] Kircher, *Musurgia universalis*, I:581–97.

[112] Quoted in Claude V. Palisca, "The Genesis of Mattheson's Style Classification," in *New Mattheson Studies*, ed. George J. Buelow and Hans Joachim Marx (Cambridge: Cambridge UP, 1983), 410.

[113] Joseph Müller-Blattau, *Die Kompositionslehre Heinrich Schützens in der Fassung seines Schülers Christoph Bernhard*, 2nd ed. (Kassel: Bärenreiter, 1963), 42–43.

[114] Braun, *Die Musik des 17. Jahrhunderts*, 179 and 229.

[115] Chorales also inspired more complex settings, employing such techniques as chorale-derived phrases treated in imitation (chorale motets); chorale used as a *cantus firmus*; chorale tune ornamented with diminutions as in Italian vocal music; even madrigal-like settings.

[116] Dietrich Bartel, *Musica poetica: Musical-Rhetorical Figures in German Baroque Music* (Lincoln: U of Nebraska P, 1997). For a concise introduction to rhetorical practice see in this volume the chapter by Joachim Knape.

[117] Bartel, *Musica poetica*, 80–82.

[118] Klaus Garber, ed., *Pegnesisches Schäfergedicht 1644–1645*, Deutsche Neudrucke, Reihe: Barock, 8 (Tübingen: Niemeyer, 1966); Garber, "Nuremberg, Arcadia on the Pegnitz: The Self-Stylization of an Urban Sodality," in *Imperiled Heritage: Tradition, History, and Utopia in Early Modern German Literature*, ed. Max Reinhart, Studies in European Cultural Transition 5 (Aldershot: Ashgate, 2000), 117–208. Pastoral poetry is dealt with further by Max Reinhart in the introduction to this volume.

[119] They are preserved in the manuscript Lüneburg, Ratsbücherei, Mus. ant. pract. KN 207/6. For Rosenmüller see Peter Wollny, "Zur stilistischen Entwicklung des geistlichen Konzerts in der Nachfolge von Heinrich Schütz," *Schütz Jahrbuch* 23 (2001): 16–17; for Weckmann, *Four Sacred Concertos*, ed. Alexander Silbiger, Recent Researches in the Music of the Baroque Era, vol. 46 (Madison: A-R Editions, 1984), xii.

[120] NG2, "Cantata (II), The German Cantata to 1800," by Friedhelm Krummacher.

[121] Snyder, *Dieterich Buxtehude*, 198–200.

[122] NG2, "Albrici, Vincenzo," by Mary Frandsen.

The imperial library at Vienna, from Edward Brown, Durch Niederland, Teutschland, Hungarn . . . gethane Reisen (Nuremberg, 1711). Courtesy of Herzog August Bibliothek, Wolfenbüttel.

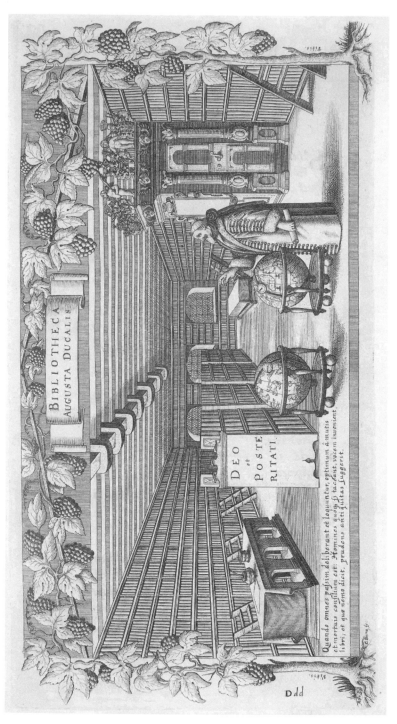

Duke August of Braunschweig-Lüneburg in his library, from Martin Gosky, Arbustum vel Arboretum Augustæum (Wolfenbüttel: Stern, 1650). Courtesy of Herzog August Bibliothek, Wolfenbüttel.

Early Modern German Libraries and Collections

Jill Bepler

Reconstructing Libraries

T HE LITERARY PRODUCTS OF ANY ERA can be fully understood only in the
light of the texts and contexts of which they form a part. As a discipline,
the history of ideas traces the movement of knowledge, transferred in texts or
by the process of instruction and education in general. The history of the
transmission of texts, both the media by which they were transmitted and the
institutions in which they were preserved, has been a focus of intellectual history over recent decades.[1] Ideally we would always like to know exactly which
texts — whether those literally being consulted or those stored in memory
from previous reading — an author had at his or her disposal during the writing process. The sources for such information are varied, incompletely preserved, and often hard to track down. The reception of the texts themselves
can be traced to a greater or lesser extent via direct and indirect references in
other texts in the form of quotations or notes. Texts were discussed and information about them disseminated in printed journals or unprinted correspondence. A degree of understanding of the historical and local contexts in which
they were read and the way in which they were used by individual readers can
be gained from those readers' marginalia and from taking note of their provenance.[2] Books and manuscripts are preserved as artifacts in libraries and
archives. These institutions themselves have checkered histories, which are
often difficult to reconstruct. The fact that texts are traded as commodities in
the form of books means that few collections have ever been static. The history of large libraries necessarily encompasses the history of a great number of
individual collectors and collections, and its reconstruction is dependent on
the archival material available, on detailed records of acquisitions, and on the
survival of earlier inventories and catalogues.[3] Library and auction catalogues
give information on the size and contents of collections and provide insight
into the popularity and geographical distribution of individual texts.[4] The
investigation of book ownership and the reconstruction of libraries provide a
necessary basis for studies in intellectual history, just as knowledge of the
organization of collections gives insights into changing ideas about the sys-
tematization of knowledge.[5] The history of collections belonging to institutions, whether ecclesiastical, academic, civic, or dynastic, and the prestige they
enjoyed at any given moment reflect the cultural climate of the times. The

composition of individual collections mirrors shifts in paradigm, from theology as the "queen of sciences" in the late Middle Ages to philosophy in the early Enlightenment, from library systems organized in hierarchical groups based on the university faculties and the liberal arts to open systems based on alphabetical author catalogues.

Collectors and Collections

In the late Middle Ages a new figure entered the European intellectual landscape: the individual lay collector whose personal prestige was in part expressed in the ownership of an identifiable corpus of artifacts, sometimes works of art, sometimes books. Individual collections began to rival those held by the institutions of the church (monasteries, cathedrals) or the state (treasuries), and it was only with the establishment of large public museums and collections in the mid-eighteenth century that they lost in significance. Throughout Germany well into the seventeenth century, libraries belonging to private individuals remained larger than collections held at universities. All major collections presently in the public domain, such as school and civic or parish libraries, owe their development to the incorporation of large private collections.[6]

The emergence of the individual collector took place on many levels of society, from the spheres of the high aristocracy down to the artisan household. The construction of identity and social prestige via consumerism, a phenomenon usually associated with the eighteenth century, can be seen in the stereotype of the *collector* in the early modern period.[7] Whether the interest was in books, art, or curiosities, the early modern collector occupied a part in a complex fabric of relationships, which combined the various participants into a common "social nexus."[8] The role of communication networks in the early modern period, especially the development of postal services,[9] the improvement of infrastructures, and the impact of foreign trade and professional commercial networks in facilitating collections, have only just begun to be explored.[10]

Among the lesser aristocracy and burgher families collections often became dynastic affairs, handed down over generations and secured by bequests. The act of collecting on a large scale was in most cases inextricably linked with travel and the viewing of other collections.[11] This was as true of university scholars of the late Middle Ages, of humanists and diplomats, of young aristocrats on their Grand Tours, as of sons of burghers traveling as pilgrims, students, or tutors.

The sixteenth century saw the advent of theories of collecting, or theories of museums, the most prominent in the German territories being the *Inscriptiones vel tituli theatri amplissimi* (Inscriptions, or Main Divisions of a Museum, 1565) of the Flemish scholar Samuel Quiccheberg (1529–67), who was put in charge of organizing the *Kunstkammer* (art or curiosity cabinet) collections of the Munich court. Quiccheberg had previously worked as a curator and librarian in Augsburg for Johann Jakob Fugger (1516–75), who kept in contact with a vast network of international agents. Quiccheberg's *Inscriptiones*, apostrophized as the first museum theory, aims at providing a system for organizing the presentation of all known types of collections, which provide the information necessary for understanding the world of phenomena. It also stresses the integral relationship between collections of material artifacts and the library.[12] Quiccheberg devotes a section of his tract to describing how books should be systematized (Roth 79–81). In her study of the interdependence of the various collections of the electors at Dresden, Helen Watanabe-O'Kelly cites Francis Bacon's *Gesta Grayorum* (1594), which defines the "four principal works and monuments" needed for the study of philosophy: a *Kunstkammer*, "a most perfect and general library," a garden, and an alchemical laboratory.[13] At least in a court context the history of book collections must always be seen in the broader framework of the genesis of other dynastic collections.[14]

In the early seventeenth century, important impulses for defining the purpose of libraries came with the publication of a number of seminal works.[15] The Jesuit Claude Clément's (1596–1642) *Musei sive bibliothecae tam privatae quam publicae* (Museums or Libraries Private and Public, 1628) was based on his experience at the Escorial in Madrid, where he taught at the Imperial College. The work is a celebration of an ideal spectacular library that, by virtue of combining aesthetic experience with scholarly learning, would serve to edify the user and the visitor. For this purpose Clément suggests an elaborate iconographical program of decoration for the various rooms of the library to enhance the *Kunstkammer* artifacts on display there.[16] The *Advis pour dresser une bibliothèque* (Advice on how to Furbish a Library, 1627) of the French physician and librarian Gabriel Naudé (1600–1653) is, by contrast, primarily concerned with providing a blueprint for promoting universal collections open to a broader scholarly public as a means of improving the general state of learning. Naudé's treatise marked a shift from the perception of the library as a static repository of knowledge to that of an institution actively engaged in producing new knowledge.[17] As librarian to Cardinal Mazarin in Paris, in charge of one of the largest collections in Europe, Naudé was sought out by scholarly visitors to the city as an authority in the book world, a role played by the brothers Dupuy a generation before him.[18]

During the Commonwealth in England the German exile Samuel Hartlib (d. 1662) and the indefatigable promoter of church unity John Durie (1596–1680) collaborated to write *The Reformed Librarie-Keeper* (1650), which advocates the public and political role of the library in reforming society as a whole. In their utopian vision of a well-administered library, librarians as "agents for the advancement of universal Learning"[19] play a central role as brokers of knowledge.

In Germany, publications on libraries were often accompanied by descriptions of actual collections. Notable examples are those by Johann Saubert and Johann Jakob Leibniz on Nuremberg collections (1646 and 1674, respectively), Hermann Conring on the Wolfenbüttel library (1661), and Christian Juncker on the library at Eisenach (1709). What emerges from a study of these works is that, because of their close links to other collections, most libraries were not just repositories for books: they also housed objects of art, medals and coins, maps and globes, curiosity cabinets, and mathematical and optical instruments.

The focus of the present essay is on books, on the various types of libraries, and on the activity of book collecting that evolved over the early modern period, specifically in Germany. Of necessity only a summary account can be given, and it must be stressed that the history of book collecting for the period, inextricably associated as it was with other modes of collecting, can be properly understood only against the background of the spread of printing and of the Reformation. In this process the library played a vital role as the repository of legitimating texts for Protestants and Catholics alike.[20]

Book Collections in the Late Middle Ages

Church Libraries

In the Middle Ages the largest libraries were in the hands of the church, and book production, collection, and distribution almost exclusively a prerogative of church institutions. In monastic scriptoria, manuscripts were produced for the use of the home monastery or nunnery. Copies were made additionally for "export" to other religious houses or for use by missionaries and in cathedral schools. By the first half of the fifteenth century, however, manuscripts were also being commercially produced in workshops, such as that belonging to Diebold Lauber (fl. 1450–71) in Hagenau.[21] The most important challenge to the monopoly of the church came in the mid-fifteenth century with the invention of printing, which effectively destroyed the inherent link between scriptorium and library and made book production and book collection two separate activities. Book production became a purely commercial enterprise.[22] By the latter half of the fourteenth century, monastic libraries were losing their key position as the main repositories of written knowledge; two new types of secular library were emerging to challenge their position: town council libraries, which in some cases were merged with parish libraries to form city libraries, and college or faculty libraries from which university libraries later developed.

Town Council Libraries

Town council libraries were small legal and administrative reference libraries for the use of the city's public servants and usually supervised by a *Stadtschreiber* (city archivist).[23] Their largely legal character underwent fundamental change in the course of time as a result of donations of large numbers of books from private collections containing works from multiple areas of interest. This was the case with one of the oldest such collections, the Nuremberg council library, first officially mentioned in 1370; by the beginning of the sixteenth century it contained not only the usual legal and historical works but humanist, religious, and scientific texts as well. This transformation began in 1429, when the theologian Konrad Kunhofer drew up his will and donated his books to the town council. In 1432 a special room was furnished to house the collection, which according to an inventory of 1443 comprised 151 volumes; by the time the first catalogue was compiled in 1486 the number had risen to 371. Several major acquisitions were made by the Nuremberg council from private collections, among them books from the library of the physician Hermann Schedel (1410–85) and, in 1546, 146 volumes from the estate of the mathematician and astronomer Regiomontanus (Johannes Müller von Königsberg, 1436–76).[24] Donations and legacies of books to town council collections came mainly from individuals who had been associated with the council in an official capacity, whereas it remained more usual for burghers and patricians to follow the medieval tradition of leaving their books to a parish library. For example, the Braunschweig notary and city archivist Gerwin von Hameln (ca. 1415–96) donated his 336 books to the Church of St. Andrew in 1495 rather than leave them to the town council he had served.[25] This tradition continued into the eighteenth century. In Halle, for example, some university professors preferred to leave their libraries to the Marienbibliothek (Marian Library) of the Stadtkirche (City Church) rather than to the university library.[26] In many cases, such as Nuremberg, the parish library and the town council library were not easily distinguished from one another; the library in Emden, now called the Johannes a Lasco Bibliothek, was housed at the Grosse Kirche (Great Church).

College Libraries

The second type of library to come into being in the fourteenth century was the college or faculty library. The arts faculty, in which students received their basic instruction, had its own library, as did the higher faculties of theology, law, and medicine. Access to these holdings was often restricted to professors.[27] The most famous college library in Germany was founded in 1412 in Erfurt, when the physician Amplonius Rating de Bercka (ca. 1365–1435) made provision for his collection of 633 manuscripts to go to the Collegium Amplonianum, which he had created in 1392 on the opening of the University of Erfurt (he became the university's second rector in 1395). Amplonius had studied in Prague and Cologne and taught in Erfurt and Vienna. From 1401 he was personal physician to the elector of Cologne, whom he accompanied to Italy. He started his manuscript collection as a student, and, like many collections of the period, it is dominated by texts concerned with philosophy, theology, and medicine. Amplonius was not a bibliophile but a scholar; his books document his travels, the development of his intellectual interests, and his needs as a practicing physician in Cologne. He bought manuscripts, copied them himself, or commissioned copies, and he was given manuscripts as gifts. Before donating his library Amplonius personally catalogued the books, thereby providing us with valuable documentation of a private library in the late Middle Ages, typically arranged into subject groups according to the standard disciplines of knowledge: the seven liberal arts, medicine, civil and canon law, and theology. All in all he had collected 3,748 treatises embracing all subjects taught at Erfurt.[28] Other college libraries were created soon after in Rostock (1419), Greifswald (1456), and Ingolstadt (1472).[29]

Reformation and Confessionalization

Monastic and Jesuit Libraries

Calls for monastic reform in the late Middle Ages were accompanied by demands for the revival of study in the monasteries and the upkeep of both libraries and scriptoria. The Sponheim abbot Johannes Trithemius (1462–1516) later characterized the library of a monastery as an accurate measure of its intellectual and moral state. The reform movement Devotio Moderna, which originated in Deventer and was propagated by the Augustinian Chorherren Stift (House of Canons Regular) in Windesheim and its subsidiaries (combined in 1400 to form the Windesheim Congregation), was predicated on the primary importance of book culture and libraries. The scribes produced manuscripts for individual use, for use by the order as a whole, and for sale *pro pretio*.[30] In this they were followed by the Brothers of the Common Life, whose most important task was the copying and, later, printing of devotional texts and their dissemination among the laity.[31]

The development of the library at Sponheim under Trithemius, a member of the Bursfeld Congregation reform movement, provides an early example of the establishment of a large monastic collection guided by humanist principles. Trithemius became abbot in 1482 and quickly set about building up the library to over 2,000 volumes.[32] Scholarly visitors were shown around by the abbot himself and were astonished not merely by the size of the collection but also by the wealth of languages represented in it beyond the Latin, Greek, and Hebrew expected of the humanist scholar. The ceiling and walls of the rooms were decorated with verses in Greek, Latin, and Hebrew. It is not surprising that visitors spoke of the Sponheim collection as Trithemius's own rather than the monastery's.[33] As it was formed around the specific scholarly interests of the abbot himself, however, the collection did not survive intact beyond his term of office.

Mostly located in relatively remote regions, monastery libraries were by nature not readily accessible to the broader public. Collections suffered, especially during the Peasants' War of 1524–25, but during the entire Reformation period because of dislocations and neglect or worse. The late sixteenth and the seventeenth century at last saw a resurgence of monastic libraries, and by the eighteenth century the library in Benediktbeuern (Upper Bavaria) held over 60,000 volumes.[34] Most calls for improvements in ecclesiastical libraries sought to raise the standard of education among priests, thus providing better pastoral care for the lay population. It was not until the founding of the Jesuit Order in the mid-sixteenth century and the subsequent Counter-Reformation that the use of books, pamphlets, and libraries became a strong focus of Catholic pastoral and missionary activity.[35] The establishment of Jesuit colleges and schools brought with it the foundation of important libraries that were central to the restorationist mission of the Counter-Reformation.

Some sixty-one Catholic colleges were founded in the German territories before 1640. Jesuit rules made careful provision for the maintenance and development of book collections. The fact that these rules, established in Coimbra in 1546, had validity for all libraries belonging to the order meant that acquisitions reflected not the dictates of individual collectors but tended to represent the interest of the order. Specific regulations prescribed that only the rector of the college make the final decision on which books were ordered, that no book on the *Index librorum prohibitorum* be placed on the shelves, that the books be catalogued both alphabetically and systematically, and that access to the collections be restricted to members of the college. Petrus Canisius (Peter de Hondt, 1521–97), author of immensely popular catechisms reprinted well into the twentieth century, was active in establishing libraries at Prague, Dillingen, Ingolstadt, and Innsbruck, and he ordered books from the Frankfurt book fair.[36] Records from Passau show that when its Jesuit college was founded in 1612, significant sums were immediately forthcoming for increasing the holdings of the library.[37]

Protestant Church and School Libraries

Jesuit schools were founded in direct response to the Protestant concentration on education and — as demanded by Martin Luther in his *An die Ratsherren aller Städte deutsches Landes* (To the Magistrates of All the Towns in Germany) of 1524 — the establishment of public and school libraries.[38] Luther's later opinions on burgeoning book production and libraries are somewhat ambivalent,[39] but in this particular tract he declares that the only way to uphold the true faith is to enable study of the Bible through solid grounding in Hebrew, Greek, and Latin: "Und last uns das gesagt seyn. Das wyr das Euangelion nicht wol warden erhallten on die sprachen"[40] (And let us take heed of this. That we will not be able to keep the gospel without languages). This call for new schools is accompanied by Luther's call for new libraries:

> Am letzten ist auch das wol zu bedencken allen den yenigen, so lieb und lust haben, das solche schulen und sprachen ynn Deutschen landen auffgericht und erhallten werden, das man fleys und koste nicht spare, gutte librareyen odder bücher heuser sonderlich ynn den großen stedten, die solichs wol vermügen, zuverschaffen.[41]

> [Finally it must also be taken into consideration by all those who are in favor of establishing such schools and languages in German territories, that one should not spare effort and cost on creating good libraries or houses for books, especially in the large cities, which can well afford it.]

Luther makes concrete suggestions about which works belong in the libraries. Traditional scholastic schoolbooks consisting of maxims, *quaestiones*, and sermons are to be replaced by editions of the Bible in as many languages as possible; likewise recommended are interpretations of the Bible; works of the ancient poets, and rhetoric for the acquisition of grammar and languages; and books on the liberal arts, law, and medicine. He adds: "Mit den fürnemsten aber sollten seyn die Chronicken und Historien, waserley sprachen man haben künde" (Among the most important, however, should be the chronicles and histories, in whatever languages are available).[42] Luther was no bibliophile, to be sure; he elsewhere recommends a strict selection of the best works available and condemns the indiscriminate accumulation of great numbers of books.[43]

Both the Reformation and the Counter-Reformation thus accorded schools and libraries the task of defending, upholding, and disseminating the teachings of the respective new or old faith.[44] The dissolution of monasteries in the wake of the Reformation meant that the fate of their book collections was often one of the immediate practical problems with which reformers were confronted. From as early as 1524, monastic collections, mostly those belonging to the mendicant orders located in the towns, were transferred to civic ownership, as, for example, in Magdeburg, Riga, and Joachimsthal.[45] Larger monastic collections were integrated into dynastic or university collections. Such was the case with the books belonging to the religious houses of the Wolfenbüttel territories, which were requisitioned by Duke Julius of Braunschweig-Lüneburg in 1572; such too the monastic libraries of Hesse, whose holdings provided the foundations of the university library at Marburg in 1532. However, many works from medieval collections perished. Vellum from the manuscripts, especially liturgical manuscripts, was recycled by bookbinders. A chance archival find from Aschersleben dated 1548 reads: "8 Thaler vor 1 Centhner vnd 18 Pfund Pergameen der alten Bucher vß der Kyrchenn verkaufft [. . .] eynem Buch bynder" (8 Talers for 1 hundredweight and 18 pounds of parchment from the old books out of the church sold to a bookbinder).[46]

The literary canon of the early modern period is reflected in the textbooks prescribed by the *Schulordnungen* (school ordinances) issued in the wake of the Reformation and throughout the period by cities and territorial rulers who sought to improve standards of education.[47] Similarly, the *Kirchenordnungen* (church ordinances) issued by the reformers paid close attention to the question of libraries, especially those drawn up for the North German territories by the Wittenberg educator Johannes Bugenhagen (1485–1558). The authorities were called upon to ensure that parish and monastic libraries were protected from harm and that each town should establish a "gemeyne Liberie" (public library) for the use of the clergy and employees in the schools.[48] Supervision of the library was assigned to the preacher, the almoner, or to the school rector, and parishioners were encouraged to donate books, or money for books, to the library. The Marienbibliothek in Halle was founded in 1552 when Matthias Scheller donated a sum of money for the purchase of the complete works of Martin Luther, "zum ahnfangk der leybereygen zu unser lieben frawen" (for the start of the little library at [the church of] Our Dear Lady). From this point, regular donations for the library can be found in the church records at Halle. The collection grew significantly and, in accordance with the precepts of Luther's *An die Ratsherren*, comprised not just theological texts but works from all disciplines. In 1610 a new building was erected to house it; by 1617 the library consisted of 5,000 volumes, and a librarian had been appointed to supervise it.[49] Many other Protestant church libraries were established in the course of the sixteenth century as clergymen left private collections to their parishes.[50] In the cities such collections grew to significant size, and by virtue of the terms of some bequests their administration often lay in the hands of civic authorities.

Institutional and Private Collections in the Early Modern Period

University Collections and Professors' Private Libraries

In 1512, equipped with significant funds from Friedrich der Weise (the Wise, 1463–1525), elector of Saxony, the humanist theologian Georg Spalatin (1484–1545), Friedrich's chief counsel, began buying books for the library of the University of Wittenberg, which had been founded by Friedrich in 1502. This collection marked the beginning of a new type of university collection that came to replace the medieval faculty library.[51] The elector not only donated books from his own personal library but was also involved in procuring books, most notably by writing in 1512 to Aldus Manutius, the famous Venetian printer (Aldine Press) to send books, which he intends "pro communi omnium utilitate, et doctorum, et discipulorum nostrae academiae tam posteriorum quam praesentium" (for the common use of all doctors as well as students of our university, present and future).[52] Spalatin remained in charge of the library during the reigns of three electors in all. In 1536, when the university statutes were rewritten, the library was provided with an annual budget and a librarian appointed. Acquisitions reveal a concerted effort to establish a universal collection suited to the needs of teachers and students alike. In 1533 the reformer and educator Philipp Melanchthon (1497–1560) urged the elector to buy books from all kinds of disciplines in Latin and German, rather than concentrating on theological books written by local authors.[53] Particular attention was paid to purchasing Hebrew works for the collections. So central was the role of the electors in building up the Wittenberg collection that Johann Friedrich (1503–54) was able to claim the university library as his personal property when he was deposed as elector of Saxony after the Battle of Mühlberg (24 April 1547) toward the end of the Schmalkaldic War. The books were transferred first to his new residence in Weimar and then to Jena to form the basis for the library of his new foundation, the University of Jena.[54]

Like those at Wittenberg and Jena, all university libraries founded in the sixteenth and seventeenth centuries depended on material support from the ruler of the territory in which they were located. The University of Helmstedt, for instance, was founded in 1576, but the library was not established until 1618, when Duke Friedrich Ulrich (1591–1634) presented the institution with the complete Wolfenbüttel library belonging to his forefathers, comprising about 4,300 volumes.[55] Several German university libraries had fewer than 2,000 volumes in the seventeenth century. The University of Altdorf, originally founded as a Gymnasium and elevated to university status in 1623, was a civic foundation of the city of Nuremberg. Its library also developed slowly, notwithstanding the university's renown in Europe. By 1601, the collection contained around 920 works, 700 of which came from a single estate.[56] By 1750, the number had risen to just over 6,900.[57] The library of the University of Vienna was put on a sound footing only when Empress Maria Theresia donated the library of the dissolved Jesuit Order to the university in 1755.[58] When the University of Kiel opened in 1665 the library had 1,800 volumes; sixty years later there were only 5,000 in the collection. The libraries at Rostock and Kiel were open only three hours per week in 1701.[59] It was not until the eighteenth century that university libraries with several thousand volumes emerged as the centers of scholarly study we know today.

Under these circumstances it is hardly surprising that the most important instruments of university teaching were professors' private libraries. Students able to afford to do so lodged with their professors, who did their most important teaching in their homes. The composition of the library belonging to Melanchthon's son-in-law, Caspar Peucer (1525–1602), professor of mathematics and later of medicine in Wittenberg, was obviously dictated by his lecturing needs. The inventory lists 1,455 titles and shows his interest in not only the classics but also contemporary works and the discussion and solution of the practical questions of his day. The largest subject categories in the collection are those in which Peucer lectured: medicine and history.[60] The history collection reflects his role as successor to Melanchthon as professor of world history.[61] His collection of legal texts was built upon his function as an advisor to Elector August prior to his twelve-year imprisonment on suspicion of Crypto-Calvinism in the crackdown by orthodox (Gnesio-) Lutherans in 1574. Peucer was forced to store his library at Bautzen, where the inventory was taken.[62]

A generation later, Johann Gerhard (1582–1637), professor of theology in Jena and author of the widely-read *Meditationes sacrae* (Sacred Meditations, 1606), was known for making his excellent library accessible to the students who lodged in his house as well as to interested scholars.[63] The collection was continued by Gerhard's oldest son, Johann Ernst Gerhard (1621–68), at whose death it contained over 6,000 volumes.[64] Johann Ernst developed his father's working theological library into a universal collection, obviously influenced by the libraries he had visited during his journeys after graduation from Wittenberg in 1649. Highlights of his visit to Paris included meetings with Gabriel Naudé, both in the Mazarin library, where he was able to buy duplicate copies for his own library, and in Naudé's private chambers, where the librarian kept his personal collection.[65] In the negotiations leading to Johann Ernst's subsequent appointment to a chair at the University of Jena his father's library was noted as an asset in his favor. The library holdings belonging to the political theorist and professor of medicine and politics at Helmstedt, Hermann Conring (1606–81), may be reconstructed from the 250-page printed auction catalogue of 1694. The auction was advertised in the Frankfurt Easter book fair catalogue and aroused great interest. The philosopher

Gottfried Wilhelm Leibniz (1646–1716), librarian of the dukes in Hanover and Wolfenbüttel and owner of a significant private library, was among the buyers. The nearly 3,300 volumes reflect the scholarly interests of their owner; the chairs he held — law and politics, science and medicine — are the most represented, with books in theology comprising only 22% of the collection.[66]

Daniel Georg Morhof (1639–91) was named professor of eloquence and poetry at the University of Kiel when it was founded in 1665 and later appointed professor of eloquence and history. Morhof's *Unterricht von der Teutschen Sprache und Poesie / deren Uhrsprung / Fortgang und Lehrsätzen* (Instruction in the German Language and Poetry, Its Origins, Development, and Principles, 1682) was one of the first critical histories of literature. His *Polyhistor sive de notitia auctorum et rerum commentarii* (Polyhistorian, or Notes on the Knowledge of Authors and Things, 1688), was based on his private teaching of *historia litteraria* at Kiel. Morhof's library played an important role in his teaching, as he taught primarily in his house and allowed his students full access to his library. Even when he taught publicly he brought along books from his private library.[67] *Historia litteraria* involved text-based teaching that incorporated aspects of experiment and observation. It contained several new elements: the discussion of the contents of libraries and archives, an awareness of the need for research, concern for editions and translations, and an introduction to bibliography.[68] All of these were taught by practical demonstrations of how to use libraries, just as other professors used their private collections of natural artifacts in their teaching.[69]

Court Libraries

By virtue of the sheer number of German territories (300 and more throughout the early modern period) the court library was destined to play a stronger role here than in other European countries. The development of court libraries is closely linked to the rise of humanism and to the role played by members of the ruling dynasties as patrons of individual scholars, authors, and universities. Libraries were part of the institutional state building of early absolutism and were viewed as a means of promoting identification with the land and the dynasty. Humanists exhorted princes to give expression to their respect for learning by founding libraries. Johannes Alexander Brassicanus (Köll, 1500–39) of Tübingen, successor to Johannes Reuchlin (1455–1522) as professor of law in Ingolstadt and later professor of rhetoric in Vienna, published an impassioned plea in 1530 for the creation of libraries. He describes how Reuchlin, as ambassador of Eberhard Duke of Württemberg to Emperor Friedrich III, had asked for an ancient Hebrew Bible manuscript rather than the usual gifts presented to visiting embassies on such occasions — horses with costly trappings or gold chalices.[70] In the same text Brassicanus gives a valuable eye-witness account of the famous Corvine collections of the Hungarian king Matthias (1440–90), second in size only to the Vatican library,[71] which he had been allowed to view on a visit to Buda shortly before its destruction in the Turkish conquest of 1526. This legendary collection consisted mainly of manuscripts, many of them written and illuminated by the best Florentine artists. It was renowned for its rich holdings of classical texts and standard works of Renaissance philosophy and became both a symbol of the humanist aspirations of a Renaissance ruler and of the precarious existence of libraries in time of war. Generations of scholars and book collectors vied for the surviving Corvine manuscripts, which had been dispersed throughout Europe.

If the fate of the Corvine library symbolized one of the greatest losses to humanist culture, the Bibliotheca Palatina (Palatine library) at Heidelberg had a similar meaning for Protestant Europe in the seventeenth century. It was one of the most famous court libraries in the German Empire; even in the Middle Ages the Palatine court had housed a large library.[72] Elector Ottheinrich (1502–59), who became a Lutheran in 1542, combined his own private collection and the Heidelberg castle library with the library of the Church of the Holy Spirit to create what became known as the Bibliotheca Palatina. Ottheinrich allocated an annual budget to ensure the library's future growth. The reputation of the Bibliotheca Palatina as a seat of humanist learning was guaranteed by the appointment of famous humanist scholars, as librarians, including the poet Paul Schede Melissus (1539–1602) and Janus Gruter (1560–1627), editor of the works of Cicero. Succeeding generations of Heidelberg electors secured important acquisitions for the library and deposited their own private collections there. One of the most significant additions came when the library of Ulrich Fugger (1526–84) was integrated into the holdings. Ulrich, younger brother of the famous book collector Johann Jakob Fugger, was the only Protestant in the Fugger family. He was a scholar of Latin, Greek, and Hebrew and a collector of priceless manuscripts that he had discovered either on his travels as a young man or, indirectly, later via agents in Italy, Greece, France, and Germany. The French humanist printer Henri Estienne (1528–98) repeatedly used manuscripts belonging to Ulrich Fugger for his editions of classical texts, for example his Xenophon edition of 1561.[73] Ulrich's extravagant expenditures on books and his lavish patronage of scholars brought about his financial downfall, leading the Augsburg authorities in 1562 to place him under house arrest and to confiscate most of his property. He was able to save his valuable library, however, and took it with him to Heidelberg in 1567 in exchange for the asylum and pension offered by Elector Friedrich IV. In 1614 the Bibliotheca Palatina was further augmented by the incorporation of the library of the Calvinist jurist and historian Marquard Freher (1565–1614) and eventually became the intellectual center of Calvinism in Germany. The court of Friedrich V (1596–1632) and his wife Elisabeth (1596–1662), daughter of James I of England, was one of the most splendid in Germany. When Friedrich, as a Calvinist, accepted the crown of Bohemia in defiance of the emperor and moved to Prague in 1619, a chain of events was set in motion that hastened early developments of the Thirty Years' War (1618–48). It was thus a highly symbolic act when in the first phase of the war Catholic forces overran Heidelberg (1623). The capture of the famous library and its transportation to Rome and incorporation into the Vatican library symbolized the capture of the Protestant enemy's very identity, the repository of his history.[74]

As leader of the Catholic League, Maximilian of Bavaria (1573–1651) was responsible for the capture of the Palatine library; at first he intended to keep it in Munich.[75] His own collections in the Bavarian capital were plundered by Swedish forces in 1632, however, an enormity that he in turn avenged by plundering Protestant libraries in Tübingen and Stuttgart in 1635. A series of spectacular acts of looting and taking of booty occasioned an enormous redistribution of library holdings throughout Europe. The rich collections of the library at the castle of Gotha in Thuringia, built by Duke Ernst the Pious of Saxony-Gotha (1601–75) in the 1640s, were stocked with books plundered in military campaigns from the libraries of Mainz, Würzburg, and Munich.[76] The North German Protestant Duke August of Braunschweig-Lüneburg (1579–1666), a contemporary of Maximilian and Ernst, took no active part in the military campaigns of the Thirty Years' War.[77] Rather than suffering losses his library grew during this period to majestic proportions and established his reputation as a book collector of European stature.

August conceived of his collection as an entity and believed that its value lay in its attempt to represent in the broadest sense the time's understanding of "universal" knowledge. In contrast to Maximilian, August accumulated a treasure trove of what at the time were distinctly nonrare items, ephemeral objects now rare only because they were printed for consumption. Broadsheets, pamphlets, almanacs, and newsletters were bound and preserved in Wolfenbüttel with the same care as major works by classical and humanist authors. August had what we now call "an expanded concept of literature" and esteemed ephemeral literature for its documentary value. Maximilian was far from wishing to preserve popular political or religious pamphlet literature. The differences between the two collectors, one a South German Catholic, the other a North German Protestant, can be understood by looking at their relationships with the Augsburg art dealer and book agent, Philipp Hainhofer (1578–1647). One example may serve to illustrate the fundamental difference between their instincts as collectors, as it contrasts Maximilian's elitist and religiously orthodox principles with Duke August's liberality. When, on a spontaneous impulse, the agent Hainhofer sent him a French almanac with political engravings concerning the dukes of Savoy, Maximilian tartly wrote back to say that he had forwarded the libelous pamphlet straight to the Vatican in Rome, which, as he put it, was the proper place for such things as were "der rechten opinion nicht gemeß" (not in accordance with true opinion).[78] The contract between Hainhofer and Duke August, on the other hand, gave the agent *carte blanche* to purchase whatever newly published small tracts and publications he came across.[79]

Maximilian, who stemmed from a line of connoisseurs, was renowned as a discriminating collector. By the end of the sixteenth century, when his father, Wilhelm V, abdicated in his favor, the Munich library had about 17,000 volumes, 10,000 of which had come from the Augsburg library of Johann Jakob Fugger (purchased by Maximilian's grandfather in 1571). As the younger son of an unimportant branch of the Lüneburg line, August by contrast had no dynastic library to inherit. His collection, which numbered 135,000 titles at his death in 1666, was entirely his own creation. Both Maximilian and August personally supervised all acquisitions for their libraries, though Maximilian employed a series of sorely tried academics who had to defer to him in all matters. Keeping track of individual acquisitions for the Munich collections was not a problem, however; in the thirty-two years between 1598 and 1630 the number of new volumes that entered the Munich collection, including dedicatory copies sent in by authors and publishers, totaled only 1,350, an average of forty-five new volumes per year.[80] August could easily average that many books a week, ordered in a single letter to one of his agents. Not only did he have no one to whom he delegated this task, he single-handedly checked to see that incoming books were complete copies, and he catalogued them according to his own system.

Their individual political, confessional, and dynastic contexts meant that the two men differed in their basic philosophy of collecting. Maximilian's strict Catholicism and his dynastic ambitions, directed toward underpinning his claim to the electorate bestowed on him when the Calvinist Elector Palatine Friedrich V fell under imperial ban, are mirrored in his acquisitions policies, in which works on religion and historiography predominate. Maximilian collected for the greater glory of the Wittelsbach dynasty. Its famous *Kunst- und Schatzkammer*, not the library, was the focus of his attention as a collector; the most precious books were not housed in the library at all but in his private chamber gallery. For his part, August took care that personal confessional and intellectual interests did not lead to an imbalance in the collection. Although he procured and even purchased valuable illuminated manuscripts, he did not pursue their acquisition with the passion of the art connoisseur that informed Maximilian's purchases of works by Dürer and his school.

Duke August sought to create a universal collection reflecting all available knowledge of his times. For this reason he saw to it that it was bruited about in the scholarly world at large, especially in the occasional poetry regularly printed in Wolfenbüttel celebrating the duke as a collector and scholar and in works describing the library itself, most notably in Hermann Conring's *De Bibliotheca Augusta* (1661).[81] August's own systematic arrangement of the books into subject groups, his innovative system of call numbers, and his catalogue all demonstrate his conscious plan.[82] After his death in 1666 his heirs made no changes to the collection, but neither were they committed to continuing its planned expansion. Despite the efforts of Leibniz, appointed librarian in 1691, to impress upon the Wolfenbüttel dukes the importance of buying contemporary works of scholarship, investments dwindled. A new building, erected in 1710 to house the collection, symbolized the monumental and ultimately historic nature of the collection, but also the fact that it was now intended to be visited and admired rather than used as a modern resource. The loan records kept since 1664 are a rich source of knowledge on the use of the holdings.[83]

In the first half of the seventeenth century the imperial library in Vienna was modest in comparison with the collections in Munich and Wolfenbüttel, although from the sixteenth century onward it could claim a series of celebrated librarians.[84] The Dutch scholar Hugo Blotius (1553–1608), appointed by Maximilian II in 1575, made the first systematic arrangement of the collection of 9,000 volumes that would become the National Library of Austria. The holdings expanded rapidly in the second half of the century, and by the 1670s, when the historian Peter Lambeccius (Lambeck, 1628–80) made his catalogues — including the *Commentariorum de Bibliotheca Caesarea Vindobonensi libri VIII* (Eight Books of Commentary on the Imperial Library at Vienna), so valuable for increasing our knowledge of older German literature — they had increased to 80,000.[85] The same can be said of the Berlin library of the electors of Brandenburg, which was chartered in 1661 and also grew to about 80,000 volumes. Both the library in Vienna and that in Berlin formed part of the showrooms for visitors to the court. Contemporary engravings show the Vienna library as a venue where people met and socialized. In Berlin rooms were refurbished to house the library in a wing of the castle above the apothecary. Special attention was paid to the decoration of the room. The shelves were painted red with black signboards showing the subject matter they contained; the spines of all the books were painted red to match the décor and create a uniform impression.[86]

Libraries of Humanists

From the early fifteenth century we find large private collections that manifest the humanist interests of their owners.[87] The scope and organization of such libraries were determined both by the intellectual and by the professional purposes they served. The preeminence of theology apparent in book lists of medieval libraries gave way to individual systems of assessing the importance of aspects of a collection.[88] The collections of Amplonius Rating in Erfurt (1435) were dominated by his medical interests. Albrecht von Eyb (1420–75) spent fourteen years in Italy, where he studied law and collected a large library of humanist texts that influenced his own later literary production.[89] In Eichstätt in 1459 he completed his *Margarita poetica* (Poetic Pearl, published 1472), an anthology of rhetorical, poetical, and historical texts by classical and humanist authors.[90] Reuchlin's library in Stuttgart, which he sent for protection to Pforzheim during the conflict between Duke Ulrich of Württemberg and the Swabian League, consisted of approximately 500 volumes including valuable Hebrew and Greek manuscripts.[91] In Schlettstadt (now Sélestat in France) the rich collections belonging to Beatus Rhenanus (1485–1547), editor of Tacitus and author of one of the first histories of Germany (1531), have survived intact and provide a rare example of a humanist library in its original surroundings.

Two cities with strong trade links to Italy were destined to become centers of humanist book collecting in the sixteenth century: Nuremberg and Augsburg. The collection of the Nuremberg physician and patrician Hartmann Schedel (1440–1514), who inherited a significant library from his cousin Hermann Schedel, mentioned above, also a physician, is typical in that it reflects his professional interests in medicine and science. The Schedel collection was dominated by classical and humanist texts and an interest in history, which inspired Hartmann to edit his lavishly illustrated encyclopedic *Weltchronik* (Chronicle of the World, 1493), known also as the *Nürnberger Chronik*. The surviving catalogue of the collection shows that Schedel owned 632 volumes divided into twenty-two subject groups.[92] Another important humanist library in Nuremberg belonged to the patrician Willibald Pirckheimer (1470–1530). Like Schedel, Pirckheimer had studied in Italy. His collection was characterized by the significant number of Greek texts he acquired in Latin translation and then edited. His interests ranged from manuscripts with fifth-century Egyptian hieroglyphs to astronomy and medicine, *Minnesang*, and works of contemporary German, Italian, French, and Spanish writers.[93] Pirckheimer died intestate, but the collection remained in possession of the family and was sold only in 1636, when due to their financial straits in the middle of the Thirty Years' War his heirs accepted an offer from Thomas Howard, Earl of Arundel (1586–1646), "Collector Earl," as he was called, who was passing through Germany on a diplomatic mission.[94] Pirckheimer was known for his willingness to lend books to other scholars with whom he corresponded.[95] It was a characteristic feature of humanist libraries like that of Pirckheimer, whose volumes carried his famous *ex libris* "sibi et amicis suis" (for the owner and his friends), that their books were shared and their contents discussed. This was usual even over vast distances, and the book in private collections and the personal letter became equal components of scholarly dialogue.[96]

One of the largest private humanist libraries belonged to Conrad Peutinger (1465–1547) in Augsburg. Peutinger was a lawyer and politician who had studied in Italy from 1482 to 1488. Appointed *Stadtschreiber* in Augsburg in 1497, he also served as the city's legal representative in its dealings with the Swabian League and at imperial diets. This position brought him into close contact with Emperor Maximilian I, who entrusted him with important political embassies and the supervision of His Majesty's ambitious literary projects. Peutinger was also a historian, and his working library amassed, over sixty years of continuous collecting, more than 6,000 titles in 2,200 volumes. The collection remained in the Peutinger family until 1718.[97] Book collecting in Augsburg in the early modern period was always associated with the name of Fugger, the enormously wealthy merchant family. When he visited Augsburg in 1551 the Englishman Roger Ascham wrote in a letter: "Here be five merchants in this town thought able to disburse as much ready money as five of the greatest kings in Christendom." Three of those merchants, he went on, belonged to the Fugger family, one of whom was Johann Jakob Fugger: "This man is learned and has gathered such a library of Greek and Latin books as is thought no man else to have."[98] Johann Jakob was able to use the communications system of the Fugger trading empire to seek out rare Greek, Hebrew, and Latin manuscripts or to commission copies to be made. In 1552 he acquired some 670 books from the Nuremberg Schedel collections, whose scientific, medical, astronomical, and geographical interests were a welcome enhancement of his own.[99] When financial ruin hit the Fugger family in the 1560s Johann Jakob was forced to sell his collection of over 11,000 printed works and 1,500 manuscripts to Duke Albrecht V of Bavaria for his court library at Munich. From 1565 on, books from the Fugger collection found their way to Munich, but in 1571 the whole collection was sold and left to Augsburg. As noted above, the collection belonging to his brother, the Protestant Ulrich Fugger, went to Heidelberg. Well into the seventeenth century, Augsburg remained an important center of book collecting and book selling, as the collections of the Welser family[100] and the activities of the agent Philipp Hainhofer show.[101]

Aristocratic Libraries

Johannes Rothe (ca. 1360–1434), a priest in Eisenach from a patrician family, asserts in his *Ritterspiegel* (Mirror of Knights, ca. 1415) that the ability to read and write are essential to every good knight.[102] In his *Ehrenbrief* (Letter of Honor) of 1462 to Palatine Duchess (*Pfalzgräfin*) Mechthild (1418–82) in Rottenburg, the Bavarian knight Jakob Püterich von Reichertshausen (1400–1469) replies in verse form to her offer to allow him to make copies of ninety-four works contained in her library. Mechthild's rich collection of manuscripts is recorded in his *Ehrenbrief*. Only twenty-three of her titles are unknown to Püterich, whereas his poem claims that 164 works from his own collections could augment Mechthild's library. Writing in 1920 Fritz Behrend tried to convey the radical difference between Mechthild and Püterich as collectors by comparing their correspondence to an imaginary meeting between two bibliophiles of his own day, one of whom collected only the works of Lessing and Schiller whereas the other concentrated on the latest products of the Expressionists and Futurists.[103] Mechthild's was the modern collection dictated by contemporary tastes; Püterich's library, in which medieval courtly romances and chivalric literature in German predominated, was backward-looking owing to his idiosyncratic method of collecting on his knightly travels throughout Europe. In keeping with his own self-fashioning he describes his methods of acquiring texts over more than forty years of searching between Brabant and Hungary: "mit stellen, rauben, auch darzue mit lehen, geschenkht, geschribn, khauft und darzue funden" (by stealing, robbing, and also by borrowing, they were given as presents, copied, bought, and also found; *Ehrenbrief* 28). Püterich expresses his love of traditional texts, above all works by Wolfram von Eschenbach, and his disdain for contemporary works: "der neuen acht ich nit" (I pay no attention to the new; *Ehrenbrief* 28).

Pre-1500 book collections belonging to noblemen were almost exclusively composed of devotional, practical, or literary works in the vernacular.[104] This changed radically in the sixteenth century with the spread of printing and the advent of the Reformation. It was also affected by the onset of academic training for members of the nobility, who now found themselves in competition with bourgeois elites for positions of administrative power at court. Renaissance handbooks propagated the ideal of an educated aristocracy, echoed in the various *Adels- und Fürstenspiegel* (mirrors of aristocracy and princes) of the next two centuries and adopted in the education of the sons of the urban elites.[105] The purchase of books and the viewing of libraries became a standard feature of the aristocratic cavalier's tour of the early modern period, recommended by the authors of apodemic handbooks, which provided guidelines for useful travel.[106]

The von Alvensleben family library, founded by Joachim von Alvensleben (1514–88), provides an example of how the Reformation and the new intellectual aspirations of the aristocracy combined to promote the establishment of large book collections that functioned less as objects of prestige than as actual working instruments; the reception of Roman law played a vital part in them.[107] Joachim's student years began at the age of twelve at the University of Wittenberg, where he studied under Luther and Melanchthon and received a thorough grounding in Greek and Latin. During his extensive travels through Italy and France he bought mainly legal works related to his studies. The collection attests to its founder's wide-ranging interests in theology — especially the debates within the Protestant party — historiography, law, philology, politics, philosophy, and medicine. The von der Schulenburg family followed the same pattern, sending its sons to university and allowing them extended journeys through France and Italy with a focus on legal training and the acquisition of the skills necessary for a career in diplomacy, administration, or military service. One of the family's earliest collectors, Daniel von der Schulenburg (1538–94), was a devoted scholar with a deep knowledge of Greek and Latin, who like Joachim von Alvensleben also studied under Luther and Melanchthon in Wittenberg. He was a close friend of the Helmstedt humanist and professor of philosophy Johannes Caselius (Bracht, 1533–1613), with whom he had shared quarters in Florence in 1561 when both were attending lectures by the famous Petrus Victorinus (Pietro Vettori) on the interpretation of Greek texts.[108] How closely related these aristocratic libraries were with those of urban elites is shown by comparing them with collections like that established by the Braunschweig syndic Johann Cammann the Younger (1584–1649), which numbered over 9,500 imprints.[109] Cammann's education and the genesis and structure of his library differ little from those of the Alvenslebens and Schulenburgs.

Libraries of the landed gentry served primarily the collector's own use. They were handed down over generations but might well be dispersed if interest in them lapsed. One of the largest aristocratic libraries of the sixteenth century, with approximately 6,300 volumes, belonged to Heinrich Rantzau (1526–98) in his castle at Breitenburg. It was the first important book collection in the North German duchies belonging to the Danish crown, not in the hands of the church. It by far outstripped the library of the dukes of Holstein in their castle at Gottorf, which in 1596 had only about 700 books. Like many of his contemporaries, Rantzau had been sent to Wittenberg at the age of twelve with his tutor, and his studies were primarily in the fields of philology, law, and rhetoric; he also is said to have lodged in Luther's house as a student.[110] His cavalier's tour followed when he joined the entourage of Emperor Charles V, traveling with the emperor's court for seven years through the Habsburg territories and the Netherlands. Like his father before him, on his return he was made *Stadthalter* (representative) of the Danish king in the royal territories of Schleswig-Holstein; as the king's "first servant" he became one of the most powerful men in the region.

Whereas his father's authority owed to his military achievements, Rantzau used his deliberately accumulated cultural capital and humanist interests and connections for representational purposes. He corresponded with the Dutch philosopher and political theorist Justus Lipsius (1547–1606) and received from him copies of his influential works *De constantia* (On Constancy, 1584) and *Politica* (1589). His other correspondents included Neo-Latin poets and historians at Protestant universities throughout the empire, among them Michael Beuther (1522–87) in Strasbourg (thought to have been the translator into High German of the *Reineke Fuchs* fable), the lawyer and philosopher Johannes Caselius in Helmstedt, the poet Paul Schede Melissus in Heidelberg, and the theologian and church historian David Chytraeus (1530–1600) in Rostock.[111] Rantzau was passionately interested in astronomy and became a patron of the Danish astronomer Tycho Brahe (1546–1601). His humanist aspirations are manifested in his program of buildings, memorial architecture, publications, portraiture, and scholarly collections, most importantly the library for which in the 1580s he furnished rooms over the chapel in a new wing of his castle at Breitenburg. His library benefited from the dissolution of monasteries after the Reformation, many of its volumes coming from the monastery at Segeberg. He often recorded the date and place of acquisition in the books themselves, and surviving volumes show that many were purchased on his regular diplomatic journeys. The terms of Rantzau's meticulously detailed last will and testament made careful provision for the maintenance and preservation of the library, which he commended to his heirs as "eine ewige Gedächtnus und Herrlichkeit, den Rantzowen zu Ehren uffgerichtet und fundieret" (an eternal monument and marvel, erected and founded in honor of the Rantzaus; Lohmeier 108). Castle Breitenburg was stormed and the library plundered by Wallenstein's forces in 1627.

The Author's Library

For early modern authors the library was one of their most important instruments. Pursuant to the theory that the poet, dramatist, or orator could achieve perfection only by the emulation of good models and that one of the best ways of raising the standard of German as a literary language was through translation, the availability of source materials was imperative. Most literary authors were professionals — theologians, lawyers, courtiers, diplomats, doctors, academics — whose occupations required a specialized working library; these libraries typically differed from those of their humanist predecessors by the number of works in vernacular languages. Most of our knowledge about the collections of early modern authors is gleaned from indirect sources, and seldom do we have an exact picture of what books they owned. Chance finds of individual provenances or small groups of books predominate, as is the case with the library belonging to the satirist Johann Fischart (1546/47–1590/91). Fifty-three of his books and broadsheets have been traced, some having come to light only in the mid 1990s, in a Salzburg collection originally owned by the

Catholic convert Christoph Besold (1577–1638), a professor of law at Tübingen.[112] They are particularly enlightening because their provenances and detailed marginalia contain biographical details on Fischart's university studies and travels, as well as notes on his reading and literary projects.[113]

Surviving library or auction catalogues can give a broader picture of former collections. The book collection of the Nuremberg cobbler Hans Sachs (1494–1576), one of the most prolific authors of the sixteenth century, is counted among the earliest documented libraries of a vernacular poet.[114] Sachs himself drew up the inventory about fifteen years before he died: "Anno salutis 1562 am 28 tag Januarij meins alters im 67 Jar hab ich Hans Sachs diese meine puecher inventirt vnd ain ides puech sunderlich verzaichnet nach dem Abc" (In the year of our salvation 1562 on the 28th day of January in my 67th year I, Hans Sachs, made an inventory of these my books and recorded each book separately according to the ABC's). In ordering the titles in his catalogue alphabetically Sachs was one of the first collectors to depart from the medieval hierarchical principle of beginning lists with the Bible, the church fathers, and other theological texts, followed by the liberal arts. With only about 115 titles Sachs did not possess a large library. His collection is significant for having been narrowly focused on works directly related to the subjects of his own pamphlets and dramas: Reformation theology and works of literature and history. The books are exclusively in German; translations of the works of Plutarch, Herodotus, Suetonius, and other classical writers are numerous, as they are for humanist authors including Petrarch and Boccaccio. However, Sachs also read the works of his contemporaries, notably Sebastian Brant (1457–1521) and the early novelist Jörg Wickram (ca. 1505–62). Given that only a few volumes from the collection can be traced today, Sachs's personal inventory is an invaluable source of information on his reading.

Another poet's library that can only be reconstructed via catalogues belonged to the satirist Johann Michael Moscherosch (1601–69).[115] Immediately after his death his heirs sold the complete library to the landgrave of Hessen-Darmstadt (most of the volumes were destroyed in the Allied bombing of Darmstadt in 1944). The inventory, taken when the books arrived in Darmstadt in 1669, is now the sole source of information on the composition of the poet's library, which comprised nearly 2,300 volumes and shows his broad reception of contemporary literature. Adolf Schmidt, writing in 1899, had at his disposal the complete collection in Darmstadt, the inventory, and the satirist's diary entries in almanacs dating between 1619 and 1630, which reveal that as a pupil at the famous Gymnasium in Strasbourg Moscherosch was already a regular customer of the bookseller Eberhard Zetzner. The subject groupings of the catalogue demonstrate the breadth of Moscherosch's interests: theology, law, medicine, politics, history and geography, rhetoric, philosophy, poetics, and other books in German, French, Italian, Spanish, and English (Schmidt 63). Schmidt further points out that the section on law was surprisingly small, considering that Moscherosch mainly earned his living by working in various administrative capacities for the upper nobility and for the city of Strasbourg, where he was responsible, among other duties, for issuing many *Polizey-Ordnungen* (city ordinances). His library seems mainly to have served his needs as an author. A study of German auction catalogues has shown that Moscherosch's *Visiones de Don Quevedo: Wunderliche und Warhafftige Gesichte Philanders von Sittewalt* (Visions of Don Quevedo: Wonderful and True Visions of Philander of Sittewalt, 2nd ed., 1642), a German version of Francisco Gómez de Quevedo's *Sueños* (1627), was one of the most popular vernacular works of literature in the seventeenth century.[116]

An author whose personal library consisted almost entirely of contemporary literature was the pastoral poet Jacob Schwieger (ca. 1630–63). Formerly a private tutor in Hamburg and Stade, Schwieger was licensed by the Danish king in 1657 to mint coinage in Glückstadt, an enterprise that failed and led to his financial ruin. The inventory taken of his assets at his death in 1664 gives a complete listing of his 211 books, a comparatively small number, though an extraordinary example of a literary author's specialist library.[117] Less than 20% of Schwieger's books were theological; indeed almost all traditional elements of a learned library were missing, with the exception of a few works on logic, rhetoric, dialectics, and poetics, which he probably used in his work as a private tutor. The bulk of his collection consisted in vernacular works by his contemporaries, the earliest being the complete works of Martin Opitz (1638). Many of the major baroque poets are present (Paul Fleming, Andreas Tscherning, Andreas Gryphius, Johann Rist, Philipp von Zesen, Georg Greflinger, Kaspar Stieler, Georg Philipp Harsdörffer, Johann Klaj, Christian Brehme, David Schirmer, Georg Neumark), and Schwieger's own preferred genre, the pastoral lyric, is especially represented with works by Sigmund von Birken, Schirmer, Greflinger, and Enoch Gläser. His most recent acquisition was obviously Johann Thomas's pastoral novel *Damon und Lisille*, published in 1663 shortly before Schwieger's death. The almost exclusive focus on literary texts in the vernacular is highly unusual and prefigures the poet's library of the late eighteenth century. Most of Schwieger's contemporaries built up predominately Latin, scholarly libraries geared primarily to their professional needs, in which their literary interests took second place.

The learned editorial apparatus with which the Silesian poet and dramatist Andreas Gryphius (1616–64) furnished his works suggests how large a library must have been at his disposal in Glogau, where he served as legal representative of the estates. He is also known to have used the library of his patron, the count of Schönborn. Gryphius's collection, bequeathed to his son Christian Gryphius (1649–1706), a minor poet, scholar, and educator, contained over 3,500 titles;[118] today only twenty-four of the volumes are extant.[119] A similarly small number of volumes survive from the collection of the most famous German baroque poet, Martin Opitz (1597–1639), sold following his death by plague at Danzig in 1639.[120] When Karl Gustav von Hille, author of *Der Teutsche Palmbaum* (The German Palm Tree, 1647), died in 1647, Duke August of Wolfenbüttel bought a number of books from Hille's widow, mostly titles in French and English purchased during his youthful travels; these are preserved today in the Wolfenbüttel collections.[121]

Similarly, Duke August acquired works belonging to his long-standing correspondent, the Stuttgart divine Johann Valentin Andreae (1586–1654), famous for his utopian tract *Christianopolis* (1619). During his lifetime Andreae sent about 600 books from his own collection to Wolfenbüttel and was further instrumental in procuring engravings, musical works, and Italian literature for the duke.[122] He arranged, for example, the purchase of books from the estate of the Tübingen mathematician and astronomer Michael Mästlin (1550–1631). Andreae's first and most valuable collection of over 12,000 books, many of them inherited from his grandfather, the reformer Jacob Andreae, were destroyed in 1634 in the great fire at Calw, where he was minister, an event he laments in his *Threni Calvenses* (Calwean Tears, 1635).

Opitz, Gryphius, Hille, and Andreae, like many of the major literary figures of the seventeenth century, were members of the Fruchtbringende Gesellschaft (Fruitbringing Society), founded in Thuringia in 1617 as a society dedicated to promoting, in the first place, the improvement of German as a literary language. Under the successive leadership of its founder Prince Ludwig of Anhalt-Köthen (1579–1650), Wilhelm of Saxon-Weimar (d. 1669), and August of Saxon-Weissenfels (d. 1680), the society admitted more than 900 members, mainly from the aristocracy but increasingly also from the professional classes. The group held no regular meetings, but its members maintained a vigorous written correspondence, both among themselves and with the head of the society. These letters, which were deposited in the society's *Ertzschrein* (archive), are now being published.[123] They reveal an incessant discussion about new publications, book and translation projects, and the exchange of books, giving a tantalizing insight into libraries of which no other trace remains today.

Much the same can be said of the archives of the Pegnesischer Blumenorden (Order of Flowers on the Pegnitz) in Nuremberg, founded in 1644 by Georg Philipp Harsdörffer (1607–58) and Johann Klaj (1616–56).[124] Later the moving force behind the society was Sigmund von Birken (1626–81), who bequeathed his own papers and private library to the Blumenorden.[125] At the center of literary life in Nuremberg was Birken's patron, the theologian and educator Johann Michael Dilherr (1604–69). Dilherr began his career at the University of Jena, where he held chairs between 1631 and 1634 in eloquence, history, and poetry. After being made rector in 1635 he succeeded Johann Gerhard as professor of theology. Dilherr was called to Nuremberg from the University of Jena in 1642 to become rector of the Egidien Gymnasium. In 1646 he was appointed main preacher of St. Sebald's Church and superintendent of Nuremberg's schools and city library. The private library that Dilherr brought with him to Nuremberg was a subject of comment by the collector Georg Andreas Will:

Als er mit seinen Büchern / welche damals schon alleine 14 Fuhren ausmachten / und 104 Centner schwer gewesen / durch die Vestung

Forchheim gefahren / und der Commendant / Hr. Graf von
Pappenheim von unserm Dilherr erfuhr / daß er der Besitzer dieses sogenannten freyen Studenten-Gutes wäre / hat der Graf zu ihm gesagt: So
muß der Herr ein vornehmer Studente seyn.[126]

[When he drove through the fortress of Forchheim with his books, which
even then made up 14 carts weighing 104 hundredweight, and the commander Count Pappenheim heard from our Dilherr that he was the
owner of this so-called toll-free student property, the count said to him:
"Well, sir, you must be a student of real distinction."]

By the time of Dilherr's death his library had grown to 8,000 volumes, nearly
all of which he bequeathed to Saint Sebald's Church.[127] As a scholarly library
his collection — which has been the subject of an exhaustive investigation —
is distinguished both by its relatively high volume (35%) of vernacular works
and by the predominance of contemporary works. The collection reflects his
role as a preacher and educator in Nuremberg, the scope of his correspondence, and the breadth of his personal interests. Dilherr's own 150 printed
works, his unpublished papers, and the manuscript annotations in his books
demonstrate how intensively he used the library. Realistic *exempla*, which
stemmed from his rich collection of works on history, botany, and foreign
countries and cultures, made his sermons and devotional works accessible and
exceptionally popular. His private library, together with the circumstance of his
being responsible for the city library, put Dilherr at the center of book collecting in Nuremberg.

A number of other baroque authors, in their professions as school rectors,
supervised the book collections of their various institutions. They included the
grammarian Christian Gueintz (1592–1650) as rector of the Gymnasium in
Halle, the dramatist Johann Sebastian Mitternacht (1613–79) in Naumburg
and Gera, the dramatist and author of political novels Christian Weise
(1642–1708) in Weissenfels and Zittau, Christian Gryphius at the Elisabeth
Gymnasium in Breslau, and his pupil Christian Stieff (1675–1751), also in
Breslau, at the Magdalena Gymnasium.

Still other literary authors were in charge of court libraries, often combining the post with that of court poet or historian. In Dresden the poets
Christian Brehme (1613–67) and David Schirmer (1623–87) functioned as
librarians for the Saxon elector. From 1652 on, Georg Neumark (1621–81),
secretary of the Fruchtbringende Gesellschaft in Weimar, combined the
functions of court poet and librarian. Adam Olearius (1599–1671), on his
return from the Holstein embassy to Moscow and Persia — which he
recorded in a travel account with the published title *Offt begehrte Beschreibung
der Newen Orientalischen Reyse* (Oft-requested Description of the Recent
Journey to the Orient, 1647) — was appointed court mathematician and
librarian at Gottorf, where he also supervised the ducal *Kunstkammer*. In this
capacity Olearius, like Schirmer in Dresden or Neumark in Weimar, was also
charged with writing libretti and devising festivities for all manner of courtly
occasions.

Women's Libraries

Little systematic research has been conducted on early modern German women's libraries or on their reading habits, and the following can therefore only present a fragmented picture, pieced together from patchwork evidence.[128] Initially nunneries maintained book collections that, like those in monasteries, had in many cases been founded in the fifteenth century as part of the reform movement of religious orders. Despite the ban on private possessions, reconstructions of libraries belonging to nunneries show that nuns were allowed to keep books in their cells and even to amass large collections, though only with permission of the abbess. After the owner's death they often came into possession of the nunnery and sometimes were of such a size as to account for the majority of books in the nunnery library. A catalogue of books from the nunnery in Marienburg from 1627 shows that Sister Clara Blomberg owned sixty texts, whereas only fifty-seven are listed for the nunnery's "gemeine Liberey" (communal library). In 1731 only 20% of the books counted in the Franciscan nunnery of the Holy Cross in Landshut were actually in the library — the rest were in the nuns' cells.[129] In keeping with the nuns' relatively limited knowledge of Latin, most of the works found in their libraries were written in the vernacular and nearly all were intended for liturgical or devotional use. It was not until the seventeenth century that the number of printed works exceeded that of manuscripts.

Many of the libraries belonging to religious orders were severely affected by the Reformation; nunneries often were forced to relinquish their collections or, as sometimes happened in the Thirty Years' War, to witness their destruction. In Protestant territories some nunneries became *Stiftshäuser* (Protestant convents from which nuns could marry), in which women from the aristocracy and patrician families received education; women who did not marry remained as *Stiftsdamen*. Significant libraries were often established by the abbesses in charge. Examples are the libraries at Quedlinburg and Gandersheim. The Quedlinburg collections had been established under the Ottonian abbesses of the ninth century, but by the thirteenth century, decline had set in. The first Protestant abbess, Anna II Countess of Stolberg-Wernigerode (1504–74), tried to revive the library by donating books to the collection. By the beginning of the seventeenth century, however, its historic holdings were considered worthless and medieval vellum manuscripts were being sold off to local bookbinders for reuse as cheap binding material. A breakthrough came in 1686 when the abbess Anna Dorothea of Saxon-Weimar used her own private collection to form the basis of a new *Stiftsbibliothek* for which she publicly solicited donations, mostly from the leading dynasties with which she was related.[130] The library continued to expand well into the eighteenth century. The abbesses Anna Sophia of Hessen-Darmstadt (1638–83) and Maria Aurora of Königsmark (1662–1728) are two prominent women poets to have made exceptional use of the Quedlinburg collections.[131]

The medieval library at Gandersheim, of which the gifted nun — both poet and playwright — Roswitha (fl. late tenth c.) speaks in the preface to her *Legends*, suffered a similar fate to that at Quedlinburg and was founded anew in 1722 by the abbess Elisabeth Ernestine Antonie of Saxon-Meiningen (1681–1766). The concern of the Protestant abbesses of the late seventeenth and early eighteenth centuries to establish libraries with a universal character is a reflection of their own intellectual aspirations, but it was also in keeping with the political function of the *Stift* as a court and the abbess's representational role as sovereign princess.[132] The core of the collections of the *Stiftshäuser* was provided by individual private collections. Most of the noble women entering them brought their own books, having come from environments in which book collecting was standard.

Individual collections belonging to women from the nobility are documented from the late medieval period on. Margaret of Savoy, duchess of Württemberg (1420–79), shared an interest in books with her sister-in-law Mechthild in Rottenburg, as mentioned above.[133] The Reformation marked the beginning of significant libraries belonging to women at court. Elisabeth of Braunschweig-Lüneburg (1510–58), who introduced the Reformation into her territories during her reign as regent, owned a significant library, as a surviving inventory from 1539 attests. Elisabeth maintained an extensive correspondence on theological topics, intervening in the controversy surrounding the Königsberg theologian Andreas Osiander and his theories of justification, which were unpopular with Lutherans and Calvinists alike. Elisabeth was herself the author of several devotional works, including a handbook for widows. Half of the books listed in her inventory are works by Reformation authors. As she converted to Lutheranism only in 1538 her acceptance of the new faith can doubtless be attributed in part to her reading.[134]

The earliest mention of a library at the courts of the counts of Schwarzburg in Thuringia occurs in an report by Count Wolrad von Waldeck (1509–78), who visited Rudolstadt in 1548 and was astounded by the number of books on Reformation theology his mother-in-law showed him in her chamber library.[135] Books often formed part of the dowry women took with them when they married, and functioned as conscious reflections and reminders of their particular cultural or religious heritage.[136] There are various records of women's book ownership at the court of Dresden. An inventory of approximately 430 books belonging to Electress Anna of Saxony (1532–48), taken three years after her death at age sixteen, reflects her staunch Lutheranism as well as her interest in medicine and husbandry.[137] The book collection belonging to Electress Magdalena Sibylle of Saxony (1587–1659) merits special mention in her funeral sermon.[138]

Devotional works in the costly bindings for which the electoral library in Saxony was noted can be traced in the collections of dynasties into which daughters of electors married. Holdings of the library at Darmstadt after the marriage of Sophia Eleonora of Saxony (1609–71) to Landgraf Georg II in 1625 provide evidence of such cultural transfer.[139] The books originally belonged to members of the Saxon dynasty, both male and female, back to the generation of Sophia Eleonora's great-grandparents. They reinforced the strong Lutheran orthodoxy in which she had been brought up and served to cement the ties between Darmstadt and Dresden at the outset of the Thirty

Years' War. Among the works belonging to the libraries of her ancestors, Sophia Eleonora was given Luther's *Psalter* (1541) and Johann Schütz's *Fünfftzig erhebliche Vrsachen, Darumb die Lutherischen* [. . .] *zu den Sacrementierern oder Caluinisten, nicht tretten* [. . .] *können* (Fifty Important Reasons Why the Lutherans Cannot Join the Sacramentalists or Calvinists, 1580).[140] When in the latter half of the seventeenth century her own daughters and granddaughters married from Darmstadt, they took with them books of similar significance. Other books from Darmstadt entered the collections of the counts of Stolberg when Luise Christine of Hessen-Darmstadt (1636–97) married into that family in 1665.[141] A generation later Magdalena Sibylle of Hessen-Darmstadt (1652–1712) took funeral sermons and other works to Stuttgart when she married the duke of Württemberg in 1673.[142] Her own library is remarkable in its representation of the languages she had at her command: German, Latin, French, Italian, Swedish, and Dutch.[143]

Most of the information available on noble women's book ownership comes from inventories taken at the time of their marriages or at their deaths, when their original families could lay claim to the inheritance of personal property. Chance finds in the archives have prompted studies of individual collections, like that of the libraries belonging to Sibylle Ursula of Braunschweig-Lüneburg (1629–71)[144] and Christine Charlotte of Ostfriesland (1645–99),[145] but a systematic investigation has yet to be undertaken.

Evidence of women's book ownership in the burgher classes is sparser still. Archival evidence from Nuremberg for the seventeenth century shows that books bequeathed by women or brought into families by marriage contained mainly devotional literature.[146] Indirect evidence of women's libraries and their reading habits can be found in the biographical sections of funeral sermons.[147] Susanna Elisabeth Zeidler's preface to her own anthology of poetry, *Jungferlicher Zeitvertreiber* (Maidenly Pastime, 1684), records her reading, "dieweil ich bey meinem einsamen Dorfleben / von aller anmuthigen Gesellschaft andern Frauenzimmers entfernet / sonst keinen Ergetzlichkeiten finden können / als habe ich in feinen Historien-Büchern / Lusterweckenden Gesängen / und dergleichen Gedichten gesuchet"[148] (for in my lonely village life, cut off from the agreeable society of other women, I could find no other pleasure than what I sought in good history books, heartening songs, and similar poems). The circle of women writers in Altenburg grouped around Margaretha Susanna von Kuntsch (1651–1717) profited from the book collections belonging to their fathers and husbands and also from the libraries of the educational institutions in the town.[149] It was not until the eighteenth century that bourgeois women came into clearer focus as potential customers of the book trade. In 1705 a *Frauen-Zimmer-Bibliotheckgen* (Ladies' Little Library) was published recommending a basic selection of books that would equip their owner for her task as head of a household.[150]

Early Reading Publics

None of the libraries in the early modern period were public in the modern sense. For contemporaries "public" signified a group of institutions and individuals engaged in the realization of the "common good," that is, those concerned with public law, the legislature and magistracy, church and educational institutions, and all *personae publicae* who by virtue of the public power and authority vested in them worked for the commonwealth.[151] This meant that as a rule collections were accessible only to members of certain educated social groups or to academics. Court libraries were at first open only to "persons of quality" and to some scholars, often acquaintances of the librarian in charge. The library ordinance issued by Duke Julius in Wolfenbüttel in 1572 is typical in its stipulation that the librarian was to allow no one into the collection without obtaining the express permission of the duke himself. Typical, however, is also the designation of the library as part of the official tour for visitors to the castle.[152] Philipp Hainhofer's travel accounts from the early seventeenth century record several such visits in Dresden, Munich, and Stettin. During his stay at the court of his patron Philipp of Pomerania-Stettin in 1617, Hainhofer recorded how his library, books, and reading formed the center of the duke's everyday life:

> Auf Kutschen mein Herr und Ich immer, so wol, alß die vorhergehende Tage in Joh. Georgii Agricolae Hirschbuch laut gelesen, ainer ain Capitel umb den andern, oder an Posttagen ain Schrifft und Zeitung um den andern; da dan I. F. G. das Italiänisch, gleich so fertig lesen, alß das Lateinische und Deutsch, auch das Frantzösische wohl verstehen, und eben nit feyren künden, aintweder conversiren, oder lesen oder schreiben müssen, so gar übers Essens kaine Ruhe, sondern alle Malzeit ainen Büschel Bücher und Schrifften neben sich liegen haben, ain Weil essen, ain Weil lesen, ain Weil conversiren und trinken, und mich nur wundert, wie diser Herr das Lesen und Schreiben ainen ganzen Tag in seinem Kopf also verbringen kann, und so gar nit mued würdt.[153]

> [In the coach, as on the preceding days, my lord and I took turns in reading aloud a chapter from Joh. Georg Agricola's book on deer, or on post days one letter or newsletter after the other, for His Highness can read Italian as easily as Latin and German and is well able to understand French, and just cannot relax and do nothing; he must either be conversing, reading, or writing. Even when eating he is not still, but during every meal he has a bushel of books and writings lying next to him; he eats a while, reads a while, converses and drinks a while, and I just wonder how this prince can get this reading and writing into his head the whole day and not be at all tired.]

How intensive this shared act of reading and writing could be can be demonstrated in sources relating to the library of the counts of Hohenlohe at Langenburg. Not only the poetically inclined Count Heinrich Friedrich and the preachers and court officials engaged in literary activities and communal reading; these interests extended to the court barber and the kitchen clerk as well.[154] Reading as a group activity is well documented as part of the role of the *Hausvater* or *Hausmutter* in educating their children and households and supervising domestic devotional practices. Sources as varied as novels[155] and funeral sermons often make mention of reading aloud in groups, but also of cases in which individual readers retreated into locked rooms and private spaces in order to be able to concentrate more fully.[156]

By the end of the sixteenth century, property lists show that even modest artisan households had small book collections. A fictive dialogue published under the title *Marckschiffer, oder Marckschiffergespräch* (Fair Vendors, or Fair Vendors' Dialogue) in 1596 confirms:

> Dem Teutschland mans zu dancken hat,
> Wie sichs befindt selbs in der Tat
> Dass jeder ihm jetzt leicht kan zeugen,
> Ein Liberey, dass ers hab eigen:
> Die man fande vor alten Zeiten
> Nur bey gross Herrn, reichen Leuthen.[157]

[We have Germany to thank for the fact, as it is truly the case, that nowadays everyone can build up a library to have as his own. In olden days these were only to be found in the houses of great men, of rich people.]

An early example of civic concern to make books freely available to the lower strata of society is the call in 1546 by the Strasbourg reformer Kaspar Hedio (1494–1552) for the establishment of public libraries with a stock of German books. Specifically it would be open on Sundays and holidays so that young artisans could read or be read to, "zur besserung unnd irer seelen heil" (for their improvement and the salvation of their souls), instead of spending their time in public houses or bowling and gambling.[158]

Notwithstanding the comparative want of public libraries, as we have seen, book collections were generally accessible to readers in the early modern period: to those at court; to members of institutions such as monasteries, schools, and universities; to wives, children, and apprentices in the households of wealthy craftsmen, clergymen, or burghers; to students in the houses of their professors; to tutors in the houses of the aristocrats they served. It was not until the mid-eighteenth century, however, with the rise of philanthropy, that the concept of a general public came into being, leading to the establishment of the circulating library and a general reading public.[159]

Notes

[1] See for example Anthony Grafton, *Commerce with the Classics: Ancient Books and Renaissance Readers* (Ann Arbor: U of Michigan P, 1997).

[2] Wolfgang Harms, "Das Buch im Sammlungszusammenhang," *Bibliothek und Wissenschaft* 33 (2000): 51; exemplary in this respect: Erika Rummel and Dale Schrag, *The Erasmus Collection in the Herzog August Bibliothek* (Wiesbaden: Harrassowitz, 2004), which identifies 40% of the owners and records their marginalia.

[3] A monumental repertorium of libraries in Germany now gives detailed information on surviving historical holdings: *Handbuch der historischen Buchbestände in Deutschland,*

27 vols., ed. Bernhard Fabian (Hildesheim: Olms, 1992–2000). Standard library histories: Aloys Bömer, "Von der Renaissance bis zum Beginn der Aufklärung," in *Handbuch der Bibliothekswissenschaft*, ed. Georg Leyh, vol. 3/1: *Geschichte der Bibliotheken*, 2nd ed., ed. Bömer (Wiesbaden: Harrassowitz, 1955): 499–681; Ladislaus Buzás, *Deutsche Bibliotheksgeschichte der Neuzeit (1500–1800)* (Wiesbaden: Reichert, 1976); Buzás, *German Library History, 800–1945* (Jefferson, NC: McFarland, 1986); Wolfgang Schmitz, *Deutsche Bibliotheksgeschichte* (Bern: Lang, 1984); Uwe Jochum, *Kleine Bibliotheksgeschichte*, 2nd ed. (Stuttgart: Reclam, 1999).

[4] Hans Gebauer, *Bücherauktionen in Deutschland im 17. Jahrhundert* (Bonn: Bouvier, 1981).

[5] Helmut Zedelmaier, *Bibliotheca universalis und bibliotheca selecta: Das Problem der Ordnung des gelehrten Wissens in der frühen Neuzeit* (Köln: Böhlau, 1992), 9–21.

[6] Harms, "Das Buch im Sammlungszusammenhang," 50.

[7] Martin Mulsow, "Konsumtheorie und Kulturtransfer: Einige Perspektiven für die Forschung zum 16. Jahrhundert," in *Kulturtransfer: Kulturelle Praxis im 16. Jahrhundert*, ed. Wolfgang Schmale (Innsbruck: Studien Verlag, 2003), 131–43, here 140.

[8] According to Mark A. Meadow, "Merchants and Marvels: Hans Jacob Fugger and the Origins of the Wunderkammer," in *Merchants and Marvels: Commerce, Science and Art in Early Modern Europe*, ed. Pamela H. Smith and Paula Findlen (London: Routledge, 2002), 182–200, here 184, "the activity of collecting provided a social nexus, in which noble, scholar, tradesman and even craftsman could participate in the same realm."

[9] Wolfgang Behringer, *Im Zeichen des Merkur: Reichspost und Kommunikationsrevolution in der Frühen Neuzeit* (Göttingen: Vandenhoeck & Ruprecht, 2003).

[10] See Meadow, "Merchants and Marvels," and Lisa Jardine, *Wordly Goods: A New History of the Renaissance* (London: Macmillan, 1996).

[11] Paula Findlen, *Possessing Nature: Museums, Collecting, and Scientific Culture in Early Modern Italy* (Berkeley: U of California P, 1994), especially the section on the traveler-collector as Ulysses, beginning at page 304.

[12] Harriet Roth, ed., *Der Anfang der Museumslehre in Deutschland: Das Traktat "Inscriptiones vel Tituli Theatri Amplissimi" von Samuel Quiccheberg* (Berlin: Akademie, 2000), 2.

[13] Helen Watanabe-O'Kelly, *Court Culture in Dresden: From Renaissance to Baroque* (Basingstoke: Palgrave, 2002), 72.

[14] Franz Georg Kaltwasser, *Die Bibliothek als Museum: Von der Renaissance bis heute, dargestellt am Beispiel der Bayerischen Staatsbibliothek* (Wiesbaden: Harrassowitz, 1999); and *Barocke Sammellust: Die Bibliothek und Kunstkammer des Herzogs Ferdinand Albrecht zu Braunschweig und Lüneburg (1636–1687)*, exhibition catalogue, ed. Jill Bepler (Weinheim: VCH Acta Humaniora, 1988).

[15] Mathilda Rovelstad, "Two Seventeenth-century Library Handbooks, Two Different Library Theories," *Libraries & Culture: A Journal of Library History* 35 (2000): 540–56.

[16] Rovelstad, "Two Seventeenth-century Library Handbooks," 548; see also Mathilde Rovelstad and E. Michael Camilli, "Emblems as Inspiration and Guidance in Baroque Libraries," *Libraries & Culture* 29 (1994): 147–65.

[17] Paul Nelles, "The Library as an Instrument of Discovery: Gabriel Naudé and the Uses of History," in *History and the Disciplines: The Reclassification of Knowledge in Early*

Modern Europe, ed. Donald R. Kelly (Rochester: U of Rochester P, 1997), 41–57, here 41.

[18] Klaus Garber, "Paris, Capital of European Late Humanism: Jacques Auguste de Thou and the Cabinet Dupuy," trans. Joe G. Delap, in *Imperiled Heritage: Tradition, History, and Utopia in Early Modern German Literature: Selected Essays by Klaus Garber*, ed. Max Reinhart, Studies in European Cultural Transition 5 (Aldershot, UK: Ashgate, 2000), 54–72.

[19] John Dury, *The Reformed Librarie-Keeper (1650)*, ed. Richard H. Popkin and Thomas F. Wright (Los Angeles: William Andrews Clark Memorial Library, 1983), 17; Jill Bepler, "Herzog August and the Hartlib Circle," in *A Treasure House of Books: The Library of Duke August of Brunswick-Wolfenbüttel*, exhibition catalogue, ed. Helwig Schmidt-Glintzer (Wiesbaden: Harrassowitz, 1998), 165–72, here 170.

[20] Paul Nelles, "The Renaissance Ancient Library Tradition and Christian Antiquity," in *Les humanistes et leur bibliothèque — Humanists and Their Libraries*, ed. Rudolf de Smet (Leuven: Peeters, 2002), 159–73.

[21] Jochum, *Kleine Bibliotheksgeschichte*, 78; Lieselotte Saurma-Jeltsch, *Bilderhandschriften aus der Werkstatt Diebold Laubers in Hagenau* (Wiesbaden: Reichert, 2001).

[22] Jochum, *Kleine Bibliotheksgeschichte*, 80–81; on this process see Uwe Neddermeyer, *Von der Handschrift zum gedruckten Buch: Schriftlichkeit und Leseinteresse im Mittelalter und in der frühen Neuzeit: Quantitative und qualitative Aspekte* (Wiesbaden: Harrassowitz, 1998).

[23] Paul Kaegbein, *Deutsche Ratsbüchereien bis zur Reformation*, Zentralblatt für Bibliothekswesen, Beiheft 77 (Leipzig: Harrassowitz, 1950).

[24] Kaegbein, *Deutsche Ratsbüchereien*, 9–18.

[25] Anette Haucap-Naß, *Der Braunschweiger Stadtschreiber Gerwin von Hameln und seine Bibliothek* (Wiesbaden: Harrassowitz, 1995).

[26] Waltraud Guth, *Bibliotheksgeschichte des Landes Sachsen-Anhalt* (Halle: Universitäts- und Landesbibliothek, 2004), 69.

[27] Schmitz, *Deutsche Bibliotheksgeschichte*, 56ff.

[28] Johannes Kadenbach, "Die Bibliothek des Amplonius Rating de Bercka: Entstehung, Wachstum, Profil," in *Die Bibliotheca Amploniana: Ihre Bedeutung im Spannungsfeld von Aristotelismus, Nominalismus und Humanismus*, ed. Andreas Speer (Berlin: de Gruyter, 1995), 16–31, here 27–29.

[29] Wolfgang Milde, "Bibliotheksgeschichte (Mittelalter)," in *Lexikon des gesamten Buchwesens*, 2nd ed. (Stuttgart: Hiersemann, 1987), 1:406–11, here 409.

[30] Thomas Kock, *Die Buchkultur der Devotio moderna: Handschriftenproduktion, Literaturversorgung und Bibliotheksaufbau im Zeitalter des Medienwechsels* (Frankfurt am Main: Lang, 1999), 23.

[31] Klaus Schreiner, "Bücher, Bibliotheken und *Gemeiner Nutzen* im Spätmittelalter und in der Frühneuzeit: Geistes- und sozialgeschichtliche Beiträge zur Frage nach der *utilitas librorum*," *Bibliothek und Wissenschaft* 9 (1975): 202–49, here 221–22; Nikolaus Staupach, "Von Deventer nach Windesheim: Buch und Bibliothek in der Frühzeit der Devotio moderna," in *Kloster und Bibliothek: Zur Geschichte des Bibliothekswesens der Augustiner-Chorherren in der Frühen Neuzeit*, ed. Rainer A. Müller (Paring: Augustiner-Chorherren-Verlag, 2000), 1–22.

[32] Klaus Arnold, *Johannes Trithemius (1462–1516)* (Würzburg: Schöningh, 1991).

[33] Susann El Kholi, "Ein Besuch bei Johannes Trithemius: Der Brief des Matthäus Herbenus an Jodokus Beissel vom 14. August 1495," *Archiv für mittelrheinische Kirchengeschichte* 56 (2004): 143–57, here 147.

[34] Buzás, *German Library History*, 193.

[35] Winfried Enderle, "Die Jesuitenbibliotheken im 17. Jahrhundert: das Beispiel der Bibliothek des Düsseldorfer Kollegs 1619–1773," *Archiv für Geschichte des Buchwesens* 41 (1994): 146–213, here 152–55.

[36] Enderle, "Die Jesuitenbibliotheken," 155.

[37] *Die Jesuiten in Passau: Schule und Bibliothek 1612–1773: 375 Jahre Gymnasium Leopoldinum und Staatliche Bibliothek* (Passau: Passavia Universitätsverlag, 1987), 234.

[38] Klaus Schreiner, "Bücher, Bibliotheken und *Gemeiner Nutzen*," 227–30.

[39] Uwe Czubatynski, *Armaria Ecclesiae: Studien zur Geschichte des kirchlichen Buchwesens* (Neustadt a.d.A.: Degener & Co, 1998), 46–55.

[40] Quoted in Herward von Schade, "Der Einfluß der Reformation auf die Entwicklung des evangelischen Bibliothekswesens," in *Beiträge zur Geschichte des Buchwesens im konfessionellen Zeitalter*, ed. Herbert G. Göpfert et al. (Wiesbaden: Harrassowitz, 1985), 154.

[41] Quoted in Schade, "Der Einfluβ der Reformation," 154.

[42] Quoted in Schade, "Der Einfluβ der Reformation," 154.

[43] Czubatynski, *Armaria Ecclesiae*, 54.

[44] Schreiner, "Bücher, Bibliotheken und *Gemeiner Nutzen*," 237.

[45] Bernd Moeller, "Die Anfänge kommunaler Bibliotheken in Deutschland," in *Studien zum städtischen Bildungswesen des späten Mittelalters und der frühen Neuzeit*, ed. Moeller et al. (Göttingen: Vandenhoeck & Ruprecht, 1983), 136–51, here 146.

[46] Siegfried Bräuer, quoted by Czubatynski, *Armaria Ecclesiae*, 54, note 26.

[47] See for example *Braunschweigische Kirchenordnungen von den ältesten Zeiten bis zum Jahr 1828*, ed. Friedrich Koldewey (Berlin: Hofmann, 1886–90).

[48] Hermann Erbacher, *Schatzkammern des Wissens: Ein Beitrag zur Geschichte der kirchlichen Bibliotheken* (Neustadt a.d.A.: Degener & Co., 1966), 60.

[49] Karsten Eisenmenger, "Die Geschichte der Marienbibliothek und ihrer Bibliothekare," in *450 Jahre Marienbibliothek zu Halle an der Saale: Kostbarkeiten und Raritäten einer alten Büchersammlung*, ed. Heinrich L. Nickel (Halle a.d.S.: Janos Stekovics, 2002), 1:4–31, here 15–17.

[50] Erbacher, *Schatzkammer*, 64.

[51] Moeller, "Die Anfänge kommunaler Bibliotheken," 145.

[52] Quoted and translated in Sachiko Kusukawa, *A Wittenberg University Library Catalogue of 1536*, Medieval & Renaissance Texts and Studies 142 (Cambridge: LP Publications, 1995), xv.

[53] Kusukawa, *A Wittenberg University Library Catalogue*, xvii.

[54] Kusukawa, *A Wittenberg University Library Catalogue*, xi.

[55] Otto von Heinemann, *Die Herzogliche Bibliothek zu Wolfenbüttel, 1550–1893: Neudruck der Ausgabe Wolfenbüttel 1894* (Amsterdam: van Heusden, 1969), 50.

[56] Gundula Werner and Eleonore Schmidt-Herrling, *Die Bibliotheken der Universität Altdorf*, Beihefte zum Zentralblatt für Bibliothekswesen 69 (Leipzig: Harrassowitz, 1937), 15; Wolfgang Mährle, *Academica Norica: Wissenschaft und Bildung an der Nürnberger Hohen Schule in Altdorf (1575–1623)* (Stuttgart: Steiner, 2000).

[57] Werner and Schmidt-Herrling, *Die Bibliotheken*, 71.

[58] Hilde de Ridder-Symoens, "Organisation und Ausstattung," in *Geschichte der Universität in Europa*, vol. 2, *Von der Reformation bis zur Französischen Revolution (1500–1800)*, ed. Walter Ruegg (Munich: Beck, 1996), 169–79, here 169.

[59] Paul Nelles, "Historia litteraria and Morhof: Private Teaching and Professorial Libraries at the University of Kiel," in *Mapping the World of Learning: The Polyhistor of Daniel Georg Morhof*, ed. Françoise Waquet (Wiesbaden: Harrassowitz, 2000), 31–56, here 50.

[60] Robert Kolb, *Caspar Peucer's Library: Portrait of a Wittenberg Professor of the Mid-sixteenth Century* (St Louis: Center for Reformation Research, 1976), 5.

[61] Kolb, *Caspar Peucer's Library*, 15.

[62] The manuscript inventory has an entry reading "Bibliotheca mea quae est Budissinae," in Kolb, *Caspar Peucer's Library*, 5.

[63] Helmut Claus, *Bibliotheca Gerhardina: Eigenart und Schicksal einer thüringischen Gelehrtenbibliothek des 17. Jahrhunderts* (Gotha: Landesbibliothek, 1968), 12.

[64] *Bibliotheca Gerhardina: Rekonstruktion der Gelehrten- und Leihbibliothek Johann Gerhards (1582–1637) und seines Sohnes Johann Ernst Gerhard (1621–1668)*, ed. Johann Anselm Steiger (Stuttgart-Bad Canstatt: Frommann-Holzboog, 2002).

[65] Claus, *Bibliotheca Gerhardina*, 18.

[66] Gebauer, *Bücherauktionen in Deutschland*, 65 and 144.

[67] Nelles, "Historia litteraria and Morhof," 52: "*Historia litteraria* was taught primarily in his house, with full access to his library. [. . .] In his teaching Morhof had nothing committed to writing; he dictated from memory, with occasional recourse to his books. Even in his public teaching Morhof was accustomed to bring the most choice and rare books from his collection into the lecture hall."

[68] Nelles, "Historia litteraria and Morhof," 43.

[69] Nelles, "Historia litteraria and Morhof," 54; also Nelles, "Historia litteraria at Helmstedt: Books, Professors and Students in the Early Enlightenment University," in *Die Praktiken der Gelehrsamkeit in der Frühen Neuzeit*, ed. Helmut Zedelmaier and Martin Mulsow (Tübingen: Niemeyer, 2001), 147–76, here 154ff.

[70] The relevant passage from Brassicanus's preface to his edition of Salvianus, *Über das wahre Urteil und die Vorsehung Gottes* (1530), is contained in German translation in *Die Kultur des Humanismus: Reden, Briefe, Traktate, Gespräche von Petrarca bis Kepler*, ed. Nicolette Mout (Munich: Beck, 1998): 104–9; on the Hebrew manuscript see Wilhelm Brambach, "Reuchlins Bibliothek," *Zeitschrift für die Geschichte des Oberrheins*, NF 37 (1923): 313–21, here 320.

[71] Csaba Csapodi, *The Corvinian Library: History and Stock* (Budapest: Akadémiai K., 1983); Martyn Rady, "The Corvina Library and the lost Royal Hungarian Archive," in *Lost Libraries: The Destruction of Great Book Collections since Antiquity*, ed. James Raven (London: Palgrave, 2004), 91–105.

[72] *Bibliotheca Palatina*, exhibition catalogue, ed. Elmar Mittler (Heidelberg: Edition Braus, 1986).

[73] Paul Lehmann, *Eine Geschichte der alten Fuggerbibliotheken* (Tübingen: Mohr-Siebeck, 1956), 1:82.

[74] Jill Bepler, "*Vicissitudo Temporum*: Some Sidelights on Book Collecting in the Thirty Years' War," *Sixteenth Century Journal* 32 (2001): 953–68, here 955–56; Uwe Jochum, "Am Ende der Sammlung: Bibliotheken im frühmodernen Staat," in *Macht des Wissens: Die Entstehung der modernen Wissensgesellschaft* (Cologne: Böhlau, 2004), 273–94, here 293.

[75] *Um Glauben und Reich: Kurfürst Maximilian I.: Beiträge zur Bayerischen Geschichte und Kunst*, ed. Hubert Glaser (Munich: Hirmer, 1980).

[76] *Ernst der Fromme (1601–1675): Staatsmann und Reformer*, ed. Roswitha Jacobsen and Hans-Jörg Ruge (Bucha bei Jena: quartus, 2002), 400.

[77] See Schmidt-Glintzer, ed., *A Treasure House of Books*.

[78] Brigitte Volk-Knüttel, "Maximilian I. von Bayern als Sammler und Auftraggeber: Seine Korrespondenz mit Philipp Hainhofer 1611–1615," in *Quellen und Studien zur Kunstpolitik der Wittelsbacher*, ed. Hubert Glaser (Munich: Hirmer, 1980), 83–128, here 112–13.

[79] Hainhofer to Duke August, 14/24 May 1618, in *Der Briefwechsel zwischen Philipp Hainhofer und Herzog August d. J. von Braunschweig-Lüneburg*, ed. Ronald Gobiet (Munich: Deutscher Kunstverlag, 1984), 239.

[80] Dieter Albrecht, *Maximilian I. von Bayern 1573–1651* (Munich: Oldenbourg, 1998), 275.

[81] Hermann Conring, *Die Bibliotheca Augusta zu Wolfenbüttel: Zugleich über Bibliotheken überhaupt*, trans. Peter Mortzfeld (Göttingen: Wallstein, 2005).

[82] Ulrich Johannes Schneider, "Der Ort der Bücher in der Bibliothek und im Katalog am Beispiel von Herzog Augusts Wolfenbütteler Büchersammlung," *Archiv für Geschichte des Buchwesens* 59 (2005): 91–104.

[83] Mechthild Raabe, *Leser und Lektüre vom 17. zum 19. Jahrhundert: die Ausleihbücher der Herzog August Bibliothek 1664–1806* (Munich: Saur, 1989–98).

[84] Paul Nelles, "Libraries," in *Encyclopedia of the Renaissance*, ed. Paul F. Grendler (New York: Charles Scribner's Sons, 1999), 3:420–24, here 422.

[85] Buzás, *German Library History*, 162.

[86] Ursula Winter, "Handschriften, seltene Drucke und Kuriositäten in der Churfürstlichen Bibliothek zu Cölln an der Spree," *Marginalien: Zeitschrift für Buchkunst und Bibliophilie* (1981): 50–68, here 52.

[87] Wolfgang Milde, "Bibliotheksgeschichte (Mittelalter)," in *Lexikon des gesamten Buchwesens*, 2nd ed. (Stuttgart: Hiersemann, 1987), 409.

[88] As Wolfgang Milde has shown by using the surviving catalogues of the Hartmann Schedel collection: "Über Bücherverzeichnisse der Humanistenzeit (Petrarca, Tommaso Parentucelli, Hartmann Schedel)," in *Bücherkataloge als buchgeschichtliche Quellen in der frühen Neuzeit*, ed. Reinhard Wittmann (Wiesbaden: Harrassowitz, 1985), 19–31, here 28–31.

[89] On Eyb's life and work see in this volume the chapter by John L. Flood.

[90] Eckhard Bernstein, "Albrecht von Eyb," in *Deutsche Dichter der Frühen Neuzeit 1450–1600*, ed. Stephan Füssel (Berlin: Schmidt, 1993), 96–110; Bernstein, "Albrecht von Eyb," in *Literatur Lexikon Autoren und Werke deutscher Sprache*, ed. Walther Killy (Gütersloh: Bertelsmann, 1989), 313–14.

[91] Brambach, "Reuchlins Bibliothek," 319; Schmitz, *Deutsche Bibliotheksgeschichte*, 68. In 1519 following Ulrich's siege of the imperial free city of Reutlingen the Swabian League expelled him.

[92] Schmitz, *Deutsche Bibliotheksgeschichte*, 67.

[93] Renate Johne, "Ex Libris Pirckheimeri: Bemerkungen zum Aufbau der Pirckheimerschen Familienbibliothek," *Marginalien: Zeitschrift für Buchkunst und Bibliophilie* 78 (1980): 61–67, here 62.

[94] Erwin Rosenthal, "Dürers Buchmalereien für Pirckheimers Bibliothek," *Jahrbuch der Preußischen Kunstsammlungen* 49 (1928): 1–54, here 51–52; Francis C. Springell, *Connoisseur & Diplomat* (London: Maggs, 1963), 105–10.

[95] Schmitz, *Deutsche Bibliotheksgeschichte*, 68.

[96] Harms, "Das Buch im Sammlungszusammenhang," 55. On humanist epistolary tradition and practice see Axel E. Walter, *Späthumanismus und Konfessionspolitik: Die europäische Gelehrtenrepublik um 1600 im Spiegel der Korrespondenzen Georg Michael Lingelsheims*, Frühe Neuzeit 95 (Tübingen: Niemeyer, 2004), especially the chapter "Die humanistische Epistolographie," 41–50.

[97] Hans-Jörg Künast and Helmut Zäh, *Die Bibliothek Konrad Peutingers: Edition der historischen Kataloge und Rekonstruktion der Bestände*, vol. 1, *Die Autographen Kataloge Peutingers: Der nicht-juristische Bibliotheksteil* (Tübingen: Niemeyer, 2003), 11–12.

[98] Lehmann, *Eine Geschichte der alten Fuggerbibliotheken*, 1:50.

[99] Lehmann, *Eine Geschichte der alten Fuggerbibliotheken*, 1:56.

[100] Hans-Jörg Künast, "Welserbibliotheken: Eine Bestandsaufnahme der Bibliotheken von Anton, Marcus und Paulus Welser," in *Die Welser: Neue Forschungen zur Geschichte und Kultur des oberdeutschen Handelshauses*, ed. Mark Häberlein und Johannes Burkhardt (Berlin: Akademie, 2002), 550–84.

[101] Jill Bepler, "*Vicissitudo Temporum.*"

[102] Schreiner, "Bücher, Bibliotheken und *Gemeiner Nutzen*," 232.

[103] *Der Ehrenbrief des Püterich von Reichertshausen*, ed. Fritz Behrend and Rudolf Wolkan (Weimar: Gesellschaft der Bibliophilen, 1920), 7.

[104] Schmitz, *Deutsche Bibliotheksgeschichte*, 52–54.

[105] Schreiner, "Bücher, Bibliotheken und *Gemeiner Nutzen*," 232–34.

[106] Jill Bepler, "Travelling and Posterity: The Archive, the Library and the Cabinet," in *Grand Tour — Adeliges Reisen und europäische Kultur vom 14. bis zum 16. Jahrhundert*, ed. Rainer Babel and Werner Paravicini (Stuttgart: Thorbeke, 2005), 193–205. For travel writing in the entire period see in this volume the chapter by Wolfgang Neuber.

[107] Werner Arnold, "Adelsbildung in Mitteldeutschland: Joachim von Alvensleben und seine Bibliothek," in *Bibliotheken und Bücher im Zeitalter der Renaissance*, ed. Werner Arnold (Wiesbaden: Harrassowitz, 1997), 167–94.

[108] Werner Arnold, *Die Bibliothek der Grafen von der Schulenburg* (Berlin: Kulturstiftung der Länder, 1994), 7, 8.

[109] Werner Arnold, "Gelehrtes Beamtentum in Braunschweig: Johann Cammann d. J. (1584–1649) und seine Bibliothek," *Wolfenbütteler Notizen zur Buchgeschichte* 25 (2000): 61–80.

[110] Wiebke Steinmetz, *Heinrich Rantzau (1526–1598): ein Vertreter des Humanismus in Nordeuropa und seine Wirkungen als Förderer der Künste* (Frankfurt am Main: Lang, 1991), 45.

[111] Dieter Lohmeier, *Heinrich Rantzau: Humanismus und Renaissance in Schleswig Holstein* (Heide: Westholsteinische Verlagsanstalt, 2000), 63.

[112] Christian Hoffmann, "Bücher und Autographen von Johann Fischart," *Daphnis* 25 (1996): 489–579, here 491.

[113] Hoffmann, "Bücher und Autographen von Johann Fischart," 500 and 504.

[114] Wolfgang Milde, "Das Bücherverzeichnis von Hans Sachs," in *Handwerker, Dichter, Stadtbürger: 500 Jahre Hans Sachs*, exhibition catalogue, ed. Dieter Merzbacher, Herzog August Bibliothek 72 (Wiesbaden: Harrassowitz, 1995), 38–55.

[115] Adolf Schmidt, "Die Bibliothek Moscheroschs," *Zeitschrift für Bücherfreunde* 2 (1898–99): 497–506.

[116] Gebauer, *Bücherauktionen in Deutschland*, 106.

[117] Dieter Lohmeier and Anke-Marie Lohmeier, "Jacob Schwieger: Lebenlauf, Gesellschaftskreis und Bücherbesitz eines Schäferdichters," *Jahrbuch der deutschen Schillergesellschaft* 19 (1975): 98–137, here 120, speak of "die Fachbibliothek eines Literaten" (the specialist library of a literary author).

[118] Extant auction catalogue, see Marian Szyrocki, "Catalogus Bibliothecae Gryphianae," in *Germanica Wratislaviensia* 69 (Wroclaw: Wydawn. Uniw. Wroclawskiego, 1986), microfiche 3.

[119] Martin Bircher, "Bücher aus dem Besitz von Martin Opitz," in *Martin Opitz: Studien zu Werk und Person*, ed. Barbara Becker-Cantarino, *Daphnis* 11 (1982): 253–62, here 253.

[120] Bircher, "Bücher aus dem Besitz von Martin Opitz." Another example is a list of twenty books belonging to the poet Paul Fleming (1609–40) donated to the Reval (Tallin) library in 1660, which have survived in the library of the Estonian Academy of Sciences in Tallin. See Robert Kyra, "Der Büchernachlaß Paul Flemings in der Bibliothek der estnischen Akademie der Wissenschaften," *Daphnis* 22 (1993): 27–39.

[121] Jill Bepler, "Karl Gustav von Hille (ca. 1590–1647): Zu seiner Biographie und zu seinen Beziehungen nach England," in *Respublica Guelfpherbytana Wolfenbütteler Beiträge zur Renaissance- und Barockforschung: Festschrift für Paul Raabe*, ed. Martin Bircher et al., *Chloe*, Beihefte zum *Daphnis* 6 (1987), 253–90.

[122] Martin Brecht, *J. V. Andreae und Herzog August zu Braunschweig-Lüneburg: Ihr Briefwechsel und ihr Umfeld* (Stuttgart-Bad Canstatt: Fromann-Holzboog, 2002), 251.

[123] *Briefe der Fruchtbringenden Gesellschaft und Beilagen: Die Zeit Fürst Ludwigs von Anhalt-Köthen 1617–1650*, ed. Klaus Conermann (Tübingen: Niemeyer, 1993–).

[124] Renate Jürgensen, *Utile cum dulci: Mit Nutzen erfreuen: Die Blütezeit des Pegnesischen Blumenordens in Nürnberg 1644–1744* (Wiesbaden: Harrassowitz, 1994).

[125] *Der Briefwechsel zwischen Sigmund von Birken (1626–1681) und Catharina Regina von Greiffenberg (1633–1694)*, ed. Hartmut Laufhütte and Dietrich Jöns (Tübingen: Niemeyer, 2005), brings important insights into the exchange of books and information between Birken and Greiffenberg.

[126] Georg Andreas Will, *Nürnbergisches Gelehrten-Lexicon* (1755–58), quoted by Renate Jürgensen, in *Bibliotheca Norica: Patrizier- und Gelehrtenbibliotheken in Nürnberg zwischen Mittelalter und Aufklärung* (Wiesbaden: Harrassowitz, 2002), 1:247.

[127] Of these, 5,400 volumes containing 19,807 separate works have survived in the Landeskirchliches Archiv in Nuremberg. See Jürgensen, *Bibliotheca Norica*, 250. The facts in this paragraph regarding Dilherr's collections derive mainly from Jürgensen.

[128] See elsewhere in this volume the related chapter by Anna Carrdus.

[129] Arnold Schromm, *Die Bibliothek des ehemaligen Zisterzienserinnenklosters Kirchheim am Ries: Buchpflege und geistiges Leben in einem schwäbischen Frauenstift* (Tübingen: Niemeyer, 1998), 50; also Charlotte Woodford, *Nuns as Historians in Early Modern Germany* (Oxford: Clarendon, 2002), 19ff.

[130] Margrid Reitzammer, "Die Geschichte der Historischen Bibliothek Quedlinburg," *Quedlinburger Annalen* 1 (1998): 15–41, here 24ff.

[131] Anna Sophia became abbess at Quedlinburg in 1680 after having served the cloister as provost since 1657; in 1658 she published *Der treue Seelenfreund Christus Jesus mit nachdenklichen Sinngemälden, anmutigen Lehrgedichten und neuen geistreichen Gesängen* (The True Friend of the Soul, Christ Jesus: With Meditative Emblems, Pleasant Poems for Edification, and New Spiritual Songs). Maria Aurora, mistress of August the Strong, elector of Saxony and king of Poland, was praised by Voltaire and renowned throughout northern Europe for her talents as a poet and painter.

[132] Johannes Arndt, "Möglichkeiten und Grenzen weiblicher Selbstbehauptung gegenüber männlicher Dominanz im Reichsgrafenstand des 17. und 18. Jahrhunderts," *Vierteljahrschrift für Sozial- und Wirtschaftsgeschichte* 77 (1990): 153–74.

[133] Martina Backes, *Das literarische Leben am kurpfälzischen Hof* (Tübingen: Niemeyer, 1992), 177ff.

[134] Ingeborg Mengel, "Ein bisher unbekanntes Bücherinventar der Herzogin Elisabeth von Braunschweig-Lüneburg aus dem Jahr 1539," *Jahrbuch der Gesellschaft für niedersächsische Kirchengeschichte* 50 (1952): 51–58.

[135] Franz-Joachim Stewing, "Von der Hofkirchen-, Hof- und Kanzleibibliothek zur fürstlichen öffentlichen Bibliothek," in *Historische Bibliotheken in Rudolstadt*, ed. Jens Henkel et al. (Rudolstadt: Thüringer Landesmuseum Heidecksburg, 1999), 25.

[136] Jill Bepler, "The Use of Prayer Books at Court: The Example of Wolfenbüttel," in *Gebetsliteratur der Frühen Neuzeit als Hausfrömmigkeit: Funktionen und Formen in Deutschland und den Niederlanden* (Wiesbaden: Harrassowitz, 2001), 47–62, here 61.

[137] Watanabe-O'Kelly, *Court Culture in Dresden*, 84.

[138] Jill Bepler, "*im dritten Gradu ungleicher Linie Seitwarts verwandt*: Frauen und dynastisches Bewußtsein in den Funeralwerken der Frühen Neuzeit," in *Dynastie und Herrschaftssicherung in der Frühen Neuzeit: Geschlechter und Geschlecht*, ed. Heide Wunder (Berlin: Dunckler & Humblot, 2002), 135–60, here 151.

[139] Adolf Schmidt, "Sächsische Einbände in der Großherzoglichen Hof- und Landesbibliothek zu Darmstadt," *Zeitschrift für Bücherfreunde* 10 (1918–19): 9–19.

[140] Schmidt, "Sächsische Einbände," 11.

[141] Bepler, "*im dritten Gradu*," 155.

[142] Jill Bepler, "*zu meinem und aller dehrer die sichs gebrauchen wollen, nutzen, trost und frommen:* Lektüre, Schrift und Gebet im Leben der fürstlichen Witwen in der Frühen Neuzeit," in *Witwenschaft in der Frühen Neuzeit: Fürstliche und adlige Witwen zwischen Fremd- und Selbstbestimmung*, ed. Martina Schattkowsky (Leipzig: Leipziger Universitätsverlag, 2003), 303–19, here 316.

[143] Wolfgang Irtenkauf, "Das Haus Württemberg und das Buch- und Bibliothekswesen," in *900 Jahre Württemberg: Leben und Leistung für Land und Volk* (Stuttgart: Kohlhammer, 1984), 623–35, here 629.

[144] Blake Lee Spahr, "Sibylle Ursula and Her Books," in *Problems and Perspectives: A Collection of Essays on Baroque Literature* (Frankfurt am Main: Lang, 1981), 85–110.

[145] Sabine Heißler, "Christine Charlotte von Ostfriesland (1645–1699) und ihre Bücher, oder lesen Frauen Anderes?," *Daphnis* 27 (1998): 335–418.

[146] Rolf Engelsing, *Der Bürger als Leser: Lesergeschichte in Deutschland 1500–1800* (Stuttgart: Metzler, 1994), 69–70.

[147] Cornelia Niekus Moore, "The Quest for Consolation and Amusement: Reading Habits of German Women in the Seventeenth Century," in *The Graph of Sex and the German Text: Gendered Culture in Early Modern Germany 1500–1700*, ed. Lynne Tatlock, Chloe, Beiheft zum *Daphnis* 19 (1994), 247–68; Moore, "Erbauungsliteratur als Gebrauchsliteratur für Frauen im 17. Jahrhundert: Leichenpredigten als Quelle weiblicher Lesegewohnheiten," in *Le livre religieux et ses pratiques — Der Umgang mit dem religiösen Buch*, ed. Hans E. Bödeker et al. (Göttingen: Vandenhoeck & Ruprecht, 1991), 291–314.

[148] *Jungferlicher Zeitvertreiber: das ist allerhand deudsche Gedichte bey häußlicher Arbeit und stiller Einsamkeit verfertiget und zusammen getragen von Susannen Elisabeth Zeidlerin*, ed. Cornelia Niekus Moore (1686; repr., Berne: Lang, 2000), 10.

[149] Anna Carrdus, *Das "weiblich Werk" in der Residenzstadt Altenburg: 1672–1720; Gedichte und Briefe von Margaretha Susanna von Kuntsch und Frauen in ihrem Umkreis* (Hildesheim: Olms, 2004), 42.

[150] Engelsing, *Der Bürger als Leser*, 71.

[151] Schreiner, "Bücher, Bibliotheken und *Gemeiner Nutzen*," 243.

[152] Otto von Heinemann, *Die Herzogliche Bibliothek zu Wolfenbüttel, 1550–1893* (1894; repr., Amsterdam: van Heusden, 1969), 295.

[153] Friedrich Ludwig von Medem, "Philipp Hainhofers Reise-Tagebuch, enthaltend Schilderungen aus Franken, Sachsen, der Mark Brandenburg und Pommern im Jahr 1617," *Baltische Studien* 2, no. 2 (1834): 1–180, here 64.

[154] Wolfgang Adam, "Lesen und Vorlesen am Langenburger Hof: Zur Lesefähigkeit und zum Buchbesitz der Diener und Beamten," in *Literatur und Volk im 17. Jahrhundert*, ed. Wolfgang Brückner (Wiesbaden: Harrassowitz, 1985), 475–88.

[155] Cornelia Niekus Moore, " 'Noch mehr, noch mehr!' Reading in the novels of Johann Beer," in *"Der Buchstab tödt — der Geist macht lebendig": Festschrift zum 60. Geburtstag von Hans-Gert Roloff*, ed. James Hardin and Jörg Jungmayr (Bern: Lang, 1992), 905–16.

[156] Moore, "Erbauungsliteratur als Gebrauchsliteratur," 297.

[157] Michael Hackenberg, "Books in Artisan Homes of Sixteenth-Century Germany," *Journal of Library History and Comparative Librarianship* 21 (1986): 72–79, here 73.

[158] Moeller, "Die Anfänge kommunaler Bibliotheken," 151.

[159] I should like to thank Werner Arnold, Jochen Bepler, and Cornelia Niekus Moore for reading versions of this contribution and making helpful suggestions.

Travel Reports in Early Modern Germany

Wolfgang Neuber

Genre

TRAVEL REPORTS (*REISEBERICHTE*) ARE RARELY TREATED as literary texts.[1] Until recently the primary scholarly focus has been on scientific data: geographical, zoological, ethnological, or botanical. Only an analysis of issues pertaining to genre and the poetics of the travel report can contribute to a fuller understanding of this highly significant early modern genre. There are several reasons that literary research has failed to examine travel reports as literature. For one, the travel report, along with other scientific and factual literature (*Sachliteratur*), to which it belonged, had no place in the poetics of the early modern period;[2] until the novel began to command attention in the late seventeenth century, poetics was concerned exclusively with versified forms. For contemporary theory, one must turn to rhetorics and theories of science, not to poetics.[3] For another, the subgenres to which the travel report belonged have typically been regarded by literary research as of lesser significance. A third is that the travel report had no independent status as a genre. Texts identifiable as travel reports were written from the fifteenth to the eighteenth centuries in various forms and usually in combination with other genres: as parts of family books, autobiographies, diaries, or letters. A fourth reason is that reports in the form of letters from abroad not only circulated for private use but sometimes found their way into print under the title *Neue Zeitungen* (New Tidings). These included reports by the explorers Columbus[4] and Vespucci. Actual publication was ultimately the decision not of the writers themselves of these "new tidings" but of territorial lords, scholarly experts, offspring of the original authors, or commissioning agents or publishers.

The genre history of the early modern travel report is thus in part a marketing history: the book market dictated what was likely to be of interest to a larger readership. The travel report's specific form, however — letter, diary, and so on — was the choice of the individual author, based on a sense of which form would be the optimal medium of communication, and therefore preceded the marketing decision. However, the writer who wished to provide his ruler with a travel report in the form of a letter, and the writer who intended to give his descendants a moral lesson in the form of a family album, had altogether different goals in mind. With respect to genre, therefore, the early modern travel report is unified only insofar as it is a report about movement within space and time; all formal differences are of secondary significance.

What are the internal unifying elements that make the various kinds of travel reports cohere as models, and how did these models specifically affect the perceptions of external reality in the early modern period?

Cosmography and Apodemics

Genre theory of the early modern travel report is situated in rhetorical theory in the doctrines of argumentation and style.[5] It must be composed in the lower style (*genus humile*). Frequent use of figurative language, characteristic of the middle style (*genus medium*) and high style (*genus grande*), signal an emotional involvement that is to be avoided, since the travel report is classified as *historia*, whose discourse (historiography) is dispassionate (*sine ira et studio*). Even in the otherwise ornate Baroque period, travel writing remains true to the compositional parameters of lower style; one does not hear of a "baroque travel report." As historiography, it is also subject to a second theoretical requirement: it must present the action in strictly chronological sequence and not rearrange the historical course of events (thus its unrelatedness to the historical novel).

This understanding of the early modern travel report as historiography regulates only one part of its textuality, however. Travel reports represent more than mere historical events. Additional essential elements include regional geographical descriptions and ethnographic observations, each of which has its own literary tradition and theoretical underpinnings. Of these categories — the historiographical, the geographical, and the ethnographical — the geographical, known in early modern Europe as cosmography, was the most important for the history of the travel report genre. Geography combined with historiography and ethnography to become one of the leading academic disciplines of Protestant scholarship in the sixteenth century.[6] All three categories were integrated for the first time in the *Warhaftige Historia*[7] (1557) of the young Hessian traveler Hans Staden (ca. 1525–ca. 1576).

This essential triadic model of geography existed already in classical rhetoric (in Cicero, Quintilian, Dionysius of Halicarnassensis, and others). Cicero says in *De oratore* (2.15.63), with regard to the writing of history, that it may neither make false statements nor suppress true ones: "Haec scilicet fundamenta nota sunt omnibus, ipsa autem exaedificatio posita est in rebus et verbis: rerum ratio ordinem temporum desiderat, regionum descriptionem" (For these fundamentals are known to all; the building itself however consists of things and words. The essence of the matter requires ordering of temporal events and geographical description). The third element, ethnography, concerned the representation of moral customs (*vita et mores*) and religious rites and beliefs (*ritus*). This coupling of historiography, geography (or topography), and ethnology lay at the heart of early modern cosmography. Conrad Celtis's *De origine, situ, moribus et institutis Norimbergae libellus* (1495) is exemplary; its very title enumerates the categories: the history and status of Nuremberg, and the customs and institutions of its inhabitants. Joachim von Watt's (1484–1551) commentary on Pomponius Mela of 1518 defines geography as a poetic genre that combines historiography and ethnography.[8] The three rhetorical-scientific categories, then — historiography, cosmology, and ethnography — constitute the topical macrostructure for the textual representation of geography in the early modern period and are key to understanding the genre of the travel report. This may be observed in a broader field to which travel writing belongs: *apodemics.*

The empirical observations made in the course of traveling in the fifteenth and sixteenth centuries called for a theory for their regulation. In the last third of the sixteenth century in the German-speaking lands, a new type of science thus arose, apodemics, which provided the topical categories to be observed in traveling and, subsequently, in composing the report.[9] Two traditions shaped apodemic theory. The one, topography, derived from classical rhetoric, specifically from the topos of praise of city (*laus urbis*). First used in cosmography, praise of city was eventually taken up in apodemic works. The second tradition came from professional medical writings on staying healthy while traveling — the literature of *Reiseregimina.*[10]

At first an independent genre, medical regimen writing increasingly melded with apodemic literature until, in the last quarter of the sixteenth century, it was completely displaced by geographical themes. The combined traditions created categories for describing everything observable in the world. For example, the name of a city or a region, along with its meaning and origin; its history, changing fortunes, and achievements; its topography and physical advantages, particularly with regard to agriculture, fishing, and trade; the region's mountains and fields, its uncultivated meadows, rivers, lakes, forests, swamps, seas, and natural boundaries. If it is a city, the description focuses on three main categories: buildings (cathedrals, churches, bridges, theaters, fortifications, walls, castles, markets, city hall, schools, universities, libraries, treasuries, warehouses, storage barns, harbors, fountains, canals, zoological gardens); people (living and dead, rulers, celebrities, scholars); and institutions, both political and social. All these categories can be further differentiated and subdivided. After about 1580, the travel report genre began to take on the full topical requirements of apodemic literature and eventually became overburdened by the demands for completeness. A later example of this inflation is the scholar and world traveler Adam Olearius's (1599–1671) *Offt begehrte Beschreibung der Newen Orientalischen Reise / So durch Gelegenheit einer Holsteinischen Legation an den König in Persien geschehen: Worinnen Derer Orter und Länder / durch welche die Reise gangen / als fürnemblich Rußland / Tartarien und Persien / sampt ihrer Einwohner Natur / Leben und Wesen fleissig beschrieben*[11] (Oft-requested Description of the New Oriental Journey, described on the occasion of a Holstein legation to the king of Persia: In which all of the locations and lands through which the journey proceeded are described, especially Russia, Turkey, and Persia, together with a description of all the nature, lives, and character of all of their inhabitants, 1647). The empirical-topical overtaxing of the travelogue in the seventeenth century redirected the genre toward the representation of the author and his adventures, a development that brought the travelogue closer to the novel.

Text and Illustrations

So far, we have described the theoretical conditions responsible for what constitutes the travel report as *text*. But when the early modern travel report is considered as a model for writing and communication, we find few examples that can be reduced to text alone. For the travel report typically does not consist only of words, but also of illustrations that contribute to the emotional impact of the text. Whereas the travel report *qua* historiography must remain objective and free of emotion, the pictures engage feelings for what is foreign, curious, or shocking. Even handwritten letters about a journey contain pictures that complement the textual descriptions. These pictures have significance not only because of their content, but because of their mere existence. This is particularly true in context of a book, where the pictures command immediate attention. In viewing them, the reader follows a mode of argumentation determined not only by the material illustrated but by the visual qualities of the illustrations themselves. In early modern Germany, pictures opened the medium of the travel book even to the illiterate. This applied to other richly illustrated genres as well, such as the prose history. Whoever heard the story and saw the pictures together even once could, more or less in one's own words, tell the story again simply by looking at the illustrations.

Of course, pictures without text are blind; they have no meaning without semantic reference.[12] However, only in connection with pictures does the text of the travel report create the full potential impact of the travel report for the reader by providing the emotional element of the foreign and of space. In Staden's *Warhaftige Historia* the woodcuts refer in some instances only to geographical conditions or animals. But the majority of the pictures portray the strangeness of the Brazilian Indian tribe, the Tupinambá, in its daily life, its material culture, and, especially, its ritual culture, including the practice of cannibalism.[13] These pictures are more than just illustrations — mere doublings, as it were — of the text. While the text often references them explicitly, they are not exhausted by the text but assume the status of a second, independent, argumentation. This argumentation is linked to the text in various ways, depending on the placement of the illustrations and their execution.

Some pictures belong to the "objective" type, presenting unfamiliar and therefore interesting objects or animals. In Staden these include the ethnographic passages that show Indian implements and exotic animals. They are closely linked on the book page with the text; their strength derives from the concreteness of their portrayals, whereas the textual description remains necessarily abstract (fig. 1). Another type of picture communicates the distance of the foreign region from the realm of the reader's experience: ships, for example, or maps detailing the location of the plot of the described action (fig. 2). A third type combines the first and the second and adds an element to the plot. Some of Staden's illustrations, for instance, place battles in a typologically reduced landscape (fig. 3); others depict ethnographic features of the daily life among the Tupinambá, in particular one long sequence of pictures portraying the ritual execution, dissection, and consumption of a prisoner (figs. 4, 5, 6). In view of the radically foreign quality of the objects depicted, the pictures must have exerted a strong emotional effect. That Staden's book follows the complex but clear structural principles discussed above places it among the state-of-the-art exemplars of contemporary scientific thought.

This accomplishment, however, cannot be ascribed entirely to Staden's own talent alone. Staden had, if not a ghost writer, certainly an adviser: Johann Eichmann (1500–1560; in the humanist manner, he called himself Dryander), whose scholarly knowledge enabled Staden to make his own experiences public. Eichmann was a friend of the family and, like Staden's father, came from Wetter in Hessia. A professor of mathematics and medicine at the University of Marburg, Eichmann had specialized in astronomy, dietetics — which embraced the entire daily existence of the human being — and anatomy. The predominance of the anatomical aspect in Staden's *Warhaftige Historia* very likely is to be attributed to the influence of Eichmann.[14]

This example serves to demonstrate that in the preparation of illustrations for travel reports it was possible that extraneous interests could be interjected. Rarely, as in Staden's case, the author was allowed some influence over the execution of the pictures; ordinarily, however, the publisher made use of a work whose author was either dead or permanently absent. The illustrations then became the exclusive product of an artist available to the publisher and who himself had not had the experiences of the author. This meant that the illustrations were the product of an act of imagination stimulated only by the text, not by direct experience of the travels. The artist was subject to only two requirements respecting the illustrations: that they do justice to the text, and that they correspond to the scientific and aesthetic expectations of the European readership. Again, market factors played a role in inventing the template for the travel report.

Vernacular and Latin

Most early modern travel reports were written and published in a European vernacular: German, Italian, French, English, Spanish, or Dutch. Still, one repeatedly encounters translations into Latin — this is as true for the Columbus epistolary report as for Vespucci's works and Staden's book — a phenomenon rare to the early modern period, for as a rule texts were translated from Latin into the vernacular. Why were so many travel reports translated into Latin, the language of scholars? Two possibilities come to mind: it may have been a publishing strategy, for the Latin version of a "trade" book could be sold beyond the borders of the given national market in all Europe; or, because Latin was the language of science, a Latin translation immediately assumed an independent stature within the scholarly world.

Sie machen eyne platten off irem haupt/ laſſen drumb her eyn krenglein von haren wie eyn mönch. Ich hab ſie offt gefragt/woher ſie das muſter der haar hetten/ Sagten ſie/ Yhre vorwätter hettens an eynem Manne geſehen/der hette Meire Humane geheyſſen/vnd hette vil wunderbarlichs dings vnter jnen gethan/vnd man wil es ſei eyn Prophet oder Apoſtel geweſen.

Weiter fragte ich ſie/womit ſie hetten die har können abſchneiden/ehe jnen die ſchiff hetten ſcheren bracht /ſagten ſie hetten eynen ſtein keil genomen/hetten eyn ander ding darunter gehalten /daruff die har abgeſchlagen/dañ die mittelſte platte hatten ſie mit eynem ſchiber /eyns gehellen ſteyns / welche ſie vil brauchen zum ſcheren/gemacht. Weiter haben ſie eyn ding von roten feddern gemacht/heyſſet kannittare/das binden ſie vmb den kopff.

Sie haben auch in den vnderſten lippen des mundes /eyn groß loch/das machen ſie von jugent auff/ wañ ſie noch jungen ſein/ſtechen ſie jnen mit eynem ſpitzen hirtzhorns knochen eyn löchl in hindurch/darin ſteckenſie dañ eyn ſteynlein oder

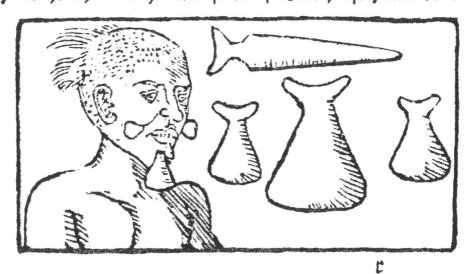

r

Figure 1. From Hans Staden, Warhaftige Historia, *1557.*

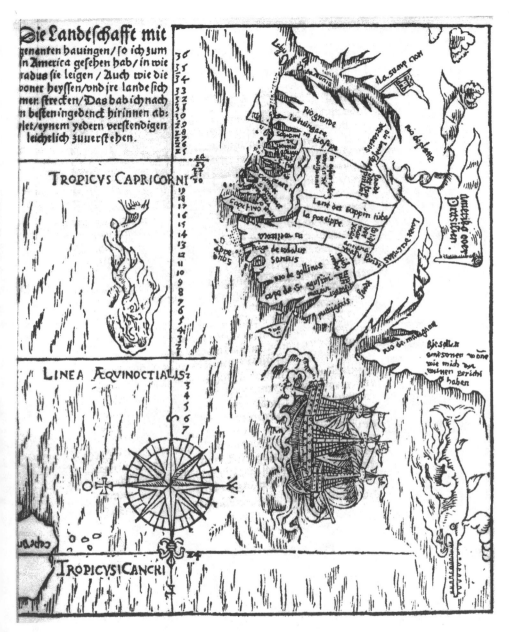

Figure 2. From Hans Staden, Warhaftige Historia, *1557.*

ren vns in den schiffen nichts thun/Aber sie wurffen vil tru-
ckenes holtzes auß irer schantze zwischen das vfer vñ schiff/
vermeynten das anzustecken/ires pfeffers der da im lande
wachsset/darin zuwerffen/ vnd vns mit dem dampffe auß
den schiffen zusagen. Aber es geriet inen nicht/ mitler weil
kam die flůt wider. Wir fůhren zů dem flecken Tammara-
ka/Die inwoner gaben vns victalia/Darmit fůhren wir wi
derumb nach der belegerung bei dem vorigen ort/hatten sie
vns die fart wider gehindert/Also/ Sie hatten beume/ wie

Figure 3. From Hans Staden, Warhaftige Historia, *1557.*

Welches nun eyn eht vnter jnen ist / dañ nimpt derwide=
eumb das holtz/der den todt schlagen sol/vnd sagt dann/ Ja
hie bin ich/ich wil dich tödten/dann die deinen haben meiner
freunde auch vil getödtet vnd gessen/antwortet er/wann ich
todt bin/so habe ich noch vil freunde/die werden mich wol
rechen/darmit schlecht er jnen/hinden auff den kopff/das jm
das birn daraus springt/ als bald nemen jn die weiber/zihen

t iij

Figure 4. From Hans Staden, Warhaftige Historia, *1557.*

in auff das fewer/kratze im die haut alle ab/machen in gang weis/stopfen jm den hinderſten mit eynem holtze zů/ auff das im nichts entgehet.

Wann im dann die haut abgefeget iſt/nimpt ſn eyn mans perſon/ ſchneidet im die beyne ober den kniehen ab/vnnd die arme an dem leibe/ dann komen die vier weiber vnd nemen die vier ſtucke/ vnd lauffen mit vmb die hütten her/machen eyn

Figure 5. From Hans Staden, Warhaftige Historia, *1557.*

eyn groß geschrey/von freuden/darnach schneiden sie jm den
rücke mit dem hindersten von dem vortheyl ab / dasselbige
theylen sie dann vnter sich / aber das ingeweyd behalten die
weiber/sieden/vnd in der brüe machen sie eynen brei / mingau
genant/ den drincken sie vnd die kinder/ das ingeweyd essen
sie / essen auch das fleysch vmb das haupt her/ das hirn in
dem heubt/die zungen/ vnnd weß sie sunst daran geniessen

Figure 6. From Hans Staden, Warhaftige Historia, *1557.*

Staden's *Warhaftige Historia* was translated into Latin in 1592.[15] A comparison of the Latin and German versions of Staden is revealing of sociological assumptions about readership and of certain related strategies of marketing. Key concepts of the German text include *Wilde* (Latin *barbari*, barbarians) and *Fest* (*solennitas*, solemnity), among others. The original German phrase "Geschlecht Wilder Leuth" (tribe of wild people) is translated in the Latin text as "multas Barbarorum nationes" (many barbarous nations); Staden's concept of *Nation*: "wohnen daselbst Nation Wilder die heissen Carios" (a nation of barbarians called Carios live there) is translated as "ubi natio Carios habitat" (there dwells the nation of the Carios). With respect to legal terms that have to do with *Nation* we see differing emphases in the two languages. The German text reads: "Was für Regiment vnd Ordnung sie haben mit der Oberkeit vnd Rechten. SJe haben sonderlich kein Regiment oder Recht / ein jede Hütte hat einen Obersten / der ist jhr König" (Regarding the kind of government and order they have with authority and laws: They have no particular government or law; each hut has a ruler, who is its king); the Latin: "De Magistratu, & legibus siue iure ipsorum. Nullis legibus, nec iure fere vllo reguntur: singularia tuguria suos habent Præfectos, quos illi Regulos vocant" (Regarding their magistracy and laws, or justice: They are governed neither by laws nor by any justice; all huts have their own prefects, whom they call kings). The four German concepts: government, order, authority, and laws are reduced to three in Latin: magistracy, laws, and justice; the ruler is specified as a prefect; the king is not technically a king but only so called. Obviously, the Latin text is more than a literal translation of the original German. The simple statement: "Die Leuthe gehen nacket" (the people walk about naked) is expanded into a judgmental commentary: "homines nudi incedentes, obscenas corporis partes nullo integunt velamine" (the people walk about naked, not covering the obscene parts of their bodies with any clothing). Passages from chapter titles show the greater tendency of the Latin text to explain and to stress the scholarly aspect:

> German: Wie das Land America oder Brasilien gelegen ist / wie ich zum theil gesehen habe. Brasilia ist ein grosses Landt / hat viel Geschlecht Wilder Leuth / dieselbigen haben viel verenderung der Sprache / vnnd seind viel seltzamer Thierer.

> [How the land of America or Brazil, as I saw it in part, is situated. Brazil is a large country, has many tribes of barbarians; they have many languages, and there are many strange animals.]

> Latin: De situ Brasiliae, quam ex parte ipsemet perlustraui, & simul de habitu seu vestitu nationis Carios. Brasilia per se ampla est Regio, multas Barbarorum nationes complectens, quae inter se linguis variant. Varia ferarum genera nutrit.

> [About the position of Brazil, through part of which I myself traveled, and also about the customs and dress of the nation of the Carios. Brazil itself is a vast region containing many nations of uncivilized peoples, who differ linguistically. It sustains many species of wild animals.]

Three points should be noted: First, the reference to customs and clothing of the Carios is found only in the Latin text, which suppresses the German adjective *seltzam* (strange), which connotes wonder. Second, the Latin completely omits from discussion the four marginalia of the brief German chapter. And third, a back translation of the previous Latin passage [see the English translation above] makes clear to what extent the Latin anticipates the syntax of modern scientific language, or, with respect to the German, how little the German has in common with modern scientific language.

These observations raise questions that touch on the social history of reading in the sense of the sociology of science. The German and Latin texts convey different information both semantically and through the cognitive guidance of pictures and marginalia. Research has only begun to explore these subjects.[16]

Alterity

Travel reports were written for various reasons: as justification of the journey and its costs, as scientific analysis of the region visited, as theologically motivated search for religious knowledge, for mercantile interests, to gather information for individuals at home or one's descendants, and so on. But all the reports, regardless of their *raison d'être*, have one thing in common: emphasis on alterity, otherness — on the exotic quality of the region, its inhabitants, animals and plants.

Not surprisingly, therefore, we find a certain disconnection between the actual activity of traveling and the subsequent one of writing the report: most early modern travels took place within the boundaries of Europe, whereas most printed travel reports, until well into the eighteenth century, described travel outside Europe. This discrepancy suggests that Europe itself was not generally deemed sufficiently "foreign" to be worthy of travel reports; the interest of European readers concentrated, therefore, on the external, exotic regions of the world.[17] Palestine was the region outside Europe represented most frequently in German printings of the fifteenth century, a fact that implies religious motivation.[18] Curiously, *Turcica* — pictorial portrayals and textual reports of the Turks or the Ottoman Empire in the broadest sense — were much less in evidence in comparison with other extra-European ethnic and regional subjects, despite the fact that the Turks had remained very much in the consciousness of Christian Europe after the conquest of Nicopolis in 1396 and, especially, of Constantinople in 1453; their constant advance westward brought about a fear that affected book publication in the Renaissance to a significant degree.[19]

If Palestine dominated fifteenth-century publications, in the sixteenth it was reports on the New Worlds, principally America and Africa.[20] Understandably, reports about the discovery of America in 1492 fared relatively badly in the book market until the end of the incunabula period.[21] The New World had been known for only a few years, and no one at the time could have grasped that a new continent had been discovered, much less its significance. This situation changed radically in the new century. According to market statistics, the works most frequently printed through the midcentury concerned America, Brazil specifically:[22]

Germany	146 Americana (of those 101 Lat.)	= 28.6%
	38 Brasiliana (of those 26 Lat.)	= 38%
Italy	125 Americana (of those 52 Lat.)	= 24.5%
	21 Brasiliana (of those 7 Lat.)	= 21%
Spain	89 Americana (of those 18 Lat.)	= 17.4%
	8 Brasiliana (of those 1 Lat.)	= 8%
France	65 Americana (of those 41 Lat.)	= 12.7%
	16 Brasiliana (of those 4 Lat.)	= 16%
Netherlands	31 Americana (of those 24 Lat.)	= 6.07%

If one disregards the strict cosmographies, it was the travel books of Columbus, Vespucci, and Cortez that accounted for the vast majority of Americana on the German market up to 1550. Travel reports on America written by Germans, some of which appeared in large printings, fall mainly in the second half of the sixteenth century.[23] Judging from the places of publication, it appears that southern Germany had an exceptional interest in travel literature in general and, after the discovery of America, particularly in reports about the New World. This interest was no doubt forged by the economic concerns of the powerful Welser family bankers (from Augsburg) in what is today Venezuela. Germany's economic influence in America faded rapidly after 1556, however, with the end of the dynastic connection between Spain and the Holy Roman Empire.

The specific subject of America in German travel reports has been well researched; lacking, however, is a comprehensive statistical study of the European publishers and their particular interest in travel reports. Nevertheless, certain cautious generalizations may be made about how the German works dealt with alterity. In the Middle Ages, what was domestic and thus one's own, as opposed to what was foreign, was primarily determined by religious discourse or rite (*ritus*). In the early modern period the distinctions were based on the conceptual pairing of *vita et mores*, life and customs. Alterity appeared increasingly as the product of anthropological rather than religious-ritualistic construction. Only toward the end of early modernity did the conceptual pairing of *vita et mores* begin to be replaced by a new, transregional, criterion: that of *Volk und Nation*.

Otherness was perceived in religious terms in various ways at different times. Islam, for example, was viewed by Christians from the eighth century until the end of the early modern era as a sect, that is, as an apostate movement vis-à-vis an originary Christian community. In his *Tractatus de moribus, condictionibus et nequicia Turcorum* (Treatise on the Customs, Circumstances, and Vileness of the Turks, 1481), Georgius of Hungary gives a biblical explanation: "Sed quod tale fuisset inicium huius secte, apparet in figura apoc. xiiij, ubi ultime persecutionis forma ponitur in figura bestie ascendentis de terra, habentis duo cornua similia agni et loquentis sicut dracco. Ista enim bestia ascendit de terra, quia a soliditate et firmitate catolice fidei orta" (But that this sect had its beginning in this manner appears in the image of the fourteenth [correct: thirteenth] chapter of the Apocalypse, where the form of the final persecution is represented as an animal that rises from the earth and has two horns like a lamb and sounds like a dragon. This beast arises out of the earth because it grew out of the foundation of the Catholic faith). Gregorius's argument was borrowed unchanged by Sebastian Franck (1499–1542) in his *Chronica vnnd beschreibung der Türckey* (1530) and essentially again by, among others, Leonhard Rauwolf (1535/40–1596) in his *Aigentliche beschreibung der Raiß* [. . .] *gegen Auffgang inn die Morgenländer* (Faithful Description of the Journey to the East in the Orient, 1582).[24] Religious signs of alterity no longer, however, were in the foreground of German travel reports of the sixteenth century, having been largely replaced by, for example, foreign customs (including cannibalism); Staden's portrayal of the tribal Americans, mentioned above, is an example. The answer to the question as to why the European reader was so interested in cannibalism is that it was seen as a symptom of world order gone awry. Evidence of this exists as late as 1700, in a travel report of Anton Sepp, which reports from the southern hemisphere of the New World:

> Dann wo in Europa Mittag / ist bey uns Mitternacht [. . .] / und also fort: Der Mittag-Wind oder Sur, ist bey ihnen warm / hier ist er frisch und kalt. Der Nord ist in Europa kalt / in America Badwarm. Und eben dieser Ursachen halber ist hier alles umgekehrt: jetzt da ich dieses schreibe um Johanni nemlichen / seynd wir Mitten im Winter / doch ohne Kälte / Frost / Schnee: Dahero wissen meine Jndianer nicht was Schnee ist / ob er weiß oder schwartz / warm oder kalt. Jn December und Januarii, wo in Europa alles zum Stein gefrieret / essen wir Feigen und brocken Lilien; Mit einem Wort / wie gesagt / alles ist hier verändert / und hat nicht übel gesprochen / der Americam die verkehrte Welt genennet.[25]

> [For where in Europe it is midday, it is midnight here, and so on: the midday wind, or Sur, is warm there; here it is fresh and cold. The north is cold in Europe, in America warm for bathing. And for precisely these reasons everything here is turned around: I am writing this on 24 June, which here is the middle of winter, but without cold, frost, or snow: my Indians therefore don't know what snow is, whether it is white or black, warm or cold. In December and January, when everything in Europe is frozen solid, we eat figs and pick lilies; in a word, as stated, everything here is changed, and he who calls America the upside-down world has not phrased the matter badly.]

There is no great revelation here. It had been known since the Middle Ages that in the southern hemisphere the seasons run counter to those in the northern hemisphere. Nor would it otherwise be noteworthy that, on St. Johannis Day (24 June) it is winter in the southern hemisphere. But the text is not merely communicating geographical knowledge. Seeing America as the world upside down implies something quite beyond the natural phenomena of the seasons; this alterity signifies the total reversal of the European order.[26] The Indians have never seen snow; they cannot remember it and therefore cannot correctly imagine it. In contrast to the Europeans they lack the capability of binary differentiation: they do not know whether snow is "weiß oder schwartz / warm oder kalt" (white or black, warm or cold). Thus they are excluded from European values even on the basis of their collective memory, and thus, as inverted Europeans, need to be set straight in their values by the genuine Europeans.

The possession of a cultural memory of Christian provenance thus emerges as the incontrovertible basis for the construction of "foreignness." But when the experience of foreignness — understood principally through the example of the history of the discovery of America — can be formulated only in the categories of what is already known to Europeans (and thus accessible to European memory), how then can the new be expressed as something uniquely so (foreign to experience)? The seeming paradox vanishes when one adds to the equation the factor of recombination of textual ingredients: that which is new appears in the rearrangement of what is familiar. The Indians behave *like* European butchers, but are *not* butchers, because they do not eat animal flesh but human flesh. The combination of things that, from the European viewpoint, cannot be connected allows, indeed produces, that which is new.

The Indians behave like European butchers who process human flesh — the principle of similarity cries out for the principle of a difference arising from the combination. Loosely formulated: everything is just like it is at home in Europe, only completely different. More precisely: it is the similarity (in rhetoric: *similitudo*) that is responsible for the departure from the norm. Sepp's travel report demonstrates this. Still completely caught up in the conception of a world upside down, he describes American plants as follows:

> Die Blumen zweiffele / ob die Europæische Flora und Chloris wurde erkennet haben: so doch denen Unsrigen nicht fast ungleich. Eine ware / wie unsrige Stein-Negelein: andere hatten die Gestalt des Blümleins je länger je lieber. Diese scheinten ein Wienerischer Saffran zu seyn: andere gleichen denen wilden Salvien.[27]
>
> [I doubt that the European Flora and Chloris would have recognized the flowers: but they were not completely different from ours. One was like our woodland pink. Others had the form of the flower called woodbine. Some seemed to be a Viennese saffron; others resembled wild sage.]

Here we find an abundance, a veritable bombardment, of remembrance. The goddess of flowers, remembered explicitly as the "European Flora and Chloris," would find herself out of place in the New World with that which belongs precisely in her realm. And yet the American flowers are similar to European flowers. Similarity, however, means difference in identity. The text reminds the reader of what is well known: of woodland pink, of woodbine, Viennese saffron, and wild sage. At the same time it marks the differences through linguistic nuances: one plant was "like" its European model, another had its "form," a third "seemed" to be a European plant, a fourth "resembled" another.

These remembrances based on the rhetorical principle of *similitudo* make it clear that more than the cultural memory of the reader is required for full comprehension. On the basis of a cultural and collective memory the imagination must, by its own volition, deform that which is remembered, must construct a distance between itself and the imagined object, must create nonidentity. In the process, however, the reader is forced to become complicit with the world upside down, which the traveler has attempted to overcome. The reader must mentally reproduce the dissimilarity between the foreign world and his own. The traveler *in situ*, on the other hand, was intent on eliminating the foreignness of the New World by using the resources of his cultural background to transform it into a world identical with the European world.

Empiricism and Verification

Much that is described in the travel report was unfamiliar to the European reader and was thus potentially suspect as being invented or false.[28] In his German translation, *Die new welt* (1533), of Simon Grynäus's Latin-language collection of travel reports, Michael Herr (d. 1550) writes that people most amazed at reports from America were those, "die sollicher ding nieh gesehen oder selbs versücht haben / die künden auch nichts dauon sagen / vnd wo etwas angezeygt wirdt / das jren verstand vbertrifft / so schuldigen sies der lugen"[29] (who have never seen or attempted such things of which there was no news; and where something is reported that goes beyond their understanding, they attribute it to a lie). Sebastian Franck's *Weltbůch* (1534), a supplement to his *Chronica*, says to the untraveled reader: "Yedoch soltu das nit gleich für luge achten / das inn vnsern landen vngewont / etwa gleich vngleüblich scheint vnd laut" (But you should not immediately think something a lie that is unfamiliar in our lands, and appears or sounds unbelievable).[30]

In order to give readers a vantage point to judge whether something is believable, and to avoid the charge of printing lies, the travel report itself sets certain criteria: First, it adheres strictly to the mode of historiographical argumentation, objectively maintaining the chronological order of events. Second, the paratexts — title pages, prefaces, headings, and subheadings — attempt to dispel any suspicion that the following reports are invented. Part of the long title of Franck's *Weltbůch* emphasizes that, although the report will contain much that is new, it may be confidently believed: "Auch etwas von new gefundenen welten vnd Jnseln / nitt auss Beroso / Joanne de monte villa / S. Brandons Histori / vnd dergleichen fabeln / sunder auß angenummnen / glaubwirdigen erfarnen / weltschreibern" (Also something of newly discovered worlds and islands, not from Berosus, or from John of Monte Villa, or St. Brendan's History, and such fables, but from accepted, credible, experienced writers about the world). In the preface to the reader, Franck reemphasizes that his report does not contain the "lugenhafft histori" (mendacious stories) of the fabulists mentioned in the title,[31] but the true accounts of world travelers who dedicated their histories to great kings and emperors.[32] Another strategy of making the reports credible is thus added: the truth of the text is guaranteed by the credibility of the person who commissioned the journey: a ruler or prince. Such a claim was not only called for theoretically, but corresponded to publication practice. The German version of the Columbus report appeared in 1497 in Strasbourg under the title *Eyn schön hübsch lesen von etlichen inßlen die do in kurtzen zyten funden synd durch den künig von hispania* (A Pleasant Reading about Some Islands that were Found in Recent Times by the King of Spain). Similarly, the titles of two Vespucci editions, likewise printed in Strasbourg (1505 and 1509), feature the names of Lord Ferdinand, King of Castile, and Lord Emanuel, King of Portugal. The ruler's authority validates the unverifiable content of the travel report.

Voyages of discovery commissioned by rulers are found only rarely in the seventeenth century, given that most of the world was presumed by now to have been discovered. This caesura lasted until the eighteenth-century explorations of the South Seas and discovery of Australia. Rather, the journeys were undertaken as legations in the service of the state, such as the aforementioned report of Adam Olearius. Most of the travel reports, however, focused on adventures. Their credibility rested again on their status as historiography and presumed the inexperience of the reader. Johann Rist devoted a large segment of his voluminous polyhistorical work, the *Alleredelste Zeit-Verkürtzung* (Most Noble Entertainment, 1668), to writings about travel. Travel writers, he says, are to be counted among the historians: "Reisebeschreiber mit unter die Historicos,"[33] and predicates the credibility of their reports on eyewitness experience. While he admits that the empirical method does not in itself guarantee the veracity of the report, he is forceful in insisting that it is the best defense for travel literature against skepticism:

> Jch sage nicht / daß in etlichen Reisebüchern / nicht unterschiedliche merckliche Fabulen werden gefunden; Sondern / daß man manchem ehrlichem Authori grossen Gewalt und Unrecht thue / in deme man jhn so freventlich wil zum Lügner machen / da man doch in der Welt nichtes bey der Hand hat / womit man jhme ein wiedriges kan erweisen.[34]
>
> [I am not saying that in certain travel books there are not to be found some curious fables, but rather that one does a great injustice to many an honorable author by making him so wickedly into a liar, simply because one has no eyewitness evidence of something in the world that can refute him.]

The requirement that a travel report must avoid the invented or untruthful is based both on the scientific (geographical and anthropological) interpretation of the world as well as on theology. In his introduction to the America report by the German soldier Ulrich Schmidel (1510–1579), the publisher Levinus Hulsius (1546–1606) writes:

> DJe Historien vnnd Relation der newen Länder vnnd Völcker / seind meines Erachtens / nit allein lustig / Sondern auch den Christen zu lesen nötig: Dann so wir wöllen die vnermeßliche wunderbahre Werck Gottes betrachten / vnd seine vnaußsprechliche Barmhertzigkeit / die er vns armen vnwürdigen Christen vielfältig bewiesen / zugemüth füren / in dem er vns nicht allein seine Erkentnůß gegeben / sonder auch mit so köstlichen Rantzion / da wir in Adam verlohren waren / vns wider erlöset hat.[35]

> [The histories and reports on the new countries and peoples are in my opinion not only amusing but also necessary for Christians to read: for in this way we can observe the unfathomable, wondrous work of God and become aware of his inexpressible mercy, which he has many times shown to us poor unworthy Christians by providing us not only with his know-ledge but with the precious ransom with which — because we had become lost through Adam — he has redeemed us.]

What is expressed here is the collective certainty of salvation, self-assurance in the consciousness of experienced grace. This is by no means a transconfessional point of view, despite the insistence that travel literature is necessary for all Christians. Precisely his further argument, that travel and the reporting of travel provide knowledge of God, is distinctly Protestant in origin; it would not have been shared by Catholics.

Confessionalism

Travel reports of the early modern period often have a decidedly confessional quality.[36] Generally speaking, travel served the revelation of the plan of salva-tion, which lent a theological ground to the empirical authority of geography. However, certain discoveries, and especially the discovery of America, chal-lenged the theological aspect of geography's authority in certain ways. Neither the Bible nor pagan literature makes any reference to an immense double con-tinent inhabited by unheard-of peoples. The biblical position, therefore, had to be expanded, an effort that took different forms, depending on whether the author was Catholic or Protestant.

Catholics viewed the discovery of the New World as a call to reevaluate and broaden the mission of salvation. Travel reports by Catholics were predominantly motivated by the purpose of explaining creation and providing witness of the increase of Catholic Christianity. Once it had become clear that the European Reformation was incontrovertible, Catholics saw missions as a kind of divine compensation: the turn away from right belief in Europe could be compensated for by the creation of new Catholics overseas.

Protestants, on the other hand, saw early modern discovery in general and the discovery of America in particular as a renewed revelation of God in current history. The world was a place where knowledge of God came to light and where natural science, especially geography, should be studied with the goal of discovering the workings of God. This could take the form of a final revelation of creation as a whole or of a demonstration — perhaps in the miraculous rescue of a lost Lutheran traveler — that God actively intervenes on behalf of a believer who has an unshakable belief in divine grace. Hans Staden's *Warhaftige Historia* was written from this viewpoint, which doubtless explains why it was printed exclusively in Protestant territories and became enormously successful: on average, it was reprinted every four years until 1715.

Reception

Its theological basis, together with its historical, geographical, anthropological, zoological, and botanical content, made the early modern travel report a privileged genre on the European, particularly the German, book market. Its reception extended into two main areas: the utilization of the various kinds of information in travel reports, and the literary structuring of early modern texts. The first area would include, in addition to all of the other cosmographical and geographical literature, Sebastian Brant's *Narrenschiff* (1494),[37] the *Faust* chapbook (1587), (especially) the *Wagnerbuch* (1593), many poems by Hans Sachs, and in the seventeenth century[38] the immense courtly novel *Arminius* (1689/90) of Daniel Casper von Lohenstein,[39] much of the polymath literature, and the Habsburg family panegyrics.[40] The second area would include the *Fortunatus* chapbook (1509) and the popular picaresque novel *Schelmuffsky* (1696) of the satirist Christian Reuter (1665–ca. 1712). However, a comprehensive history of the reception of early modern travel literature, beyond individual studies treating specific problems, remains a research desideratum. A complicating factor is that so many of the elements in travel reports are to be found in other genres as well, making it difficult to determine what is structurally unique to travel literature. There is a positive side to this challenge, however: the history of the early modern travel report will doubtless remain a rich field of research for the foreseeable future.

Translated by James Hardin

Notes

[1] See Peter J. Brenner, ed., *Der Reisebericht: Die Entwicklung einer Gattung in der deutschen Literatur* (Frankfurt am Main: Suhrkamp, 1989); also Brenner, *Der Reisebericht in der deutschen Literatur: Ein Forschungsüberblick als Vorstudie zu einer Gattungsgeschichte* (Tübingen: Niemeyer, 1990).

[2] In this volume see the chapter by Joachim Knape.

[3] See Wolfgang Neuber, "Zur Gattungspoetik des Reiseberichts: Skizze einer historischen Grundlegung im Horizont von Rhetorik und Topik," in Brenner, ed., *Der Reisebericht*, 50–67.

[4] *The First Letter of Christopher Columbus, Describing the Discovery of the New World*, in *The Bibliography of the First Letter of Christopher Columbus, Describing the Discovery of the New World*, ed. R. H. Major (Amsterdam: Meridian Publishing, 1971), 63–80.

[5] Wolfgang Neuber, *Fremde Welt im europäischen Horizont: Zur Topik der deutschen Amerika-Reiseberichte der Frühen Neuzeit*, Philologische Studien und Quellen 121 (Berlin: Schmidt, 1991) 109–65.

[6] Neuber, *Fremde Welt*, 35–58.

[7] *Warhaftige Historia vnd beschreibung eyner Landtschafft der Wilden / Nacketen / Grimmigen Menschfresser Leuthen / in der Newenwelt America gelegen / vor vnd nach Christi geburt im Land zů Hessen vnbekant / biß vff dise ij. nechst vergangene jar / Da sie Hans Staden von Homberg auß Hessen durch sein eygne erfarung erkant / vnd yetzo durch den truck an tag gibt. Dedicirt dem Durchleuchtigen Hochgebornen herrn / H. Philipsen Landtgraff zů Hessen / Graff zů Catzenelnbogen / Dietz / Ziegenhain vnd Nidda / seinem G.H. Mit eyner vorrede D. Joh. Dryandri / genant Eychman / Ordinarij Professoris Medici zů Marpurgk. Jnhalt des Büchlins volget nach den Vorreden. Getruckt zů Marpurg / im jar M. D. LVII*, facsimile reprint, ed. Günter E. Th. Bezzenberger (Kassel: Thiele und Schwarz, 1978).

[8] Gerald Strauss, *Sixteenth-Century Germany: Its Topography and Topographers* (Madison: U of Wisconsin P, 1959), 57.

[9] Neuber, *Fremde Welt*, 58–108.

[10] Wolfgang Neuber, "Der Arzt und das Reisen: Zum Anleitungsverhältnis von Regimen und Apodemik in der frühneuzeitlichen Reisetheorie," in *Heilkunde und Krankheitserfahrung in der frühen Neuzeit: Studien am Grenzrain von Literaturgeschichte und Medizingeschichte*, ed. Udo Benzenhöfer and Wilhelm Kühlmann (Tübingen: Niemeyer, 1992), 94–113.

[11] The full baroque title: *Die Offt begehrte Beschreibung Der Newen Orientalischen Reise / So durch Gelegenheit einer Holsteinischen Legation an den König in Persien geschehen: Worinnen Derer Orter und Länder / durch welche die Reise gangen / als fürnemblich Rußland / Tartarien und Persien / sampt ihrer Einwohner Natur / Leben und Wesen fleissig beschrieben / und mit vielen Kupfferstücken / so nach dem Leben gestellet / gezieret / Durch M. Adamum Olearium, Ascanium Saxonem, Fürstl: Schleßwig-Holsteinischen Hoff-mathemat. Item Ein Schreiben des WolEdeln [et]c. Johann Albrecht Von Mandelslo.*

[12] Wolfgang Neuber, "Ökonomien des Verstehens: Markt, Buch und Erkenntnis im technischen Medienwandel der Frühen Neuzeit," in *Die Verschriftlichung der Welt: Bild, Text und Zahl in der Kultur des Mittelalters und der Frühen Neuzeit*, ed. Horst Wenzel, Wilfried Seipel, and Gotthart Wunberg (Vienna: Kunsthistorisches Museum Wien, 2000), 181–211.

[13] See Franz Obermeier, *Brasilien in Illustrationen des 16. Jahrhunderts* (Frankfurt am Main: Vervuert, 2000).

[14] Wolfgang Neuber, "Marburger Menschenfresser — Hans Stadens Brasilienbericht (1557): Über die Verbindung von 'Indianern' und akademischer Anatomie" in *Marburg-Bilder: Eine Ansichtssache: Zeugnisse aus fünf Jahrhunderten*, ed. Jörg Jochen Berns (Marburg: Rathaus-Verlag, 1995–96), 1:149–64. See also Franz Obermeier,

"Hans Stadens Wahrhafftige Historia 1557 und die Literatur der Zeit," *Wolfenbütteler Notizen zur Buchgeschichte* 27 (2002): 43–80.

[15] Hans Staden, *AMERICAE TERTIA PARS Memorabilem provinciæ Brasiliæ Historiam continens* (Frankfurt am Main, 1592).

[16] Wolfgang Harms, "Lateinische Texte illustrierter Flugblätter: Der Gelehrte als möglicher Adressat eines breit wirksamen Mediums der frühen Neuzeit," in *Bildungsexklusivität und volkssprachliche Literatur — Literatur vor Lessing — nur für Experten?*, ed. Klaus Grubmüller and Günter Hess (Tübingen: Niemeyer, 1986), 74–85.

[17] Research has shown that in fifteenth-century Germany the most frequently printed works were medieval Latin encyclopedias; in Italy, on the other hand, consistent with its leading role in humanistic studies, works of ancient geographers were preferred. Travel reports published in Germany were intended mainly for entertainment, less for information. See Michael Herkenhoff, *Die Darstellung außereuropäischer Welten in Drucken deutscher Offizinen des 15. Jahrhunderts* (Berlin: Akademie, 1996), 96. This conclusion is demonstrable by comparing publishers' catalogues of prose novels. Ibid., 98.

[18] Herkenhoff, Darstellung, 277.

[19] Carl Göllner, *Die europäischen Türkendrucke des 16. Jahrhunderts*, vol. 1, *1501–1550* (Bucharest: Acad. Republicii Socialiste România, 1961); vol. 2, *1551–1600* (Bucharest: Körner, 1968); Göllner, *Die Türkenfrage in der öffentlichen Meinung Europas im 16. Jahrhundert* (Bucharest: Acad. Republicii Socialiste România, 1978).

[20] Neuber, *Fremde Welt*, 223. By 1550, 146 works on America, and 38 on Brazil had been published in the German-speaking realm. See also Marília dos Santos Lopes, *Afrika: Eine neue Welt in deutschen Schriften des 16. und 17. Jahrhunderts* (Stuttgart: Steiner, 1992).

[21] Herkenhoff, *Darstellung*, 278. The incunabula period comprises the years from the invention of the printing press to the new century, i.e., from ca. 1453 to 1500.

[22] See Friedrich Wilhelm Sixel, *Die deutschen Vorstellungen vom Indianer in der ersten Hälfte des 16. Jahrhunderts* (Città del Vaticano, 1966), 47–48.

[23] Neuber, "Die Drucke der im Original deutschen Amerikareiseberichte bis 1715: Synopse, Bibliographie und marktgeschichtlicher Kommentar," part 1, "Synopse, Bibliographie," *Frühneuzeit-Info* 2, no. 1 (1991): 76–83; part 2, "Marktgeschichtlicher Kommentar," *Frühneuzeit-Info* 2, no. 2 (1991): 12–34. Also Neuber, "Amerika in deutschen Reiseberichten des 16. und des 17. Jahrhunderts," in *Das Bild Lateinamerikas im deutschen Sprachraum*, ed. Gustav Siebenmann and Hans-Joachim König (Tübingen: Niemeyer, 1992), 37–54.

[24] Franz Babinger, "Leonhard Rauwolf: ein Augsburger Botaniker und Ostenreisender des sechzehnten Jahrhunderts," *Archiv für die Geschichte der Naturwissenschaften und der Technik*, 4 (1913): 148–61. More recently: Karl H. Dannenfeldt, *Leonard Rauwolf: Sixteenth-century Physician, Botanist, and Traveller* (Cambridge: Harvard UP, 1968).

[25] RR. PP. Antonii Sepp, und Antonii Böhm / Der Societät JESU Priestern Teutscher Nation, *Reißbeschreibung wie dieselbe aus Hispanien in Paraquariam kommen. Und Kurtzer Bericht der denckwürdigsten Sachen selbiger Landschafft / Völckern / und Arbeitung der sich alldort befindenten PP Missionariorum*, 69–70.

[26] Such a perception is obviously much older. In the letter of Columbus the trees that bear fruit in November can be understood in this manner. See Major, ed., *The First Letter of Christopher Columbus*, 63–80. Likewise, the *Utopia* of Thomas More, which

makes use of the Vespucci reports and is situated in the New World, operates with the reversal of European value systems.

[27] Sepp, *Reißbeschreibung*, 115–16.

[28] Neuber, "Die frühen deutschen Reiseberichte aus der Neuen Welt: Fiktionalitätsverdacht und Beglaubigungsstrategien," in *Der europäische Beobachter außereuropäischer Kulturen: Zur Problematik der Wirklichkeitswahrnehmung*, ed. Hans-Joachim König, Wolfgang Reinhard, and Reinhard Wendt (Berlin: Duncker & Humblot, 1989), 43–64.

[29] Michael Herr, *Die new welt der landschaften vnnd Jnsulen, so bis hie her allen Altweltbeschrybern vnbekant* (Strassburg, 1533), fol. *ij^v.

[30] Sebastian Franck, *Weltbůch: spiegel vnd bildtniß des gantzen erdbodens* (Tübingen, 1534), fol. [i]^v.

[31] The Irish saint Brendan (484–577) was a monk. A legend associated with his name reports a voyage during which he and his companions, having run aground on the back of a whale, are saved by means of a divine miracle. Berosus (ca. 300 B.C.) was a Chaldean priest, astrologer, and historian whose writings were considered specious. Mandeville describes a journey through the Orient in the years 1322–57; the work, despite its claims, presumably was not based on a journey through all the regions described. See *Sir John Mandevilles Reisebeschreibung: nach der Stuttgarter Papierhandschrift Cod. HB V 86*, trans. Michel Velser, ed. Eric John Morall (Berlin: Akademie, 1974).

[32] Franck, *Weltbůch*, fol. [i]^v.

[33] Johann Rist, *Die alleredelste Zeit-Verkürtzung Der gantzen Welt*, in *Sämtliche Werke*, vol. 6, *Epische Dichtungen*, ed. Helga Mannack, Klaus Reichelt, and Eberhard Mannack (Berlin: de Gruyter, 1976), 241–448, here 359.

[34] Rist, *Die alleredelste Zeit-Verkürtzung*, 360.

[35] Levinus Hulsius, dedication, in Ulrich Schmidel, *Wahrhafftige Historien einer wunderbaren Schiffart*, 2nd ed. (1602; repr., Graz: Akademische Druck- und Verlags-Anstalt, 1962), fol. Aij^v. Hulsius was particularly noted as a publisher of writings by Tycho Brahe and others on astronomy and astronomical instruments.

[36] Neuber, *Fremde Welt*, 47–58.

[37] Neuber, "Verdeckte Theologie: Sebastian Brant und die Südamerikaberichte der Frühzeit," in *Der Umgang mit dem Fremden*, ed. Titus Heydenreich (Munich: Fink, 1986), 9–29.

[38] Neuber, "Ansichten von der Nachtseite der Kosmographie: Amerika in der deutschen Lyrik der Frühen Neuzeit (Sachs, Quad, Opitz, Logau, Gryphius, Hofmannswaldau, Wernicke)," in *Von der Weltkarte zum Kuriositätenkabinett: Amerika im deutschen Humanismus und Barock*, ed. Karl Kohut (Frankfurt am Main: Vervuert, 1995), 44–57.

[39] Neuber, *Fremde Welt*, 283–306.

[40] Neuber, "Plus ultra — Die Überbietung der Antike durch die Entdeckung der Neuen Welt: Amerika in der deutschen Panegyrik des 17. Jahrhunderts," in *Federschmuck und Kaiserkrone: Das barocke Amerikabild in den habsburgischen Ländern*, exhibition catalogue, ed. Friedrich Polleroß, Andrea Sommer-Mathis, and Christopher F. Laferl (Vienna: Bundesministerium für Wissenschaft und Forschung, 1992), 185–93.

Illustration from Johannes Praetorius. Blockes-Berges Verrichtung.
Leipzig: Johann Scheiben, 1669.

Demonologies: Writing about Magic and Witchcraft

Gerhild Scholz Williams

DEMONOLOGIES ARE COMPREHENSIVE TRACTS, written by learned men — physicians, jurists, and theologians — reviewing the history and theology as well as the legal and medical implications and consequences of the alleged interaction of humans with demons (fallen angels). They are, on the whole, an early modern literary genre, the rational exploration of a phenomenon that appears to the modern reader anything but rational. Over the two hundred years between Institoris's (Heinrich Kramer, 1430–1505) *Malleus malefi-carum* (The Witches' Hammer) of 1487 and Johannes Praetorius's (Hans Schultz, 1630–80) *Des Blockes-Berges Verrichtung* (Witches' Sabbath on the Blocksberg) of 1668, numerous demonologies (or "witchcraft theories") were published, read, and quoted in subsequent witch tracts, sermons, broadsheets, witch trials, and laws pertaining to the practice of witchcraft. According to Walter Stephens, witchcraft theory provided a way of systematically describing preexisting ideas about relations between humans and demons, the central source of evidence being the testimony of witches on trial.[1]

Although the production and consumption of these texts was vigorous between the 1430s and the 1700s, twentieth-century historical and literary scholarship showed relatively little interest in them. In a critical assessment of the state of research on demonology as of 1977, it was found that, more often than not, demonologies had been neglected, or worse, rejected as aberrant musings of otherwise reasonable men; analysis of the structure, arguments, language, interrelations, and reception of these texts had been dismissed as unessential and uninteresting.[2] Critics had focused on nontextual realities in society, including legal practices in local communities, rather than examining the pertinent texts.[3] A reader of the research of the nineteenth and a good part of the twentieth century could not have readily determined that demonologies were central to the times in which they were produced or that they had been frequently translated and cited as authoritative sources on an issue of great interest to learned and lay audiences. During the early modern period demonology and its counterpart angelology, the study of angels, constituted a fundamental aspect of Christian cosmology and thus were integral to contemporary theology and science. The majority of scholars in the early modern period, no matter what their professional specialization and whether they supported or opposed the persecution of witches, accepted as basic the premise that demons and witches existed and that they could and did harm humankind.[4]

Since the late 1970s scholarly attitudes toward texts about the witch phenomenon have changed. Demonological writings produced between 1500 and 1700 began to attract attention as documents that could provide crucial information on early modern cultural history. These modern investigations into the phenomenon had their precursors, often divided along denominational lines, in the nineteenth century, beginning with the publication of Wilhelm Gottlieb Soldan's *Geschichte der Hexenprozesse* (History of the Witch Trials) in 1843, amended and revised in 1880 by Soldan's son-in-law, Heinrich Heppe.[5] The year 1843 also saw the publication of the first comprehensive annotated bibliography of magic and witchcraft, the *Bibliotheca magica et pneumatica* (Dictionary of Magic and Pneumatics) by Johann Georg Theodor Grässe.[6] In the early twentieth century the historian Henry Lea compiled materials for a study on witchcraft; his *oeuvre* was posthumously edited and published in 1939 by Arthur C. Howland under the title *Materials Toward a History of Witchcraft*.[7] The turn of the twentieth century also witnessed the publication of Joseph Hansen's *Zauberwahn, Inquisition und Hexenprozess im Mittelalter* (Witch Craze, Inquisition, and Witch Trials in the Middle Ages, 1900) and *Quellen und Untersuchungen zur Geschichte des Hexenwahns und der Hexenverfolgung im Mittelalter* (Sources and Investigations into the History of the Witch Craze and Persecution in the Middle Ages, 1901).[8] Lynn Thorndike's eight-volume *History of Magic and Experimental Science* (1923–58) and Russel Hope Robbins's *Encyclopedia of Magic and Demonology* (1959) remain pioneering studies in the areas of magic and history of science.[9] In the 1970s the work of the historian H. C. Erik Midelfort introduced the sociohistorical approach to modern witchcraft research.[10] Since then the field of demonological study in Europe and the United States[11] has been enriched and broadened by sociohistorical, anthropological, ethnological, and legal studies.[12] Investigations into the question of the relationship of gender and the witch phenomenon,[13] research on the history of medicine, folklore, and history of mentalities,[14] and detailed regional historical studies have further enriched this fascinating area of study.[15] Weber and Behringer have studied the phenomenon of "child witches."[16] Inquiries into literary sources and discourses associated with the history of witchcraft have been expanded by the work of Stephens and Maggi,[17] while Clark's *Thinking with Demons* (1997) takes pride of place as the most comprehensive review to date of the great varieties of demonological materials that contributed to the construction of the witch and her subsequent persecution in early modern Europe.

Magic and Demonology

To understand why learned men spent considerable intellectual effort, time, and money writing and publishing on witches and witchcraft we must try to understand their worldview. Early modern magical practices emerged from a variety of pre-Christian, non-Christian, biblical, patristic, and medieval sources. Theology, cosmology, and natural philosophy were agreed on the nature of the cosmos and mankind's place in it and on the existential danger implicit in wishing to exert control over both.[18] The association of universal order with magical words and numbers and, conversely, the conviction that the improper and illicit use of magical discourse signaled transgression and disorder, made magical practices at all times a privilege, as much feared as sought after. Moreover, magic is always, even etymologically, associated with power.[19] Its practitioners seek control — over people, animals, the weather, the stars — all the while courting a power that threatens perpetually to turn against them.[20] Historically the distinction was made between two kinds of magic, natural and demonic. Throughout the Middle Ages and the early modern period the learned considered natural magic a science that dealt with wonders and the hidden, occult properties of plants, metals, and precious stones.[21] It promised knowledge of the secrets of nature and, even more tantalizing to the learned seeker, of the knowing perception of the divine order of the universe. As an intellectual and cultural language, magic gave expression to the extraordinary. Demonic magic was a form of religion, except that it perverted the tenets of theology and religious practice.[22] Serving Satan instead of God, its practitioners invoked demons in an effort to practice *maleficia* (evils).[23] Generally, accusations of malevolent magic and witchcraft were leveled in unusual social circumstances, where neighborly envy, hatred, fear of illness, and misfortune combined with destructive results.[24]

Learned and lay people alike were always in danger of traversing the thin line between licit and illicit, white and black, divine and diabolical magic. Both types of magic presupposed the existence of a closed and finite universe, knowable only to a chosen few. Knowledge was thus potentially open to the inquiring mind even if it had not yet been revealed to everyone. The exceptional mortal, the *magus* or the witch, was believed to be able to cast an occasional glance into tantalizing secrets. The *magus*, adept in high, that is, licit magic (*scientia magica*), always stressed the special relationship of magic to philosophy and theology.[25] The desire to know prompted the association of magic with curiosity (*curiositas*). Interpreted positively this meant taking control of the universe given by God to mankind for its own; interpreted negatively curiosity became a type of hubris, of human arrogance in seeking to know what is not ours to explore.[26] When associated with God, magical powers were beneficent, their agents angels. If the same powers gained their efficacy from Satan, their agents were the fallen angels, the demons. With the help of magical languages, secret rituals, and contracts with occult powers, the aspiring human could unlock the secrets of the universe. White magic included all forms of the *natural* sciences, all theories of the universe and mankind's place in it.[27] Generally, magic included cultural practices such as geomancy, hydromancy, aeromancy, and pyromancy (divination by the four elements of earth, water, air, and fire). It was an important part of the appeal of natural magic that the four elements were thought to be inhabited by elemental spirits, life forms resembling humans and occasionally interacting with them, though not possessing a soul. Water spirits were the most closely related to humans; in rare instances, they might enter into human liaisons and even intermarry.[28]

Throughout the centuries the fascination with and fear of satanic magic and witchcraft existed alongside the passion for magic as a science and divine philosophy. The belief that magical codes could govern and influence universal energies, both good and bad, as well as human behavior and intelligence remained alive into the eighteenth century.[29] Those who were familiar with magical letters, numbers, and their cosmological interrelations could initiate contact with God or Satan. Furthermore, magic was always about keeping secrets: the learned magician shared his knowledge only with other magicians; similarly, the witch kept company with her own kind, whose ranks she strove to increase by bringing others, preferably young children, to Satan. Magical utterances and rituals could establish power over things (as in alchemical practice), over people (as in love or hate magic), and between humans and spirits (as in the torment of mortals by succubi or incubi). The inherent contradiction between the desire to know and the need of both learned and unlearned to keep secret the practice of magic led to the relentless pursuit of those presumed to be in illicit possession of such secrets, namely, people accused of being witches. In the hands of the witch, magic was thought to change from a divine science into a "semantic of deceit," a "rhetoric of seduction."[30] To keep their access licit the practitioners of white magic — the men who wanted to keep secrets — often vigorously persecuted witches.

The Witch

Any discussion of early modern magic inevitably turns to its association with witchcraft and the witch. Witch-like creatures had been feared since antiquity. Homer's Circe changes Ulysses' companions into swine. Bloodsucking creatures called *lamia* or *striga* appear in the writings of Horace and Ovid. The Old Testament (Exod. 22:18, Lev. 20:6) contains punishments and invectives against witches ("Thou shalt not suffer a witch to live"). The Latin Middle Ages speak of a *malefica* or *venefica* as a woman who inflicts evil (*maleficium*) on people, animals, and crops, while the early medieval *Canon Episcopi* (Bishop's Index, ca. 900) tells of women who fly about at night in the company of the goddess Diana.[31] The image of the witch that dominated the early modern period, however, did not emerge until the thirteenth century. Thomas Aquinas, following St. Augustine's writings about demons, noted that the devil's disciples — specifically women — practiced maleficent magic, changed themselves into animals, entered into pacts with the devil, and flew about at night. All this was done with the permission of God (*permissio dei*), the Lord of all creation and thus the master of Satan. The witch was said to have renounced consciously and voluntarily the Christian faith, the blessings of baptism and salvation. Consequently, witchcraft became associated with heresy and apostasy, except that witchcraft was considered more deadly than either crime. Not only did the witch or warlock endanger her or his own soul, but, more significantly, his or her evil doings (*maleficia*) threatened the well-being of the Christian community. By the late Middle Ages the practice of witchcraft (*crimen magiae*), understood primarily as the misuse of church rituals and violation of the sacraments, became a punishable offense both by secular and canon law. By the mid-fifteenth century the numbers of women executed for alleged witch crimes in southeastern France, Switzerland, and southwestern Germany had increased significantly. These witch trials began in Europe around 1430 and ended around 1780; the years between 1560 and 1630 saw the most vigorous persecutions.[32]

By 1484 the image of the witch as a night-flying, sexually voracious creature, engaged in all manner of evil doings, and devoted to her lord Satan, had been established. It would persist until the late eighteenth century. The papal bull *Summis desiderantes affectibus,* issued in December of that year by Innocent VIII, authorized two inquisitors, the Dominican friars Heinrich Kramer (Institoris) and Jakob Sprenger (1436–95), to identify, imprison, and prosecute the witches allegedly plaguing southwestern Germany and parts of present-day Austria. Kramer's tract *Malleus maleficarum* described how to prosecute witches effectively and established the most popular model for demonologies.[33] Almost all subsequent defenders of witch persecutions quoted Kramer's work and made use of its juridical arguments and examples. Kramer described the witch as a female engaged in *maleficia*, which consisted of manipulating weather, killing people and livestock, preventing conception, or offering newborns to Satan. She acquired her powers by openly or secretly entering into a pact — consummated by copulation — with Satan, whereupon she received the devil's mark on a hidden part of her body. To be with her own kind and to periodically renew her allegiance to Satan, she flew to the witches' Sabbath, where she ate human flesh, cooked unguents from the bodies of unbaptized children,[34] and engaged in obscene dances and indiscriminate, often incestuous sex.[35] She flew to the assembly on a broom or a goat or simply by her own power after having covered her body with concoctions made of dead babies' fat, poisonous herbs, toad's skin, and other magical ingredients.[36]

The *Malleus maleficarum* became the authoritative text on the persecution of witches in Europe.[37] Some thirty editions were published between 1486 and 1669. Although it added nothing of substance to the existing image of the witch, it contributed immeasurably over the ensuing centuries to that image's reception and dissemination across Europe.[38] The impact of the text's intensely misogynist message — that women were especially prone to falling victim to the wiles of Satan because of their weak character and sexual predilections — was far-reaching. It portrayed woman as *fides minus* (of little faith), hard to discipline, and insatiable in her sexually deviant appetites. It is important to note that even at this early stage of the witch phenomenon a tract written in opposition to the *Malleus* by the jurist from Constance Ulrich Molitor (1442–1502), *De lamiis et pitonicis mulieribus, Teutonice unholden vel hexen* (On Witches and Sorcerers; or, in German: Devils and Witches, 1489; translated into German in 1586 as *Von Unholden und Hexen* [On Devils and Witches]),[39] went through ten editions after 1490. Molitor vigorously argued against witches' ability to change into animals or fly to the Sabbath. The woodcuts that adorned one of the editions would influence the iconography of witches throughout the early modern period.

Between 1430 and 1660 the fear of witchcraft and the witch became widespread. Satan, with the permission of God and with the help of his minions — demons and witches — was imagined as setting out to visit evil on mankind, causing political, social, and religious chaos, stirring enmity between Christian nations and hatred between friends, family, and neighbors. It is calculated that about 50,000 alleged witches, the majority of them women, were executed during this period. One exception to this gender imbalance appears to have been France, where more males than females were executed. Scholarly discussion concerning the witch persecutions has been rigorous but inconclusive; more studies of specific locales and time periods are needed to assess the role of gender in the witch persecutions.[40]

While the prosecution of witches for heresy and apostasy generally fell under the jurisdiction of the church, the involvement of secular jurists became accepted juridical practice after the introduction of the imperial criminal code. This *Constitutio criminalis Carolina* (Penal Code of Charles, 1532) was a revision — known by its Latin title but retaining the German of the original — of the 1507 Bamberg Code *Peinliche Halsgerichtsordnung Kaiser Karls V.* (Code of Capital Punishment of Emperor Charles V), authored in large part by Johann von Schwarzenberg (1463/65–1528).[41] The *Constitutio criminalis Carolina* provided that criminal prosecution come under the jurisdiction of university-trained judges and legal scholars. This procedural shift weakened the influence of traditional lay courts, customarily composed of nonprofessional jurists.[42] The punishment of witchcraft and the witch was to be based on proof provided, if needed, by torture or the witch's voluntary confession that she had entered into the pact with the devil and committed *maleficia*. Magic, idolatry (devil worship), and divination were considered punishable as trespasses against the First Commandment. Punishment by death under the statutes of the *Constitutio criminalis Carolina*, however, was reserved for the proven crime of *maleficia*.

Demonologies

Resulting in part from the learned preoccupation with magic and witchcraft, the witch phenomenon left many printed documents in its wake. However, there is no single literary genre dealing with the witch or witchcraft. Instead, many different types of texts address the witch phenomenon. Witches are, for instance, the topic of sermons, broadsheets (*Newe Zeytungen*), and trial transcripts (*Urgichten*). The most compendious texts, however, are the demonologies, exploring the witch as a scientific, religious, social, and theological phenomenon. Late medieval predecessors of the early modern demonology are Johannes Nider's (1385–1438) *Formicarius* (1437), frequently cited in the *Malleus*; Geiler von Kaysersberg's (1462–1516) *Emeis* (1508); and Ulrich Tengler's (1445–1511) *New Layenspiegel* (The New Mirror for Lay People,

1511).[43] While the Catholic Church, in concert with the lay authorities, played an important role in the evolution of the witch persecutions, the Reformation did not significantly change the witch debate. Catholic and Protestant views agreed in their condemnation and punishment of the witch, although different emphases and procedures can be identified.

Martin Luther's convictions and teachings about the reality of evil in the form of Satan and his demons and witches formed the basis of Protestant demonology. While he dismissed witches' sabbaths as illusions, Luther was convinced that sexual intercourse with the devil was possible and that witches entered into a pact with the devil and practiced *maleficia*;[44] he specifically and vigorously condemned the witch's apostasy as the most serious crime against God and the Christian faith. Luther's thinking on witches consequently influenced two contrasting strands of Protestant reactions to the phenomenon: on the one hand, the call for severe punishment; on the other, moderation. Insisting on severe punishment, three writers emphasized the sinful nature of *maleficia* and the God-given duty of the magistrates to eradicate its practice and punish its practitioners: the Marburg attorney Abraham Saur in *Eine kurtze / treuwe Warnung [. . .] ob auch zu dieser unser Zeit unter uns Christen / Hexen / Zauberer und Unholden vorhanden* (A Short and Candid Warning that even in our day there are witches, magicians, and devils living among us, 1582); the Württemberg theologian Paul Frisius in *Von des Teuffels Nebelkappen* (The Devil's Hoodwink, 1583); and Samuel Meigerius, pastor at Nortorf (1532–1610), in *De panurgia lamiarum, sagarum, strigum ac Veneficarum* (On the Evil of Sorceresses, Magicians, Hags, and Witches, 1587). The Lutheran pastor Ludwig Milichius (ca. 1530–75), in *Der Zauber-Teuffel* (The Magic Devil, 1563), had advanced similar arguments emphasizing the role of godly government in witch persecutions and punishment.

Others expressed a more moderate attitude. While not denying the grave culpability of the witch, they tended to recommend prayer, religious instruction, and church discipline in the hope that these would effect a spiritual change and return the accused witch to the faith. These men — among them the Danish Lutheran theologian Nils Hemmingsen (1513–1600) in *Assertiones contra magicum incantationem* (Declarations Against the Magical Incantation, 1569) and in *Admonitio de superstitionibus magicis vitandis* (Advice for Avoiding Magical Superstitions, 1575) — were sharply critical of the often relentless will to prosecute and execute expressed by the populace and some judges. The debate about the efficacy of trial by water to identify witches belongs within this context. The suspected witch would be thrown into the water, hands and feet tied. If she floated, she was marked as a witch, since this revealed both the satanic lightness she had assumed upon entering into a pact with Satan as well as her rejection by the sanctified water; if she sank she was proven innocent, since her human, uncorrupted substance made her heavier than water. Toward the end of the sixteenth century, ordeal by water was a popular form of juridical examinations of witches, a procedure vigorously and widely discussed among jurists and physicians. In 1583 the Marburg natural philosopher and physician Wilhelm Adolph Schreiber (Scribonius, fl.

1580s) published *De examine et purgatione sagarum per aquam frigidam epistola* (Epistle on the Examination and Trying of Witches by Cold Water), which validated the procedure as legally and theologically sound. A vigorous rejection of Scribonius's thesis was advanced by Hermann Neuwalt (died 1611), professor of medicine at the University of Helmstedt, in his *Exegesis purgationis sive examinis sagarum super aquam frigidam* (Exegesis on the Trial or Examination of Witches by Cold Water, 1584). As the first tract devoted exclusively to the question of trial by water, Neuwalt's *Exegesis* was widely discussed and frequently printed. The debate between the two demonologists was subsequently included in the collection of seventeen witch tracts in German, the *Theatrum de veneficis* (Theater of Evildoings, 1586).

The witch phenomenon significantly benefited the popular interest in one of the rare literary witch documents, the *Historia von D. Johan Fausten* (History of Dr. Johann Faust). Printed for the first time in Frankfurt in 1587, this story of a scholar's pact with the devil and his destruction twenty-four years later was to have a rich reception history in European literature.[45] Johann Faust, son of a peasant, studies at the University of Wittenberg. Dissatisfied with the traditional curriculum, he turns to the Black Arts and to conjuring Satan to satisfy his inappropriate curiosity about the universe and the nature of the divine:

> [Es] stunde D. Fausti Datum dahin / das zulieben / das nicht zu lieben war / dem trachtet er Tag und Nacht nach / name an sich Adlers Flügel / wolte alle Gründ am Himmel und Erden erforschen/ dann sein Fürwitz / Freyheit und Leichtfertigkeit stache unnd reitzte jhn also / daß er auff eine zeit etliche zäuberische vocabula / figuras / characteres und coniurationes / damit er den Teufel vor sich möchte fordern / ins Werck zusetzen / und zu probiern jm fürname.[46]

> [Thus Faustus turned to loving what he should not. He yearned after (the forbidden) day and night; his spirit took on eagles' wings; he wanted to explore the heavens and the earth. His arrogance, libertine spirit, and his carelessness pushed and excited him so that, after a while, he began to put forward any number of magical words, figures, symbols and spells, in order that he might force the devil to appear before him.] (14)

He enters into a pact with Satan, signing the contract with blood. Once the agreement is reached he is joined by a devil-familiar, Mephistopheles, who instructs him in many matters of the occult sciences and also procures for his sexual pleasure many female companions, demons in the form of women. Toward the end of his twenty-four-year luxurious, expansive, and sexually licentious life, Faust expresses the wish to marry. Since marriage as a state of divine sacrament is abhorrent to Satan, Faust has to be content with the phantom of Helen of Troy, who becomes his *Schlafweib* (sleeping companion) and with whom he has a son. As the time granted to him by the pact nears its end, he gathers his students for a last meal, asks them to pray for his soul, and goes to face Satan. The devil comes at midnight to claim Faust's soul amid horrible commotion. The next day Faust's body is found in parts scattered across a dung heap. The story of Faust's life and death is told by his student and assistant Christoph Wagner, who also pledges allegiance to the devil in exchange for a life of plenty: "Sie fanden auch diese deβ Fausti Historiam auffgezeichnet/ und von jhme beschrieben" (They found Faust's story recorded and written by him). Wagner became the protagonist of a sequel to the *Faust* book, the *Wagnerbuch* (1593).

At no time, not even at the height of the prosecutions between 1580 and 1630, did all demonologists agree on the nature of the witch.[47] The physician at the court of Cleve, Johann Weyer (1515–88), saw her as an old, demented woman in need more of spiritual support and medical help than of criminal prosecution. He developed this thesis in great detail in the tract *De praestigiis daemonum* (On the Deceptions of Devils, 1663).[48] With this publication Weyer started one of the most vigorous and enduring controversies surrounding demonology in the early modern period. He argued that the moral weakness of women made them easy prey to Satan's temptations; consequently, they could neither be helped nor healed by torture or burning but only by prayer, instruction, medical intervention, and meditative isolation. By contrast, the French jurist and theorist of the absolutist state Jean Bodin (1530–96) in his *De la demonomanie des sorciers* (On the Diabolical Madness of Witches, 1580) argued vigorously in favor of witch persecutions and included a vitriolic polemic against Weyer's theses. Bodin's tract — along with its translation into German by Johann Fischart (1546–90), *Vom aussgelasnen wütigen Teuffelsheer* (On the Wild and Furious Host of Demons, 1581) — became canonical in demonological literature[49] and was cited as authoritative by demonologists as late as the early eighteenth century. At the time of the debate and during the ensuing decades scholars and theologians, even if they were somewhat supportive of Weyer, remained convinced that the devil's pact with the witch was possible, however slight a threat the witch herself actually presented. For instance, the Rostock jurist Georg Godelmann (1559–1611), in his *Disputatio de magis, veneficis et lamiis* (Disputation on Magicians, Sorceresses, and Witches, 1592), distinguished among pacts that led to real *maleficium*, those that did not, and those where the crimes were mere illusions. Misgivings about witch trials were also voiced by the Lemgo pastor Jodocus Hocker (Hieronymus Höcker, ca. 1510–66) in *Der Teufel selbs* (The Devil Himself, 1568); the pastor and theologian Hermann Hamelmann (1525–95) in *Eine Predigt zu Gandersheim [. . .] wider die Beschwerer [. . .] Zeuberer/ Nachweiser/ und Segner* (A Sermon at Gandersheim Against Conjurors, Magicians, Seers, and Prognosticators, 1572); the Bremen physician Johann Ewich (1525–88) in *De sagarum quas vulgo venificas appellant* (On Magicians, which are Commonly Called Witches, 1584); the Heidelberg University professor of Greek and mathematics Hermann Witekind (Augustin Lerchheimer von Steinfelden, 1524–1603) in *Christlich bedencken und erjinnerung von Zauberey* (Christian Admonition and Warning about the Practice of Magic, 1585); the Frankfurt jurist Johann Fichart (1511–81), in *Consilia* (Judgments,

1590); and the Zurich theologian Ludwig Lavater (1527–86), in *De spectris, lemuribus et maguis* (On Specters, Ghosts, and Magicians, 1580). The Heidelberg theologian Anton Praetorius (Johann Scultetus, 1566–1625) wrote one of the most widely read and discussed tracts, the *Gründliche[r] Bericht Von Zauberey und Zauberern* (Elementary Report on Magic and Magicians, 1598).[50] While Praetorius did not doubt the reality of the witch and of satanic influence over her, he spoke out vigorously, in general, against the treatment of women suspected of being witches and, in particular, the use of torture as an instrument to move toward confession.

Catholic demonologists did not differ much from their Protestant counterparts in their basic assumptions about the witch phenomenon. Still, it is a matter of record that some of the most damaging witch persecutions took place in the archbishoprics of Trier and Cologne, as well as in the Catholic cities of Würzburg, Bamberg, Eichstädt, Augsburg, Fulda, and Breslau. With some 2,000 recorded cases, the territories of Cologne and Westphalia reached the zenith of witch burnings. Among those who advanced the most authoritative and influential Catholic views on witches were the Trier bishop and jurist Peter Binsfeld (1546–98) in *Tractatus de confessionibus maleficorum et sagarum* (Treatise on the Confessions of Witches and Magicians, 1589), Martin del Rio (1551–1608) in *Disquisitionum magicarum libri sex* (Six Books of Disquisitions on Witches, 1599), and the French jurist Henri Boguet (1550–1619), who reported in his *Discours des sorciers* (Discourse on Sorceresses, 1602) about the prosecutions in Franche Comté. According to Stuart Clark, any differences between Catholics and Protestants lay in the remedies believed to be efficacious against witchcraft. The Catholic Church remained committed to exorcisms for help in instances of possession and to other sacramental and ritualistic support; although Protestants persecuted with comparable vigor, for these believers — who could not direct entreaties to saints, purchase indulgences, and hope for amelioration of their plight by doing good works[51] — remedies available to Catholics were off-limits. Leading Catholic voices against witch persecution included the Jesuits Friedrich von Spee (1591–1635) in *Cautio criminalis oder Rechtliches Bedencken wegen der Hexenprozesse* (Precautions in Criminal Matters, or juridical caution concerning witch trials, 1631) and Adam Tanner, theologian at Ingolstadt (1572–1632), in *Tractatus theologicus de processu adversus crimina excepta, ac speciatim adversus crimen venefici* (Treatise on the Trying of Exceptional Crimes, particularly the crime of witchcraft, 1629). In his *Cautio criminalis,* Spee, one of the great stylists of the Baroque, penned a forceful critique of trial procedures, specifically of the practice of torture in cases of witch allegations. The Lutheran theologian from Erfurt Matthäus Meyfart (1590–1642), in *Christliche erinnerung [. . .] wie das abschewliche Laster der Hexerey mit Ernst auszurotten* (Christian Admonition on seriously extinguishing the abominable sin of witchcraft, 1666), also raised his voice in defense of the woman accused of being a witch.

Finally, the phenomenon of the child-witch was reflected around 1629 in the publication of the anonymous tract *Newer Tractat von der verführten*

Kinder Zauberey (New Treatise on Children Led Astray by Magic). The idea that mothers led their daughters to Satan and that whole families swore allegiance to the devil had become commonplace by this time.

When the Leipzig author Johannes Praetorius published his tract *Blockes-Berges Verrichtung* in 1668, the number of scientific tracts devoted to the witch and her demonic proclivities had grown significantly; Praetorius's incomplete list cites about sixty. Printed witch sermons — such as Johann Greater's *Hexen oder Unholden Predigten* (Sermons on Witches and Devils, 1599), David Meder's *Acht Hexenpredigten* (Eight Sermons on Witches, 1605), or Joachim Zehner's *Fünf Predigten von den Hexen* (Five Sermons on Witches, 1613) — and pamphlets about witch trials and executions contributed to an extensive public reception of the elaborated witch image. Collections of demonologies, sermons, and discussions of controversial issues relating to the witch phenomenon were read in all quarters of Europe. Most prominent among them were the collections *Theatrum diabolorum* (Theater of Demons) of 1569 and the previously mentioned *Theatrum de veneficis* of 1586, both of which were published in German and went through several editions. The *Theatrum diabolorum* contains thirty-eight short didactic and entertaining, attractively printed devil books (the word *Teufel* [devil] usually appears in some form in the title).[52] Individual devils are assigned to specific sinful behaviors, which fall into three thematic groups: moral sins and evil habits (drinking, fashion, cursing, gambling, hunting, stinginess, sloth, arrogance, dancing, flattery, lying, swearing, and melancholy); matrimony and family; and demonology and church life, that is, the use of black magic in relation to salvation. In turn, the individual texts of the *Theatrum de veneficis* cover the whole spectrum of reactions to the witch phenomenon. These range from severe condemnation — as espoused by the Genevan pastor Lambertus Danaeus (1530–96) in *Ein Gespräch von den Zäuberern* (A Conversation about Magicians) and the pastor Jacob Vallick in *Von Zäuberern/ Hexen/ und Unholden* (On Magicians, Witches, and Devils, 1576) — to doubts that witches were capable of the deeds with which they were charged — as expressed, for example, by Witekind in *Christlich Bedencken* and Fichart in *Etliche Bedencken und Rathschläge* (Some Reservations and Advice).[53]

Several decades later the Leipzig jurist and philosopher Christian Thomasius (1655–1728), in *De crimine magiae* (On the Practice of Witchcraft, 1701), expressed comparable criticism of what he regarded as superstition and unjust persecution of those already weakened by old age and social marginalization. Finally, in *De Betoverde Weerld* (The Bewitched World, ca. 1692), the Dutch Calvinist pastor Balthasar Bekker (1634–98) moved beyond assessments critical of witch trials to outright denial of Satan's power over material things.[54] While dissertations about the efficacy of the witch and satanic contracts continued to be defended — new interest in the occult surfaced as late as the nineteenth century — the popularity of the demonologies that were written, read, and quoted with great frequency and passion either in support of or against rejections of the witch persecutions came to an end by the mid-nineteenth century.[55]

Notes

[1] Walter Stephens, *Demon Lovers: Witchcraft, Sex, and the Crisis of Belief* (Chicago: U of Chicago P, 2002). The term "witchcraft theory" comes from Stephens (323).

[2] Sydney Anglo, "Evident Authority and Authoritative Evidence: The *Malleus Maleficarum*," in *The Damned Art: Essays in the Literature of Witchcraft*, ed. Anglo (Boston: Routledge & Kegan Paul, 1977), 1–31, here 2.

[3] According to Stuart Clark, *Thinking with Demons: The Idea of Witchcraft in Early Modern Europe* (Oxford: Clarendon, 1997), vii, they had focused on "the social and institutional configurations of witch hunting, together with the patterns of prosecutions in various European regions and the local circumstances that produce them."

[4] Claudia Kauertz, *Wissenschaft und Hexenglaube: Die Diskussion des Zauber- und Hexenwesens an der Universität Helmstedt (1576–1626)*, ed. Hexenforschung (Bielefeld: Verlag für Regionalgeschichte, 2002), 25.

[5] Wilhelm Gottlieb Soldan, *Geschichte der Hexenprozesse* (Stuttgart: Cotta, 1843); on Soldan's book see Heinrich Heppe, ed., *Soldans Geschichte der Hexenprozesse* (Stuttgart: Cotta, 1880).

[6] Theodor Grässe, *Bibliotheca magica et pneumatica* (Leipzig: Engelmann, 1843).

[7] Henry Charles Lea, comp., *Materials toward a History of Witchcraft*, 3 vols., ed. Arthur C. Howland (1939; repr., New York: AMS Press, 1986).

[8] Joseph Hansen, *Zauberwahn, Inquisition und Hexenprozess im Mittelalter und die Entstehung der grossen Hexenverfolgung* (Munich: Oldenbourg, 1900); Joseph Hansen and Johannes Franck, *Quellen und Untersuchungen zur Geschichte des Hexenwahns und der Hexenverfolgung im Mittelalter mit einer Untersuchung der Geschichte des Wortes Hexe* (1901; repr., Hildesheim: Olms 1963).

[9] Lynn Thorndike, *A History of Magic and Experimental Science*, 8 vols. (New York: Macmillan, 1923–58); Russell Hope Robbins, *The Encyclopedia of Witchcraft and Demonology* (New York: Crown Publishers, 1959).

[10] H. C. Erik Midelfort, *Witch Hunting in Southwestern Germany (1562–1684)* (Stanford: Stanford UP, 1972).

[11] H. C. Erik Midelfort, "Recent Witch Hunting Research, or Where Do We Go from Here?," *The Papers of the Bibliographical Society of America* 62, no. 3 (1968): 373–420; Midelfort, "Witchcraft, Magic, and the Occult," in *Reformation Europe: A Guide to Research*, ed. Steven Ozment (St. Louis: Center for Reformation Research, 1982), 18–209.

[12] Clark, *Thinking with Demons*; Wolfgang Behringer, *Hexen und Hexenprozesse in Deutschland* (Munich: Deutscher Taschenbuch Verlag, 1988); Behringer, *Hexen: Glaube, Verfolgung, Vermarktung* (Munich: Beck, 1998); Behringer, *Hexenverfolgung in Bayern: Volksmagie, Glaubenseifer und Staatsräson in der Frühen Neuzeit* (Munich: Oldenbourg, 1987); Behringer, *Mit dem Feuer vom Leben zum Tod: Hexengesetzgebung in Bayern* (Munich: Hugendubel, 1988); Jonathan Barry, Marianne Hester, and Gareth Roberts Barry, eds., *Witchcraft in Early Modern Europe: Studies in Culture and Belief* (Cambridge: Cambridge UP, 1996); Jonathan L. Pearl, *The Crime of Crimes: Demonology and Politics in France 1590–1620* (Waterloo: Wilfried Laurier UP, 1999); Lyndal Roper, *Witch Craze: Terror and Fantasy in Baroque Germany* (New Haven: Yale UP, 2004); Gerhild Scholz Williams, *Ways of Knowing in Early Modern Germany: Johannes Praetorius as a Witness to His Time* (Aldershot: Ashgate, 2006); and Williams,

ed., *On the Inconstancy of Witches: Pierre de Lancre's "Tableau de l'inconstance des mauvais anges et Demons" (1612)*, trans. Harriet Stone and Williams (Tempe: Arizona Center for Texts and Studies, 2006).

[13] Heide Wunder, *He Is the Sun, She Is the Moon: Women in Early Modern Germany* (Cambridge: Harvard UP, 1998); Merry E. Wiesner, *Women and Gender in Early Modern Europe*, 2nd ed., New Approaches to European History 20 (Cambridge: Cambridge UP, 2000); Lyndal Roper, *Oedipus and the Devil: Witchcraft, Sexuality, and Religion in Early Modern Europe* (London: Routledge, 1994); Gerhild Scholz Williams, *Defining Dominion: The Discourses of Magic and Witchcraft in Early Modern France and Germany*, Studies in Medieval and Early Modern Civilization (Ann Arbor: Michigan UP, 1995); Sigrid Brauner, *Fearless Wives and Frightened Shrews: The Concept of the Witch in Early Modern Germany* (Amherst: U of Massachusetts P, 1995).

[14] Bengt Ankarloo and Gustav Henningsen, eds., *Early Modern European Witchcraft: Centres and Peripheries* (Oxford: Clarendon, 1990); Richard van Dülmen, *Hexenwelten: Magie und Imagination vom 16.–20. Jahrhundert* (Frankfurt am Main: Fischer Taschenbuch Verlag, 1987); Carlo Ginzburg, *Ecstasies: Deciphering the Witches' Sabbath*, trans. R. Rosenthal (New York: Pantheon Books, 1991); Peter Segl, *Der Hexenhammer: Entstehung und Umfeld des Malleus Maleficarum von 1487*, Bayreuther Historische Kolloquien 2 (Cologne: Böhlau, 1988).

[15] E. William Monter, *Witchcraft in France and Switzerland: The Borderlands During the Reformation* (Ithaca: Cornell UP, 1976); Christina Larner and Alan Macfarlane, *Witchcraft and Religion: The Politics of Popular Belief* (New York: Blackwell, 1984); J. A. Sharpe, *Instruments of Darkness: Witchcraft in England 1550–1750* (New York: Penguin, 1996); Gustav Henningsen, *The Witches' Advocate: Basque Witchcraft and the Spanish Inquisition, 1609–1614* (Reno: U of Nevada P, 1980).

[16] Hartwig Weber, *Von der verführten Kinder Zauberei: Hexenprozesse gegen Kinder im alten Württemberg* (Sigmaringen: Thorbecke, 1996); Wolfgang Behringer, "Kinderhexenprozesse: Zur Rolle von Kindern in der Geschichte der Hexenverfolgung," *Zeitschrift für Historische Forschung* 16, no. 1 (1989): 31–47.

[17] Stephens, *Demon Lovers*; Stephens, "Witches Who Steal Penises: Impotence and Illusion in Malleus Maleficarum," *Journal of Medieval and Early Modern Studies* 28, no. 3 (1998): 495–525; Armando Maggi, *Satan's Rhetoric: A Study of Renaissance Demonology* (Chicago: U of Chicago P, 2001).

[18] Ingrid Merkel and Allen G. Debus, eds., *Hermeticism and the Renaissance: Intellectual History and the Occult in Early Modern Europe* (Washington, DC: Folger Shakespeare Library, 1988); Wayne Shumaker, *The Occult Sciences in the Renaissance: A Study in Intellectual Patterns* (Berkeley: U of California P, 1972); D. P. Walker, *The Ancient Theology: Studies in Christian Platonism from the Fifteenth to the Eighteenth Century* (Ithaca: Cornell UP, 1972).

[19] The Indo-European *magh* means "to be able to" or "to help"; *maghti* "power" = *Macht* "might." The Sanskrit *magha* also means "power" or "strength" or "wealth." Thus magic, considered formally, stands for an ability, a power to execute certain actions. See Norbert Henrichs, "Scientia Magica," in *Der Wissenschaftsbegriff: Historische und systematische Untersuchungen* (Meisenheim: Anton Hain, 1970), 30–46, here 30; also Clark, *Thinking with Demons*, chapters on "Natural Magic" and "Demonic Magic," 214–50.

[20] B. P. Copenhaver, "Natural Magic, Hermeticism, and Occultism in Early Modern Science," in *Reappraisals of the Scientific Revolution*, ed. David C. Lindberg and Robert S. Westman (Cambridge: Cambridge UP, 1990), 216–301.

[21] Lorraine Daston and Catherine Park, *Wonders and the Order of Nature, 1150–1750* (New York: Zone Books, 1998). Daston and Park identify four kinds of wonders: supernatural, preternatural, artificial, and unnatural. The preternatural kind of wonders most concerned the early modern scholar.

[22] Richard Kieckhefer, *Magic in the Middle Ages* (Cambridge: Cambridge UP, 2000), 9.

[23] Valerie Flint, *The Rise of Magic in Early Medieval Europe* (Princeton: Princeton UP, 1991); Geoffrey Scarré, *Witchcraft and Magic in Sixteenth and Seventeenth Century Europe* (Atlantic Highlands: Humanities Press International, 2000), 7–8.

[24] Robin Briggs, *Witches and Neighbors: The Social and Cultural Context of European Witchcraft* (New York: Penguin, 1998), speaks of "areas of ambiguous social relations"; see also Flint, *The Rise of Magic*; Richard Kieckhefer, *European Witch Trials: Their Foundations in Popular and Learned Culture, 1300–1500* (Berkeley: U of California P, 1976).

[25] Kieckhefer, *Magic in the Middle Ages*, 3.

[26] Neil Kenny, *Curiosity in Early Modern Europe: World Histories*, Wolfenbütteler: Forschungen 81 (Wiesbaden: Harrassowitz, 1998); Jan-Dirk Müller, " 'Curiositas' und 'Erfarung' der Welt im frühen deutschen Prosaroman," in *Literatur und Laienbildung im Spätmittelalter und in der Reformationszeit*, ed. Ludger Grenzmann and Karl Stackmann (Stuttgart: Metzler, 1981), 252–73.

[27] Williams, *Defining Dominion*, 5–8.

[28] Gerhild Scholz Williams and Alexander Schwarz, *Existentielle Vergeblichkeit: Verträge in der Melusine, im Eulenspiegel and im Dr. Faustus* (Berlin: Schmidt, 2003), chapter on Melusine, 35–67.

[29] Martin Pott, *Aufklärung und Aberglaube: Die deutsche Frühaufklärung im Spiegel ihrer Aberglaubenskritik* (Tübingen: Niemeyer, 1992); William Eamon, *Science and the Secrets of Nature: Books of Secrets in Medieval and Early Modern Culture* (Princeton: Princeton UP, 1994); Brian Easlea, *Witch Hunting, Magic, and the New Philosophy: An Introduction to Debates of the Scientific Revolution, 1450–1750* (Brighton, Sussex: Harvester, 1980); Wolf-Dieter Müller-Jancke, "Von Ficino zu Agrippa: Der Magie-Begriff des Renaissance-Humanismus im Überblick," in *Epochen der Naturmystik: Hermetische Tradition im wissenschaftlichen Fortschritt*, ed. Antoine Faivre and Rolf Christian Zimmermann (Berlin: Schmidt, 1979), 5–51.

[30] Gabriele Schwab, "Seduced by Witches: Nathaniel Hawthorne's *The Scarlet Letter* in the Context of New England Witchcraft Fiction," in *Seduction and Theory: Readings of Gender, Representation, and Rhetoric*, ed. Dianne Hunter (Urbana: U of Illinois P, 1989), 172.

[31] The *Canon*, believed to have been issued by the Council of Ancyra (A.D. 314), was probably no older than the ninth century. It denied the reality of night rides with Diana. The women who believed in such an experience were considered victims of satanic delusions (Scarré, *Witchcraft and Magic*, 14).

[32] Generally, historians have identified small-scale witch panics with about 4 to 19 victims, and large-scale witch hunts with 20 or more. Persecutions exceeding 250 victims were relatively rare. Switzerland, specifically the areas around Lausanne and Geneva, saw early persecutions documented by a Lucerne chronicle that reports 200 people burned in the space of a year and a half. See Behringer, *Hexen: Glaube, Verfolgung, Vermarktung*, 38.

[33] Heinrich (Institoris) Kramer, *Malleus maleficarum*, trans. Montague Summers (1928; repr., New York: Blom, 1970); André Schnyder, "Der 'Malleus Maleficarum': Fragen und Beobachtungen zu seiner Druckgeschichte sowie zur Rezeption bei Bodin, Binsfeld und Delrio," *Archiv für Kulturgeschichte* 74, no. 2 (1992); Segl, *Der*

Hexenhammer, Wolfgang Behringer and Günter Jerouschek, eds., *Heinrich Kramer (Institoris): Der Hexenhammer: Kommentierte Übersetzung,* 2nd ed. (Munich: Deutscher Taschenbuch Verlag, 2001).

[34] Gerhild Scholz Williams, "Hexenliteratur," in *Reallexikon der deutschen Literaturwissenschaft: Neubearbeitung des Reallexikons der Deutschen Literaturgeschichte,* ed. Harald Fricke et al. (Berlin: de Gruyter, 2000), 44–46.

[35] Nicole Jacques-Chaquin and Maxime Préaud, *Le sabbat des sorciers en Europe: XVe–XIIIe siècle* (Grenoble: Millon, 1993); Ginzburg, *Ecstasies.*

[36] Scott Cunningham, *Cunningham's Encyclopedia of Magical Herbs* (St. Paul: Llewellyn, 2000); Ioan P. Couliano, *Eros and Magic in the Renaissance,* trans. Margaret Cook (Chicago: Chicago UP, 1987); Alan Charles Kors and Edward Peters, eds., *Witchcraft in Europe, 1100–1700: A Documentary History,* 2nd ed. (Philadelphia: U of Pennsylvania P, 2001).

[37] Behringer and Jerouschek, eds., *Heinrich Kramer (Institoris): Der Hexenhammer,* 11, call it the "central text of the European witch persecutions."

[38] While the *Malleus* has been credited as being the first document to have presented the elaborated witch image, recent studies have shown that this distinction belongs less to Kramer than to a number of earlier texts. However, the *Malleus* remains by far the most influential witch manual during the sixteenth and seventeenth centuries. See Jürgen Michael Schmidt, *Glaube und Skepsis: Die Kurpfalz und die abendländische Hexenverfolgung 1446–1687,* Hexenforschung 5 (Bielefeld: Verlag für Regionalgeschichte, 2000), 23–46.

[39] Ulrich Molitor, "Von Hexen und Unholden," in *Theatrum de veneficis,* ed. Abraham Saur (Frankfurt am Main: Bassaeus, 1586), 70–96.

[40] Edward Peters speaks of the "gender-debate," in Kors and Peters, eds., *Witchcraft in Europe,* 17–19.

[41] Friedrich-Christian Schroeder, ed., *Die Carolina: Die peinliche Gerichtsordnung Kaiser Karls V. von 1532* (Darmstadt: Wissenschaftliche Buchgesellschaft, 1986). Schwarzenberg, a Franconian knight in the administrative service of the bishop of Bamberg, was also charged in 1521 with composing the revision.

[42] Kauertz, *Wissenschaft und Hexenglaube,* 83–85.

[43] Schmidt, *Glaube und Skepsis;* Dieter Harmening, *Superstitio: Überlieferungs- und theoriegeschichtliche Untersuchungen zur kirchlich-theologischen Aberglaubensliteratur des Mittelalters* (Berlin: Schmidt, 1979).

[44] Kauertz, *Wissenschaft und Hexenglaube,* 35–37.

[45] Williams and Schwarz, *Existentielle Vergeblichkeit,* chapter on Faust, 109–45; Frank Baron, *Faustus on Trial: The Origins of Johann Spies's "Historia" in an Age of Witch Hunting* (Tübingen: Niemeyer, 1992).

[46] *Historia von D. Johann Fausten (1587),* ed. Stephan Füssel and Hans Joachimi Kreutzer (Stuttgart: Reclam, 1988), 14.

[47] See the essays in Hartmut Lehmann and Otto Ulbricht, eds., *Vom Unfug des Hexen-Processes: Gegner der Hexenverfolgungen von Johann Weyer bis Friedrich Spee* (Wiesbaden: Harrassowitz, 1992).

[48] George Mora, ed., *Witches, Devils, and Doctors in the Renaissance: Johann Weyer, De praestigiis daemonum,* Medieval and Renaissance Texts and Studies 73 (Binghamton: Medieval and Renaissance Texts and Studies, 1991).

[49] Jean Bodin, *De la démonomanie des sorciers* (1580; repr., Hildesheim: Olms, 1988); Bodin, *Vom ausgelasnen wütigen Teuffelsheer* (1591), trans. Johann Fischart (Graz: Akademische Verlagsanstalt, 1973).

[50] Hartmut Hegeler, *Anton Praetorius, Kämpfer gegen Hexenprozesse und Folter* (Unna: Selbstverlag, 2002).

[51] Clark, *Thinking with Demons*, 527–45.

[52] Ria Stambaugh, ed., *Teufelbücher in Auswahl*, 5 vols. (Berlin: de Gruyter, 1970–80); Heinrich Grimm, "Die deutschen 'Teufelbücher' des 16. Jahrhunderts: Ihre Rolle im Buchwesen und ihre Bedeutung," *Archiv für die Geschichte des Buchwesens* 2 (1960): 513–70.

[53] Gerhild Scholz Williams, "Invoking the Powers That Be: Types of Authority and the Production of the *Theatrum de veneficis* (1586)," in *The Construction of Authority in German Literature of the Medieval and Early Modern Periods*, ed. James F. Poag and Claire Baldwin (Chapel Hill: U of North Carolina P, 2001), 191–210.

[54] On Bekker see Lehmann and Ulbricht, eds., *Vom Unfug des Hexen-Processes*, 260–62.

[55] One of the last witches to be executed was Anna Göldi (or Göldin) from Glarus, Switzerland, in 1782. She was not burned but beheaded because of accusations of child murder and bewitchment of her employer's daughter. See Eveline Hasler, *Anna Göldin, die letzte Hexe* (Zürich: Benziger, 1982).

Part V

Lives

Parallel Lives: Heinrich Steinhöwel, Albrecht von Eyb, and Niklas von Wyle

John L. Flood

WRITING BIOGRAPHY IS ALWAYS A CHALLENGE. Facts have to be assembled, judgments balanced. When the subject is still alive it may be relatively easy to gather facts, but forming a valid judgment may be a difficult and delicate task. With historical persons the problems are almost invariably even greater. The facts are harder to ascertain, and judgments may be clouded by the accretions of history or legend. For some figures of the past, sources flow freely: the lives of Erasmus of Rotterdam, Martin Luther, or Philipp Melanchthon, for instance, can all be fairly well traced through their publications and voluminous correspondence. But for lesser personages of five centuries ago such materials are seldom abundant. Such is the case with the translators to be considered here, three contemporaries for whom — notwithstanding their historical importance for German studies — our only sources of biographical information are the relatively slender corpus of their works, scattered records of their studies and professional lives, fragmentary correspondence with contemporaries, and tenuous inferences about their awareness of and influence on one another. At best we can gain but tantalizing glimpses of late medieval lives. For the historian that is both the challenge and the reward.

At first it may seem improbable that these three men, exact contemporaries yet so different by profession, should have much in common: Heinrich Steinhöwel was a physician, Albrecht von Eyb a churchman and lawyer, Niklas von Wyle a municipal official and chancery scribe. Yet, taken together, they made a remarkable contribution to fifteenth-century German literature, introducing some of the best in Italian humanist writing to Germany and, by initiating debate about methods of translation and about German literary style, laying the foundations for one of the most important achievements of the early sixteenth century, Martin Luther's translation of the Bible into German.

Heinrich Steinhöwel

Steinhöwel was born at Weil der Stadt in 1411 or 1412 — slightly before Eyb and Wyle — probably the son of the Esslingen patrician of the same name who had settled in Weil in 1407. In April 1429, aged about eighteen, he enrolled as "Henricus Stainhäwl de Wyla" at the University of Vienna, received his bachelor's degree there in 1432, his M.A. in 1436, and taught at the university until

March 1438. That summer he studied canon law at the University of Padua. He soon turned to medicine, however, obtaining his doctorate in 1443; in December of the following year he was recorded as "lerer der ertzney" (teacher of medicine) at Heidelberg. Shortly thereafter he moved back to his native town of Weil to work as a physician, where he wrote his first work, a treatise on plague, known as his *Pestbüchlein* (Little Book on the Plague, 1473).[1] In 1449 and 1450 Steinhöwel was in Esslingen, probably employed as *Stadtarzt* (city physician). Together with the town clerk Niklas von Wyle, he supported Esslingen in its feud with Count Ulrich V of Württemberg — a typical struggle of the period between increasingly assertive town administrations and their aristocratic overlords. In July 1450 Steinhöwel took up a new appointment as municipal physician at Ulm, a post he would hold for the rest of his life. His advantageous marriage in 1454 or 1455 to an Augsburg patrician's daughter, Anastasia Egen, enhanced his social and financial station in Ulm. His acquired wealth and status as the owner of a pharmacy, the Mohrenapotheke, afforded him sufficient leisure to indulge and develop his literary interests and helped him forge links with important people in southwestern Germany,[2] including individuals with literary interests at the little courts in the area, as in Stuttgart, Urach, Rottenburg, Freiburg, and Dillingen. His association with Niklas von Wyle seems to have been of a professional nature, as town officials, rather than literary.

Steinhöwel was one of the earliest German writers to recognize the benefits of printing. At first he relied on the expertise of Günther Zainer (d. 1478), the first printer at Augsburg, fifty miles from Ulm, and he soon realized that it would be much more convenient to have a printing press on his own doorstep. In 1472 he encouraged Zainer's younger brother, Johann (d. 1523), to set up a press in Ulm, though he also continued to have books printed by Günther Zainer. The younger Zainer probably jumped at the chance to become independent, given that Steinhöwel was in a position to finance the enterprise and could keep him supplied with texts to print, and generally to assist him in developing a humanistically inspired publishing program.[3] With sufficient financial resources and ready access to an obliging local printer, Steinhöwel, whose pen was ever busy, was easily able to promote his own work, with the result that he became the most widely read German author before Luther.[4]

Steinhöwel produced at least seven works.[5] His *Pestbüchlein*, written in the mid-1440s but first printed by Johann Zainer in January 1473, was not only the first book printed at Ulm, it was the first medical book ever printed in Germany. Reprinted six times, it influenced virtually all later writers on the plague. Barely a month after the *Pestbüchlein* appeared, Zainer published Steinhöwel's *Ein tütsche Cronica von anfang der welt uncz uff keiser fridrich* (A German Chronicle from the Beginning of the World to Emperor Friedrich), commonly known as the *Tütsche Cronica* or *Deutsche Chronik*. It was an abridged translation of a mid-fourteenth-century Latin chronicle but supplemented with further information down to the reign of Friedrich III, who had become emperor in 1440. Once again Steinhöwel's work proved an invaluable source for later writers; for instance, it influenced the numerous so-called

"Chronicles of the Emperors, Kings, and Popes" printed at Augsburg by Johann Bämler and Johann Blaubirer between 1476 and 1480.[6]

By the time the *Pestbüchlein* and the *Tütsche Cronica* appeared at Ulm, Steinhöwel had already published two works of a very different nature with Günther Zainer at Augsburg, and the success of these will have left him in no doubt about the advantages of printing. One was *Apollonius*, a German translation from Latin of an ancient heroic tale (probably first written down in Greek) about Apollonius of Tyre. The oldest extant version, in Latin and dating to the fifth century A.D., was included in the twelfth-century *Gesta Romanorum* (Deeds of the Romans) and was widely known in the Middle Ages under the title *Historia Apollinii regis Tyri* (History of Apollonius, King of Tyre). Steinhöwel made his translation in 1461, but it was not printed until 1471. It was reissued by Johann Bämler at Augsburg in 1476, and some fourteen further editions appeared by the seventeenth century. Steinhöwel declares, with some humor, that he has translated the popular tale, because "eigen gedicht wer mir zeschwer" (it would be too hard for me to write a poem of my own). But his further point is that German language, writing, and even morality will profit from the direct translation of earlier ideas from Latin-language literature. He will repeat this principle in introductions to his later translations as well, including his 1471 translation of Petrarch's Latin version of the story of Griseldis from Boccaccio's *Decamerone*. This story came to be regarded in Germany as an instructive *exemplum* of marital fidelity, achieving considerable popularity in more than a dozen manuscripts.[7]

At the same time as Johann Zainer was seeing the *Tütsche Cronica* through the press, Steinhöwel was busy with his next project, *Von etlichen frauen* (On Certain Ladies), a translation of Boccaccio's *De claris mulieribus* (On Famous Women, 1361–62), a work highly esteemed in humanist circles.[8] It was in this work that Steinhöwel formulated his approach to translation: "nit von [wort] zů wort, sunder von sin zů sin" (not word by word but sense by sense). In this book, that is, he was striving above all to reproduce Boccaccio's meaning, less importance being attached to a faithful or literal reproduction of his words and style. The word-for-word versus sense-for-sense debate would inform German approaches to translation up through Luther.[9]

Finally, following the publication of his sixth project, *Spiegel menschlichen Lebens* (Mirror of Human Life, 1475), a translation of the *Speculum vitae humanae*, a work of 1471 by Rodericus Zamorensis,[10] Steinhöwel wrote the book for which he is most remembered: *Das leben des hochberümpten fabeldichters Esopi* [. . .] *mit synen fabeln* (The Life of the Famous Fable-Teller Aesop with his Fables, 1476/77). This bilingual (Latin and German) edition of some 150 of Aesop's *Fables* shows Steinhöwel to be not only a skilled translator but also a good editor in his judicious selection of fables. With its 200 woodcuts, *Esopus* has been described as one of the most beautifully illustrated books of all time.[11] As we saw with his version of Boccaccio's *De claris mulieribus*, Steinhöwel's prime concern was to convey the meaning rather than reproduce the style of the Latin original. Similarly, the preface to *Esopus* stated that it has been "geteútschet nit wort ausz wort, sunder syn ausz syn" (translated not word for word, but meaning for meaning).[12] Furthermore, he praises translators for the valuable service they render: "dz sy andern sollich kunst vnd gûtheit haben geoffenbart, die sußt ewiglichen ynen gewesen wärent verborgen" (they have revealed to others such knowledge and good things that would otherwise have been hidden from them for evermore).

In dedicating the *Spiegel menschlichen Lebens* to Duke Sigmund of Austria, Steinhöwel expresses his other great purpose in translating: to ensure that Germans have access to the pleasures of Latin literature:[13]

> Ausz disem ich bewögt, auch gemeynt hab [. . .] nit minder gût sein, ob etwaz nutzbars hochsynnigs vnd gûtes in latinischer geschrift gesetzet wäre, das in teútsche sprache zetransferieren, vnd ze bringen, vnd das die teútschen der latine vnkúnnend söllicher gûtheyt auch nit wären beraubet.
>
> [Wherefore I have thought it no less good, if there is something useful, intellectually valuable, and of good quality set down in Latin writing, to translate and render it into German, so that Germans with no knowledge of Latin should not be deprived of such good things.]

As editor and author Steinhöwel was extraordinarily productive and a major patron of the Zainer brothers, especially Johann in Ulm, generally exerting a guiding influence over his whole publishing program.[14] Zainer's dependence on Steinhöwel is suggested by the fact that the printer suffered financial collapse soon after his patron's death on 1 March 1479.

Albrecht von Eyb

Albrecht von Eyb was born into an ancient Franconian noble family at Schloss Sommersdorf, near Ansbach (Bavaria), on 24 August 1420. The third son of the family, he was destined for the church. He studied at the University of Erfurt from 1436 to 1438, but after the death of his father and at the insistence of his elder brother Ludwig he continued his education closer to home, at the Latin school at Rothenburg ob der Tauber. In 1444, after having obtained an appointment as a canon in Eichstätt, he moved to Italy, where he was to spend most of the following fifteen years, beginning with studies in Pavia, Bologna, and Padua.

He moved back to Bamberg for a few months in 1451–52, having been appointed canon at the cathedral, but returned to Bologna, where he resided until 1455. In 1459 in Pavia he was admitted to the degree of Doctor of Civil and Canon Law. He claimed that the teachers Cato Sacco, Gasparino Barzizza, and above all Baldassare Rasino had an especially profound effect on him. At Bologna he had come under the influence of the distinguished humanist Giovanni Lamola (d. 1449), and he also became acquainted with several leading scholars, including Maffeo Vegio, Lorenzo Valla, Francesco Filelfo, and especially Enea Silvio Piccolomini (1405–64), who later, as Pope Pius II (1458–64), would honor Eyb by appointing him his personal *cubicularius* (chamberlain).

On his return to Germany in 1459 Eyb became involved in ecclesiastical and political affairs and legal consultancy, specializing in matrimonial cases, especially for the defense of women. Despite its routine, his life was not without incident. Shortly after 1460 he was abducted by certain individuals who objected to his appointment to the benefice at Würzburg and was released only in return for a large ransom. It is possible that the abduction was planned by the bishop of Würzburg, whose animosity toward Eyb, a partisan of the bishop's enemy, the Hohenzollern margrave Albrecht Achilles, was well known and did not stop much short of hatred. It took two visits to Rome, in 1461 and 1462, to settle the affair. From about 1464 until his death in 1475 Eyb spent most of his time practicing law, writing legal opinions as consultant to various towns, including Nuremberg, Würzburg, Eichstätt, Kitzingen, and Augsburg, and drawing up wills, contracts, and documents relating to ecclesiastical livings and matrimonial cases. His income from his legal work, together with the proceeds of the various church appointments he held, enabled him to devote himself in later life almost entirely to literary pursuits. Between 1448 and 1459 he built up a substantial library.[15]

Eyb was neither as prolific nor as important a writer as Steinhöwel. Much of his writing was in Latin. His earliest work, never published, was *Speculum poetrie* (Mirror of Poetry, 1449), which is a moralizing assemblage of literary quotations, thematically arranged.[16] His earliest independent works, all composed in 1452 while he was living in Bamberg, are invectives and eulogies of the kind popular with humanists. The first, influenced by Enea Silvio's *Eurialus and Lucretia* (1444), is *Tractatus de speciositate Barbarae puellulae* (In Praise of the Beauty of the Young Girl Barbara). Whether she was real or a figment of his imagination is not clear; it is a free, but not vulgar, description of the physical attractions of a young girl. *Appellacio mulierum Bambergensium* (Addressing the Women of Bamberg), inspired by the Florentine scholar Leonardo Bruni Aretino's *Oratio Heliogabali ad meretrices* (Oration of Heliogabale on Harlots, 1408), is a clever satire on the allegedly lax morals of Bamberg women. This was followed by *Ad laudem et commendationem Bambergae civitatis oratio* (In Praise and Commendation of the City of Bamberg), a eulogy on the same city,[17] and by *De commendatione dignissimi et divinissimi Eucharistiae sacramento oratio* (Commendation of the Most Worthy and Divine Sacrament of the Eucharist). This piece in praise of the Eucharist was perhaps a sermon delivered on the occasion of Eyb's installation as a canon at Bamberg.

Eyb's first important work was *Margarita poetica* (Poetic Pearl), probably compiled in Italy in 1459 and foreshadowed a decade earlier in *Speculum poetrie*. Designed as a textbook of humanist rhetoric, giving advice on the composition of letters and orations, it is an anthology of humanistic texts, in which the mass of textual examples swamps any theoretical considerations. It contains excerpts of stylistic interest from Roman writers and Italian humanists and concludes with thirty orations intended to serve as models of humanistic style.[18] The concluding speech, which functions as an epilogue, contains a defense of humanistic ideals of learning in which he draws heavily on the humanist scholar and biographer Leonardo Bruni's (ca. 1370–1444, also known as Aretino) *De studiis et litteris liber* (On Studying Literature, 1422–29).[19]

Overall, Eyb regarded Cicero as the supreme stylist and quotes extensively from his works. The fourth-century Christian apologist Lactantius (240–ca. 320), later admired as "the Christian Cicero" by Italian humanists, was another favorite of his. Eyb also quotes extensively from other Latin writers on whom he had attended lectures in Italy, such as Valerius Maximus, Terence, and Plautus. Caesar, Apuleius, and Macrobius are also represented, but patristic writers scarcely figure in his works. Among medieval works he makes significant reference only to *De vita et moribus philosophorum* (On the Life and Habits of the Philosophers, 1467) of Walter Burley (ca. 1275–1344), one of the most prominent English philosophers of the fourteenth century; and from the Renaissance, Petrarch is quoted extensively. *Margarita poetica* appeared in numerous editions, printed in Nuremberg, Rome, Paris, Strasbourg, Venice, Toulouse, and Basel, and was clearly considered a useful collection. Once complete texts of the writers cited became accessible in print, Eyb's compilation became redundant.

At Eichstätt in 1459 Eyb wrote three essays, preserved only in manuscript, all dealing with the subject of women.[20] *Clarissimarum feminarum laudacio* (Praise of Famous Ladies), whose title recalls Boccaccio's *De claris mulieribus*, a work much read in southern Germany at the time, presents the great deeds of historical women as models for others. Eyb aims to show that women have been of service to the world in matters moral, literary, and social. In contrast, *Invectiva in lenam* (Invective Against the Procuress), written three days after the *Laudacio*, sets out the wicked qualities of women. Since it is dedicated to the canons of Eichstätt, it is possible that Eyb wrote the piece after they objected to his one-sided glorification of women in the *Laudacio*. The third piece, *An viro sapienti uxor sit ducenda* (Whether a Wise Man Should Marry), in effect a Latin draft for his first treatise in the vernacular, *Ob einem manne sey zunemen ein eelichs weyb oder nicht* (Whether a Man Should Take a Wife or not), stands in the tradition of the *De re uxoria* (On Married Life) written by Francesco Barbaro on the occasion of the marriage of Lorenzo Medici in 1415.

Eyb's *Ehebüchlein* (Little Book on Marriage), as the German version of this work is generally called, treats the topic of marriage with dignity and refinement in a clear, concise, and fluent prose style that has often been regarded as among the best of the period. Why it was written is not known. Having due regard for theological, moral, and legal considerations, Eyb examines the social value and the joys and sorrows of marriage, coming down decisively (but with certain reservations) in favor of the institution. The Divine Order requires marriage for the propagation of mankind, and it should be contracted for God's glory. Marriage is essential for morality; without it human society would collapse. Although married life may be beset with many difficulties, it offers the recompense of joy in offspring and companionship. To illustrate his views Eyb weaves translations of two Renaissance novellas, *Marina*[21] and *Guiscardus und Sigismunda* — two of the best German translations of the period — into the fabric of the work. The second part of the book contains the chapters "Das lob der Ee" (In Praise of Marriage) and "Das lob der frawen" (In Praise of Women), in which he recapitulates all the arguments advanced earlier. The third part offers advice on the organization of weddings. Eyb then reflects on the transience and sinfulness of human life, countering this pessimistic tone finally with a translation of the medieval legend of Albanus under the heading "Das kein sunder verzwyfelen solle" (Lest a sinner despair).[22] Even though Eyb dedicated the work to the city council of Nuremberg, there is no evidence that he envisaged marriage as passing out of the control of the church into the hands of the civil authorities. The work's popularity is evident from the publication of no fewer than twelve editions between 1472 and 1540. It is the one book of Eyb's that has attracted widespread scholarly interest in recent years.

Eyb's other work in German is *Spiegel der Sitten* (Mirror of Virtues).[23] He completed it in May 1474 but was unable to see it into print before he died on 23 or 24 July 1475.[24] The work sets forth not only the virtues but the vices too, for people could avoid the latter only if they were alerted to them. The first part of the book (fifty-four chapters) deals with the Four Cardinal Virtues and the Seven Deadly Sins, attitudes to death, and the Last Things. The second (forty-one chapters) discusses all sorts and conditions of people, from kings and princes to merchants and peasants, widows and virgins, rich and poor. The individual chapters consist largely of quotations from ancient authors, loosely strung together, drawn from many of the same florilegia (gatherings of flowers, that is, collections) and late medieval scholastic texts used already in *Margarita poetica*.[25] By augmenting the patristic and medieval material with quotations from classical and humanist authors, Eyb endeavors to reconcile medieval views with those of Italian humanism.

The final part of *Spiegel der Sitten* consists of his translation of two plays of the Roman poet Plautus, *Menaechmi* and *Bacchides*, and of the *Philogenia* of Ugolino of Pisa.[26] Breathing the air of classical antiquity, Plautus's plays had to be thoroughly remodeled. Eyb did not aim to acquaint his readers with life in classical Rome; rather he wanted to recreate the works in the context of the cultural and moral conditions of fifteenth-century Germany. The classical names have been replaced by homely German ones (thus in *Bacchides* Chrysalus, Nicobus, Philoxenus, and Parasitus become Pentz, Utz, Kuntz, and Fritz), mythological references excised, and Latin proverbs replaced by German equivalents. The purpose of including the plays is explained in Eyb's preface to the *Spiegel der Sitten*: the reader, he says, should admire "die hübschait vnd süssigkait der wörter vnd die swärlichait der synnen vnd red vnd nit die fröhlichait vnd wollust der Comedien" (the beauty and sweetness of the words [a Petrarchan echo!] and the seriousness of the meaning and the dialogue but not the merriment or pleasure the comedies afford). These translations attracted attention in the sixteenth century: Hans Sachs produced a verse version of *Menaechmi* in 1540, and Martin Glaser based a Shrovetide play on Ugolino's *Philogenia* (printed 1552).

Eyb's importance as a translator lies in the fact that, even more so than Steinhöwel, he translated freely: in his own words, "nit als gar von worten zu

worten [. . .] sunder nach dem synn vnd mainung der materien als sy am
verstendlichisten vnd besten lauten mügen" (not word for word but according
to the sense and meaning of the matter in the way that they sound most intelligible and best). It is his striving after intelligibility and his command of popular idiom that have earned him the reputation of being one of the best
German prose writers before Luther.

Early German humanism is characterized by the mingling of medieval and
humanist traditions. It is not surprising, therefore, if we find elements of both
in the work of Eyb. Whereas Max Herrmann extols Eyb as the first German
humanist to embrace not only the external form but also the inner spirit of the
new learning, Joseph Hiller regards him more as a moralist in the medieval
mold, less a humanist as such.[27] The truth doubtless lies somewhere between
the two: in some respects, Eyb was indeed a latter-day medieval moralist, but
his immersion in the *studia humanitatis* of fifteenth-century Italy left an indelible mark on much of his writing, as is evident from his frequent mention in his
works of his various Italian teachers. Some would perhaps call him a Christian
humanist. However that may be, one suspects that Eyb would not recognize
himself under the modern designation of "writer": for him humanism was
essentially a way of serving God and the law, not a literary activity for its own
sake. Hiller's assessment of Eyb may serve perhaps as an appropriate epitaph:
"As a lawyer he wanted justice, as a writer, morality, as a cleric, sanctity."[28]

Niklas von Wyle

Like Steinhöwel and Eyb, Wyle too made a significant contribution to the
growing awareness in Germany of important Italian writers, yet he is their very
antithesis. Whereas both Steinhöwel and Eyb saw it as the translator's primary
task to convey the sense, rather than the style, of a passage, Wyle advocated
close adherence to the Latin source in order to promote a gradual improvement in German style. This should not be taken to imply personal animosity
between these three translators: Wyle generously acknowledged Steinhöwel as
someone whose mastery of the subtleties of rhetoric was greater than his own.
Steinhöwel, for his part, modestly claimed no creative ability, saying that he
merely wished to turn Latin into German:

> Eigen gedicht wer mir zeschwer /
> Latin zetütschen ist min ger.[29]

[To compose original poems is too demanding, my desire is to translate
Latin into German.]

Niklas von Wyle was born at Bremgarten, Aargau, Switzerland, probably
around 1415. He enrolled at the University of Vienna in October of 1430 and
received his bachelor's degree in January of 1433, which means that he was a
contemporary of Steinhöwel there.[30] He then taught and served for a time as
notary in Zurich, where the cultured patrician Felix Hemmerli (1388–
ca. 1460) was his mentor, before becoming *Stadtschreiber* (town clerk) at

Radolfzell on Lake Constance. In 1447 he held an appointment as clerk to the council of Nuremberg for a short period, which brought him into contact with the humanist-jurist and former pupil of the great philosopher Lorenzo Valla, Dr. Gregor Heimburg (1400–1472), and his circle. In February 1448 Wyle moved to Esslingen, near Stuttgart, where, in addition to training chancery clerks and teaching suitable young people stylish expression in speech and writing,[31] he was to serve as town clerk for some twenty-two years. In this position he bore major responsibility for the conduct of the town's business and administration and was charged with undertaking a number of delicate diplomatic missions.

Though his duties in Esslingen imposed heavy burdens on him and often necessitated lengthy absences from home,[32] he somehow also found time to cultivate contacts with aristocrats and scholars and to realize his intellectual ambitions. He claimed that the only leisure time he had was at Shrovetide and at the wine harvest — and indeed it seems it was precisely these periods that he used for writing. One of the important products of his years in Esslingen was his *Colores rethoricales* (Colors of Rhetoric), written between 1464 and 1469 but left unfinished; it is prefaced with a dedication to his brother-in-law, Dr. Georg Ehinger of Ulm. This treatise deals with some of the principles of rhetoric, according to the system of the *Rhetorica ad Herennium* (Rhetoric for Herennius), a work considered in the Middle Ages to have been written by Cicero. Wyle's immediate source was not the *Rhetorica ad Herennium* itself, however, but derived from the writings of the late medieval rhetorician Nikolaus von Dybin (d. before 1387), a professor of rhetoric. Wyle's work includes a number of model letters, most of them his own, to illustrate the various rhetorical devices. This compilation, which must have influenced the scribes who worked under him at Esslingen, shows that he had one foot in the camp of the late medieval tradition of *ars dictandi* (the art of formal letter writing), a skill needed by notaries, and the other in the emulation of the Italian humanists, who prized literary style.

The years in Esslingen were the most fruitful of Wyle's life. He was able to make the acquaintance of leading persons in the area who were receptive to humanistic endeavors, including Steinhöwel, but also Jakob Püterich von Reichertshausen (1400–1469), Antonius von Pforr (d. 1483), the Württemberg counselor Dr. Georg von Absberg, and the Württemberg chancellor Johann Fünfer. Furthermore, his frequent travels on official and diplomatic business not only brought him into contact with many of the leading princes in southwestern Germany but also took him no fewer than eight times to the imperial court at Vienna or Wiener Neustadt.

From 1459 on he repeatedly received official commissions from Margrave Charles I of Baden, representing him, for instance, in November that year at the Diet of Mantua, where he delivered a speech of welcome to Enea Silvio Piccolomini, who had meanwhile been elected Pope Pius II.[33] In 1463, in his capacity as chancellor of Katharina, the margravine of Baden and sister of Emperor Friedrich III, he spent several months at the imperial court at Wiener Neustadt. In 1469, accused of damaging the interests of Esslingen in his dealings over the patronage of the monastery at Weil, Wyle chose to flee the criticism. Availing himself of his influential contacts, he quickly found new employment in the administration of the court of Duke Ulrich of Württemberg at Stuttgart as deputy to Chancellor Fünfer. His last years proved largely uneventful. He died on 13 April 1479.

Among Wyle's many literary acquaintances the most important was doubtless that of Enea Silvio Piccolomini, who had been employed as secretary in the imperial chancery at Wiener Neustadt for several years in the 1440s. More than one hundred letters by Wyle are extant, some in German, others in Latin, some of them personal ones, others merely official; several dating from 1452–57 reveal his profound admiration of Enea Silvio.[34] The correspondence began in July 1452 after Enea Silvio had seen a letter Wyle had written to Michael Pfullendorf, a mutual friend. Enea Silvio wrote congratulating Wyle on the "caracteres rotundi" (rounded humanistic hand) in which the letter had been penned and rejoicing to note that Germany was acquiring classical eloquence.[35] Wyle responded saying that Enea Silvio's writings were to him more precious than gold. Shortly before Enea Silvio's death Wyle published the first collection of the humanist's letters to be issued in Germany: *Epistole Enee siluii Poete lauriati* (Letters of Enea Silvio, Poet Laureate).[36] The collection, to which Enea Silvio's *Eurialus et Lucretia* is appended, was intended as a model for students of Latin style. The correspondence with Enea Silvio reveals that Wyle was also a painter: he sent him a painting of St. Michael in 1452 and another of St. Christopher in 1453.[37]

Wyle made what was perhaps his second most significant literary acquaintance in 1455, when he established official connections with Mechthild (1418–82), Countess Palatine of the Rhine, a leading patroness of culture.[38] She and her son, Count Eberhard the Bearded of Württemberg (1445–96), who was married to an Italian princess of the Gonzaga family, along with her sister-in-law Margaret of Savoy, all became patrons of Wyle. Mechthild was a pious and learned woman who would later help to found the University of Freiburg im Breisgau in 1460 and, together with her son, the University of Tübingen in 1477. Wyle himself praises her as "ain grosse liebhaberin aller künste" (a great admirer of all the arts), and indeed her court at Rottenburg on the Neckar, near Tübingen, became a flourishing center of literary culture, which lasted until her death. Wyle dedicated a number of his translations to her.

It is above all for his *Translationen* (also called *Translatzen* or *Tütschungen*), first published by Konrad Fyner at Esslingen in 1478, that Wyle is remembered today. This collection of eighteen of his own translations was intended to provide a selection of outstanding examples of humanistic texts that could serve as models for others. As a collection the *Translationen* do not follow any strict plan or arrangement, though the fact that the first piece, the longest and most ambitious of them all, Enea Silvio's *Eurialus and Lucretia*, is dedicated to Mechthild is a clear indication of the respect and debt he felt he owed both to the author and to his own patroness. Overwhelmingly the collection comprises works of literary and stylistic interest by Italian humanists, especially Poggio Bracciolini and Enea Silvio, and overall it was designed to exemplify everything a budding German stylist needed to know about the rules of Latin rhetoric. Almost without exception these are texts that reflect the interests of early German humanists generally; Wyle's own personal predilections are found perhaps only in the piece by his erstwhile mentor Hemmerli and the passage from Petrarch, in which he finds his misfortune at Esslingen paralleled. The wide range of topics considered and the variety of forms represented here (letter, dialogue, speech, treatise, dream account, novella) also mark out the collection as characteristic of German humanism of the period.

Not the least of his aims in producing these translations was to use them for instructional purposes in the training of chancery scribes: above all, he wanted to show his pupils the correct use of language, including the proper use of punctuation. Since suitable stylistic models could, in his view, be found only among Latin writers, whether classical or humanist, it was essential to employ these to serve as models for German style. Thus, he strove to provide renderings of the Latin that were as faithful as possible to the originals, even though he risked introducing peculiarities of Latin syntax and word order into German and sacrificing immediate intelligibility. Nevertheless, he appeals to the authority of such stylists as Leonardo Bruni, Enea Silvio, and Gregor Heimburg in support of his assertion that perseverance and growing familiarity with the best style will result in a greater awareness, appreciation, and emulation of it. Whether he himself had read Bruni's *De studiis et litteris liber* is not clear, but at least he knew of it from Enea Silvio. Bruni and Enea Silvio expected of every student of rhetoric that he should read only books making the greatest linguistic demands; by reading authors who cultivated an elegant style, the student would himself imbibe stylistic elegance. In the preface to the *Translationen* Wyle notes with approval Heimburg's view,

> daz ain yetklich tütsch, daz usz guotem zierlichem vnd wol gesatzten latine gezogen vnd recht vnd wol getran[s]feryeret wer ouch guot zierlich tütsche vnd lobes wirdig haissen vnd sin müste, vnd nit wol verbessert werden möchte.

> [that any German deriving from good, elegant, and well-formulated Latin, correctly and well-translated, must perforce be good, elegant German and appreciated as such, and could not be improved upon].

Wyle's approach to translation is radically different from that of Steinhöwel and Eyb, but it is important to remember that his advice was primarily intended for legal clerks rather than for literary practitioners in the modern sense.[39] Through his method he hoped to respond to the challenge set him by Enea Silvio to encourage a renewal of style and rhetoric in Germany. He insists that his method is to translate the Latin "vf das genewest" (as closely as possible) without any thought of whether the result will be intelligible to "dem schlechten gemainen und unernieten man" (the simple, ordinary, unlettered man). He believes the reader will gradually become accustomed to the style, and since this is modeled on good Latin the inevitable outcome must be good German style. This view, of course, reflected the prevailing opinion that Latin, a classical language and the language used for the Scriptures, was superior to the vernacular — a view that would come to be seriously challenged in the Reformation.

Wyle's translations attracted immediate attention and seem to have been well received at the courts at Rottenburg, Baden, and Stuttgart, whose members had been brought up on medieval romances and the like. For them the attraction of his writings doubtless lay less in their style than in their novel subject matter and literary qualities; and indeed, from the point of view of posterity, his main importance lies in having made some of the literary monuments of Renaissance Italy available to a wider public north of the Alps. In his dedicatory prefaces Wyle shows why the texts are of special interest, and this information affords us considerable insights into the literary tastes of the courts of the time.[40]

A year before his death, in letters to Georg von Absberg and Hans Harscher of Ulm (Steinhöwel's brother-in-law), Wyle offered some personal insight into the motivation behind his publication. The aim of his *Translationen* was to ensure that his disciples might thereby be transformed into "wolgelert latinisch manne" (learned Latinists), and he hoped with his translation of the *Colores rethoricales* to provide "etwas nutzlichs vnd guotes daz notariate antreffend" (something useful and good concerning the work of a notary). Unfortunately, his translation of Boethius's *De consolatione philosophiae* (On the Consolation of Philosophy), said to have been highly praised by Absberg, has not come down to us.[41]

Wyle's influence as a writer is somewhat intangible, though it is clear that from about 1450 to 1470 he played an important role as a focus for humanistic endeavors in Swabia and northern Switzerland. Acting upon Enea Silvio's advice, he had cultivated a wide circle of like-minded friends. Scattered remarks in his correspondence suggest that he and his friends were actively engaged in copying and exchanging manuscripts of classical and humanist texts. In particular, Wyle was a pioneer in the translation of humanist authors (notably Enea Silvio), and his example was emulated by others, such as Michael Christan (fl. 1460–82) in Constance and Wilhelm von Hirnkofen (fl. 1478) in Nuremberg. His own translation of *Eurialus et Lucretia* remained one of the most widely read pieces of narrative prose in Germany for several decades. His latinizing style as a translator influenced, among others, Heinrich Österreicher (d. 1505), abbot of Schussenried, who translated Columella's *De re rustica* (On Agricultural Matters) into German in 1491, and Johann Gottfried, translator of Cicero and Lucian. Furthermore, Wyle influenced not only the clerks who worked directly under him at Esslingen but also subsequent generations of chancery scribes for whom his own letters provided models for imitation, through reproduction in various sixteenth-century handbooks on scribal practice.[42]

Parallel Lives, Convergent Aims

Optical illusion though it is, parallel furrows in a plowed field always appear to converge at a point in the distance. Something like this seems to apply to the three writers considered here. While they were plowing separate furrows, each with a distinct approach to rendering Latin texts, somehow their efforts all converged in a new and fresh attitude to translation. Though the fifteenth-century debate over a word-for-word or meaning-for-meaning approach to translation may seem sterile now, with hindsight we recognize that these opposing views were of immense significance as part of the background to the important question of the approach to translation of the Scriptures that would help to shape the Reformation.

Though there had been fourteen printed editions of a German translation of the Bible before Martin Luther completed his own rendering of the New Testament in September 1522, these were in many respects far from satisfactory. Luther's signal achievement was that he strove to render the Scriptures accurately into natural, idiomatic German, so that his version might serve not merely as an aid to understanding the original text but even as a substitute for it. The contrast was immediately apparent to Luther's biographer Johannes Mathesius (1504–65), who recalled how in his youth he had seen ein "vndeutsche deutsche Bibel [. . .] one zweiffel auß dem Latein verdeutscht, die war dunckel vnd finster" (an un-German German Bible, doubtless translated from Latin, which was dark and obscure).[43]

It is vital to see Luther's work in the broader context of contemporary translation theory and practice in Germany, since otherwise it is difficult to appreciate the tremendous impact his translation of the Scriptures had in Germany. While Wyle believed that the only way to improve the quality of German writing was to model it closely on the style of Latin, and whereas Steinhöwel and Eyb held that the chief aim was to render the sense of the original accurately — style was incidental if not immaterial — Luther struck a happy balance between these approaches. He asserted that fidelity to the sense of the original was paramount, especially in the case of Holy Scripture, and at the same time that it was essential to ensure that it was rendered into natural, idiomatic German.[44] Defending his method in his *Sendbrief von Dolmetschen* (Open Letter on Translating, 1530), Luther asserts that Latin, Greek, or Hebrew idiom is irrelevant; the important thing is naturalness of expression in the target language:

> den man mus nicht die buchstaben inn der lateinischen sprachen fragen / wie man sol Deutsch reden / wie diese esel thun / sondern / man mus die mutter jhm hause / die kinder auff der gassen / den gemeinen man auff dem marckt drumb fragen / vnd den selbigen auff das maul sehen / wie sie reden / vnd darnach dolmetzschen so verstehen sie es den / vnd mercken / das man Deutsch mit jn redet.[45]

> [One must not be guided by the literal Latin text to find out how to express things in German, as these [popish] asses do, but one should consult the mother in the house, the children in the street, the common man in the market place, and listen to how they speak, and translate accordingly; then they will understand it and recognize that you are talking German with them.]

Natural German idiom, homely proverbial expressions, alliterative phrases, and above all, outstanding rhythmic quality make Luther's Bible language every bit as influential in German cultural history as the language of the King James Bible has been in English.[46]

Heinrich Steinhöwel, Albrecht von Eyb, and Niklas von Wyle all died during the 1470s. They all made use of the new medium of printing. Though the Bible had already begun to be printed in German, they themselves had no direct involvement in this development, yet their ideas on the art of translation may be seen to have fed into new thinking about translation and about the status of the German language in the sixteenth century.

Notes

[1] Or simply as the *Pestbuch*, but actually entitled *Büchlein der ordnung* (Little Book of Arrangements [for health]) and also referred to as *Regiment der Gesundheit* (Regimen of Health) and *Regimen wider die Pestilenz* (Regimen of the Plague).

[2] Steinhöwel can be compared with Johann Hartlieb (fl. 1450), physician and translator at the court at Munich. On Hartlieb see Alfred Karnein, *De Amore deutsch: Der Tractatus des Andreas Capellanus in der Übersetzung Johann Hartliebs* (Munich: Beck, 1970), and Reinhard Pawis, *Johann Hartliebs "Alexander"* (Munich: Artemis, 1991).

[3] On Steinhöwel and the Zainer brothers see Peter Amelung, *Der Frühdruck im deutschen Südwesten 1473–1500* (Stuttgart: Hiersemann, 1979), and Peter Amelung, *Johann Zainer the Elder and Younger* (Los Angeles: Karmiole, 1985).

[4] Gerd Dicke, "Heinrich Steinhöwel," in *Verfasserlexikon: Die deutsche Literatur des Mittelalters*, 2nd ed., ed. Kurt Ruh et al. (Berlin: de Gruyter, 1978–), 3: cols. 258–78, here 275: "St[einhöwel] ist der bis auf die Zeit Luthers meistgelesene Autor dt. Sprache."

[5] For other works uncertainly attributed to him see Dicke, "Heinrich Steinhöwel," cols. 273–75.

[6] *Gesamtkatalog der Wiegendrucke* (Leipzig: Hiersemann, 1925–), nos. 3163 and 6687, respectively.

[7] Günther Zainer's 1471 edition was followed by another in about 1473; two by Johann Zainer at Ulm during this same time; nine fifteenth-century printings; and at least eleven more in the sixteenth century. In addition to these separate printings Steinhöwel's translation was published together with other texts. On his *Griseldis* see Christa Bertelsmeier-Kierst, *"Griseldis" in Deutschland: Studien zu Steinhöwel und Arigo* (Heidelberg: Winter, 1988).

[8] Steinhöwel translated ninety-eight of the 104 lives related by Boccaccio (omitting nos. 73, 74, 81, 84, 103, and 104) but also adds one (no. 46) taken from Livy.

[9] Walter Borvitz's analysis of Steinhöwel's style of translation from the Latin original shows that he produced German sentences that are indeed "schlecht und verstentlich" (straightforward and intelligible), as he put it in his *Esopus*. He preferred the concrete to the abstract. Latin subordinate clauses are turned into main sentences, prepositional phrases become adverbs. The text is slimmed down or expanded according to the sense, contrasts implied in the Latin are sharpened or stressed. In short, there is almost no

sentence in Steinhöwel's translations that has not been changed in some way. Borvitz, *Die Übersetzungstechnik Heinrich Steinhöwels, dargestellt auf Grund seiner Verdeutschung des "Speculum vitae humanae" von Rodericus Zamorensis* (Halle/Salle: Niemeyer, 1914).

[10] Zamorensis' real name was Rodrigo Sánchez de Arévalo. Working from Günther Zainer's second edition of the Latin original, published at Augsburg in 1471, Steinhöwel completed the first part of his translation in 1473 and the second in 1474. His autograph manuscript, used by Günther Zainer as printer's copy for his edition published in 1475, still survives: Munich, Bayerische Staatsbibliothek, Cgm. 1137. Steinhöwel's manuscript is bound up with the printed edition of Niklas von Wyle's *Translationen*, a part of Steinhöwel's Aesop translation (in manuscript), and other material. This manuscript was used by Borvitz as the basis of his study, *Die Übersetzungstechnik Heinrich Steinhöwels*.

[11] Steinhöwel's influence on Aesop reception in Germany was considerable — the last edition of his text appeared in 1730. See Peter Amelung's commentary to the facsimile edition, *Der Ulmer Aesop von 1476/77: Äsops Leben und Fabeln sowie Fabeln und Schwänke anderer Herkunft: Hrsg. und ins Deutsche übersetzt von Heinrich Steinhöwel* (Ludwigsburg: Edition Libri illustri, 1995). For an authoritative and detailed analysis see Gerd Dicke, *Heinrich Steinhöwels "Esopus" und seine Fortsetzer: Untersuchungen zu einem Bucherfolg der Frühdruckzeit* (Tübingen: Niemeyer, 1994).

[12] Steinhöwel's idea-for-idea concept, though attributed by him to Horace, in fact derives from St. Jerome, translator of the Vulgate Latin version of the Bible, who readily acknowledged that, in translating from Greek into Latin, he had not rendered the text "word for word, but rather sense for sense." Steinhöwel claims to be quoting Horace but is in fact conflating Horace and Jerome. *Sancti Eusebii Hieronymi epistulae*, ed. Isidorus Hilberg, 2nd ed., Corpus Scriptorum Ecclesiasticorum Latinorum 54 (Vienna: Verlag der Österreichischen Akademie der Wissenschaften, 1996), I:508, Ep. LVII, 5, 2. On this see Werner Schwarz, "Translation into German in the fifteenth century," *The Modern Language Review* 39 (1944): 368–73.

[13] The dedication is reproduced in full in Borvitz, *Übersetzungstechnik*, 144–46, who draws attention to the fact that the ideas it contains are hardly original. The Horace reference is to *De arte poetica*, 133–34: "Nec verbo verbum curabis reddere fidus interpres" (You shall not aim to render word for word, faithful translator). Fidelity in rendering the sense of a text and the ideas it contains is the prime consideration, and more important than precise adherence to the linguistic form. What the Roman poet had actually meant was "You should be unlike a slavish translator — you should not render word for word." That is, whereas Horace was merely saying a slavish translation will not *necessarily* be a good translation, Steinhöwel asserts that a word-for-word translation can *never* be a good one. Furthermore, Horace actually says nothing of the *sense* of a passage.

[14] Thus we may suspect his hand at work behind Zainer's publication of the pseudonymous "Arigo's" German translation of Boccaccio's *Decamerone*. At one time the unidentified Arigo was thought to be Steinhöwel himself, but this is improbable, not least because Steinhöwel seems only to have translated from Latin, not from Italian. On the still unresolved problem of the identity of "Arigo" see Bertelsmeier-Kierst, *"Griseldis" in Deutschland*; Joachim Theisen, *Arigos Decameron: Übersetzungsstrategie und poetologisches Konzept* (Tübinger: Francke, 1996), and Lorenz Böninger, "Richercha sugli inizi della stampa fiorentina (1471–1473)," *La Bibliofila* 105 (2003): 225–48.

[15] For the contents of this library see Joseph Anthony Hiller, *Albrecht von Eyb: A Medieval Moralist* (1939; repr., New York: AMS Press, 1970). Eyb's copy of Anton

Koberger's Nuremberg edition of Boethius's *De consolatione philosophiae* is now in the British Library, London.

[16] The manuscript is in Gotha in the Forschungs- und Landesbibliothek, Ms. 217.

[17] Whether the second piece might represent a retraction or revocation of the first we cannot be certain. See William Hammer, "Albrecht von Eyb, Eulogist of Bamberg," *Germanic Review* 17 (1942): 14–19.

[18] Among them are pieces by Antonio Beccadelli, Cardinal Bessarion, Giovanni Lamola, Poggio Bracciolini, and four by Eyb himself (nos. 1, 16, 17, 30).

[19] See Hans Baron, ed., *Leonardo Bruni Aretino: Humanistisch-philosophische Schriften*, Quellen zur Geistesgeschichte des Mittelalters und der Renaissance 1 (Leipzig: Teubner, 1928), 5–19.

[20] For details of the manuscript see *Verfasserlexikon*, 1: col. 183.

[21] See Max Herrmann, "Die lateinische Marina," *Vierteljahrsschrift für Literaturgeschichte* 3 (1890): 1–27.

[22] This is the story of a sinful saint. The son of an incestuous union of a widower emperor and his daughter, Albanus, put out as a baby to die, is found by the childless king of Hungary who brings him up as his heir and marries him to the emperor's daughter, none other than Albanus's own mother. Albanus kills his father and mother and repents in solitude. He is murdered and his corpse occasions miraculous cures. See *Verfasserlexikon*, 1: cols. 106–8, and especially Karin Morvay, *Die Albanuslegende: Deutsche Fassungen und ihre Beziehungen zur lateinischen Überlieferung*, Medium Aevum 32 (Munich: Fink, 1977).

[23] Eyb has also been credited, but wrongly, with authorship of an anonymous version of Boccaccio's story of Griselda (*Decamerone*, X, 10). See Hans-Hugo Steinhoff, "Kein Albrecht von Eyb: Eine 'Grisardis'-Handschrift aus Philadelphia," *Zeitschrift für deutsches Altertum* 113 (1984): 132–35.

[24] It remained unpublished until his nephew, Prince-Bishop Gabriel von Eyb, commissioned the Eichstätt canon Johann Huff to prepare it for press. Huff arranged with the Augsburg publisher Johannes Rynmann to have it printed by Johann Otmar in that city, where it appeared in September 1511.

[25] Eyb relied partly on manuscripts from his own library and partly also on books obtained from elsewhere. For details see Gerhard Klecha, ed., *Albrecht von Eyb, Spiegel der Sitten* (Berlin: Schmidt, 1989).

[26] Eyb did not originally intend to include the *Bacchides* in the *Spiegel der Sitten*; it was added by Johann Huff.

[27] Hermann, "Die lateinische Marina"; Hiller says that Eyb was "a medieval moralist, a medieval thinker, rather than a 'humanist'" in *Albrecht von Eyb*, xvi.

[28] Hiller, *Albrecht von Eyb*, 29.

[29] From the preface to *Apollonius*. See Barbara Weinmayer, *Studien zur Gebrauchssituation früher deutscher Druckprosa* (Munich: Artemis, 1982), 94.

[30] See Rolf Schwenk, *Vorarbeiten zu einer Biographie des Niklas von Wyle und zu einer kritischen Ausgabe seiner ersten Translatze* (Göppingen: Kümmerle, 1978), 45–50. Unlike Steinhöwel and Wyle, Eyb never studied at Vienna, but Schwenk (51) notes that Albrecht's nephew Sigismund von Eyb enrolled there in 1435, which may just possibly have led to some contact between Albrecht and the other two translators.

[31] Schwenk, *Vorarbeiten*, 401–2, gives a list of Wyle's known pupils.

[32] Visits to Vienna alone account for nearly two years. For full details of Wyle's travels during the period when he held office at Esslingen (1448–69) see Schwenk, *Vorarbeiten*, 61–174.

[33] The address was published by Jakob Baechtold, in *Zeitschrift für Vergleichende Litteraturgeschichte und Renaissance-Litteratur*, Neue Folge, 1 (1887/88): 248–50.

[34] Wyle's extant papers are somewhat scattered; important manuscripts may be found in the Zentralbibliothek of Zurich; others are in the Dominican College Library in Washington, DC.

[35] Rudolf Wolkan, *Der Briefwechsel des Eneas Silvius Piccolomini* (Vienna: Hölder, 1909–18), 3:98–101 (no. 47). Enea had expressed similar hopes for the future in his letter of 31 January 1449 to Gregor Heimburg, in 2:79–81 (no. 25).

[36] Probably printed by Michael Greyff at Reutlingen. See Konrad Haebler, "Die Drucke der Briefsammlungen des Aeneas Silvius," *Gutenberg-Jahrbuch* 14 (1939): 138–52.

[37] See Wolkan, *Briefwechsel*, 3:116–17 (no. 58) and 438–39 (no. 251).

[38] On Mechthild see Renata Kruska, *Mechthild von der Pfalz: Im Spannungsfeld von Geschichte und Literatur*, Europäische Hochschulschriften, ser. I, vol. 1111 (Frankfurt am Main: Lang, 1989), and Martina Backes, *Das literarische Leben am kurpfälzischen Hof zu Heidelberg im 15. Jahrhundert*, Hermaea 58 (Tübingen: Niemeyer, 1992), 185–90.

[39] It has been declared to be "misguided and eccentric." Erich John Morrall, "'Selbstmord und Amor Illicitus' in der Übersetzungsliteratur von Niklas von Wyle, Arigo, Albrecht von Eyb und Johann Sieder," *Zeitschrift für deutsche Philologie* 117 (1998): 381–98.

[40] Originally the translations will have been presented to their respective dedicatees as manuscripts; the 1478 collected edition of the *Translationen*, however, was not intended for the small sophisticated court circles but for a somewhat wider public. Later, when printers in Strasbourg, Ulm, Augsburg, and Cologne brought out editions of individual texts from the collection, the ones they selected were the piquant novellas (nos. 1, 2, 3, and 13). In particular, the fascination of *Eurialus et Lucretia*, a psychological description of an illicit love impeded by social barriers, is evident from the story's subsequent popularity (some eleven separate editions between 1478 and 1594). On the popularity of such novellas see Morrall, "'Selbstmord und Amor Illicitus.'"

[41] Of these projects only the first was realized, and even that only in part, for when the *Translationen* came out in 1478 the Latin texts were not included. Only a portion of the *Colores rethoricales* appeared, and even then only half a century after his death.

[42] These included the anonymous *Formulare und deutsche Rhethorica* (Formulary and German Rhetoric, 1501), Alexander Hugen's *Rethorica und Formularium Teütsch* (Rhetoric and German Formulary, 1528), and Johann Elias Meichsner's *Hoch oder gemainer Teütscher Nation Formular* (Formulary of the Upper or General German Nation, ca. 1560). See Paul Joachimsohn, "Aus der Vorgeschichte des 'Formulare und deutsche Rhetorica,'" *Zeitschrift für deutsches Altertum* 37 (1893): 24–121.

[43] Johannes Mathesius, *Ausgewählte Werke*, vol. 3, *Luthers Leben in Predigten*, ed. Georg Loesche (Prague: Bellmann, 1906), 314. For a discussion of how Luther's Bible contributed to the standardization of German in the early modern period see elsewhere in this volume the chapter by Renate Born.

[44] Consider, for example, the woodenness of the literal translation of Matt. 6:26 (KJV: "Behold the fowls of the air: for they sow not, neither do they reap, nor gather into barns; yet your heavenly Father feedeth them") in Anton Koberger's Nuremberg Bible

of 1483, the year of Luther's birth: "Seht an die vögel des hymels. wann sy seen noch schneyden nit. noch sameln in den kasten. und ewer hymlischer vater füret sy." Compare with this the rhythm and melody of Luther's final version of 1545: "Sehet die Vogel unter dem Himel an / Sie seen nicht / sie erndten nicht / sie samlen nicht in die Schewnen / Und ewer himlischer Vater neeret sie doch."

[45] Martin Luther, *Werke* (Weimar 1883–1983), 30, ii: 637.

[46] For an assessment of Luther's place in the early history of Bible translation in Germany see John L. Flood, "Martin Luther's Bible Translation in its German and European Context," in *The Bible in the Renaissance*, ed. Richard Griffiths (Aldershot: Ashgate, 2001), 45–70.

Parallel Lives: Desiderius Erasmus and Martin Bucer

Laurel Carrington

THE PAIRING OF DESIDERIUS ERASMUS (1467/69–1536) AND MARTIN BUCER (1491–1551) presents an opportunity to view the lives of two men who had much in common, yet whose paths ultimately led them in radically different directions. Erasmus had a major influence on the young Bucer, who never lost his admiration for the older man despite later disagreements. Both entered monasteries in their early years, only to take their leave once they realized that the monastic life was not their true calling. Both devoted a large part of their lives to the cause of reform in Christendom. Temperamentally averse to divisive controversy, both sought reconciliation of the bitter conflicts that engulfed Europe during their lifetimes.

Erasmus, however, maintained his loyalty to the Roman church, whereas Bucer became the leader of the evangelical reform in Strasbourg. The consequence was that these two men, alike in so many ways, stood on opposite sides of sixteenth-century Europe's confessional fault-line, a fact that would provoke a vitriolic exchange toward the end of Erasmus's life. We might well wonder what could have brought two men of irenic temperament to this impasse. The outcome of their relationship is indicative of how poisonous the environment had become, to the point that even the best efforts at mediation and conciliation could not prevail. A close comparison of these two lives may help us better understand the lines of convergence and divergence that marked early sixteenth-century religion, scholarship, and politics.

Desiderius Erasmus of Rotterdam

Erasmus was born out of wedlock in Rotterdam in either 1467 or 1469, the son of a physician's daughter and a priest.[1] The region in which Erasmus spent his youth was marked by political instability resulting from power struggles among Duke Charles the Daring of Burgundy (1433–77), King Louis XI of France (1423–83), and Habsburg Maximilian I (1459–1519), later Holy Roman emperor.[2] There were also recurrent appearances of the dreaded Black Death, which first devastated Europe in the years between 1347 and 1350.[3]

In the century following the outbreak of the plague, which gave constant reminder of life's fragility, Europeans became exceptionally pious. Religion for most people meant receiving the sacraments and participating in a complex web of centuries-old customs: pilgrimages, prayers and masses for the dead, cults of the saints, veneration of relics, and rituals of penance. The church in its role as intermediary between heaven and earth had enormous power, and yet not all people were satisfied with what it offered them; many sought outlets for their spiritual longings beyond ordinary channels through lay associations and contact with charismatic preachers.[4] One significant manifestation of this longing in the Netherlands was the Devotio Moderna. Founded by Gerard Groote (d. 1384), the Devotio Moderna was a movement of pious clergy and laymen calling themselves the Brethren of the Common Life, who lived communally and pursued a life of prayer, fasting, and charitable works. As reflected in the *Imitatio Christi* (1418) of Thomas à Kempis (d. 1471), the movement stressed simplicity of life and a piety grounded in the love of God, in contrast to the highly sophisticated scholastic theology of the universities.[5]

Despite their awkward social circumstances, Erasmus's parents collaborated in caring for him and his older brother, Pieter.[6] Erasmus entered school first in Gouda and then in Deventer, where he remained between 1475 and 1483. Here he encountered teachers who were members of the Brethren of the Common Life, and throughout his life Erasmus would show the influence of their preference for spiritual simplicity over elaborate ceremony and scholastic theology. He also received there an early introduction to humanist learning: Alexander Hegius (1433–98), the school's headmaster from 1483, was acquainted with the renowned humanist Rudolf Agricola (Roelof Huesman, 1444–85), who paid a visit to the school during Erasmus's time there.[7] The humanist movement emphasized the importance of rhetorical skill, in contrast to abstract philosophy or systematic theology, as the means by which readers and listeners could be inspired to a love for what is good. To the humanists, knowledge pursued in isolation was sterile; in its place, they advocated a focus on knowledge that shaped one's moral life. The poets, historians, and moral philosophers of the ancient world played a vital role in this process, both in their elevating themes and their stylistic elegance. From this time on, Erasmus became devoted to literature and to learning to write with elegance and skill.

Erasmus suffered a severe crisis in the winter of 1483–84 with the death of his mother to the plague and the subsequent death of his father in Gouda. He and his brother were left to the care of guardians, whom Erasmus later bitterly accused of pressuring the boys to join a monastery. He entered the Augustinian monastery in Steyn in about 1487 and remained there for five years, a time he later described as one of deep unhappiness. Nevertheless, in Steyn he developed epistolary friendships with a circle of monks who shared his passion for the classics. In *De contemptu mundi* (On the Contempt for the World), not published until 1521 though probably composed in Steyn, Erasmus even celebrates the benefits of monastic life. The abbey's library provided an impressive assortment of works by both ancient writers and Italian humanists. In 1488, Erasmus composed a digest of Lorenzo Valla's *Elegantiae*, a grammatical analysis of Latin style, which he had encountered in his school days. In this six-volume work, Valla (1405–57), an Italian linguist and moral philosopher, had hoped to restore the beauty and clarity of the Latin language as a corrective to the grammatical distortions of Aristotelian and scholastic metaphysics. Valla was to exert a great influence on Erasmus's thinking and style. This is particularly evident in the case of Valla's *In Novum Testamentum ex divorsorum utriusque linguae codicum collatione adnotationes* (Annotations on the New Testament Collected from Various Codices in Each Language, ca. 1455), which approached interpretation of scripture through a linguistic analysis of the Greek text.

Shortly after his ordination, Erasmus received permission to serve as personal secretary to Hendrick van Bergen (1449–1502), member of a noble Burgundian family and bishop of Cambrai, who was planning to travel to Rome. Erasmus would never return to extended residence in Steyn, though it was not until 1517 that the Vatican officially released him from his vows. His new patron had close connections to the brilliant and worldly Burgundian court, but Erasmus found courtly culture distasteful. When it became clear that the promised trip to Rome was not going to materialize, he went instead to Paris in 1495 and enrolled in the university as a student of theology, where he remained for four years. Here he had his first public exposure in the world of letters with his introductory letter to a work by the humanist poet Robert Gaguin (1423–1501). The scholastic curriculum at the university held no interest for him.

In Paris, Erasmus supported himself as a tutor of Latin. Out of his tutoring experience he began compiling materials that he would eventually publish as the *Colloquia familiaria*, a collection of dialogues in a lively and often humorous style intended to introduce students to conversational Latin. The dialogues were not published until 1518; their popularity encouraged Erasmus to bring out new and expanded editions up until 1533. In this and in all of his pedagogical works, he sought to inspire his pupils to a love of learning by making the process pleasurable rather than onerous. As he added to the collection over the years, the dialogues became a framework for expressing his views on significant ethical and religious questions. In the dialogue *Peregrinatio religionis ergo* (A Pilgrimage for Religion's Sake), Erasmus is caustic in his treatment of those who abandon their responsibilities by going on pilgrimages rather than maintaining a Christian life in their own homes and communities. In another colloquy, *Proci et Puellae* (Suitors and Girls, translated as *Courtship*), he depicts a young suitor successfully persuading his sweetheart to choose marriage over her wrongheaded desire to enter a convent. Several other colloquies along the same lines uphold not only the social but also the spiritual superiority of marriage over virginity.

While in Paris he published *Adagiorum Collectanea* (A Collection of Adages, 1500), a compilation of 818 proverbs or commonplaces from ancient literature, designed to help orators and writers in developing their subjects using classical allusions.[8] Such commonplaces were extremely important to humanist writers, who would use them in several ways: as ornaments to enhance their speech, as a means of displaying their erudition, and as support for the positions they were expounding. Erasmus presents each adage along with a commentary on its meaning, a discussion of its origin, and a sample of its occurrences in the writings of the ancient authors. In putting his extraordinary erudition at the service of other writers, Erasmus placed a broad range of ancient knowledge at their ready disposal. Almost immediately after the first edition appeared he began work on a greatly enlarged edition, which he published in 1508 as *Adagiorum Chiliades* (Thousands of Adages), containing 3,260 adages, many of them in Greek, with expanded commentary. New editions appeared in 1515, 1517–18, 1520, 1526, 1528, and finally in 1533 with a collection of 4,151 adages. As this work grew over the course of Erasmus's career, it came to be an indispensable resource for students of the ancient world.

It was during his time in Paris that Erasmus began writing the *Enchiridion militis christiani* (The Handbook of the Christian Soldier, 1503), a guide to a pious life, which many readers consider one of the consummate expressions of Christian humanism. The work expresses a positive view of human nature, maintaining that people can be brought to embrace the love of Christ through proper instruction in spite of the disruption wrought by sin. The first step in accomplishing this goal is the careful reading of the language of scripture, interpreting it allegorically rather than literally. Pagan literature is valuable in teaching readers to do this because of the richness of its figurative language. Next, students must turn to renowned theologians for help in interpreting the theological lessons embedded in the text. After the apostle Paul, the interpreters Erasmus most admired were the church fathers Origen, Ambrose, Jerome, and Augustine.[9] Erasmus disparages the Scholastics: "video enim neotericos Theologos litterae nimium libenter inhaerere, et captiosis quibusdam argutiis, magis quam eruendis mysteriis operam dare, quasi vero non vere dixerit Paulus, legem nostram spiritualem esse" (I notice that modern theologians are too willing to stick to the letter and give their attention to sophistic subtleties rather than to the elucidation of the mysteries, as if Paul were not right in saying that our law is spiritual).[10]

In May 1499, Erasmus was able to travel to England under the patronage of one of his students, the young English aristocrat Lord Mountjoy. This visit marked a turning point in his life, for it was there that he made the acquaintance of two remarkable men, Thomas More (1478–1535) and John Colet (1467–1519), who would become lifelong friends and influences. More, a young lawyer and scholar with proficiency in Greek, rose to the position of lord chancellor in 1529, only to lose his life some six years later for his refusal to sign the Act of Succession.[11] At the time of Erasmus's visit, John Colet — later revered as the founder of St. Paul's school in London — was giving lectures at Oxford on the epistles of Paul. These encounters inspired Erasmus to turn his focus to the study of scripture, which he began by learning Greek. Upon returning to the Continent in 1501 he embarked on an intense study of Greek, and in 1506, when he finally made his long-awaited journey to Italy, he was able to continue these studies in the land that boasted the best teachers in Europe.[12] He obtained his doctorate at the University of Turin in September 1506, although, as he claimed in a letter to a friend, he had never aspired to become a doctor of letters.[13] He remained in Italy for almost three years, spending most of 1508 in Venice at the home of the printer Aldus Manutius (1449–1515), founder of the renowned Aldine press.[14] Here Erasmus published the first expanded edition of the *Adagia* in addition to pursuing his study of Greek.

In 1509, he received news from England of the accession of King Henry VIII (1491–1547), along with an invitation, again from Lord Mountjoy, to return to that country. The young king, whom Erasmus had met on his first visit and with whom he had since corresponded, had shown himself to be highly favorable to humanistic studies, and Erasmus's friends looked with enthusiasm to a future that would bring a flowering of patronage for humanistic learning.[15] As Erasmus traveled northward he developed a plan for a satirical oration to dedicate to his friend Thomas More, the *Moriae encomium* (Praise of Folly), which involves a pun on More's name (Greek *moria* "folly"). First published in 1511, it went through thirty-six editions during Erasmus's lifetime, delighting many readers but enraging many others.

The most famous of Erasmus's books, the *Moriae encomium* was inspired in part by the dialogues of the Greek satirist Lucian (ca. A.D. 120–after 180), taking the form of an ironic oration offered by the goddess Folly in praise of herself. At the beginning, Folly describes herself as the most widely worshiped (if not the most acknowledged) of all the gods, and the one who does the most to enhance human life. It is she who adds the touch of self-delusion that allows social bonds to flourish, for people would not be able to tolerate their spouses, their friends, or anyone else with whom they associated, "nisi vicissim inter sese nunc errant, nunc adulentur, nunc prudentes conniveant, nunc aliquot stulticiae melle sese deliniant" (if in their relations with one another they did not sometimes err, sometimes flatter, sometimes wisely overlook things, sometimes soothe themselves with the sweet salve of folly.)[16] Most of all, everyone needs the folly of self-love:

> Et ô singularem naturae sollicitudinem, ut in tanta rerum varietate paria fecit omnia! Ubi dotibus suis nonihil detraxit, ibi plusculum Philautiae solet addere, qunquam hoc ipsum stulte profecto dixi, cum haec ipsa dos sit vel maxima.[17]

> [Oh, the extraordinary solicitude of Nature! How marvelously she manages to equalize everything, even in the midst of such teeming variety! Wherever she withholds some of her gifts, just there she will add a little more self-love — but here I have made a mistake that is foolish indeed, since self-love is the greatest gift of all.]

The oration shifts from this initial playful and gentle acknowledgement of human foibles to biting satire, taking aim at warmongering monarchs, flattering advisers, greedy churchmen, hypocritical monks, and quarrelsome theologians. Here, foolishness is no longer life's mainstay, but rather its blight. No one escapes Folly's caustic tongue, least of all those who pretend to be most knowledgeable about the faith:

> Atque interim dum haec nugantur in scholis, existimant sese universam ecclesiam, alioqui ruituram, non aliter syllogismorum fulcire tibicinibus quam Atlas coelum humeris sustinet apud Poetas.[18]

[At the same time, while they are talking nonsense in the schools, they
think they are supporting the universal church, which otherwise would
collapse, with their syllogistic props in much the same way that Atlas, in
the mythology of the poets, holds up the world on his shoulders.]

The final segment, however, shows us yet another version of Folly: the foolishness of the cross. How could it be that Christ, the incarnate God, could
reject everything the world holds dear, including life itself? Yet those who
know Christ best are prepared to do the same. Folly ultimately becomes rhap-
sodic as she invokes the sublime foolishness of the mystic union with God:
"Hoc igitur quibus sentire licuit (contingit autem prepaucis), ii patiuntur quid-
dam dementiae simillimum" (So those who are granted a foretaste of this —
and very few have the good fortune — experience something which is very like
madness).[19]

During the next few years Erasmus was at the height of his influence and
productivity. His 1515 edition of the *Adagia* expands several of the adages
into lengthy essays on politics, society, and religion. One example is *Dulce bellum inexpertis* (War is sweet to those who do not know it). Erasmus argues
that of all things, war is the most vicious and contrary to the teachings of
Christ, wreaking incalculable destruction; and yet, all around him people rush
to war for frivolous reasons. This adage is one of the two most important
expressions of Erasmus's pacifism. The other, perhaps the profoundest
European argument for peace before Kant's *Zum ewigen Frieden* (Perpetual
Peace, 1795), is the book-length mock oration *Querela Pacis* (Complaint of
Peace, 1517). In this work, personified Peace deplores her neglect by virtually all of humanity. The most famous of the adages, the *Sileni Alcibiadis*
(Silenus of Alcibiadis), develops an image taken from Plato's *Symposium* that
Erasmus also introduces in the *Moria*: a figurine consisting of the Silenus figure of antiquity, appearing on the outside to be the image of a drunken satyr
but bearing within the image of a god.[20] Christ likewise at first glance is the
obscure son of a carpenter and died a shameful death; but underneath this
surface lie the sublimity of the incarnation and the redemptive power of the
cross.

The most significant work of this period, however, is the *Novum
Testamentum*, first published in March 1516 as the *Novum instrumentum*.
Erasmus had been collecting notes on the text of the New Testament for
years, dating back to his publication of Valla's *Adnotationes* in 1505. What
guided him was the belief that a true understanding of the Bible depended on
two things: a manuscript based on the most accurate ancient sources, and
knowledge of the historical and linguistic context of scripture. Erasmus
accordingly collected a set of nine Greek manuscripts, which he painstakingly
compared, noting discrepancies and using his philological expertise to discern
the likeliest reading. He also provided his own Latin translation of this new
edition of the New Testament, as an alternative to the traditional Vulgate.
The Greek text, set side by side, contains extensive notes explaining his
readings.[21]

The appearance of this work created a furor among those theologians who believed that Erasmus was tampering with sacred writings. The Vulgate, completed in the early fifth century by St. Jerome (ca. 340/42–420), was the translation officially sanctioned by the Roman church, and for Erasmus to suggest that it might be faulty was to undermine the foundation of Holy Writ itself. In addition, some critics took detailed exception to his editorial decisions. These controversies were a continuing source of frustration for Erasmus, and he responded by publishing expanded annotations in updated editions in 1519, 1522, 1527, and 1535, as well as by composing lengthy *apologiae* aimed at individual critics.[22] In his introductions to the *Novum Testamentum* — particularly the *Paraclesis* (Exhortation) to the original 1516 edition — and in the *Ratio seu methodus compendio perveniendi ad veram theologiam* (Knowledge and Method of Arriving in Brief Manner at a True Theology), a treatise on method composed in 1518 and appended to the 1519 edition, he explained his underlying philosophy and methodological principles.[23]

In addition to the *Novum Testamentum*, Erasmus published a series of paraphrases (the *Paraphrasis*) on almost all of the New Testament and, over the following decade and a half, an extensive set of critical editions of the works of the church fathers. These included Jerome (1516, in nine volumes), Cyprian (1520), Arnobius the Younger (1522), Hilary of Poitiers (1523), Irenaeus (1526, with Latin translation), Ambrose (1527), Augustine (1528, in ten volumes), Chrysostom (1530, with Latin translation), and Origen (with Latin translation; incomplete). In 1518, he republished the *Enchiridion*. Its original appearance had received small notice, but with Erasmus's established celebrity the new edition became a major breakthrough in its expression of his approach to reform and renewal in the church as well as for its focus on the inner disposition of the worshiper over the outer details of ceremonies.[24] In the *Colloquia*, which, as noted above, presented an ever-broadening critique of the popular religious practices of his time, Erasmus repeatedly takes aim at those who believe that extended pilgrimages, the cult of relics, and prayers to saints for special favors are more important than reflecting Christ's core teachings in one's personal life, above all, the teachings of Christian love, humility, and obedience to the will of God.

It is in the *Paraclesis*, however, that Erasmus offers his most compelling rendition of what he calls the *philosophia Christi*. In the first place, all things in scripture have their basis in Christ, who is the true teacher of heavenly wisdom.[25] Further, the inner life takes primacy over the details of doctrine or ceremony: "Hoc Philosophiae genus in affectibus situm verius, quam in syllogismis, vita est magis quam disputatio, afflatus potius quam eruditio, transformatio magis quam ratio" (In this kind of philosophy, located as it is more truly in the disposition of the mind than in syllogisms, life means more than debate, inspiration is preferable to erudition, transformation is a more important matter than intellectual comprehension).[26] Statements such as these would inspire a younger generation to carry out reforms that would ultimately bring Erasmus to a state of bewilderment, bitterness, and isolation.

Martin Bucer

In the summer of 1514, during a Rhine journey to Basel, Erasmus stopped in the imperial free city of Strasbourg, where he was honored by members of the town's literary circle, including the renowned writer of *Das Narrenschiff* (Ship of Fools, 1494), Sebastian Brant.[27] At his next stop in Sélestat, a small town just south of Strasbourg, he received an equally warm reception. Sélestat may have been small, but it was no backwater, for it too boasted a circle of humanist scholars that overlapped with the group at Strasbourg, and in addition a first-rate Latin school. At the center of both groups was the gentleman scholar Jacob Wimpfeling (1450–1528), who advocated a conservative reform program that was strongly influenced by Erasmus, combining elements of humanist ethical philosophy and the piety of the Devotio Moderna. This is the region where Martin Bucer began his life at about the time Erasmus was taking leave of his monastery.[28]

Our knowledge of Bucer's birth and early years is limited by a lack of primary sources. His childhood, while less disadvantageous than that of Erasmus, was equally modest in material terms. He was born in Sélestat on 11 November 1491 to the artisan Nicholas Butzer and his wife Eva. When Martin was around ten years old his parents moved to Strasbourg, leaving him in Sélestat in the care of his grandfather. Given his strong aptitude for learning, it is probable that he was sent to the Latin school, which had ties to the Brethren of the Common Life and to the school in Deventer where Erasmus had been educated.

Like Erasmus, Bucer entered monastic life in adolescence, joining the Dominican Order in 1506 as a means of continuing his education. Although he discovered that his interests did not lie with the scholastic theology that dominated the order, he nonetheless studied the works of Aristotle and Thomas Aquinas assiduously. Some ten years later, in January 1517 — at the very time when Erasmus was becoming renowned as Europe's leading intellectual — Bucer obtained a transfer to the monastery at Heidelberg. He enrolled at the city's university and became acquainted with the second generation of humanist scholars in residence there. These men were continuing the tradition established by the famous early humanists Rudolf Agricola and Conrad Celtis. Despite his fellow Dominicans' bitter opposition to humanism, Bucer studied Greek with Johannes Brenz (1499–1570), a popular lecturer in philology and philosophy who would eventually become a staunch supporter of Martin Luther and assume the leading role in the reform of Württemberg. Like Bucer, Brenz was an admirer of the work of Erasmus, particularly the *Moriae encomium*. A letter from Bucer in 1518 to the Greek scholar Beatus Rhenanus (1485–1547) of Sélestat, Erasmus's editor and collaborator, catalogues the books in his personal library. They include Erasmus's *Moriae encomium*, his *Novum instrumentum*, portions of the paraphrases, and the *Enchiridion*.[29]

Other influences began to exercise an even stronger hold on the young scholar. In April 1518, Bucer heard Luther speak at a chapter meeting of the

Augustinian Order in defense of his *Ninety-Five Theses*, which had been issued only the previous fall, on 31 October 1517. Bucer was instantly attracted to the reformer's message — that a believing Christian is justified exclusively through faith in the saving grace of Christ's sacrifice — and was thrilled to meet Luther in person. Like many other reformers and humanists at this time, Bucer believed that Luther and Erasmus were speaking with the same voice. In a letter to Rhenanus he writes about Luther: "Cum Erasmo illi conveniunt omnia, quin uno hoc praestare videtur, quod quae ille duntaxat insinuat, hic aperte docet et libere" (He concurs with Erasmus on all points, except in one thing to his advantage, that what Erasmus insinuates, Luther teaches freely and openly).[30] The following spring in Heidelberg, Bucer was awarded the Bachelor of Theology and Master of Students degrees and was ordained a priest. Hoping to meet Erasmus, he traveled to Basel, where he made the acquaintance of Johannes Froben (1460–1527), publisher of Erasmus's *Enchiridion* and *Novum Testamentum*, and the humanist Wolfgang Capito (1478–1541),[31] who had assisted Erasmus in his biblical research and who would become Bucer's collaborator in reforming Strasbourg. The desired meeting with Erasmus (at that time living in Louvain) never took place. Impressed by Luther's commentary on Paul's letter to the Galatians, Bucer undertook a correspondence with Luther and his Wittenberg colleague Philipp Melanchthon (1497–1560). In further opposition to his order, Bucer championed the humanist scholar of Hebrew, Johannes Reuchlin (1455–1522), whom the Dominicans had accused of heresy, fearing that Hebrew studies threatened Christian piety.[32]

In light of his disagreements with the Dominicans, it was not surprising when Bucer left the order in November 1520. He found friendship and refuge with Ulrich von Hutten (1488–1523), an imperial knight and humanist poet who was an avid defender of both Reuchlin and Luther, and with Franz von Sickingen (1481–1523), who would lead the abortive Knights' Revolt of 1522–23, an uprising of a group of Germany's independent-minded nobles against imperial authority.[33] He was granted release from his monastic vows in April 1521, the month in which Emperor Charles V issued the Edict of Worms in condemnation of Luther.[34] Now active in the service of Luther and his allies, Bucer began his pastoral career as a parish priest in Landstuhl in 1522.

In that year, Bucer married Elisabeth Silbereisen, a former nun, thereby unmistakably signaling his departure from the discipline of the Roman church. He left Landstuhl for a position in Wissembourg at the invitation of its prelate, Heinrich Motherer. Although the two reformers were favored by the town council, they were forced to leave Wissembourg on 1 May 1523 after the bishop of Speyer excommunicated them and demanded that the council enforce the Edict of Worms.[35] Bucer moved to Strasbourg (where his father years earlier had been granted the rights of citizenship) in response to the city council's offer of protection and permission to preach.[36] Other members of the Strasbourg clergy followed Bucer's example in marrying, while the bishop tried without success to get the council to expel Bucer and discipline the married priests. In early 1524, Bucer was appointed pastor at the church of St. Aurelia. With this position he achieved the stability and institutional support necessary to embark on what would be his life's work.

Erasmus's Debate with Luther

If Bucer's first encounter with Luther inspired him to discipleship, Erasmus's reaction was more guarded. In March 1519, Luther wrote to Erasmus acknowledging his intellectual debt to him and asking for his friendship.[37] Erasmus at first appeared to give his qualified approval to many of Luther's ideas, though he found his vehemence disquieting. However, he soon came under pressure from friends, detractors of Luther, and even from Pope Leo X to take a stand against the reformer. He struggled to retain his neutrality, but in early 1524 he composed a treatise that challenged Luther at a fundamental level: *De libero arbitrio diatribe* (A Discussion on the Freedom of the Will). Despite Luther's warning in a letter not to attack him publicly,[38] Erasmus published the work in September of that year. Thus ended the tentative truce between them.[39]

De libero arbitrio, taking up as it does the question of free will, struck directly at the crucial issue dividing Luther from the Roman church, as he later acknowledged. Erasmus opposes Luther in three major ways in this work: First, contrary to Luther's insistence on *sola scriptura* (scripture alone), Erasmus avows the integrity of a community of interpreters reaching back into the early centuries of the church's existence. Second, for all of his own criticisms of the church, he confirms his support for its authority and pledges to uphold it over all individual interpretations, including his own. Finally, he affirms his positive view of human nature in allowing for "vim humanae voluntatis, qua se possit homo applicari ad ea quae perducunt ad aeternam salutam, aut ab iisdem avertere" (a power of the human will by which man may be able to direct himself towards, or turn away from, what leads to eternal salvation).[40]

Luther was reluctant to reply, but at the urging of his allies, including Bucer, he undertook a rebuttal. Luther's *De servo arbitrio* (On the Enslaved Will, Dec. 1525) went well beyond disagreement to express personal contempt and disgust. According to Luther, scripture makes clear at many points not only that humans have no free will, but also indeed that all efforts they might make to be righteous under the illusion of free will are sinful. A deeply stung Erasmus responded with the two-volume *Hyperaspistes diatribae adversus servum arbibitrium Mart. Lutheri* (Protector of the Discussion against the Enslaved Will of Martin Luther, 1526 and 1527), but Luther did not answer. With this exchange, Erasmus made explicit his break from Luther and his reform, thus ending any lingering hopes the evangelicals might have had of enlisting him in their cause. His personal alienation in turn reflected a wider breach between humanist and evangelical reformers that would never be overcome. From this point onward Erasmus, who previously had been at the forefront of reform, found himself in a bewildering new era in which the strongest voices belonged to men of a new generation, many of whom in their youth had been his devoted admirers. One such voice was that of Martin Bucer.

Bucer and the Strasbourg Reform

In urging Luther to reply to Erasmus's challenge, Bucer made explicit his own position: the step represented his break with the humanist reform. Bucer was by now deeply involved with the reform of the church in Strasbourg[41] and had published his first significant treatise, *Das ym selbs niemant, sonder anderen leben soll, und wie der mensch dahyn kummen mög* (That No One Should Live for Himself but for Others, and How One May Do So).[42] The emphasis Bucer gives to love and service of the neighbor in this early piece would be central to his lifelong teaching and work as a reformer.

At Strasbourg he found support from his colleagues Wolfgang Capito, Caspar Hedio (1494–1552), and Matthäus Zell (1477–1548), as well as from the city's magistrates, who were essential to his success. The first German Mass in Strasbourg was conducted in 1524 by Theobald Schwarz, with communion in both kinds. Roman and German masses were celebrated side by side until January 1528, when the Mass itself was abolished. Beginning in 1524, the city's monasteries were disbanded, and in 1525 a poorhouse was established. Of particular importance were Bucer's educational reforms, which he accomplished with the help of the city magistrate Jacob Sturm (1489–1553), a key player in Reformation politics.[43] His vision was to institute a centralized system of primary and secondary education, coordinated by a school board that included both pastors and lay authorities.

For all of its early successes, Bucer's work was not to go smoothly for long. His activities alienated former friends and associates, including Wimpfeling and Rhenanus, who were dismayed at the evangelical path he had taken. In the meantime, Bucer found himself confronted with three fundamental challenges to everything he stood for: the Peasants' War of 1524–25; the migration to Strasbourg by radical reformers; and the controversy over the meaning of Christ's words of institution at the Last Supper: "This is my body."

The rebellion of the peasants against their feudal and ecclesiastical lords has its place in history as one of the most important uprisings of the laboring classes in the pre-modern world. For months, the destructive violence of the peasant armies terrorized Germany.[44] Inspired in part by Luther's preaching against the Roman church, the rebels demanded economic, social, and religious reforms. An enraged Luther responded with a pamphlet condemning the rebels and calling on the territorial princes of Germany to strike them down without mercy.[45] When peasant armies swept into Alsace in 1525, the Strasbourg preachers were called upon to act. Bucer's view of the peasants' rebellion was one of unqualified disapproval, but, unlike Luther, he attempted to negotiate with them, advocating mercy and understanding rather than slaughter. In the end, the rebels were brutally put down, but the catastrophe provided ammunition to opponents of the reform, including Erasmus, who characterized it as seditious.

Bucer's relationship with the radical reform was complex. The term itself encompasses a wide variety of sectarian groups.[46] The Anabaptists, who repudiated infant baptism, believed that the sacrament of baptism must instead mark the initiation of a confessing adult. The effect of their position was to separate the church from the wider community by seeking an exclusive church, purified of those whose morals and beliefs were not "truly Christian." Such a stance struck directly at Bucer's commitment — the core of his concept of reform — to a cooperative relationship between magistrates and church leaders to create a unified Christian community.[47] Initially, Bucer and his allies tolerated diverse opinions, preferring debate to suppression, with the result that refugees flocked to Strasbourg. Eventually, however, leaders of these groups began to preach against the Strasbourg church and became so disruptive that Bucer was forced to adopt a repressive policy toward them, in spite of his personal convictions favoring peace and reconciliation. The Strasbourg Synod, called in 1533 to establish a confession of faith and strengthen the church's organization, examined the most important leaders among the radicals, imprisoning the Anabaptist prophet Melchior Hoffmann (1495–1543) and banishing several others.[48]

None of Bucer's challenges lasted longer or was more destructive to the reform as a whole, however, than the Eucharistic controversy. It had two points of contention: the meaning of the word *is* in Christ's proclamation "This is my body," and the question of Christ's presence in the sacrament when partaken of by unbelievers. Luther insisted that *is* must be understood literally and that Christ's body and blood are physically present in the Supper. These interpretations brought him into conflict, first, with his erstwhile Wittenberg colleague Karlstadt (Andreas Rudolf Bodenstein, 1480–1541), and then somewhat later with the Zurich reformer Huldrych Zwingli (1484–1531). Karlstadt represented an exclusively spiritual understanding of the Eucharist; Zwingli argued for a symbolic interpretation of the elements of bread and wine, whereby the word *is* means *signifies*. While Luther agreed that Christ is spiritually present, he insisted on Christ's physical presence as well. The implications are profound for understanding the Eucharist as a sacrament: Luther's position implies that all participants partake of Christ's body and blood regardless of their spiritual condition, although unbelievers receive no benefit; Zwingli's implies that Christ is present only to those who believe.

Leaders in the city of Strasbourg began to consider their position when Karlstadt arrived there in 1524. In December, after much thought, Bucer professed his agreement with the symbolic interpretation of the bread and wine. The Strasbourg preachers tried to avoid an open breach with Luther, but the attempt was fruitless in light of Luther's refusal to compromise.[49] Although the impasse was deeply painful for Bucer, given his aversion to contention, by his own actions he added to its bitterness. When in late August or early September 1525 the Basel reformer Johannes Oecolampadius (1482–1531) published a defense of the spiritualist interpretation of "This is my body,"[50] Bucer openly supported him; and in 1526, following an unfriendly exchange of letters with his former Greek tutor Johannes Brenz, he published an *Apologia*. Finally, he enraged Luther and one of his allies, the Pomeranian reformer Johannes Bugenhagen (1485–1558), by inserting notes that promoted his own views of the Eucharist into German translations of the Wittenberg reformers' works that he had undertaken prior to the controversy.[51]

In 1528, however, Bucer saw an opportunity. Reading Luther's most recent statement of beliefs, he concluded that the differences between his own and Luther's positions were not as great as he had feared. He thus abandoned his Zwinglian interpretation and openly began to seek reconciliation with Luther. There were further complications, to be sure. The Marburg Colloquy of 1529 brought the Wittenberg theologians together with Zwingli, Oecolampadius, Bucer, and Hedio, but the group failed to achieve mutually acceptable language for the Last Supper.[52] At the 1530 Diet of Augsburg, for which the Wittenbergers composed the Augsburg Confession, Bucer's party arrived at a separate accord called the *Tetrapolitana* (Confession of the Four Cities), signed by the cities of Strasbourg, Constance, Lindau, and Memmingen. It was not until the Wittenberg Concord of 1536 that most Lutherans reached an agreement with Bucer's allies in South Germany; even now, the Concord did not satisfy all Zwinglians, many of whom had grown alienated from Bucer because of his concessions to Luther.[53] Despite Bucer's ultimate truce with Luther, therefore, his credibility suffered from the appearance of appeasement and casuistry.

Erasmus's Exchange with Bucer

Erasmus's experience with the Eucharistic controversy would tragically erode his relationships with friends and collaborators who were attracted to the spiritualist view. He had particularly painful exchanges with Conradus Pellicanus (Kürsner, 1478–1556), with Oecolampadius, who had helped him in his New Testament scholarship, and with the Zurich reformer Leo Jud (1482–1522), who had translated some of Erasmus's works into German.[54] Ironically, all of these men, as well as Zwingli himself, owed much of their inspiration to Erasmus's advocacy of a spiritual approach to worship. However, Erasmus deplored the reformers' tendency to construe his support for their movement from passages in his earlier works, remarking even that he would not have written the *Moriae encomium* if he had known of the storm that was coming.[55] What could have occasioned such a disturbing failure in understanding? Erasmus himself attributed it to willful misreadings, whereas his adversaries blamed his unwillingness to declare his beliefs openly. The texts that came under the most scrutiny included portions of the *Enchiridion*, the *Paraphrasis*, and the annotations to the *Novum Testamentum*. Erasmus's angry denials of his readers' conclusions were as frustrating to them as their misreadings were to him.

Erasmus added to the confusion when, in response to the publication of Oecolampadius's treatise on the Eucharist, he wrote a letter to the town council of Basel in October 1525, saying, "mea sententia doctum, diestrum, et elaboratum; adderem etiam pium, si quid pium esse posset quid pugnat cum sententia consensuque Ecclesiae: a qua dissentire periculosum esse iudico" (in my opinion the work is learned, well written, and thorough. I would also judge it pious, if anything could be so described which is at variance with the general opinion of the church, from which I consider it perilous to dissent).[56] Many readers concluded that Erasmus failed to support Oecolampadius out of fear. Leo Jud said as much in a pseudonymous pamphlet of 1526, in which he compared the views of Luther and Erasmus with those of Karlstadt, listing the *Adagia*, the *Querela pacis*, and the fifth canon of the *Enchiridion* as sources, as well as the *Adnotationes* and *Paraphrasis* on the New Testament.[57] To drive the point home, Jud quoted Erasmus's letter to the Basel town council. Erasmus responded in outrage in his pamphlet *Detectio praestigiarum* (The Uncovering of Deceptions), claiming that in giving the spirit primacy over the flesh he did not mean to suggest that the flesh did not have its place.[58] These disputes would provide the backdrop to another polemical exchange, this time between Erasmus and Bucer.

The quarrel began when Erasmus wrote an open letter, *Epistola contra pseudevangelicos* (Letter against the False Evangelicals), in December 1529. Its immediate inspiration was a recent publication by a younger Dutch scholar named Gerard Geldenhouwer (1482–1542), who claimed that Erasmus unconditionally opposed the death penalty for heretics.[59] In the context of an anxious political situation, Erasmus replied that he had never held that position and that Geldenhouwer's misrepresentation could put him in danger with any number of princes. After rebuking Geldenhouwer for his audacity, Erasmus turned his attention to the reform itself and most of its proponents. He is particularly dismayed by the manner in which the evangelical attack on the church has polarized Christendom, thus restricting the freedom to contest the very abuses the reformers claim to find most abhorrent. Toward the end of the *Epistola*, Erasmus employs an argument based on history: the early church, he claims, is not an appropriate model for people to follow today. On the one hand, that time in the church's history was not the ideal that the reformers claim it was; on the other hand, even if the ways of the early church had been ideal at the time, changing circumstances demand changes in practice. In summation he writes: "Atque utinam per quosdam vestrae professionis liceat mederi pristinis; utinam res utcunque cepta ad eam moderationem redigatur, ut quae officiunt pietati commoda prudentique curatione sanetur" (I wish that, through the agency of some who profess your conviction, healing could be sought from former conditions. I wish that this affair, however it started, might be restored to moderation, such that obstacles to piety might be cured by suitable, prudent attention).[60]

Such an attack demanded a response, and Bucer stepped forward with a lengthy defense entitled *Epistola apologetica*. He did not identify himself as the author, however, but established a collective authorship: "Qui Christi evangelion Argentorati adnunciant eiusdem professoribus et sectatoribus per Frisiam Orientalem et alias Inferioris Germaniae regiones" (Those of Strasbourg who preach the gospel of Christ, to those who profess and follow that same gospel throughout East Frisia and other regions of lower Germany).[61] The work combines a defense of the reformers' practices and doctrines with a counterattack on those of the Catholic clergy, both in their moral behavior and in their distortion of the gospel through useless and even blasphemous ceremonies. Nonetheless, Bucer endeavors to take on a mediating role by portraying the evangelicals as moderate rather than revolutionary. This strategy demands that Bucer focus at least in part on what the evangelicals have in common with the traditional church, thus drawing readers to conclude that the reformers are not cutting themselves off from the church but rather preserving and honoring it against the accumulated distortions of Rome.

Bucer treats Erasmus's accusations one by one, in each case claiming that the evangelicals have brought about no disruptive changes. In this manner he redefines the reform as indeed retaining the wheat as it destroys the tare. Bucer adopts the ethos of sobriety and reason, in contrast to Erasmus, who is openly adversarial, even to the point of employing ridicule to make his point. In consistently speaking in the *persona* of the evangelical party as a whole and adopting the first person plural as the source of his defense, Bucer presents his arguments as the product of a group united in its convictions. Despite his efforts to establish continuity with the history of the church, however, Bucer ultimately is forced to confront the undeniable division that lies at the heart of his exchange with Erasmus. He must relinquish the voice of mediation and adopt instead the resolute attitude of one who is unambiguously opposed to Rome. To Erasmus's call for moderation, discussion, and patience, Bucer gives his heart-felt concurrence, but adds: "Sed utinam agnoscantur, quae pietati vere officiunt" (Would that it were acknowledged, what those things are that are obstacles to true piety).[62]

Erasmus replied in early September 1530 with the *Epistola ad fratres Germaniae Inferioris* (Letter to the Brethren of Lower Germany) in which he recasts his earlier accusations against the reform in yet more detail, accusing the writer of the *Epistola apologetica* (whom he professes not to recognize but sarcastically nicknames "Bucephalus") of out-and-out lies. Against Bucer's imputation of unity Erasmus unwaveringly reminds his reader that the *Epistola apologetica* originated in Strasbourg, thus reducing it to the product of a particular group. He answers Bucer's dignified tone with yet more sarcasm, summarizing the views of the reformers in blunt terms in order to disrupt the language of mediation with which Bucer had attempted to formulate his party's goals; for example, he repeatedly renders Bucer's understanding of the elements in the Eucharist as nothing but bread and wine.[63]

Bucer did not confine his literary efforts during this time to polemics; in 1527, he composed commentaries on the synoptic gospels and Paul's letter to the Ephesians, and in 1528 on the Gospel of John, the book of Zephaniah, and the Psalms. The Psalms commentary in particular created controversy because he published it under a pseudonym, Aretius Felinus, to evade censorship in France. Erasmus in his *Epistola contra pseudevangelicos* attacked this ploy as an outrageous falsehood,[64] to which Bucer answered that for the sake of promoting the true gospel, such fictions were justifiable.[65] Bucer wrote his last commentary in 1536, on Paul's letter to the Romans.

The commentaries are among Bucer's most significant writings, for while he never produced a systematic theological work beyond his Catechisms,[66] he developed his doctrinal principles in his exegesis of key portions of scripture. His comment on "Therefore they could not believe" (that is, in fulfillment of the prophetic question in Isaiah 53:1: "Lord, who has believed our report, and to whom has the arm of the Lord been revealed?") includes his reflection on free will: "Quid quaeso potentius et apertius dici possit pro Dei omnia ordinantis praedestinatione et contra id quod quidam libero arbitrio tribuunt, nempe homine ex sua virtute Christo credere posse?" (I ask, what could one say more strongly and clearly in favor of God's predestining and ordaining all things, and against that which certain people attribute to free will, namely that men can believe in Christ by means of their own capability?).[67] In all of his exegetical work, Bucer shows deep respect for the church fathers, drawing upon them frequently as he departs from Luther's austere condition of *sola scriptura*.[68] However, his Latin writings suffer from a tendency toward verbosity. Like Erasmus, he had a habit of writing in haste; unlike Erasmus, he failed to rise to the highest standard of eloquence.

Erasmus's Final Years

At the time Erasmus wrote the *Epistola ad fratres* he had already moved from his home in Basel to Catholic Freiburg. As he prepared to leave, Erasmus in several letters to friends professed his shock and dismay over the destruction of images, the harassment of priests, and the banning of the Mass, all of which made it impossible for him to live there as a Catholic. Ironically, he had originally moved to Basel in 1521 from Louvain in order to escape his enemies among the theologians at the university, some of whom were among the most severe critics of his New Testament scholarship.[69] By the time Erasmus moved to Freiburg in 1529, he understandably felt like an exile and a wanderer, the victim of the extremism of Catholics and Protestants alike. The citizens of Freiburg welcomed him, yet despite their courtesy Erasmus never lost his longing to return to Basel, the place where he had accomplished his most important work and found the most satisfying companionship of his career.

Thus, in May of 1535, Erasmus journeyed to his final resting place in Basel, where he would continue to write even as serious illness became a daily burden. In August, he published a work that he had been preparing for many years, the *Ecclesiastes*, a massive treatise on the pastoral office. The *Ecclesiastes* reaffirms the sacerdotal role of the priesthood even as it focuses on the vital importance of preaching the Word of God to the pastor's flock. In this, his last major work, Erasmus summarizes his lifelong commitment to pastoral care and to the role of sound rhetorical training for priests to aid them in their task of educating the laity. As in the *Ratio seu methodus*, Erasmus develops in the *Ecclesiastes* a theology grounded in an interpretation of scripture as a work of rhetoric, which draws the recipient into the mysteries of the faith through multiple levels of meaning.[70]

For Erasmus to have undertaken such a work so late in life testifies to his continued willingness, notwithstanding his infirmity, to engage with the world. In spite of the deaths of several close friends — both John Fisher, a biblical scholar and bishop of Rochester, and Thomas More had been executed by Henry VIII in 1535 — and the continued divisions in the church, Erasmus in the *Ecclesiastes* manifests his unaltered belief in the principles of concord, the *philosophia Christi*, and the power of language to bring people to Christ. Just before he moved to Basel, in the early summer of 1535, he had published *De concordia*, a formula for concord in which he called for all authorities, sacred and secular, to join in promoting an open discussion to resolve the issues that had fractured the unity of the church. Here too, one can still discern his confidence in the healing powers of language used rightly.

The publication of the *Ecclesiastes* was followed in February 1536 by a commentary on Psalm 14, *De puritate tabernaculi* (On the Purity of the Church). By then, Erasmus knew that he was close to death. The end came in the night between 11 and 12 July 1536. The last words of a man who had enjoyed a reputation as Europe's premier Latinist were in his native Dutch: "Lieve God!"

Bucer in Maturity and Decline

During the period leading up to Erasmus's death, tensions in Europe grew as Catholics and reformers became more polarized both doctrinally and politically. The secular champion of the Roman church, Holy Roman Emperor Charles V, had in the early years of the evangelical reform found himself hampered by a conflict with the royal house of France, rebellion from many of the princes and cities of the empire, a lack of consistent support from the pope, and most serious of all, the Turkish siege of Vienna in 1529. In 1530, at a point when he had temporarily defeated his French rival and after German and Spanish troops had repulsed the Turks, Charles convened the Diet of Augsburg with the intent of resolving the religious crisis, inviting leading reformers to present their statements of belief. No one was surprised at the outcome, however, when Charles rejected both the Augsburg Confession and Bucer's *Tetrapolitana* without even the appearance of giving them serious consideration. The Diet was followed by the emperor's demand in 1531 that the Edict of Worms be upheld and that all states in the empire return to the Roman church. In response, Protestant princes formed the Schmalkaldic League as a defense.[71] War appeared to be imminent, but a renewed offensive by the Turks and further conflict with France (including a 1536 alliance between the French king and the Turks) drew Charles away from the rebellion in his empire.

Over the course of the next decade, Bucer's activities expanded beyond Strasbourg as he provided assistance to sympathetic magistrates wishing to implement reform in cities throughout the empire.[72] Between 1534 and 1537, for example, Bucher made several visits to Augsburg at the invitation of the magistrates to help establish reforms, settle disputes among the clergy, and draw up ecclesiastical ordinances. He also worked vigorously to enact reforms in Cologne, at first achieving remarkable success against a strongly united Catholic clergy, only to see his efforts struck down by the emperor eight months later, in August 1543.[73] The cause of reform in Germany had already encountered a serious setback in late 1539 with the bigamy scandal created by Philipp of Hesse (1504–67), who, appealing to the biblical precedent of Abraham and the patriarchs, demanded that Bucer sanction his second marriage while he was still married to his first wife. This put Bucer in an extremely awkward position, given that Philipp was his most important source of political support in seeking to establish the conditions for religious reform. Bucer reluctantly agreed to endorse the new marriage and attended the wedding in 1540. The resulting scandal was a serious blow to the prestige of Bucer — as well as that of Luther and Melanchthon, who were likewise influenced to support Philipp — and jeopardized Philipp's relationship with the emperor.[74]

In 1540, Charles V renewed his call for a resolution to religious divisions in Germany. Despite the struggles of the previous two decades, Bucer remained hopeful of reaching a religious accord. In subsequent negotiations, Charles agreed to allow a revised version of the Augsburg Confession to serve as the basis for discussion. For the next meeting, the Regensburg Diet of 1541, Charles's advisers enlisted leading voices of moderation on each side to draft the major points of doctrine; the agreement came to be known as the Regensburg Book. Bucer played a central role in these negotiations but was ultimately frustrated by the parties' inability to reach agreement on a number of questions, including the doctrinal authority of the church and the sacraments.[75]

The plague swept through Strasbourg in this same year, carrying away Bucer's wife and four of their children, along with his colleague Wolfgang Capito. (Bucer would eventually marry Capito's widow and have two children with her.) These deaths, as well as the poor health of Caspar Hedio and Matthäus Zell, caused Bucer to fall into a state of depression. He experienced yet another loss with the departure of John Calvin (1509–64), who was recalled to Geneva in September of 1541. Calvin had originally joined Bucer in Strasbourg in 1536 after having been expelled from Geneva, where his attempt to initiate rigorous moral and religious reforms had come into conflict with citizens who opposed such thoroughgoing changes. In Strasbourg, Bucer became Calvin's mentor and supported his teaching, preaching, and efforts at organizing reform in his native France. Calvin's fame would eventually eclipse that of his friend, but Bucer's influence on Calvin's thought remains clearly discernible. Calvin not only made use of Bucer's commentaries on the synoptic gospels in his own scholarship; he also followed Bucer's lead in questions concerning liturgy and the Eucharist.[76] Calvin's departure caused Bucer to feel especially isolated.

Nevertheless, Bucer remained a dominant figure in reformed circles. In early 1546, he reluctantly agreed to participate in a new colloquy at Regensburg (sometimes referred to as the Colloquy of Ratisbon), which opened under the cloud of impending war. It soon became obvious that Charles was using the colloquy as a ruse to justify taking up arms against the Schmalkaldic League. Meanwhile, Luther's death on 25 February was an added blow to the dispirited Protestants. Following fruitless negotiations, Bucer gave up and went home; having lost hope for compromise, he became increasingly bitter and defensive. In the war that followed, the emperor defeated the Schmalkaldic League, which was plagued by member rivalries and lack of competent leadership. Bucer believed that the League's defeat was punishment for its failure to make itself a worthy instrument of God and for its sins of self-indulgence, cowardice, and dissention.

The victorious emperor brought together both Catholic and Protestant theologians at Augsburg in 1548 for the purpose of reaching an agreement that would contain religious strife until the Council of Trent could reach a more permanent resolution. The outcome was the Augsburg Interim, which allowed for communion in both kinds by the laity, clerical marriage, and the freedom to preach the doctrine of justification by faith; however, it also mandated that the signatories retain all seven of the sacraments and the Latin Mass. Bucer refused to endorse the agreement because he believed that it forced the Protestants to sacrifice too much. On his return to Strasbourg he published *Ein Summarischer vergriff der Christlichen lehre und Religion, die man zü Strasburg hat nun in xxviii jar gelehret* (A Summary Statement of the Christian Doctrine and Religion, Which Has Now Been Taught in Strasbourg for Twenty-eight Years) as a rallying cry to the citizens of Strasbourg to uphold the reforms they had worked so hard to bring into effect. Thus, the man who had been reputed as all too willing to make sacrifices for the sake of unity finally dug in his heels. Unfortunately, he found himself in opposition to the mood of the Strasbourgers, who by this time wanted nothing more than to make peace with the emperor. On 1 March 1549, the town council voted to expel him and his associate, the Hebrew scholar Paul Fagius (Büchlein, 1504–49). Bucer departed for England shortly thereafter, never to return to the place that had been the setting for his life's greatest achievements.

Bucer chose England as his new home in part because he feared that his life was at risk in Germany, given the animus he had created in the emperor through his public opposition to the Augsburg Interim. But England also offered attractions of its own, beginning with the warm invitation from Archbishop of Canterbury Thomas Cranmer (1489–1556). He also looked forward to working with people who supported his reform efforts, chief among them Matthew Parker (1504–75), Vice-Chancellor of Cambridge University. With the accession of the boy-king Edward VI (1537–53) in January 1547, the Protestants believed that England was ready for genuine and lasting reform. Bucer was appointed professor of divinity at Cambridge, but his health was in such serious decline that he was unable to begin his lectures until early 1550. He also continued to be plagued by controversy, both with Catholic theologians whose influence remained significant among the English and with English supporters of Zwingli. After his friend and colleague

Fagius died at Cambridge (where he had been appointed professor of Hebrew) in November 1549, Bucer once more fell into depression, which was alleviated somewhat by the arrival of his family.

Notwithstanding these difficulties, Bucer gathered enough strength to compose a final major work, *De regno Christi* (Concerning the Kingdom of Christ), which he dedicated to King Edward in October 1550. In this book he presents a portrait of an ideal Christian commonwealth rooted in biblical principles. Most striking is his advocacy of an approach to governance that embraces concern for the material, moral, and spiritual well-being of the people — an approach that had guided him throughout his long career as a reformer. Bucer fell seriously ill in February 1551; he died on the first day of March.

Concluding Reflections

There are several striking points of similarity between Desiderius Erasmus and Martin Bucer, beginning with the trajectories of their lives. In youth and early adulthood each pursued his education and vocation according to the accepted paths of his generation, only to find his true calling upon encountering a mentor who introduced him to new ways of thinking. As adults, each man achieved honor and recognition in his endeavors, engaging deeply in the seminal controversies of the most important developments of his times. In later years both found frustration, disappointment, and a sense that their most cherished visions might never achieve fruition, and yet continued to produce works of major importance reflecting their profound beliefs.

Erasmus and Bucer were transitional figures in the upheavals of the sixteenth century. Today's readers generally know less about them than about the Luthers and Calvins of their time, however, since neither founded a movement identified by his name. Erasmus failed to achieve his goal of a moderate reform that would unite all Christians under the wing of the Roman church; Bucer's efforts failed to heal the divisions that afflicted Christendom. Yet to regard them from the standpoint of what they did not accomplish would be to commit an injustice against both. Their substantial achievements had a lasting impact; indeed, their efforts shaped the landscape in which Protestant reforms were carried out.

One significant effect of Erasmus's work was to make available both sacred and secular literary resources to an expanded circle of readers. His rhetorical works alone assisted in the training of young people for generations after his death, while his New Testament scholarship and editions of the church fathers proved invaluable to Catholic and Protestant theologians alike. His *philosophia Christi* provided and continues to provide inspiration to readers who are attracted to a faith grounded in tolerance and a simple love for Christ and his message.[77]

Bucer's work greatly advanced the cause of reform in Germany; indeed, it is difficult to imagine the success of the Protestant reform without him.

Similarly, it is unlikely that Calvin's ministry would have succeeded without the benefit of Bucer's mentorship and influence. Bucer played a crucial role in efforts at reconciling the parties to the Eucharistic controversy, as well as in the opening of dialogue between Catholics and Protestants. His most deeply-held belief was in a Christian community in which clergy, magistrates, and people worked together in harmony. One might say that Bucer, like Erasmus, had a positive vision of what life in the world could be for those who lived by the principles of Jesus Christ. That their efforts failed — indeed, that they themselves quarreled — is a sobering reminder of the depth of the divisions in Christendom during their lifetimes.

Notes

[1] The chief sources for Erasmus's works are *Desiderii Erasmi Roterodami opera omnia*, 10 vols., ed. Jean Leclerc (Leiden, 1703–6; repr., Hildesheim: Olms, 1961–62), hereafter cited as LB (standard reference: volume, column, column section). The following publications remain in progress: *Opera omnia Desiderii Erasmi Roterodami* (Amsterdam: North-Holland, 1969–), hereafter cited as ASD (standard reference: *ordo*, volume, page, line); and (in English) the *Collected Works of Erasmus* (Toronto: U of Toronto P, 1974–), hereafter cited as CWE (standard reference: volume, page). The critical edition of his letters is *Opus epistolarum Des. Erasmi Roterodami*, 12 vols., ed. P. S. Allen et al. (Oxford: Clarendon, 1906–58), hereafter cited as Allen (standard reference: letter [Ep] and line; volume and page only as necessary). Biographies include Léon-E. Halkin, *Erasmus: A Critical Biography*, trans. John Tonkin (Oxford: Blackwells, 1993); Cornelis Augustijn, *Erasmus: His Life, Works, and Influence* (Toronto: U of Toronto P, 1991); R. J. Schoeck, *Erasmus of Europe: The Making of a Humanist 1467–1500* (Savage, MD: Barnes & Noble Books, 1990); Margaret Mann Phillips, *Erasmus and the Northern Renaissance* (New York: Macmillan, 1950); and James D. Tracy, *Erasmus of the Low Countries* (Berkeley: U of California P, 1996). In 1524, Erasmus wrote an account of his life called the *Compendium vitae*, located in the first volume of Allen 46–52 and in CWE 4, 400–410. Some scholars have questioned its authenticity, however; see Schoeck 27 and 29, note 7.

[2] Tracy, *Erasmus of the Low Countries*, provides a good overview of the fluctuating political situation during this time.

[3] See William H. McNeill, *Plagues and Peoples* (New York: Anchor, 1976), 146–51. As we shall see, both Erasmus and Bucer experienced the loss of family members due to the plague's continuing virulence.

[4] See Steven E. Ozment, *The Reformation in the Cities: The Appeal of Protestantism to Sixteenth-century Germany and Switzerland* (New Haven: Yale UP, 1975), esp. chap. 3, sect. "Lay Defenses of the Reformation," 74–89.

[5] Erasmus would claim, however, that the Brethren were more of a hindrance than a help to those interested in learning because of the anti-intellectual quality of their piety. For discussion of this movement see Léon-E. Halkin, "La *Devotio Moderna* et Humanisme," in *Réform et Humanisme: Actes du IVᵉ Colloque de Montpellier*, ed. Jean Boisset (Montpellier: l'Université Paul Valéry, 1977), 103–12; and R. R. Post, *The*

Modern Devotion: Confrontation with Reformation and Humanism (Leiden: Brill, 1968).

[6] Erasmus does not mention his brother in the *Compendium vitae.*

[7] Agricola was a native of Groningen. After taking his Bachelor of Arts degree at Erfurt he studied at Louvain, Pavia, and, most importantly, Ferrara, where he learned Greek. See Adrie van der Laan and Fokke Akkerman, eds., *Rudolf Agricola: Letters* (Assen, The Netherlands: Koninklijke Van Gorcum; Tempe, AZ: Arizona Center for Medieval and Renaissance Studies, 2002). Schoeck, *Erasmus of Europe*, 50–51, discusses the influence this encounter had on Erasmus.

[8] The *Adagia* are available in the volumes LB II and CWE 31–36.

[9] For further discussion of Erasmus's work with the church fathers see Jan den Boeft, "Erasmus and the Church Fathers," in *The Reception of the Church Fathers in the West*, ed. Irena Backus (Leiden: Brill, 2001), 2:537–72.

[10] LB V 8D; CWE 66, 34–55.

[11] The Act of Succession, passed on 23 March 1534, recognized Princess Elizabeth, daughter of Anne Boleyn, the second wife of Henry VIII, as the true successor to the crown by declaring Henry's marriage to Catherine of Aragon invalid and their daughter Mary a bastard. All subjects were required to recognize the Act and the king's supremacy over the English church, or else be subject to a charge of treason.

[12] For further discussion of Erasmus's relationship with Italy see Auguste Renaudet, *Érasme en Italie* (Geneva: Droz, 1954); Léon-E. Halkin, "Érasme en Italie," in *Colloquia Erasmiana Turonensia*, ed. Jean Claude Margolin (Paris: Libraire Philosophique, 1972), 38–53; and Paul Oskar Kristeller, "Erasmus from an Italian Perspective," *Renaissance Quarterly* 23 (1970): 1–14.

[13] Allen, Epp 200 and 203.

[14] On the importance of the Aldine press for humanism see the chapter by Erika Rummel in this volume.

[15] Allen, Ep 215.

[16] Miller 34, ASD IV–3 94:429–30.

[17] Miller 35, ASD IV–3 96:459–62.

[18] Miller 95, ASD IV–3 154:487–90.

[19] Miller 197, ASD IV–3 193:257–194:259.

[20] In Plato's *Symposium* (221D–222A) the youth Alcibiades describes Socrates as a Silenus figure.

[21] For Erasmus's New Testament scholarship see Jerry Bentley, *Humanists and Holy Writ* (Princeton: Princeton UP, 1983), 112–219; Erika Rummel, *Erasmus's Annotations on the New Testament: From Philologist to Theologian* (Toronto: U of Toronto P, 1986); and Albert Rabil Jr., *Erasmus and the New Testament: The Mind of a Christian Humanist* (San Antonio: Trinity UP, 1972).

[22] See Erika Rummel, *Erasmus and his Catholic Critics*, 2 vols. (Nieuwkoop: De Graaf, 1989).

[23] A critical edition of the four prefaces can be found in Hajo and Annemarie Holborn, *Desiderius Erasmus Roterodamus: Ausgewählte Werke* (Munich: Beck, 1933). Manfred Hoffman provides an analysis of Erasmus's theological method, developed in the *Ratio*

and the later *Ecclesiastes,* in *Rhetoric and Theology: The Hermeneutic of Erasmus* (Toronto: U of Toronto P, 1994).

24 This work was particularly popular in Spain; see Marcel Bataillon, *Érasme et l'Espagne: recherches sur l'histoire spirituelle du XVIe siècle,* trans. Jean Claude Margolin (Geneva: Droz, 1998).

25 LB V 139D.

26 LB V 141E–F; Desiderius Erasmus, *Christian Humanism and the Reformation: Selected Writings. With the life of Erasmus, by Beatus Rhenanus,* ed. John C. Olin (New York: Harper & Row, 1965), 100.

27 Erasmus expressed his admiration for Brant in a subsequent letter to the leader of the Strasbourg circle, Jacob Wimpfeling.

28 There has long been in progress a three-part critical edition of Bucer's works: Series I: *Martin Bucers Deutsche Schriften,* ed. Gottfried Seebass (Gütersloh: Gütersloher Verlag, 1960–), henceforth cited as BDS (standard reference: volume, page, line); Series II: Martini Buceri *Opera Latina,* ed. François Wendel et al. (Paris: Presses Universitaires de France, 1954–), and continued as *Opera omnia,* ed. Robert Stupperich (Gütersloh: Bertelsmann, 1955–; also Gütersloh: Mohn, 1962–; also Leiden: Brill, 1979–), hereafter cited as BOL (standard reference: volume, page, line); and Series III: *Correspondance de Martin Bucer,* ed. Jean Rott (Leiden: Brill, 1979–), hereafter cited as BCor (standard reference: letter [Ep] and line; volume and page only as necessary). See also Jacques V. Pollet, *Martin Bucer: Études sur la Correspondance avec de nombreux textes inédits,* 2 vols. (Paris: Presses Universitaires de France, 1958–62). The most important biography of Bucer is Martin Greschat, *Martin Bucer: Ein Reformator und seine Zeit* (Munich: Beck, 1990), also available in an English translation as *Martin Bucer: A Reformer and His Times* by Stephen E. Buckwalter (Louisville: Westminster John Knox Press, 2004); see also Hastings Eells, *Martin Bucer* (New Haven: Yale UP, 1931).

29 BCor 1, Ep 3. See Friedhelm Krüger's study of Erasmian elements in Bucer's thought, *Bucer und Erasmus: Eine Untersuchung zum Einfluss des Erasmus auf die Theologie Martin Bucers (bis zum Evangelien-Kommentar von 1530)* (Wiesbaden: Steiner, 1970).

30 BCor 1, Ep 3:54–56.

31 See James M. Kittelson, *Wolfgang Capito: From Humanist to Reformer* (Leiden: Brill, 1975).

32 For an account of this controversy see Erika Rummel, *The Case against Johann Reuchlin: Religious and Social Controversy in Sixteenth-century Germany* (Toronto: U of Toronto P, 2002). In the present volume see the chapter on Neo-Latin literature by Wilhelm Kühlmann.

33 Hajo Holborn gives an account of Hutten, Sickingen, and the Knights' Revolt in *Ulrich von Hutten and the German Reformation,* trans. Roland Bainton (New York: Harper & Row, 1968).

34 On this subject see the chapter by C. Scott Dixon in this volume.

35 The Edict of Worms forbade not only the physical protection of Luther, but the abbetting of his cause in word or deed throughout the empire.

36 See Miriam U. Chrisman, *Strasbourg and the Reform: A Study in the Process of Change* (New Haven: Yale UP, 1967), and Thomas A. Brady Jr., *Ruling Class, Regime and Reformation at Strasbourg, 1520–1555* (Leiden: Brill, 1978).

[37] Allen, Ep 933.

[38] Allen, Ep 1443.

[39] There are many important works devoted to Erasmus's debate with Luther; see especially Marjorie O'Rourke Boyle, *Rhetoric and Reform: Erasmus' Civil Dispute with Luther* (Cambridge: Harvard UP, 1983); also Charles Trinkaus's introduction to CWE 76.

[40] LB IX 1220F–1221A; CWE 76 21.

[41] See Lorna Jane Abray, *The People's Reformation: Magistrates, Clergy, and Commons in Strasbourg, 1500–1598* (Ithaca: Cornell UP, 1985); William S. Stafford, *Domesticating the Clergy: The Inception of the Reformation in Strasbourg, 1522–1524* (Missoula, MT: Scholars Press for the American Academy of Religion, 1976); and René Bornert, *La Réforme Protestante du Culte à Strasbourg au XVIᵉ siècle (1523–1598)* (Leiden: Brill, 1981).

[42] BDS 1, 44–67.

[43] See Thomas A. Brady Jr., *Protestant Politics: Jacob Sturm (1489–1553) and the German Reformation* (Atlantic Highlands, NJ: Humanities Press, 1995).

[44] The scholarship on this topic is vast; see especially Bob Scribner and Gerhard Beneke, eds., *The German Peasant War of 1525: New Viewpoints* (London: Allen & Unwin, 1979); Tom Scott and Bob Scribner, eds., *The German Peasants' War: A History in Documents* (Atlantic Highlands, NJ: Humanities Press, 1991); and Peter Blickle, *The Revolution of 1525: The German Peasants' War from a New Perspective*, trans. Thomas A. Brady Jr. and H. C. Erik Midelfort (Baltimore: Johns Hopkins UP, 1981).

[45] Luther, *Wider die räuberischen und mörderischen Rotten der Bauren* (Against the Robbing and Murdering Hordes of Peasants), 1525, in *D. Martin Luthers Werke: Kritische Gesamtausgabe* (Weimar: Böhlau, 1883–1983), 18:357–61; English in *Luther's Works* (St. Louis: Concordia, 1955–), 46:45–61.

[46] The most comprehensive study of these groups is George Huntston Williams, *The Radical Reformation*, 3rd ed. (Kirksville, MO: Sixteenth Century Journal Publishers, 1992). See also James M. Stayer, *The German Peasants' War and Anabaptist Community of Goods* (Montreal: McGill-Queen's UP, 1991). See also in this volume the chapter by C. Scott Dixon.

[47] See Gottfried Hamman, *Martin Bucer, 1491–1551: Zwischen Volkskirche und Bekenntnisgemeinschaft* (Stuttgart: Steiner, 1989), and D. F. Wright, ed., *Martin Bucer: Reforming Church and Community* (Cambridge: Cambridge UP, 1994).

[48] See Marijn de Kroon, "Martin Bucer and the Problem of Tolerance," *Sixteenth Century Journal* 19, no. 2 (1988): 157–68.

[49] See Walther Köhler, *Zwingli und Luther, ihr Streit über das Abendmahl nach seinen politischen und religiösen Beziehungen* (Leipzig, 1924–53; repr., New York: Johnson, 1971).

[50] *De genuina verborum domini, hoc est corpus meum, iuxta vetustissimos authores expositione liber* (Book Concerning the Authentic Explanation of the Words "This is my body," According to the Most Ancient Authors); Basel, 1525.

[51] Erasmus took Bucer sternly to task for this subterfuge in *Epistola ad fratres* (ASD 9-1, 354:618–21).

[52] See Walther Köhler, *Das Marburger Religionsgespräch 1529: Versuch einer Rekonstruktion* (Leipzig: Heinsius, 1929).

[53] The documents relating to the Wittenberg Concord can be found in BDS 6:1.

[54] For the exchange of letters between Erasmus and Pellicanus see Allen 6, 206–21 (Epp 1637, 1638, and 1639).

[55] See *Detectio Praestigiarum*, ASD 9-1, 236:63–66.

[56] Allen 6, 206:2–5 (Ep 1636).

[57] The title of Jud's pamphlet is *Des hochgelerten Erasmi von Roterdam unnd Doctor Martin Luthers maynung vom Nachtmal unnsers herren Jhesu Christ* (The Understanding of the Highly Learned Erasmus of Rotterdam and Doctor Martin Luther of the Supper of Our Lord Jesus Christ); Augsburg: Grym, 1526.

[58] ASD 9-1, 211–62. While Erasmus in his *philosophia Christi* emphasized harmony and peace, he nonetheless frequently found himself moved to anger by what he regarded as the perversity of some of his readers.

[59] See Jacques V. Pollet, *Martin Bucer: Études sur les Relations de Bucer avec les Pays-Bas, l'Électorat de Colgne et l'Allemagne du Nord avec de nombreux textes inédits*, 2 vols. (Leiden: Brill, 1985), 1:26–34.

[60] ASD 9-1, 301:521–302:529.

[61] BOL 1, 75:2–4.

[62] BOL 1, 207:18–19.

[63] For further analysis of the exchange see Nicole Peremans, *Érasme et Bucer d'après leur Correspondance* (Paris: Société d'Editions "Les Belles Lettres," 1970), and J. Beumer, "Erasmus von Rotterdam und sein Verhältnis zu dem Deutschen Humanismus mit besonderer Rücksicht auf die konfessionellen Gegensätze," in *Scrinium Erasmianum*, ed. Joseph Coppens (Leiden: Brill, 1969), 1:165–201.

[64] ASD 9-1, 298:411–19.

[65] BOL 1, 127:19–128:7.

[66] DS 6:3.

[67] BOL 1, 2:390.

[68] See Irena Backus, "Ulrich Zwingli, Martin Bucer and the Church Fathers," in Backus, ed., *Reception of the Church Fathers*, 627–60, as well as her discussion of Bucer's sources in her introduction to BOL 2, xiii–xxxiii.

[69] For a discussion of Erasmus's problems with the Louvain theologians see the introduction to CWE 42 by John B. Payne and Albert Rabil Jr.

[70] Hoffman, *Rhetoric and Theology*, contains extensive analyses of the *Ratio* and the *Ecclesiastes*.

[71] This league was formed by Philipp of Hessen and Johann Friedrich of Saxony in the town of Schmalkalden in 1531 as a Protestant defensive force against the threats of Emperor Charles V, who had pledged to restore Europe to the Roman Catholic fold. Initially successful in the Battle of Mühlberg in 1547, Charles was forced to capitulate soon thereafter and ultimately to agree to the compromise terms of the Peace of Augsburg in 1555.

[72] See Pollet, *Martin Bucer: Études*, vol. 1 (*Études*) for details of this aspect of Bucer's career.

[73] See Pollet, *Martin Bucer: Études*, vol. 2 (*Documents*), "Dossier de l'Affaire Colonaise," 33–162, and Amy Nelson Burnett, *The Yoke of Christ: Martin Bucer and*

Christian Discipline (Kirksville, MO: Sixteenth Century Journal Publishers, 1994), 143–62.

[74] See Hastings Eells, *The Attitude of Martin Bucer toward the Bigamy of Philip of Hesse* (New Haven: Yale UP, 1924).

[75] The Regensburg Diet closed with an arrangement for an interim compromise in expectation of the next colloquy. See Volkmar Ortmann, *Reformation und Einheit der Kirche: Martin Bucers Einigungsbemühungen bei den Religionsgesprächen in Leipzig, Hagenau, Worms und Regensburg 1539–1541* (Mainz: Philipp von Zabern, 2001).

[76] See Marijn de Kroon, *Martin Bucer und Johannes Calvin: Reformatorische Perspektiven: Einleitung und Texte* (Göttingen: Vandenhoeck & Ruprecht, 1991).

[77] See Bruce E. Mansfield, *Phoenix of his Age: Interpretations of Erasmus c. 1550–1750* (Toronto: U of Toronto P, 1979).

Parallel Lives: Martin Opitz and Julius Wilhelm Zincgref

Theodor Verweyen

This essay is dedicated to Conrad Wiedemann in grateful friendship.

THE INGENIOUS IDEA OF JUXTAPOSING TWO representatives of early modern literature within one biographical sketch, such that the one casts the other into greater relief, recalls the famous prototype of parallel biography: the *Bioi paralleloi* of Plutarch (ca. 46–ca. 120), whose impact was still felt deep into the nineteenth century. Although certain of Plutarch's habits — not least his uncritical treatment of textual sources — are no longer acceptable, his concept of the life sketch or character portrait remains extremely stimulating.[1] The goal of a parallel biography of Martin Opitz and Julius Wilhelm Zincgref is to portray these early-seventeenth-century scholar-poets both personally and objectively to discover, on the one hand, what separated them and, on the other, what bound them in humanist friendship (*amicitia*). The divisive elements stem mainly from the external, or extraliterary, contexts of their lives: their social and religious backgrounds as well as the political and diplomatic spheres in which they operated; the connective elements stem from the internal world of literature itself: the poetological theory and literary ambitions of the two men. Ultimately, however, how we interpret their lives will be best explicated in terms of the cultural anthropology of early modern friendship, in which friendship appears in its premodern form of humanist *amicitia*, distinguished by a primarily intellectual, not yet individualized emancipation within an otherwise rigidly structured society.[2] This emancipating power increased proportionately to the degree of upheaval experienced by contemporary society.

Amicitia and Literary-political Aspiration

The relationship between the two authors was not free of tension, as two experiences from the years of their most intense literary production illustrate. In 1631 Julius Wilhelm Zincgref (1591–1635) published part two of his collection *Teutscher Nation Denckwürdiger Reden* (Memorable Speeches of the German Nation). Opitz contributed an alexandrine (six-foot iambic) poem — written on 21 June 1630 in Paris while on a diplomatic mission — to the preface, addressed *An Herrn D[octorem] Zincgrefen*; it is a conventional preface poem of the occasional, or casual variety common to the period between Humanism and Baroque. Opitz encourages Zincgref to demonstrate through his literary efforts within the general gloom of this unrelenting war, "was diß Edle Volck für schöne Geister trage" (what beautiful spirits this noble folk possesses), thus helping "daß Finsternuß [zu] besiegen/ Das Teutscher reden zier bißher vmbhüllet hatt" (to defeat the darkness that has enshrouded the elegance of German speeches). To underscore what he means Opitz adduces exemplary models from the threshold of the modern age, which he considers as valid as ever:

> Es ist sich zubesorgen /. . . . .
> . . . . daß dise Schreibesucht
> Der Sprache zierlichkeit wird wider in die flucht
> Verjagen wie zuvor. Es sagt mirs kein Prophete /
> Doch lehrt es mich Paris / da Ronsard nicht Poete
> Mehr heisset wie zuvor / da Bellay betteln geht/
> Da Bartas vnklar ist / da Marot nicht versteht
> Was recht Frantzösisch sey / da Jodel / da Baïff
> Nicht also reine sindt / wie jetzt der neue griff
> Vnd Hofe muster will. Heist dises nicht entlauffen
> Dem Wasser wo es quillt / vnd auß der Pfütze sauffen?[3]

[We must take care that this writing mania not again put the elegance of language to flight. It does not take a prophet to tell me this. I can see it in Paris, where Ronsard no longer is counted a poet as before, where Du Bellay goes begging, where Du Bartas has become obscure, where Marot does not understand what "real" French is, where Jodelle, where Baïf are no longer pure in terms of the new fashion and courtly model. What is all this if not running away from the water's pure source and drinking instead from a muddy puddle?][4]

Thus Opitz mobilizes his own literary experiences, gained from learning the elegant style of these classical French poets, against the stylish trends of gallant preciosity emanating from contemporary aristocratic salons. He encourages his literary comrade in arms in this first hour of the "new" German literature to uphold the original reform conceptions against their rapid obsolescence:[5]

> REcht also / liebster Freund / du lässest dich die zeiten /
> Die Sitten / disen grimm der Kriege nicht bestreiten /
> Vnd da das Vatterlandt verfolgung leiden muß /
> Bringstu es widerumb durch schreiben auff den Fuß.

[Thus it is right, dearest Friend, that you not allow the times, the customs, the evil of these wars to defeat you, so that, though our fatherland must suffer persecution, you will be able to uphold it through your writing.]

This admonition, which combines topoi of commemoration and praise, was not altogether necessary, since Zincgref shared Opitz's conception of literature as at once stable and politically adaptable. But dedications in prefaces required such conventions, due in part to the communicative nature of the practice of friendship basic to the humanist class culture;[6] in part to the evolution of a highly self-conscious literary culture; and in part simply to claims of prestige within a multitiered competitive society. Whatever the specific reason may have been, the thematizing in Opitz's poem of contemporary history and activities — the Thirty Years' War and accompanying diplomatic activities — accounts for a certain deviation from convention in this preface, though not great enough to be atypical of the genre of the *Buchbegleitgedicht* (book companion poem). Quite simply, this poem is a moving document to the era's cult of learned friendship.

A half decade earlier — this is the second of the two experiences to be mentioned — the relationship between the two poet colleagues had appeared to be anything but friendly. Opitz, back in his native Silesia since the summer of 1623,[7] was out of work. His close contacts with the Piast (Silesian and Polish dynasty) dukes of Liegnitz and Brieg brought him no material gain. In personal dedications, letters, and public statements he distanced himself vehemently from the first, so-called Strasbourg edition of his *Teutsche Poemata* (German Poems), which appeared in 1624. These poems, which Opitz had readied for publication four years earlier in Heidelberg, no longer conformed to his new stylistic standards, and he found them unfit in their present state. Zincgref, however, with the assistance of his friend, the Strasbourg scholar Matthias Bernegger (1582–1640), proceeded with his publication and had it printed in Strasbourg by Eberhard Zetzner. Accordingly, Zincgref bore the brunt of Opitz's criticisms: The first appears in a dedication copy for Georg Rudolf von Liegnitz and Brieg in 1624 in which Opitz writes that "adolescentiae suae lusus" (his adolescent games) — they had been collected and published by others despite their unreadiness for the public — will be followed by "maturiora simul et digniora" (more mature and dignified efforts). The second criticism is found in a letter of October 1624 to August Buchner (1591–1661), professor of poetry since 1616 at the University of Wittenberg. Here Opitz notes that a number of poems by other poets, "indigna luce publica et mendis plena" (unworthy of publication and full of errors), had been added arbitrarily to his own. Third, he maintains, only very discerning readers could possibly make sense of a book of poems written partly by himself, partly by others, and compiled in a disorderly and uncorrected manner. Finally, he complains in his *Buch von der Deutschen Poeterey* (1624), the groundbreaking poetics in which he describes the new stylistic principles, that the hastily published *Teutsche Poemata* contained flaws ascribable not only to his youth but also to editors overeager to spread his good name.[8] In short, it would have been better if the *Teutsche Poemata* had not been published at all.

With this massive accusation of Zincgref's edition, tinged with tones of self-criticism, Opitz shows himself to be a follower of Horace, the great representative of Augustan classicism, and thus very much a classicist himself. The motto to his *Poeterey* indeed is a quotation of the seminal lines 86–88 of Horace's *Ars poetica* and underlines the imitative crux of Opitz's aesthetics:

descriptas servare vices operumque colores
cur ego si nequeo ignoroque poeta salutor?
cur nescire pudens prave quam discere malo?

[If I fail to keep and do not understand these well-marked shifts and
shades of poetic forms, why am I hailed as poet? Why through false shame
do I prefer to be ignorant rather than to learn?][9]

Elsewhere in the *Ars poetica* the image of "limae labor" (l. 291), the time-
consuming "Mühsal des Feilens" (labor of revising) in pursuit of practical effects
through artifice, provides Opitz with a second principle of literary criticism.[10]
In his letter to Buchner, Opitz emphatically reiterates that the Strasbourg edition stemmed "a manu Zincgrefii" (from Zincgref's hand). And the public
accusations in the editorial annotations to his *Poeterey* of "mangelnde Sorgfalt"
(carelessness) and "übereilte Veröffentlichung" (premature publication) cannot have failed to affect Zincgref's reputation as an editor and scholar. While
Opitz does not explicitly mention Zincgref by name, neither does he take pains
to hide the faults from the discerning eyes of fellow scholars.

Opitz's criticism of the Strasbourg edition of course went well beyond the
internal, compositional problems of cogency and economy. At the time of
Opitz's criticism Zincgref had fled the Palatinate after Friedrich V's calamitous
campaign and was temporarily abroad in the service of the French diplomat
Guillaume Marescot. Meanwhile, with his supplementary *Außgesuchte Getichten
anderer mehr teutschen Poeten* (Selected Poems of Other German Poets) to the
1624 *Teutsche Poemata*, Zincgref dutifully tried to document the poetic tradition
that had existed in Heidelberg for two generations and was now endangered
by the war. Only such a monument, Zincgref believed, could convincingly
show the background out of which Opitz's genuinely modern principles and
practices were born.[11] Unfortunately, his plan fell flat. For Opitz looked not
to Palatine literary history but to the Fruchtbringende Gesellschaft (Fruitbringing Society, founded 1617) as the newly authoritative institution in matters of German literary style. Opitz aspired to rise to its expectations and to
champion its principles, and the *Teutsche Poemata* simply did not conform to
the society's poetological criteria. It says something about Opitz's ambitions
that he dedicated his new edition the following year to Prince Ludwig of
Anhalt, the founder of the society.[12] We may confidently refer to his stratagem
as "literary politics."

Opitz's political motives are particularly evident with respect to the new
edition, the 1625 Breslau edition, titled *Deutsche Poemata*. In the postscript of
a letter to Zincgref of 6 November 1624 Opitz begs that his long philosophical poem *Trostgedichte in Widerwertigkeit deß Krieges* (Poem of Consolation
in the Adversity of War), begun in 1621 during his exile in Denmark, continue
to be kept under wraps, as its publication could easily put his life in danger.[13]
The confessionalization that had erupted into this bloodiest of wars had also
prompted him, out of similar fears for his life, to undertake emendations to the
poems published by Zincgref in 1624.[14] The sonnet "Ein Gebet, daß Gott die
Spanier widerumb vom Rheinstrom wolle treiben" (A Prayer that God Again

Drive the Spanish from the Rhine) vividly reflects his anxiety. It expresses an anti-Habsburg view of the penetration of the Spanish troops under the general Ambrogio Spiñola from the occupied Netherlands along the Rhine into the Palatine Electorate in 1620. By 1624 Zincgref may reasonably have assumed that such sentiments, which he shared, were still held by Opitz as well. In fact, as early as his return to Silesia in 1623, Opitz had begun to prepare himself to enter the matrix of confessional politics then dominated by the House of Habsburg. He was successful in this move, though in the early months of 1625 he found himself in a position that necessitated his cooperation with the very authority that he had opposed only shortly before in his *Trostgedichte*.[15] At this juncture, therefore, we are faced with a striking divergence in the lives of the two friends: Zincgref attempts to find asylum in Strasbourg; Opitz accommodates himself to political realities in Silesia that would otherwise be offensive to his personal beliefs. These were two of the poles between which the tensions of this humanist friendship existed.

The Social Sphere

Martin Opitz, born 23 December 1597 in Bunzlau, Silesia, was six years younger than Zincgref. His father Sebastian was a butcher, following an old trade guild tradition that had in the meantime acquired Protestant roots. Notwithstanding Bunzlau's economic boom around 1600, the family's financial situation was precarious, hardly adequate for the son's long-term support — a condition exacerbated as more children were born to his father's subsequent marriages. His advancement from preparatory school to the university was possible only thanks to a scholarship from the endowment of one Martin Rothmann, who in 1595 had donated 200 thalers to assist students from impoverished families.[16] This kind of generosity was due in no small part to the attitude prevailing in late-century Lutheran Protestantism, which bore the clear imprint of the humanist educator Philipp Melanchthon that social charity should include support for education.

The circumstances into which Julius Wilhelm Zincgref was born on 3 June 1591 in Heidelberg were considerably more promising. His father, Laurentius, had moved while still young from Simmern (in the Rhenish Palatinate) to Heidelberg. A lawyer and adherent of the Calvinist-led "Second Reformation,"[17] Laurentius served as a senior member and legal adviser in the high court. His appointment by Elector Friedrich III in 1572 to the Electoral Palatinate's second-most important political body, next to the high commission, resulted in part from an evolving confessional politics that eventually produced a specifically Palatine form of civil service.[18] Among his important friends at the time of his son's birth were Georg Michael Lingelsheim (1556–1636), a member of the high commission, Petrus Denaisius (Peter Denais, 1565–1610), an assessor of the imperial chamber court in Speyer, and Marquard Freher (1565–1614), a member of the high court. All his colleagues were university educated; most were graduates of the law faculty and active in politics at the highest levels, often permanent partners or competitors of noble advisers and assessors in the high court, supreme council, or imperial chamber court. Clearly, the intellectually inclined sons of this class of state officials in the Palatinate had considerable advantages. They typically first completed a course of studies in the liberal arts faculty at one or another of the most prestigious universities in Germany or abroad;[19] they then undertook the international Grand Tour (*peregrinatio academica*), which brought them into contact with foreign intellectuals and provided opportunities to learn foreign languages (especially French) and to become familiar with diverse cultures.[20] The young Zincgref's social sphere, unlike that of the young Opitz, was professionally, academically, and culturally rich in political as well as religious stimulation.

The Confessional Frame of Reference

The lives of Zincgref and Opitz vividly illustrate to what degree that religion and its practices were territorially determined. The divisions of the once unified church and its authority (*potestas*) into many individual churches and religious centers of power over the course of the sixteenth century — this phenomenon has been aptly called "the pluralization of the *ecclesia sancta*"[21] — had nowhere produced a *pax fidei*, a peace within the community of the faithful. Quite to the contrary, the former religious and theological fronts continued to run along the same old fault lines, but now between the old church and the new confessions; within the new confessions splits proliferated between competing sectarian groups. One manifestation of these new polarities was the merciless campaign of Gnesio- (strict, genuine) Lutheranism against Philippistic (moderate) Protestantism; the events precipitated by the attack on Crypto-Calvinism in Saxony in 1574 were particularly loathsome.[22] Conditions in the territorial churches in the Palatinate, as in Silesia, around the time of Zincgref's and Opitz's birth were fraught with similar if differently motivated tensions.

Attempts at a Protestant balance between Lutherans and Reformed (adherents of the Heidelberg Catechism of 1563, the product of the vision of the pious Friedrich III) failed in the Rhenish Palatinate under the electoral administration of Johann Casimir (r. 1583–92), whereas Reformed confessionalization under Elector Friedrich III in Heidelberg largely survived the aggressive Lutheran reaction under Elector Ludwig VI (r. 1576–83). Abrupt changes in confessional loyalties always accompanied the process of confessionalization, as the temporary return of the Palatine church to the Lutheran confession in 1577 illustrates. Under secular state officials the consequences for Reformed pastors and teachers — and for professors at the University of Heidelberg — as well as for Calvinists who held public positions, could be severe. In one southwestern town in 1588 some 600 families out of a population of 6,300 chose to go into exile rather than renounce their faith.[23] The horrors of the St. Bartholomew's Day Massacre that had befallen their French brethren in 1572 contributed to the anticipation of religious persecution among the German Reformed and galvanized the collective consciousness of those bound together in confessional faith. This was the case for the young Zincgref and his family, moderate Calvinists. The condition of religious crisis was somewhat mitigated by the continuation, after Casimir's death in 1592, of his program of re-Calvinization. The last will and testament of Elector Friedrich IV in 1602, which aimed to permanently secure the Reformed faith in the Palatinate, together with the confessional politics of Elector Friedrich V after 1610, did much to shore up Casimir's initial efforts. Stability in the Calvinist church and the continuity of Calvinist life within it appeared guaranteed. However, given the unfortunate confessional experiences of preceding generations and the repeated withholding of imperial recognition of the Calvinist-Reformed faith by and after the Religious Peace of Augsburg of 1555, this stability was only relative and never free of the threat of collapse.

In the Silesia of the young Opitz a similar mix of confessional relationships obtained, despite the differences in political conditions. Opitz's birthplace belonged to the principality of Schweidnitz-Jauer, which was Lutheran around 1600, as was most of Silesia. In only a few areas, such as in the county of Glatz, the principality of Troppau, and the duchy of Oppeln, did Catholics enjoy a majority. Breslau was the residence of a Catholic bishop, though the population at large was mainly Lutheran; a few princes, Johann Christian von Brieg among them, converted to Calvinism. This religious division led to hybrid legal forms of coexistence among the confessions.[24] Many pre-Reformation customs were tenaciously upheld, such as the singing of Latin hymns in the countryside and smaller towns — unthinkable in the Calvinism of the Rhenish Palatinate — a sign of the intensely conservative character of the reform movement in Silesia. Conditions there might have provided unique opportunities for regulating conflicts of faith in the spirit of tolerance, had only the imperial disavowal of Calvinism not precluded it.[25] Although Opitz was Lutheran by birth, as he came under the influence of his gymnasial teachers he began to lean increasingly toward Calvinism. As the confessional status quo shifted with the geographical movement of the religious wars in Europe from west to east, however,[26] he had to arm himself mentally against the severe shocks that now disturbed the peaceful coexistence of the various faiths — much like what had happened in the Parisian bloodbath of 1572 or at the end of Crypto-Calvinism in Saxony in 1574.

Education

Even more emphatically than at other times, education in the age of confessionalization either reflected or opposed existing religious fixations and factored into political actions and developments. Education was in every instance a prerequisite for entry into the professional elite of the changing society and essential to what cultural anthropology calls the *intellectual emancipation* of early modern Europe.[27]

The Silesian Opitz, unlike the Palatine Zincgref, was hindered with an educational handicap from the start. Because Silesia did not have its own university its best students were obliged to go abroad to study. Lutheran students were typically sent to Wittenberg, Reformed to Heidelberg. This handicap could have its advantages, to be sure, in the sense of necessitating an attitude of give-and-take on both confessional sides. On 17 June 1619, twenty-one years of age, brilliantly talented and armed with recommendations from his Silesian patrons, Opitz, under the name Boleslaviensis Silesius, matriculated at the University of Heidelberg, the center of German Late Humanism. As a *candidatus poeseos* he embarked on the study of antiquity and oratory, both staple subjects of the rhetorical era.[28] His former teachers, several of them scholars of high repute, had prepared him well: Valentin Senftleben at the Latin School in Bunzlau (from 1605); Caspar Cunrad at the Magdalena Gymnasium in Breslau (from 1614); Tobias Scultetus and Caspar Dornau at the Schönaichianum (named after its founder, Georg von Schönaich), the elite academy in Beuthen an der Oder (from 1616 to mid-September 1617). More than anyone, it was Dornau (sometimes Latinized as Dornavius; 1577–1631), the director of the Schönaichianum, who pressed Opitz toward a career as a "worldly scholar," one who sought a balance between humanistic scholarship (in Latin), multilingualism (the prerequisite for international diplomacy), and eloquence in the mother tongue.[29]

The world Opitz entered in Heidelberg was familiar, and his transition easy, thanks to the closely knit Silesian-Palatine network. A generation before Opitz, Dornau had spent some six months in Heidelberg in conjunction with his Grand Tour of 1605. He experienced there — and his teaching career at the Schönaichianum owed much to these experiences — everything the university and court could offer for acquiring a dignified political life.[30] The educational cornerstone had been laid by the Lutheran educational reforms of 1558 under Elector Otto Heinrich (Ottheinrich, 1502–59), a bibliophile and art patron, who encouraged the modern restructuring of all university departments, including the liberal arts;[31] the establishment of professorships in Heidelberg was another sure sign of the decisive victory of German humanism. These reforms — basically unaltered by the further reforms of 1580, 1588, and 1672 — endured in their main aspects until 1786 and, as a consequence of Friedrich III's Calvinization, transformed Heidelberg into a center of Calvinist-Reformed learning and endowed the university in the years between 1559 and 1622 with a cosmopolitanism of previously unimaginable proportions.[32] Opitz was welcomed into the heart of this university and courtly culture, being offered a position as tutor in the house of the electoral privy counselor G. M. Lingelsheim. At the turn of the century Lingelsheim's house had been one of the political and literary centers of Heidelberg, frequented by the lawyers Denaisius and the elder Zincgref and by numerous Neo-Latin authors, including Paul Melissus Schede (1539–1602) and Janus Gruter (1560–1627), both of whom served as librarians at the renowned Palatina library. Lingelsheim's house was still serving this function as late as 1619, its doors now open also to the young poets Zincgref and Opitz. Opitz had arrived in Heidelberg with no specific plans for his education and profession;[33] his one-and-a-half-year stay, however, steeped in an atmosphere of humanistic scholarship and chivalric camaraderie, international exposure and political ambition, offered him valuable schooling in the art of political life.

Zincgref had comparable experiences. A native Heidelberger, born into the highest level of the civil service class, he enjoyed every educational advantage. His father's life served as an immediate example of the social benefits of higher education. Lingelsheim had sent his son Friedrich, a friend of Julius Wilhelm, to the public Paedagogium, and the elder Zincgref insisted on doing the same with his own son rather than having him educated by private tutors.[34] One of Julius Wilhelm's outstanding teachers was Melchior Adam, a Silesian, who had taught at the Paedagogium since 1601, becoming deputy headmaster and later serving as headmaster from 1613 until his death in 1622. It was Adam (ca. 1575–1622) who founded the modern genre of scholarly biography with his five volumes of *Vitae* (1615–20) of German philosophers, theologians, lawyers, and doctors. Zincgref matriculated on 5 October 1607 at his home university in the open lectures, or *auditoria*, of the liberal arts. The distinguished faculty included the eminent scholar of Greek, Aemilius Portus (Emilio Porto, 1550–1614), and the professor of eloquence and Latin poetic arts Simon Stenius (Sten, 1540–1619). His favorite lecturer was the renowned Dutch historian, ethicist, and philologist Janus Gruter, who advanced to the title of "grand patron" during his years at the university. He studied *philosophia practica* with Reinhard Bachovius (Bachoffen) von Echt (1544–1614), whose academic career was repeatedly plagued by confessional changes in Saxony and the Palatinate (from Crypto-Calvinist to Calvinist to Lutheran to Catholic and again to Calvinist).[35] It was probably von Echt, later a professor of law, who, as dean of the law faculty in 1619–20, presided in March 1620 over the conferral of the *Juris doctor* degree on Zincgref. Two others who had a significant share in his legal education were the Parisian Dionysius Gothofredus (Godefroy), who since 1604 had lectured on the humanistically informed legal theory of the *mos Gallicus* (French customary law), and Philipp Hoffmann, who held the office of university rector several times. Zincgref showed his gratitude by dedicating epigrams to all of them. The epigrams were edited and published in 1619 in the *Triga amico-poetica* (Poetry by Three Friends) by the Gymnasium professor Johann Leonhard Weidner (1588–1655), who had also collected the youthful Latin poetry of Zincgref and Friedrich Lingelsheim, in addition to his own.[36]

Zincgref's path from the liberal arts *studium generale* to a curriculum leading to the professional law degree was not as direct as the date of his doctoral degree (1620) would suggest. After his *cursus* through the liberal arts he progressed rapidly enough to the study of law; but then the detours began, and at a defining point in his life. His three-and-a-half-year-long Grand Tour (June 1612 to October 1615) had been dedicated to the study of law (matriculation at the University of Basel, July 1612; thesis defense, 1613; matriculation at the University of Orléans, 1613–14) and, typically for German Calvinists, had involved mainly western Europe (from Switzerland to France, England, and the Netherlands). He began to disappoint his friends and supporters, however, when he fell behind in his studies and was unable to take up an appropriate position in due course. In a letter to Gruter of 23 January 1618, more than two years after Zincgref's return to Heidelberg, Weidner remarked, "Julius noster quod inter Doctores juris nuperos non conspiciendus erat, demiror" (I am astonished that our Julius has been nowhere to be seen among the new doctors of law).[37] Zincgref's mother, widowed since 1610, was also troubled by her son's apparent diffidence. Nor did he, as we learn from his autobiographical poem "De seipso" (About Myself, in Weidner's *Triga*, 198–99), seriously consider, despite his excellent connections, taking a state position as expected of him, and which no doubt would have been immediately forthcoming.

According to "De seipso" he rejected the usual career path of his estate in order to enter rather a different kind of service to his *patria*.[38] His Grand Tour had introduced him to the world of European politics and international science and letters and opened his eyes to the lack of worldly sophistication of young Germans and their professors in Heidelberg. Zincgref received a startling letter from Gruter while in England in 1615; in it Gruter recommended no fewer than forty-five English and Dutch scholars to him for his studies abroad and spoke, by contrast, derisively of the "fumus palatinus" (Palatine fog) that covered the world of education back home. By *fumus*, which has a meteorological meaning of "fog" and a metaphorical meaning of "stuffy air," Gruter had found an apt image to express the inferiority of local education in comparison with elsewhere in Europe.[39] The effect of the letter on Zincgref helped to galvanize his new political will to become an active participant in current events, not only in the Palatinate but in the broader world as well.

Education and Confession

Wherever education and confession collided, education was decisive in creating the behavioral models for dealing with these conflicts. Opitz's model was different from Zincgref's in a way that has led some scholars to accuse him of being "shifty," or "more diplomat than poet," or an "opportunist and careerist." Indeed, a review of the highlights of his life lend some ostensible credence to this suspicion: 1620: Opitz composes an encomium for Friedrich V of the Palatinate, head of the Protestant Union and newly elected king of Bohemia, thus openly throwing his support to the Reformed elector's claim to being the leading Protestant challenger of the Habsburgs. 1623: Having fled into exile to Jylland (in Denmark) in 1621 following the defeat of the "Winter King" (Friedrich V), he returns to Silesia — he had never graduated from any of the three higher colleges — and resides alternately with the Protestant dukes Hans Ulrich von Schaffgotsch in Warmbrunn and Georg Rudolf in Liegnitz. Although the Silesian estates had been promised freedom of religion in an imperial decree of 1622, its guarantee is jeopardized by the rising Catholic party in Silesia. 1625: He joins a delegation of Silesian estates to Vienna under the leadership of Baron Karl Hannibal Dohna. After the failure of the Palatine-Bohemian plan Dohna had become president of the Silesian chamber and thus the most powerful champion of the Habsburg cause in Silesia. As the sole

Catholic among the Silesian aristocrats and as a loyalist to the emperor, Dohna refuses to acknowledge the claim of Friedrich V. In the course of this diplomatic mission Opitz is crowned poet laureate by Emperor Ferdinand II and receives a special accolade for his Latin and German poem of condolence, which he personally hands to the emperor, on the death of Habsburg Archduke Karl, the bishop of Breslau. 1626: He becomes private secretary to Dohna and consequently finds himself privy to extremely sensitive confessional-political affairs. A letter to Gruter of 20 November implies that he has been officially granted freedom of religion: "Patronum habeo illustrissimum burggravium de Dhona [. . .], aversum quidem a religione nostra, ita tamen mei amantem, ut benevolentiam eius praedicare satis non valeam" (I have a most illustrious patron in Count Dohna, who, though opposed to my own religion, yet loves me the more, so that I hardly am able to express how good he is).[40] 1627: Opitz is awarded a peerage through the intercession of Dohna and receives his patent of nobility in Prague from the emperor himself; henceforth he is Opitz von Boberfeld. With the expiration of the Dresden Accords of 1621, which had first guaranteed Silesian Catholics their freedom of worship, the Catholicization of Silesia is expedited and soon explodes in violence. 1628: Given the subsequent persecution of Protestants in Silesia, Opitz feels compelled to take part in Catholic rites. 1629–30: He translates the theological work *Manuale controversarium* (1623) by the Jesuit Martin Becanus (von der Breck, 1563–1624),[41] for which he receives, at the insistence of Dohna, 200 thalers from the emperor. He dedicates the first part of the newly reprinted *Deutsche Poemata* to the Reformed Prince Ludwig von Anhalt and the second part to his Catholic lord, the very person leading the persecution of the Protestants in Silesia. 1630: Dohna orders Opitz to Paris on a mission, whose purpose remains unclear to this day. Along the way he visits his old Heidelberg Reformed friends Lingelsheim and Bernegger. In Paris he finds himself at the center of the French political elite. At meetings of the city's leading intellectual society, the Cabinet Dupuy, he makes contact with members of the irenic-minded *politiques*,[42] including Jacques Auguste de Thou the Younger, son of the former president of the Cabinet Dupuy,[43] and establishes a friendship with the foremost theorist of international law, Hugo Grotius (1583–1645). 1631: Opitz translates Grotius's irenic work on religion from the original Dutch into German as *Von der Wahrheit der Christlichen Religion* (On the Truth of the Christian Religion) and dedicates his translation to the city council of Breslau. He then composes defamatory poems on Magdeburg, which had been humiliated by imperial troops, provoking howls of indignation from the Protestant camp. 1633: After the conquest of Breslau by allied Protestant forces, which puts Dohna to flight to Prague and forces the withdrawal of imperial troops from Silesia, Opitz enters the service of the Protestant Piast dukes Georg Rudolf and Johann Christian, now the most powerful princes in Silesia, as their *chargé d' affaires* in negotiating with sovereigns and military leaders. 1635–36: With the Peace of Prague, which obligates Silesia to swear loyalty to the emperor, Opitz loses his position with the Piast dukes, who go into Polish exile; he is recommended to the Catholic king

Vladislav IV of Poland and in his new position composes *Lobgedichte An die Königliche Majestät zu Polen* (Encomium to His Royal Majesty of Poland)[44] and is subsequently given an audience with the king in Danzig. He takes up residence with the Reformed preacher Bartholomäus Nigrinus even as he becomes active in King Vladislav's diplomatic corps. 1637: He is appointed royal historiographer and will remain in the service of the Polish crown until his death in 1639. Shortly before his death he visits his father, who had fled from Bunzlau, in Lissa on the German-Polish border.

That Opitz survived all of these changes unscathed as a servant to many confessional lords is in fact a testament to his character, intellect, and inexhaustible resources of knowledge, but equally to his diplomacy, his capacity for political accommodation, and not least to his ability to distance himself from, or operate within, confessional realities. It would be misguided to conclude that there was some fundamental disconnect between his personal beliefs and his political loyalties.[45] Whether the radical criticism that the Young Germans directed at Goethe, that he was simultaneously "Dichterfürst und Fürstenknecht" (poet prince and prince's knave),[46] might equally apply to Opitz is dubious at best, and impossible to answer at any rate apart from an appreciation of the historical context. The traumatic confessional struggles of the time gave rise to utopian visions about the best of all possible states (*de optimo statu reipublicae*) and irenic projects of human cooperation, even as they induced strategies of moral dissimulation and models for political survival. One notable model for survival was through imitation of the life (*imitatio vitae*) of a successful man,[47] such as that exemplified by the renowned Dutch legal historian Justus Lipsius (1547–1606), an only slightly older contemporary. Worldly men of the seventeenth century not only were conversant with Lipsius's great philosophical and political works, especially the six volumes of *Politica* (1589) and *De constantia* (On Steadfastness, 1584); they were equally impressed by the example of the great author's confessional flexibility as demonstrated in his going from one professorship at a university affiliated to one confession to another with another affiliation as developments necessitated. Although this strategy was viewed with suspicion in the intellectual circles of Late Humanism, it nevertheless was seized upon as an effective model for negotiating the dangerous political waters of the age.[48] Opitz's close relationship with the Strasbourg historian Bernegger, whose special interest was modern political science and who repeatedly lectured on Lipsius's *Politica*; his stay in Leiden in 1620 after fleeing Heidelberg; and his encounter with the dramatist Daniel Heinsius (1580–1655), one of the luminaries of Dutch Late Humanism, all would appear to comport with the Lipsian model.

Zincgref shared Opitz's intense interest in Lipsius. The personality profile that emerges of Zincgref, however, when we compare his responses to situations over approximately the same span of time, is significantly different from that of his friend.[49] 1619: He composes *Ad Fridericum Bohemiae regem* (To Friedrich, King of Bohemia), an epos of 184 hexameters,[50] which not only espouses positions congruent with official Palatine politics but indeed adjures the young ruler to accept the Bohemian crown, hoping by this appeal to rouse the politically uncommitted to action.[51] March 1620: He completes his doctoral degree in sacred and secular law (*in utroque Jure Doctoratus gradum*),[52] doubtless anticipating its usefulness, given the predicatable military actions that will be provoked by Friedrich's coronation (late October to early November 1619), but also to make himself ready to assume political office. December 1621: Following the anticipated outbreak of war he becomes general auditor, which gives him command of the Heidelberg garrison. 1622: During the siege of Heidelberg, "der Calvinisten fürnembstes Asylum vnd Ketzer Nest" (the chief Calvinist asylum and heretics' nest), as the Palatinate's enemies called it,[53] Zincgref appeals in a verse pamphlet, *Vermanung zur Dapfferkeit* (Exhortation to Bravery), to the soldierly honor of the city's defenders. In the same year, after the fall of Heidelberg in September, he flees to Strasbourg and enters the service of the French diplomat Guillaume Marescot as interpreter. 1625–26: He returns to Worms via Strasbourg and devotes himself to literary activities. December 1626 to May 1627: In St. Goar he marries Anna Nordeck, a well-to-do, intelligent, and beautiful widow, daughter of the Hessian commissar.[54] November 1628: Balthasar Venator, tutor to the sons of Lingelsheim in Strasbourg, writes to Opitz: "De Zinckgrevio diu nihil vidi, nihil audivi. Homo uxorem duxit, et, credo, negotiosus est" (No one has heard from Zincgref for a long time. He has taken a wife and, I believe, is preoccupied).[55] May 1630: A fragment of a letter from Lingelsheim to Christoph Coler (1602–58), Opitz's first biographer,[56] alludes to the political dilemma of the Calvinists: "Zincgrefius privatus vivit cum uxore in Palatinatu sub Hispanorum dominatu, ac se melioribus temporibus servat" (The private man Zincgref is living with his wife in the Palatinate, now under Spanish rule, and looks forward to better times; Schnorr von Carolsfeld 485). 1631–32: Better times appear be in store for him, as well as for the Protestant cause in general, with the entrance of Swedish King Gustav Adolf into the war.[57] 1632: Count Palatine Philipp Ludwig, the younger brother of Friedrich V, appoints Zincgref to the magistrate clerkship in Kreuznach; Ludwig's second son, the elector Karl, confirms Zincgref as magistrate clerk in the municipality of Alzey. The good times suddenly vanish, however, beginning this same year with Gustav Adolf's death on the battlefield, and reach a disastrous low point in the fall of 1634 with the defeat of the Swedes in the Battle of Nördlingen.

Zincgref's steadfastness through all these confessional and political struggles was comparable to Lingelsheim's, the guiding personality of Late Humanism in Heidelberg. How one historian has described Lingelsheim is surely applicable to Zincgref as well: "kein Vertreter einer militanten reformierten Orthodoxie mehr, doch bei aller Irenik hielt er entschieden am reformierten Glauben fest" (no representative of a militant Reformed orthodoxy, and despite all irenic leanings, he nevertheless held firm to the Reformed faith).[58] The behavioral model of changing one's confession for the sake of personal survival seems to have tempted Zincgref no more than it did Lingelsheim or Gruter, two of his intellectual fathers, or so many other Reformed scholars and diplomats in the Palatinate, for that matter. They would have preferred to leave the country or retire to private life or do whatever was necessary rather than to dissimulate or renounce their faith. This conviction by no means prevented them from promoting peace and harmony within their various Protestant and Reformed communities. In the seminal *Apologia* to the third edition (1624) of his *Facetiae pennalium* (Facetiousness of Feathery Things, 1618), Zincgref castigates the "Constantinopolitanische Kirchengezänck" (Constantinopolitan church wrangling) as an omen of the "herrlichen Reichs vnnd gantzen Lands vndergang vnnd versclafirung" (demise and enslavement of our glorious empire and country).[59] He did not intend this confessional criticism, which from the standpoint of orthodox Calvinism flirted with heresy, as an indictment of the whole system; he did not seek to depart from basic doctrine but only to avoid confessional fighting. The irenic thinking behind all this was rooted in ancient European traditions and their late-humanist adaptations. The notion of a humanistically softened Calvinism has sometimes been related to this strain of Reformed thinkers.[60] It is accurate on two counts: they remained Calvinists while holding decidedly to Reformed convictions; and Calvinism, in both theory and practice, did indeed undergo humanistic moderation. Whatever criticism was expressed, whatever modifications were sought, did not imply any kind of quietism.[61] The literary work of Zincgref is proof enough of this.

Texts and Contexts: Zincgref

Whereas *Gebrauchslyrik* (occasional verse written for ceremonial or social occasions) — another staple of the early modern period — had dominated Zincgref's early period, after his return from his Grand Tour in the fall of 1615 it diminished in interest.[62] It was his friend Weidner who decided to collect Zincgref's casual poetry — along with his own and that of Friedrich Lingelsheim — for the friendship book *Triga amico-poetica*. Zincgref did return to casual verse now and then, for instance his epitaph "De obitu Iacobi Augusti Thuani" (On the Death of Jacques Auguste de Thou, 1617), the great French *politique* and, as he calls him, "Historiae vindex" (champion of historiography).[63] His early casual poetry, extending from the "Elegia ad amicos" (Elegy to Friends, 1606) to the printing of the *Triga* (1619), reflected a vigorous engagement with the sociocultural world of Late Humanism and with its Neo-Latin linguistic instrument, whose communicative authority remained as yet uncontested and whose primary rhetorical discourse, the *genus demonstrativum*, was particularly suited for panegyric.[64]

By contrast to his early interest in occasional poetry, between 1615 and 1623 (following the fall of Heidelberg in the fall of the preceding year) Zincgref turned aggressively to the publication of independent works in both German and Latin: *Facetiae* (1618), *Emblemata* (1619), *Epos ad Fridericum* (1619), *Newe Zeitungen* (1619), *Zeitung auß der ChurPfaltz* (1621), *Vermanung zur Dapfferkeit* (1622; printed 1623), and *Quodlibetisches Weltkefig* (World Cage, Any Way You Will, 1623).[65] These works were no longer written on special occasions for individuals or small groups; no longer poetry, that is, with conventions explicitly identifiable with *ständisch* (estate-ordered) society, but as monographic responses to the politics and public issues of the day and intended for audiences well beyond the Palatinate.[66] Zincgref's two major concerns were the political struggle in the Palatinate and the advancement of German poetry, which he personifies as the *Teutsche Musa* (German Muse). These were actually two aspects of a single overriding political issue: Zincgref recognized the political unrest in the Palatinate as essentially a struggle for Calvinism and a Calvinistically led Germany, that is to say, for the liberation of Germany from Catholic Spanish influence. It was also political, as he remarked, "sintemahl es nicht ein geringes Joch ist / von einer außländischen Nation beherrschet und Tyrannisiret werden" (in the sense that it is no small burden to be dominated and tyrannized by a foreign nation).[67] Zincgref waged his battle at first with polemical fervor, for his educational experiences in other western European cultural centers had made it all too clear just how alienated and impractical Germany's educational system was. In his *Apologia* to the third edition of the satirical *Facetiae* Zincgref castigates the system's ineffectuality as a training ground for worldly service and office:

> vnd wurtzelt freylich diese durchteuffelte Schulzänckercy [. . .] in manchem also eyn / daß sie auch hernach in andern höhern facultatibus, vnnd im Politischen Wesen / ja im Regiment vnd Landsverwesung offtmahl grosse Vnheyl / zerrüttungen vnd verderben vervrsachen.[68]

> [and this devilish school bickering takes root in many who, later on, in other faculties and political institutions, indeed in the government and provincial administration, frequently cause great mischief and disruptions, even ruination].

For Zincgref, criticism of the educational system was a form of patriotism. Impractical education, according to the reader's preface to the *Facetiae*, produces "an statt wenig Gelehrter / viel Waichling vnnd verdorbene Banckerottirische Studenten vnnd Schreiber" (instead of a few scholars, many weaklings and profligate, bankrupt students and scribes) and thus undermines the military training crucial to the implementation of Palatine-German politics.[69] Zincgref renewed this attack on the militarily unfit youth five years later in the satirical-polemical pamphlet *Quodlibetisches Weltkefig*, a decision that seems to qualify it, however, as a monarchomachic work, particularly in light of the broader context of his other writings.[70] As a military judge he composed *Vermanung zur Dapfferkeit* at about the same time and for similar reasons, namely, to encourage and embolden the soldiers of his garrison who had been accused of cowardice by the local citizens:

> Drumb gehet dapffer an, Ihr meine Kriegsgenossen,
> Schlagt ritterlich darein.[71] (vv. 121–22)

> [Proceed, then, with courage, comrades in arms. Strike as becomes a knight!]

Vermanung zur Dapfferkeit is a poem that calls to action. Its urgency stems from its anti-Habsburg, antipapal feeling, combined with the resolve to defend the city against the Catholic Spanish League; the sense of historical crisis is enhanced by poetic-rhetorical means, as we shall see.

Historical reality had also provided the frame for his *Emblematum ethico-politicorum centuria* (One Hundred Ethical-Political Emblems) of 1619. In view of the Palatine-Bohemian venture, and with the *Politica* of Justus Lipsius in mind, Zincgref uses images and commentary to present an emblematic primer in governmental theory, in which civil policy (*prudentia civilis*) is complemented by military policy (*prudentia militaris*), the latter having the mandate to protect the government and the citizens. Zincgref modifies Lipsius, however, by assigning the final five emblems to represent the perspective of the "moderate absolutists" in Heidelberg Calvinism: citizens (*cives*) and ruler (*princeps*) share responsibility for the common welfare, that is, the principle of reciprocity of obligation emphatically includes participation by the citizenry, especially in times of national crisis. Given the political character of the emblem book it is understandable that Zincgref, through the high councilor Lingelsheim, sought — successfully, as it turned out — to have it published under the patronage of Friedrich V.[72] A general monarchomachic objective, as allowed for under certain circumstances by the strict Calvinist theory of sovereignty, would have run contrary to Zincgref's convictions.

Because Zincgref is responding as a poet to a pressing historical situation, it is important not only to look at what he says but also how he says it. *Vermanung zur Dapfferkeit* begins with an alexandrine couplet:

> Kein Tod ist löblicher, kein Tod wird mehr geehret,
> Als der, durch den das Heil deß Vatterlandts sich nehret.

[No death is nobler, no death more honored, than that by which the welfare of the fatherland is nourished.]

The allusion to the so-called Roman ode of Horace (3,2), specifically to the patriotic wording of line 13: "dulce et decorum est pro patria mori" (it is sweet and glorious to die for the fatherland), should be obvious enough. Zincgref's specific reference, however, is to the fragmentary song of the Greek poet Tyrtaeus (7th c. B.C.). That it was Horace himself who pointed to Tyrtaeus is apparent in lines 401–3 of the *Ars poetica*, where he invokes the *virtus bellica* of Homer and Tyrtaeus: "post hos insignis Homerus / Tyrtaeusque mares animos in Martia bella versibus exacuit" (After these [earlier poets] Homer won his renown, and Tyrtaeus with his verses fired manly hearts for battles of Mars). Such intertextuality is typical of Zincgref. The model for his *Vermanung zur Dapfferkeit* is drawn from the early Greek poetic tradition of battle counsel (*paraenesis*), with which he was familiar from the Neo-Latin translations of Philipp Melanchthon and others. Additional foreign voices, such as Horace's, are built in to achieve the greatest possible degree of persuasion (*movere*).

Zincgref employs a similar approach in the *Facetiae pennalium*, a polemic pamphlet sharing the conventions of the *facetiae* collection *Philogelos* (ca. 5th c. A.D.) and the Hellenistic *Characteres* of Aristotle's pupil Theophrastus (ca. 372–287 B.C.), both of which passed through Neo-Latin versions by

Melchior Goldast (1578–1635), Marquard Freher, and others. Zincgref scolds the scholars and students in Heidelberg in a satirical mode that draws on both contemporary and ancient critics of education. This reception of antiquity and its contemporary reworkings are keys to understanding the *Emblemata ethico-politica* as well. The book's macrostructure mirrors the early modern emblem itself, a mixed, or intermedial, tripartite genre; the commentaries to the 100 emblems are borrowed from antiquity and postantiquity, as well as from modern adaptations; quotations are based on literary and nonliterary texts of Greek and Roman antiquity, Byzantine literature, the Latin Middle Ages, legal writings, and humanist philology. Three hundred fifty of the nearly 1,300 quotations are taken from Greek texts and rendered into Latin by some fifty translators, among them the Florentine Neo-Platonist Marsilio Ficino, Erasmus, and Melanchthon, which guaranteed their wide reception. The commentaries, enriched by great diversity of genres and traditions, themselves constitute the unique textual form known since the middle of the fourth century A.D. as the cento (a poem made up of verses of other poems). Rediscovered in the Italian Renaissance, the cento was seized upon in the North by Julius Caesar Scaliger (1484–1558), the renowned French classical scholar,[73] and exploited for literary use by Lipsius in his *Politica*. Zincgref practiced the cento technique in emulation of Lipsius. The complex artifice of the emblem book satisfied the expectations of his intended audience, the *respublica litteraria*, in two ways: by responding to the poetological demand of the epoch for sophisticated invention (*fabricare*), and by demonstrating the workshop, or collective, character of mixed-genre production so esteemed in early modern literature and art. As its workshop characterization implies, other hands were involved in the making of the *Emblemata*: Matthäus Merian (1621–87), the most renowned copperplate engraver of the day, for the conception of the images (*picturae*); Gruter for advice on book sources; former university friends for the French *subscriptiones*; and Lingelsheim for facilitating publication.

Facetiae, *characteres* (textual types as understood by Theophrastus), battle paraenesis, epic verse oration, emblem, scholarly commentary, cento, pamphlet: Zincgref allows nonclassical elements (early- and late-ancient genres, textual types, subject types, and writing styles) to be amalgamated with obligatory modern forms (such as the pamphlet) and functional modes (political, critical, journalistic, even propagandistic). This holds true also for the two books of *Der Teutschen Scharpfsinnige kluge Sprüch* (Witty German Aphorisms, 1626 and 1631), written in his final phase of creativity. An enormous amount of work went into compiling these two volumes. The first alone contains some 1,635 brief narrations (the second volume added more than 450). The following one is typical:

> Hertzog Fridrich der Weiße / Churfürst in Sachsen. Als jhm etliche gerathen Erfort zuvberziehen vnd zubelägeren / es würde nicht vber fünff Mann kosten / antwortet er: Es were mit einem zu viel.[74]

> [Duke Friedrich the Wise, Electoral Prince of Saxony. When he was advised to go by way of Erfurt and lay siege there, an action that

would not cost more than five men, he answered, Even one would be too
many.]

By composing this kind of minimalist historical narrative, which formally combines situation and aphorism or wise saying (*Denkspruch*), Zincgref is referencing the apophthegm genre, cultivated most famously by that friend of Roman
worthies, Plutarch (mentioned at the outset of this chapter for his *Bioi
paralleloi*).[75] Its modern practice began with Erasmus's *Apophthegmata* of 1531
and was given its definitive description only much later by the Jesuit poet Jacob
Pontanus (Spanmüller, 1542–1626) in his *Attica bellaria* (Attic Dessert) of
1616.[76] Zincgref employs eclectic forms and traditions to create the work for
which he is best known: from imperial and regional historical accounts to
biographies, table-talks, homilies, colloquial forms, and collections of *loci communes* (commonplaces), even to oral and other unprinted materials.[77] The first
book of apophthegms in particular reflects both the acute problems of bilingual
culture since High Humanism as well as the boundaries between late-humanist
ständisch culture and popular culture. The sayings are arranged strictly according to clerical or secular speakers, much as Opitz organized the *Ausgabe letzter
Hand* (authorized edition) of his poetry into *Geistliche Poemata* and *Weltliche
Poemata* (Religious and Secular Poems); but the organization simultaneously
reflects the social status of the speakers, so that the apophthegms of the *Volk*,
the *cives* as defined in Calvinist political theory, are not only included but
indeed accorded commensurable space. The question of the *Teutsche Musa* as
an implicit "political question" is added to the "social question" as a further
determining perspective when Zincgref, reeling under the devastating loss of his
patria and its library, the very home and institutional hearth of Calvinism,
addresses the dedication to Count Philipp Moritz von Hanau:

> Demnach ich dann bey diesen trübseligen zeiten / schwermütige
> gedancken zuvertreiben / jederweilen die Teutsche Geschichten vor
> mich genommen / vnd auß denselben vnserer Landsleut *Apophthegmata*
> oder kluge reden auffgezeichnet [. . .] / zu dem end / [. . .] dem
> Vatterland zu gutem / vnnd der vhralten zugleich freythätig vnnd
> freyredigen Nation zu ehren / dieser gestalt wollen lassen außkommen.[78]
>
> [Thus in order to exorcise my melancholy in these depressing times, I
> consulted the German histories and extracted the *apophthegmata*, or wise
> sayings, of our countrymen, and have published them for the good of our
> fatherland and to honor our ancient free and free-speaking nation.]

Cultural patriotism must prevail, even if the crisis of state appears to shatter all
hope for a politically (read: Calvinistically) united Germany. By "crisis of state"
Zincgref understood the war-torn conditions in the Palatinate and other
Calvinist territories, not a threat to the state's own entity, or integrity, in the
nationalistic sense that arose in the nineteenth century. It is no wonder then
that Zincgref organized the book, and its continuation in 1631, as he did, by
selecting and combining the "clever sayings" in the spirit of Protestantism, specifically the Second Reformation. He understood it as simultaneously history

book and commemorative book in one. His interest in the recently published state novel *Argenis* (1621) — written by the Catholic Scotsman John Barclay (1582–1621) while at the papal court in Rome just before his death — was certainly of a piece with his work on the apophthegm collection. It is uncertain, however, whether he read *Argenis* as a grand epic about the subordination of church to state, that is, in the way that particularly fascinated late-humanist intellectuals suffering under the "Constantinopolitan church wrangling" mentioned above.[79]

Texts and Contexts: Opitz

Opitz translated Seneca's tragedy *Troades* (as *Die Trojanerinnen*, Trojan Women) and Barclay's *Argenis* in close temporal proximity (1625 and 1626), during a period of his life when, like Zincgref, he had no secure employment. He takes pains in his Latin dedication to the *Trojanerinnen* to make very clear, however, that his translation is not to be appreciated merely as casual poetry, but as part of a serious literary-political program:

> Sciant [. . .] hostes Musarum omnisque humanitatis, superesse etiamnum in his bellorum ciuilium quantumnis atrocissimis calamitatibus summos maximosque viros, qui literarum nostrarum, sine quibus ne res quidem publicae constare satis videntur, gloriam mirum in modum fouent ac tuentur.[80]
>
> [The enemies of the Muses and all humanity should know that even under the blows of these misfortunate civil wars — however horrible they may be — great and exalted men still live who cultivate and protect our literature in magnificent fashion, without which no state can exist.]

One of these "great and exalted men" was August Buchner, his frequent correspondent, to whom Opitz dedicates the translation. It is of vital importance that we not fail to recognize the explicit connection between crisis of state and literary program. Both Opitz and Zincgref made use of the classical literary tradition (specifically referenced in the *Trojanerinnen* by the term *Seneca tragicus*), which opens up a view on the history of an uncommonly complex literary process. Seneca's tragedy had long been cited as one example from the long *exempla* tradition before it itself ever became a model text in later reception history: four Greek plays (by Sophocles and Euripides) with subjects and characters from the corpus of sagas surrounding the Trojan War are combined in Seneca's text to escalate to an extreme the gruesomeness of events surrounding the fall of Troy, thereby to choreograph the ultimate version of "vitae hominis calamitas," the tragedy of human life. Opitz's translation belongs to this complex tradition. A great storehouse of principles and practices, transmitted through the periods of Italian and French Renaissance Humanism and directly motivated by Dutch Late Humanism, provided Opitz with the means to achieve his purposes:[81] to give expression to the contemporary experience of civil war, as modeled in post-Augustan imperial depictions of the *res tragicae*, themselves taken from the barbarian histories of mythical times; and to offer this experience as a metaphor for the modern calamity:

> [C]aptiuae nostrae [. . .] exemplo publice & in oculis omnium ostendant, non esse nouum hoc malum, vrbes validissimas integraque regna & prouincias exscindi funditus & vastari. Doceant nos quoque suum illud doloris qualecunque remedium: Moderatius ferri sortem eam posse, quam & alii ante nos passi sunt, & nunc tam multi nobiscum patiuntur. (*Weltliche Poemata* 312)

> [Our prisoners should teach by example, openly and before the eyes of everyone, that it is not an unprecedented evil that lays waste our greatest cities, kingdoms, and provinces. They should teach us the same remedy that they themselves (viz., as the chorus) have learned in sadness. Such a fate is easier to bear when others have born it before us and others now bear it with us.]

The concept of historical parallels exemplified in the dedication to Opitz's *Trojanerinnen* informs his reading of Barclay's *Argenis* as well, both with respect to form as to content. Indeed, the form-content correlation so fascinated contemporary readers that *Argenis* became the unsurpassed model, as Mikhail Bakhtin has observed,[82] for the new European novel, and would remain so well into the eighteenth century. The appeal of *Argenis* to the literary sophistication of the republic of letters made it a European bestseller for more than a century. In addition to the 1623 edition of the Neo-Latin original, Opitz mainly consulted an early French adaptation that somewhat enhanced the novel's structural lines. As a narrative form *Argenis* stemmed from two traditions: Homer's *Odyssey* and Heliodorus's prose *Aithiopica* (ca. 250 A.D.). Through use of such narrative devices as opening *in medias res,* prequel, teleological strategies, hypotactic connections, and digression (*parecbasis*), Barclay was able to draw modernizing parallels within an otherwise strict hierarchical scheme of narration. Its modernizations were not, to be sure, only a product of narrative strategy, but owed equally to the content, particularly the literary treatment of the most recent political issues. The increase in political content assured *Argenis,* as well as the whole genre, its unique character,[83] especially remarkable for its many digressions, into which themes of immediate relevance are integrated in dialogue form: theories and practice of rulership; theories of state, administration, and law; military reforms and the pros and cons of a standing army; census-taking and taxation; institutionalization and duties of diplomacy; or questions of confessionalization. *Argenis* proved to be an exemplary political novel precisely because of this kind of cataloguing, which derived in great part from the courtly system of selectivity.[84] And it was typically read as an exemplary work, as suggested by Gruter in a letter of reply to Lingelsheim on 19 June 1622, thanking him for a copy of the book and concerning the interest of "Zincgrefius noster" (our Zincgref) for the novel: "Multum tibi debeo de Barclaii Argenide, quam a capite ad calcem totam uno impetu perlegi [. . .] verum non videtur totam fabulam ideo exorsus esse: sed potius ut sub ea boni malique principis proponeret exemplar" (Many thanks for Barclay's *Argenis*, which I read from start to finish in one sitting. He seems to have begun the whole story in order to present, within its covers, master examples of the good and bad prince).[85] Gruter's focus on the exemplary in *Argenis* pertains not just to the normative elements of rulership discourse in the tradition of the *Fürstenspiegel* (mirror of princes); given the history of confessionalization, it had to do rather more specifically with whether, for the sake of creating a stable peace, the theory of the good ruler should imply a correlative state's monopoly on power. The novel as a whole was understood from the time of its publication as a *roman à clef*, since Barclay himself, in his important theoretical discussion of the novel as form in book 2, chapter 14, clearly demonstrates.[86] Barclay's handling of the dedication is further proof of this: it is dedicated to Louis XIII of France, still a minor (the Breslau publisher David Müller dedicated Opitz's translation to the sons of the duke of Brieg). As a didactic political novel *Argenis* evidently meant to show both the sovereign's obligation of and his means to absolute responsibility. The fact that the novel was read repeatedly by the power-conscious Cardinal Richelieu,[87] who had run the affairs of state for Louis since 1622, also confirms that *Argenis* was a relevant novel of state. Opitz's hastily published translation introduced Barclay's politically sensitive novel into the current debate on the crisis of state, though it had been read and discussed ever since it first appeared within the close circle of Heidelberg scholars (Zincgref, Lingelsheim, and Gruter, among others) distressed at the failed Palatine-Bohemian venture.

All of Opitz's paradigmatic works mentioned here constitute important building blocks toward a political biography deriving from a source area that has been distinctly undervalued since the Baroque: that of translation, recognized again only in recent scholarship as an independent and original accomplishment.[88] The comparatively few studies from the older research (prior to approximately 1970) that recognized the political function of literature focused mainly on works with an explicit political "message";[89] the translations of *Troades* and *Argenis* could be included, though as somewhat exceptional cases, in this corpus. One must certainly include *Trostgedichte in Widerwertigkeit deß Krieges*, still rightly considered the most significant political-moral verse composition of the century, in this core group of political texts.[90] This great work provides a powerful *memento* (4, 417–19):

> . . . . in diesen schweren Kriegen /
> In dieser bösen Zeit / in diesen letzten Zügen
> Der nunmehr-krancken Welt;
>
> [in these hard wars, in this evil time, in these final gasps of the now-so-ill world];

also a militant appeal to battle readiness (3, 213–14):

> Jetzt steht die Freyheit selbst wie gleichsam auff der Spitzen /
> Die schreyt vns sehnlich zu / die müssen wir beschützen;
>
> [Freedom herself stands now in great danger; she cries out to us fervently; we must come to her defense];

as well as a scene of shocking relevance, culminating in references to the
"Parisian Blood Wedding" (the St. Bartholomew's Massacre) of 1572, now
ghastly elevated to the cosmic level as the individual fate of the wizened
Huguenot leader Coligny (3, 110–16):

> Wie hin durch gantz Pariß die newen Hochzeit-Brunnen
> Gequollen sind durch Blut / durch Christen-Blut / gemacht /
> ·
> Der streitbare Colin ward erstlich auffgerieben /
> Auff Erden fortgeschleppt / ins Wasser eingesenckt /
> Mit Fewer halb verbrandt / in Lüfften auffgehenckt.

[As through the length of Paris the new wedding-fountains were made to
swell with blood, with Christ's blood, warring Coligny was skinned alive,
dragged along the ground, dunked in water, burned nearly to death with
fire, strung up in mid-air.]

These references, all too obviously relatable to the present, may have been
what moved Opitz to dissuade Zincgref from publishing the *Trostgedichte* back
in 1624. Not until 1633 did the political winds favor its publication. In the
meantime, not even literary disguise — the historicized depiction of ancient
civil wars, as found in Lucan's *Pharsalia* or Vergil's *Georgica* — could have
provided the necessary cover. Forgoing publicity or, in Zincgref's case, maintaining anonymity was the fate of politically critical literature in the age of
confessionalization.

Opitz resembled Zincgref and the late humanists of Heidelberg and
Strasbourg not only in the political tendencies of his youth but also in his
literary-cultural endeavors. The quality of his work, however, towered so far
above that of his colleagues, especially in the Palatinate, that they beggar comparison; his reaction to Zincgref's supplement to the 1624 Strasbourg edition
of the *Teutsche Poemata* makes this abundantly clear. The fundamental difference lay not so much, as some have claimed, in the nationalization of humanist verse through the creation of a German literary art.[91] This idea —
elucidated by Opitz in his early *Aristarchus sive de contemptu linguae
Teutonicae* (Aristarchus, or On Contempt of the German Language) of 1617
— actually came from his teacher in Beuthen, Caspar Dornau,[92] himself
inspired to it by a six-month stay in Heidelberg in 1605–6. What accounted
for the distinction between Opitz and the others lay rather in the concept of
literary theory found in the *Buch von der Deutschen Poeterey*. For the *Poeterey*
in one great motion opened up a reference system of criteria, directions, and
criticisms for the reformed art of German literature; established a concise
framework for the poetic system; and removed the long-standing uncertainty
about whether the German literary art could be taught and learned. While
Zincgref effectively adapted genres, types of texts, and compositional styles
and defined their specific-use contexts (especially political and journalistic),
Opitz formulated the entirety of a literary canon within an easily accessible
system modeled on the classical principles of *officia* (doctrine of offices) of

textbook rhetoric,[93] with its categories of *inventio, dispositio,* and *elocutio.*[94] This was hardly new, to be sure, indebted as it was to the traditions of classical and Renaissance poetics; indeed, Opitz's basic substituting of generic poetic principles in lieu of an original theory of a new kind of practice (in German) yielded only an inventory of prescriptive genres.[95] Still, his accomplishments were groundbreaking in several ways: For one, his decision to rely on generic substitutions meant that the category of genre, as compositional doctrine of versified speech, would now be guaranteed unique, systematic attention.[96] And insofar as poetics remained founded on the traditional rhetorical compositional principles of *auctoritas — exemplum — imitatio* (authority — example — imitation),[97] each genre now was assured the dignity of its own tradition. This held true for all genres and forms in the inventory of the *Poeterey:* epigram, elegy, eclogue, ode (Sapphic, Pindaric, Horatian), song, hymn, sonnet, quatrain, echo verse (later also madrigal and visual poetry), invocation, epic, tragedy, comedy, etc. Finally, this systematic organization of forms and genres, conducive on the one hand to the creation of a canon, guaranteed on the other the license to invent nonpoetic (that is, nonversified) genres, styles, and other structural types. Such deviation from the norm of regulated poetics, with its canonical forms, would eventuate in so-called "latent poetics" (such as poetics of the foreword; but other internal, or metafictional, poetics as well) and in the "genre system" that arose from these dynamic conditions. Deviation had already been apparent in Opitz's translations and adaptations of the novel, libretto, prose eclogue, consolation, etc., which made him a *classical* writer who occupied both sides of the alternatives of canon and license, norm and deviation, rather than only a *classicist* writer, in the sense of holding strictly to rhetorical imitation, or mimesis.[98]

It is Opitz, then, more than anyone else, to whom we are indebted for having laid the modern foundation for the theory of genre;[99] it is with his work that any discussion of intertextuality in German literature must begin.[100] The German Enlightenment first acknowledged Opitz as the "Vater der deutschen Dichtung" (Father of German Poetry),[101] and subsequent scholarship has upheld that claim. The name of Martin Opitz occupies an indelible place in that institution of collective memory called literary history. The same can scarcely be said of Julius Wilhelm Zincgref, his *amicus* of the early Heidelberg years.

Translated by Michael Swisher

Notes

[1] Plutarch, "Alexander," in *Plutarch's Lives,* trans. Bernadotte Perrin, Loeb Classical Library 99 (Cambridge: Harvard UP, 1986), sect. I.

[2] The sociohistorical conception of friendship described here comes from Friedrich H. Tenbruck, "Freundschaft: Ein Beitrag zu einer Soziologie der persönlichen Beziehungen," *Kölner Zeitschrift für Soziologie und Sozialpsychologie* 16 (1964): 431–56, here 447–48 and 453.

3 Zincgref, *Teutscher Nation Denckwürdiger Reden Apophthegmata genant / Anderer Theil* (Strasbourg: Glaser, 1631), fol.):(ʳ-):(2ʳ. On this question see Wilhelm Kühlmann, "Martin Opitz in Paris (1630) — Zu Text, Praetext und Kontext eines lateinischen Gedichtes an Cornelius Grotius," in *Martin Opitz (1597–1639): Nachahmungspoetik und Lebenswelt*, ed. Thomas Borgstedt and Walter Schmitz (Tübingen: Niemeyer, 2002), 208–9. For Opitz's Paris journey see Klaus Garber, "Paris, Capital of European Late Humanism: Jacques Auguste de Thou and the Cabinet Dupuy," in *Imperiled Heritage: Tradition, History, and Utopia in Early Modern German Literature*, ed. Max Reinhart (Aldershot, UK: Ashgate, 2000), 54–72.

4 The poets adduced here were all members of the famed French Pléiade literary society: Pierre de Ronsard (1524–85), Joachim Du Bellay (1522–60), Guillaume de Salluste Du Bartas (1554–90), Clément Marot (1496–1544), Etienne Jodelle (1532–73), and Jean Antoine de Baïf (1532–89).

5 The concept of *Veraltensgeschwindigkeit* (rapid obsolescence) comes from the political philosopher Hermann Lübbe, who seems first to have used it in a radio essay in the 1980s.

6 Erich Trunz introduced the still relevant term "humanistische Standeskultur" (humanist class culture) in "Der deutsche Späthumanismus um 1600 als Standeskultur" (1931), in *Deutsche Barockforschung: Dokumentation einer Epoche*, ed. Richard Alewyn, 3rd ed. (Cologne: Kiepenheuer & Witsch, 1968), 147–81.

7 See the section "Education and Confession" below for a chronological review of highlights from both poets' lives.

8 *Martin Opitz, Buch von der Deutschen Poeterey (1624)*, ed. Wilhelm Braune, revised edition by Richard Alewyn (Tübingen: Niemeyer, 1966), 21–22. Compare the introduction to Opitz's *Teutsche Poemata: Abdruck der Ausgabe von 1624*, comp. and ed. Zincgref, new edition by Georg Wittkowski (Halle a. S.: Niemeyer, 1902), x–xiv; also Heinz Entner, "Opitz' dichterische und theoretische Entwicklung von 1617 bis 1624," in *Studien zur deutschen Literatur im 17. Jahrhundert*, ed. Entner et al. (Berlin: Aufbau, 1984), 116–44, here 140: Entner speaks of a "disclaiming" ("Desavouierung").

9 Translation by H. Rushton Fairclough, in Horace, *Satires, Epistles and Ars Poetica*, Loeb Classical Library 194 (Cambridge: Harvard UP, 1929). All subsequent translations of Horace in this chapter are Fairclough's.

10 Opitz, *Buch von der Deutschen Poeterey*, [2] and 21–22.

11 Theodor Verweyen, "Über die poetische Praxis vor Opitz — am Beispiel eines Sonetts aus dem Englischen von Petrus Denaisius," *Daphnis* 13 (1984): 137–65; see also Leonard Forster, " 'Virtutis atque eruditinis consortium': Janus Gruters Plautusausgabe von 1621 und der Heidelberger Dichterkreis," in *Opitz und seine Welt: Festschrift für George Schulz-Behrend*, ed. Barbara Becker-Cantarino and Jörg-Ulrich Fechner (Amsterdam: Rodopi, 1990), 173–84, here 174–75.

12 Marian Szyrocki, *Martin Opitz* (Berlin: Rütten and Loening, 1956), 56ff.; Klaus Garber, "Martin Opitz," in *Deutsche Dichter des 17. Jahrhunderts: Ihr Leben und Werk*, ed. Harald Steinhagen and Benno von Wiese (Berlin: Schmidt, 1984), 116–84, here 140; Hans-Gert Roloff, "Martin Opitz — 400 Jahre! Ein Festvortrag," in Borgstedt and Schmitz, eds., *Martin Opitz*, 24, note 3.

13 It was eventually published in 1633. For more on the transmission of the two heretofore unknown letters between Opitz and Zincgref see Klaus Conermann and Andreas Herz, eds., "Der Briefwechsel des Martin Opitz: Ein chronologisches Repertorium," in

Wolfenbütteler Barock-Nachrichten 28 (2001): 3–133, here 44 and 83; for our purposes, see especially the first letter.

[14] *Teutsche Poemata*, 148–49; the sonnet was excluded from all editions authorized by Opitz.

[15] Roloff, "Martin Opitz — 400 Jahre!" 24–25.

[16] Szyrocki, *Martin Opitz*, 11–12.

[17] The Peace of Augsburg (1555) left many religious disagreements unsettled. Most importantly, it excluded from its terms the increasingly successful, but heterodox, Protestant confession of Calvinism. The following half of the sixteenth century — marked not only by aggressive proselytizing by Calvinists and Lutherans against the advances of the Catholic Counter-Reformation but by the rise of a Reformed alternative that emphasized principles of Christian unity and irenicism (political-philosophical doctrine of peace) — is generally identified with the period of the Second Reformation.

[18] Volker Press, *Calvinismus und Territorialstaat: Regierung und Zentralbehörden der Kurpfalz 1559–1619* (Stuttgart: Klett, 1970), 260.

[19] See in this volume the chapter by Wilhelm Kühlmann, "Education in Early Modern Germany."

[20] Dieter Mertens, "Zu Heidelberger Dichtern von Schede bis Zincgref," *Zeitschrift für deutsches Altertum* 103 (1974): 200–241, here 229.

[21] Reinhart Koselleck, *Kritik und Krise: Eine Studie zur Pathogenese der bürgerlichen Welt* (Frankfurt am Main: Suhrkamp, 1973), 13.

[22] Gnesio-Lutherans initiated persecutions of Crypto-Calvinists as early as 1560. In 1574 Elector Augustus of Wittenberg declared the Philippists to be enemies of the state and expelled or imprisoned their leaders. The Formula of Concord (1577) formalized theologically the rejection of Calvinism.

[23] See Anton Schindling and Walter Ziegler, eds., *Die Territorien des Reichs im Zeitalter der Reformation und Konfessionalisierung 1500–1650*, vol. 5, *Der Südwesten* (Münster: Aschendorff, 1993), 8–49, here 28–29.

[24] The characterization comes from Schindling and Ziegler, eds., *Die Territorien des Reichs*, vol. 2, *Der Nordosten* (1990), 118–20, here 119, note 21, who speak of "legalisierten Mischformen bekenntnismäßiger Koexistenz" (legalized hybrids of confessional coexistence).

[25] Ludwig Petry, "Politische Geschichte unter den Habsburgern," in *Geschichte Schlesiens*, vol. 2, *Die Habsburgerzeit 1526–1740*, ed. Petry and J. Joachim Menzel (Darmstadt: Bläschke, 1973), 1–135, here 62–65.

[26] Petry, "Politische Geschichte," 64.

[27] See Tenbruck, "Freundschaft."

[28] Hermann Palm, "Martin Opitz," in *Beiträge zur Geschichte der deutschen Literatur des XVI. und XVII. Jahrhunderts* (Breslau: Morgenstern, 1877), 129–260, here 157–58. For a discussion of rhetoric as cultural foundation in the early modern period see Heinrich F. Plett, "Rhetorik der Renaissance — Renaissance der Rhetorik," in *Renaissance-Rhetorik/Renaissance Rhetoric*, ed. Plett (Berlin: de Gruyter, 1993), 1–20.

[29] Robert Seidel, *Späthumanismus in Schlesien: Caspar Dornau (1577–1631): Leben und Werk* (Tübingen: Niemeyer, 1994), 307–37; here chap. 10, "Latein und Deutsch," 329.

[30] Seidel, *Späthumanismus*, 65.

[31] Fritz Trautz, "Ottheinrichs Stellung in der pfälzischen Geschichte," *Ruperto-Carola: Mitteilungen der Vereinigung der Freunde der Studentenschaft der Universität Heidelberg* 19, no. 3 (1956): 29–46.

[32] Eike Wolgast, "Das konfessionelle Zeitalter: 1500–1648," in *Die Universität Heidelberg: 1386–1986* (Berlin: Springer, 1986), 24–55, here 34–35.

[33] Seidel, *Späthumanismus*, 301. This assumption is not contradicted by the choice of rhetoric and poetry as a major course of study.

[34] Mertens, "Zu Heidelberger Dichtern," 230, with accompanying documentation.

[35] Johann Leonhard Weidner, "Hern. Ivlii Gvlielmi Zinckgrefii, Dero beyden Rechten Doctoris Leben," in *Teutscher Nation Apophthegmatvm* [. . .] *Dritter Theil* (Leyden: Heger, 1644), 109–16, here 109–10.

[36] *Triga amico-poetica* [. . .] *Editio prima procurata ab eodem Ioanne Leonhardo Weidnero* (n.p., 1619), 60–61.

[37] Quotation from Wilhelm Crecelius, *Johann Leonhard Weidner: Rektor der Lateinschule zu Elberfeld: Fortsetzer von Zincgrefs Apophthegmata* (Elberfeld: Lucas, 1886), 4.

[38] Dieter Mertens and Theodor Verweyen, "Bericht über die Vorarbeiten zu einer Zincgref-Ausgabe," *Jahrbuch für Internationale Germanistik* 4, no. 2 (1972): 125–50, here 144–45.

[39] For Gruter's letter from Heidelberg see Alexander Reifferscheid, ed., *Briefe G. M. Lingelsheims, M. Berneggers und ihrer Freunde*, vol. 1, *Quellen zur Geschichte des geistigen Lebens in Deutschland während des 17. Jahrhunderts* (Heilbronn: Henninger, 1889), 73–75, here 75. See also the "Einleitung" by Dieter Mertens and Theodor Verweyen, eds., in *Julius Wilhelm Zincgref, Facetiae Pennalium*, vol. 3 of *Gesammelte Schriften* (Tübingen: Niemeyer, 1978), viii–xl, here xiii.

[40] Reifferscheid, ed., *Briefe G. M. Lingelsheims*, 274.

[41] This work argues against or for various religious doctrines and controversial practices, including predestination, free will, infallibility of the church, and the Eucharist.

[42] The *politiques* were politically moderate jurists. The most famous work to come from their circle was Jean Bodin's *Six livres de la République* (1567).

[43] On de Thou see Garber, "Paris, Capital of European Late Humanism," esp. 59–62; in the same chapter, for Grotius and the Cabinet Dupuy, 68–69.

[44] On the exemplary character of panegyric see Theodor Verweyen, "Barockes Herrscherlob: Rhetorische Tradition, sozialgeschichtliche Aspekte, Gattungsprobleme," *Der Deutschunterricht* 28, no. 2 (1976): 25–45, with partial text.

[45] Roloff, "Martin Opitz — 400 Jahre!" 26 and passim.

[46] The Young Germans, or "Das junge Deutschland," turned literature primarily to political ends, repudiating Romanticism especially, but also many authoritative figures, including Goethe. See Theodor Verweyen and Gunther Witting, "Emanuel Geibel: 'Dichterfürst' und 'Fürstenknecht,'" in *Verehrung, Kult, Distanz: Vom Umgang mit dem Dichter im 19. Jahrhundert*, ed. Wolfgang Braungart (Tübingen: Niemeyer, 2004), 219–43, here 219–30.

[47] *Imitatio vitae* is a humanist analogy to the artistic imitation of the ancients (*imitatio veterum*).

[48] For a concentrated sketch of confessional switching among university professionals see Mertens and Verweyen, eds., *Zincgref, Gesammelte Schriften*, vol. 2, *Emblemata ethico-politica* (1993), 244. This aspect is further supported by Martin Mulsow, "Mehrfachkonversion, politische Religion und Opportunismus im 17. Jahrhundert: Ein Plädoyer für eine Indifferentismusforschung," in *Interkonfessionalität — Transkonfessionalität — binnenkonfessionelle Pluralität: Neue Forschungen zur Konfessionalisierungsthese*, eds. Kaspar von Greyerz et al. (Gütersloh: Bertelsmann, 2003), 132–50.

[49] For more on the importance of Lipsius for Zincgref see Mertens and Verweyen, "Einleitung" to *Emblemata*, esp. 20–34.

[50] This work, called an "epos," was rediscovered in the 1970s by Mertens and Verweyen in preparing the critical edition of Zincgref.

[51] Mertens and Verweyen, "Bericht über die Vorarbeiten," 147–49, discuss this in detail. Especially important is the close similarity of Zincgref's epos, which combines elements of the *parainetikon* (hortatory poem) and the *propemptikon* (departure poem), to Ludwig Camerarius's pamphlet of November 1619, *Friderici [. . .] Declaratio publica: Cur Regni Bohemiae annexarumque Provinciarum Regimen in Se susceperit.*

[52] Hans-Henrik Krummacher, " 'Laurea Doctoralis Julii Guilielmi Zincgrefii' (1620): Ein Heidelberger Gelegenheitsdruck für Julius Wilhelm Zincgref mit einem unbekannten Gedicht von Martin Opitz," in Becker-Cantarino and Fechner, eds., *Opitz und seine Welt*, 287–349, here 307–12.

[53] See the important older study by Franz Schnorr von Carolsfeld, "Julius Wilhelm Zincgrefs Leben und Schriften," *Archiv für Litteraturgeschichte* 8 (1879): 1–58 and 446–90, esp. 20.

[54] Schnorr von Carolsfeld, "Julius Wilhelm Zincgrefs Leben und Schriften," 447.

[55] Schnorr von Carolsfeld, "Julius Wilhelm Zincgrefs Leben und Schriften," 485.

[56] Originally written in Latin, the biography was translated into German and published in two volumes by Kaspar Gottlieb Lindner (Hirschberg, 1740–41) as *Umständliche Nachricht von des weltberühmten Schlesiers Martin Opitz von Boberfeld, Leben, Tode und Schriften.*

[57] Meinrad Schaab, *Geschichte der Kurpfalz*, vol. 2, *Neuzeit* (Stuttgart: Kohlhammer, 1992), 109–44, here 117–18.

[58] Press, *Calvinismus und Territorialstaat*, 371.

[59] Zincgref, *Facetiae Pennalium*, 92.

[60] See Thomas Klein, *Der Kampf um die Zweite Reformation in Kursachsen 1586–1591* (Cologne: Böhlau, 1962), 102: "[der] Kampf gegen Arminius und die fortschreitende Zersetzung des genuinen Calvinismus durch humanistisches Gedankengut"; also 153–54 and 157 on the electoral library under Christian I of Saxony (d. 1591).

[61] Quietism (Latin *quies, quietus*) is a doctrine according to which human striving yields to passive waiting upon God and the human will is accordingly annihilated.

[62] By contrast, say, to its primary role in the work of Simon Dach in Königsberg. See Albrecht Schöne, *Kürbishütte und Königsberg: Modellversuch einer sozialgeschichtlichen Entzifferung poetischer Texte: Am Beispiel Simon Dach* (Munich: Beck, 1975), 45–48.

[63] Theodor Verweyen, "Zwischenbericht über die Ausgabe der *Gesammelten Schriften* Zincgrefs," in *Literatur und Kultur im deutschen Südwesten zwischen Renaissance und Aufklärung: Neue Studien Walter E. Schäfer zum 65. Geburtstag gewidmet*, ed. Wilhelm Kühlmann, *Chloe* 22 (Amsterdam: Rodopi, 1995), 185–218, here 217–18.

[64] One of the three *genera orationis* (types of speech): *genus iudicale* (speech in court of law), *genus deliberativum* (speech of political advice), and *genus demonstrativum* (speech for occasions, hence for occasional, or casual, poetry).

[65] Mertens and Verweyen, "Bericht über die Vorarbeiten," 138–39.

[66] Mertens, "Zu Heidelberger Dichtern," 232.

[67] Zincgref, "Einleitung," *Teutsche Poemata* (1624), 1.

[68] Zincgref, *Facetiae Pennalium*, 91.

[69] Zincgref, *Facetiae Pennalium*, 3. See also the brief description of the university and sociopolitical context in Mertens, "Zu Heidelberger Dichtern," 234.

[70] Monarchomachism: a political theory developed in the 1570s and 1580s that argued for the right of subjects to resist unjust rulers. *Quodlibetisches Weltkefig* was published anonymously. On the authorship of Zincgref see Schnorr von Carolsfeld, "Zincgrefs Leben und Schriften," 67–68; Mertens and Verweyen, "Bericht über die Vorarbeiten," 140.

[71] Zincgref, *Auserlesene Gedichte Deutscher Poeten*, ed. Wilhelm Braune (Halle: Niemeyer, 1879).

[72] Zincgref, *Emblemata ethico-politica*, 1–60; "Einleitung," 27–34.

[73] Scaliger was of Italian descent (allegedly from the ruling Verona family Della Scala) but became a French citizen in mid-life.

[74] Zincgref, *Der Teutschen Scharpfsinnig kluge Sprüch* (Strasbourg: Josiae Riheln Erben, 1626), 135; see also Theodor Verweyen, "'Sie werden lachen: die Antike . . .': Traditionsbezüge zwischen früher Neuzeit und Moderne am Beispiel des Apophthegmas," *Archiv für Kulturgeschichte* 85, no. 2 (2004): 553–75.

[75] Theodor Verweyen, *Apophthegma und Scherzrede: Die Geschichte einer einfachen Gattungsform und ihrer Entfaltung im 17. Jahrhundert* (Bad Homburg: Gehlen, 1970), 78–87.

[76] Verweyen, *Apophthegma und Scherzrede*, 20–21.

[77] This list of sources will be found in the commentary volume of the edition *Julius Wilhelm Zincgref: Apophthegmata teutsch*, ed. Theodor Verweyen in collaboration with Dieter Mertens and Werner W. Schnabel (Tübingen: Niemeyer, forthcoming).

[78] Zincgref, *Scharpfsinnig kluge Sprüch*, fol. a3ᵛ.

[79] Verweyen, "Zwischenbericht," 217–18.

[80] Opitz, *Weltliche Poemata: 1644*, part 1, ed. Erich Trunz with Christine Eisner, Deutsche Neudrucke: Reihe: Barock 2 (Tübingen: Niemeyer, 1967), 312. For the etymology and semantics of *atrox* see Hans-Jürgen Schings, "*Consolatio Tragoediae*: Zur Theorie des barocken Trauerspiels," in *Deutsche Dramentheorie: Beiträge zu einer historischen Poetik des Dramas in Deutschland*, ed. Reinhold Grimm (Frankfurt am Main: Athenäum, 1971), 1:28–29 and passim.

[81] In Lipsius's standard edition but also owing much to the richly commentated edition by the Dutch philologist Petrus Scriverius. See the instructive study by Hans-Jürgen Schings, "Seneca-Rezeption und Theorie der Tragödie: Martin Opitz' Vorrede zu den *Trojanerinnen*," in *Historizität in Sprach- und Literaturwissenschaft*, ed. Walter Müller-Seidel with Hans Fromm and Karl Richter (Munich: Fink, 1974), 521–37.

[82] Bakhtin, "Die beiden stilistischen Linien des europäischen Romans," in *Die Ästhetik des Wortes*, ed Rainer Grübel (Frankfurt am Main: Suhrkamp, 1979), 251–300.

[83] This has occasioned a good deal of scholarly debate on a variety of subjects, for example over whether Grimmelshausen's *Simplicissimus* or, say, Anton Ulrich's *Aramena* is more "realistic." See the still-relevant study by Günther Müller, "Barockroman und Barockromane," *Literaturwissenschaftliches Jahrbuch der Görres-Gesellschaft* 4 (1929): 11. Concerning the question of realism in terms of structure see Richard Alewyn, "Gestalt als Gehalt: Der Roman des Barock," in *Probleme und Gestalten* (Frankfurt am Main: Suhrkamp, 1982), 117–32.

[84] Günther Müller, "Höfische Kultur der Barockzeit," in Hans Naumann and Müller, *Höfische Kultur* (Halle: Niemeyer, 1929), 81–82 and passim. See also Theodor Verweyen, "Epische *ars narrativa* im Kontext der städtischen Kultur des oberrheinischen Humanismus und des landesfürstlichen Absolutismus der Barockepoche: Wickrams *Goldtfaden* und Opitz' *Argenis*," in *Humanisten am Oberrhein: Festgabe für Dieter Mertens*, ed. Sven Lembke and Markus Müller (Leinfelden-Echterdingen: Weinbrenner, 2004), 267–302.

[85] Reifferscheid, ed., *Briefe G. M. Lingelsheims*, 127.

[86] Opitz, trans., *Argenis*, in *Gesammelte Werke: Kritische Ausgabe*, 3/1, ed. George Schulz-Behrend (Stuttgart: Hiersemann, 1970), 178–82.

[87] Koselleck, *Kritik und Krise*, 13–14.

[88] Ulrich Schulz-Buschhaus, "Emphase und Geometrie: Notizen zu Opitz' Sonettistik im Kontext des europäischen 'Petrarkismus,'" in Borgstedt and Schmitz, eds., *Martin Opitz*, 73–74. Schulz-Buschhaus's paradigmatic interpretation holds true for forms other than poetry as well.

[89] The work of Klaus Garber in particular has been effective in demonstrating this connection. Unfortunately, his political biography of Opitz (to have been called *Martin Opitz: Eine kulturpolitische Biographie*), largely completed by 1980, has not been published. I am grateful to the author for providing me with a copy of his manuscript.

[90] The following excerpts are from Opitz, *Gesammelte Werke*, 3/1, 187–266. For more on this work see especially Garber, "Opitz," in Steinhagen and von Wiese, eds., *Deutsche Dichter des 17. Jahrhunderts*, 145–63. See also Barbara Becker-Cantarino, "Daniel Heinsius' *De contemptu mortis* und Opitz' *Trostgedichte*," in Becker-Cantarino and Fechner, eds., *Opitz und seine Welt*, 37–56, as well as the penetrating study by Wilhelm Kühlmann, *Martin Opitz: Deutsche Literatur und deutsche Nation*, 2nd ed. (Heidelberg: Manutius, 2001), 37–56: "Deutschlands Ruin und der 'Trost' im Krieg."

[91] Richard Alewyn, *Vorbarocker Klassizismus und griechische Tragödie: Analyse der Antigone-Übersetzung des Martin Opitz* (1926; repr., Reihe: Libelli 79, Darmstadt: Wissenschaftliche Buchgesellschaft, 1962), 12.

[92] Heinz Entner, "Zum Kontext von Martin Opitz' *Aristarchus*," *Germanica Wratislaviensis* 17 (1982): 7–8 and passim; Seidel, *Späthumanismus*, 320–28: "Dornau und die Muttersprachendiskussion."

[93] On the systematic character of poetological reflection see Rudolf Drux, *Martin Opitz und sein poetisches Regelsystem* (Bonn: Bouvier, 1976), 39–40 and passim. See also the interesting study by Jörg Robert, "Martin Opitz und die Konstitution der Deutschen Poetik: Norm, Tradition und Kontinuität zwischen Aristarch und Buch von der Deutschen Poeterey," *Euphorion* 98 (2004): 281–322, esp. 301–7.

[94] Poetic genre occurred most significantly within the category of *dispositio* by simple substitution of poetological values for organizational arrangement. Opitz, *Poeterey*, chap. 5, 17–18 and passim.

[95] Conrad Wiedemann, "*Dispositio* und dichterische Freiheit im Barock," in *Tradition und Originalität*, ed. Walter Haug und Burghart Wachinger (Tübingen: Niemeyer, 1997), 243.

[96] Theodor Verweyen, "'Thränen des Vaterlandes / Anno 1636' von Andreas Gryphius — Rhetorische Grundlagen, poetische Strukturen, Literarizität," in *Traditionen der Lyrik: Festschrift für Hans-Henrik Krummacher*, ed. Wolfgang Düsing et al. (Tübingen: Niemeyer, 1977), 39–40 and passim.

[97] Wiedemann, "*Dispositio*," 244–45, with reference to the standard works by Wilfried Barner and Joachim Dyck.

[98] Hellmut Flashar, "Die klassizistische Theorie der Mimesis," in *Le Classicisme a Rome aux 1ers Siècles avant et après J.-C.*, ed. Flashar (Geneva: Vandœuvres, 1978), 79–97; discussion, 98–111.

[99] Wiedemann, "*Dispositio*," 245–46.

[100] Rüdiger Zymner, "Übersetzung und Sprachwechsel bei Martin Opitz," in Borgstedt and Schmitz, eds., *Martin Opitz*, 99–111. On intertextuality in early modern German writing see Wilhelm Kühlmann and Wolfgang Neuber, eds., *Intertextualität in der Frühen Neuzeit: Studien zu ihren theoretischen und praktischen Perspektiven*, Frühneuzeit-Studien 2 (Frankfurt am Main: Lang, 1994).

[101] Klaus Garber, *Martin Opitz — "der Vater der deutschen Dichtung": Eine kritische Studie zur Wissenschaftsgeschichte der Germanistik* (Stuttgart: Metzler, 1976).

SIGISMUNDUS. A.
BIRKEN DICT. BETU
LIUS. COM. PAL. CÆS.
NOB. PO. LAUR.

Nil mirare, Deas sexu constare virili,
  ac animas unum Corpus habere decem:
Has Sphyngis latebras FACIES HÆC unica pandit,
  quæ PHOEBUM sistit PIERIDESq̃ novem.

Honoris ergo offert Iacobus Sandrart Chalcographus.   M. Martinus Limburger PL.C.

Sigmund von Birken.

Duke Anton Ulrich.

Parallel Lives: Sigmund von Birken and Duke Anton Ulrich

John Roger Paas

Two German men of extraordinary literary ability, despite being born into widely separated social classes in the second quarter of the seventeenth century, were to cultivate a lasting personal and professional relationship spanning almost four decades. Like their contemporaries Marvell, Molière, and Racine, they came of age in a time of war yet directed their energies toward the world of art. Although changes in literary taste caused many later critics and readers to overlook their considerable accomplishments, in their own time they were highly respected figures; recent scholarship has reassessed their work and returned to the view that they were two of the most influential literary figures of the Baroque. These two men who led different but interconnected lives were Duke Anton Ulrich of Braunschweig-Wolfenbüttel (1633–1714) and Sigmund von Birken (1626–81), a citizen of Nuremberg.

Anton Ulrich was born into a noble family and throughout life enjoyed the rights and privileges of the upper class. His was a life of power and leisure, one over which he exercised considerable control. Birken, on the other hand, came from modest circumstances and suceeded, against enormous social and economic odds, to become one of the most influential and respected literary figures of his time in Germany. As different as these lives were, they both reflect in a revealing way broader social and political changes taking place in Germany, as well as in western society as a whole, in the early modern period. It was during the lifetimes of Birken and Anton Ulrich, for instance, that the legitimacy of the established systems of rule and privilege were being questioned throughout Europe as never before. The aristocracy — or, in places like Nuremberg, the patriciate[1] — continued to hold the reins of power and to determine political policies. But economic vitality was increasingly the product of an entrepreneurial merchant class whose wealth could buy political influence and pay for higher education for their sons. The intellectual elite of Germany arose in part from this newly wealthy *Schicht* (social level, class) and, in part, as in Birken's case, from sheer talent and a desire for social betterment. Confident in their scholarly and professional achievements, the members of the European *respublica litteraria* promoted the idea, in circulation among humanists since the early Renaissance, of a "true nobility" (*vera nobilitas*), one whose privilege was based not on blood but on merit.[2] Thus, Birken and Anton Ulrich lived on completely different social and political planes, yet, despite their differences, they shared common literary interests and enjoyed an equality of the mind. This bond determined the relationship that would endure throughout their lives.

Anton Ulrich, the younger son of Duke August the Younger of Braunschweig-Wolfenbüttel (1579–1666) and his second wife, Dorothea of Anhalt-Zerbst (1607–34), was born on 4 October 1633. He grew up within an environment of elaborate cultivation of books and learning.[3] Duke August was himself a younger son, and having been thus unburdened of many of the usual concerns of state, had been free to follow his scholarly inclination and to direct his interests toward learning and the arts. Among his contemporaries he stands out as a ruler-scholar, one with wide-ranging and deep intellectual interests. His extensive correspondence with professors and scholars throughout Europe kept Duke August abreast of current intellectual developments. He was, however, primarily an inveterate bibliophile, who had begun as early as the 1580s to assemble a personal library; as he grew older and more passionate about learning, he authorized agents throughout Europe to purchase books for his collection. At his modest residence at Hitzacker on the Elbe, east of Lüneburg, he was able to pursue his interests and to cultivate an intellectual life; even after he had taken on additional responsibilities as ruler of the duchy in 1635 and finally settled in the ducal residence at Wolfenbüttel in 1643, little changed. Harboring no ambition to expand his territory through conquest, Duke August was able to indulge himself in his scholarly and cultural pursuits.[4] He focused his energies on nurturing culture at his Renaissance-style court in Wolfenbüttel and on establishing one of the clearest outward signs of a true commitment to learning, namely, an extensive library. The collection of books and manuscripts that he was able to assemble over years of careful purchasing was unparalleled in all Europe at the time.[5]

It is not surprising that the scholarly Duke August placed special significance on the humanistic education of his children and took great care in choosing tutors for them. To Justus Georg Schottelius (1612–76), a young scholar from Wittenberg with already impeccable academic credentials — he was eventually to become the leading German grammarian of his generation — was entrusted the education of Anton Ulrich in the spring of 1638 when the boy was not yet five years of age.[6] That a scholar of such standing chose to work for Duke August rather than at a university says much about the intellectual milieu at the duke's court; it seems likely that he was persuaded to stay because of access to the great ducal library, and because of the guaranteed income and security of the position. During the greater part of the following decade he served as the primary teacher of the young prince as well as of his sisters Sibylla Ursula and Clara Augusta and their younger half-brother, Ferdinand Albrecht.

Anton Ulrich's education was both comprehensive and demanding. As was to be expected of someone receiving a solid education at the time, the young duke acquired a thorough knowledge of classical literature and Latin. In addition, he learned French, Italian, and Spanish and studied traditional subjects: geography, logic, and rhetoric. Through the influence of his musically talented stepmother, Sophie Elisabeth of Mecklenburg-Güstrow, the young prince was also able to develop his talent for music and drawing.[7] An important part of Anton Ulrich's education was his participation in theatrical pieces that Schottelius composed for public performance at court. Whereas Ferdinand Albrecht complained later in life that Schottelius had forced him to take a role in all kinds of plays before he even knew his ABC's,[8] Anton Ulrich appears to have thrived on such activities. His participation in these public performances was instrumental in the development of his public-speaking skills, and at the same time, the roles he played — always those of the politically privileged — helped to ingrain in him his proper position in society. The effect of these theatrical-pedagogical exercises on the prince was long lasting: when he was old enough to display his own literary ability, his first works of substance were short dramatic works to be performed before the court at Wolfenbüttel. The seventeen pieces that Anton Ulrich wrote between 1656 and 1669 were not simply literary exercises for the enjoyment of a limited audience. Within the framework of courtly ceremony they helped to underscore a clear message of political legitimacy.[9]

By the mid 1640s Schottelius had become known and respected as a German linguist far beyond the court at Wolfenbüttel;[10] with his career blossoming, his involvement in Anton Ulrich's education naturally diminished. With the young prince's graduation from the primary grades in 1646, Schottelius's participation in his formal education came to a close — but not before a new teacher had arrived at court: Sigmund von Birken. Although Birken was only at the beginning of his career and was professionally and socially far less skilled than Schottelius, his impact on the prince was to be profound, for he had arrived at Wolfenbüttel at a time when the adolescent Anton Ulrich was particularly impressionable. The precocious prince was twelve years old and Birken but nineteen, and through their common interest in literature they rapidly formed a personal bond that continued as long as both were alive.[11]

Birken came from simple circumstances and for years was dogged by poverty.[12] He was born Sigmund Betulius on 5 May 1626 in Wildstein (in Bohemia), where his father, Daniel Betulius, was a Lutheran village pastor.[13] It was in Bohemia that the longstanding religious and political tensions between the Protestant citizens and their Catholic overlords had precipitated the outbreak of the Thirty Years' War in 1618, and during the first decade of hostilities, the Protestant forces were constantly on the defensive. Because of the aggressive attempts of the Austrian Habsburgs to reestablish the Catholic religion throughout the territories under their control, Birken's family was forced to flee in 1629. They were fortunate to find permanent refuge in Nuremberg in late 1632, one of the few remaining bulwarks of Protestantism in southern Germany. Birken's academic abilities were recognized while he was still young, and even though he became a penniless orphan at the age of sixteen when his father died (his mother Veronica had died when he was seven), he was able to finish a thorough secondary education under Daniel Wülfer, a theologian, and Adam Zanner, a language scholar. His last teacher and mentor was Johann Michael Dilherr (1604–69), one of the leading Lutheran theologians at the time. Dilherr had been a professor of theology and rector of the University at Jena before being hired by the Nuremberg town council in 1642 to help revitalize the Lutheran religion and educational system in the city. When Birken was ready to pursue university studies the following year, he chose Dilherr's alma mater. There he studied first law and then theology, but his precarious financial circumstances forced him in 1644 to conclude his studies after only three semesters.

Birken returned to Nuremberg in 1644 just as an interest in the reformed poetic style of Martin Opitz was taking hold, and he was thus able to become involved in these developments at an early stage. Not since the time of Hans Sachs could the city boast of a poet of any renown; but in 1644 the two leading poets in Nuremberg — the patrician Georg Philipp Harsdörffer (1607–58) and Johann Klaj (1616–56), like Birken, a war refugee — founded the Pegnesischer Blumenorden (Order of the Flowers on the Pegnitz River). Like other German language societies, it had the goal of promoting German language and literature. The work that marked the literary rebirth in the city was Harsdöffer and Klaj's *Das Pegnesische Schäfergedicht* (The Shepherd Poem of the Pegnitz, 1644), a pastoral in verse and prose modeled on the *Schäfferey von der Nimfen Hercinie* (Pastoral of the Nymph Hercinie, 1630) by Martin Opitz.[14] Birken, who had come to realize that his interests lay in literary pursuits, became a member of the society the following year and, together with Klaj, wrote a kind of sequel to Harsdörffer and Klaj's *Schäfergedicht* called *Fortsetzung der Pegnitz-Schäferey* (Continuation of the Shepherd Poem of the Pegnitz, 1645).[15]

Despite the fact that by late 1645 Birken had become a member of the literary elite in Nuremberg, unfounded rumors that he led a dissolute life made it impossible for him to secure any position either within the municipal administration of the city or with a wealthy patrician. Fortunately, Harsdörffer was well connected throughout Germany and took it upon himself to help Birken find employment. Through his membership in the Fruchtbringende Gesellschaft (Fruitbringing Society), the most prestigious of the German language societies, Harsdörffer was acquainted with Schottelius, to whom he wrote and successfully recommended Birken as a tutor.

Birken arrived in Wolfenbüttel in late 1645 to begin his job of tutoring Duke August's two younger sons, for which he was to be compensated 100 talers annually and receive his room and board. In the months ahead he won their approval, and within the court community he was able to take a place among the intellectual elite. In recognition of his poetic ability he was crowned *poeta laureatus caesareus* (imperial poet laureate) on 15 June 1646, an honor that helped to solidify his reputation as a poet. But his time in Wolfenbüttel was not entirely to his liking. He did not feel capable of satisfactorily performing the necessary educational tasks on his own, and as he admitted later in his autobiography, he frequently and vehemently complained about the situation.[16] Birken was also not adept at navigating the waters at court and appears to have been pulled into petty court intrigues fueled by detractors back in Nuremberg. In October of 1646 — less than nine months after his arrival in

Wolfenbüttel — he was relieved of his pedagogical responsibilities. This was a bittersweet solution for Birken, for although he welcomed his new freedom he regretted having to leave the company of the young princes, who, during his brief tenure at court, had become very dear to him and whose presence he sorely missed. This feeling of friendship toward Anton Ulrich is reflected in the first long work that he wrote after his departure from Wolfenbüttel: *Dannebergische Helden-Beut* (The Elite of the Dannenberg Heroes, 1648), an allegorical glorification of Anton Ulrich, to whom it is dedicated.

On leaving Wolfenbüttel Birken traveled north to make the acquaintance of established fellow poets such as Johann Rist (1607–67) and Philipp von Zesen (1619–89) in Hamburg and Andreas Tscherning (1611–59) in Rostock; but his ultimate destination was far to the south in Nuremberg, where he arrived in November of 1648. His arrival coincided with an important moment in the city's history: peace negotiations ending the Thirty Years' War had just concluded in Osnabrück and Münster, and the delegates relocated to Nuremberg to work out the final details concerning the demobilization of the armies and to celebrate the end of the war. These celebrations, scheduled to begin in April of 1649, offered poets and artists in Nuremberg an excellent opportunity to find commissions for their work. As a staunch Lutheran, Birken desired to work for members of the Swedish delegation, but by the time he returned home Harsdörffer and Klaj had already made those necessary contacts for themselves. If he wished to publicly demonstrate his poetic skills before an international audience, he had little choice but to seek work among the Catholic delegates.

What must have been initially a disappointment for Birken was actually a stroke of good fortune, for through his literary endeavors during the peace celebrations he came to the attention of a wealthy Catholic nobleman, Baron (later Count) Gottlieb von Windischgrätz (1630–95). Birken would later describe him as "ein Heros der Gelehrsamkeit, nicht nur Liebhaber und Förderer der Musen, sondern auch ihr Genosse" (a demigod of erudition, not only an admirer and patron of the Muses, but also their companion).[17] Attracted by Birken's poetic talent Windischgrätz encouraged his activities; several years later, in fact, he was to engage Birken's help in preparing his own poems for publication. More important for Birken than any individual commissioned work, however, was the patronage of Windischgrätz, which laid the foundation for Birken's later work for the Habsburg court in Vienna. Owing to his intercession, Birken was ennobled by Emperor Ferdinand III in 1655.

For now, the timing of Birken's presence in Nuremberg could not have been more fortunate. Although life in the city returned to normal once the peace celebrations had ended in 1651 and the delegates had departed, Nuremberg was culturally more vibrant than it had been for years. Following the long years of political uncertainty and economic hardship, Nuremberg was experiencing a cultural rebirth. The city had a long tradition of excellence in the arts and the crafts going back well before the time of Albrecht Dürer, and on this firm foundation poetry, painting, printmaking, and printing expanded in the second half of the seventeenth century. Other German cities could also boast of famous artists and poets, but the depth and breadth of the arts in Nuremberg set it apart from all other cities.

What made Nuremberg special was the unique blend of forces that worked together to strengthen its cultural fabric. The leading members of Nuremberg society were well educated, and for those who were patricians there was an inclination to support the arts through purchases of art works for both public and private use. And, as mentioned, by the end of the war the city also had a group of able poets intent on cultivating their literary talents. In addition, Nuremberg had been one of the first cities to which Gutenberg's invention of printing with movable type had spread in the later fifteenth century, and ever since that time the city had been home to a number of enterprising printers and publishers. The city's industries were known for their high-quality products, and the printing industry was no different. Changes in taste among the reading public at about this time led to the increased illustration of books.[18] For the visual arts this change in taste was a boon, and as Nuremberg publishers catered attentively to the reading public they needed to engage a greater number of printmakers. Among those artists attracted to the city were Jacob von Sandrart (1630–1708), Joachim von Sandrart (1606–88), Mathias van Somer (fl. 1649–66), and Daniel Preisler (1627–65). The influx of such talents led to a general elevation of the cultural life in the city, and Nuremberg could with justification be called the "queen of the imperial cities."[19]

Birken was one of the earliest to take advantage of this development in the publishing industry. While still trying to make a name for himself as a poet in the late 1640s he had written anonymous verses for decorative prints and illustrated broadsheets, and over the years he continued to expand and nurture the contacts he had with printmakers and publishers. Unfortunately, he continued to be unsuccessful in his attempt to find a steady position in Nuremberg. Plagued by financial concerns he moved in 1658 to nearby Bayreuth to be close to the Brandenburg court, though the minor commissions he could obtain in this provincial location did little to improve his circumstances. His marriage of convenience that same year to the wealthy Margaretha Magdalena Müleck, his senior by sixteen years, did not help his literary career: she was not prepared to invest her assets in his poetic endeavors.

Birken was therefore careful during his years in Bayreuth to maintain intimate contact with his Nuremberg colleagues, a tactic that eventually bore fruit. After the election of Leopold I in 1658 as emperor of the Holy Roman Empire, the decision was made to have a history of the Habsburgs published. This ambitious publication project was entrusted to the publisher Michael Endter of Nuremberg, who in turn engaged Birken to undertake the mammoth task of significantly expanding and bringing up to date a sixteenth-century manuscript, *Das Österreichische Erenwerk* (The Austrian Work of Honor), that chronicled significant events in the House of Habsburg to 1555. This was a particularly demanding undertaking for Birken, for in addition to the long text the book was to be richly illustrated. The fact that he would need to work closely with the publisher and several artists as he planned the content and layout of the book necessitated his moving back to Nuremberg in 1660.

Meanwhile, the literary atmosphere in the city had changed. Klaj had died in 1656, and Harsdörffer, the moving force behind the city's literary renaissance and the founder of the Pegnesischer Blumenorden, had died two years later. No one with poetic ability had stepped forward to take their places, and the society was becoming insignificant as a German cultural institution. Into this vacuum stepped the capable and energetic Birken. In just his mid thirties in 1662, he was elected its second president and went to work reviving its original purposefulness; during his nineteen-year tenure he added more than fifty writers, including thirteen women, to its membership rolls. Over the twelve-month period following April 1660 Birken was involved in forty-five different literary projects of varying lengths.[20] Justifiably proud of his significant accomplishments, he periodically estimated his poetic output. In May of 1664, for example, he calculated that he had written 12,000 verses in many different genres over the previous twelve months.[21] A more comprehensive calculation four years later revealed the true magnitude of his poetic production. Between 1644 and 1656 he had written 53,000 verses; during the subsequent twelve years this output had soared to 400,000 verses in German and 2,000 in Latin (*Tagebücher* 1:376).

Within a short time Birken stood at the center of Nuremberg's literary community. As its second president, he reinvigorated the Pegnesischer Blumenorden through an aggressive expansion of its membership not only in the city but throughout the empire. The primary focus of his activity during the 1660s, however, was his work on the history of the Austrian Habsburgs. As he made his substantive revisions to the manuscript he worked closely with printmakers Peter Troschel, Johann Friedrich Fleischberger, and Cornelius Nicolaus Schurtz. Several large portraits and almost 200 illustrations had to be made, and Birken followed their progress from beginning to end. This entailed closely coordinating his activities with those of the artists, and in his diaries at the time he frequently noted meeting with an artist to design such things as coats of arms.[22] He also designed maps for the work and checked the portraits as they were made. Birken was intimately involved in all stages of the book's production, and when it appeared in print as *Spiegel der Ehren des Hochlöblichen Kayser- und Königlichen Ertzhaus Oesterreich* (Mirror of Honors of the Most Praiseworthy Royal and Imperial House of Austria, 1668) it was a stately folio tome of almost 1,400 pages.

By the time this book had appeared Birken had an established reputation as a literary agent or manager who could successfully oversee the entire publication process. He was conveniently situated in a city known for its printers, publishers, and printmakers, and although many of his commissions came from people in Nuremberg, it was common for people from outside the city to engage his services. Thus, when Maria Elisabeth, duchess of Schleswig-Holstein, died in May of 1664, Birken was contacted on behalf of her husband, Margrave Georg Albrecht of Brandenburg-Kulmbach, to arrange for a title plate and illustrations for the official funeral oration.[23] The resulting product was so well received that over time it led to further commissions of similar works.

One of the people to turn to Birken for help in having a book published was Anton Ulrich, who by this time was in his thirties. The two men had been carrying on a lengthy correspondence since Birken's departure from Wolfenbüttel, but then in the 1660s their lives as writers became closely connected.[24] At the death of Duke August in 1666 the leadership of the duchy passed to Anton Ulrich's elder brother, Rudolf August (1627–1704), who appointed Anton Ulrich governor. Anton Ulrich had always had strong literary interests, and since this post was largely honorary in nature he was able to pursue these interests with little interruption. His primary literary endeavors up to this time had been short dramatic pieces, but he also had poetic talent. In 1655, when he was twenty-one years old, he had presented his father with a bound collection of thirty-four devotional songs that he had written; the collection was subsequently expanded and published anonymously as *Hocherleuchtete geistliche Lieder, einer hohen Personen* (Highly Illuminating Devotional Songs by a High-ranking Person, 1665) the year before Duke August's death.

Anton Ulrich continued to revise and enlarge his collection of songs, and since it was in Nuremberg that he wished to have the work printed, it was natural for him to commission Birken to manage its production. Whereas the first edition was not illustrated, Anton Ulrich desired to have a frontispiece in the new edition, and for this work Birken turned to Georg Christoph Eimmart (1638–1705), a respected printmaker in Nuremberg. In January of 1667 Eimmart made a preliminary sketch for the frontispiece and in July he delivered the completed copperplate to Birken. Over the summer Anton Ulrich's *Christ-Fürstliches Davids-Harpfen-Spiel* (King David's Christian and Princely Harp Playing) was printed, and in the middle of September Birken received twenty Imperiales from the duke to remunerate Eimmart for his work.

Although it may seem strange that a secular ruler passed his time composing devotional songs for publication, this work fit well into Anton Ulrich's political agenda. Ever since the beginning of the Reformation the Lutheran Church had depended on the firm support of secular rulers for its continued survival. By writing devotional songs and naming King David in the title, Anton Ulrich was intentionally underscoring his divinely determined position in a political tradition extending back to Solomon and David.[25] By emphasizing this connection, the duke was portraying himself as both political and religious leader in his territory.

This work marked only the beginning of significant literary cooperation between the two men. Even before Birken had made the arrangements for the revised edition of Anton Ulrich's devotional songs, the duke had sought his help in connection with a much more ambitious project: his multivolume historical courtly novel *Die Durchleuchtige Syrerinn Aramena* (The Illustrious Syrian Woman Aramena, 1669–73). *Aramena* is a massive, intricately webbed construction involving scores of paired lovers and multiple political power centers, in which the Stoic virtues of *Standhaftigkeit* (constancy) and *Treue* (loyalty) ultimately triumph.[26] Birken's involvement in this project was to be significant, because in addition to coordinating the work of others involved in the publication of the novel, he was responsible for copyediting the entire text and even writing certain sections himself. At first he was able to devote little time to this project since he had not yet completed his work on *Spiegel der Ehren*. It was not until the fall of 1668 that Birken was finally able to turn his attention to the novel, and from that point on his diaries reveal that, although he was engaged in several smaller projects, he devoted himself to preparing Anton Ulrich's manuscript for publication. By mid-December the first, second, and third parts of *Aramena* were in Birken's hands, and he was able to send Anton Ulrich the sketch for the title plate. In January of 1669 Birken made sketches of the illustrations to appear in the first book of *Aramena*, and as work progressed he met with the artist Johann Franck (fl. 1659–90) to discuss the illustrations.[27] Sometimes the two men were also joined in their discussions by the publisher, Johann Hoffmann. By mid-May Birken's revision of the first book of the novel was complete. Although it was Birken who determined what was to be illustrated and who made the preliminary sketches, Anton Ulrich's approval was required at all stages. Birken noted on 14 August 1669 that Anton Ulrich returned nine printed sheets and twelve illustrations, presumably with his corrections (*Tagebücher* 1:489). Birken's work on the novel continued in this manner until the fifth and final volume appeared in 1673.

This multivolume project had required Birken's attention for several years, yet he had never devoted his time exclusively to it. He had continued to find time to write occasional verse and to carry on an active correspondence with many people throughout the empire. He had also structured his time so that he could work on one of his own longer works: *Guelfis oder NiderSächsischer Lorbeerhayn* (Guelfis; or, Lower Saxon Laurel Grove, 1669), a panegyrical prose eclogue dedicated to Anton Ulrich and in praise of his house.

Anton Ulrich was so pleased with Birken's editorial and managerial work that he turned to him once again when he wished to publish his second multivolume historical courtly novel: *Octavia: Römische Geschichte* (Octavia: A Roman Story, 1677–1707), an even more gigantic work of some 7,000 pages that coordinates the lives and actions of approximately 1,800 characters.[28] As with *Aramena* this work was also to be richly illustrated, and for this project Birken again hired the publisher Johann Hoffmann.[29] For the illustrations he engaged Jacob von Sandrart, the most accomplished of the Nuremberg printmakers in the second half of the seventeenth century.[30] Birken began his work on the novel in January of 1675, and in the months ahead he frequently noted in his diaries correspondence with Anton Ulrich, which contained pages of *Octavia* either to be edited or corrected.[31] Work on this novel proved to be especially demanding for Birken. One contributing factor was the deteriorating condition of his health but another was the sometimes less-than-congenial relations with the difficult publisher Hoffmann. When he finally concluded his work on the first volume he expressed in his diary, on 17 February 1677, the wish that God not place another such burden on him (*Tagebücher* 2:375).

The second volume of *Octavia* appeared in 1678, and the publication of the third in 1679 marked the end of the literary collaboration between the duke and Birken, though that did not mean the end of their friendship. They maintained their correspondence during Birken's remaining years, and Anton

Ulrich continued to act as Birken's patron by periodically sending him monetary gifts. Birken's death in 1681 brought an end to a long, fruitful, unique relationship, but Anton Ulrich's own interest in the arts continued unabated. The duke himself revised and expanded his novel until the seventh and last volume appeared in the first decade of the eighteenth century.

In Anton Ulrich's later years it was not so much literature as art and architecture that occupied most of his attention. He was appointed coregent by his brother Rudolf August in 1685 and shortly thereafter became engaged in planning a suitable residence. In 1688 he began to oversee the construction of the most ambitious baroque palace in northern Germany.[32] Like many of his peers Anton Ulrich looked to Versailles as his model. The palace that he built at Salzdahlum north of Wolfenbüttel was a clear statement of his political power, but at the same time the art gallery in the palace underscored his profound interest in and devotion to the arts.

Anton Ulrich's life came to an end in 1714, a year before the death of Louis XIV. Their passing coincided with fundamental political and intellectual change in Europe as the Baroque gave way to the Enlightenment. With time, the duke and his considerable accomplishments were virtually forgotten; as for Salzdahlum, it was deliberately destroyed.[33] Birken and his literary career had a similar fate as the culture of the Baroque was repudiated in the next century. But during their lifetimes these two men shared a common passion for art. Birken, the commoner of modest means but great intellect and energy, made a name for himself through his wide-ranging literary endeavors. Anton Ulrich, a nobleman possessed of insignificant military might but great natural talent and a love of art, found satisfaction in the Muses. Although Birken and Anton Ulrich were separated by the gulf of social class, their lives were intimately connected personally and professionally through their love of literature and art.

Notes

[1] In Birken's time the Nuremberg patriciate consisted of the city's twenty-eight oldest families, from whose ranks the city council was comprised exclusively.

[2] For an orientation to this important topic see the introduction to Manfred Lentzen's *Christoforo Landino: De vera nobilitate* (Geneva: Droz, 1970). The groundbreaking study was done by Klaus Garber, especially "Zur Statuskonkurrenz von Adel und gelehrtem Bürgertum im theoretischen Schrifttum des 17. Jahrhunderts," in *Hof, Staat und Gesellschaft in der Literatur des 17. Jahrhunderts*, ed. Elger Blühm et al. (Amsterdam: Rodopi, 1982), 115–43. Garber offers a succinct account in "The Republic of Letters and the Absolutist State: Nine Theses," thesis 2, "The Transformative Ideology of 'True Nobility,'" in *Imperiled Heritage: Tradition, History, and Utopia in Early Modern German Literature*, ed. Max Reinhart (Aldershot, UK: Ashgate, 2000), 41–53, here 43–44.

[3] The most comprehensive study of Anton Ulrich's life and literary work is Etienne Mazingue's *Anton Ulrich, duc de Braunschweig-Wolfenbuettel (1633–1714), un prince*

romancier au xviième siècle, 2 vols. (Lille: Service de Reproduction des Thèses Université de Lille III, 1974). See also the catalogue of the exhibition to commemorate the 350th anniversary of Anton Ulrich's birth: *Herzog Anton Ulrich von Braunschweig: Leben und Regieren mit der Kunst* (Braunschweig: Herzog Anton Ulrich-Museum, 1983). A good overview of the duke's literary life can be found in Blake Lee Spahr, "Herzog Anton Ulrich von Braunschweig-Lüneburg," in *Deutsche Dichter des 17. Jahrhunderts: Ihr Leben und Werk*, ed. Harald Steinhagen and Benno von Wiese (Berlin: Schmidt, 1984), 597–614; Spahr, "Anton Ulrich, Duke of Braunschweig-Lüneburg," in *Dictionary of Literary Biography*, vol. 168, *German Baroque Writers, 1661–1730*, ed. James Hardin (Detroit: Gale Research, 1996), 27–35.

[4] For a detailed discussion of the various facets of the duke's life and of his considerable accomplishments see *Sammler, Fürst, Gelehrter: Herzog August zu Braunschweig und Lüneburg 1579–1666*, Ausstellungskataloge der Herzog August Bibliothek 27 (Wolfenbüttel: Herzog August Bibliothek, 1979).

[5] In the opinion of Ferdinand Sonnenburg, *Herzog Anton Ulrich von Braunschweig als Dichter* (Berlin: Simion, 1896), 2, Duke August's library was "die reichste und wertvollste Bibliothek der Welt" (the most comprehensive and valuable library in the world). On Duke August's philosophy and habits of book collecting and on the library he established at Wolfenbüttel see in this volume the chapter by Jill Bepler.

[6] Schottelius's activities at the court in Wolfenbüttel are described in Jörg Jochen Berns, *Justus Georg Schottelius, 1612–1676: Ein Teutscher Gelehrter am Wolfenbütteler Hof*, Ausstellungskataloge der Herzog August Bibliothek 18 (Wolfenbüttel: Herzog August Bibliothek, 1976). For a more specific discussion of Anton Ulrich's education see Jörg Jochen Müller, "Fürstenerziehung im 17. Jahrhundert: Am Beispiel Herzog Anton Ulrichs von Braunschweig und Lüneburg," in *Stadt, Schule, Universität, Buchwesen und die deutsche Literatur im 17. Jahrhundert*, ed. Albrecht Schöne (Munich: Beck, 1976), 243–60. See also Sara Smart, "Justus Georg Schottelius," in *Dictionary of Literary Biography*, vol. 164, *German Baroque Writers, 1580–1660*, ed. James Hardin (Detroit: Gale Research, 1996), 292–303. Schottelius's contribution to the standardization of the German language is treated in this volume by Renate Born.

[7] Anton Ulrich's efforts at drawing and etching are described in Jürgen Hoos and Wolfgang Hofmann, "Die Entwicklung der zeichnerischen Fähigkeiten in der fürstlichen Erziehung — dargestellt am Beispiel der Handzeichnungen des jungen Ferdinand Albrecht I. von Braunschweig-Bevern (1636–1687)," an in-house scholarly study for the Hochschule für Bildende Künste, Braunschweig, 1979. Additional information about the young prince's artistic endeavors are to be found in Maria Munding, "Die fürstliche Familie," in *Sammler, Fürst, Gelehrter*, 249–52; Christian von Heusinger, "Anton Ulrichs graphische Versuche," in exhibition catalogue *Herzog Anton Ulrich von Braunschweig: Leben und Regieren mit der Kunst*, 23–25 and 30–34; John Roger Paas, "Inseparable Muses: German Baroque Poets as Graphic Artists," *Colloquia Germanica* 29 (1996): 17–21.

[8] Der Wunderliche (= Ferdinand Albrecht), *Wunderliche Begebnüssen und wunderlicher Zustand Jn dieser wunderlichen verkehrten Welt* (Bevern: Johann Heitmüller, 1678), 3.

[9] See Jörg Jochen Berns, " 'Princeps Poetarum et Poeta Principum': Das Dichtertum Anton Ulrichs als Exempel absolutistischer Rollennorm und Rollenbrechung," in *'Monarchus Poeta': Studien zum Leben und Werk Anton Ulrichs von Braunschweig-Lüneburg*, Chloe 4 (Amsterdam: Rodopi, 1985), 13–19.

[10] Two books in particular established Schottelius's renown in the early 1640s: *Teutsche Sprachkunst* (The Art of the German Language, 1641) and *Der Teutschen Sprache Einleitung* (An Introduction to the German Language, 1643), which sought to create a genuine poetic theory in terms of the unique character of the German language.

[11] Ferdinand Albrecht noted in his *Wunderliche Begebnüssen*, 3, that in contrast to Schottelius's senseless educational tactics, Birken offered useful instruction in Christian matters.

[12] For general biographies of Birken's life see Joachim Kröll, "Sigmund von Birken (1626–1681)," *Fränkische Lebensbilder* 9 (1980): 187–203; John Roger Paas, "Sigmund von Birken," in *Dictionary of Literary Biography*, vol. 164, *German Baroque Writers, 1580–1660*, ed. James Hardin (Detroit: Gale Research, 1996), 50–63.

[13] An ancestor had latinized the original name Birkener to Betulius, following the humanist practice. Later, when he was enobled in 1655, as we shall see, our author chose a version of the original name to accompany the new "von."

[14] The new genre, known as *Prosaekloge* (prose eclogue), combined the traditions of the Vergilian eclogue (all verse) and the sixteenth-century Spanish pastoral novel (with alternating prose with verse sections). For more on this genre see in this volume the introduction by Max Reinhart.

[15] Birken and Klaj's *Fortsetzung* receives detailed and broad analysis by Klaus Garber, "Nuremberg, Arcadia on the Pegnitz," in Reinhart, ed., *Imperiled Heritage*, 142–65.

[16] Sigmund von Birken, *Werke und Korrespondenz*, vol. 14, *Prosapia / Biographia*, ed. Dietrich Jöns and Hartmut Laufhütte, Neudrucke deutscher Literaturwerke, NS 41 (Tübingen: Niemeyer, 1988), 82.

[17] Birken, *Werke und Korrespondenz*, 105.

[18] The growing interest in illustrated works caused concern among publishers, who saw their production costs rise significantly. In 1669 the Endters, one of the established publishing houses in Nuremberg, wrote to the emperor to complain that they were being forced to illustrate works because print dealers were indiscriminately issuing all of their books with illustrations. See Friedrich Oldenbourg, *Die Endter: Eine Nürnberger Buchhändlerfamilie (1590–1740)* (Munich: Oldenbourg, 1911), 101. The complaint did nothing to stem the tide of illustrated works.

[19] For general information about Nuremberg's economic situation and literary position at the time see Martha White Paas, "Nürnbergs Wirtschaft im 17. Jahrhundert," in *'der Franken Rom': Nürnbergs Blütezeit in der zweiten Hälfte des 17. Jahrhunderts*, ed. John Roger Paas (Wiesbaden: Harrassowitz, 1995), 46–61; Blake Lee Spahr, "Nürnbergs Stellung im literarischen Leben des 17. Jahrhunderts," in Schöne, ed., *Stadt — Schule — Universität — Buchwesen*, 57–83.

[20] Dietrich Jöns, "Sigmund von Birken: Zum Phänomen einer literarischen Existenz zwischen Hof und Stadt," in *Literatur in der Stadt*, ed. Horst Brunner, Göppinger Arbeiten zur Germanistik 343 (Göppingen: Kümmerle, 1982), 172.

[21] Sigmund von Birken, *Die Tagebücher des Sigmund von Birken*, part 1, ed. Joachim Kröll (Würzburg: Schöningh, 1971), 88.

[22] Examples in Birken, *Tagebücher*, 1:157 (19 Jan. 1665), 186 (30 May 1666), 217 (3 Jan. 1666 and 4 Jan. 1666), 220 (17 Jan. 1666), 223 (31 Jan. 1666), 226 (14 Feb. 1666), and 245 (1 Aug. 1666).

[23] It was to be produced in Bayreuth and the oration written by Caspar von Lilien and printed by Johann Gebhard, men with whom Birken was well acquainted. For the work on the title plate he arranged to have the Nuremberg artists Franz Hieronymus Fuchs design the plate and Cornelius Nikolaus Schurtz engrave it. For the larger plates in the oration Birken secured the services of Jacob von Sandrart.

[24] Entries in Birken's diaries show clearly that over the years the duke was one of Birken's most frequent correspondents. Interestingly, however, Birken appears to have saved none of the duke's letters, whereas he carefully preserved those from most other correspondents. Birken's papers, as well as his entire personal library, are located in the archives of the Pegnesischer Blumenorden in the Germanic National Museum in Nuremberg.

[25] Berns, "Princeps Poetarum et Poeta Principum," 12.

[26] For a fascinating study of Anton Ulrich's novel and Birken's involvement in its publication see Blake Lee Spahr, *Anton Ulrich and Aramena: The Genesis and Development of a Baroque Novel*, University of California Publications in Modern Philology 76 (Berkeley: U of California P, 1966).

[27] Birken, *Tagebücher*, 1:420 (4 Jan. 1669).

[28] A discussion of the various stages of development of the novel (with mention of Birken's role) is to be found in Giles Hoyt, *The Development of Anton Ulrich's Narrative Prose on the Basis of Surviving "Octavia" Manuscripts and Prints*, Studien zur Germanistik, Anglistik und Komparatistik 33 (Bonn: Bouvier, 1977).

[29] It was not uncommon for writers to "hire" publishers, as competition among the better publishers was great at the time. In this environment, some publishers, Hoffmann among them, frequently did not pay their authors in a timely fashion; indeed, Hoffmann had a reputation for pirating editions.

[30] Although Birken dealt directly with Jacob von Sandrart, it was actually the latter's elder son Johann Jacob who engraved the plates. See *Hollstein's German Engravings, Etchings, and Woodcuts 1400–1700*, ed. John Roger Paas (Roosendaal: Sound & Vision Interactive, 1995), 40:104–25.

[31] See, for example, Sigmund von Birken, *Die Tagebücher des Sigmund von Birken*, part 2, ed. Joachim Kröll (Würzburg: Schöningh, 1974), 263 (10 Jan. 1675), 265 (16 Jan. 1675), 269 (13 Feb. 1675), 271 (6 Mar. 1675), 284 (26 June 1675).

[32] See exhibition catalogue *Herzog Anton Ulrich von Braunschweig: Leben und Regieren mit der Kunst*, 49–120.

[33] As part of his reorganization of Europe, Napoleon made his brother Jerome king of Westphalia in 1807. His territories included the dukedom of Braunschweig and, thus, the palace at Salzdahlum. In 1811 Jerome gave the palace to the city of Braunschweig with the order to complete the building of the royal residence in the city. To raise the necessary money Braunschweig demolished Salzdahlum and sold or auctioned off what was of value.

Women's Writing in the Context of Their Lives, 1520–1720

Anna Carrdus

FAR FEWER WOMEN THAN MEN WERE writing in early modern Germany and many of them remain unknown. New discoveries continually add fresh details to our view of the literary landscape — an example is the recent discovery of work by Anna Köferl. The only information we have about her is on the 1631 Nuremberg broadsheet describing the large "dolls' house" that she commissioned and then furnished over many years. Her verses appear under a woodcut by her husband, Hans Köferl, depicting the exterior of the house.[1] She tells us its size — nine feet high, five wide, four deep — and how she fitted it out with furniture, bed linen, and kitchen utensils, even with an armory, paintings, and a library. She claims to have put the leisure due to her childlessness to good use, furnishing the house to show young people how to order and equip their own eventual homes, and invites those who have not yet seen it to come and do so. As a woman writing in the early modern period, Köferl is unique in her choice of topic and highly unusual in belonging to the artisan class. Nevertheless, her dolls' house fascinatingly mirrors the full-scale building projects of noblewomen who were patrons of the arts or who collected libraries,[2] and her verses have features in common with other women's writing: a religious context (she sees her childlessness as God's will), dependence on leisure and male cooperation, didactic purpose, and a sharp focus on domestic life.

Research over the last sixty years has identified these general characteristics of early modern women's writing. In 1943 Lotte Traeger compiled a systematic list of sixteenth-century sources; in 1984 Jean M. Woods and Maria Fürstenwald published a bio-bibliographical lexicon of seventeenth- and early-eighteenth-century women writers, artists, and scholars;[3] in the late 1980s, drawing to a large extent on these sources, Barbara Becker-Cantarino and Gisela Brinker-Gabler published historical surveys of early modern women's writing.[4] Since then, numerous studies and modern editions of work by women have appeared, but research progresses slowly, often bedeviled by the difficulty of tracing women's texts and the details of their lives.

This difficulty is directly related to the secondary legal and social status of early modern women and their subordination to the male head of their family.[5] Their lack of independence helps to explain the obscurity of their lives: one has to turn to facts about a woman's father or husband in order to compile her biography. Women's lives were largely restricted to two spheres, the religious and the domestic. Their education, whether at home or in one of the few elementary schools open to girls, usually aimed to instruct them only in the interlinked duties of piety and housekeeping. Because they were to play no part in public life, girls were prohibited from all forms of higher education; this generally excluded them from learning Latin, the main language of public life and literary scholarship until the early eighteenth century. Whether a woman took up writing depended on her parents' or husband's attitude and on the extent of the leisure available to her. If she did write, she could expect her writings to circulate, if at all, not in print but only in manuscript. Many women, like Sybille Schwarz (1621–37) and Margaretha Susanna von Kuntsch (1651–1717), resisted publication out of the domestic modesty expected of them; their collected works were published posthumously by male editors — Schwarz's former teacher, Kuntsch's grandson. Few manuscript writings by women were thought worth preserving, however, with the notable exceptions of writings by rulers' consorts (wives of rulers); these were often routinely filed in court archives. Surviving texts therefore represent a mere fraction of women's output, and tracing and reassembling a woman's *oeuvre* can be arduous. Even in cases of printed writings, they often appear singly, as small pamphlets or scattered in anthologies, hymn books, or *Leichenpredigten* (printed funeral sermons); if they originally appeared in collected form, they usually survive in only a few copies held by libraries in widely separated locations.[6]

Several factors, to be sure, worked in favor of early modern women writers — above all, high social status and material prosperity — although these very factors excluded many other women from literary pursuits. Women of the ruling or lower nobility enjoyed the greatest privileges of culture and leisure. It was not unusual for them to learn Latin, French, or Italian, history, philosophy, or jurisprudence and to have tuition in music, dance, drawing, or painting. Middle-class women with prosperous and liberal-minded husbands might supplement their limited education during their adult leisure time. The obvious links between wealth, education, and leisure explain why far more women from the higher social orders than from the artisan class took up writing. Irrespective of class, however, many women who chose to write received encouragement and support from male relatives or acquaintances; this support took various forms, from advice to overseeing publication. Women also found encouragement within their domestic circles, becoming active participants through their writing in family and dynastic occasions, particularly during the seventeenth century. Typically, middle-class women wrote poems for funerals, birthdays, or weddings celebrated by members of their immediate circle; by contrast, the writings by rulers' consorts for similar occasions assumed dynastic significance in the context of court life. The religious sphere also inspired women to write. Almost without exception, women's literary pursuits had roots in the various combinations of reading, writing, and singing that formed the substance of their early religious instruction and lifelong daily devotions. Not all women who wrote in adulthood addressed religious topics, but collections of Bible passages, prayers, meditations, or sacred songs were compiled for personal use by women of the ruling, middle, and artisan classes alike, from the early sixteenth century to the early eighteenth.[7]

A variety of historical and cultural circumstances affected women's decisions to write, as well as their ability to carry out their ambition. These include the spread of printing simultaneously with the religious upheaval of the Reformation; the long conflict that followed it; the reform of vernacular poetry in the second quarter of the seventeenth century; and the so-called *querelle des femmes*, the pan-European public debate on women's education, which took on particular relevance in Germany in the early 1670s. This chronological survey will be followed by an account of the impact of domestic and religious life on women's writing.

Women Confront the Reformation, 1523–36

Women's writings give a vivid impression of the Reformation's impact on individual lives. In Nuremberg it led to the dissolution of the Klarakloster (Convent of the Poor Clares), where Caritas Pirckheimer (1467–1532) was abbess from 1503 until her death. After the city's ruling body converted to Lutheranism in 1525 she documented her convent's subsequent, and unsuccessful, struggle for survival, incorporating letters from both sides of the impassioned conflict into a first-person record of decisive conversations and often harrowing events. These included the city council's prohibition of visits by Franciscan priests — who held Mass, administered the sacraments, and heard confessions in the convent — and the forcible removal of three nuns by their families. Her account has acquired the title *Denkwürdigkeiten* (Memoirs), but it probably belongs more appropriately among the historiographical genres — chronicles, eye-witness accounts, biographies, autobiographies — practiced in German convents during the early modern period.[8]

Pirckheimer came from a wealthy patrician family in Nuremberg and received an exceptionally thorough education at home before going to the convent school and taking the veil.[9] Her illustrious brother Willibald (1470–1530), one of the city's leading men and an important intellectual force in humanist scholarship, urged her to enter into Latin correspondence with leading humanists, among them Sixtus Tucher (1459–1507), former adviser to Emperor Maximilian I and King Louis XII of France, and the poet laureate Conrad Celtis (1459–1508). All of them recognized in her the German embodiment of the ideal female humanist scholar, as represented by the figure of Magdalia in Erasmus's dialogue *Abbatis et Eruditae* (The Abbot and the Learned Woman, 1526), and compared her with other famous women who wrote in Latin, such as Paula, St. Jerome's correspondent, and Hrotsvit (ca. 935–73), canoness of the abbey of Gandersheim, whose dramas and epics were rediscovered by Celtis and edited and published by him in 1501.[10] Pirckheimer was aware of her learned reputation. Her erudition fostered the diplomatic skills she demonstrated in dealing with the city council's suppressive measures against her convent in the 1520s, including her feigned appearance of helpless humility expected of women outside humanist circles.

Pirckheimer was not the only woman from her family to benefit from a humanist education and to make a career in a convent; her six younger sisters and three of her nieces followed the same path, if with less distinction. However, the closing of so many convents during the Reformation, as well as Luther's influential teachings on marriage, which, along with childbearing, he presented as women's only destiny — *Ein Sermon von dem ehelichen Stand* (A Sermon on the Married Estate, 1519), *Vom ehelichen Leben* (On Married Life, 1519), and *Predigt vom Ehestand* (Sermon on the Married Estate, 1525)[11] — reduced the availability of this option. Although convents continued to exist and nuns to write,[12] few German women attained intellectual freedom comparable to Pirckheimer's. Rare examples include Margarete Peutinger (1481–1552), wife of the Augsburg humanist Conrad Peutinger (1465–1547), their daughters Juliana (fl. 1504) and Konstanze (fl. 1517–46), and Octavia Fulvia Morata (1526–55).[13]

Nevertheless, the fierce religious dispute that took place in print during the 1520s opened a brief window of opportunity for other women who could write. In spite of St. Paul's dictum that women should be silent in church affairs (1 Tim. 2:12),[14] some spoke out, emboldened by Luther's teachings on the priesthood of all believers. Among them were Argula von Grumbach, née von Stauff, and Katharina Zell. Although their social backgrounds were very different, their writings all reflect the intimate familiarity with the Bible that Luther fostered.

Grumbach (ca. 1492–1554) was a Bavarian aristocrat who served as lady-in-waiting (attendant to the ruler's consort) at the Munich court during her youth.[15] The first of the eight pamphlets she wrote in 1523–24 went into thirteen editions. It was a polemical open letter to theologians at the University of Ingolstadt condemning their treatment of Arsacius Seehofer, a student whom the Catholic university had forced to renounce Lutheranism under threat of torture. It conveys a strong sense of her outrage:

> Ach Gott / wie werdt jr besteen / mit ewer hohen schul / das jr so thoret vnd gewaltigklichen handelt / wider das wort gottes / vnd mit gewalt zwingt das haylig Ewangelium in der handt zu halten / dasselbig darzu zu verlaugnen / als ir dann mit Arsacius Seehofer gethon habt.[16]

> [How in God's name can you and your university expect to prevail, when you deploy such foolish violence against the Word of God; when you force someone to hold the holy gospel in their hands for the very purpose of denying it, as you did in the case of Arsacius Seehofer?]

She sent copies of this letter to the city council in Ingolstadt and to Wilhelm, duke of Bavaria, a childhood friend, with a letter reminding him of his duties as ruler that recalls Luther's *An den christlichen Adel deutscher Nation* (To the Christian Nobility of the German Nation, 1520). Her accompanying letters were published as pamphlets, as were her exhortatory letters to the citizens of Regensburg and to other noblemen: Johannes, Count Palatine of the Rhine, whom she had met at the imperial diet in Nuremberg and sought to "lobby" in the cause of reform; Adam von Thering, one of his officials; and Friedrich the Wise, Elector of Saxony. One sign of the censure her writings attracted was her husband's dismissal from his administrative post in Dietfurt; another was the scurrilous attack in doggerel verse by one Johannes of Landshut, who accused her of being "in heat" for Seehofer and ordered her back to her spindle, a woman's proper place. Grumbach's final publication was *Eyn Antwort in gedichtß weiß* (An Answer in Verse), calmly argued but satirically cast in the same doggerel, which she claims never to have used before. Indeed, her stylistic range is not fully represented by her pamphlets.[17]

Katharina Zell, née Schütz (1498–1562), was born into a well-to-do artisan family in Strasbourg.[18] In 1523 she married Matthew Zell, a priest who had adopted Lutheranism. This was one of the first clerical marriages of the Reformation and became a true working partnership: her husband called her his "helper," she saw herself as a "church mother." Like Köferl, she remained childless (two children died in infancy), which may partly account for the extraordinary energy she threw into these assumed roles. Her first publication, *Den leydenden Christglaubigen wyberen der gmein zu Kentzingen* (To the Hard-pressed, Faithful Christian Women of Kentzingen, 1524), an open letter of consolation to the wives of 150 Lutheran men expelled from this Catholic town. It is characteristic of Zell's writing that this pamphlet should be supplemented by practical help: she housed and fed some sixty of the expelled men for four weeks.

The same combination of publication and pastoral care marks two further works. One is her 1535–36 edition of the first collection of hymns in German, originally compiled by the Bohemian Brethren, followers of the reformer John Huss (ca. 1372–1415), and translated for use in the early Lutheran church by Michael Weisse (ca. 1488–1534). In line with Weisse's recommendations Zell left the text unaltered, but she added her own preface, brief instructive headings to many hymns, and new melodies to some, and had the edition printed in four inexpensive booklets so that even poorer members of Strasbourg's congregations could afford it. The other work, from 1558, is a set of meditations on Psalms 51 and 130, with a didactic commentary on the Lord's Prayer:

> *Den Psalmen Miserere / mit dem Khünig David bedacht / gebettet / und paraphrasirt von Katharina Zellin [. . .] / sampt dem Vatter unser mit seiner erklärung / zugeschickt dem Christlichen mann Juncker Felix Armbruster / zum trost in seiner kranckheit / und andern angefochtenen hertzen und Concientzen / der sünd halben betrübt & c. in truck lassen kommen.*

> [The Penitential Psalm Meditated upon, Prayed with King David, and Paraphrased by Katharina Zell, together with the Our Father and its explanation, sent to the Christian man Sir Felix Armbruster as comfort in his illness and put into print for other afflicted hearts and consciences troubled by sin.]

Zell was nursing Armbruster at the time but had written the texts earlier as a comfort to herself in hard times. Some of her personal letters — to Luther and other theologians, for example — are extant, as is the apparently improvised address she gave at her husband's burial in 1548. Like Grumbach, Zell published satirically tinged polemic: a defense (*Entschuldigung*, 1524) of her husband and the principle of clerical marriage in the face of slanderous gossip; and an open letter to the citizens of Strasbourg accusing her husband's former protégé, the cleric Ludwig Rabus (1524–92), of worldly ambition and betraying Lutheran principles (1557). She was not only widely read in Reformation literature but widely traveled, as well; she journeyed with her husband on one occasion to Switzerland and on another to Wittenberg to meet Luther.

Grumbach and Zell call regularly on scriptural authority to justify "speaking out" as female members of the laity: the prophet Joel, who foretold the Whitsun outpouring of the Holy Spirit on men and women alike (Joel 2:28–29; cf. Acts 2:17–18); women who were chosen by God as active mouthpieces: Judith (Jth. 8:11–27), Anna (Luke 2:36–38), or Mary Magdalene (John 20:1, 11–18); even Balaam's ass, a female animal (Num. 22:22–30). These biblical women were moved by divine inspiration rather than hard-won erudition and thus differed greatly from the humanist ideal embodied by Pirckheimer; like Pirckheimer, however, Grumbach and Zell were clearly aware of working within a particular female tradition. This awareness was not necessarily shared by every woman writing during the Reformation. Several women's purely personal letters on family issues raised by the Reformation found their way into print, possibly without their prior knowledge and at the hands of printers eager to profit from public interest in religious strife; other such letters have since been retrieved from archives in manuscript form.[19] All these letters are further vivid illustrations of how writing helped women to confront the Reformation.

Women Participate in Confessional Conflict, 1540–1650

Interconfessional conflict began in Germany even before the first generation of reformers had died and lasted halfway through the following century. Conflict arose not only between Catholics and Lutherans, but also between Lutheranism and other faiths. The fierce religious commitment apparent in works by Pirckheimer, Grumbach, and Zell resurfaces in writings by Elisabeth, Duchess of Braunschweig-Lüneburg, Magdalena Heymair, and Anna Ovena Hoyers.

A large body of writings by Elisabeth of Braunschweig-Lüneburg (1510–58) survives.[20] She is remembered, for example, as the first German exponent of maternal advice manuals, a genre later practiced by her daughter Anna Maria, by Benigna of Solms-Laubach (1648–1702),[21] and by certain middle-class women. The daughter of Joachim I, elector of Brandenburg, Elisabeth was fifteen when she married Erich I of Braunschweig-Lüneburg. She ruled the duchy from his death in 1540 until their son, Erich II, came of age in 1545. Her Catholic husband had tolerated her conversion to Lutheranism in 1538; as regent, however, she took steps to gain the allegiance of his Catholic subjects to her confession. Within two years she published new church ordinances, drawn up by the renowned cleric Anton Corvinus (1501–53). As her regency drew to an end she published *Ein Christlicher Sendebrieff* (A Christian Open Letter) to fortify her subjects in the Lutheran faith, and wrote a guide to rulership for her son, *Unterrichtung und Ordnung* (Instruction and Ordinance), devoting over a third of it to confessional issues, such as the need for tact when negotiating with convents. Indeed, the existence of Protestant convents in Lower Saxony today can be dated to her policies.[22] *Unterrichtung und Ordnung*, a mirror for princes, or *Fürstenspiegel*, reflects Elisabeth's desire to protect Lutheranism within the duchy beyond the end of her rule. Disappointment came for her when her son reverted to Catholicism and enforced it in the realm, though this did not destroy her hopes of cementing alliances with other Lutheran dynasties through arranging marriages for her children. However, the manual on marital life, *Ein freuntlicher und mutterlicher underricht* (A Gentle and Maternal Instruction) that she wrote for her daughter, Anna Maria (1530–68), following her marriage to Albrecht, Duke of Prussia, concentrates on spiritual and personal issues rather than on confessional politics.[23] The following extract is from the introductory section of general advice:

> [M]ein liebste tochter, wie du allezeit gehorsam gewest in meiner kegenwerdigkeit, so wolle D. L. [i.e., "Deine Liebden," a form of address used between rulers] auch nuhe in meinem abwesen irem herrn, [dem] D. L. von mir gentzlich ubergeben ist, den gehorsam in allen dingen darreichen. Darumb, mein kindt, vor allem libe des herrn wordt und negst, so habe nichts libers als deinen herrn und gemahel; nim deines berufs und standts mit fleis war; schaffe, das du selig werdest mit furcht und zitern; den got ist es warlich, der in dir wircket bede das wollen und volbringen.

> [My dearest daughter, just as you have always been obedient to me in my presence, so, beloved, will you also now in my absence proffer obedience in all things to your lord, to whom, beloved, I have completely surrendered you. Therefore, my child, above all love the Word of the Lord and then hold nothing more dear than your lord and spouse; fulfill your duty and estate with diligence; procure your salvation with fear and trembling; for truly it is God who produces within you both the will and its accomplishment.]

This intimate focus is characteristic of Elisabeth's later writings. In 1551 she published *Etliche schöne Gebet und Trostsprüche [. . .] aus der heiligen Schrifft* (A Few Fine Prayers and Comforting Sayings from the Holy Bible) for the benefit of all persecuted Lutherans and sought personal comfort in writing hymns to familiar melodies. In 1555 her Christmas present to her sister and sister-in-law was the manuscript of *Der Widwen Handbüchlein* (Consolation Manual for Widows); it was published the next year and went into four editions.

Magdalena Heymair (fl. 1566–86)[24] also wrote didactic works. Much of what little is known of her life comes from the forewords she wrote for her own publications. All her works are paraphrases of Bible extracts, presented in the form of songs to existing melodies for use in schools or the home. They include *Die Sontegliche Epistel* (The Sunday Epistles, 1566), *Das Büchlein Jesu Syrach* (The Wisdom of Jesus the Son of Sirach, or, Ecclesiasticus, 1571), *Die ApostelGeschicht* (The Acts of the Apostles, 1573), and *Das Buch Tobiae* (Tobit, 1580).[25] For many years Heymair made a living in southern Germany as a private tutor or as a schoolmistress. In about 1555 she converted from Catholicism to Lutheranism, inspired by talks about the Bible with the mother of children she was tutoring. She saw her Bible paraphrases and other texts — like "Das Geistlich A. B. C. sampt einem schönen Geistlichen Lied" (The Sacred ABC with a Fine Sacred Song), appended to *Das Büchlein Jesu Syrach* — as a means of praising God for her conversion and of laying the foundations of steadfast faith in the young. Willibald Ramsbeck, a Lutheran pastor in Cham in the Upper Palatinate, where Heymair and her husband ran a school in the 1560s, added a preface to her *Sontegliche Epistel* stressing the value of this publication within the prevailing climate of confessional conflict. Elector Frederick III's introduction of Calvinism to the area in 1559 led to Ramsbeck's dismissal and the founding of a Calvinist school that threatened the Heymairs' livelihood.[26] By 1571 they had moved to Regensburg and set up a school there.

The Heymairs ran German-language schools, humble institutions that could also admit girls but were otherwise far narrower in scope than the Latin-language schools where boys prepared for entrance to university. Pupils usually attended for a maximum of two years and received instruction in religion, reading, writing, and arithmetic. Magdalena Heymair's song versions of Bible extracts were central to the curriculum. They made religious instruction palatable to children, lent themselves well to "learning-by-heart," the main pedagogical method of the time, and served as reading primers and copy-texts for writing practice.

Pedagogical potential is inherent in the biblical texts themselves that Heymair selected for versification. Centuries before the Reformation certain New Testament passages had been identified as the core of Christian teachings and incorporated into the liturgy, with one passage from the Gospels and one from the Epistles assigned to each Sunday. Heymair wrote her *Sontegliche Epistel* in explicit emulation of *Die Sontags-Evangelia* (The Sunday Gospels) by Nikolaus Herman (1480–1561), a notable Lutheran cantor and author of devotional songs. Her collection complemented his and helped to disseminate crucial teachings in accessible form. She based her *ApostelGeschicht*, on the other hand, on the New Testament account of the earliest Christian church community, which surely must have heartened Lutherans experiencing comparable joys and trials. In her foreword she remarks that the *ApostelGeschicht* was inspired by the "Gottseligen Matronen / Frawen oder Weiber" (pious matrons, wives or women) cited in the Acts of the Apostles as specially blessed by the Holy Spirit. She adds a ten-page summary of their "acts" that serves both as an outline of the female tradition in which her work stands as well as an echo of Grumbach's and Zell's invocation of Joel's prophecy. The popularity of Heymair's works can be measured by the many editions they engendered. Three categories of text survive: prepublication manuscripts, published editions prepared by Heymair, and later editions "corrected" and expanded by

Gregor Sunderreutter (fl. 1578–86), an Augsburg pastor. They offer a rare glimpse into the dissemination of the work of an early modern woman writer.

Anna Ovena Hoyers, née Hanß (1584–1655), wrote in quite different social, geographical, and religious contexts.[27] The daughter of a wealthy land-owning farmer in the duchy of Schleswig-Holstein-Gottorf, she married a high-ranking official and had at least nine children, four of whom died young. She became involved in conflict with orthodox Lutheranism after her hus-band's death in 1622, when as an independent widow she began to read tracts by various "dissenters" and to incorporate their ideas into her writings. For example, she devoted a poem to a work of the unorthodox thinker Caspar von Schwenkfeld (1489–1561); in 1623 she provided shelter for the lay preacher Nicolaus Teting (d. 1640), a follower of the mystic Valentin Weigel (1533–88), after the Lutheran authorities in Flensburg expelled him from the town. Hoyers gathered small communities of like-minded believers around her on her properties in Schleswig-Holstein until the early 1630s, when financial difficulties increased her vulnerability as an outspoken nonconformist and forced her to leave the duchy. She eventually went into exile in Sweden and from 1648 enjoyed the protection of the widowed Queen Maria Eleonora, who provided her with refuge on a royal estate until her death. Her versifica-tion of the Book of Ruth, a biblical account of exile and widows' loyalty to one another, is dedicated to the queen.

Hoyers's work survives in her *Geistliche und Weltliche Poemata* (Sacred and Secular Poems), published in Amsterdam in 1650, and in a manuscript of over forty hymns and verse prayers prepared after her death by two of her sons.[28] Her work as a whole gives a vivid impression of her beliefs. Like the young Luther and the later reformers she admired, Hoyers was anticlerical and did not hesitate to condemn the sterile doctrines of established Lutheranism. "An die Herrn Titultrager von Hohen Schulen" (To the Gentlemen with University Titles), for example, is a satirical attack on the men responsible for Teting's expulsion from Flensburg. In "Einfältige Warheit" (Simple Truth) she insists that truth is alive in the Bible and accessible through the Holy Spirit dwelling in each individual; in this work she cites Joel's prophecy of the descent of the Holy Spirit on all people alike. Her tone ranges between the bit-ing satire of the dialect poem "De Denische Dorp-Pape" (The Danish Village Priest), which mocks clerics who skimp on their spiritual duties in favor of good living, and the tender didacticism of the *Gespräch eines Kindes mit seiner Mutter* (A Child's Conversation with Its Mother). *Gespräch* maps the true path to piety, whereby the truths explained by the mother are recognized by the child, who rejoices in them with her:

> [Kind:] Dann wer sich nicht in zeit der gnaden
> Lest warnen für der Seelen schaden /
> . . . .
> Sondern [. . .]
> [. . .] bleibt in seiner Sünden stecken /
> Denn [*sic*] wird Gott in des Satans hecken

Frontispiece to Anna Ovena Hoyers, Geistliche und
Weltliche Poemata *(1650).*

Mit Ewiger ungnad bedecken.
Mutter ist diß nicht zu beklagen?
[Mutter:] Ja kindt / das magst mit warheit sagen /
Schrecklich ist Ewig seyn verlohren /
Besser wehr das man nie gebohren.
Danck du dem lieben Gott dafür /
Der diß gibt zu erkennen dir.
Gelobet sey sein grosse gnad /
Die dir so weit gehülffen hat /
Das du diß also kanst ansehn

Vnd der Welt eitelkeit verstehn.
[Kind:] Ja Gott sey ewig lob gesagt /
Der mich daran hat frey gemacht /
Vnd lassen sehn ein bessers liecht /
Darnach ich meinen wandel richt.

[Child: For if someone does not in fit time of grace heed warning of dangers to the soul, but remains stuck fast in his sins, God will cover him in Satan's thickets with eternal disgrace. Mother, is this not lamentable?

Mother: Yes, child, you can say that in truth, it is dreadful to be lost for eternity, it would be better never to have been born. Thank the good God for enabling you to recognize this. May his great mercy be praised, which has helped you so much that you can see this and understand the futility of this world.

Child: Yes, eternal praise to God, who has delivered me from that and shown me a better light, with which I direct my path.]

Hoyers's "Gespräch" recalls the maternal advice manuals of Elisabeth of Braunschweig-Lüneburg; and other of her works fall within this same genre, such as the poem (also dedicated to her children) on the rewards of piety, "Christi Gülden Cron" (Christ's Golden Crown). The frontispiece to her published works shows a woman in conversation with a child.

Hoyers is most striking, however, as a woman who persistently used her writing to participate in public dispute. As a result of the 1642 open letter addressed to the newly persecuted fellow-believers she had left behind in Schleswig-Holstein, her published work was banned in the duchy. But her public and maternal concerns are ultimately identical, inspired by the profound devotion that finds expression in her hymns (some to melodies of her own composition), occasional poems, and prayers. Even in her acrostics the patternings of letters, often contrived from her name or presented in the form of a cross, have a meditational quality. Hoyers's work clearly reflects her sophisticated opinions about contemporary religious controversies, but her plain language and simple verse forms echo sixteenth-century literary practices.

"Opitz and the Women Poets,"[29] 1624–1720

The appearance in 1624 of Martin Opitz's *Buch von der Deutschen Poeterey* (Book of German Poetics), which launched the reform of German vernacular literature on the basis of poetic guidelines in German, with examples drawn from classical and Renaissance genres, meters, and verse forms, was welcomed not only by male writers.[30] The literary instruction previously enjoyed only by highly educated men was now accessible to women as well. Sibylle Schwarz, Catharina Regina von Greiffenberg, and Gertrud Möller were among the most notable women to begin writing within this classical tradition.

Sibylle Schwarz (1621–38) was one of Opitz's earliest and youngest women followers.[31] She began writing poetry when she was ten, but died seven years later of dysentery, a contagion spread by the movement of troops during the Thirty Years' War (soldiers had been quartered in her home town of Greifswald since 1627). Her widowed father became mayor of Greifswald in 1631. Family and university friends were the primary supporters of her poetic efforts. The domestic duties she shared with her sisters left little time for writing, but she was encouraged especially by her brother, Christian, who also taught her Dutch and Latin, and by the pastor Samuel Gerlach (1609–83). Gerlach, who was acquainted with Opitz, sent her copies of the poet's works that were circulating in manuscript; twelve years after her death it was Gerlach who published her collected poems.

As a woman Schwarz attracted public disapproval for her writing and invoked Opitz more than once to refute it. In "Ein Gesang wieder den Neidt" (A Song against Ill-will) she cites Opitz in defense of poetry and cites several famous women, including Sappho, in defense of herself. Her admiration for Opitz permeates her work. As he recommended, she practiced translation and paraphrase as means of improving the poetic use of German, working from Dutch in "Eine Tochter säuget ihre Mutter" (A Daughter Suckles Her Mother) and from Latin in "Daphne," a poem adapted from Ovid's *Metamorphoses*. She attempted several of the genres commended or cultivated by Opitz: a tragedy, "Wegen einäscherung ihres Freudenorts Fretow," following the military destruction by fire of her family's beloved coastal estate of Fretow; a biblical drama (left unfinished) on the Susanna theme; and a pastoral narrative, "Faunus," modeled on Opitz's adaptation (1626) of John Barclay's Latin novel *Argenis*. She also experimented with the full range of forms and meters in the *Poeterey*. Among her many songs and occasional poems, she composed a Pindaric ode to welcome her brother home in 1636, and among her many sonnets, sixteen are written in the Petrarchan manner introduced by Opitz into German as "Petrarquiser."[32] In his 1650 edition of her works Gerlach excuses certain imperfections of meter and language by reminding readers of Schwarz's youth, her inevitable reliance on local pronunciation, and that she was writing so soon after Opitz, that is, before German poetry had reached its present level of sophistication.

Schwarz wrote little devotional poetry, although her Lutheran faith informs much of her work: her poems on friendship, for example, blend Christian concepts of virtue into the classical notion of virtue as the source of attraction between friends. The reverse is true of the far more substantial *oeuvre* by the Austrian noblewoman Catharina Regina von Greiffenberg (1633–94),[33] who applied Opitz's principles almost exclusively to devotional writing. Greiffenberg was also strongly influenced by the Nuremberg poet Sigmund von Birken (1626–81),[34] as well as by other poets of his generation who elaborated on Opitz's guidelines and promoted vernacular literature under the auspices of the *Sprachgesellschaften* (language societies).[35] Greiffenberg belonged to the first such society for women, the Ister-Nymphen, a branch of the Ister-Gesellschaft (Society on the Ister) in lower Austria, and her seven sonnets under the rubric *Tugend-übung* (Practice of Virtue, 1675) represent a conversation between its seven members. Her many sonnets — often daring experiments with meter, rhyme, and line-length, including the dazzling use of alliteration, assonance, and compounds, which fathom the expressive potential in German poetic language — place her among the most innovative writers of her time. Lines from the sonnet "Gott-Lobende Frühlings-Lust" (God-praising Springtime-joy) exemplify her expressive use of German, not least in their defiance of adequate translation:

> Jauchzet / Bäume / Vögel singet! danzet / Blumen / Felder lacht!
> springt / ihr Brünnlein! Bächlein rauscht! spielet ihr gelinden Winde!
> walle / Lust-bewegtes Träid! süsse Flüsse fliest geschwinde!
> opffert Lob-Geruch dem Schöpffer / der euch Frisch und neu gemacht!
>
> [Exult, o trees, o birds, sing out! dance, o flowers, o fields, laugh!
> gush up, you little springs! o little brooks, rush on! play, you mild winds!
> gently wave, o joy-stirred corn! o sweet rivers, flow swiftly!
> offer up praise-incense to the Creator, who has made you fresh and new!]

It is characteristic of her poetic method "to present the concrete in vividly sensuous terms and then to interpret it in spiritual ones."[36] Recent research links Greiffenberg's sensuous imagery with her knowledge of medicine, alchemy, and theology.[37]

Greiffenberg's spiritual intensity was doubtless due in no small part to the personal adversity that she suffered as an Austrian Protestant, such as being barred by edict of the Catholic Habsburgs from attending church and taking Holy Communion. During a visit to an alternative place of worship in the town of Pressburg (Bratislava) in 1651, at the age of eighteen, she had a vision of the "Deoglorie-Licht" (light of God's glory), whereupon she devoted her life to the praise of God. This mission later came to embrace two burning ambitions: to remain celibate and (between 1666 and 1676) to convert Emperor Leopold I (r. 1658–1705) to Protestantism in the hopes of effecting radical political change. The latter met with no success; as for the former, her resolve ended in 1664 with her marriage to Hans Rudolf von Greiffenberg (ca. 1606–77), her father's half-brother and her guardian since her father's death. In addition to his role as the protector of the family's financial interests, he had been responsible for Greiffenberg's extraordinarily wide-ranging education.

Soon after her husband's death she lost their Austrian estate and emigrated to Nuremberg. Here she joined the intimate intellectual circle around Birken. As early as 1662, indeed, Birken had helped her husband to publish Greiffenberg's *Geistliche Sonnette / Lieder und Gedichte* (Sacred Sonnets, Songs, and Poems), apparently without her prior knowledge. With Birken's help until his death in 1681, and then independently, she oversaw the printing of her later publications herself. These included the 7,000-line poem *Die Sieges-Seule der Buße und Glaubens* (The Triumphal Pillar of Repentance and Faith, 1675) — a cry for Christian renewal and unification against the threat of the Turks, to which she appended her annotated translation of *Le Triomphe de la foy* (The Triumph of Faith) by Guillaume du Bartas — and her voluminous meditations on the Gospels, in prose with verse insertions, which appeared in three sets of twelve each: on Christ's incarnation, birth, and childhood (1678), on his passion (1683), and on his life, teachings, and miracles (1693).

The work of Gertrud Möller, née Eifler (1641–1705), is not widely known. Only one of her many substantial works is generally available:[38] *Erster Theil Der Parnaß-Blumen* (First Part of the Parnassian Flowers, 1672). It was unusual at the time for a collection of song texts — in this case set to music mostly by Johan Sebastian (1622–83), court musician to the elector of Brandenburg — to come complete with musical notation. Like Sebastian, Möller lived in Königsberg, where her father was a university professor and her husband a doctor. Despite having twelve children,[39] she was an active contributor in literary circles. She was much admired by Heinrich Albert (1604–51) and Simon Dach (1605–59), the leading members of Königsberg's intellectual society Kürbishütte (Pumpkin Hut); and congratulatory poems by men from the next generation of Königsberg literati preface her *Parnaß-Blumen*. One poem by these men praises the Opitzian polish of her verse; another recalls Dach's verses in honor of her marriage in 1656, in which he avowed that her poetry put his own to shame.[40] Scattered among the *Parnaß-Blumen* are a number of translations; at least half of the songs are sacred; some of the secular songs are composed in the Petrarchan manner, some are pastoral love songs, others satirical songs on sins such as pride or miserliness; the final courtship song is written in dialect, in a male persona, a rare example of bawdy comic writing by a woman. The range of meters and forms throughout the collection is impressive.

Möller won public recognition not only from Königsberg literati but also, thanks to their letters of introduction, from Birken. In 1671, at his invitation and shortly before publication of the *Parnaß-Blumen*, Möller adopted the poetic name "Mornille" and became one of the few women admitted to Nuremberg's literary society, the Pegnesischer Blumenorden (Flower Order on the Pegnitz). In a letter of thanks to Birken, the president of the society, she regrets that she has been able to cultivate her poetic talent only in the evenings, when half asleep, but assures him that belonging to the Blumenorden will spur her to greater industry.[41] Indeed, in that very year, under the authority of Birken as imperial count palatinate, Möller was proclaimed a poet laureate, an honor granted in the seventeenth century to several hundred men, among them Opitz himself, but to only a handful of women.[42]

As German vernacular literature developed along Opitzian lines and the importance of Latin waned, writing by women became more acceptable; Schwarz, Greiffenberg, and Möller were but a few of the distinguished women whose writing flourished in this new climate. Other notable names include Catharina Agricola (fl. 1628–31), whose sophisticated wedding poem of 1629 shows that she had mastered Opitz's principles of meter, and Dorothea Eleonora von Rosenthal (ca. 1600–1649), whose brief work

Poetische Gedancken an einen der Deutschen Poesie sonderbahren Beförderern (Poetic Thoughts on One of German Poetry's Outstanding Patrons, 1641) celebrates Philipp von Zesen (1619–89), as well as August Buchner (1591–1661) and Opitz, but is formally modeled on Opitz's *Schäfferey von der Nimfen Hercinie* (Pastoral on the Nymph Hercinie, 1630).[43] Among other women influenced by Opitz's followers are several whom Birken laureated and admitted to the Pegnesischer Blumenorden: Barbara Juliana Penzel (1640–74), Elisabeth von Semnitz (1629–79), Catharina Margaretha Dobenecker (1649–83), Regina Magdalena Limburger (d. 1691), and Maria Katharina Stockfleth (ca. 1633–92). Like Greiffenberg, Stockfleth was an *Ister-Nymph*. She is best known for the pastoral novel *Die Kunst- und Tugend-Gezierte Macarie* (The Artistically and Virtuously Adorned Macarie, 1669 and 1673); her husband, the pastor Heinrich Arnold Stockfleth (1643–1708), collaborated in the writing of part one, while she was sole author of part two.[44] Finally, Margaretha Susanna von Kuntsch (1651–1717), along with several other women in her circle, were indebted to an even later Opitzian author, the cleric and poet laureate Ernst Stockmann (1634–1712). They were all related to him, either by birth or by marriage, and the collection of his madrigals (1668), to which he added brief practical guidelines in his preface, inspired them to include this poetic form in their repertoire.[45] Women continued to draw support from Opitz, whether directly from his work or indirectly through his followers, until literary tastes began to change around 1720.

Querelle des femmes, 1671–1720

That far more women were writing in Germany in 1720 than in 1520 owed to the cumulative effect of encouraging influences toward the end of our period. One decisive factor in the last quarter of the seventeenth century was the positive renewal of the *querelle des femmes*.[46] The publication of catalogues of learned women was of particular influence.[47] Modeled on Boccaccio's *De claris mulieribus* (On Famous Women, ca. 1361–75), the catalogues provided lists of women of many nationalities, from ancient to early modern times, famous for their achievements in various fields, including literature. They outlined a tradition of female endeavor that began with the biblical women invoked by Grumbach, Zell, and Heymair, embraced women from classical antiquity, such as Sappho, and continued into the present. In the early seventeenth century Schwarz must have taken heart from the names of fifty-eight women in the Latin catalogue compiled by Johann Ravisius Textor in 1552.[48] From 1671 until the 1730s further catalogues appeared in increasing numbers, initially in Latin, later in German, and regularly updated with new names. Women writing in the early eighteenth century were therefore fortunate to have access to many more names, including those of living contemporaries.

Although this new wave of the *querelle des femmes* honored women's achievements, it did not advocate admitting them to higher education or public life: women were still presumed inferior to men and properly consignable to domestic roles. Nevertheless, the debate did shift public opinion in some quarters. The recognition of women in literary circles like Nuremberg's gradually spread to others where men's interests focused less on literature, more on their public roles as court officials, lawyers, clerics, or teachers. This shift was due in part to two academic dissertations on women's learning that were presented at the University of Leipzig in 1671 and published together in the same year under the title *Diatriben academicam de foeminarum eruditione* (Academic Dissertation on the Education of Women).[49] One author, Jakob Schmalz (d. before 1730), argues that it is only sensible for women in prosperous families to devote their leisure to learning, rather than to idle and morally corrupting occupations, especially if they enjoy study, and that women's "Fromme Gelehrsamkeit" (pious learning) brings glory to their nation. The other author, Johann Sauerbrey (1644–1721), glorifies Germany with a list of twenty names, among them Pirckheimer, the Peutingers, Heymair, and Möller. The practical outcome of these arguments can be seen in Altenburg, a town twenty miles south of Leipzig. Schmalz, who came from Altenburg, dedicated his dissertation to two noblewomen, well known to the area and famous for their Latin and German poetry: Margaretha Sibylla von Löser, née von Einsiedel (1642–90), and Henrietta Katharina von Gersdorf, née von Friesen (1648–1726).[50] Recent scholarship has shown that Schmalz's arguments provided encouragement not only to Margaretha Susanna von Kuntsch but to some sixteen additional middle-class women writing in or near Altenburg between 1680 and 1720.[51]

This group of Altenburger women writers bears little resemblance to what is usually thought of as a female *Sprachgesellschaft*. The seventeen women were bound together less by a love of literature than by the kinship and friendship rooted in their lives as the wives and daughters of pastors or court officials. Kuntsch was the first of her circle to start writing, and she in turn encouraged younger women, especially her daughter, Margaretha Elisabeth Stockmann (1672–1735), and her niece, Dorothea Wilhelmina Margaretha Förster (1699–1721). All of their writings, whether devotional poetry, letters, or poems on occasions such as birthdays, weddings, and funerals, are best seen as reflections of their families' solid social status. This is related to the impact of the Leipzig dissertations in Altenburg. In 1672, shortly after the dissertations appeared, the sudden demise of the ducal line of Saxony-Altenburg and the transfer of rulership to Saxony-Gotha caused a drastic decline in Altenburg's political importance. The task of reversing it by replacing lost courtly splendor with a flourishing civic culture fell to the town's middle-class elite, to which the fathers and husbands of women in Kuntsch's circle belonged. In this climate of cultural aspiration, Schmalz's argument that it was sensible for prosperous women to devote their leisure to learning and that this learning would bring glory to their nation, found peculiar resonance. As products of leisure, women's writings in the Altenburg circle served as a sign of their families' prosperity and, beyond that, of civic prosperity. At the funerals of Kuntsch and her niece, in 1717 and 1721 respectively, men from Altenburg's elite praised the women for their learning; Kuntsch, it was said, should find a place in the catalogues of learned women. The names of two women from Kuntsch's circle had indeed already appeared in a catalogue of learned women: Dorothea Gress, née Pfeiffer (ca. 1653–1728), a pastor's wife, and Juliana Patientia Schultt (1680–1701), a court official's daughter, in Georg Christian Lehms's *Teutschlands Galante Poetinnen* (Germany's Accomplished Women Poets, 1715). Here they joined women from all over Germany as sources of patriotic pride on a national scale.

These examples from Altenburg demonstrate that the potential of the *querelle des femmes* for encouragement has been underestimated. In the wake of the dissertations of 1671, women's writing could be viewed as a wholly praise-worthy, private, moral pastime that benefited public life. Indeed, certain women were bold enough to take part in the actual debate.[52] Anna Maria van Schurmann (1607–78), author of *Num foeminae christianae conveniat studium litterarum* (Whether a Christian Woman Should Be Educated, 1648), lived in the Netherlands and wrote mostly in Latin, but she was cited in Germany in arguments both for and against women's learning; Schurmann is one of the women Schwarz cites in defense of her own writing.[53] Susanna Elisabeth Zeidler (1657–ca. 1706) wrote a spirited response to a scurrilous accusation that she had claimed literary ability — which all women were said to lack — by putting her name to works allegedly written by men, while Rosina Dorothea Rücktäschel, née Schilling (ca. 1680–1744), on the other hand, addressed the theme of misogyny in her tract *Das Weib auch ein wahrer Mensch, gegen die unmenschlichen Lästerer des Weibl. Geschlechts* (Woman, also a True Human Being, against the Inhuman Slanderers of the Female Sex, 1697).[54]

One of the last catalogues to appear, Johann Caspar Eberti's *Schlesiens Hoch- und Wohlgelehrtes Frauenzimmer* (Silesia's Highly and Well-Educated Women, 1727), lists forty-five women known for their writing in Silesia. Eberti's catalogue was the starting point, furthermore, for an edition of texts by five of the women from the seventeenth century whose writing contributed to their regional culture.[55] This and the other catalogues provide the main sources for the hundreds of names listed in Woods and Fürstenwald's *Schriftstellerinnen, Künstlerinnen und gelehrte Frauen des deutschen Barock*. Still, many women writers remain unknown; many are discovered completely by surprise. One example may suffice. Sibylla Schuster, née Neithart (1639–85), is listed by Woods and Fürstenwald as the author of the tragic drama *Verkehrter, Bekehrter und wider bethörter Ophiletes* (The Wrong-headed, Reformed, and again Deluded Ophiletes, 1685). An investigation of a con-gratulatory sonnet in Schuster's *Ophiletes* turned up the name of the nearly for-gotten Agnes Heinold, née Schickart (1642–1711); Heinold, it was then learned, was the author of some sixteen further occasional poems.[56] Moreover, it is now known that Schuster and Heinold were both married to clerics in the Bavarian princely town of Oettingen. Among other interesting facts to surface about Heinold is that she received money from the town council in recogni-tion of a poem on an important civic event.

Domestic Encouragements

The support that women found within their families was an essential precondition to their writing and took diverse forms. Some women were taught or encouraged to write by male relatives and friends;[57] some were prompted to write by domestic events. Some, like Grumbach, wrote in defiance of their husbands' objections, though others, in obedience to the wishes of their fathers, suppressed a thirst for learning (at least until after they married); such was the case with Kuntsch.[58] While marital or parental disapproval conceivably forced many women to abandon writing altogether, public disapproval certainly made Schwarz and Zeidler abandon theirs, albeit only temporarily.[59] The support of male relatives or friends was therefore often crucial to the dissemination of women's writings, for, among other things, it served to protect them from adverse criticism and to shield their modesty. In this regard it is useful to distinguish between the *printing* of women's work for a narrow, often localized readership, usually in booklets of occasional poetry (for example, certain of Heinold's poems), and the *publishing* of it for the wider public, usually as a collection, such as Möller's *Parnaß-Blumen*. This distinction applies less to the sixteenth century, when Grumbach, Zell, and Heymair in fact sought the widest possible readership, than to the seventeenth, especially after the fashion for printing funeral, wedding, and other occasional poems entered its heyday at the end of the Thirty Years' War. Several of Kuntsch's poems were printed locally, yet she shrank from publishing her manuscript collection for fear of public mockery, bequeathing it instead to her family alone.[60]

The connection between paternal support and dissemination is striking in the case of Juliana Patientia Schultt, an only child.[61] Rudolph Friedrich Schultt (1644–1718), a member of the lower nobility and a court adviser, first in Glauchau, Saxony, then in Darmstadt, took sole charge of his daughter's education. He taught her to read German early (she could read the Bible when she was four) before beginning instruction in Hebrew, Greek, Latin, and French. She was well versed in arithmetic, history, geography, and genealogy, and learned to sing, to play the lute and harpsichord, and to write poetry; at the age of only nine she wrote a sonnet on the death of a friend. When she was nineteen her father allowed her to leave his care — a remarkable event at the time — to live under the spiritual guidance of August Hermann Francke (1663–1727), who was in the process of establishing a Pietist center in Halle. Here she put her education to good use teaching handwriting and music at Francke's *Gynaeceum*, a school for the daughters of noble and prosperous families.[62] Under Francke's influence Schultt rejected the bookish erudition of her father in favor of principles based on spiritual experience. This decision surfaces in a letter to her father of 13 March 1700, one of her regular letters to him or her stepmother, all of which are passionate records of her spiritual conflicts and longings:

> Sie schreiben mir / ich soll zu JEsu kommen / welches mich aber nicht
> so leicht ankömmt / weil er mir so unbekant in der lebendigen Krafft ist

/ als ein frembder Mann. Im Gehirn und Buchstaben weiß ich wohl von ihm zu reden / nur die Außübung und die Gegenwart im Hertzen mangelt mir. Sie schreiben mir von vielen Tröstungen / wenn der Glaube schwach ist. Ich aber bin noch nicht recht zerknirscht / und zum Glauben gelangt. Wie habe ich alles nur ins Gehirn gefaßt; z. E. von der Zukunft Christi in die Hertzen der Gläubigen / das ist mir ja nur so ein Wort gewesen / das ich so hergesagt / und weiter ist es nicht kommen.[63]

[You write to me that I should come to Jesus, but that's not so easy for me, because I'm as unacquainted with him in the living strength as I am with a stranger. In my brain and in the letters of the written word I can indeed speak of him, but the (living) practice and the presence in my heart are lacking. You write to me of many consolations for when faith is weak. But as yet I'm not fittingly penitent and haven't attained faith. How I've understood everything only with my brain; e.g., about the coming of Christ in the hearts of the faithful, for me that's simply been the kind of word which I just repeated, and nothing's come of it.]

But when Schultt died after two years in Halle it was with her father's approval that Francke printed these letters and some of her poems in the booklet commemorating her funeral. In 1704 two of her song texts appeared together with three of her father's in the hymn book compiled by Johann Anastasius Freylinghausen (1670–1739). His *Geistreiches Gesang-Buch* went into numerous editions and was used by Pietist congregations throughout Germany for more than a hundred years.

Among the women whose brothers fostered their writing Pirckheimer and Schwarz are the most renowned. Less known is Susanna Elisabeth Zeidler, a pastor's daughter who grew up with access to a wide range of reading material.[64] Her intellectual horizons were broadened by her slightly older brother, Johann Gottfried Zeidler (1655–1711), a poet laureate who had studied at Wittenberg and returned in 1679 to the family home in Fienstadt, near Halle, to assist his blind father. His satirical treatise on the art of divination, *Pantomysterium* (1701), contains a series of learned letters translated from French by his youngest sister, Regina (b. 1673). His support of Susanna Elisabeth's poetry is apparent in his publication gift, a collection of her poems, on the occasion of her wedding in 1686 to the pastor Andreas Haldensleben (d. 1736). The title, *Jungferlicher Zeitvertreiber* (Maidenly Pastime), reflects its origins as the work of an unmarried woman. Little is known of her life after marriage, possibly because caring for a young family prevented her from writing. A note from the prefatory material to her collection, however, explains that she habitually composed poetry while doing the housework in order to keep her mind usefully engaged. Her devotional and occasional poems are in the Opitzian tradition and are formally richly varied. Many address members of her immediate circle, including her brother, whose 1680 New Year's poem appears in the collection. It is ingeniously headed with a simple engraving of a stem from a laurel wreath signifying his sister's immortality as a poet, and proclaims his admiration of her work.

Seiner Lieben Schwester
Jungfr. Susannen Elisabeth Zeidlerin/ Poetin

ΔΕΝΔΡΟΝ ΑΠΟΛΛΩΝΟΣ
ΘΥΓΑΤΗΡ

ΠΗΝΗΙΑ
ΔΑΦΝΗ.

zum Neuen Jahr überreicht von ihren Bruder
Johann Gottfried Zeidler/ Käyserl. Edlen Poeten
und Pastore Substituto zu Fienstedt 2c.
1680.

Heading to the New Year's poem presented to Susanna Elisabeth Zeidler in
1680 by her brother Johann Gottfried. The stem from a laurel crown
signifies her immortality as a poet. From Susanna Elisabeth Zeidler,
Jungferlicher Zeitvertreiber *(1686; modern edition, 2000).*

Husbands often provided comparable support, as is clear from the lives of
Kuntsch and Susanna Elisabeth Prasch, née Keget (1661–after 1693).[65]
Prasch's marriage resembled the humanist ideal of learned partnership. Johann
Ludwig Prasch (1637–90), whose many scholarly publications earned him
national respect, was elected mayor of Regensburg in 1675 and was a delegate
to the imperial diet after 1685 (Regensburg was its seat from 1663 to 1806).
Susanna Elisabeth and Johann Ludwig married in 1683, both for the second
time; the union produced no children. In 1684 she published a treatise in
French, *Réflexions sur les Romans* (Reflections on the Novel), one of several
theoretical works on the "romantic" novel that appeared in Europe around
this time; in 1685 Johann published a novel in Latin, *Psyche Cretica* (Cretan
Psyche), that put her theory into practice, namely, that the romantic novel
should be wholly informed by Christian principles. This collaborative project
redefined the romantic novel. Prasch's work draws to some extent on the
French treatise published in 1670 by Pierre-Daniel Huët, but takes issue with
the recent fashion in France of the so-called gallant novel, which, though it
ultimately aims at moral improvement, portrays relations between the sexes in
a titillating manner. Her work enjoyed immediate acclaim in learned circles
and remained authoritative until the rise of the sentimental novel in the

mid-eighteenth century; *Psyche Cretica* reached a wider readership after it was translated into German in 1701. While it is true that women of the time were considered weaker beings, easily led astray by immoral subject matter and therefore generally prohibited from reading novels (let alone writing them),[66] Prasch and her husband subscribed to no such discrimination. He expressed a belief in the intellectual equality of the sexes and hoped that her work would prompt other women to cultivate learned virtues.

The birthday poems that Margaretha Susanna von Kuntsch gave her husband, Christoph (d. 1724), every year between 1687 and 1716 testify to his encouragement of her writing.[67] While these poems remained in manuscript until three years after her death, when her grandson published her collected work in Halle, her husband was instrumental in having other of her writings printed in their home town of Altenburg. His social position as a respected and wealthy court official — he was elevated to the lower nobility in 1708 — doubtless helped to ensure the positive reception of her work. Between 1689 and 1712 six of her poems were printed under her name in funeral booklets commemorating relatives or family friends. It was during this period that her husband adopted the active role of patron, commissioning, together with his brother, at least fifteen poems from Kuntsch. (Busy officials often commissioned poems from younger men, but seldom from a wife or sister-in-law.) Most of the poems served to fulfill his public obligation to present condolences or congratulations to fellow members of the civic elite. They were printed locally under his name or that of his brother; Kuntsch's authorship, however, is apparent from a comparison between these poems and those in the collection published by her grandson in 1720. The commissionings meant that, especially on family occasions, Kuntsch might write as many as three poems: for example, on the death of a niece one of her poems appeared under her husband's name, one under her brother-in-law's, and one under her own. A particularly poignant instance of marital support arose when Kuntsch, unusually for a woman, expressed the wish during a severe illness in 1685 to have certain of her song texts incorporated into her funeral service[68] — a wish with which her husband faithfully complied. After her death many years later, in 1717, the booklet commemorating her funeral contained two of her song texts: one was sung before the sermon, one after. This order of service followed current funeral custom, as did the inclusion in the booklet of the account of her life, which would have been read out in church. But what made the account unusual was that it was written not by the officiating pastor but by Kuntsch herself. Funeral autobiographies, especially by women, are rare. Her husband's willingness to use her texts in the funeral reinforces the image of a piously learned woman celebrated by the congregation as a source of civic pride.

While Kuntsch's husband supported her work without reservation, her grandson seems to have entertained critical doubts.[69] Christoph Gottlieb Stockmann (1698–after 1733) inherited the manuscript collection of her poetry that she had prepared for her family, and his publication of it for a broad public readership was a mark of pride. However, both the preface by Christian Friedrich Hunold (1680–1721), a well-known literary figure in Hamburg and

Halle, and the heavy-handed "corrections" undertaken by Stockmann himself —
these become apparent when the poems he published are compared with the
matching texts printed in Altenburg — indicate something other than pride.
The two men commend her subject matter while casting doubt on her artistry,
an apologetic stance often in evidence where men brought women's writing
into the public arena. While they may have undertaken the changes as a means
of disarming harsher criticism, they essentially altered Kuntsch's own, unassuming, characterization of her work as spontaneous and stylistically simple.

Domestic life not only supported women's writing; in many cases it supplied the very reasons to write. Schultt, Zeidler, and Kuntsch all wrote poems
to mark special events in the lives of relatives or friends. Kuntsch's range was
exceptionally broad: epigrammatic "reviews" of devotional works; congratulatory poems on the publication of a (male) friend's work; poems for funerals,
birthdays, namedays, and weddings (many of the latter allude with playful
bawdiness to the sexual pleasure of procreation); or entries in friendship
albums. Among the most remarkable are those on the deaths of her children.[70]
Of the fourteen children she bore between 1670 and 1693 only one daughter
lived to adulthood, eight were either stillborn or died soon after birth, three
died before they were a year old, one died at the age of seven, another at nine.
She memorializes them all in her funeral autobiography and, at far greater
length, in her poetry, where she repeatedly struggles to reconcile her grief with
faith in God's will. On only one occasion, that of the death of her nine-year-
old daughter in 1690, does her faith waver as she fiercely questions the point
of her fertility; ultimately she takes comfort in the belief that death will reunite
her with her children.

Responses to the intense grief caused by children's deaths or the deaths of
mothers in childbirth appear in writings by two women who represent polar
ends of the social spectrum: Elisabeth Graf and Aemilie Juliane, countess of
Schwarzburg-Rudolstadt. Almost nothing is known about Elisabeth Graf
(fl. 1684). The pastor and renowned devotional author Christian Scriver
(1629–93) describes her as "despised by the world" in his preface to the collection of her work that he published at her request in Magdeburg: *Funcken
Des in göttlicher und himmlischer Liebe Flammenden Hertzens* (Sparks from a
Heart Aflame with Divine and Heavenly Love, 1686).[71] Evidence suggests that
she came from the artisan class, like Köferl and Zell, and that she was widowed.
Her poetry, which Scriver says she composed while doing housework and
hastily wrote down in moments of leisure, is simple to the point of clumsiness.
Nevertheless, she is capable of writing with heartbreaking poignancy, as manifested especially in the poems on the death of her children. She seeks pious
comfort in the belief that they are well cared for in heaven, where she even
imagines Christ speaking to them, and — like Kuntsch in her poems of maternal grief — expresses a longing to join them after her own death.

Aemilie Juliane, countess of Schwarzburg-Rudolstadt, née countess of
Barby (1637–1706), is known chiefly as the author of a famous song text for
the spiritual guidance of the dying: "Wer weiß / wie nahe mir mein Ende"
(Who Knows When My End Will Come, 1686). In fact, her care for others

extended far beyond this role.[72] As a ruler's consort her domestic sphere embraced not only her family but all the inhabitants of the Thuringian principality of Schwarzburg-Rudolstadt as well. Her compilation of prayers and songs for daily use in the home during the current threat of plague and death, *Tägliche Bet-Stunden in den Hauß-Kirchen [. . .] Bey diesen gefährlichen Pest- und Sterbens-Läufften*, published in 1681, is one example of how she turned her writing to the care of her subjects; a second is her book of songs and prayers for women during pregnancy, labor, and their children's infancy: *Geistliches Weiber-Aqua-Vit* (Women's Sacred Water-of-Life, 1683). She had copies distributed free of charge to each household in the realm. This work was probably based in part on her own experiences in giving birth fifteen years earlier: she bore a healthy son, but a daughter died two days after a difficult delivery. Texts designed for use as the moment of birth drew near may have been intended to serve a therapeutic function: ever briefer clauses and phrases suggest the encouragement of the rhythmic breathing patterns nowadays recommended for the control of pain during labor.[73] Another remarkable feature of the *Geistliches Weiber-Aqua-Vit* is its large print, suitable for reading in demanding situations. This collection was especially sympathetic in an age when most prayers and songs for pregnant women were supplied by men. However, at least one other woman supplied authoritative advice. The prose manual *Die Chur-Brandenburgische Hof-Wehe-Mutter* (The Electoral Brandenburg Court Midwife, 1690), by Justina Siegmund (1636–1705), a midwife at the courts in Liegnitz, Brieg, and Berlin, went into ten editions before 1756.[74]

Finally, other rulers' consorts provide further examples of women prompted to write by domestic events. In these cases household occasions have dynastic significance: their texts contribute to the glorification of sovereignty that was central to early modern court life.[75] This is apparent in an early diary form cultivated by several women at the Darmstadt court between 1624 and 1790, including Sophia Eleonora, landgravine of Hessen-Darmstadt, née duchess of Saxony (1609–71), and her daughter-in-law, Elisabeth Dorothea, landgravine of Hessen-Darmstadt, née duchess of Saxony-Gotha (1640–1709).[76] Both women kept records of life at Darmstadt, Sophia Eleonora from 1627 to 1670, Elisabeth Dorothea from 1666 to 1709. Their diaries note day-to-day happenings and special events, such as hunting, court festivities, and visits from members of other princely dynasties, as well as occasions of vital importance to their own dynasty, such as the births and deaths of their children and the deaths of their husbands. Sophia Eleonora took part in courtly ceremonial throughout her life — dancing in ballets, for instance, like many other aristocratic women — and wrote poems for inclusion in several volumes commemorating princely deaths. Her most remarkable achievement is the folio memorial volume to her husband, which she commissioned, supervised, and had printed five years after his death. *Mausoleum* (1666) includes her own texts as well as a series of beautifully elaborate engravings, one of which depicts her in mourning with pen and paper in hand.[77] Elisabeth Dorothea collaborated in courtly festivities with equal skill and enthusiasm. To mark her husband's birthday or name day in the years from 1669 to 1672, she wrote pastoral and operatic texts for the stage containing ballet interludes, which she and other members of the family took part in.

Other rulers' consorts also wrote, organized, or performed in court festivities. Sophia Eleonora's younger sister, Magdalena Sibylla, duchess of Saxony-Altenburg, former crown princess of Denmark (1617–68), organized three days of festivities to celebrate the christening of her first son in 1654. Sophie Elisabeth, duchess of Braunschweig-Wolfenbüttel, née duchess of Mecklenburg-Güstrow (1613–76), wrote theatrical pieces to mark the birthdays of her husband, Duke August (1579–1666), bibliophile and founder of the now famous Herzog August Bibliothek, Wolfenbüttel, between 1652 and 1656.[78] Women of princely status could write to highlight their own or their husbands' positions within a dynasty, yet, like women from lower social orders, they were mainly prompted by domestic events.

Religious Encouragements

The religious sphere exerted as much influence on women's lives as the domestic during the long period between Reformation and Pietism. Some women wrote to influence other people's religious beliefs; but far more wrote on religious topics solely for their own or their families' benefit. Personal religious writings by women can never be sharply separated from domestic influences, as is apparent in funeral writings or in poems for pregnant women or on the death of children.

The church year and the Bible offered powerful religious encouragements to write.[79] Countless women wrote verse meditations on the main events of the Christian calendar — Advent, Christmas, the New Year, Easter, or Whitsun. Many texts of this kind, which arose from personal devotions and are laden with biblical references, found their way into official church hymn books. An equally widespread private devotional practice was the versification of Bible extracts, commonly for educational purposes, as it helped women to become intimately familiar with Christian teachings; this practice also, of course, provided useful training in poetic skills. Kuntsch, Förster, and Schultt all versified brief biblical texts, while Kuntsch versified whole chapters from Job, Jesus Sirach (Ecclesiasticus), the Gospels, and Paul's Epistle to the Romans.[80] Henrietta Katharina von Gersdorf, to whom Schmalz would later dedicate his Leipzig dissertation on women's learning, published a poem on the Passion in 1665 at the age of seventeen. The title page of this "Heilsame Betrachtung" (Salutary Meditation) indicates that she wrote it "zu eigener Erbauung" (for personal edification). Her later collection of spiritually uplifting songs and meditational poems, *Geistreiche Lieder und Poetische Betrachtungen*, was published posthumously in 1729, after more than thirty years of involvement in educational institutions for women in Altenburg and at the Pietist center of Halle;[81] yet it too is the product of personal engagement with biblical teachings.

Image of a piously learned woman in her study, over the inscription "Für iegliches Werck danckte Sie dem Höchsten mit einem schönen Lied" (For all his works she thanked God on high with a fine song). The four images above and below place her within the biblical tradition, showing, from left to right, Miriam and Debora; Hanna and the Virgin Mary. Frontispiece to Henrietta Katharina von Gersdorf, Geistreiche Lieder und Betrachtungen (1729). By permission of the British Library, London. Shelfmark 3425 b 29.

Many women were encouraged to write by the medieval and early modern custom of preparation for death. This discipline aimed both to ensure that individuals were spiritually ready for death at every moment of their lives as well as to diminish the fear of dying by focusing on the joys of eternal life. Kuntsch's two song texts "Auffmunterung zur seeligen Todes-Bereitung" (Encouragement to the Blessed Readiness for Death) — it contains the refrain "Schick dich zum Tod" (Prepare to die) — and "Sursum corda" (Raise Your Heart on High) are self-admonitory and, at the same time, jubilant anticipations of heavenly life.[82] A young woman in her circle, Sophia Christiana Geyer (1676–89), although only thirteen when she died, took time to prepare for death by writing two song texts for her funeral service, like Kuntsch, and by choosing five biblical texts to be inscribed on the lid and sides of her coffin.[83] Similarly, Graf wrote four "Reim-Sprüche" (Verse Mottos) for inscription on the coffin she had acquired in readiness for her death; each verse rejoices in the peace of eternal life.[84] An overlap of religious and domestic promptings is apparent in the dual function of these texts: for the women who wrote them the texts were a spiritual aid to living and dying; after death their texts aided family and friends by reminding them that they too should prepare for death and by providing personal messages of comfort. It was not unusual for women to include farewells to their parents, husbands, children, and friends.

Mothers were responsible for their children's physical and spiritual well-being; their husbands — and in prosperous families the children's private tutors — shared the latter responsibility. Hoyers, for instance, dedicated poems of spiritual guidance to her children; Kuntsch bequeathed her work to her family. When sons left home to study or to take up an independent adult life, or when daughters left to marry, women continued to contribute guidance for their religious life through letters or advice manuals. Among the writings in this genre that have survived in manuscript are Grumbach's letters to her daughter Appollonia, ill and away from home in Nuremberg in 1532, and to her wayward son Georg, also in Nuremberg, in 1538. The correspondence between the widow of a Nuremberg merchant, Magdalena Paulus Behaim, née Römer (died 1581), and her son Friedrich during his studies in Altdorf and then Padua, focuses more on practical and financial rather than on spiritual matters.[85] The famous memoirs of Glickl bas Judah Leib (1646–1724), also known as Glückel of Hameln, the widow of a Jewish merchant based in Hamburg, were written in Yiddish to her children and prefaced with spiritual advice.[86] Benigna, countess of Solms-Laubach, née countess of Promnitz (1648–1702), also covers religious and practical topics in the writings for her children in *Immer grünendes Klee-Blat Mütterlicher Vermahnungen* (Ever-fresh Clover Leaf of Maternal Exhortations), collected and published posthumously in 1717 by a courtier.[87] She insists in a letter to a son studying at university that she writes for his eyes alone and is not in favor of women writing for publication. This letter, included in *Immer grünendes Klee-Blat* under the title "Richtigster Weg-Weiser Eines Jungen Pilgrims" (Most Accurate Signpost for a Young Pilgrim), was a response to the son's request for spiritual guidance and is based on Psalm 119:9. The three texts referred to as a clover leaf in the title of the collection are manuals on the duties and responsibilities of adult life: one on rulership for her eldest son, one on a military career for a younger son, and one on marital life for a daughter. All four works reflect the combination of domestic and religious cares that determined the life of early modern women but that held broader significance for rulers' consorts, who were expected to exemplify piety for their subjects.[88] Elisabeth of Braunschweig-Lüneburg and Aemilie Juliane of Schwarzburg-Rudolstadt made use of the medium of publishing as a means of fulfilling this exemplary role. Benigna of Solms-Laubach, on the other hand, despite her public role as regent after her husband's death in 1696, preferred to write retiringly. Her advice manuals fulfill her personal duty as pious exemplar and bequeath that role to her children as one of their dynastic responsibilities. It is interesting that five of the writing mothers discussed here wrote their advice manuals as widows, with sole parental responsibility for their children's spiritual welfare.

Much of women's personal writing relates aspects of their lives to religious teachings. This is a feature of song texts and meditations as well as of more purely confessional texts, such as Kuntsch's funeral autobiography. The dissemination of texts of this kind made all their authors, whether they were rulers' consorts or members of the lower social orders, pious exemplars for others. While the exemplary function of funeral biographies had long been recognized by the Lutheran Church, the Pietist movement placed even greater emphasis on the practice, encouraging biographies and autobiographies that maintained a sharp focus on the inner, spiritual experiences of despair, remorse, repentance, and union with God.[89] Schultt vividly depicts her inner life, whether standing in despair at a spiritual "Scheideweg" (crossroads) or drawing spiritual sustenance from accounts of women's deathbed visions. Other Pietists in turn drew strength from her work and the printed accounts, in the funeral booklet, of her death.[90]

The most renowned autobiography by a Pietist woman is that of Johanna Eleonora Petersen, née baroness von und zu Merlau (1644–1724).[91] It is structured in two parts: The first, written in 1688, covers her unhappy childhood, her distaste for court life, her meeting with the founder of Pietism as a movement, Philipp Jakob Spener (1635–1705), her spiritual awakening and determination to remain celibate, and her eventual marriage to a social inferior, the Spener associate and theologian Johann Wilhelm Petersen (1649–1727). The second part, written in 1718, covers her married life and the revelatory visions that came to her in dreams and during meditation or ecstatic trance-like states; she analyzes and interprets them in detail. The entire account, published in 1718 and republished the following year, is an affirmation of God's guidance at each stage of her life. Petersen's religious influence stems from other of her publications as well, among them a commentary of several hundred pages on the Book of Revelation (1696).

The Pietist interest in women's spiritual lives was not confined to contemporaries. One of the most influential Pietist collections, Gottfried Arnold's *Unparteyische Kirchen- und Ketzer-Historie* (Impartial History of the Church and Heretics, 1700), contains an account of Hoyers's life, presumably as representative of an earlier nonconformist movement. But Arnold could, in fact, equally well have turned to women from an even earlier period and their accounts of spiritual awakenings. Zell's open letter to the citizens of Strasbourg (1557) and Heymair's foreword to *Das Büchlein Jesu Syrach* (1578) contain descriptions of their conversions from Catholicism to Lutheranism that follow a pattern discernible in other spiritual biographies and autobiographies: "external piety, internal despair leading to sickness, awakening to the true message, relief and exhilaration, response through action."[92] These links between Hoyers, Zell, Heymair, and Pietists like Schultt and Petersen suggest that a diachronic study of spiritual autobiographies by early modern women would make a valuable contribution to our understanding both of women's lives and of the religious impulses that moved them to write. Not all women's autobiographical writings sprang solely from domestic or religious experiences, to be sure: vivid accounts of occurrences in other areas of life are presented, for example, by nuns writing on the military destruction of their convents during the Thirty Years' War and by rulers' consorts who kept diary records of happenings at court.[93]

The above discussion has sketched the historical, cultural, and personal impulses that prompted early modern women to write. Many individuals have had to be omitted, including some of particular significance. These would include Maria Sibylla Merian (1647–1717), the gifted graphic artist, naturalist, and religious nonconformist who traveled to Surinam with her younger daughter, Dorothea Maria, to collect, study, and record its flora and fauna; and Maria Aurora, countess of Königsmarck (1662–1728), a mistress of August the Strong (elector of Saxony and king of Poland, 1670–1733), who was renowned throughout northern Europe for her eventful life as well as for her painterly and poetic talents.[94] Nevertheless, this chapter has placed several new figures in the literary landscape and attempted to indicate future lines of inquiry. Among these, further regional studies of women's work — in Nuremberg, Königsberg, or Oettingen, among other places — and further diachronic studies of women writing in one particular genre or tradition, or from one particular perspective, such as widowhood,[95] remain desirable. But in-depth study of many individuals' lives and works is also necessary to complete our picture of women's contribution to the literature of the early modern period.

Notes

[1] "Abriß / Entwerffung vnd Erzehlung / was in dem / von Anna Köferlin zu Nürmberg / lang zusammen getragenem Kinder-Hauß / dergleichen nie gesehen noch gemacht / anzutreffen / vnd wie ettlich hundert Stuck / alle zum gemeinen Nutz auch dienstlich / darinn zusehen," British Museum, Department of Prints and Drawings, German Broadsides, 1880-7-10-865. For a reproduction of the woodcut see Leonie von Wilckens, *Spiel, Spiele, Kinderspiel* (Nuremberg: Katalog des Germanischen Nationalmuseums Nürnberg, 1985), 67. I am indebted to David Paisey, formerly of the British Library, London, for the above information.

[2] Anke Hufschmidt, "Ilse von Saldern (1539–1607)," in *Deutsche Frauen der Frühen Neuzeit, Dichterinnen, Malerinnen, Mäzeninnen*, ed. Kerstin Merkel and Heide Wunder (Darmstadt: Wissenschaftliche Buchgesellschaft, 2000), 49–63; also Sabine Heißler, "Christine Charlotte von Ostfriesland (1645–1699) und ihre Bücher oder lesen Frauen Anderes?" *Daphnis* 27 (1998): 335–418.

[3] Lotte Traeger, "Das Frauenschrifttum in Deutschland von 1500–1650" (Ph.D. diss., Charles University, Prague, 1943), Appendix: "Bibliographie der Dichterinnen des 16. Jahrhunderts"; Jean M. Woods and Maria Fürstenwald, *Schriftstellerinnen, Künstlerinnen und gelehrte Frauen des deutschen Barock: Ein Lexikon* (Stuttgart: Metzler, 1984).

[4] Barbara Becker-Cantarino, *Der Lange Weg zur Mündigkeit: Frau und Literatur (1500–1800)* (Stuttgart: Metzler, 1987); Gisela Brinker-Gabler, ed., *Deutsche Literatur von Frauen*, vol. 1, *Vom Mittelalter bis zum Ende des 18. Jahrhunderts* (Munich: Beck, 1988).

[5] The standard social history of early modern women: Heide Wunder, *"Er ist die Sonn', sie ist der Mond": Frauen in der Frühen Neuzeit* (Munich: Beck, 1992).

[6] Reprographic reprints and the growing availablility of microfiche, microfilm, and digitalized copies offer as yet only a rather patchy solution to the problem of accessibility.

[7] For some striking examples see Jill Bepler, "Kabinettausstellung: Gebetsliteratur der Frühen Neuzeit," in *Gebetsliteratur der Frühen Neuzeit als Hausfrömmigkeit: Funktionen und Formen in Deutschland und den Niederlanden*, ed. Ferdinand van Ingen and Cornelia Niekus Moore (Wiesbaden: Harrassowitz, 2001), nos. 3–8, 11. See also Bepler's chapter in this volume.

[8] Charlotte Woodford, *Nuns as Historians in Early Modern Germany* (Oxford: Clarendon, 2002), esp. chap. 3.

[9] Ursula Hess, "Lateinischer Dialog und gelehrte Partnerschaft: Frauen als humanistische Leitbilder in Deutschland (1500–1555)," in Brinker-Gabler, ed., *Deutsche Literatur von Frauen*, 113–48, esp. 118–27.

[10] Margaret Ives and Almut Suerbaum, "The Middle Ages," in *A History of Women's Writing in Germany, Austria and Switzerland*, ed. Jo Catling (Cambridge: Cambridge UP, 2000), 13–26, esp. 14–17.

[11] Helen Watanabe-O'Kelly, "Women's Writing in the Early Modern Period," in Catling, ed., *A History of Women's Writing*, 27–44, esp. 31.

[12] Woodford, *Nuns as Historians*; Merry Wiesner-Hanks, ed., *Convents Confront the Reformation: Catholic and Protestant Nuns in Germany* (Milwaukee: Marquette UP, 1996); Hanna Dose, *Evangelischer Klosteralltag: Leben in Lüneburger Frauenkonventen 1590–1710, untersucht am Beispiel Ebstorf* (Hannover: Hahnsche Buchhandlung, 1996), esp. 230–43.

[13] On Margarete Peutinger, her daughters, and Olympia Fulvia Morata see Hess, "Lateinischer Dialog," 127–48. For a life-and-works introduction to Morata see John L. Flood, "Olympia Fulvia Morata," in *German Writers of the Renaissance and Reformation, 1280–1580*, ed. Max Reinhart and James Hardin, vol. 179 of *Dictionary of Literary Biography* (Detroit: Gale Research, 1997), 178–83.

[14] References to the Bible and the Apocrypha follow the Authorized (King James) Version.

[15] For annotated English translations of Grumbach's writings, with an introduction, see Peter Matheson, ed., *Argula von Grumbach: A Woman's Voice in the Reformation*

(Edinburgh: T&T Clark, 1995). Full details of her writings are found in the bibliography section in Silke Halbach, *Argula von Grumbach als Verfasserin reformatorischer Flugschriften* (Frankfurt am Main: Lang, 1992), 242–57. For her life and writings see most recently Hermina Joldersma, "Argula von Grumbach," in Reinhart and Hardin, eds., *German Writers*, 89–96.

[16] Argula von Grumbach, *Wie ain Christliche Frau des Adels / un Bayern durch jren / in Götlicher schrifft / wolgegründten Sendt brieffe / die Hohenschul zu Ingolstat vmb das sy aynen Ewangelischen Jüngling / zu widersprechung des wort Gottes / betrangt haben / straffet* [1523], Aiij[r]; in Matheson, ed., *Argula von Grumbach*, 76.

[17] Publication of her correspondence will throw new light on her life and work. See Matheson, ed., *Argula von Grumbach*, 4, note 7.

[18] Elsie Anne McKee, *Katharina Schütz Zell*, vol. 1, *The Life and Thought of a Sixteenth-Century Reformer*, vol. 2, *The Writings: A Critical Edition* (Leiden: Brill, 1999).

[19] For details see Charlotte Woodford, " 'Es werd nu wol zeit, das si wartet, was einem frumen ee weib zu stund': Women's Letters from the Reformation," *Daphnis* 30 (2001): 37–52.

[20] On Elisabeth of Braunschweig-Lüneburg see Barbara Becker-Cantarino, "Frauen in den Glaubenskämpfen: Öffentliche Briefe, Lieder und Gelegenheitsschriften," in Brinker-Gabler, ed., *Deutsche Literatur von Frauen*, 149–72, esp. 159–67; Merry Wiesner, "Herzogin Elisabeth von Braunschweig Lüneburg (1510–1558)," in Merkel and Wunder, eds., *Deutsche Frauen der Frühen Neuzeit*, 39–48.

[21] For details and further examples see Jill Bepler, "Die Fürstin als Betsäule — Anleitung und Praxis der Erbauung am Hof," *Morgen-Glantz* 12 (2002): 249–64, esp. 254–58.

[22] For a detailed discussion of one of these convents see Dose, *Evangelischer Klosteralltag*.

[23] A large collection of Elisabeth's letters to her son-in-law is extant.

[24] Cornelia Niekus Moore, "Biblische Weisheiten für die Jugend: Die Schulmeisterin Magdalena Heymair," in Brinker-Gabler, ed., *Deutsche Literatur von Frauen*, 172–84; Maximiliane Mayr, "Magdalena Heymair: Eine Kirchenlied-Dichterin aus dem Jahrhundert der Reformation," *Jahrbuch für Liturgik und Hymnologie* 14 (1969): 134–40.

[25] Titles and dates refer to the earliest known versions (two are manuscripts, held by the Heidelberg University Library); see the annotated bibliographies in Niekus Moore, "Biblische Weisheiten," and in Mayr, "Magdalena Heymair."

[26] See the extracts from two letters by Heymair in Mayr, "Magdalena Heymair," 139–40.

[27] Anna Ovena Hoyers, *Geistliche und Weltliche Poemata* (Amsterdam: Elsevier, 1650), ed. Barbara Becker-Cantarino (reprographic repr., Tübingen: Niemeyer, 1986), 3*-98*; Cornelia Niekus Moore, "Anna Ovena Hoyers (1584–1655)," in Merkel and Wunder, eds., *Deutsche Frauen der Frühen Neuzeit*, 65–76. For a concise account of her life and works see Barbara Becker-Cantarino, "Anna Ovena Hoyers," in *German Baroque Writers, 1580–1660*, ed. James Hardin, vol. 164 of *Dictionary of Literary Biography* (Detroit: Gale Research, 1996), 181–84.

[28] On the manuscript, with texts selected from it, see Hoyers, *Geistliche und Weltliche Poemata*, 127*-200*; Barbara Becker-Cantarino, "Die Stockholmer Liederhandschrift der Anna Ovena Hoyers," in *Barocker Lust-Spiegel: Studien zur Literatur des Barock*, ed. Martin Bircher et al. (Amsterdam: Rodopi, 1984), 329–45.

[29] The chapter heading is taken from Jean M. Woods, "Opitz and the Women Poets," in *Opitz und seine Welt*, ed. Barbara Becker-Cantarino and Jörg Ulrich Fechner (Amsterdam: Rodopi, 1990), 569–86.

[30] See the chapter in this volume by Joachim Knape.

[31] Helmut W. Ziefle, *Sibylle Schwarz: Ihr Leben und Werk* (Bonn: Bouvier, 1975); Becker-Cantarino, *Der lange Weg zur Mündigkeit*, 232–46.

[32] For more on the phenomenal influence of Petrarchism see the chapter in this volume by Gerhart Hoffmeister.

[33] Horst-Joachim Frank, *Catharina Regina von Greiffenberg: Leben und Welt der barocken Dichterin* (Göttingen: Sachse und Pohl, 1967); Kathleen Foley-Beining, *The Body and Eucharistic Devotion in Catharina Regina von Greiffenberg's "Meditations"* (Columbia, SC: Camden House, 1997); Lynne Tatlock, "Catharina Regina von Greiffenberg (1633–1694)," in Merkel and Wunder, eds., *Deutsche Frauen der Frühen Neuzeit*, 93–106.

[34] On Birken see the chapter in this volume by John Roger Paas.

[35] On language societies and related foundations see the introduction to this volume by Max Reinhart.

[36] Watanabe-O'Kelly, "Women's Writing," 37.

[37] Lynne Tatlock, Mary Lindemann, and Robert Scribner, "Sinnliche Erfahrungen und spirituelle Autorität: Aspekte von Geschlecht in Catharina Regina von Greiffenbergs Meditationen über die Empfängnis Christi und Marias Schwangerschaft," in *Geschlechterperspektiven: Forschungen zur Frühen Neuzeit*, ed. Gisela Engel and Heide Wunder (Königstein: Helmer, 1998), 178–91; Lynne Tatlock, "Scientia divinorum: Anatomy, Transformation, Incorporation in Catharina Regina von Greiffenberg's Meditations on Incarnation and the Gestation of Christ," *German History* 17 (1999): 9–24. The long-awaited publication of her correspondence with Birken will reveal other new lines of inquiry; on this project see Hartmut Laufhütte, "Ein frühneuzeitliches Briefarchiv — editorische Perspektiven und Probleme," in *"Ich an Dich": Edition, Rezeption und Kommentierung von Briefen*, ed. Werner M. Bauer et al. (Innsbruck: U Innsbruck, Institut für deutsche Sprache, Literatur und Literaturkritik, 2001), 47–62, esp. 54–56.

[38] Woods and Fürstenwald, *Schriftstellerinnen*, 70–71, cite few libraries having Möller's works. The only known copy of her substantial *Die wunder-vollen Liebes-Wercke Des DreyEinigen Großen Gottes* (Königsberg: Reusner, ca. 1680) is in the Staatsbibliothek zu Berlin — Preußischer Kulturbesitz, Abteilung Historische Drucke.

[39] Gertrud Möller, *Erster Theil Der Parnaß-Blumen / Oder Geist-und Weltliche Lieder* (Hamburg: Johann Naumann and Georg Wolff, 1672), fol. Aiij^v (information cited in one of the congratulatory verses that preface the collection).

[40] For the wedding poem see Simon Dach, *Iungite concordes mansura in foedera dextras / Oder Einfältige Hochzeit-Reime* (Königsberg: Reusner, [1656]), fol. [Aii]^r.

[41] For this letter extract, details of Möller's entry to the Pegnesischer Blumenorden, and two of her sonnets see Johann Herdegen, *Historische Nachricht von deß löblichen Hirten-und Blumen-ordens an der Pegnitz Anfang und Fortgang* (Nuremberg: Riegel, 1744), 392–402.

[42] For further details see John L. Flood, "Neglected heroines? Women poet laureates in the Holy Roman Empire," in *Bulletin of the John Rylands University Library of Manchester* 84, no. 3 (2002): 25–47, esp. 28–31.

[43] Woods, "Opitz and the Women Poets," 569, 582–83. On Agricola see Woods and Fürstenwald, *Schriftstellerinnen*, 1. On Rosenthal, with a selection of her texts, see Miroslawa Czarnecka, ed., *Dichtungen schlesischer Autorinnen des 17. Jahrhunderts* (Wroclaw: Wydawniotwo Uniwersytetu Wrocslawskiego, 1997), 63–76; also Gerhard Kosellek, "Schlesische Dichterinnen des Barock: Eine Bibliographie," in *Die oberschlesische Literaturlandschaft im 17. Jahrhundert*, ed. Kosellek (Bielefeld: Aisthesis, 2001), 503–19, esp. 509–10.

[44] For further details see Flood, "Neglected heroines?" 34–37; Woods and Fürstenwald, *Schriftstellerinnen*, 89 (on Penzel), 118 (on Semnitz), 63 (on Dobenecker), 25 (on Limburger), 122–23 (on Stockfleth). On Semnitz, with a selection of her texts, see also Czarnecka, ed., *Dichtungen schlesischer Autorinnen*, 79–190; further see Kosellek, "Schlesische Dichterinnen des Barock," 512–14. On Stockfleth and her membership in *Sprachgesellschaften* see Ute Brandes, "Studierstube, Dichterklub, Hofgesellschaft: Kreativität und kultureller Rahmen weiblicher Erzählkunst im Barock," in Brinker-Gabler, ed., *Deutsche Literatur von Frauen*, 222–47, esp. 229–36.

[45] Ernst Stockmann, *Poetische Schrifft-Lust / Oder hundert Geistliche Madrigalen* (Leipzig: Frommann, 1668); see also Anna Carrdus, ed., *Das "weiblich Werck" in der Residenzstadt Altenburg 1672–1720: Gedichte und Briefe von Margaretha Susanna von Kuntsch und Frauen in ihrem Umkreis: Mit einer Einleitung, Dokumenten, Biographien und Kommentar* (Hildesheim: Olms, 2004), 40–41. Subsequent references to the latter work will be given as: Carrdus, *WW*.

[46] Elisabeth Gössmann, "Für und wider die Frauengelehrsamkeit: Eine europäische Diskussion im 17. Jahrhundert," in Brinker-Gabler, ed., *Deutsche Literatur von Frauen*, 185–97; also Elisabeth Gössmann, ed., *Das Wohlgelahrte Frauenzimmer* (Munich: iudicium, 1984).

[47] Katharina Fietze, "Frauenbildung in der "'Querelle des femmes,'" in *Geschichte der Mädchen- und Frauenbildung*, vol. 1, *Vom Mittelalter bis zur Aufklärung*, ed. Elke Kleinau and Claudia Opitz (Frankfurt am Main: Campus, 1996), 237–51. For a survey of catalogues of learned women see Woods and Fürstenwald, *Schriftstellerinnen*, xii–xxiv.

[48] See "Ein Gesang wieder den Neidt," in Sibylle Schwarz, *Deutsche Poëtische Gedichte: Faksimiledruck nach der Ausgabe von 1650*, ed. Helmut W. Ziefle (Bern: Lang, 1980), vi–x, esp. viii; for further detail see Anna Carrdus, "Noble Models for the Middle Class: Women Writing in and around Altenburg 1671–1730," *Daphnis* 32 (2003): 611–35, esp. 611–13.

[49] See the German translation of excerpts from the dissertations in Gössmann, ed., *Das Wohlgelahrte Frauenzimmer*, 99–117.

[50] For details on both women see Carrdus, "Noble Models," 620–32.

[51] For full treatment of this topic see the introduction to the collected texts of all seventeen women, with their biographies, in Carrdus, *WW*, esp. 47–52.

[52] Work by German women who took part in the debate is still not widely known. For a collection of poems in which women thematize their underprivileged status see Gisela Brinker-Gabler, ed., *Deutsche Dichterinnen vom 16. Jahrhundert bis zur Gegenwart: Gedichte und Lebensläufe* (Frankfurt am Main: Fischer, 1978), esp. 68–111. For examples of women's participation in the *querelle des femmes* in Italy, France, and the Netherlands see Gössmann, "Für und wider die Frauengelehrsamkeit."

[53] On Schurmann see Gössmann, "Für und wider die Frauengelehrsamkeit," 194–95. For Schwarz's reference to Schurmann see Schwarz, *Deutsche Poëtische Gedichte*, viii; also Brinker-Gabler, ed., *Deutsche Dichterinnen*, 88, note 2.

[54] Susanna Elisabeth Zeidler, *Jungferlicher Zeitvertreiber, Das ist allerhand Deudsche Gedichte Bey Häußlicher Arbeit und stiller Einsamkeit verfertiget und zusammen getragen*, ed. Cornelia Niekus Moore (1686; Bern: Lang, 2000), esp. 48, 10–11. On Schilling see Woods and Fürstenwald, *Schriftstellerinnen*, 101. I am indebted to Kristina Bake, of Halle, Germany, for drawing my attention to Schilling's work.

[55] Czarnecka, ed., *Dichtungen schlesischer Autorinnen*; further, Miroslawa Czarnecka, *Die "verse-schwangere" Elysie: Zum Anteil der Frauen an der literarischen Kultur Schlesiens im 17. Jahrhundert* (Wroclaw: Wydawniotwo Uniwersytetu Wrocslawskiego, 1997); also Koselek, "Schlesische Dichterinnen des Barock."

[56] On Schuster see Woods and Fürstenwald, *Schriftstellerinnen*, 112; Birgit Neugebauer, "Agnes Heinold (1642–1711): Ein Beitrag zur Literatur von Frauen im 17. Jahrhundert," *Daphnis* 20 (1991): 601–702, esp. 602–3, 614–15. On Heinold's life and work see Neugebauer, "Agnes Heinold (1642–1711)," 606–29; and, for an appendix containing the texts of Heinold's poems, 630–702. Also on Neugebauer's rediscovery of Heinold see Watanabe-O'Kelly, "Women's Writing," 28.

[57] On this topic see Helen Watanabe-O'Kelly, " 'Sei mir dreimal mehr mit Licht bekleidet': German Poems by Women to their Mentors in the Seventeenth Century," *Colloquia Germanica* 28 (1996): 255–64.

[58] Matheson, ed., *Argula von Grumbach*, 8–9. On Kuntsch see Carrdus, *WW*, 407.

[59] Schwarz, *Deutsche Poëtische Gedichte*, iii, xxi; Zeidler, *Jungferlicher Zeitvertreiber*, 11.

[60] Carrdus, *WW*, 69, 228, 49.

[61] For Schultt's writings and biography see Carrdus, *WW*, 277–313, 425–26.

[62] Ulrike Witt, "Das Hallesche Gynäceum 1698–1740," in *Schulen machen Geschichte: 300 Jahre Erziehung in den Franckeschen Stiftungen zu Halle* (Halle: Kataloge der Franckeschen Stiftungen, 1997), 85–103.

[63] Carrdus, *WW*, 295–96.

[64] On Zeidler see the introduction in Zeidler, *Jungferlicher Zeitvertreiber*, v–xlvi.

[65] Christiane Holm, "Die verliebte Psyche und ihr galanter Brautigam: Das Roman-Projekt von Susanna Elisabeth und Johann Ludwig Prasch," in *Der galante Diskurs: Kommunikationsideal und Epochenschwelle*, ed. Thomas Borgstedt and Andreas Solbach (Dresden: Thelem, 2001), 53–85.

[66] Watanabe-O'Kelly, "Women's Writing," 33.

[67] For Kuntsch's birthday poems to her husband see her collected work in Carrdus, *WW*, 69–228, esp. 171–97; on her husband's attitude toward her work, 49–50, 407–9.

[68] Carrdus, *WW*, 78–79.

[69] On the publication of Kuntsch's collection see Carrdus, *WW*, 44–47, 52–55, 57.

[70] On Kuntsch's children see Carrdus, *WW*, 114–32, 316–19, 408; also Anna Carrdus, "Consolation Arguments and Maternal Grief in Seventeenth-Century Verse: The Example of Margarethe Susanne von Kuntsch," *German Life and Letters* 47 (1994): 137–51.

[71] The publication may have followed her death. On Graf see the preface in Elisabeth Graf, *Funcken Des in göttlicher und himmlischer Liebe Flammenden Hertzens Elisabeth Grafen Auf ihr Begehren mit einer Vorrede Ausgefertiget von C. Scriver* (Magdeburg:

Johann Daniel Müller, 1686); ibid., 45, 89, 98, 139–41 (her poems on her dead children); also Anna Carrdus, "Thränen-Tüchlein für Christliche Eltern: Consolation Books for Bereaved Parents in Sixteenth- and Seventeenth-Century Germany," *German Life and Letters* 49 (1996): 1–17, esp. 16–17.

[72] For further details see Woods and Fürstenwald, *Schriftstellerinnen*, 113–15; Judith P. Aikin, "Der Weg zur Mündigkeit in einem Frauenleben aus dem 17. Jahrhundert: Genesis und Publikationsgeschichte der geistlichen Lieder der Gräfin Aemilie Juliane von Schwarzburg-Rudolstadt," *Wolfenbütteler Barock-Nachrichten* 29 (2002): 33–59, esp. 41–47; Judith P. Aikin, "Gendered Theologies of Childbirth in Early Modern Germany and the Devotional Handbooks for Pregnant Women by Aemilie Juliana, Countess of Schwarzburg-Rudolstadt (1683)," *The Journal of Women's History* 15 (2003): 40–67; and on the role of rulers' consorts in general see Bepler, "Die Fürstin als Betsäule."

[73] Aikin, "Gendered Theologies of Childbirth," esp. 47–48.

[74] Details about this work in Kosellek, "Schlesische Dichterinnen des Barock," 514–15.

[75] See in this volume the chapter by Helen Watanabe-O'Kelly.

[76] Helga Meise, *Das archivierte Ich: Schreibkalender und höfische Repräsentation in Hessen-Darmstadt 1624–1790* (Darmstadt: Hessische Historische Kommission, 202), esp. 83–165, 346–470.

[77] Jill Bepler, Birgit Kümmel, and Helga Meise, "Weibliche Selbstdarstellung im 17. Jahrhundert: Das Funeralwerk der Landgräfin Sophia Eleonora von Hessen-Darmstadt," in Engel and Wunder, eds., *Geschlechterperspektiven*, 441–69.

[78] On Magdalena Sibylla see Carrdus, *WW*, 28–29; on Sophie Elisabeth see Sara Smart, *"Doppelte Freude der Musen": Court Festivities in Brunswick-Wolfenbüttel 1624–1700* (Wiesbaden: Harrassowitz, 1989), 51–97.

[79] For a vivid impression of the large numbers of seventeenth-century women who wrote on religious topics see entries under the names in Woods and Fürstenwald, *Schriftstellerinnen*.

[80] Carrdus, *WW*, 37–41, 72–76, 83–88, 92–93, 104–12, 247–48, 285–88.

[81] Carrdus, "Noble Models for the Middle Class," esp. 624–26; Martin H. Jung, *Frauen des Pietismus: Zehn Porträts von Johanna Regina Bengel bis Erdmuthe Dorothea von Zinzendorf* (Gütersloh: Gütersloher Verlagshaus, 1998), 27–43.

[82] Carrdus, *WW*, 70–71, 77–78; also 79–83. For examples of comparable texts see Schwarz, *Deutsche Poëtische Gedichte*, li-lii; Judith P. Aikin, "Die Letzte ihres Geschlechts: Aemilie Juliane von Schwarzburg-Rudolstadt als letzte Gräfin von Barby," *Blätter der Gesellschaft für Buchkultur und Geschichte* 5 (2001): 9–37.

[83] Carrdus, *WW*, 272–75, 392.

[84] "Folgen die Reim-Sprüche / so Sie auf ihren bereiteten Sarg schreiben lassen," in Graf, *Funcken Des in göttlicher und himmlischer Liebe Flammenden Hertzens*, 262–64.

[85] See Matheson, ed., *Argula von Grumbach*, 7–8, 25–26; Steven Ozment, ed. and narr., *Three Behaim Boys: Growing up in Early Modern Germany* (New Haven: Yale UP, 1990), 93–157.

[86] For details see Natalie Zemon Davis, *Women on the Margins: Three Seventeenth-Century Lives* (Cambridge, MA: Harvard UP, 1995), 5–62.

[87] On the religious writings by Benigna of Solms-Laubach, two of her daughters, and a granddaughter see Woods and Fürstenwald, *Schriftstellerinnen*, 119–20 and 100.

[88] Bepler, "Die Fürstin als Betsäule."

[89] On Lutheran funeral biographies see Jill Bepler, "Women in German Funeral Sermons: Models of Virtue or Slice of Life?," in *German Life and Letters* 44 (1991): 392–403. On the central role of biographies in the Pietist movement see Jeannine Blackwell, "Herzensgespräche mit Gott: Bekenntnisse deutscher Pietistinnen im 17. und 18. Jahrhundert," in Brinker-Gabler, ed., *Deutsche Literatur von Frauen*, 265–89; Ulrike Witt, *Bekehrung, Bildung und Biographie: Frauen im Umkreis des Halleschen Pietismus* (Halle: Verlag der Franckeschen Stiftungen im Niemeyer-Verlag Tübingen, 1996). For a collection of brief modern biographies see Jung, *Frauen des Pietismus.*

[90] See Carrdus, *WW*, 283–84, 397.

[91] Johanna Eleonora Petersen, *Leben, von ihr selbst mit eigener Hand aufgesetzet: Autobiographie*, ed. Prisca Guglielmetti (Leipzig: Evangelische Verlag-Anstalt, 2003). On Petersen's life and work see Blackwell, "Herzensgespräche mit Gott"; Jung, *Frauen des Pietismus*, 108–31.

[92] Merry E. Wiesner, "Katharina Zell's 'Ein Brieff an die ganze Burgerschafft der Statt Strassburg' as Theology and Autobiography," in *Colloquia Germanica* 28 (1995): 245–54, esp. 250.

[93] Charlotte Woodford, " 'Wir haben nicht gewist / was wir vor angst und schrecken thun sollen': Autobiographical Writings by Two Nuns from the Thirty Years' War," in *Autobiography by Women in German*, ed. Mererid Puw Davies, Beth Linklater, and Gisela Shaw (Oxford: Lang, 2001), 53–67; and the corresponding chapter in Woodford, *Nuns as Historians*. Also Meise, *Das archivierte Ich.*

[94] On Merian see Davis, *Women on the Margins*, 140–216; Kurt Wettengl, "Maria Sibylla Merian (1647–1717)," in Merkel and Wunder, eds., *Deutsche Frauen der Frühen Neuzeit*, 107–22. On Maria Aurora of Königsmarck see Sylvia Kraus-Meyl, *"Die berühmteste Frau zweier Jahrhunderte": Maria Aurora Gräfin von Königsmarck* (Regensburg: Pustet, 2002).

[95] For a collection of essays on various aspects of this topic see Martina Schattkowsky, ed., *Witwenschaft in der Frühen Neuzeit: Fürstliche und adlige Witwen zwischen Fremd- und Selbstbestimmung* (Leipzig: Leipziger Universitätsverlag, 2003).

Primary Literature

Abbreviations

Adams = *Desiderius Erasmus: The Praise of Folly and other Writings*. Trans. Robert M. Adams. New York: Norton, 1989.

CWE = *Collected Works of Erasmus*. Ed. Craig R. Thompson et al. 86 volumes. Toronto: U of Toronto P, 1974–2005.

LW = *Luther's Works*. Ed. Jaraslav Pelikan and Helmut T. Lehmann. 55 vols. St. Louis: Concordia Publishing House; Philadelphia: Fortress, 1955–86.

Schoolfield = *The German Lyric of the Baroque in English Translation*. Trans. George C. Schoolfield. University of North Carolina Studies in the Germanic Languages and Literatures 29. Chapel Hill: U of North Carolina P, 1961.

Tatlock = *Seventeenth Century German Prose*. Ed. Lynne Tatlock. The German Library 7. New York: Continuum, 1993.

Thomas = *German Verse from the 12th to the 20th Century in English Translation*. Trans. J. W. Thomas. University of North Carolina Studies in the Germanic Languages and Literatures 44. Chapel Hill: U of North Carolina P, 1963.

* * *

Abraham a Sancta Clara. *Auf Auf Ihr Christen*, 1683. Selection translated by Lynne Tatlock as "Arise, Arise, You Christians," in Tatlock, 86–91.

Aemilie Juliane, Countess of Schwarzburg-Rudolstadt. *Geistliches Weiber-Aqua-Vit*, 1683.

Agricola, Georg. *De re metallica*, 1530.

Agricola, Rudolf. *De laude philosophiae et reliquarum artium oratio*, 1474–79.

———. *De inventione dialectica libri tres*, 1476–79, pub. 1515.

———. *De formando studio*, 1484.

———. [Letters] Translated as *Letters* by Adrie van der Laan and Fokke Akkerman. Assen: Royal van Gorcum, 2002.

Agrippa von Nettesheim, Heinrich Cornelius. *De incertitudine & vanitate scientiarum*, 1530.

Aichinger, Gregor. *Cantiones ecclesiasticae*, 1607.

Albert, Heinrich. *Arien*, 8 books, 1638–50.

Albertanus Brixiensis. *Doctrina dicendi et tacendi* (1245), German translation as *Die Räte von der Rede*, 1472.

Albertinus, Ägidius. *Der Landstörzer: Gusman von Alfarache oder Picaro genannt*, 1615.

Alciato, Andrea. *Emblematum liber*, 1531. Translated by John F. Moffitt as *A Book of Emblems*. Jefferson, NC: McFarland & Co., 2004.

Aldrovandus, Ulissa. *De animalibus et insectis*, 1602.

Alsted, Johann Heinrich. *Encyclopaedia*, 7 vols., 1630.

Altdorfer, Albrecht. *Landscape with Castle*, ca. 1522–25.

Amerbach, Veit. *Commentaria in artem poeticam Horatii*, 1547.

Andreae, Johann Valentin. *Respublicae Christianopolitanae descriptio*, 1609.

———. *Chymische Hochzeit*, 1616. Translated by Jocelyn Godwin as *The Chemical Wedding of Christian Rosencreutz*. Grand Rapids, MI: Phanes, 1991.

———. *Turbo*, 1616.

———. *Theophilus*, 1622.

Andreas von Regensburg. *Chronik von den Fürsten zu Bayern*, 1428.

Anonymous. Cambridge Codex, 1382; partly written by Isak der Schreiber.

———. *Dukus Horant*, in Cambridge Codex.

———. *Buxheim St. Christopher*, 1423.

———. *Formulare und Tütsche rhetorica*, 1478.

———. *Ogier von Dänemark*, 1479.

———. *Großes Frankfurter Passionsspiel*, 1493.

———. *Fortunatus*, 1509.

———. *Freiburger Artikel der Singer*, 1513.

———. *Zwölf Artikel der Bauernschaft*, 1524.

———. *Luzerner Passionsspiel*, 1583.

———. *Theatrum de veneficis*, 1586.

———. *Historia von D. Johann Fausten*, 1587. The 1592 English translation, modernized by William Rose as *The Historie of the Damnable Life and Deserved Death of Doctor John Faustus* (1925). Reprint, New York: Da Capo Press, 1969.

———. *Wagnerbuch*, 1593.

———. *Triumphus Divi Michaelis Archangeli*, 1597.

———. *Lalebuch*, 1597; 1598 as *Die Schildbürger*.

———. *Ratio studiorum*, 1599.

———. *Lazarillo de Tormes* (1554), German translation, 1614.

———. *Iglauer Schulordnung*, 1615.

———. *Newer Tractat von der verführten Kinder*, 1629.

———. *Oberammergauer Passionsspiel*, 1634.

———. *Verwüstete und verödete Schäferey*, 1642.

———. *Alamodische Damen Sprichwörter*, 1648.

———. *Ballet der Glückseligkeit*, 1655.

Anonymous. *Ratio Status*, 1668.

———. *Frauen-Zimmer-Bibliotheckgen*, 1705.

Anton Ulrich of Braunschweig-Wolfenbüttel. *Orpheus*, 1659.

———. *Die Durchleuchtige Syrerinn Aramena*, 1669–73.

———. *Die Römische Octavia*, 1677–1714.

Arndt, Johann. *Vier Bücher vom Wahren Christentum*, 1610. Translated by Peter Erb as *True Christianity*. New York: Paulist Press, 1979.

Arnold, Gottfried. *Göttliche Liebes-Funken*, 1698.

———. *Unparteyische Kirchen- und Ketzer-Historie*, 1700.

Aurifaber, Johannes. *Luthers Tischreden*, 1566.

Aurpach, Johannes. *Anacreonticorum odae*, 1570.

Avancini, Nicolaus. *Curae Caesarum*, 1644.

———. *Poesis lyrica*, 1659.

Balde, Jacob. *Lyricorum libri iv, Epodon liber unus*, 1643, corrected and enlarged 1646.

———. *Sylvarum libri VII*, 1643, expanded 1646.

———. *Urania Victrix*, 1663.

Barth, Kaspar von. *Amphitreatrum gratiarum*, 1613.

———. *Erotodidascalus*, 1625.

Bebel, Heinrich. *Ars versificandi*, 1506.

———. *Facetiae*, 1508–12.

Beer, Johann. *Simplicianischer Welt-Kucker*, 1677–79.

———. *Artlicher Pokazi*, 1679.

———. *Beschreibung eines Ertz-Landstreichers Coryli*, 1679–80.

———. *Jucundus Jucundissimus*, 1680.

———. *Der Berühmte Narrenspital*, 1681.

———. *Der Politische Feuermänner-Kehrer*, 1682.

———. *Teutsche Winternächte*, 1682. Translated by John R. Russell as *German Winter Nights*. Columbia, SC: Camden House, 1998.

———. *Kurtzweilige Sommer-Täge*, 1683. Selection translated by James N. Hardin and Gerda Jordan as "The Summer Tales," in Tatlock, 256–74.

Beheim, Michael. *Pfälzische Reimchronik*, 1469–71.

Bersmann, Gregor. *De dignitate atque praestantia poetices*, 1575.

Bidermann, Jacob. *Cenodoxus*, 1602; German translation by Johann Meichel, 1635.

———. *Philemon Martyr*, after 1602, before 1614.

———. *Joseph*, 1615.

———. *Epigrammatum libri tres*, 1620.

———. *Herodiados libri tres*, 1622.

———. *Heroum et Heroidum epistolae*, 1633–34.

Bidermann, Jacob. *Utopia*, 1640.

Binsfeld, Peter. *Tractatus de confessionibus maleficorum et sagarum*, 1589.

Birken, Sigmund von. *Fortsetzung der Pegnitz-Schäferey*, 1645.

———. *Dannebergische Helden-Beut*, 1648.

———. *Ostländischer Lorbeerhäyn*, 1656.

———. *Der Donau-Strand*, 1664.

———. *Spiegel der Ehren*, 1668.

———. *Guelfis*, 1669.

———. *Chur- und Fürstlicher Sächsischer Helden-Saal*, 1677.

———. *Teutsche Rede-bind- und Dicht-Kunst*, 1679.

———. [Poetry] Selections translated by Schoolfield, 70–76.

Bisselius, Johannes. *Deliciae Veris*, 1638.

———. *Deliciae Aestatis*, 1644.

Böhme, Jakob. *Morgenröte im Aufgang*, 1634. Translated by John Sparrow as *The Aurora*. London: Watkins, 1960.

Bohse, August. *Der getreue Hoffmeister*, 1706.

Bote, Hermann von Braunschweig. *Till Eulenspiegel*, 1510/11. Translated by Paul Oppenheimer as *Till Eulenspiegel: His Adventures*. New York: Garland, 1991.

Brant, Sebastian. *Das Narrenschiff*, 1494. Translated by William Gillis as *The Ship of Fools*. London: Folio Society, 1971.

Breitinger, Johann Jacob. *Bedencken von Comoedien oder Spilen*, 1624.

Brülow, Caspar. *Moses*, 1621; German translation by Johann Merck, 1641.

Brunfels, Otto. *Aphorismi institutionis puerorum*, 1519.

Brunner, Andreas. *Nabuchodonosor*, 1635.

Brunschwig, Hieronymus. *Dies ist das Buch der chirurgia*, 1492.

Bucer, Martin. *Apologia*, 1526.

———. *Tetrapolitana*, 1530.

———. *Ein Summarischer vergriff der Christlichen lehre und Religion*, 1548.

———. *De regno Christi*, 1550. Translated as *A Treatise, how by the Worde of God, Christian mens almose ought to be distributed*, 1557. Microfilm, in *Early English Books, 1475–1640*, 309:17.

Buchholtz, Heinrich. *Hercules und Valiska*, 1659.

Buchner, August. *Kurzer Wegweiser zur deutschen Dichtkunst*, 1663.

———. *Anleitung zur Deutschen Poeterey*, 1665.

———. *Der Poet*, 1665.

Bullinger, Heinrich. *Lucretia*, 1533.

Burckhard, Jacob. *De linguae Latinae in Germania*, 1713.

Burmeister, Joachim. *Musica poetica*, 1606.

Buschius, Hermann (von dem Busche). *Spicilegium*, 1505.

———. *Vallum humanitatis*, 1518.

Calaminus, Georg. *Carminus, sive Messias in praesepi, Ecloga*, 1576.

Camerarius the Elder, Joachim. *Praecepta vitae puerilis*, ca. 1528.

———. *Commentatio explicationum omnium tragoediarum Sophoclis*, 1556.

Camerarius the Younger, Joachim. *Symbole et Emblemata*, 1590–96.

Canitz, Friedrich Rudolf Ludwig von. *Neben-Stunden unterschiedener Gedichte*, 1700.

Capito, Wolfgang. *Hebraicarum institutionum libri duo*, 1516, 1518.

Caselius, Johannes. *Pro arte poetarum oratio*, 1569.

Celtis, Conrad. *Ars versificandi et carminum*, 1486.

———. *Epitome in utramque Ciceronis rhetoricam*, 1492.

———. *Oratio in gymnasio in Ingelstadio publice recitata*, 1492. Translated by Leonard Forster as "Inaugural Address, Ingolstadt." In *Selections from Conrad Celtis, 1459–1508*, ed. Forster, 36–65. Cambridge: Cambridge UP, 1948.

———. *De origine, situ, moribus et institutis Norimbergae libellus*, 1495.

———. *Germania generalis*, ca. 1500/2.

———. *Ludus Dianae*, 1501.

———. *Opera Roswithae*, 1501.

———. *Quattuor libri amorum*, 1502.

———. [Poetry] Selections translated by Forster, 20–35.

Chelidonius, Benedictus. *Voluptatis cum Virtute disceptatio*, 1515.

Chryseus, Johannes. *Hoffteufel*, 1545.

Chytraeus, David. *Praecepta rhetoricae inventionis*, 1556.

———. *Regula vitae*, 1562.

Claius, Johannes. *Prosodiae libri tres*, 1570.

———. *Grammatica germanicae linguae*, 1578.

Clamorinus, Bartholomäus. *Thurnirbüchlein*, 1590.

Comenius, Johann Amos. *Didactica magna*, 1657.

———. *Orbis sensualium pictus*, 1658.

Conring, Hermann. *De Bibliotheca Augusta*, 1661.

Contzen, Adam. *Abissimi Regis historia*, 1628.

Copernicus, Nicolaus. *De revolutionibus orbium coelesium*, 1543.

Cordus, Euricius. *Bucolica*, 1514.

———. *Antilutheronastix*, ca. 1525.

Cramer, Daniel. *Octoginta emblemata moralia nova*, 1630.

Cranach the Elder, Lucas. *Passional Christi und Antichristi*, 1521.

———. *The Law and the Gospel*, 1529.

Crüger, Johannes. *Praxis Pietatis Melica*, 1647.

Crusius, Johann Paul. *Croesus*, 1611.

Cusa, Nicolas von. *De concordantia catholica*, 1434.

Cuspinian, Johannes. *Austria*, 1601.

Czepko, Daniel. *Sexcenta Monodisticha Sapientum*, 1640–47.

———. [Poetry] Selections translated by Schoolfield, 84–89.

Dach, Simon. [Poetry] Selections translated by Schoolfield, 90–93.

Dedekind, Friedrich. *Grobianus*, 1549.

Degler, Hans. *Adoration of the Magi*, 1604.

———. *Resurrection*, 1607.

Del Rio, Martin. *Disquisitionum magicarum libri sex*, 1599. Translated by P. G. Maxwell-Stuart as *Investigations into Magic*. Manchester: Manchester UP, 2000.

Dietterlin, Wendel. *Architectura*, 1598.

Dilherr, Johann Michael. *Heilige Sonn- und Festtags-Arbeit*, 1660.

———. *Himmel und Erden*, 1667.

Dobratzky, Gutthäter. *Wol-qualificirter Hofe-Mann*, 1664.

Dornau, Caspar. *Charidemus*, 1617.

Dürer, Albrecht. *Apocalypse*, 1498.

———. *Self-Portrait*, 1500.

———. *Philosophia*, 1502.

———. *Adam and Eve*, 1504.

———. *Dream Vision*, 1525.

———. *Underweyssung der messung*, 1525.

———. *Vier Bücher von menschlicher Proportion*, 1528.

———. [Journeys] Translated by Rudolph Tombo as *Records of Journeys to Venice and the Low Countries* (1913). New York: Dover, 1995.

Eleonore von Österreich. *Pontus und Sidonia*, 1463.

Elia Levita Bachur. *Bovo-Buch*, 1541.

Elisabeth of Braunschweig-Lüneburg. *Unterrichtung und Ordnung*, ca. 1555.

Elisabeth of Nassau-Saarbrücken. *Herpin*, before 1437.

———. *Hug Schapler*, before 1437.

———. *Loher und Maller*, before 1437.

Erasmus of Rotterdam, Desiderius. *Antibarbari*, 1493. Translated by Margaret Mann Philipps as *The Antibarbarians*, in *CWE* 23:1–122.

———. *Enchiridion militis Christiani*, 1503. Translated by Charles Fantazzias as *The Handbook of the Christian Soldier*, in *CWE* 66:1–127.

———. *Adagiorum Chiliades*, 1508; expanded editions 1515, 1517–18, 1520, 1526, 1528, 1533. Translated (including the *Adagiorum collectanea* of 1500) by R. A. B. Mynors et al. as *Adages*, in *CWE* 31–36.

———. *De pueris statim ac liberaliter instituendis declamatio*, 1509. Translated by Beert C. Verstraete as *A Declamation on the Subject of Early Liberal Education for Children*, in *CWE* 26:291–346.

———. *Laus Stultitiae*, 1511. Translated by Adams as *The Praise of Folly*, 3–87.

———. *De ratione studii ac legendi interpretandique auctores liber*, 1511–14. Translated by Brian McGregor as *On the Method of Study*, in *CWE* 24: 661–91.

———. *De duplici copia verborum ac rerum commentarii duo*, 1512. Translated by Betty I. Knott as Copia: *Foundations of the Abundant Style*, in *CWE* 24:279–659.

———. *Novum Testamentum* (*Novum instrumentum*), 1516. Foreword translated by Adams, 118–27.

———. *Querela Pacis*, 1517. Translated by Adams as *The Complaint of Peace*, 88–116.

———. *Colloquia familiaria*, 1522. Four translated by Adams as *Colloquies*, 174–227. Complete translations, in two volumes, by Craig R. Thompson, in *CWE* 39–40.

———. *De libero arbitrio diatribe*, 1524. Translated by Ernst F. Winter as *A Diatribe or Sermon Concerning Free Will*. In *Discourse on Free Will*, ed. Winter, 3–94. New York: Continuum, 2000.

———. *Dialogus Ciceronianus*, 1528. Translated by Betty I. Knott as *The Ciceronian: A Dialogue of the Ideal Latin Style*, in *CWE* 28.

———. *De civilitate morum puerilium*, 1530. Translated by Brian McGregor as *On Good Manners for Boys*, in *CWE* 25:269–89.

———. [Letters] Selections translated by Adams, 228–64. Complete translations by R. A. B. Mynors et al., in *CWE* 1–12.

Ettner, Johann Christoph. *Des getreuen Eckharts Medicinischer Maul-Affe*, 6 vols., 1694–1715.

Eyb, Albrecht von. *Ad laudem et commendationem Bambergae civitatis oratio*, 1451/2.

———. *Praecepta artis rhetoricae*, 1457.

———. *An viro sapienti uxor sit ducenda*, 1459.

———. *Clarissimarum feminarum laudacio*, 1459.

———. *Ehebüchlein*, 1472.

———. *Margarita poetica*, 1472.

Fabricius, Georg. *De re poetica libri iiii*, 1556–72.

Feyerabend, Sigmund. *Amadís de Gaula*, German translation, 1569–76, printed as *Buch der Liebe*, 13 vols., 1587.

Fichart, Johann. *Consilia*, 1590.

Finckelthaus, Gottfried. *Deutsche Gesänge*, 1640.

Fischart, Johann. *Affentheurlich naupengeheurliche Geschichtklitterung*, 1575; revised 1582.

———. *Vom ausgelasnen wütigen Teuffelsheer*, 1581.

Fleming, Paul. *Teütsche Poemata*, 1646.

———. [Poetry] Selections translated by Schoolfield, 96–105; by Thomas, 25–28.

Folz, Hans. *Jüdischer Wucher*, 1491.

Franck, Sebastian. *Chronica vnnd beschreibung der Türckey*, 1530.

———. *Weltbůch*, 1534.

———. [Letter to Campanus] Translated by George Hunston Williams as "A Letter to John Campanus by Sebastian Frank." In *Spiritual and Anabaptist Writers: Documents Illustrative of the Radical Reformation*, ed. Williams, 145–60. Philadelphia: Westminster, 1962.

Frangk, Fabian. *Ein Canzley- und Titel buechlin*, 1531.

Frischlin, Nicodemus. *Fraw Wendelgart*, 1579.

———. *Julius redivivus*, 1585.

———. *Phasma*, 1592.

———. *Priscianus vapulans*, 1592.

Gengenbach, Pamphilus. *Die Todtenfresser*, 1521.

Gerhardt, Paul. *Geistreiche Hauß- und Kirchen-Lieder*, 1707.

———. [Poetry] Selections translated by Schoolfield, 110–15; by Thomas, 22–25.

Gersdorf, Henrietta Katharina von. *Geistreiche Lieder und Poetische Betrachtungen*, 1729.

Glareanus, Henricus. *Descriptio Helvetiae*, 1514.

———. *Isagoge in musicem*, 1516.

Gnapheus, Guilhelmus. *Acolastus*, 1529. Translated by W. E. D. Atkinson as *Acolastus: A Latin Play of the 16th Century.* London, Ontario: University of Western Ontario, 1964.

Godelmann, Georg. *Disputatio de magis, veneficis et lamiis*, 1592.

Goldtwurm, Caspar. *Schemata rhetorica*, 1545.

Graf, Elisabeth. *Funcken des flammenden Hertzens*, 1686.

Greff, Joachim. *Judith*, 1536.

Greflinger, Georg. *Complementir-Büchlein*, 1645.

Gregersdorf, Georg Christoph von. *Jüngst-erbaute Schäfferey*, 1632.

Greiffenberg, Catharina Regina von. *Geistliche Sonette*, 1662.

———. *Andächtige Betrachtungen*, 3 vols., 1672, 1678, 1693. Selection translated by Lynne Tatlock as "The Most Holy and Most Healing Passion and Death of Jesus Christ," in Tatlock, 106–10.

———. [Poetry] Selections translated by Schoolfield, 120–39.

Gretser, Jacob. *Regnum humanitatis*, 3 vols., 1587–90.

Grien, Hans Baldung. *Witches' Sabbath*, 1510.

Grimmelshausen, Hans Jakob Christoffel. *Der Abentheurliche Simplicissimus Teutsch*, 1669. Translated by George Schultz-Behrend as *Simplicius Simplicissimus.* 2nd revised ed. Columbia, SC: Camden House, 1993.

———. *Der Seltzame Springinsfeld*, 1670.

———. *Trutz-Simplex: oder Ausführliche und wunderseltzame Lebensbeschreibung der Ertzbetrügerin und Landstörzerin Courasche*, 1670. Translated by Robert L. Hiller and John C. Osborne as *The Rungate Courage*. Lincoln: U of Nebraska P, 1965.

———. *Wunderbarliches Vogelnest*, 2 vols., 1672–73.

Grotius, Hugo. *Von der Wahrheit der Christlichen Religion*, German translation 1631 by M. Opitz.

Grumbach, Argula von. *Schriften*, 1523–24.

Grünewald, Mathias. *Isenheim Altarpiece*, 1515.

———. *Crying Head*, 1520.

Gryphius, Andreas. *Olivetum libri tres*, 1646.

———. *Leo Armenius*, 1650.

———. *Cardenio und Celinde*, 1657.

———. *Catharina von Georgien*, 1657.

———. *Carolus Stuardus*, 1657–63.

———. *Herr Peter Squentz*, 1658.

———. *Papinianus*, 1659.

———. *Verlibtes Gespenst* and *Die gelibte Dornrose*, 1660.

———. *Horribilicribrifax*, 1663.

———. [Poetry] Selections translated by Schoolfield, 142–67; by Thomas, 29–31.

Gueintz, Christian. *Die Deutsche Rechtschreibung*, 1645.

Günther, Johann Christian. *Gedichte*, 1724–33. Selections translated by Schoolfield, 166–73; by Thomas, 39–44.

Gutenberg, Johannes. *Gutenberg Bibel*, 1452–55.

Hallmann, Johann Christian. *Urania*, 1666.

———. *Sterbende Mariamne*, 1670.

Harsdörffer, Georg Philipp. *Frauenzimmer Gesprächspiele*, 8 vols., 1641–49.

———. *Gallia Deplorata*, 1641. Translated by Reinhart as *Lamentation for France*.

———. *Germania Deplorata*, 1641. Translated by Reinhart as *Lamentation for Germany*.

———. *Peristromata Turcica*, 1641. Translated by Max Reinhart as *Turkish Tapestries*. In *Lamentation for France and Other Polemics on War and Peace: The Latin Pamphlets of 1641–1642*, ed. Reinhart. Renaissance & Baroque: Studies & Texts. New York: Lang, forthcoming.

———. *Aulaea Romana*, 1642. Translated by Reinhart as *Roman Tapestries*.

———. *Pegnesisches Schäfergedicht*, 1644, with J. Klaj.

———. *Seelewig* (with Sigmund Theophil Staden), 1644.

———. *Poetischer Trichter*, 3 vols., 1647–53.

———. *Der Große SchauPlatz jämmerlicher Mordgeschichte*, 1650.

———. *Ars apophthegmatica*, 2 vols., 1655–56.

Harsdörffer, Georg Philipp. *Nathan und Jotham*, 2 vols., 1659.

———. [Poetry] Selections translated by Schoolfield, 176–79.

Hartlib, Samuel. *The Reformed Librarie-Keeper*, 1650, with John Durie.

Hassler, Hans Leo. *Kirchengesänge, Psalmen und geistliche Lieder*, 1608.

Haugwitz, August Adolf von. *Schuldige Unschuld: oder Maria Stuarda*, 1683.

Hausbuchmeister. *Gothaer Liebespaar*, ca. 1480–85.

Heermann, Johannes. *Devota Musica Cordis, Haus- vnd Hertz-Musica*, 1630.

Hegendorff, Christoph. *Christiana studiosae juventutis institutio*, 1526.

Heidegger, Gotthard. *Mythoscopia romantica*, 1698.

Heinrich Julius von Braunschweig. *Von Vincentio Ladislao*, 1594.

Heinsius, Daniel. *Herodes infanticida*, 1632.

Held, Jeremias. *Liber Emblematum: Kunstbuch*, 1566.

Hellwig, Johann. *Die Nymphe Noris*, 1650. Selections translated by Max Reinhart, in "Nuremberg, Arcadia on the Pegnitz," in *Imperiled Heritage: Tradition, History, and Utopia in Early Modern German Literature: Selected Essays by Klaus Garber*, ed. Reinhart, 117–208, here 165–204. Aldershot, UK: Ashgate, 2000.

Helwig, Christoph. *Kurtzer Bericht von der Didactica*, 1613, with Joachim Jungius.

Hemmingsen, Niels. *Admonitio de superstitionibus magicis vitandis*, 1575.

Herr, Michael. *Die new welt*, 1533.

Hessus, Helius Eobanus. *Bucolicon*, 1509, expanded 1528.

———. *Heroidum Christianarum epistolae*, 1514.

———. *In Martinum Lutherum elegarium libellus*, 1521.

———. *Urbs Noriberga illustrata*, 1532.

———. [Translation edition] Translated by Harry Vredeveld as *The Poetic Works of Helius Eobanus Hessus: English and Latin*. Medieval and Renaissance Texts and Studies 215. Tempe: Arizona Center for Medieval and Renaissance Studies, 2004.

Heymair, Magdalena. *Die Sontegliche Epistel*, 1566.

Hille, Karl Gustav von. *Der Teutsche Palmbaum*, 1647.

Hock, Theobald. *Schönes Blumenfeld*, 1601.

Hofmann von Hofmannswaldau, Christian. *Poetische Grab-Schrifften*, 1643. Selections translated by Schoolfield, 186–91; by Leonard Forster, in *The Penguin Book of German Verse*, 137–42. Harmondsworth, UK: Penguin, 1957.

———. *Heldenbriefe*, 1663.

———. *Deutsche Vbersetzungen vnd Getichte*, 1679.

———. [Poetry] Selections translated by Schoolfield, 186–91; by Thomas, 33–37.

Hoyers, Anna Ovena. *Geistliche und Weltliche Poemata*, 1650.

Huge, Alexander. *Rhetorica unnd Formularium teütsch*, 1528.

Hugo, Herman. *Pia desideria*, 1624.

Hunger, Wolfgang. *Emblematum libellus*, 1534.

Hunold, Christian Friedrich. *Der blutige und sterbende Jesus*, 1704.

Hutten, Ulrich von. *De arte versificatoria*, 1511.

———. *Epistolae obscurorum virorum*, 1515–17, with C. Rubeanus. Translated by Francis Griffin Stokes as *On the Eve of the Reformation: Letters of Obscure Men*. New York: Harper and Row, 1964.

———. *Aula*, 1518.

———. *Clag und vormanung*, 1520.

———. *De Guaiaci medicina et morbo gallico*, 1519. Translated by Clarence W. Mendell as "The Remarkable Medicine Guaiacum and the Cure of the Gallic Disease by Ulrich von Hutten." In *Archives of Dermatology and Syphilology* 23 (1931): 409–28, 681–704, 1045–63.

Isaac, Heinrich. *Choralis Constantinus*, 1550–55.

Jamnitzer, Christoph. *Moor's Head Drinking Cup*, ca. 1595–1600.

Jobst, Wolffgang. *Genealogia, oder Stam vnd Geburtlinia*, 1573.

Johann von Neumarkt. *Buch der Liebkosung*, 1355.

Johann von Würzburg. *Wilhelm von Österreich*, 1314; prose 1481; printed 1491.

Johannes von Soest. *Die Kinder von Limburg*, ca. 1480.

Johannes von Tepl. *Der Ackermann aus Böhmen*, 1400/1. Translated by Alexander and Elizabeth Henderson as *The Plowman from Bohemia*. New York: Unger, 1966.

Kaisersberg, Johann Geiler von. *Emeis*, 1508.

Kepler, Johann. *Mysterium cosmographicum*, 1596.

———. *Harmonices mundi*, 1619. Translated by E. J. Aiton, A. M. Duncan, and J. V. Field as *The Harmony of the World*. Philadelphia: American Philosophical Society, 1997.

Kerckmeister, Johannes. *Codrus*, 1485.

Kern, Leonhard. *Officer and Naked Woman*, 1656–59.

Kindermann, Balthasar. *Der deutsche Poet*, 1664.

Kircher, Athanasius. *Musurgia universalis*, 1650.

———. *Oedipus Aegyptiacus*, 1652.

Klaj, Johann. *Aufferstehung Jesu Christi*, 1644.

———. *Herodes der Kindermörderin*, 1645.

———. *Lobrede der Teutschen Poeterey*, 1645.

———. [Poetry] Selections translated by Schoolfield, 196–97.

Knorr von Rosenroth, Christian. *Kabbala denudata*, 2 vols., 1677–84. Translated by S. L. MacGregor Mathers as *Kabbalah Unveiled*. London: Routledge, 1951.

———. *Neuer Helicon mit seinen Neun Musen*, 1684.

———. [Poetry] Selections translated by Schoolfield, 198–99.

Konrad von Ammenhausen. *Schachzabelbuch*, 1337.

Kormart, Christoph. *Maria Stuart*, 1672.

Kramer, Heinrich. *Malleus maleficarum*, 1487.

Krüger, Bartholomäus. *Hans Clawerts Werckliche Historien*, 1587.

Kuffstein, Hans Ludwig von. *Gefängnüss der Lieb*, 1624.

Kuhlmann, Quirinus. *Himmlische Libes-küsse*, 1671.

———. *Kühlpsalter*, 1677–86.

———. [Poetry] Selections translated by Schoolfield, 202–9.

Kuhnau, Johann. *Der Schmid seines eignen Unglückes*, 1695.

———. *Musicalischen Quacksalber*, 1700. Translated by John R. Russell, with an introduction by James Hardin, as *The Musical Charlatan*. Columbia, SC: Camden House, 1997.

Lassus, Orlando de. *Neue teütsche Liedlein*, 1567.

Lauterbeck, Georg. *Regentenbuch*, 1556.

Lehmann, Christoph. *Florilegium Politicum*, 1639.

Lemnius, Simon. *Amorum libri IV*, 1542.

Lipsius, Justus. *De constantia*, 1584; German translation by A. Viritius as *Von der Bestendigkeit*, 1599.

———. *Politica*, 1589.

———. *Manuductio ad stoicam philosophiam*, 1604.

Lobwasser, Ambrosius. *Psalter*, 1573.

Locher, Jacob. *Stultifera navis*, 1497, translation of S. Brant's *Narrenschiff.*

———. *Iudicium Paridis de pomo aureo*, 1502.

Logau, Friedrich von. *Salomons von Golaw Deutscher Sinn-Getichte Drey Tausend*, 1654.

———. [Aphorisms] Translated by H. W. Longfellow as *Poetic Aphorisms from the Sinn-Gedichte of Friedrich von Logau*. Introduction by Richard E. Schade. Reprint, Lexington, KY: Polyglot, 2005.

Lohenstein, Daniel Casper von. *Ibrahim Bassa*, 1650.

———. *Cleopatra*, 1661; revised 1680.

———. *Agrippina*, 1665.

———. *Sophonisbe*, 1669; revised 1680.

———. *Ibrahim Sultan*, 1673.

———. Panegyric to C. H. von Hofmannswaldau, 1679. Translated by Linda Feldman, with Lynne Tatlock, as "Panegyric upon the Burial of Mr. Christian Hofmann von Hofmannswaldau," in Tatlock, 112–23.

———. [Poetry] Selections translated by Schoolfield, 220–25.

Löhneyß, Georg Engelhard von. *Aulico Politica*, 1622.

Luder, Peter. *Ars oratoria*, ca. 1485.

Luther, Martin. *Disputatio pro declaratione virtutis indulgentiarum* (*Ninety-Five Theses*), 1517. Translated by Project Wittenberg as *The Ninety-Five Theses of Martin Luther in English*. http://www.ctsfw.edu/etext/luther/theses/theses_e.asc.

————. *Contra scholasticam theologiam*, 1517. Translated by Harold J. Grimm as *Disputation against Scholastic Theology*, in *LW* 31:3–16.

————. *Predigt vom Ehestand*, 1519. Translated by James Atkinson as *A Sermon on the Estate of Marriage*, in *LW* 44:7–14.

————. *An den christlichen Adel deutscher Nation*, 1520. Translated by Charles M. Jacobs, revised by James Atkinson, as *To the Christian Nobility of the German Nation Concerning the Reform of the Christian Estate*, in *LW* 44:123–218.

————. *Von dem Papsttum zu Rom*, 1520. Translated by Eric W. Gritsch as *Against the Roman Papacy*, in *LW* 41:263–376.

————. *Von den guten Werken*, 1520. Translated by W. A. Lambert as *Treatise on Good Works*, in *LW* 44:21–121.

————. *Von der Babylonischen Gefangenschaft der Kirche*, 1520. Translated by A. T. W. Steinhäuser, revised by Frederick C. Ahrens and Abde Ross Wentz, as *Babylonian Captivity of the Church*, in *LW* 36:11–126.

————. *Von der Freyheyt eynisz Christen menschen*, 1520. Translated by R. S. Grignon as *Concerning Christian Liberty*. New York: Bartleby.com, 2001.

————. *Formula missae et communionis pro Ecclesia Wittembergensi*, 1523. Translated by Paul Zeller Strodach, revised by Ulrich S. Leupold, as *An Order of Mass and Communion for the Church at Wittenberg*, in *LW* 53:15–40.

————. *Wider die himmlischen Prophete*, 1524. Translated by Bernhard Erling and Conrad Bergendoff as *Against the Heavenly Prophets in the Matter of Images and Sacraments*, in *LW* 40:73–224.

————. *De servo arbitrio*, 1525. Translated by E. Gordan Rupp et al. as *On the Bondage of the Will*. In *Luther and Erasmus: Free Will and Salvation*. The Library of Christian Classics. Philadelphia: Westminster Press, 1969.

————. *Wider die räuberischen und mörderischen Rotten der andern Bauern*, 1525. Translated as *Against the Robbing and Murdering Hordes of Peasants*, in *LW* 46:45–55.

————. *Deutsche Messe und Ordnung Gottesdiensts*, 1526. Translated by Augustus Steimle, revised by Ulrich S. Leupold, as *The German Mass and Order of Service*, in *LW* 53:51–90.

————. *Der Kleine Katechismus*, 1529. Translated by Joseph Stump as *An Explanation of Luther's Small Catechism: A Handbook for Catechetical Instruction*. 2nd revised ed. Philadelphia: Muhlenberg, 1960.

————. *Der Grosse Katechismus (Deudsch Catechismus)*, 1529. Translated by Robert H. Fischer as *Large Catechism*. Philadelphia: Muhlenberg, 1959.

————. *Sendbrief von Dolmetschen*, 1530. Translated by Charles M. Jacobs, revised by E. Theodore Bachmann, as *On Translating: An Open Letter*, in *LW* 35:181–202.

————. *Die ganze Heilige Schrift deutsch*, 1545.

————. *Tischreden*, 1566. Translated by Theodore G. Tappert as *Table Talk*, in *LW* 54.

Macropedius. *Hecastus*, 1539.

Mannich, Johann. *Sacra emblemata*, 1624.

Manuel, Niklaus. *Vom Papst und seiner Priesterschaft*, 1524.

———. *Der Ablaßkrämer*, 1525.

Masen, Jacob. *Rusticus imperans*, 1654.

———. *Palaestra eloquentiae ligatae*, 1657.

Maximilian I, Emperor. *Weisskunig*, 1514.

———. *Theuerdanck*, 1517.

Melanchthon, Philipp. *De corrigendis adolescentiae studiis*, 1518.

———. *Institutiones graecae grammaticae*, 1518.

———. *Loci communes*, 1521.

———. *Elementorum rhetorices libri duo*, 1531.

———. *Erotema dialectices*, 1547.

———. [Selected writings] Translated by Ralph Keen as *A Melanchthon Reader*. New York: Lang, 1988.

———. [Selected writings] Translated by Christine F. Salazar and edited by Sachiko Kusukawa as *Melanchthon: Orations on Philosophy and Education*. Cambridge: Cambridge UP, 1999.

Mennel, Jakob. *Chronik des Hauses Österreich und der Grafen Habsburg*, 1507.

Mentel, Johannes. *Mentel Bibel*, 1466.

Merian the Elder, Matthäus. *Theatrum europaeum*, 1635–.

Meyfart, Johann Matthäus. *Teutsche rhetorica*, 1634.

Micyllus, Jacobus. *De re metrica*, 1539.

Mitternacht, Johann Christian. *Trauer-Spiel*, 1662.

———. *Politica Dramatica*, 1667.

Molitor, Ulrich. *De lamiis et pitonicis mulieribus*, 1489; German translation, as *Von Unholden und Hexen*, 1586.

Möller, Gertrud. *Parnaß-Blumen*, 1672.

Morhof, Daniel Georg. *Unterricht von der Teutschen Sprache und Poesie*, 1682.

Moscherosch, Johann Michael. *Gesichte Philanders von Sittewalt*, 1640/2. Selection translated by Lynne Tatlock as "Philander's German Supplement," in Tatlock, 138–44.

Mosellanus, Petrus. *De ratione disputandi*, 1518.

Münster, Sebastian. *Cosmographia*, 1550.

Müntzer, Thomas. *Prager Manifest*, 1521.

———. *Manifest an die Verschworenen des Allstedter Bundes*, 1525.

Murmellius, Johannes. *Versificatorie artis rudimenta*, ca. 1511.

Murner, Thomas. *Germania nova*, 1502.

Naogeorg, Thomas. *Pammachius*, 1538.

———. *Mercator seu Iudicium*, 1540.

———. *Judas Iscariotes*, 1552.

Nettesheim, Heinrich Cornelius Agrippa von. *De occulta philosophia*, 1510; pub. 1533.

Neukirch, Benjamin. *Herrn von Hoffmannswaldau und andrer Deutschen auserlesener und bißher ungedruckter Gedichte*, 7 vols., 1695–1727.

Nikolaus von Jeroschin. *Deutschordenschronik*, 1331–41.

Olearius, Adam. *Offt begehrte Beschreibung der Newen Orientalischen Reise*, 1647.

———. *Reise-Beschreibung nach Muszkau und Persien* (enlarged edition), 1696. Selection translated by Samuel H. Baron as "Households and Social Life," in Tatlock, 30–46.

Omphalius, Jakob. *De Officio*, 1550.

Opitz, Martin. *Aristarchus*, 1617.

———. *Buch von der Deutschen Poeterey*, 1624.

———. *Teutsche Poemata*, 1624.

———. *Deutsche Poemata*, 1625.

———. *Die Trojanerinnen*, 1625.

———. *Dafne* (with H. Schütz), 1627.

———. *Schäfferey von der Nimfen Hercinie*, 1630. Selection translated by Linda Feldman as "Pastorale of the Nymph Hercynia," in Tatlock, 128–34.

———. *Trostgedichte in Widerwertigkeit deß Krieges*, 1633.

———. *Judith*, 1635.

———. *Geistliche Poemata*, 1638.

———. *Weltliche Poemata: Zum viertenmal vermehret*, 1644.

———. [Poetry] Selections translated by Schoolfield, 238–45.

Osiander, Lucas. *Fünffzig geistliche Lieder und Psalmen*, 1586.

Oswald von Wolkenstein. [Songs] Selections translated by George F. Jones. In *Oswald von Wolkenstein*. New York: Twayne, 1973.

Otto von Passau. *Die vierundzwanzig Alten oder der goldene Thron der minnenden Seele*, 1418.

Paracelsus. [Selected Writings] Translated by Norbert Guterman as *Selected Writings*. Ed. Jolande Jacobi. New York: Pantheon, 1958.

Pauli, Johannes. *Schimpf und Ernst*, 1522.

Pellicanus, Conrad. *Commentaria Bibliorum*, 1532–39.

Pencz, Georg. *Rabbits Catching the Hunters*, ca. 1534–35.

Petersen, Johanna Eleonora. *Leben*, 1718.

Peutinger, Conrad. *Vitae imperatorum*, 1510.

———. *Tabula Peutingeriana*, pub. 1598.

Pfann, Johann. *Biblische Emblemata und Figuren*, 1626.

Piccolomini, Enea Silvio. *Eurialus et Lucretia*, 1444.

Piccolomini, Enea Silvio. *Tractatus de liberorum educatione*, 1450.

———. *Türkenrede*, German translation, 1455.

Pirckheimer, Caritas. *Denkwürdigkeiten*, n.d.

Pirckheimer, Willibald. *Eccius dedolatus*, 1520.

———. *Apologia seu Podagrae laus*, 1522.

———. *Hellenica*, 1532.

Plavius, Johannes. *Trawr- und Treu-Gedichten*, 1630.

Pontanus, Jacobus. *Poeticarum institutionum libri iii*, 1594.

———. *Attica bellaria*, 3 vols., 1615–20.

Postel, Christian Heinrich. *Die Wunderbahr-errettete Iphigenia*, 1699.

Praetorius, Johannes. *Des Blockes-Berges Verrichtung*, 1668.

Praetorius, Michael. *Musae Sioniae*, 1609–10.

———. *Syntagma musicum*, 1615.

Prasch, Johann Ludwig. *Psyche Cretica*, 1685.

Prasch, Susanna Elisabeth. *Réflexions sur les Romans*, 1684.

Pregitzer, Johann Ulrich. *Teutscher Regierung- und Ehren-Spiegel*, 1703.

Printz, Wolfgang Caspar. *Güldner Hund*, 1675.

Pufendorf, Samuel. *De habitu religionis Christianae ad vitam civilem*, 1682. Translated by J. Crull as *On the Nature and Qualification of Religion in Reference to Civil Society*. Indianapolis: Liberty Fund, 2002.

———. [Political writings] Selections translated in *The Political Writings of Samuel Pufendorf*. Ed. Craig L. Carr. New York: Oxford UP, 1994.

Puschmann, Adam. *Gründlicher Bericht des deutschen Meistergesanges*, 1571.

Quiccheberg, Samuel. *Inscriptiones vel tituli theatri amplissimi*, 1565.

Rachel, Joachim. *Satirische Gedichte*, 1664.

Rader, Matthäus. *Bavaria sancta*, 3 vols., 1615–27.

Ratichius, Wolfgang. *Allgemeine RednerLehr*, 1619.

———. *Allgemeine Sprachlehr*, 1619.

Rebhun, Paul. *Susanna*, 1535.

Regnart, Jakob. *Kurtzweilige teutsche Lieder zu dreyen Stimmen*, 1574, 1577, 1579.

Reichle, Hans. *Crucifixion*, 1605.

Reinkingk, Dietrich. *Biblische Policey*, 1653.

Reisch, Gregor. *Margarita philosophica*, 1503.

Reiser, Anton. *Theatromania*, 1681.

Reuchlin, Johann. *Scenica Progymnasmata* (*Henno*), 1498.

———. *De rudimentis hebraicis*, 1506.

———. *De arte cabalistica*, 1517. Translated by Martin Goodman and Sarah Goodman as *On the Art of the Kabbalah*. New York: Abaris, 1983.

Reuter, Christian. *Schelmuffsky*, 1696. Translated by Wayne Wonderley as *Christian Reuter's* Schelmuffsky. Chapel Hill: U of North Carolina P, 1962.

Rhau, Georg. *Newe deudsche geistliche Gesenge für die gemeinen Schulen*, 1544.

Rhegius, Urban. *Enchiridion odder handtbüchlin*, 1535.

Rhenanus, Beatus. *Rerum Germanicarum libri III*, 1531.

Rhodius, Theodor. *Colignius*, 1614.

Riederer, Friedrich. *Spiegel der waren Rhetoric*, 1493.

Riemer, Johann. *Der Politische Maul-Affe*, 1679.

———. *Von der erlöseten Germania*, 1679.

Rinckart, Martin. *Von Teutschen Versen*, 1645.

Rist, Johann. *Irenaromachia*, 1630, with Ernst Stapel.

———. *Das Friedejauchzende Teutschland*, 1650.

———. *Das Friedewünschende Teutschland*, 1650.

———. [Poetry] Selections translated by Schoolfield, 248–53.

Rollenhagen, Georg. *Der Reiche Mann und der arme Lazarus*, 1590.

———. *Alte newe Zeitung*, n.d. Translated by Eli Sobel as *Alte newe Zeitung: A Sixteenth-Century Collection of Fables with English Summaries*. Berkeley: U of California P, 1958.

Roritzer, Matthäus. *Geometria deutsch*, 1487/8.

Rosenthal, Dorothea Eleonora von. *Poetische Gedancken*, 1641.

Rösslin, Eucharius. *Des swangeren frauwen und hebammen Rosegarten*, 1513.

Rothe, Johannes. *Ritterspiegel*, ca. 1415.

Rubeanus, Crotus. *Epistolae obscurorum virorum*, 1515–17, with U. v. Hutten.

Rücktäschel, Rosina Dorothea. *Das Weib auch ein wahrer Mensch*, 1697.

Rüxner, Georg. *ThurnierBuch*, 1530, printed 1566.

Sabinus, Georg. *Hodeoporicon itineris Italici*, 1544.

Sachs, Hans. "Die Wittenbergisch Nachtigall," 1523.

———. *Lucretia*, 1527.

———. "Lobspruch der Stadt Nürnberg," 1530.

———. *Tragedi dess Fürsten Concreti und Gismunda*, 1545.

———. *Comedi Griselda*, 1546.

———. *Lorenzo und Lisabetha*, 1546.

———. "Summa all meiner gedicht," 1567.

———. [Shrovetide Plays] Translated by Randall W. Listerman as *Nine Carnival Plays by Hans Sachs*. Ottawa: Dovehouse, 1990.

Sambucus, Johannes. *Emblemata*, 1565.

Sattler, Johann Rudolf. *Werbungsbüchlein*, 1611.

Saubert, Johann. *Emblematum sacrorum*, 1625–30.

Schede, Paul Melissus. *Psalter*, 1572.

———. *Schediasmata*, 1586.

Schedel, Hartmann. *Weltchronik* (*Nürnberger Weltchronik*), 1493.

Scheffler, Johann (Angelus Silesius). *Geistreiche Sinn- und Schlußreime*, 1657.

———. *Heilige Seelen-Lust*, 1657.

———. *Cherubinischer Wandersmann*, 1675. Selections translated by Willard R. Trask as *The Cherubinic Wanderer*. New York: Pantheon Books, 1953.

———. [Poetry] Selections translated by Schoolfield, 256–63; by Thomas, 31–33.

Schein, Johann Hermann. *Israelsbrünnlein*, 1623.

———. *Cantional oder Gesangbuch Augspurgischer Confession*, 1627.

Schirmer, David. *Poetische Rosen-Gepüsche*, 1657.

Schlüsselfelder, Heinrich (Arigo). *Decamerone*, 1473, translation of Boccaccio.

Schnüffis, Laurentius von. [Poetry] Selections translated by Schoolfield, 208–13.

Schongauer, Martin. *Christ Carrying the Cross*, ca. 1420.

Schorer, Christoph. *Sprach- Sitten- und Tugendverderber*, 1643.

Schosser, Johannes. *Disputatio de tragoedia ex primo libro Aristotelis*, 1569.

Schott, Caspar. *Mechanica hydraulico-pneumatica*, n.d.

Schottelius, Justus Georg. *Teutsche Sprachkunst*, 1641.

———. *Der Teutschen Sprache Einleitung*, 1643.

———. *Teutsche Vers- oder Reimkunst*, 1656.

———. *Ausführliche Arbeit von der Teutschen HaubtSprache*, 1663.

———. *Ethica: Die Sittenkunst oder Wollebenskunst*, 1669.

Schrot, Martin. *Wappenbuch des Heiligen römischen Reichs*, 1580.

Schupp, Johann Balthasar. *Salomo Oder Regenten-Spiegel*, 1657.

Schurmann, Anna Maria van. *Num foeminae christianae conveniat studium litterarum*, 1648.

Schuster, Sibylla. *Verkehrter, Bekehrter und wider bethörter Ophiletes*, 1685.

Schütz, Heinrich. *Primo libro de madrigali*, 1611.

———. *Historia der frölichen und siegreichen Aufferstehung*, 1623.

———. *Cantiones sacrae*, 1625.

———. *Die Bußfertige Magdalena*, 1635, with A. Buchner.

———. *Geistliche Chor-Music*, 1648.

Schwarz, Sybille. *Deutsche Poëtische Gedichte*, 1650. Selections translated by Schoolfield, 272–75.

Schwarzenberg, Johann von. *Peinliche Halsgerichtsordnung Kaiser Karls V.*, 1507; revised 1532 as *Constitutio criminalis Carolina*.

Schwieger, Jacob. *Gründlicher Bericht von Zauberey und Zauberern*, 1598.

Seckendorff, Veit Ludwig von. *Teutscher Fürsten-Stat*, 1656.

Secundus, Johannes. *Basia*, 1539.

Secundus, Petrus Lotichius. *Elegiarum liber*, 1551. Translated by Katherine Anne O'Rourke Fraiman as "Petrus Lotichius Secundus Elegiarum liber primus." In Ph.D. dissertation, Columbia University, 1973.

Siegemund, Justina. *Die Chur-Brandenburgische Hof-Wehe-Mutter*, 1690. Translated by Lynne Tatlock as *The Court Midwife*. Chicago: U of Chicago P, 2005.

Sleidanus, Johannes. *De statu religionis Carolo V. Caesare commentarii*, 1555.

———. *De quattuor summis imperiis*, 1556.

Spangenberg, Cyriacus. *Von der Edlen und Hochberümbten Kunst der Musica*, 1598.

———. *Die Hennebergische Chronica*, 1599.

Spee von Langenfeld, Friedrich. *Cautio criminalis*, 1631.

———. *Trutznachtigall*, 1634, pub. 1649.

———. [Poetry] Selections translated by Schoolfield, 280–87.

Spener, Philipp Jacob. *Pia desideria*, 1675. Selection translated by Theodore G. Tappert as "Pia Desideria or Heartfelt Desire," in Tatlock, 94–102.

Staden, Sigmund Theophil. *Seelewig*, 1644, with G. P. Harsdörffer.

Steinhöwel, Heinrich. *Griseldis*, 1471.

———. *Pestbüchlein*, 1473.

———. *Spiegel menschlichen Lebens*, 1475.

Stiblin, Caspar. *Eudaemonensium respublica*, 1555.

Stieler, Kaspar. *Der vermeinte Printz*, 1665.

———. *Die erfreuete Unschuld*, 1666.

———. *Der betrogene Betrug*, 1667.

———. *Teutsche Sekretariat-Kunst*, 1673/4.

———. *Zeitungs Lust und Nutz*, 1695. Selection translated by Lynne Tatlock as "Newspaper's Pleasure and Profit," in Tatlock, 48–59.

———. [Poetry] Selections translated by Schoolfield, 288–93.

Stockfleth, Maria Katharina. *Die Kunst- und Tugend-Gezierte Macarie*, part 1, with H. A. Stockfleth, 1669; sole author, pt. 2, 1673.

Sturm, Johann. *Volumina poetica*, 6 vols., 1565–.

Stymmelius, Christoph. *Studentes*, 1549.

Thomas à Kempis. *De imitatione Christi*, ca. 1418/20.

Thomas, Johann. *Damon und Liselle*, 1663.

Thomasius, Christian. *De crimine magiae*, 1701.

Thüring von Ringoltingen. *Melusine*, 1456, printed 1474.

Titz, Johann Peter. *Von der Kunst Hochdeutsche Verse und Lieder zu machen*, 1642.

Trithemius, Johannes. *Annales Hiraugiensis*, 1515.

Tröster, Johann. *De remedio amoris*, 1454.

Tschesch, Theodor von. *Vitae cum Christo*, 1644.

Tschudi, Aegidius. *Chronicon Helveticum*, 1556.

Tünger, Augustin. *Facetiae Latinae et Germanicae*, 1486.

Turmair, Johannes (Aventinus). *Annalium Boiorum*, German translation as *Bayerische Chronik*, 1533, printed 1566.

Vogel, Johann. *Meditationes emblematicae*, 1648.

Vondel, Joost van den. *De Gebroeders*, 1640; German translation as *Die Sieben Brüder* by A. Gryphius, 1698.

Vossius, Gerhard Johannes. *Commentaria rhetorica*, 1630.

Wagenseil, Johann Christoph. *Buch von der Meistersinger holdseligen Kunst*, 1697.

Waldis, Burkhard. *De parabell vam vorlorn Szohn*, 1527.

Waldseemüller, Martin. *Cosmographia*, 1507.

Walter, Johann. *Geystliches gesang Buchleyn* (*Chorgesangbuch*), 1524.

Watt, Joachim von (Vadianus). *De poetica et carminis ratione*, 1518.

Weckherlin, Georg Rudolf. *Oden und Gesänge*, 1618–19.

———. *Gaistliche Gedichte*, 1648.

———. [Poetry] Selections translated by Schoolfield, 300–307.

Weidner, Johann Leonhard. *Triga amico-poetica*, 1619.

Weise, Christian. *Die drey ärgsten Ertz-Narren in der gantzen Welt*, 1672. Selection translated by Linda Feldman as "The Three Most Awful Arch-Fools in the Entire World," in Tatlock, 148–55.

———. *Politischer Redner*, 1677.

———. *Der Tochter-Mord*, 1679.

———. *Masaniello*, 1683.

———. *Die Unvergnügte Seele*, 1688.

———. *Gelehrter Redner*, 1692.

———. [Poetry] Selections translated by Schoolfield, 308–9.

Werder, Diederich von dem. *Krieg vnd Sieg Christi*, 1631.

Weyer, Johann. *De praestigiis daemonum*, 1663.

Wickram, Jörg. *Ritter Galmy uss Schottland*, 1539.

———. *Gabriotto und Reinhart*, 1551.

———. *Rollwagenbüchlein*, 1555.

———. *Von guten und bösen Nachbarn*, 1556.

———. *Der Goldtfaden*, 1557. Translated by Pierre Kaufke as *The Golden Thread: An Agreeable & Entertaining Tale of Lionel, Son of a Poor Shepherd*. Gainesville: UP of Florida, 1991.

Willich, Jodocus. *Commentaria in artem poeticam Horatii*, 1545.

Wimpfeling, Jacob. *Stylpho*, 1480.

———. *Isidoneus germanicus*, 1497.

———. *Adolescentia*, 1500.

———. *Germania*, 1502.

———. *Epithoma rerum Germanicorum*, 1505.

Witekind, Hermann. *Christlich Bedencken und Erinnerung von Zauberey*, 1585.

Wittenwiler, Heinrich. *Ring*, first decade 15th c. Translated by George Fenwick Jones as *Wittenwiler's Ring*. Chapel Hill: U of North Carolina P, 1956.

Wonnecke, Johannes. *Gart der Gesundheit*, 1485.

Wyle, Niklas von. *Colores rethoricales*, 1464–69.

———. *Translationen* (or *Translatzen*, or *Tütschungen*), 1478.

———. *Figurenlehre*, 1478.

Zasius, Johann Ulrich. *Catalogus legum antiquarum*, 1551.

Zasius, Ulrich. *Freiburger Neuen Stadtrecht*, 1520.

———. *Intellectus singulares et novi*, 1526.

Zeidler, Christian. *Monarchia optima reipublicae forma*, 1679.

Zeidler, Susanna Elisabeth. *Jungferlicher Zeitvertreiber*, 1684.

Zell, Katharina. *Entschuldigung für Matthis Zellen*, 1524.

———. *Brief an die ganze Bürgschaft der Stadt Straßburg*, 1557.

Zesen, Philipp von. *Deutscher Helicon*, 1641.

———. *Die Adriatische Rosemund*, 1645. Selection translated by Lynne Tatlock as "The Seventh Day of the Rose-Moone," in Tatlock, 2–9.

———. *Dichterisches Rosen- und Liljen-thal*, 1670.

———. [Poetry] Selections translated by Schoolfield, 312–15.

Ziegler, Kaspar. *Von den Madrigalen*, 1653.

Ziegler und Kliphausen, Heinrich Anshelm von. *Die Asiatische Banise*, 1689.

Zincgref, Julius Wilhelm. *Facetiae pennalium*, 1618.

———. *Newe Zeitungen*, 1619.

———. *Quodlibetisches Weltkefig*, 1623.

———. *Vermanung zur Dapfferkeit*, 1623.

———. *Teutscher Nation Denckwürdiger Reden*, 1628, 1631.

———. [Poetry] Selections translated by Schoolfield, 316–19.

Zwingli, Huldrych. *Von Klarheit und Gewissheit des Wortes Gottes*, 1522.

Select Secondary Literature

(The secondary bibliography consists of a selection of the works cited in the individual chapters of this volume in addition to other works pertinent to early modern German literature in its historical and cultural contexts. A certain preference is given to more recent scholarship, whether in German or English.)

Bibliographies, Collections, Handbooks, Lexica, and Dictionaries

Adam, Wolfgang, ed. *Geselligkeit und Gesellschaft im Barockzeitalter.* Wiesbaden: Harrassowitz, 1997.

Albrecht, Günter, ed. *Deutsche Schwänke in einem Band.* 4th ed. Berlin: Aufbau, 1969.

Alewyn, Richard, ed. *Deutsche Barockforschung.* 2nd ed. Cologne: Kiepenheuer & Witsch, 1966.

Ameln, Konrad, Markus Jenny, and Walter Lipphardt, eds. *Das deutsche Kirchenlied: Verzeichnis der Drucke von den Anfängen bis 1800.* Répertoire international des sources musicales, B/VIII/1. Kassel: Bärenreiter, 1975.

Angermann, Norbert, ed. *Lexikon des Mittelalters: Studienausgabe.* 9 vols. Stuttgart: Metzler, 1999.

Arnold, Klaus, Sabine Schmolinsky, and Urs Martin Zahnd, eds. *Das dargestellte ich: Studien zu Selbstzeugnissen des späteren Mittelalters und der frühen Neuzeit.* Vol. 1 of *Selbstzeugnisse des Mittelalters und der beginnenden Neuzeit.* Bochum: Winkler, 1999.

Asch, Ronald G., ed. *Der europäische Adel im Ancien Régime: Von der Krise der ständischen Monarchien bis zur Revolution (ca. 1600–1789).* Cologne: Böhlau, 2001.

Asch, Ronald G., and Adolf M. Birke, eds. *Princes, Patronage and the Nobility: The Court at the Beginning of the Modern Age c. 1450–1650.* Oxford: Oxford UP, 1991.

Babel, Rainer, and Werner Paravicini, eds. *Grand Tour — Adeliges Reisen und europäische Kultur vom 14. bis zum 16. Jahrhundert.* Stuttgart: Thorbeke, 2005.

Bachorski, Hans-Jürgen, and Werner Röcke, eds. *Weltbildwandel: Selbstdeutung und Fremderfahrung im Epochenübergang vom Spätmittelalter zur Frühen Neuzeit.* Literatur, Imagination, Realität 10. Trier: Wissenschaftlicher Verlag, 1994.

Battafarano, Italo Michele, ed. *Begrifflichkeit und Bildlichkeit in der Reformation.* Bern: Lang, 1992.

Bebb, Phillip N., and Sherrin Marshall, eds. *The Process of Change in Early Modern Europe: Essays in Honor of Miriam Usher Chrisman*. Athens: Ohio UP, 1988.

Béguerie, Pantxika, ed. *Der hübsche Martin: Kupferstiche und Zeichnungen von Martin Schongauer (ca. 1450–1491)*. Exhibition catalogue. Unterlinden Museum, Colmar, 1991.

Béhar, Pierre, and Helen Watanabe-O'Kelly, eds. *Spectacvlvm Europævm: Theatre and Spectacle in Europe (1580–1750)*. Wiesbaden: Harrassowitz, 1999.

Bennewitz, Ingrid, and Ulrich Müller, eds. *Von der Handschrift zum Buchdruck: Spätmittelalter — Reformation — Humanismus 1320–1572*. Vol. 2 of *Deutsche Literatur: Eine Sozialgeschichte*. Reinbek bei Hamburg: Rowohlt, 1991.

Benzenhöfer, Udo, and Wilhelm Kühlmann, eds. *Heilkunde und Krankheitserfahrung in der frühen Neuzeit: Studien am Grenzrain von Literaturgeschichte und Medizingeschichte*. Tübingen: Niemeyer, 1992.

Berns, Jörg-Jochen, and Thomas Rahn, eds. *Zeremoniell als höfische Ästhetik in Spätmittelalter und Früher Neuzeit*. Frühe Neuzeit 25. Tübingen: Niemeyer 1995.

Berschin, Walter, ed. *Biographie zwischen Renaissance und Barock*. Heidelberg: Mattes, 1993.

Besch, Werner, Oskar Reichmann, and Stefan Sonderegger, eds. *Sprachgeschichte: Ein Handbuch zur Geschichte der deutschen Sprache und ihrer Erforschung*. Berlin: de Gruyter, 1985.

Bezzel, Irmgard, and Bayerische Staatsbibliothek (Munich), with Herzog August Bibliothek (Wolfenbüttel), eds. *Verzeichnis der im deutschen Sprachbereich erschienenen Drucke des 16. Jahrhunderts*. Abteilung 1: 22 vols. Abteilung 2: 3 vols. Stuttgart: Hiersemann, 1983–2002.

Bietenholz, Peter G., ed. *Contemporaries of Erasmus: A Biographical Register of the Renaissance and Reformation*. 3 vols. Toronto: U of Toronto P, 1985–87.

Bircher, Martin, and Ferdinand van Ingen, eds. *Sprachgesellschaften, Sozietäten, Dichtergruppen*. Wolfenbütteler Arbeiten zur Barockforschung 7. Hamburg: Hauswedell, 1978.

Birkhan, Helmut, ed. *Die Juden in ihrer mittelalterlichen Umwelt*. Bern: Lang, 1992.

Blühm, Elger, Jörn Garber, and Klaus Garber, eds. *Hof, Staat und Gesellschaft in der Literatur des 17. Jahrhunderts*. Special issue, *Daphnis* 11, nos. 1–2 (1982).

Bödeker, Hans Erich et al., eds. *Der Umgang mit dem religiösen Buch*. Göttingen: Vandenhoeck & Ruprecht, 1991.

Bolgar, R. R., ed. *Classical Influences on European Culture: A.D. 1500–1700*. Cambridge: Cambridge UP, 1976.

Bookmann, Hartmut, ed. *Literatur, Musik und Kunst im Übergang vom Mittelalter zur Neuzeit*. Göttingen: Vandenhoeck & Ruprecht, 1995.

Brady, Thomas A. Jr., ed. *Die deutsche Reformation zwischen Spätmittelalter und Früher Neuzeit*. Schriften des Historischen Kollegs 50. Munich: Oldenbourg, 2001.

Brady, Thomas A. Jr., Heiko A. Oberman, and James D. Tracy, eds. *Handbook of European History, 1400–1600: Late Middle Ages, Renaissance, and Reformation.* 2 vols. Grand Rapids: Eerdmans, 1994.

Brauneck, Manfred, and Alfred Noe, eds. *Spieltexte der Wanderbühne.* 5 vols. Berlin: de Gruyter, 1970–99.

Brecht, Martin, ed. *Der Pietismus vom siebzehnten bis zum frühen achtzehnten Jahrhundert.* Göttingen: Vandenhoeck & Ruprecht, 1993.

Brenner, Peter J., ed. *Der Reisebericht: Die Entwicklung einer Gattung in der deutschen Literatur.* Frankfurt am Main: Suhrkamp, 1989.

Breuer, Dieter, ed. *Frömmigkeit in der Frühen Neuzeit: Studien zur religiösen Literatur des 17. Jahrhunderts in Deutschland.* Amsterdam: Rodopi, 1984.

———, ed. *Religion und Religiosität im Zeitalter des Barock.* 2 vols. Wiesbaden: Harrassowitz, 1995.

Breuer, Dieter, and Günther Kopsch. "Rhetoriklehrbücher des 16. bis 20. Jahrhunderts: Eine Bibliographie." In *Rhetorik: Beiträge zu ihrer Geschichte in Deutschland vom 16. bis 20. Jahrhundert,* ed. Helmut Schanze, 217–92. Frankfurt am Main: Athenäum, 1974.

Brink, Jean R., Allison P. Coudert, and Maryanne C. Horowitz, eds. *The Politics of Gender in Early Modern Europe.* Sixteenth Century Essays & Studies 12. Kirksville, MO: Sixteenth Century Journal Publishers, 1989.

Buck, August., ed. *Europäische Hofkultur im 16. und 17. Jahrhundert.* 3 vols. Hamburg: Hauswedell, 1981.

———, ed. *Höfischer Humanismus.* Weinheim: Acta humaniora, 1989.

———, ed. *Renaissance — Reformation: Gegensätze und Gemeinsamkeiten.* Wolfenbütteler Abhandlungen zur Renaissanceforschung 5. Wiesbaden: Harrassowitz, 1986.

———, ed. *Die Rezeption der Antike: Zum Problem der Kontinuität zwischen Mittelalter und Renaissance.* Wolfenbütteler Abhandlungen zur Renaissanceforschung 1. Hamburg: Hauswedell, 1981.

Brinker-Gabler, Gisela, ed. *Deutsche Dichterinnen vom 16. Jahrhundert bis zur Gegenwart: Gedichte und Lebensläufe.* Frankfurt am Main: Fischer, 1978.

———, ed. *Deutsche Literatur von Frauen.* Vol. 1: *Vom Mittelalter bis zum Ende des 18. Jahrhunderts.* Munich: Beck, 1988.

Brockpähler, Renate. *Handbuch zur Geschichte der Barockoper in Deutschland.* Emsdetten: Lechte, 1964.

Brückner, Wolfgang, ed. *Volkserzählung und Reformation: Ein Handbuch zur Tradierung und Funktion von Erzählstoffen und Erzählliteratur im Protestantismus.* Berlin: Schmidt, 1974.

Brunner, Horst, and Burghart Wachinger, eds. *Repertorium der Sangsprüche und Meisterlieder des 12. bis 18. Jahrhunderts.* 16 vols. Tübingen: Niemeyer, 1986–2002.

Brunner, Horst, and Werner Williams-Krapp. *Forschungen zur deutschen Literatur des Spätmittelalters: Festschrift für Johannes Janota.* Tübingen: Niemeyer, 2003.

Burke, Peter, and Roy Porter, eds. *The Social History of Language.* Cambridge: Cambridge UP, 1987.

Cameron, Euan, ed. *Early Modern Europe: An Oxford History.* Oxford: Oxford UP, 1999.

Catling, Jo, ed. *A History of Women's Writing in Germany, Austria and Switzerland.* Cambridge: Cambridge UP, 2000.

Chroniken der deutschen Städte vom 14. bis ins 16. Jahrhundert (1862). Reprint, Göttingen: Vandenhoeck & Ruprecht, 1961–69.

Classen, Albrecht. *Deutsche Liederbücher des 15. und 16. Jahrhunderts.* Münster: Waxmann, 2001.

Conermann, Klaus. *Fruchtbringende Gesellschaft: Der Fruchtbringenden Gesellschaft Geöffneter Erzschrein, das Köthener Gesellschaftsbuch Fürst Ludwigs I. von Anhalt-Köthen 1617–1650.* 3 vols. Weinheim: VCH, 1985.

Conrady, Karl Otto. "Die Erforschung der neulateinischen Literatur." *Euphorion* 49 (1955): 413–45.

Czapla, Beate, Ralf Georg Czapla, and Robert Seidel, eds. *Lateinische Lyrik der Frühen Neuzeit: Poetische Kleinformen und ihre Funktionen zwischen Renaissance und Aufklärung.* Frühe Neuzeit 77. Tübingen: Niemeyer, 2003.

Czarnecka, Mirosława, ed. *Dichtungen schlesischer Autorinnen des 17. Jahrhunderts: Eine Anthologie.* Wrocław: Wydawniotwo Uniwersytetu Wrocslawskiego, 1997.

Dackerman, Susan, ed. *Painted Prints: The Revolution of Color in Northern Renaissance & Baroque Engravings, Etchings, & Woodcuts.* Exhibition catalogue. Baltimore Museum of Art. University Park, PA: Pennsylvania State UP, 2002.

Daly, Peter M., G. Richard Dimler S.J., and Rita Haub, eds. *Emblematik und Kunst der Jesuiten in Bayern: Einfluß und Wirkung.* Imago Figurata Studies 3. Turnhout: Brepols, 2000.

Davis, Natalie Zemon, and Arlette Farge, eds. *A History of Women: Renaissance and Enlightenment Paradoxes.* Cambridge: Harvard UP, 1993.

Debus, Allen G., and Michael T. Walton, eds. *Reading the Book of Nature: The Other Side of the Scientific Revolution.* Kirksville, MO: Sixteenth Century Journal Publishers, 1998.

Die deutsche Literatur des Mittelalters: Verfasserlexikon. 12 vols. 2nd ed. Ed. Christine Stöllinger-Löser et al. Berlin: de Gruyter, 1978–2006.

Dotzauer, Winfried, ed. *Quellenkunde zur deutschen Geschichte der Neuzeit von 1500 bis zur Gegenwart.* Vol. 1: *Das Zeitalter der Glaubensspaltung (1500–1618).* Darmstadt: Wissenschaftliche Buchgesellschaft, 1987.

Dünnhaupt, Gerhart, ed. *Personalbibliographien zu den Drucken des Barock.* 2nd ed. Stuttgart: Hiersemann, 1990.

Durian-Ress, Saskia, ed. *Hans Baldung Grien in Freiburg.* Exhibition catalogue. Augustinermuseum, Freiburg, 2001.

Dyck, Cornelius J., ed. *Spiritual Life in Anabaptism.* Scottsdale, PA: Herald Press, 1995.

Eikelmann, Renate, ed. *Der Mohrenkopfpokal von Christoph Jamnitzer.* Exhibition catalogue. Bayerisches Nationalmuseum, Munich, 2000.

Enekel, Karl A. E., and Arnoud S. Q. Visser, eds. *Mundus emblematicus: Studies in Neo-Latin Emblem Books.* Imago Figurata Studies 4. Turnhout: Brepols, 2003.

Engel, Gisela, and Heide Wunder, eds. *Geschlechterperspektiven: Forschungen zur Frühen Neuzeit.* Königstein: Helmer, 1998.

Engelhardt, Markus, ed. *In Teutschland noch gantz ohnbekandt: Monteverdi-Rezeption und frühes Musiktheater im deutschsprachigen Raum.* Frankfurt am Main: Lang, 1996.

Eybl, Franz M., ed. *Enyzklopädien der frühen Neuzeit: Beiträge zu Ihrer Erforschung.* Tübingen: Niemeyer, 1995.

Fabian, Bernhard, ed. *Handbuch der historischen Buchbestände in Deutschland.* 27 vols. Hildesheim: Olms, 1992–2000.

Filedt Kok, Jan Piet, ed. *Livelier than Life: The Master of the Amsterdam Cabinet or the Housebook Master ca. 1470–1500.* Exhibition catalogue. Rijksprentenkabinet, Amsterdam. Maarssen: Schwartz, 1985.

Finscher, Ludwig, ed. *Die Musik des 15. und 16. Jahrhunderts.* Laaber: Laaber-Verlag, 1990.

Fleischer, Manfred P., ed. *The Harvest of Humanism in Central Europe.* St. Louis: Concordia, 1992.

Flood, John L. *Poets Laureate in the Holy Roman Empire.* 4 vols. Berlin: de Gruyter, 2006.

Füssel, Stephan, ed. *The Book of Books: The Luther Bible of 1534: A Cultural-Historical Introduction.* Cologne: Taschen, 2003.

———, ed. *Deutsche Dichter der frühen Neuzeit (1450–1600): Ihr Leben und Werk.* Berlin: Schmidt, 1993.

Füssel, Stephan, Gert Hübner, and Joachim Knape, eds. *Artibus: Kulturwissenschaft und deutsche Philologie des Mittelalters und der Frühen Neuzeit.* Wiesbaden: Harrassowitz, 1994.

Garber, Klaus, ed. *Handbuch des personalen Gelegenheitsschrifttums in europäischen Bibliotheken und Archiven.* Hildesheim: Olms Neue Medien, 2001–.

———, ed., *Kulturgeschichte Ostpreußens in der Frühen Neuzeit.* Tübingen: Niemeyer, 2001.

———, ed. *Kulturgeschichte Schlesiens in der Frühen Neuzeit.* 2 vols. Frühe Neuzeit 111. Tübingen: Niemeyer, 2005.

———, ed. *Nation und Literatur im Europa der Frühen Neuzeit: Akten des 1. Internationalen Osnabrücker Kongresses zur Kulturgeschichte der Frühen Neuzeit.* Frühe Neuzeit 1. Tübingen: Niemeyer, 1989.

———, ed. *Stadt und Literatur im deutschen Sprachraum der Frühen Neuzeit.* 2 vols. Frühe Neuzeit 39. Tübingen: Niemeyer, 1998.

———, ed., with Ferdinand van Ingen. *Europäische Barock-Rezeption.* Wolfenbütteler Arbeiten zur Barockforschung 20. Wiesbaden: Harrassowitz, 1991.

———, ed., with Ferdinand van Ingen, Wilhelm Kühlmann, and Wolfgang Weiß. *Europäische Barock-Rezeption.* 2 vols. Wolfenbütteler Arbeiten zur Barockforschung 20. Wiesbaden: Harrassowitz, 1991.

Garber, Klaus, ed., with Sabine Kleymann. *Kulturwissenschaftler des 20. Jahrhunderts: Ihr Werk im Blick auf das Europa der Frühen Neuzeit.* Munich: Fink, 2002.

Garber, Klaus, and Martin Klöker, eds. *Kulturgeschichte der baltischen Länder in der Frühen Neuzeit: Mit einem Ausblick in die Moderne.* Frühe Neuzeit 87. Tübingen: Niemeyer, 2003.

Garber, Klaus, Manfred Komorowski, and Axel E. Walter, eds. *Kulturgeschichte Ostpreußens in der Frühen Neuzeit.* Frühe Neuzeit 56. Tübingen: Niemeyer, 2001.

Garber, Klaus, and Heinz Wismann, eds. *Europäische Sozietätsbewegung und demokratische Tradition: Die europäischen Akademien der Frühen Neuzeit zwischen Frührenaissance und Spätaufklärung.* 2 vols. Frühe Neuzeit 26–27. Tübingen: Niemeyer, 1996.

Gardt, Andreas, Klaus J. Mattheier, and Oskar Reichmann, eds. *Sprachgeschichte des Neuhochdeutschen.* Tübingen: Niemeyer, 1995.

Geldner, Ferdinand. *Die deutschen Inkunabeldrucker: Ein Handbuch der deutschen Buchdrucker des 15. Jahrhunderts nach Druckorten.* 2 vols. Stuttgart: Hiersemann, 1968, 1970.

Gesamtkatalog der Wiegendrucke. 11 vols. Leipzig and Stuttgart: Hiersemann, 1910–2003.

Grendler, Paul, ed. *Encyclopedia of the Renaissance.* 6 vols. New York: Scribner, 1999.

———, ed. *Handbuch der deutschen Bildungsgeschichte.* Vol. 1: *15. bis 17. Jahrhundert.* Munich: Beck, 1996.

———, ed. *Staatslehre der Frühen Neuzeit.* Bibliothek der Geschichte und Politik 16. Frankfurt am Main: Deutscher Klassiker Verlag, 1995.

Grenzmann, Ludger, and Karl Stackmann, eds. *Literatur und Laienbildung im Spätmittelalter und in der Reformationszeit.* Stuttgart: Metzler, 1984.

Greschat, Martin, ed. *Zur neueren Pietismusforschung.* Darmstadt: Wissenschaftliche Buchgesellschaft, 1977.

Greschat, Martin, and Günther Lottes, eds. *Luther in seiner Zeit.* Stuttgart: Kohlhammer, 1997.

Greyerz, Kaspar von. *Religion und Kultur: Europe 1500–1800.* Darmstadt: Wissenschaftliche Buchgesellschaft, 2000.

Greyerz, Kaspar von, et al., eds. *Interkonfessionalität — Transkonfessionalität — binnenkonfessionelle Pluralität: Neue Forschungen zur Konfessionalisierungsthese.* Schriften des Vereins für Reformationsgeschichte 201. Gütersloh: Gütersloher Verlagshaus, 2003.

Griffiths, Richard, ed. *The Bible in the Renaissance.* Aldershot: Ashgate, 2001.

Grimm, Günter E., and Frank Rainer Max, eds. *Reformation, Renaissance und Barock.* Vol. 2 of *Deutsche Dichter.* Stuttgart: Reclam, 1988.

Grimm, Reinhold, ed. *Literatur und Geistesgeschichte: Festgabe für Heinz Otto Burger.* Berlin: Schmidt, 1968.

Guthmüller, Bodo, ed. *Latein und Nationalsprachen in der Renaissance.* Wolfenbütteler Arbeiten zur Renaissanceforschung 17. Wiesbaden: Harrassowitz, 1998.

Guthmüller, Bodo, and Wilhelm Kühlmann, eds. *Europa und die Türken in der Renaissance*. Tübingen: Niemeyer, 2000.

Haberkamp, Gertraut. "Werke mit Musik für die deutschsprachige Bühne des 17. Jahrhunderts — der aktuelle Quellenstand." In Engelhardt, ed., *In Teutschland noch gantz ohnbekandt*, 1–28.

Haferland, Harald, and Michael Mecklenburg, eds. *Erzählungen in Erzählungen: Phänomene der Narration in Mittelalter und Früher Neuzeit*. Forschungen zur Geschichte der älteren deutschen Literatur 19. Munich: Fink, 1996.

Hammerstein, Notker, ed. *Bildung und Wissenschaft vom 15. bis zum 17. Jahrhundert*. Vol. 64 of *Enzyklopädie Deutscher Geschichte*. Munich: Oldenbourg, 2003.

Hammerstein, Notker, and Gerrit Walther, eds. *Späthumanismus: Studien über das Ende einer kulturhistorischen Epoche*. Göttingen: Wallstein, 2000.

Hardin, James, ed. *German Baroque Writers, 1580–1660*. Vol. 164 of *Dictionary of Literary Biography*. Detroit: Gale Research, 1996.

———, ed. *German Baroque Writers, 1661–1730*. Vol. 168 of *Dictionary of Literary Biography*. Detroit: Gale Research, 1996.

Harms, Wolfgang, and Dietmar Peil, eds. *Polyvalenz und Multifunktionalität der Emblematik: Multivalence and Multifunctionality of the Emblem*. 2 vols. Mikrokosmos 35. Frankfurt am Main: Lang, 2002.

Haug, Walter, and Burghart Wachinger, eds. *Positionen des Romans im späten Mittelalter*. Tübingen: Niemeyer, 1991.

Haye, Thomas, ed. *Humanismus im Norden: Frühneuzeitliche Rezeption antiker Kultur und Literatur an Nord- und Ostsee*. Chloe 32. Amsterdam: Rodopi, 2000.

Held, Jutta, ed. *Intellektuelle in der Frühen Neuzeit*. Munich: Fink, 2002.

Henkel, Arthur, and Albrecht Schöne, eds. *Emblemata: Handbuch zur Sinnbildkunst des XVI. und XVII. Jahrhunderts*. 2nd ed. Stuttgart: Metzler, 1976.

Herding, Otto, and Robert Stupperich, eds. *Die Humanisten in ihrer politischen und sozialen Umwelt*. Deutsche Forschungsgemeinschaft: Kommission für Humanismusforschung, Mitteilung 3. Boppard: Boldt, 1976.

Hillerbrand, Hans J., ed. *The Oxford Encyclopedia of the Reformation*. 4 vols. New York: Oxford UP, 1996.

———, ed. *Radical Tendencies in the Reformation: Divergent Perspectives*. Kirksville, MO: Sixteenth Century Journal Publishers, 1987.

Hinderman, Sandra., ed. *Printing the Written Word: The Social History of Books circa 1450–1520*. Ithaca: Cornell UP, 1991.

Hoffmann, Walter, et al., eds. *Das Frühneuhochdeutsche als sprachgeschichtliche Epoche. Werner Besch zum 70. Geburtstag*. Frankfurt am Main: Lang, 1999.

Hoffmeister, Gerhart, ed. *Europäische Tradition und deutscher Literaturbarock: Internationale Beiträge zum Problem von Überlieferung und Umgestaltung*. Bern: Francke, 1973.

————, ed. *German Baroque Literature: The European Perspective*. New York: Ungar, 1983.

————, ed. *The Renaissance and Reformation in Germany: An Introduction*. New York: Ungar, 1977.

Holzhey, Helmut, and Wilhelm Schmidt-Biggemann, with Vilem Mudroch, eds. *Die Philosophie des 17. Jahrhunderts*. Vols. 4/1 and 4/2: *Das Heilige Römische Reich Deutscher Nation: Nord- und Ostmitteleuropa*. Basel: Schwabe, 2001.

Ijsewijn, Jozef. *Companion to Neo-Latin Studies*. 2 vols. Leuven: Leuven UP, 1990.

Impey, Oliver, and Arthur MacGregor, eds. *The Origins of Museums: The Cabinet of Curiosities in Sixteenth- and Seventeenth-Century Europe*. Oxford: Clarendon, 1985.

Ingen, Ferdinand van, and Cornelia Niekus Moore, eds. *Gebetsliteratur der Frühen Neuzeit als Hausfrömmigkeit: Funktionen und Formen in Deutschland und in den Niederlanden*. Wiesbaden: Harrassowitz, 2001.

Iserloh, Erwin, Josef Glazik, and Hubert Jedin, eds. *Reformation, Katholische Reform und Gegenreformation*. Vol. 4 of *Handbuch der Kirchengeschichte*. Freiburg im Breisgau: Herder, 1985.

Iserloh, Erwin, and Gerhard Müller, eds. *Martin Luther und die politische Welt*. Wiesbaden: Steiner, 1984.

Janota, Johannes. *Vom späten Mittelalter zum Beginn der Neuzeit*. Vol. 3/1 of *Geschichte der deutschen Literatur von den Anfängen bis zum Beginn der Neuzeit*. Tübingen: Niemeyer, 2004.

Jaumann, Herbert, ed. *Die europäische Gelehrtenrepublik im Zeitalter des Konfessionalismus*. Wolfenbütteler Forschungen 96. Wiesbaden: Harrassowitz, 2001.

————, ed. *Handbuch Gelehrtenkultur der Frühen Neuzeit*. Vol. 1: *Bio-bibliographisches Repertorium*. Berlin: de Gruyter, 2004.

Jung, Martin H., and Peter Walter, eds. *Theologen des 16. Jahrhunderts: Humanismus, Reformation, Katholische Erneuerung*. Darmstadt: Wissenschaftliche Buchgesellschaft, 2002.

Kaelbe, Hartmut, and Jürgen Schriewer, eds. *Vergleich und Transfer: Komparatistik in den Sozial-, Geschichts- und Kulturwissenschaften*. Frankfurt am Main: Campus, 2003.

Kemper, Hans Georg. *Deutsche Lyrik der frühen Neuzeit*. Vol. 1: *Epochen- und Gattungsprobleme: Reformationszeit*. Tübingen: Niemeyer, 1987.

Keßler, Eckhard, and Heinrich C. Kuhn, eds. *Germania latina — Latinitas teutonia: Politik, Wissenschaft, humanistische Kultur vom späten Mittelalter bis in unsere Zeit*. 2 vols. Munich: Fink, 2003.

Killy, Walther, ed. *Literatur-Lexikon: Autoren und Werke deutscher Sprache*. 14 vols. Gütersloh: Bertelsmann, 1988–93.

Kittelson, James. "Renaissance and Reformation in Germany: An Agenda for Research." *Journal of Modern History* 58 (1986): 24–140.

Klaiber, Wilbirgis. *Katholische Kontroverstheologen und Reformer des 16. Jahrhunderts: Ein Werkverzeichnis*. Münster: Aschendorff, 1978.

Kleinau, Elke, and Claudia Opitz, eds. *Geschichte der Mädchen- und Frauenbildung*. Vol. 1: *Vom Mittelalter bis zur Aufklärung*. Frankfurt am Main: Campus, 1996.

Klueting, Harm, ed. *Irenik und Antikonfessionalismus im 17. und 18. Jahrhundert*. Hildesheimer Forschungen 2. Hildesheim: Olms, 2003.

Kmetz, John, ed. *Music in the German Renaissance: Sources, Styles, and Contexts*. Cambridge: Cambridge UP, 1994.

Köhler, Hans-Joachim, et al., eds. *Flugschriften des frühen 16. Jahrhunderts auf Microfiche*. Tübingen: Zug, 1978–87.

Kohut, Karl, ed. *Von der Weltkarte zum Kuriositätenkabinett: Amerika im deutschen Humanismus und Barock*. Frankfurt am Main: Vervuert, 1995.

König, Hans-Joachim, Wolfgang Reinhard, and Reinhard Wendt, eds. *Der europäische Beobachter aussereuropäischer Kulturen: Zur Problematik der Wirklichkeitswahrnehmung*. Berlin: Duncker & Humblot, 1989.

Kosellek, Gerhard, ed. "Schlesische Dichterinnen des Barock: Eine Bibliographie." In *Die oberschlesische Literaturlandschaft im 17. Jahrhundert*, 503–19. Bielefeld: Aisthesis, 2001.

Kraye, Jill, ed. *The Cambridge Companion to Renaissance Humanism*. Cambridge: Cambridge UP, 1996.

Kreuzer, Helmut, ed. *Verschriftlichung*. Stuttgart: Metzler, 1997.

Kühlmann, Wilhelm, and Wolfgang Neuber, eds. *Intertextualität in der frühen Neuzeit: Studien zu ihren theoretischen und praktischen Perspektiven*. Frankfurt am Main: Lang, 1994.

Kühlmann, Wilhelm, Robert Seidel, and Hermann Wiegand, eds. *Humanistische Lyrik des 16. Jahrhunderts: Lateinisch und deutsch*. Bibliothek der Frühen Neuzeit 5. Frankfurt am Main: Deutscher Klassiker Verlag, 1997.

Landwehr, John. *German Emblem Books 1531–1888: A Bibliography*. Utrecht: Haentjens Dekker & Gumbert, 1972.

Langer, Andrea, and Georg Michels, eds. *Metropolen und Kulturtransfer im 15. und 16. Jahrhundert: Prag — Krakau — Danzig — Wien*. Forschungen zur Geschichte und Kultur des östlichen Mitteleuropa 12. Stuttgart: Steiner, 2001.

Lauterbach, Iris, Klaus Endemann, and Christoph Luitpold Frommel, eds. *Die Landshuter Stadtresidenz: Architektur und Ausstattung*. Munich: Zentralinstitut für Kunstgeschichte, 1998.

Langewiesche, Dieter, and Georg Schmidt, eds. *Föderative Nation: Deutschlandkonzepte von der Reformation bis zum Ersten Weltkrieg*. Munich: Oldenbourg, 2000.

Lehmann, Hartmut, ed. *Säkularisierung, Dechristianisierung, Rechristianisierung im neuzeitlichen Europa: Bilanz und Perspektiven der Forschung*. Veröffentlichungen des Max Planck Instituts für Geschichte 130. Göttingen: Vandenhoeck & Ruprecht, 1997.

Leimgruber, Nada Boskovska, ed. *Die Frühe Neuzeit in der Geschichtswissenschaft: Forschungstendenzen und Forschungserträge*. Paderborn: Schöningh, 1997.

Mahlmann-Bauer, Barbara, ed. *Scientiae et Artes: Die Vermittlung alten und neuen Wissens in Literatur, Kunst und Musik.* Wiesbaden: Harrassowitz, 2004.

Maltby, William S., ed. *Reformation Europe: A Guide to Research II.* Reformation Guides to Research 3. St. Louis: Center for Reformation Research, 1992.

Marrow, James H., and Alan Shestack, eds. *Hans Baldung Grien — Prints & Drawings.* Exhibition catalogue. National Gallery of Art, Washington, DC. New Haven: Yale University Art Gallery, 1981.

Marshall, Sherrin, ed. *Women in Reformation and Counter-Reformation Europe: Private and Public Worlds.* Bloomington: Indiana UP, 1989.

Martino, Alberto, ed. *Beiträge zur Aufnahme der italienischen und spanischen Literatur in Deutschland im 16. und 17. Jahrhundert.* Chloe 9. Amsterdam: Rodopi, 1990.

Mattheier, Klaus J., Harua Nitta, and Mitsuyo Ono, eds. *Gesellschaft, Kommunikation und Sprache Deutschlands in der frühen Neuzeit.* Munich: Iudicum, 1997.

Mehl, James V., ed. *In Laudem Caroli: Renaissance and Reformation Studies for Charles G. Nauert.* Sixteenth Century Essays and Studies 49. Kirksville, MO: Thomas Jefferson UP, 1998.

Meier, Albert, ed. *Die Literatur des 17. Jahrhunderts.* Hansers Sozialgeschichte der deutschen Literatur 2. Munich: Hanser, 1999.

Meier, Christel, ed. *Enzyklopädie im Wandel vom Hochmittelalter bis zur frühen Neuzeit.* Münstersche Mittelalter-Schriften 78. Munich: Fink, 2002.

Merkel, Kerstin, and Heide Wunder, eds. *Deutsche Frauen der Frühen Neuzeit, Dichterinnen, Malerinnen, Mäzeninnen.* Darmstadt: Wissenschaftliche Buchgesellschaft, 2000.

Moeller, Bernd, ed. *Die frühe Reformation in Deutschland als Umbruch: Wissenschaftliches Symposion des Vereins für Reformationsgeschichte 1996.* Schriften des Vereins für Reformationsgeschichte 9. Gütersloh: Gütersloher Verlagshaus, 1998.

Mommsen, Wolfgang J., ed. *Stadtbürgertum und Adel in der Reformation: Studien zur Sozialgeschichte der Reformation in Deutschland und England.* Stuttgart: Klett-Cotta, 1979.

Muchembled, Robert, and William Monter, eds. *Cultural Exchange in Early Modern Europe.* 4 vols. Cambridge: Cambridge UP, 2007.

Mühleisen, Hans-Otto, and Theo Stammen, eds. *Politische Tugendlehre und Regierungskunst: Studien zum Fürstenspiegel der Frühen Neuzeit.* Tübingen: Niemeyer, 1990.

Müller, Jan-Dirk, ed. *"Aufführung" und "Schrift" in Mittelalter und früher Neuzeit.* Stuttgart: Metzler, 1996.

———, ed. *Romane des 15. und 16. Jahrhunderts: Nach den Erstdrucken mit sämtlichen Holzschnitten.* Frankfurt am Main: Deutscher Klassiker Verlag, 1990.

Müller, Rainer A., ed. *Kloster und Bibliothek: Zur Geschichte des Bibliothekswesens der Augustiner-Chorherren in der Frühen Neuzeit.* Paring: Augustiner-Chorherren-Verlag, 2000.

Münkler, Herfried, Hans Grünberger, and Kathrin Meyer, eds. *Nationenbildung: Die Nationalisierung Europas im Diskurs humanistischer Intellektueller — Italien und Deutschland.* Politische Ideen 8. Berlin: Akademie, 1998.

Neumeister, Sebastian, and Conrad Wiedemann, eds. *Res Publica Litteraria: Die Institutionen der Gelehrsamkeit in der Frühen Neuzeit.* 2 vols. Wolfenbütteler Arbeiten zur Barockforschung 14. Wiesbaden: Harrassowitz, 1987.

Newald, Richard. *Die deutsche Literatur vom Späthumanismus zur Empfindsamkeit 1570–1750.* Vol. 5 of *Geschichte der deutschen Literatur von den Anfängen bis zur Gegenwart.* 4th ed. Munich: Beck, 1963.

Nieden, Hans-Jörg, and Marcel Nieden, eds. *Praxis Pietatis: Beiträge zu Theologie und Frömmigkeit in der Frühen Neuzeit.* Stuttgart: Kohlhammer, 1999.

Oberman, Heiko, ed. *Luther and the Dawn of the Modern Era.* Leiden: E. J. Brill, 1974.

O'Donovan, Oliver, and Joan Lockwood O'Donovan, eds. *From Irenaeus to Grotius: A Sourcebook in Christian Political Thought, 100–1625.* Grand Rapids, MI: Eerdmans, 1999.

Paas, John Roger, ed. *Effigies et Poesis: An Illustrated Catalogue of Printed Portraits with Laudatory Verses by German Baroque Poets.* 2 vols. Wiesbaden: Harrassowitz, 1988.

Packull, Werner O., and Geoffrey Dipple, eds. *Radical Reformation Studies: Essays Presented to James M. Stayer.* Aldershot: Ashgate, 1999.

Paravicini, Werner, ed. *Europäische Reiseberichte des späten Mittelalters: Eine analytische Bibliographie.* Vol. 1 of *Deutsche Reiseberichte.* Frankfurt am Main: Lang, 1994.

Patze, Hans, ed. *Geschichtsschreibung und Geschichtsbewußtsein im späten Mittelalter.* Sigmaringen: Thorbecke, 1987.

Poag, James F., and Claire Baldwin, eds. *The Construction of Authority in German Literature of the Medieval and Early Modern Periods.* Chapel Hill: U of North Carolina P, 2001.

Polenz, Peter von. *Deutsche Sprachgeschichte vom Spätmittelalter bis zur Gegenwart.* 3 vols. 2nd ed. Berlin: de Gruyter, 2000.

Puff, Helmut, and Christopher Wild, eds. *Zwischen den Disziplinen: Perspektiven der Frühneuzeitforschung.* Göttingen: Wallstein, 2003.

Reinhard, Wolfgang, ed. *Humanismus im Bildungswesen des 15. und 16. Jahrhunderts.* Mitteilung der Kommission für Humanismusforschung 12. Weinheim: Acta Humaniora, 1984.

Reinhart, Max, ed. *Infinite Boundaries: Order, Disorder, and Reorder in Early Modern German Culture.* Sixteenth Century Essays & Studies 40. Kirksville, MO: Thomas Jefferson UP, 1998.

Reinhart, Max, and Jeannine Blackwell, eds. *Cultural Contentions in Early Modern Germany.* Special double issue of *Colloquia Germanica* 28, nos. 3–4 (1995).

Reinhart, Max, and James Hardin, eds. *German Writers of the Renaissance and Reformation 1280–1580.* Vol. 179 of *Dictionary of Literary Biography.* Detroit: Gale Research, 1997.

Reynolds, L. D., and N. G. Wilson. *Scribes and Scholars: A Guide to the Transmission of Greek and Latin Literature.* 3rd ed. Oxford: Clarendon, 1991.

Röcke, Werner, and Marina Münkler, eds. *Die Literatur im Übergang vom Mittelalter zur Neuzeit.* Hansers Sozialgeschichte der deutschen Literatur 1. Munich: Hanser, 2004.

Röcke, Werner, and Ursula Schaefer, eds. *Mündlichkeit, Schriftlichkeit, Weltbildwandel: Literarische Kommunikation und Deutungsschemata von Wirklichkeit in der Literatur des Mittelalters und der Frühen Neuzeit.* Tübingen: Narr, 1996.

Rohls, Jans, and Gunther Wenz, eds. *Protestantismus und deutsche Literatur.* Göttingen: Vandenhoeck & Ruprecht, 2004.

Roloff, Hans-Gert, ed. *Die deutsche Literatur: Biographisches und bibliographisches Lexikon.* Reihe 2 (1450–1620). 3 parts. Bern: Lang, 1985–2001.

Ruh, Kurt. *Geschichte der abendländischen Mystik.* 4 vols. Munich: Beck, 1990–99.

Rupprich, Hans. *Vom späten Mittelalter bis zum Barock.* Part 1: *Das ausgehende Mittelalter, Humanismus und Renaissance 1370–1520* (1970). 2nd ed. Ed. Hedwig Heger. Munich: Beck, 1994. Part 2: *Das Zeitalter der Reformation 1520–1570.* Completed by Hedwig Heger. Munich: Beck, 1973.

Sadie, Stanley, ed. *The New Grove Dictionary of Music and Musicians.* 2nd ed. London: Oxford UP, 2001.

Schilling, Heinz, ed. *Die reformierte Konfessionalisierung in Deutschland: Das Problem der "Zweiten Reformation."* Gütersloh: Mohn, 1986.

Schindling, Anton, and Walter Ziegler, eds. *Die Territorien des Reichs im Zeitalter der Reformation und Konfessionalisierung 1500–1650.* Vol. 5: *Der Südwesten.* Münster: Aschendorff, 1993.

Schmale, Wolfgang, ed. *Kulturtransfer: Kulturelle Praxis im 16. Jahrhundert.* Innsbruck: Studien-Verlag, 2003.

Schmidt, Charles B., and Quentin Skinner, eds. *The Cambridge History of Renaissance Philosophy.* Cambridge: Cambridge UP, 1988.

Schmidt, Günter R., ed., *Glaube und Bildung: Texte zum christlichen Humanismus.* Stuttgart: Reclam, 1989.

Schmidt, Paul Gerhard. *Humanismus im deutschen Südwesten: Biographische Profile.* 2nd ed. Stuttgart: Thorbecke, 2000.

Schnell, Rüdiger, ed. *Geschlechterbeziehungen und Textfunktionen — Studien zu Eheschriften der Frühen Neuzeit.* Frühe Neuzeit 40. Tübingen: Niemeyer, 1998.

Schöne, Albrecht, ed. *Stadt, Schule, Universität, Buchwesen und die deutsche Literatur im 17. Jahrhundert.* Munich: Beck, 1976.

———, ed. *Das Zeitalter des Barock: Texte und Zeugnisse.* 2nd ed. Munich: Beck, 1968.

Schreiber, Wilhelm Ludwig. *Handbuch der Holz- und Metallschnitte des XV. Jahrhunderts.* Vol. 3 (1927). Reprint, Stuttgart: Hiersemann, 1969.

Segebrecht, Wulf, ed. *Poetische Grabschriften.* insel taschenbuch 951. Frankfurt am Main: Insel, 1987.

Siebenmann, Gustav, and Hans-Joachim König, eds. *Das Bild Lateinamerikas im deutschen Sprachraum.* Tübingen: Niemeyer, 1992.

Siebenmorgen, Harald, ed. *Leonhard Kern (1588–1662)*. Exhibition catalogue. Hällisch-Fränkisches Museum, Schwäbisch Hall. Sigmaringen: Jan Thorbecke, 1988.

Smet, Rudolf de, ed. *Les humanistes et leur bibliothèque — Humanists and Their Libraries*. Leuven: Peeters, 2002.

Smith, Pamela H., and Paula Findlen, eds. *Merchants and Marvels: Commerce, Science and Art in Early Modern Europe*. London: Routledge, 2002.

Spiewok, Wolfgang, with Danielle Buschinger and Werner Hoffmann. *Geschichte der deutschen Literatur des Spätmittelalters*. 3 vols. Greifswald: Reineke, 1997–99.

Stammen, Wolfgang, and Wolfgang E. J. Weber, eds. *Wissenssicherung, Wissensordnung und Wissensverarbeitung: Das europäische Modell der Enzyklopädien*. Colloquia Augustana 18. Berlin: Akademie, 2004.

Steinhagen, Harald, ed. *Zwischen Gegenreformation und Frühaufklärung: Späthumanismus, Barock*. Vol. 3 of *Deutsche Literatur: Eine Sozialgeschichte*. Reinbek bei Hamburg: Rowohlt, 1985.

Steinhagen, Harald, and Benno von Wiese, eds. *Deutsche Dichter des 17. Jahrhunderts: Ihr Leben und Werk*. Berlin: Schmidt, 1984.

Stolleis, Michael, ed. *Staatsdenker in der Frühen Neuzeit*. Munich: Beck, 1995.

Szarota, Elida Maria. *Das Jesuitendrama im deutschen Sprachgebiet: Eine Periochen-Edition: Texte und Kommentare*. 4 vols. Munich: Fink, 1979–87.

Tatlock, Lynne, ed. *The Graph of Sex and the German Text: Gendered Culture in Early Modern Germany 1500–1700*. Chloe 19. Amsterdam: Rodopi, 1994.

Theologische Realenzyklopädie. 35 vols. Ed. Gerhard Krause and Gerhard Müller. Berlin: de Gruyter, 1977–.

Tiemann, Barbara, ed. *Die Buchkultur im 15. und 16. Jahrhundert*. Part 2. Hamburg: Maximilian-Gesellschaft, 1999.

Ueding, Gert, ed. *Historisches Wörterbuch der Rhetorik*. 6 vols. Tübingen: Niemeyer, 1992–.

Valentin, Jean-Marie, ed. *Gegenreformation und Literatur*. Amsterdam: Rodopi, 1979.

Vierhaus, Rudolf, ed. *Frühe Neuzeit — Frühe Moderne? Forschungen zur Vielschichtigkeit von Übergangsprozessen*. Veröffentlichungen des Max-Planck-Instituts für Geschichte 104. Göttingen: Vandenhoeck & Ruprecht, 1992.

Wagener, Hans, ed. *Absurda comica: Studien zur deutschen Komödie des 16. und 17. Jahrhunderts*. Amsterdam: Rodopi, 1988.

Walter, Axel E., ed. *Regionaler Kulturraum und intellektuelle Kommunikation vom Humanismus bis ins Zeitalter des Internet: Festschrift für Klaus Garber*. Amsterdam: Rodopi, 2005.

Watanabe-O'Kelly, Helen. "The Early Modern Period (1450–1720)." In *The Cambridge History of German Literature*, ed. Watanabe-O'Kelly, 92–147. Cambridge: Cambridge UP, 1997.

Watanabe-O'Kelly, Helen, and Anne Simon. *Festivals and Ceremonies: A Bibliography of Printed Works Relating to Court, Civic and Religious Festivals in Europe 1500–1800*. London: Mansell, 2000.

Weimann, Robert, Werner Lenk, and J. J. Slomka, eds. *Renaissanceliteratur und frühbürgerliche Revolution: Studien zu den sozial- und ideologiegeschichtlichen Grundlagen europäischer Nationalliteraturen.* Berlin: Aufbau, 1976.

Weimar, Klaus, Harald Fricke, and Jan-Dirk Müller, eds. *Reallexikon: Reallexikon der deutschen Literaturwissenschaft.* 3 vols. Berlin: de Gruyter, 1997–2003.

Welzig, Werner, ed. *Katalog deutschsprachiger katholischer Predigtsammlungen.* 2 vols. Vienna: Verlag der österreichischen Akademie der Wissenschaften, 1984, 1987.

————, ed. *Predigten der Barockzeit: Texte und Kommentar.* Vienna: Verlag der österreichischen Akademie der Wissenschaften, 1995.

Westbrock, Franz Joseph, ed. *Der Brief im Zeitalter der Renaissance.* Weinheim: Acta Humaniora, 1983.

Wettengl, Kurt, ed. *Georg Flegel, 1566–1638: Stilleben.* Exhibition catalogue. Historisches Museum, Frankfurt am Main. Stuttgart: Hatje, 1993.

Wiesner, Merry E. *Women in the Sixteenth Century: A Bibliography.* St. Louis: Center for Reformation Research, 1983.

Wiesner-Hanks, Merry, ed. *Convents Confront the Reformation: Catholic and Protestant Nuns in Germany.* Milwaukee: Marquette UP, 1996.

Wilson, Katharina M., ed. *An Encyclopedia of Continental Women Writers.* Vol. 1. New York: Garland, 1991.

Wilson, Katharina M., and Frank J. Warnke, eds. *Women Writers of the Seventeenth Century.* Athens, GA: U of Georgia P, 1989.

Wittmann, Reinhard, ed. *Bücherkataloge als buchgeschichtliche Quellen in der frühen Neuzeit.* Wiesbaden: Harrassowitz, 1985.

Wolf, Herbert, ed. *Luthers Deutsch: Sprachliche Leistung und Wirkung.* Frankfurt am Main: Lang, 1996.

Woods, Jean M., and Maria Fürstenwald. *Schriftstellerinnen, Künstlerinnen und gelehrte Frauen des deutschen Barock: Ein Lexikon.* Stuttgart: Metzler, 1984.

Worstbrock, Franz Josef. *Veröffentlichungen zur Humanismusforschung.* Vol. 1: *Deutsche Antikerezeption 1450–1550.* Boppard am Rhein: Boldt, 1976.

Wunder, Heide, ed. *Dynastie und Herrschaftssicherung in der Frühen Neuzeit: Geschlechter und Geschlecht.* Berlin: Duncker & Humblot, 2002.

Zedelmaier, Helmut, and Martin Mulsow, eds. *Die Praktiken der Gelehrsamkeit in der Frühen Neuzeit.* Tübingen: Niemeyer, 2001.

General, Philosophical, Cultural, Linguistic, and Historical Studies

Admoni, Wladimir. *Historische Syntax des Deutschen.* Tübingen: Niemeyer, 1990.

Aker, Gudrun. *Narrenschiff: Literatur und Kultur in Deutschland an der Wende zur Neuzeit.* Stuttgarter Arbeiten zur Germanistik 216. Stuttgart: Heinz, 1990.

Asheim, Ivar. *Glaube und Erziehung bei Luther: Ein Beitrag zur Geschichte des Verhältnisses von Theologie und Pädagogik.* Heidelberg: Quelle & Meyer, 1961.

Axmacher, Elke. *Praxis Evangeliorum: Theologie und Frömmigkeit bei Martin Moller (1574–1606)*. Göttingen: Vandenhoeck & Ruprecht, 1989.

Bach, Heinrich. "Wo liegt die entscheidende Wirkung der 'Luthersprache' in der Entwicklung der deutschen Standardsprache?" (1984). Reprint in Wolf, ed., *Luthers Deutsch*, 126–35.

Barner, Wilfried. "Über das Negieren von Tradition: Zur Typologie literaturprogrammatischer Epochenwenden in Deutschland." In *Epochenschwelle und Epochenbewußtsein*, ed. Reinhart Herzog and Reinhart Koselleck, 3–51. Poetik und Hermeneutik 12. Munich: Fink, 1987.

Baron, Hans. *The Crisis of the Early Italian Renaissance: Civic Humanism and Republican Liberty in an Age of Classicism and Tyranny* (1955). Revised edition, Princeton: Princeton UP, 1966.

Bauer, Volker. *Die höfische Gesellschaft in Deutschland von der Mitte des 17. bis zum Ausgang des 18. Jahrhunderts*. Tübingen: Niemeyer, 1993.

Becker-Cantarino, Barbara. *Der lange Weg zur Mündigkeit: Frau und Literatur (1500–1800)*. Stuttgart: Metzler, 1987.

Bentley, Jerry H. *Humanists and Holy Writ: New Testament Scholarship in the Renaissance*. Princeton: Princeton UP, 1983.

Bernstein, Eckhard. *Ulrich von Hutten*. Reinbek bei Hamburg: Rowohlt, 1988.

Betzinger, Rudolf, and Gerhard Kettmann. "Zu Luthers Stellung im Sprachschaffen seiner Zeit" (1983). Reprint in Wolf, ed., *Luthers Deutsch*, 191–214.

Bireley, Robert. *The Refashioning of Catholicism, 1450–1700*. Washington, DC: Catholic U of America P, 1999.

Biskup, Marian, and Gerard Labuda. *Die Geschichte des deutschen Ordens in Preußen: Wirtschaft — Gesellschaft — Staat — Ideologie*. Osnabrück: Fibre, 2000.

Bleeck, Klaus, and Jörn Garber. "Nobilitas: Standes- und Privilegienlegitimation in deutschen Adelstheorien des 16. und 17. Jahrhunderts." In Blühm, J. Garber, and K. Garber, eds., *Hof, Staat und Gesellschaft*, 49–115.

Blickle, Peter. *Der Bauernkrieg: Die Revolution des gemeinen Mannes*. Munich: Beck, 1998.

———. "The Popular Reformation." In Brady, Oberman, and Tracy, eds., *Handbook of European History, 1400–1600*, 2:161–92.

———. *The Revolution of 1525: The German Peasants' War from a New Perspective*. Trans. Thomas A. Brady Jr. and H. C. Erik Midelfort. Baltimore: Johns Hopkins UP, 1981.

Blumenberg, Hans. *Säkularisierung und Selbstbehauptung*. Frankfurt am Main: Suhrkamp, 1974.

Bogner, Ralf Georg. *Die Bezähmung der Zunge: Literatur und Disziplinierung der Alltagskommunikation in der frühen Neuzeit*. Tübingen: Niemeyer, 1997.

Böhme, Günther. *Bildungsgeschichte des europäischen Humanismus*. Darmstadt: Wissenschaftliche Buchgesellschaft, 1986.

Bonfil, Robert. "Aliens Within: The Jews and Antijudaism." In Brady, Oberman, and Tracy, eds., *Handbook of European History, 1400–1600*, 1:263–302.

Borchardt, Frank L. *German Antiquity in Renaissance Myth*. Baltimore: Johns Hopkins UP, 1971.

Brady, Thomas A. Jr. *Protestant Politics: Jacob Sturm (1489–1553) and the German Reformation*. Atlantic Highlands, NJ: Humanities Press International, 1995.

———. *The Protestant Reformation in German History*. Occasional Paper No. 22. Washington, DC: German Historical Institute, 1997.

———. *Turning Swiss: Cities and Empire 1450–1550*. Cambridge: Cambridge UP, 1985.

Braudel, Fernand. *Civilization and Capitalism: 15th–18th Century*. 3 vols. Trans. Siân Reynolds. New York: Harper & Row, 1982–84.

Brecht, Martin. *Luther als Schriftsteller: Zeugnisse seines dichterischen Gestaltens*. Stuttgart: Calwer, 1990.

———. "Luther's Reformation." In Brady, Oberman, and Tracy, eds., *Handbook of European History, 1400–1600*, 2:129–60.

Breuer, Dieter. *Oberdeutsche Literatur 1565–1650: Deutsche Literaturgeschichte und Territorialgeschichte in frühabsolutistischer Zeit*. Munich: Beck, 1979.

Burckhardt, Johannes. *Das Reformationsjahrhundert: Deutsche Geschichte zwischen Medienrevolution und Institutionenbildung 1517–1617*. Stuttgart: Kohlhammer, 2002.

Burdach, Konrad. *Reformation, Renaissance, Humanismus: Zwei Abhandlungen über die Grundlage moderner Bildung und Sprachkunst*. Darmstadt: Wissenschaftliche Buchgesellschaft, 1978.

Burger, Heinz Otto. *Renaissance, Humanismus, Reformation: Deutsche Literatur im europäischen Kontext*. Bad Homburg: Gehlen, 1969.

Buzás, Ladislaus. *Deutsche Bibliotheksgeschichte der Neuzeit (1500–1800)*. Wiesbaden: Reichert, 1976.

Chrisman, Miriam U. *Strasbourg and the Reform: A Study in the Process of Change*. New Haven: Yale UP, 1967.

Conrads, Norbert. *Ritterakademien der Frühen Neuzeit: Bildung als Standesprivileg im 16. und 17. Jahrhundert*. Göttingen: Vandenhoeck & Ruprecht, 1982.

Curtius, Ernst Robert. *European Literature and the Latin Middle Ages* (1948). Trans. Willard R. Trask (1953). 7th ed. Princeton: Princeton UP, 1990.

Czubatynski, Uwe. *Armaria Ecclesiae: Studien zur Geschichte des kirchlichen Buchwesens*. Neustadt an der Aisch: Degener & Co., 1998.

Davidson, N. S. *The Counter-Reformation*. Oxford: Blackwell, 1987.

Dixon, C. Scott. *The Reformation and Rural Society: The Parishes of Brandenburg-Ansbach-Kulmbach, 1528–1603*. Cambridge: Cambridge UP, 1996.

Dülmen, Richard van. *Entstehung des frühneuzeitlichen Europa 1550–1648*. Fischer Weltgeschichte 24. Frankfurt am Main: Fischer, 1982.

————. *Kultur und Alltag in der Frühen Neuzeit.* 3 vols. Munich: Beck, 1990–94.

————. *Reformation als Revolution: soziale Bewegung und religiöser Radikalismus in der deutschen Reformation.* Munich: Deutscher Taschenbuch Verlag, 1977.

Edwards, Mark U. Jr. *Printing, Propaganda, and Martin Luther.* Berkeley: U of California P, 1994.

Ehrenpreis, Stefan, and Ute Lotz-Heumann. *Reformation und konfessionelles Zeitalter: Kontroversen um die Geschichte.* Darmstadt: Wissenschaftliche Buchgesellschaft, 2002.

Eisenstein, Elizabeth. *The Printing Press as an Agent of Social Change: Communications and Cultural Transformations in Early Modern Europe.* Vol. 2. Cambridge: Cambridge UP, 1979.

Engelsing, Rolf. *Der Bürger als Leser: Lesergeschichte in Deutschland 1500–1800.* Stuttgart: Metzler, 1994.

Evans, R. J. W. *Rudolf II and His World: A Study in Intellectual History 1576–1612.* Oxford: Oxford UP, 1973.

Febvre, Lucien. *The Problem of Unbelief in the Sixteenth Century: The Religion of Rabelais.* Trans. Beatrice Gottlieb. Cambridge: Harvard UP, 1982.

Friedell, Egon. *Kulturgeschichte der Neuzeit.* Vol. 1: *Die Krisis der europäischen Seele von der schwarzen Pest bis zum Ersten Weltkrieg.* 14th ed. dtv 30061. Munich: Deutscher Taschenbuch Verlag, 2001.

Füssel, Stephan. *Gutenberg und seine Wirkung.* Frankfurt am Main: Insel, 1999.

Garber, Jörn: *Spätabsolutismus und bürgerliche Gesellschaft: Studien zur deutschen Staats- und Gesellschaftstheorie im Übergang zur Moderne.* Frankfurt am Main: Keip, 1992.

Garber, Klaus. *Imperiled Heritage: Tradition, History, and Utopia in Early Modern German Literature: Selected Essays.* Ed. Max Reinhart. Studies in European Cultural Transition 5. Aldershot: Ashgate, 2000.

————. *Literatur und Kultur im Europa der Frühen Neuzeit.* Munich: Fink, 2006.

————. "Zur Statuskonkurrenz von Adel und gelehrtem Bürgertum im theoretis-chen Schrifttum des 17. Jahrhunderts." In Blühm, J. Garber, and K. Garber, et al., eds., *Hof, Staat und Gesellschaft,* 115–43.

Gardt, Andreas, ed. *Nation und Sprache: Die Diskussion ihres Verhältnisses in Geschichte und Gegenwart.* Berlin: de Gruyter, 2000.

Geldner, Ferdinand. *Inkunabelkunde: Eine Einführung in die Welt des frühesten Buchdrucks.* Vol. 5 of *Elemente des Buch- und Bibliothekwesens.* Wiesbaden: Reichert, 1978.

Giesecke, Michael. *Der Buchdruck der frühen Neuzeit.* Frankfurt am Main: Suhrkamp, 1991.

Gillespie, Gerald. "Renaissance, Mannerism, Baroque." In Hoffmeister, *German Baroque Literature,* 3–24.

Gleason, Elisabeth G. "Catholic Reformation, Counterreformation and Papal Reform in the Sixteenth Century." In Brady, Oberman, and Tracy, eds., *Handbook of European History, 1400–1600,* 2:317–45.

Goertz, Hans Jürgen. *Antiklerikalismus und Reformation: Sozialgeschichtliche Untersuchungen.* Göttingen: Vandenhoeck & Ruprecht, 1995.

Göllner, Carl. *Die Türkenfrage in der öffentlichen Meinung Europas im 16. Jahrhundert.* Bucharest: Acad. Republicii Socialiste România, 1978.

Götz, Ursula. *Die Anfänge der Grammatikschreibung des Deutschen in den Formularbüchern des frühen 16. Jahrhunderts.* Heidelberg: Winter, 1992.

Gow, Andrew Colin. *The Red Jews: Antisemitism in an Apocalyptic Age 1200–1600.* Leiden: Brill, 1995.

Grafton, Anthony. *Commerce with the Classics: Ancient Books and Renaissance Readers.* Ann Arbor: U of Michigan P, 1997.

———. *Defenders of the Text: The Traditions of Scholarship in an Age of Science, 1450–1800.* Cambridge: Cambridge UP, 1991.

Grane, Leif. *Martinus Noster: Luther in the German Reform Movement 1518–1521.* Mainz: von Zabern, 1994.

Grimm, Günter E. *Literatur und Gelehrtentum in Deutschland: Untersuchungen zum Wandel ihres Verhältnisses vom Humanismus bis zur Frühaufklärung.* Studien zur deutschen Literatur 75. Tübingen: Niemeyer, 1983.

Grossmann, Maria S. *Humanism in Wittenberg, 1485–1517.* Nieuwkoop: de Graaf, 1975.

Guggisberg, Hans R. *Basel in the Sixteenth Century: Aspects of the City Republic Before, During, and After the Reformation.* St. Louis: Center for Reformation Research, 1982.

Haag, Norbert. *Predigt und Gesellschaft: Die Lutherische Orthodoxie in Ulm 1640–1740.* Mainz: von Zabern, 1992.

Hagenmeier, Monika. *Predigt und Policey: Der gesellschaftspolitische Diskurs zwischen Kirche und Obrigkeit in Ulm 1624–1639.* Baden-Baden: Nomos, 1989.

Hall, Basil. *Humanists and Protestants: 1500–1900.* Edinburgh: T&T Clark, 1990.

Halporn, Barbara. *Johann Amerbach's Correspondence: Early Printing in Its Social Context.* Ann Arbor: U of Michigan P, 2000.

Harrington, Joel F. *Reordering Marriage and Society in Reformation Germany.* Cambridge: Cambridge UP, 1995.

Hartweg, Frédéric. "Die Rolle des Buchdrucks für die frühneuhochdeutsche Sprachgeschichte." In Besch, Reichmann, and Sonderegger, eds., *Sprachgeschichte,* 2:1415–34.

Herkenhoff, Michael. *Die Darstellung aussereuropäischer Welten in Drucken deutscher Offizinen des 15. Jahrhunderts.* Berlin: Akademie, 1996.

Holtz, Sabine. *Theologie und Alltag: Lehre und Leben in den Predigten der Tübinger Theologen 1550–1750.* Tübingen: Mohr, 1993.

Hsia, R. Po-Chia. *The German People and the Reformation.* Ithaca: Cornell UP, 1988.

Hsia, R. Po-Chia, and Hartmut Lehmann. *In and Out of the Ghetto: Jewish-Gentile Relations in Late Medieval and Early Modern Germany.* Cambridge: Cambridge UP, 1995.

Huber, Wolfgang. *Kulturpatriotismus und Sprachbewußtsein: Studien zur deutschen Philologie des 17. Jahrhunderts*. Frankfurt am Main: Lang, 1984.

Hundt, Markus. *Spracharbeit im 17. Jahrhundert: Studien zu Georg Philipp Harsdörffer, Justus Georg Schottelius und Christian Gueintz*. Berlin: de Gruyter, 2000.

Huppert, George. *After the Black Death: A Social History of Early Modern Europe*. Bloomington: Indiana UP, 1986.

Johns, Adrian. *The Nature of the Book: Print and Knowledge in the Making*. Chicago: U of Chicago P, 1998.

Jones, William Jervis. *Sprachhelden und Sprachverderber: Dokumente zur Erforschung des Fremdwortpurismus im Deutschen (1478–1750)*. Berlin: de Gruyter, 1995.

Kafadar, Cemal. "The Ottomans and Europe." In Brady, Oberman, and Tracey, eds., *Handbook of European History, 1400–1600*, 1:589–636.

Kaufmann, Thomas. *Universität und lutherische Konfessionalisierung*. Gütersloh: Gütersloher Verlagshaus, 1997.

Kaufmann, Thomas DaCosta. *The Mastery of Nature: Aspects of Art, Science and Humanism in the Renaissance*. Princeton: Princeton UP, 1993.

Keller, Hildegard Elisabeth. *My Secret Is Mine: Studies on Religion and Eros in the German Middle Ages*. Louvain: Peeters, 2000.

Kelly, Donald R. *History and the Disciplines: The Reclassification of Knowledge in Early Modern Europe*. Rochester, NY: U of Rochester P, 1997.

———. "*Tacitus Noster*: The *Germania* in the Renaissance and Reformation." In *Tacitus and the Tacitean Tradition*, ed. T. J. Luce and A. J. Woodman, 152–67. Princeton: Princeton UP, 1993.

Kleinschmidt, Erich. *Stadt und Literatur in der frühen Neuzeit: Voraussetzungen und Entfaltung im südwestdeutschen, elsässischen und schweizerischen Städteraum*. Cologne: Böhlau, 1982.

Knox, Dilwyn. "Erasmus' *De Civilitate* and the Religious Origins of Civility in Protestant Europe." *Archiv für Reformationsgeschichte* 86 (1995): 7–55.

Koselleck, Reinhart. *Critique and Crisis: Enlightenment and the Pathogenesis of Modern Society*. Oxford: Berg, 1988.

Krapf, Ludwig. *Germanenmythus und Reichsidee: Frühhumanistische Rezeptionsweisen der taciteischen 'Germania.'* Tübingen: Niemeyer, 1979.

Kruse, Jens-Martin. *Universitätstheologie und Kirchenreform: Die Anfänge der Reformation in Wittenberg 1516–1522*. Veröffentlichungen des Instituts für Europäische Geschichte Mainz 187. Mainz: von Zabern, 2002.

Kühlmann, Wilhelm. *Gelehrtenrepublik und Fürstenstaat: Entwicklung und Kritik des deutschen Späthumanismus in der Literatur des Barockzeitalters*. Studien und Texte zur Sozialgeschichte der Literatur 3. Tübingen: Niemeyer, 1982.

———. "Nationalliteratur und Latinität: Zum Problem der Zweisprachigkeit in der frühneuzeitlichen Literaturbewegung Deutschlands." In Garber, ed., *Nation und Literatur*, 164–206.

Kuhn, Thomas S. *The Copernican Revolution: Planetary Astronomy in the Development of Western Thought.* Cambridge: Harvard UP, 1985.

Kusukawa, Sachiko. *The Transformation of Natural Philosophy: The Case of Philip Melanchthon.* Cambridge: Cambridge UP, 1995.

Leube, Hans. *Die Reformideen in der deutschen lutherischen Kirche zur Zeit der Orthodoxie.* Leipzig: Döffling & Franke, 1924.

Lohse, Bernhard. *Der Durchbruch der reformatorischen Erkenntnis bei Luther.* Stuttgart: Steiner, 1998.

Ludwig, Walther. "De linguae Latinae in Germania fatis: Jacob Burckhardt und der neuzeitliche Gebrauch der lateinischen Sprache." *Neulateinisches Jahrbuch* 5 (2003): 185–218.

MacCulloch, Diarmaid. *The Reformation: A History.* New York: Viking, 2004.

Martin, Alfred von. *Sociology of the Renaissance.* Trans. W. L. Luetkens. Introduction by Wallace K. Ferguson. New York: Harper & Row, 1963.

McGrath, Alister. *The Intellectual Origins of the European Reformation.* Oxford: Blackwell, 1987.

Moser, Hans. "Die Kanzleisprachen." In Besch, Reichmann, and Sonderegger, eds., *Sprachgeschichte*, 1398–1407.

Moser, Hugo. "Probleme der Periodisierung des Deutschen." In *Periodisierung: Die zeitliche Gliederung der deutschen Sprachgeschichte*, ed. Thorsten Roelcke, 111–23. Frankfurt am Main: Lang, 2001.

Müller, Jan-Dirk. *Gedechtnus: Literatur und Hofgesellschaft um Maximilian I.* Forschungen zur Geschichte der älteren deutschen Literatur 2. Munich: Fink, 1982.

———. "Literaturgeschichte/Literaturgeschichtsschreibung." In *Erkenntnis der Literatur: Theorie, Konzepte, Methoden der Literaturwissenschaft*, ed. Dietrich Harth and Peter Gebhardt, 195–227. Stuttgart: Metzler, 1982.

———. "Zum Verhältnis von Reformation und Renaissance in der deutschen Literatur des 16. Jahrhunderts." In Buck, ed., *Renaissance — Reformation*, 227–53.

Münch, Paul. *Lebensformen in der Frühen Neuzeit.* Frankfurt am Main: Propyläen, 1992.

Neddermeyer, Uwe. *Von der Handschrift zum gedruckten Buch: Schriftlichkeit und Leseinteresse im Mittelalter und in der frühen Neuzeit: Quantitative und qualitative Aspekte.* Wiesbaden: Harrassowitz, 1998.

Noe, Alfred. *Der Einfluß des italienischen Humanismus auf die deutsche Literatur vor 1600.* Tübingen: Niemeyer, 1993.

Oberman, Heiko. *The Dawn of the Reformation: Essays in Late Medieval and Early Reformation Thought.* Grand Rapids, MI: Eerdmans, 1992.

Oestreich, Gerhard. *Strukturprobleme der frühen Neuzeit: Ausgewählte Aufsätze.* Ed. Brigitta Oestreich. Berlin: Duncker & Humblot, 1980.

O'Malley, John W. *Trent and All That: Renaming Catholicism in the Early Modern Era.* Cambridge: Harvard UP, 2000.

Overfield, James H. *Humanism and Scholasticism in Late Medieval Germany.* Princeton: Princeton UP, 1984.

Ozment, Steven. *The Age of Reform 1250–1550: An Intellectual and Religious History of Late Medieval and Reformation Europe.* New Haven: Yale UP, 1980.

———. *Flesh and Spirit: Private Life in Early Modern Germany.* New York: Viking, 1999.

Parker, Geoffrey. *The Thirty Years' War.* London: Routledge, 1984.

Pelikan, Jaroslav. *Reformation of Church and Dogma (1300–1700).* Chicago: U of Chicago P, 1984.

Peters, Ursula. *Literatur in der Stadt: Studien zu den sozialen Voraussetzungen und kulturellen Organisationsformen städtischer Literatur im 13. und 14. Jahrhundert.* Tübingen: Niemeyer, 1983.

Philipp, Gerhard. *Einführung ins Frühneuhochdeutsche: Sprachgeschichte — Grammatik — Texte.* Heidelberg: Quelle & Meyer, 1980.

Press, Volker. "The Habsburg Lands: the Holy Roman Empire." In Brady, Oberman, and Tracy, eds., *Handbook of European History, 1400–1600,* 1:437–66.

Rabb, Theodore K. *Renaissance Lives: Portraits of an Age.* New York: Basic Books, 2000.

Reinhard, Wolfgang. *Probleme deutscher Geschichte 1495–1806: Reichsreform und Reformation 1495–1555.* Gebhardt Handbuch deutscher Geschichte 9. Stuttgart: Kohlhammer, 2001.

———. "Zwang zur Konfessionalisierung? Prologomena zu einer Theorie des konfessionellen Zeitalters." *Zeitschrift für historische Forschung* 10 (1983): 268–77.

Reinitzer, Heimo. *Biblia deutsch: Luthers Bibelübersetzung und ihre Tradition.* Exhibition catalogue. Wolfenbüttel: Herzog August Bibliothek, 1983.

Reiss, Timothy J. *Knowledge, Discovery and Imagination in Early Modern Europe: The Rise of Aesthetic Rationalism.* Cambridge Studies in Renaissance Literature and Culture 15. Cambridge: Cambridge UP, 1997.

Rice, Eugene F. Jr., and Anthony Grafton. *The Foundations of Early Modern Europe, 1460–1559.* 2nd ed. New York: Norton, 1994.

Robisheaux, Thomas W. "The World of the Village." In Brady, Oberman, and Tracy, eds., *Handbook of European History, 1400–1600,* 1:79–112.

Röcke, Werner. "Das Ende der Geschichte: Utopie und Anti-Utopie in der Literatur des 16. Jahrhunderts." *Paragrana: Internationale Zeitschrift für Historische Anthropologie* 7 (1992): 122–39.

———. "Literaturgeschichte-Mentalitätsgeschichte." In *Literaturwissenschaft: Ein Grundkurs,* 7th ed., ed. Helmut Brackert and Jörn Stückrath, 639–49. Reinbek bei Hamburg: Rowohlt, 2001.

Rublack, Hans-Christoph. *Die Lutherische Konfessionalisierung in Deutschland.* Schriften des Vereins für Reformationsgeschichte 197. Gütersloh: Gütersloher Verlagshaus, 1992.

———. "New Patterns of Christian Life." In Brady, Oberman, and Tracy, eds., *Handbook of European History, 1400–1600,* 2:585–606.

Rublack, Ulinka. *Die Reformation in Europa*. Frankfurt am Main: Fischer, 2003.

Rummel, Erika. *The Confessionalization of Humanism in Reformation Germany*. Oxford: Oxford UP, 2000.

———. *The Humanist-Scholastic Debate in the Renaissance and Reformation*. Cambridge: Harvard UP, 1995.

———. "Voices of Reform from Hus to Erasmus." In Brady, Oberman, and Tracy, eds., *Handbook of European History, 1400–1600*, 2:61–92.

Schaeffer, Peter. "Baroque Philology: The Position of German in the European Family of Languages." In Hoffmeister, *German Baroque Literature*, 72–84.

Schilling, Heinz. *Aufbruch und Krise: Deutschland 1517–1648*. Berlin: Siedler, 1998.

———. "Confessional Europe." In Brady, Oberman, and Tracy, eds., *Handbook of European History, 1400–1600*, 2:641–81.

———. "Die Konfessionalisierung im Reich: Religiöser und gesellschaftlicher Wandel in Deutschland zwischen 1555 und 1620." *Historische Zeitschrift* 246 (1988): 1–45.

Schorn-Schütte, Luise. *Evangelische Geistlichkeit in der Frühneuzeit: Deren Anteil an der Entfaltung frühmoderner Staatlichkeit und Gesellschaft*. Quellen und Forschungen zur Reformationsgeschichte 62. Gütersloh: Gütersloher Verlagshaus, 1996.

Schöttler, Peter. "Mentalitäten, Ideologien, Diskurse: Zur sozialgeschichtlichen Thematisierung der 'dritten Ebene.'" In *Alltagsgeschichte: Zur Rekonstruktion historischer Erfahrungen und Lebensweisen*, ed. Alf Lüdtke, 85–136. Frankfurt am Main: Campus, 1989.

Scribner, Robert W. "Elements of Popular Belief." In Brady, Oberman, and Tracy, eds., *Handbook of European History, 1400–1600*, 1:231–62.

———. *For the Sake of Simple Folk: Popular Propaganda for the German Reformation*. Cambridge: Cambridge UP, 1981.

Scribner, Robert W., and C. Scott Dixon. *The German Reformation*. 2nd ed. Basingstoke: Palgrave Macmillan, 2003.

Siraisi, Nancy G. *Medieval and Early Renaissance Medicine: An Introduction to Knowledge and Practice*. Chicago: U of Chicago P, 1990.

Skalweit, Stephan. *Der Beginn der Neuzeit*. Erträge der Forschung 178. Darmstadt: Wissenschaftliche Buchgesellschaft, 1982.

Skrine, Peter. *The Baroque: Literature and Culture in Seventeenth-Century Europe*. London: Methuen, 1978.

Sottili, Agostino. "Ehemalige Studenten italienischer Renaissance-Universitäten: ihre Karrieren und soziale Rollen." In *Gelehrte im Reich: Zur Sozial- und Wirkungsgeschichte akademischer Eliten des 14. bis 16. Jahrhunderts*, Beiheft 18 of *Zeitschrift für historische Forschung*, ed. Rainer Christoph Schwinges, 41–74. Berlin: Duncker & Humblot, 1996.

Spitz, Lewis W. *The Religious Renaissance of the German Humanists*. Cambridge: Harvard UP, 1963.

Stayer, James M. *The German Peasants' War and Anabaptist Community of Goods*. Montreal: McGill-Queen's UP, 1991.

―――. "The Radical Reformation." In Brady, Oberman, and Tracy, eds., *Handbook of European History, 1400–1600*, 2:249–82.

Steiger, Johann Anselm. *Melancholie, Diätetik und Trost: Konzepte der Melancholie-Therapie im 16. und 17. Jahrhundert*. Heidelberg: Manutius, 1996.

Stolleis, Michael. "Public Law and Patriotism in the Holy Roman Empire." In Reinhart, ed., *Infinite Boundaries*, 11–33.

―――. *Staat und Staatsräson in der frühen Neuzeit: Studien zur Geschichte des öffentlichen Rechts*. suhrkamp taschenbuch wissenschaft 878. Frankfurt am Main: Suhrkamp, 1990.

Strauss, Gerald. *Nuremberg in the Sixteenth Century*. New York: Wiley, 1966.

―――. *Sixteenth-Century Germany: Its Topography and Topographers*. Madison: U of Wisconsin P, 1959.

Sträter, Udo. *Meditation und Kirchenreform in der lutherischen Kirche des 17. Jahrhunderts*. Tübingen: Mohr, 1995.

Toch, Michael. *Die Juden im mittelalterlichen Reich*. Munich: Oldenbourg, 1998.

Van Engen, John. "The Church in the Fifteenth Century." In Brady, Oberman, and Tracy, eds., *Handbook of European History, 1400–1600*, 1:305–30.

Vec, Miloš. *Zeremoniellwissenschaft im Fürstenstaat: Studien zur juristischen und politischen Theorie absolutistischer Herrschaftsrepräsentation*. Frankfurt am Main: Klostermann, 1998.

Vierhaus, Rudolf. *Germany in the Age of Absolutism*. Trans. Jonathan B. Knudsen. Cambridge: Cambridge UP, 1988.

Walter, Peter. *Theologie aus dem Geist der Rhetorik: Zur Schriftauslegung des Erasmus von Rotterdam*. Mainz: Matthias Grünewald, 1991.

Wels, Volkhard. *Triviale Künste: Die humanistische Reform der grammatischen, dialektischen und rhetorischen Ausbildung an der Wende zum 16. Jahrhundert*. Studium Litterarum 1. Berlin: Weidler, 2000.

Wiesinger, Peter. "Die sprachlichen Verhältnisse und der Weg zur allgemeinen deutschen Schriftsprache in Österreich im 18. und frühen 19. Jahrhundert." In Gardt, Mattheier, and Reichmann, eds., *Sprachgeschichte des Neuhochdeutschen*, 319–67.

Williams, George Hunston. *The Radical Reformation*. 3rd ed. Kirksville, MO: Sixteenth Century Journal Publishers, 1992.

Witt, Ronald G. "The Humanist Movement." In Brady, Oberman, and Tracy, eds., *Handbook of European History, 1400–1600*, 2:93–125.

Wittmann, Reinhard. *Geschichte des deutschen Buchhandels*. 2nd ed. Munich: Beck, 1990.

Wodianka, Stephanie. *Betrachtungen des Todes: Formen und Funktionen der 'meditatio mortis' in der europäischen Literatur*. Tübingen: Niemeyer, 2004.

Zedelmaier, Helmut. *Bibliotheca universalis und Bibliotheca selecta: Das Problem der Ordnung des gelehrten Wissens in der frühen Neuzeit*. Cologne: Böhlau, 1992.

Zeller, Winfried. *Theologie und Frömmigkeit: Gesammelte Aufsätze.* Ed. Bernd Jaspert. Marburg: Elwert, 1978.

Genres, Schools, Periods, Gender, Music, and the Visual Arts

Adam, Wolfgang. *Poetische und kritische Wälder: Untersuchungen zu Geschichte und Formen des Schreibens 'bei Gelegenheit.'* Heidelberg: Winter, 1988.

Adorno, Theodor. "Der mißbrauchte Barock." In *Ohne Leitbild: Parva aesthetica,* 133–57. Frankfurt am Main: Suhrkamp, 1967.

Aikin, Judith P. *German Baroque Drama.* Boston: Twayne, 1982.

———. *A Language for German Opera: The Development of Forms and Formulas for Recitative and Aria in Seventeenth-Century German Libretti.* Wiesbaden: Harrassowitz, 2002.

Alewyn, Richard. "Gestalt als Gehalt: Der Roman des Barock." In *Probleme und Gestalten,* 117–32. Frankfurt am Main: Suhrkamp, 1982.

———. *Vorbarocker Klassizismus und griechische Tragödie: Analyse der Antigone-Übersetzung des Martin Opitz* (1926). Reprint, Reihe Libelli 79. Darmstadt: Wissenschaftliche Buchgesellschaft, 1962.

Alexander, Robert J. *Das deutsche Barockdrama.* Sammlung Metzler 209. Stuttgart: Metzler, 1984.

Angenendt, Arno. *Geschichte der Religiosität im Mittelalter.* 2nd ed. Darmstadt: Wissenschaftliche Buchgesellschaft, 2000.

Angress, Ruth. *The Early German Epigram: A Study in Baroque Poetry.* Lexington: UP of Kentucky, 1971.

Bainton, Roland H. *Women of the Reformation in Germany and Italy.* Minneapolis: Augsburg, 1971.

Barner, Wilfried. *Barockrhetorik: Untersuchungen zu ihren geschichtlichen Grundlagen.* Tübingen: Niemeyer, 1970.

Baron, Frank. "Plautus und die deutschen Frühhumanisten." In *Studia Humanitatis,* ed. Eginhard Hora and Eckhard Keßler, 89–101. Munich: Fink, 1973.

Bartel, Dietrich. *Musica poetica: Musical-Rhetorical Figures in German Baroque Music.* Lincoln: U of Nebraska P, 1997.

Bauer, Barbara. "Multimediales Theater: Ansätze einer Poetik der Synästhesie bei den Jesuiten." In *Renaissance-Poetik,* ed. Heinrich Plett, 197–238. Berlin: de Gruyter, 1994.

Bauer, Matthias. *Der Schelmenroman.* Sammlung Metzler 282. Stuttgart: Metzler, 1994.

Baxandall, Michael. *The Limewood Sculptors of Renaissance Germany.* New Haven: Yale UP, 1980.

Beetz, Manfred. *Frühmoderne Höflichkeit: Komplimentierkunst und Gesellschaftsrituale im altdeutschen Sprachraum.* Germanistische Abhandlungen 67. Stuttgart: Metzler, 1990.

Béhar, Pierre. "Drama in the Empire." Trans. Helen Watanable-O'Kelly. In Béhar and Watanabe-O'Kelly, eds., *Spectacvlvm Europævm*, 257–87.

Benjamin, Walter. *Ursprung des deutschen Trauerspiels*. Frankfurt am Main: Suhrkamp, 1963.

Bepler, Jill, comp. *Barocke Sammellust: Die Bibliothek und Kunstkammer des Herzogs Ferdinand Albrecht zu Braunschweig und Lüneburg (1636–1687)*. Exhibition catalogue. Weinheim: VCH Acta Humaniora, 1988.

Bepler, Jill. "Kabinettausstellung: Gebetsliteratur der Frühen Neuzeit." In van Ingen and Moore, eds., *Gebetsliteratur der Frühen Neuzeit*, 291–318.

Bernstein, Eckhard. *German Humanism*. Boston: Twayne, 1983.

———. "Humanistische Intelligenz und kirchliche Reformen." In Röcke and Münkler, eds., *Die Literatur im Übergang vom Mittelalter zur Neuzeit*, 166–97.

———. "Humanistische Standeskultur." In Röcke and Münkler, eds., *Die Literatur im Übergang vom Mittelalter zur Neuzeit*, 97–129.

———. *Die Literatur des deutschen Frühhumanismus*. Sammlung Metzler 168. Stuttgart: Metzler, 1978.

Berschin, Walter. "Neulateinische Utopien im Alten Reich (1555–1741)." In Keßler and Kuhn, eds., *Germania latina — Latinitas teutonia*, 693–704.

Bevers, Holm. *Meister E. S.: Ein oberrheinischer Kupferstecher der Spätgotik*. Exhibition catalogue. Staatliche Graphische Sammlung, Munich, 1986.

Blickle, Peter. *Communal Reformation: The Quest for Salvation in Sixteenth-Century Germany*. Trans. Thomas Dunlap. Atlantic Highlands, NJ: Humanities Press International, 1992.

Bloh, Ute von. *Die illustrierten Historienbibeln: Text und Bild in Prolog und Schöpfungsgeschichte der deutschsprachigen Historienbibeln des Spätmittelalters*. Frankfurt am Main: Lang, 1991–92.

Blume, Friedrich. *Protestant Church Music: A History* (1931). New York: Norton, 1974.

Bouwsma, William J. *The Waning of the Renaissance, 1550–1640*. New Haven: Yale UP, 2000.

Bradshaw, Brandon. "Transalpine Humanism." In *The Cambridge History of Political Thought*, ed. J. H. Burns, 95–131. Cambridge: Cambridge UP, 1991.

Braun, Werner. *Die Musik des 17. Jahrhunderts*. Wiesbaden: Akademische Verlagsgesellschaft, 1981.

Brauneck, Manfred. *Die Welt als Bühne: Geschichte des europäischen Theaters*. 2 vols. Stuttgart: Metzler, 1993–96.

Brauner, Sigrid. *Fearless Wives and Frightened Shrews: The Concept of the Witch in Early Modern Germany*. Amherst: U of Massachusetts P, 1995.

Braungart, Georg. *Hofberedsamkeit: Studien zur Praxis höfisch-politischer Rede im deutschen Territorialabsolutismus*. Studien zur deutschen Literatur 96. Tübingen: Niemeyer, 1988.

Brenner, Peter J. "Der Tod des Märtyrers. 'Macht' und 'Moral' in den Trauerspielen von Andreas Gryphius." *Deutsche Vierteljahrsschrift für Literaturwissenschaft und Geistesgeschichte* 62 (1988): 246–65.

Breuer, Dieter. "Der Prediger als Erfolgsautor: Zur Funktion der Predigt im 17. Jahrhundert." *Vestigia Bibliae* 3 (1981): 31–48.

Browning, Barton W. "The Development of the Vernacular Drama." In Hoffmeister, *German Baroque Literature*, 339–56.

Burchert, Bernhard. *Die Anfänge des Prosaromans in Deutschland: Die Prosaerzählungen Elisabeths von Nassau-Saarbrücken.* Frankfurt am Main: Lang, 1987.

Burmeister, Joachim. *Musical Poetics.* Trans. Benito V. Rivera. New Haven: Yale UP, 1993.

Burnett, Stephen G. "The Regulation of Hebrew Printing in Germany, 1555–1630: Confessional Politics and the Limits of Jewish Toleration." In Reinhart, ed., *Infinite Boundaries,* 329–48.

Caemmerer, Christiane. *Siegender Cupido oder Triumphierende Keuschheit: Deutsche Schäferspiele des 17. Jahrhunderts dargestellt in einzelnen Untersuchungen.* Stuttgart-Bad Cannstatt: Frommann-Holzboog, 1998.

Catholy, Eckehard. *Das deutsche Lustspiel: Vom Mittelalter bis zum Ende der Barockzeit.* Stuttgart: Kohlhammer, 1969.

———. *Fastnachtspiel.* Sammlung Metzler 56. Stuttgart: Metzler, 1966.

———. *Das Fastnachtspiel des Spätmittelalters.* Tübingen: Niemeyer, 1961.

Chrisman, Miriam Usher. *Conflicting Visions of Reform: German Lay Propaganda Pamphlets, 1519–1530.* Atlantic Highlands, NJ: Humanities Press International, 1996.

Christensen, Carl C. *Art and the Reformation in Germany.* Athens: Ohio UP, 1979.

Colvin, Sarah. *The Rhetorical Feminine: Gender and Orient on the German Stage, 1647–1742.* Oxford: Clarendon, 1999.

Conrady, Karl Otto. *Lateinische Dichtungstradition und deutsche Lyrik des 17. Jahrhunderts.* Bonn: Bouvier, 1962.

Coreth, Anna. *Pietas Austriaca: Österreichische Frömmigkeit im Barock.* 2nd ed. Munich: Oldenbourg, 1982.

Cramer, Thomas. *Geschichte der deutschen Literatur im späten Mittelalter.* 3rd ed. Munich: Deutscher Taschenbuch Verlag, 2000.

Cuneo, Pia F. "Constructing the Boundaries of Community: Nationalism, Protestantism, and Economics in a Sixteenth-Century Broadsheet." In Reinhart, ed., *Infinite Boundaries,* 171–85.

Daly, Peter M. *Literature in the Light of the Emblem: Structural Parallels between the Emblem and Literature in the Sixteenth and Seventeenth Centuries.* 2nd rev. ed. Toronto: U of Toronto P, 1998.

Davies, Oliver. *God Within: The Mystical Tradition of Northern Europe.* New York: Paulist Press, 1988.

Davis, Natalie Zemon. *Women on the Margins: Three Seventeenth-Century Lives.* Cambridge: Harvard UP, 1995.

Dyck, Joachim. *Athen und Jerusalem: Die Tradition der argumentativen Verknüpfung von Bibel und Poesie im 17. und 18. Jahrhundert.* Munich: Beck, 1977.

———. *Ticht-Kunst: Deutsche Barockpoetik und rhetorische Tradition.* 3rd ed. Rhetorik-Forschungen 2. Tübingen: Niemeyer, 1991.

Ehrstine, Glenn. *Theatre, Culture, and Community in Reformation Bern, 1523–1555.* Studies in Medieval and Reformation Thought 85. Leiden: Brill, 2002.

Enderle, Winfried. "Die Jesuitenbibliotheken im 17. Jahrhundert: das Beispiel der Bibliothek des Düsseldorfer Kollegs 1619–1773." *Archiv für Geschichte des Buchwesens* 41 (1994): 146–213.

Erdei, Clara. *Auf dem Wege zu sich selbst: Die Meditation im 16. Jahrhundert: Eine funktionsanalytische Gattungsbeschreibung.* Wiesbaden: Harrassowitz, 1990.

Ertzdorff, Xenia von. *Romane und Novellen des 15. und 16. Jahrhunderts in Deutschland.* Darmstadt: Wissenschaftliche Buchgesellschaft, 1989.

Eybl, Franz M. *Gebrauchsfunktionen barocker Predigtliteratur.* Vienna: Braumüller, 1982.

Feistner, Edith. *Historische Typologie der deutschen Heiligenlegende des Mittelalters von der Mitte des 12. Jahrhunderts bis zur Reformation.* Wiesbaden: Reichert, 1995.

Forster, Leonard W. *The Icy Fire: Five Studies in European Petrarchism.* Cambridge: Cambridge UP, 1969.

———. "Neo-Latin Tradition and Vernacular Poetry." In Hoffmeister, *German Baroque Literature,* 87–108.

Garber, Klaus. "Begin with Goethe? Forgotten Traditions at the Threshold of the Modern Age." Trans. Karl F. Otto Jr., in Garber, *Imperiled Heritage,* 209–51.

———. *Der locus amoenus und der locus terribilis: Bild und Funktion der Natur in der deutschen Schäfer- und Landlebendichtung des 17. Jahrhunderts.* Cologne: Böhlau, 1974.

———. "Nuremberg, Arcadia on the Pegnitz: The Self-Stylization of an Urban Sodality." Trans. Karl F. Otto Jr., Michael Swisher, and Max Reinhart. In Garber, *Imperiled Heritage,* 117–208.

———. "Paris, Capital of European Late Humanism: Jacques Auguste de Thou and the Cabinet Dupuy." Trans. Joe G. Delap. In Garber, *Imperiled Heritage,* 54–72.

———. "Sozietäten, Akademien, Sprachgesellschaften." In *Europäische Enzyklopädie zu Philosophie und Wissenschaften,* ed. Hans Jörg Sandkühler, 4:366–84. Hamburg: Meiner, 1990.

———. "Utopia and the Green World: Critique and Anticipation in Pastoral Poetry." Trans. James F. Ehrman. In Garber, *Imperiled Heritage,* 73–116.

———. "'Your arts shall be: to impose the ways of peace' — Tolerance, Liberty, and the Nation in the Literature and Deeds of Humanism." Trans. Westfälisches

Landesmuseum für Kunst und Kulturgeschichte (Münster) and Michael Swisher. In Garber, *Imperiled Heritage*, 19–40.

Garber, Klaus. "Zentraleuropäischer Calvinismus und deutsche 'Barock'-Literatur: Zu den konfessionspolitischen Ursprüngen der deutschen Nationalliteratur." In Schilling, *Die reformierte Konfessionalisierung in Deutschland*, 317–48.

Gebauer, Hans. *Bücherauktionen in Deutschland im 17. Jahrhundert.* Bonn: Bouvier, 1981.

Goldbrunner, Hermann. "*Laudatio urbis:* Zu neueren Untersuchungen über das humanistische Städtelob." *Quellen und Forschungen aus italienischen Archiven und Bibliotheken* 63 (1983): 313–28.

Grant, W. Leonard. *Neo-Latin Literature and the Pastoral.* Chapel Hill: U of North Carolina P, 1965.

Grimm, Heinrich. "Die deutschen Teufelbücher des 16. Jahrhunderts: Ihre Rolle im Buchwesen und ihre Bedeutung." *Archiv für Geschichte des Buchwesens* 2 (1959): 513–70.

Hahn, Gerhard. "Literatur und Konfessionalisierung." In Röcke and Münkler, eds., *Die Literatur im Übergang vom Mittelalter zur Neuzeit*, 242–62.

Harder, Hans Bernd. *Studien zum Humanismus in den böhmischen Ländern.* Cologne: Böhlau, 1988.

Harms, Wolfgang. "Lateinische Texte illustrierter Flugblätter: Der Gelehrte als möglicher Adressat eines breit wirksamen Mediums der frühen Neuzeit." In *Bildungsexklusivität und volkssprachliche Literatur — Literatur vor Lessing — nur für Experten?*, ed. Klaus Grubmüller and Günter Hess, 74–85. Tübingen: Niemeyer, 1986.

Haude, Sigrun. "Anabaptist Women — Radical Women?" In Reinhart, ed., *Infinite Boundaries*, 313–27.

Herrmann, Hans Peter. *Naturnachahmung und Einbildungskraft: Zur Entwicklung der deutschen Poetik von 1670 bis 1740.* Ars poetica 8. Bad Homburg: Gehlen, 1970.

Hess, Daniel. "Das Gothaer Liebespaar oder die gesellschaftliche Absicherung einer gräflichen Konkubine." In *Jahreszeiten der Gefühle: Das Gothaer Liebespaar und die Minne im Spätmittelalter*, ed. Allmuth Schuttwolf, 14–20. Ostfildern-Ruit: Hatje, 1998.

Hess, Peter. *Epigramm.* Sammlung Metzler 248. Stuttgart: Metzler, 1989.

Hess, Ursula. "Lateinischer Dialog und gelehrte Partnerschaft: Frauen als humanistische Leitbilder in Deutschland (1500–1555)." In Brinker-Gabler, ed., *Deutsche Literatur von Frauen*, 1:113–48.

Hettinger, Anette, and Amalie Fößel. *Klosterfrauen, Beginen, Ketzerinnen: Religiöse Lebensformen von Frauen im Mittelalter.* Idstein: Schulz-Kirchner, 2000.

Hillerbrand, Hans J. "The 'Other' in the Age of the Reformation: Reflections on Social Control and Deviance in the Sixteenth Century." In Reinhart, ed., *Infinite Boundaries*, 245–69.

Hind, Arthur M. *An Introduction to a History of Woodcut.* 2 vols. (1935). New York: Dover, 1963.

Hoffmann, Heinz. "Neulateinische Literatur: Aufgaben und Perspektiven." *Neulateinisches Jahrbuch* 2 (2000): 57–98.

Hoffmeister, Gerhart. *Der Schelmenroman im europäischen Kontext.* Amsterdam: Rodopi, 1986.

———. *Die spanische Diana in Deutschland.* Philologische Quellen und Studien 68. Berlin: Schmidt, 1972.

Hohendahl, Peter. "Gervinus als Historiker des Barockzeitalters." In Garber, ed., *Europäische Barock-Rezeption,* 561–76.

Hojer, Gerhard, ed. *Der Italienische Bau: Materialien und Untersuchungen zur Stadtresidenz Landshut.* Exhibition catalogue. Stadtresidenz, Landshut. Landshut: Bayerische Verwaltung der Staatlichen Schlösser, Gärten und Seen, 1994.

Ijsewijn, Jozef. *Companion to Neo-Latin Studies.* Part 1: *History and Diffusion of Neo-Latin Literature.* 2nd ed. Leuven: Leuven UP, 1990. Part 2: Ijsewijn, with Dirk Sacré. *Literary, Linguistic, Philological and Editorial Questions.* 1998.

Ing, Janet: *Johann Gutenberg and His Bible: A Historical Study.* New York: Typophiles, 1990.

Jochum, Uwe. *Kleine Bibliotheksgeschichte.* 2nd ed. Stuttgart: Reclam, 1999.

Jung, Martin H. *Frauen des Pietismus: Zehn Porträts von Johanna Regina Bengel bis Erdmuthe Dorothea von Zinzendorf.* Gütersloh: Gütersloher Verlagshaus, 1998.

Jung, Werner. *Kleine Geschichte der Poetik.* Hamburg: Junius, 1997.

Jürgensen, Renate. *Utile cum dulci: Mit Nutzen erfreuen: Die Blütezeit des Pegnesischen Blumenordens in Nürnberg 1644–1744.* Wiesbaden: Harrassowitz, 1994.

Kampe, Jürgen. *Problem "Reformationsdialog": Untersuchungen zu einer Gattung im reformatorischen Medienwettstreit.* Beiträge zur Dialogforschung 14. Tübingen: Niemeyer, 1997.

King, Margaret L. *Women of the Renaissance.* Chicago: U of Chicago P, 1991.

Kingdon, Robert M. "International Calvinism." In Brady, Oberman, and Tracy, eds., *Handbook of European History, 1400–1600,* 2:229–48.

Klein, Dorothea. "Wann endet das Spätmittelalter in der Geschichte der deutschen Literatur?" In Brunner, ed., *Forschungen zur deutschen Literatur des Spätmittelalters,* 299–316.

Knape, Joachim. *Allgemeine Rhetorik: Stationen der Theoriegeschichte.* Stuttgart: Reclam, 2000.

———. *"Historie" in Mittelalter und Früher Neuzeit.* Baden-Baden: Koerner, 1984.

———. "Humanismus, Reformation, deutsche Sprache und Nation." In Gardt, ed., *Nation und Sprache,* 103–38.

Koch, Hans-Albrecht. *Das deutsche Singspiel.* Sammlung Metzler 133. Stuttgart: Metzler, 1974.

Koerner, Joseph. *The Moment of Self-Portraiture*. Chicago: U of Chicago P, 1993.

Könnecker, Barbara. *Die deutsche Literatur der Reformationszeit: Kommentar zu einer Epoche*. Munich: Winkler, 1975.

———. *Satire im 16. Jahrhundert: Epoche — Werk — Wirkung*. Munich: Beck, 1991.

Krautter, Konrad. *Die Renaissance der Bukolik in der lateinischen Literatur des 14. Jahrhunderts: Von Dante bis Petrarca*. Munich: Fink, 1983.

Kühlmann, Wilhelm. "Der Poet und das Reich: Politische, kontextuelle und ästhetische Dimensionen der humanistischen Türkenlyrik in Deutschland." In Guthmüller and Kühlmann, eds., *Europa und die Türken*, 139–248.

———. "Poeten und Puritaner: Christliche und pagane Poesie im deutschen Humanismus." *Pirckheimer-Jahrbuch* 8 (1993): 149–80.

———. "Sprachgesellschaften und nationale Utopien." In Langewiesche and Schmidt, eds., *Föderative Nation*, 245–64.

———. *Vom Humanismus zur Spätaufklärung: Ästhetische und kulturgeschichtliche Dimensionen der frühzeitlichen Lyrik und Verspublizistik in Deutschland*. Ed. Joachim Telle, Friedrich Vollhardt, and Hermann Wiegand. Tübingen: Niemeyer, 2006.

Landau, David, and Peter Parshall, *The Renaissance Print, 1470–1550*. New Haven: Yale UP, 1994.

Leaver, Robin A. "Theological Consistency, Liturgical Integrity, and Musical Hermeneutic in Luther's Liturgical Reforms." *Lutheran Quarterly* 9 (1995): 117–38.

Levack, Brian P. "The Great Witch-Hunt." In Brady, Oberman, and Tracy, eds., *Handbook of European History, 1400–1600*, 2:607–40.

Ley, Klaus. "Castiglione und die Höflichkeit: Zur Rezeption des *Cortegiano* im deutschen Sprachraum vom 16. bis zum 18 Jahrhundert." In Martino, ed., *Beiträge zur Aufnahme der italienischen und spanischen Literatur*, 3–108.

Limon, Jerzy. *Gentlemen of a Company: The Theater of the Strolling Players*. Cambridge: Cambridge UP, 1985.

Locher, Gottfried W. *Die Zwinglische Reformation im Rahmen der europäischen Kirchengeschichte*. Göttingen: Vandenhoeck & Ruprecht, 1979.

Lohmeier, Dietrich. *Weltliches und geistliches Lied des Barock: Studien zur Liedkultur in Deutschland und Scandinavien*. Amsterdam: Rodopi, 1979.

Lotz-Heumann, Ute, and Matthias Pohlig. "Confessionalization and Literature in the Empire, 1555–1700." *Central European History* 40 (2007): 35–61.

Lübbeke, Isolde. *The Thyssen-Bornemisza Collection: Early German Painting 1350–1550*. Trans. Margaret Thomas Will. London: Sotheby's Publications, 1991.

Ludwig, Walther. *Christliche Dichtung des 16. Jahrhunderts: Die "Poemata sacra" des Georg Fabricius*. Göttingen: Vandenhoeck & Ruprecht, 2001.

Meid, Volker. *Barocklyrik*. Sammlung Metzler 227. Stuttgart: Metzler, 1986.

———. *Der deutsche Barockroman*. Sammlung Metzler 128. Stuttgart: Metzler, 1974.

Mertens, Dieter, and Theodor Verweyen. "Zu Heidelberger Dichtern von Schede bis Zincgref." *Zeitschrift für deutsches Altertum* 103 (1974): 200–241.

Metzger, Michael M., and Erika A. Metzger. "The Thirty Years War and Its Impact on Literature." In Hoffmeister, *German Baroque Literature*, 38–51.

Michael, Wolfgang F. *Das deutsche Drama der Reformationszeit*. Bern: Lang, 1984.

———. *Frühformen der deutschen Bühne*. Berlin: Selbstverlag der Gesellschaft für Theatergeschichte, 1963.

Michalski, Sergiusz. *The Reformation and the Visual Arts*. London: Routledge, 1993.

Midelfort, H. C. Erik. *Witch Hunting in Southwestern Germany (1562–1684)*. Stanford: Stanford UP, 1972.

Moeller, Bernd. *Imperial Cities and the Reformation*. Trans. H. C. Erik Midelfort and Mark U. Edwards Jr. Durham: Labyrinth, 1972.

Moeller, Bernd, and Karl Stackmann. *Städtische Predigt in der Frühzeit der Reformation: Eine Untersuchung deutscher Flugschriften der Jahre 1522 bis 1529*. Abhandlungen der Akademie der Wissenschaft in Göttingen, Philologisch-Historische Klasse 3, 220. Göttingen: Vandenhoeck & Ruprecht, 1996.

Moser, Dietz-Rüdiger. *Verkündigung durch Volksgesang: Studien zur Liedpropaganda und -katechese der Gegenreformation*. Berlin: Schmidt, 1981.

Müller, Jan-Dirk. "Formen literarischer Kommunikation im Übergang vom Mittelalter zur Neuzeit." In Röcke and Münkler, eds., *Die Literatur im Übergang vom Mittelalter zur Neuzeit*, 21–53.

———. "Volksbuch/Prosaroman im 15./16. Jahrhundert — Perspektiven der Forschung." *Internationales Archiv für Sozialgeschichte der deutschen Literatur* (1985): 1–128.

Mulsow, Martin. "Konsumtheorie und Kulturtransfer: Einige Perspektiven für die Forschung zum 16. Jahrhundert." In Schmale, ed., *Kulturtransfer*, 131–43.

Münkler, Marina. "Volkssprachlicher Früh- und Hochhumanismus." In Röcke and Münkler, eds., *Die Literatur im Übergang vom Mittelalter zur Neuzeit*, 77–96.

Nagel, Bert. *Meistersang*. 2nd ed. Sammlung Metzler 12. Stuttgart: Metzler, 1971.

Nauert, Charles G. *Humanism and the Culture of Renaissance Europe*. 2nd ed. Cambridge: Cambridge UP, 2006.

Nelles, Paul. "Historia litteraria at Helmstedt: Books, Professors and Students in the Early Enlightenment University." In Zedelmaier and Mulsow, eds., *Die Praktiken der Gelehrsamkeit in der Frühen Neuzeit*, 31–56.

Neuber, Wolfgang. "Amerika in deutschen Reiseberichten des 16. und des 17. Jahrhunderts." In Siebenmann and König, eds., *Das Bild Lateinamerikas im deutschen Sprachraum*, 37–54.

———. "Der Arzt und das Reisen: Zum Anleitungsverhältnis von Regimen und Apodemik in der frühneuzeitlichen Reisetheorie." In Benzenhöfer and Kühlmann, eds., *Heilkunde und Krankheitserfahrung*, 94–113.

———. "Die frühen deutschen Reiseberichte aus der Neuen Welt: Fiktionalitätsverdacht und Beglaubigungsstrategien." In König, Reinhard, and Wendt, eds., *Der europäische Beobachter außereuropäischer Kulturen*, 43–64.

Neuber, Wolfgang. "Zur Gattungspoetik des Reiseberichts: Skizze einer historischen Grundlegung im Horizont von Rhetorik und Topik." In Brenner, ed., *Der Reisebericht*, 50–67.

Newman, Jane. *Pastoral Conventions: Poetry, Language and Thought in Seventeenth-Century Nuremberg*. Baltimore: Johns Hopkins UP, 1990.

Ottinger, Rebecca Wagner. *Music as Propaganda in the German Reformation*. Aldershot: Ashgate, 2001.

Otto, Karl F. *Die Sprachgesellschaften des 17. Jahrhunderts*. Sammlung Metzler 109. Stuttgart: Metzler, 1972.

Ozment, Steven. *Flesh and Spirit: Private Life in Early Modern Germany*. New York: Viking, 1999.

Paas, John Roger. "Inseparable Muses: German Baroque Poets as Graphic Artists." *Colloquia Germanica* 29 (1996): 17–21.

Parente, James. *Religious Drama and the Humanist Tradition: Christian Theatre in Germany and in the Netherlands, 1500–1680*. Leiden: Brill, 1987.

Parshall, Peter. "*Imago Contrafacta*: Images and Facts in the Northern Renaissance." *Art History* 16 (1993): 554–79.

Pascal, Roy. *German Literature in the 16th and 17th Centuries: Renaissance, Reformation, Baroque*. Introductions to German Literature 2. New York: Barnes & Noble, 1968.

Post, R. R. *The Modern Devotion*. Leiden: Brill, 1968.

Rädle, Fidel. "Gegenreformatorischer Humanismus: Die Schul- und Theaterkultur der Jesuiten." In Hammerstein and Walther, eds., *Späthumanismus*, 128–47.

Raitz, Walter, Werner Röcke, and Dieter Seitz. "Konfessionalisierung der Reformation und Verkirchlichung des alltäglichen Lebens." In Röcke and Münkler, eds., *Die Literatur im Übergang vom Mittelalter zur Neuzeit*, 281–316.

Reformation in Nürnberg: Umbruch und Bewahrung. Exhibition catalogue. Germanisches Nationalmuseum, Nuremberg, 1979.

Rehermann, Ernst Heinrich. *Das Predigtexempel bei protestantischen Theologen des 16. und 17. Jahrhunderts*. Göttingen: Schwartz, 1977.

Reichelt, Klaus. *Barockdrama und Absolutismus: Studien zum deutschen Drama zwischen 1650 und 1700*. Bern: Lang, 1981.

Reichstein, Frank-Michael. *Das Beginenwesen in Deutschland*. Berlin: Köster, 2001.

Reinhart, Max. "Battle of the Tapestries: A War-Time Debate in Anhalt-Köthen (Georg Philipp Harsdörffer's *Peristromata Turcica* and *Aulaea Romana*, 1641–1642)." *Daphnis* 27, nos. 2–3 (1998): 291–333.

———. "Text and Simultext: Borrowing Claudian in Seventeenth-Century Germany." *German Life and Letters*, N.S. 52, no. 3 (1999): 281–96.

Reventlow, Henning Graf. *Epochen der Bibelauslegung*. Vol. 3: *Renaissance, Reformation, Humanismus*. Munich: Beck, 1997.

Ringbom, Sixten. *From Icon to Narrative* (1965). Reprint, Doornspijk: Davaco Publishers, 1984.

Robert, Jörg. "Martin Opitz und die Konstitution der Deutschen Poetik: Norm, Tradition und Kontinuität zwischen Aristarch und Buch von der Deutschen Poeterey." *Euphorion* 98 (2004): 281–322.

Roloff, Hans-Gert. "Anfänge des deutschen Prosaromans." In *Handbuch des deutschen Romans*, ed. Helmut Koopmann, 54–79. Düsseldorf: Bagel, 1983.

———. *Kleine Schriften zur Literatur des 16. Jahrhunderts.* Ed. Christiane Caemmerer et al. Amsterdam: Rodopi, 2003.

———. "Neulateinische Literatur." In *Renaissance and Barock 1400–1700, Propyläen Geschichte der Literatur: Literatur und Gesellschaft der westlichen Welt*, 3:196–230.

Roper, Lyndal. *Oedipus and the Devil: Witchcraft, Sexuality, and Religion in Early Modern Europe.* London: Routledge, 1994.

———. *Witch Craze: Terror and Fantasy in Baroque Germany.* New Haven: Yale UP, 2004.

Rössler, Martin. *Die Liedpredigt: Geschichte einer Predigtgattung.* Göttingen: Vandenhoeck & Ruprecht, 1976.

Rötzer, Hans Gerd. *Picaro — Landstörtzer — Simplicius.* Darmstadt: Wissenschaftliche Buchgesellschaft, 1972.

Saage, Richard. *Politische Utopien der Neuzeit.* 2nd ed. Bochum: Winkler, 2000.

Saunders, Steven. *Cross, Sword, and Lyre: Sacred Music at the Imperial Court of Ferdinand II of Habsburg (1619–1637).* New York: Oxford UP, 1995.

———. "Der Kaiser als Künstler: Ferdinand III and the Politicization of Sacred Music at the Hapsburg Court." In Reinhart, ed., *Infinite Boundaries*, 187–208.

Schade, Herward von. *Der Einfluß der Reformation auf die Entwicklung des evangelischen Bibliothekswesens.* Wiesbaden: Harrassowitz, 1985.

Schade, Richard E. *Studies in Early German Comedy.* Columbia, SC: Camden House, 1988.

Schäfer, Walter Ernst. *Moral und Satire: Konturen oberrheinischer Literatur des 17. Jahrhunderts.* Frühe Neuzeit 7. Tübingen: Niemeyer, 1992.

Schattkowsky, Martina, ed. *Witwenschaft in der Frühen Neuzeit: Fürstliche und adlige Witwen zwischen Fremd- und Selbstbestimmung.* Leipzig: Leipziger Universitätsverlag, 2003.

Schmidt, Reiner. *Deutsche Ars Poetica: Zur Konstituierung einer deutschen Poetik aus humanistischem Geist im 17. Jahrhundert.* Deutsche Studien 34. Hain: Meisenheim am Glan, 1980.

Schneider, Alois. *Narrative Anleitungen zur praxis pietatis im Barock: Dargelegt am Exempelgebrauch in den "Iudicia Divina" des Jesuiten Georg Stengel (1584–1651).* Würzburg: Bayerische Blätter für Volkskunde, 1982.

Schnell, Rüdiger. *Frauendiskurs, Männerdiskurs, Ehediskurs: Textsorten und Geschlechterkonzepte in Mittelalter und Früher Neuzeit.* Frankfurt am Main: Campus, 1998.

Schnell, Rüdiger. "Prosaauflösung und Geschichtsschreibung im deutschen Spätmittelalter: Zum Entstehen des frühneuhochdeutschen Prosaromans." In Grenzmann and Stackmann, eds., *Literatur und Laienbildung*, 214–48.

———. *Sexualität und Emotionalität in der vormodernen Ehe*. Cologne: Böhlau, 2002.

Schöne, Albrecht. *Emblematik und Drama im Zeitalter des Barock*. 3rd ed. Munich: Beck, 1993.

Schreiner, Klaus. "Bücher, Bibliotheken und 'Gemeiner Nutzen' im Spätmittelalter und in der Frühneuzeit: Geistes- und sozialgeschichtliche Beiträge zur Frage nach der 'utilitas librorum.'" *Bibliothek und Wissenschaft* 9 (1975): 202–49.

Segebrecht, Wulf. *Das Gelegenheitsgedicht: Ein Beitrag zur Geschichte und Poetik der deutschen Lyrik*. Stuttgart: Metzler, 1977.

Seifert, Herbert. "Frühes italienisches Musikdrama nördlich der Alpen: Salzburg, Prag, Wien, Regensburg, und Innsbruck." In Engelhardt, ed., *In Teutschland noch gantz ohnbekandt*, 29–44.

Silver, Larry. "Forest Primeval: Albrecht Altdorfer and the German Wilderness Landscape." *Simiolus* 13 (1983): 4–43.

Sinemus, Volker. *Poetik und Rhetorik im frühmodernen deutschen Staat*. Palaestra 269. Göttingen: Vandenhoeck & Ruprecht, 1978.

Singer, Bruno. *Die Fürstenspiegel in Deutschland im Zeitalter des Humanismus und der Reformation*. Munich: Fink, 1981.

Sixel, Friedrich Wilhelm. *Die deutschen Vorstellungen vom Indianer in der ersten Hälfte des 16. Jahrhunderts*. Città del Vaticano, 1966.

Smith, Jeffrey Chipps. *German Sculpture of the Later Renaissance, c. 1520–1584: Art in an Age of Uncertainty*. Princeton: Princeton UP, 1994.

———. *The Northern Renaissance*. London: Phaidon, 2004.

———. *Nuremberg, A Renaissance City, 1500–1618*. Exhibition catalogue. Huntington Art Gallery, University of Texas. Austin: U of Texas P, 1983.

———. *Sensuous Worship: Jesuits and the Art of the Early Catholic Reformation in Germany*. Princeton: Princeton UP, 2002.

Schmitz, Claudia. *Rebellion und Bändigung der Lust: Dialogische Inszenierung konkurrierender Konzepte vom glücklichen Leben (1460–1540)*. Frühe Neuzeit 88. Tübingen: Niemeyer, 2004.

Søndergaard, Leif. "Combat between the Genders: Farcical Elements in the German 'Fastnachtspiel.'" *Ludus: Medieval and Early Renaissance Theatre and Drama* 6 (2002): 169–87.

Spiewok, Wolfgang. *Das deutsche Fastnachtsspiel: Ursprung, Funktionen, Aufführungspraxis*. 2nd ed. Greifswald: Reineke, 1997.

Steinbach, Rolf. *Die deutschen Oster- und Passionsspiele des Mittelalters: Versuch einer Darstellung und Wesensbestimmung nebst einer Bibliographie zum deutschen geistlichen Spiel des Mittelalters*. Cologne: Böhlau, 1970.

Strauss, Gerald. "Ideas of *Reformatio* and *Renovatio* from the Middle Ages to the Reformation." In Brady, Oberman, and Tracy, eds., *Handbook of European History, 1400–1600*, 2:1–30.

Strieder, Peter. "'Schri. kunst. Schri. vnd klag. dich. ser': Kunst und Künstler an der Wende vom Mittelalter zur Renaissance." *Anzeiger des Germanischen Nationalmuseums* (1983): 19–26.

Strohm, Reinhard. *The Rise of European Music, 1380–1500*. Cambridge: Cambridge UP, 1993.

Stuart, Kathy. "The Executioner's Healing Touch: Health and Honor in Early Modern German Medical Practice." In Reinhart, ed., *Infinite Boundaries*, 349–79.

Sulzer, Dieter. *Traktate zur Emblematik: Studien zu einer Geschichte der Emblemtheorien*. Ed. Gerhard Sauder. St. Ingbert: Röhrig, 1992.

Suppan, Wolfgang. *Volkslied*. 2nd ed. Sammlung Metzler, Abteilung E: Poetik 52. Stuttgart: Metzler, 1978.

Szarota, Elida Maria. *Geschichte, Politik und Gesellschaft im deutschen Drama des 17. Jahrhunderts*. Bern: Francke, 1976.

Szyrocki, Marian. *Die deutsche Literatur des Barock*. Stuttgart: Reclam, 1979.

Tenbruck, Friedrich H. "Freundschaft: Ein Beitrag zu einer Soziologie der persönlichen Beziehungen." *Kölner Zeitschrift für Soziologie und Sozialpsychologie* 16 (1964): 431–56.

Thomas, R. Hinton. *Poetry and Song in the German Baroque: A Study of the Continuo Lied*. Oxford: Clarendon, 1963.

Till, Dietmar. *Transformationen der Rhetorik: Untersuchungen zum Wandel der Rhetoriktheorie im 17. und 18. Jahrhundert*. Tübingen: Niemeyer, 2004.

Trunz, Erich. "Der deutsche Späthumanismus um 1600 als Standeskultur." In Alewyn, ed. *Deutsche Barockforschung*, 147–81.

Velten, Hans Rudolf. "Utopien im 16. Jahrhundert in Deutschland und Europe." In Röcke and Münkler, eds., *Die Literatur im Übergang vom Mittelalter zur Neuzeit*, 529–71.

Verweyen, Theodor. *Apophthegmata und Scherzrede: Die Geschichte einer einfachen Gattungsform und ihrer Entfaltung im 17. Jahrhundert*. Linguistica et Litteraria 5. Bad Homburg: Gehlen, 1970.

———. "Barockes Herrscherlob: Rhetorische Tradition, sozialgeschichtliche Aspekte, Gattungsprobleme." *Der Deutschunterricht* 28, no. 2 (1976): 25–45.

———. "Dichtungstheorie und Dichtungsverständnis bei den Nürnbergern." In *"Der Franken Rom": Nürnbergs Blütezeit in der zweiten Hälfte des 17. Jahrhunderts*, ed. John Roger Paas, 178–95. Wiesbaden: Harrassowitz, 1995.

Voßkamp, Wilhelm. *Romantheorie in Deutschland: Von Martin Opitz bis Friedrich von Blanckenburg*. Stuttgart: Metzler, 1973.

———. *Utopieforschung: Interdisziplinäre Studien zur neuzeitlichen Utopie*. 2 vols. Stuttgart: Metzler, 1982.

Wagener, Hans. "Love: From Petrarchism to Eroticism." In Hoffmeister, *German Baroque Literature*, 197–210.

Walter, Axel E. *Späthumanismus und Konfessionspolitik: Die europäische Gelehrtenrepublik um 1600 im Spiegel der Korrespondenzen Georg Michael Lingelsheims*. Frühe Neuzeit 95. Tübingen: Niemeyer, 2004.

Walther, Gerhard. *Der Heidelberger Schlossgarten.* Heidelberg: Heidelberger Verlagsanstalt, 1990.

Walz, Herbert. *Deutsche Literatur der Reformationszeit: eine Einführung.* Darmstadt: Wissenschaftliche Buchgesellschaft, 1988.

Watanabe-O'Kelly, Helen. *Court Culture in Early Modern Dresden from Renaissance to Baroque.* Basingstoke: Palgrave Macmillan, 2002.

———. " 'Sei mir dreimal mehr mit Licht bekleidet': German Poems by Women to their Mentors in the Seventeenth Century." In Reinhart and Blackwell, eds., *Cultural Contentions,* 255–64.

———. *Triumphall Shews: Tournaments at German-Speaking Courts in their European Context 1580–1750.* Berlin: Gebr. Mann, 1992.

———. "Das weibliche Publikum und die soziale Funktion des deutschen Dramas im 16. Jahrhundert." In *'Verbergendes Enthüllen': Zu Theorie und Kunst dichterischen Verkleidens,* ed. Wolfram Malte Fues and Wolfram Mauser, 67–75. Würzburg: Königshausen & Neumann, 1995.

Wegman, Rob C. *The Crisis of Music in Early Modern Europe, 1470–1530.* New York: Routledge, 2005.

Weimer, Christoph. "Luther und Cranach: Das Rechtfertigungsthema in Wort und Bild." *Luther* 74 (2003): 22–38.

Weinmayer, Barbara. *Studien zur Gebrauchssituation früher deutscher Druckprosa.* Munich: Artemis, 1982.

Wenzel, Horst. "Autobiographie." In Röcke and Münkler, eds., *Die Literatur im Übergang vom Mittelalter zur Neuzeit,* 572–95.

Wiedemann, Conrad. "Heroisch — Schäferlich — Geistlich: Zu einem möglichen Systemzusammenhang barocker Rollenhaltung." In *Dokumente des Internationalen Arbeitskreises für Barockliteratur,* 96–122. Hamburg: Hauswedell, 1978.

Wiesner, Merry E. *Women and Gender in Early Modern Europe.* 2nd ed. New Approaches to European History 20. Cambridge: Cambridge UP, 2000.

Williams, Gerhild Scholz. *Defining Dominion: The Discourses of Magic and Witchcraft in Early Modern France and Germany.* Ann Arbor: Michigan UP, 1995.

———. "Invoking the Powers That Be: Types of Authority and the Production of the *Theatrum de veneficis* (1586)." In Poag and Baldwin, eds., *The Construction of Authority in German Literature,* 191–210.

———. *Ways of Knowing in Early Modern Germany: Johannes Praetorius as a Witness to His Time.* Aldershot: Ashgate, 2006.

Witt, Ulrike. *Bekehrung, Bildung und Biographie: Frauen im Umkreis des Halleschen Pietismus.* Halle: Verlag der Franckeschen Stiftungen im Niemeyer-Verlag Tübingen, 1996.

Wolf, Gerhard. *Von der Chronik zum Weltbuch: Sinn und Anspruch südwestdeutscher Hauschroniken am Ausgang des Mittelalters.* Berlin: de Gruyter, 2002.

Wood, Christopher S. *Albrecht Altdorfer and the Origins of Landscape.* Chicago: U of Chicago P, 1993.

———. "Germany's Blind Renaissance." In Reinhart, ed., *Infinite Boundaries*, 225–44.

Woodford, Charlotte. *Nuns as Historians in Early Modern Germany*. Oxford: Clarendon, 2002.

Woods, Jean M. "Opitz and the Women Poets." In *Opitz und seine Welt: Festschrift für George Schulz-Behrend zum 12. Februar 1988*, ed. Barbara Becker-Cantarino and Jörg-Ulrich Fechner, 569–86. Amsterdam: Rodopi, 1990.

Wunder, Heide. *He Is the Sun, She Is the Moon: Women in Early Modern Germany*. Trans. Thomas Dunlap. Cambridge: Harvard UP, 1998.

Wurst, Jürgen Alexander. *Das Figurenalphabet des Meisters E. S.* Munich: Tuduv, 1999.

Individual Writers and Poets

(The following selected list seeks to give a fair representation of authors and scholarship from both the German and Neo-Latin traditions in early modern Germany. In most instances, at least one accessible scholarly edition is mentioned as an aid to approaching the author's work.)

Abraham à Sancta Clara

Edition: *Wunderlicher Traum von einem großen Narrennest*. Ed. Alois Haas. Stuttgart: Reclam, 1969.

Eybl, Franz M. *Abraham a Sancta Clara: Vom Prediger zum Schriftsteller*. Tübingen: Niemeyer, 1992.

Scherer, William F. "Abraham à Sancta Clara (Ulrich Megerle)." In Hardin, ed., *German Baroque Writers, 1661–1730*, 3–18.

Aemilie Juliane von Schwarzburg-Rudolstadt

Aikin, Judith P. "Der Weg zur Mündigkeit in einem Frauenleben aus dem 17. Jahrhundert: Genesis und Publikationsgeschichte der geistlichen Lieder der Gräfin Aemilie Juliane von Schwarzburg-Rudolstadt." *Wolfenbütteler Barock-Nachrichten* 29 (2002): 33–59.

Rodolphus Agricola

Edition: *De inventione dialectica libri tres: Drei Bücher über die Inventio dialectica: Auf der Grundlage der Edition von Alardus von Amsterdam (1539)*. Ed. and trans. Lothar Mundt. Frühe Neuzeit 11. Tübingen: Niemeyer, 1992.

Edition: *Letters: Rudolf Agricola*. Trans. and ed. Adrie van der Laan and Fokke Akkerman. Assen: Royal van Gorcum, 2002.

Akkerman, Fokke, and A. J. Vanderjagt, eds. *Rodolphus Agricola Phrisius 1444–1458*. Leiden: Brill, 1988.

Aegidius Albertinus

Edition: *Verachtung des Hoflebens und Lob des Landlebens*. Ed. Christoph E. Schweitzer. Bern: Lang, 1987.

Gemert, Guillaume van. *Die Werke des Aegidius Albertinus.* Amsterdam: APA-Holland UP, 1979.

Hoffmeister, Gerhart. "Das spanische Modell: Alemans *Guzman de Alfarache* und die Albertinische Bearbeitung." In *Der deutsche Schelmenroman im europäischen Kontext: Rezeption, Interpretation, Bibliographie,* ed. Hoffmeister, 29–48. Chloe 5. Amsterdam: Rodopi, 1987.

Larsen, Lawrence S. "Aegidius Albertinus." In Hardin, ed., *German Baroque Writers, 1580–1660,* 3–12.

Johann Valentin Andreae

Edition: *Gesammelte Schriften.* 16 vols. Ed. Wilhelm Schmidt-Biggemann et al. Stuttgart-Bad Cannstatt: Frommann-Holzboog, 1994–2003.

Beeler, Stanley W. "Johann Valentin Andreae." In Hardin, ed. *German Baroque Writers, 1580–1660,* 13–19.

Dickson, Donald R. "Johann Valentin Andreae's Utopian Brotherhoods." *Renaissance Quarterly* 49 (1996): 860–902.

Turnbull, G. H.. "Johann Valentin Andreaes' Societas christiana: A Model of Christian Society." *Zeitschrift für deutsche Philologie* 74 (1955): 151–85.

Voßkamp, Wilhelm. "Von der Staats- zur Bildungsutopie: Johann Valentin Andreaes Christianopolis." In *Innovation und Originalität,* ed. Walter Haug and Burghart Wachinger, 196–205. Tübingen: Niemeyer, 1993.

Yates, Frances A. *The Rosicrucian Enlightenment.* London: Routledge & Kegan Paul, 1972.

Anton Ulrich, Duke of Brauschweig-Lüneburg

Edition: *Werke: historisch-kritische Ausgabe.* 7 vols. Ed. Hans-Henrik Krummacher and Rolf Tarot. Stuttgart: Hiersemann, 1982–2007.

Berns, Jörg Jochen. " 'Princeps Poetarum et Poeta Principum': Das Dichtertum Anton Ulrichs als Exempel absolutistischer Rollennorm und Rollenbrechung." In *'Monarchus Poeta': Studien zum Leben und Werk Anton Ulrichs von Braunschweig-Lüneburg.* Chloe 4. Amsterdam: Rodopi, 1985.

Hoyt, Giles. *The Development of Anton Ulrich's Narrative Prose on the Basis of Surviving "Octavia" Manuscripts and Prints.* Studien zur Germanistik, Anglistik und Komparatistik 33. Bonn: Bouvier, 1977.

Kraft, Stephan. *Geschlossenheit und Offenheit der* Römischen Octavia *von Herzog Anton Ulrich: "der roman macht ahn die ewigkeit gedencken, den er nimbt kein end."* Würzburg: Königshausen, 2004.

Müller, Jörg Jochen. "Fürstenerziehung im 17. Jahrhundert: Am Beispiel Herzog Anton Ulrichs von Braunschweig und Lüneburg." In Schöne, ed., *Stadt, Schule, Universität, Buchwesen,* 243–60.

Spahr, Blake Lee. *Anton Ulrich and Aramena: The Genesis and Development of a Baroque Novel.* University of California Publications in Modern Philology 76. Berkeley: U of California P, 1966.

———. "Anton Ulrich, Duke of Brunswick-Lüneburg." In Hardin, ed., *German Baroque Writers, 1661–1730,* 26–35.

Johann Arndt

Edition (English): *True Christianity*. Trans. Peter Erb. Preface by Heiko A. Oberman. New York: Paulist Press, 1979.

Geyer, Hermann. *Verborgene Weisheit: Johann Arndts "Vier Bücher vom Wahren Christentum" als Programm einer spiritualistisch-hermetischen Theologie*. Berlin: de Gruyter, 2001.

Gruebner, Birgit. *Gott und die Lebendigkeit in der Natur: Eine Interpretation des Dritten und Vierten Buches von Johann Arndts "Wahrem Christentum."* Arbeiten zur Theologiegeschichte 4. Rheinbach: CMZ, 1998.

Schneider, Hans. "Johann Arndt als Lutheraner?" In *Die lutherische Konfessionalisierung in Deutschland*, ed. Christoph Rublack, 274–84. Gütersloh: Gütersloher Verlagshaus Mohn, 1992.

————. "Johann Arndt als Paracelsist." In *Neue Beiträge zur Paracelsus-Forschung*, ed. Peter Dilg and Hartmut Rudolph, 89–110. Stuttgart: Akademie der Diozöse Rottenburg-Stuttgart, 1995.

Johannes Aventinus

Edition: *Baierische Chronik*. Ed. Georg Leidinger. Munich: Diederichs, 1988.

Merzbacher, Friedrich. "Aventin und das Recht." *Zeitschrift für bayerische Landesgeschichte* 40, nos. 2–3 (1977): 373–90.

Strauss, Gerald. *Historian of an Age of Crisis: The Life and Work of Johannes Aventinus 1477–1534*. Cambridge: Harvard UP, 1963.

Jacob Balde

Edition: *Dichtungen, Lateinisch und Deutsch*. Trans. and ed. Max Wehrli. Cologne: Hegner, 1963.

Herzog, Urs. *Divina Poesis: Studien zu Jacob Baldes geistlicher Odendichtung*. Tübingen: Niemeyer, 1976.

Schoolfield, George C. "Jacob Balde." In Hardin, ed., *German Baroque Writers, 1580–1660*, 29–44.

Valentin, Jean-Marie, ed. *Jacob Balde und seine Zeit: Akten des Ensisheimer Kolloquiums 15–16 Okt. 1982*. Bern: Lang, 1986.

Wiegmann, Hermann. "Ingenium und Urbanitas: Untersuchungen zur literaturgeschichtlichen Position Jacob Baldes." *Germanisch-romanische Monatsschrift* 63 (1982): 22–28.

Caspar von Barth

Edition (poetry selection): In Kühlmann, Seidel, and Wiegand, eds., *Humanistische Lyrik*, 863–904 (commentary: 1484–527).

Edition: *Pornoboscodiadascalus Latinus (1624): Kaspar Barth's Neo-Latin Translation of Celestina*. Ed. Enrique Fernández. North Carolina Studies in the Romance Languages and Literatures 284. Chapel Hill: U of North Carolina P, 2006.

Hoffmeister, Johannes. *Kaspar von Barths Leben, Werke und sein Deutscher Phönix*. Beiträge zur neueren Literaturgeschichte, N.F. 19. Heidelberg: Winter, 1931.

Kühlmann, Wilhelm. In Kühlmann, *Gelehrtenrepublik*, 255–63.

Heinrich Bebel

Edition: *Comoedia de optima studio iuvenum* (1504). Trans. and ed. Wilfried Barner et al. Stuttgart: Reclam, 1982.

Mertens, Dieter. "Bebels Einstand." In *Aus südwestdeutscher Geschichte: Festschrift für Hans-Martin Maurer*, ed. Wolfgang Schmierer et al., 307–24. Stuttgart: Kohlhammer, 1994.

Johann Beer

Edition: *Sämtliche Werke*. 12 vols. Ed. Hans-Gert Roloff and Ferdinand van Ingen. Bern: Lang, 1981–2005.

Hardin, James. "Johann Beer." In Hardin, ed., *German Baroque Writers, 1661–1730*, 36–50.

Krämer, Jört. *Johann Beers Romane, Poetologie, Poetik und Rezeption niederer Texte im späten 17. Jahrhundert*. Bern: Lang, 1991.

Solbach, Andreas. *Johann Beer: Rhetorisches Erzählen zwischen Satire und Utopie*. Tübingen: Niemeyer, 2003.

———. *Johann Beer: Schriftsteller, Komponist und Hofbeamter, 1655–1700*. Frankfurt am Main: Lang, 2003.

Jakob Bidermann

Edition: *Cenodoxus*. Trans. (German) Joachim Meichel (1635). Ed. Rolf Tarot. Stuttgart: Reclam, 1965.

Edition: *Ludi theatrales, 1666*. Ed. Rolf Tarot. 2 vols. Tübingen: Niemeyer, 1967.

Best, Thomas W. "Jacob Bidermann." In Hardin, ed., *German Baroque Writers, 1580–1660*, 45–49.

Valentin, Jean-Marie. "Die Jesuitendichter Bidermann und Avancini." In Steinhagen and von Wiese, eds., *Deutsche Dichter des 17. Jahrhunderts*, 385–414.

Wehrli, Max. "Bidermann, *Cenodoxus*." In *Das deutsche Drama*, ed. Benno von Wiese, 1:13–34. Düsseldorf: Bagel, 1958.

Sixtus Birck

Edition: *Sämtliche Dramen*. Ed. Manfred Brauneck. 3 vols. Berlin: de Gruyter, 1969–80.

Casey, Paul F. *The Susanna Theme in German Literature*. Bonn: Grundmann, 1976.

Sigmund von Birken

Edition: *Prosapia/Biographia*. Vol. 14 of *Werke und Korrespondenz*. Ed. Dietrich Jöns and Hartmut Laufhütte. Neudrucke deutscher Literaturwerke, N.F. 41. Tübingen: Niemeyer, 1988.

Edition: *Die Tagebücher des Sigmund von Birken*. 2 vols. Ed. Joachim Kröll. Würzburg: Schöningh, 1971, 1974.

Edition: *Teutsche Rede-bind- und Dicht-Kunst oder Kurze Anweisung zur Teutschen Poesy. Mit Geistlichen Exempeln* (1679). Reprint, Hildesheim: Olms, 1973.

Kröll, Joachim. "Sigmund von Birken (1626–1681)." *Fränkische Lebensbilder* 9 (1980): 187–203.

Paas, John Roger. "The Publication of a Seventeenth-Century Bestseller: Sigmund von Birken's *Der Donau-Strand* (1664)." In *The German Book: Studies Presented to David L. Paisey*, ed. John L. Flood, 229–41. London: British Library, 1995.

———. "Sigmund von Birken." In Hardin, ed., *German Baroque Writers, 1580–1660*, 50–63.

Verweyen, Theodor. "Daphnes Metamorphosen: Zur Problematik der Tradition mittelalterlicher Denkformen im 17. Jahrhundert am Beispiel des 'Programma Poeticum' Sigmund von Birkens." In *Rezeption und Produktion zwischen 1570 und 1730: Festschrift für Günther Weydt*, ed. Wolfdietrich Rasch et al., 319–79. Bern: Francke, 1972.

Johannes Bocer

Edition: *Sämtliche Eklogen*. Trans. and ed. Lothar Mundt. Tübingen: Niemeyer, 1999.

Jakob Böhme

Edition: *Jacob Böhme Werke: "Morgenröte" und "De Signatura Rerum."* Ed. Ferdinand van Ingen. Bibliothek der Frühen Neuzeit 6. Bibliothek deutscher Klassiker 143. Frankfurt am Main: Deutscher Klassiker Verlag, 1997.

Classen, Albrecht. "Jakob Böhme." In Hardin, ed., *German Baroque Writers, 1580–1660*, 64–73.

Walsh, David. *The Mysticism of Innerworldly Fulfillment: A Study of Jakob Böhme*. Gainesville: U Presses of Florida, 1983.

Weeks, Andrew. *Jakob Böhme: An Intellectual Biography of the 17th Century Philosopher and Mystic*. Albany: State U of New York P, 1991.

Hermann Bote

Hayden-Roy, Priscilla A. "Hermann Bote." In Reinhart and Hardin, eds., *German Writers of the Renaissance and Reformation*, 3–13.

Wunderlich, Werner. *"Till Eulenspiegel."* UTB 1288. Munich: Fink, 1984.

Sebastian Brant

Edition: *Kleine Texte*. 3 vols. Ed. Thomas Wilhelmi. Stuttgart-Bad Cannstatt: Frommann-Holzboog, 1998.

Edition: *Das Narrenschiff: Nach der Erstausgabe (Basel 1594) mit den Zusätzen der Ausgaben von 1495 und 1499 sowie den Holzschnitten der deutschen Originalausgabe*. 3rd ed. Ed. Manfred Lemmer. Tübingen: Niemeyer, 1986.

Cleve, John Van. "Sebastian Brant." In Reinhart and Hardin, eds., *German Writers of the Renaissance and Reformation*, 14–22.

Gaier, Ulrich. *Satire: Studien zu Sebastian Brants Narrenschiff*. Tübingen: Niemeyer, 1966.

Knape, Joachim. *Dichtung, Recht und Freiheit: Studien zu Leben und Werk Sebastian Brants, 1457–1521*. Baden-Baden: Koerner, 1992.

Wiegand, Hermann. "Sebastian Brant (1457–1521): Ein streitbarer Publizist an der Schwelle der Neuzeit." In Schmidt, ed., *Humanismus im deutschen Südwesten*, 77–104.

Wilhelmi, Thomas. *Sebastian Brant: Forschungen zu seinem Leben, zum "Narrenschiff" und zum übrigen Werk.* Basel: Schwabe, 2002.

Zeydel, Edwin H. *Sebastian Brant.* New York: Twayne, 1967.

Martin Bucer

Edition: Series I: *Martin Bucers Deutsche Schriften.* Ed. Gottfried Seebass. Gütersloh: Gütersloher Verlag, 1960–. Series II: Martini Buceri *Opera Latina.* Ed. François Wendel et al. Paris: Presses Universitaires de France, 1954–. Continued as *Opera omnia.* Ed. Robert Stupperich. Gütersloh: Bertelsmann, 1955–; also Gütersloh: Mohn, 1962–; also Leiden: Brill, 1979–. Series III: *Correspondance de Martin Bucer.* Ed. Jean Rott. Leiden: Brill, 1979–.

Burnett, Amy Nelson. *The Yoke of Christ: Martin Bucer and Christian Discipline.* Kirksville, MO: Sixteenth Century Journal Publishers, 1994.

Greschat, Martin. *Martin Bucer: A Reformer and His Times.* Trans. Stephen E. Buckwalter. Louisville: Westminster Knox Press, 2004.

Krüger, Friedhelm. *Bucer und Erasmus: Eine Untersuchung zum Einfluss des Erasmus auf die Theologie Martin Bucers (bis zum Evangelien-Kommentar von 1530).* Wiesbaden: Steiner, 1970.

Strohm, Christoph. "Martin Bucer: Vermittler zwischen den Konfessionen." In Jung and Walter, eds., *Theologen des 16. Jahrhunderts,* 116–34.

Wright, D. F., ed. *Martin Bucer: Reforming Church and Community.* Cambridge: Cambridge UP, 1994.

Augustus Buchner

Edition: *Anleitung zur deutschen Poeterey* [and] *Poet.* Ed. Marian Szyrocki. Deutsche Neudrucke. Reihe: Barock 5. Tübingen: Niemeyer, 1966.

Aiken, Judith P. "August Buchner." In Hardin, ed., *German Baroque Writers, 1580–1660,* 74–80.

Andreas Heinrich Bucholtz

Edition: *Der christlichen königlichen Fürsten Herkuliskus und Herkuladisla, auch ihrer hochfürstlichen Gesellschafft anmuhtige Wunder-Geschichte.* Ed. Ulrich Maché. Bern: Lang, 1982.

Lindner, Andreas. *A. H. Bucholtz Herkules-Roman 1659/60: zur Synthese von Erbauungs- und zeitgenössischer Unterhaltungsliteratur im Barock.* Berlin: Lit, 2006.

Maché, Ulrich. "Andreas Heinrich Bucholtz." In Hardin, ed., *German Baroque Writers, 1661–1730,* 73–83.

Hermann von dem Busche

Kühlmann, Wilhelm. "Hermann von dem Busche." In Killy, ed., *Literatur-Lexikon,* 2:335–36.

Mehl, James V. "Hermann von dem Busche's *Vallum humanitatis* (1518): A German Defense of the Renaissance Studia Humanitatis." *Renaissance Quarterly* 42 (1989): 480–506.

Joachim Camerarius

Edition: *Symbola et Emblemata* (1590–1604). 2 vols. Ed. Wolfgang Harms and Ulla Britta Kuechen. Graz: Akademische Druck- und Verlags-Anstalt, 1986–88.

Baron, Frank, ed. *Joachim Camerarius (1500–1574): Beiträge zur Geschichte des Humanismus im Zeitalter der Reformation*. Munich: Fink, 1978.

Wolfgang Capito

Edition: *The Correspondence of Wolfgang Capito*. Ed. Erika Rummel and Milton Kooistra. Vol. 1: 1507–1523. Toronto: U of Toronto P, 2005.

Kittelson, James M. *Wolfgang Capito: From Humanist to Reformer*. Leiden: Brill, 1975.

Conrad Celtis

Edition: *Die "Germania generalis" des Conrad Celtis: Studien mit Edition, Übersetzung und Kommentar*. Ed. Gernot Michael Müller. Tübingen: Niemeyer, 2001.

Edition (English): *Selections from Conrad Celtis 1459–1508*. Trans. and ed. Leonard Forster. Cambridge: Cambridge UP, 1948.

Price, David. "Conrad Celtis." In Reinhart and Hardin, eds., *German Writers of the Renaissance and Reformation*, 23–33.

Robert, Jörg. *Konrad Celtis und das Projekt der deutschen Dichtung: Studien zur humanistischen Konstitution von Poetik, Philosophie, Nation und Ich*. Tübingen: Niemeyer, 2003.

Schäfer, Eckhart. *Deutscher Horaz: Conrad Celtis, Georg Fabricius, Paul Melissus, Jacob Balde*. Wiesbaden: Steiner, 1976.

Spitz, Lewis. *Conrad Celtis: The German Arch-Humanist*. Cambridge: Harvard UP, 1957.

Worstbrock, Franz-Josef. "Konrad Celtis: Zur Konstitution des humanistischen Dichters in Deutschland." In Bookmann, ed., *Literatur, Musik und Kunst*, 9–35.

Nathan Chytraeus

Edition (poetry selection): In Kühlmann, Seidel, and Wiegand, eds., *Humanistische Lyrik*, 693–705 (commentary: 1356–64).

Edition: *Io. Casae Galateus: Das ist das Buechlein von erbarn hoeflichen und holdseligen Sitten* (1597). Deutsche Neudrucke: Reihe Barock 34. Reprint of 1607 edition, Tübingen: Niemeyer 1984.

Elsmann, Thomas, ed. *Nathan Chytraeus (1543–1598): ein Humanist in Rostock und Bremen: Quellen und Studien*. Bremen: Edition Temmen, 1991.

Pettke, Sabine. *Nathan Chytraeus: Quellen zur Zweiten Reformation in Norddeutschland*. Cologne: Böhlau, 1994.

Euricius Cordus

Edition (poetry selection): In Kühlmann, Seidel, and Wiegand, eds., *Humanistische Lyrik*, 221–45 (commentary: 1080–96).

Müller, Armgard. *Das Bucolicon des Euricius Cordus und die Tradition der Gattung*. Trier: Wissenschaftlicher Verlag, 1997.

Schäfer, Eckart. "Euricius Cordus: Vergil in Hessen." In *Candide Iudex*, ed. Anna Elissa Radke, 283–313. Stuttgart: Steiner, 1998.

Wiegand, Hermann. "Euricius Cordus." In Killy, *Literatur-Lexikon* 13, 220–23.

Daniel Czepko

Edition: *Sämtliche Werke*. 7 vols. Ed. Hans-Gert Roloff and Marian Szyrocki. Berlin: de Gruyter, 1980–86.

Meier, Annemarie. *Daniel Czepko als geistlicher Dichter*. Bonn: Bouvier, 1975.

Roloff, Hans-Gert. "Daniel Czepko." In Hardin, ed., *German Baroque Writers, 1580–1660*, 81–87.

Simon Dach

Edition: *Simon Dach und der Königsberger Dichterkreis*. Ed. Alfred Kelletat. Stuttgart: Reclam, 1986.

Schöne, Albrecht. *Kurbishütte und Königsberg: Modellversuch einer sozialgeschichtlichen Entzifferung poetischer Texte: Am Beispiel Simon Dach*. Munich: Beck, 1982.

Schoolfield, George C. "Simon Dach." In Hardin, ed., *German Baroque Writers, 1580–1660*, 88–106.

Segebrecht, Wulf. "Simon Dach und die Königsberger." In Steinhagen and von Wiese, eds., *Deutsche Dichter des 17. Jahrhunderts*, 242–69.

Johann Michael Dilherr

Edition: *Drei-Ständige Sonn- und Festtag-Emblemata, oder Sinn-bilder: Johann Michael Dilherr, Georg Philipp Harsdörffer* (ca. 1660). Ed. Dietmar Peil. Reprint, Hildesheim: Olms, 1994.

Wietfeldt, James Willard. *The Emblem Literature of Johann Michael Dilherr (1604–1669)*. Nuremberg: Schriftenreihe des Stadtarchivs Nürnberg, 1955.

Caspar Dornau

Edition: *Amphitheatrum sapientiae Socraticae ioco-seriae: Schauplatz scherz- und ernsthafter Weisheiten* (1619). Ed. Robert Seidel. Texte der frühen Neuzeit 9. Reprint, Goldbach: Keip, 1995.

Seidel, Robert. *Späthumanismus in Schlesien: Caspar Dornau (1577–1631): Leben und Werk*. Tübingen: Niemeyer, 1994.

Jeremias Drexel

Breidenbach, Heribert. *Der Emblematiker Jeremias Drexel S.J. (1581–1638): mit einer Einführung in die Jesuitenemblematik und einer Bibliographie der Jesuitenemblembücher*. Urbana: U of Illinois, 1970.

Gauly, Heribert. *Das einfache Auge: die Lehre des P. Jeremias Drexel SJ über die "rechta intentio."* Mainz: Matthias-Grünewald-Verlag, 1962.

Pörnbacher, Karl. *Jeremias Drexel: Leben und Werk eines Barockpredigers.* Munich: Seitz, 1965.

Albrecht Dürer

Edition: *Vier Bücher von menschlicher Proportion: Faksimile der Erstausgabe.* London: Wagner, 1970.

Anzewelsky, Fedja. *Dürer: His Art and Life.* Trans. Heide Grieve. New York: Alpine Fine Arts Collection, 1980.

Goldberg, Gisela, Bruno Heimberg, and Martin Schawe, eds. *Albrecht Dürer: Die Gemälde der Alten Pinakothek.* Munich: Edition Braus, 1998.

Hutchison, Jane Campbell. *Albrecht Dürer: A Biography.* Princeton: Princeton UP, 1990.

Panofsky, Erwin. *The Life and Art of Albrecht Dürer* (1943). Princeton: Princeton UP, 1955.

Price, David. "Albrecht Dürer." In Reinhart and Hardin, eds., *German Writers of the Renaissance and Reformation,* 34–41.

Schütz, Karl. *Albrecht Dürer im Kunsthistorischen Museum.* Vienna: Electa, 1994.

Elisabeth von Braunschweig-Lüneburg

Wiesner, Merry. "Herzogin Elisabeth von Braunschweig Lüneburg (1510–1558)." In Merkel and Wunder, eds. *Deutsche Frauen der Frühen Neuzeit,* 39–48.

Elisabeth von Nassau-Saarbrücken

Edition: *Hug Schapler* (1500 edition). In *Romane des 15. und 16. Jahrhunderts,* ed. Jan-Dirk Müller, 177–381 (commentary: 1088–1158). Frankfurt am Main: Deutscher Klassiker Verlag, 1990.

Classen, Albrecht. "Elisabeth von Nassau-Saarbrücken." In Reinhart and Hardin, eds., *German Writers of the Renaissance and Reformation,* 42–47.

Haubrichs, Wolfgang, ed. *Zwischen Deutschland und Frankreich: Elisabeth von Lothringen, Gräfin von Nassau-Saarbrücken.* St. Ingbert: Röhrig, 2002.

Desiderius Erasmus of Rotterdam

Edition: *Opera omnia Desiderii Erasmi Roterodami.* Amsterdam: North-Holland, 1969–.

Edition (English): *Collected Works of Erasmus.* Toronto: U of Toronto P, 1974–.

Augustijn, Cornelius. *Erasmus: His Life, Works, and Influence.* Toronto: U of Toronto P, 1991.

Bainton, Roland H. *Erasmus of Christendom.* New York: Scribner, 1969.

Boeft, Jan den. "Erasmus and the Church Fathers." In *The Reception of the Church Fathers in the West,* ed. Irena Backus, 2:537–72. Leiden: Brill, 2001.

Boyle, Marjorie O'Rourke. *Rhetoric and Reform: Erasmus' Civil Dispute with Luther.* Cambridge: Harvard UP, 1983.

Holeczek, Heinz. "Erasmus von Rotterdam (1466/67–1536): Humanistische Profile — Erasmus im Profil." In Schmidt, ed., *Humanismus im deutschen Südwesten*, 125–49.

Mansfield, Bruce E. *Phoenix of His Age: Interpretations of Erasmus c. 1550–1750.* Toronto: U of Toronto P, 1979.

Rummel, Erika. *Erasmus as a Translator of the Classics.* Erasmus Studies 7. Toronto: U of Toronto P, 1985.

Schoeck, Richard J. *Erasmus of Europe: The Prince of Humanists.* 2 vols. Edinburgh: Edinburgh UP, 1990–93.

Tracy, James D. *Erasmus of the Low Countries.* Berkeley: U of California P, 1996.

Johann Christoph Ettner

Bibliography: *Johann Christoph Ettner: Eine beschreibende Bibliographie.* Ed. James Hardin. Bibliographien zur deutschen Literatur 3. Bern: Francke, 1988.

Hardin, James. "Johann Christoph Ettner." In Hardin, ed., *German Baroque Writers, 1661–1730*, 98–105.

Albrecht von Eyb

Edition: *Deutsche Schriften des Albrecht von Eyb* (1890). Reprint as *Albrecht von Eyb: Deutsche Schriften I/II.* Ed. Max Herrmann. Hildesheim: Weidmann, 1984.

Edition: *Ob einem manne sey zunemen ein eelichs weyb oder nicht* (1472). Darmstadt: Wissenschaftliche Buchgesellschaft, 1982.

Bernstein, Eckhard. "Albrecht von Eyb." In Füssel, ed., *Deutsche Dichter der Frühen Neuzeit*, 96–110.

Flood, John L. "Albrecht von Eyb." In Reinhart and Hardin, eds., *German Writers of the Renaissance and Reformation*, 48–54.

Georg Fabricius

Edition (poetry selection): In Kühlmann, Seidel, and Wiegand, eds., *Humanistische Lyrik*, 607–51 (commentary: 1311–35).

Ludwig, Walther. *Christliche Dichtung des 16. Jahrhunderts: Die "Poemata sacra" des Georg Fabricius.* Göttingen: Vandenhoeck & Ruprecht, 2001.

Schäfer, Eckart. *Deutscher Horaz: Conrad Celtis — Georg Fabricius — Paul Melissus & Jacob Balde.* Wiesbaden: Steiner, 1976.

Faustbuch

Edition: In *Romane des 15. und 16. Jahrhunderts*, ed. Jan-Dirk Müller, 829–986 (commentary: 1319–430). Bibliothek deutscher Klassiker 54. Frankfurt am Main: Deutscher Klassiker Verlag, 1990.

Johann Fischart

Edition: *Sämtliche Werke.* Ed. Hans-Gert Roloff, Ulrich Seelbach, and W. Eckehart Spengler. Bern: Lang, 1993–.

Ertz, Stefan. *Fischart und die Schiltbürgerchronik: Untersuchungen zum Lale- und Schildbürgerbuch.* Cologne: Gabel, 1989.

Wailes, Stephen L. "Johann Fischart." In Reinhart and Hardin, eds., *German Writers of the Renaissance and Reformation*, 55–62.

Paul Fleming

Edition: *Paul Flemings Deutsche Gedichte.* 2 vols. (1865). Reprint, Darmstadt: Wissenschaftliche Buchgesellschaft, 1965.

Entner, Heinz. *Paul Fleming: Ein deutscher Dichter im Dreißigjährigen Krieg.* Leipzig: Reclam, 1989.

Pohl, Maria Cäcilie. *Paul Fleming: Ich-Darstellung, Übersetzungen, Reisegedichte.* Münster: Lit, 1993.

Sperberg-McQueen, Marian. *The German Poetry of Paul Fleming: Studies in Genre and History.* Chapel Hill: U of North Carolina P, 1990.

Hans Folz

Edition: *Die alt und neu ee; Herzog von Burgund; Die zwölf buhlerischen Bauern; Kaiser Constantinus.* In *Fastnachtspiele aus dem fünfzehnten Jahrhundert.* 4 vols. Ed. Adelbert von Keller. Darmstadt: Wissenschaftliche Buchgesellschaft, 1965–66.

Delap, Joe G. "Hans Folz." In Reinhart and Hardin, eds., *German Writers of the Renaissance and Reformation*, 63–69.

Krohn, Rüdiger. "Hans Folz." In Füssel, ed., *Deutsche Dichter der frühen Neuzeit*, 111–24.

Sebastian Franck

Edition: *Sämtliche Werke: kritische Ausgabe mit Kommentar.* Vols. 1, 4, and 11 to date. Ed. Hans-Gert Roloff et al. Stuttgart-Bad Cannstatt: Frommann-Holzboog, and Bern: Lang, 1992–2005.

Hayden-Roy, Patrick. *The Inner Word and the Outer World: A Biography of Sebastian Franck.* New York: Lang, 1994.

Hayden-Roy, Priscilla A. "Sebastian Frank." In Reinhart and Hardin, eds., *German Writers of the Renaissance and Reformation*, 70–82.

Müller, Jan-Dirk, ed. *Sebastian Franck (1499–1542).* Wiesbaden: Harrassowitz, 1993.

Nikodemus Frischlin

Edition: *Julius Redivivus.* Ed. Richard E. Schade. Stuttgart: Reclam, 1983.

Edition: *Phasma.* Ed. David Price. Stuttgart-Bad Cannstatt: Fromman-Holzboog, 2007.

Holtz, Sabine, and Dieter Mertens, eds. *Nikodemus Frischlin: Poetische und prosaische Praxis unter den Bedingungen des konfessionellen Zeitalters.* Stuttgart-Bad Cannstatt: Frommann-Holzboog, 1999.

Kühlmann, Wilhelm. "Nicodemus Frischlin (1547–1590): Der unbequeme Dichter." In Schmidt, ed., *Humanismus im deutschen Südwesten*, 265–88.

Price, David. *The Polical Dramaturgy of Nikodemus Frischlin: Essays on Humanist Drama in Germany.* Chapel Hill: U of North Carolina P, 1990.

Schade, Richard E. "Philipp Nicodemus Frischlin." In Füssel, ed., *Deutsche Dichter der frühen Neuzeit*, 613–25.

Paul Gerhardt

Edition (poetry selections in English): In *The German Lyric of the Baroque in English Translation*, trans. George C. Schoolfield, 110–15. Chapel Hill: U of North Carolina P, 1961.

Axmacher, Elke. "Paul Gerhardt als lutherischer Theologe." In *450 Jahre evangelische Theologie in Berlin*, ed. Gerhard Besier and Christof Gestrich, 79–104. Göttingen: Vandenhoeck & Ruprecht, 1989.

Gillespie, Gerald. *German Baroque Poetry*, 131–35. New York: Twayne, 1971.

Metzger, Erika A. "Paul Gerhardt." In Hardin, ed., *German Baroque Writers, 1580–1660*, 113–20.

Guilielmus Gnapheus

Edition (English): *Acolastus*, 1529. Translated by W. E. D. Atkinson as *Acolastus: A Latin Play of the 16th Century*. London, Ontario: University of Western Ontario, 1964.

Rädle, Fidel. "Acolastus — der Verlorene Sohn: Zwei lateinische Bibeldramen des 16. Jahrhunderts." In *Gattungsinnovation und Motivstruktur*, ed. Theodor Wolpers, 2:15–34. Göttingen: Vandenhoeck & Ruprecht, 1992.

Catharina Regina von Greiffenberg

Edition: *Sämtliche Werke*. 10 vols. (1683). Ed. Martin Bircher. Reprint, Millwood, NY: Kraus Reprint, 1983.

Classen, Albrecht. "Catharina Regina von Greiffenberg." In Hardin, ed., *German Baroque Writers, 1661–1730*, 114–20.

Daly, Peter M. *Dichtung und Emblematik bei Catharina Regina von Greiffenberg*. Bonn: Bouvier, 1976.

Eltz-Hoffmann, Lieselotte. *Catharina Regina von Greiffenberg*. Stuttgart: Quell, 1995.

Foley-Beining, Kathleen. *The Body and Eucharistic Devotion in Catharina Regina von Greiffenberg's 'Meditations.'* Columbia, SC: Camden House, 1997.

Frank, Horst-Joachim. *Catharina Regina von Greiffenberg: Leben und Welt der barocken Dichterin*. Göttingen: Sachse und Pohl, 1967.

Tatlock, Lynne. "Catharina Regina von Greiffenberg (1633–1694)." In Merkel and Wunder, eds., *Deutsche Frauen der Frühen Neuzeit*, 93–106.

Johann Jacob Christoffel von Grimmelshausen

Edition: *Simplicissimus Teutsch*. Ed. Dieter Breuer. Bibliothek der Frühen Neuzeit 4/1. Bibliothek deutscher Klassiker 44. Frankfurt am Main: Deutscher Klassiker Verlag, 1989.

Berns, Jörg Jochen. "Die Zusammenfügung der Simplicianischen Schriften: Bermerkungen zum Zyklus-Problem." *Simpliciana: Jahrbuch der Grimmelshausen-Gesellschaft* 10 (1998): 301–25.

Breuer, Dieter. *Grimmelshausen Handbuch*. UTB 8182. Munich: Fink, 1999.

Mannack, Eberhard. "Hans Jakob Christoffel von Grimmelshausen." In Steinhagen and von Wiese, eds., *Deutsche Dichter des 17. Jahrhunderts*, 517–52.

Negus, Kenneth. *Grimmelshausen*. New York: Twayne, 1974.

Otto, Karl F. Jr., ed. *A Companion to the Works of Grimmelshausen*. Rochester, NY: Camden House, 2003.

Wagner, Hans. "*Johann Jacob Christoffel von Grimmelshausen*." In Hardin, ed., *German Baroque Writers, 1661–1730*, 121–39.

Argula von Grumbach

Halbach, Silke. *Argula von Grumbach als Verfasserin reformatorischer Flugschriften*. Frankfurt am Main: Lang, 1992.

Joldersma, Hermina. "Argula von Grumbach." In Reinhart and Hardin, eds., *German Writers of the Renaissance and Reformation*, 89–96.

Matheson, Peter, ed. *Argula von Grumbach: A Woman's Voice in the Reformation*. Edinburgh: T&T Clark, 1995.

Andreas Gryphius

Edition: *Gesamtausgabe der deutschsprachigen Werke*. 12 vols., including supplements. Ed. Hugh Powell and Marian Szyrocki. Tübingen: Niemeyer, 1963–87.

Brenner, Peter. "Der Tod des Märtyrers: 'Macht' und 'Moral' in den Trauerspielen von Andreas Gryphius." *Deutsche Vierteljahrsschrift für Literaturwissenschaft und Geistesgeschichte* 62 (1988): 246–65.

Jöns, Dietrich Walter. *Das "Sinnen-Bild": Studien zur allegorischen Bildlichkeit bei Andreas Gryphius*. Stuttgart: Metzler, 1966.

Kaminski, Nicola. *Andreas Gryphius*. Stuttgart: Reclam, 1998.

Lötscher, Jolanda. *Andreae Gryphii Horribilicribrifax Teutsch: Formanalyse und Interpretation eines deutschen Lustspiels des 17. Jahrhunderts im soziokulturellen und dichtungstheoretischen Kontext*. Bern: Lang, 1994.

Mannack, Eberhard. *Andreas Gryphius*. 2nd ed. Sammlung Metzler 76. Stuttgart: Metzler, 1986.

Mauser, Wolfram. *Dicthung, Religion und Gesellschaft im 17. Jahrhundert: Die "Sonnete" des Andreas Gryphius*. Munich: Fink, 1976.

Solbach, Andreas. "Amtsethik und lutherischer Gewissensbegriff in Andreas Gryphius' 'Papinianus.'" *Daphnis* 28 (1999): 668–72.

Spahr, Andreas. "Andreas Gryphius." In Hardin, ed., *German Baroque Writers, 1580–1660*, 131–44.

Steinhagen, Harald. *Wirklichkeit und Handeln im barocken Drama: Historisch-ästhetische Studien zum Trauerspiel des Andreas Gryphius*. Tübingen: Niemeyer, 1977.

Toscan, Daniela. *Form und Funktion des Komischen in den Komödien von Andreas Gryphius*. Bern: Lang, 2000.

Johann Christian Günther

Edition: *Werke*. Ed. Reiner Bölhoff. Bibliothek der Frühen Neuzeit 10. Bibliothek deutscher Klassiker 153. Frankfurt am Main: Deutscher Klassiker Verlag, 1998.

Metzger, Michael M. "*Johann Christian Günther.*" In Hardin, ed., *German Baroque Writers, 1661–1730*, 151–61.

Pott, Hans-Georg, ed. *Johann Christian Günther.* Paderborn: Schöningh, 1988.

Johann Christian Hallmann

Edition: *Sämtliche Werke.* 3 vols. Ed. Gerhard Spellerberg. Berlin: de Gruyter, 1975–87.

Skrine, Peter N. "Johann Christian Hallmann." In Hardin, ed., *German Baroque Writers, 1661–1730*, 175–79.

Georg Philipp von Harsdörffer

Edition: *Frauenzimmer Gesprächspiele.* 8 vols. (1641–49). Ed. Irmgard Böttcher. Deutsche Neudrucke, Reihe Barock 13–20. Reprint, Tübingen: Niemeyer, 1968–69.

Edition: *Lamentation for France and Other Polemics on War and Peace: The Latin Pamphlets of 1641–1642.* Ed. and trans. Max Reinhart. Renaissance & Baroque: Studies & Texts. New York: Lang, forthcoming.

Edition: *Pegnesisches Schäfergedicht.* Ed. Klaus Garber. Tübingen: Niemeyer, 1966.

Edition: *Poetischer Trichter / Die Teutsche Dicht-und ReimKunst / ohne Behuf der Lateinischen Sprache / in VI. Stunden einzugiessen; Samt einem Anhang von der Rechtschreibung, und Schriftscheidung, oder Distinction.* 3 vols. (1648–53). Reprint, Darmstadt: Wissenschaftliche Buchgesellschaft, 1969.

Battafarano, Italo Michele, ed. *Georg Phillip Harsdörffer: Ein deutscher Dichter und europäischer Gelehrter.* Forschungen zur europäischen Kultur 1. Bern: Lang, 1991.

Böttcher, Irmgard. "Der Nürnberger Georg Philipp Harsdörffer." In Steinhagen and von Wiese, eds., *Deutsche Dichter des 17. Jahrhunderts*, 289–346.

Forster, Leonard. "Harsdörffer's Canon of German Baroque Authors." In *Erfahrung und Überlieferung: Festschrift for C. P. Magill*, ed. H. Siefken and A. Robinson, 32–41. Cardiff: U of Wales P, 1974.

Hess, Peter. "Georg Philipp Harsdörffer." In Hardin, ed., *German Baroque Writers, 1580–1660*, 145–60.

———. *Poetik ohne Trichter: Harsdörffers "Deutsche Dicht- und Reimkunst."* Stuttgart: Heinz, 1986.

Paas, John Roger. "Poeta incarceratus: Georg Philipp Harsdörffers Zensur-Prozeß." *Germanisch-romanische Monatsschrift*, supplement 1 (1979): 155–64.

Reinhart, Max. "Battle of the Tapestries: A War-Time Debate in Anhalt-Köthen (Georg Philipp Harsdörffer's *Peristromata Turcica* and *Aulaea Romana*, 1641–1642)." *Daphnis* 27, nos. 2–3 (1998): 291–333.

Zeller, Rosmarie. *Spiel und Konversation im Barock: Untersuchungen zu Harsdörffers "Gesprächspielen."* Berlin: de Gruyter, 1974.

August Adolph von Haugwitz

Alexander, R. J. "August Adolph von Haugwitz." In Hardin, ed., *German Baroque Writers, 1661–1730*, 185–93.

Béhar, Pierre. "Nachwort." In *August Adolph von Haugwitz: Prodromus poeticus, oder: Poetischer Vortrab: 1684*, ed. Pierre Béhar, 3*–194*. Tübingen: Niemeyer, 1984.

Heitner, Robert R. "Einleitung." In *Schuldige Unschuld oder Maria Stuarda*, by Adolf August von Haugwitz, ed. Heitner, 2*–64*. Bern: Lang, 1974.

Alexander Hegius

Disse, Helmut, ed. *Alexander Hegius (ca. 1433–1498): ein münsterländischer Humanist und Pädagoge in seiner Zeit*. Ahaus: Förderkreis des Alexander-Hegius-Gymnasiums, 1999.

Kühlmann, Wilhelm. "Alexander Hegius." In Killy, ed., *Literatur-Lexikon* 5:104–5.

Agnes Heinold

Neugebauer, Birgit. "Agnes Heinold (1642–1711): Ein Beitrag zur Literatur von Frauen im 17. Jahrhundert." *Daphnis* 20 (1991): 601–702.

Heinrich Julius von Braunschweig

Edition: *Die Schauspiele des Herzogs Heinrich Julius von Braunschweig nach alten Drucken und Handschriften*. Ed. Wilhelm Ludwig Holland (1855). Reprint, Amsterdam: Rodopi, 1967.

Browning, Barton W. "Dramatic Activities and the Advent of the English Players at the Court of Heinrich Julius von Braunschweig." In *Opitz und seine Welt: Festschrift für George Schultz-Behrend*, ed. Barbara Becker-Cantarino and Jörg-Ulrich Fechner, 125–39. Amsterdam: Rodopi, 1990.

———. "Heinrich Julius of Brunswick." In Hardin, ed., *German Baroque Writers, 1580–1660*, 161–73.

Heinrich Wittenwiler

Edition: *Der Ring*. Ed. Bernhard Sowinski. Stuttgart: Helfant, 1988.

Classen, Albrecht. "Heinrich Wittenwiler." In Reinhart and Hardin, eds., *German Writers of the Renaissance and Reformation*, 326–31.

Johann Hellwig

Edition: *Die Nymphe Noris (1650)*. Ed. Max Reinhart. Columbia, SC: Camden House, 1994.

Adler, Jeremy. "Pastoral Typography: Sigmund von Birken and the 'Picture Rhymes' of Johann Hellwig." *Visible Language* 20 (1986): 121–35.

Reinhart, Max. "Ein treuer Sammler seines Vaterlands: Patriotisches Gedenken in Johann Helwigs *Sacrarium bonae memoriae Noribergensium consecratum*." In *Festschrift für Klaus Garber: Regionaler Kulturraum und intellektuelle Kommunikation: Studien zur Literatur- und Kulturgeschichte Alteuropas*, ed. Alex Walter, 733–57. Amsterdam: Rodopi, 2005.

———. "Johann Hellwig." In Hardin, ed., *German Baroque Writers, 1580–1660*, 174–80.

Eobanus Hessus

Edition: *Dichtungen der Jahre 1528–1537.* Trans. and ed. Harry Vredeveld. Bern: Lang, 1990.

Gräßer, Ingeborg. *Die Epicediendichtung des Eobanus Hessus: Lyrische Totenklage zur Zeit des Humanismus und der Reformation.* Frankfurt am Main: Lang, 1994.

Gräßer-Eberbach, Ingeborg. *Helias Eobanus Hessus: Der Poet des Erfurter Humanistenkreises.* Erfurt: Thüringen, 1993.

Ludwig, Walther. "Eobanus Hessus in Erfurt: Ein Beitrag zum Verhältnis von Humanismus und Protestantismus." *Mittellateinisches Jahrbuch* 33 (1998): 155–70.

Schäfer, Eckart. "Der deutsche Bauernkrieg in der neulateinischen Literatur." *Daphnis* 9 (1980): 1–31.

Vredeveld, Harry. "Eobanus Hessus." In Reinhart and Hardin, eds., *German Writers of the Renaissance and Reformation,* 97–110.

Magdalena Heymair

Moore, Cornelia Niekus. "Biblische Weisheiten für die Jugend: Die Schulmeisterin Magdalena Heymair." In Brinkler-Gabler, ed., *Deutsche Literatur von Frauen,* 172–84.

Christian Hoffmann von Hoffmannswaldau

Edition: *Herrn von Hoffmannswaldau und andrer Deutschen auserlesener und bißher ungedruckter Gedichte: Benjamin Neukirchs Anthologie.* 7 vols. Ed. Erika A. Metzger. Neudrucke deutscher Literaturwerke, N.F. 43. Tübingen: Niemeyer, 1975–91.

Fröhlich, Harry. *Apologien der Lust: zum Diskurs der Sinnlichkeit in der Lyrik Hoffmannswaldaus und seiner Zeitgenossen mit Blick auf die antike Tradition.* Tübingen: Niemeyer, 2005.

Metzger, Michael M. "Christian Hoffmann von Hoffmannswaldau." In Hardin, ed., *German Baroque Writers, 1661–1730,* 194–202.

Rotermund, Erwin. *Christian Hoffmann von Hoffmannswaldau.* Sammlung Metzler 29. Stuttgart: Metzler, 1963.

Hans Holbein the Younger

Ganz, Paul. *The Paintings of Hans Holbein.* London: Phaidon, 1950.

Rowlands, John. *Holbein: The Paintings of Hans Holbein the Younger — Complete Edition.* London: Phaidon, 1985.

Anna Ovena Hoyers

Becker-Cantarino, Barbara. "Anna Ovena Hoyers." In Hardin, ed., *German Baroque Writers, 1580–1660,* 181–84.

———. "Die Stockholmer Liederhandschrift der Anna Ovena Hoyers." In *Barocker Lust-Spiegel: Studien zur Literatur des Barock: Festschrift für Blake Lee Spahr,* ed. Martin Bircher et al., 329–45. Amsterdam: Rodopi, 1984.

Moore, Cornelia Niekus. "Anna Ovena Hoyers (1584–1655)." In Merkel and Wunder, eds., *Deutsche Frauen der Frühen Neuzeit*, 65–76.

Ulrich von Hutten

Edition: *Deutsche Schriften*. 2 vols. Ed. Heinz Mettke. Leipzig: VEB Bibliographisches Institut, 1972, 1974.

Edition: *Ulrich von Hutten: Die Schule des Tyrannen: Lateinische Schriften*. Trans. (German) and ed. Martin Treu. Darmstadt: Wissenschaftliche Buchgesellschaft, 1997.

Bernstein, Eckhard. *Ulrich von Hutten*. Reinbek bei Hamburg: Rowohlt, 1988.

Holborn, Hajo. *Ulrich von Hutten and the German Reformation*. Trans. Roland Bainton. New York: Harper & Row, 1968.

Mehl, James V. "Ulrich von Hutten." In Reinhart and Hardin, eds., *German Writers of the Renaissance and Reformation*, 111–23.

Overfield, James H. *Humanism and Scholasticism in Late Medieval Germany*, 247–97. Princeton: Princeton UP, 1984.

Johannes von Tepl

Edition: *Der Ackermann*. Ed. Willy Krogmann. 4th ed. Wiesbaden: Brockhaus, 1978.

Kiening, Christian. *Schwierige Modernität: Der Ackerman des Johannes von Tepl und die Ambiguität historischen Wandels*. Tübingen: Niemeyer, 1998.

Schröder, Werner. *Der Ackermann aus Böhmen: Das Werk und sein Autor*. Munich: Fink, 1985.

Winston-Allen, Anne. "Johannes von Tepl." In Reinhart and Hardin, eds., *German Writers of the Renaissance and Reformation*, 287–92.

Athanasius Kircher

Edition: *Musurgia universalis* (1650). 2 vols. Reprint, Hildesheim: Olms, 2006.

Leinkauf, Thomas. *Mundus combinatus: Studien zur Struktur der barocken Universalwissenschaft am Beispiel Athanasius Kirchers SJ (1602–1680)*. Berlin: Akademie, 1993.

Siebert, Harald. *Die große kosmologische Kontroverse: Rekonstruktionsversuche anhand des* Itinerarium exstaticum *von Athanasius Kircher SJ (1602–1680)*. Boethius 55. Stuttgart: Steiner, 2006.

Johann Klaj

Edition: *Redeoratorien und "Lobrede der Teutschen Poeterey."* Ed. Conrad Wiedemann. Deutsche Neudrucke, Reihe: Barock 4. Tübingen: Niemeyer, 1965.

Heitner, Robert R. "Johann Klaj's Popularization of Neo-Latin Drama." *Daphnis* 6, no. 3 (1977): 313–25.

Reinhart, Max. "Johann Klaj (Klajus)." In Hardin, ed., *German Baroque Writers, 1580–1660*, 195–205.

Wiedemann, Conrad. "Engel, Geist und Feuer: Zum Dichterselbstverständnis bei Johann Klaj, Catharina von Greiffenberg und Quirinus Kuhlmann." In Grimm, ed., *Literatur und Geistesgeschichte*, 85–109.

Christian Knorr von Rosenroth

Christian Knorr von Rosenroth: Dichter und Gelehrter am Sulzbacher Musenhof: Festschrift zur 300. Wiederkehr des Todestages. Sulzbach-Rosenberg: Literaturarchiv und Stadt Sulzbach-Rosenberg, 1989.

Ehrman, James F. "Christian Knorr von Rosenroth." In Hardin, ed., *German Baroque Writers, 1661–1730*, 222–29.

Quirinus Kuhlmann

Hoffmeister, Gerhart. "Quirinus Kuhlmann." In Hardin, ed., *German Baroque Writers, 1661–1730*, 230–38.

Wiedemann, Conrad. "Engel, Geist und Feuer: Zum Dichterselbstverständnis bei Johann Klaj, Catharina von Greiffenberg und Quirinus Kuhlmann." In Grimm, ed., *Literatur und Geistesgeschichte*, 85–109.

Johann Kuhnau

Edition: *Ausgewählte Werke*. 3 vols. Ed. James Hardin. Bern: Lang, 1992.

Hardin, James. "Johann Kuhnau." In Hardin, ed., *German Baroque Writers, 1661–1730*, 239–46.

Margaretha Susanna von Kuntsch

Edition: *Das "weiblich Werck" in der Residenzstadt Altenburg 1672–1720: Gedichte und Briefe von Margaretha Susanna von Kuntsch und Frauen in ihrem Umkreis: Mit einer Einleitung, Dokumenten, Biographien und Kommentar.* Ed. Anna Carrdus. Hildesheim: Olms, 2004.

Carrdus, Anna. "Margaretha Susanna von Kuntsch (1651–1717) und 16 Altenburger Dichterinnen." In Merkel and Wunder, eds., *Deutsche Frauen der Frühen Neuzeit*, 123–38.

Justus Lipsius

Edition: *Von der Beständigkeit*. Trans. Andreas Viritius (1599, 1601). Ed. Leonard Forster. Sammlung Metzler 45. Stuttgart: Metzler, 1965.

Laureys, Marc et al., eds. *The World of Justus Lipsius: A Contribution towards His Intellectual Biography*. Turnhout: Brepols, 1998.

Friedrich von Logau

Edition: *366 Sinn-Gedichte*. Ed. Werner Schmitz. Zurich: Haffmans, 1989.

Hess, Peter. "Friedrich von Logau." In Hardin, ed., *German Baroque Writers, 1580–1660*, 216–23.

Verweyen, Theodor. "Friedrich von Logau." In *Deutsche Dichter*, ed. Gunter E. Grimm and Frank Rainer Max, 2:163–73. Stuttgart: Reclam, 1988.

Jacob Locher

Hartl, Nina. *Die 'Stultifera navis': Jacob Lochers Übertragung von Sebastian Brants 'Narrenschiff.'* 2 vols. Münster: Waxmann, 2001.

Daniel Casper von Lohenstein

Edition: *Sämtliche Trauerspiele: Historisch-kritische Gesamtausgabe.* 3 vols. Ed. Klaus Günther Just. Stuttgart: Hiersemann, 1953–57.

Aikin, Judith P. *The Mission of Rome in the Dramas of Daniel Casper von Lohenstein: Historical Tragedy as Prophecy and Polemic.* Stuttgart: Akademischer Verlag Heinz, 1976.

Asmuth, Bernhard. *Daniel Casper von Lohenstein.* Sammlung Metzler 97. Stuttgart: Metzler, 1971.

Browning, Barton W. "Daniel Casper von Lohenstein." In Hardin, ed., *German Baroque Writers, 1661–1730,* 266–80.

Martino, Alberto. *Daniel Casper von Lohenstein: Geschichte seiner Rezeption.* Trans. (from Italian) Heribert Streicher. Tübingen: Niemeyer, 1978.

Müsch, Bettina. *Der politische Mensch im Welttheater des Daniel Casper von Lohenstein: eine Deutung seines Dramenwerkes.* Frankfurt am Main: Lang, 1992.

Newman, Jane O. *The Intervention of Philology: Gender, Learning, and Power in Lohenstein's Roman Plays.* Chapel Hill: U of North Carolina P, 2000.

Plume, Cornelia. *Heroinen in der Geschlechterordnung: Weiblichkeitsprojektionen bei Daniel Casper von Lohenstein und die "Querelle des femmes."* Stuttgart: Metzler, 1996.

Spellerberg, Gerhard. *Verhängnis und Geschichte: Untersuchungen zu den Trauerspielen und dem "Arminius"-Roman Daniel Caspers von Lohenstein.* Bad Homburg: Gehlen, 1970.

Wichert, Adalbert. *Literatur, Rhetorik und Jurisprudenz im 17. Jahrhundert: Daniel Casper von Lohenstein und sein Werk: Eine exemplarische Studie.* Tübingen: Niemeyer, 1991.

Peter Luder

Papers: Correspondence and manuscripts in the Österreichische National-bibliothek, Vienna, and the Bayerische Staatsbibliothek, Munich (Hartmann Schedel collection).

Baron, Frank. "Peter Luder." In Reinhart and Hardin, eds., *German Writers of the Renaissance and Reformation,* 129–34.

Kettermann, Rudolf. "Peter Luder (um 1415–1472): Die Anfänge der humanistischen Studien in Deutschland." In Schmidt, ed., *Humanismus im deutschen Südwesten,* 13–34.

Martin Luther

Edition: *D. Martin Luthers Werke: Kritische Gesamtausgabe.* Weimar: Böhlau, 1883–1983.

Edition (English): *Luther's Works.* Ed. Jaroslav Pelikan and Helmut T. Lehmann. St. Louis: Concordia, 1955–61.

Besch, Werner. *Die Rolle Luthers in der deutschen Sprachgeschichte.* Heidelberg: Winter, 1999.

Beutel, Albrecht. "Martin Luther: Mönch, Professor, Reformator." In Jung and Walter, eds., *Theologen des 16. Jahrhunderts,* 47–64.

Brecht, Martin. *Martin Luther: His Road to Reformation 1483–1521.* Trans. James L. Schaaf. Minneapolis: Fortress, 1985.

Buszin, Walter E. "Luther on Music." *Musical Quarterly* 32 (1946): 80–97.

Friedenthal, Richard. *Luther: Sein Leben und seine Zeit.* 12th ed. Serie Piper 259. Munich: Piper, 2004.

Junghans, Helmar, ed. *Leben und Werk Martin Luthers von 1526 bis 1546: Festgabe zu seinem 500. Geburtstag.* 2 vols. Göttingen: Vandenhock and Ruprecht, 1983.

Lohse, Bernhard. *Martin Luther: Eine Einführung in sein Leben und sein Werk.* Munich: Beck, 1983.

Oberman, Heiko A. *Luther: Man between God and the Devil.* Trans. Eileen Walliser-Schwarzbart. London: Fontana, 1989.

Schalk, Carl. *Luther on Music: Paradigms of Praise.* St. Louis: Condordia, 1988.

Szyrocki, Marian. *Martin Luther und seine Bedeutung für die deutsche Sprache und Literatur.* Wrocław: Wydawnictwo Uniwersytetu Wrocławskiego, 1985.

Wolf, Herbert, ed. *Luthers Deutsch: Sprachliche Leistung und Wirkung.* Frankfurt am Main: Lang, 1996.

Georg Macropedius

Best, Thomas W. *Macropedius.* New York: Twayne, 1972.

Marquard von Lindau

Edition: *Das Buch der Zehn Gebote (Venedig 1483): Textausgabe mit Einleitung und Glossar.* Ed. Jacobus Willem van Maeren. Amsterdam: Rodopi, 1984.

Blumrich, Rüdiger, ed. *Marquard von Lindau, Deutsche Predigten: Untersuchungen und Edition.* Tübingen: Niemeyer, 1994.

Jacob Masen

Best, Thomas W. "Time in Jacob Masen's *Rusticus imperans.*" *Humanistica Lovaniensia* 27 (1978): 287–94.

Kühlmann, Wilhelm. "Macht auf Widerruf: Der Bauer als Herrscher bei Jacob Masen SJ und Christian Weise." In *Christian Weise: Dichter — Gelehrter — Pädagoge,* ed. Peter Behnke and Hans-Gert Roloff, 245–60. Bern: Lang, 1994.

Maximilian I.

Füssel, Stephan. "Maximilian I." In Füssel, ed., *Deutsche Dichter der Frühen Neuzeit,* 200–216.

Mechthild von Magdeburg

Keul, Hildegund. *Mechthild von Magdeburg: Poetin — Begine — Mystikerin.* Freiburg im Breisgau: Herder Freiburg, 2007.

Tobin, Frank. *Mechthild von Magdeburg: A Medieval Mystic in Modern Eyes.* Columbia, SC: Camden House, 1995.

Niklaus Manuel

Edition: *Vom Papst und seiner Priesterschaft.* In *Deutsche Spiele und Dramen des 15. und 16. Jahrhunderts,* ed. Hellmut Thomke, 139–209. Frankfurt am Main: Deutscher Klassiker Verlag, 1996.

Ehrstine, Glenn. "Niklaus Manuel." In Reinhart and Hardin, eds., *German Writers of the Renaissance and Reformation,* 152–65.

Menz, Cäsar, and Hugo Wagner, eds. *Niklaus Manuel Deutsch: Maler, Dichter, Staatsmann.* Bern: Kunstmuseum Bern, 1979.

Meister Eckhart

Edition: *Meister Eckhart, Die deutschen und lateinischen Werke.* Ed. Bernhard Geyer, Josef Koch, and Erich Seeberg. Stuttgart: Kohlhammer, 2006.

McGinn, Bernard. *The Mystical Thought of Meister Eckhart: The Man from Whom God Hid Nothing.* New York: Crossroad, 2001.

Philipp Melanchthon

Edition: *Elementa rhetorices: Grundbegriffe der Rhetorik.* Trans. and ed. Volkhard Wels. Bibliothek seltener Texte in Studienausgaben 7. Berlin: Weidler, 2001.

Edition: *Werke in Auswahl: Studienausgabe.* 7 vols. Ed. Robert Stupperich et al. Gütersloh: Bertelsmann, 1951–75.

Arnhardt, Gerhard, and Gert-Bodo Reinert. *Philipp Melanchthon: Architekt des neuzeitlich-christlichen deutschen Schulsystems.* Donauwörth: Auer, 2001.

Hartfelder, Karl. *Philipp Melanchthon als Praeceptor Germaniae* (1889). Reprint, Nieuwkoop: de Graaf, 1972.

Jung, Martin H. "Philipp Melanchthon: Humanist im Dienste der Reformation." In Jung and Walter, eds., *Theologen des 16. Jahrhunderts,* 154–71.

Knape, Joachim. *Philipp Melanchthons Rhetorik.* Rhetorik-Forschungen 6. Tübingen: Niemeyer, 1993.

Leonhardt, Jürgen, ed. *Melanchthon und das Lehrbuch des. 16. Jahrhunderts.* Rostock: Philosophische Fakultät, 1997.

Scheible, Heinz. "Melanchthons Bildungsprogramm." In *Lebenslehren und Weltentwürfe im Übergang vom Mittelalter zur Neuzeit: Politik, Bildung, Naturkunde, Theologie,* ed. Hartmut Boockmann, Bernd Moeller, and Karl Stackmann, 233–48. Göttingen: Vandenhoeck & Ruprecht, 1989.

———. *Philipp Melanchthon: Eine Biographie.* Munich: Beck, 1997.

———. "Philipp Melanchthon (1497–1560): Melanchthons Werdegang." In Schmidt, ed., *Humanismus im deutschen Südwesten,* 221–38.

Visser, Dirk. "Philipp Melanchthon." In Reinhart and Hardin, eds., *German Writers of the Renaissance and Reformation,* 166–77.

Wartenberg, Günther, ed. *Werk und Rezeption Philipp Melanchthons in Universität und Schule bis ins 18. Jahrhundert.* Leipzig: Evangelische Verlags-Anstalt, 1999.

Maria Sibylla Merian

Davis, Natalie Zemon. *Drei Frauenleben: Glikl, Marie de l'Incarnation, Maria Sibylla Merian.* Darmstadt: Wissenschaftliche Buchgesellschaft, 1996.

Wettengl, Kurt. "Maria Sibylla Merian (1647–1717)." In Merkel and Wunder, eds., *Deutsche Frauen der Frühen Neuzeit,* 107–22.

Johann Matthäus Meyfart

Edition: *Teutsche Rhetorica oder Redekunst.* Ed. Erich Trunz. Deutsche Neudrucke, Reihe Barock 25. Tübingen: Niemeyer, 1977.

Trunz, Erich. *Johann Matthäus Meyfart: Theologe und Schriftsteller in der Zeit des dreißigjährigen Krieges.* Munich: Beck, 1987.

Jacobus Micyllus

Edition (poetry selection): In Kühlmann, Seidel, and Wiegand, eds., *Humanistische Lyrik,* 359–93 (commentary: 1159–77).

Classen, Johannes. *Jacob Micyllus Rector zu Frankfurt und Professor zu Heidelberg von 1524 bis 1558, als Schulmann, Dichter und Gelehrter.* Frankfurt am Main: Verlag für Kunst und Wissenschaft, 1859.

Johann Sebastian Mitternacht

Kelly, W. A. "Johann Sebastian Mitternacht." In Hardin, ed., *German Baroque Writers, 1661–1730,* 286–91.

Sorg, Norbert. *Restauration und Rebellion — Die deutschen Dramen Johann Sebastian Mitternachts: Ein Beitrag zur Geschichte des protestantischen Schuldramas im 17. Jahrhundert.* Freiburg im Breisgau: Hochschulverlag, 1980.

Olympia Fulvia Morata

Flood, John L. "Olympia Fulvia Morata." In Reinhart and Hardin, eds., *German Writers of the Renaissance and Reformation,* 178–83.

Müller, Uwe. "Olympia Fulvia Morata." In *Lebensbilder Schweinfurter Frauen,* ed. Barbara Vogel-Fuchs, 158–68. Schweinfurt: Stadtarchiv Schweinfurt, 1991.

Daniel Georg Morhof

Edition: *Unterricht von der teutschen Sprache und Poesie.* Ed. Henning Boetius. Ars Poetica. Texte 1. Bad Homburg: Wiedemeyer, 1969.

Koch, Hans Albrecht, and Dieter Lohmeier. "Morhof, Daniel Georg." In *Schleswig-holsteinisches biographisches Lexikon,* 4:162–66. Neumünster: Wachholtz, 1976.

Johann Michael Moscherosch

Edition: *Wunderliche und Wahrhafftige Gesichte Philanders von Sittewalt.* Ed. Wolfgang Harms. Stuttgart: Reclam, 1986.

Barber, Sigmund J. "Johann Michael Moscherosch (Philander von Sittewalt)." In Hardin, ed., *German Baroque Writers, 1580–1660,* 230–37.

Kühlmann, Wilhelm. "Johann Michael Moscherosch in den Jahren 1648–1651: Die Briefe an Johann Valentin Andreae." *Daphnis* 14, no. 2 (1985): 245–76.

Schäfer, Walter E. *Johann Michael Moscherosch: Staatsmann, Satiriker und Pädagoge im Barockzeitalter.* Munich: Beck, 1982.

Thomas Müntzer

Edition: *Quellen zu Thomas Müntzer.* 3 vols. Ed. Wieland Held et al. Leipzig: Verlag der Sächsischen Akademie der Wissenschaften, 2004.

Bloch, Ernst. *Thomas Müntzer als Theologe der Revolution* (1921). 3rd ed. Frankfurt am Main: Suhrkamp, 1967.

Friesen, Abraham. *Thomas Muentzer, a Destroyer of the Godless: The Making of a Sixteenth-Century Religious Revolutionary.* Berkeley: U of California P, 1990.

Goertz, Hans-Jürgen. *Thomas Müntzer: Mystiker, Apokalyptiker, Revolutionär.* Munich: Beck, 1989.

Scott, Tom. *Thomas Müntzer: Theology and Revolution in the German Reformation.* Basingstoke: Macmillan, 1989.

Johannes Murmellius

Kühlmann, Wilhelm. "Johannes Murmellius." In Killy, *Literatur-Lexikon* 8, 301–2.

Thomas Murner

Edition: *Deutsche Schriften mit den Holzschnitten der Erstdrucke.* 9 vols. Ed. Gustav Bebermeyer et al. Berlin: de Gruyter, 1918–31.

Gaus, Linda L. "Thomas Murner." In Reinhart and Hardin, eds., *German Writers of the Renaissance and Reformation,* 184–97.

Thomas Naogeorgus

Edition: *Sämtliche Werke.* 4 vols. Ed. Hans-Gert Roloff. Berlin: de Gruyter, 1975–87.

Michael, Wolfgang F. In Michael, *Das deutsche Drama der Reformationszeit,* 81–91.

Roloff, Hans-Gert. "Heilsgeschichte, Weltgeschehen und aktuelle Polemik: Thomas Naogeorgs 'Tragoedia nova Pammachius.'" *Daphnis* 9 (1980): 743–67.

Benjamin Neukirch

De Capua, A. G. and Ernst Alfred Philippson. "The So-Called 'Neukirch Sammlung': Some Facts." *Modern Language Notes* 79, no. 4 (1964): 405–14.

Metzger, Erika A. "Benjamin Neukirch." In Hardin, ed., *German Baroque Writers, 1661–1730,* 292–99.

Martin Opitz

Edition: *Gesammelte Werke.* 4 vols. Ed. George Schultz-Behrend. Bibliothek des Literarischen Vereins Stuttgart 295–97. Stuttgart: Hiersemann, 1968–90.

Becker-Cantarino, Barbara. "Martin Opitz." In Hardin, ed., *German Baroque Writers, 1580–1660,* 256–68.

Borgstedt, Thomas, and Walter Schütz, eds. *Martin Opitz (1597–1639): Nachahmungspoetik und Lebenswelt.* Tübingen: Niemeyer, 2002.

Drux, Rudolf. *Martin Opitz und sein poetisches Regelsystem.* Literatur und Wirklichkeit 18. Bonn: Bouvier 1976.

Faber du Faur, Curt von. "Der *Aristarchus:* Eine Neuwertung." *PMLA* 69 (1954): 566–90.

Garber, Klaus. *Martin Opitz, "der Vater der deutschen Dichtung": Eine kritische Studie zur Wissenschaftsgeschichte der Germanistik.* Stuttgart: Metzler, 1976.

———. "Martin Opitz' *Schäferei von der Nymphe Hercinie* als Ursprung der Prosaekloge und des Schäferromans in Deutschland." *Daphnis* 11, no. 3 (1982): 547–603.

Szyrocki, Marian. *Martin Opitz.* Munich: Beck, 1974.

Ulmer, Bernhard. *Martin Opitz.* New York: Twayne, 1971.

Oswald von Wolkenstein

Edition: *Die Lieder Oswalds von Wolkenstein.* Ed. Karl Kurt Klein. Tübingen: Niemeyer, 1962.

Classen, Albrecht. "Oswald von Wolkenstein." In Reinhart and Hardin, eds., *German Writers of the Renaissance and Reformation,* 198–205.

Robertshaw, Alan. *Oswald von Wolkenstein: The Myth and the Man.* Göppingen: Kümmerle, 1977.

Paracelsus

Edition: *Werke.* 5 vols. Ed. Will-Erich Peuckert. Darmstadt: Wissenschaftliche Buchgesellschaft, 1965–76.

Williams, Gerhild Scholz. "Paracelsus." In Reinhart and Hardin, eds., *German Writers of the Renaissance and Reformation,* 206–11.

Johanna Eleonora Petersen

Edition: *Leben, von ihr selbst mit eigener Hand aufgesetzet: Autobiographie.* Ed. Prisca Guglielmetti. Kleine Texte des Pietismus 8. Leipzig: Evangelische Verlag-Anstalt, 2003.

Conrad Peutinger

Lutz, Heinrich. *Conrad Peutinger: Beiträge zu einer politischen Biographie.* Abhandlungen zur Geschichte der Stadt Augsburg 9. Augsburg: Wissner, 1958.

Eneas Silvius Piccolomini

Morrall, Eric John. *Aeneas Sylvius Piccolomini (Pius II) and Niklas von Wyle: The Tale of Two Lovers, Eurialus and Lucretia.* Amsterdam: Rodopi, 1988.

Voigt, Georg. *Enea Silvio de' Piccolomini als Papst Pius II und sein Zeitalter* (1856–63). Reprint, Berlin: de Gruyter, 1967.

Caritas Pirckheimer

Barker, Paula Datsko. "Caritas Pirckheimer (1467–1532)." In Reinhart and Hardin, eds., *German Writers of the Renaissance and Reformation,* 212–17.

Hess, Ursula. "Caritas Pirckheimer (1467–1532)." In Merkel and Wunder, eds., *Deutsche Frauen der Frühen Neuzeit,* 19–38.

Krabbel, Gerta. *Caritas Pirckheimer: Ein Lebensbild aus der Zeit der Reformation.* Münster: Aschendorff, 1982.

Willibald Pirckheimer

Edition: *Eckius dedolatus — Der enteckte Eck: Lateinisch/Deutsch.* Trans. Niklas Holzberg. Stuttgart: Reclam, 1983.

Edition: *Der Schweizerkrieg.* Trans. Ernst Münch. Ed. Wolfgang Schiel. Berlin: Militärverlag der DDR, 1988.

Bernstein, Eckhard. "Willibald Pirckheimer." In Reinhart and Hardin, eds., *German Writers of the Renaissance and Reformation,* 218–25.

Holzberg, Niklas. *Willibald Pirckheimer: Griechischer Humanismus in Deutschland.* Munich: Fink, 1983.

Susanna Elisabeth Prasch

Holm, Christiane. "Die verliebte Psyche und ihr galanter Brautigam: Das Roman-Projekt von Susanna Elisabeth und Johann Ludwig Prasch." In *Der galante Diskurs: Kommunikationsideal und Epochenschwelle,* ed. Thomas Borgstedt and Andreas Solbach, 53–85. Dresden: Thelem, 2001.

Wolfgang Ratke

Ising, Erika. *Wolfgang Ratkes Schriften zur deutschen Grammatik (1612–1630).* Berlin: Akademie, 1959.

Kordes, Uwe. *Wolfgang Ratke (Ratichius, 1571–1635): Gesellschaft, Religiosität und Gelehrsamkeit im frühen 17. Jahrhundert.* Heidelberg: Winter, 1999.

Paul Rebhun

Edition: *Susanna.* Ed. Hans-Gert Roloff. Stuttgart: Reclam, 1967.

Casey, Paul F. *Paul Rebhun: A Biographical Study.* Stuttgart: Steiner, 1986.

Johannes Regiomontanus

Zinner, Ernst. *Regiomontanus: His Life and Work.* Trans. Ezra Brown. Studies in the History and Philosophy of Mathematics 1 (1968). Reprint, Amsterdam: Elsevier Science & Technology Books, 1990.

Johannes Reuchlin

Edition: *Briefwechsel: Johannes Reuchlin.* 2 vols. Trans. Adelbert Weh. Ed. Manfred Fuhrmann. Stuttgart-Bad Cannstatt: Fromann-Holzboog, 2004.

Edition: *Henno.* Trans. (German) and ed. Harry C. Schnur. Stuttgart: Reclam, 1995.

Newman, Jane O. "Textuality versus Performativity in Neo-Latin Drama: Johannes Reuchlin's *Henno.*" *Theater Journal* 38 (1986): 259–74.

Price, David. "Johannes Reuchlin." In Reinhart and Hardin, eds., *German Writers of the Renaissance and Reformation,* 231–40.

Rhein, Stefan. "Johannes Reuchlin." In Füssel, ed., *Deutsche Dichter der frühen Neuzeit*, 138–55.

Rummel, Erika. *The Case against Johann Reuchlin: Religious and Social Controversy in Sixteenth-Century Germany.* Toronto: U of Toronto P, 2002.

Christian Reuter

Edition: *Schelmuffsky.* Ed. Ilse-Marie Barth. Stuttgart: Reclam, 1997.

Schweitzer, Christoph E. "Christian Reuter." In Hardin, ed., *German Baroque Writers, 1661–1730*, 342–49.

Beautus Rhenanus

D'Amico, John F. *Theory and Practice in Renaissance Textual Criticism: Beatus Rhenanus between Conjecture and History.* Berkeley: U of California P, 1988.

Johann Riemer

Edition: *Werke.* 4 vols. Ed. Helmut Krause. Berlin: de Gruyter, 1979–87.

Alexander, R. J. "Johannes Riemer." In Hardin, ed., *German Baroque Writers, 1661–1730*, 350–56.

Krause, Helmut. *Feder contra Degen: Zur literarischen Vermittlung des bürgerlichen Weltbildes im Werk Johannes Riemer.* Berlin: Hofgarten, 1979.

Johann Rist

Edition: *Sämtliche Werke.* 7 vols. Ed. Eberhard Mannack. Berlin: de Gruyter, 1967–82.

Bepler, Jill. "Johann Rist." In Hardin, ed., *German Baroque Writers, 1580–1660*, 269–78.

Garber, Klaus. "Pétrarchisme pastoral et bourgeoisie protestante: La poésie pastorale de J. Rist et J. Schwieger." In *Le genre pastoral en Europe du XVe au XVIIe siècle*, ed. Claude Longeon, 269–97. Saint Etienne: Université de Saint Etienne, 1980.

Schade, Richard E. "Baroque Biography: Johann Rist's Self-Concept." *German Quarterly* 51 (1978): 338–45.

Georg Sabinus

Edition (poetry selection): In Kühlmann, Seidel, and Wiegand, eds., *Humanistische Lyrik*, 499–539 (commentary: 1240–70).

Kühlmann, Wilhelm, and Waldemar Straube. "Zur Historie und Pragmatik humanistischer Lyrik im alten Preußen: Von Konrad Celtis über Eobanus Hessus zu Georg Sabinus." In Garber, ed., *Kulturgeschichte Ostpreußens*, 657–736.

Hans Sachs

Edition: *Werke in zwei Bänden.* Ed. Reinhard Hahn. Berlin: Aufbau, 1992.

Bernstein, Eckhard. "Hans Sachs." In Reinhart and Hardin, eds., *German Writers of the Renaissance and Reformation*, 241–52.

———. *Hans Sachs: Mit Selbstzeugnissen und Bilddokumenten.* Reinbek bei Hamburg: Rowohlt, 1993.

Füssel, Stephan et al., eds. *Hans Sachs: Katalog zur Ausstellung.* 2nd ed. Göttingen: Gratia, 1979.

Hahn, Reinhard. "Hans Sachs." In Füssel, ed., *Deutsche Dichter der frühen Neuzeit,* 406–27.

Klein, Dorothea. *Bildung und Belehrung: Untersuchungen zum Dramenwerk des Hans Sachs.* Stuttgart: Heinz, 1988.

Könneker, Barbara. *Hans Sachs.* Sammlung Metzler 94. Stuttgart: Metzler, 1971.

Merzbacher, Dieter. *Handwerker, Dichter, Stadtbürger: 500 Jahre Hans Sachs.* Exhibition catalogue. Herzog August Bibliothek 72. Wiesbaden: Harrassowitz, 1995.

Paul Melissus Schede

Edition: *Die Psalmenübersetzungen des Paul Schede Melissus (1572).* Ed. Max Hermann Jellinek. Halle: Niemeyer, 1896.

Price, David. "Paul Melissus Schede." In Reinhart and Hardin, eds., *German Writers of the Renaissance and Reformation,* 260–64.

Schäfer, Eckhart. *Deutscher Horaz: Conrad Celtis, Georg Fabricius, Paul Melissus, Jacob Balde.* Wiesbaden: Steiner, 1976.

———. "Paulus Melissus Schedius (1539–1602): Leben in Versen." In Schmidt, ed., *Humanismus im deutschen Südwesten,* 239–63.

Hartmann Schedel

Edition: *Chronicle of the World (1493): The Complete and Annotated Nuremberg Chronicle.* Ed. Stephan Füssel. Cologne: Taschen, 2001.

Reske, Christoph. *The Production of Schedel's Nuremberg Chronicle.* Mainzer Studien zur Buchwissenschaft 10. Wiesbaden: Harrassowitz, 2000.

Johannes Scheffler (Angelus Silesius)

Edition: *Sämtliche poetische Werke.* 3 vols. Ed. Hans Ludwig Held. Munich: Hanser, 1952.

Sammons, Jeffrey L. *Angelus Silesius.* New York: Twayne, 1967.

———. "Johann Scheffler (Angelus Silesius)." In Hardin, ed., *German Baroque Writers, 1580–1660,* 279–88.

Skrine, Peter. "Angelus Silesius; or, The Art of Being an Angel." *London Germanic Studies* 1 (1980): 86–100.

Laurentius von Schnüffis

Harper, Anthony J. "Laurentius von Schnüffis." In Hardin, ed., *German Baroque Writers, 1661–1730,* 247–51.

Justus Georg Schottelius

Edition: *Ausführliche Arbeit von der Teutschen HaubtSprache.* Ed. Wolfgang Hecht. Deutsche Neudrucke. Reihe Barock 11–12. Tübingen: Niemeyer, 1967.

Berns, Jörg Jochen. *Justus Georg Schottelius 1612–1676: Ein Teutscher Gelehrter am Wolfenbütteler Hof.* Ausstellungskataloge der Herzog-August-Bibliothek 18. Wolfenbüttel: Herzog August Bibliothek, 1976.

Smart, Sara. "Justus Georg Schottelius." In Hardin, ed., *German Baroque Writers, 1580–1660,* 298–303.

———. "Justus Georg Schottelius and the Patriotic Movement." *Modern Language Review* 84, no. 1 (1989): 83–98.

Sibylle Schwarz

Edition: *Deutsche poëtische Gedicht: Faksimiledruck nach der Ausgabe von 1650.* Ed. Helmut W. Ziefle. Bern: Lang, 1980.

Becker-Cantarino, Barbara. "Sibylle Schwarz." In Hardin, ed., *German Baroque Writers, 1580–1660,* 312–15.

Clark, Susan. "Sibylle Schwarz: Prodigy and Feminist." In Wilson and Warnke, eds., *Women Writers of the Seventeenth Century,* 431–60.

Ziefle, Helmut W. *Sibylle Schwarz: Ihr Leben und Werk.* Bonn: Bouvier, 1975.

Caspar Schwenckfeld

Edition: *Corpus Schwenckfeldianorum.* 19 vols. Ed. Selena Gerhard Schultz. Norristown, PA: The Board of Publicaton of the Schwenckfelder Church, 1907–61.

Kuhn, Thomas K. "Caspar Schwenckfeld von Ossig: Reformatorischer Laientheologe und Spiritualist." In Jung and Walter, eds., *Theologen des 16. Jahrhunderts,* 191–208.

Weigelt, Horst. "Caspar von Schwenckfeld (1489–1561), Schwenckfeldianer." In *Theologische Realenzyklopädie* 30 (1999): 712–19.

Johannes Secundus

Edition: *Basia.* Ed. Georg Ellinger. Berlin: Weidmann, 1899.

Endres, Clifford. *Joannes Secundus: The Latin Love Elegy in the Renaissance.* Hamden: Anchor Books, 1981.

Perella, Nicolas James. *The Kiss Sacred and Profane: An Interpretative History of Kiss Symbolism.* Berkeley: U of California P, 1969.

Petrus Lotichius Secundus

Edition (poetry selections): In Kühlmann, Seidel, and Wiegand, eds., *Humanistische Lyrik,* 395–497 (commentary: 1178–239).

Auhagen, Ulrike, und Eckart Schäfer, eds. *Lotichius und die römische Elegie.* Tübingen: Narr, 2001.

Coppel, Bernhard. "Petrus Lotichius Secundus." In Füssel, ed., *Deutsche Dichter der frühen Neuzeit,* 529–44.

Zon, Stephen. *Petrus Lotichius Secundus, Neo-Latin Poet.* Bern: Lang, 1983.

Friedrich Spee von Langenfeld

Edition: *Cautio Criminalis, oder Rechtliches Bedenken wegen der Hexenprozesse.* 6th ed. Ed. Joachim-Friedrich Ritter. Munich: Deutscher Taschenbuch Verlag, 2000.

Edition: *Trutznachtigall.* Ed. G. Richard Dimler. Washington, DC: UP of America, 1981.

Battafarano, Italo Michele, ed. *Friedrich von Spee: Dichter, Theologe und Bekämpfer der Hexenprozesse.* Trento: Luigi Reverdito Editore, 1988.

Dimler, G. Richard. "Friedrich Spee von Langenfeld." In Hardin, ed., *German Baroque Writers, 1580–1660,* 316–20.

Keller, Karl. *Friedrich Spee von Langenfeld (1591–1635): Leben und Werk des Seelsorgers und Dichters.* Geldern: Keuck, 1990.

Philipp Jakob Spener

Edition: *Schriften.* 8 vols. Ed. Erich Beyreuther and Dietrich Blaufuß. Hildesheim: Olms, 1978–2002.

Pustejovsky, John. "Philipp Jakob Spener." In Hardin, ed., *German Baroque Writers, 1580–1660,* 321–29.

Wallmann, Johannes. *Philipp Jakob Spener und die Anfänge des Pietismus.* Tübingen: Mohr, 1970.

Heinrich Steinhöwel

Edition: *Der Ulmer Aesop von 1476/77: Äsops Leben und Fabeln sowie Fabeln und Schwänke anderer Herkunft: Hrsg. und ins Deutsche übersetzt von Heinrich Steinhöwel.* Ed. Peter Amelung. Ludwigsburg: Edition Libri illustri, 1995.

Classen, Albrecht. "Heinrich Steinhöwel." In Reinhart and Hardin, eds., *German Writers of the Renaissance and Reformation,* 276–80.

Dicke, Gerd. "Heinrich Steinhöwel." In *Verfasserlexikon: Die deutsche Literatur des Mittelalters.* 2nd ed, ed. Kurt Ruh et al., 3: cols. 258–78. Berlin: de Gruyter, 1981.

Hess, Ursula. *Heinrich Steinhöwels "Griseldis": Studien zur Text- und Überlieferungsgeschichte einer frühhumanistischen Prosanovelle.* Munich: Beck, 1975.

Caspar Stieler

Edition: *Die Dichtkunst des Spaten.* Ed. Herbert Zeman. Vienna: Österreichischer Bundesverlag, 1975.

Edition: *Die Geharnschte Venus.* Ed. Ferdinand van Ingen. Stuttgart: Reclam, 1970.

Aiken, Judith P. "Caspar Stieler." In Hardin, ed., *German Baroque Writers, 1580–1660,* 330–38.

———. *Scaramutza in Germany: The Dramatic Works of Caspar Stieler.* University Park: Pennsylvania State UP, 1989.

Johann Thomas

Edition: *Damon und Lisille.* Ed. Herbert Singer and Horst Gronemeyer. Hamburg: Maximilian Gesellschaft, 1966.

Bishop, Patricia. "Johann Thomas." In Hardin, ed., *German Baroque Writers, 1661–1730*, 374–79.

Thüring von Ringoltingen

Edition: *Melusine: in der Fassung des Buchs der Liebe (1587): Thüring von Ringoltingen.* Ed. Hans-Gert Roloff. Stuttgart: Reclam, 1991.

Edition: *Melusine.* In *Romane des 15. und 16. Jahrhunderts*, ed. Jan-Dirk Müller, 9–176 (commentary: 1012–87). Bibliothek deutscher Klassiker 54. Frankfurt am Main: Deutscher Klassiker Verlag, 1990.

Keller, Hildegard Elisabeth. "Berner Samstagsgeheimnisse: Die Vertikale als Erzählformel in der *Melusine.*" *Beiträge zur Geschichte der deutschen Sprache und Literatur* (forthcoming).

Joachim Vadianus (von Witt)

Edition: *De poetica et carminis ratione.* Ed. Peter Schäffer. 3 vols. Humanistische Bibliothek 2: 21,1–3. Munich: Fink, 1973–78.

Schaeffer, Peter. "Joachim Vadianus (Joachim Von Watt)." In Reinhart and Hardin, eds., *German Writers of the Renaissance and Reformation*, 293–302.

Johannes Vossius

Edition: *Commentariorum rhetoricorum, sive oratoriarum institutionum libri sex.* (1606). Reprint, Kronberg: Scriptor, 1974.

Johann Christoph Wagenseil

Edition: *Buch von der Meister-Singer Holdseligen Kunst* (1697). Ed. Horst Brunner. Litterae 38. Reprint, Göppingen: Kümmerle, 1975.

Burkhard Waldis

Edition: *Der Verlorene Sohn, ein Fastnachtspiel.* Ed. Gustav Milchsack. Halle: Niedermeyer, 1881.

Michael, Wolfgang F. "Burkhard Waldis." In Michael, *Das deutsche Drama der Reformationszeit*, 46–49.

Reich, Angelika. "Burkhard Waldis." In Füssel, ed., *Deutsche Dichter der frühen Neuzeit*, 377–88.

Georg Rodolf Weckherlin

Edition: *Georg Rudolf Weckherlins Gedichte.* 3 vols. Ed. Hermann Fischer (1894–1907). Reprint, Darmstadt: Wissenschaftliche Buchgesellschaft, 1968.

Meid, Volker. "Ein politischer Deutscher: Zu Weckherlins Sonett *An das Teutschland.*" In *Gedichte und Interpretationen* 1, ed. Meid, 148–58. Stuttgart: Reclam, 1982.

Schade, Richard E. "Georg Rodolf Weckherlin." In Hardin, ed., *German Baroque Writers, 1580–1660*, 353–56.

Diederich von dem Werder

Dünnhaupt, Gerhard. "Die *Friedensrede* Diederichs von dem Werder und ihr Verhältnis zur *Querela Pacis* des Erasmus von Rotterdam." In Hoffmeister, ed., *Europäische Tradition*, 371–90.

Witkowski, Georg. *Diederich von dem Werder.* Leipzig: Veit, 1887.

Christian Weise

Edition: *Sämtliche Werke.* 7 vols. Ed. John D. Lindberg. Continued by Hans-Gert Roloff. Berlin: de Gruyter, 1971–2006.

Behnke, Peter, and Hans-Gert Roloff, eds. Christian Weise. *Dichter — Gelehrter — Pädagoge: Beiträge zum Christian-Weise-Symposium aus Anlaß des 350. Geburtstages, Zittau, 1992. Jahrbuch für internationale Germanistik.* Reihe A, 37. Bern: Lang, 1994.

Haischer, Peter-Henning. "Zur Bedeutung von Parodie und Karneval in Christian Weises 'Zittauisch Theatrum.'" *Daphnis* 28 (1999): 287–321.

Skrine, Peter N. "Christian Weise." In Hardin, ed., *German Baroque Writers, 1661–1730*, 391–400.

Zeller, Konradin. *Pädagogik und Drama: Untersuchungen zur Schulcomödie Christian Weises.* Tübingen: Niemeyer, 1980.

Georg Wickram

Edition: *Sämtliche Werke.* 11 vols. Ed. Hans-Gert Roloff. Berlin: de Gruyter, 1967–92.

Haug, Walter. "Jörg Wickrams *Ritter Galmy:* Die Zähmung des Romans als Ursprung seiner Möglichkeit." In *Traditionswandel und Traditionsverhalten,* ed. Haug and Burckhart Wachinger. Tübingen: Niemeyer, 1991.

Kleinschmidt, Erich. "Jörg Wickram." In Füssel, ed., *Deutsche Dichter der frühen Neuzeit*, 494–511.

Maché, Ulrich. "Soziale Mobilität in den Romanen Jörg Wickrams." In *Virtus et Fortuna: Festschrift für Hans-Gert Roloff*, ed. Joseph P. Strelka and Jörg Jungmayr, 184–97. Bern: Lang, 1983.

Wåghäll, Elisabeth. "Georg Wickram." In Reinhart and Hardin, eds., *German Writers of the Renaissance and Reformation*, 309–16.

Jakob Wimpfeling

Edition: *Adolescentia.* Ed. Otto Herding, with Franz Josef Worstbrock. Munich: Fink, 1965.

Edition: *Jacobi Wimpfelingi opera selecta.* 3 vols. Ed. Otto Herding and Dieter Mertens. Munich: Fink, 1990.

Edition: *Stylpho: Lateinisch und deutsch.* Ed. Harry S. Schnur. Stuttgart: Reclam, 1971.

Mertens, Dieter. "Jakob Wimpfeling, Pädagogischer Humanismus." In Schmidt, ed., *Humanismus im deutschen Südwesten*, 35–57.

Overfield, James H. "Jakob Wimpfeling." In Reinhart and Hardin, eds., *German Writers of the Renaissance and Reformation*, 317–25.

Heinrich Wittenwiler

Edition (English): *Wittenweiler's Ring*. Trans. George Fenwick Jones. Chapel Hill: U of North Carolina P, 1956.

Classen, Albrecht. "Heinrich Wittenwiler." In Reinhart and Hardin, eds., *German Writers of the Renaissance and Reformation*, 326–31.

Niklas von Wyle

Edition: *Figurenlehre*. In *Rhetorica deutsch: Rhetorikschriften des 15. Jahrhunderts*, ed. Joachim Knape and Bernhard Roll, 205–32. Gratia 40. Wiesbaden: Harrassowitz, 2002.

Edition: *Translationen* (1861). Ed. Adelbert von Keller. Bibliothek des Litterarischen Vereins in Stuttgart 57. Reprint, Stuttgart: Hildesheim: Olms 1967.

Flood, John L. "Niklas von Wyle." In Reinhart and Hardin, eds., *German Writers of the Renaissance and Reformation*, 332–37.

Schwenk, Rolf. *Vorarbeiten zu einer Biographie des Niklas von Wyle und zu einer kritischen Ausgabe seiner ersten Translatze*. Göppingen: Kümmerle, 1978.

Worstbrock, Franz Josef. "Niklas von Wyle." In Füssel, ed., *Deutsche Dichter der frühen Neuzeit*, 35–50.

Katharina Schütz Zell

Edition: *Katharina Schütz Zell*. Vol. 2: *The Writings: A Critical Edition*. Ed. Elsie Anne McKee. Leiden: Brill, 1999.

McKee, Elsie Anne. *Katharina Schütz Zell*. Vol. 1: *The Life and Thought of a Sixteenth-Century Reformer*. Leiden: Brill, 1999.

Wiesner, Merry E. "Katharina Zell's 'Ein Brieff an die ganze Burgerschafft der Statt Strassburg' as Theology and Autobiography." In Reinhart and Blackwell, eds., *Cultural Contentions*, 245–54.

Philipp von Zesen

Edition: *Sämtliche Werke*. 17 vols. Ed. Ferdinand van Ingen. Berlin: de Gruyter, 1970–2003.

Ingen, Ferdinand van. *Philipp von Zesen*. Sammlung Metzler 96. Stuttgart: Metzler, 1970.

Krump, Sandra. "Zesens 'Adriatische Rosemund': Gesellschaftskritik und Poetik." *Euphorion* 94, no. 4 (2000): 359–402.

Otto, Karl F. Jr. "Philipp von Zesen." In Hardin, ed., *German Baroque Writers, 1580–1660*, 370–78.

Spriewald, Ingeborg. "Die Anwaltschaft für den Menschen im Roman bei Zesen und Grimmelshausen." In *Studien zur deutschen Literatur im 17. Jahrhundert*, ed. Werner Link, 352–438. Berlin: Aufbau, 1984.

Heinrich Anshelm von Zigler und Kliphausen

Hardin, James, and Renate Wilson. "Heinrich Anshelm von Zigler und Kliphausen." In Hardin, ed., *German Baroque Writers, 1661–1730*, 401–6.

Julius Wilhelm Zincgref

Edition: *Apophthegmata teutsch*. Ed. Theodor Verweyen in collaboration with Dieter Mertens and Werner W. Schnabel. Tübingen: Niemeyer, forthcoming.

Edition: *Gesammelte Schriften*. 3 vols. Ed. Dieter Mertens and Theodor Verweyen. Tübingen: Niemeyer, 1978–93.

Edition: *Emblemata ethico-politica*. Ed. Dieter Mertens and Theodor Verweyen. 2 vols. Tübingen: Niemeyer, 1993.

Clark, Jonathan P. "Julius Wilhelm Zincgref." In Hardin, ed., *German Baroque Writers, 1580–1660*, 379–83.

Weydt, Günter. "Apophthegmata Teutsch." In *Festschrift für Jost Trier zum 70. Geburtstag*, ed. William Foerste and Karl Heinz Borck, 164–85. Cologne: Böhlau, 1964.

Huldrych Zwingli

Edition: *Huldreich Zwinglis sämtliche Werke*. 14 vols. Ed. Emil Egli et al. Berlin: Schwetschke, 1905–91.

Baker, J. Wayne. "Huldrych Zwingli." In Reinhart and Hardin, eds., *German Writers of the Renaissance and Reformation*, 338–47.

Gabler, Ulrich. *Huldrych Zwingli: His Life and Work*. Trans. Ruth C. L. Gritsch. Philadelphia: Fortress, 1986.

Sallmann, Martin. "Huldrych Zwingli: Reformator und Humanist in Zürich." In Jung and Walter, eds., *Theologen des 16. Jahrhunderts*, 83–101.

Stephens, W. P. *The Theology of Huldrych Zwingli*. Oxford: Clarendon, 1986.

Contributors

JOHN ALEXANDER is Professor of German at Arizona State University. He has published in the area of early modern literature, in particular on German drama and theater from 1550 to 1750. Among his publications are two edited reprints and the monograph *Das Deutsche Barockdrama*, Sammlung Metzler 209 (1984).

JILL BEPLER received her doctorate from the University of Bristol and is head of the Fellowship Program at the Herzog August Bibliothek, Wolfenbüttel. She has written on travel writing and book collecting in the early modern period, including most recently *Travelling and Posterity: The Archive, the Library and the Cabinet* (2005). She has also published numerous articles on the role of women at court and on funerary literature and ritual in the early modern period.

RENATE BORN is Associate Professor of German at the University of Georgia. Her research interests are the evolution of modern standard German in the early modern period and the dialects of immigrant communities established in North America in the eighteenth and nineteenth centuries. She is the author of *Michigan German in Frankenmuth: Variation and Change in an East Franconian Dialect* (1993) and has published articles on Germanic verb morphology, language maintenance and death, and language pedagogy.

ANNA CARRDUS is Senior Lecturer in German at the University of Bristol. She has published on various aspects of the early modern period, including consolation literature, women's writing, and school theater. She is the author of *Das 'weiblich Werck' in der Residenzstadt Altenburg 1672–1720: Gedichte und Briefe von Margaretha Susanna von Kuntsch und Frauen in ihrem Umkreis* (2004).

LAUREL CARRINGTON is Professor of History at St. Olaf College. She has published numerous articles on Erasmus in the *Erasmus of Rotterdam Society Yearbook*, the *Archiv für Reformationsgeschichte*, and elsewhere. Currently, she is finishing the annotations for the *Epistola contra Pseudevangelicos* and the *Epistola ad Fratres Germaniae Inferioris* for volume 78 of the Collected Works of Erasmus series published by the University of Toronto Press and is working on a translation of Bucer's *Epistola Apologetica*.

PETER M. DALY is Professor Emeritus of German Studies at McGill University. His major research and publishing activities are in the sixteenth- and seventeenth-century literatures of Germany and England with special reference to verbal-visual relationships. This includes not only the emblem, but also modern analogues in advertising and propaganda. Together with a group of Canadian, American, and European colleagues he established the journal *Emblematica: An Interdisciplinary Journal for Emblem Studies* and the book series AMS Studies in the Emblem. He is general editor of the Index Emblematicus project and the bibliographic series Corpus Librorum Emblematum, both published by the University of Toronto Press.

C. SCOTT DIXON is Senior Lecturer in the School of Politics, International Studies and Philosophy at the Queen's University of Belfast. He has published on the social, political, and religious history of Germany in the early modern period. His books include *The Reformation and Rural Society* (1996), *The Reformation in Germany* (2002), and (as co-editor with Martina Fuchs) *The Histories of Charles V* (2005).

GRAEME DUNPHY lectures at the Universität Regensburg. He has published widely on medieval historiography, especially on Jans der Enikel; he is the general editor of the forthcoming *Encyclopedia of the Medieval Chronicle*. He has also worked on early modern literature — *Opitz's Anno: The Middle High German Annolied in the 1639 Edition of Martin Opitz* (2003) — and on modern cross-cultural literature.

JOHN L. FLOOD is Professor Emeritus of German in the University of London and past president of the Bibliographical Society. He has published extensively on medieval and early modern German literature, the history of medicine, and the history of the book. His publications include *The German Book 1450–1750* (1995), *Johannes Sinapius (1505–1560): Hellenist and Physician in Germany and Italy* (1997), and the four-volume *Poets Laureate in the Holy Roman Empire: A Bio-bibliographical Handbook* (2006).

STEPHAN FÜSSEL is Director of the Institute of the History of the Book and holder of the Gutenberg Chair at the Johannes Gutenberg Universität Mainz. He is Vice-President of the Willibald Pirckheimer Society for Renaissance and Humanist Studies, a member of the board of the International Gutenberg Society, and editor of the *Gutenberg Jahrbuch* and the *Pirckheimer Jahrbuch*. He has published widely on early printing, on bookselling and publishing from the eighteenth to the twentieth century, and on the future of communications. Among his many books are *Gutenberg und seine Wirkung* (1999) and *The Book of Books: The Luther Bible of 1534: A Cultural-Historical Introduction* (2003).

KLAUS GARBER is Professor Emeritus for the Theory and History of Modern Literature at the Universität Osnabrück, where he founded the Institut für Kulturgeschichte der Frühen Neuzeit and expanded its library into one of Europe's richest repositories for early modern literary studies. He has written or edited dozens of books on the literary and cultural history of the Baroque and the Early Modern, including histories of books and libraries, as well as on

Walter Benjamin and Richard Alewyn, who was his teacher in Bonn. His books and editions include *Der locus amoenus und der locus terribilis: Bild und Funktion der Natur in der deutschen Schäfer- und Landlebendichtung des 17. Jahrhunderts* (1974); *Martin Opitz, "der Vater der deutschen Dichtung": Eine kritische Studie zur Wissenschaftsgeschichte der Germanistik* (1976); and the ongoing publication of *Handbuch des personalen Gelegenheitsschrifttums in europäischen Bibliotheken und Archiven* (2001–). He is a co-founder of the Niemeyer monograph series Frühe Neuzeit. In 2003 he was awarded an honorary doctorate by the Universität Hamburg (his native city) for his contributions to the discovery and preservation of older German libraries in Poland, the Balkans, Russia, and Ukraine.

PETER HESS is Associate Professor of Germanic Studies at the University of Texas at Austin. He has published books on Harsdörffer's poetics (*Poetik ohne Trichter*, 1986) and on the epigram (*Epigramm*, 1989) and has written articles on early modern rhetoric, topics, poetics, and translation, as well as on numerous writers of the seventeenth century. His recent publications include studies of Logau's epigrams and of Dürer's view of Aztec culture. His latest monographs *Mapping Emerging Modernity: Crisis, Transgression, Discipline, and Ordering in Early Modern German Literature* and *Fortress Lilliput: Small Country Nationalism in an Age of Global Competition* (with John Hoberman) are forthcoming.

GERHART HOFFMEISTER is Professor Emeritus of German and Comparative Literature in the Department of Germanic, Slavic, and Semitic Languages at the University of California-Santa Barbara and was formerly chair of the Comparative Literature Program. He is the author of numerous books and essays on literature of the European Baroque and Romantic periods; co-author of *Germany 2000 Years*, vol. 3 (1992); and editor of various collections of essays, among them *European Romanticism: Literary Cross-Currents, Modes, and Models* (1990) and *A Reassessment of Weimar Classicism* (1996). His monographs include *Petrarkistische Lyrik* (1973; revised as *Petrarca*, 1997), *Deutsche und europäische Romantik* (1976; 2nd ed. 1990), *Byron und der europäische Byronismus* (1983), *Goethe und die europäische Romantik* (1984), and *Heine in der Romania* (2002).

JOACHIM KNAPE is Professor of General Rhetoric Studies at the Universität Tübingen. He has published widely on medieval, Renaissance, and early modern German literature and on the theory and history of rhetoric. He is editor of Georg Messerschmidt's *Brissonetus (1559)* (1988), *Rhetorica deutsch: Rhetorikschriften des 15. Jahrhunderts* (2002), Sebastian Brant's *Das Narrenschiff* (2005), *Aristotelische Rhetoriktradition* (2005), and *Bildrhetorik* (2007). He is author of *Historie in Mittelalter und früher Neuzeit* (1984), *Dichtung, Recht und Freiheit: Studien zu Leben und Werk Sebastian Brants (1457–1521)* (1992), and *Allgemeine Rhetorik: Stationen der Theoriegeschichte* (2000).

WILHELM KÜHLMANN is Professor of Modern German Literature and Comparative Literature at the Universität Heidelberg. His research focuses primarily on German literary and cultural history of the sixteenth through eighteenth centuries, including Neo-Latin literature, with particular attention to scientific, educational, and social history. He has published over 160 articles in journals and collections and has authored or edited over thirty-five books, among them *Gelehrtenrepublik und Fürstenstaat: Entwicklung und Kritik des deutschen Späthumanismus in der Literatur des Barockzeitalters* (1982), *Intertextualität in der frühen Neuzeit: Studien zu ihren theoretischen und praktischen Perspektiven* (co-edited with Wolfgang Neuber, 1994), *Humanistische Lyrik des 16. Jahrhunderts: lateinisch und deutsch* (compiled, edited, and translated with Robert Seidel and Hermann Wiegand, 1997), and *Vom Humanismus zur Spätaufklärung: Ästhetische und kulturgeschichtliche Dimensionen der frühzeitlichen Lyrik und Verspublizistik in Deutschland* (2006). A member of the Heidelberg Academy of Sciences, he is a chief researcher in the project Europa Humanistica under the auspices of the German Research Foundation (DFG) and the Heidelberg Academy and of the Project CAMENA — Neo-Latin Poetry and Literature on the Internet. He is an editor of the journal *Daphnis* and its book series Chloe; the yearbook *Antike und Abendland*; and of several book series, including Frühe Neuzeit, Mannheimer Beiträge zur Sprach- und Literaturwissenschaft, and Bibliotheca Neolatina.

WOLFGANG NEUBER is Professor of Early Modern German and Neo-Latin Literature at the Freie Universität Berlin. He has published extensively on early modern travel accounts, on the relation of text and image, and on the art of memory. He is co-editor (with W. Kühlmann) of *Intertextualität in der Frühen Neuzeit* (1994); *Documenta Mnemonica* (7 vols., 1998–); *Seelenmaschinen: Gattungstraditionen, Funktionen und Leistungsgrenzen der Mnemotechniken vom späten Mittelalter bis zum Beginn der Moderne* (2000); and *Cognition and the Book* (2005), and author of *Fremde Welt im europäischen Horizont* (1991).

JOHN ROGER PAAS is the William H. Laird Professor of German and the Liberal Arts at Carleton College. He has published widely on early modern German literature, with a special emphasis on popular imagery and on the poets of Nuremberg. His major work is the ongoing multivolume edition *The German Political Broadsheet 1600–1700* (1985–).

MAX REINHART is A. G. Steer Professor in Goethe Studies in the Department of Germanic and Slavic Studies at the University of Georgia. His major areas of research are Early Modern Germany and Late Goethe (post–1809). He is the founder and was first president of Frühe Neuzeit Interdisziplinär (FNI). His publications include an edition of essays by Klaus Garber, *Imperiled Heritage: Tradition, History, and Utopia in Early Modern German Literature* (2000); and an edition, with English translation, of Georg Philipp Harsdörffer's early Latin writings, *Lamentation for France and Other Polemics on War and Peace: The Latin Pamphlets of 1641–1642* (forthcoming).

HANS-GERT ROLOFF is Professor Emeritus of Mittlere Deutsche Literatur at the Technische Universität Berlin and was director of the Research Center for Mittlere Deutsche Literatur at the Freie Universität. He is the author of many scholarly and critical editions, articles, and books. His critical editions include the works of Johannes Reuchlin, Jörg Wickram, Daniel Czepko, Johann Beer, Friedrich Nicolai, Carl Hauptmann, and the New Testament in the translation of Martin Luther, as well as volumes in the series Die deutsche Literatur: biographisches und bibliographisches Lexikon. He has founded numerous periodicals and yearbooks, including *Daphnis* and the *Jahrbuch für internationale Germanistik*, as well as the monograph series Chloe and two series of critical editions: Ausgaben deutscher Literatur des XV. bis XVIII. Jahrhunderts and Berliner Ausgaben.

ERIKA RUMMEL is Professor Emerita of History at Wilfrid Laurier University. She has published numerous books on northern humanism, including *The Humanist-Scholastic Debate in the Renaissance and Reformation* (1995), *The Confessionalization of Humanism in Reformation Germany* (2000), and *Erasmus* (2004). She is currently directing the multivolume edition with translation of *The Correspondence of Wolfgang Capito* for the University of Toronto Press.

STEVEN SAUNDERS is Professor of Music at Colby College. His research interests include seventeenth-century sacred music and nineteenth-century American popular song. He is editor of *Giovanni Felice Sances: Motetti a 2, 3, 4, & 5 voci* (2003) and author of *Cross, Sword, and Lyre: Sacred Music at the Court of Ferdinand II of Habsburg* (1995).

JEFFREY CHIPPS SMITH, Kay Fortson Chair in European Art at the University of Texas at Austin, specializes in German and Netherlandish art 1400–1700. His publications include *Nuremberg, A Renaissance City, 1500–1618* (1983); *German Sculpture of the Later Renaissance, c. 1520–1580: Art in an Age of Uncertainty* (1994); *Sensuous Worship: Jesuits and the Art of the Early Catholic Reformation in Germany* (2002); *The Northern Renaissance* (2004); and *The Art of the Goldsmith in Late Fifteenth-Century Germany: The Kimbell Virgin and Her Bishop* (2006). He was the Articles Editor of *Renaissance Quarterly* from 2003 to 2006.

ANDREAS SOLBACH is Professor of German Literature at the Johannes Gutenberg-Universität Mainz. His books include *Johann Beer: Rhetorisches Erzählen zwischen Satire und Utopie* (2003). He has written numerous essays on early modern writers, such as Beer, Grimmelshausen, Gryphius, and Weise, and is editor of *Hermann Hesse und die literarische Moderne* (2004) and *Aedificatio: Erbauung im interkulturellen Kontext in der Frühen Neuzeit* (2005).

THEODOR VERWEYEN, Professor Emeritus of German Studies at the Friedrich-Alexander-Universität Erlangen-Nürnberg, is the author of numerous books including *Apophthegma und Scherzrede* (1970), *Die Parodie in der neueren deutschen Literatur* (with Gunther Witting, 1979), *Die Kontrafaktur: Vorlage und Verarbeitung in Literatur, bildender Kunst, Werbung und politischem Plakat* (with G. Witting, 1987), and *Bücherverbrennungen* (2000). He has edited anthologies of parodies and travesties (with G. Witting, 1983, 1989) and is the principal editor of the standard edition *J. W. Zincgref: Gesammelte Schriften* (with Dieter Mertens, 1978, 1993; and with D. Mertens and Werner W. Schnabel, 2007–8). He has written more than 100 articles on authors and topics in German literature from the early modern period through the twentieth century. Particular interests for the later period include Gottfried Benn, Bertolt Brecht, Günter Grass, Heinrich Mann, Peter Rühmkorf, and Reinhold Schneider, as well as questions concerning genres and intertextual *Schreibweisen* (e.g., parody, pastiche, travesty).

HELEN WATANABE-O'KELLY is Professor of German Literature at the University of Oxford and a Fellow of Exeter College. She has published widely on early modern German topics, particularly on court festivals and court culture. She is the author of *Court Culture in Dresden from Renaissance to Baroque* (2002), editor of *The Cambridge History of German Literature* (1997), and co-editor (with J. R. Mulryne and Margaret Shewring) of *Europa Triumphans: Court and Civic Festivals in Early Modern Europe* (2004).

GERHILD SCHOLZ WILLIAMS is the Barbara Schaps Thomas and David M. Thomas Professor in the Humanities in Arts and Sciences in the Department of Germanic Languages and Literatures at Washington University in St. Louis. Her publications include *Defining Dominion: The Discourses of Magic and Witchcraft in Early Modern France and Germany* (1995), *Existentielle Vergeblichkeit: Verträge in Melusine, Faust und Eulenspiegel* (with Alexander Schwarz, 2003), *Ways of Knowing in Early Modern Germany: Johannes Praetorius as a Witness to His Time* (2006), and *On the Inconstancy of Witches: Pierre de Lancre's Tableau de l'inconstance des mauvais anges et Demons (1612)* (translated with Harriet Stone, 2006). She has published many articles in books and journals on early modern German and French literature and culture and has co-edited a number of volumes, most recently, *Paracelsian Moments: Science, Medicine, & Astrology in Early Modern Europe* (with Charles D. Gunnoe, Jr., 2002).

Index

Notes

Illustrations are indicated by italicized page numbers.
Anonymous and unattributed works are indexed in three ways: by title (e.g., *Lancelot*; *Ogier von Dänemark*); by type or genre (e.g., ballet; Bibles; Easter and passion plays; legal texts and codes; political novel); and by the name of the group or organization with which the work is associated (e.g., English Players; Teutonic Order).

Abbreviations

anon.	anonymous
comp.	compiled
ed.	edition / edited by
pub. posthum.	published posthumously
repub.	republished
rev.	revised
trans.	translation / translated by